A Collection of English Prose

1660-1800

A Collection of

ENGLISH PROSE

1660-1800

Henry Pettit

PROFESSOR OF ENGLISH, UNIVERSITY OF COLORADO

HARPER & BROTHERS, PUBLISHERS, NEW YORK

Contents

A Note on the Text

Effort has been made to reproduce the best available texts contemporary with their earliest appearance. Where it has been necessary to choose between texts, selection has been held to within a few years of the first or at least of the first complete edition. Spelling and punctuation, except for occasional silent correction of obvious misprints, have been maintained as found. The use of capital letters and italic type also follows the original copy for the greater part. Only the long *s* and the ligatured letters had to be relinquished in favor of modern typographic practices. In a few instances, as in Swift and Sterne, where typographic practice is incorporated in the satire, it was impossible to retain all the niceties. It is hoped, however, that the flavor generally remains true enough to exhibit the changes of style in the latter half of the century (see Allen T. Hazen's "New Styles in Typography," in *The Age of Johnson: Essays Presented to Chauncey Brewster Tinker,* New Haven, 1949, pp. 403–409).

Acknowledgment

One of the pleasures of preparing an anthology along historical lines is the discovery of how much thoughtful help is waiting to be had for the asking. My thanks go to librarians generally and especially to those of the Cleveland Public Library, the Huntington, and the Library of Congress, as well as to the University Librarians of Georgia, Harvard, Illinois, and Wesleyan. I am indebted to Miss Marjorie Wynne of the Yale Rare Book Collections and to Miss Elizabeth Selleck of my own University. To my colleagues Chester Garrison, Karl Hulley, Leslie L. Lewis, and Earl Swisher, I am grateful for valuable advice in their various fields of special knowledge. Dr. Wilmarth Lewis, together with his associates Mr. A. Dayle Wallace and Mr. Charles H. Bennett, helped me considerately with Walpole's letters and gave me the use of their notes. The Marquis of Bristol was most cordial in regard to his copy of Hervey's *Memoirs,* and to him and to Lady Bristol I am grateful for their help in obtaining a microfilm of the manuscript and for their permission to reproduce it. I was also permitted to examine the copy of the manuscript in the Royal Archives at Windsor in order to compare the two. The director of the Clarendon Press was kind enough to permit me to use the text of Gray's letters and the notes from the definitive Toynbee-Whibley edition. Professor Frederick A. Pottle similarly responded to my request to use Boswell material from the Yale collections and to use his notes. To my colleague Professor George F. Reynolds, to Professor Lewis Knapp of Colorado College, and to the late Professor Karl J. Holzknecht of New York University I am deeply grateful for encouragement, advice, and especially for confidence. Dr. Johnson once defined pedantry as "awkward ostentation of needless learning"; such of this as I displayed my wife not only met with seasoned equanimity but returned with interest as a somewhat avid proofreader. Perhaps this is the place to say that no one I have named bears any blame for faults in the text, but as the eighteenth century printer occasionally condescended to say, "There are errors, which the reader may correct, with his pen."

HENRY PETTIT

Boulder, Colorado
June 1, 1960

xi

A Collection of English Prose
1660-1800

Samuel Pepys
1633-1703

THE DIARY
1660-1669

SEPTEMBER, 1666: THE MONTH OF THE FIRE

September 1st [*1666*]. Up and at the office all the morning, and then dined at home. Got my new closet made mighty clean against to-morrow. Sir W. Pen and my wife and Mercer and I to "Polichinelly," but were there horribly frighted to see Young Killigrew come in with a great many more young sparks; but we hid ourselves, so as we think they did not see us.[1] By and by they went away, and then we were at rest again; and so, the play being done, we to Islington, and there eat and drank and mighty merry; and so home singing, and after a letter or two at the office, to bed.

2nd (Lord's day). Some of our mayds sitting up late last night to get things ready against our feast to-day, Jane called us up about three in the morning, to tell us of a great fire they saw in the City. So I rose and slipped on my night-gowne, and went to her window, and thought it to be on the back-side of Marke-lane at the farthest; but, being unused to such fires as followed, I thought it far enough off; and so went to bed again and to sleep. About seven rose again to dress myself, and there looked out at the window, and saw the fire not so much as it was and further off. So to my closett to set things to rights after yesterday's cleaning. By and by Jane comes and tells me that she hears that above 300 houses have been burned down to-night by the fire we saw, and that it is now burning down all Fish-street, by London Bridge. So I made myself ready presently, and walked to the Tower, and there got up upon one of the high places, Sir J. Robinson's little son

---

The text is from *The Diary of Samuel Pepys,* ed. H. B. Wheatley (London, G. Bell & Sons, 1893–1899), New York, Harcourt, Brace and Co. Reprinted by permission. The original manuscript of the diary is in shorthand and was first transcribed and published in 1825. While it was not until 1684 that Pepys was made Secretary of the Admiralty, during the period covered by the excerpt from his diary he was officially Surveyor-General of the Victualing Office and actually performing as secretary of the navy. During this period the English were at war with the Dutch.

[1] Sir William Penn was commissioner of the Navy and father of the William Penn famous in American history. Henry Killigrew (b. 1637), was the son of the theatrical manager Thomas Killigrew. He was various times Groom of the Bedchamber to both Charles II and his brother James, the Duke of York, and on his father's death succeeded to the office of Master of the Revels.

going up with me; and there I did see the houses at that end of the bridge all on fire, and an infinite great fire on this and the other side the end of the bridge; which, among other people, did trouble me for poor little Michell and our Sarah on the bridge. So down, with my heart full of trouble, to the Lieutenant of the Tower, who tells me that it begun this morning in the King's baker's house in Pudding-lane, and that it hath burned St. Magnus's Church and most part of Fish-street already. So I down to the water-side, and there got a boat and through bridge, and there saw a lamentable fire. Poor Michell's house, as far as the Old Swan, already burned that way, and the fire running further, that in a very little time it got as far as the Steele-yard, while I was there. Everybody endeavouring to remove their goods, and flinging into the river or bringing them into lighters that lay off; poor people staying in their houses as long as till the very fire touched them, and then running into boats, or clambering from one pair of stairs by the water-side to another. And among other things, the poor pigeons, I perceive, were loth to leave their houses, but hovered about the windows and balconys till they were, some of them burned, their wings, and fell down. Having staid, and in an hour's time seen the fire rage every way, and nobody, to my sight, endeavouring to quench it, but to remove their goods, and leave all to the fire, and having seen it get as far as the Steele-yard, and the wind mighty high and driving it into the City; and every thing, after so long a drought, proving combustible, even the very stones of churches, and among other things the poor steeple by which pretty Mrs.———— lives, and whereof my old schoolfellow Elborough is parson, taken fire in the very top, and there burned till it fell down: I to White Hall (with a gentleman with me who desired to go off from the Tower, to see the fire, in my boat); to White Hall, and there up to the King's closett in the Chappell, where people come about me, and I did give them an account dismayed them all, and word was carried in to the King. So I

was called for, and did tell the King and Duke of Yorke what I saw, and that unless his Majesty did command houses to be pulled down nothing could stop the fire. They seemed much troubled, and the King commanded me to go to my Lord Mayor from him and command him to spare no houses, but to pull down before the fire every way. The Duke of York bid me tell him that if he would have any more soldiers he shall; and so did my Lord Arlington afterwards, as a great secret. Here meeting with Captain Cocke, I in his coach, which he lent me, and Creed with me to Paul's, and there walked along Watling-street, as well as I could, every creature coming away loaden with goods to save, and here and there sicke people carried away in beds. Extraordinary good goods carried in carts and on backs. At last met my Lord Mayor in Canning-street, like a man spent, with a handkercher about his neck. To the King's message he cried, like a fainting woman, "Lord! what can I do? I am spent: people will not obey me. I have been pulling down houses; but the fire overtakes us faster than we can do it." That he needed no more soldiers; and that, for himself, he must go and refresh himself, having been up all night. So he left me, and I him, and walked home, seeing people all almost distracted, and no manner of means used to quench the fire. The houses, too, so very thick thereabouts, and full of matter for burning, as pitch and tarr, in Thames-street; and warehouses of oyle, and wines, and brandy, and other things. Here I saw Mr. Isaake Houblon, the handsome man, prettily dressed and dirty, at his door at Dowgate, receiving some of his brothers' things, whose houses were on fire; and, as he says, have been removed twice already; and he doubts (as it soon proved) that they must be in a little time removed from his house also, which was a sad consideration. And to see the churches all filling with goods by people who themselves should have been quietly there at this time. By this time it was about twelve o'clock; and so home, and there find my guests, which was Mr. Wood and his wife Barbary Sheldon, and also Mr. Moone: she mighty fine, and her husband, for aught I see, a likely man. But Mr. Moone's design and mine, which was to look over my closett and please him with the sight thereof, which he hath long desired, was wholly disappointed; for we were in great trouble and disturbance at this fire, not knowing what to think of it. However, we had an extraordinary good dinner, and as merry as at this time we could be. While at dinner Mrs. Batelier come to enquire after Mr. Woolfe and Stanes (who, it seems, are related to them), whose houses in Fish-street are all burned, and they in a sad condition. She would not stay in the fright. Soon as dined, I and Moone away, and walked through the City, the streets full of nothing but people and horses and carts loaden with goods, ready to run over one another, and removing goods from one burned house to another. They now removing out of Canning-streete (which received goods in the morning) into Lumbard-streete, and further; and among others I now saw my little goldsmith, Stokes, receiving some friend's goods, whose house itself was burned the day after. We parted at Paul's; he home, and I to Paul's Wharf, where I had appointed a boat to attend me, and took in Mr. Carcasse and his brother, whom I met in the streete, and carried them below and above bridge to and again to see the fire, which was now got further, both below and above, and no likelihood of stopping it. Met with the King and Duke of York in their barge, and with them to Queenhithe, and there called Sir Richard Browne to them. Their order was only to pull down houses apace, and so below bridge at the water-side; but little was or could be done, the fire coming upon them so fast. Good hopes there was of stopping it at the Three Cranes above, and at Buttolph's Wharf below bridge, if care be used; but the wind carries it into the City, so as we know not by the water-side what it do there. River full of lighters and boats taking in goods,

and good goods swimming in the water, and only I observed that hardly one lighter or boat in three that had the goods of a house in, but there was a pair of Virginalls[2] in it. Having seen as much as I could now, I away to White Hall by appointment, and there walked to St. James's Parke, and there met my wife and Creed and Wood and his wife, and walked to my boat; and there upon the water again, and to the fire up and down, it still encreasing, and the wind great. So near the fire as we could for smoke; and all over the Thames, with one's face in the wind, you were almost burned with a shower of fire-drops. This is very true; so as houses were burned by these drops and flakes of fire, three or four, nay, five or six houses, one from another. When we could endure no more upon the water, we to a little ale-house on the Bankside, over against the Three Cranes, and there staid till it was dark almost, and saw the fire grow; and, as it grew darker, appeared more and more, and in corners and upon steeples, and between churches and houses, as far as we could see up the hill of the City, in a most horrid malicious bloody flame, not like the fine flame of an ordinary fire. Barbary and her husband away before us. We staid till, it being darkish, we saw the fire as only one entire arch of fire from this to the other side the bridge, and in a bow up the hill for an arch of above a mile long: it made me weep to see it. The churches, houses, and all on fire and flaming at once; and a horrid noise the flames made, and the cracking of houses at their ruine. So home with a sad heart, and there find every body discoursing and lamenting the fire; and poor Tom Hater come with some few of his goods saved out of his house, which is burned upon Fish-streete Hill. I invited him to lie at my house, and did receive his goods, but was deceived in his lying there, the newes coming every moment of the growth of the fire; so as we were forced to begin to pack up our owne goods, and prepare for their removal; and did by moonshine (it

---

[2] The virginal was a stringed instrument with a keyboard, probably in a square case without attached legs. A *pair* is used in the sense of a *set* rather than of *two*. Its name may derive from its common use by young women.

being brave dry, and moonshine, and warm weather) carry much of my goods into the garden, and Mr. Hater and I did remove my money and iron chests into my cellar, as thinking that the safest place. And got my bags of gold into my office, ready to carry away, and my chief papers of accounts also there, and my tallys into a box by themselves. So great was our fear, as Sir W. Batten hath carts come out of the country to fetch away his goods this night. We did put Mr. Hater, poor man, to bed a little; but he got but very little rest, so much noise being in my house, taking down of goods.

3rd. About four o'clock in the morning, my Lady Batten sent me a cart to carry away all my money, and plate, and best things, to Sir W. Rider's at Bednall Greene. Which I did, riding myself in my night-gowne in the cart; and, Lord! to see how the streets and the highways are crowded with people running and riding, and getting of carts at any rate to fetch away things. I find Sir W. Rider tired with being called up all night, and receiving things from several friends. His house full of goods, and much of Sir W. Batten's and Sir W. Pen's. I am eased at my heart to have my treasure so well secured. Then home, with much ado to find a way, nor any sleep all this night to me nor my poor wife. But then and all this day she and I, and all my people labouring to get away the rest of our things, and did get Mr. Tooker to get me a lighter to take them in, and we did carry them (myself some) over Tower Hill, which was by this time full of people's goods, bringing their goods thither; and down to the lighter, which lay at the next quay, above the Tower Docke. And here was my neighbour's wife, Mrs.———, with her pretty child, and some few of her things, which I did willingly give way to be saved with mine; but there was no passing with any thing through the postern,[3] the crowd was so great. The Duke of Yorke come this day by the office, and spoke to us, and did ride with his guard up and down the City to keep all quiet

———————
[3] back gate.

(he being now Generall, and having the care of all). This day, Mercer being not at home, but against her mistress's order gone to her mother's, and my wife going thither to speak with W. Hewer, met her there, and was angry; and her mother saying that she was not a 'prentice girl, to ask leave every time she goes abroad, my wife with good reason was angry, and, when she came home, bid her be gone again. And so she went away, which troubled me, but yet less than it would, because of the condition we are in, fear of coming into in a little time of being less able to keepe one in her quality. At night lay down a little upon a quilt of W. Hewer's in the office, all my owne things being packed up or gone; and after me my poor wife did the like, we having fed upon the remains of yesterday's dinner, having no fire nor dishes, nor any opportunity of dressing any thing.

4th. Up by break of day to get away the remainder of my things; which I did by a lighter at the Iron gate: and my hands so few, that it was the afternoon before we could get them all away. Sir W. Pen and I to Tower-streete, and there met the fire burning three or four doors beyond Mr. Howell's, whose goods, poor man, his trayes, and dishes, shovells, &c., were flung all along Tower-street in the kennels, and people working therewith from one end to the other; the fire coming on in that narrow streete, on both sides, with infinite fury. Sir W. Batten not knowing how to remove his wine, did dig a pit in the garden, and laid it in there; and I took the opportunity of laying all the papers of my office that I could not otherwise dispose of. And in the evening Sir W. Pen and I did dig another, and put our wine in it; and I my Parmazan cheese, as well as my wine and some other things. The Duke of Yorke was at the office this day, at Sir W. Pen's; but I happened not to be within. This afternoon, sitting melancholy with Sir W. Pen in our garden, and thinking of the certain burning of this office, without extraordinary means, I did propose for the sending up of all our workmen from Woolwich and Deptford yards (none whereof yet appeared), and to write to Sir W. Coventry[4] to have the Duke of Yorke's permission to pull down houses, rather than lose this office, which would much hinder the King's business. So Sir W. Pen he went down this night, in order to the sending them up to-morrow morning; and I wrote to Sir W. Coventry about the business, but received no answer. This night Mrs. Turner (who, poor woman, was removing her goods all this day, good goods into the garden, and knows not how to dispose of them), and her husband supped with my wife and I at night, in the office, upon a shoulder of mutton from the cook's, without any napkin or any thing, in a sad manner, but were merry. Only now and then walking into the garden, and saw how horridly the sky looks, all on a fire in the night, was enough to put us out of our wits; and, indeed, it was extremely dreadful, for it looks just as if it was at us, and the whole heaven on fire. I after supper walked in the darke down to Tower-streete, and there saw it all on fire, at the Trinity House on that side, and the Dolphin Taverne on this side, which was very near us; and the fire with extraordinary vehemence. Now begins the practice of blowing up of houses in Tower-streete, those next the Tower, which at first did frighten people more than any thing; but it stopped the fire where it was done, it bringing down the houses to the ground in the same places they stood, and then it was easy to quench what little fire was in it, though it kindled nothing almost. W. Hewer this day went to see how his mother did, and comes late home, telling us how he hath been forced to remove her to Islington, her house in Pye-corner being burned; so that the fire is got so far that way, and all the Old Bayly, and was running down to Fleete-streete; and Paul's is burned, and all Cheapside. I wrote to my father this night, but the post-house being burned, the letter could not go.

5th. I lay down in the office again upon W. Hewer's quilt, being mighty weary, and sore in my feet with going till I was hardly able to stand. About two in the morning my wife calls me up and tells me of new cryes of fire, it being come to Barkeing Church, which is the bottom of our lane. I up, and finding it so, resolved presently to take her away, and did, and took my gold, which was about £2,350, W. Hewer, and Jane, down by Proundy's boat to Woolwich;[5] but, Lord! what a sad sight it was by moone-light to see the whole City almost on fire, that you might see it plain at Woolwich, as if you were by it. There, when I come, I find the gates shut, but no guard kept at all, which troubled me, because of discourse now begun, that there is plot in it, and that the French had done it. I got the gates open, and to Mr. Shelden's, where I locked up my gold, and charged my wife and W. Hewer never to leave the room without one of them in it, night or day. So back again, by the way seeing my goods well in the lighters at Deptford, and watched well by people. Home, and whereas I expected to have seen our house on fire, it being now about seven o'clock, it was not. But to the fyre, and there find greater hopes than I expected; for my confidence of finding our Office on fire was such, that I durst not ask any body how it was with us, till I come and saw it not burned. But going to the fire, I find by the blowing up of houses, and the great helpe given by the workmen out of the King's yards, sent up by Sir W. Pen, there is a good stop given to it, as well as at Marke-lane end as ours; it having only burned the dyall of Barking Church, and part of the porch, and was there quenched. I up to the top of Barking steeple, and there saw the saddest sight of desolation that I ever saw; every where great fires, oyle-cellars, and brimstone, and other things burning. I became afeard to stay there long, and therefore down again as fast as I could, the fire being spread as far as I could see it; and to Sir W. Pen's, and there eat a piece of cold meat, having eaten nothing

---

[4] Secretary to the Duke of York.

[5] Seven miles directly east of St. Paul's Church.

since Sunday, but the remains of Sunday's dinner. Here I met with Mr. Young and Whistler; and having removed all my things, and received good hopes that the fire at our end is stopped, they and I walked into the town, and find Fanchurch-streete, Gracious-streete, and Lumbard-streete all in dust. The Exchange a sad sight, nothing standing there, of all the statues or pillars, but Sir Thomas Gresham's[6] picture in the corner. Walked into Moorefields (our feet ready to burn, walking through the towne among the hot coles), and find that full of people, and poor wretches carrying their goods there, and every body keeping his goods together by themselves (and a great blessing it is to them that it is fair weather for them to keep abroad night and day); drank there, and paid twopence for a plain penny loaf. Thence homeward, having passed through Cheapside and Newgate Market, all burned, and seen Anthony Joyce's house in fire. And took up (which I keep by me) a piece of glasse of Mercers' Chappell in the streete, where much more was, so melted and buckled with the heat of the fire like parchment. I also did see a poor cat taken out of a hole in the chimney, joyning to the wall of the Exchange, with the hair all burned off the body, and yet alive. So home at night, and find there good hopes of saving our office; but great endeavours of watching all night, and having men ready; and so we lodged them in the office, and had drink and bread and cheese for them. And I lay down and slept a good night about midnight, though when I rose I heard that there had been a great alarme of French and Dutch being risen, which proved nothing. But it is a strange thing to see how long this time did look since Sunday, having been always full of variety of actions, and little sleep, that it looked like a week or more, and I had forgot almost the day of the week.

6th. Up about five o'clock, and there met Mr. Gawden at the gate of the office

(I intending to go out, as I used, every now and then to-day, to see how the fire is) to call our men to Bishop's-gate, where no fire had yet been near, and there is now one broke out: which did give great grounds to people, and to me too, to think that there is some kind of plot in this (on which many by this time have been taken, and it hath been dangerous for any stranger to walk in the streets), but I went with the men, and we did put it out in a little time; so that that was well again. It was pretty to see how hard the women did work in the cannells,[7] sweeping of water; but then they would scold for drink, and be as drunk as devils. I saw good butts of sugar broke open in the street, and people go and take handsfull out, and put into beer, and drink it. And now all being pretty well, I took boat, and over to Southwarke, and took boat on the other side the bridge, and so to Westminster, thinking to shift myself,[8] being all in dirt from top to bottom; but could not there find any place to buy a shirt or pair of gloves, Westminster Hall being full of people's goods, those in Westminster having removed all their goods, and the Exchequer money put into vessels to carry to Nonsuch; but to the Swan, and there was trimmed; and then to White Hall, but saw nobody; and so home. A sad sight to see how the River looks: no houses nor church near it, to the Temple, where it stopped. At home, did go with Sir W. Batten, and our neighbour, Knightly (who, with one more, was the only man of any fashion left in all the neighbourhood thereabouts, they all removing their goods and leaving their houses to the mercy of the fire), to Sir R. Ford's, and there dined in an earthen platter—a fried breast of mutton; a great many of us, but very merry, and indeed as good a meal, though as ugly a one, as ever I had in my life. Thence down to Deptford, and there with great satisfaction landed all my goods at Sir G. Carteret's safe, and nothing missed I

---

[6] Gresham (1519?–1579) London financier and founder of the Royal Exchange. He endowed the college named for him in which the Royal Society met and which was later identi-

fied with the development of science.

[7] Gutters for drainage in the street.

[8] change clothes.

could see, or hurt. This being done to my great content, I home, and to Sir W. Batten's, and there with Sir R. Ford, Mr. Knightly, and one Withers, a professed lying rogue, supped well, and mighty merry, and our fears over. From them to the office, and there slept with the office full of labourers, who talked, and slept, and walked all night long there. But strange it was to see Cloath-workers' Hall on fire these three days and nights in one body of flame, it being the cellar full of oyle.

7th. Up by five o'clock; and, blessed be God! find all well; and by water to Paul's Wharfe. Walked thence, and saw all the towne burned, and a miserable sight of Paul's church, with all the roofs fallen, and the body of the quire fallen into St. Fayth's;[9] Paul's school also, Ludgate, and Fleet-street, my father's house, and the church, and a good part of the Temple the like. So to Creed's lodging, near the New Exchange, and there find him laid down upon a bed; the house all unfurnished, there being fears of the fire's coming to them. There borrowed a shirt of him, and washed. To Sir W. Coventry, at St. James's, who lay without curtains, having removed all his goods; as the King at White Hall, and every body had done, and was doing. He hopes we shall have no publique distractions upon this fire, which is what every body fears, because of the talke of the French having a hand in it. And it is a proper time for discontents; but all men's minds are full of care to protect themselves, and save their goods: the militia is in armes every where. Our fleetes, he tells me, have been in sight one of another, and most unhappily by fowle weather were parted, to our great losse, as in reason they do conclude; the Dutch being come out only to make a shew, and please their people; but in very bad condition as to stores, victuals, and men.

They are at Bullen, and our fleete come to St. Ellen's. We have got nothing, but have lost one ship, but he knows not what. Thence to the Swan, and there drank: and so home, and find all well. My Lord Bruncker, at Sir W. Batten's, and tells us the Generall[10] is sent for up, to come to advise with the King about business at this juncture, and to keep all quiet; which is great honour to him, but I am sure is but a piece of dissimulation. So home, and did give orders for my house to be made clean; and then down to Woolwich, and there find all well. Dined, and Mrs. Markham come to see my wife. So I up again, and calling at Deptford for some things of W. Hewer's, he being with me, and then home and spent the evening with Sir R. Ford, Mr. Knightly, and Sir W. Pen at Sir W. Batten's. This day our Merchants first met at Gresham College, which, by proclamation, is to be their Exchange. Strange to hear what is bid for houses all up and down here; a friend of Sir W. Rider's having £150 for what he used to let for £40 per annum. Much dispute where the Custome-house shall be; thereby the growth of the City again to be foreseen. My Lord Treasurer, they say, and others, would have it at the other end of the towne. I home late to Sir W. Pen's, who did give me a bed; but without curtains or hangings, all being down. So here I went the first time into a naked bed, only my drawers on; and did sleep pretty well: but still both sleeping and waking had a fear of fire in my heart, that I took little rest. People do all the world over cry out of the simplicity of my Lord Mayor in generall; and more particularly in this business of the fire, laying it all upon him. A proclamation is come out for markets to be kept at Leadenhall and Mile-end-greene, and several other places about the towne; and Tower-hill, and all churches to be

[9] John Evelyn speaks of this catastrophe in his *Diary:* "The ruines of the vaulted roof falling broke into St. Faith's, which being fill'd with the magazines of bookes belonging to ye stationers, and carried thither for safety, they were all consumed, burning for a weeke following."

[10] George Monk, Duke of Albemarle. Pepys reports on December 6 of the preceding year that "The Duke of Yorke is made generall of all forces by land and sea, and the Duke of Albemarle, lieutenant-generall."

set open to receive poor people.

8th.　Up and with Sir W. Batten and Sir W. Pen by water to White Hall and they to St. James's. I stopped with Sir G. Carteret to desire him to go with us, and to enquire after money. But the first he cannot do, and the other as little, or says, "when we can get any, or what shall we do for it?" He, it seems, is employed in the correspondence between the City and the King every day, in settling of things. I find him full of trouble, to think how things will go. I left him, and to St. James's, where we met first at Sir W. Coventry's chamber, and there did what business we can, without any books. Our discourse, as every thing else, was confused. The fleete is at Portsmouth, there staying a wind to carry them to the Downes, or towards Bullen, where they say the Dutch fleete is gone, and stays. We concluded upon private meetings for a while, not having any money to satisfy any people that may come to us. I bought two eeles upon the Thames, cost me six shillings. Thence with Sir W. Batten to the Cock-pit, whither the Duke of Albemarle is come. It seems the King holds him so necessary at this time, that he hath sent for him, and will keep him here. Indeed, his interest in the City, being acquainted, and his care in keeping things quiet, is reckoned that wherein he will be very serviceable. We to him; he is courted in appearance by every body. He very kind to us; I perceive he lays by all business of the fleete at present, and minds the City, and is now hastening to Gresham College, to discourse with the Aldermen. Sir W. Batten and I home (where met by my brother John, come to town to see how things are with us), and then presently he with me to Gresham College; where infinity of people, partly through novelty to see the new place, and partly to find out and hear what is become one man of another. I met with many people undone, and more that have extraordinary great losses. People speaking their thoughts variously about the beginning of the fire, and the rebuilding of the City. Then to Sir W. Batten's, and took my brother with me, and there

dined with a great company of neighbours, and much good discourse; among others, of the low spirits of some rich men in the City, in sparing any encouragement to the poor people that wrought for the saving their houses. Among others, Alderman Starling, a very rich man, without children, the fire at next door to him in our lane, after our men had saved his house, did give 2s. 6d. among thirty of them,[11] and did quarrel with some that would remove the rubbish out of the way of the fire, saying that they come to steal. Sir W. Coventry told me of another this morning in Holborne, which he shewed the King: that when it was offered to stop the fire near his house for such a reward that came but to 2s. 6d. a man among the neighbours he would give but 18d. Thence to Bednall Green by coach, my brother with me, and saw all well there, and fetched away my journall-book to enter for five days past, and then back to the office, where I find Bagwell's wife, and her husband come home. Agreed to come to their house to-morrow, I sending him away to his ship to-day. To the office and late writing letters, and then to Sir W. Pen's, my brother lying with me, and Sir W. Pen gone down to rest himself at Woolwich. But I was much frightened and kept awake in my bed, by some noise I heard a great while below stairs; and the boys not coming up to me when I knocked. It was by their discovery of people stealing of some neighbours' wine that lay in vessels in the streets. So to sleep; and all well all night.

9th (Sunday).　Up; and was trimmed, and sent my brother to Woolwich to my wife, to dine with her. I to church, where our parson made a melancholy but good sermon; and many and most in the church cried, specially the women. The church mighty full; but few of fashion, and most strangers. I walked to Bednall Green, and there dined well, but a bad venison pasty at Sir W. Rider's. Good people they are, and good discourse; and his daughter, Middleton, a fine woman, discreet. Thence home, and to church

---

[11] One penny each.

again, and there preached Dean Harding; but, methinks, a bad, poor sermon, though proper for the time; nor eloquent, in saying at this time that the City is reduced from a large folio to a decimo-tertio.[12] So to my office, there to write down my journall, and take leave of my brother, whom I sent back this afternoon, though rainy; which it hath not done a good while before. But I had no room or convenience for him here till my house is fitted; but I was very kind to him, and do take very well of him his journey. I did give him 40s. for his pocket, and so, he being gone, and, it presently rayning, I was troubled for him, though it is good for the fyre. Anon to Sir W. Pen's to bed, and made my boy Tom to read me asleep.

10th. All the morning clearing our cellars, and breaking in pieces all my old lumber, to make room, and to prevent fire. And then to Sir W. Batten's, and dined; and there hear that Sir W. Rider says that the towne is full of the report of the wealth that is in his house, and would be glad that his friends would provide for the safety of their goods there. This made me get a cart; and thither, and there brought my money all away. Took a hackney-coach myself (the hackney-coaches now standing at All-gate). Much wealth indeed there is at his house. Blessed be God, I got all mine well thence, and lodged it in my office; but vexed to have all the world see it. And with Sir W. Batten, who would have taken away my hands before they were stowed. But by and by comes brother Balty from sea, which I was glad of; and so got him, and Mr. Tooker, and the boy, to watch with them all in the office all night, while I upon Jane's coming went down to my wife, calling at Deptford, intending to see Bagwell,[13] but did not ouvrir la porte comme je did expect. So down late to Woolwich, and there find my wife out of humour and

indifferent, as she uses upon her having much liberty abroad.

11th. Lay there, and up betimes, and by water with my gold, and laid it with the rest in my office, where I find all well and safe. So with Sir W. Batten to the New Exchange by water and to my Lord Bruncker's house, where Sir W. Coventry and Sir G. Carteret met. Little business before us but want of money. Broke up, and I home by coach round the town. Dined at home, Balty and myself putting up my papers in my closet in the office. He away, I down to Deptford and there spoke with Bagwell and agreed upon to-morrow, and come home in the rain by water. In the evening at Sir W. Pen's, with my wife at supper: he in a mad, ridiculous, drunken humour; and it seems there have been some late distances between his lady and him, as my [wife] tells me. After supper, I home, and with Mr. Hater, Gibson, and Tom alone, got all my chests and money into the further cellar with much pains, but great content to me when done. So very late and weary to bed.

12th. Up, and with Sir W. Batten and Sir W. Pen to St. James's by water, and there did our usual business with the Duke of Yorke. Thence I to Westminster, and there spoke with Michell and Howlett, who tell me how their poor young ones are going to Shadwell's. The latter told me of the unkindness of the young man to his wife, which is now over, and I have promised to appear a counsellor to him. I am glad she is like to be so near us again. Thence to Martin,[14] and there did tout ce que je voudrais avec her, and drank, and away by water home and to dinner, Balty and his wife there. After dinner I took him down with me to Deptford, and there by the Bezan[15] loaded above half my goods and sent them away. So we back home, and then I found occasion to return in the dark and to Bagwell, and there . . .

---

[12] From a large-sized book to a pocket-sized one.

[13] A carpenter's pretty wife with whom Pepys was carrying on an illicit affair. As usual in his references to matters of sex he lapses into for-eign words, here into French. Pepys found employment for the husband in the navy yard.

[14] Another of Pepys's loose women.

[15] A yacht.

did do all that I desired, but though I did intend pour avoir demeurais con elle to-day last night, yet when I had done ce que je voudrais I did hate both elle and la cose, and taking occasion from the occasion of su marido's return . . . did me lever, and so away home late to Sir W. Pen's (Balty and his wife lying at my house), and there in the same simple humour I found Sir W. Pen, and so late to bed.

13th. Up, and down to Tower Wharfe; and there, with Balty and labourers from Deptford again to fetch the rest, and there eat a bit of dinner at the Globe, with the master of the Bezan with me, while the labourers went to dinner. Here I hear that this poor towne do bury still of the plague seven or eight in a day.[16] So to Sir G. Carteret's to work, and there did to my content ship off into the Bezan all the rest of my goods, saving my pictures and fine things, that I will bring home in wherrys when the house is fit to receive them: and so home, and unload them by carts and hands before night, to my exceeding satisfaction: and so after supper to bed in my house, the first time I have lain there; and lay with my wife in my old closett upon the ground, and Balty and his wife in the best chamber, upon the ground also.

14th. Up, and to work, having carpenters come to helpe in setting up bedsteads and hangings; and at that trade my people and I all the morning, till pressed by publique business to leave them against my will in the afternoon: and yet I was troubled in being at home, to see all my goods lie up and down the house in a bad condition, and strange workmen going to and fro might take what they would almost. All the afternoon busy; and Sir W. Coventry come to me, and found me, as God would have it, in my office, and people about me setting my papers to rights; and there discoursed about getting an account ready against the Parliament, and thereby did create me infinite of business, and to be

done on a sudden; which troubled me: but, however, he being gone, I about it late, and to good purpose. And so home, having this day also got my wine out of the ground again, and set in my cellar; but with great pain to keep the porters that carried it in from observing the money-chests there. So to bed as last night, only my wife and I upon a bedstead with curtains in that which was Mercer's chamber, and Balty and his wife (who are here and do us good service), where we lay last night. This day, poor Tom Pepys,[17] the turner, was with me, and Kate Joyce, to bespeake places; one for himself, the other for her husband. She tells me he hath lost £140 per annum, but have seven houses left.

15th. All the morning at the office, Harman being come to my great satisfaction to put up my beds and hangings, so I am at rest, and followed my business all day. Dined with Sir W. Batten, mighty busy about this account, and while my people were busy, wrote near thirty letters and orders with my owne hand. At it till eleven at night; and it is strange to see how clear my head was, being eased of all the matter of all these letters; whereas one would think that I should have been dazed. I never did observe so much of myself in my life. In the evening there comes to me Captain Cocke, and walked a good while in the garden. He says he hath computed that the rents of houses lost by this fire in the City comes to £600,000 per annum; that this will make the Parliament more quiet than otherwise they would have been, and give the King a more ready supply; that the supply must be by excise, as it is in Holland; that the Parliament will see it necessary to carry on the warr; that the late storm hindered our beating the Dutch fleete, who were gone out only to satisfy the people, having no business to do but to avoid us; that the French, as late in the yeare as it is, are coming; that the Dutch are really in bad condition, but that this unhappinesse of ours do give them heart; that there was a late

16 The plague which began in London in the summer of 1665 and had claimed over 60,000 victims was almost spent by the time of the fire.

17 A cousin.

difference between my Lord Arlington and Sir W. Coventry about neglect in the last to send away an express of the other's in time; that it come before the King, and the Duke of Yorke concerned himself in it; but this fire hath stopped it. The Dutch fleete is not gone home, but rather to the North, and so dangerous to our Gottenburgh fleete. That the Parliament is likely to fall foul upon some persons; and, among others, on the Vice-chamberlaine, though we both believe with little ground. That certainly never so great a loss as this was borne so well by citizens in the world; he believing that not one merchant upon the 'Change will break upon it. That he do not apprehend there will be any disturbances in State upon it; for that all men are busy in looking after their owne business to save themselves. He gone, I to finish my letters, and home to bed; and find to my infinite joy many rooms clean; and myself and wife lie in our own chamber again. But much terrified in the nights now-a-days with dreams of fire, and falling down of houses.

16th (Lord's day). Lay with much pleasure in bed talking with my wife about Mr. Hater's lying here and W. Hewer also, if Mrs. Mercer leaves her house. To the office, whither also all my people about this account, and there busy all the morning. At noon, with my wife, against her will, all undressed and dirty, dined at Sir W. Pen's, where was all the company of our families in towne; but, Lord! so sorry a dinner: venison baked in pans, that the dinner I have had for his lady alone hath been worth four of it. Thence, after dinner, displeased with our entertainment, to my office again, and there till almost midnight and my people with me, and then home, my head mightily akeing about our accounts.

17th. Up betimes, and shaved myself after a week's growth: but, Lord! how ugly I was yesterday and how fine to-day! By water, seeing the City all the way, a sad sight indeed, much fire being still in. To Sir W. Coventry, and there read over my yesterday's work: being a collection of the particulars of the excess of charge created by a war, with good content. Sir W. Coventry was in great pain lest the French fleete should be passed by our fleete, who had notice of them on Saturday, and were preparing to go meet them; but their minds altered, and judged them merchantmen, when the same day the Success, Captain Ball, made their whole fleete, and come to Brighthelmstone, and thence at five o'clock afternoon, Saturday, wrote Sir W. Coventry newes thereof; so that we do much fear our missing them. Here come in and talked with him Sir Thomas Clifford, who appears a very fine gentleman, and much set by at Court for his activity in going to sea, and stoutness every where, and stirring up and down. Thence by coach over the ruines, down Fleete Streete and Cheapside to Broad Streete to Sir G. Carteret, where Sir W. Batten (and Sir J. Minnes, whom I had not seen a long time before, being his first coming abroad) and Lord Bruncker passing his accounts. Thence home a little to look after my people at work and back to Sir G. Carteret's to dinner; and thence, after some discourse with him upon our publique accounts, I back home, and all the day with Harman and his people finishing the hangings and beds in my house, and the hangings will be as good as ever, and particularly in my new closet. They gone and I weary, my wife and I, and Balty and his wife, who come hither to-day to helpe us, to a barrel of oysters I sent from the river to-day, and so to bed.

18th. Strange with what freedom and quantity I pissed this night, which I know not what to impute to but my oysters, unless the coldness of the night should cause it, for it was a sad rainy and tempestuous night. Soon as up I begun to have some pain in my bladder and belly, as usual, which made me go to dinner betimes, to fill my belly, and that did ease me, so as I did my business in the afternoon, in forwarding the settling of my house, very well. Betimes to bed, my wife also being all this day ill in the same manner. Troubled at my wife's haire coming off so much. This day the Parliament met, and adjourned till Friday, when the King will be with them.

19th. Up, and with Sir W. Pen by coach to St. James's, and there did our usual business before the Duke of Yorke; which signified little, our business being only complaints of lack of money. Here I saw a bastard of the late King of Sweden's come to kiss his hands; a mighty modish French-like gentleman. Thence to White Hall, with Sir W. Batten and Sir W. Pen, to Wilkes's; and there did hear the many profane stories of Sir Henry Wood damning the parsons for so much spending the wine at the sacrament, cursing that ever they took the cup to themselves, and then another story that he valued not all the world's curses, for for two pence he shall get at any time the prayers of some poor body that is worth a 1,000 of all their curses; Lord Norwich drawing a tooth at a health.[18] Another time, he and Pinchbacke and Dr. Goffe, now a religious man, Pinchbacke did begin a frolick to drink out of a glass with a toad in it that he had taken up going out to shit, he did it without harm. Goffe, who knew sacke would kill the toad, called for sacke; and when he saw it dead, says he, "I will have a quick toad, and will not drink from a dead toad." By that means, no other being to be found, he escaped the health. Thence home, and dined, and to Deptford and got all my pictures put into wherries, and my other fine things, and landed them all very well, and brought them home, and got Sympson to set them all up to-night; and he gone, I and the boy to finish and set up my books, and everything else in my house, till two o'clock in the morning, and then to bed; but mightily troubled, and even in my sleep, at my missing four or five of my biggest books. Speed's Chronicle and Maps, and the two parts of Waggoner,[19] and a book of cards, which I suppose I have put up with too much care, that I have forgot where they are, for sure they are not stole. Two little pictures of sea and ships, and a little gilt frame belonging to my plate of the River, I want; but my books do heartily trouble me. Most of my gilt frames are hurt, which also troubles me, but most my books. This day I put on two shirts, the first time this year, and do grow well upon it; so that my disease is nothing but wind.

20th. Up, much troubled about my books, but cannot imagine where they should be. Up, to the setting my closett to rights, and Sir W. Coventry takes me at it, which did not displease me. He and I to discourse about our accounts, and the bringing them to the Parliament, and with much content to see him rely so well on my part. He and I together to Broad Streete to the Vice-Chamberlain, and there discoursed a while and parted. My Lady Carteret come to town, but I did not see her. He tells me how the fleete is come into the Downes. Nothing done, nor French fleete seen: we drove all from our anchors. But he says newes is come that De Ruyter[20] is dead, or very near it, of a hurt in his mouth, upon the discharge of one of his own guns; which put him into a fever, and he likely to die, if not already dead. We parted, and I home to dinner, and after dinner to the setting things in order, and all my people busy about the same work. In the afternoon, out by coach, my wife with me, which we have not done several weeks now, through all the ruines, to shew her them, which frets her much, and is a sad sight indeed. Set her down at her brother's, and thence I to Westminster Hall, and there staid a little while, and called her home. She did give me an account of great differences between her mother and Balty's wife. The old woman charges her with going abroad and staying out late, and painting in the absence of her husband, and I know not what; and they grow proud, both he and she, and do not help their father and mother out of what I help them to, which I do not like, nor my wife. So home, and to the office, to even my journall, and then home, and

[18] a toast, the occasion for swaggering exploits.

[19] Wagenaer's *Speculum Nauticum* (Leiden, 1585) or its English translation of about 1588. By "a book of cards," Pepys means a book of *charts*, or maps. Pepys was a devoted bibliophile; his library is now in the Pepysian Library, Magdalene College, Cambridge University.

[20] Michael de Ruyter (1606–1676), Admiral of the Dutch fleet.

very late up with Jane setting my books in perfect order in my closet, but am mightily troubled for my great books that I miss, and I am troubled the more for fear there should be more missing than what I find, though by the room they take on the shelves I do not find any reason to think it. So to bed.

21st. Up, and mightily pleased with the setting of my books the last night in order, and that which did please me most of all is that W. Hewer tells me that upon enquiry he do find that Sir W. Pen hath a hamper more than his own, which he took for a hamper of bottles of wine, and are books in it. I was impatient to see it, but they were carried into a wine-cellar, and the boy is abroad with him at the House, where the Parliament met to-day, and the King to be with them. At noon after dinner I sent for Harry, and he tells me it is so, and brought me by and by my hamper of books to my great joy, with the same books I missed, and three more great ones, and no more. I did give him 5s. for his pains. And so home with great joy, and to the setting of some of them right, but could not finish it, but away by coach to the other end of the town, leaving my wife at the 'Change, but neither come time enough to the Council to speak with the Duke of Yorke, nor with Sir G. Carteret, and so called my wife, and paid for some things she bought, and so home, and there after a little doing at the office about our accounts, which now draw near the time they should be ready, the House having ordered Sir G. Carteret, upon his offering them, to bring them in on Saturday next, I home, and there, with great pleasure, very late new setting all my books; and now I am in as good condition as I desire to be in all worldly respects. The Lord of Heaven make me thankfull, and continue me therein! So to bed. This day I had new stairs of main timber put to my cellar going into the yard.

22nd. To my closet, and had it new washed, and now my house is so clean as I never saw it, or any other house in my life, and everything in as good condition as ever before the fire; but with, I believe, about £20 cost one way or other, besides about £20 charge in removing my goods, and do not find that I have lost any thing but two little pictures of ships and sea, and a little gold frame for one of my sea-cards. My glazier, indeed, is so full of worke that I cannot get him to come to perfect my house. To the office, and there busy now for good and all about my accounts. My Lord Bruncker come thither, thinking to find an office, but we have not yet met. He do now give me a watch, a plain one, in the roome of my former watch with many motions which I did give him. If it goes well, I care not for the difference in worth, though I believe there is above £5. He and I to Sir G. Carteret to discourse about his account, but Mr. Waith not being there nothing could be done, and therefore I home again, and busy all day. In the afternoon comes Anthony Joyce to see me, and with tears told me his losse, but yet that he had something left that he can live well upon, and I doubt it not. But he would buy some place that he could have, and yet keepe his trade where he is settled in St. Jones's. He gone, I to the office again, and then to Sir G. Carteret, and there found Mr. Wayth, but, Lord! how fretfully Sir G. Carteret do discourse with Mr. Wayth about his accounts, like a man that understands them not one word. I held my tongue and let him go on like a passionate foole. In the afternoon I paid for the two lighters that carried my goods to Deptford, and they cost me £8. Till past midnight at our accounts, and have brought them to a good issue, so as to be ready to meet Sir G. Carteret and Sir W. Coventry to-morrow, but must work to-morrow, which Mr. T. Hater had no mind to, it being the Lord's day, but, being told the necessity, submitted, poor man! This night writ for brother John to come to towne. Among other reasons, my estate lying in money, I am afeard of any sudden miscarriage. So to bed mightily contented in dispatching so much business, and find my house in the best condition that ever I knew it. Home to bed.

23rd (Lord's day). Up, and after being trimmed, all the morning at the office with my people about me till about one o'clock, and then home, and my people with me, and Mr. Wayth and I eat a bit of victuals in my old closet, now my little dining-room, which makes a pretty room, and my house being so clean makes me mightily pleased, but only I do lacke Mercer or somebody in the house to sing with. Soon as eat a bit Mr. Wayth and I by water to White Hall, and there at Sir G. Carteret's lodgings Sir W. Coventry met, and we did debate the whole business of our accounts to the Parliament; where it appears to us that the charge of the war from September 1st, 1664, to this Michaelmas, will have been but £3,200,000, and we have paid in that time somewhat about £2,200,000, so that we owe above £900,000: but our method of accounting, though it cannot, I believe, be far wide from the mark, yet will not abide a strict examination if the Parliament should be troublesome. Here happened a pretty question of Sir W. Coventry, whether this account of ours will not put my Lord Treasurer to a difficulty to tell what is become of all the money the Parliament have given in this time for the war, which hath amounted to about £4,000,000, which nobody there could answer; but I perceive they did doubt what his answer could be. Having done, and taken from Sir W. Coventry the minutes of a letter to my Lord Treasurer, Wayth and I back again to the office, and thence back down to the water with my wife and landed him in Southwarke, and my wife and I for pleasure to Fox-hall,[21] and there eat and drank, and so back home, and I to the office till midnight drawing the letter we are to send with our accounts to my Lord Treasurer, and that being done to my mind, I home to bed.

24th. Up, and with Sir W. Batten and Sir W. Pen to St. James's, and there with Sir W. Coventry read and all approved of my letter, and then home, and after dinner, Mr. Hater and Gibson dining with me, to the office, and there very late new moulding my accounts and writing fair my letter, which I did

against the evening, and then by coach, left my wife at her brother's, and I to St. James's, and up and down to look [for] Sir W. Coventry; and at last found him and Sir G. Carteret with the Lord Treasurer at White Hall, consulting how to make up my Lord Treasurer's general account, as well as that of the Navy particularly. Here I brought the letter, but found that Sir G. Carteret had altered his account since he did give me the abstract of it: so all my letter must be writ over again, to put in his last abstract. So to Sir G. Carteret's lodgings, to speak a little about the alteration; and there looking over the book that Sir G. Carteret intends to deliver to the Parliament of his payments since September 1st, 1664, and there I find my name the very second for flags, which I had bought for the Navy, of calico, once, about 500 and odd pounds, which vexed me mightily. At last, I concluded of scraping out my name and putting in Mr. Tooker's,[22] which eased me; though the price was such as I should have had glory by. Here I saw my Lady Carteret lately come to towne, who, good lady! is mighty kind, and I must make much of her, for she is a most excellent woman. So took up my wife and away home, and there to bed, and

25th. Up betimes, with all my people to get the letter writ over, and other things done, which I did, and by coach to Lord Bruncker's, and got his hand to it; and then to the Parliament House and got it signed by the rest, and then delivered it at the House-door to Sir Philip Warwicke; Sir G. Carteret being gone into the House with his book of accounts under his arme, to present to the House. I had brought my wife to White Hall, and leaving her with Mrs. Michell, where she sat in her shop and had burnt wine sent for her, I walked in the Hall, and among other with Ned Pickering, who continues still a lying, bragging coxcombe, telling me that my Lord Sandwich may thank himself for all his misfortune; for not suffering him

[21] Foxhall, Faukeshall, or Vauxhall, a manor in Surrey, originally Fulke's Hall, from the name of its owner; now a pleasure garden for Londoners.

[22] A messenger for the navy commissioners.

and two or three good honest fellows more to take them by the throats that spoke ill of him, and told me how basely Lionell Walden hath carried himself towards my Lord, by speaking slightly of him, which I shall remember. Thence took my wife home to dinner, and then to the office, where Mr. Hater all the day putting in order and entering in a book all the measures that this account of the Navy hath been made up by, and late at night to Mrs. Turner's, where she had got my wife and Lady Pen and Pegg, and supped, and after supper and the rest of the company by design gone, Mrs. Turner and her husband did lay their case to me about their lodgings, Sir J. Minnes being now gone wholly to his owne, and now, they being empty, they doubt Sir T. Harvy or Lord Bruncker may look after the lodgings. I did give them the best advice, poor people, that I could, and would do them any kindnesse, though it is strange that now they should have ne'er a friend of Sir W. Batten or Sir W. Pen to trust to but me, that they have disobliged. So home to bed, and all night still mightily troubled in my sleepe with fire and houses pulling down.

26th. Up, and with Sir J. Minnes to St. James's, where every body going to the House, I away by coach to White Hall, and after a few turns, and hearing that our accounts come into the House but to-day, being hindered yesterday by other business, I away by coach home, taking up my wife and calling at Bennet's, our late mercer, who is come into Covent Garden to a fine house looking down upon the Exchange; and I perceive many Londoners every day come; and Mr. Pierce hath let his wife's closett, and the little blind bed-chamber, and a garret to a silke man for £50 fine,[23] and £30 per annum, and £40 per annum more for dieting the master and two prentices. So home, not agreeing for silk for a petticoat for her which she desired, but home to dinner and then back to

White Hall, leaving my wife by the way to buy her petticoat of Bennet, and I to White Hall waiting all the day on the Duke of Yorke to move the King for getting Lanyon some money at Plymouth out of some oyle prizes brought in thither, but could get nothing done, but here by Mr. Dugdale[24] I hear the great loss of books in St. Paul's Church-yarde, and at their Hall also, which they value at about £150,000; some booksellers being wholly undone, and among others, they say, my poor Kirton. And Mr. Crumlum, all his books and household stuff burned; they trusting to St. Fayth's, and the roof of the church falling, broke the arch down into the lower church, and so all the goods burned. A very great loss. His father hath lost above £1,000 in books; one book newly printed, a Discourse, it seems, of Courts. Here I had the hap to see my Lady Denham: and at night went into the dining-room and saw several fine ladies; among others, Castlemayne, but chiefly Denham again[25]; and the Duke of Yorke taking her aside and talking to her in the sight of all the world, all alone; which was strange, and what also I did not like. Here I met with good Mr. Evelyn,[26] who cries out against it, and calls it bitchering, for the Duke of Yorke talks a little to her, and then she goes away, and then he follows her again like a dog. He observes that none of the nobility come out of the country at all to help the King, or comfort him, or prevent commotions at this fire; but do as if the King were nobody; nor ne'er a priest comes to give the King and Court good council, or to comfort the poor people that suffer; but all is dead, nothing of good in any of their minds: he bemoans it, and says he fears more ruin hangs over our heads. Thence away by coach, and called away my wife at Unthanke's, where she tells me she hath bought a gowne of 15s. per yard; the same, before her face, my Lady Castlemayne this day bought also, which

---

[23] a premium agreed to for the privilege of obtaining or renewing a lease.

[24] John, son of the famous antiquarian, William Dugdale.

[25] Lady Denham was the wife of the poet, Sir John Denham, and mistress to the Duke

of York. Castlemayne, was Barbara Villiers (1641–1709), later Duchess of Cleveland, mistress of Charles II.

[26] John Evelyn (1620–1706), like Pepys, keeper of a diary. See note 9.

I seemed vexed for, though I do not grudge it her, but to incline her to have Mercer again, which I believe I shall do, but the girle, I hear, has no mind to come to us again, which vexes me. Being come home, I to Sir W. Batten, and there hear our business was tendered to the House to-day, and a Committee of the whole House chosen to examine our accounts, and a great many Hotspurs enquiring into it, and likely to give us much trouble and blame, and perhaps (which I am afeard of) will find faults enow to demand better officers. This I truly fear. Away with Sir W. Pen, who was there, and he and I walked in the garden by moonlight, and he proposes his and my looking out into Scotland about timber, and to use Pett there; for timber will be a good commodity this time of building the City; and I like the motion, and doubt not that we may do good in it. We did also discourse about our Privateer, and hope well of that also, without much hazard, as, if God blesses us, I hope we shall do pretty well toward getting a penny. I was mightily pleased with our discourse, and so parted, and to the office to finish my journall for three or four days, and so home to supper, and to bed. Our fleete abroad, and the Dutch too, for all we know; the weather very bad; and under the command of an unlucky man, I fear. God bless him, and the fleete under him!

27th. A very furious blowing night all the night; and my mind still mightily perplexed with dreams, and burning the rest of the town, and waking in much pain for the fleete. Up, and with my wife by coach as far as the Temple, and there she to the mercer's again, and I to look out Penny, my tailor, to speak for a cloak and cassock for my brother, who is coming to town; and I will have him in a canonical dress, that he may be the fitter to go abroad with me. I then to the Exchequer, and there, among other things, spoke to Mr. Falconbridge about his girle I heard sing at Nonsuch, and took him and some other 'Chequer men to the Sun Taverne, and there spent 2s. 6 d. upon them, and he sent for the girle, and she hath a pretty way of singing, but

hath almost forgot for want of practice. She is poor in clothes, and not bred to any carriage, but will be soon taught all, and if Mercer do not come again, I think we may have her upon better terms, and breed her to what we please. Thence to Sir W. Coventry's, and there dined with him and Sir W. Batten, the Lieutenant of the Tower, and Mr. Thin, a pretty gentleman, going to Gottenburgh. Having dined, Sir W. Coventry, Sir W. Batten, and I walked into his closet to consider of some things more to be done in a list to be given to the Parliament of all our ships, and time of entry and discharge. Sir W. Coventry seems to think they will soon be weary of the business, and fall quietly into the giving the King what is fit. This he hopes. Thence I by coach home to the office, and there intending a meeting, but nobody being there but myself and Sir J. Minnes, who is worse than nothing, I did not answer any body, but kept to my business in the office till night, and then Sir W. Batten and Sir W. Pen to me, and thence to Sir W. Batten's, and eat a barrel of oysters I did give them, and so home, and to bed. I have this evening discoursed with W. Hewer about Mercer, I having a mind to have her again, and I am vexed to hear him say that she hath no mind to come again, though her mother hath. No newes of the fleete yet, but that they went by Dover on the 25th towards the Gun-fleete, but whether the Dutch be yet abroad, or no, we hear not. De Ruyter is not dead, but like to do well. Most think that the gross of the French fleete are gone home again.

28th. Lay long in bed, and am come to agreement with my wife to have Mercer again, on condition she may learn this winter two months to dance, and she promises me she will endeavour to learn to sing, and all this I am willing enough to. So up, and by and by the glazier comes to finish the windows of my house, which pleases me, and the bookbinder to gild the backs of my books. I got the glass of my book-presses to be done presently, which did mightily content me, and to setting my study in a little better order; and so to my office to my people, busy about our Parliament accounts; and so to dinner, and then at them again close. At night comes Sir W. Pen, and he and I a turn in the garden, and he broke to me a proposition of his and my joining in a design of fetching timber and deals from Scotland, by the help of Mr. Pett upon the place; which, while London is building, will yield good money. I approve it. We judged a third man, that is knowing, is necessary, and concluded on Sir W. Warren, and sent for him to come to us to-morrow morning. I full of this all night, and the project of our man of war; but he and I both dissatisfied with Sir W. Batten's proposing his son to be Lieutenant, which we, neither of us, like. He gone, I discoursed with W. Hewer about Mercer, having a great mind she should come to us again, and instructed him what to say to her mother about it. And so home, to supper, and to bed.

29th. A little meeting at the office by Sir W. Batten, Sir W. Pen, and myself, being the first since the fire. We rose soon, and comes Sir W. Warren, by our desire, and with Sir W. Pen and I talked of our Scotch motion, which Sir W. Warren did seem to be stumbled at, and did give no ready answer, but proposed some thing previous to it, which he knows would find us work, or writing to Mr. Pett to be informed how matters go there as to cost and ways of providing sawyers or saw-mills. We were parted without coming to any good resolution in it, I discerning plainly that Sir W. Warren had no mind to it, but that he was surprised at our motion. He gone, I to some office business, and then home to dinner, and then to office again, and then got done by night the lists that are to be presented to the Parliament Committee of the ships, number of men, and time employed since the war, and then I with it (leaving my wife at Unthanke's) to St. James's, where Sir W. Coventry staid for me, and he and I perused our lists,

and find to our great joy that the wages, victuals, wear and tear, cast by the medium of[27] the men, will come to above [£]3,000,000; and that the extraordinaries, which all the world will allow us, will arise to more than will justify the expence we have declared to have been at since the war, viz., £320,000, he and I being both mightily satisfied, he saying to me, that if God send us over this rubb, we must take another course for a better Comptroller. So we parted, and I to my wife [at Unthanke's], who staid for the finishing her new best gowne (the best that ever I made her), coloured tabby,[28] flowered, and so took it and her home; and then I to my people, and having cut them out a little more work than they expected, viz., the writing over the lists in a new method, I home to bed, being in good humour, and glad of the end we have brought this matter to.

30th (*Lord's day*). Up, and to church, where I have not been a good while: and there the church infinitely thronged with strangers since the fire come into our parish; but not one handsome face in all of them, as if, indeed, there was a curse, as Bishop Fuller heretofore said, upon our parish. Here I saw Mercer come into the church, which I had a mind to, but she avoided looking up, which vexed me. A pretty good sermon, and then home, and comes Balty and dined with us. A good dinner; and then to have my haire cut against winter close to my head, and then to church again. A sorry sermon, and away home. [Sir] W. Pen and I to walk to talk about several businesses, and then home; and my wife and I to read in Fuller's Church History,[29] and so to supper and to bed. This month ends with my mind full of business and concernment how this office will speed with the Parliament, which begins to be mighty severe in the examining our accounts, and the expence of the Navy this war.

---

[27] i.e., computed by taking an average.
[28] taffeta weave.
[29] Thomas Fuller, *The Church History of* *Britain* (1655) from the time of the druids to the execution of Charles I in 1649.

Samuel Butler
1612-1680

CHARACTERS

A SMALL POET

Is one, that would fain make himself that, which *Nature* never meant him; like a *Fanatic*,[1] that inspires himself with his own Whimsies. He sets up Haberdasher of small Poetry, with a very small Stock, and no Credit. He believes it is Invention enough to find out other Men's Wit; and whatsoever he lights upon either in Books, or Company, he makes bold with as his own. This he puts together so untowardly, that you may perceive his own Wit has the Rickets, by the swelling Disproportion of the Joints. Imitation is the whole Sum of him; and his Vein is but an Itch or Clap, that he has catched of others; and his Flame like that of Charcoals, that were burnt before: But as he wants Judgment to understand what is best, he naturally takes the worst, as being most agreeable to his own Talent. You may know his Wit not to be natural, 'tis so unquiet and troublesome in him: For as those, that have Money but seldom, are always shaking their Pockets, when they have it; so does he, when he thinks he has got something, that will make him appear. He is a perpetual Talker; and you may know by the Freedom of his Discourse, that he came lightly by it, as Thieves spend freely what they get. He measures other Men's Wits by *their* Modesty, and his own by *his* Confidence. He makes nothing of writing Plays, because he has not Wit enough to understand the Difficulty. This makes him venture to talk and scribble, as Chowses[2] do to play with cunning Gamesters, until they are cheated and laughed at. He is always talking of Wit, as those, that have bad Voices, are always singing out of Tune; and those, that cannot play, delight to fumble on Instruments. He grows the unwiser by other Men's Harms; for the worse others write, he finds the more Encouragement to do so too. His Greediness of Praise is so eager, that he swallows any Thing, that comes in the Likeness of it, how notorious and palpable soever, and is as Shot-free against any Thing, that may lessen his good Opinion of himself—This renders him incurable, like Diseases, that grow insensible.

If you dislike him it is at your own Peril; he is sure to put in a Caveat beforehand against your Understanding; and, like a Malefactor in Wit, is always furnished with Exceptions against his Judges. This puts him upon perpetual Apologies, Excuses, and Defences, but still by Way of Defiance, in a Kind of

---

Text from *The Genuine Remains in Verse and Prose of Mr. Samuel Butler*, ed. by R. Thyer (2 vols., London, 1759), II 107–127.

[1] Dissenter from the Church of England on the Protestant side, as Baptist, Independent, Quaker, etc.

[2] cheats, swindlers.

whiffling Strain, without Regard of any
Man, that stands in the Way of his
Pageant. Where he thinks he may do it
safely, he will confidently own other
Men's Writings; and where he fears the
Truth may be discovered, he will by fee-
ble Denials and feigned Insinuations give
Men Occasion to suppose so.

If he understands *Latin* or *Greek* he
ranks himself among the Learned, despises the Ignorant, talks Criticisms out
of *Scaliger*,[3] and repeats *Martial's*[4]
baudy Epigrams, and sets up his Rest
wholly upon Pedantry. But if he be not
so well qualified, he crys down all Learning as pedantic, disclaims Study, and professes to write with as great Facility, as
if his Muse was sliding down *Parnassus*.[5]
Whatsoever he hears well said he seizes
upon by poetical Licence; and one Way
makes it his own, that is by ill repeating
of it—This he believes to be no more
Theft, than it is to take that, which others throw away. By this means his Writings are, like a Taylor's Cushion, of mo-
saic Work, made up of several Scraps
sewed together. He calls a slovenly nasty
Description *great Nature,* and dull Flat-
ness *strange Easiness.* He writes down
all that comes in his Head, and makes no
Choice, because he has nothing to do it
with, that is Judgment. He is always re-
pealing the old Laws of Comedy, and
like the *long Parliament* making *Ordi-
nances* in their Stead;[6] although they
are perpetually *thrown out* of Coffee-
Houses, and come to Nothing. He is like
an *Italian* Thief, that never robs, but
he murthers, to prevent Discovery; so
sure is he to cry down the Man from
whom he purloins, that his petty Larceny
of Wit may pass unsuspected. He is but
a Copier at best, and will never arrive
to practise by the Life: For bar him the
Imitation of something he has read, and
he has no Image in his Thoughts. Observation and Fancy, the Matter and
Form of just Wit, are above his Philoso-

phy. He appears so over concerned in all
Men's Wits, as if they were but Dispar-
agements of his own; and crys down all
they do, as if they were Encroachments
upon him. He takes Jests from the Owners and breaks them, as *Justices* do false
Weights, and Pots that want Measure.
When he meets with any Thing, that is
very good, he changes it into small
Money, like three Groats[7] for a Shilling,
to serve several Occasions. He disclaims
Study, pretends to take Things in Motion, and to shoot flying, which appears
to be very true by his often missing of
his Mark. His Wit is much troubled
with Obstructions; and he has Fits as
painful as those of the Spleen.[8] He fancies himself a dainty spruce Shepherd,
with a Flock and a fine silken Shepherdess, that follows his Pipe, as Rats did the
Conjurers in *Germany*.[9]

As for *Epithets,* he always avoids
those, that are near akin to the Sense.
Such matches are unlawful, and not fit
to be made by a *Christian* Poet; and
therefore all his Care is to chuse out
such, as will serve, like a wooden Leg,
to piece out a maim'd Verse, that wants
a Foot or two; and if they will but
rhime now and then into the Bargain, or
run upon a Letter, it is a Work of Su-
pererrogation.

For *Similitudes,* he likes the hardest
and most obscure best: For as Ladies
wear black Patches, to make their Complexions seem fairer than they are; so
when an Illustration is more obscure
than the Sense that went before it, it
must of Necessity make it appear clearer
than it did: For Contraries are best set
off with Contraries.

He has found out a Way to save the
Expence of much Wit and Sense: For he
will make less than some have prodigally
laid out upon five or six Words serve
forty or fifty Lines. This is a thrifty Invention, and very easy; and, if it were
commonly known, would much increase

---

[3] Julius Caesar Scaliger (1484–1558), Italian critic.
[4] Marcus Valerius Martialis (*c.* 40–*c.* 102),
Roman epigrammatist.
[5] Mountain in Greece sacred to the Muses.
[6] i.e., he makes his own rules; the Long
Parliament sat from 1640 to 1653 in defiance

of the monarch.
[7] Silver coins worth fourpence, or one-third
of a shilling.
[8] A medical term used loosely for hypo-
chondria.
[9] The legend of the Pied Piper of Hamelin
dates from 1284.

the Trade of Wit, and maintain a Multitude of small Poets in constant Employment. He has found out a new Sort of poetical *Georgics,* a Trick of sowing Wit like clover-grass on barren Subjects, which would yield nothing before. This is very useful for the Times, wherein, some Men say, there is no Room left for new Invention. He will take three Grains of Wit like the Elixir,[10] and projecting it upon the *Iron-Age* turn it immediately into *Gold*—All the Business of Mankind has presently vanished, the whole World has kept Holiday; there has been no Men but Heroes and Poets, no Women but Nymphs and Shepherdesses; Trees have born Fritters, and Rivers flowed Plum-Porrige.

We read that *Virgil* used to make fifty or sixty Verses in a Morning, and afterwards reduce them to ten.[11] This was an unthrifty Vanity, and argues him as well ignorant in the Husbandry of his own Poetry, as *Seneca* says he was in that of a Farm; for in plain *English* it was no better than bringing a Noble to Ninepence.[12] And as such Courses brought the *prodigal Son* to eat with Hogs: So they did him to feed with Horses,[13] which were not much better Company, and may teach us to avoid doing the like. For certainly it is more noble to take four or five Grains of Sense, and, like a Gold-Beater, hammer them into so many Leaves as will fill a whole Book; than to write nothing but Epitomies,[14] which many wise Men believe will be the Bane and Calamity of Learning.

When he writes, he commonly steers the Sense of his Lines by the Rhime that is at the End of them, as Butchers do Calves by the Tail. For when he has made one Line, which is easy enough; and has found out some sturdy hard Word, that will but rhime, he will hammer the Sense upon it, like a Piece of hot Iron upon an Anvil, into what Form he pleases.

There is no Art in the World so rich in Terms as Poetry; a whole Dictionary is scarce able to contain them: For there is hardly a Pond, a Sheep-walk, or a Gravel-pit in all *Greece,* but the antient Name of it is become a Term of Art in Poetry. By this means small Poets have such a Stock of able hard Words lying by them, as *Dryades, Hamadryades, Aonides, Fauni, Nymphoe, Sylvani, etc.* that signify nothing at all; and such a World of pedantic Terms of the same Kind, as may serve to furnish all the new Inventions and *thorough-Reformations,* that can happen between this and *Plato's* great Year.[15]

When he writes he never proposes any Scope or Purpose to himself, but gives his Genius all Freedom: For as he, that rides abroad for his Pleasure, can hardly be out of his Way; so he that writes for his Pleasure, can seldom be beside his Subject. It is an ungrateful Thing to a noble Wit to be confined to any Thing—To what Purpose did the Antients feign *Pegasus* to have Wings, if he must be confined to the Road and Stages like a Pack-Horse, or be forced to be obedient to Hedges and Ditches? Therefore he has no Respect to Decorum and Propriety of Circumstance; for the Regard of Persons, Times, and Places is a Restraint too servile to be imposed upon poetical Licence; like him that made *Plato* confess *Juvenal* to be a Philosopher, or *Persius,* that calls the *Athenians Quirites.*[16]

For *Metaphors,* he uses to chuse the

---

[10] A substance in alchemy for transmuting base metals to gold.

[11] From a passage in the life of Vergil ascribed to Donatus.

[12] i.e., wasteful extravagance; an old proverb. A noble was a coin current in England until 1461 worth 6s. 8d.

[13] The life of Vergil referred to in note 11 says that Vergil studied veterinary medicine and while employed in the stables of Augustus came to the attention of the ruler.

[14] summaries or digests.

[15] That space of time which, according to ancient astronomers, elapses before all the stars and constellations return to their former positions in respect to the equinoxes. Tycho Brahe calculated this period at 25,816 years.

[16] These are examples of anachronisms. It is not known who put Juvenal before Plato, but in another place Butler himself says: "Persius commits a very great absurdity, when laying the scene of his fourth Satyr in Greece, and bringing in Socrates reproving a young statesman, he makes him call the Grecians Quirites." Quirites were Roman citizens in their capacity as civilians.

hardest, and most far-fet[17] that he can light upon—These are the Jewels of Eloquence, and therefore the harder they are, the more precious they must be.

He'll take a scant Piece of coarse Sense, and stretch it on the Tenterhooks of half a score Rhimes, until it crack that you may see through it, and it rattle like a Drum-Head. When you see his Verses hanged up in Tobacco-Shops, you may say, in defiance of the Proverb, *that the weakest does not always go to the Wall;*[18] for 'tis well known the Lines are strong enough, and in that Sense may justly take the Wall of any, that have been written in our Language. He seldom makes a Conscience of his Rhimes; but will often take the Liberty to make *preach* rhime with *Cheat, Vote* with *Rogue,* and *Committee-Man* with *Hang.*[19]

He'll make one Word of as many Joints, as the Tin-Pudding, that a Jugler pulls out of his Throat, and chops in again—What think you of *glud-fumflam-hasta-minantes?*[20] Some of the old *Latin* Poets bragged, that their Verses were tougher than Brass, and harder than Marble;[21] what would they have done, if they had seen these? Verily they would have had more reason to wish themselves an hundred Throats, than they then had, to pronounce them.

There are some, that drive a Trade in writing in praise of other Writers, (like Rooks,[22] that bet on Gamesters Hands) not at all to celebrate the learned Author's Merits, as they would shew, but their own Wits, of which he is but the Subject. The Letchery of this Vanity has spawned more Writers than the *civil Law:* For those, whose Modesty must not endure to hear their own Praises spoken, may yet publish of themselves the most notorious Vapours[23] imaginable. For if the Privilege of Love be allowed—*Dicere quae puduit, scribere jussit Amor,*[24] why should it not be so in Self-Love too? For if it be Wisdom to conceal our Imperfections, what is it to discover our Virtues? It is not like, that *Nature* gave Men great Parts upon such Terms, as the *Fairies* use to give Money, to pinch and leave them if they speak of it. They say—*Praise is but the Shadow of Virtue;* and sure that Virtue is very foolish, that is afraid of its own Shadow.

When he writes *Anagrams,* he uses to lay the Outsides of his Verses even (like a Bricklayer) by a Line of Rhime and Acrostic, and fill the Middle with Rubbish—In this he imitates *Ben. Johnson,* but in nothing else.[25]

There was one, that lined a Hat-Case with a Paper of *Benlowse's*[26] Poetry—*Prynne*[27] bought it by Chance, and put

---

[17] far-fetched.

[18] The position of honor on foot was next the wall, a custom still observed when gentlemen in company with ladies walk on the side toward the street.

[19] A *Committee-Man* implies a Puritan, from the Committee of Both Kingdoms that fought the first of England's civil wars in 1648. Butler's choices of rhymes here all carry political implications.

[20] A coined word implying nonsense.

[21] In particular:

Exegi monumentum aere perennius
Regalique situ Pyrammidum altius.
(More durable than brass, the frame
Which here I consecrate to fame;
Higher than pyramids that rise,
With royal pride, to brave the skies.)
(Horace, *Odes,* III, xxx, 1–2, tr. Francis.)

[22] cheats; in this instance, those who lead the gullible into betting against cardsharps.

[23] personal complaints, from a medical term for nervous debility.

[24] "But what I blushed to speak, Love made me write" (Ovid, *Epistles,* IV, 10, tr. Otway).

[25] Jonson was a bricklayer by trade. Butler's use of the term *anagrams* is that of a broader use recognized in the seventeenth century than now prevalent. He used the term in this sense in *Hudibras,* III, i, 771–772:

His body, that stupendous frame,
Of all the world the anagram.

[26] Edward Benlowes (1604–1676), a religious poet who went to extremes in choice of words and syntax.

[27] William Prynne (1600?–1669), a persistent critic of the government whose punishment under Laud was to have his ears cut off and his cheeks branded. In order to suppress his activities the government imprisoned him on the Isle of Jersey where he wrote a verse description of his prison and of his meditations on rocks, seas, and gardens, named after the castle in which he was confined, "Mount Orgueil," about 1738.

a new Demi-Castor[28] into it. The first Time he wore it he felt only a singing in his Head, which within two Days turned to a Vertigo—He was let Blood in the Ear by one of the State-Physicians, and recovered; but before he went abroad he writ a Poem of Rocks and Seas, in a Stile so proper and natural, that it was hard to determine, which was ruggeder.

There is no Feat of Activity, nor Gambol of Wit, that ever was performed by Man, from him that vaults on *Pegasus,* to him that tumbles through the Hoop of an Anagram, but *Benlows* has got the Mastery in it, whether it be high-rope Wit, or low-rope Wit. He has all Sorts of *Echoes, Rebus's, Chronograms, etc.* besides *Carwitchets, Clenches,* and *Quibbles*—As for *Altars* and *Pyramids* in Poetry, he has out-done all Men that Way; for he has made a *Gridiron,* and a *Frying-Pan* in Verse, that, beside the Likeness in Shape, the very Tone and Sound of the Words did perfectly represent the Noise, that is made by those Utensils, such as the old Poet called *sartago loquendi.*[29] When he was a Captain,[30] he made all the Furniture of his Horse, from the Bit to the Crupper, in beaten Poetry, every Verse being fitted to the Proportion of the Thing, with a moral Allusion of the Sense to the Thing; as the *Bridle of Moderation, the Saddle of Content,* and *the Crupper of Constancy;* so that the same Thing was both Epigram and Emblem,[31] even as a Mule is both Horse and Ass.

Some Critics are of Opinion, that Poets ought to apply themselves to the Imitation of *Nature,* and make a Conscience of digressing from her; but he is none of these. The antient Magicians could charm down the Moon, and force Rivers back to their Springs by the Power of Poetry only; and the Moderns will undertake to turn the Inside of the Earth outward (like a Jugler's Pocket) and shake the *Chaos* out of it, make *Nature*

shew Tricks like an Ape, and the Stars run on Errands; but still it is by dint of Poetry. And if Poets can do such noble Feats, they were unwise to descend to mean and vulgar: For where the rarest and most common Things are of a Price (as they are all one to Poets) it argues Disease in Judgment not to chuse the most curious. Hence some infer, that the Account they give of things deserves no Regard, because they never receive any Thing, as they find it, into their Compositions, unless it agree both with the Measure of their own Fancies, and the Measure of their Lines, which can very seldom happen: And therefore when they give a Character of any Thing or Person, it does commonly bear no more Proportion to the Subject, than the Fishes and Ships in a Map do to the Scale. But let such know, that Poets, as well as Kings, ought rather to consider what is fit for them to give, than others to receive; that they are fain to have regard to the Exchange of Language, and write high or low, according as that runs: For in this Age, when the smallest Poet seldom goes below more the most, it were a Shame for a greater and more noble Poet not to out-throw that cut a Bar.

There was a *Tobacco-Man,* that wrapped *Spanish* Tobacco in a Paper of Verses, which *Benlows* had written against the *Pope,* which by a natural Antipathy, that his Wit has to any Thing that's Catholic, spoiled the Tobacco; for it presently turned Mundungus.[32] This Author will take an *English* Word, and, like the *Frenchman,* that swallowed Water and spit it out Wine, with a little Heaving and Straining would turn it immediately into *Latin,* as *plunder at ille Domos*—Mille *Hocopokiana,* and a thousand such.

There was a young Practitioner in Poetry, that found there was no good to be done without a Mistress: For he, that writes of Love before he hath tried it, doth but travel by the Map; and he, that

---

[28] felt hat.

[29] Literally, a frying pan of language, from Persius, *Satires,* I, 80, variously translated as a hotch-potch, a medley, or a hubbub of language.

[30] Benlowes had been captain of the horse in the Civil Wars.

[31] An illustration accompanied by verses and often with morals in prose.

[32] rank, bad tobacco.

makes Love without a Dame, does like a Gamester, that plays for Nothing. He thought it convenient therefore, first to furnish himself with a Name for his Mistress beforehand, that he might not be to seek, when his Merit or good Fortune should bestow her upon him: for every Poet is his mistresse's Godfather, and gives her a new Name, like a Nun that takes Orders. He was very curious to fit himself with a handsome Word of a tunable Sound; but could light upon none, that some Poet or other had not made use of before. He was therefore forced to fall to coining, and was several Months before he could light on one, that pleased him perfectly. But after he had overcome that Difficulty, he found a greater remaining, to get a Lady to own him. He accosted some of all Sorts, and gave them to understand, both in Prose and Verse, how incomparably happy it was in his Power to make his Mistress, but could never convert any of them. At length he was fain to make his Landress supply that Place as a Proxy, until his good Fortune, or somebody of better Quality would be more kind to him, which after a while he neither hoped nor cared for; for how mean soever her Condition was before, when he had once pretended to her, she was sure to be a Nymph and a Goddess. For what greater Honour can a Woman be capable of, than to be translated into precious Stones and Stars? No Herald in the World can go higher. Besides he found no Man can use that Freedom of Hyperbole in the Character of a Person commonly known (as great Ladies are) which we can in describing one so obscure and unknown, that nobody can disprove him. For he, that writes but one Sonnet upon any of the public Persons, shall be sure to have his Reader at every third Word cry out —What an Ass is this to call *Spanish paper and Ceruse*[33] *Lilies and Roses,* or *claps Influences*—To say, *the Graces are her waiting Women,* when they are known to be no better than her Bawdes —*that Day breaks from her Eyes,* when she looks asquint—Or that *her Breath*

perfumes the Arabian Winds, when she puffs Tobacco?

It is no mean Art to improve a Language, and find out Words, that are not only removed from common use, but rich in Consonants, the Nerves and Sinews of Speech, to raise a soft and feeble Language like ours to the Pitch of *High-Dutch,* as he did, that writ

Arts rattling Foreskins shrilling Bagpipes quell.[34]

This is not only the most elegant, but most politic Way of Writing, that a Poet can use; for I know no Defence like it to preserve a Poem from the Torture of those that lisp and stammer. He that wants Teeth may as well venture upon a Piece of tough horny Brawn as such a Line, for he will look like an Ass eating Thistles.

He never begins a Work without an Invocation of his *Muse;* for it is not fit that she should appear in public, to shew her Skill before she is entreated, as Gentlewomen do not use to sing, until they are applied to, and often desired.

I shall not need to say any Thing of the Excellence of Poetry, since it has been already performed by many excellent Persons, among whom some have lately undertaken to prove, that the civil Government cannot possibly subsist without it,[35] which for my Part, I believe to be true in a poetical Sense, and more probable to be received of it, than those strange Feats of building Walls, and making Trees dance, which Antiquity ascribes to Verse. And though *Philosophers* are of a contrary Opinion, and will not allow Poets fit to live in a Commonwealth, their Partiality is plainer than their Reasons; for they have no other Way to pretend to this Prerogative themselves, as they do, but by removing Poets, whom they know to have a fairer Title; and this they do so unjustly, that *Plato,* who first banished Poets his Republic, forgot that that very Commonwealth was poetical. I shall say nothing to them, but only desire the World to

---

[33] artificial coloring.
[34] Source unknown.

[35] An allusion to Sir William Davenant's *Preface to Gondibert* (1650).

consider, how happily it is like to be governed by those, that are at so perpetual
a civil War among themselves, that if we
should submit ourselves to their own
Resolution of this Question, and be content to allow them only fit to rule if they
could but conclude it so themselves, they
would never agree upon it—Mean while
there is no less Certainty and Agreement
in Poetry than the Mathematics; for
they all submit to the same Rules without Dispute or Controversy. But whosoever shall please to look into the Records
of Antiquity shall find their Title so un-
questioned, that the greatest Princes in
the whole World have been glad to derive their Pedigrees, and their Power
too, from Poets. *Alexander* the great had
no wise a Way to secure that Empire to
himself by *Right,* which he had gotten by
Force, then by declaring himself the Son
of *Jupiter;* and who was *Jupiter* but the
Son of a Poet? So *Caesar* and all *Rome*
was transported with Joy, when a Poet
made *Jupiter* his Colleague in the Empire; and when *Jupiter* governed, what
did the Poets, that governed Jupiter?

John Bunyan
1628-1688

THE PILGRIM'S PROGRESS:
In the Similitude of a Dream
1678

As I walk'd through the Wilderness of this World, I lighted on a certain place, where was a Denn;[1] And I laid me down in *that* place to sleep: And as I slept I dreamed a Dream. I dreamed, and behold *I saw a Man*[2] *cloathed with Rags, standing in a certain place, with his face from his own House, a Book in his hand, and a great burden upon his Back*. I looked, and saw him open the Book, and read therein; and as he read, he wept and trembled: and not being able longer to contain, he brake out with a lamentable cry; saying,[3] *What shall I do?*

In this plight therefore he went home, and refrained himself as long as he could, that his Wife and Children should not perceive his distress; but he could not be silent long, because that his trouble increased: wherefore at length he brake his mind to his Wife and Children; and thus he began to talk to them, *O my dear Wife,* saith he, *and you the Children of my bowels, I your dear friend am in my self undone, by reason of a burden that lieth hard upon me: moreover, I am for certain informed, that this our City will be burned with fire from Heaven, in which fearful overthrow, both my self, with thee, my Wife, and you my sweet babes, shall miserably come to ruine; except (the which, yet I see not) some way of escape can be found, whereby we may be delivered*. At this his Relations they were sore amazed; not for that they believed, that what he said to them was true, but because they thought, that some frenzy distemper had got into his head: therefore, it drawing towards night, and they hoping that sleep might settle his brains, with all hast they got him to bed; but the night was as troublesome to him as the day: wherefore instead of sleeping, he spent it in sighs and tears. So when the morning was come, they would know how he did; and he told them worse and worse. He also set to talking to them again, but they began to be hardened;[4] they also thought to drive away his distemper by harsh and surly carriages to him: Sometimes they would deride, sometimes they would chide, and sometimes they would quite neglect him: wherefore he began to retire himself to his Chamber to pray for, and pity them;

Text from the Locker-Lampson-Church copy of the third edition, 1679, by permission of the Huntington Library, San Marino, California (HM 102817). Notes throughout are from the text, corrected where necessary, and, as in the original, they sometimes refer to the material they precede.

[1] The Gaol.
[2] Isa. 64:6; Luke 14:33; Ps. 38:4; Heb. 2:2; Acts 16:31.
[3] His Out-cry.
[4] Carnal Physick for a Sick Soul.

and also to condole his own misery: he would also walk solitarily in the Fields, sometimes reading, and somtimes praying; and thus for some dayes he spent his time.

Now, I saw upon a time, when he was walking in the Fields, that he was (as he was wont) reading in his Book, and greatly distressed in his mind; and as he read, he burst out, as he had done before, crying, *What shall I do to be saved?*

I saw also that he looked *this* way, and *that* way, as if he would run; yet he stood still, because, (as I perceived) he could not tell which way to go. I looked then, and saw a man named *Evangelist,* coming to him, and asked, *Wherefore dost thou cry?* He answered, Sir, I perceive, by the Book in my hand, that I am condemned to die, and after that,[5] to come to judgment; and I find that I am not willing[6] to do the first, nor able to do the second.[7]

Then saith *Evangelist,* Why not willing to die? since this life is attended with so many evils? The Man answered, because I fear that this burden that is upon my back, will sink me lower then the Grave; and I shall fall into *Tophet.*[8] And Sir, if I be not fit to go to Prison, I am not fit to go to Judgment, and from thence to Execution; and the thoughts of these things make me cry.

Then saith *Evangelist,* If this be thy condition, why standest thou still? He answered, because I know not whither to go, Then he gave him a *Parchment-Roll,*[9] and there was written within, *Fly from the wrath to come.*[10]

The Man therefore read it, and looking upon *Evangelist* very carefully; said Whither must I fly? Then said *Evangelist,* pointing with his finger over a very wide Field, Do you see yonder *Wicketgate?*[11] The Man said, No. Then said the other, Do you see yonder shining light?[12] He said, I think I do. Then said *Evangelist,* Keep that light in your eye, and go up directly thereto, so shalt thou see the Gate; at which when thou knockest, it shall be told thee what thou shalt do.

So I saw in my Dream, that the Man began to run; Now he had not run far from his own door, but his Wife and Children perceiving it, began to cry after him to return: but the Man[13] put his fingers in his ears, and ran on crying, Life, Life, Eternal Life: so he looked not behind him, but fled towards the middle of the Plain.[14]

The Neighbors also came out to see him run,[15] and as he ran, some mocked, others threatened, and some cried after him to return: And among those that did so, there were two that were resolved to fetch him back by force. The name of the one was *Obstinate,* and the name of the other *Pliable.*[16] Now by this time the Man was got a good distance from them; but however they were resolved to pursue him; which they did, and in a little time they overtook him. Then saith the Man, Neighbors, *Wherefore are you come?* They said, To perswade you to go back with us; but he said, that can by no means be: You dwell, (said he,) in the City of *Destruction,* (the place also where I was born) I see it to be so; and dying there, sooner or later, you will sink lower than the Grave, into a place that burns with Fire and Brimstone: be content good Neighbors, and go along with me.

What![17] said *Obstinate, and leave our Friends, and our Comforts behind us!*

Yes,[18] said *Christian,* (for that was his name) because, that *all, which you shall forsake,* is not worthy[19] to be compared with a *little* of that that I am seeking to enjoy, and if you will go along with me, *and hold it,* you shall fare as I my self;

---

[5] Heb. 9:27.
[6] Job 16:21, 22.
[7] Ezek. 22:14.
[8] Isa. 30:33.
[9] Conviction of the necessity of flying.
[10] Matt. 3:7.
[11] Matt. 7; Ps. 119:105; II Pet. 1:29.
[12] Christ, and the way to him cannot be found without the Word.

[13] Luke 14:26.
[14] Gen. 19:27.
[15] They that fly from the wrath to come, are a Gazing-stock to the world. Jer. 20:10.
[16] Obstinate and Pliable follow him.
[17] Obstinate.
[18] Christian.
[19] II Cor. 4:18.

for there where I go is enough,[20] and to spare; Come away, and prove my words.

Obst. What are the things you seek, since you leave all *the world to find them?*

Chr. I seek an *Inheritance,*[21] *incorruptible, undefiled, and that fadeth not away;* and it is laid up in Heaven,[22] and safe there, to be bestowed at the time appointed, on them that diligently seek it. Read it so, if you will, in my Book.

Obst. *Tush,* said *Obstinate, away with your Book; will you go back with us, or no?*

Chr. No, not I, saith the other; because I have laid my hand to the Plow.[23]

Obst. *Come then, Neighbor* Pliable, *let us turn again, and go home without him; there is a company of these Craz'd-headed Coxcombs, that when they take a fancy by the end, are wiser in their own eyes then seven men that can render a reason.*

Pli. Then said *Pliable,* Don't revile; if what the good *Christian* says, is true, the things he looks after are better then ours; my heart inclines to go with my Neighbour.

Obst. *What! more fools still? be ruled by me and go back: who knows whither such a brain-sick fellow will lead you? go back, go back, and be wise.*

Chr.[24] Come with thy Neighbor *Pliable,* there are such things to be had which I spoke of, and many more Glories besides; if you believe not me, read here in this Book; and for the truth of what is exprest therein, behold, all is confirmed by the Blood of him that made it.

Pli.[25] *Well Neighbor* Obstinate (*saith* Pliable) *I begin to come to a point, I intend to go along with this good man, and to cast in my lot with him: But my good Companion, do you know the way to this desired place?*

Chr. I am directed by a man whose name is *Evangelist,* to speed me to a little Gate that is before us, where we shall receive instructions about the way.

Pli. *Come then, good Neighbor, let us be going: then they went both together.*

Obst. And I will go back to my place, said *Obstinate:* I will be no Companion of such mis-led fantastical Fellows.

Now I saw in my Dream, that when *Obstinate* was gone back, *Christian* and *Pliable* went talking[26] over the Plain; and thus they began their discourse.

Chr. Come Neighbour *Pliable,* how do you do? I am glad you are perswaded to go along with me; and had even *Obstinate* himself, but felt what I have felt of the powers, and terrors of what is yet unseen, he would not thus lightly have given us the back.

Pliable. *Come Neighbor* Christian, *since there is none but us two here, tell me now further, what the things are: and how to be enjoyed, whither we are going.*

Chr. I can better conceive of them with my mind, than speak of them with my Tongue: But yet since you are desirous to know, I will read of them in my Book.

Pli. *And do you think that the words of your Book, are certainly true?*

Chr. Yes verily, for it was made by him that cannot lie.[27]

Pli. *Well said; what things are they?*

Chr. There is an endless Kingdom[28] to be inhabited, and everlasting life to be given us; that we may inhabit that Kingdom for ever.

Pli. *Well said, and what else?*

Chr. There are Crowns of Glory to be given us; and Garments[29] that will make us shine like the Sun in the Firmament of Heaven.

Pli. *This is excellent; and what else?*

Chr. There shall be no more crying, nor sorrow;[30] for he that is owner of the place, will wipe all tears from our eyes.

Pli. *And what company shall we have there?*

Chr. There we shall be with *Sera-*

[20] Luke 15.
[21] I Pet. 1:4.
[22] Heb. 11:16.
[23] Luke 9:62.
[24] Christian and Obstinate pull for Pliable's Soul.
[25] Pliable consented to go with Christian.
[26] Talk between Christian and Pliable.
[27] Titus 1:2.
[28] Isa. 45:17; John 10:27,28,29.
[29] II Tim. 4:8; Rev. 3, 4; Matt. 13.
[30] Isa. 15:8; Rev. 7:16,17; 21:4.

phims,[31] and *Cherubins,* Creatures that will dazle your eyes to look on them: There also you shall meet with thousands, and ten thousands that have gone before us to that place; none of them are hurtful, but loving, and holy; every one walking in the sight of God; and standing in his presence with acceptance for ever: In a word, there we shall see the Elders[32] with their Golden Crowns: There we shall see the Holy Virgins[33] with their Golden Harps. There we shall see Men[34] that by the World were cut in pieces, burnt in flames, eaten of Beasts, drowned in the Seas, for the love that they bare to the Lord of the place; all well, and cloathed with immortality,[35] as with a Garment.

Pli. *The hearing of this is enough to ravish ones heart; but are these things to be enjoyed? how shall we get to be sharers hereof?*

Chr. The Lord, the Governor of that Country, hath recorded *that* in this Book:[36] The substance of which is, if we be truly willing to have it, he will bestow it upon us freely.

Pli. *Well, my good Companion, glad am I to hear of these things: Come on, let us mend our pace.*

Chr. I cannot go so fast as I would, by reason of this burden that is on my back.

Now I saw in my Dream, that just as they had ended this talk, they drew near to a very *Miry Slough* that was in the midst of the Plain, and they being heedless, did both fall suddenly into the bog. The name of the Slow was *Dispond.* Here therefore they wallowed for a time, being grievously bedaubed with the dirt; And *Christian,* because of the burden that was on his back, began to sink in the Mire.

Pli. *Then said* Pliable, *Ah, Neighbor* Christian, *where are you now?*

Chr. Truly, said *Christian,* I do not know.

Pli. At that *Pliable* began to be offended; and angerly, said to his fellow, *Is this the happiness you have told me all this while of? if we have such ill speed at our first setting out, What may we expect, 'twixt this and our journeys end?*[37] *May I get out again with my life, you shall possess the brave Country alone for me.* And with that he gave a desperate struggle or two, and got out of the Mire, on that side of the Slough which was next to his own house: So away he went, and *Christian* saw him no more.

Wherefore *Christian* was left to tumble in the Slough of *Dispond* alone; but still he endeavoured to struggle to that side of the Slough, that was still further from his own House,[38] and next to the Wicket-gate; the which he did, but could not get out, because of the burden that was upon his back: But I beheld in my Dream, that a Man came to him, whose name was *Help,* and asked him, *What he did there?*

Chr. Sir, said *Christian,* I was bid go this way, by a Man called *Evangelist,* who directed me also to yonder Gate, that I might escape the wrath to come: And as I was going thither, I fell in here.

Help. *But why did you not look for the steps?*[39]

Chr. *Fear* followed me so hard, that I fled the next way, and fell in.

Help. *Then,* said he, *Give me thy hand;*[40] *so he gave him his hand,* and he drew him out,[41] and set him upon sound ground, and bid him go on his way.

Then I stepped to him that pluckt him out, and said; Sir, Wherefore, since over this place is the way from the City of *Destruction,* to yonder *Gate,* is it, that *this* Plat is not mended, that poor Travellers might go thither with more security? And he said unto me, this *Miry*

---

31 Isa. 6:2; I Thess. 4:16,17; Rev. 5:11.
32 Rev. 4:4.
33 [Rev.] Chap. 14:1,2,3,4,5.
34 John 12:25.
35 II Cor. 5:2,3,5.
36 Isa. 55:12; John 7:37; 6:37; Rev. 21:6; 22:17.

37 It is not enough to be pliable.
38 Christian in trouble, seeks still to get further from his own House.
39 The Promises.
40 Help lifts him out.
41 Ps. 40:2.

slow, is such a place as cannot be mended: It is the descent whither the scum and filth that attends conviction for sin[42] doth continually run, and therefore is it called the *Slough of Dispond:* for still as the sinner is awakened about his lost condition, there ariseth in his soul many fears, and doubts, and discouraging apprehensions, which all of them get together, and settle in this place: And this is the reason of the badness of this ground.

It is not the pleasure of the King[43] that this place should remain so bad; his Laborers also, have by the direction of His Majesties Surveyors, been for above this sixteen hundred years, imployed about this patch of ground, if perhaps it might have been mended: yea, and to my knowledge, said he, *Here* hath been swallowed up, at least, twenty thousand Cart loads; yea millions of wholesome Instructions, that have at all seasons been brought from all places of the Kings Dominions; (and they that can tell, say, they are the best materials to make good ground of the place,) If so be it might have been mended, but it is the *Slough of Dispond* still; and so will be, when they have done what they can.

True, there are by the direction of the Law-giver, certain good and substantial steps,[44] placed even through the very midst of this *Slough;* but at such time as this place doth much spue out its filth, as it doth against change of Weather, these steps are hardly seen; or if they be, men through the dizziness of their Heads, step besides; and then they are bemired to purpose, notwithstanding the steps be there; but the ground is good[45] when they are once got in at the Gate.

Now I saw in my Dream, that by this time *Pliable*[46] was got home to his House again. So his Neighbors came to visit him;[47] and some of them called him wise Man for coming back; and some called him Fool for hazarding himself with *Christian;* others again did mock at his Cowardliness; saying, Surely since you began to venture, I would not have been so base to have given out for a few difficulties. So *Pliable* sat sneaking among them. But at last he got more confidence, and then they all turned their tables, and began to deride poor *Christian* behind his back. And thus much concerning *Pliable.*

Now as Christian was walking solitary by himself, he espied one afar off, come crossing over the field to met him;[48] and their hap was to meet *just as they were crossing the way of each other.* The Gentleman's name was, Mr. *Worldly-Wiseman,* he dwelt in the Town of *Carnal-Policy,* a very great Town, and also hard by, from whence Christian came. This man then meeting with Christian, and having some inckling of him, for Christians setting forth from the City of *Destruction,* was much noised abroad, not only in the Town where he dwelt, but also it began to be the *Town*-talk in some other places, Master *Worldly-Wiseman* therefore, having some guess of him, by beholding his laborious going, by observing his sighs and groans, and the like; began thus to enter into some talk with *Christian.*

World. *How now, good fellow, whither away after this burdened manner?*[49]

Chr. A burdened manner indeed, as ever, I think, poor creature had. And whereas you ask me, *Whither away,* I tell you, Sir, I am going to yonder Wicket-gate before me; for there, as I am informed, I shall be put into a way to be rid of my heavy burden.

Worl. *Hast thou a Wife and Children?*

Chr. Yes, but I am so laden with this burden, that I cannot take that pleasure in them as formerly: methinks, I am as if I had none.[50]

Worl. *Wilt thou hearken to me, if I give thee counsel?*

---

[42] What makes the Slough of Dispond.

[43] Isa. 35:3,4.

[44] The Promises of forgiveness and acceptance to life by Faith in Christ.

[45] I Sam. 12:23.

[46] Plyable got home, and is visited of his Neighbors.

[47] His entertainment by them at his return.

[48] Mr. Worldly-Wiseman meets with Christian.

[49] Talk betwixt Mr. Worldly-Wiseman and Christian.

[50] I Cor. 7:29.

Chr. If it be good, I will; for I stand in need of good counsel.

Worl.[51] *I would advise thee then, that thou with all speed get thy self rid of thy burden; for thou wilt never be settled in thy mind till then: nor canst thou enjoy the benefits of the blessing which God hath bestowed upon thee till then.*

Chr. That is that which I seek for, even to be rid of this heavy burden; but get it off my self I cannot: nor is there a man in our Country that can take it off my shoulders; therefore am I going this way, as I told you, that I may be rid of my burden.

Worl. *Who bid thee go this way to be rid of thy burden?*

Chr. A man that appeared to me to be a very great and honorable person; his name, as I remember is *Evangelist.*

Worl.[52] *I beshrow him for his counsel; there is not a more dangerous and troublesome way in the world, then is that unto which he hath directed thee; and that thou shalt find, if thou wilt be ruled by his counsel: Thou hast met with something (as I perceive) already; for I see the dirt of the* Slough of Dispond *is upon thee; but that Slough is the beginning of the sorrows that do attend those that go on in that way: hear me, I am older than thou! thou art like to meet with in the way which thou goest, Wearisomeness, Painfulness, Hunger, Perils, Nakedness, Sword, Lions, Dragons, Darkness; and in a word, death, and what not? These things are certainly true, having been confirmed by many testimonies. And why should a man so carelessly cast away himself, by giving heed to a stranger.*

Chr. Why, Sir, this burden upon my back is more terrible to me than are all these things which you have mentioned:[53] nay, methinks I care not what I meet with in the way, so be I can also meet with deliverance from my burden.

Worl. *How camest thou by the burden at first?*

Chr. By reading this Book in my hand.

Worl.[54] *I thought so; and it is happened unto thee as to other weak men, who meddling with things too high for them, do suddenly fall into thy distractions; which distractions do not only unman men, (as thine I perceive has done thee) but they run them upon desperate ventures, to obtain they know not what.*

Chr. I know what I would obtain. it is ease for my heavy burden.

Worl. *But why wilt thou seek for ease this way, seeing so many dangers attend it, especially, since (hadst thou but patience to hear me) I could direct thee to the obtaining of what thou desirest, without the dangers that thou in this way wilt run thy self into: yea, and the remedy is at hand. Besides, I will add, that instead of those dangers, thou shalt meet with much safety, friendship, and content.*

Chr. Pray Sir open this secret to me.

Worl.[55] *Why in yonder Village, (the Village is named* Morality) *there dwells a Gentleman, whose name is Legality, a very judicious man (and a man of a very good name) that has skill to help men off with such burdens as thine are, from their shoulders: yea, to my knowledge he hath done a great deal of good this way: Ai, and besides, he hath skill to cure those that are somewhat crazed in their wits with their burdens. To him, as I said, thou mayest go, and be helped presently. His house is not quite a mile from this place; and if he should not be at home himself, he hath a pretty young man to his Son, whose name is* Civility, *that can do it (to speak on) as well as the old Gentleman himself: There, I say, thou mayest be eased of thy burden, and if thou art not minded to go back to thy former habitation, as indeed I would not wish thee, thou mayest send for thy wife and Children to thee to this Village, where there are houses now stand empty, one of*

---

[51] Mr. Worldly-Wiseman, Counsel to Christian.

[52] Mr. Worldly-Wiseman Condemned Evangelists Counsel.

[53] The frame of the heart of young Christians.

[54] Worldly-Wiseman does not like that Men should be serious in reading the Bible.

[55] Whether Mr. Worldly-Wiseman prefers Morality before the Straight Gate.

which thou mayest have at reasonable rates: *Provision is there also cheap and good, and that which will make thy life the more happy, is, to be sure there thou shalt live by honest neighbors, in credit and good fashion.*

Now[56] was *Christian* somewhat at a stand, but presently he concluded; if this be true which this Gentleman hath said, my wisest course is to take his advice, and with that he thus farther spoke.

Chr. Sir, which is my way to this honest man's house?

Worl. *Do you see yonder high hill?*[57]

Chr. Yes, very well.

Worl. By that *Hill* you must go, and the first house you come at, is his.

So *Christian* turned out of his way to go to Mr. *Legality's* house for help: but behold, when he was got, now, hard by the *Hill,* it seemed so high, and also, that side of it that was next the way side, did hang so much over, that Christian was afraid to venture further,[58] lest the *Hill* should fall on his head: wherefore there he stood still, and wotted not what to do. Also his burden, *now,* seemed heavier to him, than while he was in his way. There came also flashes of fire[59] out of the Hill, that made *Christian* afraid that he should be burned:[60] here therefore he swet, and did quake for fear.[61] And now he began to be sorry that he had taken Mr. *Worldly-Wisemans* counsel; and with that he saw *Evangelist* coming to meet him;[62] at the sight also of whom he began to blush for shame. So *Evangelist* drew nearer, and nearer, and coming up to him, he looked upon him with a severe and dreadful countenance: and thus began to reason with *Christian.*

Evan.[63] What doest thou here? said he: at which word *Christian* knew not what to answer: wherefore, at present he stood speechless before him. Then said *Evangelist* farther, *Art not thou the man that I found crying, without the walls of the City of* Destruction?

Chr. Yes, dear Sir, I am the man.

Evan. *Did not I direct thee the way to the little Wicket-gate?*

Chr. Yes, dear Sir said *Christian.*

Evan. *How is it then that thou art so quickly turned aside, for thou art now out of the way?*

Chr. I met with a Gentleman, so soon as I had got over the *Slough of Dispond,* who perswaded me, that I might in the *Village* before me, find a man that could take off my burden.

Evan. *What was he?*

Chr. He looked like a Gentleman, and talked much to me, and got me at last to yield; so I came hither: but when I beheld this Hill, and how it hangs over the way, I suddenly made a stand, lest it should fall on my head.

Evan. *What said that Gentleman to you?*

Chr. Why, he asked me whither I was going, and I told him.

Evan. *And what said he then?*

Chr. He asked me if I had a Family, and I told him: but, said I, I am so loaden with the burden that is on my back, that I cannot take pleasure in them as formerly.

Evan. *And what said he then?*

Chr. He bid me with speed get rid of my burden, and I told him 'twas ease that I sought: And said I, I am therefore going to yonder *Gate* to receive further direction how I may get to the place of deliverance. So he said that he would shew me a better way, and short, not so attended with difficulties, as the way, Sir, that you set me: which way, said he, will direct you to a Gentleman's house that hath skill to take off these burdens: So I believed him, and turned out of that way into this, if haply I might be soon eased of my burden: but when I came to this place, and beheld things as they are, I stopped for fear, (as I said) of danger: but I now know not what to do.

Evan. *Then* (said Evangelist) *stand*

---

[56] Christian Snared by Mr. Worldly-Wisemans Word.

[57] Mount Sinai.

[58] Christian afraid that Mount Sinai would fall on his head.

[59] Exod. 19:18.

[60] [Exod. 19] Ver. 16.

[61] Heb. 12:11.

[62] Evangelist findeth Christian under Mount Sinai and looketh severely upon him.

[63] Evangelist reasons afresh with Christian.

still a little, that I may shew thee the words of God. So he stood trembling. *Then* (said Evangelist)[64] *See that ye refuse not him that speaketh; for if they escaped not who refused him that spake on Earth,[65] much more shall not we escape, if we turn away from him that speaketh from Heaven. He said moreover,[66] Now the just shall live by faith; but if any man draws back, my soul shall have no pleasure in him. He also did thus apply them, Thou art the man that art running into this misery, thou hast began to reject the counsel of the most high, and to draw back thy foot from the way of peace, even almost to the hazarding of thy perdition.*

Then *Christian* fell down at his foot as dead, crying, Wo is me, for I am undone: at the sight of which *Evangelist* caught him by the right hand, saying,[67] all manner of sin and blasphemies shall be forgiven unto men; be not faithless, but believing; then did *Christian* again a little revive, and stood up trembling, as at first, before *Evangelist.*

Then *Evangelist* proceeded, saying, *Give more earnest heed to the things that I shall tell thee of.* I will now shew thee who it was that deluded thee, and who 'twas also to whom he sent thee. The man that met thee, is one *Worldly-Wiseman,* and rightly is he so called;[68] partly, because he favoureth only the Doctrine of this World[69] (therefore he always goes to the Town of *Morality* to church) and partly because he loveth that Doctrine best, for it saveth him from the Cross;[70] and because he is of this carnal temper, therefore he seeketh to prevent my ways, though right. Now there are three things in this mans counsel that thou must utterly abhor.[71]

1. His turning thee out of the way.
2. His labouring to render the Cross odious to thee.

3. And his setting thy feet in that way that leadeth unto the administration of Death.

First, Thou must abhor his turning thee out of the way; yea, and thine own consenting thereto: because this is to reject the counsel of God, for the sake of the counsel of a *Worldly-Wiseman.* The Lord says,[72] *Strive to enter in at the strait gate,* the gate to which I send thee; *for strait is the gate that leadeth unto life, and few there be that find it.* From this little wicket-gate, and from the way thereto, hath this wicked man turned thee, to the bringing of thee almost to destruction; hate therefore his turning thee out of the way, and abhor thy self for harkning to him.

Secondly, Thou must abhor his labouring to render the Cross odious unto thee; for thou art to *prefer it before the treasures in Egypt:[73]* besides the King of Glory hath told thee, that he that will save his life shall lose it:[74] and *he that comes after him, and hates not his father and mother, and wife, and children, and brethren, and sisters; yea, and his own life also, he cannot be my Disciple.[75]* I say therefore, for a man to labour to perswade thee, that that shall be thy death, without which the truth hath said, thou canst not have eternal life, this Doctrine thou must abhor.

Thirdly, thou must hate his setting of thy feet in the way that leadeth to the ministration of death. And for this thou must consider to whom he sent thee, and also how unable that person was to deliver thee from thy burden.

He to whom thou wast sent for ease, being by name *Legality,* is the Son of the Bond woman[76] which now is, and is in bondage with her children, and is in a mystery[77] this Mount *Sinai,* which thou hast feared will fall on thy head. Now if she with her children are in bondage,

---

[64] Heb. 12:25.
[65] Evangelist convinces Christian of his Error.
[66] [Heb.] Chap. 10:38.
[67] Matt. 12; Mark 3.
[68] Mr. Worldly-Wiseman discribed by Evangelist.
[69] I John 4:5.
[70] I Cor. 6:12.

[71] Evangelist discovers the deceit of Mr. Worldly-Wiseman.
[72] Luke 13:24; Matt. 7:13,14.
[73] Heb. 11:25,26.
[74] Mark 8:34; John 13:25; Matt. 10:39.
[75] Luke 14:26.
[76] Gal. 4:21,22,23,24,25,26,27.
[77] The Bond-Woman.

how canst thou expect by them to be made free? This *Legality* therefore is not able to set thee free from thy burden. No man was as yet ever rid of his burden by him, no, nor ever is like to be: ye cannot be justified by the works of the Law; for by the deeds of the Law no man living can be rid of his burden: therefore Mr. *Worldly-Wiseman* is an alien, and Mr. *Legality* a cheat: and for his Son *Civility,* notwithstanding his simpering looks, he is but an hypocrite, and cannot help thee. Believe me, there is nothing in all this noise, that thou hast heard of this scottish man, but a design to beguile thee of thy Salvation, by turning thee from the way in which I had set thee. After this *Evangelist* called aloud to the Heavens for confirmation of what he had said; and with that there came words and fire out of the Mountain under which poor Christian stood, that made the hair of his flesh stand. The words were thus pronounced, *As many as are of the works of the Law, are under the curse; for it is written, Cursed is every one that continueth not in all things which are written in the Book of the Law to do them.*[78]

Now *Christian* looked for nothing but death, and began to cry out lamentably, even cursing the time in which he met with Mr. *Worldly-Wiseman,* still calling himself a thousand fools for hearkening to his counsel: he also was greatly ashamed to think that this Gentlemans arguments, flowing only from the flesh, should have that prevalency with him as to cause him to forsake the right way. This done, he applied himself again to *Evangelist* in words and sense as follows.

Chr.[79] Sir, what think you? is there hopes? may I now go back and go up to the *Wicket gate,* shall I not be abandoned for this, and sent back from thence ashamed. I am sorry I have hearkened to this man's counsel, but may my sin be forgiven.

Evang. Then said *Evangelist* to him, Thy sin is very great, for by it thou hast committed two evils; thou hast forsaken the way that is good, to tread in forbidden paths: yet will the man at the Gate receive thee, for he has *good will* for men;[80] only, said he, take heed that thou turn not aside again, lest thou perish from the way when his wrath is kindled but a little. Then did *Christian* address himself to go back, and *Evangelist,* after he had kist him, gave him one smile, and bid him God speed; so he went on with hast, neither spake he to any man by the way; nor if any man asked him, would he vouchsafe them an answer. He went like one that was all the while treading on forbidden ground, and could by no means think himself safe, till again he was got into the way which he left to follow Mr. *Worldly-Wiseman's* counsel: so in process of time *Christian* got up to the Gate. Now over the Gate there was Written, *Knock and it shall be opened unto you.*[81] He knocked therefore more than once or twice, saying,

May I now enter here? will he within
Open to sorry me, though I have been
An undeserving Rebel? then shall I,
Not fail to sing his lasting praise on high.

At last there came a grave person to the Gate: named *Good-will,* who asked, *Who was there? and whence he came? and what he would have?*

Chr. Here is a poor burdened sinner, I come from the City of *Destruction,* but am going to Mount *Zion,* that I may be delivered from the wrath to come; I would therefore, Sir, since I am informed that by this Gate is the way thither, know if you are *willing* to let me in.

Good-Will.[82] I am *willing* with all my heart, said he; and with that he opened the Gate.

So when *Christian* was slepping in, the other gave him a pull: Then said *Christian,* what means that? The other told him, a little distance from this Gate, there is erected a strong Castle, of which

---

[78] Gal. 3:10.
[79] Christian Enquired if he may yet be Happy.
[80] Evangelist comforts him.

[81] Matt. 7:8.
[82] The Gate will be opened to broken-hearted sinners.

Belzebub is the Captain:[83] from thence both he, and them that are with him, shoot arrows at those that come up to this Gate; if happily they may die before they can enter in. Then, said *Christian,*[84] I rejoyce and tremble. So when he was got in, the man of the Gate asked him, Who directed him thither?

Chr.[85] *Evangelist* bid me come hither and knock, (as I did;) And he said, that you, Sir, would tell me what I must do.

Good Will. *An open Door is set before thee, and no man can shut it.*

Chr. Now I begin to reap the benefits of my hazards.

Good Will. *But how is it that you came alone?*

Chr. Because none of my Neighbors saw their danger as I saw mine.

Good Will. *Did any of them know of your coming?*

Chr. Yes, my Wife and Children saw me at the first, and called after me to turn again: Also some of my Neighbors stood crying, and calling after me to return; but I put my Fingers in mine Ears, and so came on my way.

Good Will. *But did none of them follow you to perswade you to go back?*

Chr. Yes, both *Obstinate,* and *Pliable:* But when they saw that they could not prevail, *Obstinate* went railing back; but *Pliable* came with me a little way.

Good Will. *But why did he not come through?*

Chr. We indeed came both together, until we came at the *Slough of Dispond,* into the which, we also suddenly fell. And then was my Neighbor *Pliable* discouraged, and would not adventure further. Wherefore getting out again,[86] on *that side* next to his own house; he told me, I should possess the brave Country alone for him: So he went *his* way, and I came *mine.* He after *Obstinate,* and I to this Gate.

Good Will. Then said *Good Will,* Alas poor man, is the Cœlestial Glory of so small esteem with him, that he counteth it not worth running the hazards of a few difficulties to obtain it?

Chr. Truly, said *Christian,* I have said the truth of *Pliable,* and if I should also say all the truth of my self, it will appear[87] there is no betterment 'twixt him and my self. 'Tis true, he went back to his own house, but I also turned aside to go in the way of death, being perswaded thereto by the carnal arguments of one Mr. *Worldly Wiseman.*

Good Will. Oh, did he light upon you! what, he would have had you a sought for ease at the hands of Mr. *Legality;* they are both of them a very cheat: but did you take his counsel?

Chr. Yes, as far as I durst, I went to find out Mr. *Legality,* until I thought that the Mountain that stands by his house, would have fallen upon my head: wherefore there I was forced to stop.

Good Will. That Mountain has been the death of many, and will be the death of many more: 'tis well you escaped being by it dasht in pieces.

Chr. Why, truly I do not know what had become of me there, had not *Evangelist* happily met me again as I was musing in the midst of my *dumps:* but 'twas Gods mercy that he came to me again, for else I had never come hither. But now I am come, such a one as I am, more fit indeed for death by that Mountain, than thus to stand talking with my Lord: But Oh, what a favour is this to me, that yet I am admitted entrance here.

Good Will.[88] We make no objections against any, notwithstanding all that they have done before they come hither, *they in no wise are cast out;*[89] and therefore, good *Christian,* come a little way with me, and I will teach thee about the way thou must go. Look before thee;[90] dost thou see this narrow way? *THAT* is the way thou must go. It was cast up by the Patriarchs, Prophets,

---

[83] Satan envies those that enter the straight Gate.

[84] Christian Entred the Gate with Joy and trembling.

[85] Talk between Good Will and Christian.

[86] A man may have company when he sets out for Heaven, and yet go thither alone.

[87] Christian accuseth himself before the man at the Gate.

[88] Christian is comforted again.

[89] John 6:37.

[90] Christian directed yet on his way.

Christ, and his Apostles, and it is as straight as a *Rule* can make it: This is the way thou must go.

Chr. But said *Christian, is there no turnings nor windings, by which a Stranger may*[91] *lose the way?*

Good Will. Yes, there are many ways *BUTT* down upon this; and they are crooked, and wide: But *thus* thou may'st distinguish the right from the wrong, *The* right only being straight and narrow.[92]

Then I saw in my Dream,[93] That Christian asked him further, If he could not help him off with his burden that was upon his back; for as yet he had not got rid thereof, nor could he by any means get it off without help.

He told him, As to thy burden, be content to bear it, until thou comest to the *place* of Deliverance;[94] for there it will fall from thy back it self.

Then *Christian* began to gird up his loins, and to address himself to his Journey. So the other told him, that by that he was gone some distance from the Gate, he would come at the house of the *Interpreter,* at whose Door he should knock; and he would shew him excellent things. Then *Christian* took his leave of his Friend, and he again bid him God speed.

Then he went on, till he came at the house of the *Interpreter,*[95] where he *knocked* over, and over: at last one came to the dore, and asked *Who was there?*

Chr. Sir, here is a Traveller, who was bid by an acquaintance of the Goodman of this House, to call here for my profit: I would therefore speak with the Master of the House: so he called for the Master of the House; who after a little time came to *Christian,* and asked him what he would have?

Chr. Sir, said *Christian,* I am a Man that am come from the City of *Destruction,* and am going to the Mount *Zion,* and I was told by the Man that stands at the Gate, at the head of this way; that if I called here, you would shew me excellent things, such as would be an help to me in my Journey.

Inter. Then said the *Interpreter,*[96] come in, I will shew thee that which will be profitable to thee. So he commanded his man to light the Candle,[97] and bid *Christian* follow him; so he had him into a private Room, and bid his Man open a door; the which when he had done, *Christian* saw a Picture[98] of a very grave Person hang up against the wall, and this was the fashion of it,[99] *It had eyes lift up to Heaven, the best of Books in his hand, the Law of Truth was written upon its lips, the World was behind his back; it stood as if it pleaded with Men, and a Crown of Gold did hang over its head.*

Chr. *Then said* Christian, *What means this?*

Inter. The Man whose Picture this is, is one of a thousand, he can beget Children,[100] Travel in birth with Children, and Nurse them himself when they are born.[101] And whereas thou seest him with his eyes lift up to Heaven, the best of Books in his hand, and the Law of Truth writ on his Lips: it is to shew thee, that his work is to know, and unfold dark things to sinners; even as also thou seest[102] him stand as if he pleaded with Men: And whereas thou seest the World as cast behind him, and that a Crown hangs over his head; that is, to shew thee, that slighting, and dispising the things that are present, for the love that he hath to his Masters service, he is sure in the world that comes next, to have Glory for his Reward: Now, said the *Interpreter,* I have shewed thee *this* Picture first,[103] because the Man whose Picture this is, is the only Man, whom the Lord of the Place whither thou art going, hath authorized, to be thy Guide in all difficult places thou mayest meet

---

[91] Christian afraid of losing his way.

[92] Matt. 7:14.

[93] Christian weary of his Burden.

[94] There is no deliverance from the guilt, and burden of sin, but by the Death and Blood of Christ.

[95] Christian comes to the House of the Interpreter.

[96] He is entertained.

[97] Illumination.

[98] Christian sees a brave Picture.

[99] The fashion of the Picture.

[100] I Cor. 4:15.

[101] Gal. 4:19.

[102] The meaning of the Picture.

[103] Why he shewed him the Picture first.

with in the way: wherefore take good heed to what I have shewed thee, and bear well in thy mind what thou hast seen; lest in thy Journey, thou meet with some that pretend to lead thee right, but their way goes down to death.

Then he took him by the hand, and led him into a very large *Parlour* that was full of dust, because never swept; the which, after he had reviewed a little while, the *Interpreter* called for a man to *sweep:* Now when he began to sweep, the dust began so abundantly to fly about, that *Christian* had almost therewith been choaked: Then said the *Interpreter* to a *Damsel* that stood by, Bring hither the Water, and sprinkle the Room; the which when she had done, it was swept, and cleansed with pleasure.

Chr. Then said Christian, *What means this?*

Int. The *Interpreter* answered; This Parlor, is the heart of a Man that was never sanctified by the sweet Grace of the Gospel: The *dust,* is his Original Sin, and inward Corruptions that have defiled the whole Man. He that began to sweep at first, is the Law; but she that brought water, and did sprinkle it, is the Gospel: Now, whereas thou sawest that so soon as the first began to sweep, the dust did so fly about, that the Room by him could not be cleansed but that thou wast almost choaked therewith. This is to shew thee, that the Law, instead of cleansing the heart (by its working) from sin,[104] doth revive, put strength into,[105] and increase it in the soul,[106] even as it doth discover and forbid it, for it doth not give power to subdue.

Again, as thou sawest the *Damsel* sprinkle the Room with Water, upon which it was cleansed with pleasure: This is to shew thee, that when the Gospel comes in the sweet and precious influences thereof to the heart, then I say, even as thou sawest the Damsel lay the dust by sprinkling the Floor with Water, so is sin vanquished and subdued, and the

soul made clean, through the Faith of it; and consequently[107] fit for the King of Glory to inhabit.

I saw moreover in my Dream,[108] that the *Interpreter* took him by the hand, and had him into a little Room, where sat two little Children, each one in his Chair: The name of the eldest was *Passion,* and the name of the other, *Patience; Passion* seemed to be much discontent, but *Patience* was very quiet. Then *Christian* asked, What is the reason of the discontent of *Passion?*[109] The *Interpreter* answered, The Governor of them would have him stay for his best things till the beginning of the next year; but he will have all now: But[110] *Patience* is willing to wait.

Then I saw that one came to *Passion,*[111] and brought him a Bag of Treasure, and poured it down at his feet; the which he took up, and rejoyced therein, and withal, laughed *Patience* to scorn: But I beheld but a while, and he had lavished all away,[112] and had nothing left him but Rags.

Chr. Then said Christian *to the* Interpreter,[113] *Expound this matter more fully to me.*

Int. So he said, These two Lads are Figures; *Passion,* of the Men of *this* World; and *Patience,* of the Men of *that* which is to come: For as here thou seest, *Passion will have all now,* this year; that is to say, in *this* World; *So* are the Men of this World: they must have all their good things now, they cannot stay till next *Year;* that is, until the *next* World, for their Portion of good. That Proverb,[114] *A Bird in the hand is worth two in the Bush,* is of more Authority with them, then are all the Divine Testimonies of the good of the world to come. But as thou sawest, that he had quickly lavished all away, and had presently left him, nothing but Rags; So will it be with all such men at the end of this world.

Chr. Then said Christian; *Now I*

---

104 Rom. 7:6.
105 I Cor. 15:56.
106 Rom. 5:20.
107 John 15:3; Eph. 5:26; Acts 15:9; Rom. 16:25,26; John 15:13.
108 He shewed him Passion and Patience.

109 Passion will have it now.
110 Patience is for waiting.
111 Passion has his desire.
112 And quickly lavishes all away.
113 The matter expounded.
114 The Worldly man for a Bird in the hand.

see that Patience *has the best Wisdom,*[115] *and that upon many accounts.* 1. *Because he stays for the best things.* 2. *And also because he will have the glory of his, when the other hath nothing but rags.*

Int. Nay, you may add another; to wit, The glory of the *next* world will never wear out; but *these* are suddenly gone. Therefore *Passion* had not so much reason to laugh at *Patience,* because he had his good things first, as *Patience* will have to laugh at *Passion,*[116] because he had his best things *last;* for *first* must give place to *last,* because *last* must have his time to come but *last* gives place to *nothing;* for there is not another to succeed: he therefore that hath his portion *first,* must needs have a time to spend it; but he that has his portion *last,* must have it lastingly. Therefore it is said of *Dives,*[117] *In thy life thou receivedst thy good things, and likewise* Lazarus *evil things; but now he is comforted, and thou art tormented.*

Chr. *Then I perceive, 'tis not best to covet things that are now, but to wait for things to* come.

Int. You say Truth,[118] *For the things that are seen, are* Temporal; *but the things that are not see, are* Eternal: But though this be so, yet since things present, and our fleshly appetite, *are such near Neighbours one to another;* and again, because things to come, and carnal sense, are such strangers one to another: therefore it is, that the first of these so suddenly fall into *amity,* and that *distance* is so continued between the second.

Then I saw in my Dream, that the *Interpreter* took *Christian* by the hand, and led him into a place, where was a Fire burning against a Wall, and one standing by it, always casting much Water upon it to quench it: Yet did the Fire burn higher and hotter.

Then said Christian, *What means this?*

The *Interpreter* answered, This fire, is the work of Grace that is wrought in the heart; he that casts water upon it, to ex-

tinguish and put it out, is the *Devil:* but in that thou seest the fire, notwithstanding, burn higher and hotter, thou shalt also see the reason of that: So he had him about to the back-side of the Wall, where he saw a Man with a Vessel of Oyl in his hand, of the which he did also continually cast, (but secretly) into the Fire. Then said *Christian, What means this?* The *Interpreter* answered, This is *Christ,* who continually with the Oyl of his Grace, maintains the work already begun in the heart; by the means of which, notwithstanding what the Devil can do,[119] the souls of his people prove gracious still. And in that thou sawest, that the Man stood behind the Wall to maintain the fire; this is to teach thee, that it is hard for the tempted to see how this work of Grace is maintained in the soul.

I saw also that the *Interpreter* took him again by the hand, and led him into a pleasant place, where was builded a stately Palace, beautiful to behold; at the sight of which, *Christian* was greatly delighted; he saw also upon the top thereof, certain persons walking, who were cloathed all in gold. Then said *Christian,* May we go in thither? Then the *Interpreter* took him, and led him up toward the door of the Palace; and behold, at the door, stood a great company of men, as desirous to go in, but durst not. There also sat a Man, at a little distance from the door, at a Table-side, with a Book, and his Inkhorn before him, to take the Name of him that should enter therein: He saw also that in the door-way, stood many Men in armor to keep it, being resolved to do to the Men that would enter, what hurt and mischief they could. Now was *Christian* somwhat in a maze; at last, when every Man started back for fear of the armed men; *Christian* saw a man, of a very stout countenance, come up to the Man that sat there to write; saying,[120] *Set down my Name Sir;* the which when he had done, he saw the Man draw his Sword, and put an Hel-

---

[115] Patience had the best Wisdom.
[116] Things that are first must give place, but things that are last are lasting.
[117] Luke 16. Dives had his good things.
[118] II Cor. 4:18. The first things are but Temporal.
[119] II Cor. 12:9.
[120] The valiant man.

met upon his Head, and rush toward the door upon the armed men, who laid upon him with deadly force; but the Man, not at all discouraged, fell to cutting and hacking most fiercely; so after he had received and given many wounds[121] to those that attempted, to keep him out, he cut his way through them all, and pressed forward into the Palace; at which there was a pleasant voice heard from those that were within, even of those that walked upon the top of the Palace, saying,

Come in, Come in;
Eternal Glory thou shalt win.

So he went in, and was cloathed with such Garments as they. Then *Christian* smiled, and said, I think verily I know the meaning of this.

Now, said *Christian,* let me go hence: Nay stay (said the *Interpreter*) till I have shewed thee a little more, and after that, thou shalt go on thy way. So he took him by the hand again, and led him into a very dark Room, where there sat a Man in an Iron Cage.[122]

Now the Man, to look on, seemed very sad: he sat with his eyes looking down to the ground, his hands folded together; and he sighed as if he would break his heart. Then said *Christian, What means this?* At which the *Interpreter* bid him talk with the Man.

Chr. Then said *Christian* to the Man, *What art thou?* The Man answered, *I am what I was not once.*

Chr. *What wast thou once?*

Man. The *Man* said, I was once a fair and flourishing Professor,[123] both in mine own eyes, and also in the eyes of others: I once was, as I thought, fair for the Cœlestial City, and had then even joy at the thoughts that I should get thither.

Chr. *Well, but what art thou now?*

Man. I am now a Man of Dispair, and am shut up in *it,* as in *this* Iron Cage. I cannot get out; O *now* I cannot.

Chr. *But how camest thou in this condition?*

Man. I left off to watch, and be sober; I laid the reins upon the neck of my lusts; I sinned against the light of the Word, and the goodness of God: I have grieved the Spirit, and he is gone; I tempted the Devil, and he is come to me; I have provoked God to anger, and he has left me; I have so hardened my heart, that I *cannot* repent.

Then said *Christian* to the *Interpreter,* But is there no hopes for such a man as this? Ask him, said the *Interpreter.*

Chr. Then said *Christian, Is there no hope but you must be kept in this Iron Cage of Despair?*

Man. No, none at all.

Chr. *Why? The Son of the Blessed is very pitiful.*

Man. I have Crucified[124] him to my self afresh, I have despised his Person,[125] I have despised his Righteousness, I have counted his Blood an unholy thing, I have done despite to the Spirit of Grace:[126] Therefore I have shut my self out of all the Promises; and there now remains to me nothing but threatnings, dreadful threatnings, fearful threatnings of certain Judgement and firy Indignation, which shall devour me as an Adversary.

Chr. *For what did you bring your self into this condition?*

Man. For the Lusts, Pleasures, and Profits of this World; in the enjoyment of which, I did then promise my self much delight: but now even every one of those things also bite me, and gnaw me like a burning worm.

Chr. *But canst thou not now repent and turn?*

Man. God hath denied me repentance; his Word gives me no encouragement to believe; yea, himself hath shut me up in this Iron Cage: nor can all the men in the world let me out. O Eternity! Eternity! how shall I grapple with the misery that I must meet with in Eternity?

Int. Then said the *Interpreter* to *Christian,* Let this mans misery be remembred by thee, and be an everlasting caution to thee.

---

[121] Acts 14:22.
[122] Despair like an Iron Cage.
[123] Luke 8:13.

[124] Heb. 6:6.
[125] Luke 19:14.
[126] Heb. 10:28,29.

Chr. Well, said *Christian,* this is fearfull; God help me to watch and be sober; and to pray, that I may shun the cause of this mans misery. Sir, is it not time for me to go on my way now?

Int. Tarry till I shall shew thee one thing more, and then thou shalt go on thy way.

So he took *Christian* by the hand again, and led him into a Chamber, where there was one a rising out of Bed; and as he put on his Rayment, he shook and trembled. Then said *Christian,* Why doth this man thus tremble? The *Interpreter* then bid him tell to *Christian* the reason of his so doing: So he began, and said, This night as I was in my sleep, I Dreamed, and behold the Heavens grew exceeding black; also it thundred and lightned in most fearful wise, that it put me into an Agony. So I looked up in my Dream,[127] and saw the Clouds rack at an unusual rate, upon which I heard a great sound of a Trumpet, and saw also a Man sit upon a Cloud, attended with the thousands of Heaven; they were all in flaming fire, also the Heavens were on a burning flame. I heard then a voice, saying, *Arise ye Dead, and come to Judgment;* and with that the Rocks rent, the Graves opened, and the Dead that were therein came forth; some of them were exceeding glad, and looked upward; and some sought to hide themselves under the Mountains: Then I saw the Man that sat upon the Cloud, open the Book; and bid the World draw near. Yet there was by reason of a fierce flame[128] that issued out and came from before him, a convenient distance betwixt him and them, as betwixt the Judge and the Prisoners at the Bar. I heard it also proclaimed to them that attended on the Man that sat on the Cloud,[129] *Gather together the Tares, the Chaff, and Stubble, and cast them into the burning Lake;* and with that the bottomless pit opened, just whereabout I stood; out of the mouth of which there came in an abundant manner smoke, and Coals of fire, with hideous noises. It was also said to the same persons[130] *Gather my Wheat into the Garner.* And with that I saw many catch'd up[131] and carried away into the Clouds, but I was left behind. I also sought to hide my self, but I could not; for the Man that sat upon the Cloud, still kept his eye upon me: my sins also came into mind,[132] and my Conscience did accuse me on every side. Upon this I awaked from my sleep.

Chr. *But what was it that made you so afraid of this sight?*

Man. Why, I thought that the day of Judgment was come, and that I was not ready for it: but this frighted me most, that the Angels gathered up several, and left me behind; also the pit of Hell opened her mouth just where I stood: my Conscience too within afflicted me; and (as I thought,) the Judge had always his eye upon me, shewing indignation in his countenance.

Then said the *Interpreter* to *Christian, Hast thou considered all these things?*

Chr. Yes, and they put me in *hope* and *fear.*

Int. Well, keep all things so in thy mind, that they may be as a *Goad* in thy sides, to prick thee forward in the way thou must go. Then *Christian* began to gird up his loins, and to address himself to his Journey. Then said the *Interpreter,* The Comforter be always with thee good *Christian,* to guide thee in the way that leads to the City.

So *Christian* went on his way, saying,

Here I have seen things rare, and profitable;
Things pleasant, dreadful, things to make me stable
In what I have began to take in hand:
Then let me think on them, and understand
Wherefore they shewed me was, and let me be
Thankful, O good Interpreter, to thee.

---

[127] I Cor. 15; I Thess. 4; Jude 15; II Thess. 1:8; John 5:28; Rev. 20:11,12,13,14; Isa. 26:21; Mic. 7:16,17; Ps. 5:1,2,3; Dan. 7:10.
[128] Mal. 3:2,3; Dan. 7:9,10.
[129] Matt. 3:13; 13:30; Mal. 4:1.
[130] Luke 3:17.
[131] I Thess. 4:16,17.
[132] Rom. 2:14,15.

Sir William Temple
1628-1699

AN ESSAY UPON THE ANCIENT AND MODERN LEARNING
1690

Whoever converses much among the old Books, will be something hard to please among the New; yet these must have their Part too in the Leisure of an idle Man, and have many of them their Beauties as well as their Defaults. Those of Story or Relations of Matter of Fact, have a Value from their Substance, as much as from their Form; and the Variety of Events, is seldom without Entertainment or Instruction, how indifferently soever the Tale is told. Other Sorts of Writings have little of Esteem, but what they receive from the Wit, Learning, or Genius of the Authors, and are seldom met with of any Excellency, because they do but trace over the Paths that have been beaten by the Ancients, or Comment, Critick and Flourish upon them; and are at best but Copies after those Originals, unless upon Subjects never touched by them; such as are all that relate to the different Constitutions of Religions, Laws, or Governments in several Countries, with all Matters of Controversy that arise upon them.

Two Pieces that have lately pleased me (abstracted from any of these Subjects) are, one in *English* upon the *Antideluvian* World;[1] and another in *French* upon the *Plurality of Worlds*;[2] one writ by a Divine, and the other by a Gentleman, but both very finely in their several Kinds, and upon their several Subjects, which would have made very poor work in common Hands: I was so pleased with the last (I mean the Fashion of it, rather than the Matter, which is old and beaten) that I enquired for what else I could of the same hand, till I met with a small Piece concerning Poesy,[3] which gave me the same Exception to both these Authors, whom I should otherwise have been very partial to. For the first could not end his Learned Treatise without a Panegyrick of Modern Learning and Knowledge in comparison of the Ancient: And the other falls so grosly into the censure of the old Poetry and Preference of the new, that I could not read either of these Strains, without some Indignation, which no Quality among Men is so apt to raise in me as Sufficiency, the worst Composition out of the Pride and Ignorance of Mankind. But these two, being not the only Persons of the Age that defend these Opinions, it may be worth examining how far either Reason or Experience can be allowed to plead or determine in their Favour.

Text from *The Works of Sir William Temple* (London, 1720), I, 151–169.

[1] Thomas Burnet (1635?–1715), *Sacred Theory of the Earth* (1684–1689).

[2] Bernard le Bovier de Fontenelle (1657–1757), *Entretiens sur la pluralité des mondes* (1686).

[3] Fontenelle *Poésies Pastorelles* (1688).

The Force of all that I have met with upon this Subject, either in Talk or Writing is, first, as to Knowledge; that we must have more than the Ancients, because we have the Advantage both of theirs and our own, which is commonly illustrated by the Similitude of a Dwarf's standing upon a Gyant's Shoulders, and seeing more or farther than he. Next as to Wit or Genius, that Nature being still the same, these must be much at a Rate in all Ages, at least in the same Climates, as the Growth and Size of Plants and Animals commonly are; and if both these are allowed, they think the Cause is gained. But I cannot tell why we should conclude, that the Ancient Writers had not as much Advantage from the Knowledge of others, that were Ancient to them, as we have from those that are Ancient to us. The Invention of Printing has not perhaps multiplied Books, but only the Copies of them; and if we believe there were Six Hundred Thousand in the Library of *Ptolomy*,[4] we shall hardly pretend to equal it by any of ours, not, perhaps, by all put together; I mean so many Originals, that have lived any Time, and thereby given Testimony of their having been thought worth preserving. For the Scribblers are infinite, that like Mushrooms or Flies, are born and die in small circles of time; whereas Books, like Proverbs, receive their chief Value from the Stamp and Esteem of Ages through which they have passed. Besides the Account of this Library at *Alexandria,* and others very Voluminous in the lesser *Asia* and *Rome,* we have frequent mention of Ancient Writers in many of those Books which we now call Ancient, both Philosophers and Historians. 'Tis true, that besides what we have in Scripture concerning the Original and Progress of the *Jewish* Nation; all that passed in the rest of our World before the *Trojan* War, is either sunk in the Depths of Time, wrapt up in the Mysteries of Fables, or so maimed by the Want of Testimonies and loss of

Authors, that it appears to us in too obscure a Shade, to make any Judgment upon it. For the Fragments of *Manethon*[5] about the Antiquities of Ægypt, the Relations in *Justin*[6] concerning the *Scythian* Empire, and many others in *Herodotus* and *Diodorus Siculus,*[7] as well as the Records of *China,* make such Excursions beyond the Periods of Time given us by the Holy Scriptures, that we are not allowed to reason upon them. And this Disagreement it self, after so great a Part of the World became Christian, may have contributed to the Loss of many Ancient Authors. For *Solomon* tells us even in his Time, of Writing many Books there was no End; and whoever considers the Subject and the Stile of *Job,* which by many is thought more Ancient than *Moses,* will hardly think it was written in an Age or Country that wanted either Books or Learning; and yet he speaks of the Ancients then, and their Wisdom, as we do now.

But if any should so very rashly and presumptuously conclude, that there were few Books before those we have either Extant or upon Record; yet that cannot argue there was no Knowledge or Learning before those Periods of Time, whereof they give us the short Account. Books may be Helps to Learning and Knowledge, and make it more common and diffused; but I doubt, whether they are necessary ones or no, or much advance any other Science, beyond the particular Records of Actions or Registers of Time; and these perhaps might be as long preserved without them, by the Care and Exactness of Tradition in the long Successions of certain Races of Men, with whom they were intrusted. So in *Mexico* and *Peru,* before the least use or mention of Letters, there was remaining among them the Knowledge of what had passed in those mighty Nations and Governments for many Ages. Whereas in *Ireland,* that is said to have flourished in Books and Learning before they had much Progress in *Gaul* or *Brittany;*

---

[4] Alexandrian library founded in the third century B.C. and burnt in 642.

[5] Egyptian historian of the third century B.C.

[6] Marcus Junianus Justinus, Roman historian

of the third century.

[7] Greek historians of the fifth and first centuries B.C.

there are now hardly any Traces left of what passed there, before the Conquest made of that Country by the *English* in *Henry* the Second's Time. A strange but plain Demonstration, how Knowledge and Ignorance, as well as Civility and Barbarism, may succeed each other in the several Countries of the World; how much better the Records of Time may be kept by Tradition in one Country than by Writing in another; and how much we owe to those Learned Languages of *Greek* and *Latin,* without which, for ought I know, the World in all these *Western* Parts would hardly be known to have been above five or six Hundred Years old, nor any Certainty remain of what passed in it before that Time.

'Tis true, in the *Eastern* Regions, there seems to have been a general Custom of the Priests in each Country; having been either by their own Choice, or by Design of the Governments, the perpetual Conservers of Knowledge and Story. Only in *China,* this last was committed particularly to certain Officers of State, who were appointed or continued upon every Accession to that Crown, to Register distinctly the Times and memorable Events of each Reign. In *Æthiopia, Ægypt, Chaldea, Persia, Syria, Judea,* these Cares were committed wholly to the Priests, who were not less diligent in the Registers of Times and Actions, than in the Study and successive Propagation thereby of all Natural *Science* and *Philosophy.* Whether this was managed by Letters, or Tradition, or by both; 'tis certain the Ancient Colleges, or Societies of Priests, were mighty Reservoirs or Lakes of Knowledge, into which some Streams entred perhaps every Age, from the Observations or Inventions of any great Spirits or transcendent Genius's, that happened to rise among them; and nothing was lost out of these Stores, since the Part of conserving what others have gained, either in Knowledge or Empire, is as common and easy, as the other is hard and rare among Men.

In these Soils were planted and cultivated those mighty Growths of *Astronomy, Astrology, Magick, Geometry,* Natural *Philosophy,* and Ancient *Story.* From these Sources, *Orpheus, Homer, Lycurgus, Pythagoras, Plato,* and others of the Ancients, are acknowledged to have drawn all those Depths of Knowledge or Learning, which have made them so Renowned in all succeeding Ages. I make a Distinction between these Two, taking Knowledge to be properly meant of Things that are generally agreed to be true by Consent of those that first found them out, or have been since instructed in them; but Learning is the Knowledge of the different and contested Opinions of Men in former Ages, and about which they have perhaps never agreed in any; and this makes so much of one, and so little of the other in the World.

Now to judge, Whether the Ancients or Moderns, can be probably thought to have made the greatest Progress in the Search and Discoveries of the vast Region of Truth and Nature; it will be worth inquiring, What Guides have been used, and what Labours imploy'd by the one and the other in these Noble Travels and Pursuits.

The Modern Scholars have their usual Recourse to the Universities of their Countries; some few it may be to those of their Neighbours; and this, in quest of Books rather than Men for their Guides, though these are living, and those, in Comparison, but dead Instructors; which like a Hand with an Inscription, can point out the strait Way upon the Road, but can neither tell you the next Turnings, resolve your Doubts, or answer your Questions, like a Guide that has traced it over, and perhaps knows it as well as his Chamber. And who are these dead Guides we seek in our Journey? They are at best but some few Authors that remain among us, of a great many that wrote in *Greek* and *Latin,* from the Age of *Hypocrates* to that of *Marcus Antoninus,* which reaches not much above Six Hundred Years. Before that time I know none, besides some Poets, some Fables, and some few Epistles; and since that time, I know very few that can pretend to be Authors, rather than Transcribers or Commentators of the Ancient Learning: Now to consider at what Sources our Ancients drew their Water, and with what unwearied Pains: 'Tis evident, *Thales* and *Pythagoras*[8] were the Two Founders of the *Grecian* Philosophy; the First gave Beginning to the *Ionick* Sect, and the other to the *Italick;* out of which, all the others celebrated in *Greece* or *Rome* were derived or composed: *Thales* was the First of the *Sophi*, or Wise Men famous in *Greece,* and is said to have learned his *Astronomy, Geometry, Astrology, Theology,* in his Travels from his Country *Miletus* to *Egypt, Phœnicia, Crete,* and *Delphos: Pythagoras* was the Father of Philosophers, and of the Virtues, having in Modesty chosen the Name of *a Lover of Wisdom,* rather than of *Wise;* and having first introduced the Names of the Four Cardinal Virtues, and given them the Place and Rank they have held ever since in the World: Of these Two mighty Men remain no Writings at all, for those Golden Verses that go under the Name of *Pythagoras* are generally rejected as spurious, like many other Fragments of *Sybils* or old Poets, and some intire Poems that run with Ancient Names: Nor is it agreed, Whether he ever left any thing written to his Scholars or Cotemporaries; or whether all that learn'd of him, did it not by the Ear and Memory, and all that remained of him, for some succeeding Ages, were not by Tradition. But whether these ever writ or no, they were the Fountains, out of which the following *Greek* Philosophers drew all those Streams that have since watered the Studies of the Learned World, and furnished the Voluminous Writings of so many Sects, as passed afterwards under the common Name of Philosophers.

As there were Guides to those that we call Ancients, so there were others that were Guides to them, in whose Search they travelled far and laboured long.

There is nothing more agreed, than, That all the Learning of the *Greeks* was deduced Originally from *Egypt* or *Phœnicia;* but, Whether theirs might not have flourished to that Degree it did, by

the Commerce of the *Ethiopians, Chaldæans, Arabians,* and *Indians,* is not so evident, (though I am very apt to believe it) and to most of these Regions some of the *Grecians* travelled in search of those Golden Mines of Learning and Knowledge: Not to mention the Voyages of *Orpheus, Musaeus, Lucurgus, Thales, Solon, Democritus, Herodotus, Plato,* and that vain Sophist, *Apollonius,* (who was but an Ape of the Ancient Philosophers) I shall only trace those of *Pythagoras,* who seems, of all others, to have gone the farthest upon this Design, and to have brought home the greatest Treasures. He went first to *Egypt,* where he spent Two and Twenty Years in Study and Conversation, among the several Colleges of Priests, in *Memphis, Thebes* and *Heliopolis,* was initiated in all their several Mysteries, in order to gain Admittance and Instruction, in the Learning and Sciences that were there, in their highest Ascendent. Twelve Years he spent in *Babylon,* and in the Studies and Learning of the Priests or *Magi* of the *Chaldeans.* Besides these long Abodes, in those Two Regions, celebrated for Ancient Learning, and where one Author, according to their Calculations, says, He gained the Observations of innumerable Ages, He Travelled likewise upon the same scent into *Æthiopia, Arabia, India,* to *Crete,* to *Delphos,* and to all the Oracles that were Renowned in any of these Regions.

What sort of Morals some of those may have been that he went so far to seek, I shall only endeavour to Trace out, by the most ancient Accounts that are given of the *Indian Brachmans,* since those of the Learned or Sages in the other Countries occur more frequent in Story. These were all of one Race or Tribe, that was kept chast from any other Mixture, and were dedicated wholly to the Service of the Gods, to the Studies of Wisdom and Nature, and to the Counsel of their Princes. There was not only particular Care taken of their Birth and Nurture, but even from their Conception. For when a Woman among them was known to have Conceived, much Thought and Diligence was im-

[8] Greek philosophers of the sixth century B.C.

ployed about her Diet and Entertainments, so far as to furnish her with pleasant Imaginations, to compose her Mind and her Sleeps, with the best Temper, during the Time she carried her Burthen. This I take to be a Strain beyond the *Grecian* Wit, or the Constitutions even of their imaginary Lawgivers, who began their Cares of Mankind only after their Birth, and none before. Those of the *Brachmans* continued in the same Degree for their Education and Instruction, in which, and their Studies, and Discipline of their Colleges, or separate Abodes in Woods and Fields, they spent Thirty Seven Years. Their Learning and Institutions were unwritten, and only Traditional among themselves, by a perpetual Succession. Their Opinions in Natural Philosophy, were, That the World was round, that it had a Beginning, and would have an End, but reckoned both by immense Periods of Time; that the Author of it was a Spirit, or a Mind, that pervaded the whole Universe, and was diffused through all the Parts of it. They held the Transmigration of Souls, and some used Discourses of Infernal Mansions, in many Things, like those of *Plato.* Their Moral Philosophy consisted chiefly in preventing all Diseases or Distempers of the Body, from which they esteemed the perturbation of Mind, in a great measure, to arise. Then, in composing the Mind, and exempting it from all anxious Cares, esteeming the troublesome and follicitous Thoughts, about Past and Future, to be like so many Dreams, and no more to be regarded. They despised both Life and Death, Pleasure and Pain, or at least thought them perfectly indifferent. Their Justice was exact and exemplary; their Temperance so great, that they lived upon Rice or Herbs, and upon nothing that had sensitive Life. If they fell Sick, they counted it such a Mark of Intemperance, that they would frequently Die out of shame and sullenness; but many lived a Hundred and Fifty, and some Two Hundred Years.

Their Wisdom was so highly esteemed, that some of them were always imployed to follow the Courts of their Kings, to advise them upon all Occasions, and instruct them in Justice and Piety; and upon this Regard, *Calanus,* and some others, are said to have followed the Camp of *Alexander,* after his Conquest of one of their Kings. The Magical Operations, reported of them, are so wonderful, that they must either be wholly disbelieved, or will make easie way for the Credit of all those that we so often meet with in the latter Relations of the Indies. Above all the rest, their Fortitude was most admirable in their Patience and Endurance of all Evils, of Pain, and of Death; some standing, sitting, lying, without any Motion whole Days together in the scorching Sun; others standing whole Nights upon one Leg, and holding up a heavy Piece of Wood or Stone in both Hands, without ever moving, (which might be done, upon some sort of Penances usual among them.) They frequently ended their Lives by their own Choice, and not Necessity, and most usually by Fire; some upon Sickness, others upon Misfortunes, some upon meer satiety of Life; so *Calanus,* in *Alexander's* time, burnt himself publickly, upon growing old and infirm; *Zormanochages,* in the time of *Augustus,* upon his constant Health and Felicity, and to prevent his living so long as to fall into Diseases or Misfortunes. These were the *Brachmans* of *India,* by the most Ancient Relations remaining of them, and which compar'd with our Modern, (since Navigation and Trade have discovered so much of those vast Countries) make it easie to conjecture that the present *Baniams* have derived from them many of their Customs and Opinions, which are still very like them, after the course of Two Thousand Years. For how long Nations, without the Changes introduced by Conquest, may continue in the same Customs, Institutions, and Opinions, will be easily observed, in the Stories of the *Peruvians* and *Mexicans,* of the *Chineses* and *Scythians:* These last being described by *Herodotus,* to lodge always in Carts, and to feed commonly upon the Milk of

Mares, as the *Tartars* are reported to do at this time, in many Parts of those vast *Northern* Regions.

From these Famous *Indians,* it seems to me most probable, that *Pythagoras* learn'd, and transported into *Greece* and *Italy,* the greatest Part of his Natural and Moral Philosophy, rather than from the *Egyptians,* as is commonly supposed; for I have not observed any mention of the Transmigration of Souls, held among the *Egyptians,* more Ancient than the time of *Pythagoras.* On the contrary, *Orpheus* is said to have brought out of *Egypt* all his Mystical Theology, with the Stories of the *Stygian* Lake, *Charon,* the Infernal Judges, which were wrought up by the succeeding Poets (with a mixture of the *Cretan* Tales, or Traditions) into that Part of the *Pagan* Religion, so long observed by the *Greeks* and *Romans.* Now 'tis obvious, that this was in all Parts very different from the *Pythagorean* Opinion of Transmigration, which, though it was preserved long among some of the succeeding Philosophers, yet never entered into the vulgar[9] Belief of *Greece* or *Italy.*

Nor does it seem unlikely that the *Egyptians* themselves might have drawn much of their Learning from the *Indians;* for they are observed, in some Authors, to have done it from the *Æthiopians;* and Chronologers, I think, agree, that these were a Colony that came anciently from the River *Indus,* and planted themselves upon that Part of *Africa,* which from their Name was afterward called *Æthiopia,* and in probability brought their Learning and their Customs with them. The *Phœnicians* are likewise said to have been anciently a Colony that came from the *Red Sea,* and planted themselves upon the *Mediterranean,* and from thence spread so far the Fame of their Learning, and their Navigations.

To strengthen this Conjecture, of much Learning being derived from such remote and ancient Fountains as the *Indies,* and perhaps *China;* it may be asserted with great Evidence, that though we know little of the Antiquities of *India,* beyond *Alexander's* time; yet those of *China* are the oldest that any where pretend to any fair Records; for these are agreed, by the Missionary Jesuits, to extend so far above Four Thousand Years, and with such Appearance of clear and undeniable Testimonies, that those Religious Men themselves, rather than question their Truth, by finding them contrary to the vulgar Chronology of the Scripture, are content to have recourse to that of the *Septuagint,* and thereby to salve the Appearances in those Records of the *Chineses.* Now though we have been deprived the knowledge of what Course Learning may have held, and to what heights it may have soared, in that vast Region, and during so great Antiquity of Time, by reason of the Savage Ambition of one of their Kings,[10] who, desirous to begin the Period of History from his own Reign, ordered all Books to be burnt, except those of Physick and Agriculture; so that, what we have remaining besides, of that Wise and Ancient Nation, is but what was either by Chance, or by private Industry, rescued out of that publick Calamity (among which were a Copy of the Records and Successions of the Crown); yet it is observable and agreed, that as the Opinions of the Learned among them are at present, so they were anciently divided into Two Sects, whereof one held the Transmigration of Souls, and the other the Eternity of Matter, comparing the World to a great Mass of Metal, out of which some Parts are continually made up into a Thousand various Figures, and after certain Periods melted down again into the same Mass. That there were many Volumes written of old in Natural Philosophy among them; that near the Age of *Socrates,* lived their Great and Renowned *Confutius,* who began the same Design of reclaiming Men from the useless and endless Speculations of Nature, to those of Morality. But with this Difference, that the Bent of the

---

[9] common.

[10] Shih Huang Ti, founder of the Ch'in dynasty, 246 B.C.

Grecian seemed to be chiefly upon the Happiness of private Men or Families, but that of the *Chinese,* upon the good Temperament and Felicity of such Kingdoms or Governments as that was, and is known to have continued for several Thousands of Years; and may be properly called, a Government of Learned Men, since no other are admitted into Charges of the State.

For my own part, I am much inclined to believe, that in these Remote Regions, not only *Pythagoras* learn'd the first Principles, both of his Natural and Moral Philosophy; but that those of *Democritus*[11] (who travelled into *Ægypt, Chaldea,* and *India,* and whose Doctrines were after improved by *Epicurus*) might have been derived from the same Fountains; and that long before them both, *Lycurgus,*[12] who likewise travelled into *India,* brought from thence also the chief Principles of his Laws and Politicks, so much Renowned in the World.

For whoever observes the Account already given of the Ancient *Indian* and *Chinese* Learning and Opinions, will easily find among them the Seeds of all these *Grecian* Productions and Institutions: As, the Transmigration of Souls, and the four Cardinal Virtues:[13] The long Silence injoined his Scholars, and Propagation of their Doctrines by Tradition, rather than Letters, and Abstinence from all Meats that had Animal Life, introduced by *Pythagoras:* The Eternity of Matter, with perpetual Changes of Form, the Indolence of Body, and Tranquility of Mind, by *Epicurus:*[14] And among those of *Lycurgus;* the Care of Education from the Birth of Children, the austere Temperance of Diet, the patient Endurance of Toil and Pain, the Neglect or Contempt of Life, the Use of Gold and Silver only in their Temples, the Defence[15] of Commerce with Strangers, and several others, by him established among the *Spartans,* seem all to be wholly *Indian,* and different from any Race or Vein of Thought or Imagination, that have ever appeared in *Greece,* either in that Age or any since.

It may look like a Paradox, to deduce Learning from Regions accounted commonly so barbarous and rude. And 'tis true, the generality of People were always so, in those *Eastern* Countries, and their Lives wholly turned to Agriculture, to Mechanicks, or to Trades: But this does not hinder particular Races or Successions of Men, (the design of whose Thought and Time was turned wholly to Learning and Knowledge) from having been what they are represented, and what they deserve to be esteemed; since among the *Gauls,* the *Goths,* and the *Peruvians* themselves, there have been such Races of Men under the Names of *Druids, Bards, Amautas, Runers,* and other barbarous Appellations.

Besides, I know no Circumstances like to contribute more to the Advancement of Knowledge and Learning among Men, than exact Temperance in their Races, great Pureness of Air, and Equality of Climate, long Tranquility of Empire or Government: And all these we may justly allow to those *Eastern* Regions, more than any others we are acquainted with, at least till the Conquests made by the *Tartars,* upon both *India* and *China,* in the latter Centuries. However, it may be as pardonable, to derive some Parts of Learning from thence, as to go so far for the Game of *Chess,* which some Curious and Learned Men have deduced from *India* into *Europe,* by two several Roads, that is, by *Persia* into *Greece,* and by *Arabia* into *Africk* and *Spain.*

Thus much I thought might be allowed me to say, for the giving some Idea of what those Sages or Learned Men were, or may have been, who were Ancients to those that are Ancients to us. Now to observe what these have been, is more easie and obvious. The most Ancient *Grecians* that we are at all acquainted with, after *Lycurgus,* who was certainly a great Philosopher

---

[11] Greek philosopher of the fifth century B.C.
[12] Spartan legislator of the ninth century B.C.
[13] i.e., justice, prudence, temperance, and fortitude.
[14] Greek philosopher of the fourth century B.C.
[15] prohibition.

as well as Law-giver, were the seven Sages:[16] Tho' the Court of *Croesus*[17] is said to have been much resorted to, by the Sophists of *Greece,* in the happy Beginnings of his Reign. And some of these seven seem to have brought most of the Sciences out of *Ægypt* and *Phœnicia,* into *Greece;* particularly those of *Astronomy, Astrology, Geometry,* and *Arithmetick.* These were soon followed by *Pythagoras,* (who seems to have introduced Natural and Moral Philosophy) and by several of his Followers, both in *Greece* and *Italy.* But of all these, there remains nothing in Writing now among us; so that *Hyppocrates, Plato,* and *Xenophon,*[18] are the first *Philosophers,* whose Works have escaped the Injuries of Time. But that we may not conclude, the first Writers we have of the *Grecians,* were the first Learned or Wise among them; we shall find upon inquiry, that the more Ancient Sages of *Greece* appear, by the Characters remaining of them, to have been much the greater Men. They were generally Princes or Law-givers of their Countries, or at least offered and invited to be so, either of their own or of others, that desired them to frame or reform their several Institutions of Civil Government. They were commonly excellent Poets, and great Physicians: they were so learned in Natural Philosophy, that they fore-told, not only Eclipses in the Heavens, but Earthquakes at Land, and Storms at Sea, great Drowths and great Plagues, much Plenty, or much Scarcity of certain sorts of Fruits or Grain; not to mention the Magical Powers attributed to several of them, to allay Storms, to raise Gales, to appease Commotions of People, to make Plagues cease; which Qualities, whether upon any ground of Truth or no, yet if well believed, must have raised them to that strange height they were at, of common Esteem and Honour, in their own and succeeding Ages.

By all this may be determined, whether our Moderns or our Ancients may have had the greater and the better Guides, and which of them have taken the greater Pains, and with the more Application in the Pursuit of Knowledge. And, I think, it is enough to shew, that the Advantages we have, from those we call the Ancients, may not be greater, than what they had from those that were so to them.

But after all, I do not know whether the high flights of Wit and Knowledge, like those of Power and of Empire in the World, may not have been made by the pure Native Force of Spirit or Genius, in some single Men, rather than by any derived strength among them, however increased by Succession; and whether they may not have been the Atchievements of Nature, rather than the Improvements of Art. Thus the Conquests of *Ninus* and *Semiramis,* of *Alexander* and *Tamerlane,* which I take to have been the Greatest recorded in Story, were at their heigth in those Persons that began them; and so far from being increased by their Successors, that they were not preserved in their Extent and Vigour by any of them, grew weaker in every hand they passed through, or were divided into many, that set up for great Princes, out of several small ruins of the first Empires, till they withered away in Time, or were lost by the change of Names, and Forms of Families, or of Governments.

Just the same Fate seems to have attended the highest flights of Learning and of Knowledge, that are upon our Registers. *Thales, Pythagoras, Democritus, Hyppocrates, Plato, Aristotle, Epicurus,* were the first mighty Conquerors of Ignorance in our World, and made greater Progresses in the several Empires of Science, than any of their Successors have been since able to reach. These have hardly ever pretended more, than to learn what the others taught, to remember what they invented, and not able to compass that it self, they have set up for Authors, upon some Parcels of those great Stocks, or else have contented

---

[16] Solon, Thales, Pitacus, Bias, Chilon, Cleobulus, and Periander of Corinth, all of whom lived about 620–548 B.C.

[17] Lydian king of the sixth century B.C.
[18] Greek historian of the fourth century B.C.

themselves only to comment upon those Texts, and make the best Copies they could, after those Originals.

I have long thought, that the different Abilities of Men, which we call Wisdom or Prudence, for the Conduct of publick Affairs or private Life, grow directly out of that little grain of Intellect or good Sense, which they bring with them into the World; and that the Defect of it in Men, comes from some Want in their Conception or Birth.

. . . Dixitque semel Nascentibus Author, Quicquid scire licet. . . .[19]

And though this may be improved or impaired in some Degree, by accidents of Education, of Study, and of Conversation and Business, yet it cannot go beyond the reach of its Native Force, no more than Life can beyond the Period to which it was destined, by the Strength or Weakness of the seminal Virtue.

If these Speculations should be true, then I know not what Advantages we can pretend to Modern Knowledge, by any we receive from the Ancients: Nay, 'tis possible, Men may lose rather than gain by them; may lessen the Force and Growth of their own Genius, by constraining and forming it upon that of others; may have less Knowledge of their own, for contenting themselves with that of those before them. So a Man that only Translates, shall never be a Poet, nor a Painter that only Copies, nor a Swimmer that swims always with Bladders. So People that trust wholly to others Charity, and without Industry of their own, will be always poor. Besides, who can tell, whether Learning may not even weaken Invention, in a Man that has great Advantages from Nature and Birth; whether the weight and number of so many other Mens Thoughts and Notions, may not suppress his own, or hinder the Motion and Agitation of them, from which all Invention arises; as heaping on Wood, or too many Sticks, or too close together, suppresses, and

sometimes quite extinguishes a little Spark that would otherwise have grown up to a noble Flame. The strength of Mind, as well as of Body, grows more from the warmth of Exercise, than of Cloaths; nay, too much of this Foreign Heat rather makes Men faint, and their Constitutions tender or weaker, than they would be without them. Let it come about how it will, if we are Dwarfs, we are still so, though we stand upon a Gyant's Shoulders; and even so placed, yet we see less than he, if we are naturally shorter sighted, or if we do not look as much about us, or if we are dazled with the height, which often happens from weakness either of Heart or Brain.

In the growth and stature of Souls as well as Bodies, the common Productions are of indifferent sizes, that occasion no gazing nor no wonder: But tho' there are or have been sometimes Dwarfs and sometimes Gyants in the World, yet it does not follow, that there must be such in every Age nor in every Country: This we can no more conclude, than that there never have been any, because there are none now, at least in the compass of our present Knowledge or Inquiry. As I believe, there may have been Gyants at some time, and some place or other in the World, of such a Stature, as may not have been equalled perhaps again, in several Thousands of Years, or in any other Parts; so there may be Gyants in Wit and Knowledge, of so over-grown a Size, as not to be equalled again in many successions of Ages, or any compass of Place or Country. Such, I am sure, *Lucretius* esteems and describes *Epicurus* to have been, and to have risen, like a Prodigy of Invention and Knowledge, such as had not been before, nor was like to be again; and I know not why others of the Ancients may not be allowed to have been as great in their Kinds, and to have built as high, though upon different Schemes or Foundations. Because there is a Stag's Head at *Amboyse* of a most prodigious size, and a large Table at *Memorancy* cut out of the thickness of a Vine-stock, is it necessary, that there must be, every age, such a Stag in every great Forest, or such a Vine in every large Vineyard; or

---

[19] "And God told them at birth whatever they might know."

that the Productions of Nature in any kind, must be still alike, or something near it, because Nature is still the same? May there not many Circumstances concur to one Production, that do not to any other, in one or many Ages? In the growth of a Tree, there is the native Strength of the Seed, both from the Kind, and from the Perfections of its ripening, and from the Health and Vigour of the Plant that bore it. There is the Degree of Strength and Excellence, in that Vein of Earth where it first took Root: There is a Propriety of Soil, suited to the kind of Tree that grows in it; there is a great favour or dis-favour to its Growth, from Accidents of Water and of Shelter, from the Kindness or Unkindness of Seasons, till it be past the Need or the Danger of them. All these, and perhaps many others, joined with the Propitiousness of Climate, to that sort of Tree, and the length of Age it shall stand and grow, may produce an Oak, a Fig, or a Plain-Tree, that shall deserve to be renowned in Story, and shall not perhaps be parallell'd in other Countries or Times.

May not the same have happened in the Production, Growth and Size of Wit and Genius in the World, or in some Parts or Ages of it, and from many more Circumstances that contributed towards it, than what may concur to the stupendous Growth of a Tree or Animal? May there not have been, in *Greece* or *Italy* of old, such Prodigies of Invention and Learning in *Philosophy, Mathematicks, Physick, Oratory, Poetry,* that none has ever since approached them, as well as there were in *Painting, Statuary, Architecture?* and yet their unparallell'd and inimitable Excellencies in these are undisputed.

Science and Arts have run their Circles, and had their Periods in the several Parts of the World: They are generally agreed, to have held their course from *East* to *West,* to have begun in *Chaldea* and *Ægypt,* to have been Transplanted from thence to *Greece,* from *Greece* to *Rome;* to have sunk there, and after many Ages, to have revived from those Ashes and to have sprung up again, both

in *Italy* and other more *Western* Provinces of *Europe.* When *Chaldea* and *Ægypt* were Learned and Civil, *Greece* and *Rome* were as rude and barbarous as all *Ægypt* and *Syria* now are, and have been long. When *Greece* and *Rome* were at their Heights in Arts and Science, *Gaul, Germany, Britain,* were as ignorant and barbarous, as any Parts of *Greece* or *Turkey* can be now.

These, and greater Changes, are made in the several Countries of the World, and courses of time, by the Revolutions of Empire, the Devastations of Armies, the Cruelties of Conquering, and the Calamities of enslaved Nations; by the violent Inundations of Water in some Countries, and the cruel Ravages of Plagues in others. These sorts of Accidents sometimes lay them so waste, that when they rise again, 'tis from such low Beginnings, that they look like New-Created Regions, or growing out of the Original State of Mankind, and without any Records or Remembrances, beyond certain short periods of Time. Thus that vast Continent of *Norway* is said to have been so wholly desolated by a Plague, about eight or nine hundred years ago, that it was for some Ages following a very Desart, and since all over-grown with Wood: and *Ireland* was so spoiled and wasted by the Conquests of the *Scutes* and *Danes,* that there hardly remains any Story or Tradition what that Island was, how Planted or Governed above five hundred Years ago. What Changes have been made by violent Storms, and Inundations of the Sea in the Maritime Provinces of the *Low-Countries,* is hard to know, or to believe what is told, nor how ignorant they have left us of all that passed there before a certain and short period of Time.

The Accounts of many other Countries would perhaps as hardly, and as late, have waded out of the Depths of Time, and Gulphs of Ignorance, had it not been for the Assistance of those two Languages, to which we owe all we have of Learning or Ancient Records in the World. For whether we have any thing of the Old *Chaldean, Hebrew, Arabian,* that is truly Genuine or more Ancient than the *Augustan* Age, I am much in doubt; yet 'tis probable, the vast *Alexandrian* Library must have chiefly consisted of Books composed in those Languages, with the *Ægyptian, Syrian* and *Æthiopick,* or at least translated out of them by the Care of the *Ægyptian* Kings or Priests, as the *Old Testament* was, wherein the *Septuagints* imploy'd left their Name to that Famous Translation.

'Tis very true and just, all that is said of the mighty Progress that Learning and Knowledge have made in these *Western* Parts of *Europe,* within these hundred and fifty Years; but that does not conclude, it must be at greater Heighth than it had been in other Countries, where it was growing much longer periods of Time; it argues more how low it was then amongst us, rather than how high it is now.

Upon the Fall of the *Roman* Empire, almost all Learning was buried in its Ruines: The *Northern* Nations, that conquered or rather overwhelmed it by their Numbers, were too barbarous to preserve the Remains of Learning or Civility, more carefully than they did those of Statuary or Architecture, which fell before their Brutish Rage. The *Saracens* indeed, from their Conquests of *Ægypt, Syria,* and *Greece,* carried home great Spoils of Learning, as well as other Riches, and gave the Original of all that Knowledge, which flourished for some time among the *Arabians,* and has since been copied out of many Authors among them, as theirs have been out of those of the Countries they had subdued; nor indeed do Learning, Civility, Morality, seem any where to have made a greater Growth, in so short a time, than in that Empire, nor to have flourish'd more than in the Reign of their Great *Almanzor,*[20] under whose Victorious Ensigns *Spain* was conquered by the *Moors;* but the *Goths,* and all the rest of those *Scythian* Swarms that from beyond the *Danube* and the *Elb,* under so many several Names, over-run all *Europe,* took very hardly and very late any Tincture of the

Learning and Humanity that had flourished in the several Regions of it, under the Protection, and by the Example and Instructions of the *Romans,* that had so long possessed them: Those *Northern* Nations were indeed easier induced to imbrace the Religion of those they had subdued, and by their Devotion gave great Authority and Revenues, and thereby Ease to the Clergy, both Secular and Regular, through all their Conquests. Great numbers of the better sort among the oppressed Natives, finding this vein among them, and no other way to be safe and quiet under such rough Masters, betook themselves to the Profession and Assemblies of Religious Orders and Fraternities, and among those only were preserved all the poor Remainders of Learning, in these several Countries.

But these good Men, either contented themselves with their Devotion, or with the Ease of quiet Lives, or else imployed their Thoughts and Studies to raise and maintain the Esteem and Authority of that sacred Order, to which they owed the Safety and Repose, the Wealth and Honour they injoyed. And in this they so well succeeded, that the Conquerors were governed by those they had subdued, the Greatest Princes by the Meanest Priests, and the Victorious *Franks* and *Lombard* Kings fell at the Feet of the *Roman* Prelates.

Whilst the Clergy were busied in these Thoughts or Studies, the better sort among the Laity were wholly turned to Arms and to Honour, the meaner sort to Labour or to Spoil; Princes taken up with Wars among themselves, or in those of the Holy Land, or between the Popes and Emperors upon Disputes of the Ecclesiastical and Secular Powers; Learning so little in use among them, that few could write or read, besides those of the Long Robes. During this course of Time, which lasted many Ages in the *Western* Parts of *Europe,* the *Greek* Tongue was wholly lost, and the Purity of the *Roman* to that degree, that what remained of it was only a certain Jargon rather than *Latin,* that passed among the *Monks* and *Fryars* who were at all learned; and among the Students of the

---

[20] Moorish military leader of the tenth century.

several Universities, which served to carry them to *Rome* in pursuit of Preferments or Causes depending there, and little else.

When the *Turks* took *Constantinople*, about two hundred Years ago, and soon after possessed themselves of all *Greece*, the poor Natives fearing the Tyranny of those cruel Masters made their Escapes in great numbers to the neighbouring Parts of Christendom, some by the *Austrian* Territories into *Germany*, others by the *Venetian* into *Italy* and *France;* several that were Learned among these *Grecians*, (and brought many Ancient Books with them in that Language) began to teach it in these Countries; first to gain Subsistence, and afterwards Favour in some Princes or Great Mens Courts, who began to take a Pleasure or Pride in countenancing Learned Men. Thus began the Restoration of Learning in these Parts, with that of the *Greek* Tongue; and soon after, *Reuchlyn* and *Erasmus*[21] began that of the purer and ancient Latin. After them, *Buchanan*[22] carried it, I think, to the greatest Heighth of any of the Moderns before or since: The *Monkish Latin* upon this Return was laughed out of Doors, and remains only in the Inns[23] of *Germany* or *Poland;* and with the Restitution of these two Noble Languages, and the Books remaining of them, (which many Princes and Prelates were curious to recover and collect) Learning of all Sorts began to thrive in these *Western* Regions; and since that time, and in the first succeeding Century, made perhaps a greater Growth than in any other that we know of in such a compass of Time, considering into what Depths of Ignorance it was sunk before.

But why from thence should be concluded, That it has out-grown all that was Ancient, I see no reason. If a Strong and Vigorous Man at thirty Years old should fall into a Consumption, and so draw on till Fifty in the extreamest Weakness and Infirmity; after that, should begin to recover Health till sixty, so as to be again as strong as Men usually are at that Age: It might perhaps truly be said in that case, that he had grown more in Strength that last ten Years than any others of his Life; but not that he was grown to more Strength and Vigour, than he had at thirty Years old.

But what are the Sciences wherein we pretend to excel? I know of no New Philosophers, that have made Entries upon that Noble Stage for fifteen hundred Years past, unless *Des Cartes* and *Hobbs*[24] should pretend to it; of whom I shall make no Critick here, but only say, That by what appears of Learned Mens Opinions in this Age they have by no means eclipsed the Lustre of *Plato, Aristotle, Epicurus,* or others of the Ancients. For Grammar or Rhetorick, no Man ever disputed it with them; nor for Poetry, that ever I heard of, besides the New *French* Author I have mentioned;[25] and against whose Opinion there could, I think, never have been given stronger Evidence, than by his own Poems, printed together with that Treatise.

There is nothing new in *Astronomy*, to vie with the Ancients, unless it be the *Copernican* System;[26] nor in *Physick*, unless *Harvey's* Circulation of the Blood.[27] But whether either of these be modern Discoveries, or derived from old Fountains, is disputed: Nay, it is so too, whether they are true or no; for though Reason may seem to favour them more than the contrary Opinions, yet Sense can very hardly allow them; and to satisfie Mankind, both these must concur. But if they are true, yet these two great Discoveries have made no Change in the

---

[21] German humanist (1455–1522) and Dutch humanist (1466?–1536) respectively.

[22] Scottish historian (1506–1582).

[23] Law schools like the English Inns of Court.

[24] Leading philosophers of the century: René Descartes, French (1596–1650), and Thomas Hobbes, English (1588–1679).

[25] Fontenelle.

[26] The Polish astronomer Nicolaus Copernicus (1473–1543) argued that the planets circled the sun and not the earth; by Temple's time his hypothesis had been well substantiated by observations and detailed calculations.

[27] The English physician William Harvey (1578–1657) successfully demonstrated the circulation of the blood.

Conclusions of *Astronomy,* nor in the Practice of Physick, and so have been of little Use to the World, though perhaps of much Honour to the Authors.

What are become of the Charms of Musick, by which Men and Beasts, Fishes, Fowls and Serpents, were so frequently enchanted, and their very Natures changed; by which the Passions of Men were raised to the greatest Height and Violence, and then as suddenly appeased, so as they might be justly said to be turned into Lyons or Lambs, into Wolves or into Harts, by the Powers and Charms of this admirable Art? 'Tis agreed by the Learned, that the Science of Musick so admired of the Ancients is wholly lost in the World, and that what we have now is made up out of certain Notes that fell into the Fancy or Observation of a poor *Fryar,* in chanting his Mattins. So as those two Divine Excellencies of Musick and Poetry are grown, in a manner, to be little more, but the one Fidling, and the other Rhyming; and are indeed very worthy the Ignorance of the Fryar, and the Barbarousness of the *Goths* that introduced them among us.

What have we remaining of *Magick,* by which the *Indians,* the *Chaldeans,* the *Ægyptians* were so renowned, and by which Effects so wonderful, and to common Men so astonishing were produced, as made them have recourse to Spirits or Supernatural Powers, for some Account of their strange Operations? By *Magick,* I mean some excelling Knowledge of Nature, and the various Powers and Qualities in its several Productions, and the Application of certain Agents to certain Patients, which by Force of some peculiar Qualities produce Effects very different from what fall under vulgar Observation or Comprehension. These are by ignorant People called *Magick* and *Conjuring,* and such like Terms, and an Account of them much about as wise, is given by the common Learned, from *Sympathies, Antipathies, Idiosyncrasies, Talismans,* and some Scraps or Terms left us by the *Ægyptians* or *Grecians* of the Ancient Magick, but the Science

seems with several others to be wholly lost.

What Traces have we left of that admirable Science or Skill in Architecture by which such stupendous Fabricks have been raised of old, and so many of the Wonders of the World been produced, and which are so little approached by our Modern Atchievements of this Sort, that they hardly fall within our Imagination? Not to mention the Walls and Palace of *Babylon,* the Pyramids of *Ægypt,* the Tomb of *Mausolus,* or *Colosse* of *Rhodes,* the Temples and Palaces of *Greece* and *Rome:* What can be more admirable in this kind than the *Roman* Theatres, their Aqueducts, and their Bridges, among which that of *Trajan* over the *Danube* seems to have been the last Flight of the Ancient Architecture? The stupendous Effects of this Science sufficiently evince, at what Heighths the Mathematicks were among the Ancients; but if this be not enough, who ever would be satisfied, need go no further than the Siege of *Syracuse,* and that mighty Defence made against the *Roman* Power, more by the wonderful Science and Arts of *Archimedes,* and almost magical Force of his Engines, than by all the Strength of the City, or Number and Bravery of the Inhabitants.

The greatest Invention that I know of in latter Ages, has been that of the Load-Stone, and consequently, the greatest Improvement has been made in the Art of Navigation; yet there must be allowed to have been something stupendous in the Numbers, and in the Built of their Ships and Gallies of Old; and the Skill of Pilots, from the Observation of the Stars in the more serene Climates, may be judged, by the Navigations so celebrated in Story, of the *Tyrians* and *Carthaginians,* not to mention other Nations. However, 'tis to this we owe the Discovery and Commerce of so many vast Countries, which were very little, if at all, known to the Ancients, and the experimental Proof of this Terrestrial Globe, which was before only Speculation, but has since been surrounded by the Fortune and Boldness of several Navigators.

From this great, though fortuitous Invention, and the Consequence thereof, it must be allowed, that Geography is mightily advanced in these latter Ages. The vast Continents of *China,* the *East* and *West-Indies,* the long Extent and Coasts of *Africa,* with the numberless Islands belonging to them, have been hereby introduced into our Acquaintance, and our Maps, and great Increases of Wealth and Luxury, but none of Knowledge, brought among us, further than the Extent and Situation of Countrey, the Customs and Manners of so many Original Nations which we call Barbarous, and I am sure have treated them as if we hardly esteem them to be a part of Mankind. I do not doubt, but many Great and more Noble Uses would have been made of such Conquests or Discoveries, if they had fallen to the Share of the *Greeks* and *Romans* in those Ages, when Knowledge and Fame were in as great Request as endless Gains and Wealth are among us now; and how much greater Discoveries might have been made by such Spirits as theirs, is hard to guess. I am sure, ours, though great, yet look very imperfect, as to what the Face of this Terrestrial Globe would probably appear, if they had been pursued as far as we might justly have expected from the Progresses of Navigation, since the Use of the Compass, which seems to have been long at a stand : How little has been performed of what has been so often and so confidently promised, of a *North West* Passage to the *East* of *Tartary,* and *North* of *China?* How little do we know of the Lands on that side of the *Magellan Straits* that lie towards the *South-Pole,* which may be vast Islands or Continents, for ought any can yet aver, though that Passage was so long since found out ? Whether *Japan* be Island or Continent, with some Parts of *Tartary* on the *North* side, is not certainly agreed. The Lands of *Yedso* upon the *North-East* Continent have been no more than Coasted, and whether they may not join to the *Northern* Continent of *America* is by some doubted.

But the Defect or Negligence seems yet to have been greater towards the *South,* where we know little beyond thirty-five Degrees, and that only by the Necessity of doubling the *Cape of Goodhope* in our *East-India* Voyages; yet a Continent has been long since found out within fifteen Degrees to *South,* and about the Length of *Java,* which is marked by the Name of *New Holland* in the Maps, and to what Extent none knows, either to the *South,* the *East,* or the *West;* yet the Learned have been of Opinion, That there must be a Balance of Earth on that side of the Line in some Proportion to what there is on the other, and that it cannot be all *Sea* from thirty Degrees to the *South-Pole,* since we have found Land to above sixty five Degrees towards the *North.* But our Navigators that way have been confined to the Roads of Trade; and our Discoveries bounded by what we can manage to a certain Degree of Gain. And I have heard it said among the *Dutch,* that their *East-India* Company have long since forbidden, and under the greatest Penalties, any further Attempts of discovering that Continent, having already more Trade in those Parts than they can turn to Account, and fearing some more Populous Nation of *Europe* might make great Establishments of Trade in some of those unknown Regions, which might ruin or impair what they have already in the *Indies.*

Thus we are lame still in Geography it self, which we might have expected to run up to so much greater Perfection by the Use of the Compass, and it seems to have been little advanced these last hundred Years. So far have we been from improving upon those Advantages we have received from the Knowledge of the Ancients, that since the late Restoration of Learning and Arts among us, our first Flights seem to have been the highest, and a sudden Damp to have fallen upon our Wings, which has hindred us from rising above certain Heights. The Arts of Painting and Statuary began to revive with Learning in *Europe,* and made a great but short Flight; so as for these last hundred Years we have not had One Master in either of them, who deserved a Rank with those that flourished in that short Period after they began among us.

It were too great a Mortification to think, That the same Fate has happened to us, even in our Modern Learning, as if the Growth of that, as well as of Natural Bodies, had some short Periods, beyond which it could not reach, and after which it must begin to decay. It falls in one Countrey or one Age, and rises again in others, but never beyond a certain Pitch. One Man, or one Countrey, at a certain Time runs a great Length in some certain Kinds of Knowledge, but lose as much Ground in others, that were perhaps as useful and as valuable. There is a certain Degree of Capacity in the greatest Vessel, and when 'tis full, if you pour in still, it must run out some way or other, and the more it runs out on one side the less runs out at the other. So the greatest Memory, after a certain Degree, as it learns or retains more of some Things or Words, loses and forgets as much of others. The largest and deepest Reach of Thought, the more it pursues some certain Subjects the more it neglects others.

Besides, few Men or none excel in all Faculties of Mind. A great Memory may fail of Invention; both may want Judgment to Digest or Apply what they Remember or Invent. Great Courage may want Caution, great Prudence may want Vigour, yet all are necessary to make a great Commander. But how can a Man hope to excel in all Qualities, when some are produced by the Heat, others by the Coldness of Brain and Temper? The Abilities of Man must fall short on one side or other, like too scanty a Blanket when you are a-bed, if you pull it upon your Shoulders, you leave your Feet bare; if you thrust it down upon your Feet, your Shoulders are uncovered.

But what would we have, unless it be other Natures and Beings than God Almighty has given us? The Height of our Statures may be Six or Seven Foot, and we would have it Sixteen; the Length of our Age may reach to a Hundred Years, and we would have it a Thousand. We are born to grovel upon the Earth, and we would fain sore up to the Skies. We

cannot comprehend the Growth of a Kernel or Seed, the Frame of an *Ant* or *Bee;* we are amazed at the Wisdom of the one, and Industry of the other, and yet we will know the Substance, the Figure, the Courses, the Influences of all those glorious Cœlestial Bodies, and the End for which they were made; we pretend to give a clear Account how Thunder and Lightning (that great Artillery of God Almighty) is produced, and we cannot comprehend how the Voice of a Man is framed, that poor little noise we make every time we speak. The Motion of the Sun is plain and evident to some Astronomers, and of the Earth to others, yet we none of us know which of them moves, and meet with many seeming Impossibilities in both, and beyond the Fathom of Human Reason or Comprehension. Nay, we do not so much as know what Motion is, nor how a Stone moves from our Hand, when we throw it cross the Street. Of all these that most Ancient and Divine Writer gives the best Account in that short Satyr, *Vain Man would fain be wise, when he is born like a Wild Ass's Colt.*[28]

But, God be thanked, his Pride is greater than his Ignorance; and what he wants in Knowledge, he supplies by Sufficiency. When he has looked about him as far as he can, he concludes there is no more to be seen; when he is at the End of his Line, he is at the Bottom of the Ocean; when he has shot his best, he is sure, none ever did nor ever can shoot better or beyond it. His own Reason is the certain Measure of Truth, his own Knowledge, of what is possible in Nature, though his Mind and his Thoughts change every Seven Years, as well as his Strength and his Features; nay, though his Opinions change every Week or every Day, yet he is sure, or at least confident, that his present Thoughts and Conclusions are just and true, and cannot be deceived; and among all the Miseries, to which Mankind is born and subjected in the whole Course of his Life, he has this one Felicity to comfort and support him, that in all Ages, in all Things, every

---

[28] Job 11:12.

Man is always in the right. A Boy of Fifteen is wiser than his Father at Forty, the meanest Subject than his Prince or Governours; and the Modern Scholars, because they have for a Hundred Years past learned their Lesson pretty well, are much more knowing than the Ancients their Masters.

But let it be so, and proved by good Reasons, is it so by Experience too? Have the Studies, the Writings, the Productions of *Gresham* College,[29] or the late Academies of *Paris*,[30] outshined or eclipsed the *Lycaeum* of *Plato*, the Academy of *Aristotle*, the *Stoa* of *Zeno*, the Garden of *Epicurus?* Has *Harvey* outdone *Hippocrates*, or *Wilkins*,[31] *Archimedes?* Are *D'Avila's* and *Strada's*[32] Histories beyond those of *Herodotus* and *Livy?*[33] Are *Sleyden's* Commentaries[34] beyond those of *Caesar?* the Flights of *Boileau*[35] above those of *Virgil?* If all this must be allowed, I will then yield *Gondibert*[36] to have excelled *Homer*, as is pretended; and the Modern *French* Poetry, all that of the Ancients. And yet, I think, it may be as reasonably said, that the Plays in *Moor-Fields*[37] are beyond the *Olympick* Games; a *Welsh* or *Irish* Harp excels those of *Orpheus* and *Arion;* the Pyramid[38] in *London* those of *Memphis;* and the *French* Conquests in *Flanders* are greater than those of *Alexander* and *Caesar*, as their Operas and Panegyricks would make us believe.

But the Consideration of Poetry ought to be a Subject by it self. For the Books we have in Prose, Do any of the Modern we converse with appear of such a Spirit and Force, as if they would live longer than the Ancient have done? If our Wit and Eloquence, our Knowledge or Inventions would deserve it, yet our Languages would not; there is no hope of their lasting long, nor of any thing in them; they change every Hundred Years so as to be hardly known for the same, or any thing of the former Stiles to be endured by the latter; so as they can no more last like the Ancients, than excellent Carvings in Wood, like those in Marble or Brass.

The Three modern Tongues most esteemed, are *Italian, Spanish* and *French;* all imperfect Dialects of the Noble *Roman;* first mingled and corrupted with the harsh Words and Terminations of those many different and barbarous Nations, by whose Invasions and Excursions the *Roman* Empire was long infested: They were afterwards made up into these several Languages, by long and Popular Use, out of those Ruins and Corruptions of *Latin*, and the prevailing Languages of those Nations, to which these several Provinces came in time to be most and longest subjected (as the *Goths* and *Moors* in *Spain*, the *Goths* and *Lombards* in *Italy*, the *Franks* in *Gaul*) besides a mingle of those Tongues which were Original to *Gaul* and to *Spain*, before the *Roman* Conquests and Establishments there. Of these, there may be some Remainders in *Biscay* or the *Asturias;* but I doubt, whether there be any of the old *Gallick* in *France*, the Subjection there having been more universal, both to the *Romans* and *Franks*. But I do not find the Mountainous Parts on the *North* of *Spain* were ever wholly subdued, or formerly Governed, either by the *Romans, Goths,* or *Saracens*, no more than *Wales* by *Romans, Saxons,* or *Normans*, after their Conquests in our Island, which has preserved the ancient

---

[29] Sir Thomas Gresham (1519?–1579), London financier who established the Royal Exchange, endowed his home as a site for philosophical lectures and meetings.

[30] Académie Française, 1634; Académie des Inscriptions et des Belles-Lettres, 1663; Académie des Sciences, 1666.

[31] John Wilkins (1614–1672), prominent in the formation of the English Royal Society for the Advancement of Knowledge.

[32] Enrico Caterino Davila (1576–1631), Italian historian; Famianus Strada (1572–1649).

[33] Roman historian of the Augustan Age.

[34] A German work (1655) on religion and the state.

[35] Nicolas Boileau-Despréaux (1636–1711), French poet and critic.

[36] English epic by Sir William Davenant (1606–1668).

[37] New theater section of London.

[38] A monument erected in Fish-street Hill to commemorate the fire of London, as late as 1759 called "the finest modern Column in the World . . . being 24 Feet higher than Trajan's Pillar at Rome" (B. Martin, *The Natural History of England*, I, 247).

Biscayn and *British* more intire, than any Native Tongue of other Provinces, where the *Roman* and *Gothick* or *Northern* Conquests reached, and were for any time Established.

'Tis easie to imagine, how imperfect Copies these modern Languages, thus composed, must needs be of so excellent an Original, being patcht up out of the Conceptions as well as Sounds of such barbarous or inslaved People. Whereas the *Latin* was framed or cultivated by the Thoughts and Uses of the Noblest Nation that appears upon any Record of Story, and inriched only by the Spoils of *Greece,* which alone could pretend to contest it with them. 'Tis obvious enough, what rapport there is, and must ever be, between the Thoughts and Words, the Conceptions and Languages of every Country, and how great a Difference this must make in the Comparison and Excellence of Books; and how easie and just a Preference it must decree to those of the *Greek* and *Latin,* before any of the Modern Languages.

It may, perhaps, be further affirmed, in Favour of the Ancients, that the oldest Books we have, are still in their kind the best. The two most Ancient, that I know of in Prose, among those we call Profane Authors, are *Æsop's* Fables, and *Phalaris's* Epistles, both living near the same time, which was that of *Cyrus* and *Pythagoras.*[39] As the first has been agreed by all Ages since, for the greatest Master in his kind, and all others of that Sort have been but Imitations of his Original; so I think the Epistles of *Phalaris* to have more Race, more Spirit, more Force of Wit and Genius than any others I have ever seen, either Ancient or Modern. I know several Learned Men (or that usually pass for such, under the Name of Criticks) have not esteemed them Genuine, and *Politian* with

some others have attributed them to *Lucian:*[40] But I think he must have little Skill in Painting, that cannot find out this to be an Original; such Diversity of Passions, upon such Variety of Actions and Passages of Life and Government, such Freedom of Thought, such Boldness of Expression, such Bounty to his Friends, such Scorn of his Enemies, such Honour of Learned Men, such Esteem of Good, such Knowledge of Life, such Contempt of Death, with such Fierceness of Nature and Cruelty of Revenge, could never be represented but by him that possessed them; and I esteem *Lucian* to have been no more capable of Writing, than of Acting what *Phalaris* did. In all one writ, you find the Scholar or the Sophist; and in all the other, the Tyrant and the Commander.

The next to these in Time, are *Herodotus, Thucydides, Hippocrates, Plato, Xenophon,* and *Aristotle;* of whom I shall say no more, than what I think is allowed by all, that they are in their several kinds inimitable. So are *Caesar, Salust,* and *Cicero,* in theirs, who are the Ancientest of the *Latin,* (I speak still of Prose) unless it be some little of old *Cato,* upon Rustick Affairs.

The Heighth and Purity of the *Roman* Stile, as it began towards the Time of *Lucretius,* which was about that of the *Jugurthin* War; so it ended about that of *Tiberius;* and the last Strain of it seems to have been *Velleius Paterculus.*[41] The Purity of the *Greek* lasted a great deal longer, and must be allowed till *Trajan's* Time,[42] when *Plutarch* wrote, whose *Greek* is much more estimable, than the *Latin* of *Tacitus* his Contemporary. After this last, I know none that deserves the Name of *Latin,* in comparison of what went before them, especially in the *Augustan* Age; if any, 'tis the little Treatise of *Minutius Fœ-*

---

[39] The so-called letters of Phalaris (570–544 B.C.), like the fables of Aesop (620–560 B.C.) come down from texts many centuries beyond the time of their alleged authors. In 1692 Roger L'Estrange published an English text of Aesop's *Fables* and in 1695 Charles Boyle published an edition of the *Letters* of Phalaris. For subsequent developments connected with

this passage, see Swift's *Battle of the Books,* particularly "The Bookseller to the Reader" and notes.

[40] Politian, Italian humanist (1454–1494); Lucian, Greek author of the second century.

[41] Roman historian of the first century.

[42] i.e., the second century.

lix.[43] All *Latin* Books that we have till the end of *Trajan,* and all *Greek* till the end of *Marcus Antoninus,* have a true and very estimable Value. All written since that time, seem to me to have little more than what comes from the Relation of Events we are glad to know, or the Controversie of Opinions in Religion or Laws, wherein the busie World has been so much imployed.

The great Wits among the Moderns have been, in my Opinion, and in their several Kinds, of the *Italians, Boccace, Machiavel,* and *Padre Paolo;*[44] among the *Spaniards, Cervantes,* (who writ *Don Quixot*) and *Guevara;*[45] among the *French, Rablais,* and *Montagne;*[46] among the *English,* Sir *Philip Sidney, Bacon* and *Selden:*[47] I mention nothing of what is written upon the Subject of Divinity, wherein the *Spanish* and *English* Pens have been most Conversant, and most Excelled. The Modern *French* are *Voiture, Rochfaucalt's* Memoirs, *Bussy's Amours de Gaul,*[48] with several other little Relations or Memoirs that have run this Age, which are very pleasant and entertaining, and seem to have Refined the *French* Language to a Degree, that cannot be well exceeded. I doubt it may have happened there, as it does in all Works, that the more they are filed and polished, the less they have of Weight and of Strength; and as that Language has much more Fineness and Smoothness at this time, so I take it to have had much more Force, Spirit and Compass, in *Montagne's* Age.

Since those Accidents, which contributed to the Restoration of Learning, almost extinguished in the *Western* Parts of *Europe,* have been observed; it will be just to mention some that may have hindred the Advancement of it, in Proportion to what might have been expected from the mighty Growth and Progress made in the first Age after its Recovery. One great Reason may have been, that very soon after the Entry of Learning upon the Scene of *Christendom,* another was made by many of the New-Learned Men, into the Inquiries and Contests about Matters of Religion; the Manners, and Maxims, and Institutions introduced by the Clergy, for Seven or Eight Centuries past; the Authority of Scripture and Tradition; of Popes and of Councils; of the Ancient Fathers, and of the latter School-Men and Casuists; of Ecclesiastical and Civil Power. The Humour of ravelling into all these Mystical or Intangled Matters, mingling with the Interests and Passions of Princes and of Parties, and thereby heightned or enflamed, produced infinite Disputes, raised violent Heats throughout all Parts of *Christendom,* and soon ended in many Defections or Reformations from the *Roman* Church, and in several new Institutions, both Ecclesiastical and Civil, in divers Countries; which have been since Rooted and Established in almost all the *North West* Parts. The endless Disputes and litigious Quarrels upon all these Subjects, favoured and incouraged by the Interests of the several Princes ingaged in them, either took up wholly, or generally imployed the Thoughts, the Studies, the Applications, the Endeavours of all or most of the finest Wits, the deepest Scholars, and the most learned Writers that the Age produced. Many Excellent Spirits, and the most Penetrating *Genii,* that might have made admirable Progresses and Advances in many other Sciences, were sunk and

---

[43] Christian apologist of the second or third century to whose *Octavius* Temple alludes.

[44] Giovanni Boccaccio (1313–1375), author of *The Decameron;* Nicolò Machiavelli (1469–1527), author of *The Prince;* Paolo Sarpi (1552–1623), author of *The History of the Council of Trent.*

[45] Miguel de Cervantes (1547–1616); Luis Vélez de Guevara (1579–1644), novelist and dramatist.

[46] François Rabelais (1494?–1553), author of *Gargantua* and *Pantagruel;* Michel de Montaigne (1533–1592), author of *Essais.*

[47] Sidney (1554–1586); Sir Francis Bacon (1561–1626); John Selden (1584–1654), called by Milton "the chief of learned men reputed in this land," author of *Table-Talk,* which had appeared only a year before Temple's essay.

[48] Vincent Voiture (1597–1648), famous for his letters; Duc François de La Rochefoucauld (1613–1680), whose *Mémoires* were published in 1662, author of the celebrated *Maximes;* Roger de Rabutin, Comte de Bussy (1618–1693), author of *Histoire amoureuse des Gaules.*

overwhelmed in the Abyss of Disputes about Matters of Religion, without ever turning their Looks or Thoughts any other way. To these Disputes of the Pen, succeeded those of the Sword; and the Ambition of great Princes and Ministers, mingled with the Zeal, or covered with the Pretences of Religion, has for a Hundred Years past infested *Christendom* with almost a perpetual Course, or Succession, either of Civil or of Foreign Wars: The Noise and Disorders whereof have been ever the most Capital Enemies of the *Muses,* who are seated, by the Ancient Fables, upon the Top of *Parnassus;* that is, in a Place of Safety and of Quiet, from the Reach of all Noises and Disturbances of the Regions below.

Another Circumstance that may have hindred the Advancement of Learning, has been a Want or Decay of Favour in Great Kings and Princes, to Encourage or Applaud it. Upon the first Return or Recovery of this fair Stranger among us, all were fond of Seeing her, apt to Applaud her: She was lodged in Palaces instead of Cells; and the greatest Kings and Princes of the Age took either a Pleasure in courting her, or a Vanity in admiring her, and in favouring all her Train. The Courts of *Italy* and *Germany,* of *England,* of *France,* of *Popes,* and of *Emperors,* thought themselves Honoured and Adorned, by the Number and Qualities of Learned Men, and by all the Improvements of Sciences and Arts, wherein they excelled. They were invited from all Parts, for the Use and Entertainment of Kings, for the Education and Instruction of young Princes, for Advice and Assistance to the greatest Ministers; and, in short, the Favour of Learning was the Humour and Mode of the Age. *Francis* the First, *Charles* the Fifth, and *Henry* the Eighth (those Three great Rivals) agreed in this, though in nothing else. Many Nobles pursued this Vein with great Application and Success; among whom, *Picus de Mirandula,*[49] a Sovereign Prince in *Italy,*

---

[49] Count Giovanni Pico della Mirandola (1463–1494).

might have proved a Prodigy of Learning, if his Studies and Life had lasted as long as those of the Ancients: For I think all of them that writ much of what we have now remaining, lived old, whereas he dyed about Three and Thirty, and left the World in Admiration of so much Knowledge in so much Youth. Since those Reigns I have not observed in our Modern Story, any Great Princes much celebrated for their Favour of Learning, further than to serve their Turns, to justifie their Pretensions and Quarrels, or flatter their Successes. The Honour of Princes has of late struck Sail to their Interest; whereas of old, their Interests, Greatness and Conquests, were all dedicated to their Glory and Fame.

How much the Studies and Labours of Learned Men must have been damped for want of this Influence and kind Aspect of Princes, may be best conjectured from what happened on the contrary, about the *Augustan* Age, when the Learning of *Rome* was at its Height, and perhaps owed it in some Degree to the Bounty and Patronage of that Emperor, and *Mecœnas* his Favourite, as well as to the Felicity of the Empire, and Tranquility of the Age.

The Humour of Avarice, and Greediness of Wealth, have been ever, and in all Countries, where Silver and Gold have been in Price and of current Use: But if it be true in particular Men, that as Riches increase, the Desires of them do so too, May it not be true of the general Vein and Humour of Ages? May they not have turned more to this Pursuit of insatiable Gains, since the Discoveries and Plantations of the *West-Indies,* and those vast Treasures that have flowed in to these *Western* Parts of *Europe* almost every Year, and with such mighty Tides for so long a Course of Time? Where few are Rich, few care for it; where many are so, many desire it; and most in time begin to think it necessary. Where this Opinion grows generally in a Country, the Temples of Honour are soon pulled down, and all Men's Sacrifices are made to those of Fortune, The Soldier as well as the Merchant, the

Scholar as well as the Plough-Man, the Divine and the States-Man, as well as the Lawyer and Physician.

Now I think that nothing is more evident in the World, than that Honour is a much stronger Principle, both of Action and Invention, than Gain can ever be. That all the Great and Noble Productions of Wit and of Courage, have been inspired and exalted by that alone. That the Charming Flights and Labours of Poets, the deep Speculations and Studies of Philosophers, the Conquests of Emperors and Atchievements of Heroes, have all flowed from this one Source of Honour and Fame. The last Farewel that *Horace* takes of his Lyrick Poems, *Epicurus* of his Inventions in Philosophy, *Augustus* of his Empire and Government, are all of the same Strain;[50] and as their Lives were entertained, so their Age was relieved, and their Deaths softned, by the Prospect of lying down upon the Bed of Fame.

Avarice is, on the other side, of all Passions the most sordid, the most clogged and covered with Dirt and with Dross, so that it cannot raise its Wings beyond the smell of the Earth: 'Tis the Pay of Common Soldiers, as Honour is of Commanders; and yet among those themselves, none ever went so far upon the Hopes of Prey or of Spoils, as those that have been spirited by Honour or Religion. 'Tis no wonder then, that Learning has been so little advanced since it grew to be Mercenary, and the Progress of it has been fettered by the Cares of the World, and disturbed by the Desires of being rich, or the Fears of being poor; from all which, the Ancient *Philosophers,* the *Brachmans* of *India,* the *Chaldæan Magi,* and *Ægyptian* Priests, were disintangled and free.

But the last Maim given to Learning, has been by the Scorn of Pedantry, which the Shallow, the Superficial, and the Sufficient among Scholars first drew upon themselves, and very justly, by pretend-

ing to more than they had, or to more Esteem than what they had could deserve, by broaching it in all Places, at all Times, upon all Occasions, and by living so much among themselves, or in their Closets and Cells, as to make them unfit for all other Business, and ridiculous in all other Conversations. As an Infection that rises in a Town, first falls upon Children or weak Constitutions, or those that are subject to other Diseases, but spreading further by degrees, seizes upon the most Healthy, Vigorous and Strong; and when the Contagion grows very general, all the Neighbours avoid coming into the Town, or are afraid of those that are Well among them, as much as of those that are Sick. Just so it fared in the Common-wealth of Learning, some poor weak Constitutions were first infected with Pedantry, the Contagion spread in time upon some that were stronger; Foreigners that heard there was a Plague in the Country, grew afraid to come there, and avoided the Commerce of the Sound as well as of the Diseased. This Dislike or Apprehension turned, like all Fear, to Hatred, and Hatred to Scorn. The rest of the Neighbours began first to rail at Pedants, then to ridicule them; the Learned began to fear the same Fate, and that the Pigeons should be taken for Daws, because they were all in a Flock: And because the Poorest and Meanest of the Company were Proud, the Best and the Richest began to be Ashamed.

An Ingenious *Spaniard* at *Brussels* would needs have it that the History of *Don Quixot* had ruined the *Spanish* Monarchy; for before that time, Love and Valour were all Romance among them; every young Cavalier that entred the Scene, dedicated the Services of his Life, to his Honour first, and then to his Mistress. They lived and died in this romantick Vein; and the old Duke of *Alva,*[51] in his last *Portugal* Expedition, had a young Mistress, to whom the

---

[50] Horace, "I have finished a monument more durable than brass" (*Odes,* III, xxx); Epicurus, "Farewell: remember my sayings" (Diogenes Laertius, *Vita Philosophorum,* x); Augustus,

"Express your approval by applause" (Caius Suetonius Tranquillus, *De Vita Caesarum*).

[51] Spanish military commander (1508–?1583).

Glory of that Atchievement was devoted, by which he hoped to value himself, instead of those Qualities he had lost with his Youth. After *Don Quixot* appeared, and with that inimitable Wit and Humour turned all this Romantick Honour and Love into Ridicule; the *Spaniards,* he said, began to grow ashamed of both, and to laugh at Fighting and Loving; or at least otherwise than to pursue their Fortune, or satisfie their Lust; and the Consequences of this, both upon their Bodies and their Minds, this *Spaniard* would needs have pass for a great Cause of the Ruin of *Spain,* or of its Greatness and Power.

Whatever Effect the Ridicule of Knight-Errantry might have had upon that Monarchy, I believe that of Pedantry has had a very ill one upon the Common-wealth of Learning; and I wish the Vein of Ridiculing all that is Serious and Good, all Honour and Virtue, as well as Learning and Piety, may have no worse Effects on any other State: 'Tis the Itch of our Age and Climate, and has over-run both the Court and the Stage; enters a House of Lords and Commons, as boldly as a *Coffee*-House, Debates of Council as well as private Conversation; and I have known in my Life, more than one or two Ministers of State, that would rather have said a Witty thing, than done a Wise one; and made the Company Laugh, rather than the Kingdom Rejoyce. But this is enough to excuse the Imperfections of Learning in our Age, and to censure the Sufficiency of some of the Learned; and this small Piece of Justice I have done the Ancients, will not, I hope, be taken, any more than 'tis meant, for any Injury to the Moderns.

I shall conclude with a Saying of *Alphonsus* (Sirnamed the Wise) King of *Aragon;*[52]

That among so many things as are by Men possessed or pursued in the Course of their Lives, all the rest are Bawbles, besides Old Wood to Burn, Old Wine to Drink, Old Friends to Converse with, and Old Books to Read.

---

[52] Alfonso V, King of Aragon (1416–1458), born in 1385. Temple is confused with Alfonso X; the epithet of Alfonso V is The Magnanimous.

John Dryden
1631-1700

FABLES, ANCIENT AND MODERN

PREFACE

'Tis with a Poet, as with a Man who designs to build, and is very exact, as he supposes, in casting up the Cost beforehand: But, generally speaking, he is mistaken in his Account, and reckons short of the Expence he first intended: He alters his Mind as the Work proceeds, and will have this or that Convenience more, of which he had not thought when he began. So has it hapned to me; I have built a House, where I intended but a Lodge: Yet with better Success than a certain Nobleman, who beginning with a Dog-kennil, never liv'd to finish the Palace he had contriv'd.

From translating the First of *Homer's Iliads,* (which I intended as an Essay to the whole Work) I proceeded to the Translation of the Twelfth Book of *Ovid's Metamorphoses,* because it contains, among other Things, the Causes, the Beginning, and Ending, of the *Trojan* War: Here I ought in reason to have stopp'd; but the Speeches of *Ajax* and *Ulysses* lying next in my way, I could not balk 'em. When I had compass'd them, I was so taken with the former Part of the Fifteenth Book, (which is the Master-piece of the whole *Meta-morphoses*) that I enjoyn'd my self the pleasing Task of rendring it into *English.* And now I found, by the Number of my Verses, that they began to swell into a little Volume; which gave me an Occasion of looking backward on some Beauties of my Author, in his former Books: There occur'd to me the Hunting of the Boar, *Cinyras* and *Myrrha,* the good-natur'd Story of *Baucis* and *Philemon,* with the rest, which I hope I have translated closely enough, and given them the same Turn of Verse, which they had in the Original; and this, I may say without vanity, is not the Talent of every Poet: He who has arriv'd the nearest to it, is the Ingenious and Learned *Sandys,*[1] the best Versifier of the former Age; if I may properly call it by that Name, which was the former Part of this concluding Century. For *Spencer* and *Fairfax*[2] both flourish'd in the Reign of Queen *Elizabeth:* Great Masters in our Language; and who saw much farther into the Beauties of our Numbers, than those who immediately followed them. *Milton* was the Poetical Son of *Spencer,* and Mr. *Waller*[3] of *Fairfax;* for we have our Lineal Descents and

Text from *Fables, Ancient and Modern,* 1700.

[1] George Sandys (1578–1644) translated Ovid's *Metamorphoses.*

[2] Edmund Spenser (c. 1552–1599) and Edward Fairfax (c. 1580–1635); the latter translated the modern Italian epic *Gerusalemme Liberata* (1575) of Torquato Tasso under the title *Godfrey of Bulloigne.*

[3] Edmund Waller (1606–1687).

Clans, as well as other Families: *Spencer* more than once insinuates, that the Soul of *Chaucer* was transfus'd into his Body; and that he was begotten by him Two hundred years after his Decease. *Milton* has acknowledg'd to me, that *Spencer* was his Original; and many besides my self have heard our famous *Waller* own, that he deriv'd the Harmony of his Numbers from the *Godfrey of Bulloign,* which was turn'd into *English* by Mr. *Fairfax.* But to return: Having done with *Ovid* for this time, it came into my mind, that our old *English* Poet *Chaucer* in many Things resembled him, and that with no disadvantage on the Side of the Modern Author, as I shall endeavour to prove when I compare them: And as I am, and always have been studious to promote the Honour of my Native Country, so I soon resolv'd to put their Merits to the Trial, by turning some of the *Canterbury* Tales into our Language, as it is now refin'd: For by this Means both the Poets being set in the same Light, and dress'd in the same *English* Habit, Story to be compar'd with Story, a certain Judgment may be made betwixt them, by the Reader, without obtruding my Opinion on him: Or if I seem partial to my Country-man, and Predecessor in the Laurel, the Friends of Antiquity are not few: And besides many of the Learn'd, *Ovid* has almost all the *Beaux,* and the whole Fair Sex his declar'd Patrons.[4] Perhaps I have assum'd somewhat more to my self than they allow me; because I have adventur'd to sum up the Evidence: But the Readers are the Jury; and their Privilege remains entire to decide according to the Merits of the Cause: Or, if they please to bring it to another Hearing, before some other Court. In the mean time, to follow the Thrid[5] of my Discourse, (as Thoughts, according to Mr. *Hobbs,* have always some Connexion)[6] so from *Chaucer* I was led to think on *Boccace,*[7] who was not only his Contemporary, but also pursu'd the same Studies; wrote Novels in Prose, and many Works in Verse; particularly is said to have invented the Octave Rhyme, or *Stanza* of Eight Lines, which ever since has been maintain'd by the Practice of all *Italian* Writers, who are, or at least assume the Title of *Heroick Poets:* He and *Chaucer,* among other Things, had this in common, that they refin'd their Mother-Tongues; but with this difference, that *Dante* had begun to file their Language, at least in Verse, before the time of *Boccace,* who likewise receiv'd no little Help from his Master *Petrarch:* But the Reformation of their Prose was wholly owing to *Boccace* himself; who is yet the Standard of Purity in the *Italian* Tongue; though many of his Phrases are become obsolete, as in process of Time it must needs happen. *Chaucer* (as you have formerly been told by our learn'd Mr. *Rhymer*)[8] first adorn'd and amplified our barren Tongue from the *Provencall,* which was then the most polish'd of all the Modern Languages: But this Subject has been copiously treated by that great Critick, who deserves no little Commendation from us his Countrymen. For these Reasons of Time, and Resemblance of Genius, in *Chaucer* and *Boccace,* I resolv'd to join them in my present Work; to which I have added some Original Papers of my own; which whether they are equal or inferiour to my other Poems, an Author is the most improper Judge; and therefore I leave them wholly to the Mercy of the Reader: I will hope the best, that they will not be condemn'd; but if they should, I have the Excuse of an old Gentleman, who mounting on Horseback before some Ladies, when I was present, got up somewhat heavily, but desir'd of the Fair Spectators, that they would count Fourscore and eight before they judg'd him. By the Mercy of God, I am already come within Twenty Years of his Number, a Cripple in my Limbs, but what Decays are in my Mind, the Reader must determine. I think my self as vigorous as ever in the Faculties

---

[4] Presumably as the author of *Ars Amoris.*
[5] thread.
[6] Thomas Hobbes (1588–1679), English philosopher of materialism.

[7] Giovanni Boccaccio (1313–1375).
[8] Thomas Rymer (1641–1713) in *A Short View of Tragedy.*

of my Soul, excepting only my Memory, which is not impair'd to any great degree; and if I lose not more of it, I have no great reason to complain. What Judgment I had, increases rather than diminishes; and Thoughts, such as they are, come crowding in so fast upon me, that my only Difficulty is to chuse or to reject; to run them into Verse, or to give them the other Harmony of Prose, I have so long studied and practis'd both, that they are grown into a Habit, and become familiar to me. In short, though I may lawfully plead some part of the old Gentleman's Excuse; yet I will reserve it till I think I have greater need, and ask no Grains of Allowance for the Faults of this my present Work, but those which are given of course to Humane Frailty. I will not trouble my Reader with the shortness of Time in which I writ it; or the several Intervals of Sickness: They who think too well of their own Performances, are apt to boast in their Prefaces how little Time their Works have cost them; and what other Business of more importance interfer'd: But the Reader will be as apt to ask the Question, Why they allow'd not a longer Time to make their Works more perfect? and why they had so despicable an Opinion of their Judges, as to thrust their indigested Stuff upon them, as if they deserv'd no better?

With this Account of my present Undertaking, I conclude the first Part of this Discourse: In the second Part, as at a second Sitting, though I alter not the Draught, I must touch the same Features over again, and change the Dead-colouring of the Whole. In general I will only say, that I have written nothing which savours of Immorality or Profaneness; at least, I am not conscious to my self of any such Intention. If there happen to be found an irreverent Expression, or a Thought too wanton, they are crept into my Verses through my Inadvertency: If the Searchers find any in the Cargo, let them be stav'd or forfeited, like Counterbanded Goods; at least, let their Authors be answerable for them, as being but imported Merchandise, and not of my own Manufacture. On the other Side, I have endeavour'd to chuse such Fables, both Ancient and Modern, as contain in each of them some instructive Moral, which I could prove by Induction, but the Way is tedious; and they leap foremost into sight, without the Reader's Trouble of looking after them. I wish I could affirm with a safe Conscience, that I had taken the same Care in all my former Writings; for it must be own'd, that supposing Verses are never so beautiful or pleasing, yet if they contain any thing which shocks Religion, or Good Manners, they are at best, what *Horace* says of good Numbers without good Sense, *Versus inopes rerum, nugaeque canorae:*[9] Thus far, I hope, I am Right in Court, without renouncing to my other Right of Self-defence, where I have been wrongfully accus'd, and my Sense wire-drawn into Blasphemy or Bawdry, as it has often been by a Religious Lawyer, in a late Pleading against the Stage;[10] in which he mixes Truth with Falshood, and has not forgotten the old Rule, of calumniating strongly, that something may remain.

I resume the Thrid of my Discourse with the first of my Translations, which was the First *Iliad* of *Homer.* If it shall please God to give me longer Life, and moderate Health, my Intentions are to translate the whole *Ilias;* provided still, that I meet with those Encouragements from the Publick, which may enable me to proceed in my Undertaking with some Chearfulness. And this I dare assure the World before-hand, that I have found by Trial, *Homer* a more pleasing Task than *Virgil,* (though I say not the Translation will be less laborious.) For the *Grecian* is more according to my Genius, than the *Latin* Poet. In the Works of the two Authors we may read their Manners, and natural Inclinations, which are wholly different. *Virgil* was of a quiet, sedate Temper; *Homer* was violent, impetuous, and full of Fire. The chief Tal-

[9] Meaningless poetry, more sound than sense" (*Ars Poetica*, l. 322).
[10] Jeremy Collier (1650–1726), a clergyman and nonjuror, in *A Short View of the Immorality and Profaneness of the English Stage* (1698).

ent of *Virgil* was Propriety of Thoughts, and Ornament of Words: *Homer* was rapid in his Thoughts, and took all the Liberties both of Numbers, and of Expressions, which his Language, and the Age in which he liv'd allow'd him: *Homer's* Invention was more copious, *Virgil's* more confin'd: So that if *Homer* had not led the Way, it was not in *Virgil* to have begun Heroick Poetry: For, nothing can be more evident, than that the *Roman* Poem is but the Second Part of the *Ilias;* a Continuation of the same Story: And the Persons already form'd: The Manners of *Æneas,* are those of *Hector* superadded to those which *Homer* gave him. The Adventures of *Ulysses* in the *Odysseis,* are imitated in the first Six Books of *Virgil's Æneis:* And though the Accidents are not the same, (which would have argu'd him of a servile, copying, and total Barrenness of Invention) yet the Seas were the same, in which both the *Heroes* wander'd; and *Dido* cannot be deny'd to be the Poetical Daughter of *Calypso.* The Six latter Books of *Virgil's* Poem, are the Four and twenty *Iliads* contracted: A Quarrel occasion'd by a Lady, a Single Combate, Battels fought, and a Town besieg'd. I say not this in derogation to *Virgil,* neither do I contradict any thing which I have formerly said in his just Praise:[11] For his *Episodes* are almost wholly of his own Invention; and the Form which he has given to the Telling, makes the Tale his own, even though the Original Story had been the same. But this proves, however, that *Homer* taught *Virgil* to design: And if Invention be the first Vertue of an Epick Poet, then the *Latin* Poem can only be allow'd the second Place. Mr. *Hobbs,* in the Preface to his own bald Translation of the *Ilias,*[12] (studying Poetry as he did Mathematicks, when it was too late) Mr. *Hobbs,* I say, begins the Praise of *Homer* where he should have ended it. He tells us, that the first Beauty of an Epick Poem consists in Diction, that is, in the Choice of Words, and Harmony of Numbers: Now, the Words are the Colouring of the Work, which in the Order of Nature is last to be consider'd. The Design, the Disposition, the Manners, and the Thoughts, are all before it: Where any of those are wanting or imperfect, so much wants or is imperfect in the Imitation of Humane Life; which is in the very Definition of a Poem. Words indeed, like glaring Colours, are the first Beauties that arise, and strike the Sight; but if the Draught be false or lame, the Figures ill dispos'd, the Manners obscure or inconsistent, or the Thoughts unnatural, then the finest Colours are but Dawbing, and the Piece is a beautiful Monster at the best. Neither *Virgil* nor *Homer* were deficient in any of the former Beauties; but in this last, which is Expression, the *Roman* Poet is at least equal to the Grecian, as I have said elsewhere; supplying the Poverty of his Language, by his Musical Ear, and by his Diligence. But to return: Our two Great Poets, being so different in their Tempers, one Cholerick and Sanguin, the other Phlegmatick and Melancholick; that which makes them excel in their several Ways, is, that each of them has follow'd his own natural Inclination, as well in Forming the Design, as in the Execution of it. The very *Heroes* shew their Authors: *Achilles* is hot, impatient, revengeful, *Impiger, iracundus, inexorabilis, acer, etc.*[13] *Æneaes* patient, considerate, careful of his People, and merciful to his Enemies; ever submissive to the Will of Heaven, *quo fata trahunt retrahuntque, sequamur.*[14] I could please my self with enlarging on this Subject, but am forc'd to defer it to a fitter Time. From all I have said, I will only draw this Inference, That the Action of *Homer* being more full of Vigour than that of *Virgil,* according to the Temper of the Writer, is of consequence more pleasing to the Reader. One warms you by Degrees; the other sets you on fire all at once, and never intermits his Heat.

---

[11] Dryden had translated the whole of the *Aeneid* in 1697.

[12] Hobbes (see note 6) had translated both the *Iliad* and the *Odyssey* in 1676.

[13] "indefatigable, passionate, inexorable, vehement" (Horace, *Ars Poetica,* l. 121).

[14] "Let us pursue our destiny wherever it leads or restrains us" (*Aeneid,* V, 709).

'Tis the same Difference which *Longinus* makes betwixt the Effects of Eloquence in *Demosthenes,* and *Tully.* One persuades; the other commands.[15] You never cool while you read *Homer,* even not in the Second Book, (a graceful Flattery to his Countrymen;) but he hastens from the Ships, and concludes not that Book till he has made you an Amends by the violent playing of a new Machine. From thence he hurries on his Action with Variety of Events, and ends it in less Compass than Two Months. This Vehemence of his, I confess, is more suitable to my Temper: and therefore I have translated his First Book with greater Pleasure than any Part of *Virgil:* But it was not a Pleasure without Pains: The continual Agitations of the Spirits, must needs be a Weakning of any Constitution, especially in Age: and many Pauses are required for Refreshment betwixt the Heats; the *Iliad* of its self being a third part longer than all *Virgil's* Works together.

This is what I thought needful in this Place to say of *Homer.* I proceed to *Ovid,* and *Chaucer;* considering the former only in relation to the latter. With *Ovid* ended the Golden Age of the *Roman* Tongue: From *Chaucer* the Purity of the *English* Tongue began. The Manners of the Poets were not unlike: Both of them were well-bred, well-natur'd, amorous, and Libertine, at least in their Writings, it may be also in their Lives. Their Studies were the same, Philosophy, and Philology. Both of them were knowing in Astronomy, of which *Ovid's* Books of the *Roman* Feasts, and *Chaucer's* Treatise of the *Astrolabe,* are sufficient Witnesses. But *Chaucer* was likewise an Astrologer, as were *Virgil, Horace, Persius,* and *Manilius.*[16] Both writ

with wonderful Facility and Clearness; neither were great Inventors: For *Ovid* only copied the *Grecian* Fables; and most of *Chaucer's* Stories were taken from his *Italian* Contemporaries, or their Predecessors: *Boccace* his *Decameron* was first publish'd; and from thence our *Englishman* has borrow'd many of his *Canterbury* Tales: Yet that of *Palamon* and *Arcite*[17] was written in all probability by some *Italian* Wit, in a former Age; as I shall prove hereafter: The Tale of *Grizild*[18] was the Invention of *Petrarch;* by him sent to *Boccace;* from whom it came to *Chaucer: Troilus* and *Cressida* was also written by a *Lombard* Author;[19] but much amplified by our *English* Translatour, as well as beautified; the Genius of our Countrymen in general being rather to improve an Invention, than to invent themselves; as is evident not only in our Poetry, but in many of our Manufactures. I find I have anticipated already, and taken up from *Boccace* before I come to him: But there is so much less behind; and I am of the Temper of most Kings, *who love to be in Debt,* are all for present Money, no matter how they pay it afterwards: Besides, the Nature of a Preface is rambling; never wholly out of the Way, nor in it. This I have learn'd from the Practice of honest *Montaign,*[20] and return at my pleasure to *Ovid* and *Chaucer,* of whom I have little more to say. Both of them built on the Inventions of other Men; yet since *Chaucer* had something of his own, as *The Wife of Baths Tale, The Cock and the Fox,*[21] which I have translated, and some others, I may justly give our Countryman the Precedence in that Part; since I can remember nothing of *Ovid* which was wholly his. Both of them understood the Manners; under

---

[15] "The great opportunity of Demosthenes' sublimity comes where intense expression and vehement passion are involved, and where the audience is to be completely swept away. The wealth of Cicero [i.e., Tully] is appropriate when the audience is to be overawed with words, for it is best fitted for the expression of commonplaces," etc. (*On the Sublime,* XII).

[16] Also, Dryden himself is known to have had enough interest in astrology to cast his son's horoscope.

[17] "The Knight's Tale."

[18] Griselda of "The Clerk's Tale."

[19] Chaucer attributed the source of his poem to "myn auctor called Lollius" (I, 394), but no such writer is known.

[20] Michel de Montaigne (1533–1592), author of *Essais.*

[21] i.e., "The Nun's Priest's Tale." Various sources and analogues for both tales have been proposed, but essentially Dryden was correct in emphasizing their originality.

which Name I comprehend the Passions, and, in a larger Sense, the Descriptions of Persons, and their very Habits: For an Example, I see *Baucis* and *Philemon* as perfectly before me, as if some ancient Painter had drawn them; and all the Pilgrims in the *Canterbury* Tales, their Humours, their Features, and the very Dress, as distinctly as if I had supp'd with them at the *Tabard* in *Southwark:* Yet even there too the Figures of *Chaucer* are much more lively, and set in a better Light: Which though I have not time to prove; yet I appeal to the Reader, and am sure he will clear me from Partiality. The Thoughts and Words remain to be consider'd, in the Comparison of the two Poets; and I have sav'd my self one half of that Labour, by owning that *Ovid* liv'd when the *Roman* Tongue was in its Meridian; *Chaucer,* in the Dawning of our Language: Therefore that Part of the Comparison stands not on an equal Foot, any more than the Diction of *Ennius*[22] and *Ovid;* or of *Chaucer,* and our present *English.* The Words are given up as a Post not to be defended in our Poet, because he wanted the Modern Art of Fortifying. The Thoughts remain to be consider'd: And they are to be measur'd only by their Propriety; that is, as they flow more or less naturally from the Persons describ'd, on such and such Occasions. The Vulgar Judges, which are Nine Parts in Ten of all Nations, who call Conceits[23] and Jingles Wit, who see *Ovid* full of them, and *Chaucer* altogether without them, will think me little less than mad, for preferring the *Englishman* to the *Roman:* Yet, with their leave, I must presume to say, that the Things they admire are only glittering Trifles, and so far from being Witty, that in a serious Poem they are nauseous, because they are unnatural. Wou'd any Man who is ready to die for Love, describe his Passion like *Narcissus?* Wou'd

he think of *inopem me copia fecit,*[24] and a Dozen more of such Expressions, pour'd on the Neck of one another, and signifying all the same Thing? If this were Wit, was this a Time to be witty, when the poor Wretch was in the Agony of Death? This is just *John Littlewit* in *Bartholomew Fair,*[25] who had a Conceit (as he tells you) left him in his Misery; a miserable Conceit. On these Occasions the Poet shou'd endeavour to raise Pity: But instead of this, *Ovid* is tickling you to laugh. *Virgil* never made use of such Machines,[26] when he was moving you to commiserate the Death of *Dido:* He would not destroy what he was building. *Chaucer* makes *Arcite* violent in his Love, and unjust in the Pursuit of it: Yet when he came to die, he made him think more reasonably: He repents not of his Love, for that had alter'd his Character; but acknowledges the Injustice of his Proceedings, and resigns *Emilia to Palamon.* What would *Ovid* have done on this Occasion? He would certainly have made *Arcite* witty on his Death-bed. He had complain'd he was farther off from Possession, by being so near, and a thousand such Boyisms,[27] which *Chaucer* rejected as below the Dignity of the Subject. They who think otherwise, would by the same Reason prefer *Lucan*[28] and *Ovid* to *Homer* and *Virgil,* and *Martial*[29] to all Four of them. As for the Turn of Words, in which *Ovid* particularly excels all Poets; they are sometimes a Fault, and sometimes a Beauty, as they are us'd properly or improperly; but in strong Passions always to be shunn'd, because Passions are serious, and will admit no Playing. The *French* have a high Value for them; and I confess, they are often what they call Delicate, when they are introduc'd with Judgment; but *Chaucer* writ with more Simplicity, and follow'd Nature more closely, than to use them. I have thus far, to the best of my Knowledge, been

---

[22] Quintus Ennius (239–?169 B.C.), called the father of Latin poetry.

[23] figures of speech.

[24] "Plenty makes me poor"—Narcissus (Ovid, *Metamorphoses,* III, 466).

[25] By Ben Jonson.

[26] machinations or devices, suggesting the *deus ex machina* of classical drama.

[27] puerilities.

[28] Roman poet (39–65).

[29] Roman epigrammatist (40–102).

an upright Judge betwixt the Parties in Competition, not medling with the Design nor the Disposition of it; because the Design was not their own; and in the disposing of it they were equal. It remains that I say somewhat of *Chaucer* in particular.

In the first place, As he is the Father of *English* Poetry, so I hold him in the same Degree of Veneration as the *Grecians* held *Homer*, or the *Romans Virgil*: He is a perpetual Fountain of good Sense; learn'd in all Sciences; and therefore speaks properly on all Subjects: As he knew what to say, so he knows also when to leave off; a Continence which is practis'd by few Writers, and scarcely by any of the Ancients, excepting *Virgil* and *Horace*. One of our late great Poets[30] is sunk in his Reputation, because he cou'd never forgive any Conceit which came in his way; but swept like a Dragnet, great and small. There was plenty enough, but the Dishes were ill sorted; whole Pyramids of Sweet-meats, for Boys and Women; but little of solid Meat, for Men: All this proceeded not from any want of Knowledge, but of Judgment; neither did he want that in discerning the Beauties and Faults of other Poets; but only indulg'd himself in the Luxury of Writing; and perhaps knew it was a Fault, but hop'd the Reader would not find it. For this Reason, though he must always be thought a great Poet, he is no longer esteem'd a good Writer: And for Ten Impressions, which his Works have had in so many successive Years, yet at present a hundred Books are scarcely purchas'd once a Twelvemonth: For, as my last Lord *Rochester*[31] said, though somewhat profanely, *Not being of God, he could not stand.*

Chaucer follow'd Nature every where; but was never so bold to go beyond her: And there is a great Difference of being *Poeta* and *nimis Poeta*,[32] if we may believe *Catullus,* as much as betwixt a modest Behaviour and Affectation. The Verse of *Chaucer,* I confess, is not Harmonious to us; but 'tis like the Eloquence of one whom *Tacitus* commends, it was *auribus istius temporis accommodata:*[33] They who liv'd with him, and some time after him, thought it Musical; and it continues so even in our Judgment, if compar'd with the Numbers of *Lidgate* and *Gower*[34] his Contemporaries: There is the rude Sweetness of a *Scotch* Tune[35] in it, which is natural and pleasing, though not perfect. 'Tis true, I cannot go so far as he who publish'd the last Edition of him;[36] for he would make us believe the Fault is in our Ears, and that there were really Ten Syllables in a Verse where we find but Nine: But this Opinion is not worth confuting; 'tis so gross and obvious an Errour, that common Sense (which is a Rule in every thing but Matters of Faith and Revelation) must convince the Reader, that Equality of Numbers in every Verse which we call *Heroick*,[37] was either not known, or not always practis'd in *Chaucer's* Age. It were an easie Matter to produce some thousands of his Verses, which are lame for want of half a Foot, and sometimes a whole one, and which no Pronunciation can make otherwise. We can only say, that he liv'd in the Infancy of our Poetry, and that nothing is brought to Perfection at the first. We must be Children before we grow Men. There was an *Ennius,* and in process of Time a *Lucilius,* and a *Lucretius,* before *Virgil* and *Horace;* even after *Chaucer* there was a *Spencer,* a *Harrington,* a

---

[30] Abraham Cowley (1618–1667). The word "forgive" in this sentence is used in the special sense of "give up" or "forego."

[31] John Wilmot, second Earl of Rochester (1647–1680).

[32] "a poet" and "too much of a poet." The source is not Catullus but Martial (*Epigrams,* III, xliv).

[33] "appropriate to the ears of that time" (adapted from *Dialogue About the Orators,* l. 21).

[34] John Lydgate (*c.* 1370–*c.* 1431) and John Gower (*c.* 1325–1408).

[35] ballad.

[36] By Thomas Speght in 1602; reprinted in 1687. It is remarkable that the text of Chaucer's poems was, until 1721, available only in the heavy, black and almost unreadable gothic type apparently deemed appropriate to his medieval language.

[37] Iambic pentameter.

Fairfax, before *Waller* and *Denham* were in being: And our Numbers were in their Nonage till these last appear'd. I need say little of his Parentage, Life, and Fortunes: They are to be found at large in all the Editions of his Works. He was employ'd abroad, and favour'd by *Edward* the Third, *Richard* the Second, and *Henry* the Fourth, and was Poet, as I suppose, to all Three of them. In *Richard's* Time, I doubt, he was a little dipt in the Rebellion of the Commons;[38] and being Brother-in-Law to *John of Ghant,* it was no wonder if he follow'd the Fortunes of that Family; and was well with *Henry* the Fourth when he had depos'd his Predecessor. Neither is it to be admir'd, that *Henry,* who was a wise as well as a valiant Prince, who claim'd by Succession, and was sensible that his Title was not found, but was rightfully in *Mortimer,* who had married the Heir of *York;* it was not to be admir'd, I say, if that great Politician should be pleas'd to have the greatest Wit of those Times in his Interests, and to be the Trumpet of his Praises. *Augustus* had given him the Example, by the Advice of *Mecaenas,* who recommended *Virgil* and *Horace* to him; whose Praises help'd to make him Popular while he was alive, and after his Death have made him Precious to Posterity. As for the Religion of our Poet, he seems to have some little Byas towards the Opinions of *Wickliff,*[39] after *John of Gaunt* his Patron; somewhat of which appears in the Tale of *Piers Plowman:*[40] Yet I cannot blame him for inveighing so sharply against the Vices of the Clergy in his Age: Their Pride, their Ambition, their Pomp, their Avarice, their Worldly Interest, deserv'd the Lashes which he gave them, both in that, and in most of his *Canterbury Tales:* Neither has his Contemporary *Boccace,*

spar'd them. Yet both those Poets liv'd in much esteem, with good and holy Men in Orders: For the Scandal which is given by particular Priests, reflects not on the Sacred Function. *Chaucer's Monk,* his *Chanon,* and his *Fryar,* took not from the Character of his *Good Parson.* A Satyrical Poet is the Check of the Laymen, on bad Priests. We are only to take care, that we involve not the Innocent with the Guilty in the same Condemnation. The Good cannot be too much honour'd, nor the Bad too coursly us'd: For the Corruption of the Best, becomes the Worst.[41] When a Clergy-man is whipp'd, his Gown is first taken off, by which the Dignity of his Order is secur'd: If he be wrongfully accus'd, he has his Action of Slander; and 'tis at the Poet's Peril, if he transgress the Law. But they will tell us, that all kind of Satire, though never so well deserv'd by particular Priests, yet brings the whole Order into Contempt. Is then the Peerage of *England* any thing dishonour'd, when a Peer suffers for his Treason? If he be libell'd, or any way defam'd, he has his *Scandalum Magnatum*[42] to punish the Offender. They who use this kind of Argument, seem to be conscious to themselves of somewhat which has deserv'd the Poet's Lash; and are less concern'd for their Publick Capacity, than for their Private: At least, there is Pride at the bottom of their Reasoning. If the Faults of Men in Orders are only to be judg'd among themselves, they are all in some sort Parties: For, since they say the Honour of their Order is concern'd in every Member of it, how can we be sure, that they will be impartial Judges? How far I may be allow'd to speak my Opinion in this Case, I know not: But I am sure a Dispute of this Nature caus'd Mischief in abundance betwixt a King of *England* and an Archbishop of *Can-*

---

[38] Parlous years following the Peasants' Revolt of 1381.

[39] John Wycliffe (1320?–1384), English protestant against the papacy and Catholic dogma.

[40] Chaucer's canon at this time included a tale attacking the church and attributed to the Ploughman but now not accepted as Chaucer's. Dryden confused it with the poem

Piers Plowman, attributed to William Langland.

[41] An old proverb. Cf. Shakespeare's Sonnet 94: "Lilies that fester smell far worse than weeds."

[42] Law protecting high office from malicious slander. It is still current in laws protecting banks from false rumors about their security.

terbury;[43] one standing up for the Laws of his Land, and the other for the Honour (as he call'd it) of God's Church; which ended in the Murther of the Prelate, and in the whipping of his Majesty from Post to Pillar for his Penance. The Learn'd and Ingenious Dr. *Drake* has sav'd me the Labour of inquiring into the Esteem and Reverence which the Priests have had of old;[44] and I would rather extend than diminish any part of it: Yet I must needs say, that when a Priest provokes me without any Occasion given him, I have no Reason, unless it be the Charity of a *Christian,* to forgive him: *Prior laesit*[45] is Justification sufficient in the Civil Law. If I answer him in his own Language, Self-defence, I am sure, must be allow'd me; and if I carry it farther, even to a sharp Recrimination, somewhat may be indulg'd to Humane Frailty. Yet my Resentment has not wrought so far, but that I have follow'd *Chaucer* in his Character of a Holy Man,[46] and have enlarg'd on that Subject with some Pleasure, reserving to my self the Right, if I shall think fit hereafter, to describe another sort of Priests, such as are more easily to be found than the Good Parson; such as have given the last Blow to Christianity in this Age, by a Practice so contrary to their Doctrine. But this will keep cold till another time. In the mean while, I take up *Chaucer* where I left him. He must have been a Man of a most wonderful comprehensive Nature, because, as it has been truly observ'd of him, he has taken into the Compass of his *Canterbury Tales* the various Manners and Humours (as we now call them) of the whole *English* Nation, in his Age. Not a single Character has escap'd him. All his Pilgrims are severally distinguish'd from each other; and not only in their Inclinations, but in their very Phisiognomies and Persons. *Bap-*

tista Porta[47] could not have describ'd their Natures better, than by the Marks which the Poet gives them. The Matter and Manner of their Tales, and of their Telling, are so suited to their different Educations, Humours, and Callings, that each of them would be improper in any other Mouth. Even the grave and serious Characters are distinguish'd by their several sorts of Gravity: Their Discourses are such as belong to their Age, their Calling, and their Breeding; such as are becoming of them, and of them only. Some of his Persons are Vicious, and some Vertuous; some are unlearn'd, or (as *Chaucer* calls them) Lewd, and some are Learn'd. Even the Ribaldry of the Low Characters is different: The *Reeve,* the *Miller,* and the *Cook,* are several Men, and distinguish'd from each other, as much as the mincing Lady Prioress, and the broad-speaking gap-tooth'd Wife of *Bathe.* But enough of this: There is such a Variety of Game springing up before me, that I am distracted in my Choice, and know not which to follow. 'Tis sufficient to say according to the Proverb, that here is God's Plenty. We have our Fore-fathers and Great Grand-dames all before us, as they were in *Chaucer's* Days; their general Characters are still remaining in Mankind, and even in *England,* though they are call'd by other Names than those of *Moncks,* and *Fryars,* and *Chanons,* and *Lady Abbesses,* and *Nuns:* For Mankind is ever the same, and nothing lost out of Nature, though everything is alter'd. May I have leave to do my self the Justice, (since my Enemies will do me none, and are so far from granting me to be a good Poet, that they will not allow me so much as to be a Christian, or a Moral Man) may I have leave, I say, to inform my Reader, that I have confin'd my Choice to such Tales of *Chaucer,* as favour nothing of Immod-

[43] Henry II and Thomas à Becket, resulting in the assassination of the latter in 1170. Cf. T. S. Eliot, *Murder in the Cathedral.*

[44] Dr. James Drake (1667–1707), *The Ancient and Modern Stage Surveyed, or Mr. Collier's Views on the Immorality and Profaneness of the Stage Set in a True Light* (1669). Collier had gone so far as to argue that no priest, even of a heathen faith, should be satirized.

[45] "He hit me first."

[46] Chaucer's "Persoun of a Toun," the character of the good pastor in the Prologue to *The Canterbury Tales.*

[47] Giovanni Battista della Porta, author of the treatise *De Humana Physiognomia* (1586).

esty. If I had desir'd more to please than to instruct, the *Reve,* the *Miller,* the *Shipman,* the *Merchant,* the *Sumner,* and above all, the *Wife of Bathe,* in the Prologue to her Tale, would have procur'd me as many Friends and Readers, as there are *Beaux* and Ladies of Pleasure in the Town. But I will no more offend against Good Manners: I am sensible as I ought to be of the Scandal I have given by my loose Writings; and make what Reparation I am able, by this Publick Acknowledgment.[48] If any thing of this Nature, or of Profaneness, be crept into these Poems, I am so far from defending it, that I disown it. *Totum hoc indictum volo.*[49] *Chaucer* makes another manner of Apologie for his broadspeaking, and *Boccace* makes the like; but I will follow neither of them. Our Country-man, in the end of his Characters, before the *Canterbury Tales,* thus excuses the Ribaldry, which is very gross, in many of his Novels.

But first, I pray you, of your courtesy,
That ye ne arrete it nought my villany,
Though that I plainly speak in this mat-
tere
To tellen you her words, and eke her
chere:
Ne though I speak her words properly,
For this ye known as well as I,
Who shall tellen a tale after a man
He mote rehearse as nye, as ever He can:
Everich word of it been in his charge,
All speke he, never so rudely, ne large
Or else he mote tellen his tale untrue,
Or feine things, or find words new:
He may not spare, altho he were his
brother,

He mote as well say o word as another.
Christ spake himself full broad in holy
Writ,
And well I wote no Villany is it.
Eke Plato saith, who so can him rede,
The words mote been Cousin to the
dede.[50]

Yet if a Man should have enquir'd of *Boccace* or of *Chaucer,* what need they had of introducing such Characters, where obscene Words were proper in their Mouths, but very undecent to be heard; I know not what Answer they could have made: For that Reason, such Tales shall be left untold by me. You have here a *Specimen* of *Chaucer's* Language, which is so obsolete, that his Sense is scarce to be understood; and you have likewise more than one Example of his unequal Numbers, which were mention'd before. Yet many of his Verses consist of Ten Syllables, and the Words not much behind our present *English:* As for Example, these two Lines, in the Description of the Carpenter's Young Wife:

Wincing she was, as is a jolly Colt,
Long as a Mast, and upright as a Bolt.[51]

I have almost done with *Chaucer,* when I have answer'd some Objections relating to my present Work. I find some People are offended that I have turn'd these Tales into modern *English;* because they think them unworthy of my Pains, and look on *Chaucer* as a dry, old-fashion'd Wit, not worth receiving. I have often heard the late Earl of *Leicester*[52] say, that Mr. *Cowley* himself was

---

[48] As early as 1686 in "An Ode to the Pious Memory of . . . Mrs. Anne Killegrew," Dryden had apologized for making "prostitute and profligate the Muse."

[49] "I wish all that unsaid."

[50] Prologue, ll. 725–742, which may be paraphrased thus:
But first, I ask your indulgence not to think ill of me for speaking in their language and in their voices, and even to the extent of using their own words exactly. Everyone knows that whoever repeats a story, however often, must have every word at his command and tell everything, no matter how crude or extravagant

it may seem. Otherwise, he will be unfaithful to the story either by making things up or putting them in another light. He must be as exact as if his life depended on it or he may as well invent the whole thing. I do not think it is wrong of Christ himself to use everyday language in the Gospels as he does. Plato too says, to those who know how to read him correctly, that words have an inevitable association with circumstances.

[51] "The Miller's Tale," ll. 77–78. A synonym of *wincing* is *skittish.*

[52] Philip Sidney, third Earl of Leicester (1619–1698).

of that opinion; who having read him over at my Lord's Request, declar'd he had no Taste of him. I dare not advance my Opinion against the Judgment of so great an Author: But I think it fair, however, to leave the Decision to the Publick: Mr. *Cowley* was too modest to set up for a Dictatour; and being shock'd perhaps with his old Style, never examin'd into the depth of his good Sense. *Chaucer,* I confess, is a rough Diamond, and must first be polish'd e'er he shines. I deny not likewise, that living in our early Days of Poetry, he writes not always of a piece; but sometimes mingles trivial Things, with those of greater Moment. Sometimes also, though not often, he runs riot, like *Ovid,* and knows not when he has said enough. But there are more great Wits, beside *Chaucer,* whose Fault is their Excess of Conceits, and those ill sorted. An Author is not to write all he can, but only all he ought. Having observ'd this Redundancy in *Chaucer,* (as it is an easie Matter for a Man of ordinary Parts to find a Fault in one of greater) I have not ty'd my self to a Literal Translation; but have often omitted what I judg'd unnecessary, or not of Dignity enough to appear in the Company of better Thoughts. I have presum'd farther in some Places, and added somewhat of my own where I thought my Author was deficient, and had not given his Thoughts their true Lustre, for want of Words in the Beginning of our Language. And to this I was the more embolden'd, because (if I may be permitted to say it of my self) I found I had a Soul congenial to his, and that I had been conversant in the same Studies. Another Poet, in another Age, may take the same Liberty with my Writings; if at least they live long enough to deserve Correction. It was also necessary sometimes to restore the Sense of *Chaucer,* which was lost or mangled in the Errors of the Press: Let this Example suffice at present in the Story of *Palamon* and *Arcite,* where the Temple

of *Diana* is describ'd, you find these Verses, in all the Editions of our Author:

There saw I Dane *turned unto a Tree,*
I mean not the Goddess Diane,
But Venus *Daughter, which that hight*
    Dane.

Which after a little Consideration I knew was to be reform'd into this Sense, that *Daphne* the Daughter of *Peneus* was turn'd into a Tree. I durst not make thus bold with *Ovid,* lest some future *Milbourn*[53] should arise, and say, I varied from my Author, because I understood him not.

But there are other Judges who think I ought not to have translated *Chaucer* into *English,* out of a quite contrary Notion: They suppose there is a certain Veneration due to his old Language; and that it is little less than Profanation and Sacrilege to alter it. They are farther of opinion, that somewhat of his good Sense will suffer in this Transfusion, and much of the Beauty of his Thoughts will infallibly be lost, which appear with more Grace in their old Habit. Of this Opinion was that excellent Person, whom I mention'd, the late Earl of *Leicester,* who valu'd *Chaucer* as much as Mr. *Cowley* despis'd him. My Lord dissuaded me from this Attempt, (for I was thinking of it some Years before his Death) and his Authority prevail'd so far with me, as to defer my Undertaking while he liv'd, in deference to him: Yet my Reason was not convinc'd with what he urg'd against it. If the first End of a Writer be to be understood, then as his Language grows obsolete, his Thoughts must grow obscure, *multa renascuntur quae nunc cecidere; cadentque quae nunc sunt in honore vocabula, si volet usus, quem penes arbitrium est & jus & norma loquendi.*[54] When an ancient Word for its Sound and Significancy deserves to be reviv'd, I have that reasonable Veneration for Antiquity, to restore it. All beyond this is Superstition. Words are not like

---

[53] Luke Milbourne (1649–1720), author of *Notes on Dryden's Virgil* (1698), an attack on Dryden's translation.
[54] "Many words will be revived which are now obsolete and many now held in honor will disappear if custom dictates, which is the arbiter, the law, and the norm of speech" (Horace, *Ars Poetica,* ll. 70–73).

Land-marks, so sacred as never to be re-mov'd: Customs are chang'd, and even Statutes are silently repeal'd, when the Reason ceases for which they were en-acted. As for the other Part of the Argu-ment, that his Thoughts will lose of their original Beauty, by the innovation of Words; in the first place, not only their Beauty, but their Being is lost, where they are no longer understood, which is the present Case. I grant, that something must be lost in all Transfusion, that is, in all Translations; but the Sense will remain, which would otherwise be lost, or at least be maim'd, when it is scarce intelligible; and that but to a few. How few are there who can read *Chaucer,* so as to understand him perfectly? And if imperfectly, then with less Profit, and no Pleasure. 'Tis not for the Use of some old *Saxon* Friends, that I have taken these Pains with him: Let them neglect my Version, because they have no need of it. I made it for their sakes who un-derstand Sense and Poetry, as well as they; when that Poetry and Sense is put into Words which they understand. I will go farther, and dare to add, that what Beauties I lose in some Places, I give to others which had them not orig-inally: But in this I may be partial to my self; let the Reader judge, and I sub-mit to his Decision. Yet I think I have just Occasion to complain of them, who because they understand *Chaucer,* would deprive the greater part of their Coun-trymen of the same Advantage, and hoord him up, as Misers do their Gran-dam Gold, only to look on it themselves, and hinder others from making use of it. In sum, I seriously protest, that no Man ever had, or can have, a greater Venera-tion for *Chaucer,* than my self. I have translated some part of his Works, only that I might perpetuate his Memory, or at least refresh it, amongst my Country-men. If I have alter'd him any where for the better, I must at the same time ac-knowledge, that I could have done noth-ing without him: *Facile est inventis ad-dere,*[55] is no great Commendation; and

I am not so vain to think I have deserv'd a greater. I will conclude what I have to say of him singly, with this one Remark: A Lady of my Acquaintance, who keeps a kind of Correspondence with some Au-thors of the Fair Sex in *France,* has been inform'd by them, that *Mademoiselle de Scudery,*[56] who is as old as *Sibyl,* and in-spir'd like her by the same God of Po-etry, is at this time translating *Chaucer* into modern *French.* From which I gather, that he has been formerly trans-lated into the old *Provencall,* (for, how she should come to understand Old *Eng-lish,* I know not.) But the Matter of Fact being true, it makes me think, that there is something in it like Fatality; that after certain Periods of Time, the Fame and Memory of Great Wits should be renew'd, as *Chaucer* is both in *France* and *England.* If this be wholly Chance, 'tis extraordinary; and I dare not call it more, for fear of being tax'd with Su-perstition.

Boccace comes last to be consider'd, who living in the same Age with *Chaucer,* had the same Genius, and fol-low'd the same Studies: Both writ Nov-els, and each of them cultivated his Mother-Tongue: But the greatest Re-semblance of our two Modern Authors being in their familiar Style, and pleas-ing way of relating Comical Adventures, I may pass it over, because I have trans-lated nothing from *Boccace* of that Na-ture. In the serious Part of Poetry, the Advantage is wholly on *Chaucer's* Side; for though the *Englishman* has borrow'd many Tales from the *Italian,* yet it ap-pears, that those of *Boccace* were not generally of his own making, but taken from Authors of former Ages, and by him only modell'd: So that what there was of Invention in either of them, may be judg'd equal. But *Chaucer* has refin'd on *Boccace,* and has mended the Stories which he has borrow'd, in his way of telling; though Prose allows more Lib-erty of Thought, and the Expression is more easie, when unconfin'd by Num-bers. Our Countryman carries Weight,[57]

---

[55] "It is easy to add to what has already been found."

[56] Mlle. Madeleine de Scudéry (1607–1701),

French novelist. No such translation has been located.

[57] i.e., is under a handicap.

and yet wins the Race at disadvantage. I desire not the Reader should take my Word; and therefore I will set two of their Discourses on the same Subject, in the same Light, for every Man to judge betwixt them. I translated *Chaucer* first, and amongst the rest, pitch'd on the Wife of *Bath's* Tale; not daring, as I have said, to adventure on her Prologue; because 'tis too licentious: There *Chaucer* introduces an old Woman of mean Parentage, whom a youthful Knight of Noble Blood was forc'd to marry, and consequently loath'd her: The Crone being in bed with him on the wedding Night, and finding his Aversion, endeavours to win his Affection by Reason, and speaks a good Word for her self, (as who could blame her?) in hope to mollifie the sullen Bridegroom. She takes her Topiques from the Benefits of Poverty, the Advantages of old Age and Ugliness, the Vanity of Youth, and the silly Pride of Ancestry and Titles without inherent Vertue, which is the true Nobility. When I had clos'd *Chaucer,* I return'd to *Ovid,* and translated some more of his Fables; and by this time had so far forgotten the Wife of *Bath's* Tale, that when I took up *Boccace,* unawares I fell on the same Argument of preferring Virtue to Nobility of Blood, and Titles, in the Story of *Sigismonda;* which I had certainly avoided for the Resemblance of the two Discourses, if my Memory had not fail'd me. Let the Reader weigh them both; and if he thinks me partial to *Chaucer,* 'tis in him to right *Boccace.*

I prefer in our Countryman, far above all his other Stories, the Noble Poem of *Palamon* and *Arcite,* which is of the *Epique* kind, and perhaps not much inferiour to the *Ilias* or the *Æneis:* the Story is more pleasing than either of them, the Manners as perfect, the Diction as poetical, the Learning as deep and various; and the Disposition full as artful: only it includes a greater length of time; as taking up seven years at least; but *Aristotle* has left undecided the Duration of the Action; which yet is easily reduc'd into the Compass of a year, by a Narration of what preceded the Return of *Palamon* to *Athens.* I had thought for the Honour of our Nation, and more particularly for his, whose Laurel, tho' unworthy, I have worn after him, that this Story was of *English* Growth, and *Chaucer's* own: But I was undeceiv'd by *Boccace;* for casually looking on the End of his seventh *Giornata,* I found *Dioneo* (under which name he shadows himself) and *Fiametta* (who represents his Mistress, the natural Daughter of *Robert* King of *Naples*) of whom these Words are spoken. *Dioneo e Fiametta gran pezza cantarono insieme d'Arcita, e di Palamone:*[58] by which it appears that this Story was written before the time of *Boccace;* but the Name of its Author being wholly lost, *Chaucer* is now become an Original; and I question not but the Poem has receiv'd many Beauties by passing through his Noble Hands. Besides this Tale, there is another of his own Invention, after the manner of the *Provencalls,* call'd *The Flower and the Leaf;*[59] with which I was so particularly pleas'd, both for the Invention and the Moral; that I cannot hinder my self from recommending it to the Reader.

As a Corollary to this Preface, in which I have done Justice to others, I owe somewhat to my self: not that I think it worth my time to enter the Lists with one *M*———,[60] or one *B*———,[61] but barely to take notice, that such Men there are who have written scurrilously against me without any Provocation. *M*———, who is in Orders, pretends amongst the rest this Quarrel to me, that I have fallen foul on Priesthood; If I have, I am only to ask Pardon of good

---

[58] "Dioneo and Fiametta sang together a long time of Arcita and Palamone." "The Knight's Tale" is now known to be an adaptation of Boccaccio's own poem, "Teseide," probably itself derived from earlier sources.

[59] No longer considered part of the Chaucerian canon, the poem was also considered Chaucer's by Wordsworth and admired by him.

[60] Milbourne; see note 53.

[61] Sir Richard Blackmore (1650?–1729), author of *Prince Arthur* (1695). The use of the initials *M* and *B* also is an allusion to classical symbols of dull pseudocritics, Maevius and Baevius.

Priests, and am afraid his part of the Reparation will come to little. Let him be satisfied that he shall not be able to force himself upon me for an Adversary. I contemn him too much to enter into Competition with him. His own Translations of *Virgil* have answer'd his Criticisms on mine. If (as they say, he has declar'd in Print) he prefers the Version of *Ogilby*[62] to mine, the World has made him the same Compliment: For 'tis agreed on all hands, that he writes even below *Ogilby:* That, you will say, is not easily to be done; but what cannot M——— bring about? I am satisfy'd however, that while he and I live together, I shall not be thought the worst Poet of the Age. It looks as if I had desir'd him underhand to write so ill against me: But upon my honest Word I have not brib'd him to do me this Service, and am wholly guiltless of his Pamphlet. 'Tis true I should be glad, if I could persuade him to continue his good Offices, and write such another Critique on any thing of mine: For I find by Experience he has a great Stroke with the Reader, when he condemns any of my Poems to make the World have a better Opinion of them. He has taken some Pains with my Poetry; but no body will be persuaded to take the same with his. If I had taken to the Church (as he affirms, but which was never in my Thoughts) I should have had more Sense, if not more Grace, than to have turn'd my self out of my Benefice by writing Libels on my Parishioners. But his Account of my Manners and my Principles, are of a Piece with his Cavils and his Poetry: And so I have done with him for ever.

As for the City Bard, or Knight Physician,[63] I hear his Quarrel to me is, that I was the Author of *Absalom* and *Achitophel,* which he thinks is a little hard on his Fanatique[64] Patrons in *London.*

But I will deal the more civilly with his two Poems, because nothing ill is to be spoken of the Dead: And therefore Peace be to the *Manes* of his *Arthurs.* I will only say that it was not for this Noble Knight that I drew the Plan of an Epick Poem on King *Arthur* in my Preface to the Translation of *Juvenal.*[65] The Guardian Angels of Kingdoms were Machines too ponderous for him to manage; and therefore he rejected them as *Dares* did the Whirl-bats[66] of *Eryx* when they were thrown before him by *Entellus:*[67] Yet from that Preface he plainly took his Hint: For he began immediately upon the Story; though he had the Baseness not to acknowledge his Benefactor; but in stead of it, to traduce me in a Libel.

I shall say the less of Mr. *Collier,* because in many Things he has tax'd me justly; and I have pleaded Guilty to all Thoughts and Expressions of mine, which can be truly argu'd of Obscenity, Profaneness, or Immorality; and retract them. If he be my Enemy, let him triumph; if he be my Friend, as I have given him no Personal Occasion to be otherwise, he will be glad of my Repentance. It becomes me not to draw my Pen in the Defence of a bad Cause, when I have so often drawn it for a good one. Yet it were not difficult to prove, that in many Places he has perverted my Meaning by his Glosses; and interpreted my Words into Blasphemy and Baudry, of which they were not guilty. Besides that, he is too much given to Horse-play in his Raillery; and comes to Battel, like a Dictatour from the Plough. I will not say, *The Zeal of God's House has eaten him up;*[68] but I am sure it has devour'd some Part of his Good Manners and Civility. It might also be doubted, whether it were altogether Zeal, which prompted him to this rough manner of Proceeding; perhaps it became not one of his Function to rake into the Rubbish of Ancient and Modern Plays; a Divine might have employ'd his Pains to better purpose, than in the Nastiness of *Plautus*

[62] John Ogilby (1600–1676) translated Vergil in 1649.

[63] Blackmore.

[64] i.e., religious dissent from the Church of England.

[65] In 1683.

[66] loaded boxing gloves.

[67] *Aeneid,* V, 400.

[68] Ps. 69:9.

and *Aristophanes;* whose Examples, as they excuse not me, so it might be possibly suppos'd, that he read them not without some Pleasure. They who have written Commentaries on those Poets, or on *Horace, Juvenal,* and *Martial,* have explain'd some Vices, which without their Interpretation had been unknown to Modern Times. Neither has he judg'd impartially betwixt the former Age and us.

There is more Baudry in one Play of *Fletcher's* call'd *The Custom of the Country,*[69] than in all ours together. Yet this has been often acted on the Stage in my remembrance. Are the Times so much more reform'd now, than they were Five and twenty Years ago? If they are, I congratulate the Amendment of our Morals. But I am not to prejudice the Cause of my Fellow-Poets, though I abandon my own Defence:

They have some of them answer'd for themselves, and neither they nor I can think Mr. *Collier* so formidable an Enemy, that we should shun him. He has lost Ground at the latter end of the Day, by pursuing his Point too far, like the Prince of *Conde* at the Battel of *Senneph:*[70] From Immoral Plays, to No Plays; *ab abusu ad usum, non valet consequentia.*[71] But being a Party, I am not to erect my self into a Judge. As for the rest of those who have written against me, they are such Scoundrels, that they deserve not the least Notice to be taken of them. *B*——— and *M*——— are only distinguish'd from the Crowd, by being remember'd to their Infamy.

. . . *Demetri, Teque Tigelli Discipularum inter jubeo plorare cathedras.*[72]

---

[69] John Fletcher (1579–1625); written and produced in the 1620's. Pepys has three references to the play. He read it in 1664 and deemed it "a very poor one." He saw it acted in January 1667 and thought it "of all plays that ever I did see, the worst," and again in August of the same year with "the house mighty empty—more than ever I saw it—and an ill play."

[70] A pyrrhic victory of a celebrated French commander in 1674 over William of Orange, now (1689–1702) William III of England.

[71] i.e., citation of abuse has no necessary bearing on the possible usefulness of something.

[72] i.e., Demetrius, and you Tigellius, go weep over the easy chairs of your female disciples (Horace, *Satires,* I, x, 90–91). Perhaps it could be better paraphrased: The two of you go find consolation among your audiences in the women's clubs.

Jonathan Swift
1667-1745

A TALE OF A TUB

SECTION IX

A DIGRESSION CONCERNING THE ORIGINAL, THE USE AND IMPROVEMENT OF *MADNESS* IN A COMMONWEALTH

Nor shall it any ways detract from the just Reputation of this famous Sect, that its Rise and Institution are owing to such an Author as I have described *Jack*[1] to be; A Person whose Intellectuals were overturned, and his Brain shaken out of its Natural Position; which we commonly suppose to be a Distemper, and call by the Name of *Madness* or *Phrenzy*. For, if we take a Survey of the greatest Actions that have been performed in the World, under the Influence of Single Men; which are, *The Establishment of New Empires by Conquest: The Advance and Progress of New Schemes in Philosophy; and the contriving, as well as the propagating of New Religions:* We shall find the Authors of them all, to have been Persons, whose natural Reason hath admitted great Revolutions from their Dyet, their Education, the Prevalency of some certain Temper, together with the particular Influence of Air and Climate. Besides, there is something Individual in human Minds, that easily kindles at the accidental Approach and Collision of certain Circumstances, which tho' of paltry and mean Appearance, do often flame out into the greatest Emergencies of Life. For great Turns are not always given by strong Hands, but by lucky Adaption,[2] and at proper Seasons; and it is of no import, where the Fire was kindled, if the Vapor has once got up into the Brain. For the *upper Region* of Man, is furnished like the *middle Region* of the Air; The Materials are formed from Causes of the widest Difference, yet produce at last the same Substance and Effect. Mists arise from the Earth, Steams from Dunghils, Exhalations from the Sea, and Smoak from Fire; yet all Clouds are the same in Composition, as well as Consequences: and the Fumes issuing from a Jakes, will furnish as comely and useful a Vapor, as Incense from an Altar. Thus far, I suppose, will easily be granted me; and then it will follow, that as the Face of Nature never produces Rain, but when it is overcast and disturbed, so Human-Understanding, seated in the Brain, must be troubled and overspread by Vapours, as-

---

The text and original notes are from the fifth edition of 1710; the *Tale* was first published in 1704.

---

[1] Throughout the *Tale*, Swift has satirized Protestant dissent from the established Church by ridiculing the ardent enthusiasm of Jack, brother of Martin (the Anglican) and Peter (the Catholic).

[2] "the act of fitting" (Johnson's *Dictionary*).

cending from the lower Faculties, to water the Invention, and render it fruitful. Now, altho' these Vapours (as it hath been already said) are of as various Original,[3] as those of the Skies, yet the Crop they produce, differ both in Kind and Degree, meerly according to the Soil. I will produce two Instances to prove and Explain what I am now advancing.

A certain Great Prince[4] raised a mighty Army, filled his Coffers with infinite Treasures, provided an invincible Fleet, and all this, without giving the least Part of his Design to his greatest Ministers, or his nearest Favourites. Immediately the whole World was alarmed; the neighbouring Crowns, in trembling Expectations, towards what Point the Storm would burst; the small Politicians, every where forming profound Conjectures. Some believed he had laid a Scheme for Universal Monarchy: Others, after much Insight, determined the Matter to be a Project for pulling down the *Pope,* and setting up the *Reformed* Religion, which had once been his own. Some, again, of a deeper Sagacity, sent him into *Asia* to subdue the *Turk,* and recover *Palestine.* In the midst of all these Projects and Preparations; a certain *State-Surgeon;*[5] gathering the Nature of the Disease by these Symptoms, attempted the Cure, at one Blow performed the Operation, broke the Bag, and out flew the *Vapour;* nor did anything want to render it a compleat Remedy, only that the Prince unfortunately happened to Die in the Performance. Now, is the Reader exceeding curious to learn, from whence this *Vapour* took its Rise, which had so long set the Nations at a Gaze? What secret Wheel, what hidden Spring could put into Motion so wonderful an Engine? It was afterwards discovered, that the Movement of this whole Machine had been directed by an absent *Female* whose Eyes had raised a Protuberancy, and before Emission, she was removed into an Enemy's Country. What should an unhappy Prince do in such ticklish Circumstances as these? He tried in vain the Poet's never-failing Receipt of *Corpora quæque;* For,

Idque petit corpus mens unde est saucia
 amore;
Unde feritor, eo tendit, gestitq; coire.[6]
                                        LUCR.

Having to no purpose used all peaceable Endeavours, the collected part of the *Semen,* raised and enflamed, became adust,[7] converted to Choler, turned head upon the spinal Duct, and ascended to the Brain. The very same Principle that influences a *Bully* to break the Windows of a Whore, who has jilted him, naturally stirs up a Great Prince to raise mighty Armies, and dream of nothing but Sieges, Battles, and Victories.

. . . Teterrima belli
 Causa. . . .[8]

The other Instance[9] is, what I have read somewhere, in a very antient Author, of a mighty King, who for the space of above thirty Years, amused himself to take and loose Towns; beat Armies, and be beaten; drive Princes out of their Dominions; fright Children from their Bread and Butter; burn, lay waste, plunder, dragoon, massacre Subject and Stranger, Friend and Foe, Male and Female. 'Tis recorded, that the Philosophers of each Country were in grave Dispute, upon Causes Natural, Moral, and Political, to find out where they should assign an original Solution of this *Phænomenon.* At last the *Vapour* or

---

[3] "origin" (Johnson's *Dictionary*).
[4] *"This was* Harry *the Great of France"* (Swift).
[5] "Ravillac, *who stabb'd* Henry *the Great in his Coach"* (Swift).
[6] Lucretius, *De Rerum Natura,* IV, 1048 ff.; a passage concerned with the results of frustrated love.

[7] "said of the blood, when by reason of its excessive heat, the thinner parts of it steam through in vapours" (Bailey's *Dictionary*).
[8] "The foul cause of war" (Horace, *Satires,* I, iii, 107).
[9] *"This is meant of the Present* French *King"* (Swift).

Spirit, which animated the Hero's Brain, being in perpetual Circulation, seized upon that Region of Human Body, so renown'd for furnishing the *Zibeta Occidentalis,*[10] and gathering there into a Tumor, left the rest of the World for that Time in Peace. Of such mighty Consequence it is, where those Exhalations fix; and of so little, from whence they proceed. The same Spirits which in their superior Progress would conquer a Kingdom, descending upon the *Anus,* conclude in a *Fistula.*

Let us next examine the great Introducers of new Schemes in Philosophy, and search till we can find, from what Faculty of the Soul the Disposition arises in mortal Man, of taking it into his Head, to advance new Systems with such an eager Zeal, in things agreed on all hands impossible to be known: from what Seeds this Disposition springs, and to what Quality of human Nature these Grand Innovators have been indebted for their Number of Disciples. Because, it is plain, that several of the chief among them, both *Antient* and *Modern,* were usually mistaken by their Adversaries, and indeed, by all, except their own Followers, to have been Persons Crazed, or out of their Wits, having generally proceeded in the common Course of their Words and Actions, by a Method very different from the vulgar Dictates of unrefined Reason: agreeing for the most Part in their several Models, with their present undoubted Successors in the *Academy of Modern Bedlam* (whose Merits and Principles I shall farther examine in due Place.) Of this Kind were *Epicurus, Diogenes, Apollonius, Lucretius, Paracelsus, Des Cartes,* and others; who, if they were now in the World, tied fast, and separate from their Followers, would in this our undistinguishing Age, incur manifest Danger of *Phlebotomy,* and *Whips,* and *Chains,* and *dark Chambers,* and *Straw.*

For, what Man in the natural State, or Course of Thinking, did ever conceive it in his Power, to reduce the Notions of all Mankind, exactly to the same Length, and Breadth, and Heighth of his own? Yet this is the first humble and civil Design of all Innovators in the Empire of Reason. *Epicurus,* modestly hoped, that one Time or other, a certain Fortuitous Concourse of all Mens Opinions, after perpetual Justlings, the Sharp with the Smooth, the Light and the Heavy, the Round and the Square, would by certain *Clinamina,*[11] unite in the Notions of *Atoms* and *Void,* as these did in the Originals of all Things. *Cartesius*[12] reckoned to see before he died, the Sentiments of all Philosophers, like so many lesser Stars in his *Romantick* System, rapt and drawn within his own *Vortex.* Now, I would gladly be informed, how it is possible to account for such Imaginations as these in particular Men, without Recourse to my *Phænomenon* of *Vapours,* ascending from the lower Faculties to over-shadow the Brain, and there distilling into Conceptions, for which the Narrowness of our Mother-Tongue has not yet assigned any other Name, besides that of *Madness* or *Phrenzy.* Let us therefore now conjecture how it comes to pass, that none of these great Prescribers, do ever fail providing themselves and their Notions, with a Number of implicite Disciples. And, I think, the Reason is easie to be assigned: For, there is a peculiar *String* in the Harmony of Human Understanding, which in several individuals is exactly of the same Tuning. This, if you can dexterously screw up to its right Key, and then strike gently upon it; Whenever you have the Good Fortune to light among those of the same Pitch, they will by a secret necessary Sympathy, strike exactly at the same time. And in this one Circumstance, lies all the Skill or Luck of the Matter; for if you chance to jar the

---

[10] "Paracelsus, *who was so famous for Chymistry, try'd an Experiment upon human Excrement, to make a Perfume of it, which when he had brought to Perfection, he called* Zibeta Occidentalis, *or* Western-Civet, *the back Parts of Man (according to his Division mention'd* by the Author, page 160.) *being the* West" (Swift).

[11] inclination, bias (cf. Lucretius, *De Rerum Natura,* II, 292).

[12] René Descartes (1596–1650), French philosopher and rationalist.

String among those who are either above or below your own Height, instead of subscribing to your Doctrine, they will tie you fast, call you Mad, and feed you with Bread and Water. It is therefore a Point of the nicest Conduct to distinguish and adapt this noble Talent, with respect to the Differences of Persons and of Times. *Cicero* understood this very well, when writing to a Friend in *England,* with a Caution, among other Matters, to beware of being cheated by our *Hackney-Coachmen* (who it seems, in those days, were as arrant Rascals as they are now) has these remarkable words. *Est quod gaudeas te in ista loca venisse, ubi aliquid sapere viderere.*[13] For, to speak a bold Truth, it is a fatal Miscarriage, so ill to order Affairs, as to pass for a *Fool* in one Company, when in another you might be treated as a Philosopher. Which I desire *some certain Gentlemen of my Acquaintance,* to lay up in their Hearts, as a very seasonable *Innuendo.*

This, indeed, was the Fatal Mistake of that worthy Gentleman, my most ingenious Friend, Mr. *W—tt—n:*[14] A Person, in appearance ordain'd for great Designs, as well as Performances; whether you will consider his *Notions* or his *Looks.* Surely, no Man ever advanced into the Publick, with fitter Qualifications of Body and Mind, for the Propagation of a new Religion. Oh, had those happy Talents misapplied to vain Philosophy, been turned into their proper Channels of *Dreams* and *Visions,* where *Distortion* of Mind and Countenance, are of such Sovereign Use; the base detracting World would not then have dared to report, that something is amiss,

that his Brain hath undergone an unlucky Shake; which even his Brother *Modernists* themselves, like Ungrates, do whisper so loud, that it reaches up to the very Garret I am now writing in.

Lastly, Whosoever pleases to look into the Fountains of *Enthusiasm,* from whence, in all Ages, have eternally proceeded such fatning Streams, will find the Spring Head to have been as *troubled* and *muddy* as the Current; Of such great Emolument, is a Tincture of this *Vapour,* which the World calls *Madness,* that without its Help, the World would not only be deprived of those two great Blessings, *Conquests* and *Systems,* but even all Mankind would happily[15] be reduced to the same Belief in Things Invisible. Now, the former *Postulatum* being held, that it is of no Import from what Originals this *Vapour* proceeds, but either in what *Angles* it strikes and spreads over the Understanding, or upon what *Species* of Brain it ascends; It will be a very delicate Point to cut the Feather, and divide the several Reasons to a Nice and Curious Reader, how this numerical Difference in the Brain, can produce Effects of so vast a Difference from the same *Vapour,* as to be the sole Point of Individuation between *Alexander the Great, Jack of Leyden,*[16] and *Monsieur Des Cartes.* The present Argument is the most abstracted that ever I engaged in, it strains my Faculties to their highest Stretch; and I desire the Reader to attend with utmost Perpensity; For, I now proceed to unravel this knotty Point.

There is in Mankind a certain[17] * *
* * * * * * * * * * * * * * * * * *
* * * * * * * * * * * * * * * * * *

---

[13] "[Cicero's] *Epist. ad Fam. Trabatio"* (Swift): "You may well be proud of yourself for having won such position that you are looked upon as a man of some sense." It should be superfluous to point out that Swift's "Hackney-Coachmen" are Cicero's "charioteers" and that Cicero's friend Trabatius was in Gaul and not in England.

[14] William Wotton, who defended the idea of progress against Sir William Temple's cyclical theory of history during the "battle of the books."

[15] *happily] unhappily,* 1704. Textual variants

from the edition of 1710 are indicated following the single bracket.

[16] Johann Buckholdt (1509–1536), Dutch Anabaptist fanatic.

[17] "Here is another Defect in the Manuscript, but I think the Authour did wisely, and that the Matter which thus strained his Faculties, was not worth a Solution; and it were well if all Metaphysical Cobweb Problems were not otherwise answered" (Swift). There is also a marginal note in the original text: *"Hic multa desiderantur"* ("Here much is wanting").

* * * * * And this I take to be a clear Solution of the Matter.

Having therefore so narrowly past thro' this intricate Difficulty, the Reader will, I am sure, agree with me in the Conclusion; that if the *Moderns* mean by *Madness,* only a Disturbance or Transposition of the Brain, by Force of certain *Vapours* issuing up from the lower Faculties; Then has this *Madness* been the Parent of all those mighty Revolutions, that have happened in *Empire,* in *Philosophy,* and in *Religion.* For, the Brain, in its natural Position and State of Serenity, disposeth its Owner to pass his Life in the common Forms, without any Thought of subduing Multitudes to his own *Power,* his *Reasons* or his *Visions;* and the more he shapes his Understanding by the Pattern of Human Learning, the less he is inclined to form Parties after his particular Notions; because that instructs him in his private Infirmities, as well as in the stubborn Ignorance of the People. But when a Man's Fancy gets *astride* on his Reason, when Imagination is at Cuffs[18] with the Senses, and common Understanding, as well as common Sense, is Kickt out of Doors; the first Proselyte he makes, is Himself, and when that is once compass'd, the Difficulty is not so great in bringing over others; A strong Delusion always operating from *without,* as vigorously as from *within.* For, Cant and Vision are to the Ear and the Eye, the same that Tickling is to the Touch. Those Entertainments and Pleasures we most value in Life, are such as *Dupe* and play the Wag with the Senses. For, if we take an Examination of what is generally understood by *Happiness,* as it has Respect, either to the Understanding or the Senses, we shall find all its Properties and Adjuncts will herd under this short Definition: That, *it is a perpetual Possession of being well Deceived.* And first, with Relation to the Mind or Understanding; 'tis manifest, what mighty Advantages Fiction has over Truth; and the Reason is just at our Elbow; because Imagination can build nobler Scenes, and produce more wonderful Revolutions than Fortune or Nature will be at Expence to furnish. Nor is Mankind so much to blame in his Choice, thus determining him, if we consider that the Debate meerly lies between *Things past,* and *Things conceived;* and so the Question is only this; Whether Things that have Place in the *Imagination,* may not as properly be said to *Exist,* as those that are seated in the *Memory;* which may be justly held in the Affirmative, and very much to the Advantage of the former, since This is acknowledged to be the *Womb* of Things, and the other allowed to be no more than the *Grave.* Again, if we take this Definition of Happiness, and examine it with Reference to the Senses, it will be acknowledged wonderfully adapt.[19] How fading and insipid do all Objects accost us that are not convey'd in the Vehicle of *Delusion?* How shrunk is every Thing, as it appears in the Glass of Nature? So, that if it were not for the Assistance of Artificial *Mediums,* false Lights, refracted Angles, Varnish, and Tinsel; there would be a mighty Level in the Felicity and Enjoyments of Mortal Men. If this were seriously considered by the World, as I have a certain Reason to suspect it hardly will; Men would no longer reckon among their high Points of Wisdom, the Art of exposing weak Sides, and publishing Infirmities; an Employment in my Opinion, neither better nor worse than that of *Unmasking,* which I think, has never been allowed fair Usage, either in the *World* or the *Play-House.*

In the Proportion that Credulity is a more peaceful Possession of the Mind, than Curiosity, so far preferable is that Wisdom, which converses about the Surface, to that pretended Philosophy which enters into the Depth of Things, and then comes gravely back with Informations and Discoveries, that in the inside they are good for nothing. The two Senses, to which all Objects first address themselves, are the Sight and the Touch; These never examine farther than the Colour, the Shape, the Size, and what-

---

[18] at odds. [19] adept.

ever other Qualities dwell, or are drawn by Art upon the Outward of Bodies; and then comes Reason officiously, with Tools for cutting, and opening, and mangling, and piercing, offering to demonstrate, that they are not of the same consistence quite thro'. Now, I take all this to be the last Degree of perverting Nature; one of whose Eternal Laws it is, to put her best Furniture[20] forward. And therefore, in order to save the Charges of all such expensive Anatomy for the Time to come; I do here think fit to inform the Reader, that in such Conclusions as these, Reason is certainly in the Right; and that in most Corporeal Beings, which have fallen under my Cognizance, the *Outside* hath been infinitely preferable to the *Inn*:[21] Whereof I have been farther convinced from some late Experiments. Last Week I saw a Woman *flay'd*, and you will hardly believe, how much it altered her Person for the worse. Yesterday I ordered the Carcass of a *Beau* to be stript in my Presence; when we were all amazed to find so many unsuspected Faults under one Suit of Cloaths: Then I laid open his *Brain*, his *Heart*, and his *Spleen;* But, I plainly perceived at every Operation, that the farther we proceeded, we found the Defects encrease upon us in Number and Bulk: from all which, I justly formed this Conclusion to my self; That whatever Philosopher or Projector can find out an Art to sodder and patch up the Flaws and Imperfections of Nature, will deserve much better of Mankind, and teach us a more useful Science, than that so much in present Esteem, of widening and exposing them (like him who held *Anatomy* to be the ultimate End of *Physick*.) And he, whose Fortunes and Dispositions have placed him in a convenient Station to enjoy the Fruits of this noble Art; He that can with *Epicurus* content his Ideas with the *Films* and *Images* that fly off upon his Senses from the *Superficies*[22] of Things; Such a Man truly wise, creams off Nature, leaving the Sower and the Dregs,

for Philosophy and Reason to lap up. This is the sublime and refined Point of Felicity, called, *the Possession of being well deceived;* The Serene Peaceful State of being a Fool among Knaves.

But to return to *Madness.* It is certain, that according to the System I have above deduced; every *Species* thereof proceeds from a Redundancy of *Vapours;* therefore, as some Kinds of *Phrenzy* give double Strength to the Sinews, so there are of other *Species,* which add Vigor, and Life, and Spirit to the Brain: Now, it usually happens, that these active Spirits, getting Possession of the Brain, resemble those that haunt other waste and empty Dwellings, which for want of Business, either vanish, and carry away a Piece of the House, or else stay at home and fling it all out of the Windows. By which are mystically display'd the two principal Branches of *Madness,* and which some Philosophers not considering so well as I, have mistook to be different in their Causes, overhastily assigning the first to Deficiency, and the other to Redundance.

I think it therefore manifest, from what I have here advanced, that the main Point of Skill and Address, is to furnish Employment for this Redundancy of *Vapour,* and prudently to adjust the Season of it; by which means it may certainly become of Cardinal and Catholick Emolument in a Commonwealth. Thus one Man chusing a proper Juncture, leaps into a Gulph, from whence proceeds a Hero, and is called the Saver of his Country; Another atchieves the same Enterprise, but unluckily timing it, has left the Brand of *Madness,* fixt as a Reproach upon his Memory; Upon so nice a Distinction are we taught to repeat the Name of *Curtius* with Reverence and Love; that of *Empedocles,* with Hatred and Contempt. Thus, also it is usually conceived, that the Elder *Brutus* only personated the *Fool* and *Madman,* for the Good of the Publick: but this was nothing else, than a Redundancy of the same *Vapor,* long

---

[20] "equipage; embellishments; decorations" (Johnson's *Dictionary*).

[21] *Inn*] *In*, 1704.

[22] "the surface or outermost part of a thing, the outside" (Bailey's *Dictionary*).

misapplied, called by the *Latins, Ingenium par negotiis:*[23] Or, (to translate it as nearly as I can) a sort of *Phrenzy,* never in its right Element, till you take it up in Business of the State.

Upon all which, and many other Reasons of equal Weight, though not equally curious; I do here gladly embrace an Opportunity I have long sought for, of Recommending it as a very noble Undertaking, to Sir *E——d S——r,* Sir *C——r M——ve,* Sir *J——n B——ls, J——n H——w,* Esq;[24] and other Patriots concerned, that they would move for Leave to bring in a Bill, for appointing Commissioners to Inspect into *Bedlam,*[25] and the Parts adjacent; who shall be empowered to *send for Persons, Papers, and Records:* to examine into the Merits and Qualifications of every Student and Professor; to observe with utmost Exactness their several Dispositions and Behaviour; by which means, duly distinguishing and adapting their Talents, they might produce admirable Instruments for the several Offices in a State, * * * * * * * * * * * * * * * *Civil* and *Military;* proceeding in such Methods as I shall here humbly propose. And, I hope the Gentle Reader will give some Allowance to my great Solicitudes in this important Affair, upon Account of that high Esteem I have ever born that honourable Society, whereof I had some Time the Happiness to be an unworthy Member.

Is any Student tearing his Straw in piece-meal, Swearing and Blaspheming, biting his Grate, foaming at the Mouth, and emptying his Pispot in the Spectator's Faces? Let the Right Worshipful, the *Commissioners of Inspection,* give him a Regiment of Dragoons, and send him into *Flanders* among the *Rest.* Is another eternally talking, sputtering, gaping, bawling, in a Sound without Period or Article? What wonderful Talents are here mislaid! Let him be furnished immediately with a green Bag and Papers, and *three Pence*[26] in his Pocket, and away with Him to *Westminster-Hall.* You will find a Third, gravely taking the Dimensions of his Kennel; A Person of Foresight and Insight, tho' kept quite in the Dark; for why, like *Moses, Ecce cornut a erat ejus facies.*[27] He walks duly in one Pace, intreats your Penny with due Gravity and Ceremony; talks much of hard Times, and Taxes, and the *Whore of Babylon;* Bars up the woodden Window of his Cell constantly at eight a Clock: Dreams of *Fire,* and *Shop-lifters,* and *Court Customers,* and *Priviledg'd Places.* Now, what a Figure would all these Acquirements amount to, if the Owner were sent into the *City* among his Brethren! Behold a Fourth, in much and deep Conversation with himself, biting his Thumbs at proper Junctures; His Countenance chequered with Business and Design; sometimes walking very fast, with his Eyes nailed to a Paper that he holds in his Hands: A great Saver of Time, somewhat thick of Hearing, very short of Sight, but more of Memory. A Man ever in Haste, a great Hatcher and Breeder of Business, and excellent at the Famous Art of *whispering Nothing.* A huge Idolater of Monosyllables and Procrastination; so ready to *Give* his Word to every Body, that he never *keeps* it. One that has forgot the common *Meaning* of Words, but an admirable Retainer of the *Sound.* Extreamly subject to the *Loosness,* for his *Occasions* are perpetually *calling him away.* If you approach his Grate in his familiar Intervals; *Sir,* says he, *Give me a Penny, and I'll sing you a Song: But give me the Penny first.* (Hence comes the common Saying, and commoner Practice of parting with Money for a *Song.*)

---

[23] "Tacit." (Swift). An anomaly, not found in these exact terms in Tacitus, meaning the improvement of natural endowments by activity of one sort or another.

[24] The text of an edition in 1720 gives these names in full: Sir Edmund Seymour, Sir Christopher Musgrave, Sir John Bowls, and John How, Esq., all prominent Parliamentary Tories.

[25] Site of the Hospital of St. Mary of Bethlehem in London, a royal asylum for lunatics.

[26] *"A Lawyer's Coach-hire"* (Swift).

[27] *"Cornutus, is either Horned or Shining, and by this Term,* Moses *is described in the vulgar* Latin *of the Bible"* (Swift) (Exod. 34:29–30).

What a compleat System of *Court-Skill* is here described in every Branch of it, and all utterly lost with wrong Application? Accost the Hole of another Kennel, first stopping your Nose, you will behold a surley, gloomy, nasty, slovenly Mortal, raking in his own Dung, and dabling in his Urine. The best Part of his Diet, is the Reversion of his own Ordure, which exspiring into Steams, whirls perpetually about, and at last re-infunds.[28] His Complexion is of a dirty Yellow, with a thin scattered Beard, exactly agreeable to that of his Dyet upon its first Declination;[29] like other Insects, who having their Birth and Education in an Excrement, from thence borrow their Colour and their Smell. The Student of this Apartment is very sparing of his Words, but somewhat over-liberal of his Breath; He holds his Hand out ready to receive your Penny, and immediately upon Receipt, withdraws to his former Occupations. Now, is it not amazing to think, the Society of *Warwick-Lane,*[30] should have no more Concern, for the Recovery of so useful a Member, who, if one may judge from these Appearances, would become the greatest Ornament to that Illustrious Body? Another Student struts up fiercely to your Teeth, puffing with his Lips; half squeezing out his Eyes, and very graciously holds you out his Hand to kiss. The *Keeper* desires you not to be afraid of this Professor, for he will do you no Hurt: To him alone is allowed the Liberty of the Anti-Chamber, and the *Orator* of the Place gives you to understand, that this solemn Person is a *Taylor* run mad with Pride. This considerable Student is adorned with many other Qualities, upon which, at present, I shall not farther enlarge. * * *Heark in your Ear*[31] * * * * * * * * I am strangely mistaken, if all his Address, his Motions, and his Airs, would not then be very natural, and in their proper Element.

I shall not descend so minutely, as to insist upon the vast Number of *Beaux, Fidlers, Poets,* and *Politicians,* that the World might recover by such a Reformation? But what is more material, besides the clear Gain redounding to the Commonwealth, by so large an Acquisition of Persons to employ, whose Talents and Acquirements, if I may be so bold to affirm it, are now buried, or at least misapplied: It would be a mighty Advantage accruing to the Publick from this Enquiry, that all these would very much excel, and arrive at great Perfection in their several Kinds; which, I think, is manifest from what I have already shewn; and shall inforce by this one plain Instance; That even, I myself, the Author of these momentous Truths, am a Person, whose Imaginations are hard-mouth'd, and exceedingly disposed to run away with his *Reason,* which I have observed from long Experience, to be a very light Rider, and easily shook off; upon which Account, my Friends will never trust me alone, without a solemn Promise, to vent my Speculations in this, or the like manner, for the universal Benefit of Human kind; which, perhaps, the gentle, courteous, and candid Reader, brimful of that *Modern* Charity and Tenderness, usually annexed to his *Office,* will be very hardly persuaded to believe.

---

[28] The phrase *infundibulum reinum* was used in anatomy for "the pelvis or basin of the reins [bowels], thro' which the urine passes to the ureters and bladder" (Bailey's *Dictionary*). Swift thus uses an appropriate term for reversal of direction.

[29] descent.

[30] Royal College of Physicians.

[31] "*I cannot conjecture what the Author means here, or how this Chasm could be fill'd, tho' it is capable of more than one Interpretation*" (Swift).

A FULL AND TRUE ACCOUNT
of the Battel Fought
Last Friday, Between the Antient and the Modern Books in St. James's Library

The following Discourse, as it is un-questionably of the same Author, so it seems to have been written about the same time with the former, I mean, the Year 1697, when the famous Dispute was on Foot, about *Antient and Modern Learning.* The Controversy took its Rise from an Essay of Sir *William Temple's,*[32] upon that Subject; which was answer'd[33] by *W. Wotton,* B.D. with an Appendix by Dr. *Bently,*[34] endeavouring to destroy the Credit of *Æsop* and *Phalaris,* for Authors, whom Sir William Temple had in the Essay before-mentioned, highly commended. In that Appendix, the Doctor falls hard upon a new Edition[35] of *Phalaris,* put out by the Honourable *Charles Boyle* (now *Earl of Orrery*) to which, Mr. *Boyle,* replyed at large, with great Learning and Wit;[36] and the Doctor, voluminously, rejoyned.[37] In this Dispute, the Town highly resented to see a Person of Sir *William Temple's* Character and Merits, roughly used by the two Reverend Gentlemen aforesaid, and without any manner of Provocation. At length, there appearing no End of the Quarrel, our Author tells us, that the BOOKS in *St. James's* Library, looking upon themselves as Parties principally concerned, took up the Controversie, and came to a decisive Battel; But, the Manuscript, by the Injury of Fortune, or Weather, being in several Places imperfect, we cannot learn to which side the Victory fell.

I must warn the Reader, to beware of applying to Persons what is here meant, only of Books in the most literal Sense. So, when *Virgil* is mentioned, we are not to understand the Person of a famous Poet, call'd by that Name, but only certain Sheets of Paper, bound up in Leather, containing in Print, the Works of the said Poet, and so of the rest.

Satyr is a sort of Glass, *wherein Beholders do generally discover every body's Face but their Own; which is the chief Reason for that kind Reception it meets in the World, and that so very few are offended with it. But if it should happen otherwise, the Danger is not great; and, I have learned from long Experience, never to apprehend Mischief from those Understandings, I have been able to provoke; For, Anger and Fury, though they add Strength to the* Sinews *of the Body, yet are found to relax those of the* Mind, *and to render all its Efforts feeble and impotent.*

There is a Brain *that will endure but one* Scumming: *Let the Owner gather it with discretion, and manage his little*

The text and original notes are from the edition of 1710.

[32] *Essay upon the Ancient and Modern Learning* (1690).
[33] *Reflections upon Ancient and Modern Learning* (1694).
[34] Richard Bentley's contribution appeared in the second edition (1697) of Wotton's *Reflections.* Bentley was custodian of the king's library at St. James's.
[35] 1695.
[36] Dr. *Bentley's Dissertations on the Epistles of Phalaris, and the Fables of Æsop, Examin'd* (1698).
[37] *A Dissertation upon the Epistles of Phalaris* (1699).

Stock with Husbandry; but of all things, let him beware of bringing it under the Lash *of his* Betters; *because, That will make it all bubble up into Impertinence, and he will find no new Supply:* Wit, *without knowledge, being a Sort of* Cream, *which gathers in a Night to the Top, and by a skilful Hand, may be soon* whipt *into* Froth; *but once scumm'd away, what appears underneath will be fit for nothing, but to be thrown to the* Hogs.

[THE BATTLE OF THE BOOKS]

Whoever examines with due Circumspection into the *Annual Records* of *Time,* will find it remarked, that *War is the Child of Pride,* and *Pride the Daughter of Riches;*[38] The former of which Assertions may be soon granted; but one cannot so easily subscribe to the latter: For *Pride* is nearly related to Beggary and *Want,* either by Father or Mother, and sometimes by both; And, to speak naturally, it very seldom happens among Men to fall out, when all have enough: Invasions usually travelling from *North* to *South,* that is to say, from Poverty upon Plenty. The most antient and natural Grounds of Quarrels, are *Lust* and *Avarice;* which, tho' we may allow to be Brethren or collateral Branches of *Pride,* are certainly the Issues of *Want.* For, to speak in the Phrase of Writers upon the Politicks, we may observe in the Republick of *Dogs,* (which in its Original seems to be an Institution of the *Many*) that the whole State is ever in the profoundest Peace, after a full Meal; and, that Civil Broils arise among them, when it happens for one great *Bone* to be seized on by some *leading Dog,* who either divides it among the *Few,* and then it falls to an *Oligarchy,* or keeps it to Himself, and then it runs up to a *Tyranny.* The same reasoning also, holds Place among them, in those Dissensions we behold upon a Turgescency in any of their Females. For, the Right of Pos-session lying in common (it being impossible to establish a Property in so delicate a Case) Jealousies and Suspicions do so abound, that the whole Commonwealth of that Street, is reduced to a manifest *State of War,* of every *Citizen* against every *Citizen;* till some One of more Courage, Conduct, or Fortune than the rest, seizes and enjoys the Prize; Upon which, naturally arises Plenty of Heart-burning, and Envy, and Snarling against the *Happy Dog.* Again, if we look upon any of these Republicks engaged in a Forein War, either of Invasion or Defence, we shall find, the same Reasoning will serve, as to the Grounds and Occasions of each; and, that *Poverty,* or *Want,* in some Degree or other, (whether Real, or in Opinion, which makes no Alteration in the Case) has a great Share, as well as *Pride,* on the Part of the Aggressor.

Now, whoever will please to take this Scheme, and either reduce or adapt it to an Intellectual State, or Commonwealth of Learning, will soon discover the first Ground of Disagreement between the two great Parties at this Time in Arms; and may form just Conclusions upon the Merits of either Cause. But the Issue or Events of this War are not so easie to conjecture at: For, the present Quarrel is so enflamed by the warm Heads of either Faction, and the Pretensions *somewhere or other* so exorbitant, as not to admit the least Overtures of Accommodation: This Quarrel first began (as I have heard it affirmed by an old Dweller in the Neighborhood) about a small Spot of Ground, *lying* and *being* upon one of the two Tops of the Hill *Parnassus;*[39] the highest and largest of which, had it seems, been time out of Mind, in quiet Possession of certain Tenants, call'd the *Antients;* And the other was held by the *Moderns.* But, these disliking their present Station, sent certain Ambassadors to the *Antients,* complaining of a great Nuisance, how the Height of that Part of *Parnassus,* quite spoiled the Prospect

---

[38] "Riches produceth Pride; Pride is War's Ground, c. Vid. Ephem. de *Mary Clarke;* opt. Edit." (marginal note). The reference is to a contemporary almanac.

[39] A mountain sacred to the Muses, one part of which was especially reserved to Apollo, the other to Dionysus (Bacchus).

of theirs, especially towards the *East;* and therefore, to avoid a War, offered them the Choice of this Alternative; either that the *Antients* would please to remove themselves and their Effects down to the lower Summity,[40] which the *Moderns* would graciously surrender to them, and advance in their Place; or else, that the said *Antients* will give leave to the *Moderns* to come with Shovels and Mattocks, and level the said Hill, as low as they shall think it convenient. To which, the *Antients* made Answer: How little they expected such a Message as this, from a Colony, whom they had admitted out of their own Free Grace, to so near a Neighborhood. That, as to their own Seat, they were *Aborigines* of it, and therefore, to talk with them of a Removal or Surrender, was a Language they did not understand. That, if the Height of the Hill, on their side, shortned the Prospect of the *Moderns,* it was a Disadvantage they could not help, but desired them to consider, whether that Injury (if it be any) were not largely recompenced by the *Shade* and *Shelter* it afforded them. That, as to the levelling or digging down, it was either Folly or Ignorance to propose it, if they did, or did not know, how that side of the Hill was an entire Rock, which would break their Tools and Hearts; without any Damage to itself. That they would therefore advise the *Moderns,* rather to raise their own side of the Hill, than dream of pulling down that of the *Antients,* to the former of which, they would not only give Licence, but also largely contribute. All this was rejected by the *Moderns,* with much Indignation, who still insisted upon one of the two Expedients; And so this Difference broke out into a long and obstinate War, maintain'd on the one Part, by Resolution, and by the Courage of certain Leaders and Allies; but, on the other, by the greatness of their Number, upon all Defeats, affording continual Recruits. In this Quarrel, whole Rivulets of *Ink* have been exhausted, and the Virulence of both Parties enormously augmented.

Now, it must here be understood, that *Ink* is the great missive Weapon, in all Battels of the Learned, which, convey'd thro' a sort of Engine, call'd a *Quill,* infinite Numbers of these are darted at the Enemy, by the Valiant on each side, with equal Skill and Violence, as if it were an Engagement of *Porcupines.* This malignant Liquor was compounded by the Engineer, who invented it, of two Ingredients, which are *Gall* and *Copperas,*[41] by its Bitterness and Venom, to *Suit* in some Degree, as well as to *Foment* the Genius of the Combatants. And as the *Grecians,* after an Engagement, when they could not *agree* about the Victory, were wont to set up Trophies on both sides, the beaten Party being content to be at the same Expence, to keep it self in Countenance (A laudable and antient Custom, happily reviv'd of late, in the Art of War) so the *Learned,* after a sharp and bloody Dispute, do on both sides hang out their Trophies too, which-ever comes by the worst. These Trophies have largely inscribed on them the Merits of the Cause; a full impartial Account of such a Battel, and how the Victory fell clearly to the Party that set them up. They are known to the World under several Names; As, *Disputes, Arguments, Rejoynders, Brief Considerations, Answers, Replies, Remarks, Reflexions, Objections, Confutations.* For a very few Days they are fixed up in all Publick Places, either by themselves or their Representatives,[42] for Passengers to gaze at: From whence the chiefest and largest are removed to certain Magazines, they call, *Libraries,* there to remain in a Quarter purposely assign't them, and from thenceforth, begin to be called, *Books of Controversie.*

In these Books, is wonderfully instilled and preserved, the Spirit of each Warrier, while he is alive; and after his Death, his Soul transmigrates there, to inform them. This, at least, is the more common Opinion; But, I believe, it is with Libraries, as with other Cœmeteries, where some Philosophers affirm, that a certain Spirit, which they call

---

[40] summit.
[41] ferrous sulphate, used in making ink.

[42] *"Their Title Pages"* (marginal note).

Brutum hominis,[43] hovers over the Monument, till the Body is corrupted, and turns to *Dust,* or to *Worms,* but then vanishes or dissolves: So, we may say, a restless Spirit haunts over every *Book,* till *Dust* or *Worms* have seized upon it; which to some, may happen in a few Days, but to others, later; And therefore, *Books* of Controversy, being of all others, haunted by the most disorderly Spirits, have always been confined in a separate Lodge from the rest; and for fear of mutual violence against each other, it was thought Prudent by our Ancestors, to bind them to the Peace with strong Iron Chains. Of which Invention, the original Occasion was this: When the Works of *Scotus*[44] first came out, they were carried to a certain great Library, and had Lodgings appointed them; But this Author was no sooner settled, than he went to visit his Master *Aristotle,* and there both concerted together to seize *Plato* by main Force, and turn him out from his antient Station among the *Divines,* where he had peaceably dwelt near Eight Hundred Years. The Attempt succeeded, and the two Usurpers have reigned ever since in his stead: But to maintain Quiet for the future, it was decreed, that all *Polemicks* of the larger Size, should be held fast with a Chain.

By this Expedient, the publick Peace of Libraries, might certainly have been preserved, if a new Species of controversial Books had not arose of late Years, instinct with a most malignant Spirit, from the War above-mentioned, between the *Learned,* about the higher Summity of *Parnassus.*

When these Books were first admitted into the Publick Libraries, I remember to have said upon Occasion, to several Persons concerned, how I was sure, they would create Broyls where-ever they came, unless a World of Care were taken: And therefore, I advised, that the Champions of each side should be coupled together, or otherwise mixt, that like the blending of contrary Poysons, their Malignity might be employ'd among themselves. And it seems, I was neither an ill Prophet, nor an ill Counsellor; for it was nothing else but the Neglect of this Caution, which gave Occasion to the terrible Fight that happened on *Friday* last between the *Antient* and *Modern Books* in the *King's Library.* Now, because the Talk of this Battel is so fresh in every body's Mouth, and the Expectation of the Town so great to be informed in the Particulars: I, being possessed of all Qualifications requisite in an *Historian,* and retained by neither Party; have resolved to comply with the urgent *Importunity of my Friends,* by writing down a full impartial Account thereof.

The *Guardian* of the *Regal Library,* a Person of great Valor, but chiefly renowned for his *Humanity,*[45] had been a fierce Champion for the *Moderns,* and in an Engagement upon *Parnassus,* had vowed, with his own Hands, to knock down two of the *Antient* Chiefs,[46] who guarded a small Pass on the superior Rock; but endeavouring to climb up, was cruelly obstructed by his own unhappy Weight, and tendency towards his Center; a Quality, to which, those of the *Modern* Party, are extreme subject; For, being light-headed, they have in Speculation, a wonderful Agility, and conceive nothing too high for them to mount; but in reducing to Practice, discover a mighty Pressure about their Posteriors and their Heels. Having thus failed in

---

[43] Cf. Thomas Vaughan, *Anthroposophia Theomagica* (1650), p. 58: "This vanish or ascent of the inward *Ethereall* Principles doth not presently follow their separation: For that part of man which *Paracelsus* calls *Homo Syderens,* and more appositly *Brutum hominis* . . . which is the *Astral Man,* hovers sometimes about the *Dormitories* of the Dead."

[44] John Duns Scotus (*c.*1265–*c.*1308), a Franciscan monk, one of the founders of scholasticism.

[45] "*The Honourable Mr. Boyle, in the Preface to his Edition of Phalaris, says he was refus'd a manuscript by the Library-Keeper,* pro solita Humanitate sua [by virtue of his singular humanity]" (Swift). The "Library-Keeper" was Richard Bentley, who is referred to above in the passage, "The Bookseller to the Reader" (p. 84).

[46] Æsop and Phalaris, whose works Bentley and Wotton declared spurious.

his Design, the disappointed Champion bore a cruel Rancour to the *Antients,* which he resolved to gratifie, by shewing all Marks of his Favour to the *Books* of their Adversaries, and lodging them in the fairest Apartments; when at the same time, whatever *Book* had the boldness to own it self for an Advocate of the *Antients,* was buried alive in some obscure Corner, and threatned upon the least Displeasure, to be turned out of Doors. Besides, it so happened, that about this time, there was a strange Confusion of Place among all the *Books* in the Library; for which several Reasons were assigned. Some imputed it to a great heap of *learned Dust,* which a perverse Wind blew off from a Shelf of *Moderns* into the *Keeper's* Eyes. Others affirmed, He had a Humour to pick the *Worms* out of the *Schoolmen,*[47] and swallow them fresh and fasting; whereof some fell upon his *Spleen,* and some climbed up into his Head, to the great Perturbation of both. And lastly, others maintained, that by walking much in the dark about the Library, he had quite lost the Situation of it out of his Head; And therefore, in replacing his *Books,* he was apt to mistake, and clap *Des-Cartes*[48] next to *Aristotle;* Poor *Plato* had got between *Hobbes*[49] and the *Seven Wise Masters,*[50] and *Virgil* was hemm'd in with *Dryden* on one side, and *Withers*[51] on the other.

Mean while, those *Books* that were Advocates for the *Moderns,* chose out one from among them, to make a Progress thro' the whole Library, examine the Number and Strength of their Party, and concert their Affairs. This Messenger performed all things very industriously, and brought back with him a List of their Forces,[52] in all Fifty Thousand, consisting chiefly of *light Horse, heavy-armed Foot,* and *Mercenaries;* Whereof the *Foot* were in general but sorrily armed, and worse clad; Their *Horses* large, but extremely out of Case and Heart; However, some few by trading among the *Antients,* had furnisht themselves tolerably enough.

While Things were in this Ferment; *Discord* grew extremely high, hot Words passed on both sides, and ill blood was plentifully bred. Here a solitary *Antient,* squeezed up among a whole Shelf of *Moderns,* offered fairly to dispute the Case, and to prove by manifest Reasons, that the Priority was due to them, from long Possession, and in regard of their Prudence, Antiquity, and above all, their great Merits towards the *Moderns.* But these denied the Premises and seemed very much to wonder, how the *Antients* could pretend to insist upon their Antiquity, when it was so plain (if they went to that) that the *Moderns* were much the more *Antient* of the two. As for any Obligations they owed to the *Antients,*[53] they renounced them all. *'Tis true,* said they, *we are informed, some few of our Party have been so mean to borrow their Subsistence from You; But the rest, infinitely the greater Number (and especially, we* French *and* English*) were so far from stooping to so base an Example, that there never passed, till this very hour, six Words between us. For, our* Horses *are of our own breeding, our* Arms *of our own forging, and our* Cloaths *of our own cutting out and sowing. Plato* was by chance upon the next Shelf, and observing those that spoke to be in the ragged Plight, mentioned a while ago; their *Jades* lean and foundred, their *Weapons* of rotten Wood, their *Armour* rusty, and nothing

---

[47] The scholastic philosophers who flourished from the eleventh to the fifteenth century.

[48] See note 12.

[49] Thomas Hobbes (1588–1679), English philosopher.

[50] A collection of Oriental tales which had considerable currency in the seventeenth and eighteenth centuries.

[51] George Wither (1588–1677), an English satirical poet.

[52] Throughout *The Battel,* epic poets are represented as full-armed cavalry, lyric poets as light-horse, philosophers as bowmen, historians as foot-soldiers, mathematicians as engineers, and dragoons as scientists, particularly physicians.

[53] "According to the Modern Paradox" (marginal note).

but Raggs underneath; he laugh'd loud, and in his pleasant way, swore, *By G——, he believ'd them.*

Now, the *Moderns* had not proceeded in their late Negotiation, with Secrecy enough to escape the Notice of the Enemy. For, those Advocates, who had begun the Quarrel, by setting first on Foot the Dispute of Precedency, talkt so loud of coming to a Battel, that *Temple* happened to over-hear them, and gave immediate Intelligence to the *Antients;* who thereupon drew up their scattered Troops together, resolving to act upon the defensive; Upon which, several of the *Moderns* fled over to their Party, and among the rest, *Temple* himself. This *Temple* having been educated and long conversed among the *Antients,* was, of all the *Moderns,* their greatest Favorite, and became their greatest Champion.

Things were at this Crisis, when a material Accident fell out. For, upon the highest Corner of a large Window, there dwelt a certain *Spider* swollen up to the first Magnitude, by the Destruction of infinite Numbers of *Flies,* whose Spoils lay scattered before the Gates of his Palace, like human Bones before the Cave of some Giant. The Avenues to his Castle were guarded with Turk-pikes,[54] and Palissadoes, all after the *Modern* way of Fortification. After you had passed several Courts, you came to the Center, wherein you might behold the *Constable* himself in his own Lodgings, which had Windows fronting to each Avenue, and Ports to sally out upon all Occasions of Prey or Defence. In this Mansion he had for some Time dwelt in Peace and Plenty, without Danger to his *Person* by *Swallows* from above, or to his *Palace* by *Brooms* from below: When it was the Pleasure of Fortune to conduct thither a wandring *Bee,* to whose Curiosity a broken Pane in the Glass had discovered itself; and in he went, where expatiating a while, he at last happened to alight upon one of the outward Walls of the *Spider's* Cittadel; which yielding to the unequal Weight, sunk down to the very Foundation. Thrice he endeavoured

to force his Passage, and Thrice the Center shook. The *Spider* within, feeling the terrible Convulsion, supposed at first, that *Nature* was approaching to her final Dissolution; or else, that *Beelzebub* with all his Legions, was come to revenge the Death of many thousands of his Subjects, whom his Enemy had slain and devoured. However, he at length valiantly resolved to issue forth, and meet his Fate. Mean while, the *Bee* had acquitted himself of his Toils, and posted securely at some Distance, was employed in cleansing his Wings, and disengaging them from the ragged Remnants of the Cobweb. By this Time the *Spider* was adventured out, when beholding the Chasms, and Ruins, and Dilapidations of his Fortress, he was very near at his Wit's end, he stormed and swore like a Mad-man, and swelled till he was ready to burst. At length, casting his Eye upon the *Bee,* and wisely gathering Causes from Events, (for they knew each other by Sight) *A Plague split you,* said he, *for a giddy Son of a Whore; Is it you, with a Vengeance, that have made this Litter here? Could not you[55] look before you, and be d——n'd? Do you think I have nothing else to do (in the Devil's Name) bu to Mend and Repair after your Arse? Good Words, Friend,* said the *Bee,* (having now pruned himself, and being disposed to drole) *I'll give you my Hand and Word to come near your Kennel no more; I was never in such a confounded Pickle since I was born. Sirrah,* replied the *Spider, if it were not for breaking an old Custom in our Family, never to stir abroad against an Enemy, I should come and teach you better Manners. I pray, have Patience,* said the *Bee, or you will spend your Substance, and for ought I see, you may stand in need of it all, towards the Repair of your House. Rogue, Rogue,* replied the *Spider, yet, methinks, you should have more Respect to a Person, whom all the World allows to be so much your Betters. By my Troth,* said the *Bee, the Comparison will amount to a very good Jest, and you will do me a Favour, to let me know the Reasons, that*

---

[54] *Turk-pikes*] *Turn-pikes,* 1704; Turkish spears in either event.

[55] *Could not you*] *Could you not,* 1704.

all the World is pleased to use in so hopeful a Dispute. At this, the *Spider* having swelled himself into the Size and Posture of a Disputant, began his Argument in the true Spirit of Controversy, with a Resolution to be heartily scurrilous and angry, to urge on his own Reasons, without the least Regard to the Answers or Objections of his Opposite; and fully predetermined in his Mind against all Conviction.

Not to disparage my self, said he, *by the Comparison with such a Rascal; What art thou but a Vagabond without House or Home, without Stock or Inheritance? Born to no Possession of your own, but a Pair of Wings, and a Drone-Pipe. Your Livelihood is an universal Plunder upon Nature; a Freebooter over Fields and Gardens; and for the sake of Stealing, will rob a Nettle as readily as a Violet. Whereas I am a domestick Animal, furnisht with a Native Stock within my self. This large Castle (to shew my Improvements in the Mathematicks)*[56] *is all built with my own Hands, and the Materials extracted altogether out of my own Person.*

I am glad, answered the *Bee,* to hear *you grant at least, that I am come honestly by my Wings and my Voice, for then, it seems, I am obliged to Heaven alone for my Flights and my Musick; and Providence would never have bestowed on me two such Gifts, without designing them for the noblest Ends. I visit, indeed, all the Flowers and Blossoms of the Field and the Garden, but whatever I collect from thence, enriches my self, without the least Injury to their Beauty, their Smell, or their Taste. Now, for you and your Skill in Architecture, and other Mathematicks, I have little to say: In that Building of yours, there might, for ought I know, have been Labor and Method enough, but by woful Experience for us both, 'tis too plain, the Materials are nought, and I hope, you will henceforth take Warning, and consider Duration and matter, as well as method and Art. You, boast, indeed, of*

being obliged to no other Creature, but of drawing, and spinning out all from your self; That is to say, if we may judge of the Liquor in the Vessel by what issues out, You possess a good plentiful Store of Dirt and Poison in your Breast; And, tho' I would by no means, lessen or disparage your genuine Stock of either, yet, I doubt you are somewhat obliged for an Encrease of both, to a little foreign Assistance. Your inherent Portion of Dirt, does not fail of Acquisitions, by Sweepings exhaled from below: and one Insect furnishes you with a share of Poison to destroy another. So that in short, the Question comes all to this; Whether[57] *is the nobler Being of the two. That which by a lazy Contemplation of four Inches round; by an over-weening Pride, which feeding and engendering on it self, turns all into Excrement and Venom; producing nothing at all, but Fly-bane and a Cobweb: Or That, which, by an universal Range, with long Search, much Study, true Judgment, and Distinction of Things, brings home Honey and Wax.*

This Dispute was managed with such Eagerness, Clamor, and Warmth, that the two Parties of *Books* in Arms below, stood Silent a while, waiting in Suspense what would be the Issue; which was not long undetermined: For the *Bee* grown impatient at so much loss of Time, fled strait away to a bed of Roses, without looking for a Reply; and left the Spider like an Orator, *collected* in himself, and just prepared to burst out.

It happened upon this Emergency, that *Æsop* broke silence first. He had been of late most barbarously treated by a strange Effect of the *Regent's Humanity,*[58] who had tore off his Title-page, sorely defaced one half of his Leaves, and chained him fast among a Shelf of *Moderns.* Where soon discovering how high the Quarrel was like to proceed, He tried all his Arts, and turned himself to a thousand Forms: At length in the borrowed Shape of an *Ass,* the *Regent* mistook Him for a *Modern;* by

---

[56] The Moderns prided themselves on their progress in mathematics. Cf. William Wotton's *Reflections upon Ancient and Modern Learning* (1694), chap. XIV.

[57] "which of two" (Johnson's *Dictionary*).

[58] See note 45, above.

which means, he had Time and Opportunity to escape to the *Antients,* just when the *Spider* and the *Bee* were entring into their Contest; to which He gave His Attention with a world of Pleasure; and when it was ended, swore in the loudest Key, that in all his Life, he had never known two Cases so parallel and adapt[59] to each other, as That in the Window, and this upon the Shelves. The *Disputants,* said he, *have admirably managed the Dispute between them, have taken in the full Strength of all that is to be said on both sides, and exhausted the Substance of every Argument* pro *and* con. *It is but to adjust the Reasonings of both to the present Quarrel, then to compare and apply the Labors and Fruits of each, as the* Bee *has learnedly deduced them; and we shall find the Conclusion fall plain and close upon the* Moderns *and* Us. *For, pray Gentlemen, was ever any thing so* Modern *as the* Spider *in his Air, his Turns, and his Paradoxes? He argues in the Behalf of* You *his Brethren, and Himself, with many Boastings of his native Stock, and great Genius; that he Spins and Spits wholly from himself, and scorns to own any Obligation or Assistance from without. Then he displays to you his great Skill in Architecture, and Improvement in the Mathematicks. To all this, the* Bee, *as an Advocate, retained by us the* Antients, *thinks fit to Answer; that if one may judge of the great Genius or Inventions of the* Moderns, *by what they have produced, you will hardly have Countenance to bear you out in boasting of either. Erect your Schemes with as much Method and Skill as you please; yet, if the materials be nothing but Dirt, spun out of your own Entrails (the Guts of* Modern *Brains) the Edifice will conclude at last in a* Cobweb: *The Duration of which, like that of other* Spiders *Webs, may be imputed to their being forgotten, or neglected, or hid in a Corner. For any Thing else of Genuine, that the* Moderns *may pretend to, I cannot recollect; unless it be a large Vein of Wrangling and Satyr, much of a Nature and Substance with the* Spider's *Poison; which, however, to*[60] *pretend to spit wholly out of themselves, is improved by the same Arts, by feeding upon the* Insects *and* Vermin *of the Age. As for* Us, *the* Antients, *We are content with the* Bee, *to pretend to Nothing of our own, beyond our* Wings *and our* Voice: *that is to say, our* Flights *and our* Language; *For the rest, whatever we have got, has been by infinite Labor, and search, and ranging thro' every Corner of Nature: The Difference is, that instead of* Dirt *and* Poison, *we have rather chose to fill our Hives with* Honey *and* Wax, *thus furnishing Mankind with the two Noblest of Things, which are* Sweetness *and* Light.

'Tis wonderful to conceive the Tumult arisen among the *Books,* upon the Close of this long Descant of *Æsop;* Both Parties took the Hint, and heightened their Animosities so on a sudden, that they resolved it should come to a Battel. Immediately, the two main Bodies withdrew under their several Ensigns, to the farther Parts of the Library, and there entered into Cabals, and Consults upon the present Emergency. The *Moderns* were in very warm Debates upon the Choice of their *Leaders,* and nothing less than the Fear impending from their Enemies, could have kept them from Mutinies upon this Occasion. The Difference was greatest among the *Horse,* where every private *Trooper* pretended to the Chief Command, from *Tasso*[61] and *Milton,* to *Dryden* and *Withers.* The *Light-Horse* were Commanded by *Cowly,*[62] and *Despreaux.*[63] There, came the *Bowmen* under their valiant Leaders, *Des-Cartes, Gassendi,*[64] and *Hobbes,* whose Strength was such, that they could shoot their Arrows beyond the *Atmos-*

---

[59] suitable.

[60] *to*] *they,* 1704.

[61] Torquato Tasso (1544–1595), Italian epic poet.

[62] Abraham Cowley (1618–1667), English poet.

[63] Nicolas Boileau (1636–1711), French critic and poet.

[64] Pierre Gassendi (1592–1655), French anti-Aristotelian philosopher.

phere, never to fall down again, but turn like that of *Evander,*[65] into *Meteors,* or like the *Canon-ball* into *Stars. Paracelsus*[66] brought a *Squadron* of *Stink-Pot-Flingers* from the snowy Mountains of *Rhoetia.* There, came a vast Body of *Dragoons,* of different Nations, under the leading of *Harvey,*[67] their great *Aga:*[68] Part armed with *Scythes,* the Weapons of Death; Part with *Launces* and long *Knives,* all steept in Poison; Part shot *Bullets* of a most malignant Nature, and used *white Powder* which infallibly killed without *Report.* There, came several Bodies of *heavy-armed Foot,* all *Mercenaries,* under the Ensigns of *Guiccardine,*[69] *Davila,*[70] *Polydore Virgil,*[71] *Buchanan,*[72] *Mariana,*[73] *Cambden,*[74] and others. The *Engineers* were commanded by *Regiomontanus*[75] and *Wilkins.*[76] The rest were a confused Multitude, led by *Scotus, Aquinas,*[77] and *Bellarmine;*[78] of mighty Bulk and Stature, but without either Arms, Courage, or Discipline. In the last Place, came infinite Swarms of *Calones,*[79] a disorderly Rout led by *Lestrange;*[80] Rogues and Raggamuffins, that follow the Camp for nothing but the Plunder; All without *Coats* to cover them.

The Army of the *Antients* was much fewer in Number; *Homer* led the *Horse,* and *Pindar* the *Light-Horse; Euclid* was chief *Engineer: Plato* and *Aristotle* commanded the *Bow men, Herodotus* and *Livy* the *Foot, Hippocrates* the *Dragoons.* The *Allies,* led by *Vossius*[81] and *Temple,* brought up the Rear.

All things violently tending to a decisive Battel; *Fame,* who much frequented, and had a large Apartment formerly assigned her in the *Regal Library,* fled up strait to *Jupiter,* to whom she delivered a faithful account of all that passed between the two Parties below. (For, among the Gods, she always tells Truth.) *Jove* in great concern, convokes a Council in the *Milky-Way.* The Senate assembled, he declares the Occasion of convening them; a bloody Battel just impendent between two mighty Armies of *Antient* and *Modern* Creatures, call'd *Books,* wherein the Celestial Interest was but too deeply concerned. *Momus,*[82] the Patron of the *Moderns,* made an Excellent Speech in their Favor, which was answered by *Pallas* the Protectress of the *Antients.* The Assembly was divided in their affections; when *Jupiter* commanded the Book of Fate to be laid before Him. Immediately were brought by *Mercury,* three large Volumes in Folio, containing Memoirs of all Things past, present, and to come. The Clasps were of Silver, double Gilt; the Covers, of Celestial Turky-leather, and the Paper such as here on Earth might almost pass for Vellum. *Jupiter* having silently read the Decree, would communicate the Import to none, but presently shut up the Book.

---

[65] A legendary Arcadian strong man, son of Hermes.

[66] Theophrastus Bombastus von Mohenheim (1493?–1541), called Paracelsus, Swiss physician and experimental philosopher.

[67] William Harvey (1587–1657), discoverer of the circulation of the blood. In his *Essay upon the Ancient and Modern Learning,* Sir William Temple had questioned the practical value of this discovery.

[68] chief officer, a Moslem title of distinction.

[69] Francesco Guicciardini (1483–1540), Florentine historian.

[70] Enrico Davila (1576–1631), Italian historian.

[71] Polydore Vergil (1470?–?1555), Italian historian of England.

[72] George Buchanan (1506–1582), Scottish historian and poet.

[73] Juan de Mariana (1536–?1624), Spanish historian.

[74] William Camden (1551–1623), English antiquary and historian.

[75] Johann Müller (1436–1476) of Königsberg, German mathematician and astronomer.

[76] John Wilkins (1614–1672), English mathematician and one of the founders of the Royal Society.

[77] St. Thomas Aquinas (c.1225–1274), Italian scholastic philosopher.

[78] Cardinal Robert Bellarmine (1542–1621), Italian defender of the Roman Catholic Church against Protestantism.

[79] *"These are Pamphlets which are not bound or cover'd"* (Swift).

[80] Sir Roger L'Estrange (1616–1704), English journalist and pamphleteer, translator of Cicero and Seneca.

[81] Isaac Vossius (1618–1689), Dutch classical scholar, canon of Windsor from 1673, editor of the works of several ancient authors.

[82] The classical god of mockery.

Without the Doors of this Assembly, there attended a vast Number of light, nimble Gods, menial Servants to *Jupiter:* These are his ministring Instruments in all Affairs below. They travel in a Caravan, more or less together, and are fastened to each other like a Link of Gally-slaves, by a light Chain, which passes from them to *Jupiter's* great Toe: And yet in receiving or delivering a Message, they may never approach above the lowest Step of his Throne, where he and they whisper to each other thro' a long hollow Trunk. These Deities are call'd by mortal Men, *Accidents,* or *Events;* but the Gods call them, *Second Causes. Jupiter* having delivered his Message to a certain Number of these Divinities, they flew immediately down to the Pinnacle of the Regal Library, and consulting a few Minutes, entered unseen, and disposed the Parties according to their Orders.

Mean while, *Momus* fearing the worst, and calling to mind an antient Prophecy, which bore no very good Face to his Children the *Moderns;* bent his Flight to the Region of a malignant Deity, call'd *Criticism.* She dwelt on the Top of a snowy Mountain in *Nova Zembla;* there *Momus* found her extended in her Den, upon the Spoils of numberless Volumes half devoured. At her right Hand sat *Ignorance,* her Father and Husband, blind with Age; at her left, *Pride,* her Mother, dressing her up in the Scraps of Paper herself had torn. There, was *Opinion* her Sister, light of Foot, hoodwinkt,[83] and headstrong, yet giddy and perpetually turning. About her play'd her Children, *Noise* and *Impudence, Dullness* and *Vanity, Positiveness, Pedantry,* and *Ill-Manners.* The Goddess herself had Claws like a Cat: Her Head, and Ears, and Voice, resembled those of an *Ass;* Her Teeth fallen out before;[84] Her Eyes turned inward, as if she lookt only upon herself: Her Diet was the overflowing of her own *Gall:* Her *Spleen* was so large, as to stand prominent like a Dug of the first Rate, nor wanted Excrescencies in form of Teats, at which a Crew of ugly Monsters were greedily sucking; and, what is wonderful to conceive, the bulk of Spleen encreased faster than the Sucking could diminish it. *Goddess,* said *Momus, can you sit idly here, while our devout Worshippers, the* Moderns, *are this Minute entring into a cruel Battel, and, perhaps, now lying under the Swords of their Enemies; Who then hereafter, will ever sacrifice, or build Altars to our Divinities? Haste therefore to the* British Isle, *and, if possible, prevent their Destruction, while I make Factions among the Gods, and gain them over to our Party.*

Momus having thus delivered himself, staid not for an answer, but left the Goddess to her own Resentment; Up she rose in a Rage, and as it is the Form upon such Occasions, began a Soliloquy. *'Tis I* (said she) *who give Wisdom to Infants and Idiots; By Me, Children grow wiser than their Parents. By Me,* Beaux *become Politicians; and* School-boys, *Judges of Philosophy. By Me, Sophisters debate, and conclude upon the Depths of Knowledge; and Coffee-house Wits instinct by Me, can correct an Author's Style, and display his minutest Errors, without understanding a Syllable of his Matter or his Language. By Me, Striplings spend their Judgment, as they do their Estate, before it comes into their Hands. 'Tis I, who have deposed Wit and Knowledge from their Empire over* Poetry, *and advanced my self in their stead. And shall a few* upstart Antients *dare oppose me?—But, come, my aged Parents, and you, my Children dear, and thou my beauteous Sister; let us ascend my Chariot, and hast to assist our devout* Moderns, *who are now sacrificing to us a* Hecatomb,[85] *as I perceive by that grateful Smell, which from thence reaches my Nostrils.*

The Goddess and her Train having mounted the Chariot, which was drawn by *tame Geese,* flew over infinite Regions, shedding her Influence in due Places, till at length, she arrived at her beloved Island of *Britain;* but in hover-

---

[83] blindfolded.
[84] in front.

[85] A large number of oxen.

ing over its *Metropolis,* what Blessings did she not let fall upon her Seminaries of *Gresham* and *Covent-Garden?*[86] And now she reach'd the fatal Plain of St. *James's* Library, at what time the two Armies were upon the Point to engage; where entring with all her Caravan, unseen, and landing upon a Case of Shelves, now desart, but once inhabited by a Colony of *Virtuoso's,*[87] she staid a while to observe the posture of both Armies.

But here, the tender Cares of a Mother began to fill her Thoughts, and move in her Breast. For, at the Head of a Troop of *Modern Bow-men,* she cast her Eyes upon her Son *W—tt—n;* to whom the Fates had assigned a very short Thread. *W—tt—n,* a young Hero, whom an unknown Father of mortal Race, begot by stollen Embraces with this Goddess. He was the Darling of his Mother, above all her Children, and she resolved to go and comfort Him. But first, according to the good old Custom of Deities, she cast about to change her Shape; for fear the Divinity of her Countenance might dazzle his Mortal Sight, and over-charge the rest of his Senses. She therefore gathered up her Person into an *Octavo*[88] Compass: Her Body grew white and arid, and split in pieces with Driness; the thick turned into Pastboard, and the thin into Paper, upon which, her Parents and Children, artfully strowed a Black Juice, or Decoction of Gall and Soot, in Form of Letters; her Head, and Voice, and Spleen, kept their primitive Form, and that which before, was a Cover of Skin, did still continue so. In which Guise, she march'd on towards the *Moderns,* undistinguishable in Shape and Dress from the *Divine B—ntl—y, W—tt—n's* dearest Friend. *Brave W—tt—n,* said the God-

dess, *Why do our Troops stand idle here, to spend their present Vigour and Opportunity of this Day? Away, let us haste to the Generals, and advise to give the Onset immediately.* Having spoke thus, she took the ugliest of her Monsters, full glutted from her Spleen, and flung it invisibly into his Mouth; which flying strait up into his Head, squeez'd out his Eye-Balls, gave him a distorted Look, and half over-turned his Brain. Then she privately ordered two of her beloved Children, *Dulness* and *Ill-Manners,* closely to attend his Person in all Encounters. Having thus accoutred him, she vanished in a Mist, and the *Hero* perceived it was the Goddess, his Mother.

The destined Hour of Fate, being now arrived, the Fight began; whereof, before I dare adventure to make a particular Description, I must, after the Example of other Authors, petition[89] for a hundred Tongues, and Mouths, and Hands, and Pens; which would all be too little to perform so immense a Work. Say, Goddess, that presidest over History; who it was that first advanced in the Field of Battel. *Paracelsus,* at the Head of his *Dragoons,* observing *Galen* in the adverse Wing, darted his Javelin with a mighty Force, which the brave *Antient* received upon his Shield, the Point breaking in the second fold. * * *
* * * * * * * * * * * * * * * * *
* * * * * * * * * * * * * * * * *90

They bore the wounded *Aga,* on their Shields to his Chariot * * * * * * * *
* * * * * * * * * * * * * * * * *
* * * * * * * * * * * * * * * *91

Then Aristotle observing Bacon[92] advance with a furious Mien, drew his Bow to the Head, and let fly his Arrow, which mist the valiant *Modern,* and went hizzing over his Head; but *Des-Cartes* it hit; The Steel Point quickly

---

[86] Gresham College, London, was identified with experimental science. Covent Garden, a part of London, was probably a school of acting; in 1732 it became the site of a theater.

[87] "a man skilled in antique or natural curiosities" (Johnson's *Dictionary*).

[88] A relatively small book, in which the sheets of paper of which it is made are folded into eight leaves.

[89] i.e., by an address to the Muse or Muses, after the manner of epic and other poets.

[90] *"Hic-pauca desunt"* ["Here a little is missing"] (marginal note).

[91] *"Desunt non nulla"* ["Nothing here"] (marginal note).

[92] Francis Bacon (1561–1626), English philosopher and scientist.

found a *Defect* in his *Head-piece;* it pierced the Leather and the Past-board, and went in at his Right Eye. The Torture of the Pain, whirled the valiant *Bow-man* round, till Death, like a Star of superior Influence, drew him into his own Vortex. *[93] when *Homer* appeared at the Head of the Cavalry, mounted on a furious Horse, with Difficulty managed by the Rider him self, but which no other Mortal durst approach; He rode among the Enemies Ranks, and bore down all before him. Say, Goddess, whom he slew first, and whom he slew last. First, *Gondibert*[94] advanced against Him, clad in heavy Armour, and mounted on a staid sober Gelding, not so famed for his Speed as his Docility in kneeling, whenever his Rider would mount or alight. He had made a Vow to *Pallas,* that he would never leave the Field, till he had spoiled *Homer*[95] of his Armour; Madman, who had never once *seen* the Wearer, nor understood his Strength. Him *Homer* overthrew, Horse and Man to the Ground, there to be trampled and choak'd in the Dirt. Then, with a long Spear, he slew *Denham,*[96] a stout *Modern,* who from his Father's side, derived his Lineage from *Apollo,* but his Mother was of *Mortal* Race. He fell, and bit the Earth. The Celestial Part Apollo took, and made it a Star, but the Terrestrial lay wallowing upon the Ground. Then *Homer* slew *W—sl—y*[97] with a kick of his Horse's heel; He took *Perrault*[98] by mighty Force out of his Saddle, then hurl'd him at *Fontenelle,*[99] with the same Blow dashing out both their Brains.

On the left Wing of the Horse, *Virgil* appeared in shining Armor, compleatly fitted to his Body; He was mounted on a dapple grey Steed, the slowness of whose Pace, was an Effect of the highest Mettle and Vigour. He cast his Eye on the adverse Wing, with a desire to find an Object worthy of his valour, when behold, upon a sorrel Gelding of a monstrous Size, appear'd a Foe, issuing from among the thickest of the Enemy's Squadrons; but his Speed was less than his Noise; for his Horse, old and lean, spent the Dregs of his Strength in a high Trot, which tho' it made slow advances, yet caused a loud Clashing of his Armor, terrible to hear. The two Cavaliers had now approached within the Throw of a Lance, when the Stranger desired a Parley, and lifting up the Vizard of his Helmet, a Face hardly appeared from within, which after a pause, was known for that of the renowned *Dryden.*[100] The brave *Antient* suddenly started, as one possess'd with Surprize and Disappointment together: For, the Helmet was nine times too large for the Head, which appeared Situate far in the hinder Part, even like the Lady in a Lobster,[101] or like a Mouse under a Canopy of State, or like a shriveled Beau from within the Pent-house of a modern Perewig: And the voice was suited to the Visage, sounding weak and remote. *Dryden* in a long Harangue soothed up the good *Antient,* called him *Father,* and by a large deduction of Genealogies, made it plainly appear, that they were nearly related. Then he humbly proposed an Exchange of Armor, as a lasting Mark of Hospitality

---

[93] *"Ingens hiatus hic in MS"* ["Important gap here in the manuscript"] (marginal note).

[94] Hero of an unfinished epic of the same name in heroic quatrains by Sir William Davenant (1606–1668). Even the author was bored with the poem.

[95] *"Vid Homer"* (marginal note).

[96] *"Sir John Denham's Poems are very unusual, extremely Good, and very Indifferent, so that his Detractors said he was not the real Author of* Cooper's Hill" (Swift).

[97] Samuel Wesley (1662–1735), rector of Epworth, father of the famous Wesleys, John and Charles, and author of a long poem, *The*

Life of Christ (1693).

[98] Charles Perrault (1628–1703), author of *Parallèle des anciens et des modernes.*

[99] Bernard le Bovier de Fontenelle (1657–1757), author of *Entretiens sur la pluralité des mondes,* referred to by Sir William Temple as one of the occasions of his *Essay upon the Ancient and Modern Learning.*

[100] John Dryden (1631–1700) had translated Vergil's poetry.

[101] According to a folk tradition the outlines of a woman's figure could be seen on the stomach of a lobster.

between them. *Virgil* consented (for the Goddess *Diffidence* came unseen, and cast a Mist before his Eyes)[102] tho' his was of Gold, and cost a hundred Beeves, the others but of rusty Iron. However, this glittering Armor became the *Modern* yet worse than his Own. Then, they agreed to exchange Horses; but when it came to the Trial, *Dryden* was afraid, and utterly unable to mount. *[103]

Lucan[104] appeared upon a fiery Horse, of admirable Shape, but head-strong, bearing the Rider where he list, over the Field; he made a mighty Slaughter among the Enemy's Horse; which Destruction to stop, *Bl—ckm—re,*[105] a famous *Modern* (but one of the *Mercenaries*) strenuously opposed himself; and darted a Javelin, with a strong Hand, which falling short of its Mark, struck deep in the Earth. Then *Lucan* threw a Lance; but *Æsculapius*[106] came unseen, and turn'd off the Point. *Brave* Modern, *said* Lucan, *I perceive some God protects you, for never did my Arm so deceive me before; But, what Mortal can contend with a God? Therefore, let us Fight no longer, but present Gifts to each other.* Lucan then bestowed the *Modern a Pair of Spurs,* and *Bl—ckm—re gave Lucan a Bridle.* *[107]

Creech;[108] But, the Goddess *Dulness* took a Cloud, formed into the Shape of *Horace,* armed and mounted, and placed it in a flying Posture before Him. Glad was the Cavalier, to begin a Combat with a flying Foe, and pursued the Image, threatning loud; till at last it led him to the peaceful Bower of his Father *Ogleby,*[109] by whom he was disarmed, and assigned to his Repose.

Then *Pindar* slew ———, and ———, and *Oldham,*[110] and ———[111] and *Afra*[112] the *Amazon* light of foot; Never advancing in a direct Line, but wheeling with incredible Agility and Force, he made a terrible Slaughter among the Enemies *Light-Horse.* Him, when *Cowley* observed, his generous Heart burnt within him, and he advanced against the fierce *Antient,* imitating his Address, and Pace and Career, as well as the Vigour of his Horse, and his own Skill would allow. When the two Cavaliers had approach'd within the Length of three Javelins; first *Cowley* threw a Lance, which miss'd *Pindar,* and passing into the Enemy's Ranks, fell ineffectual to the Ground. Then *Pindar* darted a Javelin, so large and weighty, that scarce a dozen *Cavaliers, as Cavaliers* are in our degenerate Days, could raise it from the Ground; yet he threw it with Ease, and it went by an unerring Hand, singing through the air; Nor could the *Modern* have avoided present Death, if he had not luckily opposed the Shield that had been given him by *Venus.* And now both Hero's drew their Swords, but the *Modern* was so aghast and disordered, that he knew not where he was; his Shield dropt from his Hands; thrice he fled, and thrice he could not escape; at last he turned, and lifting up his Hands, in the Posture of a Suppliant, *God-like* Pindar, said he, *spare my Life, and possess my Horse with these Arms: besides the Ransom which my friends will give, when they hear I am alive, and your Prisoner. Dog,* said Pindar, *Let your Ransom stay with your Friends: But your Carcass shall be left for the Fowls of the Air, and the* Beasts of the Field. With that, he raised his Sword, and with a mighty Stroak, cleft the wretched *Modern* in twain, the Sword

---

[102] "Vid. Homer" (marginal note).

[103] *"Alter hiatus in MS"* ["Another hiatus in the manuscript"] (marginal note).

[104] Roman poet (39–65), author of *Pharsalia,* a heroic poem describing the conflict between Caesar and Pompey.

[105] Sir Richard Blackmore (1650?–1729), English physician and author of lengthy epics.

[106] God of medicine.

[107] *"Pauca desunt"* ["A little is missing"] (marginal note).

[108] Thomas Creech (1659–1700), translator of Lucretius and Horace.

[109] John Ogilby (1600–1676), translator of Vergil and Homer.

[110] John Oldham (1653–1683), author of Pindaric odes, classical imitations, and satires.

[111] Names omitted in the original.

[112] Aphra Behn (1640–1689), author of sensational plays and novels.

pursuing the Blow; and one half lay panting on the Ground, to be trod in pieces by the Horses Feet, the other half was born by the frighted Steed thro' the Field. This *Venus*[113] took, and wash'd it seven times in *Ambrosia,* then struck it thrice with a Sprig of *Amarant;*[114] upon which, the Leather grew round and soft, and the Leaves turned into Feathers, and being gilded before, continued gilded still; so it became a *Dove,* and She harness'd it to her Chariot. *[115]

[THE EPISODE OF B—NTL—Y AND W—TT—N]

Day being far spent, and the numerous Forces of the *Moderns* half inclining to a Retreat, there issued forth from a Squadron of their *heavy armed Foot,* a Captain, whose Name was *B—ntl—y;* in Person, the most deformed of all the Moderns; Tall, but without Shape or Comeliness; Large, but without Strength or Proportion. His Armour was patch'd up of a thousand incoherent Pieces; and the Sound of it, as he march'd, was loud and dry, like that made by the Fall of a Sheet of Lead, which an *Etesian* Wind[116] blows suddenly down from the Roof of some Steeple. His Helmet was of old rusty Iron, but the Vizard was Brass, which tainted by his Breath, corrupted into Copperas, nor wanted Gall from the same Fountain; so, that whenever provoked by Anger or Labour, an atramentous[117] Quality, of most malignant Nature, was seen to distil from his Lips. In his right Hand he grasp'd a Flail,[118] and (that he might never be unprovided of an *offensive* Weapon) a Vessel full of *Ordure* in his Left: Thus, compleatly arm'd, he advanc'd with a slow and heavy Pace, where the *Modern* Chiefs were holding a Consult upon the Sum of Things; who, as he came onwards, laugh'd to behold his crooked Leg, and hump Shoulder, which his Boot and Armour vainly endeavouring to hide were forced to comply with, and expose. The Generals made use of him for his Talent of Railing; which kept within Government, proved frequently of great Service to their Cause, but at other times did more Mischief than Good; For at the least Touch of Offence, and often without any at all, he would, like a wounded Elephant, convert it against his Leaders. Such, at this Juncture, was the Disposition of *B—ntl—y,* grieved to see the Enemy prevail, and dissatisfied with every Body's Conduct but his own. He humbly gave the *Modern* Generals to understand, that he conceived, with great Submission, they were all a Pack of *Rogues,* and *Fools,* and *Sons of Whores, and d—mn'd Cowards,* and *confounded Loggerheads,* and *illiterate Whelps,* and *nonsensical Scoundrels;* That if Himself had been constituted General, those *presumptuous* Dogs,[119] the *Antients,* would long before this, have been beaten out of the Field. *You,* said he, *sit here idle, but, when I, or any other valiant* Modern, *kill an Enemy, you are sure to seize the Spoil. But, I will not march one Foot against the Foe, till you all swear to me, that, whomever I take or kill, his Arms I shall quietly possess. B—ntl—y* having spoke thus, *Scaliger*[120] bestowing him a sower Look; *Miscreant* Prater, said he, *Eloquent only in thine own Eyes, Thou railest without Wit, or Truth, or Discretion. The Malignity of thy Temper perverteth Nature, Thy* Learning *makes thee more* Barbarous, *thy Study of* Hu-

---

[113] *"I do not approve of the Author's Judgment in this, for I think* Cowley's *Pindaricks are much preferable to his* Mistress" (Swift).

[114] An imaginary flower that never fades.

[115] *"Hiatus valdè deflendus in MS"* ["An important hiatus occurs in the manuscript"] (marginal note).

[116] A periodic wind of annual recurrence.

[117] inky, black.

[118] *"The Person here spoken of, is famous*

for letting fly at every Body without Distinction, and using mean and foul Scurrilities" (Swift).

[119] "Vid. Homer. de Thersite" (marginal note). Thersites was the most deformed and scurrilous of the Greeks at Troy.

[120] Joseph Justus Scaliger (1540–1609), outstanding scholar of the Renaissance and founder of historical criticism.

manity, *more* Inhuman; *Thy* Converse *amongst Poets more* groveling, miry, *and* dull. *All Arts of* civilizing *others, render thee* rude *and* untractable; Courts *have taught thee* ill Manners, *and* polite Conversation *has finish'd thee a* Pedant. *Besides, a greater Coward burtheneth not the Army. But never despond, I pass my Word, whatever Spoil thou takest, shall certainly be thy own; though, I hope, that vile Carcass will first become a prey to Kites and Worms.*

B—ntl—y durst not reply; but half choaked with Spleen and Rage, withdrew, in full Resolution of performing some great Achievment. With him, for his Aid and Companion, he took his beloved *W—tt—n;* resolving by Policy or Surprize, to attempt some neglected Quarter of the *Antients* Army. They began their March over Carcasses of their slaughtered Friends; then to the Right of their own Forces: then wheeled Northward, till they came to *Aldrovandus's* Tomb,[121] which they pass'd on the side of the declining Sun. And now they arrived with Fear towards the Enemy's Out-guards; looking about, if haply, they might spy the Quarters of the Wounded, or some straggling Sleepers, unarm'd and remote from the rest. As when two *Mongrel-Curs,* whom *native Greediness,* and *domestick Want,* provoke, and join in Partnership, though fearful, nightly to invade the Folds of some rich Grazier; They, with Tails depress'd, and lolling Tongues, creep soft and slow; mean while, the conscious *Moon,* now in her *Zenith,* on their guilty Heads, darts perpendicular Rays; Nor dare they bark, though much provok'd at her refulgent Visage, whether seen in Puddle by Reflexion, or in Sphear direct; but one surveys the Region round, while t'other scours the Plain, if haply, to discover at distance from the Flock, some *Carcass* half devoured, the Refuse of gorged Wolves, or ominous Ravens. So march'd

this lovely, loving Pair of Friends, nor with less Fear and Circumspection: when, at distance, they might perceive two shining Suits of Armor, banging upon an Oak, and the Owners not far off in a profound Sleep. The two Friends drew Lots, and the pursuing of this Adventure, fell to *B—ntl—y;* On he went, and in his Van *Confusion* and *Amaze;* while *Horror* and *Affright* brought up the Rear. As he came near; Behold two Hero's of the *Antients* Army, *Phalaris* and *Æsop,* lay fast asleep: *B—ntl—y* would fain have dispatch'd them both, and stealing close, aimed his Flail at *Phalaris's* Breast. But then, the Goddess *Affright* interposing, caught the *Modern* in her icy Arms, and dragg'd him from the Danger she foresaw; For both the dormant Hero's happened to turn at the same Instant, tho' soundly Sleeping, and busy in a Dream. For *Phalaris* was just that Minute dreaming,[122] how a most vile *Poetaster* had lampoon'd him, and how he had got him roaring in his *Bull.* And *Æsop* dream'd, that as he and the *Antient Chiefs* were lying on the Ground, a *Wild Ass* broke loose, ran about trampling and kicking, and dunging in their Faces, *B—ntl—y* leaving the two Hero's asleep, seized on both their Armors, and withdrew in quest of his Darling *W—tt—n.*

He, in the mean time, had wandred long in search of some Enterprize, till at length, he arrived at a small *Rivulet,* that issued from a Fountain hard by, call'd in the Language of mortal Men, *Helicon.*[123] Here he stopt, and, parch'd with thirst, resolved to alay it in this limpid Stream. Thrice, with profane Hands, he essay'd to raise the Water to his Lips, and thrice it slipt all thro' his Fingers. Then he stoop'd prone on his Breast, but e'er his Mouth had kiss'd the liquid Crystal, *Apollo* came, and, in the Channel, held his *Shield* betwixt the *Modern* and the Fountain, so that he

---

[121] Ulisse Aldrovandi (1522–1605), Italian scientist. His great work on natural history was not published until after his death, hence Swift's allusion to it as his tomb.

[122] "*This is according to* Homer, *who tells the Dreams of those who were kill'd in their sleep*" (Swift).

[123] A mountain in Boeotia sacred to the Muses. From it flowed the inspiring fountains of Hippocrene and Aganippe.

drew up nothing but *Mud*. For, altho'
no Fountain on Earth can compare with
the Clearness of *Helicon,* yet there lies
at Bottom, a thick sediment of *Slime* and
Mud; For, so *Apollo* begg'd of *Jupiter,*
as a Punishment to those who durst attempt to taste it with unhallowed Lips,
and for a Lesson to all, not to *draw too
deep,* or *far from the Spring.*

At the Fountain Head, *W—tt—n* discerned two Hero's; The one he could
not distinguish, but the other was soon
known for *Temple,* General of the *Allies*
to the *Antients.* His Back was turned,
and he was employ'd in Drinking large
Draughts in his Helmet, from the Fountain, where he had withdrawn himself
to rest from the Toils of the War.
W—tt—n, observing him, with quaking
Knees, and trembling Hands, spoke thus
to Himself: *Oh, that I could kill this
Destroyer of our Army, what Renown
should I purchase among the Chiefs! But
to issue out against Him, Man for
Man, Shield against Shield, and Launce
against Launce;*[124] *what* Modern *of us
Dare? For, he fights like a God, and
Pallas or Apollo are ever at his Elbow.
But, Oh,* Mother! *if what Fame reports, be true, that I am the Son of so
great a Goddess, grant me to Hit* Temple *with this Launce, that the Stroak
may send Him to Hell, and that I may
return in Safety and Triumph, laden
with his Spoils.* The first Part of his
Prayer, the Gods granted, at the Intercession of His *Mother* and of *Momus;*
but the rest, by a perverse Wind sent
from *Fate,* was scattered in the Air.
Then *W—tt—n* grasp'd his Launce, and
brandishing it thrice over his head,
darted it with all his Might, the *Goddess,* his *Mother,* at the same time, adding Strength to his Arm. Away the
Launce went hizzing, and reach'd even
to the Belt of the averted *Antient,* upon
which, lightly grazing, it fell to the
Ground. *Temple* neither felt the
Weapon touch him, nor heard it fall;
And *W—tt—n,* might have escaped to
his Army, with the Honor of having re-
mitted his Launce against so great a
Leader, unrevenged; But, *Apollo* enraged, that a Javelin, flung by the Assistance of so foul a *Goddess,* should pol-
lute his Fountain, put on the shape of
———,[125] and softly came to young
Boyle, who then accompanied *Temple:*
He pointed, first to the Launce, then to
the distant *Modern* that flung it, and
commanded the young Hero to take immediate Revenge. *Boyle,* clad in a suit
of Armor which had been *given him by
all the Gods,* immediately advanced
against the trembling Foe, who now fled
before him. As a young Lion, in the *Lib-
yan Plains,* or *Araby Desart,* sent by his
aged Sire to hunt for Prey, or Health,
or Exercise; He scours along, wishing to
meet some Tiger from the Mountains,
or a furious Boar; If Chance, a *Wild
Ass,* with Brayings importune, affronts
his Ear, the generous Beast, though
loathing to distain his Claws with Blood
so vile, yet much provok'd at the offensive Noise; which *Echo,* foolish Nymph,
like her *ill judging Sex,* repeats much
louder, and with more Delight than *Phil-
omela's* Song:[126] He vindicates the
Honor of the Forest, and hunts the
noisy, long-ear'd Animal. So *W—tt—n*
fled, so *Boyle* pursued. But *W—tt—n*
heavy-arm'd, and slow of foot, began
to slack his Course; when his Lover
B—ntl—y appeared, returning laden
with the Spoils of the two sleeping *Antients. Boyle* observed him well, and soon
discovering the Helmet and Shield of
Phalaris, his Friend, both which he had
lately with his own Hands, new polish'd
and gilded; Rage sparkled in His Eyes,
and leaving his Pursuit after *W—tt—n,*
he furiously rush'd on against this new
Approacher. Fain would he be revenged
on both; but both now fled different
Ways: And as a Woman in a little
House, that gets a painful Livelihood by
Spinning;[127] if chance her *Geese* be
scattered o'er the Common, she courses
round the Plain from side to side, com-

---

[124] *"Vid. Homer"* (marginal note).
[125] Name omitted in the original.

[126] The song of the nightingale.
[127] *"Vid. Homer"* (marginal note).

pelling here and there, the Straglers to the Flock; They cackle loud and flutter o'er the Champain.[128] So *Boyle* pursued, so fled this Pair of Friends: finding at length, their Flight was vain, they bravely joyn'd, and drew themselves in *Phalanx*. First, *B—ntl—y* threw a Spear with all his Force, hoping to pierce the Enemy's Breast; But *Pallas* came unseen, and in the Air took off the Point, and clap'd on one of Lead, which after a dead Bang against the Enemy's Shield, fell blunted to the Ground. Then *Boyle* observing well his Time, took a Launce of wondrous Length and sharpness; and as this Pair of Friends compacted stood close Side to Side, he wheel'd him to the right, and with unusual Force, darted the Weapon. *B—ntl—y* saw his Fate approach, and flanking down his Arms, close to his Ribs, hoping to save his Body; in went the Point, passing through

Arm and Side, nor stopt, or spent its Force, till it had also pierc'd the valiant *W—tt—n,* who going to sustain his dying Friend, shared his Fate. As, when a skilful Cook has truss'd a Brace of *Woodcocks,* He, with Iron Skewer, pierces the tender Sides of both, their Legs and Wings close pinion'd to their Ribs; So was this pair of Friends transfix'd, till down they fell, joyn'd in their Lives, joyn'd in their Deaths; so closely joyn'd, that *Charon*[129] would mistake them both for one, and waft them over *Styx* for half his Fare. Farewel, beloved, loving Pair; Few Equals have you left behind: And happy and immortal shall you be, if all my Wit and Eloquence can make you.

And, now *[130]

A MEDITATION UPON A BROOM-STICK

ACCORDING TO THE STYLE AND MANNER OF THE HONBLE ROBERT BOYLE'S MEDITATIONS[131]

[The following story of the composition of *A Meditation upon a Broom-Stick* while Swift was attached to the household of the Earl of Berkeley was first recorded by Thomas Sheridan in his *Life of . . . Swift* (1784) in these words:

He passed much of his time at Lord Berkeley's, officiating as Chaplain to the family, and attending Lady Berkeley in her private devotions. After which, the Doctor, by her desire, used to read to her some moral or religious discourse.

The Countess had at this time taken a great liking to Mr. Boyle's Meditations, and was determined to go through them in that manner; but as Swift had by no means the same relish for that kind of writing which her Ladyship had, he soon grew weary of the task; and a whim coming into his head, resolved to get rid of it in a way which might occasion some sport in the family; for which they had as high a relish as himself. The next time he was employed in reading one of these Meditations, he took an opportunity of conveying away the book, and dexter-

---

The text is from the first edition, 1710.

[128] *This is also, after the manner of* Homer; *the Woman's getting a painful Livelihood by Spinning, has nothing to do with the Similitude, nor would be excusable without such an Authority"* (Swift).

[129] A god of hell who ferried the dead across the rivers Styx and Acheron.

[130] *"Desunt cætera"* ["The rest is missing"] (marginal note).

[131] Robert Boyle (1627–1691), chemist. The style of his *Reflections upon Several Subjects,* which Swift is parodying here, had also been parodied in Samuel Butler's *Occasional Reflections on Dr. Charlton's Feeling a Dog's Pulse in Gresham College.*

ously inserted a leaf, on which he had written his own Meditation on a Broom-stick; after which, he took care to have the book restored to its proper place, and in his next attendance on my Lady, when he was desired to proceed to the next Meditation, Swift opened upon the place where the leaf had been inserted, and with great composure of countenance read the title, "A Meditation on a Broom-stick." Lady Berkeley, a little surprised at the oddity of the title, stopped him, repeating the words, "A Meditation on a Broom-stick!" bless me, what a strange subject! But there is no knowing what useful lessons of instruction this wonderful man may draw, from things apparently the most trivial. Pray let us hear what he says upon it. Swift then, with an inflexible gravity of countenance, proceeded to read the Meditation, in the same solemn tone which he had used in delivering the former. Lady Berkeley, not at all suspecting a trick, in the fulness of her prepossession, was every now and then, during the reading of it, expressing her admiration of this extraordinary man, who could draw such fine moral reflections from so contemptible a subject; with which, though Swift must have been inwardly not a little tickled, yet he preserved a most perfect composure of features, so that she had not the least room to suspect any deceit. Soon after, some company coming in, Swift pretended business, and withdrew, foreseeing what was to follow. Lady Berkeley, full of the subject, soon entered upon the praises of those heavenly Meditations of Mr. Boyle. But, said she, the Doctor has just been reading one to me, which has surprised me more than all the rest. One of the company asked which the Meditations she meant. She answered directly, in the simplicity of her heart, I mean that excellent Meditation on a Broom-stick. The company looked at each other with some surprise, and could scarce refrain from laughing. But they all agreed that they had never heard of such a Meditation before. Upon my word, said my Lady, there it is, look into that book, and convince yourselves. One of them opened the book, and found it there indeed, but in Swift's hand-writing; upon which a general burst of laughter ensued; and my Lady, when the first surprise was over, enjoyed the joke as much as any of them; saying, what a vile trick has that rogue played me! But it is his way, he never baulks his humour in any thing. The affair ended in a great deal of harmless mirth, and Swift, you may be sure, was not asked to proceed any farther in the Meditations.]

This single Stick, which you now behold Ingloriously lying in that neglected Corner, I once knew in a Flourishing State in A Forest, it was full of Sap, full of Leaves, and full of Boughs; but now, in vain does the busie Art of Man pretend to Vye with Nature, by tying that wither'd Bundle of Twigs to its sapless Trunk; 'tis now at best but the Reverse of what it was, a Tree turn'd upside down, the Branches on the Earth, and the Root in the Air; 'tis now handled by every Dirty Wench, condemn'd to do her Drudgery, and by a Capricious kind of Fate, destin'd to make other Things Clean, and be Nasty it self: At Length, worn to the Stumps in the Service of the Maids, 'tis either thrown out of Doors, or condemn'd to its last use of kindling Fires. When I beheld this, I sigh'd, and said within my self, **Surely Man**[132] **is a Broom-stick**; Nature sent him into the World Strong and Lusty, in a Thriving Condition, wearing his own Hair on his Head, the proper Branches of this Reasoning Vegetable, till the Axe of Intemperance has lopt off his Green Boughs, and left him a wither'd Trunk: He then flies unto Art, and puts on a *Peruque,* valuing himself upon an Unnatural Bundle of Hairs, all cover'd with Powder that never grew on his Head; but now should this our *Broom-Stick* pretend to enter the Scene, proud of those *Birchen* Spoils it never bore, and all cover'd with Dust, tho' the Sweepings of the Finest Lady's Chamber, we should be apt to Ridicule and Despise its Vanity, Partial Judges that we are! of Our own Excellencies, and other Men's Faults.

---

[132] *man*] *mortal man* in subsequent editions.

But a *Broom-stick,* perhaps you'll say, is an Emblem of a Tree standing on its Head; and pray what is Man, but a Topsy-turvy Creature, his Animal Faculties perpetually a Cock-Horse [the][133] Rational; His Head where his Heels should be; groveling on the Earth, and yet with all his Faults, he sets up to be an universal Reformer and Corrector of Abuses, a Remover of Grievances, rakes into every Slut's Corner of Nature, bringing hidden Corruptions to the Light, and raises a mighty Dust where there was none before, sharing deeply all the while, in the very same Pollutions he pretends to sweep away: His last Days are spent in Slavery to Women, and generally the least deserving; 'till worn to the Stumps, like his Brother *Bezom,*[134] he's either kickt out of Doors, or made use of to kindle Flames, for others to warm Themselves by.

TRAVELS into several Remote Nations of the World by Captain Lemuel Gulliver

PART III. A VOYAGE TO LAPUTA, BALNIBARBI, LUGGNAGG, GLUBBDUBDRIBB AND JAPAN

CHAPTER I

The Author sets out on his Third Voyage; is taken by Pyrates. The Malice of a Dutchman. *His Arrival at an Island. He is received into* Laputa.

I had not been at Home above ten Days, when Captain *William Robinson,* a *Cornish* Man, Commander of the *Hopewell,* a stout Ship of Three Hundred Tuns, came to my House. I had formerly been Surgeon of another Ship where he was Master, and a fourth Part Owner, in a Voyage to the *Levant;*[135] He had always treated me more like a Brother than an inferior Officer, and hearing of my Arrival made me a Visit, as I apprehended only out of Friendship, for nothing passed more than what is usual after long Absences. But repeating his Visits often, expressing his Joy to find me in good Health, asking whether I were now settled for Life, adding that he intended a Voyage to the *East-Indies,* in two Months; at last he plainly invited me, though with some Apologies, to be Surgeon of the Ship; that I should have another Surgeon under me besides our two Mates; that my Sallary should be double to the usual Pay; and that having experienced my Knowledge in Sea-Affairs to be at least equal to his, he would enter into any Engagement to follow my Advice, as much as if I had share in the Command.

He said so many other obliging Things, and I knew him to be so honest a Man, that I could not reject his Proposal; the Thirst I had of seeing the World, notwithstanding my past Misfortunes, continuing as violent as ever. The only Difficulty that remained, was to persuade my Wife, whose Consent, however, I at last obtained by the Prospect of Advantage she proposed to her Children.

We set out the 5th Day of *August,* 1706. and arrived at Fort *St. George*[136] the 11th of *April,* 1707. stayed there

---

The text is that of the second edition, 1726, with a few significant changes from the second edition, "corrected," of 1727, and one material addition from the text of 1735.

---

[133] *the*] *and,* 1710; the phrase *mounted on his* was substituted later for *a Cock-Horse and.*

The present reading assumes a typographical error in reading the manuscript.

[134] besom, broom.

[135] "the Mediterranean sea, or countries on the east side of it, or to the east of Italy" (Bailey's *Dictionary*).

[136] Site of the modern city of Madras.

three Weeks to refresh our Crew, many of whom were sick. From thence we went to *Tonquin*,[137] where the Captain resolved to continue some Time because many of the Goods he intended to buy were not ready, nor could he expect to be dispatched in some Months. Therefore in hopes to defray some of the Charges he must be at, he bought a Sloop, loaded it with several sorts of Goods, wherewith the *Tonquinese* usually trade to the neighbouring Islands, and putting fourteen Men on Board, whereof three were of the Country, he appointed me Master of the Sloop, and gave me Power to traffick for two Months, while he transacted his Affairs at *Tonquin*.

We had not sailed above three Days, when a great Storm arising, we were driven five Days to the North-North-East, and then to the East; after which we had fair Weather, but still with a pretty strong Gale from the West. Upon the tenth Day we were chased by two Pyrates, who soon overtook us; for my Sloop was so deep loaden, that she sailed very slow, neither were we in a Condition to defend our selves.

We were boarded about the same Time by both the Pyrates, who enter'd furiously at the Head of their Men, but finding us all prostrate upon our Faces, (for so I gave order,) they pinioned us with strong Ropes, and setting a Guard upon us, went to search the Sloop.

I observed among them a *Dutch-man*, who seemed to be of some Authority, though he was not Commander of either Ship. He knew us by our Countenances to be *Englishmen*, and jabbering to us in his own Language, swore we should be tied Back to Back, and thrown into the Sea. I spoke *Dutch* tolerably well; I told him who we were, and begged him, in consideration of our being Christians and Protestants, of neighbouring Countries, in strict Alliance,[138] that he would move the Captains to take some Pity on us.

This inflamed his Rage; he repeated his Threatnings, and, turning to his Companions, spoke with great Vehemence, in the *Japanese* Language, as I suppose, often using the Word *Christianos*.

The largest of the two Pyrate Ships was commanded by a *Japanese* Captain, who spoke a little *Dutch*, but very imperfectly. He came up to me, and after several Questions, which I answered in great Humility, he said we should not die. I made the Captain a very low Bow, and then turning to the *Dutch-man*, said, I was sorry to find more Mercy in a Heathen, than in a Brother Christian. But I had soon Reason to repent those foolish Words, for that malicious Reprobate, having often endeavoured in vain to persuade both the Captains that I might be thrown into the Sea, (which they would not yield to after the Promise made me, that I should not die,) however prevailed so far as to have a Punishment inflicted on me, worse in all human Appearance than Death it self. My Men were sent by an equal Division into both the Pirate-Ships, and my Sloop new manned. As to my self, it was determined that I should be set a drift in a small Canoe, with Paddles and a Sail, and four Days Provisions, which last the *Japanese* Captain was so kind to double out of his own Stores, and would permit no Man to search me. I got down into the Canoe, while the *Dutchman* standing upon the Deck, loaded me with all the Curses and injurious Terms his Language could afford.

About an Hour before we saw the Pirates, I had taken an Observation, and found we were in the Latitude of 46 N. and of Longitude 183.[139] When I was at some Distance from the Pirates, I discovered by my Pocket-Glass several Islands to the South-East. I set up my Sail, the Wind being fair, with a Design to reach the nearest of those Islands, which I made a Shift to do in about

---

[137] A small country located between China and Laos.

[138] Great Britain and Holland had marked the commercial rivalry of the seventeenth century but from 1701 had been bound by agreements preventing war though not individual

acts of violence. The Dutch had exclusive trading rights with the Japanese.

[139] It was customary at this time to measure longitude continuously from west to east; 183° would thus be 177°W according to present practice.

three Hours. It was all rocky; however, I got many Birds Eggs, and striking Fire I kindled some Heath and dry Sea-Weed, by which I roasted my Eggs. I eat no other Supper, being resolved to spare my Provisions as much as I could. I passed the Night under the Shelter of a Rock, strowing some Heath under me, and slept pretty well.

The next Day I sailed to another Island, and thence to a third and fourth, sometimes using my Sail, and sometimes my Paddles. But not to trouble the Reader with a particular Account of my Distresses, let it suffice, that on the 5th Day I arrived at the last Island in my Sight, which lay South-South-East to the former.

This Island was at a greater Distance than I expected, and I did not reach it in less than five Hours. I encompassed it almost round before I could find a convenient Place to land in, which was a small Creek, about three Times the Wideness of my Canoe. I found the Island to be all rocky, only a little intermingled with Tufts of Grass, and sweet-smelling Herbs. I took out my small Provisions, and after having refreshed my self, I secured the Remainder in a Cave, whereof there were great Numbers. I gathered plenty of Eggs upon the Rocks, and got a Quantity of dry Sea-Weed and parched Grass, which I designed to kindle the next Day, and roast my Eggs as well as I could. (For I had about me my Flint, Steel, Match,[140] and Burning-Glass.) I lay all Night in the Cave where I had lodged my Provisions. My Bed was the same dry Grass and Seaweed which I intended for Fewel. I slept very little, for the Disquiets of my Mind prevailed over my Weariness, and kept me awake. I considered how impossible it was to preserve my Life in so desolate a Place, and how miserable my End must be. Yet I found my self so listless and desponding, that I had not the Heart to rise, and before I could get Spirits enough to creep out of my Cave, the Day was far advanced. I walked a while among the

Rocks; the Sky was perfectly clear, and the Sun so hot, that I was forced to turn my Face from it: When all on a sudden it became obscured, as I thought, in a Manner very different from what happens by the Interposition of a Cloud. I turned back, and perceived a vast Opake Body between me and the Sun, moving forwards towards the Island: It seemed to be about two Miles high, and hid the Sun six or seven Minutes; but I did not observe the Air to be much colder, or the Sky more darkned, than if I had stood under the Shade of a Mountain. As it approached nearer over the Place where I was, it appeared to be a firm Substance, the Bottom flat, smooth, and shining very bright from the Reflection of the Sea below. I stood upon a Height about two hundred Yards from the Shoar, and saw this vast Body descending almost to a Parallel with me, at less than an *English* Mile distance. I took out my Pocket-Perspective,[141] and could plainly discover Numbers of People moving up and down the Sides of it, which appeared to be sloping, but what those People were doing, I was not able to distinguish.

The natural Love of Life gave me some inward Motions of Joy, and I was ready to entertain a Hope, that this Adventure might some Way or other help to deliver me from the desolate Place and Condition I was in. But at the same Time the Reader can hardly conceive my Astonishment, to behold an Island in the Air, inhabited by Men, who were able, (as it should seem) to raise, or sink, or put it into a Progressive Motion, as they pleased. But not being at that Time in a Disposition to philosophise upon this Phœnomenon, I rather chose to observe what Course the Island would take, because it seemed for a while to stand still. Yet soon after it advanced nearer, and I could see the Sides of it encompassed with several Gradations of Galleries and Stairs, at certain Intervals, to descend from one to the other. In the lowest Gallery I beheld some People fishing with long Angling Rods, and others looking

---

[140] Material to be ignited either by sparks struck from the flint and steel or by rays of the sun concentrated by the burning glass.

[141] "a glass through which things are viewed" (Bailey's *Dictionary*).

on. I waved my Cap, (for my Hat was long since worn out,) and my Handkerchief towards the Island; and, upon its nearer Approach, I called and shouted with the utmost Strength of my Voice, and then looking circumspectly, I beheld a Crowd gathered to that Side which was most in my View. I found by their pointing towards me, and to each other, that they plainly discovered me, although they made no Return to my Shouting. But I could see four or five Men running in great Haste up the Stairs to the Top of the Island, who then disappeared. I happened rightly to conjecture, that these were sent for Orders to some Person in Authority upon this Occasion.

The Number of People increased, and in less than half an Hour the Island was moved and raised in such a Manner, that the lowest Gallery appeared in a Parallel of less than an Hundred Yards distance from the Height where I stood. I then put my self into the most supplicating Postures, and spoke in the humblest Accent, but received no Answer. Those who stood nearest over-against me, seemed to be Persons of Distinction, as I supposed by their Habit. They conferred earnestly with each other, looking often upon me. At length one of them called out in a clear, polite, smooth Dialect, not unlike in Sound to the *Italian;* and therefore I returned an Answer in that Language, hoping at least that the Cadence might be more agreeable to his Ears. Although neither of us understood the other, yet my Meaning was easily known, for the People saw the Distress I was in.

They made Signs for me to come down from the Rock, and go towards the Shoar, which I accordingly did; and the flying Island being raised to a convenient Height, the Verge[142] directly over me, a Chain was let down from the lowest Gallery, with a Seat fasten'd to the Bottom, to which I fixed my self, and was drawn up by Pullies.

CHAPTER II

The Humours and Dispositions of the Laputians *described. An Account of their* Learning. Of the King and his Court. The Authors Reception there. The Inhabitants subject to Fears and Disquietudes. An Account of the Women.

At my alighting I was surrounded by a Crowd of People; but those who stood nearest seemed to be of better Quality. They beheld me with all the Marks and Circumstances of Wonder; neither, indeed, was I much in their Debt, having never till then seen a Race of Mortals so singular in their Shapes, Habits, and Countenances. Their Heads were all reclined[143] either to the Right, or the Left; one of their Eyes turned inward, and the other directly up to the Zenith. Their outward Garments were adorned with the Figures of Suns, Moons, and Stars, interwoven with those of Fiddles, Flutes, Harps, Trumpets, Guittars, Harpsicords, and many more Instruments of Musick, unknown to us in *Europe*. I observed here and there many in the Habit of Servants, with a blown Bladder fasten'd like a Flail to the End of a short Stick, which they carried in their Hands. In each Bladder was a small Quantity of dried Pease, or little Pebbles, (as I was afterwards informed.) With these Bladders they now and then flapped the Mouths and Ears of those who stood near them of which Practice I could not then conceive the Meaning: It seems the Minds of these People are so taken up with intense Speculations, that they neither can speak, nor attend to the Discourses of others, without being rouzed by some external Taction[144] upon the Organs of Speech and Hearing; for which Reason, those Persons who are able to afford it always keep a *Flapper* (the Original is *Climenole*)[145] in their Family, as one of their Domesticks, nor ever walk abroad or make Visits without him. And the Business of this Officer is, when two or three more Persons are in Company, gently to strike with his Bladder the Mouth of him who is to speak, and the right Ear of him or them to

---

[142] brink. Cf. Milton's "verge of Heaven" (*Paradise Lost,* VI, 865).

[143] bent.

[144] "act of touching" (Bailey's *Dictionary*).

[145] This is an example of Swift's parodying of inane uses of etymology.

whom the Speaker addresseth himself. This *Flapper* is like-wise employed diligently to attend his Master in his Walks, and, upon occasion, to give him a soft Flap on his Eyes, because he is always so wrapped up[146] in Cogitation, that he is in manifest Danger of falling down every Precipice, and bouncing his Head against every Post, and in the Streets of justling others, or being justled himself into the Kennel.[147]

It was necessary to give the Reader this Information, without which he would be at the same Loss with me, to understand the Proceedings of these People, as they conducted me up the Stairs, to the Top of the Island, and from thence to the Royal Palace. While we were ascending, they forgot several Times what they were about, and left me to my self, till their Memories were again rouzed by their *Flappers;* for they appeared altogether unmoved by the Sight of my foreign Habit and Countenance, and by the Shouts of the Vulgar, whose Thoughts and Minds were more disengaged.

At last we enter'd the Palace, and proceeded into the Chamber of Presence, where I saw the King seated on his Throne, attended on each Side by Persons of Prime Quality. Before the Throne, was a large Table filled with Globes and Spheres, and Mathematical Instruments of all Kinds. His Majesty took not the least Notice of us, although our Entrance was not without sufficient Noise, by the Concourse of all Persons belonging to the Court. But he was then deep in a Problem, and we attended at least an Hour, before he could solve it. There stood by him on each Side, a young Page, with Flaps in their Hands, and when they saw he was at Leisure, one of them gently struck his Mouth, and the other his right Ear, at which he started like one awaked on the sudden, and looking towards me, and the Company I was in, recollected the Occasion of our coming, whereof he had been informed before. He spoke some Words,

whereupon immediately a young Man with a Flap came up to my Side, and flapt me gently on the right Ear, but I made Signs, as well as I could, that I had no Occasion for such an Instrument; which as I afterwards found gave his Majesty and the whole Court a very mean Opinion of my Understanding. The King, as far as I could conjecture, asked me several Questions, and I addressed my self to him in all the Languages I had. When it was found, that I could neither understand, nor be understood, I was conducted, by the King's Order, to an Apartment in his Palace, (this Prince being distinguished above all his Predecessors for his Hospitality to Strangers,) where two Servants were appointed to attend me. My Dinner was brought, and four Persons of Quality, whom I remember'd to have seen very near the King's Person, did me the Honour to dine with me. We had two Courses, of three Dishes each. In the first Course there was a Shoulder of Mutton, cut into an Æquilateral Triangle, a Piece of Beef into a Rhomboides,[148] and a Pudding into a Cycloid.[149] The second Course was two Ducks, trussed up into the Form of Fiddles, Sausages and Puddings resembling Flutes and Hautboys,[150] and a Breast of Veal in the Shape of a Harp. The Servants cut our Bread into Cones, Cylinders, Parallelograms, and several other mathematical Figures.

While we were at Dinner, I made bold to ask the Names of several Things in their Language, and those noble Persons, by the Assistance of their *Flappers,* delighted to give me Answers, hoping to raise my Admiration of their great Abilities, if I could be brought to converse with them. I was soon able to call for Bread, and Drink, or whatever else I wanted.

After Dinner my Company withdrew, and a Person was sent to me by the King's Order, attended by a *Flapper.* He brought with him Pen, Ink, and Paper, and three or four Books, giving me to understand by Signs, that he was

---

[146] rapt, carried away.
[147] "the watercourse of a street" (Johnson's *Dictionary*).

[148] rhomboid.
[149] arc.
[150] oboes.

sent to teach me the Language. We sat together four Hours, in which Time I wrote down a great Number of Words in Columns, with the Translation over against them. I likewise made a Shift to learn several short Sentences. For my Tutor would order one of my Servants to fetch something, or turn about, to make a Bow, to sit, or stand, or walk, and the like. Then I took down the Sentence in writing. He shewed me also in one of his Books, the Figures of the Sun, Moon, and Stars, the Zodiack, the Tropics, and Polar Circles, together with the Denominations of many Figures of Planes and Solids. He gave me the Names and Descriptions of all the musical Instruments, and the general Terms of Art in playing on each of them. After he had left me, I placed all my Words with their Interpretations in Alphabetical Order. And thus in a few Days, by the help of a very faithful Memory, I got some Insight into their Language.

The Word, which I interpret the *Flying* or *Floating Island,* is in the Original *Laputa,*[151] whereof I could never learn the true Etymology. *Lap* in the old obsolete Language signifieth *High,* and *Untuh* a *Governor,* from which, they say, by Corruption was derived *Laputa* from *Lapuntuh.* But I do not approve of this Derivation, which seems to be a little strained. I ventured to offer to the Learned among them a Conjecture of my own, that *Laputa* was *quasi Lap outed, Lap* signifying properly the Dancing of the Sun-Beams in the Sea, and *outed* a Wing; which, however, I shall not obtrude, but submit to the judicious Reader.

Those to whom the King had entrusted me, observing how ill I was clad, ordered a Taylor to come next Morning, and take my Measure for a Suit of Clothes. This Operator did his Office after a different manner from those of his Trade in *Europe.* He first took my Altitude by a Quadrant, and then with Rule and Compasses, described the Dimensions and Outlines of my whole Body, all which he enter'd upon Paper,

and in six Days brought my Clothes very ill made, and quite out of shape, by happening to mistake a Figure in the Calculation. But my Comfort was, that I observed such Accidents very frequent, and little regarded.

During my Confinement for want of Clothes, and by an Indisposition that held me some Days longer, I much enlarged my Dictionary; and when I went next to Court, was able to understand many Things the King spoke, and to return him some kind of Answers. His Majesty had given Orders that the Island should move North-East and by East, to the Vertical Point over *Lagado,* the Metropolis of the whole Kingdom below upon the firm Earth. It was about ninety Leagues distant, and our Voyage lasted four Days and an half. I was not in the least sensible of the progressive Motion made in the Air by the Island. On the second Morning, about Eleven a-Clock, the King himself in Person, attended by his Nobility, Courtiers, and Officers, having prepared all their musical Instruments, played on them for three Hours without Intermission, so that I was quite stunned with the Noise; neither could I possibly guess the Meaning till my Tutor informed me. He said that the People of their Island had their Ears adapted to hear the Musick of the Spheres,[152] which always played at certain Periods, and the Court was now prepared to bear their Part in what ever Instrument they most excelled.

In our Journey towards *Lagado* the capital City, his Majesty ordered that the Island should stop over certain Towns and Villages, from whence he might receive the Petitions of his Subjects. And to this Purpose several Packthreads were let down with small Weights at the Bottom. On these Packthreads the People strung their Petitions, which mounted up directly like the Scraps of Paper fastned by School-Boys at the End of the String that holds their Kite. Sometimes we received Wine and Victuals from below, which were drawn up by Pullies.

---

151 Cf. note 145, above.
152 heavenly music. Cf. Dryden's "Ode to

the Pious Memory of Mrs. Anne Killegrew."

The Knowledge I had in Mathematicks gave me great Assistance in acquiring their Phraseology, which depended much upon that Science and Musick; and in the latter I was not unskilled. Their Ideas are perpetually conversant in Lines and Figures. If they would, for Example, praise the Beauty of a Woman, or any other Animal, they describe it by Rhombs, Circles, Parallelograms, Ellipses, and other Geometrical Terms, or by Words of Art drawn from Musick, needless here to repeat. I observed in the King's Kitchen all Sorts of mathematical and musical Instruments, after the Figures of which they cut up the Joints that were served to his Majesty's Table.

Their Houses are very ill built, the Walls bevil,[153] without one Right Angle in any Apartment; and this Defect ariseth from the Contempt they bear to practical Geometry, which they despise, as Vulgar and Mechanick, those Instructions they give being too refined for the Intellectuals of their Work-men; which occasions perpetual Mistakes. And although they are dextrous enough upon a Piece of Paper in the Management of the Rule, the Pencil, and the Divider, yet in the common Actions and Behaviour of Life, I have not seen a more clumsy, awkward, and unhandy People, nor so slow and perplexed in their Conceptions upon all other Subjects, except those of Mathematicks and Musick. They are very bad Reasoners, and vehemently given to Opposition, unless when they happen to be of the right Opinion, which is seldom their Case. Imagination, Fancy, and Invention,[154] they are wholly Strangers to, nor have any Words in their Language by which those Ideas can be expressed; the whole Compass of their Thoughts and Mind being shut up within the two forementioned Sciences.

Most of them, and especially those who deal in the Astronomical Part, have great Faith in judicial Astrology,[155] although they are ashamed to own it publickly. But what I chiefly admired, and thought altogether unaccountable, was the strong Disposition I observed in them towards News and Politicks, perpetually enquiring into publick Affairs, giving their Judgments in Matters of State, and passionately disputing every Inch of a Party Opinion. I have indeed observed the same Disposition among most of the Mathematicians I have known in *Europe,* although I could never discover the least Analogy between the two Sciences, unless those People suppose, that because the smallest Circle hath as many Degrees as the largest, therefore the Regulation and Management of the World require no more Abilities than the handling and turning of a Globe. But, I rather take this Quality to spring from a very common Infirmity of human Nature, inclining us to be more curious and conceited in Matters where we have least Concern, and for which we are least adapted either by Study or Nature.

These People are under continual Disquietudes, never enjoying a Minute's Peace of Mind; and their Disturbances proceed from Causes which very little affect the rest of Mortals.[156] Their Apprehensions arise from several Changes they dread in the celestial Bodies. For Instance; That the Earth by the continual Approaches of the Sun towards it, must in Course of Time be absorbed or swallowed up. That the Face of the Sun will, by degrees, be encrusted with its own Effluvia, and give no more Light to the World. That the Earth very narrowly escaped a Brush from the Tail of the last Comet, which would have infallibly reduced it to Ashes; and that the next, which they have calculated for one

---

[153] "An angle that is not square, is called a bevil angle" (Johnson's *Dictionary*).

[154] Swift opposes these qualities to the enumerative characteristics of mathematics and music.

[155] "a science or art that pretends to judge of and foretel future events, by considering the positions and influences of stars" (Bailey's *Dictionary*).

[156] Swift probably means the people other than those on the Flying Island, though he may also be implying that the repose of ordinary men is not disturbed by abstract predictions.

and thirty Years hence, will probably destroy us. For, if in its Perihelion[157] it should approach within a certain Degree of the Sun, (as by their Calculations they have Reason to dread), it will Conceive a Degree of Heat ten thousand times more intense than that of red-hot glowing Iron; and in its Absence from the Sun, carry a blazing Tail ten hundred thousand and fourteen Miles long; through which, if the Earth should pass at the Distance of one hundred thousand Miles from the *Nucleus* or main Body of the Comet, it must in its Passage be set on fire, and reduced to Ashes. That the Sun daily spending its Rays without any Nutriment to supply them, will at last be wholly consumed and annihilated; which must be attended with the Destruction of this Earth, and of all the Planets that receive their Light from it.

They are so perpetually alarmed with the Apprehensions of these and the like impending Dangers, that they can neither sleep quietly in their Beds, nor have any Relish for the common Pleasures or Amusements of Life. When they meet an Acquaintance in the Morning, the first Question is about the Sun's Health, how he looked at his Setting and Rising, and what Hopes they have to avoid the Stroke of the approaching Comet. This Conversation they are apt to run into with the same Temper that Boys discover, in delighting to hear terrible Stories of Spirits and Hobgoblins, which they greedily listen to, and dare not go to Bed for fear.

The Women of the Island have Abundance of Vivacity; they contemn their Husbands, and are exceedingly fond of Strangers, whereof there is always a considerable Number from the Continent below, attending at Court, either upon Affairs of the several Towns and Corporations, or their own particular Occasions, but are much despised, because they want the same Endowments. Among these the Ladies chuse their Gallants: But the Vexation is, that they act with too much Ease and Security, for the Husband is always so wrapt[158] in Speculation, that the Mistress and Lover may proceed to the greatest Familiarities before his Face, if he be but provided with Paper and Implements, and without his Flapper at his Side.

The Wives and Daughters lament their Confinement to the Island, although I think it the most delicious Spot of Ground in the World; and although they live here in the greatest Plenty and Magnificence, and are allowed to do whatever they please, they long to see the World, and take the Diversions of the Metropolis, which they are not allowed to do without a particular Licence from the King; and this is not easy to be obtained, because the People of Quality have found, by frequent Experience, how hard it is to persuade their Women to return from below. I was told that a great Court-Lady, who had several Children, is married to the Prime Minister,[159] the richest Subject in the Kingdom, a very graceful Person, extremely fond of her, and lives in the finest Palace of the Island, went down to *Lagado,* on the Pretence of Health, there hid her self for several Months, till the King sent a Warrant to search for her, and she was found in an obscure Eating house all in Rags, having pawned her Clothes to maintain an old deformed Footman, who beat her every Day, and in whose Company she was taken much against her Will. And although her Husband received her with all possible Kindness, and without the least Reproach, she soon after contrived to steal down again, with all her Jewels, to the same Gallant, and hath not been heard of since.

This may, perhaps, pass with the Reader rather for an *European* or *English* Story, than for one of a Country so remote: But he may please to consider, that the Caprices of Womenkind are not

---

[157] The point in the orbit of a comet nearest the sun.

[158] See note 146, above.

[159] Undoubtedly intended to be taken as Robert Walpole.

limited by any Climate or Nation, and that they are much more uniform than can be easily imagined.

In about a Month's Time I had made a tolerable Proficiency in their Language, and was able to answer most of the King's Questions, when I had the Honour to attend him. His Majesty discovered not the least Curiosity to enquire into the Laws, Government, History, Religion, or Manners of the Countries where I had been, but confined his Questions to the State of Mathematicks, and received the Account I gave him, with great Contempt and Indifference, though often rouzed by his *Flapper* on each Side.

CHAPTER III

A Phenomenon solved by modern Philosophy and Astronomy. The Laputians great Improvements in the latter. The King's Method of suppressing Insurrections.

I desired leave of this Prince to see the Curiosities of the Island, which he was graciously pleased to grant, and ordered my Tutor to attend me. I chiefly wanted to know to what Cause in Art, or in Nature, it owed its several Motions, whereof I will now give a Philosophical Account to the Reader.

The flying or floating Island is exactly circular, its Diameter 7837 Yards,[160] or about four Miles and an half, and consequently contains ten thousand Acres. It is three hundred Yards thick. The Bottom or under Surface, which appears to those who view it from below, is one even regular Plate of Adamant,[161] shooting up to the Height of about two hundred Yards. Above it lie the several Minerals in their usual Order, and over all is a Coat of rich Mould ten or twelve Foot deep. This declivity of the upper Surface, from the Circum-

ference to the Center, is the natural Cause why all the Dews and Rains which fall upon the Island, are conveyed in small Rivulets towards the Middle, where they are emptied into four large Basons, each of about half a Mile in Circuit, and two hundred Yards distant from the Center. From these Basons the Water is continually exhaled by the Sun in the Daytime, which effectually prevents their over-flowing. Besides, as it is in the Power of the Monarch to raise the Island above the Region of Clouds and Vapours, he can prevent the falling of Dews and Rains when ever he pleases: For the highest Clouds cannot rise above two Miles, as Naturalists agree, at least they were never known to do in that country.

At the Center of the Island there is a Chasm about fifty Yards in Diameter, from whence the Astronomers descend into a large Dome, which is therefore called *Flandona Gagnole,* or the *Astronomers Cave,* situated at the Depth of a hundred Yards beneath the upper Surface of the Adamant. In this Cave are twenty Lamps continually burning, which from the Reflection of the Adamant cast a strong Light into every Part. The Place is stored with great Variety of Sextants, Quadrants, Telescopes, Astrolabes,[162] and other Astronomical Instruments. But the greatest Curiosity, upon which the Fate of the Island depends, is a Load-stone[163] of a prodigious Size, in Shape resembling a Weaver's Shuttle. It is in Length six Yards, and in the thickest Part at least three Yards over. This Magnet is sustained by a very strong Axle of Adamant passing through its Middle, upon which it plays, and is poized so exactly, that the weakest Hand can turn it. It is hooped round with an hollow Cylinder of Adamant, four Foot deep, as many thick, and twelve Yards in Diameter, placed Horizontally, and supported by eight Adamantine Feet,

[160] The diameter of the earth had been calculated at just about this number of miles by Sir Isaac Newton.

[161] "a stone, imagined by writers, of impenetrable hardness" (Johnson's *Dictionary*). Brilliance was also a characteristic of adamant,

which strongly resembles the diamond and also at times was said to be possessed of magnetic properties, though it is not used in this latter sense by Swift.

[162] Instruments for taking altitudes.

[163] magnet.

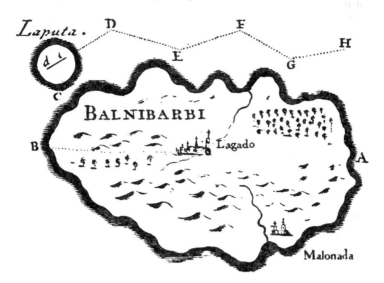

each six Yards high. In the middle of the Concave Side there is a Groove twelve Inches deep, in which the Extremities of the Axle are lodged, and turned round as there is Occasion.

The Stone cannot be moved from its Place by any Force, because the Hoop and its Feet are one continued Piece with that Body of Adamant, which constitutes the Bottom of the Island.

By Means of this Load-stone, the Island is made to rise and fall, and move from one Place to another. For, with Respect to that Part of the Earth over which the Monarch presides, the Stone is endued at one of its Sides with an attractive Power, and at the other with a repulsive. Upon placing the Magnet erect with its attracting End towards the Earth, the Island descends; but when the repelling Extremity points downwards, the Island mounts directly upwards. When the Position of the Stone is oblique, the Motion of the Island is so too. For in this Magnet the Forces always act in Lines parallel to its Direction.

By this oblique Motion the Island is conveyed to different Parts of the Monarch's Dominions. To explain[164] the manner of its Progress, let $A\ B$ represent a Line drawn cross the Dominions of

Balnibarbi, let the Line $c\ d$ represent the Load-stone, of which let d be the repelling End, and c the attracting End; the Island being over C, let the Stone be placed in the Position $c\ d$, with its repelling End downwards, then the Island will be driven upwards obliquely towards D. When it is arrived at D, let the Stone be turned upon its Axle till its attracting End points towards E, and then the Island will be carried obliquely towards E; where, if the Stone be again turned upon its Axle till it stands in the Position $E\ F$, with its repelling Point downwards, the Island will rise obliquely towards F; where, by directing the attracting End towards G, the Island may be carried to G, and from G to H, by turning the Stone, so as to make its repelling Extremity point directly downwards. And thus by changing the Situation of the Stone as often as there is Occasion, the Island is made to rise and fall by Turns in an oblique Direction; and by those alternate Risings and Fallings (the Obliquity being not considerable) is conveyed from one Part of the Dominions to the other.

But it must be observed, that this Island cannot move beyond the Extent of the Dominions below, nor can it rise above the Height of four Miles. For which the Astronomers (who have writ-

---

[164] What follows is an obvious parody of common scientific explanations.

112 Jonathan Swift

ten large Systems concerning the Stone)
assign the following Reason;[165] That the
magnetick Virtue does not extend beyond
the Distance of four Miles, and that the
Mineral which acts upon the Stone in
the Bowels of the Earth, and in the Sea
about six Leagues distant from the
Shoar, is not diffused through the whole
Globe, but terminated with the Limits
of the King's Dominions; and it was easy
from the great Advantage of such a superior Situation, for a Prince to bring
under his Obedience whatever Country
lay within the Attraction of that Magnet.

When the Stone is put parallel to the
Plane of the Horizon, the Island standeth still; for in that Case, the Extremities
of it being at equal Distance from the
Earth, act with equal Force, the one in
drawing downwards, the other in pushing upwards, and consequently no Motion can ensue.

This Load-stone is under the Care of
certain Astronomers, who from Time to
Time give it such Positions as the Monarch directs. They spend the greatest
Part of their Lives in observing the celestial Bodies, which they do by the Assistance of Glasses far excelling ours in
Goodness. For, although their largest
Telescopes do not exceed three Feet, they
magnify much more than those of a
Hundred with us, and shew the Stars
with greater Clearness.[166] For this Advantage hath enabled them to extend the
Discoveries much farther than our Astronomers in *Europe;* for they have made
a Catalogue of ten thousand fixed Stars;
whereas the largest of ours do not contain above one third Part of that Number.[167] They have likewise discovered
two lesser Stars, or *Satellites,* which re-

volve about *Mars,*[168] whereof the inner-
most is distant from the Center of the
primary Planet exactly three of his Diameters, and the outer-most five; the former revolves in the Space of ten Hours,
and the latter in twenty one and an half;
so that the Squares of their periodical
Times are very near in the same Proportion with the Cubes of their Distance
from the Center of *Mars,* which evidently shews them to be governed by the
same Law of Gravitation, that influences
the other Heavenly Bodies.[169]

They have observed ninety three different Comets, and settled their Periods
with great Exactness. If this be true,
(and they affirm it with great Confidence,) it is much to be wished that
their Observations were made publick,
whereby the Theory of Comets, which
at present is very lame and defective,
might be brought to the same Perfection
with other Parts of Astronomy.

The King would be the most absolute
Prince in the Universe, if he could but
prevail on a Ministry to join with him;
but these having their Estates below on
the Continent, and considering that the
Office of a Favourite hath a very uncertain Tenure, would never consent to the
enslaving their Country.

If any Town should engage in Rebellion or Mutiny, fall into violent Factions, or refuse to pay the usual Tribute,
the King hath two Methods of reducing
them to Obedience. The first and the
mildest Course is by keeping the Island
hovering over such a Town, and the
Lands about it, whereby he can deprive
them of the Benefit of the Sun and the
Rain, and consequently afflict the Inhabitants with Death and Diseases. And
if the Crime deserve it, they are at the

---

[165] The "reason" will be seen to be a fallacy, that of begging the question or of arguing in a circle, concluding what has been advanced as a premise to the conclusion.

[166] This sentence was added in the edition of 1735. It is identical with a manuscript note in Charles Ford's interleaved copy of the first edition made between 1733 and 1735, except that Ford's copy has "Yards" after "Hundred." The allusion is unquestionably to the newly invented reflecting telescope and perhaps to that presented to the Royal Society in 1723

by John Hadley, which magnified 230 diameters although only slightly over five feet long.

[167] John Flamsteed's *British Catalogue of Stars* (1725) lists about 3000 stars.

[168] The two satellites of Mars now recognized were not discovered by scientists until 1877. Swift was probably less of an inspired prophet than an unusually adept amateur in the use of scientific laws for the prediction of such discoveries, as the laws were already known.

[169] Swift is here using an actual relationship known as Kepler's third law.

same Time pelted from above with great Stones, against which they have no Defence but by creeping into Cellars or Caves, while the Roofs of their Houses are beaten to Pieces. But if they still continue obstinate, or offer to raise Insurrections, he proceeds to the last Remedy, by letting the Island drop directly upon their Heads, which makes a universal Destruction both of Houses and Men. However, this is an Extremity to which the Prince is seldom driven, neither indeed is he willing to put it in Execution, nor dare his Ministers advise him to an Action, which, as it would render them odious to the People, so it would be a great Damage to their own Estates, which lie all below, for the Island is the King's Demesn.

But there is still indeed a more weighty Reason, why the Kings of this Country have been always averse from executing so terrible an Action, unless upon the utmost Necessity. For if the Town intended to be destroyed should have in it any tall Rocks, as it generally falls out in the larger Cities, a Situation probably chosen at first with a View to prevent such a Catastrophe; or if it abound in high Spires or Pillars of Stone, a sudden Fall might endanger the Bottom or Under-Surface of the Island, which, although it consists, as I have said, of one entire Adamant two hundred Yards thick, might happen to crack by too great a Choque,[170] or burst by approaching too near the Fires from the Houses below, as the Backs both of Iron and Stone will often do in our Chimneys. Of all this the People are well apprized, and understand how far to carry their Obstinacy, where their Liberty or Property is concerned. And the King, when he is highest provoked, and most determined to press a City to Rubbish, orders the Island to descend with great Gentleness, out of a Pretence of Tenderness to his People, but indeed for fear of breaking the Adamantine Bottom; in which Case, it is the Opinion of all their Philosophers, that the Load-stone could no

longer hold it up, and the whole Mass would fall to the Ground.

By a fundamental Law of this Realm, neither the King, nor either of his two elder Sons, are permitted to leave the Island;[171] nor the Queen, till she is past Child-bearing.

[On leaving Laputa, Gulliver visits the Grand Academy of Lagado and the Island of Sorcerers before arriving at Luggnagg.]

CHAPTER X

The Luggnuggians *commended. A particular Description of the* Struldbrugs, *with many Conversations between the Author and some eminent Persons upon that Subject.*

The *Luggnuggians* are a polite and generous People, and although they are not without some share of that Pride which is peculiar to all *Eastern* Countries, yet they shew themselves courteous to Strangers, especially such who are countenanced by the Court. I had many Acquaintance among Persons of the best Fashion, and being always attended by my Interpreter, the Conversation we had was not disagreeable.

One Day in much good Company I was asked by a Person of Quality, whether I had seen any of their *Struldbrugs* or *Immortals.* I said I had not, and desired he would explain to me what he meant by such an Appellation applyed to a mortal Creature. He told me, that sometimes, though very rarely, a Child happened to be born in a Family with a red circular Spot in the Forehead, directly over the left Eyebrow, which was an infallible Mark that it should never dye. The Spot, as he described it, was about the compass of a Silver Three-pence, but in the course of Time grew larger, and changed its Colour; for at twelve Years old it became Green, so continued till five and Twenty, then

---

170 shock.
171 An English law of 1701, repealed in 1715, required the consent of Parliament for the king to leave the British Isles.

turned to a deep Blue; at Five and Forty it grew Coal Black, and as large as an *English* Shilling, but never admitted any farther Alteration. He said these Births were so rare, that he did not believe there could be above Eleven Hundred *Struldbrugs* of both Sexes in the whole Kingdom, of which he computed about fifty in the Metropolis, and among the rest a young Girl born about three Years ago. That these Productions were not peculiar to any Family but a meer effect of Chance, and the Children of the *Struldbruggs* themselves, were equally mortal with the rest of the People.

I freely own my self to have been struck with inexpressible Delight upon hearing this Account: And the Person who gave it me happening to understand the *Balnibarbian* Language, which I spoke very well, I could not forbear breaking out into expressions perhaps a little too Extravagant. I cryed out as in a Rapture; Happy Nation where every Child hath at least a chance for being immortal! Happy People who enjoy so many living Examples of antient Virtue, and have Masters ready to instruct them in the Wisdom of all former Ages! But, happiest beyond all comparison are those excellent *Struldbruggs,* who born exempt from that universal Calamity of human Nature, have their Minds free and disingaged, without the weight and depression of Spirits caused by the continual Apprehension of Death. I discovered my Admiration that I had not observed any of these illustrious Persons at Court: the black Spot on the Fore-head, being so remarkable a Distinction, that I could not have easily overlooked it: And it was impossible that his Majesty, a most Judicious Prince, should not provide himself with a good number of such wise and able Councellours. Yet perhaps the Virtue of those Reverend Sages was too strict for the Corrupt and Libertine Manners of a Court. And we often find by Experience that young Men are too opinionative and volatile to be guided by the sober Dictates of their Seniors. However, since the King was pleased to allow me Access to his Royal Person, I was resolved upon the very first occasion to deliver my Opinion to him on this Matter freely, and at large by the help of my Interpreter; and whether he would please to take my Advice or no, yet in one thing I was determined, that his Majesty having frequently offered me an Establishment in this Country, I would with great thankfulness accept the Favour, and pass my Life here in the Conversation of those superior Beings the *Struldbruggs,* if they would please to admit me.

The Gentleman to whom I addressed my Discourse, because (as I have already observed) he spoke the Language of *Balnibarbi,* said to me with a sort of a Smile, which usually ariseth from Pity to the Ignorant, that he was glad of any occasion to keep me among them, and desired my Permission to explain to the Company what I had spoke. He did so, and they talked together for some time in their own Language, whereof I understood not a Syllable, neither could I observe by their Countenances what impression my Discourse had made on them. After a short Silence the same Person told me, that his Friends and mine (so he thought fit to express himself) were very much pleased with the judicious Remarks I had made on the great Happiness and Advantages of immortal Life, and they were desirous to know in a particular manner, what Scheme of Living I should have formed to my self, if it had fallen to my Lot to have been born a *Struldbrugg.*

I answered, it was easy to be Eloquent on so copious and delightful a Subject, especially to me who have been often apt to amuse my self with Visions of what I should do if I were a King, a General, or a great Lord: And upon this very Case I had frequently run over the whole System how I should employ my self, and pass the time if I were sure to live for ever.

That, if it had been my good Fortune to come into the World a *Struldbrugg,* as soon as I could discover my own Happiness by understanding the difference between Life and Death, I would first resolve by all Arts and Methods whatsoever to procure my self Riches. In the pursuit of which by Thrift and Management, I might reasonably expect in about two Hundred Years, to be the Wealthiest Man in the Kingdom. In the second place, I would from my earliest Youth apply myself to the study of Arts and Sciences, by which I should arrive in time to excel all others in Learning. Lastly I would carefully record every Action and Event of Consequence that happened in the Publick, impartially draw the Characters of the several Successions of Princes, and great Ministers of State, with my own Observations on every Point. I would exactly set down the several changes in Customs, Languages, Fashions, Dress, Dyet and Diversions. By all which Acquirements, I should be a living Treasury of Knowledge and Wisdom, and certainly become the Oracle of the Nation.

I would never marry after threescore, but live in an hospitable manner, yet still on the saving side. I would entertain myself in forming and directing the Minds of hopeful young Men, by convincing them from my own Remembrance, Experience and Observation, fortified by numerous Examples, of the usefulness of Virtue in publick and private Life. But, my Choice and constant Companions should be a sett of my own immortal Brother hood, among whom I would elect a dozen from the most Ancient down to my own Contemporaries. Where any of these wanted Fortunes, I would provide them with convenient Lodges round my own Estate, and have some of them always at my Table, only mingling a few of the most valuable among you Mortals, whom length of Time would harden me to lose with little or no Reluctance, and treat your Posterity after the same manner, just as a Man diverts himself with the Annual Succession of Pinks and Tulips in his Garden, without regretting the loss of those which withered the preceeding Year.

These *Struldbruggs* and I would mutually communicate our Observations and Memorials through the Course of Time, remark the several Gradations by which Corruption steals into the World, and oppose it in every step, by giving perpetual Warning and Instruction to Mankind; which, added to the strong Influence of our own Example, would probably prevent that continual Degeneracy of Human Nature so justly complained of in all Ages.

Add to all this, the pleasure of seeing the various Revolutions of States and Empires, the Changes in the lower and upper World, antient Cities in Ruins, and obscure Villages become the Seats of Kings. Famous Rivers lessening into shallow Brooks, the Ocean leaving one Coast dry, and over-whelming another: The Discovery of many Countries yet unknown. Barbarity over-running the politest Nations, and the most barbarous become civilized. I should then see the Discovery of the *Longitude*,[172] the *perpetual Motion*, the *Universal Medicine*, and many other great Inventions brought to the utmost Perfection.

What wonderful Discoveries should we make in Astronomy, by outliving and confirming our own Predictions, by observing the Progress and Returns of Comets, with the changes of Motion in the Sun, Moon and Stars.

I enlarged upon many other Topicks which the natural desire of endless Life and sublunary Happiness could easily furnish me with. When I had ended, and the Sum of my Discourse had been interpreted as before, to the rest of the Company, there was a good deal of Talk among them in the Language of the Country, not without some Laughter at my Expence. At last the same Gentleman who had been my Interpreter said, he was desired by the rest to set me right in a few Mistakes, which I had fallen into through the common Imbecillity of human Nature, and upon that allowance was less answerable for them. That, this Breed of *Struldbruggs* was peculiar to their Country; for there were no such People either in *Balnibarbi* or *Japan*, where he had the Honour to be Embas-

---

[172] Prompted by men of science and commerce, Parliament had appointed a committee in 1714 to encourage studies leading to a solution to the problem of determining longitude at sea.

sador from his Majesty, and found the Natives in both these Kingdoms very hard to believe that the Fact was possible, and it appeared from my Astonishment when he first mentioned the matter to me, that I received it as a thing wholly new, and scarcely to be credited. That in the two Kingdoms above mentioned, where during his Residence he had converse very much, he observed long Life to be the universal Desire and Wish of Mankind. That whoever had one Foot in the Grave, was sure to hold back the other as strongly as he could. That the eldest had still hopes of living one Day longer, and looked on Death as the greatest Evil, from which Nature always prompted him to retreat; only in this Island of *Luggnagg,* the Appetite for living was not so eager, from the continual Example of the *Struldbruggs* before their Eyes.

That the System of Living contrived by me was unreasonable and unjust, because it supposed a Perpetuity of Youth, Health, and Vigour, which no Man could be so foolish to Hope, however extravagant he may be in his Wishes. That the Question therefore was not whether a Man would chuse to be always in the Prime of Youth, attended with Prosperity and Health, but how he would pass a perpetual Life under all the usual Disadvantages which old Age brings along with it. For although few Men will avow their Desires of being immortal upon such hard Conditions, yet in the two Kingdoms before-mentioned of *Balnibarbi* and *Japan,* he observed that every Man desired to put off Death for sometime longer, let it approach ever so late, and he rarely heard of any Man who died willingly, except he were incited by the Extremity of Grief or Torture. And he appealed to me whether in those Countries I had travelled as well as my own, I had not observed the same general Disposition.

After this Preface he gave me a particular Account of the *Struldbruggs* among them. He said they commonly acted like Mortals, till about thirty Years old, after which by degrees they grew melancholy and dejected, encreas-

ing in both till they came to four-score. This he learned from their own Confession; for otherwise there not being above two or three of that Species born in an Age, were too few to form a general Observation by. When they came to fourscore Years, which is reckoned the Extremity of living in this Country, they had not only all the Follies and Infirmities of other old Men, but many more which arose from the dreadful Prospects of never dying. They were not only Opinionative, Peevish, Covetous, Morose, Vain, Talkative, but uncapable of Friendship, and dead to all natural Affection, which never descended below their Grand-children. Envy and impotent Desires are their prevailing Passions. But those Objects against which their Envy seems principally directed, are the Vices of the younger sort, and the Deaths of the old. By reflecting on the former, they find themselves cut off from all possibility of Pleasure; and whenever they see a Funeral, they lament and repine that others are gone to an Harbour of Rest, to which they themselves never can hope to arrive. They have no Remembrance of any thing but what they learned and observed in their Youth and middle Age, and even that is very imperfect. And for the Truth or Particulars of any Fact, it is safer to depend on common Traditions than upon their best Recollections. The least miserable among them appear to be those who turn to Dotage, and entirely lose their Memories; these meet with more Pity and Assistance, because they want many bad Qualities which abound in others.

If a *Struldbrugg* happen to marry one of his own kind, the Marriage is dissolved of course by the Courtesy of the Kingdom, as soon as the younger of the two come to be four-score. For the Law thinks it a reasonable Indulgence, that those who are condemned without any Fault of their own to a perpetual Continuance in the World, should not have their Misery doubled by the Load of a Wife.

As soon as they have compleated the term of eighty Years, they are look'd on as dead in Law; their Heirs immediately succeed to their Estates, only a small Pittance is reserved for their Support, and the poor ones are maintained at the publick Charge. After that Period they are held incapable of any Employment of Trust or Profit, they cannot purchase Lands or take Leases, neither are they allowed to be Witnesses in any Cause, either Civil or Criminal, not even for the Decision of Meers[173] and Bounds.

At Ninety they lose their Teeth and Hair, they have at that age no Distinction of Taste, but eat and drink whatever they can get, without Relish or Appetite. The Diseases they were subject to still continuing without encreasing or diminishing. In talking they forget the common Appellation of things, and the Names of Persons, even of those who are their nearest Friends and Relations. For the same reason they never can amuse themselves with reading, because their Memory will not serve to carry them from the beginning of a Sentence to the end; and by this Defect they are deprived of the only Entertainment whereof they might otherwise be capable.

The Language of this Country being always upon the Flux, the *Struldbruggs* of one Age do not understand those of another, neither are they able after two hundred Years to hold any Conversation (farther than by a few general Words) with their Neighbours the Mortals, and thus they lye under the Disadvantage of living like Foreigners in their own Country.

This was the Account given me of the *Struldbruggs,* as near as I can remember. I afterwards saw five or six of different Ages, the youngest not above two hundred Years old, who were brought me at several times by some of my Friends; but although they were told that I was a great Traveller, and had seen all the World, they had not the least Curiosity to ask me a Question; only desired I would give them *Slumskudask,* or a Token of Remembrance, which is a modest way of begging, to avoid the Law that strictly forbids it, be-

cause they are provided for by the Publick, although indeed with a very scanty Allowance.

They are deprived and hated by all sort of People; when one of them is born, it is reckoned ominous, and their Birth is recorded very particularly; so that you may know their Age by consulting the Registry, which however hath not been kept above a thousand Years past, or at least hath been destroyed by time or publick Disturbances. But the usual way of computing how old they are is by asking them what Kings or great Persons they can remember, and then consulting History, for infallibly the last Prince, in their Mind, did not begin his Reign after they were four-score Years old.

They were the most mortifying Sight I ever beheld, and the Women more horrible than the Men. Besides the usual Deformities in extreme old Age, they acquired an additional Ghastliness in Proportion to their Number of Years, which is not to be described, and among half a Dozen I soon distinguished which was the eldest, although there was not above a Century or two between them.

The Reader will easily believe, that from what I had heard and seen, my keen Appetite for Perpetuity of Life was much abated. I grew heartily ashamed of the pleasing Visions I had formed, and thought no Tyrant could invent a Death into which I would not run with Pleasure from such a Life. The King heard of all that had passed between me and my Friends upon this Occasion, and rallied me very pleasantly, wishing I would send a Couple of *Struldbruggs* to my own Country, to arm our People against the Fear of Death; but this it seems is forbidden by the fundamental Laws of the Kingdom, or else I should have been well content with the Trouble and Expence of transporting them.

I could not but agree that the Laws of this Kingdom, relating to the *Struldbruggs,* were founded upon the strongest Reasons, and such as any other Country would be under the Necessity of enacting in the like Circumstances. Otherwise, as Avarice is the necessary Consequent of old Age, those Immortals would in time

---

[173] "a line or boundary, dividing plough'd lands in a common" (Bailey's *Dictionary*).

become Proprietors of the whole Nation, and engross the Civil Power, which, for want of Abilities to manage, must end in the Ruin of the Publick.

CHAPTER XI

The Author leaves Luggnagg, *and sails to* Japan. *From thence he returns in a* Dutch *Ship to* Amsterdam, *and from* Amsterdam *to* England.

I thought this Account of the *Struldbruggs* might be some Entertainment to the Reader, because it seems to be a little out of the common Way, at least, I do not remember to have met the like in any Book of Travels that hath come to my Hands:[174] And if I am deceived, my Excuse must be, that it is necessary for Travellers, who describe the same Country, very often to agree in dwelling on the same Particulars, without deserving the Censure of having borrowed or transcribed from those who wrote before them.

There is indeed a perpetual Commerce between this Kingdom and the great Empire of *Japan*, and it is very probable that the *Japanese* Authors may have given some Account of the *Struldbruggs* but my Stay in *Japan* was so short, and I was so intirely a Stranger to that Language, that I was not qualified to make any Enquiries. But I hope the *Dutch*, upon this Notice, will be curious and able enough to supply my Defects.

His Majesty having often pressed me to accept some Employment in his Court, and finding me absolutely determined to return to my Native Country, was pleased to give me his Licence to depart, and honoured me with a Letter of Recommendation under his own Hand to the Emperor of *Japan*. He likewise presented me with four hundred forty four large Pieces of Gold (this Nation delighting in even Numbers) and a red Diamond, which I sold in *England* for eleven hundred Pounds.

On the sixth Day of *May*, 1709, I took a solemn Leave of his Majesty, and all my Friends. This Prince was so gracious, as to order a Guard to conduct me to *Glanguenstald,* which is a Royal Port to the *South-West* Part of the Island. In six Days I found a Vessel ready to carry me to *Japan,* and spent fifteen Days in the Voyage. We landed at a small Port-Town called *Xamoschi,* situated on the *South-East* Part of *Japan;* the Town lies on the *Western* Point, where there is a narrow Streight, leading *Northward* into a long Arm of the Sea, upon the *North-West* Part of which *Yedo,*[175] the Metropolis, stands. At Landing, I shewed the Custom-house Officers my Letter from the King of *Luggnagg* to his Imperial Majesty. They knew the Seal perfectly well; it was as broad as the Palm of my Hand. The Impression was, *A King lifting up a Lame Beggar from the Earth.* The Magistrates of the Town hearing of my Letter, received me as a Publick Minister; they provided me with Carriages and Servants, and bore my Charges to *Yedo,* where I was admitted to an Audience, and delivered my Letter, which was opened with great Ceremony, and explained to the Emperor by an Interpreter, who then gave me notice, by his Majesty's Order, that I should signify my Request, and whatever it were, it should be granted for the sake of his Royal Brother of *Luggnagg.* This Interpreter was a Person employed to transact Affairs with the *Hollanders;* he soon conjectured by my Countenance that I was an *European,* and therefore repeated his Majesty's Commands in *Low-Dutch,* which he spoke perfectly well. I answered, (as I had before determined,) that I was a *Dutch* Merchant, shipwrecked in a very remote Country, from whence I travelled by Sea and Land to *Luggnagg,* and then took Shipping for

---

[174] He might have seen, as Swift probably had, "An Account of the Bramines in the Indies" by John Marshall in *The Philosophical Transactions of the Royal Society* for January 1701 (XXII, 729–735), in which it was stated: "That upon the Hills by Casmere there are men that live some hundreds of Years, and can hold their breaths, and lye in Trances for several years together, if they but be kept warm."

[175] Now Tokyo.

Japan, where I knew my Countrymen often traded, and with some of these I hoped to get an Opportunity of returning into *Europe:* I therefore most humbly entreated his Royal Favour to give Order, that I should be conducted in Safety to *Nangasac:*[176] To this I added another Petition, that for the sake of my Patron the King of *Luggnagg,* his Majesty would condescend to excuse my performing the Ceremony imposed on my Countrymen of *trampling upon the Crucifix,*[177] because I had been thrown into his Kingdom by my Misfortunes, without any Intention of Trading. When this latter Petition was interpreted to the Emperor, he seemed a little surprized, and said, he believed I was the first of my Countrymen who ever made any Scruple in this Point, and that he began to doubt whether I was a real *Hollander,* or no, but rather suspected I must be a CHRISTIAN. However, for the Reasons I had offered, but chiefly to gratify the King of *Luggnagg,* by an uncommon Mark of his Favour, he would comply with the *Singularity* of my Humour; but the Affair must be managed with Dexterity, and his Officers should be commanded to let me pass, as it were, by Forgetfulness. For he assured me, that if the Secret should be discovered by my Countrymen, the *Dutch,* they would cut my Throat in the Voyage. I returned my Thanks by the Interpreter, for so unusual a Favour, and some Troops being at that Time on their March to *Nangasac,* the Commanding Officer had Orders to convey me safe thither, with particular Instructions about the Business of the *Crucifix.*

On the 9th Day of *June,* 1709. I arrived at *Nangasac,* after a very long and troublesome Journey. I soon fell into Company of some *Dutch* Sailors, belonging to the *Amboyna* of *Amsterdam,* a stout Ship of 450 Tuns. I had lived long in *Holland,* pursuing my Studies at *Leyden,* and I spoke *Dutch* well. The Sea-

men soon knew from whence I came last; they were curious to enquire into my Voyages and Course of Life. I made up a Story as short and probable as I could, but concealed the greatest Part. I knew many Persons in *Holland;* I was able to invent Names for my Parents, whom I pretended to be obscure People in the Province of *Gelderland.* I would have given the Captain (one *Theodorus Vangrult*) what he pleased to ask for my Voyage to *Holland;* but understanding I was a Surgeon, he was contented to take half the usual Rate, on Condition that I would serve him in the way of my Calling. Before we took Shipping, I was often asked by some of the Crew, whether I had performed the Ceremony above-mentioned: I evaded the Question by general Answers, that I had satisfied the Emperor and Court in all Particulars. However, a malicious Rogue of a Skipper[178] went to an Officer, and pointing to me, told him, I had not yet *trampled on the Crucifix:* But the other, who had received Instructions to let me pass, gave the Rascal twenty Strokes on the Shoulders with a Bamboo, after which I was no more troubled with such Questions.

Nothing happened worth mentioning in this Voyage. We sailed with a fair Wind to the *Cape of Good Hope,* where we staid only to take in fresh Water. On the 16th of *April* we arrived safe to *Amsterdam,* having lost only three Men by Sickness in the Voyage, and a fourth who fell from the Fore-mast into the Sea, not far from the Coast of *Guinea.* From Amsterdam I soon after set sail for *England,* in a small Vessel belonging to that City.

On the 10th of *April,* 1710, we put in at the *Downs.* I landed the next Morning, and saw once more my native Country, after an Absence of five Years and six Months compleat. I went strait to *Redriff,* where I arrived the same Day at Two in the Afternoon, and found my Wife and Family in good Health.

---

[176] Nagasaki. "It is the only port of Japan open to strangers. The Dutch factors reside in an island near, and are never suffered to come within the city, except on the arrival of their ships" (Clement Cruttwell's *New Universal* *Gazetteer,* 1798).

[177] It is reported that persons suspected of having been converted to Christianity were subjected to this rite.

[178] shipboy.

A MODEST PROPOSAL for Preventing the Children of Poor People from Being a Burden to their Parents or the Country

It is a melancholly Object to those, who walk through this great Town or travel in the Country, when they see the *Streets,* the *Roads* and *Cabbin-Doors* crowded with *Beggars* of the Female Sex, followed by three, four, or six Children, *all in Rags,* and importuning every Passenger for an Alms. These *Mothers* instead of being able to work for their honest livelyhood, are forced to employ all their time in Stroling to beg Sustenance for their *helpless Infants,* who, as they grow up, either turn *Thieves* for want of work, or leave their *dear Native Country, to fight for the Pretender*[179] *in Spain,* or sell themselves to the *Barbadoes.*

I think it is agreed by all Parties, that this prodigious number of Children in the Arms, or on the Back, or at the *heels* of their *Mothers,* and frequently of their *Fathers, is in the present deplorable state of the Kingdom,* a very great additional grievance; and therefore whoever could find out a fair, cheap and easy method of making these Children sound and useful Members of the common-wealth would deserve so well of the publick, as to have his Statue set up for a preserver of the Nation.

But my Intention is very far from being confined to provide only for the Children of *professed Beggars,* it is of a much greater Extent, and shall take in the whole Number of Infants at a certain Age, who are born of Parents in effect as little able to support them, as those who demand our Charity in the Streets.

As to my own part, having turned my Thoughts, for many Years, upon this important Subject, and maturely weighed the several *Schemes of our Projectors,* I have always found them grossly mistaken in their computation. It is true, a Child *just dropt from it's Dam,* may be supported by her Milk, for a Solar Year with little other Nourishment, at most not above the Value of two Shillings, which the Mother may certainly get, or the Value in *Scraps,* by her lawful Occupation of begging; and it is exactly at one Year Old that I propose to provide for them in such a manner, as, instead of being a Charge upon their *Parents,* or the *Parish,* or *wanting Food and Raiment* for the rest of their Lives, they shall, on the Contrary, contribute to the Feeding and partly to the Cloathing of many Thousands.

There is likewise another great Advantage in my Scheme, that it will prevent those *voluntary Abortions,* and that horrid practice of *Women murdering their Bastard Children,* alas! too frequent among us, Sacrificing the *poor innocent Babes,* I doubt, more to avoid the Expence than the Shame, which would move Tears and Pity in the most Savage and inhuman breast.

The number of Souls in this Kingdom being usually reckoned one Million and a half, Of these I calculate there may be about two hundred thousand Couple whose Wives are Breeders; from which number I substract[180] thirty Thousand Couples, who are able to maintain their own Children, although I apprehend there cannot be so many, under *the present Distresses of the Kingdom;* but this being granted, there will remain an hundred and seventy thousand Breeders. I again Substract fifty Thousand, for those

---

The text is taken from the first edition, 1729.

[179] The son of James II, claimant for restoring the Stuarts to the throne, since the Revolution settlement of 1689 which limited the crown to a Protestant succession. Swift is here implying that the Pretender's forces were thrown in with those of the Catholic Philip V of Spain in the current war with Great Britain.

[180] An accepted spelling in Swift's day. See Bailey's *Dictionary.*

Women who miscarry, or whose Children die by accident, or disease within the Year. There only remain an hundred and twenty thousand Children of poor Parents annually born: The question therefore is, How this number shall be reared, and provided for, which, as I have already said, under the present Situation of Affairs, is utterly impossible by all the Methods hitherto proposed; for we can *neither employ them in Handicraft or Agriculture;* we neither build Houses, (I mean in the Country) nor cultivate Land: They can very seldom pick up a Livelyhood *by Stealing* till they arrive at six years Old; except where they are of towardly parts; although, I confess, they learn the Rudiments much earlier; during which time they can however be properly looked upon only as *Probationers,* as I have been informed by a principal Gentleman in the County of *Cavan,* who protested to me, that he never knew above one or two Instances under the Age of six, even in a part of the Kingdom *so removed for the quickest proficiency in that Art.*

I am assured by our Merchants, that a Boy or a Girl before twelve years Old, is no saleable Commodity, and even when they come to this Age, they will not yield above three Pounds, or three Pounds and half a Crown at most on the Exchange, which cannot turn to Account either to the Parents or Kingdom, the Charge of Nutriment and Rags having been at least four times that Value.

I shall now therefore humbly propose my own Thoughts, which I hope will not be lyable to the least Objection.

I have been assured by a very knowing *American* of my acquaintance in *London,* that a young healthy Child well Nursed is at a year Old a most delicious nourishing and wholesome Food, whether *Stewed, Roasted, Baked,* or *Boiled,* and I make no doubt that it will equally serve in a *Fricasie,* or a *Ragoust.*

I do therefore humbly offer it to *publick consideration,* that of the Hundred and twenty thousand Children, already computed, twenty thousand may be reserved for Breed, whereof only one fourth part to be Males; which is more

than we allow to *Sheep, black Cattle,* or *Swine,* and my Reason is, that these Children are seldom the Fruits of Marriage, *a Circumstance not much regarded by our Savages,* therefore, *one Male* will be sufficient to serve *four Females.* That the remaining Hundred thousand may at a year Old be offered in Sale to the *Persons of Quality* and *Fortune,* through the Kingdom, always advising the Mother to let them Suck plentifully in the last Month, so as to render them Plump, and Fat for a good Table. A Child will make two Dishes at an Entertainment for Friends, and when the Family dines alone, the fore or hind Quarter will make a reasonable Dish, and seasoned with a little Pepper or Salt will be very good Boiled on the fourth Day, especially in *Winter.*

I have reckoned upon a Medium, that a Child just born will weigh 12 pounds, and in a solar Year if tolerably nursed, encreaseth to 28 Pounds.

I grant this food will be somewhat dear, and therefore very *proper for Landlords,* who, as they have already devoured most of the Parents seem to have the best Title to the Children.

Infant's flesh will be in Season throughout the Year, but more plentiful in *March,* and a little before and after, for we are told by a grave Author an eminent *French* Physician, that *Fish being a prolifick Diet,* there are more Children born in *Roman Catholick Countries* about nine Months after *Lent,* than at any other Season, therefore reckoning a Year after *Lent,* the Markets will be more glutted than usual, because the Number of *Popish Infants,* is at least three to one in this Kingdom, and therefore it will have one other Collateral advantage, by lessening the Number of Papists among us.

I have already computed the Charge of nursing a Begger's Child (in which list I reckon all *Cottagers, Labourers,* and four fifths of the *Farmers*) to be about two Shillings *per Annum,* Rags included, and I believe no Gentleman would repine to give Ten Shillings for the *Carcass of a good fat Child,* which, as I have said will make four Dishes of excellent Nutritive Meat, when he hath only some particular Friend, or his own Family to Dine with him. Thus the Squire will learn to be a good Landlord, and grow popular among his Tenants, the Mother will have Eight Shillings neat profit, and be fit for Work till she produces another Child.

Those who are more thrifty (*as I must confess the Times require*) may flea[181] the Carcass; the skin of which, Artificially dressed, will make admirable *Gloves for Ladies,* and *Summer Boots for fine Gentlemen.*

As to our City of *Dublin,* Shambles[182] may be appointed for this purpose, in the most convenient parts of it, and Butchers we may be assured will not be wanting, although I rather recommend buying the Children alive, and dressing them hot from the Knife, as we [do] *roasting Pigs.*

A very worthy Person, *a true Lover of his Country,* and whose Virtues I highly esteem, was lately pleased, in discoursing on this matter, to offer a refinement upon my Scheme. He said, that many Gentlemen of this Kingdom, having of late destroyed their Deer, he conceived that the want of Venison might be well supplied by the Bodies of young Lads and Maidens, not exceeding fourteen Years of Age, nor under twelve, so great a Number of both Sexes in every Country being now ready to Starve, for want of Work and Service: And these to be disposed of by their Parents if alive, or otherwise by their nearest Relations. But with due deference to so excellent a friend, and so deserving a Patriot, I cannot be altogether in his Sentiments, for as to the Males, my *American* acquaintance assured me from frequent Experience, that their flesh was generally Tough and Lean, like that of our Schoolboys, by a continual exercise, and their Taste disagreeable, and to Fatten them would not answer the Charge. Then as to the Females, it would, I think with humble Submission, *be a loss to the Pub-*

lick, because they soon would become Breeders themselves: And besides it is not improbable that some scrupulous People might be apt to Censure such a Practice, (although indeed very unjustly) as a little bordering upon Cruelty, which, I confess, hath always been with me the strongest objection against any Project, how well so ever intended.

But in order to justify my friend, he confessed, that this expedient was put into his Head by the famous *Sallmanaazor,*[183] a Native of the island *Formosa,* who came from thence to *London,* above twenty Years ago, and in Conversation told my Friend, that in his Country any young Person happened to be put to Death, the Executioner sold the Carcass to *Persons of Quality,* as a prime Dainty, and that, in his Time, the Body of a plump Girl of fifteen, who was crucifyed for an attempt to Poison the Emperor, was sold to his Imperial *Majesty's prime Minister of State,* and other great *Mandarins* of the Court, *in Joints from the Gibbet,*[184] at four hundred Crowns. Neither indeed can I deny, that if the same Use were made of several plump Girls in this Town, who, without one single Groat to their Fortunes, cannot stir abroad without a Chair, and appear at a *Play-House,* and *Assemblies* in Foreign fineries, which they never will pay for; the Kingdom would not be the worse.

Some Persons of a desponding Spirit are in great concern about that vast Number of poor People, who are Aged, Diseased, or Maimed, and I have been desired to imploy my Thoughts what Course may be taken, to ease the Nation of so grievous an Incumbrance. But I am not in the least pain upon that matter, because it is very well known, that they are every Day *dying,* and *rotting,* by *cold* and *famine,* and *filth,* and *vermin,* as fast as can be reasonably expected. And as to the younger Labourers, they are now in almost as hopeful a Condition. They cannot get work, and consequently pine away for want of Nourishment, to

---

181 flay.
182 "a place where butchers attend to sell meat" (Bailey's *Dictionary*).

183 George Psalmanazar (1679?–1763), author of a fictitious "Description" of Formosa (1704).
184 gallows.

a degree, that if at any Time they are accidently hired to common Labour, they have not strength to perform it, and thus the Country and themselves are happily delivered from the Evils to come.

I have too long digressed, and therefore shall return to my Subject, I think the Advantages by the Proposal which I have made are obvious and many, as well as of the highest Importance.

For *First*, as I have already observed, it would greatly lessen *the Number of Papists*, with whom we are Yearly overrun, being the principal Breeders of the Nation, as well as our most dangerous Enemies, and who stay at home on purpose with a Design *to deliver the Kingdom to the Pretender*, hoping to take their Advantage by the Absence *of so many good Protestants*, who have chosen rather to leave their Country, than stay at home, and pay Tithes against their Conscience, to an *Episcopal Curate.*

Secondly, the poorer Tenants will have something valuable of their own which by Law may be made lyable to Distress, and help to pay their Landlord's Rent, their Corn and Cattle being already seized, and *Money a Thing unknown.*

Thirdly, whereas the Maintenance of an hundred thousand Children, from two Years old, and upwards, cannot be computed at less than Ten Shillings a piece *per Annum*, the Nation's Stock will be thereby encreased fifty thousand Pounds *per Annum*, besides the Profit of a new Dish, introduced to the Tables of all *Gentlemen of Fortune* in the Kingdom, who have any Refinement in Taste, and the Money will circulate among our Selves, the Goods being entirely of our own Growth and Manufacture.

Fourthly, The constant Breeders, besides the gain of eight Shillings Ster. *per Annum*, by the Sale of their Children, will be rid of the Charge of maintaining them after the first Year.

Fifthly, This Food would likewise bring great *Custom to Taverns*, where the Vintners will certainly be so prudent as to procure the best receipts for dressing it to Perfection, and consequently have their Houses frequented by all the *fine Gentlemen*, who justly value themselves upon their Knowledge in good Eating, and a skillful Cook, who understands how to oblige his Guests, will contrive to make it as expensive as they please.

Sixthly, This would be a great Inducement to Marriage, which all wise Nations have either encouraged by Reward, or enforced by Laws and Penalties. It would encrease the Care and Tenderness of Mothers towards their Children, when they were sure of a Settlement for Life, to the poor Babes, provided in some sort by the Publick, to their Annual Profit instead of Expence; we should soon see an honest Emulation among the married Women, *which of them could bring the fattest Child to the Market.* Men would become as *fond* of their Wives, during the Time of their Pregnancy, as they are now of their *Mares* in Foal, their *Cows* in Calf, or *Sows* when they are ready to farrow, nor offer to beat or kick them (as is too *frequent* a Practice) for fear of a Miscarriage.

Many other Advantages might be enumerated. For Instance, the Addition of some thousand Carcasses in our Exportation of Barrell'd Beef. The Propagation of *Swines Flesh*, and Improvement in the Art of making good *Bacon*, so much wanted among us by the great Destruction of *Pigs*, too frequent at our Tables, which are no way comparable in Taste, or Magnificence to a well grown, fat Yearly Child, which roasted whole will make a considerable Figure at a *Lord Mayor's Feast*, or any other Publick Entertainment. But this, and many others, I omit being studious of Brevity.

Supposing that one thousand Families in this City, would be constant Customers for Infants Flesh, besides others who might have it at *merry Meetings*, particularly at *Weddings* and *Christenings*, I compute that *Dublin* would take off annually about twenty thousand Carcasses, and the rest of the Kingdom (where probably they will be sold somewhat cheaper) the remaining eighty Thousand.

I can think of no one Objection, that

will possibly be raised against this Proposal, unless it should be urged that the Number of People will be thereby much lessened in the Kingdom, This I freely own, and 'twas indeed one principal Design in offering it to the World. I desire the Reader will observe, that I calculate my Remedy, *for this one individual Kingdom of* IRELAND, *and for no other that ever was, is, or, I think, ever can be upon Earth.* Therefore let no Man talk to me of other Expedients: *Of Taxing our Absentees at five Shillings a Pound: Of using neither Cloaths, nor Houshold Furniture, except what is of our own Growth and Manufacture: Of utterly rejecting the Materials and Instruments that promote Foreign Luxury: Of curing the Expensiveness of Pride, Vanity, Idleness, and Gaming in our Women: Of introducing a Vein of Parcimony, Prudence and Temperance: Of learning to love our Country, wherein we differ even from* LAPLANDERS, *and the Inhabitants of* TOPINAMBOO:[185] *Of quitting any longer like the Jews, who were murdering one another at the very Moment their City was taken: Of being a little cautious not to sell our Country and Consciences for nothing: Of teaching Landlords to have at least one Degree of Mercy towards their Tenants.* Lastly, *Of putting a Spirit of Honesty, Industry, and Skill into our Shop-keepers, who, if a Resolution could now be taken to buy only our Native Goods, would immediately unite to cheat and exact upon us in the Price, the Measure, and the Goodness, nor could ever yet be brought to make one fair Proposal of just Dealing, though often and earnestly invited to it.*

Therefore I repeat, let no Man talk to me of these and the like Expedients, till he hath at least some Glimpse of Hope, that there will ever be some hearty and sincere Attempt to put *them in Practice.*

But as to my self, having been wearied out for many Years with offering vain, idle, visionary Thoughts, and at length utterly despairing of Success, I fortunately fell upon this Proposal, which, as it is wholly new, so it hath something Solid and Real, of no Expence and little Trouble, full in our own Power, and whereby we can incur no Danger in *disobliging* ENGLAND. For this kind of Commodity will not bear Exportation, the flesh being of too tender a Consistence, to admit a long Continuance in Salt, *although perhaps I cou'd name a Country, which would be glad to eat up our whole Nation without it.*

After all, I am not so violently bent upon my own Opinion, as to reject any Offer, proposed by wise Men, which shall be found equally Innocent, Cheap, Easy, and Effectual. But before something of that Kind shall be advanced in Contradiction to my Scheme, and offering a better, I desire the Author or Authors, will be pleased maturely to consider two Points. *First,* As Things now stand, how they will be able to find Food and Raiment for a hundred Thousand useless Mouths and Backs. And *Secondly,* There being a round Million of Creatures in Humane Figure, throughout this Kingdom, whose whole Subsistence put into a common Stock, would leave them in Debt two Millions of Pounds *Ster.* adding those, who are Beggers by Profession, to the Bulk of Farmers, Cottagers and Labourers, with their Wives and Children, who are Beggers in Effect; I desire those Politicians, who dislike my Overture, and may perhaps be so bold to attempt an Answer, that they will first ask the Parents of these Mortals, Whether they would not at this Day think it a great Happiness to have been sold for Food at a Year Old, in the manner I prescribe, and thereby have avoided such a perpetual Scene of Misfortunes, as they have since gone through, by the *Oppression of Landlords,* the Impossibility of paying Rent without Money or Trade, the Want of common Sustenance, with neither House nor Cloaths to cover them

[185] Brazil. "In Brazil, Tupinambá is the generic designation of various Tupí tribes that in the sixteenth century occupied the coast of Brazil" (Samuel Putnam, translator, *The Masters and the Slaves* by Gilberto Freyre, 1946).

from these Inclemencies of Weather, and the most inevitable Prospect of intailing the like, or greater Miseries, upon their Breed for ever.

I profess in the Sincerity of my Heart, that I have not the least Personal Interest in endeavouring to promote this necessary Work, having no other Motive than the *Publick Good of my Country, by advancing our Trade, providing for Infants, relieving the Poor, and giving some Pleasure to the Rich.* I have no Children, by which I can propose to get a single Penny; the youngest being nine Years Old, and my Wife past Childbearing.

Sir Richard Steele
1672-1729

THE TATLER
By Isaac Bickerstaff, Esq.

No. 1 [INTRODUCTORY]

Quicquid agunt Homines nostri Farrago Libelli.[1]

TUESDAY, APRIL 12. 1709.

Tho' the other Papers which are pub-lish'd for the Use of the good People of England *have certainly very wholesom Effects, and are Laudable in their par-ticular Kinds, they do not seem to come up to the main Design of such Narra-tions, which, I humbly presume, should be principally intended for the Use of Politick Persons, who are so publick-spir-ited as to neglect their own Affairs to look into Transactions of State. Now these Gentlemen, for the most Part, be-ing Persons of strong Zeal and weak In-tellects, It is both a Charitable and Nec-essary Work to offer something, whereby such worthy and well-affected Members of the Commonwealth may be instructed, after their Reading,* what to think: *Which shall be the End and Purpose of this my Paper, wherein I shall from Time to Time Report and Consider all Matters of what Kind soever that shall occur to Me, and publish such my Ad-vices and Reflections every* Tuesday,

Thursday, and Saturday, *in the Week, for the Convenience of the Post. I re-solve also to have something which may be of Entertainment to the Fair Sex, in Honour of whom I have invented the Title of this Paper. I therefore earnestly desire all Persons, without Distinction, to take it in for the present* Gratis, *and hereafter at the Price of one Penny, for-bidding all Hawkers to take more for it at their Peril. And I desire all Persons to consider, that I am at a very great Charge for proper Materials for this Work, as well as that before I resolv'd upon it I had settled a Correspondence in all Parts of the Known and Knowing World. And for as much as this Globe is not trodden upon by mere Drudges of Business only, but that Men of Spirit and Genius are justly to be esteem'd as considerable Agents in it, we shall not upon a Dearth of News present you with musty Foreign Edicts, or dull Proclama-tions, but shall divide our Relation of the Passages which occur in Action or Discourse throughout this Town, as well*

Text from the collected edition of 1710–1711, in octavo. Isaac Bickerstaff had been used as early as 1708 as Swift's pseudonym in satiriz-ing the predictions of Partridge's almanacs. It is to Swift's hoax that Steele refers in the article *"From my own Apartment"* at the end of *Tatler* No. 1.

---

[1] Whate'er men do, or say, or think, or dream, Our motley paper seizes for its theme.
(Juvenal, *Satires*, I, 85–86, tr. Pope.)

as elsewhere, under such Dates of Places as may prepare you for the Matter you are to expect, in the following Manner:

All Accounts of Gallantry, Pleasure, and Entertainment, *shall be under the Article[2] of* White's Chocolate-house;[3] Poetry, *under that of* Will's Coffee-house;[4] Learning *under the Title of* Græcian;[5] Foreign *and* Domestick News, *you will have from St.* James's Coffee-house;[6] *and what else I have to offer on any other Subject, shall be dated from my own* Apartment.

I once more desire my Reader to consider, That as I cannot keep an Ingenious Man to go daily to Will's, *under Twopence each Day merely for his Charges; to* White's, *under Sixpence; nor to the Græcian, without allowing him some Plain* Spanish,[7] *to be as able as others at the Learned Table; and that a good Observer cannot speak with even* Kidney[8] *at St.* James's *without clean Linnen: I say, these Considerations will, I hope, make all Persons willing to comply with my Humble Request (when my Gratis Stock is exhausted) of a Penny a Piece; especially since they are sure of some Proper Amusement, and that it is impossible for me to want Means to entertain 'em, having, besides the Force of my own Parts, the Power of Divination, and that I can, by casting a Figure,[9] tell you all that will happen before it comes to pass.*

But this last Faculty I shall use very sparingly, and speak but of few Things 'till they are pass'd, for fear of divulging Matters which may offend our Superiors.

White's Chocolate-house, April 7.

The deplorable Condition of a very pretty Gentleman, who walks here at the Hours when Men of Quality first appear, is what is very much lamented. His History is, That on the 9th of *September, 1705.* being in his One and twentieth Year, he was washing his Teeth at a Tavern Window in *Pall-Mall,* when a fine Equipage pass'd by, and in it a young Lady who look'd up at him; away goes the Coach, and the young Gentleman pull'd off his Night-Cap, and instead of rubbing his Gums, as he ought to do, out of the Window,[10] 'till about Four a Clock sits him down, and spoke not a Word 'till Twelve at Night; after which, he began to enquire, If any Body knew the Lady ————. The Company ask'd, What Lady? But he said no more, 'till they broke up at Six in the Morning. All the ensuing Winter he went from Church to Church every Sunday, and from Play-house to Play-house every Night in the Week, but could never find the Original of the Picture which dwelt in his Bosom. In a Word, his Attention to any Thing, but his Passion, was utterly gone. He has lost all the Money he ever play'd for, and been confuted in every Argument he has enter'd upon since the Moment he first saw her. He is of a Noble Family, has naturally a very good Air, is of a frank, honest Temper: But this Passion has so extreamly maul'd him, that his Features are set and uniform'd, and his whole Visage is deaden'd by a long Absence of Thought. He never appears in any Alacrity, but when rais'd by Wine; at which Time he is sure to come hither, and throw away a great deal of Wit on Fellows, who have no Sense further than just to observe, That our poor Lover has most Understanding when he is drunk, and is least in his Senses when he is sober.

Will's Coffee-house, April 8.

On *Thursday* last was acted, for the Benefit of Mr. *Betterton,*[11] the Celebrated Comedy, call'd *Love for Love.*[12] Those excellent Players, Mrs. *Barry,*

---

[2] "a particular part of a discourse, treatise, account, etc." (Bailey's *Dictionary*).

[3] Established in 1698 on St. James's Street, White's had a reputation for gambling.

[4] In Covent Garden.

[5] In the Strand.

[6] In St. James's Street, this house was a particular favorite of the Whigs.

[7] wine.

[8] Mr. Kidney, headwaiter at St. James's, is mentioned in several papers of *The Tatler*.

[9] i.e., reading the future.

[10] As there were no drains inside the houses, this may have been a common practice which Steele is gently satirizing.

[11] Thomas Betterton (1635?–1710), a celebrated actor, particularly of tragic roles.

[12] A play be William Congreve of 1695. The profits from this performance went to Betterton.

Mrs. *Bracegirdle,* and Mr. *Dogget,* tho' not at present concerned in the House,[13] acted on that Occasion. There has not been known so great a Concourse of Persons of Distinction as at that Time; the Stage it self was covered with Gentlemen and Ladies, and when the Curtain was drawn, it discovered even there a very splendid Audience. This unusual Encouragement, which was given to a Play for the Advantage of so great an Actor, gives an undeniable Instance, That the true Relish for Manly Entertainments and Rational Pleasures is not wholly lost. All the Parts were acted to Perfection; the Actors were careful of their Carriage, and no one was guilty of the Affectation to insert Witticisms of his own, but a due Respect was had to the Audience, for encouraging this accomplish'd Player. It is not now doubted but Plays will revive, and take their usual Place in the Opinion of Persons of Wit and Merit, notwithstanding their late Apostacy in Favour of Dress and Sound. This Place is very much altered since Mr. *Dryden* frequented it; where you used to see *Songs, Epigrams,* and *Satyrs,* in the Hands of every Man you met, you have now only a Pack of Cards; and instead of the Cavils about the Turn of the Expression, the Elegance of the Style, and the like, the Learned now dispute only about the Truth of the Game. But however, the Company is altered, all have shewn a great Respect for Mr. *Betterton:* And the very Gaming Part of this House have been so much touch'd with a Sense of the Uncertainty of Human Affairs, (which alter with themselves every Moment) that in this Gentleman, they pitied *Mark Anthony* of *Rome, Hamlett* of *Denmark, Mithridates* of *Pontus, Theodosius* of *Greece,* and *Henry* the Eighth of *England.*[14] It is well known, he has been in the Condition of each of those illustrious Personages for several Hours together, and behaved himself in those high Stations, in all the Changes of the Scene, with suitable Dignity. For these Reasons, we intend to repeat this Favour to him on a proper Occasion, lest he who can instruct us so well in personating Feigned Sorrows, should be lost to us by suffering under Real Ones. The Town is at present in very great Expectation of seeing a Comedy[15] now in Rehearsal, which is the 25th Production of my Honoured Friend Mr. *Thomas D'Urfey;* who, besides his great Abilities in the Dramatick, has a peculiar Talent in the Lyrick Way of Writing, and that with a Manner wholly new and unknown to the Antient *Greeks* and *Romans,* wherein he is but faintly imitated in the Translations of the Modern *Italian* Opera's.

St. James's Coffee-house, April 11.[16]

Letters from the *Hague* of the 16th say, That Major General *Cadogan* was gone to *Brussels,* with Orders to disperse proper Instructions for assembling the whole Force of the Allies in *Flanders* in the Beginning of the next Month. The late Offers concerning Peace, were made in the Style of Persons who think themselves upon equal Terms: But the Allies have so just a Sense of their present Advantages, that they will not admit of a Treaty, except *France* offers what is more suitable to her present Condition. At the same Time we make Preparations, as if we were alarm'd by a greater Force than that which we are carrying into the Field. Thus this Point seems now to be argued Sword in Hand. This was what a Great General alluded to, when being ask'd the Names of those who were to be Plenipotentiaries for the ensuing Peace; answer'd, with a serious Air, *There are about an Hundred thousand of us.* Mr. *Kidney,* who has the Ear of the greatest Politicians that come

---

[13] Elizabeth Barry (d. 1713), Anne Bracegirdle (d. 1748), and Thomas Doggett (d 1721), all famous actors who had retired from the stage and returned for this tribute to their former colleague.

[14] Characters Betterton had portrayed on the stage.

[15] *Modern Prophets.*

[16] The following item of news relates to war with the French and is typical of the sober news which made up part of *The Tatler* in its early numbers.

hither, tells me, There is a Mail come in to Day with Letters, dated *Hague, April* 19. N.S.[17] which say, a Design of bringing Part of our Troops into the Field at the Latter End of this Month, is now alter'd to a Resolution of marching towards the Camp about the 20th of the next. There happen'd t'other Day, in the Road of *Scheveling,* an Engagement between a Privateer of *Zealand* and one of *Dunkirk.* The *Dunkirker,* carrying 33 Pieces of Cannon, was taken and brought into the *Texel.* It is said, the Courier of Monsieur *Rouille* is return'd to him from the Court of *France.* Monsieur *Vendosme* being reinstated in the Favour of the Dutchess of *Burgundy,* is to command in *Flanders.*

Mr. *Kidney* added, That there were Letters of the 17th from *Ghent,* which give an Account, that the Enemy had form'd a Design to surprize two Battalions of the Allies which lay at *Alost;* but those Battalions receiv'd Advice of their March, and retir'd to *Dendermond.* Lieutenant General *Wood* appear'd on this Occasion at the Head of 5000 Foot, and 1000 Horse, upon which the Enemy withdrew, without making any further Attempt.

From my own Apartment.

I am sorry I am oblig'd to trouble the Publick with so much Discourse upon a Matter which I at the very first mentioned as a Trifle, *viz.* the Death of Mr. *Partridge,*[18] under whose Name there is an *Almanack* come out for the Year 1709. In one Page of which it is asserted by the said *John Partridge,* That he is still living, and not only so, but that he was also living some Time before, and even at the Instant when I writ of his Death. I have in another Place, and in a Paper by it self, sufficiently convinc'd this Man that he is dead, and if he has any Shame, I don't doubt but that by this Time he owns it to all his Acquaintance: For tho' the Legs and Arms, and whole Body of that Man may still appear and perform their animal Functions; yet since, as I have elsewhere observ'd, his Art is gone, the Man is gone. I am, as I said, concern'd, that this little Matter should make so much Noise; but since I am engag'd, I take my self oblig'd in Honour to go on in my Lucubrations, and by the Help of these Arts of which I am Master, as well as my Skill in Astrological Speculations, I shall, as I see Occasion, proceed to confute other dead Men, who pretend to be in Being, that they are actually deceased. I therefore give all Men fair Warning to mend their Manners, for I shall from Time to Time print Bills of Mortality; and I beg the Pardon of all such who shall be named therein, if they who are good for Nothing shall find themselves in the Number of the Deceased.

No. 95   [OF DOMESTIC FELICITIES]

Interea dulces pendent circum Oscula Nati,
Casta Pudicitiam servat Domus.[19]

VIRG.

FROM TUESD. NOV. 15. TO THURSD. NOV. 17. 1709.

From my own Apartment, November 16.

There are several Persons who have many Pleasures and Entertainments in their Possession which they do not enjoy. It is therefore a kind and good Office to acquaint them with their own Happiness, and turn their Attention to such Instances of their good Fortune which they are apt to overlook. Persons

[17] New Style, meaning the date according to the Gregorian calendar, which had been in use on the Continent since about 1582 and which was about eleven days ahead of the calendar still in use in England until 1750.

[18] See note on the text, p. 126.

[19] His cares are eas'd with intervals of bliss;
His little children climbing for a kiss,
Welcome their father's late return at night;
His faithful bed is crown'd with chaste delight.
(Vergil, *Georgics,* II, 523, tr. Dryden.)

in the married State often want such a Monitor, and pine away their Days, by looking upon the same Condition in Anguish and Murmur, which carries with it in the Opinion of others a Complication of all the Pleasures of Life, and a Retreat from its Inquietudes.

I am led into this Thought by a Visit I made an old Friend, who was formerly my Schoolfellow. He came to Town last Week with his Family for the Winter, and yesterday Morning sent me Word his Wife expected me to Dinner. I am as it were at Home at that House, and every Member of it knows me for their Well-wisher. I cannot indeed express the Pleasure it is, to be met by the Children with so much Joy as I am when I go thither: The Boys and Girls strive who shall come first, when they think it is I that am knocking at the Door; and that Child which loses the Race to me, runs back again to tell the Father it is Mr. *Bickerstaff*. This Day I was led in by a pretty Girl, that we all thought must have forgot me; for the Family has been out of Town these Two Years. Her knowing me again was a mighty Subject with us, and took up our Discourse at the first Entrance. After which they began to rally me upon a Thousand little Stories they heard in the Country about my Marriage to one of my Neighbour's Daughters: Upon which the Gentleman my Friend said, "Nay, if Mr. *Bickerstaff* marries a Child of any of his old Companions, I hope mine shall have the Preference; there's Mrs. *Mary* is now Sixteen, and would make him as fine a Widow as the best of them: But I know him too well; he is so enamoured with the very Memory of those who flourished in our Youth, that he will not so much as look upon the modern Beauties. I remember, old Gentleman, how often you went Home in a Day to refresh your Countenance and Dress, when *Teraminta* reigned in your Heart. As we came up in the Coach, I repeated to my Wife some of your Verses on her." With such Reflections on little Passages which happened long ago, we passed our Time during a chearful and elegant Meal. After Dinner, his Lady left the Room,

as did also the Children. As soon as we were alone, he took me by the Hand; Well, my good Friend, says he, I am heartily glad to see thee; I was afraid you would never have seen all the Company that dined with you to Day again. Do not you think the good Woman of the House a little altered, since you followed her from the Play-house, to find out who she was, for me? I perceived a Tear fall down his Cheek as he spoke, which moved me not a little. But to turn the Discourse, said I, She is not indeed quite that Creature she was when she returned me the Letter I carried from you; and told me, She hoped, as I was a Gentleman, I would be employ'd no more to trouble her who had never offended me, but would be so much the Gentleman's Friend as to disswade him from a Pursuit which he could never succeed in. You may remember, I thought her in earnest, and you were forced to employ your Cousin *Will*. who made his Sister get acquainted with her for you. You cannot expect her to be for ever Fifteen. Fifteen? replied my good Friend: Ah! You little understand, you that have lived a Batchelor, how great, how exquisite, a Pleasure there is in being really beloved! It is impossible that the most beauteous Face in Nature should raise in me such pleasing Ideas, as when I look upon that excellent Woman. That Fading in her Countenance is chiefly caused by her watching with me in my Fever. This was followed by a Fit of Sickness, which had like to have carried her off last Winter. I tell you sincerely, I have so many Obligations to her, that I cannot with any sort of Moderation think of her present State of Health. But as to what you say of Fifteen, she gives me every Day Pleasures beyond what I ever knew in the Possession of her Beauty when I was in the Vigour of Youth. Every Moment of her Life brings fresh Instances of her Complacency to my Inclinations, and her Prudence in Regard to my Fortune. Her Face is to me much more beautiful than when I first saw it; there is no Decay in any Feature which I cannot trace from the very Instant it was occasioned, by some anxious Concern for my Welfare and Interests. Thus at the same Time, methinks, the Love I conceived towards her for what she was, is heightened by my Gratitude for what she is. The Love of a Wife is as much above the idle Passion commonly called by that Name, as the loud Laughter of Buffoons is inferior to the elegant Mirth of Gentlemen. Oh! she is an inestimable Jewel. In her Examination of her Houshold Affairs, she shows a certain Fearfulness to find a Fault, which makes her Servants obey her like Children; and the meanest we have, has an ingenuous Shame for an Offence, not always to be seen in Children in other Families. I speak freely to you, my old Friend, ever since her Sickness, Things that gave me the quickest Joy before, turn now to a certain Anxiety. As the Children play in the next Room, I know the poor Things by their Steps, and am considering what they must do, should they lose their Mother in their tender Years. The Pleasure I used to take in telling my Boy Stories of the Battles, and asking my Girl Questions about the Disposal of her Baby,[20] and the Gossiping[21] of it, is turned into inward Reflection and Melancholy.

He would have gone on in this tender Way, when the good Lady entered, and with an inexpressible Sweetness in her Countenance told us, she had been searching her Closet for something very good to treat such an old Friend as I was. Her Husband's Eyes sparkled with Pleasure at the Chearfulness of her Countenance; and I saw all his Fears vanish in an Instant. The Lady observing something in our Looks which showed we had been more serious than ordinary, and seeing her Husband receive her with great Concern under a forced Chearfulness, immediately guessed at what we had been talking of; and applying her self to me, said, with a Smile, Mr. *Bickerstaff*, don't believe a Word of what he tells you, I shall still live to have you for my Second, as I have often promised you, unless he takes more Care

of himself than he has done since his coming to Town. You must know, he tells me, That he finds *London* is a much more healthy Place than the Country; for he sees several of his old Acquaintance and School-fellows are here, young Fellows with fair full-bottomed Periwigs. I could scarce keep him this Morning from going out open-breasted. My Friend, who is always extremely delighted with her agreeable Humour, made her sit down with us. She did it with that Easiness which is peculiar to Women of Sense; and to keep up the good Humour she had brought in with her, turned her Raillery upon me. Mr. *Bickerstaff*, you remember you followed me one Night from the Play-house; supposing you should carry me thither to morrow Night, and lead me into the Front-Box. This put us into a long Field of Discourse about the Beauties, who were Mothers to the present, and shined in the Boxes Twenty Years ago. I told her, I was glad she had transferred so many of her Charms, and I did not question but her eldest Daughter was within half a Year of being a Toast.[22]

We were pleasing our selves with this fantastical Preferment of the young Lady, when on a sudden we were alarm'd with the Noise of a Drum, and immediately entered my little God-son to give me a Point of War.[23] His Mother, between Laughing and Chiding, would have put him out of the Room; but I would not part with him so. I found, upon Conversation with him, tho' he was a little noisy in his Mirth, that the Child had excellent Parts, and was a great Master of all the Learning on t'other Side Eight Years old. I perceived him a very great Historian in *Æsop's* Fables; but he frankly declared to me in his Mind, That he did not delight in that Learning, because he did not believe they were true; for which Reason, I found he had very much turned his Studies for about a Twelvemonth past, into the Lives and Adventures of Don *Bellianis* of *Greece, Guy* of

---

[20] doll.
[21] Acting as godparent at baptism.
[22] "a celebrated woman whose health is often

drank" (Bailey's *Dictionary*).
[23] a martial air; written music was formerly indicated by *points* rather than by *notes*.

Warwick, the *Seven Champions,* and other Historians of that Age.[24] I could not but observe the Satisfaction the Father took in the Forwardness of his Son; and that these Diversions might turn to some Profit, I found the Boy had made Remarks, which might be of Service to him during the Course of his whole Life. He would tell you the Mismanagements of *John Hickathrift,* find Fault with the passionate Temper in *Bevis* of *Southampton,* and love St. *George* for being the Champion of *England;*[25] and by this Means, had his Thoughts insensibly moulded into the Notions of Discretion, Virtue, and Honour. I was extolling his Accomplishments, when the Mother told me, That the little Girl who led me in this Morning, was in her Way a better Scholar than he. *Betty* (says she) deals

chiefly in Fairies and Sprights; and sometimes in a Winter Night, will terrify the Maids with her Accounts, till they are afraid to go up to Bed.

I sat with them till it was very late, sometimes in merry, sometimes in serious Discourse, with this particular Pleasure, which gives the only true Relish to all Conversation, a Sense that every one of us liked each other. I went Home, considering the different Conditions of a married Life and that of a Batchelor; and I must confess, it struck me with a secret Concern, to reflect, that whenever I go off,[26] I shall leave no Traces behind me. In this pensive Mood I returned to my Family; that is to say, to my Maid, my Dog and my Cat, who only can be the better or worse for what happens to me.

No. 112 [ON RECREATION]

*Accedat Suavitas quaedam oportet Sermonum, atque Morum, haud-
quaquam mediocre Condimentum Amicitiae. Tristitia autem, & in
omni Re Severitas absit. Habet illa quidem Gravitatem, sed Amicitia
remissior esse debet, & liberior, & dulcior, & ad omnem Comitatem
Facilitatemque proclivior.*[27]

TULL.

FROM SATURDAY DEC. 24. TO TUESDAY
DEC. 27. 1709.

Sheer-Lane, December 26.

As I was looking over my Letters this Morning, I chanced to cast my Eye upon the following one, which came to my Hands about Two Months ago from an old Friend of mine, who, as I have since learned, was the Person that writ the agreeable Epistle inserted in my Paper of the Third of the last Month. It is of the same Turn with the other, and may

be looked upon as a Specimen of *Right Country Letters.*

Sir,

This sets out to you from my Summer-House upon the Terras, where I am enjoying a few Hours Sunshine, the scanty sweet Remains of a fine Autumn. The Year is almost at the lowest; so that in all Appearance, the rest of my Letters between this and Spring will be dated from my Parlour-Fire, where the little fond Prattle of a Wife and Children

[24] *The Honour of Chivalrie* (an English translation of *Don Belianus de Grecia*), *Guy of Warwick,* and *Famous Historie of the Seaven Champions of Christendom* are all legendary romances of a warlike cast.

[25] More legendary heroes of English stories appealing to young people.

[26] "to depart from a post" (Johnson's *Dictionary*); hence, to die.

[27] "There should be added a certain sweetness of discourse and manners, which is no inconsiderable sauce to friendship. But by all means throw out sadness and severity in everything. There is something of gravity indeed in it; but friendship requires a greater remissness, freedom, and pleasantness, and an inclination to good temper and affability." (Cicero, *Of Friendship*, XVIII, 66.)

will so often break in upon the Connexion of my Thoughts, that you'll easily discover it in my Style. If this Winter should prove as severe as the last, I can tell you before-hand, that I am likely to be a very miserable Man, through the perverse Temper of my eldest Boy. When the Frost was in its Extremity, you must know, that most of the Blackbirds, Robins, and Finches, of the Parish (whose Musick had entertained me in the Summer) took Refuge under my Roof. Upon this, my Care was, to rise every Morning before Day to set open my Windows for the Reception of the Cold and the Hungry, whom at the same Time I relieved with a very plentiful Alms, by strewing Corn and Seeds upon the Floors and Shelves. But Dicky, without any Regard to the Laws of Hospitality, considered the Casements as so many Traps, and used every Bird as a Prisoner at Discretion. Never did Tyrant exercise more various Cruelties: Some of the poor Creatures he chased to Death about the Room; others he drove into the Jaws of a Blood-thirsty Cat; and even in his greatest Acts of Mercy, either clipped the Wings, or singed the Tails, of his innocent Captives. You'll laugh, when I tell you I sympathized with every Bird in its Misfortunes; but I believe you'll think me in the Right for bewailing the Child's unlucky Humour. On the other Hand, I am extremely pleased to see his younger Brother carry an universal Benevolence towards every Thing that has Life. When he was between Four and Five Years Old, I caught him weeping over a beautiful Butterfly, which he chanced to kill as he was playing with it; and I am informed, that this Morning he has given his Brother Three Halfpence (which was his whole Estate) to spare the Life of a Tom-Tit. These are at present the Matters of greatest Moment within my Observation, and I know are too trifling to be communicated to any but so wise a Man as your self, and from one who has the Happiness to be,

Your most Faithful,
And most Obedient Servant.

The best Critick that ever wrote, speaking of some Passages in *Homer* which appear extravagant or frivolous, says indeed that they are Dreams; but the Dreams of *Jupiter*. My Friend's Letter appears to me in the same Light. One sees him in an idle Hour; but at the same Time in the idle Hour of a wise Man. A great Mind has something in it too severe and forbidding, that is not capable of giving it self such little Relaxations, and of condescending to these agreeable Ways of Trifling. *Tully*, when he celebrates the Friendship of *Scipio* and *Lelius*,[28] who were the greatest, as well as the politest, Men of their Age, represents it as a beautiful Passage in their Retirement, that they used to gather up Shells on the Sea-Shore, and amuse themselves with the Variety of Shape and Colour, which they met with in those little unregarded Works of Nature. The great *Agesilaus* could be a Companion to his own Children, and was surprised by the Ambassadors of[29] *Sparta,* as he was riding among them upon an Hobby-Horse. *Augustus* indeed had no Play-Fellows of his own begetting; but is said to have passed many of his Hours with little *Moorish* Boys at a Game of Marbles, not unlike our modern Taw. There is (methinks) a Pleasure in seeing great Men thus fall into the Rank of Mankind, and entertain themselves with Diversions and Amusements that are agreeable to the very weakest of the Species. I must frankly confess, that it is to me a Beauty in *Cato's* Character, that he would drink a chearful Bottle with a Friend; and I cannot but own, that I have seen with great Delight one of the most celebrated Authors of the last Age feeding the Ducks in St. *James's* Park.[30] By Instances of this Nature, the Heroes,

---

[28] Cicero's *Laelius, sive de Amicitia.*
[29] probably a mistake for *to*, as Agesilaus was king of Sparta.
[30] Thought to be Charles de Saint-Denis, Seigneur de Saint-Evremond (1610?–1703), French refugee who was patronized by the English monarchs and named Governor of Duck Island in St. James's Park, an obvious sinecure.

and Statesmen, the Philosophers, become as it were familiar with us, and grow the more amiable, the less they endeavour to appear awful. A Man who always acts in the Severity of Wisdom, or the Haughtiness of Quality, seems to move in a personated Part: It looks too Constrained and Theatrical for a Man to be always in that Character which distinguishes him from others. Besides that, the Slackening and Unbending our Minds on some Occasions, makes them exert themselves with greater Vigour and Alacrity, when they return to their proper and natural State.

As this innocent Way of passing a leisure Hour is not only consistent with a great Character, but very graceful in it, so there are Two Sorts of People to whom I would most earnestly recommend it. The First, are those who are uneasy out of Want of Thought; the Second, are those who are so out of a Turbulence of Spirit. The First are the impertinent, and the Second the dangerous Part of Mankind.

It grieves me to the very Heart, when I see several young Gentlemen, descended of honest Parents, run up and down hurrying from one End of the Town to the other, calling in at every Place of Resort, without being able to fix a Quarter of an Hour in any, and in a particular Haste without knowing for what. It would (methinks) be some Consolation, if I could perswade these precipitate young Gentlemen to compose this Restlesness of Mind, and apply themselves to any Amusement, how trivial soever, that might give them Employment, and keep them out of Harm's Way. They cannot imagine how great a Relief it would be to them, if they could grow sedate enough to play for Two or Three Hours at a Game of Push-pin.[31] But these busie, idle Animals, are only their own Tormentors: The Turbulent and Dangerous are for embroiling Councils, stirring up Seditions, and subverting Constitutions, out of a meer Restlesness of Temper, and an Insensibility of all the Pleasures of Life that are calm and

innocent. It is impossible for a Man to be so much employed in any Scene of Action, as to have great and good Affairs enough to fill up his whole Time; there will still be Casms and empty Spaces, in which a working Mind will employ it self to its own Prejudice, or that of others, unless it can be at Ease in the Exercise of such Actions as are in themselves indifferent. How often have I wished, for the Good of the Nation, That several famous Politicians could take any Pleasure in feeding Ducks. I look upon an able Statesman out of Business like a huge Whale, that will endeavour to overturn the Ship, unless he has an empty Cask to play with.

But to return to my good Friend and Correspondent, I am afraid we shall both be laughed at, when I confess, that we have often gone out into the Field to look upon a Bird's-Nest; and have more than once taken an Evening's Walk together on purpose to see the Sun set. I shall conclude with my Answer to his foregoing Letter:

Dear Sir,

I Thank you for your obliging Letter, and your Kindness to the Distressed, who will, doubtless, express their Gratitude to you themselves the next Spring. As for Dick the Tyrant, I must desire you will put a Stop to his Proceedings; and at the same Time take Care, that his little Brother be no Loser by his Mercy to the Tom-Tit. For my own Part, I am excluded all Conversation with Animals that delight only in a Country Life, and am therefore forced to entertain my self as well as I can with my little Dog and Cat. They both of 'em sit by my Fire every Night, expecting my coming Home with Impatience; and at my Entrance, never fail of running up to me, and bidding me welcome, each of 'em in his proper Language. As they have been bred up together from their Infancy, and seen no other Company, they have learned each others Manners, so that the Dog often gives himself the Airs of a Cat, and the Cat, in several of her Motions and Gestures, affects the Behaviour of the little Dog. When they are

31 "a child's play, in which pins are pushed alternately" (Johnson's *Dictionary*).

at *Play, I often make one with them;*
and sometimes please my self with con-
sidering, how much Reason and Instinct
are capable of delighting each other.
Thus, you see, I have communicated to
you the material Occurrences in my

Family, with the same Freedom that you
use to me; as I am with the same Sin-
cerity and Affection,

Your most Faithful
Humble Servant,
Isaac Bickerstaff.

No. 145 [OF OGLERS]

Nescio quis teneros Oculus mihi fascinet Agnos.[32]

VIRG.

FROM SATURD. MAR. 11. TO TUESD.
MAR. 14. 1709.

White's Chocolate house, March 13.

This Evening was allotted for taking
into Consideration a late Request of
Two indulgent Parents, touching the
Care of a young Daughter, whom they
design to send to a Boarding-School, or
keep at Home, according to my Determination; but I am diverted from that
Subject by Letters which I have received
from several Ladies, complaining of a
certain Sect of professed Enemies to the
Repose of the Fair Sex, called *Oglers.*
These are, it seems, Gentlemen who
look with deep Attention on one Object
at the Play-houses, and are ever staring
all round them in Churches. It is urged
by my Correspondents, that they do all
that is possible to keep their Eyes off
these Insnarers; but that, by what Power
they know not, both their Diversions and
Devotions are interrupted by them in
such a Manner, as that they cannot attend either, without stealing Looks at the
Persons whose Eyes are fixed upon them.
By this Means, my Petitioners say, they
find themselves grow insensibly less offended, and in Time enamoured, of these
their Enemies. What is required of me
on this Occasion, is, That as I love and
study to preserve the better Part of
Mankind, the Females, I would give
them some Account of this dangerous
Way of Assault, against which there is
so little Defence, that it lays Ambush for

the Sight it self, and makes them see-
ingly, knowingly, willingly, and forcibly
go on to their own Captivity.

This Representation of the present
State of Affairs between the Two Sexes
gave me very much Alarm; and I had no
more to do, but to recollect what I had
seen at any one Assembly for some Years
last past, to be convinced of the Truth
and Justice of this Remonstrance. If
there be not a Stop put to this evil Art,
all the Modes of Address, and the elegant Embellishments of Life, which
arise out of the noble Passion of Love,
will of Necessity decay. Who would be
at the Trouble of Rhetorick, or study
the *Bon Mien,*[33] when his Introduction
is so much easier obtained, by a sudden
Reverence in a downcast Look at the
meeting the Eye of a Fair Lady, and beginning again to ogle her as soon as she
glances another Way? I remember very
well, when I was last at an Opera, I
could perceive the Eyes of the whole
Audience cast into particular cross Angles one upon another, without any Manner of Regard to the Stage, though King
Latinus[34] was himself present when I
made that Observation. It was then very
pleasant to look into the Hearts of the
whole Company; for the Balls of Sight
are so form'd, that one Man's Eyes are
Spectacles to another to read his Heart
with. The most ordinary Beholder can
take Notice of any violent Agitation in
the Mind, any pleasing Transport, or
any inward Grief, in the Person he looks

---

[32] "I do not know what eye bewitches my
gentle lambs" (Vergil, *Eclogues,* III, 103).
[33] "good behaviour and address" (Bailey's

Dictionary).
[34] A character in an opera.

at; but one of these Oglers can see a studied Indifference, a concealed Love, or a smother'd Resentment, in the very Glances that are made to hide those Dispositions of Thought. The Naturalists tell us, That the Rattle-Snake will fix himself under a Tree where he sees a Squirrel playing; and when he has once got the Exchange of a Glance from the pretty Wanton, will give it such a sudden Stroke on its Imagination,[35] that tho' it may play from Bough to Bough, and strive to avert its Eyes from it for some Time, yet it comes nearer and nearer by little Intervals of looking another Way, 'till it drops into the Jaws of the Animal, which it knew gazed at it for no other Reason but to ruin it. I did not believe this Piece of Philosophy 'till that Night I was just now speaking of; but I then saw the same Thing pass between an Ogler and a Coquet. *Mirtillo,* the most learned of the former, had for some Time discontinued to visit *Flavia,* no less eminent among the latter. They industriously avoided all Places where they might probably meet, but Chance brought them together to the Playhouse, and seated them in a direct Line over-against each other, she in a Front Box, he in the Pit next the Stage. As soon as *Flavia* had received the Looks of the whole Crowd below her with that Air of Insensibility, which is necessary at the first Entrance, she began to look round her, and saw the Vagabond *Mirtillo,* who had so long absented himself from her Circle; and when she first discover'd him, she looked upon him with that Glance, which, in the Language of Oglers, is call'd the *Scornful,* but immediately turned her Observation another Way, and returned upon him with the *Indifferent.* This gave *Mirtillo* no small Resentment; but he used her accordingly. He took Care to be ready for her next Glance. She found his Eyes full in the Indolent, with his Lips crumpled up in the Posture of one Whistling. Her Anger at this Usage immediately appeared in every Muscle of her Face; and after many Emotions, which glisten'd in

her Eyes, she cast them round the whole House, and gave 'em Softnesses in the Face of every Man she had ever seen before. After she thought she had reduced all she saw to her Obedience, the Play began and ended their Dialogue. As soon as the first Act was over, she stood up, with a Visage full of dissembled Alacrity and Pleasure, with which she overlooked the Audience, and at last came to him. He was then placed in a Side-way with his Hat slouching over his Eyes, and gazing at a Wench in the Side-Box, as talking of that Gipsie to the Gentleman who sat by him. But as she was fixed upon him, he turned suddenly with a full Face upon her, and with all the Respect imaginable, made her the most obsequious Bow in the Presence of the whole Theatre. This gave her a Pleasure not to be concealed, and she made him the Recovering or Second Courtesie, with a Smile that spoke a perfect Reconciliation. Between the ensuing Acts, they talk'd to each other with Gestures and Glances so significant, that they ridiculed the whole House in this silent Speech, and made an Appointment that *Mirtillo* should lead her to her Coach.

The peculiar Language of one Eye, as it differs from another, as much as the Tone of one Voice from another, and the Fascination or Enchantment which is lodged in the Optick Nerves of the Persons concerned in these Dialogues, is, I must confess, too nice a Subject for one who is not an Adept in these Speculations: But I shall, for the Good and Safety of the Fair Sex, call my learned Friend Sir *William Read*[36] to my Assistance, and, by the Help of his Observations on this Organ, acquaint them when the Eye is to be believed, and when distrusted. On the contrary, I shall conceal the true Meaning of the Looks of Ladies, and indulge in them all the Art they can acquire in the Management of their Glances: All which is but too little against Creatures who triumph in Falshood, and begin to forswear with their Eyes, when their Tongues can be no longer believed.

---

[35] i.e., hypnotic trance.   [36] Queen Anne's oculist.

A very clean well-behav'd young Gentleman, who is in a very good Way in Cornhill, has writ to me the following Lines, and seems in some Passages of his Letter (which I omit) to lay it very much to Heart, that I have not spoken of a supernatural Beauty whom he sighs for, and complains to in most elaborate Language. Alas! What can a Monitor do? All Mankind live in Romance.

Royal-Exchange, Mar. 11.
Mr. *Bickerstaff*.
Some Time since you were pleased to mention the Beauties in the *New-Exchange* and *Westminster-Hall*, and in my Judgment were not very impartial; for if you were pleased to allow there was one Goddess in the *New-Exchange*, and Two Shepherdesses in *Westminster-Hall*, you very well might say, there was and is at present one Angel in the *Royal-Exchange*: And I humbly beg the Favour of you to let Justice be done her, by inserting this in your next *Tatler*; which will make her my good Angel, and me your most humble Servant,

A. B.

No. 148 [OF AFFECTATIONS IN FOOD]

. . . Gustus Elementa per omnia quaerunt,
Nunquam Animo Pretiis obstantibus . . .[37]
JUV.

FROM SATURD. MAR. 18. TO TUESD. MAR. 21. 1709.

From my own Apartment, March 20.

Having intimated in my last Paper, that I design to take under my Inspection the Diet of this great City, I shall begin with a very earnest and serious Exhortation to all my well-disposed Readers, that they would return to the Food of their Forefathers, and reconcile themselves to Beef and Mutton. This was the Diet which bred that hardy Race of Mortals who won the Fields of *Cressy* and *Agincourt*.[38] I need not go up so high as the History of *Guy* Earl of *Warwick*, who is well known to have eaten up a Dun Cow of his own killing.[39] The Renowned King *Arthur* is generally looked upon as the first who ever sat down to a whole roasted Ox (which was certainly the best Way to preserve the Gravy); and it is further added, that he and his Knights sat about it at his Round Table, and usually consumed it to the very Bones before they would enter upon any Debate of Moment. The Black Prince was a professed Lover of the Brisket; not to mention the History of the Sirloin, or the Institution of the Order of Beef-Eaters, which are all so many evident and undeniable Marks of the great Respect which our Warlike Predecessors have paid to this excellent Food. The Tables of the ancient Gentry of this Nation were covered thrice a Day with hot Roast-Beef; and I am credibly informed by an Antiquary who has searched the Registers in which the Bills of Fare of the Court are recorded, that instead of Tea and Bread and Butter, which have prevailed of late Years, the Maids of Honour in Queen *Elizabeth's* Time were allowed Three Rumps of Beef for their Breakfast. Mutton has likewise been in great Repute among our valiant Countrymen, but was formerly observed to be the Food rather of Men of nice and delicate Appetites, than those of strong and robust Constitutions. For which Reason, even to this Day, we use the Word Sheep-Biter[40] as a Term of Reproach, as we do Beef-Eater in a respectful and honourable Sense. As for

---

[37] They ransack every element for choice
Of every fish and fowl, at any price.
(Juvenal, *Satires*, XI, 14–15, tr. Congreve.)
[38] Two English victories (1346 and 1415) over the French in the Hundred Years' War.
[39] Cf. Samuel Butler's *Hudibras*, I, ii, 305–306.
[40] "a petty thief" (Johnson's *Dictionary*).

the Flesh of Lamb, Veal, Chicken, and other Animals under Age, they were the Invention of sickly and degenerate Palates, according to that wholesome Remark of *Daniel*[41] the Historian, who takes Notice, That in all Taxes upon Provisions, during the Reigns of several of our Kings, there is nothing mentioned besides the Flesh of such Fowl and Cattle as were arrived at their full Growth, and were mature for Slaughter. The Common People of this Kingdom do still keep up the Tast[e] of their Ancestors; and it is to this that we in a great Measure owe the unparallel'd Victories that have been gained in this Reign: for I would desire my Reader to consider, what Work our Countrymen would have made at *Blenheim* and *Ramillies*,[42] if they had been fed with Fricacies and Ragousts.

For this Reason we at present see the florid Complexion, the strong Limb, and the hale Constitution, are to be found chiefly among the meaner Sort of People, or in the wild Gentry, who have been educated among the Woods or Mountains: Whereas many great Families are insensibly fallen off from the Athletick Constitution of their Progenitors, and are dwindled away into a pale, sickly, Spindle-legged, Generation of Valetudinarians.

I may perhaps be thought extravagant in my Notion; but I must confess, I am apt to impute the Dishonours that sometimes happen in great Families to the inflaming kind of Diet which is so much in Fashion. Many Dishes can excite Desire without giving Strength, and heat the Body without nourishing it: As Physicians observe, That the poorest and most dispirited Blood is most subject to Fevers. I look upon a *French* Ragoust to be as pernicious to the Stomach as a Glass of Spirits; and when I have seen a young Lady swallow all the Instigations[43] of high Soups, seasoned Sauces, and forced Meats, I have wondered at the Despair or tedious Sighing of her Lovers.

The Rules among these false Delicates, are to be as Contradictory as they can be to Nature.

Without expecting the Return of Hunger, they eat for an Appetite, and prepare Dishes not to allay, but to excite it.

They admit of nothing at their Tables in its natural Form, or without some Disguise.

They are to eat every Thing before it comes in Season, and to leave it off as soon as it is good to be eaten.

They are not to approve any Thing that is agreeable to ordinary Palates; and nothing is to gratify their Senses, but what would offend those of their Inferiors.

I remember I was last Summer invited to a Friend's House, who is a great Admirer of the *French* Cookery, and (as the Phrase is) *eats well*. At our sitting down, I found the Table covered with a great Variety of unknown Dishes. I was mightily at a Loss to learn what they were, and therefore did not know where to help my self. That which stood before me I took to be a roasted Porcupine, however did not care for asking Questions; and have since been informed, that it was only a larded Turkey. I afterwards passed my Eye over several Hashes, which I do not know the Names of to this Day; and hearing that they were Delicacies, did not think fit to meddle with them.

Among other Dainties, I saw something like a Pheasant, and therefore desired to be helped to a Wing of it; but to my great Surprize, my Friend told me it was a Rabbet, which is a Sort of Meat I never cared for. At last I discovered, with some Joy, a Pig at the lower End of the Table, and begged a Gentleman that was near it to cut me a Piece of it. Upon which the Gentleman of the House said, with great Civility, I am sure you will like the Pig, for it was whipped to Death. I must confess, I heard him with Horror, and could not eat of an Animal that had died so

---

41 Samuel Daniel (1562–1619), poet and author of a history of England.
42 Two English victories (1704 and 1706) over the French in the War of the Spanish Succession.
43 allurements.

Tragical a Death. I was now in great Hunger and Confusion, when, me-thought, I smelled the agreeable Savour of Roast-Beef, but could not tell from which Dish it arose, though I did not question but it lay disguised in one of them. Upon turning my Head, I saw a noble Sirloin on the Side-Table smoking in the most delicious Manner. I had Recourse to it more than once, and could not see, without some Indignation, that substantial *English* Dish banished in so ignominious a Manner, to make Way for *French* Kickshaws.

The Desert was brought up at last, which in Truth was as extraordinary as any Thing that had come before it. The whole, when ranged in its proper Order, looked like a very beautiful Winter-Piece. There were several Pyramids of Candy'd Sweetmeats, that hung like Icicles, with Fruits scattered up and down, and hid in an artificial Kind of Frost. At the same Time there were great Quantities of Cream beaten up into a Snow, and near them little Plates of Sugar-Plumbs, disposed like so many Heaps of Hail-stones, with a Multitude of Congelations in Jellies of various Colours. I was indeed so pleased with the several Objects which lay before me, that I did not care for displacing any of them, and was half angry with the rest of the Company, that for the Sake of a Piece of Lemon-Peel, or a Sugar-Plumb, would spoil so pleasing a Picture. In-deed, I could not but smile to see several of them cooling their Mouths with Lumps of Ice, which they had just before been burning with Salts and Peppers.

As soon as this Show was over I took my Leave, that I might finish my Dinner at my own House: For as I in every Thing love what is simple and natural, so particularly in my Food; Two plain Dishes, with Two or Three good-natured, chearful, ingenious Friends, would make me more pleased and vain, than all that Pomp and Luxury can bestow. For it is my Maxim, That he keeps the greatest Table, who has the most valuable Company at it.

No. 218 [OF TULIPOMANIA]

Scriptorum Chorus omnis amat Nemus & fugit Urbes.[44]

HOR.

FROM TUESD. AUG. 29. TO THURSD. AUG. 31. 1710.

From my own Apartment, Aug. 30.

I Chanced to rise very early one particular Morning this Summer, and took a Walk into the Country to divert my self among the Fields and Meadows, while the Green was new, and the Flowers in their Bloom. As at this Season of the Year every Lane is a beautiful Walk, and every Hedge full of Nose-gays, I lost my self with a great deal of Pleasure among several Thickets and Bushes that were filled with a great Variety of Birds, and an agreeable Con-fusion of Notes, which form'd the pleasantest Scene in the World to one who had pass'd a whole Winter in Noise and Smoak. The Freshness of the Dews that lay upon every Thing about me, with the cool Breath of the Morning, which inspired the Birds with so many delightful Instincts, created in me the same Kind of animal Pleasure, and made my Heart overflow with such secret Emotions of Joy and Satisfaction as are not to be described or accounted for. On this Occasion I could not but reflect upon a beautiful Simile in *Milton*:[45]

As one who long in populous City pent,
Where Houses thick, and Sewers, annoy the Air,

[44] The tribe of writers to a man, admire The peaceful grove, and from the town retire.

(Horace, *Epistles*, II, ii, 77, tr. Francis.)
[45] *Paradise Lost*, IX, 445–451.

*Forth issuing on a Summer's Morn, to
    breath
Among the pleasant Villages, and Farms
Adjoin'd, from each Thing met conceives
    Delight:
The Smell of Grain, or tedded Grass, or
    Kine,
Or Dairy, each rural Sight, each rural
    Sound.*

Those who are conversant in the Writings of polite Authors, receive an additional Entertainment from the Country, as it revives in their Memories those charming Descriptions with which such Authors do frequently abound.

I was thinking of the foregoing beautiful Simile in *Milton,* and applying it to my self, when I observ'd to the Windward of me a black Cloud falling to the Earth in long Trails of Rain, which made me betake my self for Shelter to a House which I saw at a little Distance from the Place where I was walking. As I sat in the Porch, I heard the Voices of Two or Three Persons, who seem'd very earnest in Discourse. My Curiosity was raised when I heard the Names of *Alexander the Great* and *Artaxerxes;* and as their Talk seem'd to run on ancient Heroes, I concluded there could not be any Secret in it; for which Reason I thought I might very fairly listen to what they said.

After several Parallels between great Men, which appeared to me altogether groundless and chimerical, I was surprized to hear one say, That he valued the *Black Prince* more than the Duke of *Vendosme.*[46] How the Duke of *Vendosme* should become a Rival of the *Black Prince's,* I could not conceive: And was more startled when I heard a Second affirm with great Vehemence, That if the Emperor of *Germany* was not going off, he should like him better than either of them. He added, That though the Season was so changeable, the Duke of *Marlborough* was in blooming Beauty. I was wondering to my self from whence they had receiv'd this odd Intelligence, especially when I heard them mention the Names of several other great Generals, as the Prince of *Hesse,* and the King of *Sweden,* who, they said, were both running away. To which they added, what I entirely agreed with them in, That the Crown of *France* was very weak, but that the Mareschal *Villars* still kept his Colours. At last one of them told the Company, If they would go along with him, he would show them a Chimney-Sweeper and a Painted Lady in the same Bed, which he was sure would very much please them. The Shower which had driven them, as well as my self, into the House, was now over: And as they were passing by me into the Garden, I asked them to let me be one of their Company.

The Gentleman of the House told me, if I delighted in Flowers, it would be worth my while, for that he believed he could show me such a Blow of Tulips as was not to be matched in the whole Country.

I accepted the Offer, and immediately found that they had been talking in Terms of Gardening, and that the Kings and Generals they had mention'd were only so many Tulips, to which the Gardiners, according to their usual Custom, had given such high Titles and Appellations of Honour.

I was very much pleas'd and astonish'd at the glorious Show of these gay Vegetables, that arose in great Profusion on all the Banks about us. Sometimes I consider'd them with the Eye of an ordinary Spectator as so many beautiful Objects, varnish'd over with a natural Gloss, and stained with such a Variety of Colours, as are not to be equalled in any artificial Dyes or Tinctures.[47] Sometimes I considered every Leaf as an elaborate Piece of Tissue, in which the Threads and Fibres were woven together into different Configurations, which gave a different Colouring to the Light as it glanced on the several Parts of the Surface. Sometimes I considered the whole Bed of Tulips, according to the Notion

---

[46] These and the following political names need not be specifically identified to appreciate the jest of which they are part.

[47] Isaac Newton's *Opticks* (1704), among other similar publications, had stimulated interest in the nature of color.

of the greatest Mathematician and Philosopher that ever lived, as a Multitude of Optick Instruments, designed for the separating Light into all those various Colours of which it is composed.

I was awakened out of these my Philosophical Speculations, by observing the Company often seemed to laugh at me. I accidentally praised a Tulip as one of the finest that I ever saw; upon which they told me, 'twas a common Fool's-Coat. Upon that I praised a Second, which it seems was but another Kind of Fool's-Coat. I had the same Fate with Two or Three more; for which Reason I desired the Owner of the Garden to let me know which were the finest of the Flowers, for that I was so unskilful in the Art, that I thought the most beautiful were the most valuable, and that those which had the gayest Colours were the most beautiful. The Gentleman smiled at my Ignorance: He seemed a very plain honest Man, and a Person of good Sense, had not his Head been touched with that Distemper which *Hippocrates* calls the *Tulippo-Mania,* Τυλιππομανία;[48] insomuch that he would talk very rationally on any Subject in the World but a Tulip.

He told me, That he valued the Bed of Flowers which lay before us, and was not above Twenty Yards in Length, and Two in Breadth, more than he would the best Hundred Acres of Land in *England;* and added, That it would have been worth twice the Money it is, if a foolish Cook-Maid of his had not almost ruined him the last Winter, by mistaking an Handful of Tulip-Roots for an Heap of Onions, and by that Means (says he) made me a Dish of Porridge, that cost me above 1000*l.* Sterling. He then showed me what he thought the finest of his Tulips, which I found received all their Value from their Rarity and Oddness, and put me in Mind of your great Fortunes, which are not always the greatest Beauties.

I have often looked upon it as a Piece of Happiness, that I have never fallen into any of these fantastical Tast[e]s, nor esteemed any Thing the more for its being uncommon and hard to be met with. For this Reason, I look upon the whole Country in Spring-time as a spacious Garden, and make as many Visits to a Spot of Daizies, or a Bank of Violets, as a Florist does to his Borders and Parterres. There is not a Bush in Blossom within a Mile of me which I am not acquainted with, nor scarce a Daffodil or Cowslip that withers away in my Neighbourhood without my missing it. I walked Home in this Temper of Mind through several Fields and Meadows with an unspeakable Pleasure, not without reflecting on the Bounty of Providence, which has made the most pleasing and most beautiful Objects the most ordinary and most common.

No. 229   [OF A FRY OF LITTLE AUTHORS]

Quaesitam Meritis sume Superbiam.[49]
HOR.

FROM SATURD. SEPT. 23. TO TUESD. SEPT. 26. 1710.

From my own Apartment, Sept. 25.

The whole Creation preys upon it self: Every living Creature is inhabited. A Flea has a Thousand invisible Insects that teaze him as he jumps from Place to Place, and revenge our Quarrels upon him. A very ordinary Microscope shows us, that a Louse is it self a very lousy Creature. A Whale, besides those Seas and Oceans in the several Vessels of his Body, which are filled with innumerable Shoals of little Animals, carries about it a whole World of Inhabitants; insomuch

---

[48] The attribution of these remarks to the father of medicine is of course purely imaginary; similarly the setting of the name in Greek characters is but part of the sport, as it is not a Greek word.

[49] With conscious pride . . .
    Assume the honours justly thine.
(Horace, *Odes,* III, xxx, 14, tr. Francis.)

that, if we believe the Calculations some have made, there are more living Creatures which are too small for the naked Eye to behold about the Leviathan,[50] than there are of visible Creatures upon the Face of the whole Earth. Thus every nobler Creature is as it were the Basis and Support of Multitudes that are his Inferiors.

This Consideration very much comforts me, when I think on those numberless Vermin that feed upon this Paper, and find their Sustenance out of it; I mean, the small Wits and Scribblers that every Day turn a Penny by nibbling at my Lucubrations. This has been so advantageous to this little Species of Writers, that, if they do me Justice, I may expect to have my Statue erected in *Grub-street,* as being a common Benefactor to that Quarter.

They say, when a Fox is very much troubled with Fleas, he goes into the next Pool with a little Lock of Wool in his Mouth, and keeps his Body under Water till the Vermin get into it, after which he quits the Wool, and diving, leaves his Tormentors to shift for themselves, and get their Livelihood where they can. I would have these Gentlemen take Care that I do not serve them after the same Manner; for though I have hitherto kept my Temper pretty well, it is not impossible but I may some Time or other disappear; and what will then become of them? Should I lay down my Paper, What a Famine would there be among the Hawkers, Printers, Booksellers and Authors? It would be like Dr. B——s's[51] dropping his Cloak, with the whole Congregation hanging upon the Skirts of it. To enumerate some of these my doughty Antagonists, I was threatened to be answered Weekly *Tit* for *Tat:*[52] I was undermined by the *Whisperer,*[53] haunted by *Tom Brown's Ghost,*[54] scolded at by a *Female Tatler,*[55] and slandered by another of the same

Character, under the Title of *Atalantis.*[56] I have been *annotated, retattled, examined,* and *condoled:* But it being my standing Maxim, Never to speak ill of the Dead; I shall let these Authors rest in Peace, and take great Pleasure in thinking that I have sometimes been the Means of their getting a Belly-full. When I see my self thus surrounded by such formidable Enemies, I often think of the Knight of the *Red Cross* in *Spencer's Den of Error,*[57] who after he has cut off the Dragon's Head, and left it wallowing in a Flood of Ink, sees a Thousand monstrous Reptiles making their Attemps upon him, one with many Heads, another with none, and all of them without Eyes.

The same so sore annoyed has the Knight,
That well nigh choaked with the deadly Stink,
His Forces fail, ne can no longer fight;
Whose Courage when the Fiend perceived to shrink,
She poured forth out of her Hellish Sink
Her fruitful cursed Spawn of Serpents small,
Deformed Monsters, foul, and black as Ink;
Which swarming all about his Legs did crawl,
And him encombred sore, but could not hurt at all.

As gentle Shepherd in sweet Even-tide,
When ruddy Phœbus *gins to welk in West,*
High on an Hill, his Flock to viewen wide,
Marks which do bite their hasty Supper best;
A Cloud of combrous Gnats do him molest,
All striving to infix their feeble Stings,

---

[50] whale.
[51] Daniel Burgess (1645–1713), a dissenting minister.
[52] *Titt for Tatt,* a short-lived periodical, March 2–11, 1710.
[53] Apparently only one number was published, that of October 11, 1709.
[54] There are no copies of this extant.
[55] This ran to 115 numbers, July 8, 1709–March 29, 1710.
[56] There are no copies of this extant.
[57] *The Faerie Queene,* I, i, 13.

That from their Noyance he no where
  can rest;
But with his clownish Hands their
  tender Wings
He brusheth oft, and oft doth mar their
  Murmurings.

If ever I should want such a Fry of little Authors to attend me, I shall think my Paper in a very decaying Condition. They are like Ivy about an Oak, which adorns the Tree at the same Time that it eats into it; or like a great Man's Equipage, that do Honour to the Person on whom they feed. For my Part, when I see my self thus attacked, I do not consider my Antagonists as malicious, but hungry, and therefore am resolved never to take any Notice of them.

As for those who detract from my Labours without being prompted to it by an empty Stomach, in Return to their Censures I shall take Pains to excel, and never fail to perswade my self, that their Enmity is nothing but their Envy or Ignorance.

Give me Leave to conclude, like an old Man and a Moralist, with a Fable: The Owls, Bats, and several other Birds of Night, were one Day got together in a thick Shade, where they abused their Neighbours in a very sociable Manner. Their Satyr at last fell upon the Sun, whom they all agreed to be very troublesome, impertinent, and inquisitive. Upon which the Sun, who overheard them, spoke to them after this Manner: Gentlemen, I wonder how you dare abuse one that you know could in an Instant scorch you up, and burn every Mother's Son of you: But the only Answer I shall give you, or the Revenge I shall take of you, is, to *shine on*.

No. 271 [CONCLUSIVE]

FROM SATURDAY DEC. 30 TO TUESDAY
JAN. 2. 1710.

The Printer having informed me, that there are as many of these Papers printed as will make Four Volumes, I am now come to the End of my Ambition in this Matter, and have nothing further to say to the World under the Character of *Isaac Bickerstaff*. This Work has indeed for some Time been disagreeable to me, and the Purpose of it wholly lost by my being so long understood as the Author. I never designed in it to give any Man any secret Wound by my Concealment, but spoke in the Character of an old Man, a Philosopher, an Humorist, an Astrologer, and a Censor, to allure my Reader with the Variety of my Subjects, and insinuate, if I could, the Weight of Reason with the Agreeableness of Wit. The general Purpose of the whole has been to recommend Truth, Innocence, Honour, and Virtue, as the chief Ornaments of Life; but I considered, that Severity of Manners was absolutely necessary to him who would censure others,

and for that Reason, and that only, chose to talk in a Mask. I shall not carry my Humility so far as to call my self a vicious Man; but at the same Time must confess, my Life is at best but pardonable. And with no greater Character than this, a Man would make but an indifferent Progress in attacking prevailing and fashionable Vices, which Mr. *Bickerstaff* has done with a Freedom of Spirit that would have lost both its Beauty and Efficacy, had it been pretended to be Mr. *Steele*.

As to the Work it self, the Acceptance it has met with is the best Proof of its Value; but I should err against that Candour which an honest Man should always carry about him, if I did not own, that the most approved Pieces in it were written by others, and those which have been most excepted against by my self. The Hand that has assisted me in those noble Discourses upon the Immortality of the Soul, the glorious Prospects of another Life, and the most sublime Idea's of Religion and Virtue, is a Person[58] who

---

[58] Joseph Addison.

is too fondly my Friend ever to own them; but I should little deserve to be his, if I usurped the Glory of them. I must acknowledge at the same Time, that I think the finest Strokes of Wit and Humour in all Mr. *Bickerstaff's* Lucubrations are those for which he is also beholden to him.

As for the Satyrical Parts of these Writings, those against the Gentlemen who profess Gaming are the most licentious; but the main of them I take to come from losing Gamesters, as Invectives against the Fortunate; for in very many of them, I was very little else but the Transcriber. If any have been more particularly marked at, such Persons may impute it to their own Behaviour, (before they were touched upon) in publickly speaking their Resentment against the Author, and professing they would support any Man who should insult him. When I mention this Subject, I hope Major-General *Davenport,* Brigadier *Bisset,* and my Lord *Forbes,*[59] will accept of my Thanks for their frequent good Offices, in professing their Readiness to partake any Danger that should befal me in so just an Undertaking, as the Endeavour to banish Fraud and Couzenage from the Presence and Conversation of Gentlemen.

But what I find is the least excusable Part of all this Work, is, That I have, in some Places in it, touched upon Matters which concern both the Church and State. All I shall say for this is, That the Points I alluded to are such as concerned every Christian and Free-holder in *England;* and I could not be cold enough to conceal my Opinion on Subjects which related to either of those Characters. But Politicks apart. I must

confess, it has been a most exquisite Pleasure to me to frame Characters of Domestick Life, and put those Parts of it which are least observed into an agreeable View; to enquire into the Seeds of Vanity and Affectation, to lay before my Readers the Emptiness of Ambition: In a Word, to trace Humane Life through all its Mazes and Recesses, and show much shorter Methods than Men ordinarily practise, to be happy, agreeable, and great.

But to enquire into Men's Faults and Weaknesses has something in it so unwelcome, that I have often seen People in Pain to act before me, whose Modesty only make them think themselves liable to Censure. This, and a Thousand other nameless Things, have made it an irksome Task to me to personate Mr. *Bickerstaff* any longer; and I believe it does not often happen, that the Reader is delighted where the Author is displeased.

All I can now do for the further Gratification of the Town, is to give them a faithful Index and Explication of Passages and Allusions, and sometimes of Persons intended in the several scattered Parts of the Work. At the same Time, the succeeding Volumes shall discover which of the whole have been written by me, and which by others, and by whom, as far as I am able, or permitted.

Thus I have voluntarily done what I think all Authors should do when call'd upon. I have published my Name to my Writings, and given my self up to the Mercy of the Town (as *Shakespear* expresses it) with all my Imperfections on my Head. The indulgent Readers

Most Obliged,
Most Obedient
Humble Servant,
Richard Steele.

[59] These three men are military acquaintances of Steele.

THE SPECTATOR

No. 2   [ABOUT OUR COMPANY]

> . . . *Ast Alii sex*
> *Et plures uno conclamant ore.*[60]
> JUV.

FRIDAY, MARCH 2. 1711.

The first of our Society is a Gentleman of *Worcestershire,* of antient Descent, a Baronet, his Name Sir ROGER DE COVERLY. His great Grandfather was Inventor of that famous Country-Dance which is call'd after him. All who know that Shire, are very well acquainted with the Parts and Merits of Sir ROGER. He is a Gentleman that is very singular in his Behaviour, but his Singularities proceed from his good Sense, and are Contradictions to the Manners of the World, only as he thinks the World is in the wrong. However, this Humour creates him no Enemies, for he does nothing with Sowrness or Obstinacy; and his being unconfined to Modes and Forms, makes him but the readier and more capable to please and oblige all who know him. When he is in Town he lives in *Soho-Square:* It is said he keeps himself a Batchelour by reason he was crossed in Love, by a perverse beautiful Widow of the next County to him. Before this Disappointment, Sir ROGER was what you call a fine Gentleman, had often supped with my Lord *Rochester*[61] and Sir *George Etherege,*[62] fought a Duel upon his first coming to Town, and kick'd Bully *Dawson*[63] in a publick Coffee-house for calling him Youngster. But being ill used by the abovementioned Widow, he was very serious for a Year and a half; and tho' his Temper being naturally jovial, he at last got over it, he grew careless of himself and never dressed afterwards; he continues to wear a Coat and Doublet of the same Cut that were in Fashion at the Time of his Repulse, which, in his merry Humours, he tells us, has been in and out twelve Times since he first wore it. 'Tis said Sir ROGER grew humble in his Desires after he had forgot this cruel Beauty, insomuch that it is reported he has frequently offended in Point of Chastity with Beggars and Gypsies: But this is look'd upon by his Friends rather as Matter of Raillery than Truth. He is now in his Fifty sixth Year, cheerful, gay, and hearty, keeps a good House both in Town and Country; a great Lover of Mankind; but there is such a mirthful Cast in his Behaviour, that he is rather beloved than esteemed: His Tenants grow rich, his Servants look satisfied, all the young Women profess Love to him, and the young Men are glad of his Company: When he comes into a House he calls the Servants by their Names, and talks all the way up Stairs to a Visit. I must not omit that Sir ROGER is a Justice of the *Quorum;*[64] that he fills the Chair at a Quarter-Session with great Abilities, and three Months ago gain'd universal Applause by explaining a Passage in the Game-Act.

The Gentleman next in Esteem and Authority among us, is another Batchelour, who is a Member of the *Inner-*

Text from the original editions in folio half-sheets.

[60] "Six, or more if you please, speak out as in one voice" (Juvenal, *Satires*, VII, 167–168).

[61] John Wilmot, Earl of Rochester (1647–1680), fashionable and rakish author and patron of literature in the Restoration.

[62] Sir George Etherege (1635?–?1691), wit and dramatist, friend of Rochester, known as "Gentle George."

[63] A swaggering sharper of Whitefriars.

[64] "*a justice of the peace* and *quorum* is one without whom the rest of the justices cannot act in some cases" (Bailey's *Dictionary*).

Temple;[65] a Man of great Probity, Wit, and Understanding; but he has chosen his Place of Residence rather to obey the Direction of an old humoursome Father than in Pursuit of his own Inclinations. He was plac'd there to study the Laws of the Land, and is the most learned of any of the House in those of the Stage. *Aristotle* and *Longinus* are much better understood by him than *Littleton* or *Cooke*.[66] The Father sends up every Post Questions relating to Marriage-Articles, Leases, and Tenures, in the Neighbourhood; all which Questions he agrees with an Attorney to answer and take care of in the Lump: He is studying the Passions themselves, when he should be inquiring into the Debates among Men which arise from them. He knows the Argument of each of the Orations of *Demosthenes* and *Tully,* but not one Case in the Reports of our own Courts. No one ever took him for a Fool, but none, except his intimate Friends, know he has a great deal of Wit. This Turn makes him at once both disinterested and agreeable: As few of his Thoughts are drawn from Business, they are most of them fit for Conversation. His Taste of Books is a little too just for the Age he lives in; he has read all, but approves of very few. His Familiarity with the Customs, Manners, Actions, and Writings of the Antients, makes him a very delicate Observer of what occurs to him in the present World. He is an excellent Critick, and the Time of the Play, is his Hour of Business; exactly at five he passes through *New-Inn,* crosses through *Russel-Court,* and takes a Turn at *Will's* till the Play begins; he has his Shooes rubb'd and his Perriwig powder'd at the Barber's as you go into the *Rose.*[67] It is for the Good of the Audience when he is at a Play, for the Actors have an Ambition to please him.

The Person of next Consideration is Sir ANDREW FREEPORT, a Merchant of great Eminence in the City of *London:*

A Person of indefatigable Industry, strong Reason, and great Experience. His Notions of Trade are noble and generous, and (as every rich Man has usually some sly Way of Jesting, which would make no great Figure were he not a rich Man,) he calls the Sea the *British Common.* He is acquainted with Commerce in all its Parts, and will tell you that it is a stupid and barbarous Way to extend Dominion by Arms; for true Power is to be got by Arts and Industry. He will often argue, that if this Part of our Trade were well cultivated, we should gain from one Nation; and if another, from another. I have heard him prove, that Diligence makes more lasting Acquisitions than Valour, and that Sloth has ruin'd more Nations than the Sword. He abounds in several frugal Maxims, among which the greatest Favourite is, 'A Penny saved is a Penny got.' A General Trader of good Sense, is pleasanter Company than a general Scholar; and Sir ANDREW having a natural unaffected Eloquence, the Perspicuity of his Discourse gives the same Pleasure that Wit would in another Man. He has made his Fortunes himself; and says that *England* may be richer than other Kingdoms, by as plain Methods as he himself is richer than other Men; tho' at the same Time I can say this of him, that there is not a Point in the Compass but blows home a Ship in which he is an Owner.

Next to Sir ANDREW in the Club-room sits Captain SENTRY, a Gentleman of great Courage, good Understanding, but invincible Modesty. He is one of those that deserve very well, but are very awkard at putting their Talents within the Observation of such as should take notice of them. He was some Years a Captain, and behaved himself with great Gallantry in several Engagements and at several Sieges; but having a small Estate of his own, and being next Heir to Sir ROGER, he has quitted a Way of Life in which

---

[65] London residence of students of civil law.

[66] Lord Chief Justice Sir Edward Coke (1552–1634) supplemented a treatise on tenures by Sir Thomas Littleton (1402–1481) in a volume entitled *The First Part of the Institutes of the Lawes of England, or a Com-* *mentarie upon Littleton* (1628), which was considered indispensable to the study of English law.

[67] The Rose Tavern adjoined Drury Lane Theatre.

no Man can rise suitably to his Merit, who is not something of a Courtier as well as a Souldier. I have heard him often lament, that in a Profession where Merit is placed in so conspicuous a View, Impudence should get the Better of Modesty. When he has talked to this Purpose I never heard him make a sower Expression, but frankly confess that he left the World because he was not fit for it. A strict Honesty and an even regular Behaviour, are in themselves Obstacles to him that must press through Crowds who endeavour at the same End with himself, the Favour of a Commander. He will however in this Way of Talk excuse Generals for not disposing according to Mens Desert, or enquiring into it: For, says he, that great Man who has a Mind to help me, has as many to break through to come at me, as I have to come at him: Therefore he will conclude, that the Man who would make a Figure, especially in a military Way, must get over all false Modesty, and assist his Patron against the Importunity of other Pretenders by a proper Assurance in his own Vindication. He says it is a civil Cowardice to be backward in asserting what you ought to expect, as it is a military Fear to be slow in attacking when it is your Duty. With this Candour does the Gentleman speak of himself and others. The same Frankness runs through all his Conversation. The military Part of his Life has furnish'd him with many Adventures, in the Relation of which he is very agreeable to the Company; for he is never over-bearing, tho' accustomed to command Men in the utmost Degree below him; nor ever too obsequious, from an Habit of obeying Men highly above him.

But that our Society may not appear a Set of Humourists unacquainted with the Gallantries and Pleasures of the Age, we have among us the gallant WILL. HONEYCOMB, a Gentleman who according to his Years should be in the Decline of his Life, but having ever been very careful of his Person, and always had a very easy Fortune, Time has made but very little Impression, either by Wrinkles on his Forehead, or Traces in his Brain. His Person is well turn'd, of a good Height. He is very ready at that Sort of Discourse with which Men usually entertain Women. He has all his Life dressed very well, and remembers Habits as others do Men. He can smile when one speaks to him, and laughs easily. He knows the History of every Mode, and can inform you from which of the French King's Wenches our Wives and Daughters had this Manner of curling their Hair, that Way of placing their Hoods; whose Frailty was covered by such a Sort of Petticoat, and whose Vanity to shew her Foot made that Part of the Dress so short in such a Year. In a Word, all his Conversation and Knowledge has been in the female World: As other Men of his Age will take Notice to you what such a Minister said upon such and such an Occasion, he will tell you when the Duke of *Monmouth*[68] danced at Court such a Woman was then smitten, another was taken with him at the Head of his Troop in the *Park*. In all these important Relations, he has ever about the same Time received a kind Glance or a Blow of a Fan from some celebrated Beauty, Mother of the present Lord such-a-one. If you speak of a young Commoner that said a lively thing in the House, he starts up, 'He has good Blood in his Veins, *Tom Mirabell*[69] begot him, the Rogue cheated me in that Affair; that young Fellow's Mother used me more like a Dog than any Woman I ever made Advances to.' This Way of Talking of his very much enlivens the Conversation among us of a more sedate Turn; and I find there is not one of the Company but my self, who rarely speak at all, but speaks of him as of that Sort of Man who is usually called a well-bred fine Gentleman. To conclude his Character, where Women are not concerned, he is an honest worthy Man.

I cannot tell whether I am to account him whom I am next to speak of, as one of our Company; for he visits us but seldom, but when he does it adds to every

---

[68] Illegitimate son of Charles II and Lucy Walter.

[69] Dapper hero of Congreve's *The Way of the World* (1700).

Man else a new Enjoyment of himself. He is a Clergyman,[70] a very philosophick Man, of general Learning, great Sanctity of Life, and the most exact good Breeding. He has the Misfortune to be of a very weak Constitution, and consequently cannot accept of such Cares and Business as Preferments in his Function would oblige him to: He is therefore among Divines what a Chamber-Councellor is among Lawyers. The Probity of his Mind, and the Integrity of his Life, create him Followers, as being eloquent or loud advances others. He seldom introduces the Subject he speaks upon; but we are so far gone in Years, that he observes, when he is among us, an Earnestness to have him fall on some divine Topick, which he always treats with much Authority, as one who has no Interests in this World, as one who is hastening to the Object of all his Wishes, and conceives Hope from his Decays and Infirmities. These are my ordinary Companions.

No. 38   [OF SOCIAL AFFECTATION]

. . . Cupias non placuisse nimis.[71]
MART.

FRIDAY, APRIL 13. 1711.

A Late Conversation which I fell into, gave me an Opportunity of observing a great deal of Beauty in a very handsome Woman, and as much Wit in an ingenious Man, turned into Deformity in the one, and Absurdity in the other, by the meer Force of Affectation. The Fair One had something in her Person upon which her Thoughts were fixed, that she attempted to shew to Advantage in every Look, Word, and Gesture. The Gentleman was as diligent to do Justice to his fine Parts,[72] as the Lady to her beauteous Form: You might see his Imagination on the Stretch[73] to find out something uncommon, and what they call bright, to entertain her; while she writhed herself into as many different Postures to engage him. When she laugh'd, her Lips were to sever at a greater Distance than ordinary to shew her Teeth: Her Fan was to point to somewhat at a Distance, that in the Reach she may discover the Roundness of her Arm; then she is utterly mistaken in what she saw, falls back, smiles at her own Folly, and is so wholly discompos'd, that her Tucker is to be adjusted, her Bosom expos'd, and the whole Woman put into new Airs and Graces. While she was doing all this, the Gallant had Time to think of something very pleasant to say next to her, or make some unkind Observation on some other Lady to feed her Vanity. These unhappy Effects of Affectation, naturally led me to look into that strange State of Mind which so generally discolours the Behaviour of most People we meet with.

The learned Dr. *Burnet,* in his Theory of the Earth,[74] takes Occasion to observe, That every Thought is attended with Consciousness and Representativeness; and Mind has nothing presented to it, but what is immediately followed by a Reflection or Conscience, which tells you whether that which was so presented is graceful or unbecoming. This Act of the Mind discovers it self in the Gesture, by a proper Behaviour in those whose Consciousness goes no further than to direct them in the just Progress of their present Thought or Action; but betrays an Interruption in every second Thought, when the Consciousness is em-

---

[70] The clergyman is never named.

[71] "One would not please too much" (Martial, *Epigrams,* VI, xxix, 8).

[72] "qualities; powers; faculties; or accomplishments" (Johnson's **Dictionary).**

[73] "utmost reach of power" (Bailey's *Dictionary*).

[74] Thomas Burnet, *The Sacred Theory of the Earth* (1684–1690).

ploy'd in too fondly approving a Man's own Conceptions; which sort of Consciousness is what we call Affectation.

As the Love of Praise is implanted in our Bosoms as a strong Incentive to worthy Actions, it is a very difficult Task to get above a Desire of it for things that should be wholly indifferent. Women, whose Hearts are fixed upon the Pleasure they have in the Consciousness that they are the Objects of Love and Admiration, are ever changing the Air of their Countenances, and altering the Attitude of their Bodies, to strike the Hearts of their Beholders with new Sense of their Beauty. The dressing Part of our Sex, whose Minds are the same with the sillyer Part of the other, are exactly in the like uneasy Condition to be regarded for a well-tied Cravat, an Hat cocked with an unusual Briskness, a very well-chosen Coat, or other Instances of Merit, which they are impatient to see unobserved.

But this apparent Affectation, arising from an ill govern'd Consciousness, is not so much to be wonder'd at in such loose and trivial Minds as these: But when you see it reign in Characters of Worth and Distinction, it is what you cannot but lament, not without some Indignation. It creeps into the Heart of the wise Man, as well as that of the Coxcomb. When you see a Man of Sense look about for Applause, and discover an itching Inclination to be commended; lay Traps for a little Incense,[75] even from those whose Opinion he values in nothing but his own Favour; Who is safe against this Weakness? or who knows whether he is guilty of it or not? The best Way to get clear of such a light Fondness for Applause, is, to take all possible Care to throw off the Love of it upon Occasions that are in themselves laudable; but, as it appears, we hope for no Praise from them. Of this Nature are all Graces in Mens Persons, Dress, and bodily Deportment; which will naturally be winning and attractive if we think not of them, but lose their Force in proportion to our Endeavour to make them such. When our Consciousness turns upon

the main Design of Life, and our Thoughts are employ'd upon the chief Purpose either in Business or Pleasure; we shall never betray an Affectation, for we cannot be guilty of it: But when we give the Passion for Praise an unbridled Liberty; our Pleasure in little Perfections, robs us of what is due to us for great Virtues and worthy Qualities. How many excellent Speeches and honest Actions are lost, for want of being indifferent where we ought? Men are oppress'd with regard to their Way of speaking and acting; instead of having their Thought bent upon what they shou'd do or say, and by that Means bury a Capacity for great things, by their fear of failing in indifferent things. This, perhaps, cannot be call'd Affectation; but it has some Tincture of it, at least so far, as that their Fear of erring in a thing of no Consequence, argues they wou'd be too much pleas'd in performing it.

It is only from a thorough Disregard to himself in such Particulars, that a Man can act with a laudable Sufficiency:[76] His Heart is fix'd upon one Point in view; and he commits no Errours, because he thinks nothing an Errour but what deviates from that Intention.

The wild Havock Affectation makes in that Part of the World which shou'd be most polite, is visible wherever we turn our Eyes: It pushes Men not only into Impertinencies in Conversation, but also in their premeditated Speeches. At the Bar it torments the Bench, whose Business it is to cut off all Superfluities in what is spoken before it by the Practitioner; as well as several little Pieces of Injustice which arise from the Law it self. I have seen it make a Man run from the Purpose before a Judge, who was, when at the Bar himself, so close and logical a Pleader, that with all the Pomp of Eloquence in his Power, he never spoke a Word too much.

It might be born even here, but it often ascends the Pulpit it self; and the Declaimer, in that sacred Place, is frequently so impertinently witty, speaks of

---

[75] A metaphor for *flattery*.

[76] pride.

the last Day it self with so many quaint Phrases, that there is no Man who understands Raillery, but must resolve to sin no more: Nay, you may behold him sometimes in Prayer for a proper Delivery of the great Truths he is to utter, humble himself with so very well turn'd phrase, and mention his own Unworthiness in a Way so very becoming, that the Air of the pretty Gentleman is preserv'd, under the Lowliness of the Preacher.

I shall end this with a short Letter I writ the other Day to a very witty Man, over-run with the Fault I am speaking of.

Dear Sir,

I Spent some Time with you the other Day, and must take the Liberty of a Friend to tell you of the unsufferable Affectation you are guilty of in all you say and do. When I gave you an Hint of it,

you ask'd me whether a Man is to be cold to what his Friends think of him? No; but Praise is not to be the Entertainment of every Moment: He that hopes for it must be able to suspend the Possession of it till proper Periods of Life, or Death it self. If you would not rather be commended than be Praiseworthy, contemn little Merits; and allow no Man to be so free with you, as to praise you to your Face. Your Vanity by this Means will want its Food. At the same time your Passion for Esteem will be more fully gratify'd; Men will praise you in their Actions: Where you now receive one Compliment, you will then receive twenty Civilities. Till then you will never have of either, further than
Sir,
Your humble Servant.

No. 49 [OF CONVERSATION]

. . . Hominem pagina nostra sapit.[77]
MART.

THURSDAY, APRIL 26. 1711.

It is very natural for a Man who is not turned for Mirthful Meetings of Men, or Assemblies of the fair Sex, to delight in that sort of Conversation which we find in Coffee-houses. Here a Man, of my Temper, is in his Element; for, if he cannot talk, he can still be more agreeable to his Company, as well as pleased in himself, in being only an Hearer. It is a Secret known but to few, yet of no small use in the Conduct of Life, that when you fall into a Man's Conversation, the first thing you should consider is, whether he has a greater Inclination to hear you, or that you should hear him. The latter is the more general Desire, and I know very able Flatterers that never speak a word in Praise of the Persons from whom they obtain daily Favours, but still practise a skilful Attention to whatever is uttered by those with whom they converse. We are very

Curious to observe the Behaviour of Great Men and their Clients; but the same Passions and Interests move Men in lower Spheres; and I (that have nothing else to do, but make Observations) see in every Parish, Street, Lane, and Alley of this Populous City, a little Potentate that has his Court, and his Flatterers who lay Snares for his Affection and Favour, by the same Arts that are practised upon Men in higher Stations.

In the Place I most usually frequent, Men differ rather in the time of Day in which they make a Figure, than in any real Greatness above one another. I, who am at the Coffee-house at Six in a Morning, know that my Friend *Beaver* the Haberdasher has a Levy of more undissembled Friends and Admirers, than most of the Courtiers or Generals of *Great Britain.* Every Man about him has, perhaps, a News Paper in his Hand, but none can pretend to guess what Step will be taken in any one Court of *Europe,* 'till Mr. *Beaver* has thrown down his Pipe, and declares what Measures the Allies must enter into upon this new Pos-

---

[77] "Men and manners I describe" (Martial, *Epigrams*, X, iv, 10).

ture of Affairs. Our Coffee-house is near one of the Inns of Court, and *Beaver* has the Audience and Admiration of his Neighbours from Six 'till within a Quarter of Eight, at which time he is interrupted by the Students of the House; some of whom are ready Dress'd for *Westminster,* at Eight in a Morning, with Faces as busie as if they were retain'd in every Cause there; and others come in their Night-Gowns[78] to Saunter away their Time, as if they never designed to go thither. I do not know that I meet, in any of my Walks, Objects which move both my Spleen and Laughter so effectually, as those Young Fellows at the *Grecian, Squire's, Searle's,* and all other Coffee-houses adjacent to the Law, who rise early for no other purpose but to publish their Laziness. One would think these young *Virtuoso's*[79] take a gay Cap and Slippers, with a Scarf and Party-colour'd Gown, to be Ensigns[80] of Dignity; for the vain Things approach each other with an Air, which shows they regard one another for their Vestments. I have observed, that the Superiority among these proceeds from an Opinion of Gallantry and Fashion: The Gentleman in the Strawberry Sash, who presides so much over the rest, has, it seems, subscribed to every Opera this last Winter, and is supposed to receive Favours from one of the Actresses.

When the Day grows too busie for these Gentlemen to enjoy any longer the Pleasures of their *Deshabilé,* with any manner of Confidence, they give Place to Men who have Business or good Sense in their Faces, and come to the Coffee-house either to transact Affairs or enjoy Conversation. The Persons to whose Behaviour and Discourse I have most regard, are such as are between these two sorts of Men: Such as have not Spirits too Active to be happy and well pleased in a private Condition, nor Complexions too warm to make them neglect the Duties and Relations of Life. Of these sort of Men consist the worthier Part of Mankind; of these are all good Fathers, gen-

erous Brothers, sincere Friends, and faithful Subjects. Their Entertainments are derived rather from Reason than Imagination; Which is the Cause that there is no Impatience or Instability in their Speech or Action. You see in their Countenances they are at home, and in quiet Possession of the present Instant, as it passes, without desiring to Quicken it by gratifying any Passion, or prosecuting any new Design. These are the Men formed for Society, and those little Communities which we express by the Word *Neighbourhoods.*

The Coffee-house is the Place of Rendezvous to all that live near it, who are thus turned to relish calm and ordinary Life. *Eubulus*[81] presides over the middle Hours of the Day, when this Assembly of Men meet together. He enjoys a great Fortune handsomely, without launching into Expence, and exerts many noble and useful Qualities, without appearing in any publick Employment. His Wisdom and Knowledge are serviceable to all that think fit to make use of them; and he does the Office of a Council, a Judge, an Executor, and a Friend to all his Acquaintance, not only without the Profits which attend such Offices, but also without the Deference and Homage which are usually paid to them. The giving of Thanks is displeasing to him. The greatest Gratitude you can show him, is to let him see you are the better Man for his Services; and that you are as ready to oblige others, as he is to oblige you.

In the private Exigencies of his Friends he lends, at legal Value, considerable Sums, which he might highly increase by rolling in the Publick Stocks. He does not consider in whose Hands his Mony will improve most, but where it will do most Good.

Eubuls has so great an Authority in his little Diurnal[82] Audience, that when he shakes his Head at any Piece of publick News, they all of them appear dejected; and, on the contrary, go home to their Dinners with a good Stomach and chearful Aspect, when *Eubulus* seems to

---

78 "a loose gown used for an undress" (Johnson's *Dictionary*).
79 dilettantes.
80 signs.
81 the name signifies lucky.
82 daily.

intimate that Things go well. Nay, their Veneration towards him is so great, that when they are in other Company they speak and act after him; are Wise in his Sentences, and are no sooner sat down at their own Tables, but they hope or fear, rejoice or despond as they saw him do at the Coffee-house. In a word, every Man is *Eubulus* as soon as his Back is turn'd.

Having here given an Account of the several Reigns that succeed each other from Day-break 'till Dinner-time, I shall mention the Monarchs of the Afternoon on another occasion, and shut up the whole Series of them with the History of *Tom*[83] the Tyrant; who, as first Minister of the Coffee-house, takes the Government upon him between the Hours of Eleven and Twelve at Night, and gives his Orders in the most Arbitrary manner to the Servants below him, as to the Disposition of Liquors, Coal and Cinders.

No. 143   [OF CHEERFUL RESOLUTION]

Non est vivere sed valere Vita.[84]

MARTIAL.

TUESDAY, AUGUST 14. 1711.

It is an unreasonable thing some Men expect of their Acquaintance. They are ever complaining that they are out of Order, or Displeas'd, or they know not how, and are so far from letting that be a Reason for retiring to their own Homes, that they make it their Argument for coming into Company. What has any body to do with Accounts of a Man's being Indispos'd but his Physician? If a Man laments in Company, where the rest are in Humour enough to enjoy themselves, he should not take it ill if a Servant is order'd to present him with a Porringer of Cawdle[85] or Posset-Drink,[86] by way of Admonition that he go Home to Bed. That part of Life which we ordinarily understand by the Word Conversation, is an Indulgence to the Sociable Part of our Make, and should incline us to bring our proportion of Good Will or good Humour among the Friends we meet with, and not to trouble them with Relations which must of necessity oblige them to a real or feign'd Affliction. Cares, Distresses, Diseases, Uneasinesses and Dislikes of our own, are by no means to be obtruded upon our Friends. If we would consider how little of this Vicissitude of Motion and Rest, which we call Life, is spent with Satisfaction, we should be more tender of our Friends, than to bring them little Sorrows which do not belong to them. There is no real Life, but chearful Life, therefore Valetudinarians should be Sworn, before they enter into Company, not to say a Word of themselves 'till the Meeting breaks up. It is not here pretended, that we should be always fit with Chaplets of Flowers round our Heads, or be crowned with Roses, in order to make our Entertainment agreeable to us; but if (as it is usually observed) they who resolve to be Merry, seldom are so, it will be much more unlikely for us to be well pleased, if they are admitted who are always complaining they are sad. Whatever we do we should keep up the Chearfulness of our Spirits, and never let them sink below an Inclination at least to be well pleased: The Way to this is to keep our Bodies in Exercise, our Minds at Ease. That insipid State, wherein neither are in Vigour, is not to be accounted any part of our Portion of Being. When we are in the Satisfaction of some Innocent Pleasure, or pursuit of

---

[83] Headwaiter at White's Coffee House.

[84] "For life is only, when blest with health" (Martial, *Epigrams,* VI, lxx, 15).

[85] "a drink made of milk, with ale, wine, eggs, sugar, and spice" (Bailey's *Dictionary*); usually spelled *caudle.*

[86] "milk curdled with wine . . ." (Johnson's *Dictionary*).

some laudable Design, we are in the Possession of Life, of Human Life. Fortune will give us Disappointments enough, and Nature is attended with Infirmities enough, without our adding to the unhappy side of our Account by our Spleen or ill Humour. Poor *Cottilus*[87] among so many real Evils, a Chronical Distemper, and a narrow Fortune, is never heard to complain; that equal Spirit of his, which any Man may have, that, like him, will conquer Pride, Vanity and Affectation, and follow Nature, is not to be broken, because it has no Points to contend for: To be anxious for nothing but what Nature demands as necessary, if it is not the way to an Estate, is the way to what Men aim at by getting an Estate. This Temper will preserve Health in the Body, as well as Tranquility in the Mind. *Cottilus* sees the World in an hurry with the same Scorn that a Sober Person sees a Man Drunk. Had he been contented with what he ought to have been, how could, says he, such a one have met with such a Disappointment? If another had valued his Mistress for what he ought to have loved her, he had not been in her Power. If her Virtue had had a part of his Passion, her Levity had been his Cure; she could not then have been false and amiable at the same time.

Since we cannot promise our selves constant Health, let us endeavour at such a Temper as may be our best Support in the Decay of it. *Uranius*[88] has arrived at that Composure of Soul, and wrought himself up to such a neglect of every thing with which the generality of Mankind is enchanted, that nothing but acute Pains can give him Disturbance, and against those too he will tell his intimate Friends he has a Secret which gives him present Ease. *Uranius* is so thoroughly perswaded of another Life, and endeavours so sincerely to secure an Interest in it, that he looks upon Pain but as a quickening of his Pace to an Home, where he shall be better provided for than in his present Apartment. Instead of the melancholy Views which others

are apt to give themselves, he will tell you that he has forgot he is Mortal, nor will he think of himself as such. He thinks at the time of his Birth he entered into an Eternal Being, and the short Article of Death he will not allow an interruption of Life, since that Moment is not of half the Duration as is his ordinary Sleep. Thus is his being one uniform and consistent Series of chearful Diversions and moderate Cares, without fear or hope of Futurity. Health to him is more than Pleasure to another Man, and Sickness less affecting to him, than Indisposition is to others.

I must confess, if one does not regard Life after this manner, none but Ideots can pass it away with any tollerable Patience. Take a Fine Lady who is of a Delicate Frame, and you may observe from the Hour she rises a certain Weariness of all that passes about her. I know more than one who is much too nice to be quite alive. They are sick of such strange frightful People that they meet, one is so awkard and another so disagreeable, that it looks like a Penance to breath the same Air with them. You see this is so very true that a great part of Ceremony and Good-breeding among the Ladies, turns upon their Uneasiness; and I'll undertake, if the How-d'ye Servants[89] of our Women were to make a weekly Bill of Sickness, as the Parish Clerks do of Mortality, you would not find in an Account of seven Days, one in thirty that was not downright Sick or indisposed, or but a very little better than she was, and so forth.

It is certain that to enjoy Life and Health as a constant Feast we should not think Pleasure necessary, but, if possible, to arrive at an Equality of Mind. It is as mean to be overjoy'd upon occasions of Good Fortune, as to be dejected in Circumstances of Distress. Laughter in one Condition is as unmanly as Weeping in the other. We should not form our Minds to expect Transport on every Occasion, but know how to make it Enjoyment to be out of Pain. Ambition, Envy,

---

[87] The name signifies morbid cynicism.
[88] The Muse of Astronomy; the name signifies heavenly or magnanimous qualities.

[89] Messengers sent to inquire about the state of health of one's friends.

vagrant Desire, or impertinent Mirth will take up our Minds, without we can possess our selves in that Sobriety of Heart which is above all Pleasures, and can be felt much better than described: But the ready way, I believe, to the right Enjoyment of Life, is by a Prospect towards another to have but a very mean Opinion of it. A Great Author[90] of our time has set this in an excellent Light, when with a Philosophick Pity of Human Life he spoke of it in his Theory of the Earth in the following manner.

For what is this Life but a Circulation of little mean Actions? We lie down, and rise again; Dress and undress; feed and wax hungry; Work or Play, and are weary; and then we lie down again, and the Circle returns. We spend the Day in Trifles, and when the Night comes we throw our selves into the Bed of Folly, amongst Dreams and broken Thoughts and wild Imaginations. Our Reason lies asleep by us, and we are for the time as arrant Brutes as those that sleep in the Stalls or in the Field. Are not the Capacities of Man higher than these? And ought not his Ambition and Expectations to be greater? Let us be Adventurers for another World: 'Tis at least a fair and noble Chance; and there is nothing in this worth our Thoughts or our Passions. If we should be disappointed we are still no worse than the rest of our Fellow-Mortals; and if we succeed in our Expectations, we are Eternally Happy.

No. 266 [OF PROSTITUTION]

Id vero est quod ego mihi puto palmarium
Me reperisse, quomodo adolescentulus
Meretricum ingenia, & mores possit noscere
Mature ut cum cognorit perpetuo oderat.[91]

                    TER.

FRIDAY, JANUARY 4. 1712.

No Vice or Wickedness, which People fall into from Indulgence to Desire, which are natural to all, ought to place them below the Compassion of the virtuous Part of the World; which indeed often makes me a little apt to suspect the Sincerity of their Virtue, who are too warmly provoked at other Peoples personal Sins. The unlawful Commerce of the Sexes is of all other the hardest to avoid; and yet there is no one which you shall hear the rigider Part of Womankind speak of with so little Mercy. It is very certain that a modest Woman cannot abhor the Breach of Chastity too much; but pray let her hate it for herself, and only pity it in others. WILL. HONEYCOMB calls these over-offended Ladies, the outragiously virtuous.

I do not design to fall upon Failures in general, with relation to the Gift of Chastity, but at present only enter upon that large Field, and begin with the Consideration of poor and publick Whores. The other Evening passing along near *Covent-Garden,* I was jogged on the Elbow as I turned into the Piazza, on the right Hand coming out of *James-street,* by a slim young Girl of about Seventeen, who with a pert Air asked me if I was for a Pint of Wine. I do not know but I should have indulged my Curiosity in having some Chat with her, but that I am informed the Man of the *Bumper*[92]

---

[90] Thomas Burnet (1635?–1715).

[91] "This I conceive to be my masterpiece, that I have discovered how inexperienced youth may detect the artifices of bad women, and by knowing them early, detest them for ever"

(Terence, *The Eunuch,* V, iv, 8–11).

[92] Steele's friend, the actor and noted raconteur Richard Estcourt (1668–1712), had just opened *The Bumper Tavern* in James Street.

knows me; and it would have made a Story for him not very agreeable to some Part of my Writings, though I have in others so frequently said that I am wholly unconcerned in any Scene I am in, but meerly as a Spectator. This Impediment being in my Way, we stood under in one of the Arches by Twilight; and there I could observe as exact Features as I had ever seen, the most agreeable Shape, the finest Neck and Bosom, in a Word, the whole Person of a Woman exquisitly beautiful. She affected to allure me with a forced Wantonness in her Look and Air; but I saw it checked with Hunger and Cold: Her Eyes were wan and eager, her Dress thin and tawdry, her Mein genteel and childish. This strange Figure gave me much Anguish of Heart, and to avoid being seen with her I went away, but could not forbear giving her a Crown. The poor thing sighed, curtisied, and with a Blessing, expressed with the utmost Vehemence, turned from me. This Creature is what they call *newly come upon the Town,* but who, I suppose, falling into cruel Hands, was left in the first Month from her Dishonour, and exposed to pass through the Hands and Discipline of one of those Hags of Hell whom we call Bawds. But least I should grow too suddenly grave on this Subject, and be my self outragiously good, I shall turn to a Scene in one of *Fletcher's* Plays, where this Character is drawn, and the Œconomy of Whoredom most admirably described. The Passage I would point to is in the third Scene of the second Act of the *Humorous Lieutenant. Leucippe,* who is Agent for the King's Lust, and bawds at the same Time for the whole Court, is very pleasantly introduced, reading her Minutes as a Person of Business, with two Maids, her Under-Secretaries, taking Instructions at a Table before her. Her Women, both those under her present Tutelage, and those which she is laying Wait for, are alphabetically set down in her Book; and as she is looking over the Letter *C,* in a muttering Voice, as if between Soliloquy and speaking out, she says,

Her Maiden-head will yield me; let me see now;
She is not Fifteen they say: For her Complexion—
Cloe, Cloe, Cloe, *here I have her,*
Cloe, *the Daughter of a Country Gentleman;*
Her Age upon Fifteen. Now her Complexion,
A lovely brown; here 'tis; Eyes black and rolling,
The Body neatly built; she strikes a Lute well,
Sings most enticingly: These Helps consider'd,
Her Maiden-head will amount to some three hundred,
Or three hundred and fifty Crowns; 'twill bear it handsomly.
Her Father's poor, some little Share deducted,
To buy him a Hunting-Nag. . . .

These Creatures are very well instructed in the Circumstances and Manners of all who are any Way related to the fair one whom they have a Design upon. As *Cloe* is to be purchased with fifty Crowns, and the Father taken off with a Pad; the Merchant's Wife next to her, who abounds in Plenty, is not to have downright Money, but the mercenary Part of her Mind is engaged with a Present of Plate and a little Ambition: She is made to understand that it is a Man of Quality who dies for her. The Examination of a young Girl for Business, and the crying down her Value for being a slight thing, together with every other Circumstance in the Scene, are inimitably excellent, and have the true Spirit of Comedy; tho' it were to be wished the Author had added a Circumstance which should make *Leucippe's* Baseness more odious.

It must not be thought a Digression from my intended Speculation, to talk of Bawds in a Discourse upon Wenches; for a Woman of the Town is not thoroughly and properly such, without having gone through the Education of one of these Houses: But the compassionate Case of very many is, that they are taken into such Hands without any the least Suspicion, previous Temptation, or Admonition to what Place they are going. The last Week I went to an Inn in the City, to enquire for some Provisions which were sent by a Waggon out of the Country; and as I waited in one of the Boxes till the Chamberlain had looked over his Parcels, I heard an old and a young Voice repeating the Questions and Responses of the Church-Catechism. I thought it no Breach of good Manners to peep at a Crevise, and look in at People so well employed; but who should I see there but the most artful Procuress in the Town, examining a most beautiful Country-Girl, who had come up in the same Waggon with my things, *Whether she was well educated, could forbear playing the Wanton with Servants and idle Fellows, of which this Town,* says she, *is too full:* At the same Time, *Whether she knew enough of Breeding; as that if a Squire or a Gentleman, or one that was her Betters, should give her a civil Salute, she could curtsie and be humble nevertheless. Her innocent forsooths, yes's, and't please you's, and she would do her Endeavour,* moved the good old Lady to take her out of the Hands of a Country Bumkin her Brother, and hire her for her own Maid. I stay'd till I saw them all marched out to take Coach; the Brother loaded with a great Chees, he prevailed upon her to take for her Civilities to Sister. This poor Creature's Fate is not far off that of her's whom I spoke of above; and it is not to be doubted, but after she has been long enough a Prey to Lust she will be delivered over to Famine; the Ironical Commendation of the Industry and Charity of these antiquated Ladies. These Directors of Sin, after they can no longer commit it, makes up the Beauty of the inimitable Dedication to the *Plain Dealer,*[93] and is a Masterpiece of Raillery on this Vice: But to understand all the Purleues of this Game the better, and to illustrate this Subject in future Discourses, I must venture myself, with my Friend WILL, into the Haunts of Beauty and Gallantry; from pampered Vice in the Habitations of the Wealthy, to distressed indigent Wickedness expelled the Harbours of the Brothel.

No. 454   [OF A DAY IN LONDON]

Sine me, Vacivom tempus ne quod duim mihi Laboris.[94]
TER. HEAU.

MONDAY, AUGUST II. 1712.

It is an inexpressible Pleasure to know a little of the World, and be of no Character or Significancy in it. To be ever unconcerned, and ever looking on new Objects with an endless Curiosity, is a Delight known only to those who are turned for Speculation: Nay they who enjoy it, must value things only as they are the Objects of Speculation, without drawing any worldly Advantage to themselves from them, but just as they are what contribute to their Amusement, or the Improvement of the Mind. I lay one Night last Week at *Richmond;* and being restless, not out of Dissatisfaction, but a certain busy Inclination one sometimes has, I arose at Four in the Morning, and took Boat for *London,* with a Resolution to rove by Boat and Coach for the next Four and twenty Hours, till the many different Objects I must needs meet with should tire my Imagination, and give me an Inclination to a Repose more profound than I was at that Time

---

[93] A restoration comedy by William Wycherley.

[94] "Give me leave to allow me no respite from labor." Terence, *The Self-Tormentor,* I, i, 38–39.

capable of. I beg People's Pardon for an odd Humour I am guilty of, and was often that Day, which is saluting any Person whom I like, whether I know him or not. This is a Particularity would be tolerated in me, if they considered that the greatest Pleasure I know I receive at my Eyes, and that I am obliged to an agreeable Person for coming abroad into my View, as another is for a Visit of Conversation at their own Houses.

The Hours of the Day and Night are taken up in the Cities of *London* and *Westminster* by People as different from each other as those who are born in Different Centuries. Men of Six a Clock give Way to those of Nine, they of Nine to the Generation of Twelve, and they of Twelve disappear, and make Room for the fashionable World, who have made Two a Clock the Noon of the Day.

When we first put off from Shore, we soon fell in with a Fleet of Gardiners bound for the several Market-Ports of *London;* and it was the most pleasing Scene imaginable to see the Chearfulness with which those industrious People ply'd their Way to a certain Sale of their Goods. The Banks on each Side are as well peopled, and beautified with as agreeable Plantations, as any Spot on the Earth; but the *Thames* it self, loaded with the Product of each Shore, added very much to the Landskip. It was very easy to observe by their Sailing, and the Countenances of the ruddy Virgins who were Supercargoes, the Parts of the Town to which they were bound. There was an Air in the Purveyors for *Covent-Garden,* who frequently converse with Morning Rakes, very unlike the seemly Sobriety of those bound for *Stocks-Market.*

Nothing remarkable happen'd in our Voyage; but I landed with Ten Sail of Apricock Boats at *Strand-Bridge,* after having put in at *Nine-Elmes,* and taken in Melons, consign'd by Mr. *Cuffe* of that Place, to *Sarah Sewell* and Company, at their Stall in *Covent-Garden.* We arriv'd at *Strand-Bridge* at Six of the Clock, and were unloading; when the Hackney-Coachmen of the foregoing Night took their Leave of each other at the *Dark-House,* to go to Bed before the Day was too far spent. Chimney Sweepers pass'd by us as we made up to the Market and some Raillery happen'd between one of the Fruit-Wenches and those black Men, about the Devil and *Eve,* with Allusion to their several Professions. I could not believe any Place more entertaining than *Covent-Garden;* where I strolled from one Fruit Shop to another, with Crowds of agreeable young Women around me, who were purchasing Fruit for their respective Families. It was almost Eight of the Clock before I could leave that Variety of Objects. I took Coach and followed a young Lady, who tripped into another just before me, attended by her Maid. I saw immediately she was of the Family of the *Vainloves.* There are a Sett of these, who, of all things affect the Play of *Blindman's-Buff,* and leading Men into Love for they know not whom, who are fled they know not where. This Sort of Woman is usually a janty Slattern; she hangs on her Cloaths, plays her Head, varies her Posture, and changes Place incessantly; and all with an Appearance of striving at the same time to hide her self, and yet give you to understand she is in Humour to laugh at you. You must have often seen the Coachmen make Signs with their Fingers as they drive by each other, to intimate how much they have got that Day. They can carry on that Language to give Intelligence where they are driving. In an Instant my Coachman took the Wink to pursue, and the Lady's Driver gave the Hint that he was going through *Long-Acre* towards St. *James's:* While he whipp'd up *James-street,* we drove for *King-street,* to save the Pass at St. *Martin's Lane.* The Coachmen took Care to meet, justle, and threaten each other for Way, and be intangled at the End of *Newport-street* and *Long-Acre.* The Fright, you must believe, brought down the Lady's Coach Door, and obliged her, with her Mask off, to enquire into the Bustle, when she sees the Man she would avoid. The Tackle of the Coach-Window is so bad she cannot draw it up again, and she drives on sometimes wholly discovered, and sometimes half escaped, according to the Accident of Carriages in her Way. One of these Ladies keeps her Seat in an Hackney-Coach as well as the best Rider does on a managed Horse. The laced Shooe of her Left Foot, with a careless Gesture, just appearing on the opposite Cushion, held her both firm, and in a proper Attitude to receive the next Jolt.

As she was an excellent Coach-Woman, many were the Glances at each other which we had for an Hour and an Half in all Parts of the Town by the Skill of our Drivers; till at last my Lady was conveniently lost with Notice from her Coachman to ours to make off, and he should hear where she went. This Chace was now at an End, and the Fellow who drove her came to us, and discovered that he was ordered to come again in an Hour, for that she was a Silk-Worm. I was surprized with this Phrase, but found it was a Cant among the Hackney Fraternity for their best Customers, Women who ramble twice or thrice a Week from Shop to Shop, to turn over all the Goods in Town without buying any thing. The Silk-Worms are, it seems, indulged by the Tradesmen; for tho' they never buy, they are ever talking of new Silks, Laces and Ribbands, and serve the Owners in getting them Customers, as their common Dunners[95] do in making them pay.

The Day of People of Fashion began now to break, and Carts and Hacks were mingled with Equipages of Show and Vanity; when I resolved to walk it out of Cheapness; but my unhappy Curiosity is such, that I find it always my Interest to take Coach, for some odd Adventure among Beggars, Ballad Singers, or the like, detains and throws me into Expence. It happen'd so immediately; for at the Corner of *Warwick-street,* as I was listning to a new Ballad, a ragged Rascal, a Beggar who knew me, came up to me, and began to turn the Eyes of the good Company upon me, by telling me he was extreme poor, and should die in the Streets for want of Drink, except I immediately would have the Charity to give him Six-pence to go into the next Ale-house and save his Life. He urged, with a melancholy Face, that all his Family had died of Thirst. All the Mob have Humour, and two or three began to take the Jest; by which Mr. *Sturdy* carried his Point, and let me sneak off to a Coach. As I drove along, it was a pleasing Reflection to see the World so prettily chequer'd since I left *Richmond,* and the Scene still filling with Children of a new Hour. This Satisfaction encreased as I moved towards the City; and gay Signs, well disposed Streets, magnificent publick Structures, and wealthy Shops, adorn'd with contented Faces, made the Joy still rising till we came into the Centre of the City, and Centre of the World of Trade, the *Exchange of London.* As other Men in the Crowds about me were pleased with their Hopes and Bargains, I found my Account in observing them, in Attention to their several Interests. I, indeed, look'd upon my self as the richest Man that walk'd the *Exchange* that Day; for my Benevolence made me share the Gains of every Bargain that was made. It was not the least of the Satisfactions in my Survey, to go up Stairs, and pass the Shops of agreeable Females; to observe so many pretty Hands busy in the Foldings of Ribbands, and the utmost Eagerness of agreeable Faces in the Sale of Patches, Pins, and Wires, on each Side the Counters, was an Amusement, in which I should longer have indulged my self, had not the dear Creatures called to me to ask what I wanted, when I could not answer, only *To look at you.* I went to one of the Windows which opened to the Area below, where all the several Voices lost their Distinction, and rose up in a confused Humming; which created in me a Reflection that could not come into the Mind of any but of one a little too studious; for I said to my self, with a kind of Pun in Thought, *What Nonsense is all the Hurry of this World to those who are above it?* In these, or not much wiser Thoughts, I had like to have lost my Place at the Chop-House; where

---

[95] Those "employed in soliciting petty debts" (Johnson's *Dictionary*); a *dun,* according to Johnson, was "a clamorous, importunate, troublesome creditor."

every Man, according to the natural Bashfulness or Sullenness of our Nation, eats in a publick Room a Mess of Broth, or Chop of Meat, in dumb Silence, as if they had no Pretence to speak to each other on the Foot of being Men, except they were to each other's Acquaintance.

I went afterwards to *Robin's*,[96] and saw People who had din'd with me at the Five-penny Ordinary just before, give Bills for the Value of large Estates; and could not but behold with great Pleasure, Property lodged in, and transferr'd in a Moment from such as would never be Masters of half as much as is seemingly in them, and given from them every Day they live. But before Five in the Afternoon I left the City, came to my common Scene of *Covent-Garden*, and pass'd the Evening at *Wills*[97] in attending the Discourses of several Sets of People, who reliev'd each other within my Hearing on the Subjects of Cards, Dice, Love, Learning and Politicks. The last Subject kept me till I heard the Streets in the Possession of the Bell man, who had now the World to himself, and cry'd, *Past Two of Clock*. This rous'd me from my Seat, and I went to my Lodging, led by a Light,[98] whom I put into the Discourse of his private Oeconomy, and made him give me an Account of the Charge, Hazard, Profit and Loss of a Family that depended upon a Link,[99] with a Design to end my trivial Day with the Generosity of Six-pence, instead of a third Part of that Sum. When I came to my Chamber I writ down these Minutes; but was at a Loss what Instruction I should propose to my Reader from the Enumeration of so many insignificant Matters and Occurrences; and I thought it of great Use, if they could learn with me to keep their Minds open to Gratification, and ready to receive it from any thing it meets with. This one Circumstance will make every Face you see give you the Satisfaction you now take in beholding that of a Friend; will make every object a pleasing one; will make all the Good which arrives to any Man, an Encrease of Happiness to your self.

---

[96] A coffee house in Exchange Alley.
[97] A coffee house in Covent Garden.
[98] A man carrying a light to help one through the streets at night.
[99] "a torch made of pitch and hards [refuse of flax]" (Johnson's *Dictionary*).

Joseph Addison

1672-1719

THE TATLER

No. 220 [OF A RELIGIOUS THERMOMETER]

Insani sanus Nomen ferat, æquus iniqui,
Ultra quam satis est, Virtutem si petat ipsam.[1]

HOR.

FROM SATURD. SEPT. 2. TO TUESD. SEPT. 5. 1710.

From my own Apartment, Sept. 4.

Having received many Letters filled with Compliments and Acknowledgments for my late useful Discovery of the Political Barometer,[2] I shall here Communicate to the Publick an Account of my Ecclesiastical Thermometer, the latter giving as manifest Prognostications of the Changes and Revolutions in Church, as the former does of those in State, and both of them being absolutely necessary for every prudent Subject who is resolved to keep what he has, and get what he can.

The Church Thermometer, which I am now to treat of, is supposed to have been invented in the Reign of *Henry* the Eighth,[3] about the Time when that Re-ligious Prince put some to Death for owning the Pope's Supremacy, and others for denying Transubstantiation. I do not find, however, any great Use made of this Instrument till it fell into the Hands of a learned and vigilant Priest or Minister,[4] (for he frequently wrote himself both one and the other) who was some Time Vicar of *Bray*.[5] This Gentleman lived in his Vicaridge to a good old Age; and after having seen several Successions of his neighbouring Clergy either burnt or banish'd, departed this Life with the Satisfaction of having never deserted his Flock, and died Vicar of *Bray*. As this Glass was first designed to calculate the different Degrees of Heat in Religion, as it raged in Popery, or as it cooled and grew temperate in the Reformation, it was marked at several Distances, after the Manner our ordinary Thermometer

---

Text from the collected edition of 1710–1711, in octavo.

[1] Thus good, or bad, to one extreme betray
Th'unbalanc'd Mind, and snatch the Man away;
For Vertue's self may too much Zeal be had;
The worst of Madmen is a Saint run mad.

(Horace, *Epistles*, I, vi, 15–16, tr. Pope.)

[2] Described in *Tatler* No. 214 by Steele.

[3] Henry VIII (1491–1547) of England, under whom the Church of England and that of Rome became independent entities.

[4] i.e., depending on whether the ruling mode was for High Church or Low.

[5] A small seaport in Ireland.

is to this Day, *viz. Extream Hot, sultry Hot, very Hot, Hot, Warm, Temperate, Cold, just Freezing, Frost, hard Frost, great Frost, extream Cold.*

It is well known, that *Toricellius*,[6] the Inventor of the common Weather-Glass, made the Experiment in a long Tube which held Thirty two Foot of Water; and that a more modern Virtuoso[7] finding such a Machine altogether unweildy and useless, and considering that Thirty two Inches of Quicksilver weighed as much as so many Foot of Water in a Tube of the same Circumference, invented that sizeable Instrument which is now in Use. After this Manner, that I might adapt the Thermometer I am now speaking of to the present Constitution of our Church, as divided into *High* and *Low,* I have made some necessary Variations both in the Tube and the Fluid it contains. In the first Place, I ordered a Tube to be cast in a Planetary Hour, and took Care to seal it Hermetically, when the Sun was in Conjunction with *Saturn.* I then took the proper Precautions about the Fluid, which is a Compound of Two very different Liquors; one of them a Spirit drawn out of a strong heady Wine; the other a particular Sort of Rock Water, colder than Ice, and clearer than Chrystal. The Spirit is of a red fiery Colour, and so very apt to ferment, that unless it be mingled with a Proportion of the Water, or pent up very close, it will burst the Vessel that holds it, and fly up in Fume and Smoak. The Water on the contrary is of such a subtle piercing Cold, that unless it be mingled with a Proportion of the Spirits, it will sink through almost every Thing that it is put into, and seems to be of the same Nature as the Water mentioned by *Quintus Curtius*,[8] which, says the Historian, could be contained in nothing but in the Hoof, or (as the *Oxford* Manuscript has it) in the Skull of an Ass. The Thermometer is marked according to the following Fig-

ure, which I set down at length, not only to give my Reader a clear Idea of it, but also to fill up my Paper.

> *Ignorance.*
> *Persecution.*
> *Wrath.*
> *Zeal.*
> *CHURCH.*
> *Moderation.*
> *Lukewarmness.*
> *Infidelity.*
> *Ignorance.*

The Reader will observe, that the Church is placed in the Middle Point of the Glass, between *Zeal* and *Moderation,* the Situation in which she always flourishes, and in which every good *Englishman* wishes her who is a Friend to the Constitution of his Country. However, when it mounts to *Zeal,* it is not amiss; and when it sinks to *Moderation,* is still in a most admirable Temper. The worst of it is, that when once it begins to rise, it has still an Inclination to ascend, insomuch that it is apt to climb from *Zeal* to *Wrath,* and from *Wrath* to *Persecution,* which always ends in *Ignorance,* and very often proceeds from it. In the same Manner it frequently takes its Progress through the lower Half of the Glass; and when it has a Tendency to fall, will gradually descend from *Moderation* to *Lukewarmness,* and from *Lukewarmness* to *Infidelity,* which very often terminates in *Ignorance,* and always proceeds from it.

It is a common Observation, that the ordinary Thermometer will be affected by the breathing of People who are in the Room where it stands; and indeed, it is almost incredible to conceive how the Glass I am now describing will fall by the Breath of a Multitude crying *Popery;* or on the contrary, how it will rise when the same Multitude (as it sometimes happens) cry out in the same Breath, *The Church is in Danger.*

---

[6] Evangelista Torricelli (1608–1647), Italian physicist, discoverer of the principle of the barometer.

[7] "a man skilled in . . . natural curiosities"

(Johnson's *Dictionary*).

[8] Quintus Curtius Rufus, Roman author of a *History of Alexander the Great.*

As soon as I had finished this my Glass, and adjusted it to the above-mentioned Scale of Religion, that I might make proper Experiments with it, I carried it under my Cloak to several Coffee-houses, and other Places of Resort about this great City. At St. *James's* Coffee-house, the Liquor stood at *Moderation;* but at *Will's,* to my extream Surprize, it subsided to the very lowest Mark on the Glass. At the *Grecian* it mounted but just one Point higher; at the *Rainbow,* it still ascended Two Decrees[9]: *Child's* fetched it up to *Zeal,* and other adjacent Coffee-houses to *Wrath.*

It fell into the lower Half of the Glass as I went further into the City, till at length it settled at *Moderation,* where it continued all the Time I stay'd about the *Change,* as also whilst I passed by the *Bank.* And here I cannot but take Notice, that through the whole Course of my Remarks, I never observed my Glass to rise at the same Time that the Stocks did.

To compleat the Experiment, I prevailed upon a Friend of mine, who works under me in the Occult Sciences, to make a Progress with my Glass through the whole Island of *Great Britain;* and after his Return, to present me with a Register of his Observations. I guessed beforehand at the Temper of several Places he passed through, by the Characters they have had Time out of Mind. Thus that facetious Divine, Dr. *Fuller,*[10] speaking of the Town of *Banbury* near a Hundred Years ago, tells us, it was a Place famous for Cakes and *Zeal,* which I find by my Glass is true to this Day as to the latter Part of this Description; though I must confess, it is not in the same Reputation for Cakes that it was in the Time of that learned Author; and thus of other Places. In short, I have now by me, digested in an Alphabetical Order, all the Counties, Corporations and Boroughs, in *Great Britain,* with their respective Tempers, as they stand related to my Thermometer: But this I shall keep to my self, because I would by no Means do any Thing that may seem to influence any ensuing Elections.

The Point of Doctrine which I would propagate by this my Invention, is the same which was long ago advanced by that able Teacher *Horace,* out of whom I have taken my Text for this Discourse: We should be careful not to overshoot our selves in the Pursuits even of Virtue. Whether *Zeal* or *Moderation* be the Point we aim at, let us keep Fire out of the one, and Frost out of the other. But alas! the World is too wise to want such a Precaution. The Terms *High-Church* and *Low-Church,* as commonly used, do not so much denote a Principle, as they distinguish a Party. They are like Words of Battle, that have nothing to do with their original Signification, but are only given out to keep a Body of Men together, and to let them know Friends from Enemies.

I must confess, I have considered with some little Attention the Influence which the Opinions of these great National Sects have upon their Practice; and do look upon it as one of the unaccountable Things of our Times, that Multitudes of honest Gentlemen, who entirely agree in their Lives, should take it in their Heads to differ in their Religion.

No. 249   [TRAVELS OF A SHILLING]

Per varios Casus, per tot Discrimina Rerum,
Tendimus. . . .[11]

VIRG.

---

[9] The references are to the degrees of dissent that would be attributed to those who frequented the coffee houses and the places of business. "Decrees," so spelled, but whether it is an intentional pun, or a printer's error is not now to be determined.

[10] Thomas Fuller (1608–1661), English clergyman and biographer.

[11] "Through various hazards and events we move" (Vergil, *Aeneid,* I, 204, tr. Dryden).

From my own Apartment, November 10.

I was last Night visited by a Friend[12] of mine who has an inexhaustible Fund of Discourse, and never fails to entertain his Company with a Variety of Thoughts and Hints that are altogether new and uncommon. Whether it were in Complaisance to my Way of Living, or his real Opinion, he advanced the following Paradox, That it required much greater Talents to fill up and become a retired Life, than a Life of Business. Upon this Occasion he rallied very agreeably the busie Men of the Age, who only valued themselves for being in Motion, and passing through a Series of trifling and insignificant Actions. In the Heat of his Discourse, seeing a Piece of Money lying on my Table, I defie (says he) any of these active Persons to produce half the Adventures that this Twelvepenny-Piece has been engaged in, were it possible for him to give us an Account of his Life.

My Friend's Talk made so odd an Impression upon my Mind, that soon after I was a-Bed I fell insensibly into a most unaccountable *Resverie,*[13] that had neither Moral nor Design in it, and cannot be so properly called a Dream as a Delirium.

Methoughts the Shilling that lay upon the Table reared it self upon its Edge, and turning the Face towards me, opened its Mouth, and in a soft Silver Sound gave me the following Account of his Life and Adventures:

I was born, says he, on the Side of a Mountain, near a little Village of *Peru,* and made a Voyage to *England* in a Ingot, under the Convoy of Sir *Francis Drake.* I was, soon after my Arrival, taken out of my *Indian* Habit, refined, naturalized, and put into the *British* Mode, with the Face of Queen *Elizabeth* on one Side, and the Arms of

the Country on the other. Being thus equipped, I found in me a wonderful Inclination to ramble, and visit all the Parts of the new World into which I was brought. The People very much favoured my natural Disposition, and shifted me so fast from Hand to Hand, that before I was Five Years old, I had travelled into almost every Corner of the Nation. But in the Beginning of my Sixth Year, to my unspeakable Grief, I fell into the Hands of a miserable old Fellow, who clapped me into an Iron Chest, where I found Five Hundred more of my own Quality who lay under the same Confinement. The only Relief we had, was to be taken out and counted over in the fresh Air every Morning and Evening. After an Imprisonment of several Years, we heard some Body knocking at our Chest, and breaking it open with an Hammer. This we found was the old Man's Heir, who, as his Father lay a dying, was so good as to come to our Release: He separated us that very Day. What was the Fate of my Companions I know not: As for my self, I was sent to the Apothecary's Shop for a Pint of Sack. The Apothecary gave me to an Herb-Woman, the Herb-Woman to a Butcher, the Butcher to a Brewer, and the Brewer to his Wife, who made a Present of me to a Nonconformist Preacher. After this Manner I made my Way merrily through the World; for, as I told you before, we Shillings love nothing so much as travelling. I sometimes fetched in a Shoulder of Mutton, sometimes a Play-Book, and often had the Satisfaction to treat a Templer[14] at a Twelvepenny Ordinary,[15] or carry him with Three Friends to *Westminster-Hall.*

In the Midst of this pleasant Progress which I made from Place to Place, I was arrested by a superstitious old Woman, who shut me up in a greasy Purse, in Pursuance of a foolish Saying, That

[12] Jonathan Swift, who twice mentions this paper in his *Journal to Stella* (November 30, 1710, and December 14, 1710).

[13] reverie; dream.

[14] A student in law.

[15] "an eating or victualling house, where persons may eat at so much *per meal*" (Bailey's *Dictionary*).

while she kept a Queen *Elizabeth's* Shilling about her, she should never be without Money. I continued here a close Prisoner for many Months, till at last I was exchanged for Eight and Forty Farthings.

I thus rambled from Pocket to Pocket till the Beginning of the Civil Wars, when, to my Shame be it spoken, I was employed in raising Soldiers against the King: For being of a very tempting Breadth, a Serjeant made Use of me to inveigle Country Fellows, and list them in the Service of the Parliament.

As soon as he had made one Man sure, his Way was to oblige him to take a Shilling of a more homely Figure, and then practise the same Trick upon another. Thus I continued doing great Mischief to the Crown, till my Officer chancing one Morning to walk Abroad earlier than ordinary, sacrificed me to his Pleasures, and made Use of me to seduce a Milk-Maid. This Wench bent me, and gave me to her Sweetheart, applying more properly than she intended the usual Form of, *To my Love and from my Love.* This ungenerous Gallant marrying her within few Days after, pawned me for a Dram of Brandy, and drinking me out next Day, I was beaten flat with an Hammer, and again set a running.

After many Adventures, which it would be tedious to relate, I was sent to a young Spendthrift, in Company with the Will of his deceased Father. The young Fellow, who I found was very extravagant, gave great Demonstrations of Joy at the receiving the Will; but opening it, he found himself disinherited and cut off from the Possession of a fair Estate, by Vertue of my being made a Present to him. This put him into such a Passion, that after having taken me in his Hand, and cursed me, he squirred[16] me away from him as far as he could fling me. I chanced to light in an unfre-

quented Place under a dead Wall, where I lay undiscovered and useless, during the Usurpation of *Oliver Cromwell.*

About a Year after the King's Return, a poor Cavalier that was walking there about Dinner-time fortunately cast his Eye upon me, and, to the great Joy of us both, carried me to a Cook's Shop, where he dined upon me, and drank the King's Health. When I came again into the World, I found that I had been happier in my Retirement than I thought, having probably by that Means escaped wearing a monstrous Pair of Breeches.[17]

Being now of great Credit and Antiquity, I was rather looked upon as a Medal than an ordinary Coin; for which Reason a Gamester laid hold of me, and converted me to a Counter, having got together some Dozens of us for that Use. We led a melancholy Life in his Possession, being busy at those Hours wherein Current Coin is at rest, and partaking the Fate of our Master, being in a few Moments valued at a Crown, a Pound, or a Sixpence, according to the Situation in which the Fortune of the Cards placed us. I had at length the good Luck to see my Master break,[18] by which Means I was again sent Abroad under my primitive Denomination of a Shilling.

I shall pass over many other Accidents of less Moment, and hasten to that fatal Catastrophe when I fell into the Hands of an Artist[19] who conveyed me under Ground, and with an unmerciful Pair of Sheers cut off my Titles, clipped my Brims, retrenched my Shape, rubbed me to my inmost Ring, and in short, so spoiled and pillaged me, that he did not leave me worth a Groat. You may think what a Confusion I was in to see my self thus curtailed and disfigured. I should have been ashamed to have shown my Head, had not all my old Acquaintance been reduced to the same shameful Figure, excepting some few that were punched through the Belly. In the midst

---

[16] threw.

[17] The two shields on a Cromwell shilling were deprecated as "breeches," which they somewhat resembled.

[18] "become bankrupt" (Bailey's *Dictionary*).

[19] An outlaw who salvaged silver by trimming the edges of coins.

of this general Calamity, when every Body thought our Misfortune irretrievable, and our Case desperate, we were thrown into the Furnace together, and (as it often happens with Cities rising out of a Fire) appeared with greater Beauty and Lustre than we could ever boast of before. What has happened to me since this Change of Sex[20] which you now see, I shall take some other Opportunity to relate. In the mean Time I shall only repeat Two Adventures, as being very extraordinary, and neither of them having ever happened to me above once in my Life. The First was, my being in a Poet's Pocket, who was so taken with the Brightness and Novelty of my Appearance, that it gave Occasion to the finest Burlesque Poem in the *British* Language, entituled from me, *The Splendid Shilling*.[21] The Second Adventure, which I must not omit, happened to me in the Year 1703, when I was given away in Charity to a blind Man; but indeed this was by a Mistake, the Person who gave me having heedlesly thrown me into the Hat among a Pennyworth of Farthings.

THE SPECTATOR

No. 1 [INTRODUCTORY]

*Non fumum ex fulgore, sed ex fumo dare lucem
Cogitat, ut speciosa dehinc miracula promat.*[22]
HOR.

TO BE CONTINUED EVERY DAY.
THURSDAY, MARCH 1. 1711

I have observed, that a Reader seldom peruses a Book with Pleasure 'till he knows whether the Writer of it be a black or a fair Man, of a mild or cholerick Disposition, Married or a Batchelor, with other Particulars of the like nature, that conduce very much to the right Understanding of an Author. To gratify this Curiosity, which is so natural to a Reader, I design this Paper, and my next, as Prefatory Discourses to my following Writings, and shall give some Account in them of the several Persons that are engaged in this Work. As the chief Trouble of Compiling, Digesting and Correcting will fall to my Share, I must do my self the Justice to open the Work with my own History.

I was born to a small Hereditary Estate, which I find, by the Writings of the Family, was bounded by the same Hedges and Ditches in *William* the Conqueror's Time that it is at present, and has been delivered down from Father to Son whole and entire, without the Loss or Acquisition of a single Field or Meadow, during the Space of six hundred Years. There goes a Story in the Family, that when my Mother was gone

---

Text from the original editions in folio half-sheets.

[20] It is apparent from what follows that the portrait of Queen Elizabeth has been replaced by that of one of the kings prior to the accession of Queen Anne in 1702.

[21] By John Philips (1676–1709).

[22] One with a flash begins, and ends in smoke;
Another out of smoke brings glorious light,
And (without raising expectation high)
Surprises us with daring miracles.
(Horace, *Ars Poetica*, ll. 143–144,
tr. Roscommon.)

with Child of me about three Months, she dreamt that she was brought to Bed of a Judge: Whether this might proceed from a Law-Suit which was then depending in the Family, or my Father's being a Justice of the Peace, I cannot determine; for I am not so vain as to think it presaged any Dignity that I should arrive at in my future Life, though that was the Interpretation which the Neighbourhood put upon it. The Gravity of my Behaviour at my very first Appearance in the World, and all the Time that I sucked, seemed to favour my Mother's Dream: For, as she has often told me, I threw away my Rattle before I was two Months old, and would not make use of my Coral 'till they had taken away the Bells from it.

As for the rest of my Infancy, there being nothing in it remarkable, I shall pass it over in Silence. I find, that, during my Nonage, I had the Reputation of a very sullen Youth, but was always a Favourite of my School-Master, who used to say, *that my Parts*[23] *were solid and would wear well.* I had not been long at the University, before I distinguished myself by a most profound Silence: For during the Space of eight Years, excepting in the publick Exercises of the College, I scarce uttered the Quantity of an hundred Words; and indeed do not remember that I ever spoke three Sentences together in my whole Life. Whilst I was in this Learned Body I applied my self with so much Diligence to my Studies, that there are very few celebrated Books, either in the Learned or the Modern Tongues, which I am not acquainted with.

Upon the Death of my Father I was resolved to travel into Foreign Countries, and therefore left the University,

with the Character of an odd unaccountable Fellow, that had a great deal of Learning, if I would but show it. An insatiable Thirst after Knowledge carried me into all the Countries of *Europe,* where there was any thing new or strange to be seen; nay, to such a Degree was my Curiosity raised, that having read the Controversies of some great Men concerning the Antiquities of *Egypt,* I made a Voyage to *Grand Cairo,* on purpose to take the Measure of a Pyramid; and as soon as I had set my self right in that Particular, returned to my Native Country with great Satisfaction.

I have passed my latter Years in this City, where I am frequently seen in most publick Places, tho' there are not above half a dozen of my select Friends that know me; of whom my next Paper shall give a more particular Account. There is no Place of Publick Resort, wherein I do not often make my Appearance; sometimes I am seen thrusting my Head into a Round of Politicians at *Will's,*[24] and listning with great Attention to the Narratives that are made in those little Circular Audiences. Sometimes I smoak a Pipe at *Child's;* and whilst I seem attentive to nothing but the *Post-Man,*[25] overhear the Conversation of every Table in the Room. I appear on *Sunday* Nights at *St. James's* Coffee-House, and sometimes join the little Committee of Politicks in the Inner-Room, as one who comes there to hear and improve. My Face is likewise very well known at the *Grecian,* the *Cocoa-Tree,* and in the Theaters both of *Drury-Lane,* and the *Hay-Market.*[26] I have been taken for a Merchant upon the *Exchange* for above these ten Years, and sometimes pass for a *Jew* in the Assembly of Stock-Jobbers[27] at *Jonathan's.* In short, where ever I see a Cluster of

---

[23] "qualities; powers; faculties; or accomplishments" (Johnson's *Dictionary*).

[24] The coffee houses: Will's, St. James's, and the Grecian were used in *The Tatler* (see No. 1 by Steele); Child's, frequented by physicians and clergymen, was in St. Paul's Churchyard; the Cocoa-Tree was a Tory house in Pall Mall; Jonathan's was in Change Alley.

[25] A newspaper (1695–1730): *The Postman and the Historical Account,* etc.

[26] The Haymarket Theatre had opened in 1706 and was soon to become the home of Italian opera.

[27] "a low wretch who gets money by buying and selling shares in the funds" (Johnson's *Dictionary*).

People I always mix with them, tho' I never open my Lips but in my own Club.

Thus I live in the World, rather as a Spectator of Mankind, than as one of the Species; by which means I have made my self a Speculative Statesman, Soldier, Merchant and Artizan, without ever medling with any Practical Part in Life. I am very well versed in the Theory of an Husband, or a Father, and can discern the Errors in the Œconomy, Business, and Diversion of others, better than those who are engaged in them; as Standers-by discover Blotts,[28] which are apt to escape those who are in the Game. I never espoused any Party with Violence, and am resolved to observe an exact Neutrality between the Whigs and Tories, unless I shall be forc'd to declare my self by the Hostilities of either side. In short, I have acted in all the parts of my Life as a Looker-on, which is the Character I intend to preserve in this Paper.

I have given the Reader just so much of my History and Character, as to let him see I am not altogether unqualified for the Business I have undertaken. As for other Particulars in my Life and Adventures, I shall insert them in following Papers, as I shall see occasion. In the mean time, when I consider how much I have seen, read and heard, I begin to blame my own Taciturnity; and since I have neither Time nor Inclination to communicate the Fulness of my Heart in Speech, I am resolved to do it in Writing; and to Print my self out, if possible, before I Die. I have been often told by my Friends, that it is Pity so many useful Discoveries which I have made, should be in the Possession of a Silent Man. For this Reason therefore, I shall publish a Sheet full of Thoughts every Morning, for the Benefit of my Contemporaries; and if I can any way contribute to the Diversion or Improvement of the Country in which I live, I shall

leave it, when I am summoned out of it, with the secret Satisfaction of thinking that I have not Lived in vain.

There are three very material Points which I have not spoken to in this Paper, and which, for several important Reasons, I must keep to my self, at least for some Time: I mean, an Account of my Name, my Age, and my Lodgings. I must confess I would gratify my Reader in any thing that is reasonable; but as for these three Particulars, though I am sensible they might tend very much to the Embellishment of my Paper, I cannot yet come to a Resolution of communicating them to the Publick. They would indeed draw me out of that Obscurity which I have enjoy'd for many Years, and expose me in Publick Places to several Salutes and Civilities, which have been always very disagreeable to me; for the greatest Pains I can suffer, are the being talked to, and being stared at. It is for this Reason likewise, that I keep my Complexion and Dress, as very great Secrets; tho' it is not impossible, but I may make Discoveries of both in the Progress of the Work I have undertaken.

After having being thus particular upon my self, I shall in to-Morrow's Paper give an Account of those Gentlemen who are concerned with me in this Work. For, as I have before intimated, a Plan of it is laid and concerted (as all other Matters of Importance are) in a Club. However, as my Friends have engaged me to stand in the Front, those who have a mind to correspond with me, may direct their Letters *To the Spectator,* at Mr. *Buckley's*[29] in *Little Britain.* For I must further acquaint the Reader, that tho' our Club meets only on *Tuesdays* and *Thursdays,* we have appointed a Committee to sit every Night, for the Inspection of all such Papers as may contribute to the Advancement of the Publick Weal.

---

[28] "a blot *in Back-gammon* [occurs] when a single man lies open to be taken up" (Bailey's *Dictionary*).

[29] Samuel Buckley, printer of *The Spectator.*

No. 26   [A VISIT TO WESTMINSTER ABBEY]

Pallida mors aequo pulsat pede pauperum tabernas
Regumque turres, o beate Sexti,
Vitae summa brevis spem nos vetat inchoare lungam.
Jam te premet nox, fabulaeque manes;
Et domus exilis Plutonia. . . .[30]

HOR.

FRIDAY, MARCH 30. 1711.

When I am in a serious Humour, I very often walk by my self in *Westminster* Abbey; where the Gloominess of the Place, and the Use to which it is applied, with the Solemnity of the Building, and the Condition of the People who lye in it, are apt to fill the Mind with a kind of Melancholy, or rather Thoughtfulness, that is not disagreeable. I yesterday pass'd a whole Afternoon in the Church-yard, the Cloysters, and the Church, amusing my self with the Tomb-stones and Inscriptions that I met with in those several Regions of the Dead. Most of them recorded nothing else of the buried Person, but that he was born upon one Day and died upon another: The whole History of his Life, being comprehended in those two Circumstances that are common to all Mankind. I could not but look upon these Registers of Existence, whether of Brass or Marble, as a kind of Satyr upon the departed Persons; who had left no other Memorial of them, but that they were born and that they died. They put me in mind of several Persons mentioned in the Battles of Heroic Poems, who have sounding Names given them, for no other Reason but that they may be killed, and are celebrated for nothing but being knocked on the Head.

Γλαῖχον τε, Μέδοητά, Θερσιλοχόν τε.

HOM.

Glaucumque,   Medontaque,   Thersilo-
chumque.[31]

VIRG.

The Life of these Men is finely described in Holy Writ, by *the Path of an Arrow*[32] which is immediately closed up and lost.

Upon my going into the Church, I entertain'd my self with the digging of a Grave; and saw in every Shovel-full of it that was thrown up, the Fragment of a Bone or Skull intermixt with a kind of fresh mouldering Earth that some time or other had a Place in the Composition of an humane Body. Upon this, I began to consider with my self what innumerable Multitudes of People lay confus'd together under the Pavement of that ancient Cathedral; how Men and Women, Friends and Enemies, Priests and Soldiers, Monks and Prebendaries, were crumbled amongst one another, and blended together in the same common Mass; how Beauty, Strength, and Youth, with Old-age, Weakness, and Deformity, lay undistinguish'd in the same promiscuous Heap of Matter.

After having thus surveyed this great Magazine of Mortality, as it were in the Lump, I examined it more particularly

---

[30] With equal pace impartial fate
Knocks at the palace as the cottage gate;
   Nor should our sum of life extend
Our growing hopes beyond their destin'd end,
   When sunk to Pluto's shadowy coasts,
Opprest with darkness and the fable ghosts.
(Horace, *Odes*, I, iv, 13–17, tr. Francis.)

[31] "Glaucus, and Medon, and Thersilochus," heroes lost in the war of Troy (*Iliad*, XVII, 216; *Aeneid*, VI, 483).

[32] The passage is in the *Apocrypha, The Wisdome of Solomon*, v, 12: "Or like as when an arrow is shot at a mark, it parteth the aire, which immediately cometh together again; so that a man cannot know where it went through . . ." (edition of 1637). These verses form a portion of the morning lesson for the day which celebrates the conversion of St. Paul, and of the evening lesson for All Saints' Day.

by the Accounts which I found on several of the Monuments that are raised in every Quarter of that ancient Fabrick. Some of them were covered with such extravagant Epitaphs, that, if it were possible for the dead Person to be acquainted with them, he would blush at the Praises which his Friends had bestow'd upon him. There are others so excessively modest, that they deliver the Character of the Person departed in Greek or Hebrew, and by that Means are not understood once in a Twelvemonth. In the poetical Quarter, I found there were Poets that had no Monuments, and Monuments that had no Poets. I observed indeed that the present War had filled the Church with many of these uninhabited Monuments, which had been erected to the Memory of Persons whose Bodies were perhaps buried in the Plains of *Blenheim* or in the Bosom of the Ocean.

I could not but be very much delighted with several modern Epitaphs, which are written with great Elegance of Expression and Justness of Thought, and therefore do Honour to the Living as well as to the Dead. As a Foreigner is very apt to conceive an Idea of the Ignorance or Politeness of a Nation from the Turn of their publick Monuments and Inscriptions, they should be submitted to the Perusal of Men of Learning and Genius before they are put in Execution. Sir *Cloudesly Shovel's*[33] Monument has very often given me great Offence: Instead of the brave rough English Admiral, which was the distinguishing Character of that plain gallant Man, he is represented on his Tomb by the Figure of a Beau, dress'd in a long Perriwig, and reposing himself upon Velvet Cushions under a Canopy of State. The Inscription is answerable to the Monument; for instead of celebrating the many remarkable Actions he had performed in the Service of his Country, it acquaints us only with the Manner of his Death, in which it was impossible for him to reap any Honour. The *Dutch,* whom we are apt to despise for want of Genius, shew an infinitely greater Taste of Antiquity and Politeness in their Buildings and Works of this Nature, than what we meet with in those of our own Country. The Monuments of their Admirals, which have been erected at the publick Expense, represent 'em like themselves; and are adorn'd with rostral[34] Crowns and naval Ornaments, with beautiful Festoons of Shells and Coral.

But to return to our Subject. I have left the Repository of our English Kings for the Contemplation of another Day, when I shall find my Mind disposed for so serious an Amusement. I know that Entertainments of this Nature, are apt to raise dark and dismal Thoughts in timorous Minds and gloomy Imaginations; but for my own Part, though I am always serious, I do not know what it is to be melancholy; and can therefore take a View of Nature in her deep and solemn Scenes, with the same Pleasure as in her most gay and delightful ones. By this Means I can improve my self with those Objects, which others consider with Terrour. When I look upon the Tombs of the Great, every Emotion of Envy dies in me; when I read the Epitaphs of the Beautiful, every inordinate Desire goes out; when I meet with the Grief of Parents upon a Tomb-stone, my heart melts with Compassion; when I see the Tomb of the Parents themselves, I consider the Vanity of grieving for those whom we must quickly follow: When I see Kings lying by those who deposed them, when I consider rival Wits plac'd Side by Side, or the holy Men that divided the World with their Contests and Disputes, I reflect with Sorrow and Astonishment on the little Competitions, Factions, and

---

[33] A naval leader (1650–1707) who after effecting the destruction of the French Mediterranean fleet was lost at sea in a wreck off the Scilly Isles on his return trip. A further irony of which Addison could not have been aware was that many years later a dying woman confessed that she had extinguished what life remained to the Admiral when his body had been washed ashore so that she could secure a ring from his hand.

[34] Pertaining to formal appearances on public platforms or rostra.

Debates of Mankind. When I read the several Dates of the Tombs, of some that dy'd Yesterday, and some six hundred Years ago, I consider that great Day when we shall all of us be Contemporaries, and make our Appearance together.

No. 106 [A VISIT TO SIR ROGER'S]

. . . *Hinc tibi Copia*
Manabit ad plenum, benigno
Ruris honorum opulenta cornu.[35]

HOR.

MONDAY, JULY 2. 1711.

Having often received an Invitation from my Friend Sir ROGER DE COVERLY to pass away a Month with him in the Country, I last Week accompanied him thither, and am settled with him for some Time at his Country-house, where I intend to form several of my ensuing Speculations. Sir ROGER, who is very well acquainted with my Humour, lets me rise and go to bed when I please, dine at his own Table or in my Chamber as I think fit, sit still and say nothing without bidding me be merry. When the Gentlemen of the Country come to see him, he only shews me at a Distance: As I have been walking in his Fields I have observed them stealing a Sight of me over an Hedge, and have heard the Knight desiring them not to let me see them, for that I hated to be stared at.

I am the more at Ease in Sir ROGER'S Family, because it consists of sober and staid Persons; for as the Knight is the best Master in the World, he seldom changes his Servants; and as he is beloved by all about him, his Servants never care for leaving him: By this Means his Domesticks are all in Years, and grown old with their Master. You would take his Valet de Chambre for his Brother, his Butler is grey-headed, his Groom is one of the gravest Men that I have ever seen, and his Coachman has the Looks of a Privy-Counsellor.[36] You see the Goodness of the Master even in the old House-dog, and in a grey Pad that is kept in the Stable with great Care and Tenderness out of regard to his past Services, tho' he has been useless for several Years.

I could not but observe with a great deal of Pleasure the Joy that appeared in the Countenances of these ancient Domesticks upon my Friend's Arrival at his Country-Seat. Some of them could not refrain from Tears at the Sight of their old Master; every one of them press'd forward to do something for him, and seemed discouraged if they were not employed. At the same Time the good old Knight, with a mixture of the Father and the Master of the Family, tempered the Enquiries after his own Affairs with several Kind Questions relating to themselves. This Humanity and good Nature engages every Body to him, so that when he is pleasant upon any of them, all his Family are in good Humour, and none so much as the Person whom he diverts himself with: On the Contrary, if he coughs or betrays any Infirmity of old Age, it is easy for a Stander-by to observe a secret Concern in the Looks of all his Servants.

My worthy Friend has put me under the particular Care of his Butler, who is a very prudent Man, and, as well as the rest of his Fellow-Servants, wonderfully

[35] Here plenty's liberal horn shall pour
Of fruits for thee a copious show'r,
Rich honours of the quiet plain.

(Horace, *Epistles*, I, xvii, 14–16.)
[36] Similar in dignity to an official of the American president's cabinet.

desirous of pleasing me, because they have often heard their Master talk of me as of his particular Friend.

My chief Companion when Sir ROGER is diverting himself in the Woods or the Fields, is a very venerable Man, who is ever with Sir ROGER, and has lived at his House in the Nature of a Chaplain above thirty Years. This Gentleman is a Person of good Sense and some Learning, of a very regular Life and obliging Conversation: He heartily loves Sir ROGER, and knows that he is very much in the old Knight's Esteem; so that he lives in the Family rather as a Relation than a Dependant.

I have observed in several of my Papers, that my Friend Sir ROGER, amidst all his good Qualities, is something of an Humourist; and that his Virtues, as well as Imperfections, are as it were tinged by a certain Extravagance, which makes them particularly his, and distinguishes them from those of other Men. This Cast of Mind, as it is generally very innocent in itself, so it renders his Conversation highly agreeable, and more delightful than the same Degree of Sense and Virtue would appear in their common and ordinary Colours. As I was walking with him last Night, he ask'd me, How I liked the good Man whom I have just now mentioned? and without staying for my Answer, told me, That he was afraid of being insulted with *Latin* and *Greek* at his own Table; for which Reason, he desired a particular Friend of his at the University to find him out a Clergyman rather of plain Sense than much Learning, of a good Aspect, a clear Voice, a sociable Temper, and, if possible, a Man that understood a little of Back-Gammon. My Friend,

says Sir ROGER, found me out this Gentleman, who, besides the Endowments I required of him, is, they tell me, a good Scholar though he does not shew it. I have given him the Parsonage of the Parish; and because I know his Value, have settled upon him a good Annuity during his Life. If he out-lives me, he shall find that he was higher in my Esteem than perhaps he thinks he is. He has now been with me thirty Years; and though he does not know I have taken Notice of it, has never in all that Time asked any thing of me for himself, tho' he is every Day sollicting me for something in Behalf of one or other of my Tenants his Parishioners. There has not been a Law-Suit in the Parish since he has lived among them: If any Dispute arises, they apply themselves to him for the Decision; if they do not acquiesce in his Judgment, which I think never happened above once or twice at most, they appeal to me. At his first settling with me, I made him a present of all the good Sermons that have been printed in *English,* and only begged of him that every *Sunday* he would pronounce one of them in the Pulpit. Accordingly, he has digested them into such a Series, that they follow one another naturally, and make a continued System of practical Divinity.

As Sir ROGER was going on in his Story, the Gentleman we were talking of came up to us; and upon the Knight's asking him who preached to Morrow (for it was *Saturday* Night) told us, the Bishop of St. *Asaph*[37] in the Morning, and Doctor *South*[38] in the Afternoon. He then shewed us his List of Preachers for the whole Year, where I saw with a great deal of Pleasure Archbishop *Tillotson,* Bishop *Saunderson,* Doctor *Barrow,*

[37] An amusing touch in view of Sir Roger's conservatism as the Bishop of St. Asaph at this time was the newly appointed William Fleetwood, an exceptionally zealous Whig who owed his appointment only to the personal regard of Queen Anne to whom, in spite of his politics, he was "my bishop." Because of the incongruity of having Sir Roger's chaplain use the sermons of an outstanding Whig, some editors have supposed Addison must have been referring to Fleetwood's predecessor, but such

a likelihood is quite unsound, besides discounting Addison's propensity for humor.

[38] Robert South (1634–1716), canon of Christ Church, was sufficiently well known as a High Church man that his conservatism in this regard was doubtless considered by Addison as an effective balance to take the curse off the use of Fleetwood in the morning service. In addition, South's sermons were known for their wit.

Doctor *Calamy*,[39] with several living Authors who have published Discourses of practical Divinity. I no sooner saw this venerable Man in the Pulpit, but I very much approved of my Friend's insisting upon the Qualifications of a good Aspect and a clear Voice; for I was so charmed with the Gracefulness of his Figure and Delivery, as well as with the Discourses he pronounced, that I think I never passed any Time more to my Satisfaction. A Sermon repeated after this Manner, is like the Composition of a Poet in the Mouth of a graceful Actor.

I could heartily wish that more of our Country-Clergy would follow this Example; and instead of wasting their Spirits in laborious Compositions of their own, would endeavour, after a handsome Elocution and all those other Talents that are proper to enforce what has been penn'd by greater Masters. This would not only be more easy to themselves, but more edifying to the People.

No. 108   [FISHERMAN WILL]

Gratis anhelans, multa agendo nihil agens.[40]
PHÆD.

WEDNESDAY, JULY 4. 1711.

As I was Yesterday Morning walking with Sir ROGER before his House, a Country-Fellow brought him a huge Fish, which, he told him, Mr. *William Wimble* had caught that very Morning; and that he presented it, with his Service, to him, and intended to come and dine with him. At the same Time he delivered a Letter, which my Friend read to me as soon as the Messenger left him.

Sir ROGER,

I desire you to accept of a Jack,[41] which is the best I have caught this Season. I intend to come and stay with you a Week, and see how the Perch bite in the *Black River*.[42] I observed, with some Concern, the last Time I saw you upon the Bowling-Green, that your Whip wanted a Lash to it: I will bring half a Dozen with me that I twisted last Week, which I hope will serve you all the Time you are in the Country. I have not been out of the Saddle for six Days last past, having been at *Eaton*[43] with Sir *John's* eldest Son. He takes to his Learning hugely.

I am,
SIR,
Your humble Servant,
Will. Wimble.

This extraordinary Letter, and Message that accompanied it, made me very curious to know the Character and Quality of the Gentleman who sent them; which I found to be as follows: *Will. Wimble* is younger Brother to a Baronet, and descended of the ancient Family of the *Wimbles*. He is now between Forty and Fifty; but being bred to no Business and born to no Estate, he generally lives with his elder Brother as Superintendant of his Game. He hunts a Pack of Dogs better than any Man in the Country, and is very famous for finding out a Hare.

---

[39] John Tillotson (1630–1694), Robert Sanderson (1587–1663), Isaac Barrow (1630–1677), and Edmund Calamy (1600–1666), were all famous preachers of the English church. Calamy was a nonconformist, Barrow an eminent mathematician and scholar, Sanderson's life is among those Isaac Walton wrote, and Tillotson a very popular archbishop of Canterbury who owed his position to the revolution.

[40] "Out of breath to no purpose, and very busy about nothing" (Phaedrus, *Fables*, II, v, 3).

[41] "a young pike-fish" (Bailey's *Dictionary*).

[42] A fictional reference.

[43] Eton, a distinguished preparatory school opposite Windsor on the Thames.

He is extremely well versed in all the little Handicrafts of an idle Man: He makes a *May*-fly[44] to a Miracle; and furnishes the whole Country with Angle-Rods. As he is a good-natur'd officious Fellow, and very much esteemed upon Account of his Family, he is a welcome Guest at every House, and keeps up a good Correspondence among all the Gentlemen about him. He carries a Tulip-Root in his Pocket from one to another, or exchanges a Puppy between a couple of Friends that live perhaps in the opposite Sides of the County. *Will.* is a particular Favourite of all the young Heirs, whom he frequently obliges with a Net that he has weaved, or a Setting-dog that he has *made* himself:[45] He now and then presents a Pair of Garters of his own knitting to their Mothers or Sisters, and raises a great deal of Mirth among them, by enquiring as often as he meets them *how they wear?* These Gentleman-like Manufactures and obliging little Humours, make *Will.* the Darling of the Country.

Sir ROGER was proceeding in the Character of him, when we saw him make up to us, with two or three Hazle-twigs in his Hand that he had cut in Sir ROGER's Woods, as he came through them, in his Way to the House. I was very much pleased to observe on one Side the hearty and sincere Welcome with which Sir ROGER received him, and on the other the secret Joy which his Guest discovered at Sight of the good old Knight. After the first Salutes were over, *Will.* desired Sir ROGER to lend him one of his Servants to carry a Set of Shuttle-cocks he had with him in a little Box to a Lady that liv'd about a Mile off, to whom it seems he had promised such a Present for above this half Year. Sir ROGER's Back was no sooner turn'd, but honest *Will.* begun to tell me of a large Cock-Pheasant that he had sprung in one of the neighbouring Woods, with two or three other Adventures of the same Na-

ture. Odd and uncommon Characters are the Game that I look for, and most delight in; for which Reason I was as much pleased with the Novelty of the Person that talked to me, as he could be for his Life with the springing of a Pheasant, and therefore listned to him with more than ordinary Attention.

In the Midst of his Discourse the Bell rung to Dinner, where the Gentleman I have been speaking of had the Pleasure of seeing the huge Jack, he had caught, served up for the first Dish in a most sumptuous Manner. Upon our sitting down to it he gave us a long Account how he had hooked it, played with it, foiled it, and at length drew it out upon the Bank, with several other Particulars that lasted all the first Course. A Dish of Wild-fowl that came afterwards furnished Conversation for the rest of the Dinner, which concluded with a late Invention of *Will's* for improving the Quail-Pipe.[46]

Upon withdrawing into my Room after Dinner, I was secretly touched with Compassion towards the honest Gentleman that had dined with us; and could not but consider with a great deal of Concern, how so good an Heart and such busy Hands were wholly employed in Trifles; that so much Humanity should be so little beneficial to others, and so much Industry so little advantageous to himself. The same Temper of Mind and Application to Affairs might have recommended him to the publick Esteem, and have raised his Fortune in another Station of Life. What Good to his Country or himself might not a Trader or Merchant have done with such useful tho' ordinary Qualifications?

Will. Wimble's is the Case of many a younger Brother of a great Family, who had rather see their Children starve like Gentlemen, than thrive in a Trade or Profession that is beneath their Quality. This Humour fills several Parts of *Europe* with Pride and Beggary. It is the

---

[44] An artificial lure for fish.

[45] "a dog taught to find game, and point it out to the sportsman" (Johnson's *Dictionary*).

[46] "a pipe with which fowlers allure quails" (Johnson's *Dictionary*).

Happiness of a trading Nation, like ours, that the younger Sons, tho' uncapable of any liberal Art or Profession, may be placed in such a Way of Life, as may perhaps enable them to vie with the best of their Family: Accordingly we find several Citizens that were launched into the World with narrow Fortunes, rising by an honest Industry to greater Estates than those of their elder Brothers. It is not improbable but *Will.* was formerly tried at Divinity, Law, or Physick; and that finding his Genius did not lie that Way, his Parents gave him up at length to his own Inventions: But certainly, however improper he might have been for Studies of a higher Nature, he was perfectly well turned for the Occupations of Trade and Commerce. As I think this is a Point which cannot be too much inculcated, I shall desire my Reader to compare what I have here written with what I have said in my Twenty first Speculation.[47]

No. 112   [SUNDAY IN THE COUNTRY]

'Αθανάτους μέν πρῶτα θεὺς, νομω ῶς διάκειται,
Τιμᾶ. . . .[48]

PYTH.

MONDAY, JULY 9. 1711.

I am always very well pleased with a Country *Sunday;* and think, if keeping holy the Seventh Day had been only a human Institution, it would have been the best Method that could have been thought of for the polishing and civilizing of Mankind. It is certain the Country-People would soon degenerate into a kind of Savages and Barbarians, were there not such frequent Returns of a stated Time, in which the whole Village meet together with their best Faces, and in their cleanliest Dress, to converse with one another upon indifferent Subjects, hear their Duties explained to them, and join together in Adoration of the supreme Being. *Sunday* clears away the Rust of the whole Week, not only as it refreshes in their Minds the Notions of Religion, but as it puts both the Sexes upon appearing in their most agreeable Forms, and exerting all such Qualities as are apt to give them a Figure in the Eye of the Village. A Country-Fellow distinguishes himself as much in the *Church-yard,* as a Citizen does upon the *Change,* the whole Parish-Politicks being generally discuss'd in that Place either after Sermon or before the Bell rings.

My Friend Sir ROGER being a good Churchman, has beautified the Inside of his Church with several Texts of his own chusing: He has likewise given a handsome Pulpit-Cloth, and railed in the Communion-Table at his own Expence. He has often told me that at his coming to his Estate he found the Parish very irregular; and that in order to make them kneel and join in the Responses, he gave every one of them a Hassock and a Common-prayer Book; and at the same Time employed an itinerant Singing-Master, who goes about the Country for that purpose, to instruct them rightly in the Tunes of the Psalms; upon which they now very much value themselves, and indeed out-do most of the Country Churches that I have ever heard.

As Sir ROGER is Landlord to the

---

[47] In *Spectator* No. 21 Addison had deplored what he considered the overcrowding of "the three great Professions of Divinity, Law, and Physick," and strongly recommended that young men engage in commercial enterprise.

[48] "First, in obedience to thy country's rites, worship the immortal gods." (Pythagoras, *Carmina Aurea,* ll. 1–2).

whole Congregation, he keeps them in very good Order, and will suffer no Body to sleep in it besides himself; for if by Chance he has been surprized into a short Nap at Sermon, upon recovering out of it he stands up and looks about him, and if he sees any Body else nodding, either wakes them himself, or sends his Servant to them. Several other of the old Knight's Particularities break out upon these Occasions: Sometimes he will be lengthening out a Verse in the Singing-Psalms half a Minute after the rest of the Congregation have done with it; sometimes, when he is pleased with the Matter of his Devotion, he pronounces *Amen* three or four times to the same Prayer; and sometimes stands up when every Body else is upon their Knees, to count the Congregation, or see if any of his Tenants are missing.

I was Yesterday very much surprized to hear my old Friend, in the Midst of the Service, calling out to one *John Mathews* to mind what he was about, and not disturb the Congregation. This *John Mathews,* it seems is remarkable for being an idle Fellow, and at that Time was kicking his Heels for his Diversion. This Authority of the Knight, though exerted in that odd Manner which accompanies him in all Circumstances of Life, has a very good Effect upon the Parish, who are not polite enough to see any thing ridiculous in his Behaviour; besides that, the general good Sense and Worthiness of his Character, make his Friends observe these little Singularities as Foils that rather set off than blemish his good Qualities.

As soon as the Sermon is finished, no Body presumes to stir till Sir ROGER is gone out of the Church. The Knight walks from his Seat in the Chancel, between a double Row of his Tenants, that stand bowing to him on each Side; and every now and then inquires how such an one's Wife or Mother, or Son, or Father do whom he does not see at the Church; which is understood as a secret Reprimand to the Person that is absent.

The Chaplain has often told me, that upon a Catechizing-day, when Sir ROGER has been pleased with a Boy that answers well, he has ordered a Bible to be given him next Day for his Encouragement; and sometimes accompanies it with a Flitch of Bacon to his Mother. Sir ROGER has likewise added five Pounds a Year to the Clerk's Place; and that he may encourage the young Fellows to make themselves perfect in the Church-Service, has promised upon the Death of the present Incumbent, who is very old, to bestow it according to Merit.

The fair Understanding between Sir ROGER and his Chaplain, and their mutual Concurrence in doing Good, is the more remarkable, because the very next Village is famous for the Differences and Contentions that rise between the Parson and the 'Squire, who live in a perpetual State of War. The Parson is always preaching at the 'Squire, and the 'Squire, to be revenged on the Parson never comes to Church. The 'Squire has made all his Tenants Atheists and Tithe-Stealers; while the Parson instructs them every *Sunday* in the Dignity of his Order, and insinuates to them in almost every Sermon, that he is a better Man than his Patron. In short, Matters are come to such an Extremity, that the 'Squire has not said his Prayers either in publick or private this half Year; and that the Parson threatens him, if he does not mend his Manners, to pray for him in the Face of the whole Congregation.

Feuds of this Nature, though too frequent in the Country, are very fatal to the ordinary People; who are so used to be dazled with Riches, that they pay as much Deference to the Understanding of a Man of an Estate, as of a Man of Learning; and are very hardly brought to regard any Truth, how important soever it may be, that is preached to them, when they know there are several Men of five hundred a Year who do not believe it.

No. 125 [OF PARTY]

Ne pueri, ne tanta animis assuescite bella:
Neu patriae validas in fiscera vertite vires.[49]

VIR.

TUESDAY, JULY 24. 1711.

My worthy Friend Sir ROGER, when we are talking of the Malice of Parties, very frequently tells us an Accident that happened to him when he was a School-boy, which was at the time when the Feuds ran high between the Round-heads and Cavaliers.[50] This worthy Knight being then but a Stripling, had Occasion to enquire which was the Way to St. *Ann's* Lane, upon which the Person whom he spoke to, instead of answering his Question, called him a young Popish Cur, and asked him who had made *Ann* a Saint? The Boy being in some Confusion, enquired of the next he met, which was the way to *Ann's* Lane, but was called a Prick-eared Curr for his Pains, and instead of being shown the Way was told, that she had been a Saint before he was born, and would be one after he was hang'd. Upon this, says Sir ROGER, I did not think fit to repeat the former Question, but going into every Lane of the Neighbourhood, asked what they called the Name of that Lane. By which ingenious Artifice he found out the Place he enquired after, without giving Offence to any Party. Sir ROGER generally closes this Narrative with Reflections on the Mischief that Parties do in the Country; how they spoil good Neighbourhood, and make honest Gentlemen hate one another; besides that they manifestly tend to the Prejudice of the Land-Tax, and the Destruction of the Game.

There cannot a greater Judgment befall a Country than such a dreadful Spirit of Division as rends a Government into two distinct People, and makes them greater Strangers and more averse to one another, than if they were actually two different Nations. The Effects of such a Division are pernicious to the last degree, not only with regard to those Advantages which they give the Common Enemy, but to those private Evils which they produce in the Heart of almost every particular Person. This Influence is very fatal both to Mens Morals, and their Understandings; It sinks the Virtue of a Nation, and not only so, but destroys even Common Sense.

A furious Party Spirit, when it rages in its full Violence, exerts it self in Civil War and Blood-shed; and when it is under its greatest Restraints naturally breaks out in Falshood, Detraction, Calumny, and a partial Administration of Justice. In a word, It fills a Nation with Spleen and Rancour, and extinguishes all the Seeds of Good-nature, Compassion and Humanity.

Plutarch[51] says very finely that a Man should not allow himself to hate even his Enemies, because, says he, if you indulge this Passion in some Occasions, it will rise of it self in others; if you hate your Enemies, you will contract such a vicious Habit of Mind, as by Degrees will break out upon those who are your Friends, or those who are indifferent to you. I might here observe how admirably this Precept of Morality (which derives the Malignity of Hatred from the Passion it self, and not from its Object) answers to that great Rule[52] which was dictated to the World about an hundred years before this Philosopher writ; but instead of

---

[49] This thirst of kindred blood, my sons, detest,
Nor turn your force against your country's breast.
(Vergil, *Aeneid*, VI, 833–834, tr. Dryden.)
[50] The Puritans of the seventeenth century were known as Roundheads because of their custom of wearing their hair cut short; the Cavaliers were those faithful to the king's cause.
[51] *De capienda ex inimicis utilitate* (*Moralia,* II, 91).
[52] The golden rule (Matt. 7:12; Luke 6:31).

that, I shall only take notice, with a real Grief of Heart, that the Minds of many good Men among us appear sowered with Party-Principles, and alienated from one another in such a manner, as seems to me altogether inconsistent with the Dictates either of Reason or Religion. Zeal for a Publick Cause is apt to breed Passions in the Hearts of virtuous Persons, to which the Regard of their own private Interest would never have betrayed them.

If this Party Spirit has so ill an Effect on our Morals, it has likewise a very great one upon our Judgments. We often hear a poor insipid Paper or Pamphlet cryed up, and sometimes a noble Piece depretiated by those who are of a different Principle from the Author. One who is actuated by this Spirit is almost under an Incapacity of discerning either real Blemishes or Beauties. A Man of Merit in a different Principle, like an Object seen in two different Mediums,[53] appears crooked or broken, however streight and entire it may be in it self. For this Reason there is scarce a Person of any Figure in *England* who does not go by two Characters altogether different, and as opposite to one another as Light and Darkness. Knowledge and Learning suffer in a very particular manner from this strange Prejudice, which at present prevails amongst all Ranks and Degrees in the *British* Nation. As Men formerly became eminent in learned Societies by their Parts and Acquisitions, they now distinguish themselves by the Warmth and Violence with which they espouse their respective Parties. Books are valued upon the like Considerations: An Abusive, Scurrilous Style passes for Satyr, and a dull Scheme of Party Notions is called fine Writing.

There is one Piece of Sophistry practised by both Sides, and that is the taking every scandalous Story that has been ever whispered or invented of a Private Man, for a known undoubted Truth, and raising suitable Speculations upon it. Calum-

nies that have been never proved, or have been often refuted, are the ordinary Postulatums of these infamous Scriblers, upon which they proceed as upon first Principles granted by all Men, though in their Hearts they know they are false, or at best very doubtful. When they have laid these Foundations of Scurrility, it is no wonder that their Superstructure is every way answerable to them. If this shameless Practice of the present Age endures much longer, Praise and Reproach will cease to be Motives of Action in good Men.

There are certain Periods of Time in all Governments when this inhuman Spirit prevails. *Italy* was long torn in pieces by the *Guelfes* and *Gibellines,* and *France* by those who were for and against the League,[54] but it is very unhappy for a Man to be born in such a stormy and tempestuous Season. It is the restless Ambition of Artful Men that thus breaks a People into Factions, and draws several well-meaning People to their Interest, by a Specious Concern for their Country. How many honest Minds are filled with uncharitable and barbarous Notions, out of their Zeal for the Publick Good? What Cruelties and Outrages would they not commit against Men of an adverse Party, whom they would honour and esteem, if instead of considering them as they are represented, they knew them as they are? Thus are Persons of the greatest Probity seduced into shameful Errors and Prejudices, and made bad Men even by that noblest of Principles, the Love of their Country. I cannot here forbear mentioning the Famous *Spanish* Proverb, *If there were neither Fools nor Knaves in the World, all People would be of one Mind.*

For my own part, I could heartily wish that all Honest Men would enter into an Association, for the Support of one another against the Endeavours of those whom they ought to look upon as their common Enemies, whatsoever side

---

[53] This refers to the experiment of putting a stick half into water and observing the apparent bent or broken condition, a classic demonstration of the untrustworthiness of sense evidence.

[54] An organization of French Catholics in 1576 by the Duke of Guise, ostensibly to resist Calvinism, but actually to overthrow the rule of Henry III.

they may belong to. Were there such an honest Neutral Body of Forces, we should never see the worst of Men in great Figures of Life, because they are useful to a Party; nor the best unregarded, because they are above practising those Methods which would be grateful to their Faction. We should then single every Criminal out of the Herd, and hunt him down, however formidable and overgrown he might appear: On the contrary, we should shelter distressed Innocence, and defend Virtue, however beset with Contempt or Ridicule, Envy or Defamation. In short, we should not any longer regard our Fellow-Subjects as Whigs or Tories, but should make the Man of Merit our Friend, and the Villain our Enemy.

No. 251   [THE CRIES OF LONDON]

. . . Linguae centum sunt, oraque centum,
Ferrea vox. . . .[55]

VIRG.

TUESDAY, DECEMBER 18. 1711.

There is nothing which more astonishes a Foreigner and frights a Country Squire, than the *Cries of London*. My good Friend, Sir ROGER, often declares, that he cannot get them out of his Head, or go to sleep for them the first Week that he is in Town. On the contrary, WILL. HONEYCOMB calls them the *Ramage de la Ville*,[56] and prefers them to the Sounds of Larks and Nightingales, with all the Music of the Fields and Woods. I have lately received a Letter from some very odd Fellow upon this Subject, which I shall leave with my Reader, without saying any thing further of it.

SIR,
I am a Man out of all Business, and would willingly turn my Head to any thing for an honest Livelihood. I have invented several Projects for raising many Millions of Mony without burthening the Subject, but I cannot get the Parliament to listen to me, who look upon me, forsooth, as a Crack and a Projector; so that despairing to enrich either my self or my Country by this Publick-spiritedness, I would make some Proposals to you relating to a Design, which I have very much at Heart, and which may procure me an handsom Subsistance, if you will be pleased to recommend it to the Cities of *London* and *Westminster*.

The Post I would aim at is to be Comptroller general of the *London* Cries, which are at present under no manner of Rules or Discipline. I think I am pretty well qualified for this Place, as being a Man of very strong Lungs, of great Insight into all the Branches of our *British* Trades and Manufactures, and of a competent Skill in Musick.

The Cries of *London* may be divided into Vocal and Instrumental. As for the latter, they are at present under a very great Disorder. A Freeman of *London* has the Privilege of disturbing a whole Street for an hour together, with the twancking of a Brass Kettle or a Frying-Pan. The Watchman's Thump at Midnight startles us in our Beds, as much as the breaking in of a Thief. The Sowgelder's Horn has indeed something musical in it, but this is seldom heard within the Liberties.[57] I would therefore propose, that no Instrument of this nature should be made use of, which I have not tuned and licensed, after having care-

---

[55] A hundred mouths, a hundred tongues,
And throats of brass inspir'd with iron lungs.
(Vergil, *Aeneid*, VI, 625–626, tr. Dryden.)

[56] "the babble of the city."
[57] Suburban areas subject to municipal authority.

fully examined in what manner it may affect the Ears of her Majesty's liege Subjects.

Vocal Cries are of a much larger Extent, and indeed so full of Incongruities and Barbarisms, that we appear a distracted City, to Foreigners, who do not comprehend the Meaning of such Enormous Outcries. Milk is generally sold in a Note above *Elah*,[58] and in Sounds so exceedingly shrill, that it often sets our Teeth an edge. The Chimney Sweeper is contained to no certain pitch; he sometimes utters himself in the deepest Base, and sometimes in the sharpest Treble; sometimes in the highest, and sometimes in the lowest Note of the Gamut. The same Observation might be made on the Retailers of Small-cole,[59] not to mention broken Glasses or Brickdust. In these, therefore, and the like Cases, it should be my Care to sweeten and mellow the Voices of these itinerant Tradesmen, before they make their appearance in our Streets; as also to accommodate their Cries to their respective Wares; and to take care in particular that those may not make the most noise, who have the least to sell, which is very observable in the Venders of Cardmatches, to whom I cannot but apply that old Proverb of *Much Cry but little Wool*.

Some of these last-mentioned Musicians are so very loud in the Sale of these trifling Manufactures, that an honest Splenetick Gentleman of my Acquaintance bargained with one of them never to come into the Street where he lived; But what was the effect of this Contract? why, the whole Tribe of Cardmatchmakers which frequent that Quarter, passed by his Door the very next Day, in hopes of being bought off after the same manner.

It is another great Imperfection in our *London* Cries, that there is no just Time nor Measure observed in them. Our News should indeed be Published in a very quick time, because it is a Commodity that will not keep cold. It should not however be cried with the same Pre-

cipitation as *Fire:* Yet this is generally the case: A Bloody Battel alarms the Town from one end to another in an Instant. Every Motion of the *French* is Published in so great an hurry, that one would think the Enemy were at our Gates. This likewise I would take upon me to regulate in such a manner, that there should be some Distinction made between the spreading of a Victory, a March, or an Incampment, a *Dutch,* a *Portugal,* or a *Spanish* Mail. Nor must I omit under this Head, those excessive Alarms with which several boisterous Rusticks infest our Streets in Turnip Season; and which are more inexcusable, because these are Wares which are in no danger of Cooling upon their Hands.

There are others who affect a very slow time, and are in my Opinion much more tuneable than the former; the Cooper in particular swells his last Note in an hollow Voice, that is not without its Harmony; nor can I forbear being inspired with a most agreeable Melancholy, when I hear that sad and solemn Air with which the Publick is very often asked, if they have any Chairs to mend. Your own Memory may suggest to you many other lamentable Ditties of the same nature, in which the Musick is wonderfully languishing and melodious.

I am always pleased with that particular time of the Year which is proper for the pickling of Dill and Cucumbers; but alas this Cry, like the Song of the Nightingales, is not heard above two Months. It might therefore be worth while, to consider whether the same Air might not in some Cases be adapted to other Words.

It might likewise deserve our most serious Consideration, how far, in a well regulated City, those Humourists are to be tolerated, who not contented with the traditional Cries of their Fore-fathers, have invented particular Songs and Tunes of their own: Such as was, not many Years since, the Pastry-man, commonly known by the Name of the Colly-Molly-Puff; and such as is at this Day

---

[58] "the highest note in the scale of music" (Bailey's *Dictionary*).

[59] "little wood coal [charcoal] used in lighting fires" (Bailey's *Dictionary*).

the Vender of Powder and Washballs, who, if I am rightly inform'd, goes under the Name of *Powder-Watt.*

I must not here omit one particular Absurdity which runs through this whole Vociferous Generation, and which renders their Cries very often not only incommodious, but altogether useless to the Publick, I mean that Idle Accomplishment which they all of them aim at, of Crying so as not to be understood. Whether or no they have learned this from several of our affected Singers, I will not take upon me to say; but most certain it is, that People know the Wares they deal in rather by their Tunes than by their Words; insomuch that I have sometimes seen a Country Boy run out to buy Apples of a Bellows-mender, and Gingerbread from a Grinder of Knives and Scissars. Nay, so strangely infatuated are some very eminent Artists of this particular Grace in a Cry, that none but their Acquaintance are able to guess at their Profession; for who else can

know, that *Work if I had it,* should be the Signification of a Corn-Cutter.

For-as-much therefore as Persons of this Rank are seldom Men of Genius or Capacity, I think it would be very proper that some Man of good Sense and sound Judgment should preside over these Publick Cries, who should permit none to lift up their Voices in our Streets, that have not tuneable Throats, and are not only able to overcome the Noise of the Croud, and the rattling of Coaches, but also to vend their respective Merchandizes in apt Phrases, and in the most distinct and agreeable Sounds. I do therefore humbly recommend my self as a Person rightly qualified for this Post; and if I meet with fitting Encouragement, shall communicate some other Projects which I have by me, that may no less conduce to the Emolument of the Publick.

I am,
SIR, &c.
Ralph Crotchett.

No. 409   [OF LITERARY TASTE]

. . . Musaeo contingere cuncta depore.[60]
LUCR.

THURSDAY, JUNE 19. 1712.

Gratian[61] very often recommends *the fine Taste,* as the utmost Perfection of an accomplished Man. As this Word arises very often in Conversation, I shall endeavour to give some Account of it, and to lay down Rules how we may know whether we are possessed of it, and how we may acquire that fine Taste of Writing, which is so much talked of among the Polite World.

Most Languages make use of this Metaphor, to express that Faculty of the Mind, which distinguishes all the most concealed Faults and nicest Perfections in Writing. We may be sure this Metaphor would not have been so general in

all Tongues, had there not been a very great Conformity between that Mental Taste, which is the Subject of this Paper, and that Sensitive Taste which gives us a Relish of every different Flavour that affects the Palate. Accordingly we find, that there are as many Degrees of Refinement in the intellectual Faculty, as in the Sense, which is marked out by this common Denomination.

I knew a Person who possessed the one in so great a Perfection, that after having tasted ten different Kinds of Tea, he would distinguish, without seeing the colour of it, the particular Sort which was offered him; and not only so, but any two sorts of them that were mixt together in an equal Proportion; nay, he

---

[60] "To grace each subject with enlivening wit" (Lucretius, *De Rerum Natura,* I, 933).

[61] Baltasar Gracián (1601–1658), a Spanish literary critic.

has carried the Experiment so far, as upon tasting the Composition of three different sorts, to name the Parcels from whence the three several Ingredients were taken. A Man of a fine Taste in Writing will discern after the same manner, not only the general Beauties and Imperfections of an Author, but discover the several Ways of thinking and expressing himself, which diversify him from all other Authors, with the several Foreign infusions of Thought and Language, and the particular Authors from whom they were borrowed.

After having thus far explained what is generally meant by a fine Taste in Writing, and shown the Propriety of the Metaphor which is used on this Occasion, I think I may define it to be *that Faculty of the Soul, which discerns the Beauties of an Author with Pleasure, and the Imperfections with Dislike.* If a Man would know whether he is possessed of this Faculty, I would have him read over the celebrated Works of Antiquity, which have stood the Test of so many different Ages and Countries; or those Works among the Moderns, which have the Sanction of the Politer Part of our Contemporaries. If upon the Perusal of such Writings he does not find himself delighted in an extraordinary manner, or, if upon reading the admired Passages in such Authors, he finds a Coldness and Indifference in his Thoughts, he ought to conclude, not (as is too usual among tasteless Readers) that the Author has not those Perfections which have been admired in him, but that he himself wants the Faculty of discovering them.

He should, in the second place, be very careful to observe, whether he tastes the distinguishing Perfections, or, if I may be allowed to call them so, the Specifick Qualities of the Author whom he peruses; whether he is particularly pleased with *Livy* for his manner of telling a Story, with *Sallust* for his entering into those internal Principles of Action which arise from the Characters and Manners of the Persons he describes, or with *Tacitus* for his displaying those outward Motives of Safety and Interest, which

give birth to the whole Series of Transactions which he relates.

He may likewise consider, how differently he is affected by the same Thought, which presents it self in a great Writer, from what he is when he finds it delivered by a Person of an ordinary Genius. For there is as much difference in apprehending a Thought cloathed in *Cicero's* Language, and that of a common Author, as in seeing an Object by the Light of a Taper, or by the Light of the Sun.

It is very difficult to lay down Rules for the acquirement of such a Taste as that I am here speaking of. The Faculty must in some degree be born with us, and it very often happens, that those who have other Qualities in Perfection are wholly void of this. One of the most eminent Mathematicians of the Age has assured me, that the greatest Pleasure he took in reading *Virgil*, was in examining *Æneas* his Voyage by the map; as I question not but many a Modern Compiler of History would be delighted with little more in that Divine Author, than in the bare matters of Fact.

But notwithstanding this Faculty must in some measure be born with us, there are several Methods for Cultivating and Improving it, and without which it will be very uncertain, and of little use to the Person that possesses it. The most natural Method for this Purpose is to be conversant among the Writings of the most Polite Authors. A Man who has any Relish for fine Writing, either discovers new Beauties, or receives stronger Impressions from the Masterly Stroaks of a great Author every time he peruses him: Besides that he naturally wears himself into the same manner of Speaking and Thinking.

Conversation with Men of a Polite Genius is another Method for improving our Natural Taste. It is impossible for a Man of the greatest Parts to consider any thing in its whole Extent, and in all its variety of Lights. Every Man, besides those general Observations which are to be made upon an Author, forms several Reflections that are peculiar to his own manner of thinking; so that

Conversation will naturally furnish us with Hints which we did not attend to, and make us enjoy other Mens Parts and Reflections as well as our own. This is the best Reason I can give for the Observation which several have made, that Men of great Genius in the same way of Writing seldom rise up singly, but at certain Periods of Time appear together, and in a Body; as they did at *Rome* in the Reign of *Augustus,* and in *Greece* about the Age of *Socrates.* I cannot think that either *Corneille, Racine, Moliere, Boileau, la Fontaine, Bruyere, Bossu,* or the *Daciers,* would have written so well as they have done, had they not been Friends and Contemporaries.[62]

It is likewise necessary for a Man who would form to himself a finished Taste of good Writing to be well versed in the Works of the best *Criticks* both Ancient and Modern. I must confess that I could wish there were Authors of this kind, who, beside the Mechanical Rules which a Man of very little Taste may discourse upon, would enter into the very Spirit and Soul of fine Writing and shew us the several Sources of that Pleasure which rises in the Mind upon the Perusal of a noble Work. Thus altho' in Poetry it be absolutely necessary that the Unities of Time, Place and Action, with other Points of the same Nature, should be thoroughly explained and understood; there is still something more essential to the Art, something that elevates and astonishes the Fancy, and gives a Greatness of Mind to the Reader, which few of the Criticks besides *Longinus* have consider'd.

Our general Taste in *England* is for Epigram, turns of Wit, and forced Conceits,[63] which have no manner of influence, either for the bettering or enlarging the Mind of him who reads them, and have been carefully avoided by the greatest Writers, both among the Ancients and Moderns. I have endeavoured in several of my Speculations to banish this *Gothic* Taste which has taken Possession among us. I entertained the Town for a Week together with an Essay upon Wit,[64] in which I endeavoured to detect several of those false kinds which have been admir'd in the different Ages of the World; and at the same time to shew wherein the nature of true Wit consists. I afterwards gave an Instance of the great force which lies in a natural Simplicity of Thought to affect the Mind of the Reader, from such Vulgar Pieces as have little else besides this single Qualification to recommend them.[65] I have likewise examined the Works of the greatest Poet which our Nation or perhaps any other has produced, and particularized most of those rational and manly Beauties which give a value to that Divine Work.[66] I shall next *Saturday* enter upon an Essay *on the Pleasures of the Imagination,* which though it shall consider that Subject at large, will perhaps suggest to the Reader what it is that gives a Beauty to many Passages of the finest Writers both in Prose and Verse. As an Undertaking of this nature is entirely new, I question not but it will be receiv'd with Candour.

No. 411   [OF PLEASURES OF THE IMAGINATION]

Avia Pieridum peragro loca, nullius ante
Trita solo; juvat integros accedere fonteis;
Atque haurire: . . .[67]

                              LUCR.

---

[62] These are all French authors of the seventeenth century.

[63] Figures of thought or speech.

[64] Addison's "Essay upon Wit" takes up six papers of *The Spectator,* Nos. 58–63.

[65] *Spectator* No. 70 acclaims literature dis-

playing "Simplicity of Thought, above that which I call the Gothick Manner in Writing."

[66] John Milton's *Paradise Lost* had been discussed in *The Spectator* in a series of eighteen Saturday papers beginning with No. 267.

[67] In wild unclear'd, to Muses a retreat,

SATURDAY, JUNE 21. 1712.

Our Sight is the most perfect and most delightful of all our Senses. It fills the Mind with the largest Variety of Ideas, converses with its Objects at the greatest Distance, and continues the longest in Action without being tired or satiated with its proper Enjoyments. The sense of Feeling can indeed give us a Notion of Extension, Shape, and all other Ideas that enter at the Eye, except Colours; but at the same time it is very much streightned and confined in its Operations, to the number, bulk, and distance of its particular Objects. Our Sight therefore seems designed to supply all these Defects, and may be considered as a more delicate and diffusive kind of Touch, that spreads it self over an infinite Multitude of Bodies, comprehends the largest Figures, and brings into our reach some of the most remote Parts of the Universe.

It is this Sense which furnishes the Imagination with its Ideas; so that by the Pleasures of the Imagination or Fancy (which I shall use promiscuously) I here mean such as arise from visible Objects, either when we have them actually in our view, or when we call up their Ideas into our Minds by Paintings, Statues, Descriptions, or any of the like Occasion. We cannot indeed have a single Image in the Fancy that did not make its first Entrance through the Sight; but we have the Power of retaining, altering and compounding those Images, which we have once received, into all the varieties of Picture and Vision that are most agreeable to the Imagination; for by this Faculty a Man in a Dungeon is capable of entertaining himself with Scenes and Landskips more beautiful than any that can be found in the whole Compass of Nature.

There are few Words in the *English* Language which are employed in a more loose and uncircumscribed Sense than those of the *Fancy* and the *Imagination*. I therefore thought it necessary to fix and determine the Notion of these two Words, as I intend to make use of them in the Thread of my following Speculations, that the Reader may conceive rightly what is the Subject which I proceed upon. I must therefore desire him to remember, that by the Pleasures of the Imagination, I mean only such Pleasures as arise originally from Sight, and that I divide these Pleasures into two kinds: My Design being first of all to Discourse of those Primary Pleasures of the Imagination, which entirely proceed from such Objects as are present to the Eye; and in the next place to speak of those Secondary Pleasures of the Imagination which flow from the Ideas of visible Objects, when the Objects are not actually before the Eye, but are called up into our Memories, or form'd into agreeable Visions of Things that are either Absent or Fictitious.

The Pleasures of the Imagination, taken in their full Extent, are not so gross as those of Sense, nor so refined as those of the Understanding. The last are, indeed, more preferable, because they are founded on some new Knowledge or Improvement in the Mind of Man; yet it must be confest, that those of the Imagination are as great and as transporting as the other. A beautiful Prospect delights the Soul, as much as a Demonstration; and a Description in *Homer* has charmed more Readers than a Chapter in *Aristotle*. Besides, the Pleasures of the Imagination have this Advantage, above those of the Understanding, that they are more obvious, and more easie to be acquired. It is but opening the Eye, and the Scene enters. The Colours paint themselves on the Fancy, with very little Attention of Thought or Application of Mind in the Beholder. We are struck, we know not how, with the Symmetry of any thing we see, and immediately assent to the Beauty of an Object, without enquiring into the particular Causes and Occasions of it.

A Man of a Polite[68] Imagination, is let into a great many Pleasures that the

O'er ground untrod before, I devious roam,
And deep-enamoured into latent springs
Presume to peep at coy virgin Naiads.

(Lucretius, *De Rerum Natura*, I, 925–927).
    [68] "accomplished" (Bailey's *Dictionary*).

Vulgar are not capable of receiving. He can converse with a Picture, and find an agreeable Companion in a Statue. He meets with a secret Refreshment in a Description and often feels a greater Satisfaction in the Prospect of Fields and Meadows, than another does in the Possession. It gives him, indeed, a kind of Property in everything he sees, and makes the most rude uncultivated Parts of Nature administer to his Pleasures: So that he looks upon the World, as it were, in another Light, and discovers in it a Multitude of Charms, that conceal themselves from the generality of Mankind.

There are, indeed, but very few who know how to be idle and innocent, or have a Relish of any Pleasures that are not Criminal; every Diversion they take is at the Expence of some one Virtue or another, and their very first Step out of Business is into Vice or Folly. A Man should endeavour, therefore, to make the Sphere of his innocent Pleasures as wide as possible, that he may retire into them with Safety, and find in them such a Satisfaction as a wise Man would not blush to take. Of this Nature are those of the Imagination, which do not require such a Bent of Thought as is necessary to our more serious Employments, nor, at the same time, suffer the Mind to sink into that Negligence and Remissness, which are apt to accompany our more sensual Delights, but, like a gentle Exercise to the Faculties, awaken them from Sloth and Idleness, without putting them upon any Labour or Difficulty.

We might here add, that the Pleasures of the Fancy are more conducive to Health, than those of the Understanding, which are worked out by Dint of Thinking, and attended with too violent a Labour of the Brain. Delightful Scenes, whether in Nature, Painting, or Poetry, have a kindly Influence on the Body, as well as the Mind, and not only serve to clear and brighten the Imagination, but are able to disperse Grief and Melancholly, and to set the Animal Spirits in pleasing and agreeable Motions. For this reason Sir *Francis Bacon,* in his Essay upon Health, has not thought it improper to prescribe to his Reader a Poem or a Prospect, where he particularly dissuades him from knotty and subtile Disquisitions, and advises him to pursue Studies, that fill the Mind with splendid and illustrious Objects, as Histories, Fables, and Contemplations of Nature.

I have in this Paper, by way of Introduction, settled the Notion of those Pleasures of the Imagination, which are the Subject of my present Undertaking, and endeavoured, by several Considerations, to recommend to my Reader the Pursuit of those Pleasures. I shall, in my next Paper, examine the several Sources from whence these Pleasures are derived.

No. 414   [OF ART AND NATURE]

. . . Alterius Sic
Altera poscit opem res & conjurat amice.[69]

WEDNESDAY, JUNE 25. 1712.

If we consider the Works of Nature and Art, as they are qualified to entertain the Imagination, we shall find the last very defective, in Comparison of the former; for though they may sometimes appear as Beautiful or Strange, they can have nothing in them of that Vastness and Immensity, which afford so great an Entertainment to the Mind of the Beholder. The one may be as Polite and Delicate as the other, but can never shew her self so August and Magnificent in the Design. There is something more bold and masterly in the rough careless Strokes of Nature, than in the nice Touches and Embellishments of Art.

---

[69] "But mutually they crave each other's aid" (Horace, *Ars Poetica,* ll. 410–411, tr. Roscommon).

The Beauties of the most stately Garden or Palace lie in a narrow Compass, the Imagination immediately runs them over, and requires something else to gratifie her; but, in the wide Fields of Nature, the Sight wanders up and down without Confinement, and is fed with an infinite variety of Images, without any certain Stint or Number. For this Reason we always find the Poet in love with a Country-Life, where Nature appears in the greatest Perfection, and furnishes out all those Scenes that are most apt to delight the Imagination.

Scriptorum chorus omnis amat nemus & fugit Urbes.[70]

HOR.

Hic Secura quies, & nescia fallere vita,
Dives opum variarum; hic latis otia fundis,
Speluncae, vivique lacus, hic frigida Tempe,
Mugitusque boum, mollesque sub arbore sumni.[71]

VIR.

But tho' there are several of these wild Scenes, that are more delightful than any artificial Shows; yet we find the Works of Nature still more pleasant, the more they resemble those of Art: For in this case our Pleasure arises from a double Principle; from the Agreeableness of the Objects to the Eye, and from their Similitude to other Objects: We are pleased as well with comparing their Beauties, as with surveying them, and can represent them to our Minds, either as Copies or Originals. Hence it is that we take Delight in a Prospect which is well laid out, and diversified with Fields and Meadows, Woods and Rivers, in those accidental Landskips of Trees, Clouds and Cities, that are sometimes found in the Veins of Marble, in the curious Fret-work of Rocks and Grottos, and, in a Word, in any thing that hath such a Variety or Regularity as may seem the Effect of Design, in what we call the Works of Chance.

If the Products of Nature rise in Value, according as they more or less resemble those of Art, we may be sure that artificial Works receive a greater Advantage from their Resemblance of such as are natural; because here the Similitude is not only pleasant, but the Pattern more perfect. The prettiest Landskip I ever saw, was one drawn on the Walls of a dark Room, that stood opposite on one side to a navigable River, and on the other to a Park.[72] The Experiment is very common in Opticks. Here you might discover the Waves and Fluctuations of the Water in strong and proper Colours, with the Picture of a Ship entering at one end, and sailing by Degrees through the whole Piece. On another there appeared the Green Shadows of Trees, waving to and fro with the Wind, and Herds of Deer among them in Miniature, leaping about upon the Wall. I must confess, the Novelty of such a sight may be one occasion of its Pleasantness to the Imagination, but certainly the chief Reason is its near Resemblance to Nature, as it does not only, like other Pictures, give the Colour and Figure, but the Motion of the Things it represents.

We have before observed, that there is generally in Nature something more Grand and August, than what we meet with in the Curiosities of Art. When, therefore, we see this imitated in any measure, it gives us a nobler and more exalted kind of Pleasure than what we

---

[70] The tribe of writers to a man, admire
The peaceful grove, and from the town retire.
   (Horace, *Epistles*, II, ii, 77, tr. Francis.)
   [71] Here easy quiet, a secure retreat,
A harmless life that knows not how to cheat,
With home-bred plenty the rich owner bless,
And rural pleasures crown his happiness.
Unvex'd with quarrels, undisturb'd with noise,
The country king his peaceful realm enjoys:
Cool grots and living lakes, the flow'ry pride

Of meads, and streams that through the valley
   glide;
And shady groves that easy sleep invite,
And, after toilsome days, a sweet repose at
   night.
(Vergil, *Georgics*, II, 467–470, tr. Dryden.)
   [72] This passage describes a camera obscura, a darkened room with a small aperture which afforded entertainment by providing a primitive television.

receive from the nicer and more accurate Productions of Art. On this Account our *English* Gardens are not so entertaining to the Fancy as those in *France* and *Italy,* where we see a large Extent of Ground covered over with an agreeable mixture of Garden and Forest, which represent every where an artificial Rudeness much more charming than that Neatness and Elegancy which we meet with in those of our own Country. It might, indeed, be of ill Consequence to the Publick, as well as unprofitable to private Persons, to alienate so much Ground from Pasturage, and the Plow, in many Parts of a Country that is so well peopled, and cultivated to a far greater advantage. But why may not a whole Estate be thrown into a kind of Garden by frequent Plantations, that may turn as much to the Profit, as the Pleasure, of the Owner? A Marsh overgrown with Willows, or a Mountain shaded with Oaks, are not only more beautiful, but more beneficial, than when they lie bare and unadorned. Fields of Corn make a pleasant Prospect, and if the Walks were a little taken care of that lie between them, if the natural Embroidery of the Meadows were helpt and improved by some small Additions of Art, and the several Rows of Hedges set off by Trees and Flowers, that the Soil was capable of receiving, a Man might make a pretty Landskip of his own Possessions.

Writers, who have given us an Account of *China,* tell us, the Inhabitants of that Country laugh at the Plantations of our *Europeans,* which are laid out by the Rule and Line; because, they say, any one may place Trees in equal Rows and uniform Figures. They chuse rather to shew a Genius in Works of this Nature, and therefore always conceal the Art by which they direct themselves. They have a Word, it seems, in their Language, by which they express the particular Beauty of a Plantation that thus strikes the Imagination at first Sight, without discovering what it is that has so agreeable an Effect. Our *British* Gardeners, on the contrary, instead of humouring Nature, love to deviate from it as much as possible. Our Trees rise in Cones, Globes, and Pyramids. We see the Marks of the Scissars upon every Plant and Bush. I do not know whether I am singular in my Opinion, but, for my own part, I would rather look upon a Tree in all its Luxuriancy and Diffusion of Boughs and Branches, than when it is thus cut and trimmed into a Mathematical Figure; and cannot but fancy that an Orchard in Flower looks infinitely more delightful, than all the little Labyrinths of the most finished Parterre.[73] But as our great Modellers of Gardens have their Magazines of Plants to dispose of, it is very natural for them to tear up all the Beautiful Plantations of Fruit Trees, and contrive a Plan that may most turn to their own Profit, in taking off their Evergreens, and the like Moveable Plants, with which their Shops are plentifully stocked.

No. 417 [OF IMAGINING THINGS STRONGLY]

Quem tu Melpomene semel
Nascentem placido lumine videris,
    Non illum labor Istmius
Clarabit pugilem, non equus impiger, &c.
Sed quae Tibur aquæ fertile perfluunt,
    Et Spissae nemorum comae
Fingent Æolio carmine nobilem.[74]

                                    HOR.

[73] garden.
[74] He on whose birth the lyric queen / Of numbers smil'd, shall never grace / The Isthmian gauntlet, or be seen / First in the fam'd Olympic race. / But him the streams that warbling flow / Rich Tibur's fertile meads along, / And shady groves, his haunts shall know

SATURDAY, JUNE 28. 1712.

We may observe, that any single Circumstance of what we have formerly seen often raises up a whole Scene of Imagery, and awakens a Thousand Ideas that before slept in the Imagination; such a particular Smell or Colour is able to fill the Mind, on a sudden, with the Picture of the Fields or Gardens where we first met with it, and to bring up into View all the Variety of Images that once attended it. Our Imagination takes the Hint, and leads us unexpectedly into Cities or Theatres, Plains or Meadows. We may further observe, when the Fancy thus reflects on the Scenes that have past in it formerly, those, which were at first pleasant to behold, appear more so upon Reflection, and that the Memory heightens the Delightfulness of the Original. A *Cartesian*[75] would account for both these Instances in the following Manner.

The Sett of Ideas, which we received from such a Prospect or Garden, having entered the Mind at the same time, have a Sett of Traces belonging to them in the Brain, bordering very near upon one another; when, therefore, any one of these Ideas arises in the Imagination, and consequently dispatches a flow of Animal Spirits[76] to its proper Trace, these Spirits, in the violence of their Motion, run not only into the Trace, to which they were more particularly directed, but into several of those that lie about it: By this means they awaken other Ideas of the same Sett, which immediately determine a new Dispatch of Spirits, that in the same manner open other Neighbouring Traces, till at last the whole Sett of them is blown up, and the whole Prospect or Garden flourishes in the Imagination. But because the Pleasure we received from these Places far surmounted, and overcame the little Disagreeableness we found in them, for this

Reason there was at first a wider Passage worn in the Pleasure Traces, and, on the contrary, so narrow a one in those that belonged to the disagreeable Ideas, that they were quickly stopt up, and rendered incapable of receiving any Animal Spirits, and consequently of exciting any unpleasant Ideas in the Memory.

It would be in vain to enquire, whether the Power of Imagining Things strongly proceeds from any greater Perfection in the Soul, or from any nicer Texture in the Brain of one Man than of another. But this is certain, that a noble Writer should be born with this Faculty in its full Strength and Vigour, so as to be able to receive lively Ideas from outward Objects, to retain them long, and to range them together, upon occasion, in such Figures and Representations as are most likely to hit the Fancy of the Reader. A Poet should take as much Pains in forming his Imagination, as a Philosopher in cultivating his Understanding. He must gain a due Relish of the Works of Nature, and be throughly conversant in the various Scenary of a Country Life.

When he is stored with Country Images, if he would go beyond Pastoral, and the lower kinds of Poetry, he ought to acquaint himself with the Pomp and Magnificence of Courts. He should be very well versed in every thing that is noble and stately in the Productions of Art, whether it appear in Painting or Statuary, in the great Works of Architecture that are in their present Glory, or in the Ruins of those that flourished in former Ages.

Such Advantages as these help to open a Man's Thoughts, and to enlarge his Imagination, and will therefore have their Influence on all Kinds of Writing, if the Author knows how to make right use of them. And among those of the learned Languages that excell in this Talent, the most perfect in their several

The master of th'Aeolian song.
(Horace, *Odes*, IV, iii, 1–4, 10–12, tr. Atterbury.)
[75] A follower of the French philosopher René Descartes, who would attempt to explain the operation of the mind in terms of cause

and effect.
[76] "a fine subtil juice or humour in animal bodies, supposed to be the great instrument of muscular motion, sensation, etc., as distinguished from natural and vital" (Bailey's *Dictionary*).

Kinds, are perhaps *Homer, Virgil,* and *Ovid.* The first strikes the Imagination wonderfully with what is Great, the second with what is Beautiful, and the last with what is Strange. Reading the *Iliad* is like travelling through a Country uninhabited, where the Fancy is entertained with a thousand Savage Prospects of vast Desarts, wide uncultivated Marshes, huge Forests, mis-shapen Rocks and Precipices. On the contrary, the *Æneid* is like a well ordered Garden, where it is impossible to find out any Part unadorned, or to cast our Eyes upon a single Spot, that does not produce some beautiful Plant or Flower. But when we are in the *Metamorphosis,* we are walking on enchanted Ground, and see nothing but Scenes of Magick lying round us.

Homer is in his Province, when he is describing a Battel or a Multitude, a Heroe or a God. *Virgil* is never better pleas'd, than when he is in his *Elysium,* or copying out an entertaining Picture. *Homer's* Epithets generally mark out what is Great, *Virgil's* what is Agreeable. Nothing can be more Magnificent than the Figure that *Jupiter* makes in the First *Iliad,* nor more Charming than that of *Venus* in the First *Æneid.*

῏Η᾿ καὶ κυανέῃσιν ἐπ᾿ ὀφρύσι νεῦσε Κρονίων
᾿Αμβρόσιαι δ᾿ ἄρα χαῖται ἐπιρρώσαντο ἄνακτος
Κρατὸς ἀπ αθανατοιο μεγαν δ᾿ἐλέλιξεν
      ῎Ολυμπον.[77]

Dixit, & avertens rosea cervice refulsit:
Ambrosiaeque comae divinum vertice
  odorem
Spiravere: Pedes vestis defluxit ad imos:
Et vera incessu patuit Dea. . . .[78]

Homer's Persons are most of them Godlike and Terrible: *Virgil* has scarce admitted any into his Poem, who are not beautiful, and has taken particular Care to make his Heroe so.

> . . . *lumenque juventae*
> *Purpureum, & lætos oculis afflavit honores.*[79]

In a Word, *Homer* fills his Readers with Sublime Ideas, and, I believe, has raised the Imagination of all the good Poets that have come after him. I shall only instance *Horace,* who immediately takes Fire at the first Hint of any Passage in the *Iliad* or *Odyssee,* and always rises above himself, when he has *Homer* in his View. *Virgil* has drawn together, into his *Æneid,* all the pleasing Scenes that his Subject is capable of admitting, and in his *Georgics* has given us a Collection of the most delightful Landskips that can be made out of Fields and Woods, Herds of Cattle, and Swarms of Bees.

Ovid, in his *Metamorphosis,* has shewn us how the Imagination may be affected by what is Strange. He describes a Miracle in every Story, and always gives us the Sight of some new Creature at the end of it. His Art consists chiefly in well-timing his Description, before the first Shape is quite worn off, and the new one perfectly finish'd; so that he every where entertains us with something we never saw before, and shews Monster after Monster, to the end of the *Metamorphosis.*

If I were to name a Poet that is a perfect Master in all these Arts of working on the Imagination, I think *Milton* may pass for one: And if his *Paradise Lost* falls short of the *Æneid* or *Iliad* in this respect, it proceeds rather from the Fault of the Language in which it is written, than from any Defect of Genius in the

---

[77] He spoke, and awful bends his sable brows;
Shakes his ambrosial curls, and gives the nod,
The stamp of fate, and sanction of the god:
High heav'n with trembling the dread signal took,
And all Olympus to the centre shook.
      (Homer, *Iliad,* I, 528, tr. Pope.)
[78] Thus having said, she turn'd and made appear
Her neck refulgent, and dishevel'd hair;

Which, flowing from her shoulders, reach'd the ground,
And widely spread ambrosial scents around:
In length of train descends her sweeping gown,
And by her graceful walk the queen of love is known.
      (Vergil, *Aeneid,* I, 406, tr. Dryden.)
[79] And gave his rolling eyes a sparkling grace,
And breath'd a youthful vigour on his face.
      (Vergil, *Aeneid,* I, 594, tr. Dryden.)

Author. So Divine a Poem in *English,* is like a stately Palace built of Brick, where one may see Architecture in as great a Perfection as in one of Marble, tho' the Materials are of a coarser Nature. But to consider it only as it regards our present Subject: What can be conceiv'd greater than the Battel of Angels, the Majesty of Messiah, the Stature and Behaviour of Satan and his Peers? What more beautiful than *Pandæmonium,* Paradise, Heaven, Angels, *Adam* and *Eve?* What more strange, than the Creation of the World, the several Metamorphoses of the fallen Angels, and the surprising Adventures that their Leader meets with in his Search after Paradise? No other Subject could have furnished a Poet with Scenes so proper to strike the Imagination, as no other Poet could have painted those Scenes in more strong and lively Colours.

No. 418   [OF TERROR AND PITY]

. . . ferat & rubus asper amonum.[80]
VIRG.

MONDAY, JUNE 30. 1712.

The Pleasures of these Secondary Views of the Imagination, are of a wider and more universal Nature than those it has, when joined with Sight; for not only what is Great, Strange or Beautiful, but any Thing that is Disagreeable when look'd upon, pleases us in an apt Description. Here, therefore, we must enquire after a new Principle of Pleasure, which is nothing else but the Action of the Mind, which *compares* the Ideas that arise from Words, with the Ideas that arise from the Objects themselves; and why this Operation of the Mind is attended with so much Pleasure, we have before considered. For this Reason therefore, the Description of a Dung-hill is pleasing to the Imagination, if the Image be presented to our Minds by suitable Expressions; tho', perhaps, this may be more properly called the Pleasure of the Understanding than of the Fancy, because we are not so much delighted with the Image that is contained in the Description, as with the Aptness of the Description to excite the Image.

But if the Description of what is Little, Common or Deformed, be acceptable to the Imagination, the Description of what is Great, Surprising or Beautiful, is much more so; because here we are not only delighted with *comparing* the Representation with the Original, but are highly pleased with the Original it self. Most Readers, I believe, are more charmed with *Milton's* Description of Paradise, than of Hell; they are both, perhaps, equaly perfect in their Kind, but in the one the Brimstone and Sulphur are not so refreshing to the Imagination, as the Beds of Flowers, and the Wilderness of Sweets in the other.

There is yet another Circumstance which recommends a Description more than all the rest, and that is, if it represents to us such Objects as are apt to raise a secret Ferment in the Mind of the Reader, and to work, with Violence, upon his Passions. For, in this Case, we are at once warmed and enlightned, so that the Pleasure becomes more Universal, and is several ways qualified to entertain us. Thus, as in Painting, it is pleasant to look on the Picture of any Face, where the Resemblance is hit, but the Pleasure encreases, if it be the Picture of a Face that is beautiful, and is still greater, if the Beauty be softned with an Air of Melancholly or Sorrow. The two leading Passions that the more serious Parts of Poetry endeavour to stir up in us, are Terror and Pity. And here, by the way, one would wonder how it comes to pass, that such Passions as are very unpleasant at all other times, are

---

[80] "The rugged thorn shall bear the fragrant rose" (Vergil, *Eclogues,* III, 89).

very agreeable when excited by proper Descriptions. It is not strange, that we should take Delight in such Passages as are apt to produce Hope, Joy, Admiration, Love, or the like Emotions in us, because they never rise in the Mind without an inward Pleasure that attends them. But how comes it to pass, that we should take delight in being terrified or dejected by a Description, when we find so much Uneasiness in the Fear or Grief that we receive from any other Occasion?

If we consider, therefore, the Nature of this Pleasure, we shall find that it does not arise so properly from the Description of what is Terrible, as from the Reflection we make on our selves at the time of reading it. When we look on such hideous Objects, we are not a little pleased to think we are in no Danger of them. We consider them at the same time, as Dreadful and Harmless; so that the more frightful Appearance they make, the greater is the Pleasure we receive from the Sense of our own Safety. In short, we look upon the Terrors of a Description, with the same Curiosity and Satisfaction that we survey a dead Monster.

>   . . . Informe cadaver
> Protrabitur, nequeunt expleri corda tuendo
> Terribiles oculos: vultum, villosaque setis
> Pectora semiferi, atque extinctos faucibus
>   ignes.[81]
>   VIRG.

It is for the same Reason that we are delighted with the reflecting upon Dangers that are past, or in looking on a Precipice at a distance, which would fill us with a different kind of Horrour, if we saw it hanging over our Heads.

In the like manner, when we read of Torments, Wounds, Deaths, and the like dismal Accidents, our Pleasure does not flow so properly from the Grief that such melancholly Descriptions give us, as from the secret Comparison which we make between our selves and the Person that suffers. Such Representations teach us to set a just Value upon our own Condition, and make us prize our good Fortune which exempts us from the like Calamities. This is, however, such a kind of Pleasure as we are not capable of receiving, when we see a Person actually lying under the Tortures that we meet with in a Description; because, in this Case, the Object presses too close upon our Senses, and bears so hard upon us, that it does not give us time or leisure to reflect on our selves. Our Thoughts are so intent upon the Miseries of the Sufferer, that we cannot turn them upon our own Happiness. Whereas, on the contrary, we consider the Misfortunes we read in History or Poetry, either as past, or as fictitious, so that the Reflection upon our selves rises in us insensibly, and over-bears the Sorrow we conceive for the Sufferings of the Afflicted.

But because the Mind of Man requires something more perfect in Matter, than what it finds there, and can never meet with any Sight in Nature which sufficiently answers its highest Ideas of Pleasantness; or, in other Words, because the Imagination can fancy to it self Things more Great, Strange, or Beautiful, than the Eye ever saw, and is still sensible of some Defect in what it has seen; on this account it is the part of a Poet to humour the Imagination in its own Notions, by mending and perfecting Nature where he describes a Reality, and by adding greater Beauties than are put together in Nature, where he describes a Fiction.

He is not obliged to attend her in the slow Advances which she makes from one Season to another, or to observe her Conduct, in the successive Production of Plants and Flowers. He may draw into his Description all the Beauties of the Spring and Autumn, and make the whole Year contribute something to render it the more agreeable. His Rose-trees, Woodbines, and Jessamines, may flower

---

[81] They drag him from his den.
    The wond'ring neighbourhood, with glad surprise,
    Behold his shagged breast, his giant size,
His mouth that flames no more, and his extinguish'd eyes.
(Vergil, *Aeneid*, VIII, 264–267, tr. Dryden.)

together, and his Beds be covered at the same time with Lillies, Violets, and Amaranths. His Soil is not restrained to any particular Sett of Plants, but is proper either for Oaks or Mirtles, and adapts it self to the Products of every Climate. Oranges may grow wild in it; Myrrh may be met with in every Hedge, and if he thinks it proper to have a Grove of Spices, he can quickly command Sun enough to raise it. If all this will not furnish out an agreeable Scene, he can make several new Species of Flowers, with richer Scents and higher Colours, than any that grow in the Gardens of Nature. His Consorts[82] of Birds may be as full and harmonious, and his Woods as thick and gloomy as he pleases. He is at no more Expence in a long Vista, than a short one, and can as easily throw his Cascades from a Precipice of half a Mile high, as from one of twenty Yards. He has his choice of the Winds, and can turn the Course of his Rivers in all the variety of *Meanders,* that are most delightful to the Reader's Imagination. In a word, he has the modelling of Nature in his own Hands, and may give her what Charms he pleases, provided he does not reform her too much, and run into Absurdities, by endeavouring to excell.

No. 419   [OF THE FAIRIE WAY OF WRITING]

. . . mentis gratissimus Error.[83]
HOR.

TUESDAY, JULY I. 1712.

There is a kind of Writing, wherein the Poet quite loses sight of Nature, and entertains his Reader's Imagination with the Characters and Actions of such Persons as have many of them no Existence, but what he bestows on them. Such are Fairies, Witches, Magicians, Demons, and departed Spirits. This Mr. *Dryden* calls *the Fairie way of Writing,*[84] which is, indeed, more difficult than any other that depends on the Poet's Fancy, because he has no Pattern to follow in it, and must work altogether out of his own Invention.

There is a very odd turn of Thought required for this sort of Writing, and it is impossible for a Poet to succeed in it, who has not a particular Cast of Fancy, and an Imagination naturally fruitful and superstitious. Besides this, he ought to be very well versed in Legends and Fables, antiquated Romances, and the Traditions of Nurses and old Women, that he may fall in with our natural Prejudices, and humour those Notions which we have imbibed in our Infancy. For, otherwise, he will be apt to make his Fairies talk like People of his own Species, and not like other Setts of Beings, who converse with different Objects, and think in a different manner from that of Mankind;

Sylvis deducti caveant, me Judice, Fauni
Ne velut inanti triviis ac pæne forenses
Aut nimium teneris juvenentur versi-
bus. . . .[85]

I do not say with Mr. *Bays* in the *Rehearsal,*[86] that Spirits must not be confined to speak Sense, but it is certain their Sense ought to be a little discoloured, that it may seem particular, and proper to the Person and the Condition of the Speaker.

These Descriptions raise a pleasing kind of Horrour in the Mind of the Reader, and amuse his Imagination with the Strangeness and Novelty of the Persons who are represented in them. They

---

[82] concerts.

[83] "A most pleasing vagary of the mind" (Horace, *Epistles,* II, ii, 140).

[84] This phrase is not found in Dryden.

[85] Let not the wood-born satyr fondly sport With am'rous verses, as if bred at court. (Horace, *Ars Poetica,* ll. 244–266, tr. Francis.)

[86] The Duke of Buckingham's play (1671) in which Dryden, as poet laureate, was satirized in the character of Mr. Bays.

bring up into our Memory the Stories we have heard in our Child-hood, and favour those secret Terrours and Apprehensions to which the Mind of Man is naturally subject. We are pleased with surveying the different Habits and Behaviours of Foreign Countries, how much more must we be delighted and surprised when we are led, as it were, into a new Creation, and see the Persons and Manners of another Species? Men of cold Fancies, and Philosophical Dispositions, object to this kind of Poetry, that it has not Probability enough to affect the Imagination. But to this it may be answered, that we are sure, in general, there are many Intellectual Beings in the World besides ourselves, and several Species of Spirits, that are subject to different Laws and Œconomies from those of Mankind; when we see, therefore, any of these represented naturally, we cannot look upon the Representation as altogether impossible; nay, many are prepossest with such false Opinions, as dispose them to believe these particular Delusions; at least, we have all heard so many pleasing Relations in favour of them, that we do not care for seeing through the Falshood, and willingly give our selves up to so agreeable an Imposture.

The Ancients have not much of this Poetry among them, for, indeed, almost the whole Substance of it owes its Original to the Darkness and Superstition of later Ages, when pious Frauds were made use of to amuse Mankind, and frighten them into a Sense of their Duty. Our Forefathers looked upon Nature with more Reverence and Horrour, before the World was enlightened by Learning and Philosophy, and loved to astonish themselves with the Apprehensions of Witchcraft, Prodigies, Charms and Enchantments. There was scarce a Village in *England* that had not a Ghost in it, the Church-yards were all haunted, every large Common had a Circle of Fairies belonging to it, and there was scarce a Shepherd to be met with who had not seen a Spirit.

Among all the Poets of this Kind our *English* are much the best, by what I have yet seen, whether it be that we abound with more Stories of this Nature, or that the Genius of our Country is fitter for this sort of Poetry. For the *English* are naturally Fanciful, and very often disposed by that Gloominess and Melancholly of Temper, which is so frequent in our Nation, to many wild Notions and Visions, to which others are not so liable.

Among the *English, Shakespear* has incomparably excelled all others. That noble Extravagance of Fancy, which he had in so great Perfection, thoroughly qualified him to touch this weak superstitious Part of his Reader's Imagination; and made him capable of succeeding, where he had nothing to support him besides the Strength of his own Genius. There is something so wild and yet so solemn in the Speeches of his Ghosts, Fairies, Witches, and the like Imaginary Persons, that we cannot forbear thinking them natural, tho' we have no Rule by which to judge of them, and must confess, if there are such Beings in the World, it looks highly probable they should talk and act as he has represented them.

There is another sort of Imaginary Beings, that we sometimes meet with among the Poets, when the Author represents any Passion, Appetite, Virtue or Vice, under a visible Shape, and makes it a Person or an Actor in his Poem. Of this Nature are the Descriptions of Hunger and Envy in *Ovid,* of Fame in *Virgil,* and of Sin and Death in *Milton.* We find a whole Creation of the like shadowy Persons in *Spencer,* who had an admirable talent in Representations of this kind. I have discoursed of these Emblematical Persons in former Papers, and shall therefore only mention them in this Place. Thus we see how many ways Poetry addresses it self to the Imagination, as it has not only the whole Circle of Nature for its Province, but makes new Worlds of its own, shews us Persons that are not to be found in Being, and represents even the Faculties of the Soul, with her several Virtues and Vices, in a sensible Shape and Character.

I shall, in my two following Papers, consider in general, how other kinds of Writing are qualified to please the Imagination, with which I intend to conclude this Essay.

No. 420 [OF THE NEW PHILOSOPHY]

. . . Quocunque volunt mentem Auditoris agunto.[87]

HOR.

WEDNESDAY, JULY 2. 1712.

As the Writers in Poetry and Fiction borrow their several Materials from outward Objects, and join them together at their own Pleasure, there are others who are obliged to follow Nature more closely, and to take entire Scenes out of her. Such are Historians, natural Philosophers, Travellers, Geographers, and, in a Word, all who describe visible Objects of a real Existence.

It is the most agreeable Talent of an Historian, to be able to draw up his Armies and fight his Battels in proper Expressions, to set before our Eyes the Divisions, Cabals, and Jealousies of Great Men, and to lead us Step by Step into the several Actions and Events of his History. We love to see the Subject unfolding it self by just Degrees, and breaking upon us insensibly, that so we may be kept in a pleasing Suspence, and have Time given us to raise our Expectations, and to side with one of the Parties concerned in the Relation. I confess this shews more the Art than the Veracity of the Historian, but I am only to speak of him as he is qualified to please the Imagination. And in this respect *Livy* has, perhaps, excelled all who ever went before him, or have written since his Time. He describes every thing in so lively a manner, that his whole History[88] is an admirable Picture, and touches on such proper Circumstances in every Story, that his Reader becomes a kind of Spectator, and feels in himself all the variety of Passions, which are correspondent to the several Parts of the Relation.

But among this Sett of Writers, there are none who more gratifie and enlarge the Imagination, than the Authors of the new Philosophy, whether we consider their Theories of the Earth or Heavens,[89] the Discoveries they have made by Glasses,[90] or any other of their Contemplations on Nature. We are not a little pleased to find every green Leaf swarm with Millions of Animals, that at their largest Growth are not big enough to be Visible. There is something very engaging to the Fancy, as well as to our Reason, in the Treatises of Metals, Minerals, Plants and Meteors. But when we survey the whole Earth at once, and the several Planets that lie within its Neighbourhood, we are filled with a pleasing Astonishment, to see so many Worlds hanging one above another, and sliding round their Axles in such an amazing Pomp and Solemnity. If, after this, we contemplate those wide Fields of *Ether,* that reach in height as far as from *Saturn* to the fixt Stars, and run abroad almost to an Infinitude, our Imagination finds its Capacity filled with so immense a Prospect, and puts it self upon the Stretch to comprehend it. But if we yet rise higher and consider the fixt Stars as so many vast Oceans of Flame, that are

---

[87] "And raise men's passions to what height he will" (Horace, *Ars Poetica,* l. 100, tr. Roscommon).

[88] i.e., of Rome.

[89] Addison may have particularly had in mind the two works which prompted Sir William Temple's *Essay upon the Ancient and Modern Learning* (1690): Thomas Burnet's *Sacred Theory of the Earth* and Bernard de Fontenelle's *Entretiens sur la pluralité des mondes.*

[90] Both telescopes and microscopes.

each of them attended with a different Sett of Planets, and still discover new Firmaments and Lights, that are sunk farther in those unfathomable Depths of *Ether,* so as not to be visible to the naked Eye, we are lost in such a Labarynth of Suns and Worlds, and confounded with the Immensity and Magnificence of Nature.

Nothing is more pleasant to the Fancy, than to enlarge it self, by Degrees, in its Contemplation of the various Proportions that its several Objects bear to each other, when it compares the Body of Man to the Bulk of the whole Earth, the Earth to the Circle it describes round the Sun, that Circle to the Sphere of the fixt Stars, the Sphere of the fixt Stars to the Circuit of the whole Creation, the whole Creation it self to the Infinite Space that is every where diffused about it; or when the Imagination works downward, and considers the Bulk of a Human Body, in respect of an Animal, a hundred times less than a Mite, the particular Limbs of such an Animal, the different Springs that actuate the Limbs, the Spirits that set these Springs a going, and the proportionable Minuteness of these several Parts, before they have arrived at their full Growth and Perfection. But if, after all this, we take the least Particle of these Animal Spirits, and consider its Capacity of being wrought into a World, that shall contain within those narrow Dimensions a Heaven and Earth, Stars and Planets, and every different Species of living Creatures, in the same Analogy and Proportion they bear to each other in our own Universe; such a Speculation, by reason of its Nicety, appears ridiculous to those who have not turned their Thoughts that way, tho', at the same time, it is founded on no less than the Evidence of a Demonstration. Nay, we might yet carry it farther, and discover in the smallest Particle of this little World, a new inexhausted Fund of Matter, capable of being spun out into another Universe.

I have dwelt the longer on this Subject, because I think it may shew us the proper Limits, as well as the Defectiveness, of our Imagination; how it is confined to a very small Quantity of Space, and immediately stopt in its Operations, when it endeavours to take in any thing that is very great, or very little. Let a Man try to conceive the different Bulk of an Animal, which is twenty, from another which is a hundred times less than a Mite, or to compare, in his Thoughts, a length of a thousand Diameters of the Earth, with that of a Million, and he will quickly find that he has no different Measures in his Mind, adjusted to such extraordinary Degrees of Grandeur or Minuteness. The Understanding, indeed, opens an infinite Space on every side of us, but the Imagination, after a few faint Efforts, is immediately at a stand, and finds her self swallowed up in the Immensity of the Void that surrounds it: Our Reason can pursue a Particle of Matter through an infinite variety of Divisions, but the Fancy soon loses sight of it, and feels in it self a kind of Charm, that wants to be filled with Matter of a more sensible Bulk. We can neither widen nor contract the Faculty to the Dimensions of either Extreme: The Object is too big for our Capacity, when we would comprehend the Circumference of a World, and dwindles into nothing, when we endeavour after the Idea of an Atome.

It is possible this Defect of Imagination may not be in the Soul it self, but as it acts in Conjunction with the Body. Perhaps there may not be room in the Brain for such a variety of Impressions, or the Animal Spirits may be incapable of figuring them in such a manner, as is necessary to excite so very large or very minute Ideas. However it be, we may well suppose that Beings of a higher Nature very much excell us in this respect, as it is probable the Soul of Man will be infinitely more perfect hereafter in this Faculty, as well as in all the rest; insomuch that, perhaps, the Imagination will be able to keep Pace with the Understanding, and to form in it self distinct Ideas of all the different Modes and Quantities of Space.

Alexander Pope
1688-1744

THE GUARDIAN

No. 15 [ON EASIE WRITING]

. . . sibi quivis
Speret idem, sudet multum, frustraque laboret,
Ausus idem. . . .[1]

HOR.

SATURDAY, MARCH 28. 1713.

I came yesterday into the Parlour, where I found Mrs. *Cornelia,* my Lady's third Daughter, all alone, reading a Paper, which, as I afterwards found, contained a Copy of Verses upon Love and Friendship. She, I believe, apprehended that I had glanced my Eye upon the Paper, and by the Order and Disposition of the Lines might distinguish that they were Poetry; and therefore, with an innocent Confusion in her Face, she told me I might read them if I pleased, and so withdrew. By the Hand, at first sight, I could not guess whether they came from a Beau or a Lady; but having put on my Spectacles, and perused them carefully, I found by some peculiar Modes in Spelling, and a certain Negligence in Grammar, that it was a Female Sonnet. I have since learned, that she hath a Correspondent in the Country who is as bookish as herself; that they write to one another by the Names of *Astrea* and *Dorinda,* and are mightily admired for their easie Lines. As I should be loath to have a Poetess in our Family, and yet am unwilling harshly to cross the Bent of a young Lady's Genius, I chose rather to throw together some Thoughts upon that kind of Poetry which is distinguished by the Name of *Easie,* than to risque the Fame of Mrs. *Cornelia's* Friend, by exposing her Work to publick View.

I have said, in a foregoing Paper, that every Thought which is agreeable to Nature, and expressed in a Language suitable to it, is written with Ease; which I offered in answer to those who ask for Ease in all Kinds of Poetry; and it is so far true, as it states the Notion of easie Writing in general, as that is opposed to what is forced or affected. But as there is an easie Mein, an easie Dress, peculiarly so called; so there is an easie sort of Poetry. In order to write easily, it is necessary, in the first place, to think easily. Now, according to different Subjects, Men think differently; Anger, Fury,

Text from the original papers in folio half-sheets, 1713.

[1] All men will try, and hope to write as well,
And (without much pains) be undeceived.
(Horace, *Ars Poetica,* l. 240, tr. Roscommon.)

and the rough Passions, awaken strong Thoughts: Glory, Grandeur, Power, raise great Thoughts: Love, Melancholy, Solitude, and whatever gently touches the Soul, inspires easie Thoughts.

Of the Thoughts suggested by these gentle Subjects, there are some which may be set off by Style and Ornament: Others there are, which the more simply they are conceived, and the more clearly they are expressed, give the Soul proportionably the more pleasing Emotions. The Figures of Stile[2] added to them serve only to hide a Beauty, however gracefully they are put on, and are thrown away like Paint upon a fine Complexion. But here not only Liveliness of Fancy is requisite to exhibit a great variety of Images; but also of Niceness of Judgment to cull out those, which, without the Advantage of Foreign Art,[3] will shine by their own intrinsick Beauty. By these means, whatsoever seems to demand Labour being rejected, that only which appears to be easie and natural will come in; and so Art will be hid by Art, which is the Perfection of easie Writing.

I will suppose an Author to be really possessed with the Passion which he writes upon, and then we shall see how he would acquit himself. This I take to be the safest way to form a Judgment of him; since if he be not truely moved, he must at least work up his Imagination as near as possible to resemble Reality. I choose to instance in Love, which is observed to have produced the most finished Performances in this Kind. A Lover will be full of Sincerity, that he may be believed by his Mistress; he will therefore think simply, he will express himself perspicuously, that he may not perplex her; he will therefore write unaffectedly. Deep Reflections are made by an Head undisturbed; and Points of Wit and Fancy are the Work of an Heart at Ease: These two Dangers then, into which Poets are apt to run, are effectually removed out of the Lover's way. The selecting proper Circumstances, and placing them in agreeable Lights, are the finest Secrets of all Poetry; but the Recollection of little Circumstances is the Lover's sole Meditation, and relating them pleasingly the Business of his Life. Accordingly we find that the most celebrated Authors of this Rank excel in Love-Verses. Out of ten thousand instances I shall name one, which I think the most delicate and tender I ever saw.

To my self I sigh often, without knowing why;
And when absent from Phyllis, *methinks I could die.*

A Man who hath ever been in Love will be touched at the reading of these Lines; and every one, who now feels that Passion, actually feels that they are true.

From what I have advanced it appears, how difficult it is to write easily. But when easie Writings fall into the Hands of an ordinary Reader, they appear to him so natural and unlaboured, that he immediately resolves to write, and fancies that all he hath to do is to take no Pains. Thus he thinks indeed simply, but the Thoughts, not being chosen with Judgment, are not beautiful; he, it is true, expresses himself plainly, but flatly withal. Again, if a Man of Vivacity takes it in his Head to write in this Way, what Self-denial must he undergo, when bright Points of Wit occur to his Fancy? How difficult will he find it to reject florid Phrases, and pretty Embellishments of Style? So true it is, that Simplicity of all things is the hardest to be copied, and Ease to be acquired with the greatest Labour. Our Family knows very well how ill Lady *Flame* looked, when she imitated Mrs. *Jane* in a plain Black Suit. And, I remember, when *Frank Courtly* was saying the other Day, that any Man might write easie, I only ask'd him, If he thought it possible that Squire *Hawthorn* should ever come into a Room as he did? He made me a very handsome Bow, and answered with a Smile, *Mr.* IRONSIDE,[4] *you have convinced me.*

I shall conclude this Paper, by observ-

---

[2] figures of speech.
[3] i.e., of affectation.

[4] Nestor Ironside is the fictitious author of *The Guardian.*

ing that *Pastoral* Poetry, which is the most considerable Kind of easie Writing, hath the oftenest been attempted with ill Success of any sort whatsoever. I shall therefore, in a little time, communicate my Thoughts upon that Subject to the Publick.

No. 40   [AN EXERCISE IN COMPARATIVE LITERATURE]

Compulerantque Greges Corydon & Thyrsis in unum.
Exillo Corydon, Corydon est tempore nobis.[5]

MONDAY, APRIL 27. 1713.

I designed to have troubled the Reader with no farther Discourses of *Pastorals,* but being informed that I am taxed of Partiality in not mentioning an Author, whose Eclogues are published in the same Volume with Mr. *Philips's;*[6] I shall employ this Paper in Observations upon him, written in the free Spirit of Criticism, and without Apprehension of offending that Gentleman, whose Character it is, that he takes the greatest Care of his Works before they are published, and has the least Concern for them afterwards.

I have laid it down as the first Rule of Pastoral, that its Idea should be taken from the Manners of the *Golden Age,* and the Moral form'd upon the Representation of Innocence; 'tis therefore plain that any Deviations from that Design degrade a Poem from being true Pastoral. In this view it will appear that *Virgil* can only have two of his Eclogues allowed to be such: His First and Ninth must be rejected, because they describe the Ravages of Armies, and Oppressions of the Innocent; *Corydon's* criminal Passion for *Alexis* throws out the Second; the Calumny and Railing in the Third are not proper to that State of Concord; the Eighth represents unlawful Ways of procuring Love by Inchantments, and introduces a Shepherd whom an inviting Precipice tempts to Self-Murder. As to the Fourth, Sixth, and Tenth, they are given up by *Heinsius, Salmasius, Rapin,*[7] and the Criticks in general. They likewise observe that but eleven of all the *Idyllia* of *Theocritus* are to be admitted as Pastorals; and even out of that Number the greater Part will be excluded for one or other of the Reasons abovementioned. So that when I remark'd in a former Paper, that *Virgil's* Eclogues, taken all together, are rather *Select Poems* than *Pastorals;* I might have said the same thing, with no less Truth, of *Theocritus.* The Reason of this I take to be yet unobserved by the Criticks, *viz. They never meant them all for Pastorals.* Which it is plain *Philips* hath done, and in that Particular excelled both *Theocritus* and *Virgil.*

As Simplicity is the distinguishing Characteristick of Pastoral, *Virgil* hath been thought guilty of too Courtly a Stile; his Language is perfectly pure, and he often forgets he is among Peasants. I have frequently wonder'd that since he was so conversant in the Writings of *Ennius,*[8] he had not imitated the Rusticity of the *Doric,* as well, by the help of the old obsolete *Roman* Language, as *Philips* hath by the antiquated *English:*

[5] Their sheep and goats together graz'd the plains—
Since when, 'tis Corydon among the swains,
Young Corydon without a rival reigns.
  (Vergil, *Eclogues*, VII, 2, tr. Dryden.)
[6] Ambrose Philips (1675?–1749), whose pastorals had appeared with Pope's in Tonson's *Poetical Miscellanies: The Sixth Part* (1709).
[7] Daniel Heinsius (1580–1655), Claudius Salmasius (1588–1653), and René Rapin (1621–1687), famous critics.
[8] One of the earliest Latin poets, born in Greece about 239 B.C., among whose verses it became proverbial to seek for pearls of poetry. The comparison of Philips to Ennius and later to Spenser is intended to heighten the ridiculousness of Philips's style.

For Example, might he not have said *Quoi* instead of *Cui; Quoijum* for *Cujum; volt* for *vult*, &c. as well as our Modern hath *Welladay* for *Alas, Whilome* for *of Old, make mock* for *deride,* and *witless Younglings* for *simple Lambs*, &c. by which Means he had attained as much of the Air of *Theocritus,* as *Philips* hath of *Spencer.*[9]

Mr. *Pope*[10] hath fallen into the same Error with *Virgil*. His Clowns do not converse in all the Simplicity proper to the Country: His Names are borrow'd from *Theocritus* and *Virgil,* which are improper to the Scene of his Pastorals. He introduces *Daphnis, Alexis* and *Thyrsis* on *British* Plains, as *Virgil* had done before him on the *Mantuan;* whereas *Philips,* who hath the strictest Regard to Propriety, makes choice of Names peculiar to the Country, and more agreeable to a Reader of Delicacy; such as *Hobbinol, Lobbin, Cuddy,* and *Colin Clout.*

So easie as Pastoral Writing may seem, (in the Simplicity we have described it) yet it requires *great Reading,* both of the *Ancients* and *Moderns,* to be a Master of it. *Philips* hath given us manifest Proofs of his Knowledge of Books; it must be confessed his Competitor hath imitated some single Thoughts of the Ancients well enough, if we consider he had not the Happiness of an University Education; but he hath dispersed them, here and there, without that Order and Method which Mr. *Philips* observes, whose whole third Pastoral is an Instance how well he hath studied the fifth of *Virgil,* and how judiciously reduced *Virgil's* Thoughts to the Standard of Pastoral; as his Contention of *Colin Clout* and the *Nightingale* shows with what Exactness he hath imitated *Strada.*

When I remarked it as a principal Fault to introduce Fruits and Flowers of a Foreign Growth, in Descriptions where the Scene lies in our Country, I did not design that Observation should extend also to Animals, or the Sensitive Life; for *Philips* hath with great Judgement described *Wolves* in *England* in his first Pastoral. Nor would I have a Poet slavishly confine himself (as Mr. *Pope* hath done) to one particular Season of the Year, one certain time of the Day, and one unbroken Scene in each Eclogue. 'Tis plain *Spencer* neglected this Pedantry, who in his Pastoral of *November* mentions the mournful Song of the Nightingale:

Sad Philomel *her Song in Tears doth steep.*

And Mr. *Philips,* by a Poetical Creation, hath raised up finer Beds of Flowers than the most industrious Gardiner; his Roses, Lillies and Daffadils blow in the same Season.

But the better to discover the Merits of our two Contemporary Pastoral Writers, I shall endeavour to draw a Parallel of them, by setting several of their particular Thoughts in the same light, whereby it will be obvious how much *Philips* hath the Advantage. With what Simplicity he introduces two Shepherds singing alternately.

Hobb.   *Come,* Rosalind, *O come, for without thee*
         What Pleasure can the Country have for me:
         Come, Rosalind, *O come; my brinded Kine,*
         My snowy Sheep, my Farm, and all is thine.

Lanq.   *Come* Rosalind, *O come; here shady Bowers*
         Here are cool Fountains, and here springing Flow'rs.
         Come, Rosalind; *Here ever let us stay,*
         And sweetly wast our live-long Time away.

---

9 The allusion here is to Spenser's archaisms.

10 Pope can speak of himself in this essay as it appeared anonymously. His pretended preference for Philips's poems, while giving himself all the best of the argument, is but part of the fun.

Our other Pastoral Writer,[11] in expressing the same Thought, deviates into downright Poetry.

Streph.   *In Spring the Fields, in Autumn Hills I love,*
        At Morn the Plains, at Noon the shady Grove,
        But Delia *always; forc'd from* Delia's *Sight,*
        Nor Plains at Morn, nor Groves at Noon delight.

Daph.   Sylvia's *like Autumn ripe, yet mild as* May,
        More bright than Noon, yet fresh as early Day;
        Ev'n Spring displeases, when she shines not here.
        But blest with her, 'tis Spring throughout the Year.

In the first of these Authors, two Shepherds thus innocently describe the Behaviour of their Mistresses.

Hobb.   *As* Marian *bath'd, by chance I passed by,*
        She blush'd, and at me cast a side-long Eye:
        Then swift beneath the Crystal Wave she try'd
        Her beauteous Form, but all in vain, to hide.

Lanq.   *As I to cool me bath'd one sultry Day,*
        Fond Lydia *lurking in the Sedges lay.*
        The Wanton laugh'd, and seem'd in Haste to fly;
        Yet often stopp'd, and often turn'd her Eye.

The other Modern (who it must be confessed hath a knack of Versifying) hath it as follows.

Streph.   *Me gentle* Delia *beckons from the Plain,*
        Then, hid in Shades, eludes her eager Swain;

[11] Pope himself.

        But feigns a Laugh, to see me search around,
        And by that Laugh the willing Fair is found.

Daph.   *The sprightly* Sylvia *trips along the Green,*
        She runs, but hopes she does not run unseen;
        While a kind Glance at her Pursuer flyes,
        How much at Variance are her Feet and Eyes!

There is nothing the Writers of this kind of Poetry are fonder of, than Descriptions of Pastoral Presents. *Philips* says thus of a Sheephook.

Of Season'd Elm; where Studs of Brass appear,
To speak the Giver's Name, the Month and Year.
The Hook of polish'd Steel, the Handle turn'd,
And richly by the Graver's Skill adorn'd.

The other of a Bowl embossed with Figures.

    . . . where wanton Ivy twines,
And swelling Clusters bend the curling Vines;
Four Figures rising from the Work appear,
The various Seasons of the rolling Year;
And what is That which binds the radiant Sky,
Where twelve bright Signs in beauteous Order lie.

The Simplicity of the Swain in this Place, who forgets the Name of the *Zodiack,* is no ill Imitation of *Virgil;* but how much more plainly and unaffectedly would *Philips* have dressed this Thought in his *Doric?*

And what That hight, which girds the Welkin sheen,
Where twelve gay Signs in meet array are seen.

If the Reader would indulge his Curiosity any farther in the Comparison of Particulars, he may read the first Pastoral of *Philips* with the second of his Contemporary, and the fourth and sixth of the former, with the fourth and first of the latter; where several Parallel Places will occur to every one.

Having now shown some Parts, in which these two Writers may be compared, it is a Justice I owe to Mr. *Philips,* to discover those in which no Man can compare with him. First, That *beautiful Rusticity,* of which I shall only produce two Instances, out of a hundred not yet quoted.

O woful Day! O Day of Woe, quoth he,
And woful I, who live the Day to see!

That Simplicity of Diction, the Melancholy Flowing of the Numbers, the Solemnity of the Sound, and the easie Turn of the Words, in this *Dirge* (to make use of our Author's Expression) are extreamly Elegant.

In another of his Pastorals, a Shepherd utters a *Dirge* not much inferior to the former, in the following Lines.

Ah me the while! ah me! the luckless Day,
Ah luckless Lad! the rather might I say;
Ah silly I! more silly than my Sheep,
Which on the flowry Plains I once did keep.

How he still Charms the Ear with these artful Repetitions of the Epithets; and how significant is the last Verse! I defy the most common Reader to repeat them, without feeling some Motions of Compassion.

In the next Place I shall rank his *Proverbs,* in which I formerly observed he excells: For Example,

A rolling Stone is ever bare of Moss;
And, to their Cost, green Years old Proverbs cross.
—— He that late lyes down, as late will rise,
And, Sluggard-like, till Noon-day snoring lyes.

Against Ill-Luck *all cunning Fore-sight fails;*
Whether we sleep or wake it nought avails.
—— Nor fear, from upright *Sentence,* Wrong.

Lastly, His *Elegant Dialect,* which alone might prove him the eldest Born of *Spencer,* and our only true *Arcadian;* I should think it proper for the several Writers of Pastoral, to confine themselves to their several *Counties. Spencer* seems to have been of this Opinion: for he hath laid the Scene of one of his Pastorals in *Wales,* where with all the Simplicity natural to that Part of our Island, one Shepherd bids the other *Good-morrow* in an unusual and elegant Manner.

Diggon Davy, *I bid hur God-day:*
Or Diggon *hur is, or I mis-say.*

Diggon answers,

Hur was hur while it was Day-light;
But now hur is a most wretched Wight,
&c.[12]

But the most beautiful Example of this kind that I ever met with, is in a very valuable Piece, which I chanced to find among some old Manuscripts, entituled, *A Pastoral Ballad;* which I think, for its Nature and Simplicity, may (notwithstanding the Modesty of the Title) be allowed a Perfect Pastoral: It is composed in the *Somersetshire* Dialect, and the Names such as are proper to the Country People. It may be observed, as a further Beauty of this Pastoral, the Words *Nymph, Dryad, Naiad, Fawn, Cupid,* or *Satyr,* are not once mentioned through the whole. I shall make no Apology for inserting some few Lines of this excellent Piece. *Cicily* breaks thus into the Subject, as she is going a Milking;

Cicily.   Rager *go vetch tha Kee, or else tha Zun,*
Will quite be go, be vore c'
have half a don.

---

[12] These are the opening lines of the ninth eclogue of Spenser's *The Shepheardes Calender.*

Roger. *Thou shouldst not ax ma
tweece, but I've a be
To dreave our Bull to Bull tha
Parson's Kee.*

It is to be observed, that this whole Dialogue is formed upon the Passion of Jealousie; and his mentioning the Parson's Kine naturally revives the Jealousie of the Shepherdess *Cicily*, which she expresses as follows:

Cicily. *Ah Rager, Rager, chez was
zore avraid
Ween in yond Vield you kiss'd
tha Parsons Maid:
Is this the Love that once to me
you zed,
When from tha Wake thou
brought'st me Gingerbread?*
Roger. *Cicily thou charg'st me false,—
I'll zwear to thee,
Tha Parson's Maid is still a
Maid for me.*

In which Answer of his are express'd at once that *Spirit of Religion,* and that *Innocence of the Golden Age,* so necessary

to be observed by all Writers of Pastoral.

At the Conclusion of this Piece, the Author reconciles the Lovers, and ends the Eclogue the most Simply in the World.

*So Rager parted vor to vetch tha Kee,
And vor her Bucket in went Cicily.*

I am loath to show my Fondness for Antiquity so far as to prefer this ancient *British* Author to our present *English* Writers of Pastoral; but I cannot avoid making this obvious Remark, that both *Spencer* and *Philips* have hit into the same Road with this old *West Country* Bard of ours.

After all that hath been said, I hope none can think it any Injustice to Mr. *Pope,* that I forbore to mention him as a Pastoral Writer; since upon the whole, he is of the same Class with *Moschus* and *Bion,*[13] whom we have excluded that Rank; and of whose Eclogues, as well as some of *Virgil's,* it may be said, that according to the Description we have given of this sort of Poetry, they are by no means *Pastorals,* but *something Better.*

No. 132 [OF SICKNESS]

WEDNESDAY, AUGUST 12, 1713.

Dear Sir,

You formerly observed to me, that nothing made a more ridiculous Figure in a Man's Life, than the Disparity we often find in him Sick and Well. Thus one of an unfortunate Constitution is perpetually exhibiting a miserable Example of the Weakness of his Mind, or of his Body, in their Turns. I have had frequent Opportunities of late to consider my self in these different Views, and hope I have received some Advantage by it. If what Mr. *Waller*[14] says be true, that

*The Soul's dark Cottage, batter'd and
decay'd,*

*Lets in new Light thro' Chinks that
Time has made:*[15]

Then surely Sickness, contributing no less than old Age to the shaking down this Scaffolding of the Body, may discover the inclosed Structure more plainly. Sickness is a sort of early old Age; it teaches us a Diffidence in our Earthly State, and inspires us with the Thoughts of a future, better than a thousand Volumes of Philosophers and Divines. It gives so warning a Concussion[16] to those Props of our Vanity, our Strength and Youth, that we think of fortifying our selves within, when there is so little dependance on our Outworks. Youth, at the very best, is but a Betrayer of Human Life in a gentler and smoother

---

[13] Greek poets of the third century B.C. who with Theocritus are pre-eminent for pastoral writings.
[14] Edmund Waller (1606–1687).

[15] These lines adapted from Vergil were said by Waller's son to have been "the last verses my dear father made."
[16] blow.

manner than Age: 'Tis like a Stream that nourishes a Plant upon its Bank, and causes it to flourish and blossom to the Sight, but at the same time is undermining it at the Root in secret. My Youth has dealt more fairly and openly with me; it has afforded several Prospects of my Danger, and given me an Advantage not very common to young Men, that the Attractions of the World have not dazzled me very much; and I began where most People end, with a full Conviction of the Emptiness of all sorts of Ambition, and the unsatisfactory Nature of all human Pleasures.

When a smart Fit of Sickness tells me this Scurvy Tenement of my Body will fall in a little time, I am e'en as unconcern'd as was that honest *Hibernian,* who (being in Bed in the great Storm some Years ago, and told the House would tumble over his Head) made Answer, *What care I for the House? I am only a Lodger.*

I fancy 'tis the best time to die when one is in the best Humour, and so excessively weak as I now am, I may say with Conscience, that I'm not at all uneasie at the Thought that many Men, whom I never had any Esteem for, are likely to enjoy this World after me. When I reflect what an inconsiderable little Atome every single Man is, with respect to the whole Creation, methinks 'tis a Shame to be concerned at the Removal of such a trivial Animal as I am. The Morning after my *Exit,* the Sun will rise as bright as ever, the Flowers smell as sweet, the Plants spring as green, the World will proceed in its old Course, People will laugh as heartily, and Marry as fast, as they were used to do. *The Memory of Man* (as it is elegantly exprest in the Wisdom of *Solomon*) *passeth away as the remembrance of a Guest that tarrieth but one Day.*[17] There are Reasons enough, in the fourth Chapter of the same Book, to make any young Man contented with the Prospect of Death. *For honourable Age is not that which standeth in length of Time, or is measured by number of Years. But Wisdom is the gray Hair to Men, and an unspotted Life is old Age.* He was taken away speedily, lest that *Wickedness should alter his Understanding, or Deceit beguile his Soul.*

I am,
Yours.

---

[17] v, 14; the exact words are: "For the hope of the ungodly is like dust that is blowen away with ye wind, like a thinne froth that is driven away with ye storme: like as the smoke which is dispersed here and there with a tempest, and passeth away as the remembrance of a guest that tarieth but a day."

George Berkeley, Bishop of Cloyne 1685-1753

THE GUARDIAN

No. 49 [NATURAL AND FANTASTIC PLEASURES]

. . . quae possit facere & servare beatum.[1]

THURSDAY, MAY 7. 1713.

It is of great Use to consider the Pleasures which constitute Human Happiness, as they are distinguished into Natural and Fantastical. *Natural Pleasures* I call those, which, not depending on the Fashion and Caprice of any particular Age or Nation, are suited to Human Nature in general, and were intended by Providence as Rewards for the using our Faculties agreeably to the Ends for which they were given us. *Fantastical Pleasures* are those which having no natural Fitness to delight our Minds, presuppose some particular Whim or Taste accidentally prevailing in a Sett of People, to which it is owing that they please.

Now I take it, that the Tranquility and Cheerfulness with which I have passed my Life, are the Effect of having, ever since I came to Years of Discretion, continued my Inclinations to the former sort of Pleasures. But, as my Experience can be a Rule only to my own Actions, it may probably be a stronger Motive to induce others to the same Scheme of Life, if they would consider that we are prompted to Natural Pleasures by an Instinct impressed on our Minds by the Author of our Nature, who best understands our Frames, and consequently best knows what those Pleasures are which will give us the least Uneasiness in the Pursuit, and the greatest Satisfaction in the Enjoyment of them. Hence it follows, that the Objects of our Natural Desires are cheap or easie to be obtained, it being a Maxim that holds throughout the whole System of created Beings, that, *Nothing is made in vain,* much less the Instincts and Appetites of Animals, which the Benevolence, as well as Wisdom of the Deity, is concerned to provide for. Nor is the Fruition of those Objects less pleasing than the Acquisition is easie; and the Pleasure is heightened by the Sense of having answered some Natural

---

Text from original edition, half-sheet folio, 1713.

[1] "To make men happy and to keep them so" (Horace, *Epistles,* I, vi, 2, tr. Creech).

End, and the Consciousness of acting in concert with the Supreme Governor of the Universe.

Under Natural Pleasures I comprehend those which are universally suited, as well to the Rational as the Sensual Part of our Nature. And of the Pleasures which affect our Senses, those only are to be esteemed Natural that are contained within the Rules of Reason, which is allowed to be as necessary an Ingredient of Human Nature as Sense. And, indeed, Excesses of any kind are hardly to be esteemed Pleasures, much less *Natural Pleasures*.

It is evident, that a Desire terminated in Mony is fantastical; so is the Desire of outward Distinctions, which bring no Delight of Sense, nor recommend us as useful to Mankind; and the Desire of things meerly because they are New or Foreign. Men, who are indisposed to a due Exertion of their higher Parts,[2] are driven to such Pursuits as these from the Restlessness of the Mind, and the sensitive Appetites being easily satisfied. It is, in some sort, owing to the Bounty of Providence, that disdaining a cheap and vulgar Happiness, they frame to themselves imaginary Goods, in which there is nothing can raise Desire but the Difficulty of obtaining them. Thus Men become the Contrivers of their own Misery, as a Punishment on themselves for departing from the Measures of Nature. Having by an habitual Reflection on these Truths made them Familiar, the Effect is, that I, among a number of Persons who have debauched their Natural Taste, see things in a peculiar Light, which I have arrived at, not by any uncommon force of Genius or acquired Knowledge, but only by unlearning the false Notions instilled by Custom and Education.

The various Objects that compose the World were by Nature formed to delight our Senses; and as it is this alone that makes them desirable to an uncorrupted Taste, a Man may be said naturally to possess them, when he possesseth those Enjoyments which they are fitted by Nature to yield. Hence it is usual with me to consider my self, as having a natural Property in every Object that administers Pleasure to me. When I am in the Country, all the fine Seats near the Place of my Residence, and to which I have Access, I regard as *mine*. The same I think of the Groves and Fields where I walk, and muse on the Folly of the *civil* Landlord in *London*, who has the fantastical Pleasure of draining dry Rent into his Coffers, but is a Stranger to fresh Air and Rural Enjoyments. By these Principles I am possessed of half a dozen of the finest Seats[3] in *England*, which in the Eye of the Law belong to certain of my Acquaintance, who, being Men of Business, chuse to live near the Court.

In some great Families, where I chuse to pass my time, a Stranger would be apt to rank me with the other Domesticks;[4] but in my own Thoughts, and Natural Judgment, I am Master of the House, and he who goes by that Name is my Steward, who eases me of the Care of providing for my self the Conveniencies and Pleasures of Life.

When I walk the Streets, I use the foregoing natural Maxim, (*viz*. That he is the true Possessor of a thing who enjoys it, and not he that owns it without the Enjoyment of it,) to convince my self that I have a Property in the gay Part of all the gilt Chariots that I meet, which I regard as Amusements designed to delight my Eyes, and the Imagination of those kind People who sit in them gaily attired only to please me. I have a real, and they only an imaginary Pleasure from their exterior Embellishments. Upon the same Principle, I have discovered that I am the *natural* Proprietor of all the Diamond Necklaces, the Crosses, Stars, Brocades, and embroidered Cloaths, which I see at a Play or Birth-Night,[5] as giving more natural Delight to the Spectator than to those that

2 "qualities; powers; faculties; or accomplishments" (Johnson's *Dictionary*).
3 dwellings.
4 servants.
5 "the night annually kept in memory of any one's birth" (Johnson's *Dictionary*).

wear them. And I look on the Beaus and Ladies as so many Parraquets[6] in an Aviary, or Tulips in a Garden, designed purely for my Diversion. A Gallery of Pictures, a Cabinet or Library that I have free Access to, I think my own. In a Word, all that I desire is the Use of things, let who will have the keeping of them. By which Maxim I am grown one of the richest Men in *Great Britain;* with this difference, that I am not a Prey to my own Cares, or the Envy of others.

The same Principles I find of great use in my private Œconomy. As I cannot go to the Price of History-painting, I have purchased at easie Rates several beautifully designed Pieces of Landschape and Perspective, which are much more pleasing to a natural Taste than unknown Faces or *Dutch* Gambols,[7] tho' done by the best Masters. My Couches, Beds, and Window-Curtains are of *Irish* Stuff, which those of that Nation work very fine and with a delightful mixture of Colours. There is not a Piece of China in my House; but I have Glasses of all sorts, and some tinged with the finest Colours, which are not the less pleasing because they are Domestick and cheaper than Foreign Toys. Every thing is neat, intire, and clean, and fitted to the Taste of one who had rather be *happy* than *be thought rich.*

Every Day, numberless innocent and natural Gratifications occur to me, while I behold my Fellow-Creatures labouring in a toilsome and absurd pursuit of Trifles; one, that he may be called by a particular Appellation; another, that he may wear a particular Ornament,[8] which I regard as a bit of Riband that has an agreeable Effect on my Sight, but is so far from supplying the Place of Merit

where it is not, that it serves only to make the want of it more Conspicuous. Fair Weather is the Joy of my Soul; about Noon I behold a blue Sky with Rapture, and receive great Consolation from the rosie dashes of Light which adorn the Clouds of the Morning and Evening. When I am lost among green Trees, I do not envy a great Man with a Crowd at his Levée.[9] And I often lay aside Thoughts of going to an Opera, that I may enjoy the silent Pleasure of walking by Moon-light, or viewing the Stars sparkle in their azure Ground; which I look upon as part of my Possessions, not without a secret Indignation at the Tastlesness of mortal Men, who, in their Race thro' Life, overlook the real Enjoyments of it.

But the Pleasure which naturally affects a Human Mind with the most lively and transporting Touches, I take to be the Sense that we act in the Eye of infinite Wisdom, Power and Goodness, that will Crown our Virtuous Endeavours here, with a Happiness hereafter, large as our Desires, and lasting as our immortal Souls. This is a perpetual Spring of Gladness in the Mind. This lessens our Calamities, and doubles our Joys. Without this the highest State of Life is insipid, and with the lowest is a Paradise. What unnatural Wretches then are those, who can be so stupid as to imagine a Merit, in endeavouring to rob Virtue of her Support, and Man of his present as well as future Bliss? But, as I have frequently taken Occasion to animadvert on that Species of Mortals, so I propose to repeat my Animadversions on them, till I see some Symptoms of Amendment.

---

[6] The French original of the modern contraction *parrot.*

[7] games.

[8] official decoration; the Order of the Garter, or similar mark of distinction, seems implicit.

[9] "the concourse of those who croud round a man of power in a morning" (Johnson's *Dictionary*).

Lady Mary Wortley Montagu
1689-1762

LETTERS

LETTER VIII

TO MR. P————[1]

Vienna, Sept. 14, O.S. [1716][2]

Perhaps you'll laugh at me, for thanking you very gravely for all the obliging concern you express for me. 'Tis certain that I may, if I please, take the fine things you say to me for wit and raillery, and, it may be, it would be taking them right. But I never, in my life, was half so well disposed to take you in earnest, as I am at present, and that distance which makes the continuation of your friendship improbable, has very much encreased my faith in it. I find that I have (as well as the rest of my sex) whatever face I set on't, a strong disposition to believe in miracles. Don't fancy, however, that I am infected by the air of these popish countries; I have, indeed, so far wandered from the discipline of the church of England, as to have been last Sunday at the Opera, which was performed in the garden of the *Favorita,*[3] and I was so much pleased with it, I have not yet repented my seeing it. Nothing of that kind ever was more magnificent; and I can easily believe, what I am told, that the decorations and habits cost the Emperor[4] thirty thousand pounds sterling. The stage was built over a very large canal, and at the beginning of the second act, divided into two parts, discovering the water, on which there immediately came, from different parts, two fleets of little gilded vessels, that gave the representation of a naval fight. It is not easy to imagine the beauty of this scene, which I took particular notice of. But all the rest were perfectly fine in their kind. The story of the Opera is the Inchantment of *Alcina,*[5] which gives op-

Text from the first edition, *Letters of The Right Honourable Lady M——y W——y M——e,* 3 vols., 1763. This late publication accounts for the reduction in capitalization as well as for modern spellings and punctuation as compared with printing in the early part of the century when the letters were actually written. The title of the edition, in accordance with fashion, printed only the first and last letters of Lady Mary's name.

[1] Alexander Pope (1688–1744), English poet and intimate friend for the time of Lady Mary.

[2] Old Style, that is, the English date; the continental date would have been September 25, N[ew] S[tyle].

[3] A prominent government building which gave its name to a quarter of Vienna.

[4] Charles VI, Emperor of the Holy Roman Empire from 1711 to his death in 1740.

[5] Very likely this was an early version of

portunities of great variety of machines and changes of the scenes, which are performed with a surprising swiftness. The theatre is so large that 'tis hard to carry the eye to the end of it, and the habits[6] in the utmost magnificence to the number of one hundred and eight. No house could hold such large decorations; but the ladies all sitting in the open air, exposes them to great inconveniences; for there is but one canopy for the imperial family; and the first night it was represented, a shower of rain happening, the opera was broke off, and the company crouded away in such confusion, that I was almost squeezed to death.—But if their opera's are thus delightful, their comedies are, in as high a degree, ridiculous. They have but one play-house, where I had the curiosity to go to a German comedy, and was very glad it happened to be the story of Amphitrion. As that subject has been already handled by a Latin, French and English poet,[7] I was curious to see what an Austrian author would make of it. I understand enough of that language to comprehend the greatest part of it, and besides I took with me a lady that had the goodness to explain to me every word. The way is to take a box, which holds four, for yourself and company. The fixed price is a gold ducat. I thought the house very low and dark; but I confess the comedy admirably recompensed that defect. I never laughed so much in my life. It begun with *Jupiter's* falling in love out of a peep-hole in the clouds, and ended with the birth of *Hercules.* But what was most pleasant, was the use Jupiter made of his metamorphosis; for you no sooner saw him under the figure of *Amphitrion,* but instead of flying to *Alcmena,* with the raptures Mr. *Dryden* puts into his mouth, he sends for Amphitrion's taylor, and cheats him of a laced coat, and his banker of a bag of money, a Jew of a diamond ring, and bespeaks a great supper in his name; and the greatest part of the comedy turns upon poor Amphitrion's being tormented by these people for their debts. *Mercury* uses *Sofia* in the same manner. But I could not easily pardon the liberty the poet has taken of larding his play with, not only indecent expressions, but such gross words as I don't think our mob would suffer from a mountebank. Besides, the two Sofia's very fairly let down their breeches in the direct view of the boxes, which were full of people of the first rank that seemed very well pleased with their entertainment, and assured me this was a celebrated piece. I shall conclude my letter with this remarkable relation, very well worthy the serious consideration of Mr. Collier.[8] I won't trouble you with farewell compliments, which I think generally as impertinent, as curtisies at leaving the room when the visit has been too long already.

LETTER XXIV

Belgrade, Feb. 12, O.S. 1717.
I did verily intend to write you a long letter from Peterwaradin,[9] where I expected to stay three or four days, but the Bassa[10] here was in such haste to see us, that he dispatched the courier back (which Mr. W————[11] had sent to know the time he would send the convoy

---

an opera by Tommaso Albinoni, of which the earliest records otherwise date from 1725. Handel's opera on this same theme was not performed until 1735 in Covent Garden, London.

6 costumes.

7 Ovid, Molière, and Dryden.

8 Jeremy Collier (1650–1726), author of *A Short View of the Immorality and Profaneness of the English Stage* (1698).

9 Petrovaradin, in what is now Yugoslavia; about 40 miles northwest of Belgrade on the Dunav river, in the borderland between possessions of the Empire and of the Turks.

10 "a title of honour and command among the Turks; viceroy of a province; the general of an army" (Johnson's *Dictionary*).

11 Her husband, the ambassador, Edward Wortley Montagu.

to meet us) without suffering him to pull off his boots. My letters were not thought important enough to stop our journey, and we left Peterwaradin the next day, being waited on by the chief officers of the garrison, and a considerable convoy of Germans and Rascians.[12] The Emperor has several regiments of these people; but, to say the truth, they are rather plunderers than soldiers; having no pay, and being obliged to furnish their own arms and horses; they rather look like vagabond gypsies, or stout beggars, than regular troops. I cannot forbear speaking a word of this race of creatures, who are very numerous all over Hungary. They have a patriarch of their own at Grand Cairo, and are really of the Greek church, but their extreme ignorance gives their priests occasion to impose several new notions upon them. These fellows letting their hair and beard grow inviolate, make exactly the figure of the Indian Bramins. They are heirs-general to all the money of the layety; for which, in return, they give them formal passports signed and sealed for Heaven; and the wives and children only inherit the house and cattle. In most other points they follow the Greek church.—This little digression has interrupted my telling you we passed over the fields of *Carlowitz,* where the last great victory was obtained by Prince Eugene over the Turks.[13] The marks of that glorious bloody day are yet recent, the field being yet strewed with the skulls and carcasses of unburied men, horses and camels. I could not look, without horror, on such numbers of mangled human bodies, nor without reflecting on the injustice of war, that makes murther,[14] not only necessary, but meritorious. Nothing

seems to be a plainer proof of the *irrationality* of mankind (whatever fine claims we pretend to reason) than the rage with which they contest for a small spot of ground, when such vast parts of fruitful earth lie quite uninhabited. 'Tis true, custom has now made it unavoidable; but can there be a greater demonstration of want of reason, than a custom being firmly established, so plainly contrary to the interest of man in general? I am a good deal inclined to believe Mr. *Hobbs,*[15] that the *state of nature,* is a *state of war;* but thence I conclude human nature not rational, if the word reason means common sense, as I suppose it does. I have a great many admirable arguments to support this reflection; I won't however trouble you with them, but return, in a plain stile, to the history of my travels.

We were met at Betsko (a village in the midway between Belgrade and Peterwaradin) by an Aga of the Janizaries,[16] with a body of Turks, exceeding the Germans by one hundred men, though the Bassa had engaged to send exactly the same number. You may judge by this of their fears. I am really persuaded, that they hardly thought the odds of one hundred men set them even with the Germans; however, I was very uneasy till they were parted, fearing some quarrel might arise notwithstanding the *parole*[17] given. We came late to Belgrade, the deep snows making the ascent to it very difficult. It seems a strong city, fortified, on the east side, by the Danube; and on the south, by the river *Save,* and was formerly the barrier of Hungary. It was first taken by Solyman the Magnificent;[18] and since, by the Emperor's forces, led by the Elector of Bavaria.[19]

---

[12] Serbians.

[13] Forces under the command of Prince Eugene of Savoy won the Battle of Peterwaradin August 5, 1716.

[14] murder.

[15] Thomas Hobbes, *Leviathan* (1651), chap. 13.

[16] An officer of the Turkish guards.

[17] promise of truce.

[18] Suleiman I, the most celebrated of the Ottoman sultans, reigned from 1520 to 1566; he invaded Hungary in 1521, taking Belgrade and five years later all of the country up to Vienna.

[19] In 1688 by the forces of Maximilian Emanuel, Elector of Barvaria. It was retaken by the Turks in 1690. Three months after Lady Mary's visit the city was once again taken, this time by the army of Prince Eugene of Savoy for the Emperor

The Emperor held it only two years, it being retaken by the Grand Vizier. It is now fortified with the utmost care and skill the Turks are capable of, and strengthened by a very numerous garrison, of their bravest Janizaries, commanded by a Bassa *Seraskier* (*i.e.* General;) though this last expression is not very just; for to say truth, the Seraskier is commanded by the Janizaries. These troops have an absolute authority here, and their conduct carries much more the aspect of rebellion, than the appearance of subordination. You may judge of this by the following story, which at the same time, will give you an idea of the *admirable* intelligence of the Governor of Peterwaradin, though so few hours distant. We were told by him at Peterwaradin, that the garrison and inhabitants of Belgrade were so weary of the war, they had killed their Bassa about two months ago, in a mutiny, because he had suffered himself to be prevailed upon, by a bribe of five purses (five hundred pound sterling) to give permission to the Tartars to ravage the German frontiers. We were very well pleased to hear of such favourable dispositions in the people; but when we came hither, we found the governor had been ill informed, and the real truth of the story to be this. The late Bassa fell under the displeasure of his soldiers, for no other reason, but restraining their incursions on the Germans. They took it into their heads from that mildness, that he had intelligence with the enemy, and sent such information to the Grand Signior at Adrianople; but, redress not coming quick enough from thence, they assembled themselves in a tumultuous manner, and by force dragged their Bassa before the Cadi and Mufti, and there demanded justice in a mutinous way; one crying out, Why he protected the Infidels? Another, Why he squeezed them of their money? The Bassa easily guessing their purpose, calmly replied to them, that they asked him too many questions, and that he had but one life, which must answer for all. They then immediately fell upon him with their scymitars, (without waiting the sentence of their heads of the law) and in a few moments cut him in pieces. The present Bassa has not dared to punish the murder; on the contrary, he affected to applaud the actors of it, as grave fellows, that knew how to do themselves justice. He takes all pretences of throwing money amongst the garrison, and suffers them to make little excursions into Hungary, where they burn some poor Rascian houses.

You may imagine, I cannot be very easy in a town which is really under the government of an insolent soldiery.— We expected to be immediately dismissed, after a night's lodging here; but the Bassa detains us till he receives orders from Adrianople, which may, possibly, be a month a coming. In the mean time, we are lodged in one of the best houses, belonging to a very considerable man amongst them, and have a whole chamber of Janizaries to guard us. My only diversion is the conversation of our host *Achmet-beg,* a title something like that of Count in Germany. His father was a great Bassa, and he has been educated in the most polite Eastern learning, being perfectly skilled in the Arabic and Persian languages, and an extraordinary scribe, which they call *Effendi.* This accomplishment makes way to the greatest preferments; but he has had the good sense to prefer an easy, quiet secure life, to all the dangerous honours of the Port.[20] He sups with us every night, and drinks wine very freely. You cannot imagine how much he is delighted with the liberty of conversing with me. He has explained to me many pieces of Arabian poetry, which, I observe, are in numbers, not unlike ours, generally of an alternate verse, and of a very musical sound. Their expressions of love are very passionate and lively. I am so much pleased with them, I really believe I should learn to read Arabic, if I was to stay here a few months. He has a very good library of their books of all kinds; and, as he tells me, spends the greatest part of his life

---

[20] Name by which the Turkish empire was known.

there. I pass for a great scholar with him, by relating to him some of the Persian tales,[21] which I find are genuine. At first, he believed I understood Persian. I have frequent disputes with him, concerning the difference of our customs, particularly the confinement of women. He assures me, there is nothing at all in it; only, says he, we have the advantage, that when our wives cheat us, no body knows it. He has wit, and is more polite than many Christian men of quality. I am very much entertained with him.—He has had the curiosity to make one of our servants set him an alphabet of our letters, and can already write a good roman hand. But these amusements do not hinder my wishing heartily to be out of this place; though the weather is colder than I believe it ever was any where, but in Greenland.—We have a very large stove constantly kept hot, and yet the windows of the room are frozen on the inside.—God knows when I may have an opportunity of sending this letter; but I have written it, for the discharge of my own conscience; and you cannot now reproach me, that one of yours make ten of mine.

Adieu.

LETTER XXXI

TO MRS. S. C.[22]

Adrianople, April 1, O.S.

In my opinion, dear S. I ought rather to quarrel with you, for not answering my Nimeguen[23] letter of August, till December, than to excuse my not writing again till now. I am sure there is on my side a very good excuse for silence, having gone such tiresome land-journies, though I don't find the conclusion of them so bad as you seem to imagine. I am very easy here, and not in the solitude you fancy me. The great number of Greeks, French, English and Italians, that are under our protection, make their court to me from morning till night; and I'll assure you, are, many of them, very fine ladies; for there is no possibility for a Christian to live easily under this government, but by the protection of an Ambassador—and the richer they are, the greater is their danger.

Those dreadful stories you have heard of the *Plague,* have very little foundation in truth. I own, I have much ado to reconcile myself to the sound of a word, which has always given me such terrible ideas; though I am convinced there is little more in it, than in a fever. As a proof of this, let me tell you, that we passed through two or three towns most violently infected. In the very next house where we lay, (in one of those places) two persons died of it. Luckily for me, I was so well deceived, that I knew nothing of the matter; and I was made believe, that our second cook had only a great cold. However, we left our doctor to take care of him, and yesterday they both arrived here in good health; and I am now let into the secret, that he has had the *Plague.* There are many that escape it, neither is the air ever infected. I am persuaded that it would be as easy a matter to root it out here, as out of Italy and France; but it does so little mischief, they are not very solicitous about it, and are content to suffer this distemper, instead of our variety, which they are utterly unacquainted with.

A propos of distempers, I am going to tell you a thing, that will make you wish yourself here. The *small-pox,* so fatal, and so general amongst us, is here entirely harmless, by the invention of *engrafting,* which is the term they give it. There is a set of old women, who make it their business to perform the operation, every autumn, in the month of September, when the great heat is abated. People send to one another to know if any

---

[21] Persian tales and the *Arabian Nights* had been translated into English; Ambrose Philips had produced some versions of the Persian in 1714.

[22] Miss Sara Chiswell, an old friend of Lady Mary's of about eighty years of age.

[23] A city in Holland.

of their family has a mind to have the small pox; they make parties for this purpose, and when they are met (commonly fifteen or sixteen together) the old woman comes with a nut-shell full of the matter of the best sort of small-pox, and asks what veins you please to have opened. She immediately rips open that, you offer to her, with a large needle (which gives you no more pain than a common scratch) and puts into the vein, as much matter as can lie upon the head of her needle, and after that, binds up the little wound with a hollow bit of shell, and in this manner opens four or five veins. The Grecians have commonly the Superstition of opening one in the middle of the forehead, one in each arm, and one on the breast, to mark the sign of the cross; but this has a very ill effect, all these wounds leaving little scars, and is not done by those that are not superstitious, who chuse to have them in the legs, or that part of the arm that is concealed. The children or young patients play together all the rest of the day, and are in perfect health to the eighth. Then the fever begins to seize them, and they keep their beds two days, very seldom three. They have very rarely above twenty or thirty in their faces, which

never mark, and in eight days time are as well as before their illness. Where they are wounded, there remains running sores during the distemper, which I don't doubt is a great relief to it. Every year thousands undergo this operation, and the French Ambassador says pleasantly, that they takes the small-pox here by way of diversion, as they take the waters in others countries. There is no example of any one that has died in it, and you may believe I am well satisfied of the safety of this experiment, since I intend to try it on my dear little son. I am patriot enough to take pains to bring this useful invention into fashion in England, and I should not fail to write to some of our Doctors very particularly about it, if I knew any one of them that I thought had virtue enough to destroy such a considerable branch of their revenue, for the good of mankind. But that distemper is too beneficial to them, not to expose to all their resentment, the hardy wight that should undertake to put an end to it. Perhaps, if I live to return, I may, however, have courage to war with them. Upon this occasion, admire the heroism in the heart of,

Your friend, &c. &c.

LETTER XXXVI

TO MR. POPE

Belgrade-Village, June 17, O.S.
I hope, before this time, you have received two or three of my letters. I had yours but yesterday, though dated the third of February, in which you suppose me to be dead and buried. I have already let you know that I am still alive; but to say truth, I look upon my present circumstances to be exactly the same with those of departed spirits. The heats of Constantinople have driven me to this place, which perfectly answers the description of the Elysian fields. I am in the middle of a wood, consisting chiefly of fruit trees, watered by a vast number of fountains, famous for the excellency of their water, and divided into many

shady walks, upon short grass, that seems to me artificial; but, I am assured, is the pure work of nature—within view of the Black-sea, from whence we perpetually enjoy the refreshment of cool breezes, that make us insensible of the heat of the summer. The village is only inhabited by the richest amongst the Christians, who meet every night at a fountain, forty paces from my house, to sing and dance. The beauty and dress of the women, exactly resemble the ideas of the antient nymphs, as they are given us by the representations of the poets and painters. But what persuades me more fully of my decease, is the situation of my own mind, the profound ignorance I am in, of what passes among the living (which only comes to me by chance) and the

great calmness with which I receive it.
Yet I have still a hankering after my
friends and acquaintances left in the
world, according to the authority of that
admirable author.

That spirits departed are wonderous kind
To friends and relations left behind,
    Which no body can deny.[24]

Of which solemn truth I am a *dead* instance. I think *Virgil* is of the same opinion, that in human souls there will still
be some remains of human passions:

—*Curae non ipsae in morte relinquunt.*[25]

And 'tis very necessary to make a perfect
Elysium, that there should be a river
Lethe, which I am not so happy as to
find. To say truth, I am sometimes very
weary of the singing and dancing, and
sunshine, and wish for the smoke and
impertinencies in which you toil; though
I endeavour to persuade myself that I
live in a more agreeable variety than
you do; and that *Monday,* setting of
partridges; *Tuesday,* reading English;
Wednesday, studying in the Turkish language, (in which, by the way, I am already very learned;) *Thursday,* classical
authors; *Friday,* spent in writing; *Saturday,* at my needle, and *Sunday,* admitting of visits and hearing of music, is a
better way of disposing of the week,
than, *Monday* at the drawing-room;
Tuesday, Lady Mohun's;[26] *Wednesday,*
at the opera; *Thursday,* the play; *Friday,* Mrs. Chetwynd's,[27] &c. a perpetual
round of hearing the same scandal, and
seeing the same follies acted over and
over, which here affect me no more than
they do other dead people. I can now
hear of displeasing things with pity and
without indignation. The reflection on
the great gulph between you and me,
cools all news that come hither. I can
neither be sensibly touched with joy or
grief, when I consider that, possibly, the
cause of either is removed, before the letter comes to my hands. But (as I said
before) this indolence does not extend
to my few friendships; I am still warmly
sensible of yours and Mr. *Congreve's,*[28]
and desire to live in your remembrance,
though dead to all the world beside.

LETTER XXXVII

Belgrade Village, June 17, O.S.
I heartily beg your ladyship's pardon;
but I really could not forbear laughing
heartily at your letter, and the commissions you are pleased to honour me with.
You desire me to buy you a Greek slave,
who is to be mistress of a thousand good
qualities. The Greeks are *subjects* and
not *slaves.* Those who are to be bought
in that manner, are either such as are
taken in war, or stolen by the Tartars,
from Russia, Circassia or Georgia, and
are such miserable awkward poor
wretches, you would not think any of
them worthy to be your house maids.
'Tis true, that many thousands were
taken in the *Morea;*[29] but they have
been, most of them, redeemed by the
charitable contributions of the Christians,
or ransomed by their own relations at
Venice. The fine slaves, that wait upon
the great ladies, or serve the pleasures of
the great men, are all bought at the age
of eight or nine years old, and educated
with great care to accomplish them in
singing, dancing, embroidery, &c. they

---

[24] The last line of these verses is the refrain
to which many verses on different subjects
were set. There are several such poems using
this refrain in *The Vocal Miscellany,* 2 vols.,
1738, although none with the verses before the
refrain as they are here.

[25] "Such concerns as these are not relinquished in death" (Vergil, *Aeneid,* VI, 444).

[26] A widow whose remarriage, to a relative
of one of Pope's friends, had just been announced.

[27] A not clearly identified acquaintance of
the circle of Lady Mary and Pope.

[28] William Congreve (1670–1729), the English playwright and close friend of Pope.

[29] Peloponnesus.

are commonly *Circassians,* and their patron never sells them, except it is as a punishment for some very great fault. If ever they grow weary of them, they either present them to a friend, or give them their freedom. Those that are exposed to sale at the markets, are always either guilty of some crime, or so entirely worthless, that they are of no use at all. I am afraid you will doubt the truth of this account, which, I own, is very different from our common notions in England; but it is no less truth for all that. —Your whole letter is full of mistakes from one end to the other. I see you have taken your ideas of Turkey from that worthy author *Dumont,*[30] who has writ with equal ignorance and confidence. 'Tis a particular pleasure to me here, to read the voyages to the Levant, which are generally so far removed from truth, and so full of absurdities, I am very well diverted with them. They never fail giving you an account of the women, whom, 'tis certain they never saw, and talking very wisely of the genius of the men, into whose company they are never admitted; and very often describe *Mosques,* which they dared not even peep into. The Turks are very proud, and will not converse with a stranger, they are not assured is considerable in his own country. I speak of the men of distinction; for, as to the ordinary fellows, you may imagine what ideas their conversation can give of the general genius of the people.

As to the Balm of *Mecca,*[31] I will certainly send you some; but it is not so easily got as you suppose it, and I cannot in conscience advise you to make use of it. I know not how it comes to have such universal applause. All the ladies of my acquaintance at London and Vienna, have begged me to send pots of it to them. I have had a present of a small quantity (which I'll assure you is very valuable) of the best sort, and with great joy applied it to my face, expecting some wonderful effect to my advantage. The next morning the change, indeed, was wonderful; my face was swelled to a very extraordinary size, and all over as red as my Lady H———'s. It remained in this lamentable state three days, during which you may be sure I passed my time very ill. I believed it would never be otherwise; and to add to my mortification, Mr. W——y reproached my indiscretion without ceasing. However, my face is since in *statu quo;* nay, I am told by the ladies here, that 'tis much mended by the operation, which I confess I cannot perceive in my looking-glass. Indeed, if one was to form an opinion of this balm from their faces, one should think very well of it. They all make use of it, and have the loveliest bloom in the world. For my part, I never intend to endure the pain of it again; let my complexion take its natural course, and decay in its own due time. I have very little esteem for medicines of this nature; but do as you please, Madam; only remember, before you use it, that your face will not be such as you will care to shew in the drawing room for some days after. If one was to believe the women in this country, there is a surer way of making one's self beloved, than by becoming handsome, though you know that's our method. But they pretend to the knowledge of secrets, that, by way of enchantment, give them the entire empire over whom they please. For me, who am not very apt to believe in wonders, I cannot find faith for this. I disputed the point last night with a lady, who really talks very sensibly on any other subject; but she was downright angry with me, in

---

[30] Jean Dumont, *New Voyage to the Levant: Containing an Account of the Most Remarkable Curiosities in Germany, France, Italy . . . and Turkey* (1696).

[31] Balm of Mecca is defined in Chambers' *Cyclopedia* (1751) as: "a dry, white gum, resembling white coppera, especially when old. It is brought from Mecca by the returns of the caravans of pilgrims and Mahometan merchants, who travel thither out of devotion to the birth-place of their prophet. It has all the virtues of the balm of Gilead, or Judea; and is probably the same, only hardened, and its colour altered." The only "virtue" of the balms, according to Chambers, was to heal wounds. Lady Mary's friends evidently used it as a beauty salve.

that she did not perceive she had per-suaded me of the truth of forty stories she told me of this kind; and, at last, mentioned several ridiculous marriages, that there could be no other reason as-signed for. I assured her, that in Eng-land, where we were entirely ignorant of all magick, where the climate is not half so warm, nor the women half so hand-some, we were not without our ridicu-lous marriages; and that we did not look upon it, as any thing supernatural, when a man played the fool for the sake of a woman. But my arguments could not convince her against (as she said) her certain knowledge. To this she added, that she scrupled making use of *charms* herself; but that she could do it when-ever she pleased; and staring me in my face, said, (with a very learned air) that no enchantments would have their effects upon me, and that there were some peo-ple exempt from their power, but very few. You may imagine how I laughed at this discourse: but all the women are of the same opinion. They don't pretend to any commerce with the devil, but only that there are certain compositions adapted to inspire love. If one could send over a ship-load of them, I fancy it would be a very quick way of raising an estate. What would not some ladies of our acquaintance give for such merchan-dize? Adieu, my dear lady—I cannot conclude my letter with a subject that affords more delightful scenes to the im-agination. I leave you to figure to your-self, the extreme court that will be made to me, at my return, if my travels should furnish me with such a useful piece of learning. I am, dear Madam,

Your, &c. &c.

Ambrose Philips
1675?-1749

THE FREE-THINKER

No. 92 [A WINTER EVENING TALE]

Da spatium vitae, multos da, Jupiter, annos:
Hoc recto vultu, solum hoc, & pallidus optas.
Sed Quam continuis & quantis longa senectus
Plena malis! . . .[1]

JUVEN.

FRIDAY, FEBRUARY 6. 1718.

To entice Young Ladies to delight in Reading, and to lead them insensibly into the Paths of Philosophy, I have lately given them Two Winter-Evening Tales; to which I shall add a Third of so Gen eral an Instruction, that it may serve for a Lesson to the whole Sex, from the Princess down to the Country-Nymph.

There was, upon a Time, an old Queen, so very far stricken in Years, that her Majesty was Toothless and Bald. Her Head shook and trembled perpetually, like the Leaves of an Aspin; and her Sight was so dim, that Spectacles were no longer of any Use to her: Her Mouth was almost hid by the near Approach of her Nose to her Chin: Her Stature was so diminished, that she was shrunk into a shapeless Heap; and her Back so bowed that you would have thought she had been crooked from her Infancy.

A *Fairy,* who had assisted at the Birth of this Queen, came to her, and said; Do you desire to grow Young again? Most earnestly, reply'd the Queen: I would part with all my Jewels, to be but Twenty. Then (continues the *Fairy*) it will be necessary to make an Exchange, and to transfer your Age and Infirmities to some One, who will be contented to spare you her Youth and Health. To whom therefore shall we give your Hundred Years?

Hereupon, the Queen gave Orders, to make diligent Enquiry, through the Kingdom, for a Person, who might be willing to barter Youth for Age, upon a valuable Consideration. When these Orders were publickly known, a great many poor People from all Parts flocked to the Court; all of them desirous to be made

---

Text from first collected edition, 1721.

[1] Jove grant me length of life, and years good store
Heap on my bended back, I ask no more.

Both sick and healthful, young and old conspire
In this one silly mischievous desire.
Mistaken blessing which old age they call,
'Tis a long, nasty, darksome hospital.
(Juvenal, *Satires,* X, 188–191, tr. Dryden.)

Old and Rich: But, when they had seen the Queen at Dinner, hideous in her Infirmities, trembling and coughing over a Mess of Water-Gruel, and doating ever and anon, as she spoke; not One was inclinable to take up the Burden of her Years. They chose rather to live by Begging, and to enjoy their Youth and Health in Rags. There came likewise a Crowd of Ambitious Persons; to whom she promised great Dignities and the highest Honours: But, when they had seen her; what will all our Grandeur avail, said they, when we shall appear so frightful, as to be ashamed to shew our selves in Publick?

At last, there came a Young Country-Girl (whose Name was *Mopsy*) in full Bloom; and she demanded the Crown, as an Equivalent for her Youth and Beauty. The Queen immediately grew Angry: But to what Purpose? She was bent upon renewing her Vigour at any Price; and said to *Mopsy*; Let us divide my Kingdom, and share alike; You shall reign over the One Half, and I will content my self with the Other: This will be Power enough in Conscience for you, who are but a little mean Peasant. No, replies the Girl; I am not so easily satisfy'd: Let me enjoy my obscure Condition, and my Rosy Complexion; and much Good may it do your Majesty with your Hundred Years, and your Wrinkles, and more than one Foot in the Grave. But then, says the Queen, what should I be able to do without my Kingdom? You would Laugh, you would Dance, you would Sing, like me; answers the young Gipsy; and immediately she broke out into Laughter, and Danced, and Sung. The Queen, who was far from being in a Condition to imitate her Jollity, said; and what would you do in my Place? You, who are neither accustomed to old Age, nor Empire? I cannot well say, answers this Country Lass, what I should do: But I have a Month's Mind to try it a little; for I have always heard, it is a Fine Thing to be a Queen.

When the Two Parties seemed now disposed to an Agreement, and were ready to strike the Bargain, in comes the *Fairy;* and, addressing her self to *Mopsy*,

said: Are you willing to make Trial of the Condition of an Old Queen; and see first how you like it, before you resolve upon the Change in good Earnest? With all my Heart, replies the Girl. Her Forehead is instantly furrowed with Wrinkles; her chesnut Hair turns white; she grows peevish and morose; her Head shakes; her Teeth are loose; and she is already an Hundred Years old. The *Fairy* then opens a little Box, and lets out a Multitude of Officers and Courtiers of both Sexes, richly apparelled; who soon shot up into the full Stature of Men and Women, and paid their Homage to the New Queen. She is conducted to her Chair of State; and a costly Banquet is immediately set before her: But, alas, she has no Appetite, and cannot bear the Fumes of the Table: Her Limbs fail her, when she tries to walk: She is aukward, and bashful, and in a Maze; she knows not how to speak, nor which way to turn her self; she calls for a Looking Glass, and is startled at her own Deformity; and she coughs till her Sides ake.

In the mean time the True Queen stood in a Corner of the Room by her self: she laughs, and begins to grow Handsome. Her Temples are shaded with Hair, and she renews her Teeth: Her Cheeks glow with Youth, and her Forehead is fair and smooth. And now she begins to recollect her Youthful Airs, and her Virgin Coyness; and to set her Person out to the best Advantage. But, she is troubled to find her self but meanly habited; her Coats short and scanty; and her Wastecoat of a coarse Woollen Stuff: She was not used to be thus poorly equipt; and one of her own Guards, who took her for some rude Creature, went to turn her out of the Palace.

Then said *Mopsy* to her; I perceive, you are not a little Uneasy in my Condition; and I am much more weary of yours: Take your Crown again; and give me back my Russet Garment. The Exchange was soon made: As soon the Queen withered; and the Virgin Peasant bloomed afresh. The Restitution was hardly compleated on Both sides; when each began to repent: But, it was too late: For the *Fairy* had now condemned them Both to remain in their proper State.

The Queen bewailed her self daily upon the smallest indisposition: Alas, (would she say) if I was *Mopsy* at this time, I should sleep indeed in a Cottage, and feed upon Chesnuts; but then, by Day I should dance in the Shade with the Shepherds to the sweet Musick of the Pipe. What am I the happier for lying in an embroidered Bed, where I am never free from Pain? Or for any Numerous Attendants, who have not the Power to relieve me?

Her Grief, for having forfeited her Choice, encreased her Indispositions; and the Physicians, (who were Twelve in Number) constantly attending her, soon brought her Distempers to a Height. Briefly, she died at the end of Two Months. *Mopsy* was in the midst of a Dance with her Companions, on the Bank of a running Sream, when Tidings came of the Queen's Death: Then she blessed her self, that she had escaped from Royalty, more through good Fortune and Impatience, than through Forecast and Resolution.

Daniel Defoe
c. 1660-1731

From THE LIFE AND STRANGE SURPRISING ADVENTURES OF ROBINSON CRUSOE

[ALL FOR A LOAF OF BREAD]

I was now in the Months of *November* and *December*,[1] expecting my Crop of Barley and Rice. The Ground I had manur'd or dug up for them was not great; for as I observ'd, my Seed of each was not above the Quantity of half a Peck; for I had lost one whole Crop by sowing in the dry Season; but now my Crop promis'd very well, when on a sudden I found I was in Danger of losing it all again by Enemies of several sorts, which it was scarce possible to keep from it; as first, the Goats, and wild Creatures which I call'd Hares, who tasting the Sweetness of the Blade, lay in it Night and Day, as soon as it came up, and eat it so close, that it could get no time to shoot up into Stalk.

This I saw no Remedy for, but by making an Enclosure about it with a Hedge, which I did with a great deal of Toil; and the more, because it requir'd Speed. However, as my Arable Land was but small, suited to my Crop, I got it totally well fenced in about three Weeks time; and shooting some of the Creatures in the Day-time, I set my Dog to guard it in the Night, tying him up to a Stake at the Gate, where he would stand and bark all Night long; so in a little time the Enemies forsook the Place, and the Corn[2] grew very strong, and well, and began to ripen apace.

But as the Beasts ruined me before, while my Corn was in the Blade, so the Birds were as likely to ruine me now, when it was in the Ear; for going along by the Place to see how it throve, I saw my little Crop surrounded with Fowls of I know not how many sorts, who stood as it were watching till I should be gone. I immediately let fly among them (for I always had my Gun with me.) I had no sooner shot but there rose up a little Cloud of Fowls, which I had not seen at all, from among the Corn it self.

This touch'd me sensibly, for I foresaw, that in a few Days they would devour all my Hopes, that I should be starv'd, and never be able to raise a Crop at all, and what to do I could not tell: However, I resolv'd not to lose my Corn, if possible, tho' I should watch it Night and Day. In the first Place, I went among it to see what Damage was al-

---

Text from the third edition, 1719; first published in the same year.

[1] Crusoe's island was in the tropics, off the east coast of Brazil.
[2] grain.

ready done, and found they had spoil'd a good deal of it; but that as it was yet too green for them, the Loss was not so great, but that the Remainder was like to be a good Crop if it could be sav'd.

I staid by it to load my Gun, and then coming away I could easily see the Thieves sitting upon all the Trees about me, as if they only waited till I was gone away, and the Event proved it to be so; for as I walk'd off as if I was gone, I was no sooner out of their Sight, but they dropt down one by one into the Corn again. I was so provok'd that I could not have Patience to stay till more came on, knowing that every Grain that they eat now, was, *as it might be said,* a Peck-loaf to me in the Consequence; but coming up to the Hedge, I fir'd again, and kill'd three of them. This was what I wish'd for; so I took them up, and serv'd them as we serve notorious Thieves in *England,* (*viz.*) Hang'd them in Chains for a Terror to others. It is impossible to imagine almost, that this should have such an Effect as it had; for the Fowls would not only not come at the Corn, but in short they forsook all that Part of the Island, and I could never see a Bird near the Place as long as my Scare-Crows hung there.

This I was very glad of, you may be sure; and about the latter end of *December,* which was our second Harvest of the Year, I reap'd my Crop.

I was sadly put to it for a Scythe or a Sickle to cut it down, and all I could do was to make one as well as I could out of one of the broad Swords or Cutlasses, which I sav'd among the Arms out of the Ship. However, as my first Crop was but small, I had no great Difficulty to cut it down: in short, I reap'd it my way, for I cut nothing off but the Ears, and carry'd it away in a great Basket which I had made, and so rubb'd it out with my Hands; and at the End of all my Harvesting, I found that out of my half Peck of Seed, I had near two Bushels of Rice, and above two Bushels and half of Barley, *that is to say,* by my Guess, for I had no Measure at that time.

However, this was a great Encouragement to me; and I foresaw that in time,

it would please God to supply me with Bread: And yet here I was perplex'd again, for I neither knew how to grind or make Meal of my Corn, or indeed how to clean it and part it; nor if made into Meal, how to make Bread of it; and if how to make it, yet I knew not how to bake it: these things being added to my Desire of having a good Quantity for Store, and to secure a constant Supply, I resolv'd not to taste any of this Crop, but to preserve it all for Seed against the next Season, and in the mean time to employ all my Study and Hours of working to accomplish this great Work of providing myself with Corn and Bread.

It might be truly said, that now I work'd for my Bread. 'Tis a little wonderful, and what I believe few People have thought much upon, (*viz.*) the strange Multitude of little things necessary in the Providing, Producing, Curing, Dressing, Making and Finishing this one Article of Bread.

I that was reduced to a meer State of Nature, found this to my daily Discouragement, and was made more and more sensible of it every Hour, even after I had got the first Handful of Seed-Corn, which, as I have said, came up unexpectedly, and indeed to a Surprise.

First, I had no Plow to turn up the Earth, no Spade or Shovel to dig it. Well, this I conquer'd, by making a wooden Spade, as I observ'd before; but this did my Work in but a wooden manner; and tho' it cost me a great many Days to make it, yet for want of Iron it not only wore out the sooner, but made my Work the harder, and made it be perform'd much worse.

However, this I bore with, and was content to work it out with Patience, and bear with the Badness of the Performance. When the Corn was sow'd, I had no Harrow, but was forced to go over it my self, and drag a great heavy Bough of a Tree over it, to Scratch it, as it may be call'd, rather than Rake or Harrow it.

When it was growing and grown, I have observ'd already how many things I wanted, to fence it, secure it, mow or reap it, cure and carry it Home, thrash, part it from the Chaff, and save it. Then I wanted a Mill to grind it, Sieves to dress it, Yeast and Salt to make it into Bread, and an Oven to bake it; and yet all these things I did without, as shall be observ'd; and yet the Corn was an inestimable Comfort and Advantage to me too. All this, as I said, made every thing laborious and tedious to me, but that there was no help for; neither was my time so much Loss to me, because as I had divided it, a certain Part of it was every Day appointed to these Works; and as I resolv'd to use none of the Corn for Bread till I had a greater Quantity by me, I had the next six Months to apply myself wholly by Labour and Invention to furnish myself with Utensils proper for the performing all the Operations necessary for the making the Corn (when I had it) fit for my use.

But first, I was to prepare more Land, for I had now Seed enough to sow above an Acre of Ground. Before I did this, I had a Weeks-work at least to make me a Spade, which when it was done was but a sorry one indeed, and very heavy, and requir'd double Labour to work with it; however I went thro' that, and sow'd my Seed in two large flat Pieces of Ground, as near my House as I could find them to my Mind, and fenc'd them in with a good Hedge, the Stakes of which were all cut of that Wood which I had set before, and knew it would grow, so that in one Year's time I knew I should have a Quick or Living Hedge, that would want but little Repair. This Work was not so little as to take me up less than three Months, because great Part of that time was of the wet Season, when I could not go abroad.

Within Doors, *that is,* when it rained, and I could not go out, I found Employment on the following Occasions; always observing, that all the while I was at work I diverted myself with talking to my Parrot, and teaching him to Speak; and I quickly learned him to know his own Name, and at last to speak it out pretty loud, POLL, which was the first Word I ever heard spoken in the Island by any Mouth but my own. This therefore was not my Work, but an Assistant to my Work; for now, as I said, I had a great Employment upon my Hands, as follows, (*viz.*) I had long study'd, by some Means or other, to make myself some Earthen Vessels, which indeed I wanted sorely, but knew not where to come at them: However, considering the Heat of the Climate, I did not doubt but if I could find out any such Clay, I might botch up some such Pot, as might, being dry'd in the Sun, be hard enough, and strong enough to bear handling, and to hold any Thing that was dry, and required to be kept so; and as this was necessary in the preparing Corn, Meal, &c. which was the Thing I was upon, I resolved to make some as large as I could, and fit only to stand like Jars to hold what should be put into them.

It would make the Reader pity me, or rather laugh at me, to tell how many awkward Ways I took to raise this Paste, what odd mishapen ugly things I made, how many of them fell in, and how many fell out, the Clay not being stiff enough to bear its own Weight; how many crack'd by the over violent Heat of the Sun, being set out too hastily; and how many fell in Pieces with only removing, as well before as after they were dry'd; and in a word, how after having laboured hard to find the Clay, to dig it, to temper it, to bring it home and work it, I could not make above two large earthen ugly things, I cannot call them Jarrs, in about two Months Labour.

However, as the Sun bak'd these two very dry and hard, I lifted them very gently up, and set them down again in two great Wicker-Baskets, which I had made on purpose for them, that they might not break; and as between the Pot and the Basket there was a little room to spare, I stuff'd it full of the Rice and Barley Straw, and these two Pots being to stand always dry, I thought would hold my dry Corn, and perhaps the Meal, when the Corn was bruised.

Tho' I miscarried so much in my Design for large Pots, yet I made several smaller things with better Success; such as little round Pots, flat Dishes, Pitchers and Pipkins,[3] and any things my Hand turn'd to, and the Heat of the Sun bak'd them strangely hard.

But all this would not answer my End, which was to get an Earthen Pot to hold what was Liquid, and bear the Fire, which none of these could do. It happen'd after some time, making a pretty large Fire for cooking my Meat, when I went to put it out after I had done with it, I found a broken Piece of one of my Earthen-ware Vessels in the Fire, burnt as hard as a Stone, and red as a Tile. I was agreeably surpriz'd to see it, and said to my self, that certainly they might be made to burn whole, if they would burn broken.

This set me to studying how to order my Fire, so as to make it burn me some Pots. I had no notion of a Kiln, such as the Potters burn in, or of glazing them with Lead, tho' I had some Lead to do it with; but I plac'd three large Pipkins, and two or three Pots in a Pile one upon another, and plac'd my Fire-wood all round it with a great Heap of Embers under them; I ply'd the Fire with fresh Fuel round the out-side, and upon the top, till I saw the Pots in the inside red hot quite thro', and observ'd that they did not crack at all; when I saw them clear red, I let them stand in that Heat about 5 or 6 Hours, till I found one of them, tho' it did not crack, did melt or run, for the Sand which was mixed with the Clay melted by the Violence of the Heat, and would have run into Glass if I had gone on; so I slack'd my Fire gradually, till the Pots began to abate of the red Colour, and watching them all Night, that I might not let the Fire abate too fast, in the Morning I had three very good, I will not say handsome Pipkins, and two other Earthen Pots, as hard burnt as could be desir'd; and one of them perfectly glaz'd with the Running of the Sand.

After this Experiment, I need not say that I wanted no sort of Earthen Ware

for my Use; but I must needs say, as to the Shapes of them, they were very indifferent, as any one may suppose, when I had no way of making them, but as the Children make Dirt-Pyes, or as a Woman would make Pyes that never learnt to raise Paste.

No Joy at a thing of so mean a Nature was ever equal to mine, when I found I had made an Earthen Pot that would bear the Fire; and I had hardly Patience to stay till they were cold, before I set one upon the Fire again, with some Water in it, to boil me some Meat, which it did admirably well; and with a Piece of a Kid I made some very good Broth, though I wanted Oatmeal, and several other Ingredients requisite to make it so good as I would have had it been.

My next Concern was, to get me a Stone Mortar to stamp or beat some Corn in; for as to the Mill, there was no thought at arriving to that Perfection of Art, with one Pair of Hands. To supply this Want I was at a great Loss; for of all Trades in the World I was as perfectly unqualified for a Stone-Cutter, as for any whatever; neither had I any Tools to go about it with. I spent many a Day to find out a great Stone big enough to cut hollow, and make fit for a Mortar, and could find none at all; except what was in the solid Rock, and which I had no way to dig or cut out; nor indeed were the Rocks in the Island of Hardness sufficient, but were all of a sandy crumbling Stone, which would neither bear the Weight of a heavy Pestle, or would break the Corn without filling it with Sand; so after a great deal of Time lost in Searching for a Stone, I gave it over, and resolv'd to look out for a great Block of hard Wood, which I found indeed much easier; and getting one as big as I had Strength to stir, I rounded it, and form'd it on the Outside with my Axe and Hatchet, and then with the help of Fire and infinite Labour; made a hollow Place in it, as the *Indians* in *Brasil* make their *Canoes*. After this, I made a great heavy Pestle or Beater, of the Wood call'd the Iron-

---

[3] small jars.

Wood, and this I prepared and laid by against I had my next Crop of Corn, when I propos'd to myself to grind, or rather pound, my Corn into Meal to make my Bread.

My next Difficulty was to make a Sieve, or Search, to dress my Meal, and to part it from the Bran, and the Husk, without which I did not see it possible I could have any Bread. This was a most difficult thing, so much as but to think on; for to be sure I had nothing like the necessary thing to make it; I mean fine thin Canvas, or Stuff to search the Meal through. And here I was at a full Stop for many Months; nor did I really know what to do; Linnen I had none left, but what was meer Rags; I had Goats Hair, but neither knew I how to weave it, or spin it; and had I known how, here was no Tools to work it with; all the Remedy that I found for this, was, That at last I did remember I had among the Seamens Cloaths which were sav'd out of the Ship, some Neckcloths of Callicoe or Muslin; and with some Pieces of these I made three small Sieves, but proper enough for the Work; and thus I made shift for some Years; how I did afterwards, I shall shew in its Place.

The baking Part was the next thing to be consider'd, and how I should make Bread when I came to have Corn; for first I had no Yeast; as to that Part, as there was no supplying the Want, so I did not concern my self much about it: But for an Oven, I was indeed in great Pain: at length I found out an Experiment for that also, which was this; I made some Earthen Vessels very broad, but not deep; that is to say, about two Foot Diameter, and not above nine Inches deep: these I burnt in the Fire, as I had done the other, and laid them by; and when I wanted to bake, I made a great Fire upon my Hearth, which I had pav'd with some square Tiles of my own making and burning also; but I should not call them square.

When the Fire-wood was burnt pretty much into Embers, or live Coals, I drew them forward upon this Hearth, so as to cover it all over, and there I let them

lie, till the Hearth was very hot; then sweeping away all the Embers, I set down my Loaf, or Loaves, and whelming down the Earthen Pot upon them, drew the Embers all round the Outside of the Pot, to keep in, and add to the Heat; and thus, as well as in the best Oven in the World, I bak'd my Barley-Loaves, and became in little time a meer Pastry-Cook into the Bargain; for I made myself several Cakes of the Rice and Puddings; indeed I made no Pies, neither had I any Thing to put into them, supposing I had, except the Flesh either of Fowls or Goats.

It need not be wondered at, if all these things took me up most Part of the third Year of my Abode here; for it is to be observ'd, That in the Intervals of these Things, I had my new Harvest and Husbandry to manage; for I reap'd my Corn in its Season, and carried it Home as well as I could, and laid it up in the Ear, in my large Baskets, till I had Time to rub it out; for I had no Floor to thrash it on, or Instrument to thrash it with.

And now indeed my Stock of Corn increasing, I really wanted to build my Barns bigger. I wanted a Place to lay it up in; for the Increase of the Corn now yielded me so much, that I had of the Barley about twenty Bushels, and of the Rice as much, or more; insomuch, that now I resolv'd to begin to use it freely; for my Bread had been quite gone a great while; also I resolv'd to see what Quantity would be sufficient for me a whole Year, and to sow but once a Year.

Upon the whole, I found that the forty Bushels of Barley and Rice was much more than I could consume in a Year; so I resolv'd to sow just the same Quantity every Year that I sowed the last, in hopes that such a Quantity would fully provide me with Bread, &c.

[THE PROPER SHAPE OF A BOAT]

All the while these Things were doing, you may be sure my Thoughts run many times upon the Prospect of Land which I had seen from the other Side of the Island, and I was not without secret Wishes that I were on Shore there, fancying the seeing the main Land, and in an inhabited Country, I might find some Way or other to convey my self farther, and perhaps at last find some Means of Escape.

But all this while I made no Allowance for the Dangers of such a Condition, and how I might fall into the Hands of Savages, and perhaps such as I might have Reason to think far worse than the Lions and Tigers of *Africa.* That if I once came into their Power, I should run a Hazard more than a Thousand to One of being kill'd, and perhaps of being eaten; for I had heard that the People of the *Carribean* Coasts were Cannibals, or Man-eaters; and I knew by the Latitude, that I could not be far off from that Shore. That suppose they were not Cannibals, yet that they might kill me, as many *Europeans* who had fallen into their Hands had been served, even when they had been ten or twenty together, much more I that was but one, and could make little or no Defence. All these things, I say, which I ought to have consider'd well of, and did cast up in my Thoughts afterwards, yet took up none of my Apprehensions at first; but my Head run mightily upon the Thought of getting over to the Shore.

Now I wish'd for my Boy *Xury,* and the Long-Boat with the Shoulder of Mutton Sail, with which I sail'd above a thousand Miles on the Coast of *Africk;* but this was in vain. Then I thought I would go and look at our Ship's Boat, which, as I have said, was blown up upon the Shore a great Way in the Storm, when we were first cast away. She lay almost where she did at first, but not quite; and was turn'd by the Force of the Waves and the Winds, almost Bottom upward, against a high Ridge of Beachy rough Sand; but no Water about her as before.

If I had had Hands to have refitted her, and to have launch'd her into the Water, the Boat would have done well enough, and I might have gone back into the *Brasils* with her easily enough; but I might have foreseen, that I could no

more turn her, and set her upright upon her Bottom, than I could remove the Island. However, I went to the Woods and cut Levers and Rollers, and brought them to the Boat, resolv'd to try what I could do; suggesting to myself, that if I could but turn her down, I might easily repair the Damage she had receiv'd, and she would be a very good Boat, and I might go to Sea in her very easily.

I spar'd no Pains indeed, in this Piece of fruitless Toil, and spent, I think, three or four Weeks about it; at last finding it impossible to heave it up with my little Strength, I fell to digging away the Sand to undermine it, and so to make it fall down, setting Pieces of Wood to thrust and guide it right in the Fall.

But when I had done this, I was unable to stir it up again, or to get under it, much less to move it forward towards the Water; so I was forc'd to give it over; and yet, though I gave over the Hopes of the Boat, my desire to venture over for the Main increased, rather than decreased, as the Means for it seem'd impossible.

This at length put me upon thinking, Whether it was not possible to make myself a *Canoe,* or *Periagua,* such as the Natives of those Climates make, even without Tools, or, as I might say, without Hands, *viz.* of the Trunk of a great Tree. This I not only thought possible, but easy, and pleas'd myself extreamly with the Thoughts of making it, and with my having much more Convenience for it than any of the *Negroes* or *Indians;* but not at all considering the particular Inconveniences which I lay under, more than the *Indians* did, *viz.* Want of Hands to move it, when it was made, into the Water; a Difficulty much harder for me to surmount, than all the Consequences of want of Tools could be to them: For what was it to me, That when I had chosen a vast Tree in the Woods, I might with much Trouble cut it down, if after I might be able with my Tools to hew and dub the Out-side into the proper Shape of a Boat, and burn or cut out the Inside to make it hollow, so to make a Boat of it, if after all this, I must leave it just there where

I found it, and was not able to launch it into the Water.

One would have thought, I could not have had the least Reflection upon my Mind of my Circumstance, while I was making this Boat, but I should have immediately thought how I should get it into the Sea; but my Thoughts were so intent upon my Voyage over the Sea in it, that I never once consider'd how I should get it off of the Land; and it was really in its own Nature more easy for me to guide it over forty five Miles of Sea, than about forty five Fathom[4] of Land, where it lay, to set it a float in the Water.

I went to work upon this Boat the most like a Fool that ever Man did, who had any of his Senses awake. I pleas'd myself with the Design, without determining whether I was ever able to undertake it; not but that the Difficulty of launching my Boat came often into my Head; but I put a stop to my own Enquiries into it, by this foolish Answer which I gave myself, *Let's first make it, I'll warrant I'll find some Way or other to get it along, when 'tis done.*

This was a most preposterous Method; but the Eagerness of my Fancy prevail'd, and to work I went. I fell'd a Cedar Tree: I question much whether *Solomon* ever had such a one for the Building of the Temple at *Jerusalem*. It was five Foot ten Inches Diameter at the lower Part next the Stump, and four Foot eleven Inches Diameter at the End of twenty two Foot, after which it lessen'd for a while, and then parted into Branches: It was not without infinite Labour that I fell'd this Tree: I was twenty Days hacking and hewing at it at the Bottom. I was fourteen more getting the Branches and Limbs, and the vast spreading Head of it cut off, which I hack'd and hew'd through with Axe and Hatchet, and inexpressible Labour: After this, it cost me a Month to shape it, and dub it to a Proportion, and to something like the Bottom of a Boat, that it might swim upright as it ought to

do. It cost me near three Months more to clear the Inside, and work it out so, as to make an exact Boat of it: This I did indeed without Fire, by mere Mallet and Chissel, and by the dint of hard Labour, till I had brought it to be a very handsome *Periagua,* and big enough to have carried six and twenty Men, and consequently big enough to have carried me and all my Cargo.

When I had gone through this Work, I was extremely delighted with it. The Boat was really much bigger than I ever saw a *Canoe,* or *Periagua,* that was made of one Tree, in my Life. Many a weary Stroke it had cost, you may be sure; and there remained nothing but to get it into the Water; and had I gotten it into the Water, I make no question, but I should have began the maddest Voyage and the most unlikely to be perform'd, that ever was undertaken.

But all my Devices to get it into the Water fail'd me, though they cost me infinite Labour too. It lay about one hundred Yards from the Water, and not more. But the first Inconvenience was, it was up Hill towards the Creek: well, to take away this Discouragement, I resolv'd to dig into the Surface of the Earth, and so make a Declivity: This I begun, and it cost me a prodigious deal of Pains; but who grudges Pains, that have their Deliverance in View? But when this was work'd through, and this Difficulty manag'd, it was still much at one; for I could no more stir the *Canoe,* than I could the other Boat.

Then I measur'd the Distance of Ground, and resolv'd to cut a Dock, or Canal, to bring the Water up to the *Canoe,* seeing I could not bring the *Canoe* down to the Water: Well, I began this Work, and when I began to enter into it, and calculate how deep it was to be dug, how broad, how the Stuff to be thrown out, I found, that by the number of Hands I had, being none but my own, it must have been ten or twelve Years before I should have gone through with it; for the Shore lay high, so that at the upper End it must have been at least twenty Foot deep; so at length, tho' with

---

[4] A measure of six feet.

great Reluctancy, I gave this Attempt over also.

This griev'd me heartily, and now I saw, tho' too late, the Folly of beginning a Work before we count the Cost, and before we judge rightly of our own Strength to go through with it.

[REFLECTIONS OCCASIONED BY AN ANNIVERSARY]

In the middle of this Work, I finish'd my fourth Year in this Place, and kept my Anniversary with the same Devotion, and with as much Comfort as ever before; for by a constant Study, and serious Application of the Word of God, and by the Assistance of his Grace, I gain'd different Knowledge from what I had before. I entertain'd different Notions of things. I look'd now upon the World as a thing remote, which I had nothing to do with, no Expectation from, and indeed no Desires about: In a word, I had nothing indeed to do with it, nor was ever like to have; so I thought it look'd as we may perhaps look upon it hereafter, *viz.* as a Place I had lived in, but was come out of it; and well might I say, as Father *Abraham* to *Dives, Between me and thee is a great Gulph fixed.*[5]

In the first Place, I was removed from all the Wickedness of the World here: I had neither the *Lust of the Flesh, the Lust of the Eye, or the Pride of Life.* I had nothing to covet; for I had all that I was now capable of enjoying: I was Lord of the whole Manor; or if I pleas'd, I might call myself King, or Emperor over the whole Country which I had Possession of. There were no Rivals: I had no Competitor, none to dispute Sovereignty or Command with me. I might have rais'd Ship Loadings of Corn; but I had no use for it; so I let as little grow as I thought enough for my Occasion. I had Tortoise or Turtles enough; but now and then one was as much as I could put to any use. I had Timber enough to have built a Fleet of Ships. I had Grapes enough to have made Wine, or to have cur'd into Raisins, to have loaded that Fleet when they had been built.

But all I could make use of, was, All that was valuable. I had enough to eat, and to supply my Wants, and, what was all the rest to me? If I kill'd more Flesh than I could eat, the Dog must eat it, or the Vermin. If I sow'd more Corn than I could eat, it must be spoil'd. The Trees that I cut down, were lying to rot on the Ground: I could make no more use of them than for Fewel, and that I had no Occasion for, but to dress my Food.

In a Word, the Nature and Experience of Things dictated to me upon just Reflection, that all the good Things of this World, are no farther good to us, than they are for our Use; and that whatever we may heap up indeed to give others, we enjoy just as much as we can use, and no more. The most covetous griping Miser in the World would have been cured of the Vice of Covetousness, if he had been in my Case; for I possessed infinitely more than I knew what to do with. I had no room for Desire, except it was of things which I had not, and they were but Trifles, tho' indeed of great use to me. I had, as I hinted before, a Parcel of Money, as well Gold as Silver, about thirty six Pounds Sterling: Alas! there the nasty sorry useless Stuff lay; I had no manner of Business for it; and I often thought with myself, that I would have given a Handful of it for a Gross of Tobacco-Pipes, or for a Handmill to grind my Corn; nay, I would have given it all for Sixpenny-worth of *Turnip* and *Carrot* Seed out of *England,* or for a Handful of *Pease* and *Beans,* and a Bottle of Ink: *As it was,* I had not the least Advantage by it, or Benefit from it; but there it lay in a Drawer, and grew mouldy with the Damp of the Cave, in the wet Season; and if I had had the Drawer full of Diamonds, it had been the same Case; and they had been of no manner of Value to me, because of no Use.

[5] Luke 16:26 (apparently from memory as it is not exactly phrased).

I had now brought my State of Life to be much easier in itself than it was at first, and much easier to my Mind, as well as to my Body. I frequently sat down to my Meat with Thankfulness, and admired the Hand of God's Providence, which had thus spread my Table in the Wilderness. I learned to look more upon the bright Side of my Condition, and less upon the dark Side; and to consider what I enjoy'd, rather than what I wanted; and this gave me sometimes such secret Comforts, that I cannot express them; and which I take Notice of here, to put those discontented People in mind of it, who cannot enjoy comfortably what God has given them, because they see, and covet something that he has not given them. All our Discontents about what we want, appeared to me to spring from the Want of Thankfulness for what we have.

Another Reflection was of great Use to me, and doubtless would be so to any one that should fall into such Distress as mine was; and this was to compare my present Condition with what I at first expected it should be; nay, with what it would certainly have been, if the good Providence of God had not wonderfully ordered the Ship to be cast up nearer to the Shore, where I not only could come at her, but could bring what I got out of her to the Shore, for my Relief and Comfort; without which, I had wanted for Tools to work, Weapons for Defence, or Gun-powder and Shot for getting my Food.

I spent whole Hours, I may say whole Days, in representing to myself in the most lively Colours, how I must have acted, if I had got nothing out of the Ship; how I could not have so much as got any Food, except Fish and Turtles; and that as it was long before I found any of them, I must have perish'd first: That I should have liv'd, if I had not perish'd, like a meer Savage: that if I had kill'd a Goat, or a Fowl, by any Contrivance, I had no way to flea[6] or open them, or part the Flesh from the Skin and the Bowels, or to cut it up; but must gnaw it with my Teeth, and pull it with my Claws like a Beast.

These Reflections made me very sensible of the Goodness of Providence to me, and very thankful for my present Condition, with all its Hardships and Misfortunes: And this Part also I cannot but recommend to the Reflection of those who are apt in their Misery to say, *Is any Affliction like mine!* Let them consider, how much worse the Cases of some People are, and their Case might have been, if Providence had thought fit.

I had another Reflection which assisted me also to comfort my Mind with Hopes; and this was comparing my present Condition with what I had deserv'd, and had therefore Reason to expect from the Hand of Providence. I had liv'd a dreadful Life, perfectly destitute of the Knowledge and Fear of GOD. I had been well instructed by Father and Mother; neither had they been wanting to me in their early Endeavours, to infuse a religious Awe of GOD into my Mind, a Sense of my Duty, and of what the Nature and End of my Being requir'd of me. But alas! falling early into the Sea-faring Life, which of all the Lives is the most destitute of the Fear of GOD, tho' his Terrors are always before them; I say, falling early into the Sea-faring Life, and into Sea-faring Company, all that little Sense of Religion which I had entertain'd, was laugh'd out of me by my Mess mates, by a harden'd despising of Dangers, and the Views of Death, which grew habitual to me, by my long Absence from all manner of Opportunities to converse with any thing but what was like myself, or to hear any thing that was good, or tended towards it.

So void was I of every thing that was good, or of the least Sense of what I was, or was to be, that in the greatest Deliverances I enjoy'd, such as my Escape from *Salle,*[7] my being taken up by the *Portuguese* Master of the Ship, my being planted so well in the *Brasils,* my receiving the Cargo from *England,* and the

---

[6] to skin.

[7] Salé on the coast of Morocco, where Crusoe had been captive of the Moors for two years early in the story.

like, I never had once the Word *Thank God,* so much as on my Mind, or in my Mouth; nor in the greatest Distress, had I so much as a Thought to pray to him; or so much as to say, *Lord have Mercy upon me;* no nor to mention the Name of GOD, unless it was to swear by, and blaspheme it.

I had terrible Reflections upon my Mind for many Months, as I have already observ'd, on the Account of my wicked and hardned Life past; and when I look'd about me, and consider'd what particular Providences had attended me since my coming into this Place, and how God had dealt bountifully with me; had not only punish'd me less than my Iniquity had deserv'd, but had so plentifully provided for me; this gave me great Hopes that my Repentance was accepted, and that God had yet Mercy in store for me.

With these Reflections I work'd my Mind up, not only to Resignation to the Will of God in the present Disposition of my Circumstances, but even to a sincere Thankfulness for my Condition; and that I who was yet a living Man, ought not to complain, seeing I had not the due Punishment of my Sins; that I enjoy'd so many Mercies which I had no reason to have expected in that Place; that I ought never more to repine at my Condition, but to rejoyce, and to give daily Thanks for that daily Bread which nothing but a croud of Wonders could have brought. That I ought to consider I had been fed even by Miracle, even as great as that of feeding *Elijah* by Ravens;[8] nay, by a long Series of Miracles, and that I could hardly have nam'd a Place in the unhabitable Part of the World where I could have been cast more to my Advantage: A Place, where as I had no Society, which was my Affliction on one hand, so I found no ravenous Beasts, no furious Wolves or Tygers to threaten my Life, no venomous Creatures or poisonous, which I might feed on to my hurt, no Savages to murder and devour me.

In a Word, as my Life was a Life of Sorrow one way, so it was a Life of

Mercy another; and I wanted nothing to make it a Life of Comfort, but to be able to make my Sense of God's Goodness to me, and Care over me in this Condition, be my daily Consolation; and after I did make a just Improvement of these things, I went away and was no more sad.

I had now been here so long, that many things which I brought on Shore for my Help, were either quite gone, or very much wasted and near spent.

[NOT QUITE NAKED]

My Ink, as I observ'd, had been gone for some time, all but a very little, which I eek'd out with Water a little and a little, till it was so pale it scarce left any Appearance of black upon the Paper: As long as it lasted I made use of it to minute down the Days of the Month on which any remarkable thing happen'd to me; and first by casting up Times past, I remember that there was a strange Concurrence of Days in the various Providences which befel me, and which, if I had been superstitiously inclin'd to observe Days as Fatal or Fortunate, I might have had Reason to have look'd upon with a great deal of Curiosity.

First, I had observ'd, that the same Day that I broke away from my Father and my Friends, and run away to *Hull* in order to go to Sea, the same Day afterwards I was taken by the *Salle* Man of War, and made a Slave.

The same Day of the Year that I escaped out of the Wreck of that Ship in *Yarmouth* Roads, that same Day-Year afterwards I made my escape from *Salle* in the Boat.

The same Day of the Year I was born on, (*viz.*) the 30th of *September,* the same Day I had my Life so miraculously saved 26 Years after, when I was cast on Shore in this Island; so that my wicked Life and my solitary Life begun both on a Day.

The next thing to my Ink's being wasted, was that of my Bread, I mean the Bisket which I brought out of the Ship: this I had husbanded to the last

---

[8] I Kings 17:6.

degree, allowing myself but one Cake of Bread a Day for above a Year, and yet I was quite without Bread for near a Year before I got any Corn of my own; and great Reason I had to be thankful that I had any at all, the getting it being, as has been already observed, next to miraculous.

My Cloaths began to decay too mightily: As to Linnen, I had had none a good while, except some chequer'd Shirts which I found in the Chests of the other Seamen, and which I carefully preserv'd, because many times I could bear no other Cloaths on but a Shirt; and it was a very great help to me that I had among all the Mens Cloaths of the Ship almost three dozen of Shirts. There were also several thick Watch-coats of the Seamens, which were left indeed, but they were too hot to wear; and tho' it is true, that the Weather was so violent hot that there was no need of Cloaths; yet I could not go quite naked; no, tho' I had been inclined to it, which I was not, nor could not abide the Thoughts of it, tho' I was all alone.

The Reason why I could not go quite naked, was, I could not bear the Heat of the Sun so well when quite naked, as with some Cloaths on; nay, the very Heat frequently blister'd my Skin; whereas with a Shirt on, the Air itself made some Motion, and whistling under that Shirt, was twofold cooler than without it: No more could I ever bring myself to go out in the Heat of the Sun without a Cap or a Hat; the Heat of the Sun beating with such Violence as it does in that Place, would give me the Headach presently, by darting so directly on my Head, without a Cap or a Hat on; so that I could not bear it; whereas if I put on my Hat, it would presently go away.

Upon those Views I began to consider about putting the few Rags I had, which I called Cloaths, into some Order: I had worn out all the Waistcoats I had, and my Business was now to try if I could

not make Jackets out of the great Watch-coats which I had by me, and with such other Materials as I had; so I set to work a Tayloring, or rather indeed a Botching; for I made most piteous Work of it. However, I made shift to make two or three new Waistcoats, which I hoped would serve me a great while; as for Breeches or Drawers, I made but a very sorry shift indeed, till afterward.

I have mentioned, that I saved the Skins of all the Creatures that I kill'd, I mean four-footed ones, and I had hung them up stretch'd out with Sticks in the Sun, by which means some of them were so dry and hard that they were fit for little, but others it seems were very useful. The first thing I made of these was a great Cap for my Head, with the Hair on the Outside to shoor off the Rain; and this I perform'd so well, that after this I made me a Suit of Cloaths wholly of these Skins, that is to say, a Waistcoat and Breeches open at Knees, and both loose, for they were rather wanting to keep me cool than to keep me warm. I must not omit to acknowledge that they were wretchedly made; for if I was a bad *Carpenter,* I was a worse *Taylor.* However, they were such as I made very good shift with; and when I was abroad, if it happen'd to rain, the Hair of my Waistcoat and Cap being outermost, I was kept very dry.

After this I spent a great deal of Time and Pains to make me an Umbrella; I was indeed in great want of one, and had a great mind to make one; I had seen them made in the *Brasils,* where they are very useful in the great Heats which are there: And I felt the Heats every jot as great here, and greater too, being nearer the Equinox;[9] besides, as I was obliged to be much abroad, it was a most useful thing to me, as well for the Rains as the Heats. I took a world of Pains at it, and was a great while before I could make any thing likely to hold; nay, after I thought I had hit the way, I spoil'd 2 or 3 before I made one to my

---

[9] Crusoe evidently means the equator, as equinox refers to a time of the year when the day and night are of equal length. Defoe's use of the word is not in eighteenth-century dictionaries.

mind; but at last I made one that answer'd indifferently well: the main difficulty I found was to make it to let down: I could make it to spread, but if it did not let down too, and draw in, it was not portable for me any way but just over my Head, which would not do. However, at last, as I said, I made one to answer, and cover'd it with Skins, the Hair upwards, so that it cast off the Rains like a Penthouse, and kept off the Sun so effectually, that I could walk out in the hottest of the Weather with greater Advantage than I could before in the coolest, and when I had no need of it, could close it and carry it under my Arm.

Thus I lived mighty comfortably, my Mind being entirely composed by resigning to the Will of God, and throwing myself wholly upon the Disposal of his Providence. This made my Life better than sociable; for when I began to regret the want of Conversation, I would ask myself, whether thus conversing mutually with my own Thoughts, and, as I hope I may say, with even God himself by Ejaculations, was not better than the utmost Enjoyment of humane Society in the World?

William Law
1686-1761

A SERIOUS CALL TO A DEVOUT
AND HOLY LIFE

CHAPTER 14 [THE CHARACTERS OF MUNDANUS AND CLASSICUS]

Mundanus[1] is a man of excellent parts, and clear apprehension. He is well advanc'd in age, and has made a great figure in business. Every part of *trade* and business that has fallen in his way, has had some improvement from him; and he is always contriving to carry every method of doing any thing well, to its greatest height. *Mundanus* aims at the greatest perfection in every thing. The *soundness* and *strength* of his mind, and his just way of thinking upon things, makes him intent upon removing all imperfections.

He can tell you all the defects and errors in all the common methods, whether of *trade, building,* or improving *land,* or *manufactures.* The clearness and strength of his understanding, which he is constantly improving, by continual exercise in these matters, by often digesting his thoughts in writing, and trying every thing every way, has render'd him a great master of most concerns in human life.

Thus has *Mundanus* gone on, increasing his *knowledge* and *judgment,* as fast as his years came upon him.

The one only thing which has not fallen under his improvement, nor receiv'd any benefit from his judicious mind, is his *devotion:* This is just in the same *poor* state it was, when he was only six years of age; and the *old man* prays now, in that little form of words, which his mother us'd to hear him repeat night and morning.

This *Mundanus,* that hardly ever saw the poorest *utensil,* or ever took the meanest *trifle* into his hand, without considering how it might be *made,* or *us'd* to better advantage, has gone all his life long praying in the same manner, as when he was a *child;* without ever considering how much *better,* or *oftner* he might pray; without considering how improveable the spirit of devotion is, how many helps a wise and reasonable man may call to his assistance, and how necessary it is, that our prayers should be enlarg'd, vary'd, and suited to the particular state and condition of our lives.

If *Mundanus* sees a book of *devotion,* he passes it by, as he does a *spelling-book,*

Text from first edition, 1729.

[1] *Mundanus* signifies worldliness; hence, man of practical affairs, a hard-headed businessman.

because he remembers that he learn'd to *pray* so many years ago under his *mother,* when he learnt to *spell.*

Now how poor and pitiable is the conduct of this man of sense, who has so much judgment and understanding in every thing, but that which is the *whole wisdom* of man?

And how miserably do many people, more or less imitate this conduct?

All which seems to be owing to a strange infatuated state of negligence, which keeps people from considering what *devotion* is. For if they did but once proceed so far, as to *reflect* about it, or ask themselves any questions concerning it, they would soon see, that the spirit of *devotion* was like any other *sense* or *understanding,* that is only to be improv'd by *study, care, application,* and the *use* of such *means* and *helps,* as are necessary to make a man a proficient in any art, or science.

Classicus[2] is a man of learning, and well vers'd in all the best authors of antiquity. He has read them so much, that he has enter'd into their spirit, and can very ingeniously imitate the manner of any of them. All their thoughts are his thoughts, and he can express himself in their language. He is so great a friend to this improvement of the mind, that if he lights of a young scholar, he never fails to advise him concerning his studies.

Classicus tells his young man, he must not think that he has done enough, when he has only learnt *languages;* but that he must be daily conversant with the best authors, read them again and again, catch their spirit by living with them, and that there is no other way of becoming like them, or of making himself a man of *taste* and *judgment.*

How wise might *Classicus* have been, and how much good might he have done in the world, if he had but thought as *justly* of *devotion,* as he does of *learning?*

He never, indeed, says any thing *shocking* or *offensive* about *devotion,* be-

cause he never *thinks,* or *talks* about it. It suffers nothing from him, but neglect and disregard.

The two Testaments would not have had so much as a place amongst his Books, but that they are both to be had in *Greek.*

Classicus thinks that he sufficiently shews his regard for the holy Scripture, when he tells you, that he has no other Books of piety besides them.

It is very well, *Classicus,* that you prefer the Bible to all other Books of piety; he has no judgment, that is not thus far of your opinion.

But if you will have no other book of piety besides the *Bible,* because it is the best, How comes it, *Classicus,* that you don't content your self with *one* of the *best* Books amongst the *Greeks* and *Romans?* How comes it that you are so greedy and eager after *all* of them? How comes it that you think the knowledge of one is a necessary help to the knowledge of the other? How comes it that you are so earnest, so laborious, so expensive of your time and money, to restore *broken periods,* and *scraps* of the ancients?

How comes it that you read so many *Commentators* upon *Cicero, Horace,* and *Homer,* and not one upon the Gospel? How comes it that you love to read a man? How comes it that your love of *Cicero,* and *Ovid,* makes you love to read an *author* that writes like them; and yet your *esteem* for the *Gospel* gives you no desire, nay, prevents your reading such Books, as breathe the very spirit of the Gospel?

How comes it that you tell your *young scholar,* he must not content himself with barely understanding his authors, but must be continually reading them *all,* as the only means of entering into their spirit, and forming his own judgment according to them?

Why then must the Bible lye alone in your study? Is not the spirit of the saints, the piety of the holy followers of Jesus Christ, as good and necessary a means of entering into the spirit and *taste* of the Gospel, as the reading of the antients is of entering into the spirit of antiquity?

Is the spirit of poetry only to be got

---

[2] *Classicus* signifies scholarly attributes; hence, an inhabitant of an ivory tower, an "egghead."

by much reading of Poets and Orators? And is not the spirit of devotion to be got in the same way, by frequent reading the holy thoughts, and pious strains of devout men?

Is your young Poet to search after *every line,* that may give new wings to his fancy, or direct his imagination? And is it not as reasonable for him, who desires to improve in the divine life, that is, in the love of heavenly things, to search after every strain of devotion, that may move, kindle, and inflame the holy ardour of his soul?

Do you advise your *Orator* to translate the best Orations, to commit much of them to memory, to be frequently exercising his talent in this manner, that habits of thinking and speaking justly may be form'd in his mind? And is there not the same benefit and advantage to be made by books of devotion? Should not a man use them in the same way, that habits of devotion, and aspiring to God in holy thoughts, may be well form'd in his soul?

Now the reason why *Classicus* does not *think* and *judge* thus reasonably of devotion, is owing to his never thinking of it in any other manner, than as the repeating a *form* of *words.* It never in his life enter'd into his head, to think of devotion as a *state of the heart,* as an *improveable talent* of the mind, as a *temper* that is to *grow* and *increase* like our *reason* and *judgment,* and to be form'd in us by such a regular diligent use of proper means, as are necessary to form any other wise habit of mind.

And it is for want of this, that he has been content all his life, with the *bare letter* of Prayer, and eagerly bent upon entering into the *spirit* of *heathen poets* and *orators.*

And it is much to be lamented, that numbers of *scholars* are *more* or *less* chargeable with this excessive folly; so negligent of improving their devotion, and so desirous of other poor accomplishments, as if they thought it a nobler talent, to be able to write an *epigram* in the *turn* of *Martial,* than to *live,* and *think,* and *pray* to God, in the spirit of St. *Austin.*

And yet, to correct this temper, and fill a man with a quite contrary spirit, there seems to be no more requir'd, than the *bare* belief of the truth of Christianity.

And if you was to ask *Mundanus,* and *Classicus,* or any man of business, or learning, whether *piety* is not the highest perfection of man, or *devotion* the greatest attainment in the world, they must both be forced to answer in the affirmative, or else give up the truth of the Gospel.

For to set any accomplishment against devotion, or to think any thing, or all things in the world, bears any proportion to its excellency; is the same absurdity in a Christian, as it would be in a *Philosopher* to prefer a *meals meat,* to the greatest improvement in knowledge.

For as *Philosophy* professes purely the search and enquiry after knowledge, so *Christianity* supposes, intends, desires and aims at nothing else, but the raising fallen man to a divine life, to such habits of holiness, such degrees of devotion, as may fit him to enter amongst the holy inhabitants of the kingdom of heaven.

He that does not believe this of Christianity, may be reckon'd an infidel; and he that believes thus much, has *faith* enough to give him a right *judgment* of the *value* of things, to support him in a *sound mind,* and enable him to conquer all the temptations which the world shall lay in his way.

John, Baron Hervey of Ickworth

1696-1743

From MEMOIRS OF THE REIGN OF GEORGE II

[DEATH OF THE QUEEN, 1737]

On Wednesday the 9th of Nov. the Queen was taken ill in the Morning at her new Library in St. James's Park: she call'd her Complaint the Cholick, her Stomach & Bowels giving her great pain. She came home, took Daffy's-Elixir by Dr. Tesier[1] the German & House Physician's advice, but was such great Pain, & so uneasy with frequent Reachings[2] to vomit that she went into Bed. However when the Clock struck two, & the King proposed sending Ld. Grantham[3] to dismiss the Company & declare there would be no Drawingroom, she according to the Custom of the Family, not caring to own, or at least to have it generally known how ill she was, told the K.[4] she was much better, that she would get up, & see the Company as usual. As soon as she came into the Drawingroom she came up to Ld. H.[5] &
say'd *is it not intolerable at my Age[6] to be plagued with a new Distemper? here is this nasty Cholick that I had at Hamptoncourt come again.* The Queen had twice this Summer at Hamptoncourt been seized with a vomiting & purging which had lasted in the most violent manner for three or four Hours & then left her so easy, & well that she had play'd the same night in the Drawingroom as usual & talk'd with almost the same Cherfullness. This made Ld. H. less allarm'd than he otherwise would have been at her present Disorder, for she look'd extreamly ill, & complain'd much more than was her Custom to do when she suffer'd most. Ld. H. ask'd her what she had taken & when she told him, he reply'd, *for God sake Madam go to your own Room, what have you to do here?* She then went & talk'd a little to the rest of the Company, & coming back again to Ld. H. say'd *I am not able*

Text from manuscript in the possession of the Marquis of Bristol and reproduced through his courtesy.

[1] George Lewis Tesier (d. 1742).

[2] retchings.

[3] Henry d'Auverquerque, first Earl of Grantham (1672–1754), the Queen's Lord Chamberlain, referred to on another occasion by Hervey as "an old stupid Dutchman, whose vocabulary did not consist of above twenty words, and even these he did not understand the meaning of."

[4] George II (1683–1760). He had been king of England ten years. On one occasion, Hervey wrote of him: "I do not believe there ever lived a man to whose temper benevolence was so absolute a stranger."

[5] Hervey regularly refers to himself in the third person.

[6] 54.

to entertain People. Would to God (reply'd Ld. H.) *the King would have done talking of the Dragon of Wantley[7] & release you.* (This was a new silly Farce which every body at this time went to see) At last the K. went away, telling the Q. as he went by, that she had overlook'd the Ds. of Norfolk.[8] The Q. made her excuse for having done so to the Ds. of Norfolk the last Person she ever spoke to in public, & then retired, going immediately in to Bed, where she grew worse every moment.

At seven a Clock when Ld. H. return'd to St. James's from Monsr. de Gambier's the french Embassador's where he dined that day, he went up to the Q.'s Apartment & found her in bed, with the Ps.[9] Caroline only in the Room: the K. being gone, as usual at that hour, to play in the Ps. Emely's Apartment. The Q. ask'd Ld. H. what he used to take in his violent Fits of the Cholick; & Ld. H. imagining the Q.'s Pain to proceed from a Goutish Humour in her Stomach that should be driven from that dangerous Seat into her Limbs, told her nothing ever gave him immediate ease but strong things: to which the Q. reply'd.—Pshaw—You think now like all the other Fools, that this is the Pain of an old nasty Gout. But her Vomittings, or rather her reachings, together with such accute Pain continuing in a degree that she could not lye one moment quiet, she say'd about an hour after to Ld. H. *give me what you will, I will take it.* & the Ps. Caroline bidding him not lose this Oportunity, he only say'd to the Q. he would fetch the strongest thing he could get, telling her at the same time that his former experience of violent fits of the Cholick was such that he was sure all the Angels in Heaven together could not procure her immediate Ease without it.

He fetch'd some Snake-root & Brandy, & asking Dr. Tesier who was in the outward Room whether he might venture to give it her; Dr. Tesier who was naturally timid, & made more so by the manner in which he had been talk'd to, in the K.'s Illness last year, say'd the Q.'s Pulse was very high & feverish, & as she was unused to drinking any thing strong, he could not affirm that this very strong Cordial would do her no hurt. Ld. H. then ask'd him, if he should propose to the K. to call in another Physician, & if he had any Objection to Broxholme;[10] & Dr. Tesier saying he wish'd it extreamly but did not dare to propose it him-self to the K., Ld. H. told Ps. Caroline what had pass'd, that he did not dare to take upon him to give the Snake-Root, without Tesier's Consent; & would if she approved propose to the K. that Dr. Broxholm might be call'd in.

The Ps. Carolina consented, & Ld. H. speaking to the K. who was now return'd from Ps. Emely's Apartment, & began to be allarm'd, Dr. Broxholme was immediately sent for by Ld. H. When he came, Tesier & He agree'd to give the Q. immediately some Snake-Root with Sr. Walter Rawleigh's Cordial; but this Cordial being long in preparing, & Ranby[11] House-Surgeon to the K. a sensible Fellow & a Favorite of Ld. H.'s, telling Ld. H. that insisting on these occasions upon a Cordial with this Name or tother Name was mere Quackery, & that no Cordial was better than another in these Cases but in Proportion to it's Strength; Ld. H. got some Usquebaugh immediately, & telling Ps. Caroline what Ranby had say'd, the Usquebaugh was

---

[7] By Henry Carey, at Covent Garden.

[8] The Duchess of Norfolk had earlier in the year played a diplomatic hand in the quarrel between the King and his son. Hervey told of the Prince's taking her town house: "The Prince took the Duke of Norfolk's house in St. James's Square for his town dwelling . . . but before the Duke of Norfolk would consent to the Prince having his house, the Duchess of Norfolk came to Hampton Court to ask the Queen, whom she saw in private, if it would be disagreeable to her and the King; and the Queen assuring the Duchess of Norfolk it would not, and thanking her for the civility she had shown to the King and her, the Duke of Norfolk let the Prince know his house was at His Royal Highness's service."

[9] Princess.

[10] Noel Broxholme (1689–1748), who had been recently called in by the Prince to attend the birth of a child.

[11] John Ranby (1703–1773).

immediately given to the Q. who kept it about half an Hour, which was about 29 Minutes longer than she had kept any thing else, but then brought it up. Soon after the Snake-Root & Sr. Walter-Rawleigh's Cordial arrived from the Apothecary's; it was taken & thrown up about an Hour after. All these strong things, twice Daffy's Elixir, Mint-water Usquebaugh, Snake-Root & Sr. W. R.,'s Cordial, had without easing the Q.'s Pain so encreased her Fever, that the Drs. order'd Ranby to bleed her twelve ounces immediately. She took a Glyster[12] but it came from her just as it went into her.

The Ps. Caroline had been extremely ill all this Summer at Hamptoncourt of Rheumatic Pains & growing every Day worse, notwithstanding all the Medicines that had been given her, in what the Physicians call a regular way; Ld. H. upon her coming to town had persuaded her to take Ward's Pill; a *Nostrum* belonging to one Ward, an excellent Medicine, not only in Rheumatisms but in several Cases, which all the Physicians & Surgeons for being so endeavour'd to decry.

Ps. Caroline persuaded by Ld. H. had taken this Medicine since her Arrival in London, with the Privity[13] rather than Consent of the K. & Q. & keeping it a Secret to every body else. But in four times taking only, she had found such Benefit, that notwithstanding she had been unable to walk or get up from her Chair without help when she began it; she was now quite free from Pain & could walk almost as well as she ever could have done in her Life. This Medicine vomits, purges, & sweat's in a great degree.

However her Recovery being not yet perfect, the K. & Q. were both extreamly solicitous to have her go to bed which she did not do till two a Clock in the Morning.

The K. inconveniently both to himself & the Q. lay on the Q.'s Bed all night in his Nightgown, where he could not sleep, nor she turn about easyly.

Early in the morning the Q. was blooded 12. ounces more upon which her Fever that had been very high all night abated, & every body but her-self, thought she was better.

When the K. went to his own side to change his Linnen she told the Ps. Caroline, it signify'd nothing what they did to her for she should certainly dye: & added, *poor Caroline! you are very ill too, we shall soon meet again in another Place.*

Her vomitting was suspended for a few Hours this Morning, but nothing pass'd downwards, & two Glysters she took return'd immediately & pure.

However on this Amendment as every Body call'd it, but few really thought it, the K. resolved to have his Levé,[14] & that the Pss. should see the Company at the usual Hour of the Q.'s going out, in her Drawingroom; & to show what od & inconsistent Particulars we are all composed of, this being the Day the foreign Ministers came to Court, the K. in the midst of all his real & great Concern for the Q. sent to his Pages to bid them be sure to have his last new Ruffles sow'd on, upon the Shirt he was to put on that Day at his publick Dressing: such sort of Particulars will seem very trifling to those who do not think like me that trifling Circumstances often let one more into People's Tempers & Characters than those Parts of their Conduct that are of greater Importance, from wch. one frequently knows no more of their natural turn of Mind than one does of their natural Gate whilst they are dancing.[15]

Mrs. Herbert sister in Law to Ld. Pembroke[16] happen'd to be the Bedchamber-Woman in waiting this Week on the Q. & tho she was a personal, &

---

[12] More commonly *clyster:* "an injection into the anus" (Johnson's *Dictionary*).

[13] "consciousness; joint knowledge; private concurrence" (Johnson's *Dictionary*).

[14] public audience.

[15] Cf. Pope's couplet from *An Essay on Criticism* (1711):

True ease in writing comes from art, not chance,
As those move easiest who have learned to dance.

[16] Henry Herbert, ninth Earl of Pembroke (1693–1751), had been made Groom of the Stole in 1735 with a stipend of £3000 a year.

warm Enemy, & had long been so, to Sr.
R. W.[17] yet she was so sensible, so well-
bred so handy, so cherfull, & so agreable
to the Q. that the Q. desired her if she
should continue ill longer than that week
that Mrs. Herbert would continue in
waiting.

Mrs. Herbert, Mrs. Selwin[18] & Mrs.
Brudnal[19] were the only Bedchamber
Women who attended the Q. during her
whole Illness, Lady Sundon[20] being very
ill at the Bath; & the rest absent elsewhere. None of the Ladys of her Bedchamber were admitted to her at all.

Ld. H. ask'd the D. of Newcastle[21]
this Morning, if he would not send for
Sr. R. W. & the D. of Newcastle say'd
he had mention'd it, but that the Ps.
Emely had told him the K. & Q. would
both dislike he should. But his Grace
added he would write that Night to
Houghton,[22] to say how the Q. was, &
disguise nothing.

He did so & Ps. Emely added a
Postscript in the Letter, softening the
State of Things, & begging Sr. R. W.
by all means not to think of coming to
town.

Ld. H. wrote that Night softening
nothing, & advising him by all means to
come, & did not then tell Sr. Rt. what
he thought he plainly perceived, that the
Ps. Emely & the D. of Newcastle had
no mind he should come. The Ps. Emely
hoping I believe that the Q. would not
take his staying at Houghton well, & the
D. of Newcastle, join'd to that Reason,
proposing perhaps by Sr. Rt.'s absence
to have the K. more to himself. If that
was his Scheme, he was disappointed for
after this Day, the K. saw no Minister,
nor any one Man Servant that belong'd
to him but Ld. H. who was never out of
the Q.'s Apartment, for above four or
5 hours at most at a time during her
whole Illness, & sometimes not two in

the 24. & never went from the K. without his desiring him to come back as
soon as he could.

This Evening whilst the Ps. Caroline
& he were alone with the Q. she complaining & they comforting, She often
say'd;—*I have an ill which no body
knows of.* Which they both understood
to mean nothing more than that she felt
what she could not describe, & more
than any body imagined. Ps. Caroline's
extreme Concern & almost continual
Weeping, gave her a return of her Rheu-
matism, which settled in her Back, &
added to this, she had from this violent
& perpetual Weeping a frequent Bleeding at her Nose & in great Quantitys.
The K. & Q. therefore both persuaded
her to go to bed & insisted on her doing
so about Midnight, Ld. H. promising
her to sit up & giving his Word he
would frequently come & inform her
how the Q. was, exactly & without the
least Disguise.

This Night two more Physicians were
call'd in, Sr. Hans Slone & Dr. Hulse:[23]
who order'd Blisters & a Purge; the
Purge came up like every other thing,
soon after she had swallow'd it. & the
Blisters tho a Remedy to wch the King
& Q. had often declared themselves very
averse, were put upon her Legs.

Ld. H. went once or twice in the
Night as he had promised to Ps.
Caroline, the K. sat up in the Q.'s Room
& Ps. Emely lay on a Couch in Mrs.
Herbert's. At six a Clock on Friday
Morning the Q. was again blooded;
upon which her Fever went almost en-
tirely off; but the total Stoppage & fre-
quent Vomittings still continued.

On Friday Ld. H. again desired the
D. of Newcastle to send an Express for
Sr. R. W. which his Grace at last
thought fit to do; but sending the Messenger round by Euston where the D. of

[17] Sir Robert Walpole (1676–1745), Prime Minister.
[18] 1691–1777; "a simple cunning woman" (Hervey).
[19] Mrs. Brudenell, the Queen's chambermaid, reputedly very ill-tempered.
[20] A woman much disliked by the Prime Minister; she died in 1742.

[21] Thomas Pelham-Holles, first Duke of Newcastle (1693–1768), Secretary of State; referred to by Hervey on another occasion as Walpole's "echo."
[22] Walpole's residence in Norfolk.
[23] Sir Hans Sloane (1660–1753), "a physician by profession, a very dull fellow" (Hervey); Edward Hulse (1682–1759).

Grafton then was, & the Messenger by accident, or order, loitering on the Road, Sr. R. W. had not these Letters till Saturday Evening, & set not out for London till Sunday morning.

On Friday Ld. H. hearing the P.[24] was come from Kew to Carlton-house in Pell-mell[25] suspected, he had done so in order to come to St. James's to enquire after the Q. & perhaps to ask to see her; & that no Resolution on such a step might be taken by the K. in a hurry; Ld. H. told the K. his Conjecture, & ask'd his My.[26] in case it should prove a true one what he would have done. The K. say'd, if the Puppy should in one of his impertinent, affected, airs of Duty & Affection, dare to come to St. James's I order you to go to the Scoundrel & tell him I wonder at his Impudence for daring to come here; that he has my orders already & knows my Pleasure, & bid him go about his Busyness; for his poor Mother is not in a Condition to see him act his false whining cringing tricks now, nor am I in a humour to bear his impertinence, & bid him trouble me with no more Messages but get out of my House.

About an hour or two afterward whilst Ld. H. was sitting with the Duke[27] drinking tea in the Q.'s Apartment a message came by one of the Q.'s Pages to the Duke to tell him Lady Pembroke the Q.'s Lady then in waiting desired to speak with his R. H.[28] in the Passage. Ld. H. telling the D. he suspected this might prove something relative to the Prince, say'd he would go with him. Accordingly he went, & Lady Pembroke told the Duke, Ld. North[29] had just been with her from the P. to desire her in the P.'s Name, to let the K. & Q. know his R. H. was in the utmost affliction upon hearing of the Q.'s Illness, was come to London in order to hear more frequently how she did; & that the

only thing that could alleviate his great Concern at this time was to be admitted to the Honour of seeing her.

The D. say'd, I am not a proper Person Madam to take the Charge of this Message, but there is Ld. H. who is the only one of Papa's Servants that see's him at present, & is just going to him, if you will deliver it to him he will certainly let the King know.

Accordingly Lady Pembroke repeated the Message over again to Ld. H. & Ld. H. assured her he would take the first Opportunity to acquaint the K. with it.

When Ld. H. told the K. what had pass'd, his My. flew into as great a Rage as he could have done had he not been prepared. This (say'd he) is like one of the scoundrels tricks. It is just a Peice with his kneeling down in the Dirt before the Mob to kiss her Hand at the Coach Door when she came from Hamptoncourt to see the Ps. tho he had not spoke one word to her during her whole Visit: I always hated the Rascal, but now I hate him yet worse than ever. He wants now to come to disturb his poor dying Mother; but she shall not see him, you have hear'd her, & all my Daughters have hear'd her very often this year at Hamptoncourt desire me if she should be ill & out of her Senses, that I would never let that Villain come near her, & whilst she had her Senses she was sure she should never desire it. No, no, he shall not come & act any of his silly Plays here, besides suposing the Q. loved him as much as she hates him, it would be as improper for her to see him in that Case as it is now; she is not in a Condition to bear the Emotion; therefore my Ld. you know my Thoughts, I have told you already the Answer I would have given, you have but to tell it my Ld. North, & be sure not to forget to say I will be plagued with no more Messages.

Ld. H. told the K. if he deliver'd a

[24] Frederick, Prince of Wales (1707–1751), heir apparent, who helped to establish the tradition that the sons of the Hanoverian kings regularly quarreled with their fathers. Differences between father and son were augmented by political schemers.

[25] Pall Mall, where the Prince was living.

[26] Majesty.

[27] Frederick's younger brother, William, Duke of Cumberland (1721–1765).

[28] His Royal Highness.

[29] Francis, seventh Lord North (1704–1790), Lord of the Bedchamber to the Prince of Wales.

verbal Message only, that the P. & his People would certainly engraft a thousand Lyes upon it, & without a possibility of being disproved.

It is no matter for that reply'd the K. I will not honor him with another written message nor have the Apearance of giving my-self at this time so much trouble about him.—Nor would I have your My. (answer'd Ld. H.) but if you will give me leave, as for the help of my own Memory, to put your My's Commands down in writing, & only let me read that Paper, without delivering it, yr. Majy. will at once show that you will neither honor them with a written Message nor trust them with a verbal one.—You are in the right say'd the K. do so, put down in writing what you are to say; & pray see who are in the Rooms & take two People of Quality & Credit along with you, to be by when you read the Paper to Ld. North, that they may be witnesses to what passes, for else that Pack of Knaves & Lyars (Cartouche's Gang[30] as the poor Q. always calls them) are capable of reporting you to have say'd things you never thought of.

Ld. H. went immediately to put down what he was to say in writing & desired the D. of Newcastle & Ld. Pembroke to go along with him to Ld. North, & telling them that he had already named them to the K. for that purpose, acquainting them at the same time with all the material Part of what I have already related, concerning this transaction.

Ld. Pembroke, Ld. H. chose as a Man of Credit, & the D. of Newcastle, because he thought it would mortify him to play Subaltern in an Occurrence where Ld. H. acted the Principal Part; a Petitesse[31] in Ld. H.'s way of thinking, but one he liked to indulge.

The Message Ld. H. drew was as follows.—

Message deliver'd by Ld. Hervey by word of mouth to Ld. North at St. James's Friday *Nov. 11. 1737.* In the Presence of the Duke of Newcastle & Ld. Pembroke.

I have acquainted the King with the Message sent to Lady Pembroke & his Majy. has order'd me to say, that in the present Situation & Circumstances his Majy. does not think fit, that the Prince should see the Queen, & therefore expects he should not come to St. James's.

The K. thought this Draught[32] much too mild (but after a little Persuasion consented to it; as also (at Ld. H.'s request) to see the D. of Newcastle & Ld. Pembroke only for a Minute, to read this Paper to them, to tell them he had order'd Ld. H. to deliver this Message, & to order them to be present when he did so. & the K. again in their Presence, repeated his Commands to Ld. H. to be sure not to give a Copy of that Paper, with his Reasons, already mention'd why he would not have it done, as well as those for his ordering the D. of Newcastle & Ld. Pembroke to be witnesses to what pass'd at this Interview: cutting Ld. Pembroke very short who would have offer'd some Palliatives to the wording of the Message, & telling him my Ld. you are always for softening, & I think it is much too soft already for such a Villain & a Scoundrel it is much softer than I order'd Ld. Hervey to prepare it.—So pray go & let it be given this Moment, & be sure I am plagued with no more Impertinence of this sort, for I will neither have the poor Q. disturb'd with these silly Messages, nor will I be troubled with them again my-self.

When Ld. H. deliver'd the Message Lord North desired he might have a Copy of it in writing, to wch. Ld. Pembroke answer'd that Ld. H. had the K.'s positive Commands not to give it in writing; & Ld. H. added that he would read it as often as Ld. North pleased: & after hearing it 3. or 4. times, Ld. North took his Leave.

In the afternoon the Q. say'd to the King, she wonder'd *the Griff* (the Nick-

---

[30] Louis Dominique Bourguignon, called Cartouche (1693–1721), was the celebrated chief of a gang of French thieves.

[31] indignity.
[32] draft.

name of the P.) had not sent to ask to see her yet; it would be so like one of his *Paroitres*,[33] but sooner or later I am sure one shall be plagued with some Message of that sort, because he will think it will have a good air in the World to ask to see me & perhaps hopes, I shall be fool enough to let him come & give him the Pleasure of seeing my last Breath go out of my Body, by wch. means he would have ye Joy of knowing I was dead 5 Mins. sooner than he could know it in Pel-mell.

The K. then bid her not be under any Aprehensions of a trouble of this kind, for that he had already taken Care to prevent it, & then related to her every Circumstance of the Message he had received & the answer he had return'd by Ld. H. The K. told the Q. too, that if she had the least Mind to see her Son, he had no Objection to it, & beg'd her to do just what she liked. I am so far (say'd the Q.) from desiring to see him, that nothing but yr. absolute Commands should ever make me consent to it. For what should I see him? for him to tell me a hundred lyes, to give myself at this time a great deal of trouble to no purpose. If anything I could say to him would alter his Behaviour I would see him with all my Heart. But I know that is impossible, whatever advice I gave him he would thank me for, pleureroit comme un veau[34] all the while I was speaking, & swear to follow my directions, & would laugh at me the moment he was out of the room and do just the contrary of all I bid him the moment I was dead. There is no hope of mending him; it is a sad wretch, and therefore if I should grow worse & be weak enough to talk of seeing him I beg you will conclude that I doot[35] and rave, and insist upon your promising me now that I shall not see him. The whole of Friday the Q. grew worse every hour. When the King came into the Room he whisper'd to her that he was afraid her distress proceeded from a thing he had promised never to speak of again; but

that now his Duty to her call'd upon him to tell the Physicians all he knew: & all he apprehended; she beg'd & entreated him with great Ernestness that he would not; & spoke with more warmth & Pevishness than she show'd at any other Minute during her whole Illness. However he sent for Ranby the Surgeon & told him he apprehended the Q. had a Rupture at her Navel & bid him examine her: the Q. carry'd her desire to conceal this Complaint so far, that when Ranby came to feel her, she lay'd his Hand on the Pit of her Stomach & say'd all her Pain was there; but Ranby slipping his Hand lower, kept it there in spight of her some little time & then without saying one word to the Q. went & spoke softly to the K. at the Chimney; upon wch. the Q. started up & sitting in her Bed say'd to Ranby with great eagerness, I am sure now, you lying Fool, you are telling the K. I have a Rupture.—I am so (say'd Ranby) & there is no more time to be lost, yr. Majy. has conceal'd it too long already; & I beg another Surgeon may be call'd in immediately. The Q. made no answer but lay down again, turn'd her Head to the other side, & as the K. told me, he thinks it was the only Tear he saw her shed whilst she was ill. The K. bid Ranby send immediately for old Busier[36] the Surgeon whom (tho fourscore years old) the K. & Q. had a great Opinion of & prefer'd to every other man of his Profession.

Busier not being immediately to be found, & the K. very impatient, he bid Ranby go & bring the first Surgeon of any Note & Credit he could find, & whilst Ranby was absent on this errand, the K. told Ld. H. the whole History of this Rupture.

The first Symptoms I ever perceived of it (say'd he) were 14 years ago just after the Q. lay in of Louisa; & she then told me, when I spoke to her of it, that it was nothing more than what was common for almost every Woman to have after a hard Labour, or after having

[33] affectations.
[34] "He would cry like a calf."
[35] "dote . . . to be delirious" (Johnson's
Dictionary).
[36] Paul Busier.

many Children: this made me easy, & it grew better & continued better afterward for several Years: when it grew worse again, I persuaded her to consult some Surgeon, which she declined, & was so uneasy whenever I spoke to her on this Subject, that I knew not how to press her: but when I came from Hannover the last time but one, I found it so much worse than ever, that I again spoke to her, told her it was certainly a Rupture & that she ran great Risques in taking no Care of it: she was so very uneasy upon my saying this, telling me it was no such thing, & that I fancy'd she had a nasty Distemper which she was sure she had not, & spoke so much more pevishly to me on this Occasion, than she had ever done in her Life upon any other, that upon my renewing my Solicitations to her, to let some Body see it, & her growing every time I mention'd it, more & more hurt & angry, I at last told her, I wish'd she might not repent her Obstinacy, but promised her I never would mention this Subject to her again as long as I lived.

The K. in as plain Insinuations as he could without saying it in direct terms, did intimate to Ld. H. that the Q. had received what he had say'd to her on this Subject upon his Return from Hannover, as if she had reproach'd him with being grown weary of her Person & endeavouring to find Blemishes in it, that did not belong to Her.

I do firmly believe, she carry'd her Abhorrence to being known to have a Rupture so far, that she would have dy'd without declaring it, or letting it be known, had not the K. told it in spight of her.

And tho People may think this weakness, little of a piece with the Greatness of the rest of her Character yet they will judge partially who interpret this Delicacy, to be merely an ill-timed Coquetry at 54, that would hardly have been excusable at 25:—She knew better than any body else, that her Power over the King was not preserved independent, as most People thought, of the Charms of

her Person; & as her Power over him, was the principal Object of her Pursuit; she fear'd very reasonably the Loss, or the weakening of any Tye by which she held him; several things she afterward say'd to the K. in her Illness which both the K. & the Ps. Caroline told me again plainly demonstrated how strongly these Apprehensions of making her Person distastefull to the K. work'd upon her.

When Ranby return'd he brought one Shipton[37] with him, a City-Surgeon, & one of the most eminent, & most able of the whole Profession; by this time too Busier arrived, & these three attended her constantly. After they had examined the Q. they all told the K. she was in the utmost danger. Busier proposed making the Operation of cutting a hole at her Navel wide enough to thrust the Gutt back into it's place; wch. Ranby opposed, saying that all the Guts, upon such an Operation would come out of the Body in a Moment into the Bed; & that he thought he felt at the bottom of the swelling (wch. was of an immense size) a Softness which he took to be a disposition to making Matter, & which they might encourage by warm fomentations till the swelling might break of it-self, or at least allow them by a slight Touch of a Lancet to open it without danger. Shipton enclining to Ranby's Opinion, this method was pursued.

In the mean time Ld. H. telling the K. that he had heard it say'd among some Lawyers, that if the Q. dy'd Richmond-Gardens would come to the P.; the K. order'd Ld. H. to go immediately to my Ld. Chancellour[38] & ask his Opinion upon it; Ld. H. accordingly went to Westminster-Hall where my Ld. Chancellour then was trying a Cause in the Court of Chancery; Ld. H. sent for him off the Bench, & Ld. Chancellour stopping the Proceedings, retired into a private Room with Ld. H., & told Ld. H. he would look into the Deeds & Acts of Parlt. by which Richmond was settled on the Q. & should then be able to give his Opinion more

---

[37] John Shipton (d. 1748).

[38] Philip Yorke, first Earl of Hardwicke (1690–1764).

particularly, but in the mean time, bid Ld. H. tell the K. whatever the Settlement was it could not be alter'd by any Will the Q. should make; & that whatever she dy'd possess'd of, that was unsettled would go to the K. if she dy'd without a Will, or even with one, if that will was not made in consequence of Powers given her by his Majy.

This Answer made the K. easy as to every thing belonging to the Q. except Richmond; & when my Ld. Chancellour had examined all the Settlements relating to that; it came out, that Richmond would belong to the K. for his Life, but that after his Death nothing could prevent it's going to the P.

The K. told the Q. of this Transaction to set her mind at ease from Doubts she had concieved, & Fears she had form'd of the Prince being any way pecuniaryly the better for her Death.

About six a clock this Saturday Evening the Surgeons lanced the Swelling just at her Navel & lett out some matter; but not enough to abate the swelling in any material degree, or give them any great hope of her Recovery.

The Princess Caroline's Nose bled so violently & almost constantly this whole Day, that she was but little in the Q.'s Bedchamber, but stay'd in the outward Room of her Majy.'s Apartment & was again blooded with much Difficulty, for Ranby was forced to prick her in both Arms, & even at both, the Blood was so thick he could get but little.

However her Mother being so ill, no persuasions could prevail with her to go to her own side to bed; she lay all night on a Couch in the outward Room, Ps. Emely sat up with the Q. the K. went to bed, & Ld. H. lay on a Matrass on the Floor at the foot of Ps. Caroline's Couch.

About four a Clock on Sunday Morning the Q. complaining that her Wound was extremely painfull & desiring to have it dress'd Ranby & Shipton were call'd in to her, & upon opening the Wound declared it had already begun to mortify; Hulse whose turn it was that Night to sit up was sent for into the Q.'s Bedchamber & acquainted by the

Surgeons with the Situation she was in; Hulse came to the Ps. Caroline & told her this terrible & dreaded News; upon wch. she bid him & Ranby go immediately & inform the K.

All this pass'd in the Room without Ld. H.'s waking who was fallen asleep quite exhausted by Concern & Watching. Ps. Caroline as soon as the Surgeons & Hulse were gone to the K. waked Ld. H. & told him if ever he saw the Q. again it must be immediately for that the Physicians & Surgeons had declared the Mortification already begun & were gone to tell the K. that it was impossible for her to live many Hours.

When Hulse and Ranby came back to Ps. Caroline (the K. being already up & gone to the Q.) Ps. Caroline & Ld. H. ask'd Hulse if there was no possibility left of her Recovery; & he answer'd—none. Ld. H. then ask'd Ranby if they were never decieved in the signs of a Mortification; to which Ranby shaking his Head reply'd *we know them but too well.* The Q. finding the Wound still so uneasy, sent again to have them open & dress it. But Hulse say'd it was to no Purpose to do any thing more; & Ranby assured the Ps. Caroline he could do nothing that would not give the Q. more Pain without a Possibility of doing her Majy. any good.

However the Q. insisting on having the Wound clean'd at least the K. who had told the Q. all the Surgeons had told him came out, call'd in Ranby & Hulse & made them comply with her Request. Ld. H. went in with them, just to see the Q. once more look'd at her through his Tears for a Moment & then return'd to his Matrass.

As soon as the Surgeons had apply'd some of their lenient Ointments & Anodyne Preparations, they left the Room, came to Ld. H. & confirm'd their former report of the impossibility of her holding out many Hours.

No body now remain'd in the Room with the Q. but the K. the Duke & her four Daughters[39] of whom she took

[39] Emily (1711–1786); Caroline (1713–1757); Mary (1723–1772); Louisa (1724–1751).

Leave in form desiring they would not leave her till she expired. She told the K. she had nothing to say to him; for as I have always (say'd she) told you my thoughts of Things & People as fast as they arose, I have nothing left to communicate to you. The People I love & those I do not; the People I like & dislike; & those I would wish you to be kind to, you know as well as my-self; & I am persuaded it would therefore be a useless trouble both to you & me at this time to ad any particular Recomendations.

To the Ps. Emely she say'd nothing very particular, to the Ps. Caroline she recommended the Care of her two younger Sisters, & say'd poor Caroline it is a fine Legacy I leave you; the trouble of educating these two young things. As for you William (continued She to the Duke) you know I have always loved you tenderly & placed my chief hope in you; show your Gratitude to me in your Behaviour to the K. Be a Suport to your Father, & double your Attention to make up for the Disappointment & Vexation he must recieve from your profligate & worthless Brother. It is in you only I hope, for keeping up the Credit of our Family when your Father shall be no more: attempt nothing ever against your Brother, & endeavour to mortify him no way but by showing superior merit.

She then spoke of the different Tempers & Dispositions of her two youngest Daughters & the different manner in which they ought to be treated, cautioning the Ps. Caroline not to let the Vivacity of the Ps. Louisa (the youngest) draw her into any Inconveniences & desiring her to give all the Aid she could to suport the meak & mild disposition of the Ps. Mary.

She then took a Rhuby Ring off her Finger which the King had given her at her Coronation, & putting it upon his say'd this is the last thing I have to give you—naked I came to you & naked I go from you—I had every thing, I ever possess'd, from you, & to you whatever I have I return, my Will you will find

a very short one, I give all I have to You. She then ask'd for her keys & gave them to him; all this & many more things of the like nature, whilst she expatiated on the several Rules, & Instructions she gave to her Children, according to their different Ages, Situations, & Dispositions, pass'd in this Interview; all which the K. & the Ps. Caroline related to me: who told me there were no dry Eyes during this Conference in the Room but the Queen's, who as they could percieve, shed in all this touching Scene, not one Tear.

It is not necessary to examine whether the Q.'s reasoning was good or bad in wishing the K. in case she died should marry again. It is certain she did wish it, had often said so when he was present & when he was not present & when she was in health & gave it now as her advice to him when she was dying; upon which his sobs began to rise & his tears to fall with double vehemence: whilst in the midst of this passion, wiping his eyes, & sobbing between every word, with much ado he got out this answer. Non j'aurai des maitresses.[40] To which the Q. made no other reply than Ah! mon Dieu, cela n'empeche pas.[41] I know this episode will hardly be credited, but it is literally true.[42]

When she had finish'd all she had to say on these Subjects, she say'd she fancy'd she could sleep, the K. say'd many kind things to her & kiss'd her Face & her Hands a hundred Times; but even at this time, on her asking for her Watch (which hung by the Chimney) in order to give it him to take care of her Seal, the natural Brusquerie of his Temper (even in these moments) broke out, which show'd how addicted he was to snapping without being angry, & that he was often capable of using those worst whom he loved best; for on this Proposal of giving him the Watch to take Care of the Seal with the Q.'s Arms—in the midst of Sobs & Tears, he raised & quicken'd his Voice & say'd ah! my God! let it alone, the Q. has always such strange Fancys—who should med-

---

[40] "No, I will have mistresses."

[41] "Oh, heavens! that won't hinder you."
[42] The king did not marry again.

dle with your Seal? is it not as safe there as in my Pocket?

The Q. after this fell into a sort of dosing; during which time the K. often say'd she is dying, she will go away in this Sleep; it is over she will suffer no more. However when she waked, she say'd she found herself refresh'd and much better, adding I know it is only a Reprieve to make me suffer longer, & therefore I wish it was at an end; for I can not recover, but my nasty Heart will not break yet. She then added that she believed she should not dye till Wednesday[43] for that all the remarkable Occurrences of her Life had happen'd on that Day, that she had been born of a Wednesday married on a Wednesday, & brought to bed of her first Child on a Wednesday; that she had heard the first news of the Late King's Death on a Wednesday & been crown'd on a Wednesday, & for this Reason believed she should dye of a Wednesday. This I own show'd a Weakness in her but one wch. at this time might be excused, as most People's minds are a little weaken'd on these Occasions, & few People even of the strongest minds are altogether exempt from some little Taint of that Weakness call'd Superstition; many People have more of it than they care to let others know they have; & some more of it than they know them-selves.

On Sunday Morning about nine a Clock the Surgeons upon opening the Queen's wound found the Mortification was not spread, & upon cutting off what was already mortify'd declared she might recover: this appear'd so inconsistent with their Declarations some few hours before, & in my Opinion show'd so much Ignorance, that if a Life of this Consequence, committed to the Care of four of the best Physicians, & three of the best Surgeons in England received no better Assistance from their Skill, how natural it is to deplore the Situation of those whose Safety depends on the Sagacity of these Professions; & how reasonable to despise those who put their trust in such aids. Not that I am so unjust to Surgery as to put that Science

upon the same Foot with Physick: & for my own part I firmly believe there was not ye least Mortification begun, when they ignorantly pronounced there was; & that what they cut off was not mortify'd, & only declared so, to conceal the mistake they had made the night before in saying it was.

On Monday Morning Sr. Rt. W. arrived from Houghton, the Q. had mention'd him but twice during her Illness, once to say she hoped they would not send for him, & the Day before he came, upon hearing he had been sent for, to ask if he was come. The King when she ask'd that Question desired to know if she had any thing she wanted to say to him, to wch she answer'd—no, nothing, my asking if he was come, was meer Curiosity.

Ld. H. told the King Sr. Rt. was in the outward Room, upon which his Majy. order'd Ld. H. to bring him in; Sr. Robt. with some Difficulty from his great Bulk & natural awkwardness knelt down & kiss'd his Majy.'s Hand, but with much less difficulty (for he was at present thoroughly frighted) dropt some very proper Tears & ask'd, *how is the Queen?* to which the King reply'd *come & see your-self, my good Sr. Rt.* & then carry'd him to the Q.'s Bedside. The Interview was short, but what the Q. say'd was material, for these were her Words; My good Sr. Rt. you see me in a very indifferent Situation, I have nothing to say to you but to recommend the King my Children & the Kingdom to your Care.—As soon as Sr. Rt. came out of the Room he told Ld. H. what had pass'd; who asking of him what he thought of the Queen; say'd my Ld. she is as much dead as if she was in her Coffin; if ever I heard a Corps speak it was just now in that Room. He then repeated again what the Q. had say'd to him in the presence of the K. & the Princesses, which Ld. H. found made a great Impression on his Pride whatever it did on his Tenderness; for he repeated it to every Body he saw for a fortnight after.

Vain of this Reception, & presuming upon the Strength of it, he came in the Evening without being sent for into the

---

[43] It is now Sunday.

Room where Ld. H. used to be with the K. whenever his Majy. was not with the Q. Ld. H. knew the K. would not like this, but was afray'd to tell Sr. Rt. so; lest Sr. Rt. should think him proud of an Honour he was not to partake; & Fool enough to be pleased with a Distinction, which had no other Consequence than making those who thought it of more importance than he knew it was, envy fear & hate him; & indeed the Nature of Ld. H.'s Interest with the K. was such as might make him many Enemys but few Friends; for as it was much easyer to make the K. hate than love, so Ld. H. (had he been disposed to it) could with very little Industry have prejudiced his Majy. against whom he thought fit, but with no Pains whatever could bring him to bestow any material marks of Favour on those he loved best.

When the K. found Sr. Rt. W. in the Evening in this Room, he gave him a very cold Reception, & every time Sr. Rt. spoke & offer'd his Advice, or told his Opinion with regard to the Q.'s Illness or the manner in which she was treated his Majy. gave him very short Answers not in the smoothest Terms. The next Morning however the K. found him there again, & with him the D. of Grafton[44] whom the K. had not yet seen since his Return from the Country; he spoke very coldly to both, & going soon back to the Q.'s Bedchamber he complain'd there that the outward-Room was so full of People one could not stir for them. Upon which the Princess Caroline by the Q.'s Order immediately sent to bid the Room be cleared of every body who did not use to be there; & from this time no body attempted to come there any more.

Monday & Tuesday, the Queen was what the Doctors, Surgeons, & Courtiers call'd better; there being no threatening Symptoms in her Wound, & her Vomitings being much slacken'd; but nothing passing through her, those who judg'd by essential Circumstances, & not on the hourly variation of trifles, whatever they might say from fashion or to please, could not in reality believe the Queen's Condition more hopefull, or less dangerous, whilst that main Point of the internal Stoppage continued in the same Situation, & whenever the K. used to tell her how much better the Doctors & Surgeons say'd she was & the Hopes they gave him, the moment his back was turn'd she used to look at the Princesses, shake her Head & bid them not flatter themselves, & often in the Day used to tell them, believe me my dear Children it wont do, at 25, I might have struggled through it, but at 55, I can not resist.

During this time the Prince's Family had by little & little under the Pretense first of inquiring of the Q.'s Health from the Prince or Princess, & afterwards for them-selves got into possession of coming every Day & all Day to St. James's, till there was no part of the Day in which there were not three or four of them dangling in that Part of the Q.'s State Apartment where the Lady of the Bedchamber sat to receive all those who came to inquire about the Queen & give the *no-Intelligence* of the Doctors verdict on her Majesty's Situation.

This Evasion of the King's Order (which tho it only litterally forbid those who went to the Prince's Court coming into the King's Presence was certainly meant to forbid them coming to St. James's) made the K. extreamly angry, & more especially because the K. knew they only came to inquire if the Q. was better, in hopes of hearing she was worse; & as the Q. her-self say'd (when she heard of their being dayly & hourly there) to watch her last Breath, in order to have the merit to their Master of bringing the first News of her Death.

The K. sent Ld. H. to Sr. Rt. W. to know what way he should take to prevent these scoundrels (as he call'd them) coming every Day to St. James's in defiance of his order to insult him & the Q. in their present Distress. Sr. R. W. ask'd Ld. H. what he would advise on this

44 Charles Fitzroy, second Duke of Grafton (1683–1757), referred to on another occasion by Hervey as "the King's Lord Chamberlain, an English editon of the Queen's [see note 3 above], very little improved, whose only pleasure was hunting."

Occasion & Ld. H. who was always ready to give the P. a Slap, & knew how uneasy their coming to St. James's made the Q. say'd that he thought they ought to be forbidden; but Sr. R. W. who had no mind unnecessarily to shock the P., especially at this time, when he thought the Spur[45] that used to urge him on to those attacks was going to be blunted; told Ld. H. that the Prince's Servants would certainly pretend they came out of Respect & concern for the Q. that therefore there would be an Air of Hardness in forbidding them at this Time, since no body could disprove that pretended Motive; he added too, that they had not transgress'd the litteral Sense of the order which only forbid them the King's presence; & as the K. might very well be suposed to know nothing of their coming, he thought it would be better for the K. just at this Time not to mix any marks of Resentment against his Son, with those of Affection for his Wife, nor give People a handle to say no Situation of distress can soften him enough to make him forget to hate one Moment.

This Advice Ld. H. convey'd to the K. who took it with as much Reluctance as his Ldsp.[46] brought it: tho not with so good an Excuse to him-self for sacrificing his Inclination to his Fear: especially when he found it made the Q. so uneasy that she often ask'd if no body would turn those Ravens out of the House, who were only there to watch her Death & would gladly tear her to pieces whilst she was alive;—I hope at least it will not be thought proper to let them come into my Room, if they should have a mind to it. The Q. guess'd very truely the Reason of their coming, for the Prince all this while used to sit up at his House in Pall-mall almost the whole night & every night, sending messengers continually to St. James's, showing the

utmost impatience for their return & saying with equal Prudence & humanity to the People who were with him;— *make sure we shall soon have good news. She can not hold out much longer,* & talk all Day along in the same Strain to every body about him; this the D. of Marlborough told Harry Fox & Harry Fox to Ld. H., & some time after the D. of Marlborough told it to Ld. H. him-self; poor Mr. Hamilton only, when he was told such Remarks were spread, doubted the truth of them, & say'd the P. was in the utmost concern for his Mother; but when Lady Archibald[47] was ask'd if the P. was really concern'd for the Queen, she laugh'd & say'd he is very decent.

Many Letters were written & great Care was taken by the Princesses to prevent the Ps. Royal[48] making her Mother's Illness an Excuse for coming to England at this time, every body knowing the very indifferent Reception she would meet with on her Arrival from her Father, who not being apt to retain much Affection for people who gave him any Trouble or put him to any Expence, & as little addicted to speak of them in a softer manner than he thought of them, had often lately express'd himself upon the Ps. Royal's Chapter in terms not altogether so paternal with regard to the affection they contain'd as with regard to the authority: & positive Orders were sent to Horace Walpole[49] if Persuasion fail'd to stop her by Force, wch Orders he communicated to ye P. of Orange[50] who immediately told them (tho desired not) to his Wife; the Consequence of wch was her venting all the Passion & Anger raised against those who had sent the Orders on him who received them.

On Wednesday Morning the Queen sent for Sr. R. W. who saw her alone but not for above a quarter of an hour;

---

[45] i.e., the Queen.

[46] Lordship.

[47] Lady Archibald Hamilton (*c.* 1700–1752), of the prince's entourage.

[48] Anne (1709–1759), eldest daughter to Caroline, had married the Prince of Orange in 1734 and was residing in Holland.

[49] 1678–1757, younger brother to Sir Robert and uncle to the more famous Horace, the letter-writer; envoy and minister plenipotentiary to the government at The Hague from 1734 to 1740.

[50] See note 48 above.

what really pass'd I know not but by Conjecture; but have reason to think it was only to desire Sr. Rt. W. to examine what was to become of Richmond after her Death; Sr. R. told the K. this was all; & at first he told Ld. H. so too; the K. also told Ld. H. that the Q. had told him this was all she had sent for him for. But when Sr. Rt. went from the Q. to the K. the K. (as Sr. Rt. told Ld. H.) used him worse than ever he had done in his Life & when Sr. R. told him he had been sent for by the Q. the K. forbid him going any more without first acquainting him; & say'd he would not have the Q. plagued now with Busyness, adding that she was too weak to bear it; which was very true, but he himself, whenever he was in the Room, was always asking her so many Questions, talking so fast & in so loud a Voice, & teazing her to eat & drink so many different things, that the Princesses, by Ld. H.'s advice got the Doctors to make it one of the Articles in their written Prescription for the Q. that she should not be talk'd to, more than was absolutely necessary, & always in the lowest Voice, & this Prescription with the rest, after it had been shown to the K. was pin'd up on the curtain of the Q.'s Bed; but this Prescription had as little effect on the K. as the rest of their Prescriptions had on her.

Sr. Rt. waited at night at St. James's till Ld. H. came from the K. & then ask'd him if he could comprehend what had put the K. into such a devilish humour in the morning when the Q. was so much better; Ld. H. say'd he could as little comprehend any turns in the K.'s temper, as he could Sr. Rt.'s giving into the ill-founded Opinion of thinking the Q. better; for till a Passage is open'd (continued he) I can not think her vomiting a little more or a little less of any Consequence; or that it signifys much that the external Circumstances of her Wound are something less threatening, when all the internal Symptoms remain just in the same unknown & dangerous Condition they were.

Oh! my Lord (say'd Sr. Robt.) if this Woman should dye what a Scene of Confusion will here be? who can tell into what hands the K. will fall? or who will have the Management of him? I defy the ablest Person in this Kingdom to foresee what will be the Consequence of this great Event. For my own part (reply'd Ld. H.) I have not the least doubt how it will be; he will cry for her for a fortnight, forget her in a Month, have two or three Women that he will pass his Time with; but whilst they have most of his Time, a little of his Money, less of his Confidence & no Power, you will have all the Credit, more Power than ever you had, & govern him more absolutely than ever you did. Your Credit before was through the Medium of the Q. & all Power through a Medium must be weaker than when it operates directly; besides Sr. all Princes must now & then be decieved by their Ministers, & as the K. is much easyer decieved than the Q. so your Task, whenever that Task is decieving, will be much less difficult than it was before. In the first Place because the K. is naturally much less suspicious than the Q. in the next because he is less penetrating, & lastly because he cares much less to converse with different People, & will hear no body talk to him of Busyness but your-self.—Oh! my Lord interrupted Sr. Rt. tho he will hear no body but me you do not know how often he refuses to hear me when it is on a Subject he does not like: but by the Q. I can fetch him round with Time to those Subjects again; she can make him do the same thing in another Shape; & when I give her her Lesson, can make him propose the very thing as his own Opinion which a week before he had rejected as mine. The many Oportunitys she has; the Credit she has with him, the Knowledg of his temper, the being constantly at him; & the Opinion he has both of her Judgment & her Pursuit of his Interest & his Pleasure as her first Objects make this Part easy for her, but I have not the same materials to act it, & can not do without somebody that has Leisure to operate slowly upon him, which is the only way he can be effectually operated upon; for he is neither to be persuaded nor convinced; he will do nothing to oblige any body nor ever own or think he has been in the wrong; & I have told the Q. a thousand times that it is not to be wonder'd at, that he should be of that mind, when She, whom he believes sooner than any other Body in the world, never heard him broach the most absurd Opinion, or declare the most extravagant design that She did not tell him he was in the right.—Notwithstanding all this reply'd Ld. H. I am convinced if the Q. should dye (which I firmly believe she will) that you will have him faster than ever, & yet I am sincere enough to own to you I heartyly wish she may recover. This Conversation lasted two or three Hours & kept Ld. H. out of bed much longer than he desired, this being the first Night since the Q. was ill that he had been dismiss'd so early or had a prospect of passing so many Hours undisturb'd. The K. had been particularly anxious this whole Day upon what the Q. had say'd with regard to her dying of a Wednesday which could not be much wonder'd at since a mind much less addicted to Superstition than his Majy.'s might have been a little affected by a smaller Hint wch had fallen from one they loved in such Circumstances, & on an Occasion of so much Importance to them. Could it then be surprising that a man who believed in Ghosts & Witches should not be proof against a Weakness that might have appear'd in one exempt from many more, than his Majesty's best Friends can deny him to labour under.

On Thursday the Q.'s Vomitings return'd with as much Violence as ever, & in the Afternoon one of the Guts burst in such a Manner that all her Excrement came out at the Wound in her Belly, tho the Surgeons could not by any probing certainly tell whereabouts in the Gut the Fracture was.

The running of the wound was in such immense Quantitys that it went through all the Quilts of the Bed, & flow'd all over the Floor; some ignorant People about her who knew not from what Cause this discharge proceeded,

told the Q. they hoped this Evacuation would do her good, to which the Q. reply'd very calmly she hoped so too, for that it was all the Evacuation she should ever have.

Every Day once at least & sometimes oftener from the first of her being under the Surgeons Hands they were forced, or thought them-selves so, to make some new Incision, & every Operation of this kind which before she underwent she always used to ask the K. if he approved what the Surgeons proposed to do, & when he say'd they had told him it was necessary, & that he hoped she wold consent to any thing they thought so, She always submitted immediately, & with the utmost Patience & resignation & Resolution suffer'd them to cut & probe as deep & as long as they thought fit.

She ask'd Ranby once whilst he was dressing her wound if he would not be glad to be officiating in the same manner to his old cross Wife that he hated so much; & if any involuntary Groans or Complainings broke from her during the Operations, she used immediately after to bid the Surgeons not mind her, & make them excuses for interrupting them with her silly Complaints when She knew they were doing all they could to help her.

On Wednesday some wise some pious & a great many busy meddling impertinent People about the Court asking in whispers every body they met whether the Q. had had any body to pray by her, wondering at the irreligion of the Q. for thinking she could pray as well for herself as any body could pray for her, & at those about her for not putting her in mind of so essential a Duty; Sr. R. W. desired Ps. Emely to propose to the K. or Q. that the Archbishop[51] should be sent for in order to stop People's Impertinences upon this Subject; & when the Ps. Emely made some Difficulty about taking upon her to make this Proposal to the K. or Q., Sr. Rt. in the presence of a dozen People (who really wish'd this divine Physician for the Q.'s

---

[51] John Potter (1674–1747), who had but that year succeeded William Wake; referred to on another occasion by Hervey as "honest Potter."

Soul might be sent for, upon the foot of her Salvation,) very prudently added by way of stimulating the Ps. Emely, pray Madam let this Farce be play'd, the Arch-bishop will act it very well, you may bid him be as short as you will, it will do the Q. no hurt, no more than any good, & it will satisfy all the wise & good Fools who will call us all Atheists if we dont pretend to be as great Fools as they are.

After this eloquent & discreet Persuasion the whole Company staring with the utmost astonishment at Sr. R. W. some in admiration of his Piety & others of his Prudence the Ps. Emely spoke to the K., the K. to the Q. & the Archbishop was sent for; who continued afterward, to pray by her Morning & Evening, at which Ceremony her Children always assisted, but the K., constantly went out of the Room before his Episcopal Grace was admitted; but all this was thrown away for the People that had whisper'd & wonder'd & clamour'd at no Prayers were now just as busy & as whispering & as wondering about no Sacrament. Some Fools say'd the Q. had not Religion enough to ask to receive the Sacrament, some other Fools say'd she had ask'd for it & that the Archbiship had refused to give it her unless she would first be reconciled to her Son; & this many Ideots believed & many who were not Ideots told in hopes of finding Credit from those that were: there were some who were impertinent enough to ask the Archbishop him-self why he would not advise the Q. to be reconciled to the P. & more than hinted to him, that he would be wanting in his Duty if he did not; to which his Grace very decently & properly answer'd that whenever the Q. had done him the Honour to talk to him upon that unhappy Division in the Family she had always done it with so much Sense & Goodness that he never thought she wanted any Advice. The Q. desired the Arch-Bishop if she dy'd to take care of Dr. Butler,[52] her Clerk of the Closet; & he was the only Body I ever heard of

her recommending particularly & by name all the while she was ill her Servants in general she recommended to the K. & in general to him say'd he knew whom she like & disliked, but did not that I know of, name any body to him in particular.

From the time of the bursting of the Gut the Physicians & Surgeons, who had hitherto without any disguise or Reserve talk'd over all the Particulars of the Q.'s Case to any body that ask'd them any Questions, were absolutely forbidden by the K. to reveal this Circumstance, or to give any other answer for the future to any body whatever who inquired concerning the Q.'s Health, than the general one of her being much as she was. Had these restrictive Orders been issued by his Majy. on the first discovery of the Q.'s Rupture, considering her delicacy on this point & his Passion for a Mistery, on every point, it would have been easy to account for this Edict being given out; but after her Case had been talk'd over for five Days as publickly & as minutely as if she had been desected before St. James's Gate, I own I was at a Loss to comprehend why these orders were issued, especially when this circumstance was not by the Physicians or Surgeons pronounced so inevitably mortal as I should have thought it natural for them to judge it. The K. told it to Ld. H. & Ranby to Sr. R. W. Ld. H. ventured to reveal it to the Ps. Caroline, but the K. not telling it him-self to any of his Children none of the rest of them knew it, but were extreamly surprised, as well as the rest of the Court, at the sudden costiveness[53] of the Physicians & Surgeons in their present Accounts of the Q.'s Situation.

During this time the K. talk'd perpetually to Ld. H. the Physicians & Surgeons, & his Children who were the only People he ever saw out of the Q.'s Room of the Q.'s good Qualitys, his Fondness for her, his anxiety for her Welfare, & the irreparable Loss her Death would be to him, & repeated every Day & many times in the Day all her

---

[52] Joseph Butler, Bishop of Durham (1692-1752).

[53] reserve.

Merits in every Capacity with Regard to him & every other Body she had to do with; he say'd she was the best Wife, the best Mother, the best Companion, the best Friend, & the best Woman that ever was born; that she was the wisest, the most agreable, & the most usefull body man or woman that he had ever been acquainted with. That he firmly believed she never since he first knew her, ever thought of any thing she was to do or to say, but with the view of doing or saying it in the manner which would be most agreable or most serviceable to him; that he had never seen her out of humour in his Life; that he had pass'd more Hours with her than he believed any other two People in the world had ever pass'd together, & that he never had been tired in her Company one minute; & that he was sure he could have been happy with no other Woman upon Earth for a wife, & that if she had not been his wife, he had rather have had her for his mistress than any woman he had ever been acquainted with; that he believed she never had had a thought of People or things which she had not communicated to him, that she had the best Head, the best Heart & the best temper that God-almighty had ever given to any human Creature man or woman; & that she had not only soften'd all his Leisure hours, but been of more use to him as a Minister, than any other Person had ever been to him or to any other Prince; that with a Patience, which he knew he was not master of, she had listen'd to the Nonsense of all the impertinent Fools that wanted to talk to him, & had taken all that trouble off his Hands, reporting nothing to him that was unnecessary or would have been tedious for him to hear, & never forgetting any thing that was material, usefull, or entertaining to him to know. He say'd that join'd to all the Softness & delicacy of her own Sex she had all the personal as well as political Courage of the firmest & bravest men: that not only he & her Family but the whole Nation would feel the Loss of her, if she dy'd & that as to all the *brilliant*

& *enjouement*[54] of the Court, there would be an End of it when she was gone; & that there would be no bearing a Drawingroom, when the only body that ever enlivened it (and one that always enlivened it) was no longer there.—Poor Woman how she always found something obliging agreable & pleasing to say to every body, & always sent People away from her better satisfy'd than they came, comme elle soutenoit sa Dignité avec Grace, avec Politesse, avec Douceur![55]—These were the terms in which he was for ever now talking of the Q. & in which he likewise talk'd to her; & yet so unaccountable were the sudden Sallys of his Temper, & so little was he able or willing to command them, that in the midst of all this flow of Tenderness he hardly ever went into her Room that he did not even in this moving Situation, snub her for something or other she say'd or did; when her constant uneasyness from the Sickness in her Stomach & the Soreness of her Wound, made her shift her Posture every Minute, he would say to her, how the Devil should you sleep when you will never lye still a Moment; you want to rest, & the Doctors tell you nothing can do you so much good, & yet you are always moving about: no body can sleep in that manner, & that is always your way, you never take the proper Method to get what you want & then you wonder you have it not.—And as the Doctors say'd she might eat or drink any thing she had a mind to, or could swallow, the K. was ever proposing something or other, which she never refused, tho she knew it would only lye burning in her Stomach for half an hour or an Hour & then come up again; when she could get things down, notwithstanding these effects, which to other People she say'd she knew they would have, her Complaisance to him made her always swallow them; & when he thank'd her for so doing, she used to answer it is the last Service I can do you: but when her Stomach recoil'd so that it was impossible for her to force any thing down her

---

[54] brilliance and entertainment.
[55] "with what grace, good manners, and gentleness, she bore herself."

throat which he had given her & that she only tasted it & gave it away; he used pevishly to say my God how is it possible you should not know whether you like a thing or not? if you do not like it why do you call for it? & if you do why will you give it away? to which she would only answer, I am very silly, & very whimsical, for a Dégout[56] takes me in a moment for what I think a minute before I have a mind to.

Notwithstanding the constant Pain she was in, & her great want of Rest, the Physicians never gave her Opium but one Night; she her-self was not much inclined to take it, & the Physicians thinking it might possibly from it's binding Quality prevent the relief she so much wanted, were not very forward to prescribe it: she had not rested with it all night, & when the King came into her Room in the Morning, as she lay with her Eyes fix'd at a Point in the Air, as People often do in those situations when they are neither enough at ease to shutt their Eyes & Sleep, nor enough themselves to prevent their thoughts wandering, or to see the things they seem to look at; the King with a loud & quick Voice, say'd to her *Mon Dieu qu'est-ce que vous regardez? comment peut-on fixer ses yeux comme ca? vos yeux ressemblent a ceux d'un Veau à qui on vient de couper la Gorge?*[57]

There was besides this mixture of Brutality & tenderness towards the Q. at this time in the K.'s Conduct & Conversation, another mixture full as natural to him & much less extraordinary, which was the mixing constantly some Praises of him-self with those he bestow'd on her. He never talk'd of her being a good Wife without giving strong hints of his deserving a good one & being at least as good a Husband; & gave People to understand when he commended her Understanding that he did not think it the worse for her having

kept him Company so many years: he plainly show'd too that he not only wish'd other People should believe, but did him-self believe that her whole Behavior to him was the natural effect of an amourous Attachment to his Person, & an adoration of his great Genius. When he mention'd his present Fears for the Q. he always interwove an account of the Intrepidity with which he waited his own Fate the year before both in the Storm & during his Illness afterward; giving tiresome Accounts with what resolution & Presence of Mind he talk'd to his Pages on Shipboard during the Tempest; & for a proof of his own Courage & the want of the same magnanimity in them; told us that when he saw La Chaux one of his Pages pale & trembling in the corner of the Cabin he say'd to him—comment as tu peur?[58]— to wch La Chaux (say'd he) reply'd *oui Sire vraiment & je crois qu'il n'y a que votre Majy dans le Vaisseau qui ne l'a pas.*[59]—from which History, the Conclusion the K. proposed one should draw, was much less natural, than that which most People draw, wch. was that his Majy. had a mind to seem on that Occasion to have more Courage than he had, & that the Valet de-Chambre very adroitly made his Court by pretending to have less.

As to his Behavior during his Illness what fears he had I know not, but the Q. & every body about him say'd he always seem'd to think him-self much worse than he was; & for the accounts of his Pevishness & Impatience they could with great difficulty, according to his own Confession, exceed Reality for he him-self told me that he found such an abominable forwardness in him-self, that in the Intermissions of it (which was not easy to catch) he had told his Pages not to mind him when he was unreasonably chiding & swearing at them, for that it was part of his distemper &

---

56 loathing.

57 "What in heaven's name are you looking at? How can you stare like that? Your eyes look like a calf's whose throat has just been cut."

58 "Are you afraid?"

59 "Yes, sir, very much, and I am sure your Majesty is the only one on board who is not."

that he could not help it. There was a mixture of good nature & good-sense in this Apology that I own, I who knew him, should rather have taken for an accidental distemper than the other, for it was much less of a Piece with his Conduct in health, than what he endeavour'd to excuse.

One Night whilst the Q. was ill as he was sitting in his Night-Gown & night-cap in a great Chair with his Legs upon a Stool, & no body in the room with him but the Ps. Emely who lay upon a Couch & Ld. H. who sat by the fire; he talk'd in this Strain of his own Courage in the Storm & his Illness, till the Ps. Emely (as Ld. H. thought) fell fast asleep, whilst Ld. H. as tired as he was of the present Conversation, & this last week's watching was left alone to act civil auditor & adroit Courtier, to aplaud what he heard & every now & then to ask such proper Questions as led the K. into giving some more particular detail of his own Magnanimity. The K. turning towards Ps. Emely & seeing her Eyes shutt, cry'd, *poor good Child her Duty, Affection, & attendance on her Mother have quite exhausted her Spirits;* & soon after he went into the Q.'s Room. As soon as his Back was turn'd Ps. Emely started up, & say'd is he gone? how tiresome he is?—Ld. H. who had no mind to trust her R. Hs. with singing her Fathers Praises in duetto with her;—reply'd only—I thought yr. R. Hs. had been asleep.—No—say'd the P. Emely, I only shut my Eyes that I might not join in the ennuyant[60] Conversation, & wish I could have shut my Ears too—in the first Place I am sick to death of hearing of his great Courage every day of my Life—in the next Place, one thinks now of Mama & not of him; who cares for his old Storm?—I believe too it is a great Lye, & that he was as much afray'd as I should have been; for all what he says now.—& as to his not being afray'd when he was ill, I know that is a Lye,

for I saw him—& I heard all his Sighs & his Groans, when he was in no more danger than I am at this moment; he was talking too for ever of dying, & that he was sure he should not recover.—All this, considering the kind things she had heard the K. say the minute before when he imagined her asleep, Ld. H. thought a pretty extraordinary return for her to make for that paternal Goodness, or would have thought it so in any body but her; & look'd upon this openness to him whom she did not love yet less to be accounted for, unless he could have imagined it was to draw him in to eccho her & then to relate what he say'd as if he had say'd it unaccompany'd.

Whilst she was going on with the Panegyrick on the K. which I have related, the K. return'd, upon which she began to rub her Eyes as if she had that Instand raised her Head from her Pillows.—& say'd I have really slept very heartly—how long had Papa been out of the room?—The K. who had very little or rather no Suspicion in his Composition took these Appearances for Realitys & say'd it is time for us all to take a little Rest, we will all go to bed, for by staying here we do the poor Q. no good, & our-selves hurt: & so dismissing Ld. H. they all retired.

I will relate no farther Particulars how the two following Days pass'd, as such a Narration would be only recapitulating a Diary of the two former, without any material Variation. The Q. grew so perceptibly weaker every Hour that every one she lived was more than was expected; She ask'd Dr. Tesier on Sunday in the Evening with no seeming Impatience under any Article of her present Circumstances but their duration; how long he thought it was possible for all this to last? To wch he answer'd; je crois que votre Majy sera bien tôt soulagée[61] & she calmly reply'd—Tant mieux.[62] About 10. a Clock on Sunday night the K. being in bed & asleep on the Floor at the Feet of the

---

[60] tiresome.

[61] "I think your Majesty will soon be comfortable."

[62] "So much the better."

Q.'s Bed, & the Ps. Emely on a Couch-Bed in a Corner of ye Room, the Q. began to rattle in ye Throat, & Mrs. Purcel[63] giving the allarm that she was expiring, all in the Room started up, Ps. Caroline was sent for, & Ld. H. but before the last arrived the Q. was just dead; all she say'd before she dy'd was—I have now got an Asthma—open ye Window—then she say'd—*pray*—upon wch the Ps. Emely began to read some Prayers of which she scarce repeated ten Words before the Q. expired. The Ps. Caroline held a looking-Glass to her Lips & finding there was not ye least Damp upon it urg'd 'tis over; & say'd not one Word more, nor shed as yet one Tear on the arrival of a Misfortune the Dread of wch. had cost her so many.

The K. kiss'd the Face & Hands of the lifeless Body several times but in a few Minutes left the Q.'s Apartment & went to that of his Daughters, accompany'd only by them, then, advising them to go to bed, & take care of themselves he went to his own Side; & as soon as he

was in bed sent for Ld. H. to come & sit by him: where after talking sometime & more calmly than one could have expected, of the manner of the Q.'s Death, he dismiss'd Ld. H. & sent for one of his Pages to sit up in his Room all Night: & by the by as he ordered one of them for sometime after the death of the Queen to lye in his room, & that I am very sure he believed many stories of Ghosts & Witches and Apparitions, I take this order (with good deference to his magnanimity on other occasions) to have been the result of the same way of thinking that makes many weak minds fancy themselves more secure from any supernatural danger in the light than in the dark, & in company than alone.

Ld. H. went back to the Ps. Caroline's bedchamber where he stayed till five o'clock in the morning, endeavouring to lighten her Grief by indulging it, & not by that silly way of trying to divert what can not be remov'd, or to bring comfort to such Affliction as time only can alleviate.

John Wesley
1703-1791

From JOURNAL

[PREACHING IN THE FIELDS, 1739]

Thursday, March 29, I left London, and in the evening expounded to a small company at Basingstoke. Saturday 31, in the evening I reached Bristol, and met Mr. Whitefield[1] there. I could scarce reconcile myself at first to this *strange way* of preaching in the fields, of which he set me an example on Sunday: having been all my life, till very lately, so tenacious of every point relating to decency and order, that I should have thought the saving of souls *almost a sin,* if it had not been done *in a church.*

April 1, In the evening (Mr. Whitefield being gone), I begun expounding our Lord's sermon on the Mount,[2] (one pretty remarkable precedent of *field-preaching,* I suppose *there were churches* at that time also), to a little society which was accustomed to meet once or twice a week in Nicholas-street.

Monday 2, At four in the afternoon, I submitted to *be more vile,* and proclaimed in the highways the glad tidings of salvation, speaking from a little eminence, in a ground adjoining to the city, to about three thousand people. The Scripture on which I spoke was this, (Is it possible, any one should be ignorant, that it is fulfilled in every true minister of Christ?) *The Spirit of the Lord is upon me, because he hath anointed me to preach the Gospel to the poor. He hath sent me to heal the broken-hearted; to preach deliverance to the captives, and recovery of sight to the blind: to set at liberty them that are bruised, to proclaim the acceptable year of the Lord.*[3]

At seven I began expounding the Acts of the Apostles, to a society meeting in Baldwin-street; and the next day, the Gospel of St. John, in the chapel at Newgate; where I also daily read the morning service of the church.

Wednesday 4, At Baptist Mills, (a sort of a suburb or village, about half a mile from Bristol), I offered the Grace of God to about fifteen hundred persons, from these words, *I will heal their backsliding, I will love them freely.*[4]

In the evening, three women agreed to meet together weekly, with the same intention as those at London, viz. *To confess their faults one to another, and pray one for another, that they might be healed.* At eight, four young men agreed to meet, in pursuance of the same design. How dare any man deny this to be, as to the substance of it, a means of grace, ordained by God? Unless he will affirm,

---

Text from the first American edition, 1830, in a copy in the possession of the library of the University of Georgia.

[1] George Whitefield (1714–1770), popular Methodist preacher.
[2] Matt. 5–7; Luke 6:20–49.
[3] Luke 4:18.
[4] Hos. 14:4.

with Luther in the fury of his Solifidianism,[5] that St. James's epistle is *an epistle of straw?*

Thursday 5, At five in the evening I began at a society in Castle street, expounding the epistle to the Romans; and the next evening, at a society in Gloucester-lane, the first Epistle of St. John, on Saturday evening at Weavers-hall also I begun expounding the epistle to the Romans, and declared that Gospel to all, which is the *power of God unto salvation, to every one that believeth.*

Sunday 8, At seven in the morning, I preached to about a thousand persons at Bristol, and afterwards to about fifteen hundred, on the top of Hannam-mount in Kingswood. I called to them in the words of the evangelical prophet, *Ho! every one that thirsteth, come ye to the waters; come and buy wine and milk without money and without price.*[6] About five thousand were in the afternoon at Rosegreen (on the other side of Kingswood) ; among whom I stood and cried, in the name of the Lord, *If any man thirst, let him come unto me and drink. He that believeth on Me, as the Scripture hath said, out of his belly shall flow rivers of living water.*

Tuesday 10, I was desired to go to Bath; where I offered to about a thousand souls the free Grace of God to *heal their backslidings,* and in the morning to, I believe more than two thousand. I preached to about the same number at Baptist-mills, in the afternoon, on Christ, *made of God unto us, wisdom and righteousness, and sanctification and redemption.*

Saturday 14, I preached at the Poorhouse; three or four hundred were within, and more than twice that number without: to whom I explained those comfortable words, *When they had nothing to pay he frankly forgave them both.*[7]

Sunday 15, I explained at seven, to five or six thousand persons, the story of the pharisee and the publican.[8] About

three thousand were present at Hannammount. I preached at Newgate, after dinner to a crowded congregation. Between five and six we went to Rosegreen: it rained hard at Bristol, but not a drop fell upon us, while I declared to about five thousand, *Christ our wisdom, and righteousness, and sanctification, and redemption.* I concluded the day by shewing at the society in Baldwin-street, that his *blood cleanseth us from all sin.*

Tuesday 17, At five in the afternoon, I was at a little society in the Back-lane. The room in which we were was propped beneath; but the weight of people made the floor give way, so that, in the beginning of the expounding, the post which propped it fell down with a great noise. But the floor sunk no further, so that after a little surprise at first, they quietly attended to the things, that were spoken.

Thence I went to Baldwin-street, and expounded, as it came in course, the fourth chapter of the Acts. We then called upon God to confirm his word. Immediately one that stood by, to our no small surprise, cried out aloud, with the utmost vehemence, even as in the agonies of death. But we continued in prayer, till *a new song was put in her mouth, a thanksgiving unto our God.* Soon after, two other persons (well known in this place, as labouring to live in all good conscience towards all men) were seized with strong pain, and constrained to *roar for the disquietness of their heart.* But it was not long before they likewise burst forth into praise to God their Saviour. The last who called upon God as out of the belly of hell, was I——— E———,[9] a stranger in Bristol. And in a short space, he also was overwhelmed with joy and love, knowing that God had healed his backslidings. So many living witnesses hath God given, that *his hand is still stretched out to heal, and that signs and wonders are even now wrought, by His holy child Jesus.*

---

[5] The doctrine that faith alone, without works, is necessary to justification.
[6] Isa. 55:1.

[7] Luke 7:42.
[8] Matt. 9.
[9] Not otherwise identified.

Monday 4, Many came to me and earnestly advised me, "Not to preach abroad in the afternoon, because there was a combination of several persons, who threatened terrible things." This report being spread abroad brought many thither, of *the better sort of people* (so called) and added, I believe, more than a thousand, to the ordinary congregation. The scripture to which, not my choice, but the Providence of God directed me was, *Fear not thou, for I am with thee: be not dismayed, for I am thy God. I will strengthen thee, yea I will help thee, yea, I will uphold thee with the right hand of my righteousness.*[10] The power of God came with his word: so that none scoffed, or interrupted, or opened his mouth.

Tuesday 5, There was great expectation at Bath, of what a noted man[11] was to do to me there: And I was much entreated, "Not to preach; because no one knew what might happen." By this report I also gained a much larger audience, among whom were many of the rich and great. I told them plainly, *The Scripture* had *concluded* them *all under sin,* high and low, rich and poor, one with another. Many of them seemed to be not a little surprised, and were sinking a-pace into seriousness, when their champion appeared, and coming close to me, asked, "By what authority I did these things?" I replied, by the authority of Jesus Christ, conveyed to me by the (now) Archbishop of Canterbury,[12] when he laid his hands upon me, and said, "Take thou authority to preach the Gospel." He said, "This is contrary to Act of Parliament. This is a Conventicle."[13] I answered, "Sir, the Conventicles mentioned in that Act (as the preamble shews) are seditious meetings. But this is not such. Here is no shadow of sedition. Therefore it is not contrary to that Act." He replied, "I say it is. And beside, your preaching frightens people out of their wits." "Sir, did you ever hear me preach?" "No." "How then can you judge of what you never heard?" "Sir, by common report. Common report is enough." "Give me leave, Sir, to ask, Is not your name Nash?" "My name is Nash." "Sir, I dare not judge of you by common report. I think it is not enough to judge by." Here he paused a while, and having recovered himself, asked, "I desire to know, what this people comes here for?" On which one replied, "Sir, leave him to me. Let an old woman answer him." "You, Mr. Nash, take care of your body. We take care of our souls, and for the food of our souls we come here." He replied not a word, but walked away.

As I returned, the street was full of people, hurrying to and fro, and speaking great words. But when any of them asked, "Which is he?" and I replied, "I am he," they were immediately silent. Several ladies following me into Mr. Merchant's house, the servant told me, "There were some wanted to speak with me." I went to them, and said, "I believe, ladies, the maid mistook: you only wanted to look at me." I added, "I do not expect that the rich and great should want either to speak with *me,* or to hear *me,* for I speak the plain truth; a thing *you* hear little of, and do not desire to hear." A few more words passed between us, and I retired.

Thursday 20, After preaching to a small, attentive congregation, I rode to Wednesbury.[14] At twelve I preached in a ground near the middle of the town,

---

[10] Isa. 41:10.

[11] As is made clear later, this was the famous Richard (Beau) Nash, master of ceremonies and of gaming in this popular rendezvous of the wealthy.

[12] Wesley had been ordained September 19, 1725, by John Potter, then Bishop of Oxford, later (1737) Archbishop of Canterbury.

[13] Nash implies that Wesley was conducting a religious meeting not in conformity with the Church of England and hence prohibited by the Conventicle Act.

[14] A village in Staffordshire.

to a far larger congregation than was expected, on *Jesus Christ, the same yesterday, and to-day, and for ever.* I believe every one present felt the power of God. And no creature offered to molest us either going or coming; but *the Lord fought for* us, and we *held our peace.*

I was writing at Francis Ward's[15] in the afternoon, when the cry arose, that "the mob had beset the house." We prayed that God would disperse them. And it was so: one went this way, and another that: so that in half an hour not a man was left. I told our brethren, "Now is the time for us to go." But they pressed me exceedingly to stay; so, that I might not offend them, I sat down, though I foresaw what would follow. Before five the mob surrounded the house again, in greater numbers than ever. The cry of one and all was, "Bring out the minister; we will have the minister." I desired one to take their captain by the hand, and bring him into the house. After a few sentences interchanged between us, the lion was become a lamb. I desired him to go and bring one or two more of the most angry of his companions. He brought in two, who were ready to swallow the ground with rage; but in two minutes they were as calm as he. I then bade them make way, that I might go out among the people. As soon as I was in the midst of them I called for a chair, and standing up, asked, "What do any of you want with me?" Some said, "We want you to go with us to the Justice." I replied, "That I will with all my heart." I then spoke a few words, which God applied; so that they cried out with might and main, "The gentleman is an honest gentleman, and we will spill our blood in his defence." I asked, "Shall we go to the Justice tonight or in the morning?" Most of them cried, "To-night, to-night." On which I went before, and two or three hundred followed, the rest returning whence they came.

The night came on before we had walked a mile, together with heavy rain. However, on we went to Bentley-Hall, two miles from Wednesbury. One or two ran before to tell Mr. Lane,[16] "They had brought Mr. Wesley before his worship." Mr. Lane replied, "What have I to do with Mr. Wesley? Go, and carry him back again." By this time the main body came up, and began knocking at the door. A servant told them, "Mr. Lane was in bed." His son followed, and asked, "What was the matter?" One replied, "Why, an't please you, they sing psalms all day; nay, and make folks rise at five in the morning. And what would your worship advise us to do?" "To go home," said Mr. Lane, "and be quiet."

Here they were at a full stop, till one advised, "to go to Justice Persehouse, at Walsal." All agreed to this. So we hastened on, and about seven [o'clock] came to his house. But Mr. P—— likewise sent word, "That he was in bed." Now they were at a stand again; but at last they all thought it the wisest course to make the best of their way home. About fifty of them undertook to convoy me. But we had not gone a hundred yards, when the mob of Walsal came, pouring in like a flood, and bore down all before them. The Darlaston mob made what defence they could; but they were weary, as well as outnumbered; so that, in a short time, many being knocked down, the rest ran away, and left me in their hands.

To attempt speaking was vain, for the noise on every side was like the roaring of the sea. So they dragged me along till we came to the town: where seeing the door of a large house open, I attempted to go in; but a man catching me by the hair, pulled me back into the middle of the mob. They made no more stop till they had carried me through the main street from one end of the town to the other. I continued speaking all the time to those within hearing, feeling no pain or weariness. At the west end of the town, seeing a door half open, I made toward it, and would have gone in, but a gentleman in the shop would not suffer me, saying, "They would pull the house down to the ground." However, I stood at the door, and asked, "Are you willing to hear me speak?" Many cried

---

[15] Unidentified.　　　　　　[16] The justice of the peace.

out, "No, no! knock his brains out! down with him! kill him at once!" Others said, "Nay, but we will hear him first." I began asking, "What evil have I done!—which of you all have I wronged in word or deed?" And continued speaking for above a quarter of an hour, till my voice suddenly failed. Then the floods began to lift up their voice again; many crying out, "Bring him away, Bring him away."

In the mean time my strength and my voice returned, and I broke out aloud into prayer. And now the man who had just before headed the mob, turned and said, "Sir, I will spend my life for you; follow me, and not one soul here shall touch a hair of your head." Two or three of his fellows confirmed his words, and got close to me immediately. At the same time the gentleman in the shop cried out, "For shame, for shame, let him go." An honest butcher, who was a little farther off, said, "It was a shame they should do thus;" and pulled back four or five one after another, who were running on the most fiercely. The people then, as if it had been by common consent, fell back to the right and left; while those three or four men took me between them, and carried me through them all. But on the bridge the mob rallied again: we therefore went on one side, over the mill-dam, and thence through the meadows; till a little before ten, God brought me safe to Wednesbury, having lost only one flap of my waistcoat, and a little skin from one of my hands.

I never saw such a chain of providences before; so many convincing proofs that the hand of God is on every person and thing, over-ruling all as it seemeth Him good.

The poor woman of Darlaston, who had headed that mob, and sworn that none should touch me, when she saw her followers give way, ran into the thickest of the throng, and knocked down three or four men, one after another. But many assaulting her at once, she was overpowered, and had probably been killed in a few minutes, (three men keeping her down, and beating her with all their might), had not a man called out to one of them, "Hold; Tom, hold!"

"Who is there?" said Tom. "What, honest Munchin? Nay, then, let her go." So they held their hands, and let her get up, and crawl home as well as she could.

From the beginning to the end I found the same presence of mind, as if I had been sitting in my own study. But I took no thought for one moment before another: only once it came into my mind, that if they should throw me into the river it would spoil the papers that were in my pocket. For myself, I did not doubt but I should swim across, having but a thin coat and a light pair of boots.

The circumstances that follow, I thought, were particularly remarkable: 1, That many endeavoured to throw me down while we were going down-hill on a slippery path to the town, as well judging, that if I were once on the ground, I should hardly rise any more. But I made no stumble at all, nor the least slip, till I was entirely out of their hands: 2, That although many strove to lay hold on my collar or clothes to pull me down, they could not fasten at all: only one got fast hold on the flap of my waistcoat, which was soon left in his hand. The other flap, in the pocket of which was a bank-note, was torn but half off. 3, That a lusty man, just behind, struck at me several times with a large oaken stick; with which, if he had struck me once on the back part of my head, it would have saved him all farther trouble; but every time the blow was turned aside I know not how, for I could not move to the right-hand or left. 4, That another came rushing through the press, and raising his arm to strike, on a sudden let it drop, and only stroked my head, saying, "What soft hair he has." 5, That I stopped exactly at the Mayor's door, as if I had known it (which the mob doubtless thought I did), and found him standing in the shop, which gave the first check to the madness of the people. 6, That the very first men, whose hearts were turned, were the heroes of the town, the captains of the rabble on all occasions, one of them having been a prize-fighter at the bear-garden. 7, That from first to last, I heard none give a reviling word, or call me by any opprobrious name whatever. But the cry of one and all was, "The preacher! the parson! the minister!" 8, That no creature, at least within my hearing, lay any thing to my charge, either true or false; having in the hurry quite forgot to provide themselves with an accusation of any kind. And, lastly, that they were utterly at a loss what they should do with me; none proposing any determinate thing, only, "Away with him; kill him at once."

By how gentle degrees does God prepare us for his will! Two years ago a piece of a brick grazed my shoulders. It was a year after that the stone struck me between the eyes. Last month I received one blow, and this evening two; one before we came into the town, and one after we were gone out. But both were as nothing; for though one man struck me on the breast with all his might, and the other on the mouth with such a force that the blood gushed out immediately; I felt no more pain from either of the blows, than if they had touched me with a straw.

It ought not to be forgotten, that when the rest of the society made all haste to escape for their lives, four only would not stir, William Stitch, Edward Slater, John Griffiths, and Joan Parks: these kept with me, resolving to live or die together. And none of them received one blow but William Stitch, who held me by the arm from one end of the town to the other. He was then dragged away and knocked down; but he soon rose and got to me again. I afterwards asked him, "What he expected when the mob came upon us?" He said, "To die for Him who had died for us; and he felt no hurry or fear, but calmly waited till God should require his soul of him."

I asked J. P——, if she were not afraid when they tore her from me? She said, "No; no more than I am now. I could trust God for you as well as for myself. From the beginning I had a full persuasion that God would deliver you. I knew not how, but I left that to Him, and was as sure as if it were already done." I asked, if the report were true, that she had fought for me. She said, "No; I knew God would fight for his

children."—And shall these souls perish at the last?

When I came back to Francis Ward's, I found many of our brethren waiting upon God. Many also whom I never had seen before came to rejoice with us. And the next morning, as I rode through the town in my way to Nottingham, every one I met expressed such a cordial affection, that I could scarce believe what I saw and heard.

I cannot close this head without inserting as great a curiosity in its kind, as I believe was ever yet seen in England, which had its birth within a very few days of this remarkable occurrence at Walsal:

Staffordshire.
To all High-Constables, Petty-Constables, and other of his Majesty's Peace-officers, within the said county, and particularly to the Constable of Tipton," (near Walsal.)

Whereas, we his Majesty's Justices of the peace, for the said county of Stafford, have received information, that several disorderly persons, styling themselves Methodist preachers, go about, raising routs and riots, to the great damage of his Majesty's liege people, and against the peace of our Sovereign Lord the King:

These are in his Majesty's name, to command you and every one of you, within your respective districts, to make diligent search after the said Methodist preachers, and to bring him or them before some of us his said Majesty's Justices of the peace, to be examined concerning their unlawful doings.

Given under our hands and seals this day of October, 1743.
JOHN LANE,
WM. PERSEHOUSE.

N.B. The very Justices to whose houses I was carried, and who severally refused to see me!

Saturday 22, I rode from Nottingham to Epworth, and on Monday set out for Grimsby. But at Ferry we were at a full stop: The boatmen telling us, "We could not pass the Trent: It was as much as our lives were worth to put from shore before the storm abated." We waited an hour. But being afraid it would do much hurt, if I should disappoint the congregation at Grimsby, asked the men, "If they did not think it possible, to get to the other shore?" They said, "They could not tell; but if we would venture our lives, they would venture theirs." So we put off, having six men, two women, and three horses in the boat, Many stood, looking after us on the river side: in the middle of which we were, when in an instant, the side of the boat was under water, and the horses and men rolling one over another. We expected the boat to sink every moment, but I did not doubt being able to swim ashore. The boatmen were amazed as well as the rest; but they quickly recovered and rowed for life. And soon after our horses leaping overboard, lightened the boat, and we all came unhurt to land.

They wondered what was the matter I did not rise (for I lay along in the bottom of the boat; and I wondered too, till upon examination I found, that a large iron crow,[17] which the boatmen sometimes used, was (none knew how) run through the string of my boot, which pinned me down that I could not stir. So that if the boat had sunk, I should have been safe enough from swimming any further.

The same day, and as near as we could judge the same hour, the boat in which my brother[18] was crossing the Severn, at the New Passage, was carried away by the wind, and in the utmost danger of splitting upon the rocks. But the same God, when all human hope was past, delivered them as well as us.

In the evening, the house at Grimsby not being able to contain one-fourth of the congregation, I stood in the street, and exhorted every prodigal to *arise and go to his father*. One or two endeavoured to interrupt, but they were soon stilled by their own companions. The next day, Tuesday 25, one in the town promised us the use of a large room. But he was prevailed upon to retract his promise before the hour of preaching came. I then designed going to the Cross,[19] but the rain prevented; so that we were a little at a loss, till we were offered a very convenient place, by a woman who was a sinner. I there declared him (about one o'clock,) whom God hath exalted, to give repentance and remission of sins. And God so confirmed the word of his grace, that I marvelled any one could withstand Him.

However, the prodigal held out till the evening, when I enlarged upon her sins and faith, who *washed* our *Lord's feet with tears, and wiped them with the hairs of her head*. She was then utterly broken in pieces, (as, indeed, was well nigh the whole congregation,) and came after me to my lodging, crying out, "O, Sir! *What must I do to be saved?"* Being now informed of her case, I said, "Escape for your life; return instantly to your husband." She said, "But how can it be? Which way can I go? He is above a hundred miles off. I have just received a letter from him, and he is at New-castle-upon-Tyne." I told her, "I am going for Newcastle in the morning; you may go with me. William Blow shall take you behind him."[20] And so he did. Glory be to the Friend of sinners! He hath plucked one more brand out of the fire. Thou poor sinner, thou hast received a prophet in the name of a prophet; and thou art found of Him that sent him.

Wednesday 26, I enlarged upon those deep words, *Repent and believe the Gospel*. When I had done, a man stood forth in the midst, one who had exceedingly troubled his brethren, vehemently maintaining (for the plague had spread hither also,) that they ought not to pray, to sing, to communicate; to search the Scriptures, or to trouble themselves about works, but only to believe and *be still,* and said with a loud voice, "Mr. Wesley, let me speak a few words. Is it not said, *A certain man had two sons? And he*

---

[17] crowbar.
[18] Charles Wesley (1707–1788), like his brother, was a Methodist preacher; he is especially remembered for his many hymns.
[19] crossroads.
[20] i.e., on horseback.

said unto the younger, Go and work in my vineyard. And he answered, I will not: but afterwards he repented and went?[21] I am he. I said yesterday, 'I will not go to hear him; I will have nothing to do with him.' But I repent. Here is my hand. By the grace of God, I will not leave you as long as I live."

William Blow, Mrs. S., and I set out at six. During our whole journey to Newcastle, I scarce observed her to laugh or even smile once. Nor did she ever complain of any thing, or appeared moved in the least with those trying circumstances which many times occurred in our way. A steady seriousness, or sadness rather, appeared in her whole behaviour and conversation, as became one that felt the burthen of sin, and was groaning after salvation. In the same spirit, by all I could observe or learn, she continued during her stay at Newcastle. Not long after, her husband removed from thence, and wrote to her to follow him. She set out in a ship bound for Hull. A storm met them by the way. The ship sprung a leak. But though it was near the shore, on which many people flocked together, yet the sea ran so exceeding high, that it was impossible to make any help. Mrs. S. was seen standing on the deck, as the ship gradually sunk; and afterwards, hanging by her hands on the ropes, till the masts likewise disappeared. Even then for some moments they could observe her floating upon the waves, till her clothes, which buoyed her up, being thoroughly wet, she sunk—I trust into the ocean of God's mercy.

---

[21] Matt. 21:28.

Colley Cibber
1671-1757

AN APOLOGY for the Life of
Mr. Colley Cibber, Comedian

CHAPTER I

*The Introduction. The Author's
Birth. Various Fortune at School. Not
lik'd by those he lov'd there. Why. A
Digression upon Raillery. The Use and
Abuse of it. The Comforts of Folly.
Vanity of Greatness. Laughing, no bad
Philosophy.*

You[1] know, Sir, I have often told you,
that one time or other I should give the
Publick some Memoirs of my own Life;
at which you have never fail'd to laugh,
like a Friend, without saying a word to
dissuade me from it; concluding, I suppose, that such a wild Thought could not
possibly require a serious Answer. But
you see I was in earnest. And now you
will say, the World will find me, under
my own Hand, a weaker Man than perhaps I may have pass'd for, even among
my Enemies.—With all my Heart! my
Enemies will then read me with
Pleasure, and you, perhaps, with Envy,
when you find that Follies, without the
Reproach of Guilt upon them, are not
inconsistent with Happiness.—But why

make my Follies publick? Why not? I
have pass'd my Time very pleasantly
with them, and I don't recollect that
they have ever been hurtful to any other
Man living. Even admitting they were
injudiciously chosen, would it not be
Vanity in me to take Shame to myself
for not being found a Wise Man?
Really, Sir, my Appetites were in too
much haste to be happy, to throw away
my Time in pursuit of a Name[2] I was
sure I could never arrive at.

Now the Follies I frankly confess, I
look upon as, in some measure, discharged; while those I conceal are still
keeping the Account open between me
and my Conscience. To me the Fatigue
of being upon a continual Guard to hide
them, is more than the Reputation of
being without them can repay. If this be
Weakness, *defendit numerus*,[3] I have
such comfortable Numbers on my side,
that were all Men to blush, that are not
Wise, I am afraid, in Ten, Nine Parts
of the World ought to be out of Countenance: But since that sort of Modesty
is what they don't care to come into,
why should I be afraid of being star'd

Text from the second edition, 1740; first
published in the same year.

[1] Cibber never identified the patron to whom
the *Apology* is addressed, but it was thought

by the editor R. H. Lowe to have been Henry
Pelham, brother to the powerful Duke of
Newcastle.

[2] reputation.

[3] "There is strength in numbers."

at, for not being particular? Or if the Particularity lies in owning my Weakness, will my wisest Reader be so inhuman as not to pardon it? But if there should be such a one, let me, at least, beg him to shew me that strange Man, who is perfect! Is any one more unhappy, more ridiculous, than he who is always labouring to be thought so, or that is impatient, when he is not thought so? Having brought myself to be easy, under whatever the World may say of my Undertaking, you may still ask me, why I give myself all this trouble? Is it for Fame, or Profit to myself, or Use or Delight to others? For all these Considerations I have neither Fondness nor Indifference: If I obtain none of them, the Amusement, at worst, will be a Reward that must constantly go along with the Labour. But behind all this, there is something inwardly inciting, which I cannot express in few Words; I must therefore a little make bold with your Patience.

A Man who has pass'd above Forty Years of his Life upon a Theatre, where he has never appear'd to be Himself, may have naturally excited the Curiosity of his Spectators to know what he really was, when in no body's Shape but his own; and whether he, who by his Profession had so long been ridiculing his Benefactors, might not, when the Coat of his Profession was off, deserve to be laugh'd at himself; or from his being often seen in, the most flagrant, and immoral Characters; whether he might not see as great a Rogue, when he look'd into the Glass himself, as when he held it to others.

It was doubtless, from a Supposition that this sort of Curiosity wou'd compensate their Labours, that so many hasty Writers have been encourag'd to publish the Lives of the late Mrs. Old-

field, Mr. *Wilks,* and Mr. *Booth,*[4] in less time after their Deaths than one could suppose it cost to transcribe them.

Now, Sir, when my Time comes, lest they shou'd think it worth while to handle my Memory with the same Freedom, I am willing to prevent its being so odly besmear'd (or at best but flatly white-wash'd) by taking upon me to give the Publick This, as true a Picture of myself as natural Vanity will permit me to draw: For, to promise you that I shall never be vain, were a Promise that, like a Looking-glass too large, might break itself in the making: Nor am I sure I ought wholly to avoid that Imputation, because if Vanity be one of my natural Features, the Portrait wou'd not be like me without it. In a word, I may palliate, and soften, as much as I please; but upon an honest Examination of my Heart, I am afraid the same Vanity which makes even homely People employ Painters to preserve a flattering Record of their Persons, has seduced me to print off this *Chiaro Oscuro*[5] of my Mind.

And when I have done it, you may reasonably ask me, of what Importance can the History of my private Life be to the Publick? To this, indeed, I can only make you a ludicrous Answer, which is, That the Publick very well knows, my Life has not been a private one; that I have been employ'd in their Service, ever since many of their Grandfathers were young Men; And tho' I have voluntarily laid down my Post, they have a sort of Right to enquire into my Conduct, (for which they have so well paid me) and to call for the Account of it, during my Share of Administration in the State of the Theatre. This Work, therefore, which, I hope, they will not expect a Man of hasty Head shou'd confine to any regular

---

[4] Biographies of the actors Anne Oldfield (1683–1730), Robert Wilks (1665?–1732), and Barton Booth (1681–1733) had appeared immediately after their deaths; indeed, Donald Stauffer (*The Art of Biography in Eighteenth Century England,* 2 vols., 1941) cites evidence of Benjamin Victor's *Memoirs of the Life of Barton Booth, Esq.* having appeared two years before Booth's death, although it is apparent

from Stauffer's entry of the evidence that he had not himself seen an earlier edition than that of 1733. The publisher Curll played an active hand in this kind of journalistic exploitation of the gossip which the deaths of famous actors stirred publicly.

[5] More commonly in the eighteenth century. *clare obscure:* "light and shade in painting" (Bailey's *Dictionary*).

Method: (For I shall make no scruple of leaving my History, when I think a Digression may make it lighter, for my Reader's Digestion.) This Work, I say, shall not only contain the various Impressions of my Mind, (as in *Louis the Fourteenth* his Cabinet[6] you have seen the growing Medals of his Person from Infancy to Old Age,) but shall likewise include with them the *Theatrical History of my Own Time,* from my first Appearance on the Stage to my last *Exit.*

If then what I shall advance on that Head, may any ways contribute to the Prosperity or Improvement of the Stage in Being, the Publick must of consequence have a Share in its Utility.

This, Sir, is the best Apology I can make for being my own Biographer. Give me leave therefore to open the first Scene of my Life, from the very Day I came into it; and tho' (considering my Profession) I have no reason to be asham'd of my Original; yet I am afraid a plain dry Account of it, will scarce admit of a better Excuse than what my Brother *Bays* makes for Prince *Prettyman* in the *Rehearsal,*[7] viz. *I only do it, for fear I should be thought to be no body's Son at all;* for if I have led a worthless Life, the Weight of my Pedigree will not add an Ounce to my intrinsic Value. But be the Inference what it will, the simple Truth is this.

I was born in *London,* on the *6th* of *November* 1671, in *Southampton-Street,* facing *Southampton-House.* My Father, *Caius Gabriel Cibber,* was a Native of *Holstein,* who came into *England* some time before the Restoration of King *Charles* II. to follow his Profession, which was that of a Statuary, &c. The *Basso Relievo* on the Pedestal of the Great Column in the City,[8] and the two Figures of the *Lunaticks,*[9] the *Raving*

and the *Melancholy,* over the Gates of *Bethlehem-Hospital,* are no ill Monuments of his Fame as an Artist. My Mother was the Daughter of *William Colley,* Esq; of a very ancient Family of *Glaiston* in *Rutlandshire,* where she was born. My Mother's Brother, *Edward Colley,* Esq; (who gave me my Christian Name) being the last Heir Male of it, the Family is now extinct. I shall only add, that in *Wright's* History of *Rutlandshire,* publish'd in 1684, the *Colley's* are recorded as Sheriffs and Members of Parliament from the Reign of *Henry* VII. to the latter End of *Charles* I. in whose Cause chiefly Sir *Antony Colley,* my Mother's Grandfather, sunk his Estate from Three Thousand to about Three Hundred *per Annum.*

In the Year 1682, at little more than Ten Years of Age, I was sent to the Free-School of *Grantham* in *Lincolnshire,* where I staid till I got through it, from the lowest Form to the uppermost. And such Learning as that School could give me, is the most I pretend to (which, tho' I have not utterly forgot, I cannot say I have much improv'd by Study) but even there I remember I was the same inconsistent Creature I have been ever since! always in full Spirits, in some small Capacity to do right, but in a more frequent Alacrity to do wrong; and consequently often under a worse Character than I wholly deserv'd: A giddy Negligence always possess'd me, and so much, that I remember I was once whipp'd for my *Theme,* tho' my Master told me, at the same time, what was good of it was better than any Boy's in the Form. And (whatever Shame it may be to own it) I have observ'd the same odd Fate has frequently attended the course of my later Conduct in Life. The unskilful openness, or in the plain Terms, the Indiscretion I have always

---

[6] Louis XIV's cabinet of medals was a room in the private suite of the monarch at Versailles in which among paintings and mirrors were cases of coins, medals, and cameos of rare and beautiful character. The greater part of the collection is now in the French National Gallery in Paris.

[7] *The Rehearsal* (1671), a play by George

Villiers, Duke of Buckingham, satirizing the poet laureate, John Dryden, as "Bayes"; the passage which is paraphrased by Cibber is found at III, iv, 63–65.

[8] A monument to the fire of London.

[9] Now in the Victoria and Albert Museum in South Kensington.

acted with from my Youth, has drawn more ill-will towards me, than Men of worse Morals and more Wit might have met you. My Ignorance, and want of Jealousy of Mankind has been so strong, that it is with Reluctance I even yet believe any Person, I am acquaint with, can be capable of Envy, Malice, or Ingratitude; And to shew you what a Mortification it was to me, in my very boyish Days, to find myself mistaken, give me leave to tell you a School Story.

A great Boy, near the Head taller than my self, in some wrangle at Play had insulted me; upon which I was foolhardy enough to give him a Box on the Ear; the Blow was soon return'd with another, that brought me under him, and at his Mercy. Another Lad, whom I really lov'd, and thought a good-natur'd one, cry'd out with some warmth, to my Antagonist (while I was down) Beat him, beat him soundly! This so amaz'd me, that I lost all my Spirits to resist, and burst into Tears! When the Fray was over I took my Friend aside, and ask'd him, How he came to be so earnestly against me? To which, with some glouting[10] Confusion, he reply'd, Because you are always jeering, and making a Jest of me to every Boy in the School. Many a Mischief have I brought upon myself by the same Folly in riper Life. Whatever Reason I had to reproach my Companion's declaring against me, I had none to wonder at it, while I was so often hurting him: Thus I deserv'd his Enmity, by my not having Sense enough to know I *had* hurt him; and he hated me, because he had not Sense enough to know, that I never *intended* to hurt him.

As this is the first remarkable Error of my Life I can recollect, I cannot pass it by without throwing out some further Reflections upon it; whether flat or spirited, new or common, false or true, right or wrong, they will be still my own, and consequently like me; I will therefore boldly go on; for I am only

oblig'd to give you my *own,* and not a *good* Picture, to shew as well the Weakness, as the Strength of my Understanding. It is not on what I write, but on my Reader's Curiosity I relie to be read through: At worst, tho' the Impartial may be tir'd, the Ill-natur'd (no small number) I know will see the bottom of me.

What I observ'd then, upon my having undesignedly provok'd my School-Friend into an Enemy, is a common Case in Society; Errors of this kind often sour the Blood of Acquaintance into an inconceivable Aversion, where it is little suspected. It is not enough to say of your Raillery, that you intended no Offence; if the Person you offer it to has either a wrong Head, or wants a Capacity to make that distinction, it may have the same effect as the Intention of the grossest Injury: And in reality, if you know his Parts are too slow to return it in kind, it is a vain and idle Inhumanity, and sometimes draws the Aggressor into difficulties not easily got out of: Or to give the Case more scope, suppose your Friend may have a passive Indulgence for your Mirth, if you find him silent at it; tho' you were as intrepid as *Caesar,* there can be no excuse for your not leaving it off. When you are conscious that your Antagonist can give as well as take, then indeed the smarter the Hit the more agreeable the Party: A Man of chearful Sense, among Friends will never be grave upon an Attack of this kind, but rather thank you that you have given him a Right to be even with you: There are few Men (tho' they may be Masters of both) that on such occasions had not rather shew their Parts[11] than their Courage, and the Preference is just; a Bull-Dog may have one, and only a Man can have the other. Thus it happens, that in the coarse Merriment of common People, when the Jest begins to swell into earnest; for want of this Election you may observe, he that has least wit generally gives the first Blow.

---

[10] "To glout . . . (a low word of which I find no etymology) To pout; to look sullen. It is still used in Scotland" (Johnson's *Dictionary*).

[11] Here this favorite word of the century seems to mean *ingenuity* rather than the usual definition of it as given in the dictionaries of the period,

Now, as among the Better sort, a readiness of Wit is not always a Sign of intrinsick Merit; so the want of that readiness is no Reproach to a Man of plain Sense and Civility, who therefore (methinks) should never have these lengths of Liberty taken with him. Wit there becomes absurd, if not insolent; ill-natur'd I am sure it is, which Imputation a generous Spirit will always avoid, for the same Reason that a Man of real Honour will never send a Challenge to a Cripple. The inward Wounds that are given by the inconsiderate Insults of Wit, to those that want it, are as dangerous as those given by Oppression to Inferiors; as long in healing, and perhaps never forgiven. There is besides (and little worse than this) a mutual Grossness in Raillery, that sometimes is more painful to the Hearers that are not concern'd in it, than to the Persons engaged. I have seen a couple of these clumsy Combatants drub one another with as little Manners or Mercy as if they had two Flails in their Hands; Children at Play with Case-knives could not give you more Apprehension of their doing one another a Mischief, And yet, when the Contest has been over, the Boobys have look'd round them for Approbation, and upon being told they were admirably well match'd, have sat down (bedawb'd as they were) contented, at making it a drawn Battle. After all that I have said, there is no clearer way of giving Rules for Raillery than by Example.

There are two Persons now living,[12] who tho' very different in their manner, are, as far as my Judgment reaches, complete Masters of it; one of a more polite and extensive Imagination, the other of a Knowledge more closely useful to the Business of Life: The one gives you perpetual Pleasure, and seems always to be taking it; the other seems to take none, till his Business is over, and then gives you as much as if Pleasure were his only Business. The one enjoys his Fortune, the other thinks it first necessary to make it; though that he will enjoy it then, I cannot be positive, because when a Man

has once pick'd up more than he wants, he is apt to think it a Weakness to suppose he has enough. But as I don't remember ever to have seen these Gentlemen in the same Company, you must give me leave to take them separately.

The first of them, then, has a Title, and ———— no matter what; I am not to speak of the great, but the happy part of his Character, and in this one single light; not of his being an illustrious, but a delightful Companion.

In Conversation he is seldom silent but when he is attentive, nor ever speaks without exciting the Attention of others; and tho' no Man might with less Displeasure to his Hearers engross the Talk of the Company, he has a Patience in his Vivacity that chuses to divide it, and rather gives more Freedom than he takes; his sharpest Replies having a mixture of Politeness that few have the command of; his Expression is easy, short, and clear; a stiff or studied Word never comes from him; it is in a simplicity of Style that he gives the highest Surprize, and his Ideas are always adapted to the Capacity and Taste of the Person he speaks to: Perhaps you will understand me better if I give you a particular Instance of it. A Person at the University, who from being a Man of Wit, easily became his Acquaintance there, from that Acquaintance found no difficulty in being made one of his Chaplains: This Person afterwards leading a Life that did no great Honour to his Cloth, obliged his Patron to take some gentle notice of it; but as his Patron knew the Patient was squeamish, he was induced to sweeten the Medicine to his Taste, and therefore with a smile of good-humour told him, that if to the many Vices he had already, he would give himself the trouble to add one more, he did not doubt but his Reputation might still be set up again. Sir *Crape,* who could have no Aversion to so pleasant a Dose, desiring to know what it might be, was answered, *Hypocrisy, Doctor, only a little Hypocrisy!* This plain Reply can need no Comment; but

---

[12] Although unidentified by Cibber, the first of these persons seems to resemble the urbane Earl of Chesterfield; Cibber's editor R. H. Lowe rejected the attribution of the second person to Bubb Doddington as unlike him.

ex pede Herculem,[13] he is every where proportionable. I think I have heard him since say, the Doctor thought Hypocrisy so detestable a Sin that he dy'd without committing it. In a word, this Gentleman gives Spirit to Society the Moment he comes into it, and whenever he leaves it, they who have Business have then leisure to go about it.

Having often had the Honour to be my self the But of his Raillery, I must own I have received more Pleasure from his lively manner of raising the Laugh against me, than I could have felt from the smoothest flattery of a serious Civility. Tho' Wit flows from him with as much ease as common Sense from another, he is so little elated with the Advantage he may have over you, that whenever your good Fortune gives it against him, he seems more pleas'd with it on your side than his own. The only advantage he makes of his Superiority of Rank is, that by always waving it himself, his inferior finds he is under the greater Obligation not to forget it.

When the Conduct of social Wit is under such Regulations, how delightful must those *Convivia,* those Meals of Conversation be, where such a Member presides; who can with so much ease (as *Shakespear* phrases it)[14] *set the Table in a roar.* I am in no pain that these imperfect Out-lines will be apply'd to the Person I mean, because every one who has the Happiness to know him, must know how much more in this particular Attitude is wanting to be like him.

The other Gentleman, whose bare Interjections of Laughter have humour in them, is so far from having a Title, that he has lost his real name, which some Years ago he suffer'd his Friends to railly him out of; in lieu of which they have equipp'd him with one they thought had a better sound in good Company. He is the first Man of so sociable a Spirit, that I ever knew capable of quitting the Allurements of Wit and Pleasure, for a strong Application to Business; in his Youth (for there was

a Time when he was young) he set out in all the hey-day Expences of a modish Man of Fortune; but finding himself over-weighted with Appetites, he grew restiff, kick'd up in the middle of the Course, and turn'd his back upon his Frolicks abroad, to think of improving his Estate at home: In order to which he clapt Collars upon his Coach-Horses, and that their Mettle might not run over other People, he ty'd a Plough to their Tails, which tho' it might give them a more slovenly Air, would enable him to keep them fatter in a foot pace, with a whistling Peasant beside them, than in a full trot, with a hot-headed Coachman behind them. In these unpolite Amusements he has laugh'd like a Rake, and look'd about him like a Farmer for many Years. As his Rank and Station often find him in the best Company, his easy Humour, whenever he is called to it, can still make himself the Fiddle of it.

And tho' some say, he looks upon the Follies of the World like too severe a Philosopher, yet he rather chuses to laugh than to grieve at them; to pass his time therefore more easily in it, he often endeavours to conceal himself, by assuming the Air and Taste of a Man in fashion; so that his only Uneasiness seems to be, that he cannot quite prevail with his Friends to think him a worse Manager, than he really is; for they carry their Raillery to such a height, that it sometimes rises to a Charge of downright Avarice against him. Upon which Head, it is no easy matter to be more merry upon him, than he will be upon himself. Thus while he sets that Infirmity in a pleasant Light, he so disarms your Prejudice, that if he has it not, you can't find in your Heart to wish he were without it. Whenever he is attack'd where he seems to lie so open, if his Wit happens not to be ready for you, he receives you with an assenting Laugh, till he has gain'd time enough to whet it sharp enough for a Reply, which seldom turns out to his disadvantage. If you are

---

[13] "from the foot of Hercules," meaning that as Hercules is known by his foot so this anecdote should portray the character of the man

of the world with which Cibber is here occupied.

[14] *Hamlet,* V, i, 211.

too strong for him (which may possibly happen from his being oblig'd to defend the weak side of the Question) his last Resource is to join in the Laugh, till he has got himself off by an ironical Applause of your Superiority.

If I were capable of Envy, what I have observ'd of this Gentleman would certainly incline me to it; for sure to get through the necessary Cares of Life, with a Train of Pleasures at our Heels, in vain calling after us, to give a constant Preference to the Business of the Day, and yet be able to laugh while we are about it, to make even Society the subservient Reward of it, is a State of Happiness which the gravest Precepts of moral Wisdom will not easily teach us to exceed. When I speak of Happiness, I go no higher than that which is contain'd in the World we now tread upon; and when I speak of Laughter, I don't simply mean that which every Oaf is capable of, but that which has its sensible Motive and proper Season, which is not more limited than recommended by that indulgent Philosophy,

Cum ratione insanire.[15]

When I look into my present Self, and afterwards cast my Eye round all my Hopes, I don't see any one Pursuit of them that should so reasonably rouze me out of a Nod in my Great Chair, as a call to those agreeable Parties I have sometimes the Happiness to mix with, where I always assert the equal Liberty of leaving them, when my Spirits have done their best with them.

Now, Sir, as I have been making my way for above Forty Years through a Crowd of Cares, (all which, by the Favour of Providence, I have honestly got rid of) is it a time of Day for me to leave off these Fooleries, and to set up a new Character? Can it be worth my while to waste my Spirits, to bake my Blood, with serious Contemplations, and perhaps impair my Health, in the fruitless Study of advancing myself into

the better Opinion of those very—very few Wise Men that are as old as I am? No, the Part I have acted in real Life, shall be all of a piece,

> . . . *Servetur ad imum,*
> *Qualis ab incepto processerit.*[16]
> HOR.

I will not go out of my Character, by straining to be wiser than I *can* be, or by being more affectedly pensive than I *need* be; whatever I am, Men of Sense will know me to be, put on what Disguise I will; I can no more put off my Follies, than my Skin; I have often try'd, but they stick too close to me; nor am I sure my Friends are displeased with them; for, besides that in this Light I afford them frequent matter of Mirth, they may possibly be less uneasy at their *own* Foibles, when they have so old a Precedent to keep them in Countenance. Nay, there are some frank enough to confess, they envy what they laugh at; and when I have seen others, whose Rank and Fortune have laid a sort of Restraint upon their Liberty of pleasing their Company, by pleasing themselves, I have said softly to myself,—Well, there is some Advantage in having neither Rank nor Fortune! Not but there are among them a third Sort, who have the particular Happiness of unbending into the very Wantonness of Good-humour, without depreciating their Dignity: He that is not Master of that Freedom, let his Condition be never so exalted, must still want something to come up to the Happiness of his Inferiors who enjoy it. If *Socrates* cou'd take pleasure in playing at *Even or Odd* with his Children, or *Agesilaus* divert himself in riding the Hobby-horse with them, am I oblig'd to be as eminent as either of them before I am as frolicksome? If the Emperor *Adrian,* near his death, cou'd play with his very Soul, his *Animula,* &c. and regret that it cou'd be no longer companionable; if Greatness, at the same time was not the Delight he was so loth

---

[15] "To be insane systematically" (Terence, *Eunuchus,* I, i, 18).

[16] From his first entrance to the closing scene

Let him one equal character maintain.
(Horace, *Ars Poetica,* ll. 127–128, tr. Francis.)

to part with, sure then these chearful Amusements I am contending for, must have no inconsiderable share in our Happiness; he that does not chuse to live his own way, suffers others to chuse for him. Give me the Joy I always took in the End of an old Song,

My Mind, my Mind is a Kingdom to me![17]

If I can please myself with my own Follies, have not I a plentiful Provision for Life? If the World thinks me a Trifler, I don't desire to break in upon their Wisdom; let them call me any Fool, but an Unchearful one; I live as I write; while my Way amuses me, it's as well as I wish it; when another writes better, I can like him too, tho' he shou'd not like me. Not our great Imitator[18] of *Horace* himself can have more Pleasure in writing his Verses, than I have in reading them, tho' I sometimes find myself there (as *Shapespear* terms it) *dispraisingly*[19] spoken of: If he is a little free with me, I am generally in good Company, he is as blunt with my Betters; so that even here I might laugh in my turn. My Superiors, perhaps, may be mended by him; but, for my part, I own myself incorrigible: I look upon my Follies as the best part of my Fortune, and am more concern'd to be a good Husband of Them, than of That; nor do I believe I shall ever be rhim'd out of them. And, if I don't mistake, I am supported in my way of thinking by *Horace* himself, who, in excuse of a loose Writer, says,

Praetulerim scriptor delirus, inersque videri,
Dum mea delectent, mala me, aut denique fallant,
Quam sapere, et ringi . . .[20]

which, to speak of myself as a loose Philosopher, I have thus ventur'd to imitate:

Me, while my laughing Follies can deceive,
Blest in the dear Delirium let me live,
Rather than wisely know my Wants and grieve.

We had once a merry Monarch[21] of our own, who thought chearfulness so valuable a Blessing, that he would have quitted one of his Kingdoms where he cou'd not enjoy it; where, among many other Conditions they had ty'd him to, his sober Subjects wou'd not suffer him to laugh on a *Sunday;* and tho' this might not be the avow'd Cause of his Elopement,[22] I am not sure, had he had no other, that this alone might not have serv'd his turn; at least, he has my hearty Approbation either way; for had I been under the same Restriction, tho' my staying were to have made me his Successor, I shou'd rather have chosen to follow him.

How far his Subjects might be in the right, is not my Affair to determine; perhaps they were wiser than the Frogs in the Fable,[23] and rather chose to have a Log, than a Stork for their King; yet I hope it will be no Offence to say, that King *Log* himself must have made but a very simple Figure in History.

The Man who chuses never to laugh, or whose becalm'd Passions know no Motion, seems to me only in the quiet State of a green Tree; he vegetates, 'tis true, but shall we say he lives? Now, Sir, for Amusement.—Reader, take heed! for I find a strong impulse to talk impertinently; if therefore you are not as fond of seeing, as I am of shewing myself in all my Lights, you may turn over two Leaves together, and leave what follows to those who have more Curiosity, and less to do with their Time, than you

---

[17] Variant of a song found in William Byrd's *Psalmes, Sonets, and Songs of Sadnes and Pietie* (1588).

[18] Alexander Pope, who had ridiculed Cibber as the chief of dunces in *The Dunciad*.

[19] *Othello*, III, iii, 72.

[20] Horace, *Epistles*, II, ii, 128–130.

[21] Charles II.

[22] The allusion is to Charles's flight in 1650 from his Scottish Presbyterian subjects to the freedom of the Highlanders.

[23] One of Aesop's fables; the frogs, being discontented with a log for a monarch because of its inactivity, were sent a stork which ate them two at a meal, the moral being that a tyrant is worse than no ruler at all.

have.—As I was saying then, let us, for Amusement, advance this, or any other Prince, to the most glorious Throne, mark out his Empire in what Clime you please, fix him on the highest Pinnacle of unbounded Power; and in that State let us enquire into his degree of Happiness; make him at once the Terror and the Envy of his Neighbours, send his Ambition out to War, and gratify it with extended Fame and Victories; bring him in triumph home, with great unhappy Captives behind him, through the Acclamations of his People, to repossess his Realms in Peace. Well, when the Dust has been brusht from his Purple, what will he do next? Why, this envy'd Monarch (who, we will allow to have a more exalted Mind than to be delighted with the trifling Flatteries of a congratulating Circle) will chuse to retire, I presume, to enjoy in private the Contemplation of his Glory; an Amusement, you will say, that well becomes his Station! But there, in that pleasing Rumination, when he has made up his new Account of Happiness, how much, pray, will be added to the Balance more than as it stood before his last Expedition? From what one Article will the Improvement of it appear? Will it arise from the conscious Pride of having done his weaker Enemy an Injury? Are his Eyes so dazzled with false Glory, that he thinks it a less Crime in him to break into the Palace of his Princely Neighbour, because he gave him time to defend it, than for a Subject feloniously to plunder the House of a private Man? Or is the Outrage of Hunger and Necessity more enormous than the Ravage of Ambition? Let us even suppose the wicked Usage of the World, as to that Point, may keep his Conscience quiet; still, what is he to do with the infinite Spoil that his imperial Rapine has brought home? Is he to sit down, and vainly deck himself with the Jewels which he has plunder'd from the Crown of another, whom Self-defence had compell'd to oppose him? No, let us not debase his Glory into so low a Weakness. What Appetite, then, are these shining Treasures food for? Is their vast Value in seeing his vulgar Subjects stare at

them, wise Men smile at them, or his Children play with them? Or can the new Extent of his Dominions add a Cubit to his Happiness? Was not his Empire wide enough before to do good in? And can it add to his Delight that now no Monarch has such room to do mischief in? But farther; if even the great *Augustus,* to whose Reign such Praises are given, cou'd not enjoy his Days of Peace, free from the Terrors of repeated Conspiracies, which lost him more Quiet to suppress, than his Ambition cost him to provoke them. What human Eminence is secure? In what private Cabinet then must this wondrous Monarch lock up his Happiness, that common Eyes are never to behold it? Is it, like his Person, a Prisoner to its own Superiority? Or does he at last poorly place it in the Triumph of his injurious Devastations? One Moment's Search into himself will plainly shew him, that real and reasonable Happiness can have no Existence without Innocence and Liberty. What a Mockery is Greatness without them? How lonesome must be the Life of that Monarch, who, while he governs only by being fear'd, is restrain'd from letting down his Grandeur sometimes to forget himself, and to humanize him into the Benevolence and Joy of Society? To throw off his cumbersome Robe of Majesty to be a Man without Disguise, to have a sensible Taste of Life in its Simplicity, till he confess, from the sweet Experience, that *dulce est desipere in loco,*[24] was no Fool's Philosophy. Or if the gawdy Charms of Pre-eminence are so strong that they leave him no Sense of a less pompous, tho' a more rational Enjoyment, none sure can envy him, but those who are the Dupes of an equally fantastick Ambition.

My Imagination is quite heated and fatigued, in dressing up this Phantome of Felicity; but I hope it has not made me so far misunderstood, as not to have allow'd, that in all the Dispensations of Providence, the Exercise of a great and virtuous Mind is the most elevated State of Happiness: No, Sir, I am not for set-

---

[24] "It's fun to cut up when you can" (Horace, *Odes,* IV, xii, 28).

ting up Gaiety against Wisdom; nor for preferring the Man of Pleasure to the Philosopher; but for shewing, that the Wisest, or greatest Man, is very near an unhappy Man, if the unbending Amusements I am contending for, are not sometimes admitted to relieve him.

How far I may have over-rated these Amusements, let graver Casuists decide; whether they affirm, or reject, what I have asserted, hurts not my Purpose; which is not to give Laws to others; but to shew by what Laws I govern myself: If I am misguided, 'tis Nature's Fault, and I follow her, from this Persuasion; That as Nature has distinguish'd our Species from the mute Creation, by our Risibility, her Design must have been, by that Faculty, as evidently to raise our Happiness, as by our *Os Sublime*[25] (our erected Faces) to lift the Dignity of our Form above them.

Notwithstanding all I have said, I am afraid there is an absolute Power, in what is simply call'd our Constitution, that will never admit of other Rules for Happiness, than her own; from which (be we never so wise or weak) without Divine Assistance, we only can receive it; So that all this my Parade, and Grimace of Philosophy, has been only making a mighty Merit of following my own Inclination. A very natural Vanity! Thought it is some sort of Satisfaction to know it does not impose upon me. Vanity again! However, think It what you will that has drawn me into this copious Digression, 'tis now high time to drop it: I shall therefore in my next Chapter return to my School, from whence, I fear, I have too long been Truant.

---

[25] Ovid, *Metamorphoses*, I, 85: "face." Cibber plays on a parallel with scientific nomenclature for bones of the body, as for in- stance: os pubis, os sacrum, os ischium, os hyoides, etc. In this sense, man's face is his "sublime bone."

Samuel Richardson
1689-1761

From PAMELA; or, Virtue Rewarded

And Distress indeed! For here I am still! And every thing has been worse and worse! Oh! the poor unhappy *Pamela!*—Without any Resource left, and ruin'd in all my Contrivances. But, Oh! my dear Parents, rejoice with me, even in this low Plunge of my Distress; for your poor *Pamela* has escap'd from an Enemy worse than any she ever met with; an Enemy she never thought of before; and was hardly able to stand against. I mean, the Weakness and Presumption, both in one, of her own Mind! which had well nigh, had not divine Grace interposed, sunk her into the lowest last Abyss of Misery and Perdition! I will proceed, as I have Opportunity, with my sad Relation: For my Pen and Ink (in my now doubly secur'd Closet) is all that I have, besides my own Weakness of Body, to employ myself with: And, till yesterday Evening, I have not been able to hold a Pen.

I took with me but one Shift, besides what I had on, and two Handkerchiefs, and two Caps, which my Pocket held, (for it was not for me to incumber myself) and all my Stock of Money, which was but five or six Shillings, to set out for I knew not where; and got out of the Window, not without some Difficulty, sticking a little at my Shoulders and Hips; but I was resolv'd to get out, if possible. And it was further from the Leads[1] than I thought, and I was afraid I had sprain'd my Ancle; and when I had dropt from the Leads to the Ground, it was still further off; but I did pretty well there; at least, I got no Hurt to hinder me from pursuing my Intentions: So being now on the Ground, I hid my Papers under a Rose-bush, and cover'd them over with Mould, and there they still lie, as I hope. Then I hy'd away to the Pond: The Clock struck Twelve, just as I got out; and it was a dark misty Night, and coldish; but I felt none then.

When I came to the Pond-side, I flung in my Upper-coat, as I had design'd, and my Neck-handkerchief, and a round ear'd Cap, with a Knot;[2] and then with great Speed ran to the Door, and took the Key[3] out of my Pocket, my poor Heart beating all the Time against my Bosom, as if it would have forc'd its way out: And beat it well might! For I then, too late, found, that I was most miserably disappointed; for the wicked Woman[4] had taken off that Lock, and

Text from the first edition 1740.

[1] "flat roof to walk on" (Johnson's *Dictionary*).

[2] To cover her proposed flight, Pamela wants to leave the impression that she has been drowned in the pond.

[3] To the door in the garden wall.

[4] The housekeeper, Mrs. Jewkes, who has the responsibility for keeping Pamela from escaping.

put another on; so that my Key would not open it. I try'd and try'd, and feeling about, I found a Padlock besides, on another Part of the Door. O then how my Heart sunk!—I dropt down with Grief and Confusion, unable to stir or support myself for a while. But my Fears awakening my Resolution, and knowing that my Attempt would be as terrible for me, as any other Danger I could then encounter, I clamber'd up upon the Ledges of the Door, and the Lock, which was a great wooden one, reaching the Top of the Door with my Hands; and little thinking I could climb so well, made shift to lay hold on the Top of the Wall with my Hands; but, alas for me! nothing but ill Luck!—no Escape for poor *Pamela!* The Wall being old, the Bricks I held by, gave way, just as I was taking a Spring to get up, and down came I, and received such a Blow upon my Head, with one of the Bricks, that it quite stunn'd me; and I broke my Shins and my Ancle besides, and beat off the Heel of one of my Shoes.

In this dreadful way, flat upon the Ground, lay poor I, for I believe five or six Minutes; and when I would have got up, I could hardly stand; for I found I had bruis'd my left Hip and Shoulder, and was full of Pain with it; and besides my Head bled, and ak'd with the Blow I had with the Brick.—Yet this I valued not! but crawl'd a good way, upon my Feet and Hands, in Search of a Ladder, I just recollected to have seen against the Wall two Days before, on which the Gardener was nailing a Nectarine Branch, that was blown off from the Wall: But no Ladder could I find, and the Wall was very high. What now, thinks I, must become of the poor miserable *Pamela!*—Then I began to wish myself most heartily again in my Closet, and to repent of my Attempt, which I now censur'd as rash, because it did not succeed.

God forgive me! but a sad Thought came just then into my Head!—I tremble to think of it! Indeed my Apprehensions of the Usage I should meet

with, had like to have made me miserable for ever! O my dear, dear Parents, forgive your poor Child; but being then quite desperate, I crept along till I could get up on my Feet, tho' I could hardly stand; and away limp'd I!—What to do, but to throw myself into the Pond, and so put a Period to all my Griefs in this World!—But, Oh! to find them infinitely aggravated (had I not, by God's Grace, been with-held) in a miserable *Eternity!* As I have escap'd this Temptation, (blessed be God for it!) I will tell you my Conflicts on this dreadful Occasion, that God's Mercies may be magnify'd in my Deliverance, that I am yet on this Side the dreadful Gulph, from which there can be no Redemption.

It was well for me, as I have since thought, that I was so maim'd, as made me the longer before I got to the Water; for this gave me some Reflection, and abated that Liveliness of my Passions, which possibly might otherwise have hurry'd me, in my first Transport of Grief, (on my seeing no way to escape, and the hard Usage I had Reason to expect from my dreadful Keepers) to throw myself in without Consideration; but my Weakness of Body made me move so slowly, that it gave Time for a little Reflection, a Ray of Grace, to dart in upon my benighted Mind; and so, when I came to the Pond-side, I sat myself down on the sloping Bank, and began to ponder my wretched Condition: And thus I reason'd with myself.

Pause here a little, *Pamela,* on what thou are about, before thou takest the dreadful Leap; and consider whether there be no Way yet left, no Hope, if not to escape from this wicked House, yet from the Mischiefs threatened thee in it.

I then consider'd, and after I had cast about in my Mind, every thing that could make me hope, and saw no Probability; a wicked Woman devoid of all Compassion! a horrid Helper just arriv'd in this dreadful *Colbrand!*[5] an angry and resenting Master,[6] who now hated me, and threaten'd the most afflicting Evils! and, that I should, in all Probability, be

---

[5] An infamous Swiss character who adds to Pamela's persecution.

[6] Her abductor, called throughout Mr. B.

depriv'd even of the Opportunity I now had before me, to free myself from all their Persecutions—What hast thou to do, distressed Creature, said I to myself, but throw thyself upon a merciful God, (who knows how innocently I suffer) to avoid the merciless Wickedness of those who are determin'd on my Ruin?

And then thought I, (and Oh! that Thought was surely of the Devil's Instigation; for it was very soothing and powerful with me) these wicked Wretches, who now have no Remorse, no Pity on me, will then be mov'd to lament their Misdoings; and when they see the dead Corpse of the unhappy *Pamela* dragg'd out to these slopy Banks, and lying breathless at their Feet, they will find that Remorse to wring their obdurate Hearts, which now has no Place there!—And my Master, my angry Master, will then forget his Resentments, and say, O this is the unhappy *Pamela!* that I have so causelessly persecuted and destroy'd! Now do I see she preferr'd her Honesty to her Life, will he say, and is no Hypocrite, nor Deceiver; but really was the innocent Creature she pretended to be! Then, thinks I, will he, perhaps, shed a few Tears over the poor Corse of his persecuted Servant; and, tho' he may give out, it was Love and Disappointment, and that too, (in order to hide his own Guilt) for the unfortunate Mr. *Williams,*[7] perhaps, yet will he be inwardly griev'd, and order me a decent Funeral, and save me, or rather this Part of me, from the dreadful Stake, and the Highway Interrment; and the young Men and Maidens all around my dear Father's, will pity poor *Pamela;* but O! I hope I shall not be the Subject of their Ballads and Elegies; but that my Memory, for the sake of my dear Father and Mother, may quickly slide into Oblivion!

I was once rising, so indulgent was I to this sad way of thinking, to throw myself in: But again, my Bruises made me slow; and I thought, What art thou about to do, wretched *Pamela?* how knowest thou, tho' the Prospect be all dark to thy short-sighted Eye, what God

may do for thee, even when all human Means fail? God Almighty would not lay me under these sore Afflictions, if he had not given me Strength to grapple with them, if I will exert it as I ought: And who knows, but that the very Presence I so much dread, of my angry and designing Master, (for he has had me in his Power before, and yet I have escap'd) may be better for me, than these persecuting Emissaries of his, who, for his Money, are true to their wicked Trust, and are harden'd by that, and a long Habit of Wickedness, against Compunction of Heart? God can touch his Heart in an Instant; and if this should not be done, I can then but put an End to my Life, by some other Means, if I am so resolved.

But how do I know, thought I, that even these Bruises and Maims that I have gotten, while I pursu'd only the laudable Escape I had meditated, may not kindly furnish me with the Opportunity I now am tempted to precipitate myself upon, and of surrendering up my Life, spotless and unguilty, to that merciful Being who gave it!

Then, thought I, who gave thee, presumptuous as thou art, a Power over thy Life? Who authoriz'd thee to put an End to it, when the Weakness of thy Mind suggests not to thee a Way to preserve it with Honour? How knowest thou what Purposes God may have to serve, by the Trials with which thou are now tempted? Art *thou* to put a Bound to God's Will, and to say, Thus much will I bear, and no more? And, wilt thou *dare* to say, that if the Trial be augmented, and continued, thou wilt sooner die than bear it?

This Act of Despondency, thought I, is a Sin, that, if I pursue it, admits of no Repentance, and can therefore claim no Forgiveness.—And wilt thou, for shortening thy transitory Griefs, *heavy* as they are, and *weak* as thou fanciest thyself, plunge both Body and Soul into everlasting Misery? Hitherto, *Pamela,* thought I, thou art the innocent, the suffering *Pamela;* and wilt thou be the guilty Aggressor? and, because wicked Men persecute thee, wilt thou fly in the

---

[7] The village curate who is fond of Pamela.

Face of the Almighty, and bid Defiance to his Grace and Goodness, who can still turn all these Sufferings to thy Benefits? And how do I know, but that God, who sees all the lurking Vileness of my Heart, may not have permitted these Sufferings on that very Score, and to make me rely solely on his Grace and Assistance, who perhaps have too much prided myself in a vain Dependence on my own foolish Contrivances? Then again, thought I, wilt thou suffer in *one* Moment all the good Lessons of thy poor honest Parents, and the Benefit of their Example, (who have persisted in doing their Duty with Resignation to the Divine Will, amidst the extremest Degrees of Disappointment, Poverty and Distress, and the Persecutions of an ingrateful World, and merciless Creditors) to be thrown away upon thee; and bring down, as in all Probability this thy Rashness will, their grey Hairs with Sorrow to the Grave, when they shall understand that their beloved Daughter, slighting the Tenders of Divine Grace, desponding in the Mercies of a gracious God, has blemish'd, in this *last Act,* a *whole* Life, which they had hitherto approv'd and delighted in?

What then, presumptuous *Pamela,* dost thou here, thought I? Quit with Speed these guilty Banks, and flee from these dashing Waters, that even in their sounding Murmurs, this still Night, reproach thy Rashness! Tempt not God's Goodness on the mossy Banks, that have been Witnesses of thy guilty Intentions; and while thou hast Power left thee, avoid the tempting Evil, lest thy grand Enemy, now repuls'd by Divine Grace, and due Reflection, return to the Charge with a Force that thy Weakness may not be able to resist! And lest one rash Moment destroy all the Convictions, which now have aw'd thy rebellious Mind into Duty and Resignation to the Divine Will!

And so saying, I arose; but was so stiff with my Hurts, so cold with the moist Dew of the Night, and the wet Banks on which I had sat, as also the Damps arising from so large a Piece of Water, that with great Pain I got from the Banks of this Pond, which now I think of with Terror; and bending my limping Steps towards the House, refug'd myself in the Corner of an Outhouse, where Wood and Coals are laid up for Family Use, till I should be found by my cruel Keepers, and consign'd to a wretched Confinement, and worse Usage than I had hitherto experienc'd; and there behind a Pile of Fire-wood I crept, and lay down, as you may imagine, with a Mind just broken, and a Heart sensible to nothing but the extremest Woe and Dejection.

This, my dear Father and Mother, is the Issue of your poor *Pamela's* fruitless Enterprize; and God knows, if I had got out at the Back-door, whether I had been at all in better Case, moneyless, friendless, as I am, and in a strange Place!—But blame not your poor Daughter too much: Nay, if ever you see this miserable Scribble, all bathed and blotted with my Tears, let your Pity get the better of your Blame! But I know it will.—And I must leave off for the present—For, Oh! my Strength and my Will are at present very far unequal to one another.—But yet, I will add, that tho' I should have prais'd God for my Deliverance, had I been freed from my wicked Keepers, and my designing Master; yet I have more abundant Reason to praise God, that I have been deliver'd from a worse Enemy, *myself!*

I will continue my sad Relation.

It seems Mrs. *Jewkes* awaked not till Day-break, and not finding me in Bed, she call'd me; and no Answer being return'd, she relates, that she got out of Bed, and run to my Closet; and not finding me, searched under the Bed, and in another Closet, finding the Chamber-door as she had left it, quite fast, and the Key, as usual, about her Wrist. For if I could have got out at the Chamber-door, there were two or three Passages, and Doors to them all, double lock'd and barr'd, to go thro', into the great Garden; so that if I would escape, there was no Way but that of the Window; and that very Window, because of the

Summer-parlour under it; for the other Windows were a great way from the Ground.

She says, she was excessively frighted, and instantly rais'd the *Swiss,* and the two Maids, who lay not far off; and finding every Door fast, she said, I must be carry'd away, as St. *Peter* was out of Prison, by some Angel. It is a Wonder she had not a worse Thought!

She says, she wept and wrung her Hands, and took on sadly, running about like a mad Woman, little thinking I could have got out of the Closet Window, between the Iron Bars; and indeed I don't know if I could do so again. But at last finding that Casement open, they concluded it must be so; and so they ran out into the Garden, and found, it seems, my Footsteps in the Mould of the Bed which I dropt down upon from the Leads: And so speeded away, all of them, that is to say, Mrs. *Jewkes, Colbrand* and *Nan,* towards the Back-door, to see if that was fast, while the Cook was sent to the Out-offices to raise the Men, and make them get Horses ready, to take each a several way to pursue me.

But it seems, that finding that Door double-lock'd and padlock'd, and the Heel of my Shoe, and the broken Bricks, they verily concluded I was got away by some Means, over the Wall; and then, they say, Mrs. *Jewkes* seem'd like a distracted Woman: Till at last, *Nan* had the Thought to go towards the Pond, and there seeing my Coat, and Cap and Handkerchief in the Water, cast almost to the Banks by the dashing of the Waves, she thought it was me, and screaming out, run to Mrs. *Jewkes,* and said, O Madam, Madam! here's a piteous Thing!—Mrs.[8] *Pamela* lies drown'd in the Pond!—Thither they all ran! and finding my Cloaths, doubted not I was at the Bottom; and they all, *Swiss* among the rest, beat their Breasts, and made most dismal Lamentations; and Mrs. *Jewkes* sent *Nan* to the Men, to bid them get the Drag-net ready, and leave the Horses, and come to try to find the poor Innocent! as she, it seems, *then*

call'd me, beating her Breast, and lamenting my hard Hap; but most what would become of them, and what Account they should give to my Master.

While every one was thus differently employ'd, some weeping and wailing, some running here and there, *Nan* came into the Wood-house; and there lay poor I; so weak, so low, and dejected, and withal so stiff with my Bruises, that I could not stir nor help myself to get upon my Feet. And I said, with a low voice, (for I could hardly speak) Mrs. *Ann,*[9] Mrs. *Ann!*—The Creature was sadly frighted, but was taking up a Billet to knock me on the Head, believing I was some Thief, as she said; but I cry'd, out, O Mrs. *Ann,* Mrs. *Ann,* help me, for Pity's sake, to Mrs. *Jewkes!* for I cannot get up!—Bless me, said she, what! you, Madam!—Why our Hearts are almost broke, and we were going to drag the Pond for you, believing you had drown'd yourself. Now, said she, you'll make us all alive again!

And, without helping me, she run away to the Pond, and brought all the Crew to the Wood-house.—The wicked Woman, as she entered, said, Where is she?—Plague of her Spells, and her Witchcrafts! She shall dearly repent of this Trick, if my Name be *Jewkes;* and coming to me, took hold of my Arm so roughly, and gave me such a Pull, as made me squeal out, (my Shoulder being bruis'd on that Side) and drew me on my Face. O cruel Creature! said I, if you knew what I had suffer'd, it would move you to pity me!

Even *Colbrand* seem'd to be concern'd, and said, Fie, Madam, fie! you see she is almost dead! You must not be so rough with her. The Coachman *Robin* seem'd to be sorry for me too, and said, with Sobs, What a Scene is here! Don't you see she is all bloody in her Head, and cannot stir?—Curse of her Contrivances! said the horrid Creature; she has frighted me out of my Wits, I'm sure. How the D——l came you here?—O! said I, ask me now no Questions, but let the Maids carry me up to my Prison;

---

and there let me die decently, and in Peace! For indeed I thought I could not live two Hours.

The still more inhuman Tygress said, I suppose you want Mr. *Williams* to pray by you, don't you? Well, I'll send for my Master this Minute; let him come and watch you himself, for me; for there's no such thing as holding you, I'm sure!

So the Maids took me up between them, and carry'd me to my Chamber; and when the Wretch saw how bad I was, she began a little to relent—while every one wonder'd (at what I had neither Strength nor Inclination to tell them) how all this came to pass; which they imputed to Sorcery and Witchcraft.

I was so weak, when I had got up Stairs, that I fainted away, with Dejection, Pain and Fatigue; and they undress'd me, and got me to Bed, and Mrs. *Jewkes* order'd *Nan* to bathe my Shoulder, and Arm, and Ancle, with some old Rum warm'd; and they cut the Hair a little from the back Part of my Head, and wash'd that; for it was clotted with Blood, from a pretty long, but not deep Gash; and put a Family Plaister upon it; for if this Woman has any good Quality, it is, it seems, in a Readiness and Skill to manage in Cases, where sudden Misfortunes happen in a Family.

After this, I fell into a pretty sound and refreshing Sleep, and lay till Twelve o'Clock, tolerably easy, considering I was very feverish and aguishly inclin'd; and she took a good deal of Care to fit me to undergo more Trials, which I had hop'd would have been more happily ended: But Providence did not see fit.

She would make me rise about Twelve; but I was so weak, I could only sit up till the Bed was made, and went into it again; and was, as they said, delirious some Part of the Afternoon.

But having a tolerable Night on *Thursday*, I was a good deal better on *Friday*, and on *Saturday* got up, and eat[10] a little Spoon-meat,[11] and my Feverishness seem'd to be gone, and I was so pick'd up by Evening, that I begg'd her Indulgence in my Closet, to be left to myself; which she consented to, it being double-barr'd the Day before, and I assuring her that all my Contrivances, as she call'd them, were at an End. But first she made me tell her the whole Story of my Enterprize; which I did, very faithfully, knowing now that nothing could stand me in any stead, or contribute to my Safety and Escape: And she seem'd full of Wonder at my Resolution and Venturesomeness; but told me frankly, that I should have found a hard Matter to get quite off; for that she was provided with a Warrant from my Master, (who is a Justice of Peace in this County, as well as the other) to get me apprehended, if I *had* got away, on Suspicion of wronging him, let me have been where I would.

O how deep-laid are the Mischiefs designed to fall on my devoted Head!—Surely, surely, I cannot be worthy all this Contrivance!—This too well shews me the Truth of what was hinted to me formerly at the other House, that my Master swore he would *have* me! O preserve me, Heaven! from being his, in his own wicked Sense of the Adjuration!

I must add, that now this Woman sees me pick up so fast, she uses me worse, and has abridg'd me of Paper all but one Sheet, which I am to shew her written or unwritten on Demand, and has reduc'd me to one Pen; yet my hidden Stores stand me in stead. But she is more and more snappish and cross; and tauntingly calls me Mrs. *Williams,* and any thing that she thinks will vex me.

---

[10] A regular past tense, for the modern *ate*.   [11] "liquid food; nourishment taken with a spoon" (Johnson's *Dictionary*).

Philip Dormer Stanhope, Fourth Earl of Chesterfield

1694-1773

LETTERS

LETTER CXXII

London, June the 21st, O.S.[1] 1748.
Dear Boy,

Your very bad enunciation runs so much in my head, and gives me such real concern, that it will be the subject of this, and, I believe, of many more letters. I congratulate both you and myself, that I was informed of it (as I hope) in time to prevent it; and shall ever think myself, as hereafter you will, I am sure, think yourself, infinitely obliged to Sir Charles Williams,[2] for informing me of it. Good God! if this ungraceful and disagreeable manner of speaking had, either by your negligence or mine, become habitual to you, as in a couple of years more it would have been, what a figure would you have made in company, or in a public assembly? Who would have liked you in the one, or have attended to you in the other? Read what Cicero and Quintilian say of Enunciation, and see what a stress they lay upon the gracefulness of it; nay, Cicero goes further, and even maintains, that a good figure is necessary for an Orator; and, particularly, that he must not be *vastus;* that is, overgrown and clumsy. He shows by it, that he knew mankind well, and knew the powers of an agreeable figure and a graceful manner. Men, as well as women, are much oftener led by their hearts, than by their understandings. The way to the heart is, thorough the senses; please their eyes and their ears, and the work is half done. I have frequently known a man's fortune decided for ever by his first address. If it is pleasing, people are hurried involuntarily into a persuasion that he has a merit, which possibly he has not; as, on the other hand, if it is ungraceful, they are

---

Text from first edition, with a few minor corrections from the third, both published in 1774.

[1] Old Style, meaning the English calendar, as opposed to the calendar in use on the Continent, which was advanced eleven days.

[2] Envoy to the Court of Poland-Saxony at Dresden.

immediately prejudiced against him; and unwilling to allow him the merit which, it may be, he has. Nor is this sentiment so unjust and unreasonable as at first it may seem; for, if a man has parts,[3] he must know of what infinite consequence it is to him to have a graceful manner of speaking, and a genteel and pleasing address:[4] he will cultivate and improve them to the utmost. Your figure is a good one; you have no natural defect in the organs of speech; your address may be engaging, and your manner of speaking graceful, if you will; so that, if they are not so, neither I, nor the world, can ascribe it to any thing but your want of parts. What is the constant and just observation, as to all actors upon the stage? Is it not, that those who have the best sense always speak the best, though they may happen not to have the best voices? They will speak plainly, distinctly, and with the proper emphasis, be their voices ever so bad. Had Roscius spoken *quick, thick,* and *ungracefully,* I will answer for it, that Cicero would not have thought him worth the oration which he made in his favour. Words were given us to communicate our ideas by; and there must be something inconceivably absurd, in uttering them in such a manner, as that either people cannot understand them, or will not desire to understand them. I tell you, truly and sincerely, that I shall judge of your parts by your speaking gracefully or ungracefully. If you have parts, you will never be at rest till you have brought yourself to a habit of speaking most gracefully; for I aver, that it is in your power. You will desire Mr. Harte,[5] that you may read aloud to him, every day; and that he will interrupt and correct you, every time that you read too fast, do not observe the proper stops, or lay a wrong emphasis. You will take care to open your teeth when you speak; to articulate every word distinctly; and to beg of Mr.

Harte, Mr. Eliot,[6] or whomever you speak to, to remind, and stop you, if ever you fall into the rapid and unintelligible mutter. You will even read aloud to yourself, and tune your utterance to your own ear; and read at first much slower than you need to do, in order to correct yourself of that shameful trick of speaking faster than you ought. In short, you will make it your business, your study, and your pleasure, to speak well, if you think right. Therefore, what I have said in this, and in my last, is more than sufficient, if you have sense; and ten times more would not be sufficient, if you have not: so here I rest it.

Next to graceful speaking, a genteel carriage,[7] and a graceful manner of presenting yourself, are extremely necessary, for they are extremely engaging; and carelessness in these points is much more unpardonable, in a young fellow, than affectation. It shows an offensive indifference about pleasing. I am told by one here, who has seen you lately, that you are awkward in your motions, and negligent of your person: I am sorry for both; and so will you, when it will be too late, if you continue so some time longer. Awkwardness of carriage is very alienating; and a total negligence of dress, and air, is an impertinent insult upon custom and fashion. You remember Mr.———[8] very well, I am sure, and you must consequently remember his extreme awkwardness; which, I can assure you, has been a great clog to his parts and merit, that have, with much difficulty, but barely counterbalanced it at last. Many, to whom I have formerly commended him, have answered me, That they were sure he could not have parts, because he was so awkward; so much are people, as I observed to you before, taken by the eye. Women have great influence, as to a man's fashionable character; and an awkward man will never have their votes; which, by the

---

[3] "qualities; powers; faculties; or accomplishments" (Johnson's *Dictionary*).

[4] "manner of carrying one's self in company" (Bailey's *Dictionary*).

[5] The Rev. Walter Harte (1709–1774), tutor to young Stanhope.

[6] Edward Eliot (1727–1804), at the moment a companion of Stanhope.

[7] bearing.

[8] Not identified; Dobrée says, "Possibly Lyttleton."

way, are very numerous, and much oftener counted than weighed. You should therefore give some attention to your dress, and to the gracefulness of your motions. I believe, indeed, that you have no perfect model for either, at Leipsig, to form yourself upon; but, however, do not get a habit of neglecting either: and attend properly to both, when you go to Courts; where they are very necessary, and where you will have good masters, and good models for both. Your exercises of riding, fencing, and dancing, will civilize and fashion your body and your limbs, and give you, if you will but take it, *l'air d'un honnête homme.*[9]

I will now conclude, with suggesting one reflection to you; which is, that you should be sensible[10] of your good fortune, in having one who interests himself enough in you, to inquire into your faults, in order to inform you of them. Nobody but myself would be so solicitous, either to know or correct them; so that you might consequently be ignorant of them yourself; for our own self-love draws a thick veil between us and our faults. But when you hear yours from me, you may be sure that you hear them from one, who, for your sake only, desires to correct them; from one whom you cannot suspect of any partiality but in your favour; and from one who heartily wishes that his care of you, as a Father, may, in a little time, render every care unnecessary but that of a Friend.

Adieu.

P.S. I condole with you for the untimely and violent death of the tuneful Matzel.[11]

LETTER CXXIX

London, September the 5th, O.S., 1748.

Dear Boy,

I have received yours, with the enclosed German letter to Mr. Grevenkop,[12] which he assures me is extremely well written, considering the little time that you have applied yourself to that language. As you have now got over the most difficult part, pray go on diligently, and make yourself absolutely master of the rest. Whoever does not entirely possess a language, will never appear to advantage, or even equal to himself, either in speaking or writing it. His ideas are fettered, and seem imperfect or confused, if he is not master of all the words and phrases necessary to express them. I therefore desire, that you will not fail writing a German letter, once every fortnight, to Mr. Grevenkop; which will make the writing of that language familiar to you: and, moreover, when you shall have left Germany, and be arrived at Turin, I shall require you to write even to me in German; that you may not forget, with ease, what you have with difficulty learned. I likewise desire, that, while you are in Germany, you will take all opportunities of conversing in German, which is the only way of knowing that, or any other language, accurately. You will also desire your German master to teach you the proper titles and superscriptions to be used to people of all ranks; which is a point so material, in Germany, that I have known many a letter returned unopened, because one title in twenty has been omitted in the direction.

St. Thomas's day now draws near, when you are to leave Saxony and go to Berlin; and I take it for granted, that, if any thing is yet wanting, to complete your knowledge of the state of that Electorate, you will not fail to procure it before you go away. I do not mean, as you will easily believe, the number of churches, parishes, or towns; but I mean the constitution, the revenues, the troops, and the trade of that Electorate. A few questions, sensibly asked, of sensible

---

[9] "the appearance of a gentleman."
[10] aware.
[11] A bullfinch which had belonged to Sir Charles Williams.
[12] Gaspar Grevenkop, Chesterfield's secretary.

people, will procure you the necessary informations; which I desire you will enter in your little book. Berlin will be entirely a new scene to you, and I look upon it, in a manner, as your first step into the great world: take care that step be not a false one, and that you do not stumble at the threshold. You will there be in more company than you have yet been; Manners and Attentions will therefore be more necessary. Pleasing in company, is the only way of being pleased in it yourself. Sense and Knowledge are the first and necessary foundations for pleasing in company; but they will by no means do alone, and they will never be perfectly welcome, if they are not accompanied with Manners and Attentions. You will best acquire these by frequenting the companies of people of fashion; but then you must resolve to acquire them, in those companies, by proper care and observation; for I have known people, who, though they have frequented good company all their lifetime, have done it in so inattentive and unobserving a manner, as to be never the better for it, and to remain as disagreeable, as awkward, and as vulgar, as if they had never seen any person of fashion. When you go into good company (by good company is meant the people of the first fashion of the place) observe carefully their turn,[13] their manners, their address; and conform your own to them. But this is not all neither: go deeper still; observe their characters, and pry, as far as you can, into both their hearts and their heads. Seek for their particular merit, their predominant passion, or their prevailing weakness; and you will then know what to bait your hook with, to catch them. Man is a composition of so many, and such various ingredients, that it requires both time and care to analyse him: for though we have, all, the same ingredients in our general composition, as Reason, Will, Passions, and Appetites; yet the different proportions and combinations of them, in each individual, produce that infinite variety of characters, which, in some particular or other, distinguishes every individual from another. Reason ought to direct the whole, but seldom does. And he who addresses himself singly to another man's reason, without endeavouring to engage his heart in his interest also, is no more likely to succeed, than a man who should apply only to a King's nominal Minister, and neglect his Favourite. I will recommend to your attentive perusal, now that you are going into the world, two books, which will let you as much into the characters of men, as books can do. I mean, *Les Réflexions Morales de Monsieur de la Rochefoucault,* and *Les Caractères de La Bruyère:*[14] but remember, at the same time, that I only recommend them to you as the best general maps, to assist you in your journey, and not as marking out every particular turning and winding that you will meet with. There, your own sagacity and observation must come to their aid. La Rochefoucault is, I know, blamed, but I think without reason, for deriving all our actions from the source of self-love. For my own part, I see a great deal of truth, and no harm at all, in that opinion. It is certain, that we seek our own happiness in every thing we do; and it is as certain, that we can only find it in doing well, and in conforming all our actions to the rule of right reason, which is the great law of Nature. It is only a mistaken self-love that is a blameable motive, when we take the immediate and indiscriminate gratification of a passion, or appetite, for real happiness. But am I blameable, if I do a good action, upon account of the happiness which that honest consciousness will give me? Surely not. On the contrary, that pleasing consciousness is a proof of my virtue. The reflection, which is the most censured in Monsieur de la Rochefoucault's book, as a very ill-natured one, is this; *On trouve dans le malheur de son meilleur ami, quelque chose qui ne déplait pas.*[15] And why not? Why may I not feel a very tender and real concern

---

[13] "form, cast, shape, manner" (Johnson's *Dictionary*).

[14] François de La Rochefoucauld, *Réflexions ou sentences et Maximes morales* (1665);

Jean de La Bruyère, *Les Caractères* (1688).

[15] "One finds in the misfortune of one's best friend something not unpleasing."

for the misfortune of my friend, and yet at the same time feel a pleasing consciousness at having discharged my duty to him, by comforting and assisting him to the utmost of my power in that misfortune? Give me but virtuous actions, and I will not quibble and chicane[16] about the motives. And I will give any body their choice of these two truths, which amount to the same thing: He, who loves himself best, is the honestest man; or, The honestest man loves himself best.

The characters of La Bruyere are pictures from the life; most of them finely drawn, and highly coloured. Furnish your mind with them first; and when you meet with their likeness, as you will every day, they will strike you the more. You will compare every feature with the original; and both will reciprocally help you to discover the beauties and the blemishes.

As women are a considerable, or at least a pretty numerous part of company; and as their suffrages go a great way toward establishing a man's character, in the fashionable part of the world (which is of great importance to the fortune and figure he proposes to make in it) it is necessary to please them. I will therefore, upon this subject, let you into certain *Arcana*,[17] that will be very useful for you to know, but which you must, with the utmost care, conceal; and never seem to know. Women, then, are only children of a larger growth; they have an entertaining tattle, and sometimes wit; but for solid, reasoning good sense, I never in my life knew one that had it, or who reasoned or acted consequentially for four-and-twenty hours together. Some little passion or humour always breaks in upon their best resolutions. Their beauty neglected, or controverted, their age increased, or their supposed understandings depreciated, instantly kindles their little passions, and overturns any system of consequential conduct, that, in their most reasonable moments, they might have been capable

of forming. A man of sense only trifles with them, plays with them, humours and flatters them, as he does with a sprightly, forward child; but he neither consults them about, nor trusts them with, serious matters; though he often makes them believe that he does both; which is the thing in the world that they are proud of; for they love mightily to be dabbling in business (which, by the way, they always spoil;) and being justly distrustful, that men in general look upon them in a trifling light, they almost adore that man, who talks more seriously to them, and who seems to consult and trust them: I say, who seems; for weak men really do, but wise ones only seem to do it. No flattery is either too high or too low for them. They will greedily swallow the highest, and gratefully accept of the lowest; and you may safely flatter any woman, from her understanding, down to the exquisite taste of her fan. Women, who are either indisputably beautiful, or indisputably ugly, are best flattered upon the score of their understandings: but those who are in a state of mediocrity, are best flattered upon their beauty, or at least their graces; for every woman, who is not absolutely ugly, thinks herself handsome; but not hearing often that she is so, is the more grateful, and the more obliged to the few who tell her so: whereas a decided and conscious beauty looks upon every tribute, paid to her beauty, only as her due; but wants to shine, and to be considered on the side of her understanding: and a woman, who is ugly enough to know that she is so, knows that she has nothing left for it but her understanding, which is, consequently, (and probably in more senses than one) her weak side. But these are secrets, which you must keep inviolably, if you would not, like Orpheus, be torn to pieces by the whole sex:[18] on the contrary, a man, who thinks of living in the great world, must be gallant, polite, and attentive to please the women. They have, from the weakness of men, more or less influence in all Courts: they abso-

16 Avoid the issue by using trickery.
17 secrets.
18 In Greek legend, Orpheus stole into the intimate confidences of women and was destroyed to prevent his betraying their secrets.

lutely stamp every man's character in the *beau monde,* and make it either current, or cry it down, and stop it in payments. It is, therefore, absolutely necessary to manage, please, and flatter them; and never to discover the least marks of contempt, which is what they never forgive: but in this they are not singular, for it is the same with men; who will much sooner forgive an injustice than an insult. Every man is not ambitious, or covetous, or passionate; but every man has pride enough in his composition to feel and resent the least slight and contempt. Remember, therefore, most carefully to conceal your contempt, however just, wherever you would not make an implacable enemy. Men are much more unwilling to have their weaknesses and their imperfections known, than their crimes; and, if you hint to a man, that you think him silly, ignorant, or even ill-bred, or awkward, he will hate you more, and longer, than if you tell him, plainly, that you think him a rogue. Never yield to that temptation, which, to most young men, is very strong, of exposing other people's weaknesses and infirmities, for the sake either of diverting the company, or of showing your own superiority. You may get the laugh on your side by it, for the present; but you will make enemies by it for ever; and even those who laugh with you then, will, upon reflection, fear, and consequently hate you: besides that, it is ill-natured; and that a good heart desires rather to conceal, than expose, other people's weaknesses or misfortunes. If you have wit, use it to please, and not to hurt: you may shine, like the sun in the temperate zones, without scorching. Here it is wished for; under the Line[19] it is dreaded.

These are some of the hints, which my long experience in the great world enables me to give you; and which, if you attend to them, may prove useful to you in your journey through it. I wish it may be a prosperous one; at least, I am sure that it must be your own fault if it is not.

Make my compliments to Mr. Harte, who, I am very sorry to hear, is not well. I hope by this time he is recovered.

Adieu.

---

[19] i.e., the Tropic of Cancer, 22.5° N latitude.

Tobias Smollett
1721-1771

From THE ADVENTURES OF
RODERICK RANDOM

CHAPTER XXVII. [THE PRACTICE OF MEDICINE ABOARD SHIP]

I acquire the friendship of the surgeon, who procures a warrant[1] for me, and makes me a present of cloathes—a battle between a midshipman and me—the surgeon leaves the ship—the captain comes on board with another surgeon—a dialogue between the captain and Morgan[2]—the sick are ordered to be brought upon the quarter-deck and examined—the consequences of that order—a madman accuses Morgan, and is set at liberty by command of the captain, whom he instantly attacks and pummels without mercy.

While I was busied with my friend in this practice,[3] the doctor chanced to pass by the place where we were, and stopping to observe me, appeared very well satisfied with my method of application; and afterwards sent for me to his cabbin, where, having examined me touching my skill in surgery, and the particulars of my fortune, interested himself so far in my behalf, as to promise his assistance in procuring a warrant for me, seeing I had been already found qualified at Surgeon's hall, for the station I now filled on board; and this he the more cordially engaged in, when he understood I was nephew to lieutenant Bowling, for whom he expressed a particular regard.— In the mean time, I could learn from his discourse, that he did not intend to go to sea again with captain Oakhum, having, as he thought, been indifferently used by him during the last voyage.

While I lived tollerably easy, in expectation of preferment, I was not altogether without mortifications, which I not only suffered from the rude insults of the sailors, and petty officers, among whom I was known by the name of *Loblolly Boy;*[4] but also from the disposition of Morgan, who, though friendly in the main, was often very troublesome with his pride, which expected a good deal of submission from me, and delighted in recapitulating the favours I had received at his hands.

About six weeks after my arrival on board, the surgeon bidding me follow him into his cabbin, presented a warrant

---

Text from the first edition, 1748.

[1] A license to practice aboard ship.

[2] First mate of *The Thunder,* the ship on which the present action takes place.

[3] Roderick, who is telling his own story, has newly come aboard and through the intervention of Mr. William Thomson, the second mate, has been employed as assistant to the ship's surgeon.

[4] A derisive allusion to the Scottish origins of Roderick; loblolly was boiled oatmeal.

to me, by which I was appointed surgeon's third mate on board the Thunder.—This he had procured by his interest at the Navy-office; as also another for himself, by virtue of which he was removed into a second rate. I acknowledged his kindness in the strongest terms my gratitude could suggest, and professed my sorrow at the prospect of losing such a valuable friend, to whom I hoped to have recommended myself still further, by my respectful and diligent behaviour.—But his generosity rested not here;—for, before he left the ship, he made me a present of a chest and some cloaths, that enabled me to support the rank to which he had raised me.—I found my spirit revive with my good fortune; and now I was an officer, resolved to maintain the dignity of my station, against all opposition or affronts; nor was it long before I had occasion to exert my resolution; my old enemy the midshipman (whose name was Crampley) entertaining an implacable animosity against me, for the disgrace he had suffered on my account,[5] had since that time taken all opportunities of reviling and ridiculing me, when I was not intitled to retort his bad usage.—And even after I had been rated on the books, and mustered as surgeon's mate, did not think fit to restrain his insolence.—In particular, being one day present, while I dressed a wound in a sailor's leg, he began to sing a song, which I thought highly injurious to the honour of my country, and therefore signified my resentment, by observing, that the Scots always laid their account in finding enemies among the ignorant, insignificant and malicious.[6]—This unexpected piece of assurance enraged him to such a degree, that he lent me a blow on the face, which I verily thought had demolished my cheekbone; I was not slow in returning the obligation, and the affair began to be very serious, when by accident Mr. Morgan, and one of the master's mates, coming

that way, interposed, and inquiring into the cause, endeavoured to promote a reconciliation; but finding us both exasperated to the uttermost, and bent against accommodation, they advised us, either to leave our difference undecided till we should have an opportunity of terminating it on shore, like gentlemen, or else chuse a proper place on board, and bring it to an issue by boxing. This last expedient was greedily embraced; and being forthwith conducted to the ground proposed, we stript in a moment, and began a very furious contest, in which I soon found myself inferior to my antagonist, not so much in strength and agility, as in skill, which he had acquired in the school at Hockley in the Hole and Tottenham-Court.[7]—Many cross-buttocks did I sustain, and pegs on the stomach without number, till at last, my breath being quite gone, as well as my vigour wasted, I grew desperate, and collecting all my spirits in one effort, threw in at once head, hands, and feet with such violence, that I drove my antagonist three paces backward into the main hatch-way, down which he fell, and pitching upon his head and right shoulder, remained without sense and motion.—Morgan looking down, and seeing him lie in that condition, cried, "Up on my conscience, as I am a Christian sinner (look you) I believe his pattles are all ofer; but I take you all to witness that there was no treachery in the case, and that he has suffered by the chance of war."—So saying, he descended to the deck below, to examine into the situation of my adversary; and left me very little pleased with my victory, as I found myself not only terribly bruised, but likewise in danger of being called to account for the death of Crampley: But this fear vanished when my fellow-mate, having by bleeding him in the jugular, brought him to himself, and assured himself of the state of his body, called up to me, to be under no con-

---

[5] On being taken forcibly aboard *The Thunder* by a press gang, Roderick had appealed in vain to the mercies of the midshipman who now found himself in an inferior position to Roderick.

[6] i.e., settled their score by picking on those they knew they could beat.

[7] Tough areas of London.

cern, for the midshipman had received no other damage than as pretty a luxation[8] of the *os humeri,* as one would desire to see on a summer's day.—Upon this information, I crawled down to the cockpit, and acquainted Thomson[9] with the affair, who, providing himself with bandages, &c. necessary for the occasion, went up to assist Mr. Morgan in the reduction of the dislocation.—When this was successfully performed, they wished me joy of the event of the combat; and the Welchman,[10] after observing, that in all likelihood, the ancient Scots and Britons were the same people, bid me "Praise Cot for putting mettle in my pelly, and strength in my limbs to support it."—I acquired such reputation by this recounter (which lasted twenty minutes) that every body became more cautious of his behaviour towards me; though Crampley with his arm in a sling, talked very high, and threatened to seize the first opportunity of retrieving on shore, the honour he had lost by an accident, from which I could justly claim no merit.

About this time, captain Oakhum, having received sailing orders, came on board, and brought along with him a surgeon of his own country, who soon made us sensible of the loss we suffered in the departure of doctor Atkins; being grossly ignorant, and intolerably assuming, false, vindictive, and unforgiving; a merciless tyrant to his inferiors, an abject sycophant to those above him. In the morning after the captain came on board, our first mate, according to custom, went to wait on him with a sick list, which when this grim commander had perused, he cried with a stern countenance, "Blood and oons! sixty-one sick people on board of my ship!—Harkee you, sir, I'll have no sick in my ship, by G—d." The Welchman replied, he should be very glad to find no sick people

on board; but while it was otherwise, he did no more than his duty in presenting him with a list.—"You and your list may be d——n'd, (said the captain, throwing it at him) I say, there shall be no sick in this ship while I have the command of her."—Mr. Morgan being nettled at this treatment, told him, his indignation ought to be directed to Got Almighty, who visited his people with distempers, and not to him, who contributed all in his power towards their cure. The Bashaw[11] not being used to such behaviour in any of his officers, was enraged to fury at this satirical insinuation, and stamping with his foot, called him insolent scoundrel, threatening to have him pinioned to the deck, if he should presume to utter another syllable. But the blood of Caractacus[12] being thoroughly heated, disdained to be restricted by such a command, and began to manifest itself in, "Captain Oakoum, I am a shentleman of birth and parentage (look you) and peradventure, I am moreover——." Here his harrangue was broke off by the captain's steward, who being Morgan's countryman, hurried him out of the cabbin before he had time to exasperate his master to a greater degree, which would certainly have been the case; for the indignant Welchman, could hardly be hindered by his friend's arguments and intreaties, from re-entering the presence chamber, and defying captain Oakhum to his teeth.—He was, however, appeased at length, and came down to the birth,[13] where finding Thomson and me at work preparing medicines, he bid us leave off our lapour and go to play, for the captain, by his sole word and power and command, had driven sickness a pegging to the tevil, and there was no more malady on poard. So saying, he drank off a gill of brandy, sighed grievously three times, poured forth an ejaculation of "Got pless my

---

[8] "the act of disjointing; any thing disjointed" (Johnson's *Dictionary*); the *os humeri* is the upper arm. Put in simple terms, Crampley suffered a dislocated shoulder.

[9] Second mate to the captain of *The Thunder;* see note 3 above.

[10] Morgan, the first mate.

[11] i.e. Turkish tyrant.

[12] Morgan proudly traced his pedigree back to Caractacus, Welsh king of the Britons (first century A.D.).

[13] berth.

heart, liver, and lungs!" and then began to sing a Welch song with great earnestness of visage, voice and gesture.—I could not conceive the meaning of this singular phænomenon, and saw by the looks of Thomson, who at the same time, shook his head, that he suspected poor Cadwallader's[14] brains were unsettled. He perceiving our amazement, told us, he would explain the mystery; but at the same time, bid us take notice, that he had lived poy, patchelor, married man and widower, almost forty years, and in all that time, there was no man nor mother's son in the whole world, who durst use him so ill as captain Oakhum had done. Then he acquainted us with the dialogue that passed between them, as I have already related it; and had no sooner finished this narration, than he received a message from the surgeon, to bring the sick-list to the quarter-deck, for the captain had ordered all the patients thither to be reviewed.—This inhuman order shocked us extremely, as we knew it would be impossible to carry some of them on the deck, without imminent danger of their lives; but as we likewise knew it would be to no purpose for us to remonstrate against it, we repaired to the quarter-deck in a body, to see this extraordinary muster; Morgan observing by the way, that the captain was going to send to the other world, a great many evidences to testify against himself.—When we appeared upon deck, the captain bid the doctor, who stood bowing at his right hand, look at these lazy, lubberly sons of bitches, who were good for nothing on board, but to eat the king's provision, and encourage idleness in the skulkers.—The surgeon grinned approbation, and taking the list, began to examine the complaints of each as they could crawl to the place appointed.— The first who came under his cognizance, was a poor fellow just freed of a fever, which had weakened him so much, that he could hardly stand.—Mr. Mack-

shane (for that was the doctor's name) having felt his pulse, protested he was as well as any man in the world; and the captain delivered him over to the boatswain's mate, with orders that he should receive a round dozen at the gangway immediately, for counterfeiting himself sick when he was not;—but before the discipline could be executed, the man dropt down on the deck, and had well nigh perished under the hands of the executioner.—The next patient to be considered, laboured under a quartan ague,[15] and being then, in his interval of health, discovered no other symptoms of distemper, than a pale meagre countenance, and emaciated body; upon which, he was declared fit for duty, and turned over to the boatswain;—but being resolved to disgrace the doctor, died upon the forecastle next day, during his cold fit.—The third complained of a pleuretic stitch,[16] and spitting of blood, for which doctor Mackshane prescribed exercise at the pump to promote expectoration; but whether this was improper for one in his situation, or that it was used to excess, I know not, but in less than half an hour, he was suffocated with a deluge of blood that issued from his lungs.—A fourth, with much difficulty climbed to the quarter-deck, being loaded with a monstrous ascites[17] or dropsy, that invaded his chest so much, he could scarce fetch his breath; but his disease being interpreted into fat, occasioned by idleness and excess of eating, he was ordered, with a view to promote perspiration and enlarge his chest, to go aloft immediately: It was in vain for this unwieldy wretch, to alledge his utter incapacity, the boatswain's driver was commanded to whip him up with a cat and nine tails: The smart of this application made him exert himself so much, that he actually arrived at the foot-hook-shrouds,[18] but when the enormous weight of his body had nothing else to support it than his weakened arms, either out of

---

[14] Ancient fighting king of Wales (seventh century) who had spirit but not enough strength to prevail over the enemy.

[15] an intermittent fever, recurring every fourth day.

[16] A painful inflammation of the membrane covering the lung.

[17] An abdominal swelling.

[18] principal ropes supporting the masts, fastened into the ship's timbers.

spite or necessity, he quitted his hold, and plumped into the sea, where he must have been drowned, had not a sailor who was in a boat along-side, saved his life, by keeping him afloat, till he was hoisted on board by a tackle.—It would be tedious and disagreeable to describe the fate of every miserable object that suffered by the inhumanity and ignorance of the captain and surgeon, who so wantonly sacrificed the lives of their fellow-creatures. Many were brought up in the height of fevers, and rendered delirious by the injuries they suffered in the way.—Some gave up the ghost in the presence of their inspectors; and others, who were ordered to their duty, languished a few days at work, among their fellows, and then departed without any ceremony.—On the whole, the number of sick was reduced to less than a dozen; and the authors of this reduction were applauding themselves for the service they had done to their king and country, when the boatswain's mate informed his honour, that there was a man below lashed to his hammock by the direction of the doctor's mate, and that he begged hard to be released; affirming, he had been so maltreated only for a grudge Mr. Morgan bore to him, and that he was as much in his senses as any man aboard.—The captain hearing this, darted a severe look at the Welchman, and ordered the man to be brought up immediately: Upon which, Morgan protested with great fervency, that the person in question was as mad as a March-hare; and begged for the love of Got, they would at least keep his arms pinioned during his examination, to prevent him from doing mischief.—This request the commander granted for his own sake, and the patient was produced, who insisted upon his being in his right wits with such calmness and strength of argument, that every body present was in-

clined to believe him, except Morgan, who affirmed there was no trusting to appearances; for he himself had been so much imposed upon by his behaviour two days before, that he had actually unbound him with his own hands, and had well nigh been murdered for his pains: this was confirmed by the evidence of one of the waiters, who declared, he had pulled this patient from the doctor's mate, whom he had gotten down and almost strangled.—To this the man answered, that the witness was a creature of Morgan's, and was suborned to give his testimony against him by the malice of the mate, whom the defendant had affronted, by discovering[19] to the people on board, that Mr. Morgan's wife kept a gin-shop in Rag-Fair.—This anecdote produced a laugh at the expence of the Welchman, who shaking his head with some emotion, said, "Ay, ay, 'tis no matter.—Got knows, 'tis an arrant falshood."—Captain Oakhum, without any further hesitation, ordered the fellow to be unfettered; at the same time, threatening to make Morgan exchange situations with him for his spite; but the Briton no sooner heard the decision in favour of the madman, than he got up the mizzen-shrouds, crying to Thomson and me to get out of his reach, for we should see him play the tevil with a vengeance. We did not think fit to disregard this caution, and accordingly got up on the poop, whence we behold the maniac (as soon as he was released) fly at the captain like a fury, crying, "I'll let you know, you scoundrel, that I am commander of this vessel"—and pummel him without mercy. The surgeon, who went to the assistance of his patron, shared the same fate; and it was with the utmost difficulty, that he was mastered at last, after having done great execution among those who opposed him.

---

[19] disclosing.

From TRAVELS THROUGH FRANCE AND ITALY

LETTER XXXVIII   [CROSSING THE ALPS]

TO DR. S——[20] AT NICE

Turin, *March 18, 1765.*

Dear Sir,

I am just returned[21] from an excursion to Turin, which is about thirty leagues from hence,[22] the greater part of the way lying over frightful mountains covered with snow. The difficulty of the road, however, reaches no farther than Coni, from whence there is an open highway through a fine plain country, as far as the capital of Piedmont,[23] and the traveller is accommodated with chaise and horses to proceed either post, or by cambiatura,[24] as in other parts of Italy. There are only two ways of performing the journey over the mountains from Nice; one is to ride a mule-back, and the other to be carried in a chair. The former I chose, and set out with my servant on the seventh day of February at two in the afternoon. I was hardly clear of Nice, when it began to rain so hard that in less than an hour the mud was half a foot deep in many parts of the road. This was the only inconvenience we suffered, the way being in other respects practicable enough; for there is but one small hill to cross on this side of the village of L'Escarene, where we arrived about six in the evening. The ground in this neighbourhood is tolerably cultivated, and the mountains are planted to the tops with olive trees. The accommodation here is so very bad, that I had no inclination to be a bed longer than was absolutely necessary for refreshment; and therefore I proceeded on my journey at two in the morning, conducted by a guide, whom I hired for this purpose at the rate of three livres[25] a day. Having ascended one side, and descended the other, of the mountain called Braus, which took up four hours, though the road is not bad, we at six reached the village of Sospello, which is agreeably situated in a small valley, surrounded by prodigious high and barren mountains. This little plain is pretty fertile, and being watered by a pleasant stream, forms a delightful contrast with the hideous rocks that surround it. Having reposed myself and my mules two hours at this place, we continued our journey over the second mountain, called Brovis, which is rather more considerable than the first, and in four hours arrived at La Giandola, a tolerable inn situated betwixt the high road and a small river, about a gun-shot from the town of Brieglie, which we leave on the right. As we jogged along in the grey of the morning, I was a little startled at two figures which I saw before me, and began to put my pistols in order. It must be observed that these mountains are infested with *contrabandiers,* a set of smuggling peasants, very bold and desperate, who make a traffic of selling tobacco, salt, and other

---

Text from first edition, 1766.

[20] Smollett relates the *Travels* in the form of letters to recipients, for the most part, as in this instance, unidentified, and possibly not intended to imply real persons.

[21] arrived.

[22] i.e., from Nice.

[23] Turin.

[24] Two methods of paying for a trip, according to whether one paid each time the horses were changed (post) or for the completed trip (cambiatura).

[25] "At present, the French crown is but equal to 27 d. ½ sterling on which footing the *livre* is but equivalent to 10 d. ½ sterling" (Chambers' *Cyclopaedia,* 1752); thus, three French livres would be 2s. 7½d. sterling. This rate of exchange is further borne out by Smollett's later mention in this letter to "forty sols . . . [as] nearly equal to two shillings sterling."

merchandise, which have not payed duty, and sometimes lay travellers under contribution.[26] I did not doubt but there was a gang of these free-booters at hand; but as no more than two persons appeared, I resolved to let them know we were prepared for defence, and fired one of my pistols, in hope that the report of it, echoed from the surrounding rocks, would produce a proper effect: but, the mountains and roads being entirely covered with snow to a considerable depth, there was little or no reverberation, and the sound was not louder than that of a pop-gun, although the piece contained a good charge of powder. Nevertheless, it did not fail to engage the attention of the strangers, one of whom immediately wheeled to the left about, and being by this time very near me, gave me an opportunity of contemplating his whole person. He was very tall, meagre, and yellow, with a long hooked nose, and small twinkling eyes. His head was cased in a woollen night-cap, over which he wore a flapped hat; he had a silk handkerchief about his neck, and his mouth was furnished with a short wooden pipe, from which he discharged wreathing clouds of tobacco-smoke. He was wrapped in a kind of capot of green bays,[27] lined with wolf-skin, had a pair of monstrous boots, quilted on the inside with cotton, was almost covered with dirt, and rode a mule so low that his long legs hung dangling within six inches of the ground. This grotesque figure was so much more ludicrous than terrible, that I could not help laughing; when taking his pipe out of his mouth, he very politely accosted me by name. You may easily guess I was exceedingly surprised at such an address on the top of the mountain Brovis: but he forthwith put an end to it, by discovering himself to be the marquis M. whom I had the honour to be acquainted with at Nice. After having rallied him upon his equipage, he gave me to understand he had set out from Nice the morning of the same day that I departed; that he

was going to Turin, and that he had sent one of his servants before him to Coni with his baggage. Knowing him to be an agreeable companion, I was glad of this encounter, and we resolved to travel the rest of the way together. We dined at La Giandola, and in the afternoon rode along the little river Roida, which runs in a bottom between frightful precipices, and in several places forms natural cascades, the noise of which had well-nigh deprived us of the sense of hearing; after a winding course among these mountains, it discharges itself into the Mediterranean at Vintimiglia, in the territory of Genoa. As the snow did not lie on these mountains, when we cracked our whips, there was such a repercussion of the sound as is altogether inconceivable. We passed by the village of Saorgio, situated on an eminence, where there is a small fortress which commands the whole pass, and in five hours arrived at our inn, on this side the Col de Tende, where we took up our quarters, but had very little reason to boast of our entertainment. Our greatest difficulty, however, consisted in pulling off the marquis's boots, which were of the kind called Seafarot, by this time so loaded with dirt on the outside, and so swelled with the rain within, that he could neither drag them after him as he walked, nor disencumber his legs of them, without such violence as seemed almost sufficient to tear him limb from limb. In a word, we were obliged to tie a rope about his heel, and all the people in the house assisting to pull, the poor marquis was drawn from one end of the apartment to the other before the boot would give way: at last his legs were happily disengaged, and the machines carefully dried and stuffed for next day's journey.

We took our departure from hence at three in the morning, and at four, began to mount the Col de Tende, which is by far the highest mountain[28] in the whole journey: it was now quite covered with snow, which at the top of it was near

---

[26] demand payment for free passage.
[27] A long coat of beige (bays), that is, unbleached wool.

[28] The Col di Tenda is slightly over 6000 feet above sea level.

twenty feet thick. Half way up, there are quarters for a detachment of soldiers, posted here to prevent smuggling, and an inn called La Ca, which in the language of the country signifies the house. At this place, we hired six men to assist us in ascending the mountain, each of them provided with a kind of hough to break the ice, and make a sort of steps for the mules. When we were near the top, however, we were obliged to alight, and climb the mountain, supported each by two of those men, called Coulants, who walk upon the snow with great firmness and security. We were followed by the mules, and though they are very sure footed animals, and were frost-shod for the occasion, they stumbled and fell very often; the ice being so hard that the sharp headed nails in their shoes could not penetrate. Having reached the top of this mountain, from whence there is no prospect but of other rocks and mountains, we prepared for descending on the other side by the Leze, which is an occasional sledge made of two pieces of wood, carried up by the Coulants for this purpose. I did not much relish this kind of carriage, especially as the mountain was very steep, and covered with such a thick fog that we could hardly see two or three yards before us. Nevertheless, our guides were so confident, and my companion, who had passed the same way on other occasions, was so secure, that I ventured to place myself on this machine, one of the coulants standing behind me, and the other sitting before, as the conductor, with his feet paddling among the snow, in order to moderate the velocity of its descent. Thus accommodated, we descended the mountain with such rapidity, that in an hour we reached Limon, which is the native place of almost all the muleteers who transport merchandise from Nice to Coni and Turin. Here we waited full two hours for the mules, which travelled with the servants by the common road. To each of the coulants we paid forty sols, which are nearly equal to two shillings sterling. Leaving Limon, we were in two hours quite disengaged from the gorges of the mountains, which are partly covered with wood and pasturage, though altogether inaccessible, except in summer; but from the foot of the Col de Tende, the road lies through a plain all the way to Turin. We took six hours to travel from the inn where we had lodged over the mountain to Limon, and five hours from thence to Coni. Here we found our baggage, which we had sent off by the carriers one day before we departed from Nice; and here we dismissed our guides, together with the mules. In winter, you have a mule for this whole journey at the rate of twenty livres; and the guides are payed at the rate of two livres a day, reckoning six days, three for the journey to Coni, and three for their return to Nice. We set out so early in the morning in order to avoid the inconveniencies and dangers that attend the passage of this mountain. The first of these arises from your meeting with long strings of loaded mules in a slippery road, the breadth of which does not exceed a foot and an half. As it is altogether impossible for two mules to pass each other in such a narrow path, the muleteers have made doublings or elbows in different parts, and when the troops of mules meet, the least numerous is obliged to turn off into one of these doublings, and there halt until the others are past. Travellers in order to avoid this disagreeable delay, which is the more vexatious, considering the excessive cold, begin the ascent of the mountain early in the morning before the mules quit their inns. But the great danger of travelling here when the sun is up, proceeds from what they call the Valanches.[29] These are balls of snow detached from the mountains which over top the road, either by the heat of the sun, or the humidity of the weather. A piece of snow thus loosened from the rock, though perhaps not above three or four feet in diameter, increases sometimes in its descent to such a degree, as to become two hundred paces in length, and rolls down with such rapidity, that the traveller is crushed to death before he can make three steps on the road. These dreadful heaps drag every thing along with them in their descent. They tear up huge trees by the roots, and if they

---

[29] avalanches.

chance to fall upon a house, demolish it to the foundation. Accidents of this nature seldom happen in the winter while the weather is dry; and yet scarce a year passes in which some mules and their drivers do not perish by the valanches. At Coni we found the countess C————[30] from Nice, who had made the same journey in a chair, carried by porters. This is no other than a common elbow-chair of wood, with a straw bottom, covered above with waxed cloth, to protect the traveller from the rain or snow, and provided with a footboard upon which the feet rest. It is carried like a sedan-chair; and for this purpose six or eight porters are employed at the rate of three or four livres a head per day, according to the season, allowing three days for their return. Of these six men, two are between the poles carrying like common chairmen, and each of these is supported by the other two, one at each hand: but as those in the middle sustain the greatest burthen, they are relieved by the others in a regular rotation. In descending the mountain, they carry the poles on their shoulders, and in that case, four men are employed, one at each end.

At Coni, you may have a chaise to go with the same horses to Turin, for which you pay fifteen livres, and are a day and a half on the way. You may post it, however, in one day, and then the price is seven livres ten sols per post,[31] and ten sols to the postilion.[32] The method we took was that of cambiatura. This is a chaise with horses shifted at the same stages that are used in posting: but as it is supposed to move slower, we pay but five livres per post, and ten sols to the postilion. In order to quicken its pace, we gave ten sols extraordinary to each postilion, and for this gratification, he drove us even faster than the post. The chaises are like those of Italy, and will take on near two hundred weight of baggage.

Coni is situated between two small streams, and though neither very large nor populous, is considerable for the strength of its fortifications. It is honoured with the title of the Maiden-Fortress, because though several times besieged, it was never taken. The prince of Conti invested it in the war of 1744; but he was obliged to raise the siege, after having given battle to the king of Sardinia. The place was gallantly defended by the baron Leutrum, a German protestant, the best general in the Sardinian service: but what contributed most to the miscarriage of the enemy, was a long tract of heavy rains, which destroyed all their works, and rendered their advances impracticable.

I need not tell you that Piedmont is one of the most fertile and agreeable countries in Europe, and this the most agreeable part of Piedmont, though it now appeared to disadvantage from the rigorous season of the year: I shall only observe that we passed through Sabellian, which is a considerable town, and arrived in the evening at Turin. We entered this fine city by the gate of Nice, and passing through the elegant Piazza di San Carlo, took up our quarters at the Bona Fama, which stands at one corner of the great square, called La Piazza Castel.

Were I even disposed to give a description of Turin, I should be obliged to postpone it till another opportunity, having no room at present to say any thing more, but that I am always

Yours.

---

[30] Unidentified.
[31] Place where the horses are changed.
[32] guide.

Henry Fielding
1707-1754

From TOM JONES, the History of a Foundling

An Apology for all Heroes who have good Stomachs, with a Description of a Battle of the amorous Kind.

[BOOK IX] CHAPTER V

Heroes, notwithstanding the high Ideas, which by the Means of Flatterers they may entertain of themselves, or the World may conceive of them, have certainly more of mortal than divine about them. However elevated their Minds may be, their Bodies at least (which is much the major Part of most) are liable to the worst Infirmities and subject to the vilest Offices of human Nature. Among these latter the Act of Eating, which hath by several wise Men been considered as extremely mean and derogatory from the Philosophic Dignity, must be in some Measure performed by the greatest Prince, Heroe, or Philosopher upon Earth; nay, sometimes Nature hath been so frolicksome as to exact of these dignified Characters, a much more exorbitant Share of this Office, than she hath obliged those of the lowest Order to perform.

To say the Truth, as no known Inhabitant of this Globe is really more than Man, so none need be ashamed of submitting to what the Necessities of Man demand; but when those great Personages I have just mentioned, condescend to aim at confining such low Offices to themselves; as when by hoarding or destroying, they seem desirous to prevent any others from eating, they then surely become very low and despicable.

Now after this short Preface, we think it no Disparagement to our Heroe to mention the immoderate Ardour with which he laid about him at this Season. Indeed it may be doubted, whether *Ulysses,* who by the Way seems to have had the best Stomach of all the Heroes in that eating Poem of the Odyssey, ever made a better Meal. Three Pounds at least of that Flesh which formerly had contributed to the Composition of an Ox, was now honoured with becoming Part of the individual Mr. *Jones.*

This Particular we thought ourselves obliged to mention, as it may account for our Heroe's temporary Neglect of his fair Companion;[1] who eat[2] but very little, and was indeed employed in Considerations of a very different Nature, which passed unobserved by *Jones,* till he had entirely satisfied that Appetite which a Fast of twenty-four Hours had procured him; but his Dinner was no sooner ended, than his Attention to other Matters revived; with these Matters therefore we shall now proceed to acquaint the Reader.

Mr. *Jones,* of whose personal Accomplishments we have hitherto said very

Text from the first edition, 1749.

---

[1] In accord with the adventurous romances which Fielding is parodying, Tom has just rescued his "fair Companion" from the clutches of a villain who seemed about to tie her to a tree and now, as customary, the novelist has the problem of disposing of the spoils of victory.

[2] ate.

little, was in reality, one of the handsomest young Fellows in the World. His Face, besides being the Picture of Health, had in it the most apparent Marks of Sweetness and Good-Nature. These Qualities were indeed so characteristical in his Countenance, that while the Spirit and Sensibility in his Eyes, tho' they must have been perceived by an accurate Observer, might have escaped the Notice of the less discerning, so strongly was this Good-nature painted in his Look, that it was remarked by almost every one who saw him.

It was, perhaps, as much owing to this, as to a very fine Complection, that his Face had a Delicacy in it almost inexpressible, and which might have given him an Air rather too effeminate, had it not been joined to a most masculine Person and Mein; which latter had as much in them of the *Hercules,* as the former had of the *Adonis.* He was besides active, genteel, gay and good-humoured, and had a Flow of Animal Spirits,[3] which enlivened every Conversation where he was present.

When the Reader hath duly reflected on these many Charms which all centered in our Heroe, and considers at the same Time the fresh Obligations which Mrs. *Waters* had to him, it will be a Mark of more Prudery than Candour to entertain a bad Opinion of her, because she conceived a very good Opinion of him.

But whatever Censures may be passed upon her, it is my Business to relate Matters of Fact with Veracity. Mrs. *Waters* had, in Truth, not only a good Opinion of our Heroe, but a very great Affection for him. To speak out boldly at once, she was in Love, according to the present universally received Sense of that Phrase, by which Love is applied indiscriminately to the desirable Objects of all our Passions, Appetites, and Senses, and is understood to be that Preference which we give to one Kind of Food rather than to another.

But tho' the Love to these several Objects may possibly be one and the same in all Cases, its Operations however must be allowed to be different; for how much soever we may be in Love with an excellent Surloin of Beef, or Bottle of *Burgundy;* with a Damask Rose, or *Cremona* Fiddle; yet do we never smile, nor ogle, nor dress, nor flater, nor endeavour by any other Arts or Tricks to gain the Affection of the said Beef, &c. Sigh indeed we sometimes may; but it is generally in the Absence, not in the Presence of the beloved Object. For otherwise we might possibly complain of their Ingratitude and Deafness, with the same Reason as *Pasiphae*[4] doth of her Bull, whom she endeavoured to engage by all the Coquetry practised with good Success in the Drawing Room, on the much more sensible, as well as tender, Hearts of the fine Gentlemen there.

The contrary happens, in that Love which operates between Persons of the same Species, but of different Sexes. Here we are no sooner in Love, than it becomes our principal Care to engage the Affection of the Object beloved. For what other Purpose indeed are our Youth instructed in all the Arts of rendering themselves agreeable? If it was not with a View to this Love, I question whether any of those Trades which deal in setting off and adorning the Human Person would procure a Livelihood. Nay, those great Polishers of our Manners, who are by some thought to teach what principally distinguishes us from the Brute Creation, even Dancing-Masters themselves, might possibly find no Place in Society. In short, all the Graces which young Ladies and young Gentlemen too learn from others; and the many Improvements which, by the Help of a Looking-glass, they add of their own, are in Reality those very *Spicula & Facies Amoris,* so often mentioned by *Ovid;*[5] or, as they are sometimes called in our own Language, *The whole Artillery of Love.*

Now Mrs. *Waters* and our Heroe had no sooner sat down together, than the former began to play this Artillery upon the latter. But here, as we are about to

---

[3] i.e., was animated.

[4] Wife of Minos in the Greek legend; she fell in love with a white bull and mothered the Minotaur.

[5] "the arms and armament of love"; Ovid is the classical authority on matters of love.

attempt a Description hitherto unessayed either in Prose or Verse, we think proper to invoke the Assistance of certain Aerial Beings, who will, we doubt not, come kindly to our Aid on this Occasion.

"Say then, you Graces, you that inhabit the heavenly Mansions of *Seraphina's*[6] Countenance; for you are truly Divine, are always in her Presence, and well know all the Arts of charming. Say, what were the weapons now used to captivate the Heart of Mr. *Jones.*"

"First, from two lovely blue Eyes, whose bright Orbs flashed Lightning at their Discharge, flew forth two pointed Ogles. But happily for our Heroe, hit only a vast Piece of Beef which he was then conveying into his Plate, and harmless spent their Force. The fair Warrior perceived their Miscarriage, and immediately from her fair Bosom drew forth a deadly Sigh. A Sigh, which none could have heard unmoved, and which was sufficient at once to have swept off a dozen Beaus; so soft, so sweet, so tender, that the insinuating Air must have found its subtle Way to the Heart of our Hope, had it not luckily been driven from his Ears by the coarse Bubbling of some bottled Ale, which at that Time he was pouring forth. Many other Weapons did she assay; but the God of Eating (if there be any such Deity; for I do not confidently assert it) preserved his Votary; or perhaps it may not be *Dignus vindice nodus,*[7] and the present Security of *Jones* may be accounted for by natural Means: For as Love frequently preserves from the Attacks of Hunger, so may Hunger possibly, in some Cases, defend us against Love.

The Fair One, enraged at her frequent Disappointments, determined on a short Cessation of Arms. Which Interval she employed in making ready every Engine of Amorous Warfare for the renewing of the Attack, when Dinner should be over.

No sooner then was the Cloth removed, than she again began her Operations. First, having planted her Right Eye side-ways against Mr. *Jones,* she shot from its Corner a most penetrating Glance; which, tho' great Part of its Force was spent before it reached our Heroe, did not vent itself absolutely without Effect. This the Fair One perceiving, hastily withdrew her Eyes, and leveled them downwards as if she was concerned for what she had done: Tho' by this Means she designed only to draw him from his Guard, and indeed to open his Eyes, through which she intended to surprize his Heart. And now, gently lifting up those two bright Orbs which had already begun to make an Impression on poor *Jones,* she discharged a Volley of small Charms at once from her whole Countenance in a Smile. Not a Smile of Mirth, nor of Joy; but a Smile of Affection, which most Ladies have always ready at their Command, and which serves them to show at once their Good-Humour, their pretty Dimples, and their white Teeth.

This Smile our Heroe received full in his Eyes, and was immediately staggered with its Force. He then began to see the Designs of the Enemy, and indeed to feel their Success. A Parley now was set on Foot between the Parties; during which the artful Fair so slily and imperceptibly carried on her Attack, that she had almost subdued the Heart of our Heroe, before she again repaired to Acts of Hostility. To confess the Truth, I am afraid Mr. *Jones* maintained a Kind of *Dutch* Defense,[8] and treacherously delivered up the Garrison without duly weighing his Allegiance to the fair *Sophia.*[9] In short, no sooner had the amorous Parley ended, and the Lady had unmasked the Royal Battery, by carelessly letting her Handkerchief drop from her Neck, than the Heart of Mr. *Jones* was entirely taken, and the fair Conqueror enjoyed the usual Fruits of her Victory."

Here the Graces think proper to end their Description, and here we think proper to end the Chapter.

---

[6] An angel.

[7] "a problem worth defending" (Horace, *Ars Poetica,* l. 191).

[8] i.e., half-hearted.

[9] Sophia Western, the romantic heroine of the novel, from whom Tom is temporarily separated as characteristic of a romance.

Samuel Johnson
1709-1784

THE RAMBLER

No. 85   [THE NECESSITY OF ACTION]

TUESDAY, JANUARY 8, 1751

Otia si tollas periere Cupidinis *arcus*
Contemptaeque jacent, et sine Luce
Faces.[1]

OVID.

Many Writers of Eminence in Physick have laid out their Diligence upon the Consideration of those Distempers to which Men are more remarkably exposed by particular States of Life, and very learned Treatises have been produced upon the Maladies of the Camp, the Sea, and the Mines. There is, indeed, scarcely any Employment which a Man accustomed to anatomical Enquiries, and medical Refinements, would not find Reasons for declining as dangerous to Health, did not his Learning and Experience inform him, that almost every Occupation, however formidable and threatening, is happier and safer than a Life of Sloth.

The Necessity of Action is not only demonstrable from the Fabrick of the Body, but evident from Observation on the universal Practice of Mankind, who for the Preservation of Health, in those whose Rank or Wealth exempts them from the Necessity of lucrative Labour, have invented Sports and Diversions, though not of equal Use to the World with manual Trades, yet of equal Fatigue to those that practise them, and differing only from the Drudgery of the Husbandman or Manufacturer, as they are the Acts of Choice, and therefore performed without the painful Sense of Compulsion. The Huntsman rises early, persues his Game through all the Dangers and Obstructions of the Chase, swims Rivers, and scales Precipices, returns home no less harrassed than the Soldier, and has, perhaps, sometimes incurred no less Hazard of Wounds or Death: Yet he has no Motive to incite his Ardour; he is neither subject to the Commands of a General, nor the Penalties of Neglect and Disobedience; nor has either Profit or Honour to expect from his Perils and his Conquests: He toils without the Hope either of mural or civick Garlands, and must content himself without any higher Praise than that of his Companions.

But such indeed is the Constitution of Man, that Labour may be with great Justice stiled its own Reward; nor will any external Incitements be requisite, if it be considered how much Happiness is gained, and how much Misery is escaped by frequent and violent Agitation of the Body.

Text from the original sheets as dated individually.

[1] At busy hearts in vain love's arrows fly;
Dim, scorn'd, and impotent, his torches lie.
(*Remedy for Love*, ll. 139–140.)

Ease is the utmost that can be hoped from a sedentary and unactive Habit; Ease, a neutral State between Pain and Pleasure. The Dance of Spirits, the Bound of Vigour, the Readiness of Enterprize, and Defiance of Fatigue, are reserved for him that braces his Nerves, and hardens his Fibres, that keeps his Limbs pliant with Motion, and by frequent Exposure fortifies his Frame against the common Accidents of Cold and Heat.

With Ease, however, if it could be secured, many would be content; but nothing terrestrial can be kept at a Stand. Ease, if it is not rising into Pleasure, will be falling towards Pain, and whatever Hope the Dreams of Speculation may suggest of observing the Proportion between Nutriment and Labour, and keeping the Body in a healthy State by Supplies exactly equal to its Waste, we know, that in Effect the vital Powers, unexcited by Motion, grow gradually languid, that as their Vigour fails Obstructions are generated, and that from Obstructions proceed most of those Pains that wear us away slowly with periodical Tortures, and though they sometimes suffer Life to be long, condemn it to be useless; that chain us down on the Couch of Misery, and mock us with the Hopes of Death.

Exercise, indeed, cannot secure us from that Dissolution to which we are decreed; but while the Soul and Body continue united, it can make the Association pleasing, and can give probable Hopes that they shall be disjoined by an easy Separation. It was a Principle among the Ancients, that acute Diseases are from Heaven, and chronical from ourselves; the Dart of Death indeed falls from Heaven, but we poison it by our own Misconduct; to dye is the Fate of Man, but to dye with lingering Anguish is generally his Folly.

It is indeed necessary to that Perfection of which our present State is capable, that the Mind and Body should both be kept in Action; that neither the Faculties of the one nor of the other be suffered to grow lax or torpid for Want of Use; that neither Health be purchased by voluntary Submission to Ignorance, nor Knowledge cultivated at the Expense of that Health, which must enable it either to give Pleasure to its Possessor or Assistance to others. It is too frequently the Pride of Students to despise those Amusements and Recreations which give to the rest of Mankind Strength of Limbs and Cheerfulness of Heart. Solitude and Contemplation are indeed seldom consistent with such Skill in common Exercises or Sports as is necessary to make them practised with Delight, and no Man is willing to do that of which the Necessity is not pressing and immediate, when he knows that his Awkwardness must make him ridiculous.

Ludere qui nescit, campestribus abstinet Armis,
Indoctusque Pilae, Discive, Trochive quiescit,
Ne spissae Risum tollant impunè Coronae.[2]

Thus the Man of Learning is often resigned, almost by his own Consent, to Languor and to Pain; and while in the Prosecution of his Studies he suffers the Weariness of Labour, is subject by his Course of Life to the Maladies of Idleness.

It was, perhaps, from the Observation of this great Omission in those who are employed about intellectual Objects, that *Locke* has, in his *System of Education*,[3] so warmly urged the Necessity of a manual Trade to Men of all Ranks and Professions, that when the Mind is weary with its proper Labours, it may be relaxed by a slighter Attention to some mechanical Operation; and while the vital Functions are resuscitated and awakened by vigorous Motion, the Understanding may be retained from that

---

[2] He that's unskilful will not toss a bull,
Nor run, nor wrestle, for he fears the fall;
He justly fears to meet deserv'd disgrace,
And that the ring will hiss the baffled ass.

(Horace, *Ars Poetica*, ll. 379–381, tr. Creech.)
[3] John Locke (1632–1704), *Some Thoughts concerning Education* (1693), para. 201.

Vagrance and Dissipation by which it too often relieves itself, after a long Intenseness of Thought, unless some Allurement be presented that may engage Attention without Anxiety.

There is so little Reason for expecting any frequent Conformity to *Locke's* Precept, that it is not necessary to enquire whether the Practice of manual Arts might not give Occasion to petty Emulation, and trivial Ambition; and whether, if our Divines and Physicians were taught the Lathe and the Chizzel, they might not think more of their Tools than their Books; as *Nero* neglected the Care of his Empire for his Chariot and his Fiddle. It is certainly dangerous to be too much pleased with little Things; but what is there which may not be perverted? Let us, however, remember how much worse Employment might have been found for those Hours, which a manual Occupation appears to engross; let us compute the Profit with the Loss, and when we reflect how often a Genius is allured from his Studies, consider that perhaps by the same Attractions he is sometimes withheld from Debauchery, and recalled from Malice, from Ambition, from Envy, and from Lust.

I have always admired the Wisdom of those by whom our Female Education was instituted, for having contrived, that every Woman of whatever Condition should be taught some Arts of Manufacture, by which the Vacuities of recluse and domestick Leisure may always be filled up; since the Weakness of their Sex, and the general System of Life, exclude them from many Employments which by diversifying the Circumstances of Men, preserve them from being cankered by the Rust of their own Thoughts. I know not how much of the Virtue and Happiness of the World may be the Consequence of this judicious Regulation. Perhaps, the most powerful

Fancy might be unable to figure the Confusion and Slaughter that would be produced by so many piercing Eyes and vivid Understandings, turned loose at once upon Mankind, with no other Business than to sparkle and intrigue, to perplex and to destroy.

For my Part, whenever Chance brings within my Observation a Knot of Misses busy at their Needles, I consider myself as in the School of Virtue; and though I have no extraordinary Skill in Plainwork or Embroidery, look upon their Operations with, at least, as much Satisfaction as their Governess, because I regard them as providing a Security against the most dangerous Ensnarers of the Soul, by enabling themselves to exclude Idleness from their solitary Moments, and with Idleness her attendant Train of Passions, Fancies, and Chimeras, Fears, Sorrows and Desires. *Ovid* and *Cervantes* inform, that Love has no Power but over those whom he catches unemployed; and *Hector,* in the *Iliad,* when he sees *Andromache* overwhelmed with Terrors, sends her for Consolation to the Loom and the Distaff.[4]

It is certain that any wild Wish or vain Imagination never takes such firm Possession of the Mind, as when it is found empty and unoccupied; for the old peripatetick Principle, that *Nature abhors a Vacuum,* may be properly applied to the Intellect; it will embrace any Thing however absurd or criminal rather than be wholly without an Object. Perhaps every Man may date the Predominance of those Desires that disturb his Life and contaminate his Conscience, from some unhappy Hour when too much Leisure exposed him to their Incursions, for he has lived with little Observation either on himself or others, who does not know that to be idle is to be vicious.

---

[4] Near the end of the sixth book.

No. 117 [THE HISTORY OF A GARRET]

TUESDAY, APRIL 30, 1751

Ὄσσαν ἐπ᾽ Οὐλύμπῳ μέμασαν θέμεν᾽ αὐτὰρ
ἐπ᾽ Ὄσσῃ
Πήλιον εἰνοσίφυλλον, ιν᾽ ὁρανὸς
αμζατὸς ἔιη.[5]

                                    HOM.

To the RAMBLER
Sir,

Nothing has more retarded the Advancement of Learning than the Disposition of vulgar Minds to ridicule and vilify what they cannot comprehend. All Industry must be excited by Hope; and as the Student often proposes no other Reward to himself than Praise, he is easily discouraged by Contempt and Insult. He who brings with him into a clamorous Multitude the Timidity of Recluse Speculation, and has never hardened his Front in publick Life, nor accustomed his Passions to the Vicissitudes and Accidents, the Triumphs and Defeats of mixed Conversation, will blush at the Stare of petulant Incredulity, and suffer himself to be driven, by a Burst of Laughter, from the Fortresses of Demonstration. The Mechanist will be afraid to assert before hardy Contradiction, the Possibility of tearing down Bulwarks with a Silkworm's thread; and the Astronomer of relating the Rapidity of Light, the Distance of the fixed Stars, and the Height of the lunar Mountains.

If I could by any Efforts have shaken off this Cowardice, I had not sheltered myself under a borrowed Name, nor applied to you for the Means of communicating to the Public the Theory of a Garret, a Subject which, except some Slight and transient Strictures, has been hitherto neglected by those who were best qualified to adorn it, either for

Want of Leisure to prosecute the various Researches in which a nice Discussion must necessarily engage them, or because it requires such Diversity of Knowledge, and such Extent of Curiosity as is scarcely to be found in any single Intellect; or because they having more Sagacity than myself, foresaw the Tumults which would be raised against them, and knowing that it was vain to write what they durst not publish, confined their Knowledge to their own Breasts, and abandoned Prejudice and Folly to the Direction of Chance.

That the Professors of Literature[6] generally reside in the highest Stories has been immemorially observed. The Wisdom of the Ancients was well acquainted with the intellectual Advantages of an elevated Situation; why else were the *Muses* stationed on *Olympus* or *Parnassus* by those who could with equal Right have raised them Bowers in the Vale of *Tempe,* or erected their Altars among the Flexures of *Meander?*[7] Why was *Jove* himself nursed upon a Mountain? or why did the Goddesses, when the Prize of Beauty was contested, try the Cause upon the Top of *Ida?* Such were the Fictions by which the great Masters of the earlier Ages endeavoured to inculcate to Posterity the Importance of a Garret, which, though they have been long obscured by the Negligence and Ignorance of succeeding Times, were well enforced by the celebrated Symbol of *Pythagoras,* Ἀνεμων πνεόντων, την ἠχὼ προσκύνει, when **the** Wind blows worship its Echo. This could not but be understood by his Disciples as an inviolable Injunction to live in a Garret, which I have always found frequently visited by the Echo and the Wind. Nor was the Tradition wholly obliterated in the Age of *Augustus,* for

---

[5] The gods they challenge, and affect the skies;
Heav'd on Olympus tott'ring Ossa stood;
On Ossa, Pelion nods with all his wood.
        (*Odyssey,* XI, 315–316, tr. Pope.)
The lines are also quoted by Longinus in his critical treatise *On the Sublime,* a classical

essay which became increasingly popular through the eighteenth century in England.
   [6] authors.
   [7] A river in what is now Turkey, known anciently for its windings, hence supplying the word *meander.*

Tibullus evidently congratulates himself upon his Garret, not without some Allusion to the *Pythagorean* Precept.

Quam jurat immites ventos *audire
  cubantem . . .
Aut, gelidas hybernus aquas cu fuderit
  auster,
Securum somnos, imbre juvante, sequi.*[8]

And it is impossible not to discover the Fondness of *Lucretius* for a Garret in his Description of the lofty Towers of serene Learning, and the Pleasure with which a wise Man looks down upon the confused and erratic State of the World moving below him.

*Sed nil dulcius est, bene quam munita
  tenere
Edita doctrina sapientum templa serena;
Despicere unde queas alios, passimq;
  videre
Errare, atque viam palanteis quaerere
  vitae.*[9]

The Institution has, indeed, continued to our own Time, the Garret is still the usual Receptacle of the Philosopher and Poet; but this like many ancient Customs is perpetuated only by an accidental Imitation without Knowledge of the original Reason for which it was established; *Causa latet res est notissima.*[10] Conjectures have, indeed, been advanced concerning these Habitations of Literature, but without much Satisfaction to the judicious Enquirer. Some have imagined that the Garret is generally chosen by the Wits, as most easily rented, and concluded that no Man rejoices in his aerial Abode, but on the Days of Payment. Others suspect that a Garret is chiefly convenient, as it is remoter than any other Part of the House from the outer Door, which is often observed to be infested by Visitants,[11] who talk incessantly of Beer, or Linen, or a Coat, and repeat the same Sounds every Morning and sometimes again in the Afternoon, without any Variation, except that they grow daily more importunate and clamorous, and raise their Voices in Time from mournful Murmurs to raging Vociferations, and whose eternal Monotony is always detestable to a Man whose chief Pleasure is to enlarge his Knowledge and vary his Ideas. Others talk of Freedom from Noise, and Abstraction from common Business or Amusements; and some yet more visionary, tell us that the Faculties are enlarged by open Prospects, and that the Fancy is more at Liberty, when the Eye ranges without Confinement.

These Conveniencies may perhaps all be found in a well chosen Garret, but surely they cannot be supposed sufficiently important to have operated unvariably upon different Climates, distant Ages, and separate Nations. Of an universal Practice, there must still be presumed an universal Cause, which however recondite and abstruse, may be perhaps reserved to make me illustrous by its Discovery, and you by its Promulgation.

It is universally known that the Faculties of the Mind, are invigorated or weakened by the state of the Body, and that the Body is in a great Measure regulated by the various Compressions of the ambient Element. The Effects of the Air in the Production or Cure of corporal Maladies have been acknowledged from the Time of *Hippocrates,* but no Man has yet sufficiently considered how far it may influence the Operations of the Mind, though every Day affords Instances of local Understanding, of Wits and Reasoners, whose Faculties are adapted to some single Spot, and who when they are removed to any other

---

[8] How sweet in sleep to pass the careless hours,
Lull'd by the beating winds and dashing show'rs.
  (*Elegies*, I, i, 46–48.)
[9] 'Tis sweet thy lab'ring steps to guide
To virtue's heights, with wisdom well supply'd,
And all the magazines of learning fortify'd:
From thence to look below on human kind,
Bewildered in the maze of life, and blind.
  (Lucretius, *De Rerum Natura*, II, 7–10,
    tr. Dryden.)
[10] "The cause is secret, but the effect is known."
[11] i.e., bill collectors.

Place sink at once into Silence and Stupidity. I have discovered by a long Series of Observations, that Invention and Elocution suffer great Impediments from dense and impure Vapours, and that the Tenuity of a defecated Air at a proper Distance from the Surface of the Earth, accelerates the Fancy, and sets at Liberty these intellectual Powers which were before shackled by too strong Attraction, and unable to expand themselves under the Pressure of a gross Atmosphere. I have found Dulness to quicken into Sentiment in a thin Ether, as Water, though not very hot, boils in a Receiver partly exhausted; and Heads in Appearance empty have teemed with Notions upon rising Ground, as the flaccid Sides of a Football would have swelled out into Stiffness and Extension.

For this Reason I never think myself qualified to judge decisively of any Man's Faculties, whom I have only known in one Degree of Elevation, but take some Opportunity of attending him from the Cellar to the Garret, and try upon him all the various Degrees of Rarefaction and Condensation, Tension and Laxity. If he is neither vivacious aloft nor serious below, I then consider him as hopeless; but as it seldom happens that I do not find the Temper to which the Texture of his Brain is fitted, I accommodate him in Time with a Tube of Mercury, first marking the Point most favourable to his Intellects, according to Rules which I have long studied, and which I may, perhaps, reveal to Mankind in a complete Treatise of barometrical Pneumatology.

Another Cause of the Gayety and Sprightliness of the Dwellers in Garrets, is probably the Encrese of that vertiginous Motion, with which we are carried round by the diurnal Revolution of the Earth. The power of Agitation upon the Spirits is well known; every Man has felt his Heart lighten'd in a rapid Vehicle or on a galloping Horse; and nothing is plainer than that he who towers to the fifth Story, is whirled through more Space by every Circumrotation, than another

that grovels upon the Ground-floor. The Nations between the Tropicks, are known to be fiery, inconstant, inventive, and fanciful, because living at the utmost Length of the Earth's Diameter, they are carried about with more Swiftness than those whom Nature has placed nearer to the Poles; and therefore, as it becomes a wise Man to struggle with the Inconveniences of his Country, whenever Celerity and Acuteness are requisite, we must actuate our Languor by taking a few Turns round the Center in a Garret.

If you imagine that I ascribe to Air and Motion Effects which they cannot produce, I desire you to consult your own Memory, and consider whether you have never known a Man acquire Reputation in his Garret, which when Fortune or a Patron had placed him upon the first Floor, he was unable to maintain, and who never recovered his former Vigour of Understanding till he was restored to his native Situation. That a Garret will make every Man a Wit I am very far from supposing; I know there are some who would continue Blockheads even on the Summit of the *Andes,* or on the Pike[12] of *Teneriffe.* But let not any Man be considered as unimproveable till this potent Remedy has been tried; for, perhaps, he was formed to be great only in a Garret, as the Joiner of *Aretæus*[13] was a Madman in every Place but his own Shop.

I think a frequent Removal to various Distances from the Center so necessary to a just Estimate of intellectual Abilities, and consequently of so great Use in Education, that if I hoped that the Public could be persuaded to so expensive an Experiment, I would propose that there should be a Cavern dug and a Tower erected like those which *Bacon* describes in *Solomon's* House,[14] for the Expansion and Concentration of Understanding, according to the Exigence of different Employments, or Constitutions. Perhaps some that fume away in Meditations upon Time and Space in the Tower, might compose Tables of Interest at a certain Depth; and he that upon level

[12] peak.

[13] A Greek physician of the first century.
[14] In *The New Atlantis* (1626).

Ground stagnates in Narrative, might, at the Height of half a Mile, ferment into Merriment, sparkle with Repartee, and froth with Declamation.

Addison observes that we may find the Heat of *Virgil*'s Climate, in some Lines of his *Georgic;* so, when I read a Composition, I immediately determine the Height of the Author's Habitation. As an elaborate Performance is commonly said to smell of the Lamp, my Commendation of a noble Thought, a sprightly Sally, or a bold Figure, is to pronounce it fresh from the Garret; an Expression which would break from me upon the Perusal of most of your Papers, did I not believe that you have quitted the Garret and ascended to the Cockloft.

HYPERTATUS.[15]

No. 137   [ON HUMANIZING THE INTELLECTUAL]

TUESDAY, JULY 9, 1751

Dum vitant stulti-vitia, in contraria currunt.[16]

HOR.

That Wonder is the Effect of Ignorance has been often observed. That awful Stilness of Attention with which the Mind is overspread, at the first View of an unexpected Effect, or an uncommon Performance ceases when we have Leisure to disentangle Complications and investigate Causes. Wonder is a Pause of Reason, a sudden Cessation of the mental Progress, which lasts only while the Understanding is fixed upon some single Idea, and is at an End when it recovers Force enough to divide the Object into its Parts, or mark the intermediate Gradations from the first Motive to the last Consequence.

It may be remarked with equal Truth, that Ignorance is often the Effect of Wonder. It is common for those who have never accustomed themselves to the Labour of Enquiry, nor invigorated their Confidence by any Conquests over Difficulty, to sleep in the gloomy Quiescence of Astonishment, without any Effort to animate Languor, or dispel Obscurity. What they cannot immediately conceive, they consider as too high to be reached, or too extensive to be comprehended, and therefore content themselves with the Gaze of Ignorance, forbear to attempt what they have no Hopes of performing, and resign the Pleasure of rational Contemplation to more pertinacious Study, or more active Faculties.

Among the Productions of Art, there are many of a Form so different from that of their first Materials, and many consisting of Parts so numerous and so nicely adapted to each other, that it is not possible to consider them without Amazement. But when we enter the Shops of Artificers, and observe the various Tools by which every Operation is facilitated, and trace the Progress of a Manufacture through the different Hands that contribute to its Perfection, in Succession to each other, we soon discover that every single Man has an easy Task, and that the Extremes, however remote, of natural Rudeness and artificial Elegance, are joined by a regular Concatenation of Effects, of which every one is introduced by that which precedes it, and equally introduces that which is to follow.

The same is the State of intellectual and manual Performances. A long Calculation or a complex Diagram affrights the timorous and unexperienced from a second View; but if we have Skill sufficient to analise them into simple Principles, it will generally be discovered that our Fear was groundless. *Divide and conquer* is a Principle equally just in Science as in Policy. Complication is a Species of Confederacy, which, while it continues united, bids Defiance to the most active and vigorous Intellect, but

---

[15] A coined word suggesting a person in an elevated position.

[16] Whilst fools one vice condemn,

They run into the opposite extreme.
(Horace, *Satires,* I, ii, 24, tr. Creech.)

of which every Member is separately weak, and which may therefore be quickly subdued if it can once be broken.

The chief Art of Learning, as *Locke*[17] has observed, is to attempt but little at a Time. The farthest Excursions of the Mind are made by short Flights frequently repeated, the most lofty Fabricks of Science are formed by the continued Accumulation of single Propositions.

It often happens, whatever be the Cause, that this Impatience of Labour or Dread of Miscarriage seizes those who are most distinguished for Quickness of Apprehension; and that they who might with greatest Reason promise themselves Victory, are least willing to hazard the Encounter. This Diffidence, where the Attention is not laid asleep by Laziness, or dissipated by Pleasures, can arise only from confused and general Views, such as Negligence snatches in haste, or from the Disappointment of Hopes formed by Arrogance without Reflection. To expect that the Intricacies of Science will be pierced by a careless Glance, or the Eminences of Fame ascended without Labour, is to expect a peculiar Privilege or Power denied to the rest of Mankind; but to suppose that the Maze is insecutable[18] by Diligence, or the Heights inaccessible by Perseverance, is to submit tamely to the Tyranny of Fancy, and enchain the Mind in voluntary Shackles.

It is the usual Ambition of the Heroes in Literature to enlarge the Boundaries of Knowledge, and to discover and conquer new Regions of the intellectual World. To the Success of such Undertakings perhaps some Degree of fortuitous Happiness is necessary which no Man can promise or procure to himself, and therefore Doubt and Irresolution may be forgiven in him that ventures into the untrodden Abysses of Truth, and attempts to find his Way through the Fluctuations of Uncertainty, and the Conflicts of Contradiction. But when nothing more is required than to pursue a Path already beaten, and to trample Obstacles which others have demolished, why should any Man so much suspect his own Powers as to imagine them unequal to the Attempt?

It were to be wished that those who devote their Lives to Study would resolve at once to believe nothing too great for their Attainment, and to consider nothing as too little for their Regard, to extend their Notice alike to Nature and to Life, and unite some Knowledge of the living World to their Acquaintance with past Ages and remote Events.

Nothing has so much exposed Men of Learning to Contempt and Ridicule as their Ignorance of Things which are known to all but themselves, and their Inability to conduct common Negotiations, or to extricate their Affairs from trivial Perplexities. Those who have been taught to consider the Institutions of the Schools, as giving the last Perfection to human Abilities, are surprised to see Men wrinkled with Science, yet wanting to be instructed in minute Circumstances of Propriety or necessary Forms of daily Transaction; and quickly shake off their Reverence for Modes of Education, which they find to produce no Superiority above the rest of Mankind. Books, says *Bacon, can never teach the Use of Books.*[19] The Student must learn by Commerce with Mankind to reduce his Speculations to Practice, and accommodate his Knowledge to the Purposes of Life.

It is too common for those who have been bred to scholastic Professions, and passed much of their Time in Academies, where nothing but Learning confers Honours, to disregard every other Qualification and to imagine that they shall find Mankind ready to pay Homage to their Knowledge, and to croud about them for Counsel and Instruction. They, therefore, step out from their Cells into the open World, with all the Confidence of Authority and the Dignity of Importance; they look round about them at

---

[17] In *Some Thoughts concerning Education.* See note 3.

[18] unpursuable. The word is not in Johnson's *Dictionary,* although *insecution* is there defined as "pursuit" but noted as "not in use."

[19] Bacon's actual words were, "Studies . . . teach not their own use," in his essay "Of Studies" (1597).

once with Ignorance and Scorn, on a Race of Beings to whom they are equally unknown and equally contemptible, but whose Manners they must imitate, and with whose Opinions they must comply if they desire to pass their Time happily among them.

To lessen that Disdain with which Scholars are always inclined to look on the common Business of the World, and the Unwillingness with which they condescend to learn what is not to be found in any System of Philosophy, it may be necessary to consider that tho' Admiration is excited by abstruse Researches and remote Discoveries, we cannot hope to give Pleasure, or to conciliate Affection, but by softer Accomplishments, and by Qualities more easily communicable to those about us. He that can only converse upon Questions, of which only a small Part of Mankind has Knowledge sufficient to be curious, must pass his Days in unsocial Silence, and live in the Crowd of Life without a Companion; he that can only be useful in great Occasions, may die without exerting his Abilities, and stand a helpless Spectator of a thousand Vexations which fret away the Happiness of Life, and which nothing is required to remove but general Address and Readiness of Expedients.

No Degree of Knowledge attainable by Man is able to set him above the Want of hourly Assistance, or the Desire of fond Endearments, and tender Officiousness;[20] and, therefore, no Man should think it unnecessary to learn those Arts by which Friendship may be gained. Kindness is preserved by a constant Reciprocation of Benefits, or Interchange of Pleasures, but such Benefits only can be bestowed, as others are capable to receive, and such Pleasures only imparted, as others are qualified to enjoy.

By this Descent from the Pinacles of Art no Honour will be lost, for the Condescensions of Learning are always overpaid by Gratitude; an elevated Genius employed in little Things appears, to use the Simile of *Longinus*,[21] like the Sun in his Evening Declination, he remits his Splendor but retains his Magnitude, and pleases more, though he dazzles less.

No. 152 [ON QUALITIES OF THE EPISTOLARY STYLE]

SATURDAY, AUGUST 31, 1751.

Tristia mæstum
Vultum verba decent, iratum plena
minarum.[22]

HOR.

"It was the Wisdom, says *Seneca,* of ancient Times, to consider what is most useful as most illustrious." If this Rule be observed with Regard to Works of Genius, there is scarcely any Species of Composition which deserves more to be cultivated than the epistolary Stile, since none is of more various or frequent Use, through the whole Subordination of human Life.

It has happened, however, that among the numerous Writers which our Nation has produced, perhaps always equal in Force and Genius, and of late in Elegance and Accuracy to those of any other Country, very few have yet endeavoured to distinguish themselves by the Publication of Letters, except such as have been written in the Discharge of publick Trusts, and during the Transaction of great Affairs, which though they may afford Precedents to the Minister, and Memorials to the Historian, are of very little Use as Examples of the familiar Stile, or Models of private Correspondence.

If it be enquired by Foreigners how this Deficiency could happen in the Literature of a Country, where every Man indulges himself with so little Danger in Speaking and Writing, may we not without the Imputation of Bigotry or Arrogance inform them, that it may

20 "service" (Johnson's *Dictionary*).
21 *On the Sublime*, IX, 13.
22 Disastrous words can best disaster show;
In angry phrase the angry passions glow.
(Horace, *Ars Poetica*, l. 105, tr. Elphinston.)

be justly ascribed to our Contempt of Trifles, and to our due Sense of the Dignity of the Publick, that we do not think it reasonable to fill the World with Volumes from which nothing can be learned, nor expect that the Employments of the busy, or the Amusements of the gay, should give Way to Narratives of our private Affairs, to our Complaints of Absence, Expressions of Fondness, or Declarations of Fidelity.

A very slight Perusal of the epistolary Writings by which the Wits of *France* have signalized themselves, will prove that other Nations need not be discouraged from the like Attempts by the Consciousness of Inability; for surely it is not very difficult to relate trifling Occurrences, to magnify familiar Incidents, to repeat adulatory Professions, to accumulate servile Hyperboles, and to produce all that can be found in the despicable Remains of *Voiture* and *Scarron*.[23]

Yet as much of Life must be passed in Affairs which become considerable only by their frequent Occurrence, and much of the Pleasure which our Condition allows must be produced by giving Elegance to Trifles, it is necessary to learn how to become little without becoming mean, to maintain the necessary Intercourses of Civility, and fill up the Vacuities of Action by agreeable Appearances. It had therefore been of some Advantage if such of our Writers as have most excelled in the Art of decorating Insignificance, had supplied us with a few Sallies of innocent Gaiety, Effusions of honest Tenderness, or Exclamations of unimportant Hurry.

Precept has generally been posterior to Performance. No Man has taught the Art of composing any Work of Genius but by the Example of those who performed it without any other Help than Vigour of Imagination, and Rectitude of Judgment. As we have few Letters,

we have likewise few Criticisms upon the epistolary Stile. The Observations with which *Walsh*[24] has introduced his Pages of Inanity are such as give him very little Claim to the Rank which *Dryden* has assigned him amongst the Criticks. *Letters,* says he, *are intended as Resemblances of Conversation, and the chief Excellencies of Conversation are good Humour and good Breeding.* This Remark, equally valuable for its Novelty and Propriety, he dilates and enforces with an Appearance of compleat Acquiescence in his own Discovery.

No Man was ever in Doubt about the moral Qualities of a Letter. It has been always known that he who endeavours to please must appear pleased, and he who would not provoke Rudeness must not practise it. The Question among those who endeavour to establish Rules for epistolary Performances is only how Gaiety or Civility may be most properly expressed; as among the Criticks in History it is not contested whether Truth ought to be preserved, but by what Mode of Diction it is best adorned.

As Letters are written on all Subjects, in all States of Mind, and on all Occasions, the epistolary Stile cannot be reduced to any settled Rules, or described by any single Characteristic, and perhaps we may safely disentangle our Minds from critical Embarrasments, by determining that a Letter has no Pecularity but in its Form, and that nothing is necessary to be refused Admission into a Letter which is proper in any other Method of treating the same Subject. The Qualities of the epistolary Stile most frequently required are Ease and Simplicity, an even Flow of unlaboured Diction, and an artless Arrangement of obvious Sentiments. But these Directions however strongly they may be inculcated by the Speculatist, are no sooner applied to actual Use, than their Scantiness and Imperfection become evident.

---

[23] Vincent Voiture (1598–1648) and Paul Scarron (1610–1660), outstanding for their contributions to the French intellectual milieu of their times.

[24] William Walsh, Preface to *Letters and Poems Amorous and Gallant* (1692): "The Stile of Letters ought to be free, easy and natural; as near approaching to familiar Conversation as possible. The two best Qualities in Conversation are good Humour and good Breeding."

Letters are written to the great and to the mean, to the learned and the ignorant, at Rest and in Distress, in Sport and in Passion. Nothing can be more improper than Ease and Laxity of Expression, when the Importance of the Subject impresses Solicitude, or the Dignity of the Person exacts Reverence.

That Letters should be written with strict Conformity to Nature is true, because nothing but Conformity to Nature can make any Composition beautiful or just. But it is natural to depart from Familiarity of Language upon Occasions not familiar; whatever elevates the Sentiments will consequently raise the Expression; whatever fills us with Hope or Terror will produce some Perturbation of Images, and some figurative Distortions of Phrase. Wherever we are studious to please we are afraid of trusting our first Thoughts, and endeavour to recommend our Opinion by studied Ornaments, by Accuracy of Method, and Elegance of Stile.

If the Personages of the comick Scene, be allowed by *Horace* to raise their Language in the Transports of Anger to the turgid Vehemence of Tragedy, the epistolary Writer may without Censure comply with the Varieties of his Matter. If great Events are to be related, he may with all the Solemnity of an Historian, deduce them from their Causes, connect them with their Concomitants, and trace them to their Consequences. If a disputed Position is to be established, or a remote Principle to be investigated, he may detail his Reasonings with all the Nicety of syllogistick Method. If a Menace is to be averted, or a Benefit implored, he may without any Violation of the Edicts of Criticism, call every Power of Rhetorick to his Assistance, and try every Inlet at which Passion enters the Heart.

Those Letters that have no other End than the Entertainment of the Correspondent are perhaps more properly to be regulated by critical Precepts, because the Matter and Stile are equally arbitrary, and Rules are always more necessary, as there is more Power of Choice. In Letters of this Kind, some conceive Art graceful, and others think Negligence amiable; some model them by the Sonnet, and will allow them by no Means of delighting, but the soft Lapse of calm Mellifluence, others adjust them by the Epigram, and expect pointed Sentences and forcible Periods. The one Party considers Exemption from Faults as the Height of Excellence, the other looks upon Neglect of Excellence as the most disgusting Fault; one avoids Censure, the other aspires to Praise; one is always in Danger of Insipidity, the other continually on the Brink of Affectation.

When the Subject has no intrinsick Dignity it must necessarily owe all its Attractions to artificial Embellishments, and may properly catch at all the Advantages which the Art of Writing can bestow. He that, like *Pliny,* sends his Friend a Portion[25] for his Daughter, will without *Pliny's* Eloquence or Addres, find Means of exciting Gratitude, and securing Acceptance, but he that has no other Present to make but a Garland, a Ribbon, or some petty Curiosity, must endeavour to recommend it by his Manner of giving it.

The Purpose for which Letters are written when there is no Intelligence to communicate, or Business to transact, is to preserve in the Minds of the absent either Love or Esteem; to excite Love we must communicate Pleasure, and to raise Esteem we must discover Abilities. Pleasures will generally be given, as Abilities are discovered by Scenes of Imagery and Points of Conceit,[26] unexpected Sallies and artful Compliments. Trifles will always require Exuberance of Ornament; the Building which has no Strength can be valued only for the Art of its Decorations. The Stone must be polished with Care, which hopes to be valued as a Diamond, and Words ought surely to be laboured when they are intended to stand for Things.

---

[25] "part of an inheritance given to a child" (Johnson's *Dictionary*).

[26] figures of speech.

From THE ADVENTURER

No. 120   [CONSOLATIONS OF AFFLICTION]

SATURDAY, DECEMBER 29, 1753.

> *. . . Ultima semper*
> *Expectanda dies homini, dicique beatus*
> *Ante obitum nemo supremaque funera*
> *debet.*[27]
>
> OVID.

> But no frail man, however great or high,
> Can be concluded blest before he die.
>
> ADDISON.

The numerous miseries of human life have extorted in all ages an universal complaint. The wisest of men terminated all his experiments in search of happiness, by the mournful confession, that "all is vanity;" and the antient patriarchs lamented, that "the days of their pilgrimage were few and evil."

There is, indeed, no topick on which it is more superfluous to accumulate authorities, nor any assertion of which our own eyes will more easily discover, or our sensations more frequently impress the truth, than, that misery is the lot of man, that our present state is a state of danger and infelicity.

When we take the most distant prospect of life, what does it present us but a chaos of unhappiness, a confused and tumultuous scene of labour and contest, disappointment and defeat? If we view past ages in the reflection of history, what do they offer to our meditation but crimes and calamities? One year is distinguished by a famine, another by an earthquake; kingdoms are made desolate, sometimes by wars, and sometimes by pestilence; the peace of the world is interrupted at one time by the caprices of a tyrant, at another by the rage of a conqueror. The memory is stored only with vicissitudes of evil; and the happiness, such as it is, of one part of mankind, is found to arise commonly from

sanguinary success, from victories which confer upon them the power, not so much of improving life by any new enjoyment, as of inflicting misery on others, and gratifying their own pride by comparative greatness.

But by him that examines life with a more close attention, the happiness of the world will be found still less than it appears. In some intervals of publick prosperity, or to use terms more proper, in some intermissions of calamity, a general diffusion of happiness may seem to overspread a people; all is triumph and exultation, jollity and plenty; there are no publick fears and dangers, and "no complainings in the streets." But the condition of individuals is very little mended by this general calm: pain and malice and discontent still continue their havock; the silent depredation goes incessantly forward; and the grave continues to be filled by the victims of sorrow.

He that enters a gay assembly, beholds the cheerfulness displayed in every countenance, and finds all sitting vacant and disengaged, with no other attention than to give or to receive pleasure; would naturally imagine, that he had reached at last the metropolis of felicity, the place sacred to gladness of heart, from whence all fear and anxiety were irreversibly excluded. Such, indeed, we may often find to be the opinion of those, who from a lower station look up to the pomp and gaiety which they cannot reach: but who is there of those who frequent these luxurious assemblies, that will not confess his own uneasiness, or cannot recount the vexations and distresses that prey upon the lives of his gay companions?

The world, in its best state, is nothing more than a larger assembly of beings, combining to counterfeit happiness which

---

Conducted by John Hawkesworth (1715?–1773); text from Johnson's *Works*, ed. Sir John Hawkins (1787), vol. IX.

[27] *Metamorphoses*, III, 137.

they do not feel, employing every art and contrivance to embellish life, and to hide their real condition from the eyes of one another.

The species of happiness most obvious to the observation of others, is that which depends upon the goods of fortune; yet even this is often fictitious. There is in the world more poverty than is generally imagined; not only because many whose possessions are large have desires still larger, and many measure their wants by the gratifications which others enjoy; but great numbers are pressed by real necessities which it is their chief ambition to conceal, and are forced to purchase the appearance of competence and cheerfulness at the expense of many comforts and conveniencies of life.

Many, however, are confessedly rich, and many more are sufficiently removed from all danger of real poverty: but it has been long ago remarked, that money cannot purchase quiet; the highest of mankind can promise themselves no exemption from that discord or suspicion, by which the sweetness of domestick retirement is destroyed; and must always be even more exposed, in the same degree as they are elevated above others, to the treachery of dependents, the calumny of defamers, and the violence of opponents.

Affliction is inseparable from our present state; it adheres to all the inhabitants of this world in different proportions indeed, but with an allotment which seems very little regulated by our own conduct. It has been the boast of some swelling moralists, that every man's fortune was in his own power, that prudence supplied the place of all other divinities, and that happiness is the unfailing consequence of virtue. But, surely, the quiver of Omnipotence is stored with arrows, against which the shield of human virtue, however adamantine it has been boasted, is held up in vain: we do not always suffer by our crimes; we are not always protected by our innocence.

A good man is by no means exempt from the danger of suffering by the crimes of others; even his goodness may raise him enemies of implacable malice and restless perseverance: the good man has never been warranted by Heaven from the treachery of friends, the disobedience of children, or the dishonesty of a wife; he may see his cares made useless by profusion, his instructions defeated by perverseness, and his kindness rejected by ingratitude; he may languish under the infamy of false accusations, or perish reproachfully by an unjust sentence.

A good man is subject, like other mortals, to all the influences of natural evil; his harvest is not spared by the tempest, nor his cattle by the murrain;[28] his house flames like others in a conflagration; nor have his ships any peculiar power of resisting hurricanes: his mind, however elevated, inhabits a body subject to innumerable casualties, of which he must always share the dangers and the pains; he bears about him the seeds of disease, and may linger away a great part of his life under the tortures of the gout or stone; at one time groaning with insufferable anguish, at another dissolved in listlessness and languor.

From this general and indiscriminate distribution of misery, the moralists have always derived one of their strongest moral arguments for a future state; for since the common events of the present life happen alike to the good and bad, it follows from the justice of the Supreme Being, that there must be another state of existence, in which a just retribution shall be made, and every man shall be happy and miserable according to his works.

The miseries of life may, perhaps, afford some proof of a future state, compared as well with the mercy as the justice of God. It is scarcely to be imagined, that Infinite Benevolence would create a being capable of enjoying so much more than is here to be enjoyed, and qualified by nature to prolong pain by remembrance, and anticipate it by terror, if he was not designed for something nobler and better than a state,

---

28 "the plague in cattle" (Johnson's *Dictionary*).

in which many of his faculties can serve only for his torment; in which he is to be importuned by desires that never can be satisfied, to feel many evils which he had no power to avoid, and to fear many which he shall never feel: there will surely come a time, when every capacity of happiness shall be filled, and none shall be wretched but by his own fault.

In the mean time, it is by affliction chiefly that the heart of man is purified, and that the thoughts are fixed upon a better state. Prosperity, allayed and imperfect as it is, has power to intoxicate the imagination, to fix the mind upon the present scene, to produce confidence and elation, and to make him who enjoys affluence and honours forget the hand by which they were bestowed. It is seldom that we are otherwise, than by affliction, awakened to a sense of our own imbecillity, or taught to know how little all our acquisitions can conduce to safety or to quiet; and how justly we may ascribe to the superintendence of a higher Power, those blessings which in the wantonness of success we considered as the attainments of our policy or courage.

Nothing confers so much ability to resist the temptations that perpetually surround us, as an habitual consideration of the shortness of life, and the uncertainty of those pleasures that solicit our pursuit; and this consideration can be inculcated only by affliction. "O Death! how bitter is the remembrance of thee, to a man that lives at ease in his possessions!" If our present state were one continued succession of delights, or one uniform flow of calmness and tranquillity, we should never willingly think upon its end; death would then surely surprise us as "a thief in the night;" and our task of duty would remain unfinished, till "the night came when no man can work."

While affliction thus prepares us for felicity, we may console ourselves under its pressures, by remembering, that they are no particular marks of divine displeasure; since all the distresses of persecution have been suffered by those, "of whom the world was not worthy;" and the Redeemer of Mankind himself was "a man of sorrows and acquainted with grief."

THE IDLER

No. 86   [DISTRESSES OF APARTMENT-HUNTING]

SATURDAY, DECEMBER 8, 1759.

To the Idler.
Sir,
   I am a young lady newly married to a young gentleman. Our fortune is large, our minds are vacant, our dispositions gay, our acquaintances numerous, and our relations splendid. We considered that marriage, like life, has its youth; that the first year is the year of gaiety and revel, and resolved to see the shews and feel the joys of *London* before the increase of our family should confine us to domestick cares and domestick pleasures.

   Little time was spent in preparation; the coach was harnessed, and a few days brought us to *London,* and we alighted at a lodging provided for us by Miss *Biddy Trifle,* a maiden niece of my husband's father, where we found apartments on a second floor, which my cousin told us would serve us till we could please ourselves with a more commodious and elegant habitation, and which she

Text from Johnson's *Works,* ed. Sir John Hawkins (1787), vol. VIII; the Idler papers originally appeared in 1758–1760 in the *Universal Chronicle.*

had taken at a very high price, because it was not worth the while to make a hard bargain for so short a time.

Here I intended to lie concealed till my new clothes were made, and my new lodging hired; but Miss *Trifle* had so industriously given notice of our arrival to all her acquaintance, that I had the mortification next day of seeing the door thronged with painted coaches and chairs with coronets,[29] and was obliged to receive all my husband's relations on a second floor.

Inconveniences are often balanced by some advantage: the elevation of my apartments furnished a subject for conversation, which, without some such help, we should have been in danger of wanting. Lady *Stately* told us how many years had passed since she climbed so many steps. Miss *Airy* ran to the window, and thought it charming to see the walkers so little in the street; and Miss *Gentle* went to try the same experiment, and screamed to find herself so far above the ground.

They all knew that we intended to remove, and therefore all gave me advice about a proper choice. One street was recommended for the purity of its air, another for its freedom from noise, another for its nearness to the park, another because there was but a step from it to all places of diversion, and another, because its inhabitants enjoyed at once the town and country.

I had civility enough to hear every recommendation with a look of curiosity while it was made, and of acquiescence when it was concluded, but in my heart felt no other desire than to be free from the disgrace of a second floor, and cared little where I should fix, if the apartments were spacious and splendid.

Next day a chariot was hired, and Miss *Trifle* was dispatched to find a lodging. She returned in the afternoon, with an account of a charming place, to which my husband went in the morning to make the contract. Being young and

unexperienced, he took with him his friend *Ned Quick,* a gentleman of great skill in rooms and furniture, who sees, at a single glance, whatever there is to be commended or censured. Mr. *Quick,* at the first view of the house, declared that it could not be inhabited, for the sun in the afternoon shone with full glare on the windows of the dining-room.

Miss *Trifle* went out again, and soon discovered another lodging, which Mr. *Quick* went to survey, and found, that, whenever the wind should blow from the east, all the smoke of the city would be driven upon it.

A magnificent set of rooms was then found in one of the streets near *Westminster-Bridge,* which Miss *Trifle* preferred to any which she had yet seen; but Mr. *Quick,* having mused upon it for a time, concluded that it would be too much exposed in the morning to the fogs that rise from the river.

Thus Mr. *Quick* proceeded to give us every day new testimonies of his taste and circumspection; sometimes the street was too narrow for a double range of coaches; sometimes it was an obscure place, not inhabited by persons of quality. Some places were dirty, and some crowded; in some houses the furniture was ill suited, and in others the stairs were too narrow. He had such fertility of objections that Miss *Trifle* was at last tired, and desisted from all attempts for our accommodation.

In the mean time I have still continued to see my company on a second floor, and am asked twenty times a day when I am to leave those odious lodgings, in which I live tumultuously without pleasure, and expensively without honour. My husband thinks so highly of Mr. *Quick,* that he cannot be persuaded to remove without his approbation; and Mr. *Quick* thinks his reputation raised by the multiplication of difficulties.

In this distress to whom can I have recourse? I find my temper vitiated by daily disappointment, by the sight of

---

[29] Symbols of aristocracy. "The coronet of a duke is adorned with strawberry leaves; that of a marquis has leaves with pearls interposed; that of an earl raises the pearls above the leaves; that of a viscount is surrounded with only pearls; that of a baron has only four pearls" (Johnson's *Dictionary*).

pleasures which I cannot partake, and the possession of riches which I cannot enjoy. Dear Mr. *Idler,* inform my husband that he is trifling away, in superfluous vexation, the few months which custom has appropriated to delight; that matrimonial quarrels are not easily reconciled between those that have no children; that wherever we settle he must always find some inconvenience; but nothing is so much to be avoided as a perpetual state of enquiry and suspense.

I am, Sir,
Your humble servant,
PEGGY HEARTLESS.

INTRODUCTION TO . . . CLOATHING FRENCH PRISONERS OF WAR

The Committee entrusted with the money contributed to the relief of the subjects of *France,* now prisoners in the *British* dominions, here lay before the publick an exact account of all the sums received and expended, that the donors may judge how properly their benefactions have been applied.

Charity would lose its name, were it influenced by so mean a motive as human praise: it is therefore not intended to celebrate by any particular memorial, the liberality of single persons, or distinct societies; it is sufficient that their works praise them.

Yet he who is far from seeking honour, may very justly obviate censure. If a good example has been set, it may lose its influence by misrepresentation; and to free charity from reproach, is itself a charitable action.

Against the relief of the *French* only one argument has been brought; but that one is so popular and specious, that if it were to remain unexamined, it would by many be thought irrefragable. It has been urged, that charity, like other virtues, may be improperly and unseasonably exerted; that while we are relieving *Frenchmen,* there remain many *English-men* unrelieved; that while we lavish pity on our enemies, we forget the misery of our friends.

Grant this argument all it can prove, and what is the conclusion?—That to relieve the *French* is a good action, but that a better may be conceived. This is all the result, and this all is very little. To do the best can seldom be the lot of man; it is sufficient if, when opportunities are presented, he is ready to do good. How little virtue could be practiced, if beneficence were to wait always for the most proper objects, and the noblest occasions; occasions that may never happen, and objects that may never be found.

It is far from certain, that a single *Englishman* will suffer by the charity to the *French.* New scenes of misery make new impressions; and much of the charity which produced these donations, may be supposed to have been generated by a species of calamity never known among us before. Some imagine that the laws have provided all necessary relief in common cases, and remit the poor to the care of the publick; some have been deceived by fictitious misery, and are afraid of encouraging imposture; many have observed want to be the effect of

Written by Johnson for a member of the Committee, Thomas Hollis, in the midst of the Seven Years' War (1756–1763); text from Johnson's *Works,* ed. Sir John Hawkins (1787), vol. X. Its full title is *Introduction to the Proceedings of the Committee appointed to manage the Contributions begun at London, December 18, 1759 for Cloathing French Prisoners of War.*

vice, and consider casual almsgivers as patrons of idleness. But all these difficulties vanish in the present case: we know that for the Prisoners of War there is no legal provision; we see their distress, and are certain of its cause; we know that they are poor and naked, and poor and naked without a crime.

But it is not necessary to make any concessions. The opponents of this charity must allow it to be good, and will not easily prove it not to be the best. That charity is best, of which the consequences are most extensive: the relief of enemies has a tendency to unite mankind in fraternal affection; to soften the acrimony of adverse nations, and dispose them to peace and amity: in the mean time, it alleviates captivity, and takes away something from the miseries of war. The rage of war, however mitigated, will always fill the world with calamity and horror: let it not then be unnecessarily extended; let animosity and hostility cease together; and no man be longer deemed an enemy, than while his sword is drawn against us.

The effects of these contributions may, perhaps, reach still further. Truth is best supported by virtue: we may hope from those who feel or who see our charity, that they shall no longer detest as heresy that religion, which makes its professors the followers of Him, who has commanded us to "do good to them that hate us."

From A JOURNEY TO THE WESTERN ISLANDS OF SCOTLAND

SKY. ARMIDEL.[30]

In the morning, September the twentieth [1773], we found ourselves on the edge of the sea. Having procured a boat, we dismissed our Highlanders, whom I would recommend to the service of any future travellers, and were ferried over to the isle of Sky. We landed at *Armidel,* where we were met on the sands by Sir Alexander Macdonald,[31] who was at that time there with his lady, preparing to leave the island, and reside at Edinburgh.

Armidel is a neat house, built where the *Macdonalds* had once a seat, which was burnt in the commotions that followed the Revolution. The walled orchard, which belonged to the former house, still remains. It is well shaded by tall ash trees, of a species, as Mr. Janes[32] the fossilist informed me, uncommonly valuable. This plantation is very properly mentioned by Dr. *Campbell,*[33] in his new account of the state of *Britain,* and deserves attention; because it proves that the present nakedness of the *Hebrides* is not wholly the fault of nature.

As we sat at Sir Alexander's table, we were entertained, according to the ancient usage of the North, with the melody of the bagpipe. Every thing in those countries has its history. As the bagpiper was playing, an elderly Gentle-

---

Text from the first edition, 1775.

[30] The Isle of Skye is in the Inner Hebrides; Boswell and Johnson disembarked at Armidel on their arrival from the mainland.

[31] Johnson and Boswell had dined with Sir Alexander and his lady in London April 6, 1772, when Lady Macdonald had claimed "*Rasselas* . . . the finest Novel she had ever read" (*Private Papers of James Boswell,* ed. Geoffrey Scott and Frederick A. Pottle, 1930).

[32] Not otherwise identified.

[33] John Campbell, *A Political Survey of Great Britain* (2 vols., 1774).

man informed us, that in some remote time, the *Macdonalds* of Glengary having been injured, or offended by the inhabitants of *Culloden,* and resolving to have justice or vengeance, came to *Culloden* on a Sunday, where finding their enemies at worship, they shut them up in the church, which they set on fire; and this, said he, is the tune that the piper played while they were burning.

Narrations like this, however uncertain, deserve the notice of a traveller, because they are the only records of a nation that has no historians, and afford the most genuine representation of the life and character of the ancient Highlanders.

Under the denomination of *Highlander* are comprehended in Scotland all that now speak the Erse language, or retain the primitive manners, whether they live among the mountains or in the islands; and in that sense I use the name, when there is not some apparent reason for making a distinction.

In *Sky* I first observed the use of Brogues, a kind of artless shoes, stitched with thongs so loosely, that though they defend the foot from stones, they do not exclude water. Brogues were formerly made of raw hides, with the hair[34] inwards, and such are perhaps still used in rude and remote parts; but they are said not to last above two days. Where life is somewhat improved, they are now made of leather tanned with oak bark, as in other places, or with the bark of birch, or roots of tormentil, a substance recommended in defect of bark, about forty years ago, to the Irish tanners, by one to whom the parliament of that kingdom voted a reward. The leather of *Sky* is not completely penetrated by vegetable matter, and therefore cannot be very durable.

My inquiries about brogues, gave me an early specimen of Highland information. One day I was told, that to make brogues was a domestick art, which every man practiced for himself, and that a pair of brogues was the work of an hour.

I supposed that the husband made brogues as the wife made an apron, till next day it was told me, that a brogue-maker was a trade, and that a pair would cost half a crown. It will easily occur that these representations may both be true, and that, in some places, men may buy them, and in others make them for themselves; but I had both the accounts in the same house within two days.

Many of my subsequent inquiries upon more interesting topicks ended in the like uncertainty. He that travels in the Highlands may easily saturate his soul with intelligence, if he will acquiesce in the first account. The Highlander gives to every question an answer so prompt and peremptory, that skepticism itself is dared into silence, and the mind sinks before the bold reporter in unresisting credulity; but, if a second question be ventured, it breaks the enchantment; for it is immediately discovered, that what was told so confidently was told at hazard, and that such fearlessness of assertion was either the sport of negligence, or the refuge of ignorance.

If individuals are thus at variance with themselves, it can be no wonder that the accounts of different men are contradictory. The traditions of an ignorant and savage people have been for ages negligently heard, and unskilfully related. Distant events must have been mingled together, and the actions of one man given to another. These, however, are deficiencies in story, for which no man is now to be censured. It were enough, if what there is yet opportunity of examining were accurately inspected, and justly represented; but such is the laxity of Highland conversation, that the inquirer is kept in continual suspense, and by a kind of intellectual retrogradation, knows less as he hears more.

In the islands the plaid is rarely worn. The law by which the Highlanders have been obliged to change the form of their dress,[35] has, in all the places that we have visited, been universally obeyed. I

---

[34] The word *skin* in the first edition was corrected to read *hair* in a list of errata published with the edition.

[35] As a result of the Jacobite Rebellion of 1745.

have seen only one gentleman completely clothed in the ancient habit, and by him it was worn only occasionally and wantonly.[36] The common people do not think themselves under any legal necessity of having coats; for they say that the law against plaids was made by Lord Hardwicke, and was in force only for his life: but the same poverty that made it then difficult for them to change their clothing, hinders them now from changing it again.

The fillibeg,[37] or lower garment, is still very common, and the bonnet almost universal; but their attire is such as produces, in a sufficient degree, the effect intended by the law, of abolishing the dissimilitude of appearance between the Highlanders and the other inhabitants of Britain; and, if dress be supposed to have much influence, facilitates their coalition with their fellow-subjects.

What we have long used we naturally like, and therefore the Highlanders were unwilling to lay aside their plaid, which yet to an unprejudiced spectator must appear an incommodious and cumbersome dress; for hanging loose upon the body, it must flutter in a quick motion, or require one of the hands to keep it close. The Romans always laid aside the gown when they had any thing to do. It was a dress so unsuitable to war, that the same word which signified a gown signified peace. The chief use of a plaid seems to be this, that they could commodiously wrap themselves in it, when they were obliged to sleep without a better cover.

In our passage from *Scotland* to *Sky,* we were wet for the first time with a shower. This was the beginning of the Highland winter, after which we were told that a succession of three dry days was not to be expected for many months. The winter of the *Hebrides* consists of little more than rain and wind. As they are surrounded by an ocean never frozen, the blasts that come to them over the water are too much softened to have the power of congelation.[38] The salt loughs, or inlets of the sea, which shoot very far into the island, never have any ice upon them, and the pools of fresh water will never bear the walker. The snow that sometimes falls, is soon dissolved by the air, or the rain.

This is not the description of a cruel climate, yet the dark months are here a time of great distress; because the summer can do little more than feed itself, and winter comes with its cold and its scarcity upon families very slenderly provided.

POPE

[THE EARLY YEARS]

Alexander Pope was born in London, May 22, 1688, of parents whose rank or station was never ascertained: we are informed that they were of *gentle blood;* that his father was of a family of which the Earl of Downe[39] was the head, and that his mother was the daughter of William Turner, Esquire, of York, who

Text follows that of Johnson's *Works,* ed. Sir John Hawkins (1787), vol. IV; it was originally published in 1781 as part of *The Lives of the Most Eminent English Poets.*

[36] carelessly.
[37] kilt.
[38] "act of turning fluids to solids" (Johnson's *Dictionary*).

[39] This is now known to be wrong, as many of the apparent facts at Johnson's disposal necessarily were, but George Sherburn says in his authentic record *The Early Career of Alexander Pope* (1934) that "Johnson's life of Pope . . . is easily the most satisfactory of the lives of the poet yet written."

had likewise three sons, one of whom had the honour of being killed, and the other of dying, in the service of Charles the First; the third was made a general officer in Spain, from whom the sister inherited what sequestrations and forfeitures had left in the family.

This, and this only, is told by Pope; who is more willing, as I have heard observed, to shew what his father was not, than what he was. It is allowed that he grew rich by trade; but whether in a shop or on the Exchange was never discovered, till Mr. Tyers told, on the authority of Mrs. Racket, that he was a linen-draper in the Strand. Both parents were papists.[40]

Pope was from his birth of a constitution tender and delicate; but is said to have shewn remarkable gentleness and sweetness of disposition. The weakness of his body continued through his life; but the mildness of his mind perhaps ended with his childhood. His voice, when he was young, was so pleasing, that he was called in fondness the *little Nightingale*.

Being not sent early to school, he was taught to read by an aunt; and when he was seven or eight years old, became a lover of books. He first learned to write by imitating printed books; a species of penmanship in which he retained great excellence through his whole life, though his ordinary hand was not elegant.

When he was about eight, he was placed in Hampshire under Taverner, a Romish priest, who, by a method very rarely practised, taught him the Greek and Latin rudiments together. He was now first regularly initiated in poetry by the perusal of Ogylby's *Homer*,[41] and Sandys' *Ovid*:[42] Ogylby's assistance he never repaid with any praise; but of Sandys he declared, in his notes to the *Iliad,* that English poetry owed much of its present beauty to his translations.

Sandys very rarely attempted original composition.

From the care of Taverner, under whom his proficiency was considerable, he was removed to a school at Twyford near Winchester, and again to another school about Hyde-park Corner; from which he used sometimes to stroll to the playhouse, and was so delighted with theatrical exhibitions, that he formed a kind of play from Ogylby's *Iliad,* with some verses of his own intermixed, which he persuaded his school-fellows to act, with the addition of his master's gardener, who personated *Ajax*.

At the two last schools he used to represent himself as having lost part of what Taverner had taught him, and on his master at Twyford he had already exercised his poetry in a lampoon. Yet under those masters he translated more than a fourth part of the *Metamorphoses*. If he kept the same proportion in his other exercises, it cannot be thought that his loss was great.

He tells of himself, in his poems, that *he lisp'd in numbers;*[43] and used to say that he could not remember the time when he began to make verses. In the style of fiction it might have been said of him as of Pindar, that, when he lay in his cradle, *the bees swarmed about his mouth.*

About the time of the Revolution,[44] his father, who was undoubtedly disappointed by the sudden blast of popish prosperity, quitted his trade, and retired to Binfield in Windsor Forest, with about twenty thousand pounds; for which, being conscientiously determined not to entrust it to the government, he found no better use than that of locking it up in a chest, and taking from it what his expences required; and his life was long enough to consume a great part of it, before his son came to the inheritance.

---

[40] Roman Catholics.

[41] John Ogilby's *Iliad* (1660) and *Odyssey* (1665).

[42] George Sandys's translation of the *Metamorphoses* was completed in America and published in London in 1626.

[43] *An Epistle from Mr. Pope to Dr. Arbuth-* *not* (1735), 1. 128, the "numbers" being poetic measures.

[44] i.e., 1688–1689, when the retirement of the Catholic monarch James II and the recognition of William and Mary insured Protestant succession to the throne and brought about an act requiring the removal of Catholics from London to a distance of ten miles.

To Binfield Pope was called by his father when he was about twelve years old; and there he had for a few months the assistance of one Deane, another priest, of whom he learned only to construe a little of *Tully's Offices*.[45] How Mr. Deane could spend, with a boy who had translated so much of *Ovid,* some months over a small part of *Tully's Offices,* it is now vain to enquire.

Of a youth so successfully employed, and so conspicuously improved, a minute account must be naturally desired; but curiosity must be contented with confused, imperfect, and sometimes improbable intelligence. Pope, finding little advantage from external help, resolved thenceforward to direct himself, and at twelve formed a plan of study which he completed with little other incitement than the desire of excellence.

His primary and principal purpose was to be a poet, with which his father accidentally concurred, by proposing subjects, and obliging him to correct his performances by many revisals; after which the old gentleman, when he was satisfied, would say, *these are good rhymes.*

In his perusal of the English poets he soon distinguished the versification of Dryden, which he considered as the model to be studied, and was impressed with such veneration for his instructer, that he persuaded some friends to take him to the coffee-house which Dryden frequented, and pleased himself with having seen him.

Dryden died May 1, 1701,[46] some days before Pope was twelve; so early must he therefore have felt the power of harmony, and the zeal of genius. Who does not wish that Dryden could have known the value of the homage that was paid him, and foreseen the greatness of his young admirer?

The earliest of Pope's productions is his *Ode on Solitude,* written before he was twelve, in which there is nothing more than other forward boys have attained, and which is not equal to Cowley's performances at the same age.

His time was now spent wholly in reading and writing. As he read the Classicks, he amused himself with translating them; and at fourteen made a version of the first book of the *Thebais,*[47] which, with some revision, he afterwards published. He must have been at this time, if he had no help, a considerable proficient in the Latin tongue.

By Dryden's Fables, which had then been not long published, and were much in the hands of poetical readers, he was tempted to try his own skill in giving Chaucer a more fashionable appearance, and put *January and May,* and the *Prologue of the Wife of Bath,* into modern English. He translated likewise the Epistle of *Sappho to Phaon* from Ovid, to complete the version, which was before imperfect; and wrote some other small pieces, which he afterwards printed.

He sometimes imitated the English poets, and professed to have written at fourteen his poem upon *Silence,* after Rochester's *Nothing.* He had now formed his versification, and in the smoothness of his numbers surpassed his original: but this is a small part of his praise; he discovers such acquaintance both with human life and public affairs, as is not easily conceived to have been attainable by a boy of fourteen in *Windsor Forest.*

Next year he was desirous of opening to himself new sources of knowledge, by making himself acquainted with modern languages; and removed for a time to London, that he might study French and Italian, which, as he desired nothing more than to read them, were by diligent application soon dispatched. Of Italian learning he does not appear to have ever made much use in his subsequent studies.

He then returned to Binfield, and delighted himself with his own poetry. He tried all styles, and many subjects. He wrote a comedy, a tragedy, an epick poem, with panegyricks on all the princes

---

[45] The *De Officiis* (*Of Moral Duties*) of Cicero was the first classical book printed from movable type (1465).

[46] 1700.

[47] *The Thebiad,* an epic poem by the Latin poet Publius Papinius Statius.

of Europe; and, as he confesses, *thought himself the greatest genius that ever was.* Self-confidence is the first requisite to great undertakings; he, indeed, who forms his opinion of himself in solitude, without knowing the powers of other men, is very liable to errour; but it was the felicity of Pope to rate himself at his real value.

Most of his puerile productions were, by his maturer judgement, afterwards destroyed; *Alcander,* the epick poem, was burnt by the persuasion of Atterbury.[48] The tragedy was founded on the legend of *St. Genevieve.* Of the comedy there is no account.

Concerning his studies it is related, that he translated Tully *on old Age;* and that, besides his books of poetry and criticism, he read *Temple's Essays* and *Locke on human Understanding.* His reading, though his favourite authors are not known, appears to have been sufficiently extensive and multifarious; for his early pieces shew, with sufficient evidence, his knowledge of books.

He that is pleased with himself easily imagines that he shall please others. Sir William Trumbal, who had been ambassador at Constantinople, and secretary of state, when he retired from business, fixed his residence in the neighbourhood of Binfield. Pope, not yet sixteen, was introduced to the statesman of sixty, and so distinguished himself, that their interviews ended in friendship and correspondence. Pope was, through his whole life, ambitious of splendid acquaintance, and he seems to have wanted neither diligence nor success in attracting the notice of the great; for from his first entrance into the world, and his entrance was very early, he was admitted to familiarity with those whose rank or station made them most conspicuous.

From the age of sixteen the life of Pope, as an author, may be properly computed. He now wrote his pastorals,

which were shewn to the Poets and Criticks of that time; as they well deserved, they were read with admiration, and many praises were bestowed upon them and upon the Preface, which is both elegant and learned in a high degree; they were, however, not published till five years afterwards.

Cowley, Milton, and Pope, are distinguished among the English Poets by the early exertion of their powers; but the works of Cowley alone were published in his childhood, and therefore of him only can it be certain that his puerile performances received no improvement from his maturer studies.

At this time began his acquaintance with Wycherley,[49] a man who seems to have had among his contemporaries his full share of reputation, to have been esteemed without virtue, and caressed without good-humour. Pope was proud of his notice; Wycherley wrote verses in his praise, which he was charged by Dennis[50] with writing to himself, and they agreed for a while to flatter one another. It is pleasant to remark how soon Pope learned the cant of an author, and began to treat criticks with contempt, though he had yet suffered nothing from them.

But the fondness of Wycherley was too violent to last. His esteem of Pope was such, that he submitted some poems to his revision; and when Pope, perhaps proud of such confidence, was sufficiently bold in his criticisms, and liberal in his alterations, the old scribbler was angry to see his pages defaced, and felt more pain from the detection than content from the amendment of his faults. They parted; but Pope always considered him with kindness, and visited him a little time before he died.

Another of his early correspondents was Mr. Cromwell,[51] of whom I have learned nothing particular but that he used to ride a hunting in a tye-wig. He was fond, and perhaps vain, of amusing

---

[48] Francis Atterbury, Bishop of Rochester, exiled in 1723 for alleged complicity in the Jacobite cause.

[49] William Wycherley (1640?–1716), the dramatist.

[50] John Dennis (1657–1734), the critic.

[51] Henry Cromwell, with whom Pope corresponded in the years 1709–1711. The "tye-wig" which he is said to have worn while hunting was a wig on which the hair was drawn together in the back and tied with a ribbon.

himself with poetry and criticism; and sometimes sent his performances to Pope, who did not forbear such remarks as were now-and-then unwelcome. Pope, in his turn, put the juvenile version of *Statius* into his hands for correction.

Their correspondence afforded the publick its first knowledge of Pope's Epistolary Powers; for his Letters were given by Cromwell to one Mrs. Thomas, and she many years afterwards sold them to Curll,[52] who inserted them in a volume of his Miscellanies.

Walsh,[53] a name yet preserved among the minor poets, was one of his first encouragers. His regard was gained by the Pastorals, and from him Pope received the council by which he seems to have regulated his studies. Walsh advised him to correctness, which, as he told him, the English poets had hitherto neglected, and which therefore was left to him as a basis of fame; and, being delighted with rural poems, recommended to him to write a pastoral comedy, like those which are read so eagerly in Italy; a design which Pope probably did not approve, as he did not follow it.

Pope had now declared himself a poet; and thinking himself entitled to poetical conversation, began at seventeen, to frequent Will's, a coffee-house on the north side of Russel-street in Covent-garden, where the wits of that time used to assemble, and where Dryden had, when he lived, been accustomed to preside.

During this period of his life he was indefatigably diligent, and insatiably curious; wanting health for violent, and money for expensive pleasures, and having certainly excited in himself very strong desires of intellectual eminence, he spent much of his time over his books; but he read only to store his mind with facts and images, seizing all that his authors presented with undistinguishing voracity, and with an appetite for knowledge too eager to be nice. In a mind like his, however, all the faculties were at once involuntarily improving. Judgement is forced upon us by experience. He that reads many books must compare one opinion or one style with another; and when he compares, must necessarily distinguish, reject, and prefer. But the account given by himself of his studies was, that from fourteen to twenty he read only for amusement, from twenty to twenty-seven for improvement and instruction; that in the first part of this time he desired only to know, and in the second he endeavoured to judge.

The Pastorals, which had been for some time handed about among poets and criticks, were at last printed (1709) in Tonson's Miscellany, in a volume which began with the Pastorals of Philips,[54] and ended with those of Pope.

The same year was written the *Essay on Criticism;* a work which displays such extent of comprehension, such nicety of distinction, such acquaintance with mankind, and such knowledge both of ancient and modern learning, as are not often attained by the maturest age and longest experience. It was published about two years afterwards; and being praised by Addison in the *Spectator*[55] with sufficient liberality, met with so much favour as enraged Dennis,[56] "who," he says, "found himself attacked, without any manner of provocation on his side, and attacked in his person, instead of his writings, by one who was wholly a stranger to him, at a time when all the world knew he was persecuted by fortune; and not only saw that this was attempted in a clandestine manner, with the utmost falsehood and calumny, but found that all this was done by a little affected hypocrite, who had nothing in his mouth at the same time but truth, candour, friendship, good-nature, humanity, and magnanimity."

How the attack was clandestine is not easily perceived, nor how his person is

---

[52] Edmund Curll, a publisher who used sensationalism to promote the sale of his books.

[53] William Walsh (1663–1708).

[54] Ambrose Philips (1675?–1749). See Pope's essay comparing his pastorals with those of Philips to his own advantage in *The Guardian*

above, pp. 197–201.

[55] No. 253.

[56] —to publish *Reflections Critical and Satyrical upon a Late Rhapsody, call'd An Essay upon Criticism* (1711), from which the quotations which follow are derived.

depreciated; but he seems to have known something of Pope's character, in whom may be discovered an appetite to talk too frequently of his own virtues.

The pamphlet is such as rage might be expected to dictate. He supposes himself to be asked two questions; whether the Essay will succeed, and who or what is the author.

Its success he admits to be secured by the false opinions then prevalent; the author he concludes to be *young and raw*.

"First, because he discovers a sufficiency beyond his little ability, and hath rashly undertaken a task infinitely above his force. Secondly, while this little author struts, and affects the dictatorian air, he plainly shews, that at the same time he is under the rod; and while he pretends to give law to others, is a pedantick slave to authority and opinion. Thirdly, he hath, like school-boys, borrowed both from living and dead. Fourthly, he knows not his own mind, and frequently contradicts himself. Fifthly, he is almost perpetually in the wrong."

All these positions he attempts to prove by quotations and remarks; but his desire to do mischief is greater than his power. He has, however, justly criticised some passages, in these lines:

There are whom heaven has bless'd with store of wit,
Yet want as much again to manage it;
For wit and judgement ever are at strife . . .

It is apparent that *wit* has two meanings, and that what is wanted, though called *wit,* is truly judgement. So far Dennis is undoubtedly right; but, not content with argument, he will have a little mirth, and triumphs over the first couplet in terms too elegant to be forgotten. "By the way, what rare numbers are here! Would not one swear that this youngster had espoused some antiquated Muse, who had sued out a divorce on account of impotence from some superannuated sinner; and, having been p—xed[57] by her

former spouse, has got the gout in her decrepit age, which makes her hobble so damnably." This was the man who would reform a nation sinking into barbarity.

In another place Pope himself allowed that Dennis had detected one of those blunders which are called *bulls*. The first edition had this line:

What is this wit—
Where wanted, scorn'd; and envied where acquir'd?

"How," says the critick, "can wit be *scorn'd* where it is not? Is not this a figure frequently employed in Hibernian[58] land? The person that wants this wit may indeed be scorned, but the scorn shews the honour which the contemner has for wit." Of this remark Pope made the proper use, by correcting the passage.

I have preserved, I think, all that is reasonable in Dennis's criticism; it remains that justice be done to his delicacy. "For his acquaintance (says Dennis) he names Mr. Walsh, who had by no means the qualification which this author reckons absolutely necessary to a critick, it being very certain that he was, like this Essayer, a very indifferent poet; he loved to be well-dressed; and I remember a little young gentleman whom Mr. Walsh used to take into his company, as a double foil to his person and capacity. —Enquire between *Sunninghill* and *Oakingham*[59] for a young, short, squab gentleman, the very bow of the God of Love, and tell me whether he be a proper author to make personal reflections?— He may extol the antients, but he has reason to thank the gods that he was born a modern; for had he been born of Grecian parents, and his father consequently had by law had the absolute disposal of him, his life had been no longer than that of one of his poems, the life of half a day.—Let the person of a gentleman of his parts be never so contemptible, his inward man is ten times more ridiculous; it being impossible that his

---

[57] poxed; meaning disfigured from syphilis.
[58] Ireland; a blunder was sometimes referred to as an Irish bull.
[59] Villages on either side of Binfield.

outward form, though it be that of downright monkey, should differ so much from human shape, as his unthinking immaterial part does from human understanding." Thus began the hostility between Pope and Dennis, which, though it was suspended for a short time, never was appeased. Pope seems, at first, to have attacked him wantonly; but though he always professed to despise him, he discovers, by mentioning him very often, that he felt his force or his venom.

Of this Essay Pope declared that he did not expect the sale to be quick, because *not one gentleman in sixty, even of liberal education, could understand it.* The gentlemen, and the education of that time, seem to have been of a lower character than they are of this. He mentioned a thousand copies as a numerous impression.

Dennis was not his only censurer; the zealous papists thought the monks treated with too much contempt, and Erasmus too studiously praised; but to these objections he had not much regard.

The *Essay* has been translated into French by *Hamilton,* author of the *Comte de Grammont,* whose version was never printed, by *Robotham,* secretary to the King for Hanover, and by *Resnel;* and commented by Dr. Warburton,[60] who has discovered in it such order and connection as was not perceived by Addison, nor, as is said, intended by the author.

Almost every poem, consisting of precepts, is so far arbitrary and immethodical, that many of the paragraphs may change places with no apparent inconvenience; for of two or more positions, depending upon some remote and general principle, there is seldom any cogent reason why one should precede the other. But for the order in which they stand, whatever it be, a little ingenuity may easily give a reason. *It is possible,* says Hooker,[61] *that by long circumduction, from any one truth all truth may be inferred.* Of all homogeneous truths, at least of all truths respecting the same general end, in whatever series they may be produced, a concatenation by intermediate ideas may be formed, such as, when it is once shewn, shall appear natural; but if this order be reversed, another mode of connection equally specious may be found or made. Aristotle is praised for naming Fortitude first of the cardinal virtues, as that without which no other virtue can steadily be practised; but he might, with equal propriety, have placed Prudence and Justice before it, since without Prudence Fortitude is mad; without Justice, it is mischievous.

As the end of method is perspicuity, that series is sufficiently regular that avoids obscurity; and where there is no obscurity, it will not be difficult to discover method.

In the *Spectator*[62] was published the *Messiah,* which he first submitted to the perusal of Steele, and corrected in compliance with his criticisms.

It is reasonable to infer, from his Letters, that the verses on the *Unfortunate Lady* were written about the time when his *Essay* was published. The Lady's name and adventures I have sought with fruitless enquiry.

I can therefore tell no more than I have learned from Mr. Ruffhead,[63] who writes with the confidence of one who could trust his information. She was a woman of eminent rank and large fortune, the ward of an unkle, who, having given her a proper education, expected like other guardians that she should make at least an equal match; and such he proposed to her, but found it rejected in favour of a young gentleman of inferior condition.

Having discovered the correspondence between the two lovers, and finding the young lady determined to abide by her own choice, he supposed that separation might do what can rarely be done by arguments, and sent her into a foreign

---

[60] William Warburton (1698–1779) edited Pope's works in nine volumes, 1751.

[61] Richard Hooker, *Of the Lawes of Ecclesiasticall Politie* (1593), Bk. II, chap. i, sec. 2: The actual words are: "By long circuit of deduction it may be that even all truth out of any truth may be concluded."

[62] No. 378.

[63] Owen Ruffhead, *Life of Pope* (1769).

country, where she was obliged to converse only with those from whom her unkle had nothing to fear.

Her lover took care to repeat his vows; but his letters were intercepted and carried to her guardian, who directed her to be watched with still greater vigilance; till of this restraint she grew so impatient, that she bribed a woman-servant to procure her a sword, which she directed to her heart.

From this account, given with evident intention to raise the Lady's character, it does not appear that she had any claim to praise, nor much to compassion. She seems to have been impatient, violent, and ungovernable. Her unkle's power could not have lasted long; the hour of liberty and choice would have come in time. But her desires were too hot for delay, and she liked self-murder better than suspence.

Nor is it discovered that the unkle, whoever he was, is with much justice delivered to posterity as a *false Guardian;* he seems to have done only that for which a guardian is appointed; he endeavoured to direct his niece till she should be able to direct herself. Poetry has not often been worse employed than in dignifying the amorous fury of a raving girl.

Not long after, he wrote the *Rape of the Lock,* the most airy, the most ingenious, and the most delightful of all his compositions, occasioned by a frolick of gallantry, rather too familiar, in which Lord Petre cut off a lock of Mrs. Arabella Fermor's hair. This, whether stealth or violence, was so much resented, that the commerce of the two families, before very friendly, was interrupted. Mr. Caryl,[64] a gentleman who, being secretary to King James's Queen, had followed his Mistress into France, and who being the author of *Sir Solomon Single,* a comedy, and some translations, was entitled to the notice of a Wit, solicited Pope to endeavour a reconciliation by a ludicrous poem, which might bring both the parties to a better temper. In compliance with Caryl's request, though his name was for a long time marked only by the first and last letter, C——l, a poem of two cantos was written (1711), as is said, in a fortnight, and sent to the offended Lady, who liked it well enough to shew it; and, with the usual process of literary transactions, the author, dreading a surreptitious edition, was forced to publish it.

The event is said to have been such as was desired; the pacification and diversion of all to whom it related, except Sir *George Brown,* who complained with some bitterness that, in the character of *Sir Plume,* he was made to talk nonsense. Whether all this be true, I have some doubt; for at Paris, a few years ago, a niece of Mrs. Fermor, who presided in an English Convent, mentioned Pope's work with very little gratitude, rather as an insult than an honour; and she may be supposed to have inherited the opinion of her family.

At its first appearance it was termed by Addison *merum sal.*[65] Pope, however, saw that it was capable of improvement; and, having luckily contrived to borrow his machinery from the *Rosicrucians,*[66] imparted the scheme with which his head was teeming to Addison, who told him that his work, as it stood, was *a delicious little thing,* and gave him no encouragement to retouch it.

This has been too hastily considered as an instance of Addison's jealousy; for as he could not guess the conduct of the new design, or the possibilities of pleasure comprised in a fiction of which there had been no examples, he might very reasonably and kindly persuade the author to acquiesce in his own prosperity, and forbear an attempt which he considered as an unnecessary hazard.

Addison's counsel was happily rejected. Pope foresaw the future efflorescence of imagery then budding in his mind, and resolved to spare no art, or industry of cultivation. The soft luxuri-

---

[64] John Caryll, one of Pope's close friends; Johnson has confused Caryll with his uncle.
[65] "inimitable wit."
[66] Members of a society devoted to occult lore.

ance of his fancy was already shooting, and all the gay varieties of diction were ready at his hand to colour and embellish it.

His attempt was justified by its success. The *Rape of the Lock* stands forward, in the classes of literature, as the most exquisite example of ludicrous poetry. Berkeley[67] congratulated him upon the display of powers more truly poetical than he had shewn before; with elegance of description and justness of precepts, he had now exhibited boundless fertility of invention.

He always considered the intermixture of the machinery with the action as his most successful exertion of poetical art. He indeed could never afterwards produce any thing of such unexampled excellence. Those performances, which strike with wonder, are combinations of skilful genius with happy casualty; and it is not likely that any felicity, like the discovery of a new race of preternatural[68] agents, should happen twice to the same man.

Of this poem the author was, I think, allowed to enjoy the praise for a long time without disturbance. Many years afterwards Dennis published some remarks upon it, with very little force, and with no effect; for the opinion of the publick was already settled, and it was no longer at the mercy of criticism.

About this time he published the *Temple of Fame,* which, as he tells Steele in their correspondence, he had written two years before; that is, when he was only twenty-two years old, an early time of life for so much learning and so much observation as that work exhibits.

On this poem Dennis afterwards published some remarks, of which the most reasonable is, that some of the lines represent *motion* as exhibited by *sculpture.*

Of the Epistle from *Eloisa to Abelard,* I do not know the date. His first inclination to attempt a composition of that

tender kind arose, as Mr. Savage[69] told me, from his perusal of Prior's *Nut-brown Maid.* How much he has surpassed Prior's work it is not necessary to mention, when perhaps it may be said with justice, that he has excelled every composition of the same kind. The mixture of religious hope and resignation gives an elevation and dignity to disappointed love, which images merely natural cannot bestow. The gloom of a convent strikes the imagination with far greater force than the solitude of a grove.

This piece was, however, not much his favourite in his latter years, though I never heard upon what principle he slighted it.

In the next year (1713) he published *Windsor Forest;* of which part was, as he relates, written at sixteen, about the same time as his Pastorals, and the latter part was added afterwards: where the addition begins, we are not told. The lines relating to the Peace confess their own date. It is dedicated to Lord Landsdowne,[70] who was then high in reputation and influence among the Tories; and it is said, that the conclusion of the poem gave great pain to Addison, both as a poet and a politician. Reports like this are often spread with boldness very disproportionate to their evidence. Why should Addison receive any particular disturbance from the last lines of *Windsor Forest?* If contrariety of opinion could poison a politician, he would not live a day; and, as a poet, he must have felt Pope's force of genius much more from many other parts of his works.

The pain that Addison might feel it is not likely that he would confess; and it is certain that he so well suppressed his discontent, that Pope now thought himself his favourite; for, having been consulted in the revisal of *Cato,*[71] he introduced it by a Prologue; and, when Dennis published his Remarks, under-

---

[67] George Berkeley, the philosopher. See pp. 203–205.

[68] "different from what is natural" (Johnson's *Dictionary*).

[69] Richard Savage (1697?–1743), a friend of Johnson's during his early years in London.

[70] George Granville, Baron Lansdowne (1667–1735); the Treaty of Utrecht, by which the war with Spain was brought to a close, was the work of the Tory government.

[71] Addison's tragedy.

took not indeed to vindicate but to revenge his friend, by a *Narrative of the
Frenzy of John Dennis.*

There is reason to believe that Addison gave no encouragement to this disingenuous hostility; for, says Pope, in a
Letter to him, "indeed your opinion, that
'tis entirely to be neglected, would be my
own in my own case; but I felt more
warmth here than I did when I first saw
his book against myself (though indeed
in two minutes it made me heartily
merry)." Addison was not a man on
whom such cant of sensibility could make
much impression. He left the pamphlet
to itself, having disowned it to Dennis,
and perhaps did not think Pope to have
deserved much by his officiousness.

This year was printed in the *Guardian*
the ironical comparison between the Pastorals of Philips and Pope; a composition
of artifice, criticism, and literature, to
which nothing equal will easily be
found. The superiority of Pope is so ingeniously dissembled, and the feeble lines
of Philips so skilfully preferred, that
Steele, being deceived, was unwilling to
print the paper lest Pope should be offended. Addison immediately saw the
writer's design; and, as it seems, had
malice enough to conceal his discovery,
and to permit a publication which, by
making his friend Philips ridiculous,
made him for ever an enemy to Pope.

It appears that about this time Pope
had a strong inclination to unite the art
of Painting with that of Poetry, and put
himself under the tuition of Jervas.[72]
He was near-sighted, and therefore not
formed by nature for a painter: he tried,
however, how far he could advance, and
sometimes persuaded his friends to sit. A
picture of Betterton,[73] supposed to be
drawn by him, was in the possession of
Lord Mansfield: if this was taken from

the life, he must have begun to paint earlier; for Betterton was now dead. Pope's
ambition of this new art produced some
encomiastick verses to Jervas, which certainly shew his power as a poet; but I
have been told that they betray his ignorance of painting.

He appears to have regarded Betterton
with kindness and esteem; and after his
death published, under his name, a version into modern English of Chaucer's
Prologues, and one of his Tales, which,
as was related by Mr. Harte,[74] were believed to have been the performance of
Pope himself by Fenton,[75] who made him
a gay offer of five pounds, if he would
shew them in the hand of Betterton.

[THE TRANSLATIONS OF HOMER]

The next year (1713) produced a
bolder attempt, by which profit was
sought as well as praise. The poems
which he had hitherto written, however
they might have diffused his name, had
made very little addition to his fortune.
The allowance which his father made
him, though, proportioned[76] to what he
had, it might be liberal, could not be
large; his religion hindered him from the
occupation of any civil employment,[77]
and he complained that he wanted even
money to buy books.

He therefore resolved to try how far
the favour of the publick extended, by
soliciting a subscription to a version of
the *Iliad,* with large notes.

To print by subscription was, for some
time, a practice peculiar to the English.
The first considerable work, for which
this expedient was employed, is said to
have been Dryden's *Virgil;* and it had
been tried again with great success when
the *Tatlers* were collected into volumes.

---

[72] Charles Jervas (1675?–1739), a portrait
painter; Pope made frequent use of his London
residence, "next Door to the Right Hon. the
Lord Viscount Townshend's," in Cleveland
Court.

[73] Thomas Betterton (1635?–1710), a famous English actor.

[74] Walter Harte (1709–1774), friend of
Pope's and Johnson's, and a one-time tutor to

the illegitimate son of the Earl of Chesterfield.

[75] Elijah Fenton (1683–1730), playwright
and assistant to Pope in his edition of Shakespeare's works and in the translation of the
Odyssey.

[76] in proportion.

[77] As a Catholic, he was not entitled to
service in the government.

There was reason to believe that Pope's attempt would be successful. He was in the full bloom of reputation, and was personally known to almost all whom dignity of employment or splendour of reputation had made eminent; he conversed indifferently with both parties, and never disturbed the publick with his political opinions; and it might be naturally expected, as each faction then boasted its literary zeal, that the great men, who on other occasions practised all the violence of opposition, would emulate each other in their encouragement of a poet who had delighted all, and by whom none had been offended.

With those hopes, he offered an English *Iliad* to subscribers, in six volumes in quarto, for six guineas; a sum, according to the value of money at that time, by no means inconsiderable, and greater than I believe to have been ever asked before. His proposal, however, was very favourably received; and the patrons of literature were busy to recommend his undertaking, and promote his interest. Lord Oxford,[78] indeed, lamented that such a genius should be wasted upon a work not original; but proposed no means by which he might live without it. Addison recommended caution and moderation, and advised him not to be content with the praise of half the nation, when he might be universally favoured.

The greatness of the design, the popularity of the author, and the attention of the literary world, naturally raised such expectations of the future sale, that the booksellers made their offers with great eagerness; but the highest bidder was *Bernard Lintot,* who became proprietor on condition of supplying, at his own expence, all the copies which were to be delivered to subscribers or presented to friends, and paying two hundred pounds for every volume.[79]

Of the Quartos it was, I believe, stipulated that none should be printed but for the author, that the subscription might not be depreciated; but Lintot impressed the same pages upon a small Folio, and paper perhaps a little thinner; and sold exactly at half the price, for half a guinea each volume, books so little inferior to the Quartos, that, by a fraud of trade, those Folios, being afterwards shortened by cutting away the top and bottom, were sold as copies printed for the subscribers.

Lintot printed two hundred and fifty on royal paper in Folio, for two guineas a volume; of the small Folio, having printed seventeen hundred and fifty copies of the first volume, he reduced the number in the other volumes to a thousand.

It is unpleasant to relate that the bookseller, after all his hopes and all his liberality, was, by a very unjust and illegal action, defrauded of his profit. An edition of the English *Iliad* was printed in Holland in Duodecimo, and imported clandestinely for the gratification of those who were impatient to read what they could not yet afford to buy. This fraud could only be counteracted by an edition equally cheap and more commodious; and Lintot was compelled to contract his Folio at once into a Duodecimo, and lose the advantage of an intermediate gradation. The notes, which in the Dutch copies were placed at the end of each book, as they had been in the large volumes, were now subjoined to the text in the same page, and are therefore more easily consulted. Of this edition two thousand five hundred were first printed, and five thousand a few weeks afterwards; but indeed great numbers were necessary to produce considerable profit.

Pope, having now emitted his proposals, and engaged not only his own reputation, but in some degree that of his friends who patronised his subscription, began to be frighted at his own undertaking; and finding himself at first embarrassed with difficulties, which retarded and oppressed him, he was for a

---

78 Robert Harley, first Earl of Oxford (1661–1724), who until the death of Queen Anne was one of the principal secretaries of state; at the time (1714) proposals to publish a translation of the *Iliad* were circulated, Oxford was in prison on a charge of high treason.

79 Accurate details of the publication of the *Iliad,* as of all Pope's works, are presented in *Alexander Pope: A Bibliography* (1922, 1927) by R. H. Griffith.

time timorous and uneasy; had his nights disturbed by dreams of long journeys through unknown ways, and wished, as he said, *that somebody would hang him*.

This misery, however, was not of long countinuance; he grew by degrees more acquainted with Homer's images and expressions, and practice increased his facility of versification. In a short time he represents himself as dispatching regularly fifty verses a day, which would shew him by an easy computation the termination of his labour.

His own diffidence was not his only vexation. He that asks a subscription soon finds that he has enemies. All who do not encourage him defame him. He that wants money will rather be thought angry than poor; and he that wishes to save his money conceals his avarice by his malice. Addison had hinted his suspicion that Pope was too much a Tory; and some of the Tories suspected his principles because he had contributed to the *Guardian,* which was carried on by *Steele.*

To those who censured his politicks were added enemies yet more dangerous, who called in question his knowledge of Greek, and his qualifications for a translator of Homer. To these he made no publick opposition; but in one of his Letters escapes from them as well as he can. At an age like his, for he was not more than twenty-five, with an irregular education, and a course of life of which much seems to have passed in conversation, it is not very likely that he overflowed with Greek. But when he felt himself deficient he sought assistance; and what man of learning would refuse to help him? Minute enquiries into the force of words are less necessary in translating Homer than other poets, because his positions are general, and his representations natural, with very little dependence on local or temporary customs, on those changeable scenes of artificial life, which, by mingling original with accidental notions, and crowding the mind with images which time effaces, produce ambiguity in diction, and obscurity in books. To this open display of unadulterated nature it must be ascribed, that Homer has fewer passages of doubtful meaning than any other poet either in the learned or in modern languages. I have read of a man, who being, by his ignorance of Greek, compelled to gratify his curiosity with the Latin printed on the opposite page, declared that from the rude simplicity of the lines literally rendered, he formed nobler ideas of the Homeric majesty than from the laboured elegance of polished versions.

Those literal translations were always at hand, and from them he could easily obtain his author's sense with sufficient certainty: and among the readers of Homer the number is very small of those who find much in the Greek more than in the Latin, except the musick of the numbers.

If more help was wanting, he had the poetical translation of *Eobanus Hessus,*[80] an unwearied writer of Latin verses; he had the French Homers of *La Valterie* and *Dacier,*[81] and the English of *Chapman, Hobbes,* and *Ogylby.*[82] With Chapman, whose work, though now totally neglected, seems to have been popular almost to the end of the last century, he had very frequent consultations, and perhaps never translated any passage till he had read his version, which indeed he has been sometimes suspected of using instead of the original.

Notes were likewise to be provided; for the six volumes would have been very little more than six pamphlets without them. What the mere perusal of the text could suggest, Pope wanted no assistance to collect or methodize; but more was necessary; many pages were to be filled, and learning must supply materials to wit and judgement. Something might be gathered from Dacier; but no man loves to be indebted to his contemporaries, and

[80] Helius Eobanus Hessus (1488–1540) had turned the *Iliad* into Latin.

[81] La Valterie's translation appeared in 1681, that by Anne Lefebvre Dacier in 1711–1716.

[82] George Chapman's in 1598–1614, Thomas Hobbes's in 1676, and John Ogilby's in 1660–1665.

Dacier was accessible to common readers. Eustathius[83] was therefore necessarily consulted. To read Eustathius, of whose work there was then no Latin version, I suspect Pope, if he had been willing, not to have been able; some other was therefore to be found, who had leisure as well as abilities; and he was doubtless most readily employed who would do much work for little money.

The history of the notes has never been traced. Broome,[84] in his preface to his poems, declares himself the commentator *in part upon the Iliad;* and it appears from Fenton's Letter, preserved in the Museum, that Broome was at first engaged in consulting Eustathius; but that after a time, whatever was the reason, he desisted; another man of Cambridge was then employed, who soon grew weary of the work; and a third, that was recommended by *Thirlby,* is now discovered to have been *Jortin,*[85] a man since well known to the learned world, who complained that Pope, having accepted and approved his performance, never testified any curiosity to see him, and who professed to have forgotten the terms on which he worked. The terms which Fenton uses are very mercantile: *I think at first sight that his performance is very commendable, and have sent word for him to finish the 17th book, and to send it with his demands for his trouble. I have here enclosed the specimen; if the rest come before the return, I will keep them till I receive your order.*

Broome then offered his service a second time, which was probably accepted, as they had afterwards a closer correspondence. Parnell[86] contributed the Life of Homer, which Pope found so harsh, that he took great pains in correcting it; and by his own diligence, with such help as kindness or money could procure him, in somewhat more than five years he completed his version of the *Iliad,* with the notes. He began it in 1712, his twenty-fifth year; and concluded it in 1718, his thirtieth year.

When we find him translating fifty lines a day, it is natural to suppose that he would have brought his work to a more speedy conclusion. The *Iliad,* containing less than sixteen thousand verses, might have been dispatched in less than three hundred and twenty days by fifty verses in a day. The notes, compiled with the assistance of his mercenaries, could not be supposed to require more time than the text. According to this calculation, the progress of Pope may seem to have been slow; but the distance is commonly very great between actual performances and speculative possibility. It is natural to suppose, that as much as has been done to-day may be done to-morrow; but on the morrow some difficulty emerges, or some external impediment obstructs. Indolence, interruption, business, and pleasure, all take their turns of retardation; and every long work is lengthened by a thousand causes that can, and ten thousand that cannot, be recounted. Perhaps no extensive and multifarious performance was ever effected within the term originally fixed in the undertaker's mind. He that runs against Time, has an antagonist not subject to casualties.

The encouragement given to this translation, though report seems to have over-rated it, was such as the world has not often seen. The subscribers were five hundred and seventy-five. The copies for which subscriptions were given were six hundred and fifty-four; and only six hundred and sixty were printed. For those copies Pope had nothing to pay; he therefore received, including the two hundred pounds a volume, five thousand three hundred and twenty pounds four shillings, without deduction, as the books were supplied by Lintot.

By the success of his subscription Pope was relieved from those pecuniary distresses with which, notwithstanding his popularity, he had hitherto struggled. Lord Oxford had often lamented his disqualification for publick employment, but

---

[83] Eustathius of Thessalonica, Byzantine scholar (d. *c.* 1193), best known for his commentary on the *Iliad* and *Odyssey*.
[84] William Broome (1689–1745).

[85] John Jortin (1698–1770), at that time an undergraduate student; Thirlby was his tutor.
[86] Thomas Parnell (1679–1718), the poet.

never proposed a pension. While the translation of Homer was in its progress, Mr. Craggs,[87] then secretary of state, offered to procure him a pension, which, at least during his ministry, might be enjoyed with secrecy. This was not accepted by Pope, who told him, however, that, if he should be pressed with want of money, he would send to him for occasional supplies. Craggs was not long in power, and was never solicited for money by Pope, who disdained to beg what he did not want.

With the product of this subscription, which he had too much discretion to squander, he secured his future life from want, by considerable annuities. The estate of the Duke of Buckingham[88] was found to have been charged with five hundred pounds a year, payable to Pope, which doubtless his translation enabled him to purchase.

It cannot be unwelcome to literary curiosity, that I deduce thus minutely the history of the English *Iliad*. It is certainly the noblest version of poetry which the world has ever seen; and its publication must therefore be considered as one of the great events in the annals of Learning.

[Here a short passage citing Pope's workmanship is omitted.]

The *Iliad* was published volume by volume, as the translation proceeded; the four first books appeared in 1715. The expectation of this work was undoubtedly high, and every man who had connected his name with criticism, or poetry, was desirous of such intelligence as might enable him to talk upon the popular topick. Halifax,[89] who, by having been first a poet, and then a patron of poetry, had acquired the right of being a judge, was willing to hear some books while they were yet unpublished. Of this rehearsal Pope afterwards gave the following account.

"The famous Lord Halifax was rather a pretender to taste than really possessed of it.—When I had finished the two or three first books of my translation of the *Iliad,* that Lord desired to have the pleasure of hearing them read at his house—Addison, Congreve, and Garth,[90] were there at the reading. In four or five places, Lord Halifax stopt me very civilly, and with a speech each time, much of the same kind, 'I beg your pardon, Mr. Pope; but there is something in that passage that does not quite please me. Be so good as to mark the place, and consider it a little at your leisure.—I am sure you can give it a little turn.'—I returned from Lord Halifax's with Dr. Garth, in his chariot; and, as we were going along, was saying to the Doctor, that my Lord had laid me under a good deal of difficulty by such loose and general observations; that I had been thinking over the passages almost ever since, and could not guess at what it was that offended his Lordship in either of them. Garth laughed heartily at my embarrassment; said, I had not been long enough acquainted with Lord Halifax to know his way yet; that I need not puzzle myself about looking those places over and over, when I got home. 'All you need do (says he) is to leave them just as they are; call on Lord Halifax two or three months hence, thank him for his kind observations on those passages, and then read them to him as altered. I have known him much longer than you have, and will be answerable for the event.' I followed his advice; waited on Lord Halifax some time after; said, I hoped he would find his objections to those passages removed; read them to him exactly as they were at first: and his Lordship was extremely pleased with them, and cryed out, *Ay, now they are perfectly right: nothing can be better.*"

It is seldom that the great or the wise suspect that they are despised or cheated. Halifax, thinking this a lucky opportu-

[87] James Craggs (1685–1720) succeeded Addison as secretary of state.

[88] John Sheffield, Duke of Buckingham, died in February 1721; Pope edited his literary works (1723).

[89] Charles Montagu, first Earl of Halifax (1661–1715).

[90] Sir Samuel Garth (1661–1719), author of *The Dispensary* (1699), a mock heroic poem.

nity of securing immortality, made some advances of favour and some overtures of advantage to Pope, which he seems to have received with sullen coldness. All our knowledge of this transaction is derived from a single Letter (Dec. 1, 1714), in which Pope says, "I am obliged to you, both for the favours you have done me, and those you intend me. I distrust neither your will nor your memory, when it is to do good; and if I ever become troublesome or solicitous, it must not be out of expectation, but out of gratitude. Your Lordship may cause me to live agreeably in the town, or contentedly in the country, which is really all the difference I set between an easy fortune and a small one. It is indeed a high strain of generosity in you to think of making me easy all my life, only because I have been so happy as to divert you some few hours: but, if I may have leave to add it is because you think me no enemy to my native country, there will appear a better reason; for I must of consequence be very much (as I sincerely am) yours &c."

These voluntary offers, and this faint acceptance, ended without effect. The patron was not accustomed to such frigid gratitude, and the poet fed his own pride with the dignity of independence. They probably were suspicious of each other. Pope would not dedicate till he saw at what rate his praise was valued; he would be *troublesome out of gratitude, not expectation.* Halifax thought himself entitled to confidence; and would give nothing, unless he knew what he should receive. Their commerce had its beginning in hope of praise on one side, and of money on the other, and ended because Pope was less eager of money than Halifax of praise. It is not likely that Halifax had any personal benevolence to Pope; it is evident that Pope looked on Halifax with scorn and hatred.

The reputation of this great work failed of gaining him a patron; but it deprived him of a friend. Addison and he were now at the head of poetry and criticism; and both in such a state of elevation, that, like the two rivals in the Roman state, one could no longer bear an equal, nor the other a superior. Of the gradual abatement of kindness between friends, the beginning is often scarcely discernible by themselves, and the process is continued by petty provocations, and incivilities sometimes peevishly returned, and sometimes contemptuously neglected, which would escape all attention but that of pride, and drop from any memory but that of resentment. That the quarrel of those two wits should be minutely deduced, is not to be expected from a writer to whom, as Homer says, *nothing but rumour has reached, and who has no personal knowledge.*

Pope doubtless approached Addison, when the reputation of their wit first brought them together, with the respect due to a man whose abilities were acknowledged, and who, having attained that eminence to which he was himself aspiring, had in his hands the distribution of literary fame. He paid court with sufficient diligence by his Prologue to *Cato,* by his abuse of Dennis, and with praise yet more direct, by his poem on the *Dialogues on Medals,*[91] of which the immediate publication was then intended. In all this there was no hypocrisy; for he confessed that he found in Addison something more pleasing than in any other man.

It may be supposed, that as Pope saw himself favoured by the world, and more frequently compared his own powers with those of others, his confidence increased, and his submission lessened; and that Addison felt no delight from the advances of a young wit, who might soon contend with him for the highest place. Every great man, of whatever kind be his greatness, has among his friends those who officiously, or insiduously, quicken his attention to offences, heighten his disgust, and stimulate his resentment. Of

---

[91] The title of Pope's *Verses occasioned by Mr. Addison's Treatise of Medals* (1720) was changed in the edition of 1735 to *Epistle V.*

To Mr. Addison, Occasioned by his Dialogues on Medals; the verses commemorate Addison's essay on ancient coins.

such adherents Addison doubtless had many, and Pope was now too high to be without them.

From the emission and reception of the Proposals for the *Iliad,* the kindness of Addison seems to have abated. Jervas the painter once pleased himself (Aug. 20, 1714) with imagining that he had re-established their friendship; and wrote to Pope that Addison once suspected him of too close a confederacy with Swift, but was now satisfied with his conduct. To this Pope answered, a week after, that his engagements to Swift were such as his services in regard to the subscription demanded, and that the Tories never put him under the necessity of asking leave to be grateful. *But,* says he, *as Mr. Addison must be the judge in what regards himself, and seems to have no very just one in regard to me, so I must own to you I expect nothing but civility from him.* In the same Letter he mentions Philips, as having been busy to kindle animosity between them; but, in a Letter to Addison, he expresses some consciousness of behaviour, inattentively deficient in respect.

Of Swift's industry in promoting the subscription there remains the testimony of Kennet,[92] no friend to either him or Pope.

"Nov. 2, 1713, Dr. Swift came into the coffee-house, and had a bow from every body but me, who, I confess, could not but despise him. When I came to the antichamber to wait, before prayers, Dr. Swift was the principal man of talk and business, and acted as master of requests. —Then he instructed a young nobleman that the *best Poet in England* was Mr. *Pope* (a papist), who had begun a translation of *Homer* into English verse, for which *he must have them all subscribe;* for, says he, the author *shall not* begin to print till *I have* a thousand guineas for him."

About this time it is likely that Steele, who was, with all his political fury,

good-natured and officious,[93] procured an interview between these angry rivals, which ended in aggravated malevolence. On this occasion, if the reports be true, Pope made his complaint with frankness and spirit, as a man undeservedly neglected or opposed; and Addison affected a contemptuous unconcern, and, in a calm even voice, reproached Pope with his vanity, and, telling him of the improvements which his early works had received from his own remarks and those of Steele, said, that he, being now engaged in publick business, had no longer any care for his poetical reputation; nor had any other desire, with regard to Pope, than that he should not, by too much arrogance, alienate the publick.

To this Pope is said to have replied with great keenness and severity, upbraiding Addison with perpetual dependance, and with the abuse of those qualifications which he had obtained at the publick cost, and charging him with mean endeavours to obstruct the progress of rising merit. The contest rose so high, that they parted at last without any interchange of civility.

The first volume of *Homer* was (1715) in time published; and a rival version of the first *Iliad,* for rivals the time of their appearance inevitably made them, was immediately printed, with the name of Tickell.[94] It was soon perceived that, among the followers of Addison, Tickell had the preference, and the criticks and poets divided into factions. *I,* says Pope, *have the town, that is, the mob, on my side; but it is not uncommon for the smaller party to supply by industry what it wants in numbers.—I appeal to the people as my rightful judges, and, while they are not inclined to condemn me, shall not fear the high-flyers[95] at Button's.* This opposition he immediately imputed to Addison, and complained of it in terms sufficiently resentful to Craggs, their common friend.

When Addison's opinion was asked,

[92] Basil Kennett (1674–1715), a miscellaneous writer.

[93] "kind" (Johnson's *Dictionary*).

[94] Thomas Tickell (1686–1740); Pope's first book of the *Iliad* came out June 6 and the version attributed to Tickell, but not certainly his, was brought out two days later.

[95] Persons who carry their opinions "to extravagance" (Johnson's *Dictionary*), meaning, in this context, Whigs.

he declared the versions to be both good, but Tickell's the best that had ever been written; and sometimes said that they were both good, but that Tickell had more of *Homer*.

Pope was now sufficiently irritated; his reputation and his interest were at hazard. He once intended to print together the four versions of Dryden, Maynwaring,[96] Pope, and Tickell, that they might be readily compared, and fairly estimated. This design seems to have been defeated by the refusal of Tonson, who was the proprietor of the other three versions.

Pope intended at another time a rigorous criticism of Tickell's translation, and had marked a copy, which I have seen, in all places that appeared defective. But while he was thus meditating defence or revenge, his adversary sunk before him without a blow; the voice of the publick were not long divided, and the preference was universally given to Pope's performance.

He was convinced, by adding one circumstance to another, that the other translation was the work of Addison himself; but if he knew it in Addison's lifetime, it does not appear that he told it. He left his illustrious antagonist to be punished by what has been considered as the most painful of all reflections, the remembrance of a crime perpetrated in vain.

The other circumstances of their quarrel were thus related by Pope.

"Philips seemed to have been encouraged to abuse me in coffee-houses, and conversations: and Gildon[97] wrote a thing about Wycherley, in which he had abused both me and my relations very grossly. Lord Warwick[98] himself told me one day, that it was in vain for me to endeavour to be well with Mr. Addison; that his jealous temper would never admit of a settled friendship between us: and, to convince me of what he had said, assured me, that Addison had encouraged

Gildon to publish those scandals, and had given him ten guineas after they were published. The next day, while I was heated with what I had heard, I wrote a Letter to Mr. Addison, to let him know that I was not unacquainted with this behaviour of his; that if I was to speak severely of him, in return for it, it should be not in such a dirty way, that I should rather tell him, himself, fairly of his faults, and allow his good qualities; and that it should be something in the following manner: I then adjoined the first sketch of what has since been called my satire on Addison. Mr. Addison used me very civilly ever after."

The verses on Addison, when they were sent to Atterbury, were considered by him as the most excellent of Pope's performances; and the writer was advised, since he knew where his strength lay, not to suffer it to remain unemployed.

This year (1715) being, by the subscription, enabled to live more by choice, having persuaded his father to sell their estate at Binfield, he purchased, I think only for his life, that house at Twickenham to which his residence afterwards procured so much celebration, and removed thither with his father and mother.

Here he planted the vines and the quincunx[99] which his verses mention; and being under the necessity of making a subterraneous passage to a garden on the other side of the road, he adorned it with fossile bodies, and dignified it with the title of a grotto; a place of silence and retreat, from which he endeavoured to persuade his friends and himself that cares and passions could be excluded.

A grotto is not often the wish or pleasure of an Englishman, who has more frequent need to solicit than exclude the sun; but Pope's excavation was requisite as an entrance to his garden, and, as some men try to be proud of their defects, he extracted an ornament from

[96] Arthur Maynwaring (1668–1712).

[97] Charles Gildon's *Memoirs of William Wycherley* (1718) had spoken slightingly of Pope's father as a "Rustick Parent."

[98] The Earl of Warwick, son of the widowed

Countess of Warwick to whom Addison was married in 1716; he was friendly with Pope.

[99] A popular garden design with trees planted in the center and at the four corners.

an inconvenience, and vanity produced a grotto where necessity enforced a passage. It may be frequently remarked of the studious and speculative, that they are proud of trifles, and that their amusements seem frivolous and childish; whether it be that men conscious of great reputation think themselves above the reach of censure, and safe in the admission of negligent indulgences, or that mankind expect from elevated genius an uniformity of greatness, and watch its degradation with malicious wonder, like him who having followed with his eye an eagle into the clouds, should lament that she ever descended to a perch.

While the volumes of his *Homer* were annually published, he collected his former works (1717) into one quarto volume, to which he prefixed a Preface, written with great spriteliness and elegance, which was afterwards reprinted, with some passages subjoined that he at first omitted; other marginal additions of the same kind he made in the later editions of his poems. Waller[100] remarks, that poets lose half their praise, because the reader knows not what they have blotted. Pope's voracity of fame taught him the art of obtaining the accumulated honour both of what he had published, and what he had suppressed.

In this year his father died suddenly, in his seventy-fifth year, having passed twenty-nine years in privacy. He is not known but by the character which his son has given him. If the money with which he retired was all gotten by himself, he had traded very successfully in times when sudden riches were rarely attainable.

The publication of the *Iliad* was at last completed in 1720. The splendor and success of this work raised Pope many enemies, that endeavoured to depreciate his abilities. Burnet,[101] who was afterwards a Judge of no mean reputation,

censured him in a piece called *Homerides* before it was published. Ducket likewise endeavoured to make him ridiculous. Dennis was the perpetual persecutor of all his studies. But, whoever his criticks were, their writings are lost; and the names which are preserved, are preserved in the *Dunciad*.

In this disastrous year (1720) of national infatuation, when more riches than Peru can boast were expected from the South Sea,[102] when the contagion of avarice tainted every mind, and even poets panted after wealth, Pope was seized with the universal passion, and ventured some of his money. The stock rose in its price; and he for a while thought himself *the Lord of thousands*. But this dream of happiness did not last long; and he seems to have waked soon enough to get clear with the loss only of what he once thought himself to have won, and perhaps not wholly of that.

Next year he published some select poems of his friend Dr. Parnell, with a very elegant Dedication to the Earl of Oxford; who, after all his struggles and dangers, then lived in retirement, still under the frown of a victorious faction, who could take no pleasure in hearing his praise.

He gave the same year (1721) an edition of *Shakespeare*. His name was now of so much authority, that Tonson thought himself entitled, by annexing it, to demand a subscription of six guineas for Shakespeare's plays in six quarto volumes; nor did his expectation much deceive him; for of seven hundred and fifty which he printed, he dispersed a great number at the price proposed. The reputation of that edition indeed sunk afterwards so low, that one hundred and forty copies were sold at sixteen shillings each.

On this undertaking, to which Pope was induced by a reward of two hundred and seventeen pounds twelve shillings,

---

[100] Edmund Waller (1606–1687); Johnson had in mind the following couplet from Waller's verses "Upon the Earl of Roscommon's Translation of Horace":
Poets lose half the praise they should have got
Could it be known what they discreetly blot.

[101] Sir Thomas Burnet (1694–1753) was aided by George Duckett (1684–1732) in this attack on Pope; the purpose was presumably political.
[102] An infamous financial speculation in South Sea stocks ended in 1720 when the bubble burst.

he seems never to have reflected afterwards without vexation; for Theobald,[103] a man of heavy diligence, with very slender powers, first, in a book called *Shakespeare Restored,* and then in a formal edition, detected his deficiencies with all the insolence of victory; and, as he was now high enough to be feared and hated, Theobald had from others all the help that could be supplied, by the desire of humbling a haughty character.

From this time Pope became an enemy to editors, collaters, commentators, and verbal criticks; and hoped to persuade the world, that he miscarried in this undertaking only by having a mind too great for such minute employment.

Pope in his edition[104] undoubtedly did many things wrong, and left many things undone; but let him not be defrauded of his due praise. He was the first that knew, at least the first that told, by what helps the text might be improved. If he inspected the early editions negligently, he taught others to be more accurate. In his Preface he expanded with great skill and elegance the character which had been given of Shakespeare by Dryden; and he drew the publick attention upon his works, which, though often mentioned, had been little read.

Soon after the appearance of the *Iliad,* resolving not to let the general kindness cool, he published proposals for a translation of the *Odyssey,* in five volumes, for five guineas. He was willing, however, now to have associates in his labour, being either weary with toiling upon another's thoughts, or having heard, as Ruffhead relates, that Fenton and Broome had already begun the work, and liking better to have them confederates than rivals.

In the patent,[105] instead of saying that he had *translated* the *Odyssey,* as he had said of the *Iliad,* he says that he had *undertaken* a translation: and in the proposals the subscription is said to be not solely for his own use, but for that of *two of his friends who have assisted him in this work.*

In 1723, while he was engaged in this new version, he appeared before the Lords at the memorable trial of Bishop Atterbury,[106] with whom he had lived in great familiarity, and frequent correspondence. Atterbury had honestly recommended to him the study of the popish controversy, in hope of his conversion; to which Pope answered in a manner that cannot much recommend his principles, or his judgement. In questions and projects of learning, they agreed better. He was called at the trial to give an account of Atterbury's domestick life, and private employment, that it might appear how little time he had left for plots. Pope had but few words to utter, and in those few he made several blunders.

His Letters to Atterbury express the utmost esteem, tenderness, and gratitude: *perhaps,* says he, *it is not only in this world that I may have cause to remember the Bishop of Rochester.* At their last interview in the Tower, Atterbury presented him with a Bible.

Of the *Odyssey* Pope translated only twelve books; the rest were the work of Broome and Fenton: the notes were written wholly by Broome, who was not over-liberally rewarded. The Publick was carefully kept ignorant of the several shares; and an account was subjoined at the conclusion, which is now known not to be true.

The first copy of Pope's books, with those of Fenton, are to be seen in the Museum. The parts of Pope are less interlined than the *Iliad;* and the latter books of the *Iliad* less than the former. He grew dexterous by practice, and every sheet enabled him to write the next with more facility. The books of Fenton have very few alterations by the hand of Pope. Those of Broome have not been found; but Pope complained, as it is reported, that he had much trouble in correcting them.

---

[103] Lewis Theobald (1688–1744), who was castigated by Pope as "piddling Tibbald."

[104] Johnson also had edited Shakespeare (1765).

[105] "a writ conferring some exclusive right or privilege" (Johnson's *Dictionary*); this was a letter announcing the intention of publishing, and hence seems to have been assumed by Johnson to lay claim to the territory.

[106] See note 48, above.

His contract with Lintot was the same as for the *Iliad,* except that only one hundred pounds were to be paid him for each volume. The number of subscribers was five hundred and seventy-four, and of copies eight hundred and nineteen; so that his profit, when he had paid his assistants, was still very considerable. The work was finished in 1725; and from that time he resolved to make no more translations.

The sale did not answer Lintot's expectation; and he then pretended to discover something of fraud in Pope, and commenced or threatened a suit in Chancery.

On the English *Odyssey* a criticism was published by Spence,[107] at that time Prelector of Poetry at Oxford; a man whose learning was not very great, and whose mind was not very powerful. His criticism, however, was commonly just; what he thought, he thought rightly; and his remarks were recommended by his coolness and candour. In him Pope had the first experience of a critick without malevolence, who thought it as much his duty to display beauties as expose faults; who censured with respect, and praised with alacrity.

[THE MIDDLE YEARS]

With this criticism Pope was so little offended, that he sought the acquaintance of the writer, who lived with him from that time in great familiarity, attended him in his last hours, and compiled memorials of his conversation. The regard of Pope recommended him to the great and powerful, and he obtained very valuable preferments in the Church.

Not long after, Pope was returning home from a visit in a friend's coach, which, in passing a bridge, was overturned into the water; the windows were closed, and being unable to force them

open, he was in danger of immediate death, when the postilion snatched him out by breaking the glass, of which the fragments cut two of his fingers in such a manner, that he lost their use.

Voltaire, who was then in England, sent him a Letter of Consolation. He had been entertained by Pope at his table, where he talked with so much grossness that Mrs. Pope[108] was driven from the room. Pope discovered, by a trick, that he was a spy for the Court, and never considered him as a man worthy of confidence.

He soon afterwards (1727) joined with Swift, who was then in England, to publish three volumes of Miscellanies, in which amongst other things he inserted the *Memoirs of a Parish Clerk,* in ridicule of Burnet's importance in his own History,[109] and a *Debate upon Black and White Horses,* written in all the formalities of a legal process by the assistance, as is said, of Mr. Fortescue,[110] afterwards Master of the Rolls. Before these Miscellanies is a preface signed by Swift and Pope, but apparently written by Pope; in which he makes a ridiculous and romantick complaint of the robberies committed upon authors by the clandestine seizure and sale of their papers. He tells, in tragick strains, how *the cabinets of the Sick and the closets of the Dead have been broke open and ransacked;* as if those violences were often committed for papers of uncertain and accidental value, which are rarely provoked by real treasures; as if epigrams and essays were in danger where gold and diamonds are safe. A cat, hunted for his musk, is, according to Pope's account, but the emblem of a wit winded by booksellers.

His complaint, however, received some attestation; for the same year the Letters written by him to Mr. Cromwell, in his youth, were sold by Mrs. Thomas[111] to Curll, who printed them.

In these Miscellanies was first pub-

---

[107] Joseph Spence (1699–1768) published an *Essay on Pope's Odyssey* in two parts (1726 and 1727); as prelector, he was public lecturer.

[108] The poet's mother.

[109] Gilbert Burnet (1643–1715), author of *The History of My Own Times,* published

posthumously, beginning in 1724.

[110] William Fortescue, one of Pope's best friends.

[111] Elizabeth Thomas (1667–1731), Henry Cromwell's mistress.

lished the *Art of Sinking in Poetry,* which, by such a train of consequences as usually passes in literary quarrels, gave in a short time, according to Pope's account, occasion to the *Dunciad.*

In the following year (1728) he began to put Atterbury's advice in practice; and shewed his satirical powers by publishing the *Dunciad,* one of his greatest and most elaborate performances, in which he endeavoured to sink into contempt all the writers by whom he had been attacked, and some others whom he thought unable to defend themselves.

At the head of the Dunces he placed poor Theobald, whom he accused of ingratitude; but whose real crime was supposed to be that of having revised *Shakespeare* more happily than himself. This satire had the effect which he intended, by blasting the characters which it touched. Ralph,[112] who, unnecessarily interposing in the quarrel, got a place in a subsequent edition, complained that for a time he was in danger of starving, as the booksellers had no longer any confidence in his capacity.

The prevalence of this poem was gradual and slow: the plan, if not wholly new, was little understood by common readers. Many of the allusions required illustration; the names were often expressed only by the initial and final letters, and, if they had been printed at length, were such as few had known or recollected. The subject itself had nothing generally interesting, for whom did it concern to know that one or another scribbler was a dunce? If therefore it had been possible for those who were attacked to conceal their pain and their resentment, the *Dunciad* might have made its way very slowly in the world.

This, however, was not to be expected: every man is of importance to himself, and therefore, in his own opinion, to others; and, supposing the world already acquainted with all his pleasures and his

pains, is perhaps the first to publish injuries or misfortunes, which had never been known unless related by himself, and at which those that hear them will only laugh; for no man sympathises with the sorrows of vanity.

The history of the *Dunciad* is very minutely related by Pope himself, in a Dedication which he wrote to Lord Middlesex in the name of Savage.[113]

"I will relate the war of the *Dunces* (for so it has been commonly called), which began in the year 1727, and ended in 1730.

"When Dr. Swift and Mr. Pope thought it proper, for reasons specified in the Preface to their Miscellanies, to publish such little pieces of theirs as had casually got abroad, there was added to them the *Treatise of the Bathos,* or the *Art of Sinking in Poetry.* It happened that in one chapter of this piece the several pieces of bad poets were ranged in classes, to which were prefixed almost all the letters of the alphabet (the greatest part of them at random); but such was the number of poets eminent in that art, that some one or other took every letter to himself: all fell into so violent a fury, that, for half a year or more, the common newspapers (in most of which they had some property, as being hired writers) were filled with the most abusive falsehoods and scurrilities they could possibly devise; a liberty no way to be wondered at in those people, and in those papers, that for many years, during the uncontrouled license of the press, had aspersed almost all the great characters of the age; and this with impunity, their own persons and names being utterly secret and obscure.

"This gave Mr. Pope the thought, that he had now some opportunity of doing good, by detecting and dragging into light these common enemies of mankind; since, to invalidate this universal slander, it sufficed to shew what contemptible

---

[112] James Ralph (1695?–1762), writer and journalist, came to England from America with Benjamin Franklin in 1724; his attack on Pope in 1728 is said to have been for the purpose of attracting attention to himself.

[113] The poet Richard Savage (1697?–1743) is generally thought to have been Pope's informant concerning the activities of struggling Grub Street authors.

men were the authors of it. He was not without hopes, that, by manifesting the dulness of those who had only malice to recommend them, either the booksellers would not find their account in employing them, or the men themselves, when discovered, want courage to proceed in so unlawful an occupation. This it was that gave birth to the *Dunciad;* and he thought it an happiness, that, by the late flood of slander on himself, he had acquired such a peculiar right over their names as was necessary to this design.

"On the 12th of March, 1729, at St. James's, that poem was presented to the King and Queen (who had before been pleased to read it) by the right honourable Sir Robert Walpole; and some days after the whole impression was taken and dispersed by several noblemen and persons of the first distinction.

"It is certainly a true observation, that no people are so impatient of censure as those who are the greatest slanderers, which was wonderfully exemplified on this occasion. On the day the book was first vended, a crowd of authors besieged the shop; intreaties, advices, threats of law and battery, nay cries of treason, were all employed to hinder the coming-out of the *Dunciad:* on the other side, the booksellers and hawkers made as great efforts to procure it. What could a few poor authors do against so great a majority as the publick? There was no stopping a torrent with a finger; so out it came.

"Many ludicrous circumstances attended it. The *Dunces* (for by this name they were called) held weekly clubs, to consult of hostilities against the author: one wrote a Letter to a great minister, assuring him Mr. Pope was the greatest enemy the government had; and another bought his image in clay, to execute him in effigy; with which sad sort of satisfaction the gentlemen were a little comforted.

"Some false editions of the book having an owl in their frontispiece, the true one, to distinguish it, fixed in its stead an ass laden with authors. Then another surreptitious one being printed with the same ass, the new edition in octavo re-turned for distinction to the owl again. Hence arose a great contest of booksellers against booksellers, and advertisements against advertisements; some recommending the edition of the owl, and others the edition of the ass; by which names they came to be distinguished, to the great honour also of the gentlemen of the *Dunciad.*"

Pope appears by this narrative to have contemplated his victory over the *Dunces* with great exultation; and such was his delight in the tumult which he had raised, that for a while his natural sensibility was suspended, and he read reproaches and invectives without emotion, considering them only as the necessary effects of that pain which he rejoiced in having given.

It cannot however be concealed that, by his own confession, he was the aggressor; for nobody believes that the letters in the *Bathos* were placed at random; and it may be discovered that, when he thinks himself concealed, he indulges the common vanity of common men, and triumphs in those distinctions which he had affected to despise. He is proud that his book was presented to the King and Queen by the right honourable Sir Robert Walpole; he is proud that they had read it before; he is proud that the edition was taken off by the nobility and persons of the first distinction.

The edition of which he speaks was, I believe, that which, by telling in the text the names and in the notes the characters of those whom he had satirised, was made intelligible and diverting. The criticks had now declared their approbation of the plan, and the common reader began to like it without fear; those who were strangers to petty literature, and therefore unable to decypher initials, and blanks, had now names and persons brought within their view; and delighted in the visible effect of those shafts of malice, which they had hitherto contemplated, as shot into the air.

Dennis, upon the fresh provocation now given him, renewed the enmity, which had for a time been appeased by mutual civilities; and published remarks, which he had till then suppressed, upon the *Rape of the Lock*. Many more grumbled in secret, or vented their resentment in the newspapers by epigrams or invectives.

Ducket, indeed, being mentioned as loving Burnet with *pious passion,* pretended that his moral character was injured, and for some time declared his resolution to take vengeance with a cudgel. But Pope appeased him, by changing *pious passion* to *cordial friendship,* and by a note, in which he vehemently disclaims the malignity of meaning imputed to the first expression.

Aaron Hill,[114] who was represented as diving for the prize, expostulated with Pope in a manner so much superior to all mean solicitation, that Pope was reduced to sneak and shuffle, sometimes to deny, and sometimes to apologize; he first endeavours to wound, and is then afraid to own that he meant a blow.

The *Dunciad,* in the complete edition, is addressed to Dr. Swift: of the notes, part was written by Dr. Arbuthnot;[115] and an apologetical Letter was prefixed, signed by Cleland,[116] but supposed to have been written by Pope.

After this general war upon Dulness, he seems to have indulged himself awhile in tranquillity; but his subsequent productions prove that he was not idle. He published (1731) a poem on *Taste,* in which he very particularly and severely criticises the house, the furniture, the gardens, and the entertainments of *Timon,* a man of great wealth and little taste. By *Timon* he was universally supposed, and by the Earl of Burlington,[117] to whom the poem is addressed, was privately said, to mean the Duke of Chandos;[118] a man perhaps too much delighted with pomp and show, but of a temper

kind and beneficent, and who had consequently the voice of the publick in his favour.

A violent outcry was therefore raised against the ingratitude and treachery of Pope, who was said to have been indebted to the patronage of Chandos for a present of a thousand pounds, and who gained the opportunity of insulting him by the kindness of his invitation.

The receipt of the thousand pounds Pope publickly denied; but from the reproach which the attack on a character so amiable brought upon him, he tried all means of escaping. The name of Cleland was again employed in an apology, by which no man was satisfied; and he was at last reduced to shelter his temerity behind dissimulation, and endeavour to make that disbelieved which he never had confidence openly to deny. He wrote an exculpatory letter to the Duke, which was answered with great magnanimity, as by a man who accepted his excuse without believing his professions. He said, that to have ridiculed his taste, or his buildings, had been an indifferent action in another man; but that in Pope, after the reciprocal kindness that had been exchanged between them, it had been less easily excused.

Pope, in one of his Letters, complaining of the treatment which his poem had found, *owns that such criticks can intimidate him, nay almost persuade him to write no more, which is a compliment this age deserves.* The man who threatens the world is always ridiculous; for the world can easily go on without him, and in a short time will cease to miss him. I have heard of an idiot, who used to revenge his vexations by lying all night upon the bridge. *There is nothing,* says

[114] 1683–1750, dramatist, poet, and essayist, included in early editions of the *Dunciad,* II, 283 ff., among the aspirants for dulness who dived into the muddy waters of Fleet-ditch for the prize of "a pig of lead."

[115] John Arbuthnot (1667–1735), physician to Queen Anne and author of *The History of John Bull* (1712).

[116] William Cleland (1674?–1741), a friend of Pope's.

[117] Richard Boyle, third Earl of Burlington

and fourth Earl of Cork (1695–1753), an active practitioner of Palladium architecture.

[118] James Brydges, first Duke of Chandos (1673–1744), a wealthy patron of the arts. George Sherburn has adequately demonstrated that Johnson was wrong in accepting the attribution (see " 'Timon's Villa' and Cannons," *Huntington Library Bulletin,* October 1935); F. W. Bateson reviews the evidence in *Poems of Alexander Pope,* gen. ed. John Butt, vol. III, pt. 2, app. B (1951).

Juvenal, *that a man will not believe in his own favour.* Pope had been flattered till he thought himself one of the moving powers in the system of life. When he talked of laying down his pen, those who sat round him intreated and implored, and self-love did not suffer him to suspect that they went away and laughed.

The following year deprived him of Gay, a man whom he had known early, and whom he seemed to love with more tenderness than any other of his literary friends. Pope was now forty-four years old; an age at which the mind begins less easily to admit new confidence, and the will to grow less flexible, and when therefore the departure of an old friend is very acutely felt.

In the next year he lost his mother, not by an unexpected death, for she had lasted to the age of ninety-three; but she did not die unlamented. The filial piety of Pope was in the highest degree amiable and exemplary; his parents had the happiness of living till he was at the summit of poetical reputation, till he was at ease in his fortune, and without a rival in his fame, and found no diminution of his respect or tenderness. Whatever was his pride, to them he was obedient; and whatever was his irritability, to them he was gentle. Life has, among its soothing and quiet comforts, few things better to give than such a son.

One of the passages of Pope's life, which seems to deserve some enquiry, was a publication of Letters between him and many of his friends, which falling into the hands of *Curll,* a rapacious bookseller of no good fame, were by him printed and sold. This volume containing some Letters from noblemen, Pope incited a prosecution against him in the House of Lords for breach of privilege, and attended himself to stimulate the resentment of his friends. *Curll* appeared at the bar, and, knowing himself in no great danger, spoke of Pope with very little reverence. *He has,* said Curll, *a knack at versifying, but in prose I think myself a match for him.* When the orders of the House were examined, none of them appeared to have been infringed;

Curll went away triumphant, and Pope was left to seek some other remedy.

Curll's account was, that one evening a man in a clergyman's gown, but with a lawyer's band, brought and offered to sale a number of printed volumes, which he found to be Pope's epistolary correspondence; that he asked no name, and was told none, but gave the price demanded, and thought himself authorised to use his purchase to his own advantage.

That Curll gave a true account of the transaction, it is reasonable to believe, because no falshood was ever detected; and when some years afterwards I mentioned it to Lintot,[119] the son of Bernard, he declared his opinion to be, that Pope knew better than any body else how Curll obtained the copies, because another parcel was at the same time sent to himself, for which no price had ever been demanded, as he made known his resolution not to pay a porter, and consequently not to deal with a nameless agent.

Such care had been taken to make them publick, that they were sent at once to two booksellers; to Curll, who was likely to seize them as a prey; and to Lintot, who might be expected to give Pope information of the seeming injury. Lintot, I believe, did nothing; and Curll did what was expected. That to make them publick was the only purpose may be reasonably supposed, because the numbers offered to sale by the private messengers shewed that hope of gain could not have been the motive of the impression.

It seems that Pope, being desirous of printing his Letters, and not knowing how to do, without imputation of vanity, what has in this country been done very rarely, contrived an appearance of compulsion; that when he could complain that his Letters were surreptitiously published, he might decently and defensively publish them himself.

Pope's private correspondence, thus promulgated, filled the nation with praises of his candour, tenderness, and

---

[119] Henry Lintot, whose father published Pope's Homer.

benevolence, the purity of his purposes, and the fidelity of his friendship. There were some Letters which a very good or a very wise man would wish suppressed; but, as they had been already exposed, it was impracticable now to retract them.

From the perusal of those Letters, Mr. Allen[120] first conceived the desire of knowing him; and with so much zeal did he cultivate the friendship which he had newly formed, that when Pope told his purpose of vindicating his own property by a genuine edition, he offered to pay the cost.

This however Pope did not accept; but in time solicited a subscription for a Quarto volume, which appeared (1737) I believe, with sufficient profit. In the Preface he tells, that his Letters were reposited in a friend's library, said to be the Earl of Oxford's, and that the copy thence stolen was sent to the press. The story was doubtless received with different degrees of credit. It may be suspected that the Preface to the Miscellanies was written to prepare the publick for such an incident; and to strengthen this opinion, James Worsdale,[121] a painter, who was employed in clandestine negotiations, but whose veracity was very doubtful, declared that he was the messenger who carried, by Pope's direction, the books to Curll.

When they were thus published and avowed, as they had relation to recent facts, and persons either then living or not yet forgotten, they may be supposed to have found readers; but as the facts were minute, and the characters, being either private or literary, were little known, or little regarded, they awakened no popular kindness or resentment: the book never became much the subject of conversation; some read it as contemporary history, and some perhaps as a model of epistolary language; but those who read it did not talk of it. Not much therefore was added by it to fame or envy; nor do I remember that it produced either publick praise, or publick censure.

It had however, in some degree, the recommendation of novelty. Our language has few Letters, except those of statesmen. Howel[122] indeed, about a century ago, published his Letters, which are commended by *Morhoff*,[123] and which alone of his hundred volumes continue his memory. Loveday's[124] Letters were printed only once; those of Herbert and Suckling[125] are hardly known. Mrs. Phillips's[126] [*Orinda's*] are equally neglected; and those of Walsh[127] seem written as exercises, and were never sent to any living mistress or friend. Pope's epistolary excellence had an open field; he had no English rival, living or dead.

Pope is seen in this collection as connected with the other contemporary wits, and certainly suffers no disgrace in the comparison: but it must be remembered, that he had the power of favouring himself: he might have originally had publication in his mind, and have written with care, or have afterwards selected those which he had most happily conceived, or most diligently laboured: and I know not whether there does not appear something more studied and artificial in his productions than the rest, except one long Letter by Bolingbroke, composed with all the skill and industry of a pro-

---

[120] Ralph Allen (1694–1764) of Bath, who became acquainted with Pope in 1736; he had become wealthy by effecting an improvement in the mail service.

[121] James Worsdale, for a time apprenticed to the famous painter Kneller and later employed by Henry Thrale, one of Johnson's friends.

[122] James Howell (1594?–1666), *Epistolae Ho-elianae: Familiar Letters* (1650).

[123] Daniel George Morhof (1639–1691), *De Ratione Conscriberandarum Epistolarum*.

[124] Robert Loveday's posthumous *Letters, Domestick and Forrein, to several Persons, occasionally distributed in subjects Philosophicall, Historicall, and Morall* (1659).

[125] George Herbert's letters to his mother had appeared in Izaac Walton's *Life* (1670); Sir John Suckling's letters had been included in his *Last Remains* (1659).

[126] Katharine Philips (1631–1664), *Letters from Orinda to Poliarchus*.

[127] See note 24.

fessed author. It is indeed not easy to distinguish affectation from habit; he that has once studiously formed a style, rarely writes afterwards with complete ease. Pope may be said to write always with his reputation in his head; Swift perhaps like a man who remembered that he was writing to Pope; but Arbuthnot like one who lets thoughts drop from his pen as they rise into his mind.

Before these Letters appeared, he published the first part of what he persuaded himself to think a system of Ethicks, under the title of an *Essay on Man;* which, if his Letter to Swift (of Sept. 14, 1725) be rightly explained by the commentator, had been eight years under his consideration, and of which he seems to have desired the success with great solicitude. He had now many open and doubtless many secret enemies. The *Dunces* were yet smarting with the war; and the superiority which he publickly arrogated, disposed the world to wish his humiliation.

All this he knew, and against all this he provided. His own name, and that of his friend to whom the work is inscribed, were in the first editions carefully suppressed; and the poem, being of a new kind, was ascribed to one or another, as favour determined, or conjecture wandered; it was given, says Warburton, to every man, except him only who could write it. Those who like only when they like the author, and who are under the dominion of a name, condemned it; and those admired it who are willing to scatter praise at random, which while it is unappropriated excites no envy. Those friends of Pope, that were trusted with the secret, went about lavishing honours on the newborn poet, and hinting that Pope was never so much in danger from any former rival.

To those authors whom he had personally offended, and to those whose opinion the world considered as decisive, and whom he suspected of envy or malevolence, he sent his essay as a present before publication, that they might defeat their own enmity by praises, which they could not afterwards decently retract.

With these precautions, in 1733 was published the first part of the *Essay on Man.* There had been for some time a report that Pope was busy upon a System of Morality; but this design was not discovered in the new poem, which had a form and a title with which its readers were unacquainted. Its reception was not uniform; some thought it a very imperfect piece, though not without good lines. While the author was unknown, some, as will always happen, favoured him as an adventurer, and some censured him as an intruder; but all thought him above neglect; the sale increased, and editions were multiplied.

The subsequent editions of the first Epistle exhibited two memorable corrections. At first, the poet and his friend

Expatiate freely o'er this scene of man,
A mighty maze *of walks without a plan.*

For which he wrote afterwards,

A mighty maze, *but not without a plan:*

for, if there were no plan, it was in vain to describe or to trace the maze.

The other alteration was of these lines;

And spite of pride, *and in thy reason's spite,*
One truth is clear, whatever is, is right:

but having afterwards discovered, or been shewn, that the *truth* which subsisted *in spite of reason* could not be very *clear,* he substituted

And spite of pride, *in erring reason's spite.*

To such oversights will the most vigorous mind be liable, when it is employed at once upon argument and poetry.

The second and third Epistles were published; and Pope was, I believe, more and more suspected of writing them; at last, in 1734, he avowed the fourth, and claimed the honour of a moral poet.

In the conclusion it is sufficiently acknowledged, that the doctrine of the *Es-*

say on Man was received from Boling-broke,[128] who is said to have ridiculed Pope, among those who enjoyed his confidence, as having adopted and advanced principles of which he did not perceive the consequence, and as blindly propagating opinions contrary to his own. That those communications had been consolidated into a scheme regularly drawn, and delivered to Pope, from whom it returned only transformed from prose to verse, has been reported, but hardly can be true. The Essay plainly appears the fabrick of a poet: what Bolingbroke supplied could be only the first principles; the order, illustration, and embellishments, must all be Pope's.

These principles it is not my business to clear from obscurity, dogmatism, or falsehood; but they were not immediately examined; philosophy and poetry have not often the same readers; and the Essay abounded in splendid amplifications and sparkling sentences, which were read and admired, with no great attention to their ultimate purpose; its flowers caught the eye, which did not see what the gay foliage concealed, and for a time flourished in the sunshine of universal approbation. So little was any evil tendency discovered, that, as innocence is unsuspicious, many read it for a manual of piety.

Its reputation soon invited a translator. It was first turned into French prose, and afterwards by Resnel[129] into verse. Both translations fell into the hands of Crousaz,[130] who first, when he had the version in prose, wrote a general censure, and afterwards reprinted Resnel's version, with particular remarks upon every paragraph.

Crousaz was a professor of Switzerland, eminent for his treatise of Logick,

and his *Examen de Pyrrhonisme,* and, however little known or regarded here, was no mean antagonist. His mind was one of those in which philosophy and piety are happily united. He was accustomed to argument and disquisition, and perhaps was grown too desirous of detecting faults; but his intentions were always right, his opinions were solid, and his religion pure.

His incessant vigilance for the promotion of piety disposed him to look with distrust upon all metaphysical systems of Theology, and all schemes of virtue and happiness purely rational; and therefore it was not long before he was persuaded that the positions of Pope, as they terminated for the most part in natural religion, were intended to draw mankind away from revelation, and to represent the whole course of things as a necessary concatenation of indissoluble fatality; and it is undeniable, that in many passages a religious eye may easily discover expressions not very favourable to morals, or to liberty.

About this time Warburton[131] began to make his appearance in the first ranks of learning. He was a man of vigorous faculties, a mind fervid and vehement, supplied by incessant and unlimited enquiry, with wonderful extent and variety of knowledge, which yet had not oppressed his imagination, nor clouded his perspicacity. To every work he brought a memory full fraught, together with a fancy fertile of original combinations, and at once exerted the powers of the scholar, the reasoner, and the wit. But his knowledge was too multifarious to be always exact, and his pursuits were too eager to be always cautious. His abilities gave him an haughty confidence, which he disdained to conceal or mollify;

[128] Henry St. John, first Viscount Bolingbroke, who with Lord Oxford had shared Tory control of England from 1710 to the death of Queen Anne in 1714 and had lived for some years after in exile. Maynard Mack reviews the influence of Bolingbroke on the *Essay on Man* in *Poems of Alexander Pope,* gen. ed. John Butt, vol. III, pt. 1 (1950).
[129] The Abbé Resnel, a French translator.
[130] Jean Pierre de Crousaz (1663–1748),

Swiss writer who is credited with the introduction of the philosophy of Descartes and Locke to Lausanne; an ardent opponent of the philosophy of Leibniz and Bayle, he attacked Pope's optimism in his *Examen de l'essai de M. Pope sur l'homme* (1737).
[131] William Warburton (1698–1779), Bishop of Gloucester, critic and editor of Pope's works (1751).

and his impatience of opposition disposed him to treat his adversaries with such contemptuous superiority as made his readers commonly his enemies, and excited against the advocate the wishes of some who favoured the cause. He seems to have adopted the Roman Emperor's determination, *oderint dum metuant;*[132] he used no allurements of gentle language, but wished to compel rather than persuade.

His style is copious without selection, and forcible without neatness; he took the words that presented themselves: his diction is coarse and impure, and his sentences are unmeasured.

He had, in the early part of his life, pleased himself with the notice of inferior wits, and corresponded with the enemies of Pope. A Letter was produced, when he had perhaps himself forgotten it, in which he tells *Concanen,*[133] "Dryden *I observe borrows for want of leasure, and* Pope *for want of genius:* Milton *out of pride, and Addison out of modesty."* And when Theobald published *Shakespeare,* in opposition to Pope, the best notes were supplied by Warburton.

But the time was now come when Warburton was to change his opinion, and Pope was to find a defender in him who had contributed so much to the exaltation of his rival.

The arrogance of Warburton excited against him every artifice of offence, and therefore it may be supposed that his union with Pope was censured as hypocritical inconstancy; but surely to think differently, at different times, of poetical merit, may be easily allowed. Such opinions are often admitted, and dismissed, without nice examination. Who is there that has not found reason for changing his mind about questions of greater importance?

Warburton, whatever was his motive, undertook, without solicitation, to rescue Pope from the talons of Crousaz, by freeing him from the imputation of favouring fatality, or rejecting revelation; and from month to month continued a vindication of the *Essay on Man,* in the literary journal of that time called *The Republick of Letters.*[134]

Pope, who probably began to doubt the tendency of his own work, was glad that the positions, of which he perceived himself not to know the full meaning, could by any mode of interpretation be made to mean well. How much he was pleased with his gratuitous defender, the following Letter evidently shews:

March 24, 1743.

Sir,

I have just received from Mr. R. two more of your Letters. It is in the greatest hurry imaginable that I write this; but I cannot help thanking you in particular for your third Letter, which is so extremely clear, short, and full, that I think Mr. Crousaz ought never to have another answer, and deserved not so good an one. I can only say, you do him too much honour, and me too much right, so odd as the expression seems; for you have made my system as clear as I ought to have done, and could not. It is indeed the same system as mine, but illustrated with a ray of your own, as they say our natural body is the same still when it is glorified. I am sure I like it better than I did before, and so will every man else. I know I meant just what you explain; but I did not explain my own meaning so well as you. You understand me as well as I do myself; but you express me better than I could express myself. Pray accept the sincerest acknowledgements. I cannot but wish these Letters were put together in one Book, and intend (with your leave) to procure a translation of part, at least, of all of them into French; but I shall not proceed a step without your consent and opinion, &c.

By this fond and eager acceptance of an exculpatory comment, Pope testified

---

[132] "Let them hate me as long as they respect me." (Suetonius, *Caligula,* XXX).

[133] Matthew Concanen (1701–1749), a minor poet, to whom Warburton had written the letter quoted January 2, 1727.

[134] The name was changed from *The Present State of the Republick of Letters* in 1736 to *The Works of the Learned;* Warburton's vindication appears in IV, 425, and V, 56, 89, 159, and 330.

that, whatever might be the seeming or real import of the principles which he had received from Bolingbroke, he had not intentionally attacked religion; and Bolingbroke, if he meant to make him without his own consent an instrument of mischief, found him now engaged with his eyes open on the side of truth.

It is known that Bolingbroke concealed from Pope his real opinions. He once discovered them to Mr. Hooke,[135] who related them again to Pope, and was told by him that he must have mistaken the meaning of what he heard; and Bolingbroke, when Pope's uneasiness incited him to desire an explanation, declared that Hooke had misunderstood him.

Bolingbroke hated Warburton, who had drawn his pupil from him; and a little before Pope's death they had a dispute, from which they parted with mutual aversion.

From this time Pope lived in the closest intimacy with his commentator, and amply rewarded his kindness and his zeal; for he introduced him to Mr. Murray,[136] by whose interest he became preacher at Lincoln's Inn, and to Mr. Allen, who gave him his niece and his estate, and by consequence a bishoprick. When he died, he left him the property of his works; a legacy which may be reasonably estimated at four thousand pounds.

Pope's fondness for the *Essay on Man* appeared by his desire of its propagation. Dobson,[137] who had gained reputation by his version of Prior's *Solomon*, was employed by him to translate it into Latin verse, and was for that purpose some time at Twickenham; but he left his work, whatever was the reason, unfinished; and, by Benson's[138] invitation, undertook the longer task of *Paradise Lost*. Pope then desired his friend to find a scholar who should turn his Essay into Latin prose; but no such performance has ever appeared.

Pope lived at this time *among the Great,* with that reception and respect to which his works entitled him, and which he had not impaired by any private misconduct or factious partiality. Though Bolingbroke was his friend, Walpole was not his enemy; but treated him with so much consideration as, at his request, to solicit and obtain from the French Minister an abbey for Mr. Southcot, whom he considered himself as obliged to reward, by this exertion of his interest, for the benefit which he had received from his attendance in a long illness.

It was said, that, when the Court was at Richmond, Queen Caroline had declared her intention to visit him. This may have been only a careless effusion, thought on no more: the report of such notice, however, was soon in many mouths; and, if I do not forget or misapprehend Savage's account, Pope, pretending to decline what was not yet offered, left his house for a time, not, I suppose, for any other reason than lest he should be thought to stay at home in expectation of an honour which would not be conferred. He was therefore angry at Swift, who represents him as *refusing the visits of a Queen,* because he knew that what had never been offered had never been refused.

Beside the general system of morality, supposed to be contained in the *Essay on Man,* it was his intention to write distinct poems upon the different duties or conditions of life; one of which is the Epistle to Lord Bathurst (1733) on the *Use of Riches,* a piece on which he declared great labour to have been bestowed.

---

[135] Probably Nathaniel Hooke (d. 1763), a miscellaneous writer who assisted the Duchess of Marlborough in the preparation of her memoirs.

[136] William Murray, first Earl of Mansfield (1705–1793), from 1756 Lord Chief Justice of the King's Bench.

[137] "Dobson translated the first book [*Solomon*] as a school-exercise when at Winchester College" (Joseph Warton); Johnson speaks later of his spending some time at the house of Pope translating the *Essay on Man.*

[138] William Benson (1682–1754), a prominent patron of letters.

Into this poem some incidents are historically thrown, and some known characters are introduced, with others of which it is difficult to say how far they are real or fictitious; but the praise of *Kyrl, the Man of Ross,* deserves particular examination, who, after a long and pompous enumeration of his publick works and private charities, is said to have diffused all those blessings from *five hundred a year.* Wonders are willingly told, and willingly heard. The truth is, that *Kyrl* was a man of known integrity, and active benevolence, by whose solicitation the wealthy were persuaded to pay contributions to his charitable schemes; this influence he obtained by an example of liberality exerted to the utmost extent of his power, and was thus enabled to give more than he had. This account Mr. Victor received from the minister of the place, and I have preserved it, that the praise of a good man, being made more credible, may be more solid. Narrations of romantick and impracticable virtue will be read with wonder, but that which is unattainable is recommended in vain; that good may be endeavoured, it must be shewn to be possible.

This is the only piece in which the author has given a hint of his religion, by ridiculing the ceremony of burning the pope, and by mentioning with some indignation the inscription on the Monument.

When this poem was first published, the dialogue, having no letters of direction, was perplexed and obscure. Pope seems to have written with no very distinct idea; for he calls that an *Epistle to Bathurst,* in which Bathurst is introduced as speaking.

He afterwards (1734) inscribed to Lord Cobham his *Characters of Men,* written with close attention to the operations of the mind and modifications of life. In this poem he has endeavoured to establish and exemplify his favourite theory of the *Ruling Passion,* by which he means an original direction of desire to some particular object, an innate affection which gives all action a determinate and invariable tendency, and operates upon the whole system of life, either openly, or more secretly by the intervention of some accidental or subordinate propension.

Of any passion, thus innate and irresistible, the existence may reasonably be doubted. Human characters are by no means constant; men change by change of place, of fortune, of acquaintance; he who is at one time a lover of pleasure, is at another a lover of money. Those indeed who attain any excellence commonly spend life in one pursuit; for excellence is not often gained upon easier terms. But to the particular species of excellence men are directed, not by an ascendant planet or predominating humour, but by the first book which they read, some early conversation which they heard, or some accident which excited ardour and emulation.

It must be at least allowed that this *ruling Passion,* antecedent to reason and observation, must have an object independent on human contrivance; for there can be no natural desire of artificial good. No man therefore can be born, in the strict acceptation, a lover of money; for he may be born where money does not exist: nor can he be born, in a moral sense, a lover of his country; for society, politically regulated, is a state contradistinguished from a state of nature; and any attention to that coalition of interests which makes the happiness of a country is possible only to those whom enquiry and reflection have enabled to comprehend it.

This doctrine is in itself pernicious as well as false: its tendency is to produce the belief of a kind of moral predestination, or over-ruling principle which cannot be resisted; he that admits it is prepared to comply with every desire that caprice or opportunity shall excite, and to flatter himself that he submits only to the lawful dominion of Nature, in obeying the resistless authority of his *ruling Passion.*

Pope has formed his theory with so little skill, that, in the examples by which he illustrates and confirms it, he has confounded passions, appetites, and habits.

To the *Characters of Men* he added soon after, in an Epistle supposed to have been addressed to Martha Blount,[139] but which the last edition has taken from her, the *Characters of Women*. This poem, which was laboured with great diligence, and in the author's opinion with great success, was neglected at its first publication, as the commentator supposes, because the publick was informed, by an advertisement, that it contained *no Character drawn from the Life;* an assertion which Pope probably did not expect or wish to have been believed, and which he soon gave his readers sufficient reason to distrust, by telling them, in a note, that the work was imperfect, because part of his subject was *Vice too high* to be yet exposed.

The time however soon came, in which it was safe to display the Dutchess of Marlborough[140] under the name of *Atossa;* and her character was inserted with no great honour to the writer's gratitude.

He published from time to time (between 1730 and 1740) Imitations of different poems of Horace, generally with his name, and once as was suspected without it. What he was upon moral principles ashamed to own, he ought to have suppressed. Of these pieces it is useless to settle the dates, as they had seldom much relation to the times, and perhaps had been long in his hands.

This mode of imitation, in which the ancients are familiarised, by adapting their sentiments to modern topicks, by making Horace say of Shakespeare what he originally said of Ennius, and accommodating his satires on Pantolabus and Nomentanus to the flatterers and prodigals of our own time, was first practised in the reign of Charles the Second by Oldham and Rochester, at least I remember no instances more ancient. It is a kind of middle composition between translation and original design, which pleases when the thoughts are unexpectedly applicable, and the parallels lucky.[141] It seems to have been Pope's favourite amusement; for he has carried it further than any former poet.

He published likewise a revival, in smoother numbers, of Dr. Donne's Satires, which was recommended to him by the Duke of Shrewsbury[142] and the Earl of Oxford. They made no great impression on the publick. Pope seems to have known their imbecillity, and therefore suppressed them while he was yet contending to rise in reputation, but ventured them when he thought their deficiences more likely to be imputed to Donne than to himself.

The Epistle to Dr. Arbuthnot, which seems to be derived in its first design from Boileau's Address *à son Esprit,* was published in January 1735, about a month before the death of him to whom it is inscribed. It is to be regretted, that either honour or pleasure should have been missed by Arbuthnot; a man estimable for his learning, amiable for his life, and venerable for his piety.

Arbuthnot was a man of great comprehension, skilful in his profession, versed in the sciences, acquainted with ancient literature, and able to animate his mass of knowledge by a bright and active imagination; a scholar with great brilliance of wit; a wit, who, in the crowd of life, retained and discovered a noble ardour of religious zeal.

In this poem Pope seems to reckon with the publick. He vindicates himself from censures; and with dignity, rather then arrogance, enforces his own claims to kindness and respect.

Into his poem are interwoven several paragraphs which had been before printed as a fragment, and among them

---

[139] 1690–1763, Pope's closest female friend, to whom it was once rumored he was about to be married.

[140] The most recent editor, F. W. Bateson (*The Poems of Alexander Pope,* gen. ed. John Butt, vol. III, pt. 2, 1951), considers the general eighteenth-century attribution of the character of Atossa incorrect and believes Atossa was intended as a portrait of the Duchess of Buckinghamshire.

[141] Johnson himself had adapted Juvenal's third satire to *London* and his tenth to *The Vanity of Human Wishes.*

[142] Charles Talbot (1660–1718).

the satirical lines upon Addison, of which the last couplet has been twice corrected. It was at first,

Who would not smile if such a man there be?
Who would not laugh if Addison were he?

Then,

Who would not grieve if such a man there be?
Who would not laugh if Addison were he?

At last it is,

Who but must laugh if such a man there be?
Who would not weep if Atticus were he?

He was at this time at open war with Lord Hervey, who had distinguished himself as a steady adherent to the Ministry; and, being offended with a contemptuous answer to one of his pamphlets, had summoned Pulteney to a duel. Whether he or Pope made the first attack, perhaps cannot now be easily known: he had written an invective against Pope, whom he calls *Hard as thy heart, and as thy birth obscure;* and hints that his father was a *hatter*. To this Pope wrote a reply in verse and prose: the verses are in this poem; and the prose, though it was never sent, is printed among his Letters, but to a cool reader of the present time exhibits nothing but tedious malignity.

His last Satires, of the general kind, were two Dialogues, named, from the year in which they were published, *Seventeen Hundred and Thirty-eight.* In these poems many are praised and many are reproached. Pope was then entangled in the opposition; a follower of the Prince of Wales,[143] who dined at his house, and the friend of many who obstructed and censured the conduct of the Ministers. His political partiality was too plainly shewn: he forgot the prudence with which he passed, in his earlier years, uninjured and unoffending through much more violent conflicts of faction.

In the first Dialogue, having an opportunity of praising Allen of Bath,[144] he asked his leave to mention him as a man not illustrious by any merit of his ancestors, and called him in his verses *low-born Allen.* Men are seldom satisfied with praise introduced or followed by any mention of defect. Allen seems not to have taken any pleasure in his epithet, which was afterwards softened into *humble Allen.*

In the second Dialogue he took some liberty with one of the *Foxes,* among others; which *Fox,*[145] in a reply to Lyttelton,[146] took an opportunity of repaying, by reproaching him with the friendship of a lampooner, who scattered his ink without fear or decency, and against whom he hoped the resentment of the Legislature would quickly be discharged.

About this time Paul Whitehead,[147] a small poet, was summoned before the Lords for a poem called *Manners,* together with Dodsley[148] his publisher. Whitehead, who hung loose upon society, sculked and escaped; but Dodsley's shop and family made his appearance necessary. He was, however, soon dismissed; and the whole process was probably intended rather to intimidate Pope, than to punish Whitehead.

Pope never afterwards attempted to join the patriot with the poet, nor drew his pen upon statesmen. That he desisted from his attempts of reformation is imputed, by his commentator, to his despair of prevailing over the corruption of the

[143] Who, as Hervey's *Memoirs* makes clear, was not on good terms with his father, George II.

[144] See note 120 above.

[145] Henry Fox (1705–1774), later first Baron Holland, a prominent Whig politician.

[146] George Lyttelton (1709–1773), secretary to the Prince of Wales in 1737.

[147] Whitehead (1710–1774) wrote the political satire *State Dunces* (1733) in imitation of Pope's *Dunciad.*

[148] Robert Dodsley (1703–1764), author, editor, and one of the most prolific patrons of letters as publisher of the century.

time. He was not likely to have been ever of opinion, that the dread of his satire would countervail the love of power or of money; he pleased himself with being important and formidable, and gratified sometimes his pride, and sometimes his resentment; till at last he began to think he should be more safe if he were less busy.

The *Memoirs of Scriblerus,* published about this time, extend only to the first book of a work projected in concert by Pope, Swift, and Arbuthnot, who used to meet in the time of Queen Anne, and denominated themselves the *Scriblerus Club.* Their purpose was to censure the abuses of learning by a fictitious Life of an infatuated Scholar. They were dispersed; the design was never completed; and Warburton laments its miscarriage, as an event very disastrous to polite letters.

If the whole may be estimated by this specimen, which seems to be the production of Arbuthnot, with a few touches perhaps by Pope, the want of more will not be much lamented; for the follies which the writer ridicules are so little practised, that they are not known; nor can the satire be understood but by the learned: he raises phantoms of absurdity, and then drives them away. He cures diseases that were never felt.

For this reason this joint production of three great writers has never obtained any notice from mankind; it has been little read, or when read has been forgotten, as no man could be wiser, better, or merrier, by remembering it.

The design cannot boast of much originality; for, besides its general resemblance to *Don Quixote,* there will be found in it particular imitations of the History of Mr. *Ouffle.*[149]

Swift carried so much of it into Ireland as supplied him with hints for his *Travels;* and with those the world might have been contented, though the rest had been suppressed.

Pope had sought for images and sentiments in a religion not known to have been explored by many other of the English writers; he had consulted the modern writers of Latin poetry, a class of authors whom Boileau endeavoured to bring into contempt, and who are too generally neglected. Pope, however, was not ashamed of their acquaintance, nor ungrateful for the advantages which he might have derived from it. A small selection from the Italians, who wrote in Latin, had been published at London, about the latter end of the last century, by a man who concealed his name, but whom his Preface shews to have been well qualified for his undertaking. This collection Pope amplified by more than half, and (1740) published it in two volumes, but injuriously omitted his predecessor's preface. To these books, which had nothing but the mere text, no regard was paid, the authors were still neglected, and the editor was neither praised nor censured.

He did not sink into idleness; he had planned a work, which he considered as subsequent to his *Essay on Man,* of which he has given this account to Dr. Swift.

March 25, 1736.
If ever I write any more Epistles in verse, one of them shall be addressed to you. I have long concerted it, and begun it; but I would make what bears your name as finished as my last work ought to be, that is to say, more finished than any of the rest. The subject is large, and will divide into four Epistles, which naturally follow the *Essay on Man;* viz. 1. Of the Extent and Limits of Human Reason and Science. 2. A View of the useful and therefore attainable, and of the unuseful and therefore unattainable, Arts. 3. Of the Nature, Ends, Application, and Use of different Capacities. 4. Of the Use of *Learning,* of the *Science,* of the *World,* and of *Wit.* It will conclude with a satire against the Misapplication of all these, exemplified by Pictures, Characters, and Examples.

This work in its full extent, being now afflicted with an asthma, and finding the powers of life gradually declining, he

---

[149] *Historie des imaginations extravagantes de M. Oufle* (1710) by Laurent Dordelon.

had no longer courage to undertake; but, from the materials which he had provided, he added, at Warburton's request, another book to the *Dunciad,* of which the design is to ridicule such studies as are either hopeless or useless, as either pursue what is unattainable, or what, if it be attained, is of no use.

When this book was printed (1742) the laurel had been for some time upon the head of Cibber; a man whom it cannot be supposed that Pope could regard with much kindness or esteem, though in one of the Imitations of *Horace* he has liberally enough praised the *Careless Husband.* In the *Dunciad,* among other worthless scribblers, he had mentioned Cibber; who, in his *Apology,* complains of the great poet's unkindness as more injurious, *because,* says he, *I never have offended him.*

It might have been expected that Pope should have been, in some degree, mollified by this submissive gentleness; but no such consequence appeared. Though he condescended to commend Cibber once, he mentioned him afterwards contemptuously in one of his Satires, and again in his Epistle to Arbuthnot; and in the fourth book of the *Dunciad* attacked him with acrimony, to which the provocation is not easily discoverable. Perhaps he imagined that, in ridiculing the Laureat, he satirised those by whom the laurel had been given, and gratified that ambitious petulance with which he affected to insult the great.

The severity of this satire left Cibber no longer any patience. He had confidence enough in his own powers to believe that he could disturb the quiet of his adversary, and doubtless did not want instigators, who, without any care about the victory, desired to amuse themselves by looking on the contest. He therefore gave the town a pamphlet, in which he declares his resolution from that time never to bear another blow without returning it, and to tire out his adversary by perseverance, if he cannot conquer him by strength.

The incessant and unappeasable malignity of Pope he imputes to a very distant cause. After the *Three Hours after Marriage* had been driven off the stage, by the offence which the mummy and crocodile gave the audience, while the exploded scene was yet fresh in memory, it happened that Cibber played *Bayes* in the *Rehearsal;* and, as it had been usual to enliven the part by the mention of any recent theatrical transactions, he said, that he once thought to have introduced his lovers disguised in a Mummy and a Crocodile. "This," says he, "was received with loud claps, which indicated contempt of the play." Pope, who was behind the scenes, meeting him as he left the stage, attacked him, as he says, with all the virulence of a *Wit out of his senses;* to which he replied, "that he would take no other notice of what was said by so particular a man than to declare, that, as often as he played that part, he would repeat the same provocation."

He shews his opinion to be, that Pope was one of the authors of the play which he so zealously defended; and adds an idle story of Pope's behaviour at a tavern.

The pamphlet was written with little power of thought or language, and, if suffered to remain without notice, would have been very soon forgotten. Pope had now been enough acquainted with human life to know, if his passion had not been too powerful for his understanding, that, from a contention like his with Cibber, the world seeks nothing but diversion, which is given at the expence of the higher character. When Cibber lampooned Pope, curiosity was excited; what Pope would say of Cibber nobody enquired, but in hope that Pope's asperity might betray his pain and lessen his dignity.

He should therefore have suffered the pamphlet to flutter and die, without confessing that it stung him. The dishonour of being shewn as Cibber's antagonist could never be compensated by the victory. Cibber had nothing to lose; when Pope had exhausted all his malignity upon him, he would rise in the esteem both of his friends and his enemies. Silence only could have made him despicable; the blow which did not appear to be felt, would have been struck in vain.

But Pope's irascibility prevailed, and he resolved to tell the whole English world that he was at war with Cibber; and to shew that he thought him no common adversary, he prepared no common vengeance; he published a new edition of the *Dunciad,* in which he degraded *Theobald* from his painful pre-eminence, and enthroned *Cibber* in his stead. Unhappily the two heroes were of opposite characters, and Pope was unwilling to lose what he had already written; he has therefore depraved his poem by giving to Cibber the old books, the cold pedantry, and sluggish pertinacity of Theobald.

Pope was ignorant enough of his own interest, to make another change, and introduced Osborne[150] contending for the prize among the booksellers. Osborne was a man intirely destitute of shame, without sense of any disgrace but that of poverty. He told me, when he was doing that which raised Pope's resentment, that he should be put into the *Dunciad;* but he had the fate of *Cassandra;*[151] I gave no credit to his prediction, till in time I saw it accomplished. The shafts of satire were directed equally in vain against Cibber and Osborne; being repelled by the impenetrable impudence of one, and deadened by the impassive dulness of the other. Pope confessed his own pain by his anger; but he gave no pain to those who had provoked him. He was able to hurt none but himself; by transferring the same ridicule from one to another, he destroyed its efficacy; for, by shewing that what he had said of one he was ready to say of another, he reduced himself to the insignificance of his own magpye, who from his cage calls cuckold at a venture.[152]

Cibber, according to his engagement, repaid the *Dunciad* with another pamphlet, which, Pope said, *would be as good as a dose of hartshorn*[153] *to him;* but his tongue and his heart were at variance. I have heard Mr. Richardson[154] relate, that he attended his father the painter on a visit, when one of Cibber's pamphlets came into the hands of Pope, who said, *These things are my diversion.* They sat by him while he perused it, and saw his features writhen with anguish; and young Richardson said to his father, when they returned, that he hoped to be preserved from such diversion as had been that day the lot of Pope.

From this time, finding his diseases more oppressive, and his vital powers gradually declining, he no longer strained his faculties with any original composition, nor proposed any other employment for his remaining life than the revisal and correction of his former works; in which he received advice and assistance from Warburton, whom he appears to have trusted and honoured in the highest degree.

He laid aside his Epick Poem, perhaps without much loss to mankind; for his hero was *Brutus* the Trojan, who, according to a ridiculous fiction, established a colony in Britain. The subject therefore was of the fabulous age; the actors were a race upon whom imagination has been exhausted, and attention wearied, and to whom the mind will not easily be recalled, when it is invited in blank verse, which Pope had adopted with great imprudence, and I think without due consideration of the nature of our language. The sketch is, at least in part, preserved by Ruffhead;[155] by which it appears, that Pope was thoughtless enough to model the names of his heroes with terminations not consistent with the time or country in which he places them.

He lingered through the next year; but perceived himself, as he expresses it, *going down the hill.* He had for at least

[150] Thomas Osborne (d. 1767), a prominent publisher of the midcentury.

[151] A character in Greek legend whose fate is that her prophecies are not believed.

[152] i.e., abuses anyone at random.

[153] i.e., a reviving whiff of ammonia (formerly obtained from hartshorn).

[154] Jonathan (1694–1771), who edited his father's *Theory of Painting.*

[155] in his *Life of Pope* (1769).

five years been afflicted with an asthma, and other disorders, which his physicians were unable to relieve. Towards the end of his life he consulted Dr. Thomson, a man who had, by large promises, and free censures of the common practice of physick, forced himself up into sudden reputation. Thomson declared his distemper to be a dropsy, and evacuated part of the water by tincture of jalap;[156] but confessed that his belly did not subside. Thomson had many enemies, and Pope was persuaded to dismiss him.

While he was yet capable of amusement and conversation, as he was one day sitting in the air with Lord Bolingbroke and Lord Marchmont,[157] he saw his favourite Martha Blount at the bottom of the terrace, and asked Lord Bolingbroke to go and hand her up. Bolingbroke, not liking his errand, crossed his legs, and sat still; but Lord Marchmont, who was younger and less captious, waited on the Lady; who, when he came to her, asked, *What, is he not dead yet?* She is said to have neglected him, with shameful unkindness, in the latter time of his decay; yet, of the little which he had to leave, she had a very great part. Their acquaintance began early; the life of each was pictured on the other's mind; their conversation therefore was endearing, for when they met, there was an immediate coalition of congenial notions. Perhaps he considered her unwillingness to approach the chamber of sickness as female weakness, or human frailty; perhaps he was conscious to himself of peevishness and impatience, or, though he was offended by her inattention, might yet consider her merit as overbalancing her fault; and, if he had suffered his heart to be alienated from her, he could have found nothing that might fill her place; he could have only shrunk within himself; it was too late to transfer his confidence or fondness.

In May 1744, his death was approaching; on the sixth, he was all day delirious, which he mentioned four days afterwards as a sufficient humiliation of the vanity of man; he afterwards complained of seeing things as through a curtain, and in false colours; and one day, in the presence of Dodsley, asked what arm it was that came out from the wall. He said that his greatest inconvenience was inability to think.

Bolingbroke sometimes wept over him in this state of helpless decay; and being told by Spence, that Pope, at the intermission of his deliriousness, was always saying something kind either of his present or absent friends, and that his humanity seemed to have survived his understanding, answered, *It has so.* And added, *I never in my life knew a man that had so tender a heart for his particular friends, or more general friendship for mankind.* At another time he said, *I have known Pope these thirty years, and value myself more in his friendship than* —his grief then suppressed his voice.

Pope expressed undoubting confidence of a future state. Being asked by his friend Mr. Hooke, a papist, whether he would not die like his father and mother, and whether a priest should not be called, he answered, *I do not think it essential, but it will be very right; and I thank you for putting me in mind of it.*

In the morning, after the priest had given him the last sacraments, he said, "There is nothing that is meritorious but virtue and friendship, and indeed friendship itself is only a part of virtue."

He died in the evening of the thirtieth day of May, 1744, so placidly, that the attendants did not discern the exact time of his expiration. He was buried at Twickenham, near his father and mother, where a monument has been erected to him by his commentator, the Bishop of Gloucester.

He left the care of his papers to his executors, first to Lord Bolingbroke, and if he should not be living to the Earl of Marchmont, undoubtedly expecting

---

156 A purgative drug from the root of a West Indian nightshade plant.
157 Hugh Hume (1708–1794), third Earl of Marchmont, an outstanding politician whose friendship Pope cultivated during the last years of his life.

them to be proud of the trust, and eager to extend his fame. But let no man dream of influence beyond his life. After a decent time Dodsley the bookseller went to solicit preference as the publisher, and was told that the parcel had not been yet inspected; and whatever was the reason, the world has been disappointed of what was *reserved for the next age.*

He lost, indeed, the favour of Bolingbroke by a kind of posthumous offence. The political pamphlet called *The Patriot King* had been put into his hands that he might procure the impression of a very few copies, to be distributed according to the author's direction among his friends, and Pope assured him that no more had been printed than were allowed; but, soon after his death, the printer brought and resigned a complete edition of fifteen hundred copies, which Pope had ordered him to print, and to retain in secret. He kept, as was observed, his engagement to Pope better than Pope had kept it to his friend; and nothing was known of the transaction, till, upon the death of his employer, he thought himself obliged to deliver the books to the right owner, who, with great indignation, made a fire in his yard, and delivered the whole impression to the flames.

Hitherto nothing had been done which was not naturally dictated by resentment of violated faith; resentment more acrimonious, as the violator had been more loved or more trusted. But here the anger might have stopped; the injury was private, and there was little danger from the example.

Bolingbroke, however, was not yet satisfied; his thirst of vengeance excited him to blast the memory of the man over whom he had wept in his last struggles; and he employed Mallet,[158] another friend of Pope, to tell the tale to the publick, with all its aggravations. Warburton, whose heart was warm with his legacy, and tender by the recent separa-tion, thought it proper for him to interpose; and undertook, not indeed to vindicate the action, for breach of trust has always something criminal, but to extenuate it by an apology. Having advanced what cannot be denied, that moral obliquity is made more or less excusable by the motives that produce it, he enquires what evil purpose could have induced Pope to break his promise. He could not delight his vanity by usurping the work, which, though not sold in shops, had been shewn to a number more than sufficient to preserve the author's claim; he could not gratify his avarice, for he could not sell his plunder till Bolingbroke was dead; and even then, if the copy was left to another, his fraud would be defeated, and, if left to himself, would be useless.

Warburton therefore supposes, with great appearance of reason, that the irregularity of his conduct proceeded wholly from his zeal for Bolingbroke, who might perhaps have destroyed the pamphlet, which Pope thought it his duty to preserve, even without its author's approbation. To this apology an answer was written in a *Letter to the most impudent man living.*

He brought some reproach upon his own memory by the petulant and contemptuous mention made in his will of Mr. Allen, and an affected repayment of his benefactions. Mrs. Blount, as the known friend and favourite of Pope, had been invited to the house of Allen, where she comported herself with such indecent arrogance, that she parted from Mrs. Allen in a state of irreconcileable dislike, and the door was for ever barred against her. This exclusion she resented with so much bitterness as to refuse any legacy from Pope, unless he left the world with a disavowal of obligation to Allen. Having been long under her dominion, now tottering in the decline of life, and unable to resist the violence of her temper, or, perhaps with the prejudice of a lover, persuaded that she had suffered improper treatment, he complied with her demand, and polluted his will with female resentment. Allen accepted the legacy, which he gave to the Hospital at Bath; observ-

---

158 David Mallet (*né* Malloch) (1705?–1765), a minor writer.

ing that Pope was always a bad accomptant,[159] and that, if to 150 *l.* he had put a cypher more, he had come nearer to the truth.

[A GENERAL VIEW OF HIS CHARACTER]

The person of Pope is well-known not to have been formed by the nicest model. He has, in his account of the *Little Club,* compared himself to a spider, and by another is described as protuberant behind and before. He is said to have been beautiful in his infancy; but he was of a constitution originally feeble and weak; and as bodies of a tender frame are easily distorted, his deformity was probably in part the effect of his application. His stature was so low, that, to bring him to a level with common tables, it was necessary to raise his seat. But his face was not displeasing, and his eyes were animated and vivid.

By natural deformity, or accidental distortion, his vital functions were so much disordered, that his life was a *long disease.* His most frequent assailant was the headach, which he used to relieve by inhaling the steam of coffee, which he very frequently required.

Most of what can be told concerning his petty peculiarities was communicated by a female domestick of the Earl of Oxford, who knew him perhaps after the middle of life. He was then so weak as to stand in perpetual need of female attendance; extremely sensible of cold, so that he wore a kind of fur doublet, under a shirt of a very coarse warm linen with fine sleeves. When he rose, he was invested in boddice made of stiff canvass, being scarce able to hold himself erect till they were laced, and he then put on a flannel waistcoat. One side was contracted. His legs were so slender, that he enlarged their bulk with three pair of stockings, which were drawn on and off by the maid; for he was not able to dress or undress himself, and neither went to bed nor rose without help. His weakness made it very difficult for him to be clean.

His hair had fallen almost all away; and he used to dine sometimes with Lord Oxford, privately, in a velvet cap. His dress of ceremony was black with a tyewig, and a little sword.

The indulgence and accommodation which his sickness required, had taught him all the unpleasing and unsocial qualities of a valetudinary man. He expected that every thing should give way to his ease or humour, as a child, whose parents will not hear her cry, has an unresisted dominion in the nursery.

C'est que l'enfant toûjours est homme,
C'est que l'homme est toûjours enfant.[160]

When he wanted to sleep he *nodded in company;* and once slumbered at his own table while the Prince of Wales was talking of poetry.

The reputation which his friendship gave procured him many invitations; but he was a very troublesome inmate. He brought no servant, and had so many wants, that a numerous attendance was scarcely able to supply them. Wherever he was, he left no room for another, because he exacted the attention, and employed the activity of the whole family. His errands were so frequent and frivolous, that the footmen in time avoided and neglected him; and the Earl of Oxford discharged some of the servants for their resolute refusal of his messages. The maids, when they had neglected their business, alleged that they had been employed by Mr. Pope. One of his constant demands was of coffee in the night, and to the woman that waited on him in his chamber he was very burthensome; but he was careful to recompense her want of sleep; and Lord Oxford's servant declared, that in a house where her business was to answer his call, she would not ask for wages.

He had another fault, easily incident to those who, suffering much pain, think themselves entitled to whatever pleasures they can snatch. He was too indulgent

---

[159] accountant.

[160] "A child is always a man; a man is always a child."

to his appetite; he loved meat highly seasoned and of strong taste; and, at the intervals of the table, amused himself with biscuits and dry conserves. If he sat down to a variety of dishes, he would oppress his stomach with repletion, and though he seemed angry when a dram was offered him, did not forbear to drink it. His friends, who knew the avenues to his heart, pampered him with presents of luxury, which he did not suffer to stand neglected. The death of great men is not always proportioned to the lustre of their lives. Hannibal, says Juvenal, did not perish by a javelin or a sword; the slaughters of Cannae were revenged by a ring.[161] The death of Pope was imputed by some of his friends to a silver saucepan, in which it was his delight to heat potted lampreys.[162]

That he loved too well to eat, is certain; but that his sensuality shortened his life will not be hastily concluded, when it is remembered that a conformation so irregular lasted six and fifty years, notwithstanding such pertinacious diligence of study and meditation.

In all his intercourse with mankind, he had great delight in artifice, and endeavoured to attain all his purposes by indirect and unsuspected methods. *He hardly drank tea without a stratagem.* If, at the house of his friends, he wanted any accommodation, he was not willing to ask for it in plain terms, but would mention it remotely as something convenient; though, when it was procured, he soon made it appear for whose sake it had been recommended. Thus he teazed Lord Orrery[163] till he obtained a screen. He practised his arts on such small occasions, that Lady Bolingbroke used to say, in a French phrase, that *he plaid the politician about cabbages and turnips.* His unjustifiable impression[164] of the *Patriot King,* as it can be imputed to no particular motive, must have proceeded from his general habit of secrecy and cunning; he caught an opportunity of a sly trick, and

pleased himself with the thought of outwitting Bolingbroke.

In familiar or convivial conversation, it does not appear that he excelled. He may be said to have resembled Dryden, as being not one that was distinguished by vivacity in company. It is remarkable, that, so near his time, so much should be known of what he has written, and so little of what he has said: traditional memory retains no sallies of raillery, nor sentences of observation; nothing either pointed or solid, either wise or merry. One apophthegm only stands upon record. When an objection raised against his inscription for Shakespeare was defended by the authority of *Patrick,* he replied— *horresco referens*[165]—that *he would allow the publisher of a Dictionary to know the meaning of a single word, but not of two words put together.*

He was fretful, and easily displeased, and allowed himself to be capriciously resentful. He would sometimes leave Lord Oxford silently, no one could tell why, and was to be courted back by more letters and messages than the footmen were willing to carry. The table was indeed infested by Lady Mary Wortley, who was the friend of Lady Oxford, and who, knowing his peevishness, could by no intreaties be restrained from contradicting him, till their disputes were sharpened to such asperity, that one or the other quitted the house.

He sometimes condescended to be jocular with servants or inferiors; but by no merriment, either of others or his own, was he ever seen excited to laughter.

Of his domestick character, frugality was a part eminently remarkable. Having determined not to be dependent, he determined not to be in want, and therefore wisely and magnanimously rejected all temptations to expence unsuitable to his fortune. This general care must be universally approved; but it sometimes appeared in petty artifices of parsimony,

---

[161] i.e., by poison carried in a ring.

[162] An eel-like fish.

[163] John Boyle, fifth Earl of Orrery (1707–1762), a friend of long standing of both Pope and Swift, author of *Remarks on the Life and Writings of Jonathan Swift.*

[164] The number of copies printed.

[165] "shudder to think of it" (Vergil, *Aeneid,* II, 204).

such as the practice of writing his compositions on the back of letters, as may be seen in the remaining copy of the *Iliad,* by which perhaps in five years five shillings were saved; or in a niggardly reception of his friends, and scantiness of entertainment, as, when he had two guests in his house, he would set at supper a single pint upon the table; and having himself taken two small glasses would retire and say, *Gentlemen, I leave you to your wine.* Yet he tells his friends, that *he has a heart for all, a house for all, and, whatever they may think, a fortune for all.*

He sometimes, however, made a splendid dinner, and is said to have wanted no part of the skill or elegance which such performances require. That this magnificence should be often displayed, that obstinate prudence with which he conducted his affairs would not permit; for his revenue, certain and casual, amounted only to about eight hundred pounds a year, of which however he declares himself able to assign one hundred to charity.

Of this fortune, which as it arose from publick approbation was very honourably obtained, his imagination seems to have been too full: it would be hard to find a man, so well entitled to notice by his wit, that ever delighted so much in talking of his money. In his Letters, and in his Poems, his garden and his grotto, his quincunx and his vines, or some hints of his opulence, are always to be found. The great topick of his ridicule is poverty; the crimes with which he reproaches his antagonists are their debts, their habitation in the Mint, and their want of a dinner. He seems to be of an opinion not very uncommon in the world, that to want money is to want every thing.

Next to the pleasure of contemplating his possessions, seems to be that of enumerating the men of high rank with whom he was acquainted, and whose notice he loudly proclaims not to have been obtained by any practices of meanness or servility; a boast which was never denied to be true, and to which very few poets have ever aspired. Pope never set genius to sale; he never flattered those whom he did not love, or praised those whom he did not esteem. Savage however remarked, that he began a little to relax his dignity when he wrote a distich for *his Highness's dog.*[166]

His admiration of the Great seems to have increased in the advance of life. He passed over peers and statesmen to inscribe his *Iliad* to Congreve, with a magnanimity of which the praise had been compleat had his friend's virtue been equal to his wit. Why he was chosen for so great an honour, it is not now possible to know; there is no trace in literary history of any particular intimacy between them. The name of Congreve appears in the Letters among those of his other friends, but without any observable distinction or consequence.

To his latter works, however, he took care to annex names dignified with titles, but was not very happy in his choice; for, except Lord Bathurst, none of his noble friends were such as that a good man would wish to have his intimacy with them known to posterity: he can derive little honour from the notice of Cobham, Burlington, or Bolingbroke.

Of his social qualities, if an estimate be made from his Letters, an opinion too favourable cannot easily be formed; they exhibit a perpetual and unclouded effulgence of general benevolence, and particular fondness. There is nothing but liberality, gratitude, constancy, and tenderness. It has been so long said as to be commonly believed, that the true characters of men may be found in their Letters, and that he who writes to his friend lays his heart open before him. But the truth is, that such were simple friendships of the *Golden Age,* and are now the friendships only of children. Very few can boast of hearts which they dare lay open to themselves, and of which, by whatever accident exposed, they do not shun a distinct and continued view; and,

---

[166] *Epigram engraved on the Collar of a Dog which I gave to His Royal Highness*

I am his Highness' Dog at *Kew;*
Pray tell me Sir, whose Dog are you?

certainly, what we hide from ourselves we do not shew to our friends. There is, indeed, no transaction which offers stronger temptations to fallacy and sophistication than epistolary intercourse. In the eagerness of conversation the first emotions of the mind often burst out, before they are considered; in the tumult of business, interest and passion have their genuine effect; but a friendly Letter is a calm and deliberate performance, in the cool of leisure, in the stillness of solitude, and surely no man sits down to depreciate by design his own character.

Friendship has no tendency to secure veracity; for by whom can a man so much wish to be thought better than he is, as by him whose kindness he desires to gain or keep? Even in writing to the world there is less constraint; the author is not confronted with his reader, and takes his chance of approbation among the different dispositions of mankind; but a Letter is addressed to a single mind, of which the prejudices and partialities are known; and must therefore please, if not by favouring them, by forbearing to oppose them.

To charge those favourable representations, which men give of their own minds, with the guilt of hypocritical falsehood, would shew more severity than knowledge. The writer commonly believes himself. Almost every man's thoughts, while they are general, are right; and most hearts are pure, while temptation is away. It is easy to awaken generous sentiments in privacy; to despise death when there is no danger; to glow with benevolence when there is nothing to be given. While such ideas are formed they are felt, and self-love does not suspect the gleam of virtue to be the meteor of fancy.

If the Letters of Pope are considered merely as compositions, they seem to be premeditated and artificial. It is one thing to write, because there is something which the mind wishes to discharge; and another, to solicit the imagination, because ceremony or vanity requires something to be written. Pope confesses his early Letters to be vitiated with *affectation and ambition:* to know whether he

disentangled himself from these perverters of epistolary integrity, his book and his life must be set in comparison.

One of his favourite topicks is contempt of his own poetry. For this, if it had been real, he would deserve no commendation; and in this he was certainly not sincere, for his high value of himself was sufficiently observed; and of what could he be proud but of his poetry? He writes, he says, when *he has just nothing else to do;* yet Swift complains that he was never at leisure for conversation, because he *had always some poetical scheme in his head.* It was punctually required that his writing-box should be set upon his bed before he rose; and Lord Oxford's domestick related, that, in the dreadful winter of Forty,[167] she was called from her bed by him four times in one night, to supply him with paper, lest he should lose a thought.

He pretends insensibility to censure and criticism, though it was observed by all who knew him that every pamphlet disturbed his quiet, and that his extreme irritability laid him open to perpetual vexation; but he wished to despise his criticks, and therefore hoped that he did despise them.

As he happened to live in two reigns when the Court paid little attention to poetry, he nursed in his mind a foolish disesteem of Kings, and proclaims that *he never sees Courts.* Yet a little regard shewn him by the Prince of Wales melted his obduracy; and he had not much to say when he was asked by his Royal Highness, *how he could love a Prince while he disliked Kings?*

He very frequently professes contempt of the world, and represents himself as looking on mankind, sometimes with gay indifference, as on emmets of a hillock, below his serious attention; and sometimes with gloomy indignation, as on monsters more worthy of hatred than of pity. These were dispositions apparently counterfeited. How could he despise those whom he lived by pleasing, and on whose approbation his esteem of himself

---

167 The winter of 1739–1740 was spectacularly severe.

was superstructed? Why should he hate those to whose favour he owed his honour and his ease? Of things that terminate in human life, the world is the proper judge; to despise its sentence, if it were possible, is not just; and if it were just, is not possible. Pope was far enough from this unreasonable temper; he was sufficiently *a fool to Fame,* and his fault was, that he pretended to neglect it. His levity and his sullenness were only in his Letters; he passed through common life, sometimes vexed, and sometimes pleased, with the natural emotions of common men.

His scorn of the great is repeated too often to be real; no man thinks much of that which he despises; and as falsehood is always in danger of inconsistency, he makes it his boast at another time that he lives among them.

It is evident that his own importance swells often in his mind. He is afraid of writing, lest the clerks of the Post-office should know his secrets; he has many enemies; he considers himself as surrounded by universal jealousy; *after many deaths, and many dispersions, two or three of us,* says he, *may still be brought together, not to plot, but to divert ourselves, and the world too, if it pleases;* and they can live together, and *shew what friends wits may be, in spite of all the fools in the world.* All this while it was likely that the clerks did not know his hand; he certainly had no more enemies than a publick character like his inevitably excites; and with what degree of friendship the wits might live, very few were so much fools as ever to enquire.

Some part of this pretended discontent he learned from Swift, and expresses it, I think, most frequently in his correspondence with him. Swift's resentment was unreasonable, but it was sincere; Pope's was the mere mimickry of his friend, a fictitious part which he began to play before it became him. When he was only twenty-five years old, he related that *a glut of study and retirement had thrown him on the world,* and that there was danger lest *a glut of the world should throw him back upon study and*

retirement. To this Swift answered with great propriety, that Pope had not yet either acted or suffered enough in the world to have become weary of it. And, indeed, it must be some very powerful reason that can drive back to solitude him who has once enjoyed the pleasures of society.

In the Letters both of Swift and Pope there appears such narrowness of mind, as makes them insensible of any excellence that has not some affinity with their own, and confines their esteem and approbation to so small a number, that whoever should form his opinion of the age from their representation, would suppose them to have lived amidst ignorance and barbarity, unable to find among their contemporaries either virtue or intelligence, and persecuted by those that could not understand them.

When Pope murmurs at the world, when he professes contempt of fame, when he speaks of riches and poverty, of success and disappointment, with negligent indifference, he certainly does not express his habitual and settled sentiments, but either wilfully disguises his own character, or, what is more likely, invests himself with temporary qualities, and sallies out in the colours of the present moment. His hopes and fears, his joys and sorrows, acted strongly upon his mind; and if he differed from others, it was not by carelessness; he was irritable and resentful; his malignity to Philips, whom he had first made ridiculous, and then hated for being angry, continued too long. Of his vain desire to make Bentley contemptible, I never heard any adequate reason. He was sometimes wanton in his attacks; and, before Chandos, Lady Wortley, and Hill, was mean in his retreat.

The virtues which seem to have had most of his affection were liberality and fidelity of friendship, in which it does not appear that he was other than he describes himself. His fortune did not suffer his charity to be splendid and conspicuous; but he assisted Dodsley with a hundred pounds, that he might open a shop; and of the subscription of forty pounds a year, that he raised for Savage, twenty were paid by himself. He was accused of loving money, but his love was eagerness to gain, not solicitude to keep it.

In the duties of friendship he was zealous and constant: his early maturity of mind commonly united him with men older than himself; and therefore, without attaining any considerable length of life, he saw many companions of his youth sink into the grave; but it does not appear that he lost a single friend by coldness or by injury; those who loved him once, continued their kindness. His ungrateful mention of Allen, in his will, was the effect of his adherence to one whom he had known much longer, and whom he naturally loved with greater fondness. His violation of the trust reposed in him by Bolingbroke could have no motive inconsistent with the warmest affection; he either thought the action so near to indifferent that he forgot it, or so laudable that he expected his friend to approve it.

It was reported, with such confidence as almost to enforce belief, that in the papers intrusted to his executors was found a defamatory Life of Swift, which he had prepared as an instrument of vengeance, to be used if any provocation should be ever given. About this I enquired of the Earl of Marchmont, who assured me that no such piece was among his remains.

The religion in which he lived and died was that of the Church of Rome, to which in his correspondence with Racine he professes himself a sincere adherent. That he was not scrupulously pious in some part of his life, is known by many idle and indecent applications of sentences taken from the Scriptures; a mode of merriment which a good man dreads for its profaneness, and a witty man disdains for its easiness and vulgarity. But to whatever levities he has been betrayed, it does not appear that his principles were ever corrupted, or that he ever lost his belief of Revelation. The positions which

he transmitted from Bolingbroke he seems not to have understood, and was pleased with an interpretation that made them orthodox.

A man of such exalted superiority, and so little moderation, would naturally have all his delinquencies observed and aggravated: those who could not deny that he was excellent, would rejoice to find that he was not perfect.

Perhaps it may be imputed to the unwillingness with which the same man is allowed to possess many advantages, that his learning has been depreciated. He certainly was in his early life a man of great literary curiosity; and when he wrote his *Essay on Criticism* had, for his age, a very wide acquaintance with books. When he entered into the living world, it seems to have happened to him as to many others, that he was less attentive to dead masters; he studied in the academy of Paracelsus,[168] and made the universe his favourite volume. He gathered his notions fresh from reality, not from the copies of authors, but the originals of Nature. Yet there is no reason to believe that literature ever lost his esteem; he always professed to love reading; and Dobson, who spent some time at his house translating his *Essay on Man,* when I asked him what learning he found him to possess, answered, *More than I expected.* His frequent references to history, his allusions to various kinds of knowledge, and his images selected from art and nature, with his observations on the operations of the mind and the modes of life, shew an intelligence perpetually on the wing, excursive, vigorous, and diligent, eager to pursue knowledge, and attentive to retain it.

From this curiosity arose the desire of travelling, to which he alludes in his verses to Jervas, and which, though he never found an opportunity to gratify it, did not leave him till his life declined.

Of his intellectual character, the constituent and fundamental principle was

---

[168] Theophrastus Bombastus von Hohenheim (1493?–1541), called Paracelsus, was a Swiss physician who related all things in a Platonic scheme.

Good Sense, a prompt and intuitive perception of consonance and propriety. He saw immediately, of his own conceptions, what was to be chosen, and what to be rejected; and, in the works of others, what was to be shunned, and what was to be copied.

But good sense alone is a sedate and quiescent quality, which manages its possessions well, but does not increase them; it collects few materials for its own operations, and preserves safety, but never gains supremacy. Pope had likewise genius; a mind active, ambitious, and adventurous, always investigating, always aspiring; in its widest searches still longing to go forward, in its highest flights still wishing to be higher; always imagining something greater than it knows, always endeavouring more than it can do.

To assist these powers, he is said to have had great strength and exactness of memory. That which he had heard or read was not easily lost; and he had before him not only what his own meditations suggested, but what he had found in other writers, that might be accommodated to his present purpose.

These benefits of nature he improved by incessant and unwearied diligence; he had recourse to every source of intelligence, and lost no opportunity of information; he consulted the living as well as the dead; he read his compositions to his friends, and was never content with mediocrity when excellence could be attained. He considered poetry as the business of his life; and, however he might seem to lament his occupation, he followed it with constancy; to make verses was his first labour, and to mend them was his last.

From his attention to poetry he was never diverted. If conversation offered any thing that could be improved, he committed it to paper; if a thought, or perhaps an expression more happy than was common, rose to his mind, he was careful to write it; an independent distich was preserved for an opportunity of insertion; and some little fragments have been found containing lines, or parts of lines, to be wrought upon at some other time.

He was one of those few whose labour is their pleasure. He was never elevated to negligence, nor wearied to impatience; he never passed a fault unamended by indifference, nor quitted it by despair. He laboured his works first to gain reputation, and afterwards to keep it.

Of composition there are different methods. Some employ at once memory and invention, and, with little intermediate use of the pen, form and polish large masses by continued meditation, and write their productions only when, in their own opinion, they have completed them. It is related of Virgil, that his custom was to pour out a great number of verses in the morning, and pass the day in retrenching exuberances and correcting inaccuracies. The method of Pope, as may be collected from his translation, was to write his first thoughts in his first words, and gradually to amplify, decorate, rectify, and refine them.

With such faculties, and such dispositions, he excelled every other writer in *poetical prudence;* he wrote in such a manner as might expose him to few hazards. He used almost always the same fabric of verse; and, indeed, by those few essays which he made of any other, he did not enlarge his reputation. Of this uniformity the certain consequence was readiness and dexterity. By perpetual practice, language had in his mind a systematical arrangement; having always the same use for words, he had words so selected and combined as to be ready at his call. This increase of facility he confessed himself to have perceived in the progress of his translation.

But what was yet of more importance, his effusions were always voluntary, and his subjects chosen by himself. His independence secured him from drudging at a task, and labouring upon a barren topick: he never exchanged praise for money, nor opened a shop of condolence or congratulation. His poems, therefore, were scarce ever temporary. He suffered coronations and royal marriages to pass without a song, and derived no opportunities from recent events, nor any popularity from the accidental disposition of his readers. He was never reduced to the necessity of soliciting the sun to shine upon a birth-day, of calling the Graces and Virtues to a wedding, or of saying what multitudes have said before him. When he could produce nothing new, he was at liberty to be silent.

His publications were for the same reason never hasty. He is said to have sent nothing to the press till it had lain two years under his inspection: it is at least certain, that he ventured nothing without nice examination. He suffered the tumult of imagination to subside, and the novelties of invention to grow famil-iar. He knew that the mind is always enamoured of its own productions, and did not trust his first fondness. He con-sulted his friends, and listened with great willingness to criticism; and, what was of more importance, he consulted him-self, and let nothing pass against his own judgement.

He professed to have learned his po-etry from Dryden, whom, whenever an opportunity was presented, he praised through his whole life with unvaried lib-erality; and perhaps his character may re-ceive some illustration, if he be compared with his master.

Integrity of understanding and nicety of discernment were not allotted in a less proportion to Dryden than to Pope. The rectitude of Dryden's mind was suf-ficiently shewn by the dismission of his poetical prejudices, and the rejection of unnatural thoughts and rugged numbers. But Dryden never desired to apply all the judgement that he had. He wrote, and professed to write, merely for the people; and when he pleased others, he contented himself. He spent no time in struggles to rouse latent powers; he never attempted to make that better which was already good, nor often to mend what he must have known to be faulty. He wrote, as he tells us, with very little consideration; when occasion or necessity called upon him, he poured out what the present moment happened to supply, and, when once it had passed the press, ejected it from his mind; for when he had no pecuniary interest, he had no further solicitude.

Pope was not content to satisfy; he de-sired to excel, and therefore always en-deavoured to do his best: he did not court the candour, but dared the judge-ment of his reader, and, expecting no in-dulgence from others, he shewed none to himself. He examined lines and words with minute and punctilious observation, and retouched every part with indefati-gable diligence till he had left nothing to be forgiven.

For this reason he kept his pieces very long in his hands, while he considered and reconsidered them. The only poems which can be supposed to have been writ-ten with such regard to the times as might hasten their publication, were the two satires of *Thirty-eight;* of which Dodsley told me, that they were brought to him by the author, that they might be fairly copied. "Almost every line," he said, "was then written twice over; I gave him a clean transcript, which he sent some time afterwards to me for the press, with almost every line written twice over a second time."

His declaration, that his care for his works ceased at their publication, was not strictly true. His parental attention never abandoned them; what he found amiss in the first edition, he silently cor-rected in those that followed. He appears to have revised the *Iliad,* and freed it from some of its imperfections; and the *Essay on Criticism* received many im-provements after its first appearance. It will seldom be found that he altered without adding clearness, elegance, or vigour. Pope had perhaps the judgement of Dryden; but Dryden certainly wanted the diligence of Pope.

In acquired knowledge, the superiority must be allowed to Dryden, whose edu-cation was more scholastick, and who before he became an author had been al-lowed more time for study, with better means of information. His mind has a larger range, and he collects his images and illustrations from a more extensive circumference of science. Dryden knew more of man in his general nature, and Pope in his local manners. The notions of Dryden were formed by comprehen-sive speculation; and those of Pope by minute attention. There is more dignity in the knowledge of Dryden, and more certainty in that of Pope.

Poetry was not the sole praise of either; for both excelled likewise in prose; but Pope did not borrow his prose from his predecessor. The style of Dryden is capricious and varied; that of Pope is cautious and uniform; Dryden obeys the motions of his own mind; Pope constrains his mind to his own rules of composition. Dryden is sometimes vehement and rapid; Pope is always smooth, uniform, and gentle. Dryden's page is a natural field, rising into inequalities, and diversified by the varied exuberance of abundant vegetation; Pope's is a velvet lawn, shaven by the scythe, and levelled by the roller.

Of genius, that power which constitutes a poet; that quality without which judgement is cold, and knowledge is inert; that energy which collects, combines, amplifies, and animates; the superiority must, with some hesitation, be allowed to Dryden. It is not to be inferred that of this poetical vigour Pope had only a little, because Dryden had more; for every other writer since Milton must give place to Pope; and even of Dryden it must be said, that, if he has brighter paragraphs, he has not better poems. Dryden's performances were always hasty, either excited by some external occasion, or extorted by domestick necessity; he composed without consideration, and published without correction. What his mind could supply at call, or gather in one excursion, was all that he sought, and all that he gave. The dilatory caution of Pope enabled him to condense his sentiments, to multiply his images, and to accumulate all that study might produce, or chance might supply. If the flights of Dryden therefore are higher, Pope continues longer on the wing. If of Dryden's fire the blaze is brighter, of Pope's the heat is more regular and constant. Dryden often surpasses expectation, and Pope never falls below it. Dryden is read with frequent astonishment, and Pope with perpetual delight.

This parallel will, I hope, when it is well considered, be found just; and if the reader should suspect me, as I suspect myself, of some partial fondness for the memory of Dryden, let him not too hastily condemn me; for meditation and enquiry may, perhaps, shew him the reasonableness of my determination.

[THE CHARACTERISTICS OF HIS WRITINGS]

The Works of Pope are now to be distinctly examined, not so much with attention to slight faults or petty beauties, as to the general character and effect of each performance.

It seems natural for a young poet to initiate himself by Pastorals, which, not professing to imitate real life, require no experience, and, exhibiting only the simple operation of unmingled passions, admit no subtle reasoning or deep enquiry. Pope's pastorals are not however composed but with close thought; they have reference to the times of the day, the seasons of the year, and the periods of human life. The last, that which turns the attention upon age and death, was the author's favourite. To tell of disappointment and misery, to thicken the darkness of futurity, and perplex the labyrinth of uncertainty, has been always a delicious employment of the poets. His preference was probably just. I wish, however, that his fondness had not overlooked a line in which the *Zephyrs* are made *to lament in silence*.

To charge these pastorals with want of invention, is to require what never was intended. The imitations are so ambitiously frequent, that the writer evidently means rather to shew his literature than his wit. It is surely sufficient for an author of sixteen not only to be able to copy the poems of antiquity with judicious selection, but to have obtained sufficient power of language, and skill in metre, to exhibit a series of versification, which had in English poetry no precedent, nor has since had an imitation.

The design of *Windsor Forest* is evidently derived from *Cooper's Hill*,[169]

---

[169] By Sir John Denham (1642).

with some attention to Waller's poem on *The Park;* but Pope cannot be denied to excel his masters in variety and elegance, and the art of interchanging description, narrative, and morality. The objection made by Dennis is the want of plan, of a regular subordination of parts terminating in the principal and original design. There is this want in most descriptive poems, because as the scenes, which they must exhibit successively, are all subsisting at the same time, the order in which they are shewn must by necessity be arbitrary, and more is not to be expected from the last part than from the first. The attention, therefore, which cannot be detained by suspense, must be excited by diversity, such as his poem offers to its reader.

But the desire of diversity may be too much indulged; the parts of *Windsor Forest* which deserve least praise are those which were added to enliven the stillness of the scene, the appearance of Father Thames, and the transformation of *Lodona.* Addison had in his *Campaign* derided the *Rivers* that *rise from their oozy beds* to tell stories of heroes, and it is therefore strange that Pope should adopt a fiction not only unnatural but lately censured. The story of *Lodona* is told with sweetness; but a new metamorphosis is a ready and puerile expedient; nothing is easier than to tell how a flower was once a blooming virgin, or a rock an obdurate tyrant.

The *Temple of Fame* has, as Steele warmly declared, *a thousand beauties.* Every part is splendid; there is great luxuriance of ornaments; the original vision of Chaucer was never denied to be much improved; the allegory is very skillfully continued, the imagery is properly selected, and learnedly displayed: yet, with all this comprehension of excellence, as its scene is laid in remote ages, and its sentiments, if the concluding paragraph be excepted, have little relation to general manners or common life, it never obtained much notice, but is turned si-

lently over, and seldom quoted or mentioned with either praise or blame.

That the *Messiah* excels the *Pollio*[170] is no great praise, if it be considered from what original the improvements are derived.

The *Verses on the unfortunate Lady* have drawn much attention by the illaudable singularity of treating suicide with respect; and they must be allowed to be written in some parts with vigorous animation, and in others with gentle tenderness; nor has Pope produced any poem in which the sense predominates more over the diction. But the tale is not skillfully told; it is not easy to discover the character of either the Lady or her Guardian. History relates that she was about to disparage herself by a marriage with an inferior; Pope praises her for the dignity of ambition, and yet condemns the unkle to detestation for his pride; the ambitious love of a niece may be opposed by the interest, malice, or envy of an unkle, but never by his pride. On such an occasion a poet may be allowed to be obscure, but inconsistency never can be right.

The *Ode* for *St. Cecilia's Day* was undertaken at the desire of Steele: in this the author is generally confessed to have miscarried, yet he has miscarried only as compared with Dryden; for he has far outgone other competitors. Dryden's plan is better chosen; history will always take stronger hold of the attention than fable: the passions excited by Dryden are the pleasures and pains of real life, the scene of Pope is laid in imaginary existence; Pope is read with calm acquiescence, Dryden with turbulent delight; Pope hangs upon the ear, and Dryden finds the passes of the mind.

Both the odes want the essential constituent of metrical compositions, the stated recurrence of settled numbers. It may be alleged, that Pindar is said by Horace to have written *numeris lege solutis:*[171] but as no such lax performances have been transmitted to us, the

[170] W. J. Mackee, *Pollio: an Elegiac Ode; written in the Wood near R—— Castle* (1762).

[171] "in unpredictable meter" (*Odes,* IV, ii, 12).

meaning of that expression cannot be fixed; and perhaps the like return might properly be made to a modern Pindarist, as Mr. Cobb[172] received from Bentley, who, when he found his criticisms upon a Greek Exercise, which Cobb had presented, refuted one after another by Pindar's authority, cried out at last, *Pindar was a bold fellow, but thou art an impudent one.*

If Pope's ode be particularly inspected, it will be found that the first stanza consists of sounds well chosen indeed, but only sounds.

The second consists of hyperbolical common-places, easily to be found, and perhaps without much difficulty to be as well expressed.

In the third, however, there are numbers, images, harmony, and vigour, not unworthy the antagonist of Dryden. Had all been like this—but every part cannot be the best.

The next stanzas place and detain us in the dark and dismal regions of mythology, where neither hope nor fear, neither joy nor sorrow, can be found: the poet however faithfully attends us; we have all that can be performed by elegance of diction, or sweetness of versification; but what can form avail without better matter?

The last stanza recurs again to common-places. The conclusion is too evidently modelled by that of Dryden; and it may be remarked that both end with the same fault, the comparison of each is literal on one side, and metaphorical on the other.

Poets do not always express their own thoughts; Pope, with all this labour in the praise of Musick, was ignorant of its principles, and insensible of its effects.

One of his greatest though of his earliest works is the *Essay on Criticism,* which, if he had written nothing else, would have placed him among the first criticks and the first poets, as it exhibits every mode of excellence that can embellish or dignify didactick composition, selection of matter, novelty of arrangement, justness of precept, splendour of illustration, and propriety of digression. I know not whether it be pleasing to consider that he produced this piece at twenty, and never afterwards excelled it: he that delights himself with observing that such powers may be soon attained, cannot but grieve to think that life was ever after at a stand.

To mention the particular beauties of the Essay would be unprofitably tedious: but I cannot forbear to observe, that the comparison of a student's progress in the sciences with the journey of a traveller in the Alps,[173] is perhaps the best that English poetry can shew. A simile, to be perfect, must both illustrate and ennoble the subject; must shew it to the understanding in a clearer view, and display it to the fancy with greater dignity; but either of these qualities may be sufficient to recommend it. In didactick poetry, of which the great purpose is instruction, a simile may be praised which illustrates, though it does not ennoble; in heroicks, that may be admitted which ennobles, though it does not illustrate. That it may be complete, it is required to exhibit, independently of its references, a pleasing image; for a simile is said to be a short episode. To this antiquity was so attentive, that circumstances were sometimes added, which, having no parallels, served only to fill the imagination, and produced what Perrault ludicrously called *comparisons with a long tail.* In their similies the greatest writers have sometimes failed; the ship-race, compared with the chariot-race, is neither illustrated nor aggrandised; land and water make all the difference: when Apollo, running after Daphne, is likened to a greyhound chasing a hare, there is nothing gained; the ideas of pursuit and flight are too plain to be made plainer; and a god and the daughter of a god are not represented much to their advantage by a hare and dog. The simile of the Alps has no useless parts, yet affords a striking picture

---

[172] Samuel Cobb (1675–1713), translator and versifier; Isaac Watts considered his *Ode attempted in the Style of Pindar* the "best and truest *Pindaric* that ever I read."

[173] ll. 222–235.

by itself; it makes the foregoing position better understood, and enables it to take faster hold on the attention; it assists the apprehension, and elevates the fancy.

Let me likewise dwell a little on the celebrated paragraph, in which it is directed that *the sound should seem an echo to the sense;* a precept which Pope is allowed to have observed beyond any other English poet.

This notion of representative metre, and the desire of discovering frequent adaptations of the sound to the sense, have produced, in my opinion, many wild conceits and imaginary beauties. All that can furnish this representation are the sounds of the words considered singly, and the time in which they are pronounced. Every language has some words framed to exhibit the noises which they express, as *thump, rattle, growl, hiss.* These however are but few, and the poet cannot make them more, nor can they be of any use but when sound is to be mentioned. The time of pronunciation was in the dactylick measures of the learned languages capable of considerable variety; but that variety could be accommodated only to motion or duration, and different degrees of motion were perhaps expressed by verses rapid or slow, without much attention of the writer, when the image had full possession of his fancy; but our language having little flexibility, our verses can differ very little in their cadence. The fancied resemblances, I fear, arise sometimes merely from the ambiguity of words; there is supposed to be some relation between a *soft* line and a *soft* couch, or between *hard* syllables and *hard* fortune.

Motion, however, may be in some sort exemplified; and yet it may be suspected that even in such resemblances the mind often governs the ear, and the sounds are estimated by their meaning. One of the most successful attempts has been to describe the labour of Sisyphus:

With many a weary step, and many a groan,
Up a high hill he heaves a huge round stone;

The huge round stone, resulting with a bound,
Thunders impetuous down, and smoaks along the ground.

Who does not perceive the stone to move slowly upward, and roll violently back? But set the same numbers to another sense;

While many a merry tale, and many a song,
Chear'd the rough road, we wish'd the rough road long.
The rough road then, returning in a round,
Mock'd our impatient steps, for all was fairy ground.

We have now surely lost much of the delay, and much of the rapidity.

But, to shew how little the greatest master of numbers can fix the principles of representative harmony, it will be sufficient to remark that the poet, who tells us, that

When Ajax strives . . . the words move slow.
Not so when swift Camilla scours the plain,
Flies o'er th' unbending corn, and skims along the main;

when he had enjoyed for about thirty years the praise of Camilla's lightness of foot, tried another experiment upon *sound* and *time,* and produced this memorable triplet;

Waller was smooth, but Dryden taught to join
The varying verse, the full resounding line,
The long majestick march, and energy divine.

Here are the swiftness of the rapid race, and the march of slow-paced majesty, exhibited by the same poet in the same sequence of syllables, except that the exact prosodist will find the line of *swiftness* by one time longer than that of *tardiness.*

Beauties of this kind are commonly fancied; and when real are technical and nugatory, not to be rejected, and not to be solicited.

To the praises which have been accumulated on *The Rape of the Lock* by readers of every class, from the critick to the waiting-maid, it is difficult to make any addition. Of that which is universally allowed to be the most attractive of all ludicrous compositions, let it rather be now enquired from what sources the power of pleasing is derived.

Dr. Warburton, who excelled in critical perspicacity, has remarked that the preternatural agents are very happily adapted to the purposes of the poem. The heathen deities can no longer gain attention: we should have turned away from a contest between Venus and Diana. The employment of allegorical persons always excites conviction of its own absurdity; they may produce effects, but cannot conduct actions; when the phantom is put in motion, it dissolves: thus *Discord* may raise a mutiny; but *Discord* cannot conduct a march, nor besiege a town. Pope brought into view a new race of Beings, with powers and passions proportionate to their operation. The Sylphs and Gnomes act at the toilet and the tea-table; what more terrifick and more powerful phantoms perform on the stormy ocean, or the field of battle, they give their proper help, and do their proper mischief.

Pope is said, by an objector, not to have been the inventor of this petty nation; a charge which might with more justice have been brought against the author of the *Iliad,* who doubtless adopted the religious system of his country; for what is there but the names of his agents which Pope has not invented? Has he not assigned them characters and operations never heard of before? Has he not, at least, given them their first poetical existence? If this is not sufficient to denominate his work original, nothing original ever can be written.

In this work are exhibited, in a very high degree, the two most engaging powers of an author. New things are made familiar, and familiar things are made new. A race of aerial people, never heard of before, is presented to us in a manner so clear and easy, that the reader seeks for no further information, but immediately mingles with his new acquaintance, adopts their interests, and attends their pursuits, loves a Sylph, and detests a Gnome.

That familiar things are made new, every paragraph will prove. The subject of the poem is an event below the common incidents of common life; nothing real is introduced that is not seen so often as to be no longer regarded; yet the whole detail of a female-day is here brought before us invested with so much art of decoration, that, though nothing is disguised, every thing is striking, and we feel all the appetite of curiosity for that from which we have a thousand times turned fastidiously away.

The purpose of the poet is, as he tells us, to laugh at *the little unguarded follies of the female sex.* It is therefore without justice that Dennis[174] charges the *Rape of the Lock* with the want of a moral, and for that reason sets it below the *Lutrin,* which exposes the pride and discord of the clergy. Perhaps neither Pope nor Boileau has made the world much better than he found it; but, if they had both succeeded, it were easy to tell who would have deserved most from publick gratitude. The freaks, and humours, and spleen, and vanity of women, as they embroil families in discord, and fill houses with disquiet, do more to obstruct the happiness of life in a year than the ambition of the clergy in many centuries. It has been well observed, that the misery of man proceeds not from any single crush of overwhelming evil, but from small vexations continually repeated.

It is remarked by Dennis likewise, that the machinery is superfluous; that, by all the bustle of preternatural operation, the main event is neither hastened nor retarded. To this charge an efficacious answer is not easily made. The Sylphs cannot be said to help or to op-

---

[174] John Dennis, *Remarks on Mr. Pope's Rape of the Lock* (1728).

pose; and it must be allowed to imply some want of art, that their power has not been sufficiently intermingled with the action. Other parts may likewise be charged with want of connection; the game at *ombre* might be spared, but if the Lady had lost her hair while she was intent upon her cards, it might have been inferred that those who are too fond of play will be in danger of neglecting more important interests. Those perhaps are faults; but what are such faults to so much excellence!

The Epistle of *Eloise to Abelard* is one of the most happy productions of human wit: the subject is so judiciously chosen, that it would be difficult, in turning over the annals of the world, to find another which so many circumstances concur to recommend. We regularly interest ourselves most in the fortune of those who most deserve our notice. Abelard and Eloise were conspicuous in their days for eminence of merit. The heart naturally loves truth. The adventures and misfortunes of this illustrious pair are known from undisputed history. Their fate does not leave the mind in hopeless dejection; for they both found quiet and consolation in retirement and piety. So new and so affecting is their story, that it supersedes invention, and imagination ranges at full liberty without straggling into scenes of fable.

The story, thus skilfully adopted, has been diligently improved. Pope has left nothing behind him, which seems more the effect of studious perseverance and laborious revisal. Here is particularly observable the *curiosa felicitas*,[175] a fruitful soil, and careful cultivation. Here is no crudeness of sense, nor asperity of language.

The sources from which sentiments, which have so much vigour and efficacy, have been drawn, are shewn to be the mystick writers by the learned author[176] of the *Essay on the Life and Writings of Pope;* a book which teaches how the

brow of Criticism may be smoothed, and how she may be enabled, with all her severity, to attract and to delight.

The train of my disquisition has now conducted me to that poetical wonder, the translation of the *Iliad;* a performance which no age or nation can pretend to equal. To the Greeks translation was almost unknown; it was totally unknown to the inhabitants of Greece. They had no recourse to the Barbarians for poetical beauties, but sought for every thing in Homer, where, indeed, there is but little which they might not find.

The Italians have been very diligent translators; but I can hear of no version, unless perhaps Anguillara's Ovid[177] may be excepted, which is read with eagerness. The *Iliad* of Salvini every reader may discover to be punctiliously exact; but it seems to be the work of a linguist skilfully pedantick; and his countrymen, the proper judges of its power to please, reject it with disgust.

Their predecessors the Romans have left some specimens of translation behind them, and that employment must have had some credit in which Tully and Germanicus[178] engaged; but unless we suppose, what is perhaps true, that the plays of Terence were versions of Menander, nothing translated seems ever to have risen to high reputation. The French, in the meridian hour of their learning, were very laudably industrious to enrich their own language with the wisdom of the ancients; but found themselves reduced, by whatever necessity, to turn the Greek and Roman poetry into prose. Whoever could read an author, could translate him. From such rivals little can be feared.

The chief help of Pope in this arduous undertaking was drawn from the versions of Dryden. Virgil had borrowed much of his imagery from Homer; and part of the debt was now paid by his translator. Pope searched the pages of Dryden for happy combinations of heroic

175 A paradox, "Carefully contrived good fortune"; it is more skillfully expressed by Pope in the *Essay on Criticism* as "a happiness as well as care."
176 Joseph Warton (1722–1800).

177 Giovanni Andrea dell-Angiullara translated Ovid's *Metamorphoses* (Venice, 1561). The *Iliad* was translated into Italian by Maria Salvini (1653–1729).
178 Roman emperor (15 B.C.–A.D. 19).

diction; but it will not be denied that he added much to what he found. He cultivated our language with so much diligence and art, that he has left in his *Homer* a treasure of poetical elegances to posterity. His version may be said to have tuned the English tongue; for since its appearance no writer, however deficient in other powers, has wanted melody. Such a series of lines so elaborately corrected, and so sweetly modulated, took possession of the publick ear; the vulgar was enamoured of the poem, and the learned wondered at the translation.

But in the most general applause discordant voices will always be heard. It has been objected by some, who wish to be numbered among the sons of learning, that Pope's version of Homer is not Homerical; that it exhibits no resemblance of the original and characteristick manner of the Father of Poetry, as it wants his awful simplicity, his artless grandeur, his unaffected majesty. This cannot be totally denied; but it must be remembered that *necessitas quod cogit defendit;*[179] that may be lawfully done which cannot be forborn. Time and place will always enforce regard. In estimating this translation, consideration must be had of the nature of our language, the form of our metre, and, above all, of the change which two thousand years have made in the modes of life and the habits of thought. Virgil wrote in a language of the same general fabrick with that of Homer, in verses of the same measure, and in an age nearer to Homer's time by eighteen hundred years; yet he found, even then, the state of the world so much altered, and the demand for elegance so much increased, that mere nature would be endured no longer; and perhaps, in the multitude of borrowed passages, very few can be shewn which he has not embellished.

There is a time when nations emerging from barbarity, and falling into regular subordination, gain leisure to grow wise, and feel the shame of ignorance and the craving pain of unsatisfied curiosity.

To this hunger of the mind plain sense is grateful; that which fills the void removes uneasiness, and to be free from pain for a while is pleasure; but repletion generates fastidiousness; a saturated intellect soon becomes luxurious, and knowledge finds no willing reception till it is recommended by artificial diction. Thus it will be found, in the progress of learning, that in all nations the first writers are simple, and that every age improves in elegance. One refinement always makes way for another, and what was expedient to Virgil was necessary to Pope.

I suppose many readers of the English *Iliad,* when they have been touched with some unexpected beauty of the lighter kind, have tried to enjoy it in the original, where, alas! it was not to be found. Homer doubtless owes to his translator many *Ovidian* graces not exactly suitable to his character; but to have added can be no great crime, if nothing be taken away. Elegance is surely to be desired, if it be not gained at the expence of dignity. A hero would wish to be loved, as well as to be reverenced.

To a thousand cavils one answer is sufficient; the purpose of a writer is to be read, and the criticism which would destroy the power of pleasing must be blown aside. Pope wrote for his own age and his own nation: he knew that it was necessary to colour the images and point the sentiments of his author; he therefore made him graceful, but lost him some of his sublimity.

The copious notes with which the version is accompanied, and by which it is recommended to many readers, though they were undoubtedly written to swell the volumes, ought not to pass without praise: commentaries which attract the reader by the pleasure of perusal have not often appeared; the notes of others are read to clear difficulties, those of Pope to vary entertainment.

It has however been objected, with sufficient reason, that there is in the commentary too much of unseasonable levity and affected gaiety; that too many appeals are made to the Ladies, and the ease which is so carefully preserved is some-

---

[179] The Latin is translated in the following clause.

times the ease of a trifler. Every art has its terms, and every kind of instruction its proper style; the gravity of common criticks may be tedious, but is less despicable than childish merriment.

Of the *Odyssey* nothing remains to be observed: the same general praise may be given to both translations, and a particular examination of either would require a large volume. The notes were written by Broome, who endeavoured not unsuccessfully to imitate his master.

Of the *Dunciad* the hint is confessedly taken from Dryden's *Mac Flecknoe;* but the plan is so enlarged and diversified as justly to claim the praise of an original, and affords perhaps the best specimen that has yet appeared of personal satire ludicrously pompous.

That the design was moral, whatever the author might tell either his readers or himself, I am not convinced. The first motive was the desire of revenging the contempt with which Theobald had treated his *Shakespeare,* and regaining the honour which he had lost, by crushing his opponent. Theobald was not of bulk enough to fill a poem, and therefore it was necessary to find other enemies with other names, at whose expence he might divert the publick.

In this design there was petulance and malignity enough; but I cannot think it very criminal. An author places himself uncalled before the tribunal of Criticism, and solicits fame at the hazard of disgrace. Dulness or deformity are not culpable in themselves, but may be very justly reproached when they pretend to the honour of wit or the influence of beauty. If bad writers were to pass without reprehension, what should restrain them? *impune diem consumpserit ingens Telephus;*[180] and upon bad writers only will censure have much effect. The satire which brought Theobald and Moore into contempt, dropped impotent from Bentley, like the javelin of Priam.

All truth is valuable, and satirical criticism may be considered as useful when it rectifies error and improves judgement; he that refines the publick taste is a publick benefactor.

The beauties of this poem are well known; its chief fault is the grossness of its images. Pope and Swift had an unnatural delight in ideas physically impure, such as every other tongue utters with unwillingness, and of which every ear shrinks from the mention.

But even this fault, offensive as it is, may be forgiven for the excellence of other passages; such as the formation and dissolution of Moore, the account of the Traveller, the misfortune of the Florist, and the crouded thoughts and stately numbers which dignify the concluding paragraph.

The alterations which have been made in the *Dunciad,* not always for the better, require that it should be published, as in the last collection, with all its variations.

The *Essay on Man* was a work of great labour and long consideration, but certainly not the happiest of Pope's performances. The subject is perhaps not very proper for poetry, and the poet was not sufficiently master of his subject; metaphysical morality was to him a new study, he was proud of his acquisitions, and, supposing himself master of great secrets, was in haste to teach what he had not learned. Thus he tells us, in the first Epistle, that from the nature of the Supreme Being may be deduced an order of beings such as mankind, because Infinite Excellence can do only what is best. He finds out that these beings must be *somewhere,* and that *all the question is whether man be in a wrong place.* Surely if, according to the poet's Leibnitian reasoning,[181] we may infer that man ought to be, only because he is, we may allow that his place is the right place, because he has it. Supreme Wisdom is not less infallible in disposing than in creating. But what is meant by *somewhere* and *place,* and *wrong place,* it had been vain to ask Pope, who probably had never asked himself.

Having exalted himself into the chair

---

[180] Shall this man's elegies and t'other's play
Unpunished murder a long summer's day?
Huge Telephus, a formidable page,
Cries vengeance.
　　(Juvenal, *Satires,* I, 4, tr. Dryden.)
[181] A reference to the philosophy of Leibniz.

of wisdom, he tells us much that every man knows, and much that he does not know himself; that we see but little, and that the order of the universe is beyond our comprehension; an opinion not very uncommon; and that there is a chain of subordinate beings *from infinite to nothing,* of which himself and his readers are equally ignorant. But he gives us one comfort, which, without his help, he supposes unattainable, in the position *that though we are fools, yet God is wise.*

This Essay affords an egregious instance of the predominance of genius, the dazzling splendour of imagery, and the seductive powers of eloquence. Never were penury of knowledge and vulgarity of sentiment so happily disguised. The reader feels his mind full, though he learns nothing; and when he meets it in its new array, no longer knows the talk of his mother and his nurse. When these wonder-working sounds sink into sense, and the doctrine of the Essay, disrobed of its ornaments, is left to the powers of its naked excellence, what shall we discover? That we are, in comparison with our Creator, very weak and ignorant; that we do not uphold the chain of existence, and that we could not make one another with more skill than we are made. We may learn yet more; that the arts of human life were copied from the instinctive operations of other animals; that if the world be made for man, it may be said that man was made for geese. To these profound principles of natural knowledge are added some moral instructions equally new; that self-interest, well understood, will produce social concord; that men are mutual gainers by mutual benefits; that evil is sometimes balanced by good; that human advantages are unstable and fallacious, of uncertain duration, and doubtful effect; that our true honour is, not to have a great part, but to act it well; that virtue only is our own; and that happiness is always in our power.

Surely a man of no very comprehensive search may venture to say that he has heard all this before; but it was never till now recommended by such a blaze of embellishment, or such sweetness of melody. The vigorous contraction of some thoughts, the luxuriant amplification of others, the incidental illustrations, and sometimes the dignity, sometimes the softness of the verses, enchain philosophy, suspend criticism, and oppress judgement by overpowering pleasure.

This is true of many paragraphs; yet if I had undertaken to exemplify Pope's felicity of composition before a rigid critick, I should not select the *Essay on Man;* for it contains more lines unsuccessfully laboured, more harshness of diction, more thoughts imperfectly expressed, more levity without elegance, and more heaviness without strength, than will easily be found in all his other works.

The *Characters of Men and Women* are the product of diligent speculation upon human life; much labour has been bestowed upon them, and Pope very seldom laboured in vain. That his excellence may be properly estimated, I recommend a comparison of his *Characters of Women* with Boileau's Satire; it will then be seen with how much more perspicacity female nature is investigated, and female excellence selected; and he surely is no mean writer to whom Boileau shall be found inferior. The *Characters of Men,* however, are written with more, if not with deeper, thought, and exhibit many passages exquisitely beautiful. The *Gem and the Flower* will not easily be equalled. In the women's part are some defects; the character of *Atossa* is not so neatly finished as that of *Clodio;* and some of the female characters may be found perhaps more frequently among men; what is said of *Philomede* was true of *Prior.*

In the Epistles to Lord Bathurst and Lord Burlington, Dr. Warburton has endeavoured to find a train of thought which was never in the writer's head, and, to support his hypothesis, has printed that first which was published last. In one, the most valuable passage is perhaps the Eulogy on *Good Sense,* and the other the *End of the Duke of Buckingham.*

The Epistle to Arbuthnot, now arbitrarily called the *Prologue to the Satires,* is a performance consisting, as it seems, of many fragments wrought into one design, which by this union of scattered beauties contains more striking paragraphs than could probably have been brought together into an occasional work. As there is no stronger motive to exertion than self-defence, no part has more elegance, spirit, or dignity, than the poet's vindication of his own character. The meanest passage is the satire upon *Sporus.*

Of the two poems which derived their names from the year, and which are called the *Epilogue to the Satires,* it was very justly remarked by Savage, that the second was in the whole more strongly conceived, and more equally supported, but that it had no single passages equal to the contention in the first for the dignity of Vice, and the celebration of the triumph of Corruption.

The Imitations of Horace seem to have been written as relaxations of his genius. This employment became his favourite by its facility; the plan was ready to his hand, and nothing was required but to accommodate as he could the sentiments of an old author to recent facts or familiar images; but what is easy is seldom excellent; such imitations cannot give pleasure to common readers; the man of learning may be sometimes surprised and delighted by an unexpected parallel; but the comparison requires knowledge of the original, which will likewise often detect strained applications. Between Roman images and English manners there will be an irreconcileable dissimilitude, and the works will be generally uncouth and party-coloured; neither original nor translated, neither ancient nor modern.

Pope had, in proportions very nicely adjusted to each other, all the qualities that constitute genius. He had *Invention,* by which new trains of events are formed, and new scenes of imagery displayed, as in the *Rape of the Lock;* and by which extrinsick and adventitious embellishments and illustrations are connected with a known subject, as in the *Essay on Criticism.* He had *Imagination,* which strongly impresses on the writer's mind, and enables him to convey to the reader, the various forms of nature, incidents of life and energies of passion, as in his *Eloisa, Windsor Forest,* and the *Ethick Epistles.* He had *Judgement,* which selects from life or nature what the present purpose requires, and, by separating the essence of things from its concomitants, often makes the representation more powerful than the reality: and he had colours of language always before him, ready to decorate his matter with every grace of elegant expression, as when he accommodates his diction to the wonderful multiplicity of Homer's sentiments and descriptions.

Poetical expression includes sound as well as meaning; *Musick,* says Dryden, *is inarticulate poetry;* among the excellences of Pope, therefore, must be mentioned the melody of his metre. By perusing the works of Dryden, he discovered the most perfect fabrick of English verse, and habituated himself to that only which he found the best; in consequence of which restraint, his poetry has been censured as too uniformly musical, and as glutting the ear with unvaried sweetness. I suspect this objection to be the cant of those who judge by principles rather than perception; and who would even themselves have less pleasure in his works, if he had tried to relieve attention by studied discords, or affected to break his lines and vary his pauses.

But though he was thus careful of his versification, he did not oppress his powers with superfluous rigour. He seems to have thought with Boileau, that the practice of writing might be refined till the difficulty should overbalance the advantage. The construction of his language is not always strictly grammatical; with those rhymes which prescription had conjoined he contented himself, without regard to Swift's remonstrances, though there was no striking consonance; nor was he very careful to vary his terminations, or to refuse admission at a small distance to the same rhymes.

To Swift's edict for the exclusion of Alexandrines and Triplets he paid little regard; he admitted them, but, in the opinion of Fenton, too rarely; he uses them more liberally in his translation than his poems.

He has a few double rhymes; and always, I think, unsuccessfully, except once in the *Rape of the Lock*.

Expletives he very early ejected from his verses; but he now and then admits an epithet rather commodious than important. Each of the six first lines of the *Iliad* might lose two syllables with very little diminution of the meaning; and sometimes, after all his art and labour, one verse seems to be made for the sake of another. In his latter productions the diction is sometimes vitiated by French idioms, with which Bolingbroke had perhaps infected him.

I have been told that the couplet by which he declared his own ear to be most gratified was this:

Lo, where Mœotis sleeps, and hardly flows
The freezing Tanais through a waste of snows.

But the reason of this preference I cannot discover.

It is remarked by Watts,[182] that there is scarcely a happy combination of words, or a phrase poetically elegant in the English language, which Pope has not inserted into his version of Homer. How he obtained possession of so many beauties of speech, it were desirable to know. That he gleaned from authors, obscure as well as eminent, what he thought brilliant or useful, and preserved it all in a regular collection, is not unlikely. When, in his last years, Hall's Satires[183] were shewn him, he wished that he had seen them sooner.

New sentiments and new images others may produce; but to attempt any further improvement of versification will be dangerous. Art and diligence have now done their best, and what shall be added will be the effort of tedious toil and needless curiosity.

After all this, it is surely superfluous to answer the question that has once been asked, Whether Pope was a poet; otherwise than by asking in return, If Pope be not a poet, where is poetry to be found? To circumscribe poetry by a definition will only shew the narrowness of the definer though a definition which shall exclude Pope will not easily be made. Let us look round upon the present time, and back upon the past; let us enquire to whom the voice of mankind has decreed the wreath of poetry; let their productions be examined, and their claims stated, and the pretensions of Pope will be no more disputed. Had he given the world only his version, the name of poet must have been allowed him: if the writer of the *Iliad* were to class his successors, he would assign a very high place to his translator, without requiring any other evidence of Genius.

[A short conclusion, including commendatory verses by other hands, is omitted.]

---

[182] Isaac Watts (1674–1748), the dissenting minister and hymn writer; one of Johnson's favorite authors.
[183] John Hall (1627–1656).

Horace Walpole, fourth Earl of Orford 1717-1797

THE WORLD

NUMBER XIV [ON LETTER WRITING]

BY ADAM FITZ-ADAM.[1]

Thursday, *April* the 5th, 1753.

I do not doubt but it is already observed that I write fewer letters to myself than any of my predecessors. It is not from being less acquainted with my own merit, but I really look upon myself as superior to such little arts of fame. Compliments, which I should be obliged to shroud under the name of a third person, have very little relish for me. If I am not considerable enough to pronounce ex cathedrâ that I Adam Fitz-Adam know how to rally the follies and decide upon the customs of the world with more wit, humour, learning and taste than any man living, I have in vain undertaken the scheme of this paper. Who would be regulated by the judgment of a man who is not the most self-sufficient person alive? Why did all the pretty women in England, in the reign of queen Anne, submit the government of their fans, hoods, hoops and patches to the Specta-tor, but because he pronounced himself the best critic in fashions? Why did half the nation imbibe their politics from the Craftsman,[2] but because Caleb d'Anvers assured them that he understood the maxims of government and the constitution of his country better than any minister or patriot of the time? Throned as I am in a perfect good opinion of my own abilities, I scorn to taste the satisfaction of praise from my own pen—and (to be humble for once) I own, if there is any species of writing of which I am not perfect master, it is the epistolary. My deficience in this particular is happily common to me with the greatest men: I can even go farther, and declare that it is the Fair part of the creation which excells in that province. Ease without affectation, the politest expression, the happiest art of telling news or trifles, the most engaging turns of sentiment or passion, are frequently found in letters from women, who have lived in a sphere at all above the vulgar; while on the

Text from first edition, 1753.

[1] Fictional author of *The World*, meaning the son of man, a worldling.

[2] A political periodical (1726–1736), conducted by Nicholas Amhurst under the pseudonym of Caleb D'Anvers in opposition to the policies of Horace's father, Sir Robert Walpole, England's first prime minister.

other side, orators write affectedly, ministers obscurely, poets floridly, learned men pedantically, and soldiers tolerably when they can spell. One would not have one's daughter write like Eloisa,[3] because one would not have one's daughter feel what she felt; yet who ever wrote so movingly, so to the heart? The amiable madame de Sevigné[4] is the standard of easy engaging writing: to call her the pattern of eloquent writing will not be thought an exaggeration, when I refer my readers to her accounts of the death of marshal Turenne: some little fragments of her letters, in the appendix to Ramsay's life of that hero, give a stronger picture of him than the historian was able to do in his voluminous work. If this Fair One's epistles are liable to any censure, it is for a fault in which she is not likely to be often imitated, the excess of tenderness for her daughter.

The Italians are as proud of a person of the same sex: Lucretia Gonzaga[5] was so celebrated for the eloquence of her letters and the purity of their style, that her very notes to her servants were collected and published. I have never read the collection: one or two billets that I have met with, have not entirely all the delicacy of madame de Sevigné. In one to her footman the signora Gonzaga reprehends him for not readily obeying dame Lucy her housekeeper; and in another, addressed to the same Mrs. Lucy, she says, "If Livia will not be obedient, turn up her coats and whip her till her flesh be black and blew, and the blood run down to her heels." To be sure this sounds a little oddly to English ears, but may be very elegant, when modulated by the harmony of Italian liquids.

Several worthy persons have laid down rules for the composition of letters, but I fear it is an art which only nature can teach. I remember in one of those books (it was written by a German) there was a strict injunction not to mention your-self before you had introduced the person of your correspondent; that is, you must never use the monosyllable *I* before the pronoun *You.* The Italians have stated expressions to be used to different ranks of men, and know exactly when to subscribe themselves the devoted or the most devoted slave of the illustrious or most eminent person to whom they have the honour to write. It is true, in that country they have so clogged correspondence with forms and civilities, that they seldom make use of their own language, but generally write to one another in French.

Among many instances of beautiful letters from ladies, and of the contrary from our sex, I shall select two, which are very singular in their kind. The comparison, to be sure, is not entirely fair; but when I mention some particulars of the male author, one might expect a little more elegance, a little better orthography, a little more decorum, and a good deal less absurdity, than seem to have met in one head, which had seen so much of the world, which pretended so much to literature, and which had worn so long one of the first crowns in Europe. This personage was the emperor Maximilian,[6] grandfather of Charles the Vth. His reign was long, sometimes shining, often unprosperous, very often ignominious. His fickleness, prodigality and indigence were notorious. The Italians called him *Pochi-danari,* or the *penny-less;* a quality not more habitual to him than his propensity to repair his shattered fortunes by the most unbecoming means. He served under our Henry the eighth, as a common soldier, at the siege of Terouenne for a hundred crowns a day: he was bribed to the attempt against Pisa and bribed to give it over. In short, no potentate ever undertook to engage him in a treaty, without first offering him money. Yet this vagabond monarch, as if the annals of his reign were too glorious to be described by a plebeian pen, or as

---

[3] Referring to Eloisa's correspondence with Abelard, subject of Pope's heroic epistle *Eloisa to Abelard* (1717).

[4] Marie de Rabutin-Chantal, Marquise de Sévigné (1626–1696).

[5] The letters of Lady Lucrezia Gonzaga Manfrona were written by Ortensio Lando (1512–1553) and first appeared in Venice in 1552.

[6] Maximilian I, Holy Roman Emperor 1493–1519.

if they were worthy to be described at all, took the pains to write his own life in Dutch verse. There was another book of his composition in a different way, which does not reflect much more lustre upon his memory than his own Dutch epic; this was what he called his *livre rouge*,[7] and was a register of seventeen mortifications which he had received from Louis the twelfth of France, and which he intended to revenge on the first opportunity. After a variety of shifts, breach of promises, alliances, and treaties, he almost duped his vain cotemporary Henry the eighth, with a proposal of resigning the empire to him, while himself was meditating, what he thought, an accession of dignity even to the imperial diadem: in short, in the latter part of his life Maximilian took it into his head to canvas for the papal Tiara. Several methods were agitated to compass this object of his ambition: one, and not the least ridiculous, was to pretend that the patriarchal dignity was included in the imperial; and by virtue of that definition he really assumed the title of Pontifex Maximus, copying the pagan lords of Rome on his way to the sovereignty of the christian church. Money he knew was the surest method, but the least at his command: it was to procure a supply of that necessary ingredient that he wrote the following letter to his daughter Margaret, duchess dowager of Savoy, and governess of the Netherlands.[8]

Tres chiere & tres amèe fylle, je entendu l'avis que vous m'avez donnè per Guyllain Pingun notre garderobes, dont avons encore mieux pensè. Et ne trouvons point pour nulle resun bon que nous nous devons franchement marier, maes avons plus avant mys notre deliberation & volontè dejamès plus hanter faem nue. Et envoyons demain Monsr. deGurce Evesque à Rome devers le pape pour trouver fachon que nous puyssuns accorder avec ly de nous prendre pour ung coadjuteur, affin que apres sa mort pouruns estre assurè de avoer le papat, & de-

venir prester, & apres estre saint, & que yl vous sera de necessitè que apres ma mort vous serès contraint de me adorer, dont je me troverè bien glorioes. Je envoye sur ce ung poste devers le roy d'Arogon pour ly prier qu'y nous voulle ayder pour à ce parvenir, dont il est aussy content, moynant que je resigne l'empir à nostre comun fyls Charls, de sela aussy je me suys contentè. Je commance aussy practiker les Cardinaulx, dont ii C. ou iii C. mylle ducats me ferunt ung grand service, aveque la partialitè qui est deja entre eos. Le roy d'Arogon à mandè à son ambaxadeur que yl veulent favouryser le papat à nous. Je vous prie, tenès cette matere empu secret, ossi bien en brieff jours je creins que yl faut que tout le monde le sache, car bien mal esti possible de pratiker ung tel sy grand matere secretement, pour laquell yl faut avoer de tant de gens & de argent, succurs & pratike, & a Diù, faet de la main de votre bon pere Maximilianus futur pape, le XVIII jour de setembre. Le papa a encor les vyevers dubls, & ne peult longement fyvre.

This curious piece, which it is impossible to translate (for what language can give an adequate idea of very bad old German French?) is to be found in the fourth volume of letters of Louis XIIth, printed at Brussels by Fr. Foppens in 1712. It will be sufficient to inform such of my readers as do not understand French, that his imperial majesty acquaints his beloved daughter that he designs never to frequent naked women any more, but to use all his endeavours to procure the papacy, and then to turn priest, and at length become a saint, that his dear daughter may be obliged to pray to him, which he shall reckon matter of exceeding glory. He expresses great want of two or three hundred thousand ducats to facilitate the business, which he desires may be kept very secret, though he does not doubt but all the world will know it in two or three days; and concludes with signing himself *future Pope*.

---

[7] "red book."

[8] Walpole cites his source for the following letter and makes his own summary translation immediately after reprinting the French text.

As a contrast to this scrap of imperial folly, I shall present my readers with the other letter I mentioned. It was written by the lady Anne,[9] widow of the earls of Dorset and Pembroke (the life of the former of whom she wrote), and heiress of the great house of Clifford-Cumberland, from which, among many noble reversions, she enjoyed the borough of Appleby. Sir Joseph Williamson, secretary of state to Charles the second, wrote to name a candidate to her for that borough: the brave countess, with all the spirit of her ancestors, and with all the eloquence of independent Greece, returned this laconic answer.

I have been bullied by an usurper, I have been neglected by a court, but I will not be dictated to by a subject; your man sha'n't stand.

ANNE, DORSET, PEMBROKE, *and*
MONTGOMERY.

From CORRESPONDENCE

[LETTER ADDRESSED] TO GEORGE MONTAGU ESQ AT ATTERBURY, OXFORDSHIRE.

Strawberry hill
June 29. 1770.

Since the Sharp Mountain will not come to the little Hill, the little hill must go to the Mont-aigu.[10] In Short, what do you think of seeing me walk into your parlour a few hours after this Epistle? I had not time to notify myself sooner. The case is, Princess Amalie[11] has insisted on my going with her to, that is, meeting her, at Stowe[12] on Monday for a week. She mentioned it some time ago, & I thought I had parried it, but having been with her at Park-place these two or three days, She has commanded it so positively, that I could not refuse. Now as it woud be extremely inconvenient to my Indolence to be dressed up in weepers & hatbands[13] by six o'clock in the morning, & lest I shoud be taken for chief Mourner going to Beckford's funeral,[14] I trust you will be charitable enough to give me a bed at Atterbury for one night, whence I can arrive at Stowe in a decent time, & caparisoned, as I ought to be, when I have lost a Brother-inlaw & am to meet a Princess. Dont

---

Text from the original manuscript letters, through the courtesy of Dr. Wilmarth Lewis, who has also afforded the use of his notes, many of which are reproduced.

---

[9] Lady Anne Clifford (1590–1676), by virtue of two marriages, was able to style herself Countess Dowager of Pembroke, Dorset and Montgomery; her reputation for direct action is well characterized in the letter Walpole quotes.

[10] A pun in French on the name Montagu, meaning "sharp mountain."

[11] Amelia Sophia Eleanora (1711–1786), first encountered in Hervey's *Memoirs* as "Emely." She was then 26 years of age; she is now 59.

[12] Stowe, in Buckinghamshire, was the seat of Richard Grenville-Temple (1711–1779), first Earl Temple, a famous showplace throughout the century. Engravings of its buildings and gardens were made by Rigaud and Baron and published in 1739, and at least two books of description appeared: *A Dialogue upon the Gardens of Viscount Cobham, at Stowe* by William Gilpin (1748) and *A Description of the Most Noble House and Gardens . . . at Stow, in Buckinghamshire* by George Bickham (1756).

[13] "Mourning for his brother-in-law the Earl Cholmondeley" (W. S. Lewis).

[14] William Beckford (b. 1709), Lord Mayor of London and father of the Gothic novelist who was at this time a boy of 10 years of age. "He d[ied] 21 June and was buried at Fonthill 30 June 1770" (W. S. Lewis).

take me for a Lausun,[15] & think all this favour portends a *second* marriage between our family & the blood Royal;[16] nor that my Visit to Stowe implies my espousing Miss Wilkes.[17] I think I shall die as I am, neither higher nor lower; and above all things, no more politics. Yet I shall have many a private smile to myself, as I wander among all those consecrated & desecrated buildings, & think what company I am in, & of all that is past—but I must shorten my letter, or you will not have finished it when I arrive. Adieu!

Yrs—acoming! acoming!
HW.

[ANOTHER TO THE SAME]

Strawberry hill. 1770.
Saturday night July 7th.

After making an Inn of your house, it is but decent to thank you for my Entertainment, & to acquaint you wth the result of my journey. The Party passed off much better than I expected. A Princess at the head of a very small Set for five days together did not promise well.

However She was very good humoured, & easy, and dispensed with a large quantity of Etiquette. Lady Temple[18] is good nature itself, My Lord[19] was very civil, Lord Besborough[20] is made to suit all sorts of people, Lady Mary Coke[21] respects royalty too much not to be very condescending,[22] Lady Ann Howard[23] & Mrs. Middleton[24] filled up the drawing-room, or rather made it out, & I was so determined to carry it off as well as I coud, & happened to be in such good Spirits, & took such care to avoid politics, that we laughed a great deal,[25] & had not a cloud the whole time.

We breakfasted at half an hour after nine; but the Princess did not appear till it was finished; then we walked in the garden or drove about it in cabriolets,[26] till it was time to dress: dined at three, which tho properly proportioned to the smallness of the company to avoid ostentation, lasted a vast while, as the Princess eats and talks a great deal; then again into the garden till past seven, when we came in, drank tea & coffee, & played at Pharaoh[27] till ten, when the Princess retired, & we went to supper, & before twelve to bed. You see there was great

[15] "Antonin-Nompar de Caumont (1633–1723), Duc de Lauzun; while he was a royal favourite a marriage was projected between him and Mlle de Montpensier, Louis XIV's cousin, despite great disparity of birth" (W. S. Lewis).

[16] "HW's most outspoken admission up to this time of the marriage of his niece Lady Waldegrave and the Duke of Gloucester" (W. S. Lewis).

[17] "Mary (1750–1802), unm[arried] dau[ghter] of John Wilkes, a political ally of Lord Temple's" (W. S. Lewis).

[18] Anne Chambers (*c.* 1709–1777), married in 1737.

[19] See note 12 above.

[20] William Ponsonby (1704–1793), second Earl of Bessborough.

[21] Mary Campbell (1727–1811), married Edward, Viscount Coke, in 1747. "Lady Mary has a day-by-day account of the party in her *Journals* . . . which agrees with HW's substantially" (W. S. Lewis).

[22] "To condescend . . . To depart from the privileges of superiority by a voluntary sub-

mission; to sink willingly to equal terms with inferiours; to sooth by familiarity" (Johnson's *Dictionary*).

[23] "Lady Anne Howard (1744–99), dau[ghter] of 4th E[arl] of Carlisle by his 2d wife; Lady of the Bedchamber to Princess Amelia" (W. S. Lewis).

[24] "Catharine (d. 1784), unm[arried] dau[ghter] and heir of Sir William Middleton, 3d B[arone]t, of Belsay Castle; Bedchamber woman to Princess Amelia" (W. S. Lewis).

[25] "'The party is merrier than perhaps you would imagine. H. R. H. and Mr Walpole are admirable company' (Coke, *Journals* III, 253)" (W. S. Lewis).

[26] "a gig; a one horse chair, a light carriage" (Noah Webster's *American Dictionary*, 1828); the cabriolet came into fashion too late to be defined in Johnson's *Dictionary*.

[27] A card game. "Lord Bessborough held the bank and won our money" (W. S. Lewis, quoting Coke's *Journal*). The game of *pharaon*, of which this is doubtless a version, is described in detail in the French *Encyclopédie* of 1765.

sameness & little vivacity in all this. It was a little broken by fishing,[28] & going round the park one of the mornings; but in reality the number of buildings & variety of Scenes in the garden made each day different from the rest: and my meditations on so historic a Spot prevented my being tired. Every acre brings to one's mind some instance of the parts or pedantry, of the taste or want of taste, of the ambition, or love of fame, or greatness, or miscarriages of those that have inhabited, decorated, planned or visited the place.[29] Pope, Congreve, Vanbrugh, Kent, Gibbs, Ld Cobham, Ld Chesterfield, the Mob of Nephews, the Lyttletons, Grenvilles, Wests, Leonidas Glover & Wilkes, the late Prince of Wales, the King of Denmark, Princess Amelie, & the proud Monuments of Ld Chatham's services, now inshrined there, then anathematized there, & now again commanding there, with the Temple of friendship like the temple of Janus, sometimes open to war, & sometimes shut up in factious Cabals, all these images croud upon ones memory & add visionary personages to the charming scenes, that are so enriched with fanes & temples, that the real prospects are little less than Visions themselves.

On Wednesday night a Small Vauxhall[30] was acted for us at the grotto in the Elysian fields,[31] which was illuminated with lamps, as were the thickets & two little barks on the lake. With a little Exaggeration I could make you believe that nothing ever was so delightfull. The Idea was really pretty, but as my feelings have lost something of their romantic Sensibility, I did not quite enjoy such an Entertainment al fresco[32] so much as I shoud have done twenty years ago. The Evening was more than cool & the destined Spot any thing but dry. There were not half lamps enough, & no music but an ancient militia-man who play'd cruelly on a squeaking tabor & pipe. As our Procession descended the vast flight of steps into the garden, in which was assembled a croud of people from Buckingham & the neighbouring villages to see the Princess & the Show, the Moon shining very bright, I coud not help laughing, as I surveyed our troop, which instead of tripping lightly to such an Arcadian Entertainment, were hobbling down, by the balustrades, wrapped up in Cloaks & great coats for fear of catching cold.[33] The Earl you know is bent double, the Countess very lame, I am a miserable walker, & the Princess, tho as strong as

---

[28] "This morning the Princess ordered me to attend her to the great water to fish; in two hours I catched three score; two large carp and above twenty considerable perch; the rest small. The Princess catched about forty, but none so large as mine, to the great mortification of the page who attended her" (W. S. Lewis, quoting Coke's *Journal*).

[29] Among those mentioned by Walpole, Alexander Pope (1688–1744) memorialized a visit to Stowe in 1731 in his *Epistle to Burlington;* a cenotaph in memory of the dramatist William Congreve (1670–1729) stood in the gardens; the achievement of Sir John Vanbrugh (1664–1726), the dramatist and architect, in planning the gardens of Stowe was signalized by a pyramid sixty feet high; "James Kent (1682–1754), architect . . . designed the column to Lord Cobham at Stowe" (W. S. Lewis); the Lytteltons: George, first Baron Lyttelton (1709–1773), and Thomas, second (1744–1779), who had taken part in a masque at Stowe five summers before Walpole's visit, were descendants of Sir Richard Temple

(1634–1697), as were the Wests: Gilbert (1703–1756), distinguished author of the *Odes of Pindar* (1749) and his brother, Temple (1713–1757), a prominent vice-admiral of the navy; "Richard Glover (1712–85) [was] author of *Leonidas* and friend of George Grenville" (W. S. Lewis); John Wilkes (1727–1797), the tempestuous politician and sometime lord mayor of London, until the year before Walpole's visit, had been long and staunchly supported by Lord Temple; William Pitt (1708–1778), the first Earl of Chatham, who had brought England to the peak of its European power by his conduct of the continental wars in 1758–1760, had found frequent support in as well as use for the services of both Temple and Grenville.

[30] An implied comparison with the entertainments of Vauxhall Gardens in London.

[31] A portion of the gardens.

[32] in the open air, between daylight and dark.

[33] "Mr. Walpole thought it rather too cold, and having some apprehension of the consequence, desired when we came back to the

a Brunswic Lion, makes no figure in going down fifty stone stairs. Except Lady Ann—& by courtesy, Lady Mary, were none of us young enough for a Pastoral. We supped in the grotto, which is as proper to this climate, as a SeaCoal fire would be in the dogdays at Tivoli.[34]

But the chief Entertainment of the week, at least what was so to the Princess, is an Arch which Lord Temple has erected to her honour in the most enchanting of all picturesque Scenes. It is inscribed on one side, Ameliae Sophiae Aug. & has a medalion of her on the Other. It is placed on an eminence at the top of the Elysian fields, in a grove of orange trees. You come to it on a sudden, & are startled with delight on looking thro it: you at once see thro a glade river winding at bottom; from which a thicket rises, arched over with trees, but opened, & discovering a hillock full of haycocks, beyond which in front is the Palladian bridge, & again over that, a larger hill crowned with the castle. It is a tall landscape, framed by the Arch & the overbowering trees, & comprehending more beauties of light, shade & buildings, than any picture of Albano[35] I ever saw.

Between the flattery & the prospect the Princess was really in Elysium: She visited her arch four & five times every day, & coud not satiate herself with it. The Statues of Apollo & the Muses stand on each side of the arch. One day She found[36] in Apollo's hand the following lines, which I had written for her & communicated to Ld Temple;

Tother day with a beautifull frown on her brow
To the rest of the Gods said the Venus of Stow,[37]

What a fuss is here made with that Arch just erected!
How *our* temples are slighted, our altars neglected!
Since yon Nymph has appear'd, *we* are noticed no more:
All resort to *her* Shrine, all *her* presence adore.
And what's more provoking, before all our faces
Temple thither has drawn both the Muses & Graces.
Keep your temper, dear child, Phoebus cried with a smile,
Nor this happy, this amiable festival spoil.
Can your Shrine any longer with garlands be drest?
When a true Goddess reigns, all the false are supprest.

If you will keep my counsel, I will own to you, that originally the two last lines were much better, but I was forced to alter them out of decorum, not to be too Pagan upon the occasion; in short, here they are as in the first sketch,

Recollect, once before that our Oracles ceas'd,
When a real Divinity rose in the East.

So many heathen Temples[38] around, had made me talk as a Roman Poet woud have done; but I corrected my verses, & have made them insipid enough to offend nobody. Good night. I am rejoyced to be once more in the gay solitude of my own little Temple.

Yrs ever
HW.

---

house a glass of cherry brandy by way of prevention" (W. S. Lewis, quoting Coke's *Journals*).

[34] "Lord Temple sat by the Princess and talked to her all the time; Lady Temple, Lord Bessborough, and myself sang 'God Save our Noble King, etc.' I was in hopes the people would have joined us, but they were very silent" (W. S. Lewis, quoting Coke's *Journals*).

[35] "Stowe invariably reminded HW of Albano's landscapes [Francesco Albano, 1578–

1660]" (W. S. Lewis).

[36] "Not so in Lady Mary: 'After dinner the coffee was ordered at the Princess's arch. . . . While they drank their coffee, I observed Apollo held a paper in his hand, but not being able to reach it, I desired Lord Temple's assistance, who with some difficulty took it from the hand of Apollo'" (W. S. Lewis).

[37] A building in the gardens, designed by the architect William Kent (1684–1748).

[38] A pun on the name of his hosts.

TO THE COUNTESS OF UPPER OSSORY[39]

Jan. 15, 1797

My dear Mme.

You distress me infinitely by shewing my idle Notes, which I cannot conceive can amuse anybody. My old fashioned Breeding impels me every now & then to reply to the Letters you honour me with writing, but in truth very unwillingly, for I seldom can have anything particular to say; I scarce go out of my House; and then only to two or three very private Places, where I see nobody that really knows anything, and what I learn comes from Newspapers, that collect Intelligence from Coffeehouses, consequently, what I neither believe nor report. At Home I see only a few charitable Elders, except about Fourscore Nephews and Nieces of various Ages, who are each brought to me once a Year, to stare at me as the Methusalah of the family, and they can only speak of their own Cotemporaries, which interest me no more than if they talked of their Dolls, or Bats and Balls. Must not the Result of all this, Madam, make me a very entertaining Correspondent? and can such Letters be worth shewing? or can I have any Spirit when so old and reduced to dictate? Oh, my good Madam, dispense with me from such a Task, and think how it must add to it to apprehend such Letters being shewn. Pray send me no more such Laurels, which I desire no more than their Leaves when decked with a Scrap of Tinsel, and stuck on Twelfth Cakes[40] that lye on the Shopboards of Pastry Cooks at Christmas: I shall be quite content with a Sprig of Rosemary thrown after me, when the Parson of the Parish commits my Dust to Dust. Till then pray, Mme., accept the resignation of your

Ancient servant,
O.[41]

[39] Anne Lidell (1738–1804), who had been divorced by the second Duke of Grafton in 1769 as a result of what *The Complete English Peerage* of 1775 called "a violent itch for play."

[40] "A large cake used at the festivities of Twelfth-night, usually frosted and otherwise ornamented, and with a bean or coin introduced to determine the 'king' or 'queen' of the feast" (*Oxford English Dictionary*).

[41] O[rford], the title he had come into six years earlier; "Walpole died six weeks following the date of this letter. It is interesting to note from the original letter that although at the time he was dying he arranged to have it returned to him" (W. S. Lewis). So far as is known, this was his last letter.

Joseph Warton

1722-1800

ESSAY ON THE GENIUS AND WRITINGS OF POPE

Text from the fifth edition, corrected, 1806; originally a part of the first volume, 1756.

[SECTION IV: OF THE RAPE OF THE LOCK]

The RAPE OF THE LOCK, now before us, is the fourth, and most excellent of the heroi-comic poems.[1] The subject was a quarrel occasioned by a little piece of gallantry of Lord Petre, who, in a party of pleasure, found means to cut off a favourite lock of Mrs. Arabella Fermor's hair. POPE was desired to write it, in order to put an end to the quarrel it produced, by Mr. Caryl, who had been secretary to Queen Mary, author of Sir Solomon Single, a comedy, and of some translations in Dryden's Miscellanies. POPE was accustomed to say, "What I wrote fastest always pleased most." The first sketch of this exquisite piece, which Addison called MERUM SAL,[2] was written in less than a fortnight, in two cantos only: but it was so universally applauded, that, in the next year, our poet enriched it with the machinery of the sylphs, and extended it to five cantos; when it was printed with a letter to Mrs. Fermor, far superior to any of Voiture.[3]

The insertion of the machinery of the sylphs in proper places, without the least appearance of its being awkwardly stitched in, is one of the happiest efforts of judgment and art. He took the idea of these invisible beings, so proper to be employed in a poem of this nature, from a little French book entitled, Le Comte de Gabalis,[4] of which is given the following account in an entertaining writer. "The Abbé Villars, who came from Thoulouse to Paris, to make his fortune by preaching, is the author of this diverting work. The five dialogues of which it consists, are the result of those gay conversations in which the Abbé was engaged with a small circle of men, of fine wit and humour, like himself. When this book first appeared, it was universally read, as innocent and amusing. But at length its consequences were perceived, and reckoned dangerous, at a time when this sort of curiosities began to gain credit. Our

[1] Warton has been discussing examples of "heroi-comic" poetry: Alessandro Tassoni's La Secchia Rapita (1614), Nicolas Boileau-Despréaux's Le Lutrin (1672), and Sir Samuel Garth's The Dispensary (1699).

[2] pure wit.

[3] Vincent Voiture (1598–1648), whose letters were published after his death.

[4] A series of five discourses by the Abbé de Montfaucon de Villars in 1680, translated in the same year into English by Philip Ayres and A. Lovell, a book which Pope acknowledged as a source of his supernatural machinery in the prefatory letter to the second edition of The Rape of the Lock (1714).

devout preacher was denied the chair, and his book forbidden to be read. It was not clear whether the author intended to be ironical, or spoke all seriously. The second volume, which he promised, would have decided the question; but the unfortunate Abbé was soon afterwards assassinated by ruffians on the road to Lyons. The laughers gave out, that the gnomes and sylphs, disguised like ruffians, had shot him, as a punishment for revealing the secrets of the Cabala; a crime not to be pardoned by these jealous spirits, as Villars himself has declared in his book."[5]

It may not be improper to give a specimen of this author's manner, who has lately been well imitated in the way of mixing jest with earnest, in an elegant piece called HERMIPPUS REDIVIVUS.[6] The Comte de Gabalis being about to initiate his pupil into the most profound mysteries of the Rosicrusian philosophy, advises him to consider seriously, whether or no he had courage and resolution sufficient to RENOUNCE all those obstacles which might prevent his arising to that height which the figure of his nativity promised. "Le mot de RENONCER, (says the scholar,) m'effraya, & je ne doutai point qu'il n'allât me proposer de renoncer au baptême ou au paradis. Ainsi ne sçachant comme me tirer de ce mauvais pas; Renoncer, lui dis-je, Monsieur quoi, faut il renoncer à quelque chose? Vraiment, reprit-il, il le faut bien; & il le faut si nécessairement, qu'il faut commencer par-là. Je ne sçai si vous pourrez vous résoudre: mais je sçai bien que la sagesse n'habite point dans un corps sujet au péché, comme elle n'entre point dans une ame prevenue d'erreur ou de malice. Les sages ne vous admettront jamais à leur compagnie, si vous ne renoncez dès à présent à une chose qui ne peut compatir avec la sagesse. *Il faut,* ajoûta-t-il tout bas en se baissant à mon oreille, *il faut renoncer à tout commerce charnel avec les femmes.*"[7] On a diligent perusal of this book, I cannot find that POPE has borrowed any particular circumstances relating to these spirits, but merely the general idea of their existence.

These machines are vastly superior to the allegorical personages of Boileau and Garth;[8] not only on account of their novelty, but for the exquisite poetry, and oblique satire, which they have given the poet an opportunity to display. The business and petty concerns of a fine lady, receive an air of importance from the notion of their being perpetually overlooked, and conducted, by the interposition of celestial agents.

It is judicious to open the poem, by introducing the Guardian Sylph warning Belinda against some secret impending danger. The account which Ariel gives of the nature, office, and employment, of these inhabitants of air, is finely fancied; into which several strokes of satire are thrown with great delicacy and address.

Think what an equipage thou hast in air,
And view with scorn two pages and a
    chair.

The transformation of women of different tempers into different kinds of spirits, cannot be too much applauded.

---

[5] "Mélanges d'Histoire de Littérature. By Dom Noel Dargoune, disguised under the name of Vigneul Marville. Tom. prem. [Vol. I] pag. 275. edit. Rotterdam, 1700" (Warton).

[6] *Hermippus Redivivus, or the Sage's Triumph over Old Age and the Grave,* by John Henry Cohausen (1743).

[7] *"Le Comte de Gabalis, ou Entretiens sur les Sciences Secretes.* 2e Entretiens, page 30. à Amsterdam, 1671" (Warton's note). "The word 'renounce' frightened me, and I wondered whether he might not be going to suggest that I renounce baptism or the hereafter. Not knowing how to keep from such a false step, I said to Him: Renounce what, Monsieur; one usually renounces something. Truly, he replied, that is right; and it is necessary that one must begin with that itself. I do not know if you have the strength of mind: but I know very well that wisdom is not usual in a sinful body, as it cannot enter a soul preoccupied with error or evil. Wise men will never admit you to their company if you do not renounce immediately that which is incompatible with wisdom. *It is necessary,* he added, whispering in my ear, *it is necessary to renounce all carnal commerce with women."*

[8] The reference is to *Le Lutrin* and *The Dispensary.*

The sprites of fiery Termagants, in flame
Mount up, and take a salamander's name.
Soft yielding minds to water glide away,
And sip with Nymphs, their elemental tea.
The graver Prude sinks downward to a gnome,
In search of mischief still on earth to roam.
The light Coquettes in sylphs aloft repair,
And sport and flutter in the fields of air.

The description of the toilette, which succeeds, is judiciously given in such magnificent terms as dignify the offices performed at it. Belinda dressing, is painted in as pompous a manner as Achilles arming. The canto ends with a circumstance artfully contrived to keep this beautiful machinery in the reader's eye: for after the poet has said, that the fair heroine

Repairs her smiles, awakens ev'ry grace,
And calls forth all the wonders of her face,

He immediately subjoins,

The busy sylphs surround their darling care;
These set the head, and those divide the hair:
Some fold the sleeve, whilst others plait the gown;
And Betty's prais'd for labours not her own.

The mention of the LOCK, on which the poem turns, is rightly reserved to the second canto. The sacrifice of the Baron to implore success to his undertaking, is another instance of our poet's judgment, in heightening the subject. The succeeding scene of sailing upon the Thames is most gay and delightful, and impresses very pleasing pictures upon the imagination. Here, too, the machinery is again introduced with much propriety. Ariel summons his denizens of air, who are thus painted with a rich exuberance of fancy:

Some to the sun their insect wings unfold,
Waft on the breeze, or sink in clouds of gold:
Transparent forms, too thin for mortal sight,
Their fluid bodies half dissolv'd in light.
Loose to the wind their airy garments flew,
Thin glittering textures of the filmy dew,
Dipt in the richest tincture of the skies,
Where light disports in ever-mingling dyes;
While every beam new transient colours flings;
Colours, that change whene'er they wave their wings.

Ariel afterwards enumerates the functions and employments of the sylphs, in the following manner; where some are supposed to delight in more gross, and others in more refined, occupations.

Ye know the spheres and various tasks, assign'd
By laws eternal to th' aërial kind.
Some in the fields of purest æther play,
And bask and brighten in the blaze of day;
Some guide the course of wand'ring orbs on high,
Or roll the planets through the boundless sky;
Some, less refin'd, beneath the moon's pale light,
Pursue the stars, that shoot across the night,
Or suck the mists in grosser air below,
Or dip their pinions in the painted bow,
Or brew fierce tempests on the wintry main,
Or o'er the glebe distil the kindly rain.

Those who are fond of tracing images and sentiments to their source, may, perhaps, be inclined to think, that the hint of ascribing tasks and offices to such imaginary beings, is taken from the Fairies and the Ariel of Shakespeare: let the impartial critic determine which has the superiority of fancy. The employment of Ariel, in the TEMPEST,[9] is said to be,

. . . To tread the ooze
Of the salt deep;
To run upon the sharp wind of the
    north;
To do . . . business in the veins of th'
    earth,
When it is bak'd with frost;
. . . To dive into the fire; to ride
On the curl'd clouds.

And again,

. . . In the deep nook, where once
Thou call'd'st me up at midnight, to
    fetch dew
From the still-vext Bermoothes. . . .

Nor must I omit that exquisite song, in which his favourite and peculiar pastime is expressed.

    Where the bee sucks, there suck I;
In a cowslip's bell I lie;
There I couch when owls do cry.
On the bat's back I do fly,
After sun-set, merrily:
Merrily, merrily, shall I live now,
Under the blossom that hangs on the
    bough.

With what wildness of imagination, but yet with what propriety, are the amusements of the fairies pointed out in the MIDSUMMER NIGHT'S DREAM:[10] amusements proper for none but fairies!

. . . 'Fore the third part of a minute,
    hence:
Some to kill cankers in the musk-rose
    buds:
Some war with rear-mice for their leath-
    ern wings,
To make my small elves coats; and some
    keep back
The clamorous owl, that nightly hoots,
    and wonders

At our queint spirits. . . .

Shakespeare only could have thought of the following gratifications for Titania's lover; and they are fit only to be offered, to her lover, by a fairy queen.

Be kind and courteous to this gentleman;
Hop in his walks, and gambol in his eyes;
Feed him with apricocks and dewberries,
With purple grapes, green figs, and mul-
    berries.
The honey-bags steal from the humble
    bees,
And for night-tapers crop their waxen
    thighs,
And light them at the fiery glow-worm's
    eyes,
To have my love to bed, and to arise:
And pluck the wings from painted but-
    terflies,
To fan the moon-beams from his sleep-
    ing eyes.

If it should be thought, that Shakespeare has the merit of being the first who assigned proper employments to imaginary persons in the foregoing lines, yet it must be granted, that by the addition of the most delicate satire to the most lively fancy, POPE, in the following passage, has excelled any thing in Shakespeare, or perhaps in any other author.

Our humbler province is to tend the fair;
Not a less pleasing, though less glorious
    care;
To save the powder from too rough a
    gale,
Nor let th' imprison'd essences exhale;
To draw fresh colours from the vernal
    flow'rs,
To steal from rainbows, ere they drop
    in show'rs,
A brighter wash; to curl their waving
    hairs,
Assist their blushes, and inspire their
    airs;
Nay, oft in dreams invention we bestow,
To change a flounce, or add a furbelow.

    The seeming importance given to ev-

[9] I, ii, 298–302, 223–224, 267–269; V, i, 101–107.

[10] II, ii, 3–8; III, i, 171–180.

ery part of female dress, each of which is committed to the care and protection of a different sylph, with all the solemnity of a general appointing the several posts in his army, renders the following passage admirable, on account of its politeness, poignancy, and poetry.

Haste then, ye spirits, to your charge repair;
The fluttering fan be Zephyretta's care;
The drops to thee, Brillante, we consign;
And, Momentilla, let the watch be thine:
Do thou, Crispissa, tend the fav'rite lock:
Ariel himself shall be the guard of Shock.

The celebrated raillery of Addison on the hoop-petticoat,[11] has nothing equal to the following circumstance; which marks the difficulty of guarding a part of dress of such high consequence.

To fifty chosen sylphs, of special note,
We trust th' important charge, the PETTICOAT:
Oft have we known that sevenfold fence to fail,
Tho' stiff with hoops, and arm'd with ribs of whale:
Form a strong line about the silver bound,
And guard the wide circumference around.

RIDET HOC, INQUAM, VENUS IPSA; RIDENT
SIMPLICES NYMPHAE, FERUS ET CUPIDO.[12]

Our poet still rises in the delicacy of his satire, where he employs, with the utmost judgment and elegance, all the implements and furniture of the toilette, as instruments of punishment to those spirits who shall be careless of their charge:

of punishment such as sylphs alone could undergo. Each of the delinquents

Shall feel sharp vengeance soon o'ertake his sins;
Be stopp'd in vials, or transfix'd with pins;
Or plung'd in lakes of bitter washes lie;
Or wedg'd whole ages in a bodkin's eye;
Gums and pomatums shall his flight restrain,
While clogg'd he beats his silken wings in vain;
Or allum-styptics, with contracting pow'r,
Shrink his thin essence like a shrivel'd flow'r;
Or, as Ixion fix'd, the wretch shall feel
The giddy motion of the whirling mill;
In fumes of burning chocolate shall glow,
And tremble at the sea that froths below.

If Virgil has merited such perpetual commendation for exalting his bees by the majesty and magnificence of his diction, does not POPE deserve equal praises for the pomp and lustre of his language on so trivial a subject?

The same mastery of language appears in the lively and elegant description of the game at Ombre, which is certainly imitated from the Scacchia of Vida,[13] and as certainly equal to it, if not superior. Both of them have elevated and enlivened their subjects, by such similies as the epic poets use; but as Chess is a play of a far higher order than Ombre, POPE had a more difficult task than Vida, to raise this his inferior subject into equal dignity and gracefulness. Here again our poet artfully introduces his machinery:

Soon as she spreads her hand, th' aërial guard
Descend, and sit on each important card;
First Ariel perch'd upon a mattadore.

The majesty with which the kings of spades and clubs, and the knaves of dia-

[11] *The Spectator*, No. 127.
[12] Yes; Venus herself laughs, the nymphs with smiles, The simple nymphs! behold thy wiles.
(Horace, *Odes*, II, viii, 13–14, tr. Francis.)
[13] Marco Girolamo Vida, *Scacchia Ludus* (*A Game of Chess*) (1515).

monds and clubs, are spoken of, is very amusing to the imagination: and the whole game is conducted with great art and judgment. I question whether Hoyle[14] could have played it better than Belinda. It is finely contrived that she should be victorious; as it occasions a change of fortune in the dreadful loss she was speedily to undergo, and gives occasion to the poet to introduce a moral reflection from Virgil, which adds to the pleasantry of the story. In one of the passages where POPE has copied Vida, he has lost the propriety of the original, which arises from the different colours of the *men* at Chess.

Thus, when dispers'd a routed army runs, &c.

Non aliter, campis legio se buxea utrinque
Composuit, duplici digestis ordine tur-
    mis,
Adversisque ambae fulsere coloribus
    alae;
Quam Gallorum acies, Alpino frigore
    lactea
Corpora, si tendant albis in prælia signis,
Auroræ populos contra, et Phæthonte
    perustos
Insano Æthiopas, et nigri Memnonis
    alas.[15]

To this scene succeeds the tea-table. It is, doubtless, as hard to make a coffee-pot shine in poetry as a plough: yet POPE has succeeded in giving elegance to so familiar an object, as well as Virgil. The guardian spirits are again active, and importantly employed:

Strait hover round the fair her airy
    band;
Some, as she sipp'd, the fuming liquor
    fann'd.

Then follows an instance of assiduity fancied with great delicacy:

Some o'er her lap their careful plumes
    display'd,
Trembling, and conscious of the rich
    brocade.

But nothing can excel the behavior of the sylphs, and their wakeful solicitude for their charge, when the danger grows more imminent, and the catastrophe approaches.

Swift to the Lock a thousand sprites re-
    pair.[16]

The methods by which they endeavoured to preserve her from the intended mischief, are such only as could be executed by a sylph; and have therefore an admirable propriety, as well as the utmost elegance.

A thousand wings by turns blow back
    the hair,
And thrice they TWITCH'D the diamond
    in her ear;
Thrice she look'd back, and thrice the foe
    drew near.

Still farther to heighten the piece, and to preserve the characters of his machines to the last, just when the fatal forfex was spread,

Ev'n then, before the fatal engine clos'd,
A wretched sylph too fondly inter-
    pos'd;—
Fate urg'd the sheers, and cut the sylph
    in twain,
(But airy substance soon unites again.)—

Which last line is an admirable parody

[14] Edmond Hoyle, author of *A Short Treatise on the Game of Whist* (1742), *The Accurate Gamester's Companion* (1748), and similar books of instruction for card games; source of the expression "according to Hoyle." [15] ll. 74–80: "The wooden legion disposed itself on each side of the field, the troops distributed in orderly double file, both divisions gleaming in contrasting colors; not unlike the battle line of the Gauls, their bodies white as Alpine frost, when they move into battle with white standards against the eastern hordes, and the Ethiopians scorched by the hot sun, and the squadrons of black Memnon." [16] "It is remarkable that Madame de Sévigné has mentioned the sylphs as invisible attendants, and as interested in the affairs of the ladies, in the 101st, 104th, 195th, of her Letters" (Warton).

on that passage of Milton, which, perhaps oddly enough, describes Satan wounded:

The griding sword, with discontinuous wound,
Pass'd thro' him; but th' ethereal substance clos'd,
Not long divisible. . . .[17]

The parodies are some of the most exquisite parts of this poem. That which follows from the "Dum juga montis aper,"[18] of Virgil, contains some of the most artful strokes of satire, and the most poignant ridicule imaginable.

While fish in streams, or birds delight in air,
Or in a coach and six the British fair,
As long as Atalantis shall be read,
Or the small pillow grace a lady's bed,
While visits shall be paid on solemn days,
When numerous wax-lights in bright order blaze,
While nymphs take treats, or assignations give,
So long my honor, name, and praise, shall live.

The introduction of frequent parodies on serious and solemn passages of Homer and Virgil, give much life and spirit to heroi-comic poetry. "Tu dors, Prelat! tu dors!" in Boileau, is the "Ευδεις Ατρεος" of Homer,[19] and is full of humour. The wife of the barber talks in the language of Dido in her expostulations to her Æneas, at the beginning of the second canto of the Lutrin. POPE's parodies of the speech of Sarpedon, in Homer,[20] and of the description of Achilles's sceptre,[21] together with the scales of Jupiter,[22]

from Homer, Virgil, and Milton, are judiciously introduced in their several places; are, perhaps, superior to those Boileau or Garth have used; and are worked up with peculiar pleasantry. The mind of the reader is engaged by novelty, when it so unexpectedly finds a thought, or object, it had been accustomed to survey in another form, suddenly arrayed in a ridiculous garb. A mixture of comic and ridiculous images, with serious and important ones, adds, also, no small beauty to this species of poetry. As in the following passages, where real and imaginary distresses are coupled together:

Not youthful kings, in battle seiz'd alive;
Not scornful virgins, who their charms survive;
Not ardent lovers, robb'd of all their bliss;
Not ancient ladies, when refus'd a kiss;
Not tyrants fierce, that unrepenting die;

Nay, to carry the climax still higher,

Not Cynthia, when her manteau's pinn'd awry,
E'er felt such rage, resentment, and despair.

This is much superior to a similar passage in the Dispensary, which POPE might have in his eye:

At this the victors own such ecstacies,
As Memphian priests if their Osiris sneeze;
Or champions with Olympic clangor fir'd;
Or simp'ring prudes, with spritely Nantz inspir'd;
Or Sultans, rais'd from dungeons to a crown;

---

[17] *Paradise Lost*, VI, 329–331.
[18] Vergil, *Eclogues*, V, 76 ff. This suggestion of a possible source of Pope's lines apparently originated in Warburton's edition of Pope (1751). Geoffrey Tillotson's edition (1940) of *The Rape of the Lock* gives Dryden's translation of the *Aeneid*, I, 854, as another possible source.
[19] *Le Lutrin*, I, 73: "You are sleeping, prel-

ate! you are sleeping!"; *Iliad*, II, 23 and 60: "Are you asleep, Atreus?"
[20] *The Rape of the Lock*, V, 9–34; *Iliad*, XII, 371 ff.
[21] *The Rape of the Lock*, IV, 133–138; *Iliad*, I, 309 ff.; and Dryden's *Aeneid*, IX, 402.
[22] *The Rape of the Lock*, V, 71–74; *Iliad*, VIII, 87 ff.; *Aeneid*, XII, 725 ff.; and *Paradise Lost*, IV, 996 ff.

Or fasting zealots, when the sermon's done.[23]

These objects have no reference to Garth's subject, as almost all of POPE'S have, in the passage in question, where some female foible is glanced at. In this same canto, the cave of SPLEEN, the pictures of her attendants, ILL-NATURE *and* AFFECTATION, the effects of the vapour that hung over her palace, the imaginary diseases she occasions, the speech of Umbriel, a gnome, to this malignant deity, the vial of female sorrows, the speech of Thalestris to aggravate the misfortune, the breaking the vial, with its direful effects, and the speech of the disconsolate Belinda; all these circumstances are poetically imagined, and are far superior to any of Boileau and Garth. How much in character is it for Belinda to mark a very dismal and solitary situation, by wishing to be conveyed

Where the gilt chariot never marks the way,
Where none learn Ombre, none e'er taste Bohea.

Nothing is more common in the poets, than to introduce omens as preceding some important and dreadful event. Virgil has strongly described those that preceded the death of Dido. The rape of Belinda's LOCK must necessarily also be attended with alarming prodigies. With what exquisite satire are they enumerated!

Thrice from my trembling hand the patch-box fell;
The tottering china shook without a wind.

And still more to aggravate the direfulness of the impending evil,

Nay, Poll sate mute, and Shock was most unkind!

The chief subject of the fifth and last canto, is the battle that ensues, and the

endeavours of the ladies to recover the hair. This battle is described, as it ought to be, in very lofty and pompous terms: a game of romps was never so well dignified before. The weapons made use of are the most proper imaginable: the lightning of the ladies eyes, intolerable frowns, a pinch of snuff, and a bodkin. The machinery is not forgot:

Triumphant Umbriel on a sconce's height,
Clapp'd his glad wings, and sate to view the fight.

Again, when the snuff is given to the Baron,

The gnomes direct, to ev'ry atom just,
The pungent grains of titillating dust.

Boileau and Garth have also each of them enlivened their pieces with a mock-fight. But Boileau has laid the scene of his action in a neighbouring bookseller's shop, where the combatants encounter each other by chance. This conduct is a little inartificial; but has given the satirist an opportunity of indulging his ruling passion, the exposing the bad poets with which France at that time abounded. Swift's Battle of the Books, at the end of the Tale of a Tub, is evidently taken from this battle of Boileau, which is excellent in its kind. The fight of the physicians, in the Dispensary, is one of its most shining parts. There is a vast deal of propriety, as well as pleasantry, in the weapons Garth has given to his warriors. They are armed, much in character, with caustics, emetics, and cathartics; with buckthorn, and steel-pills; with syringes, bed-pans, and urinals. The execution is exactly proportioned to the deadliness of such irresistible weapons; and the wounds inflicted are suitable to the nature of each different instrument said to inflict them.

We are now arrived at the grand catastrophe of the poem: the invaluable Lock which is so eagerly sought, is irrecoverably lost! And here our poet has made a judicious use of that celebrated

---

[23] "Cant. V. ad. calc." (Warton).

fiction of Ariosto, that all things lost on earth are treasured in the moon. How such a fiction can properly have place in an epic poem, it becomes the defenders of this agreeably extravagant writer to justify; but in a comic poem, it appears with grace and consistency. The whole passage in Ariosto is full of wit and satire; for wit and satire were, perhaps, the chief and characteristical of the many striking excellencies of Ariosto.[24] In this repository in the lunar sphere, says the sprightly Italian, were to be found,

Le lachrime, e i sospiri de gli amanti,
L'inutil' tempo, che si perde a gioco,
E l' otio lungo d'huomini ignoranti,
Vani disegni, che non han mai loco,
I vani desiderii sono tanti,
Che la piu parte ingombra di quel loco,
Cio che in summa qua giu perdesti mai,
La su saltendo ritrovar potrai.

It is very remarkable, that the poet had the boldness to place among these imaginary treasures, the famous deed of gift of Constantine to Pope Silvester. "If (says he) I may be allowed to say this,

Questo era il dono (se pero dir lece)
Che Constantino al buon Silvestre fece."

It may be observed in general, to the honour of the poets, both ancient and modern, that they have ever been some of the first who have detected and opposed the false claims, and mischievous usurpations, of superstition and slavery. Nor can this be wondered at, since these two are the greatest enemies, not only to all true happiness, but to all true genius.

The denouement, as a pedantic disciple of Bossu[25] would call it, of this poem, is

well conducted. What is become of this important LOCK OF HAIR? It is made a constellation with that of Berenice, so celebrated by Callimachus. As it rises to heaven,

The sylphs behold it kindling as it flies,
And pleas'd pursue its progress through
    the skies.

One cannot sufficiently applaud the art of the poet, in constantly keeping in the reader's view, the machinery of the poem, to the very last. Even when the Lock is transformed, the sylphs, who had so carefully guarded it, are here once again artfully mentioned, as finally rejoicing in its honourable transformation.

In reading the Lutrin, I have always been struck with the impropriety of so serious a conclusion as Boileau has given to so ludicrous a poem. PIETY and JUSTICE are beings rather too awful to have any concern in the celebrated Desk. They appear as much out of place and season, as would the archbishop of Paris in his pontifical robes in an harlequin entertainment.

POPE does not desert his favourite Lock, even after it becomes a constellation; and the uses he assigns to it are, indeed, admirable, and have a reference to the subject of the poem:

This the beau monde shall from the
    Mall survey,
And hail with music its propitious ray;
This the blest lover shall for *Venus* take,
And send up prayers from Rosamunda's
    lake;
This Partridge soon shall view in cloud-
    less skies,

---

[24] At this point Warton quotes in a footnote a passage from Hume's *Four Dissertations*, London, 1757 (Diss. IV, p. 212), in the same vein as his own remarks about Ariosto. The selections in Italian which follow are from the *Orlando Furioso*, Bk. XXXIV, st. 75 and 80 (tr. Hoole):

The frequent tears that lovers' eyes suffuse;
The sighs they breathe: the days that game-
    sters lose.
The leisure given which fools so oft neglect;

The weak designs the mortal breast assail,
In countless numbers fill th'encumber'd vale.
For know, whate'er is lost by human kind,
Ascending here you treasur'd safe may
    find. . . .
This (let me dare to speak) that present
    show'd,
Which on Sylvester Constantine bestow'd.

[25] René Le Bossu (1631–1689), author of a critical essay on the epic: *Traité du poème épique* (1675).

When next he looks through Galileo's
    eyes;
And hence th' egregious wizard shall
    foredoom
The fate of Louis, and the fall of Rome.

This is at once, DULCE LOQUI, and RI-
DERE DECORUM.[26]

Upon the whole, I hope it will not be
thought an exaggerated panegyric to say,
that the RAPE OF THE LOCK is the BEST
SATIRE extant; that it contains the truest and liveliest picture of modern life;
and that the subject is of a more elegant
nature, as well as more artfully conducted, than that of any other heroi-
comic poem. POPE here appears in the
light of a man of gallantry, and of a
thorough knowledge of the world; and,
indeed, he had nothing, in his carriage
and deportment, of that affected singularity, which has induced some men of
genius to despise, and depart from, the
established rules of politeness and civil
life. For all poets have not practised the
sober and rational advice of Boileau:

Que les vers ne soient pas votre eternel
    emploi:
Cultivez vos amis, soyez homme de foi.
C'est peu d' etre agréable et charmant
    dans un livre;
Il fait savoir encore, et converser, et
    vivre.[27]

Our nation can boast also, of having
produced one or two more poems of the
burlesque kind, that are excellent; particularly the SPLENDID SHILLING,[28] that
admirable copy of the solemn irony of
Cervantes, who is the father and unri-
valled model of the true mock-heroic:
and the MUSCIPULA,[29] written with the
purity of Virgil, whom the author so
perfectly understood, and with the pleasantry of Lucian: to which I cannot forbear adding, the SCRIBLERIAD of Mr.
Cambridge,[30] the MACHINÆ GESTICU-
LANTES of Addison,[31] the HOBBINOL of
Somerville,[32] and the TRIVIA of Gay.[33]

If some of the most candid among the
French critics begin to acknowledge, that
they have produced nothing, in point of
SUBLIMITY and MAJESTY, equal to the
Paradise Lost, we may also venture to
affirm, that, in point of DELICACY, ELE-
GANCE, and fine-turned RAILLERY, on
which they have so much valued themselves, they have produced nothing equal
to the RAPE OF THE LOCK. It is in this
composition POPE principally appears a
POET, in which he has displayed more
imagination than in all his other works
taken together. It should, however, be
remembered, that he was not the FIRST
former and creator of those beautiful
machines, the sylphs, on which his claim
to imagination is chiefly founded. He
found them existing ready to his hand;
but has, indeed, employed them with singular judgment and artifice.

---

[26] "To prate with joy, to laugh with ease"
(Horace, *Epistles*, I, vii, 27, tr. Francis).

[27] Let not your only business be to write;
Be virtuous, just, and in your friends delight.
'Tis not enough your poems be admired;
But strive your conversation be desired.
    (*Art poétique*, IV, 121–124, tr. Soame.)

[28] By John Philips, 1701.

[29] *Muscipula, sive Cambro-muo-machia*
(1709) by Edward Holdsworth, translated into
English as *The Mouse-Trap: or, The Welsh*

Engagement with the Mice and again as *Taf-
fia's Masterpiece.*

[30] Richard Owen Cambridge, *The Scribleriad*
(1751).

[31] Joseph Addison, *Machinae Gesticulantes;
Anglice: A Puppet Show* (1698).

[32] William Somervile, *Hobbinol, or The
Rural Games* (1740).

[33] John Gay, *Trivia; or, The Art of Walking the Streets of London* (1716).

David Hume
1711-1776

OF TRAGEDY

It seems an unaccountable pleasure, which the spectators of a well-wrote tragedy receive from sorrow, terror, anxiety, and other passions, which are in themselves disagreeable and uneasy. The more they are touched and affected, the more are they delighted with the spectacle, and as soon as the uneasy passions cease to operate, the piece is at an end. One scene of full joy and contentment and security is the utmost, that any composition of this kind can bear; and it is sure always to be the concluding one. If in the texture of the piece, there be interwoven any scenes of satisfaction, they afford only faint gleams of pleasure, which are thrown in by way of variety, and in order to plunge the actors into deeper distress, by means of that contrast and disappointment. The whole art of the poet is employed, in rouzing and supporting the compassion and indignation, the anxiety and resentment of his audience. They are pleased in proportion as they are afflicted; and never are so happy as when they employ tears, sobs, and cries to give vent to their sorrow, and relieve their heart, swoln with the tenderest sympathy and compassion.

The few critics, who have had some tincture of philosophy, have remarked this singular phænomenon, and have endeavoured to account for it.

L'Abbe *Dubos*,[1] in his reflections on poetry and painting, asserts, that nothing is in general so disagreeable to the mind as the languid, listless state of indolence, into which it falls upon the removal of every passion and occupation. To get rid of this painful situation, it seeks every amusement and pursuit; business, gaming, shows, executions; whatever will rouze the passions, and take its attention from itself. No matter, what the passion is: Let it be disagreeable, afflicting, melancholy, disordered; it is still better, than that insipid languor, which arises from perfect tranquillity and repose.

It is impossible not to admit this account, as being, at least, in part satisfactory. You may observe, when there are several tables of gaming, that all the company run to those, where the deepest play is, even tho' they find not there the finest players. The view, or at least, imagination of high passions, arising from great loss or gain, affects the spectators by sympathy, gives them some touches of the same passions, and serves them for a momentary entertainment. It makes the time pass the easier with them, and is some relief to that oppression, under which men commonly labour, when left entirely to their own thoughts and meditations.

We find, that common lyars always

Text from first edition, 1757, of *Four Dissertations*, of which it is the third.

[1] Jean Baptiste Dubos, *Réflexions critiques sur la Poésie et sur la Peinture* (1719).

magnify, in their narrations, all kinds of danger, pain, distress, sickness, deaths, murders, and cruelties; as well as joy, beauty, mirth, and magnificence. It is an absurd secret, which they have for pleasing their company, fixing their attention, and attaching them to such marvellous relations, by the passions and emotions, which they excite.

There is, however, a difficulty of applying to the present subject, in its full extent, this solution, however ingenious and satisfactory it may appear. It is certain, that the same object of distress which pleases in a tragedy, were it really set before us, would give the most unfeigned uneasiness, tho' it be then the most effectual cure of languor and indolence. Monsieur *Fontenelle*[2] seems to have been sensible of this difficulty; and accordingly attempts another solution of the phænomenon; at least, makes some addition to the theory abovementioned.

"Pleasure and pain," says he, "which are two sentiments so different in themselves, differ not so much in their cause. From the instance of tickling, it appears, that the movement of pleasure pushed a little too far, becomes pain; and that the movement of pain, a little moderated, becomes pleasure. Hence it proceeds, that there is such a thing as a sorrow, soft and agreeable: It is a pain weakened and diminished. The heart likes naturally to be moved and affected. Melancholy objects suit it, and even disastrous and sorrowful, provided they are softened by some circumstance. It is certain, that on the theatre the representation has almost the effect of reality; but yet it has not altogether that effect. However we may be hurried away by the spectacle; whatever dominion the senses and imagination may usurp over the reason, there still lurks at the bottom a certain idea of falshood in the whole of what we see. This idea, tho' weak and disguised, suffices to diminish the pain which we suffer from the misfortunes of those whom we love, and to reduce that affliction to such a pitch as converts it into a pleasure. We weep for the misfortune of a hero, to whom we are attached: In the same instant we comfort ourselves, by reflecting, that it is nothing but a fiction: And it is precisely, that mixture of sentiments, which composes an agreeable sorrow, and tears that delight us. But as that affliction, which is caused by exterior and sensible objects, is stronger than the consolation, which arises from an internal reflection, they are the effects and symptoms of sorrow, which ought to prevail in the composition."

This solution seems just and convincing; but perhaps it wants still some new addition, in order to make it answer fully the phænomenon, which we here examine. All the passions, excited by eloquence, are agreeable in the highest degree, as well as those which are moved by painting and the theatre. The epilogues of *Cicero* are, on this account chiefly, the delight of every reader of taste; and it is difficult to read some of them without the deepest sympathy and sorrow. His merit as an orator, no doubt, depends much on his success in this particular. When he had raised tears in his judges and all his audience, they were then the most highly delighted, and expressed the greatest satisfaction with the pleader. The pathetic description of the butchery made by *Verres* of the *Sicilian* captains is a master-piece of this kind:[3] But I believe none will affirm, that the being present at a melancholy scene of that nature would afford any entertainment. Neither is the sorrow here softened by fiction: For the audience were convinced of the reality of every circumstance. What is it then, which in this case raises a pleasure from the bosom of uneasiness, so to speak; and a pleasure,

---

[2] Bernard le Bovier, de Fontenelle; the passage which follows is a translation from his *Réflexions sur la Poétique* (1691), sec. 36.

[3] In the year 70 B.C., Cicero, acting as public prosecutor for Sicily, impeached the Roman proconsul Verres by presenting the witnesses against him. As a result of the maneuver, the speeches (*In Verrem*), to which Hume refers, were not delivered, but remain a splendid tribute to Cicero's oratorical composition notwithstanding.

which still retains all the features and outward symptoms of distress and sorrow?

I answer: This extraordinary effect proceeds from that very eloquence, with which the melancholy scene is represented. The genius required to paint objects in a lively manner, the art employed in collecting all the pathetic circumstances, the judgment displayed in disposing them; the exercise, I say, of these noble talents, along with the force of expression, and beauty of oratorial numbers, diffuse the highest satisfaction on the audience, and excite the most delightful movements. By this means, the uneasiness of the melancholy passions is not only overpowered and effaced by something stronger of an opposite kind; but the whole movement of those passions is converted into pleasure, and swells the delight, which the eloquence raises in us. The same force of oratory, employed on an uninteresting subject, would not please half so much, or rather would appear altogether ridiculous; and the mind, being left in absolute calmness and indifference, would relish none of those beauties of imagination or expression, which, if joined to passion, give it such exquisite entertainment. The impulse or vehemence, arising from sorrow, compassion, indignation, receives a new direction from the sentiments of beauty. The latter, being the predominant emotions, seize the whole mind, and convert the former into themselves, or at least, tincture them so strongly as totally to alter their nature: And the soul, being, at the same time, rouzed by passion, and charmed by eloquence, feels on the whole a strong movement, which is altogether delightful.

The same principle takes place in tragedy; along with this addition, that tragedy is an imitation, and imitation is always of itself agreeable. This circumstance serves still farther to smooth the motions of passion, and convert the whole feeling into one uniform and strong enjoyment. Objects of the greatest terror and distress please in painting, and please more than the most beautiful objects, that appear calm and indifferent. The affection,[4] rouzing the mind, excites a large stock of spirit and vehemence; which is all transformed into pleasure by the force of the prevailing movement. It is thus the fiction of tragedy softens the passion, by an infusion of a new feeling, not merely by weakening or diminishing the sorrow. You may by degrees weaken a real sorrow, till it totally disappears; yet in none of its gradations will it ever give pleasure; except, perhaps, by accident, to a man sunk under lethargic indolence, whom it rouzes from that languid state.

To confirm this theory, it will be sufficient to produce other instances, where the subordinate movement is converted into the predominant, and gives force to it, tho' of a different, and even sometimes tho' of a contrary nature.

Novelty naturally excites the mind and attracts our attention; and the movements, which it causes, are always converted into any passion, belonging to the object, and join their force to it. Whether an event excites joy or sorrow, pride or shame, anger or goodwill, it is sure to produce a stronger affection, when new and unusual. And tho' novelty, of itself, be agreeable, it enforces the painful, as well as agreeable passions.

Had you any intention to move a person extremely by the narration of any event, the best method of encreasing its effect would be artfully to delay informing him of it, and first excite his curiosity and impatience before you let him into the secret. This is the artifice, practiced by *Iago* in the famous scene of *Shakespeare;*[5] and every spectator is sensible, that *Othello's* jealousy acquires additional force from his preceding impatience, and that the subordinate passion is here readily transformed into the predominant.

---

[4] Apparently in the sense of "good-will to any object" (Johnson's *Dictionary*), although Hume's use of the term also implies an innate faculty which is not present in any of the definitions given by Johnson of the term.

[5] *Othello*, III, iii.

Difficulties encrease passions of every kind; and by rouzing our attention, and exciting our active powers, they produce an emotion, which nourishes the prevailing affection.

Parents commonly love that child most, whose sickly infirm frame of body has occasioned them the greatest pains, trouble, and anxiety in rearing him. The agreeable sentiment of affection here acquires force from sentiments of uneasiness.

Nothing endears so much a friend as sorrow for his death. The pleasure of his company has not so powerful an influence.

Jealousy is a painful passion, yet without some share of it, the agreeable affection of love has difficulty to subsist in its full force and violence. Absence is also a great source of complaint amongst lovers, and gives them the greatest uneasiness: Yet nothing is more favorable to their mutual passion than short intervals of that kind. And if long intervals be pernicious, it is only because, thro' time, men are accustomed to them, and they cease to give uneasiness. Jealousy and absence in love compose the *dolce piccante*[6] of the *Italians,* which they suppose so essential to all pleasure.

There is a fine observation of the elder *Pliny,*[7] which illustrates the principle here insisted on. *It is very remarkable,* says he, *that the last works of celebrated artists, which they left imperfect, are always the most prized, such as the* Iris *of* Aristides, *the* Tyndarides *of* Nicomachus, *the* Medea *of* Timomachus, *and the* Venus *of* Appelles. *These are valued even above their finished productions: The broken lineaments of the piece and the half formed idea of the painter are carefully studied; and our very grief for that curious hand, which had been stopped by death, is an additional encrease to our pleasure.*

These instances (and many more might be collected) are sufficient to afford us some insight into the analogy of nature, and to show us, that the pleasure, which poets, orators, and musicians give us, by exciting grief, sorrow, indignation, compassion, is not so extraordinary nor paradoxical, as it may at first sight appear. The force of imagination, the energy of expression, the power of numbers, the charms of imitation; all these are naturally, of themselves, delightful to the mind; and when the object presented lays also hold of some affection, the pleasure still rises upon us, by the conversion of this subordinate movement, into that which is predominant. The passion, tho', perhaps, naturally, and when excited by the simple appearance of a real object, it may be painful; yet is so smoothed, and softened, and mollified, when raised by the finer arts, that it affords the highest entertainment.

To confirm this reasoning, we may observe, that if the movements of the imagination be not predominant above those of the passion, a contrary effect follows; and the former, being now subordinate, is converted into the latter, and still farther encreases the pain and affliction of the sufferer.

Who could ever think of it as a good expedient for comforting an afflicted parent, to exaggerate, with all the force of oratory, the irreparable loss, which he has met with by the death of a favorite child? The more power of imagination and expression you here employ, the more you encrease his despair and affliction.

The shame, confusion, and terror of *Verres,* no doubt, rose in proportion to the noble eloquence and vehemence of *Cicero:* So also did his pain and uneasiness. These former passions were too strong for the pleasure arising from the beauties of elocution; and operated, tho' from the same principle, yet in a contrary manner, to the sympathy, compassion, and indignation of the audience.

Lord *Clarendon,*[8] when he approaches the catastrophe of the royal party, supposes, that his narration must then become infinitely disagreeable; and he hur-

---

[6] "gentle sting."

[7] *Natural History,* Bk. xxxv, chap. 40, sec. 20.

[8] Edward Hyde, Earl of Clarendon (1609–1674), in *The True Historical Narrative of the Rebellion and Civil Wars in England.*

ries over the King's death, without giving us one circumstance of it. He considers it as too horrid a scene to be contemplated with any satisfaction, or even without the utmost pain and aversion. He himself, as well as the readers of that age, were too deeply interested in the events, and felt a pain from subjects, which an historian and a reader of another age would regard as the most pathetic and most interesting, and by consequence, the most agreeable.

An action, represented in tragedy, may be too bloody and atrocious. It may excite such movements of horror as will not soften into pleasure; and the greatest energy of expression bestowed on descriptions of that nature serves only to augment our uneasiness. Such is that action represented in the *ambitious Stepmother,*[9] where a venerable old man, raised to the height of fury and despair, rushes against a pillar, and striking his head upon it, besmears it all over with mingled brains and gore. The *English* theatre abounds too much with such images.

Even the common sentiments of compassion require to be softened by some agreeable affection, in order to give a thorough satisfaction to the audience. The mere suffering of plaintive virtue, under the triumphant tyranny and oppression of vice, forms a disagreeable spectacle, and is carefully avoided by all masters of the theatre. In order to dismiss the audience with entire satisfaction and contentment, the virtue must either convert itself into a noble courageous despair, or the vice receive its proper punishment.

Most painters appear in this light to have been very unhappy in their subjects. As they wrought for churches and convents, they have chiefly represented such horrible subjects as crucifixions and martyrdoms, where nothing appears but tortures, wounds, executions, and passive suffering, without any action or affection. When they turned their pencil from this ghastly mythology, they had recourse commonly to *Ovid,* whose fictions, tho' passionate and agreeable, are scarce natural or probable enough for painting.

The same inversion of that principle, which is here insisted on, displays itself in common life, as in the effects of oratory and poetry. Raise so the subordinate passion that it becomes the predominant, it swallows up that affection, which it before nourished and encreased. Too much jealousy extinguishes love: Too much difficulty renders us indifferent: Too much sickness and infirmity disgusts a selfish and unkind parent.

What so disagreeable as the dismal, gloomy, disastrous stories, with which melancholy people entertain their companions? The uneasy passion, being there raised alone, unaccompanied with any spirit, genius, or eloquence, conveys a pure uneasiness, and is attended with nothing that can soften it into pleasure or satisfaction.

---

[9] A tragedy by Nicholas Rowe in 1700.

Edward Young
1683-1765

CONJECTURES ON ORIGINAL COMPOSITION

Dear Sir,[1]

We confess the follies of youth without a blush; not so, those of age. However, keep me a little in countenance, by considering, that age wants amusements more, tho' it can justify them less, than the preceding periods of life. How you may relish the pastime here sent you, I know not. It is miscellaneous in its nature, somewhat licentious in its conduct; and, perhaps, not over important in its end. However, I have endeavoured to make some amends, by digressing into subjects more important, and more suitable to my season of life. A serious thought standing single among many of a lighter nature, will sometimes strike the careless wanderer after amusement only, with useful awe: as monumental marbles scattered in a wide pleasure-garden (and such there are) will call to recollection those who would never have sought it in a churchyard-walk of mournful yews.

To one such monument I may conduct you, in which is a hidden lustre, like the sepulchral lamps of old; but not like those will This be extinguished, but shine the brighter for being produced, after so long concealment, into open day.

You remember that your worthy patron, and our common friend,[2] put some questions on the *Serious Drama,* at the same time when he desired our sentiments on *Original,* and on *Moral* Composition. Tho' I despair of breaking thro' the frozen obstructions of age, and care's incumbent cloud, into that flow of thought, and brightness of expression, which subjects so polite require; yet will I hazard some conjectures on them.

I begin with *Original* Composition; and the more willingly, as it seems an original subject to me, who have seen nothing hitherto written on it: But, first, a few thoughts on Composition in general. Some are of opinion, that its growth, at present, is too luxuriant; and that the Press is overcharged. Overcharged, I think, it could never be, if none were admitted, but such as brought their Imprimatur[3] from *sound Understanding,* and the *Public Good.* Wit, indeed, however brilliant, should not be permitted to gaze self-enamoured on its useless Charms, in that Fountain of

---

Text from second edition, in same year as first, 1759.

---

[1] The title of this selection continues: *In a Letter to the Author of Sir Charles Grandison,* who is Samuel Richardson (1689–1761); *The* *History of Sir Charles Grandison* (1753–1754) was his most recent novel.

[2] That this reference to a common friend is polite pretext is clear from Richardson's letters to Young.

[3] license to print.

Fame (if so I may call the Press), if beauty is all that it has to boast; but, like the first *Brutus*,[4] it should sacrifice its most darling offspring to the sacred interests of virtue, and real service of mankind.

This restriction allowed, the more composition the better. To men of letters, and leisure, it is not only a noble amusement, but a sweet refuge; it improves their parts,[5] and promotes their peace: It opens a back-door out of the bustle of this busy, and idle world, into a delicious garden of moral and intellectual fruits and flowers; the key of which is denied to the rest of mankind. When stung with idle anxieties, or teazed with fruitless impertinence, or yawning over insipid diversions, then we perceive the blessing of a letter'd recess. With what a gust do we retire to our disinterested, and immortal friends in our closet, and find our minds, when applied to some favourite theme, as naturally, and as easily quieted, and refreshed, as a peevish child (and peevish children are we all till we fall asleep) when laid to the breast? Our happiness no longer lives on charity; nor bids fair for a fall, by leaning on that most precarious, and thorny pillow, another's pleasure, for our repose. How independent of the world is he, who can daily find new acquaintance, that at once entertain, and improve him, in the little world, the minute but fruitful creation, of his own mind?

These advantages *Composition* affords us, whether we write ourselves, or in more humble amusement peruse the works of others. While we bustle thro' the thronged walks of public life, it gives us a respite, at least, from care; a pleasing pause of refreshing recollection. If the country is our choice, or fate, there it rescues us from *sloth* and *sensuality,* which, like obscene vermin, are apt grad-

ually to creep unperceived into the delightful bowers of our retirement, and to poison all its sweets. Conscious guilt robs the rose of its scent, the lilly of its lustre; and makes an *Eden* a deflowered, and dismal scene.

Moreover, if we consider life's endless evils, what can be more prudent, than to provide for consolation under them? A consolation under them the wisest of men have found in the pleasures of the pen. Witness, among many more, *Thucydides, Xenophon, Tully, Ovid, Seneca, Pliny* the younger, who says, *In uxoris infirmitate, & amicorum periculo, aut morte turbatus, ad studia, unicum doloris levamentum, confugio.*[6] And why not add to these their modern equals, *Chaucer, Rawleigh, Bacon, Milton, Clarendon,* under the same shield, unwounded by misfortune, and nobly smiling in distress?

Composition was a cordial to these under the frowns of fortune; but evils there are, which her smiles cannot prevent, or cure. Among these are the languors of old age. If those are held honourable, who in a hand benumbed by time have grasped the just sword in defence of their country; shall they be less esteemed, whose unsteady pen vibrates to the last in the cause of religion, of virtue, of learning? Both These are happy in *this,* that by fixing their attention on objects most important, they escape numberless little anxieties, and that *tedium vitae*[7] which often hangs so heavy on its evening hours. May not this insinuate some apology for my spilling ink, and spoiling paper, so late in life?

But there are, who write with vigor, and success, to the world's delight, and their own renown. These are the glorious fruits where genius prevails. The mind of a man of genius is a fertile and pleasant field, pleasant as *Elysium*,[8] and fertile as *Tempe;*[9] it enjoys a perpetual

---

[4] Lucius Junius Brutus (d. 509 B.C.), who condemned his sons to death for conspiracy against the government; not to be confused with the Brutus who participated in the assassination of Julius Caesar nearly five hundred years later.

[5] "qualities; powers; faculties; or accomplishments" (Johnson's *Dictionary*).

[6] "In the illness of my wife and the dangers of my friends, or in my own trouble with death, I turn to studies for mitigation of sorrow" (Pliny, *Letters*, VIII, 19).

[7] "weariness with life."

[8] Greek classical heaven.

[9] Idyllic valley in Greece, celebrated by Vergil.

spring. Of that spring, *Originals* are the fairest flowers: *Imitations* are of quicker growth, but fainter bloom. *Imitations* are of two kinds; one of nature, one of authors: The first we call *Originals,* and confine the term *Imitation* to the second. I shall not enter into the curious enquiry of what is, or is not, strictly speaking, *Original,* content with what all must allow, that some compositions are more so than others; and the more they are so, I say, the better. *Originals* are, and ought to be, great favourites, for they are great benefactors; they extend the republic of letters, and add a new province to its dominion: *Imitators* only give us a sort of duplicates of what we had, possibly much better, before; increasing the mere drug of books, while all that makes them valuable, *knowledge* and *genius,* are at a stand. The pen of an *original* writer, like *Armida's*[10] wand, out of a barren waste calls a blooming spring: Out of that blooming spring an *Imitator* is a transplanter of laurels, which sometimes die on removal, always languish in a foreign soil.

But suppose an *Imitator* to be most excellent (and such there are), yet still he but nobly builds on another's foundation; his debt is, at least, equal to his glory; which therefore, on the balance, cannot be very great. On the contrary, an *Original,* tho' but indifferent (its *Originality* being set aside), yet has something to boast; it is something to say with him in *Horace,*

Meo *sum Pauper in aere;*[11]

and to share ambition with no less than *Caesar,* who declared he had rather be the first in a village, than the second at *Rome.*

Still farther: An *Imitator* shares his crown, if he has one, with the chosen object of his imitation; an *Original* enjoys an undivided applause. An *Original* may be said to be of a *vegetable* nature; it rises spontaneously from the vital root of genius; it *grows,* it is not *made: Imita-*

tions are often a sort of *manufacture* wrought up by those *mechanics, art,* and *labour,* out of pre-existent materials not their own.

Again: We read *Imitation* with somewhat of his languor, who listens to a twice-told tale: Our spirits rouze at an *Original;* that is a perfect stranger, and all throng to learn what news from a foreign land: And tho' it comes, like an *Indian* prince, adorned with feathers only, having little of weight; yet of our attention it will rob the more solid, if not equally new: Thus every telescope is lifted at a new-discovered star; it makes a hundred astronomers in a moment, and denies equal notice to the sun. But if an *Original,* by being as excellent, as new, adds admiration to surprize, then are we at the writer's mercy; on the strong wing of his imagination, we are snatched from *Britain* to *Italy,* from climate to climate, from pleasure to pleasure; we have no home, no thought, of our own; till the magician drops his pen: And then falling down into ourselves, we awake to flat realities, lamenting the change, like the beggar who dreamt himself a prince.

It is with thoughts, as it is with words; and with both, as with men; they may grow old, and die. Words tarnished, by passing thro' the mouths of the vulgar, are laid aside as inelegant, and obsolete. So thoughts, when become too common, should lose their currency; and we should send new metal to the mint, that is, new meaning to the press. The division of tongues at *Babel* did not more effectually debar men from *making themselves a name* (as the Scripture speaks,) than the too great concurrence, or union of tongues will do for ever. We may as well grow good by another's virtue, or fat by another's food, as famous by another's thought. The world will pay its debt of praise but once; and instead of applauding, explode a second demand, as a cheat.

If it is said, that most of the *Latin* classics, and all the *Greek,* except, perhaps, *Homer, Pindar,* and *Anacreon,* are

---

[10] A fascinating heroine of Tasso's *Jerusalem Delivered* (1575) with magical powers.

[11] . . . My stock is little.
But that stock my own. . . .
(*Epistles,* II, ii, 12, tr. Francis.)

in the number of *Imitators,* yet receive our highest applause; our answer is, That they, tho' not *real,* are *accidental Originals;* the works they imitated, few excepted, are lost: They, on their father's decease, enter as lawful heirs, on their estates in fame: The fathers of our copyists are still in possession; and secured in it, in spite of *Goths,* and Flames, by the perpetuating power of the Press. Very late must a modern *Imitator's* fame arrive, if it waits for their decease.

An *Original* enters early on reputation: *Fame,* fond of new glories, sounds her trumpet in triumph at its birth; and yet how few are awaken'd by it into the noble ambition of like attempts? Ambition is sometimes no vice in life; it is always a virtue in Composition. High in the towering *Alps* is the fountain of the *Po;* high in fame, and in antiquity, is the fountain of an *Imitator's* undertaking; but the river, and the imitation, humbly creep along the vale. So few are our *Originals,* that, if all other books were to be burnt, the letter'd world would resemble some metropolis in flames, where a few incombustible buildings, a fortress, temple, or tower, lift their heads, in melancholy grandeur, amid the mighty ruin. Compared with this conflagration, old *Omar*[12] lighted up but a small bonfire, when he heated the baths of the Barbarians, for eight months together, with the famed *Alexandrian* library's inestimable spoils, that no profane book might obstruct the triumphant progress of his holy *Alcoran* round the globe.

But why are *Originals* so few? not because the writer's harvest is over, the great reapers of antiquity having left nothing to be gleaned after them; nor because the human mind's teeming time is past, or because it is incapable of putting forth unprecedented births; but because illustrious examples *engross, prejudice,* and *intimidate.* They *engross* our attention, and so prevent a due inspection of ourselves; they *prejudice* our judg-

ment in favour of their abilities, and so lessen the sense of our own; and they *intimidate* us with the splendor of their renown, and thus under diffidence bury our strength. Nature's impossibilities, and those of diffidence, lie wide asunder.

Let it not be suspected, that I would weakly insinuate any thing in favour of the moderns, as compared with antient authors; no, I am lamenting their great inferiority. But I think it is no *necessary* inferiority; that it is not from divine destination, but from some cause far beneath the moon: I think that human souls, thro' all periods, are equal; that due care, and exertion, would set us nearer our immortal predecessors than we are at present; and he who questions and confutes this, will show abilities not a little tending toward a proof of that equality, which he denies.

After all, the first ancients had no merit in being *Originals:* They could *not* be *Imitators.* Modern writers have a *choice* to make; and therefore have a merit in their power. They may soar in the regions of *liberty,* or move in the soft fetters of easy *imitation;* and *imitation* has as many plausible reasons to urge, as *Pleasure* had to offer to *Hercules.* Hercules made the choice of an hero, and *so* became immortal.

Yet let not assertors of classic excellence imagine, that I deny the tribute it so well deserves. He that admires not antient authors, betrays a secret he would conceal, and tells the world, that he does not understand them. Let us be as far from neglecting, as from copying, their admirable compositions: Sacred be their rights, and inviolable their fame. Let our understanding feed on theirs; they afford the noblest nourishment: But let them nourish, not annihilate, our own. When we read, let our imagination kindle at their charms; when we write, let our judgment shut them out of our thoughts; treat even *Homer* himself, as his royal admirer was treated by the cynic; bid him stand aside, nor shade our Composi-

[12] The second Mahommedan calif of whom legend reports that he destroyed the rich library of Alexandria in the year 641. The *Alcoran* in this sentence is better known in the western world as the *Koran.*

tion from the beams of our own genius; for nothing *Original* can rise, nothing immortal, can ripen, in any other sun.

Must we then, you say, not imitate antient authors? Imitate them, by all means; but imitate aright. He that imitates the divine *Iliad,* does not imitate *Homer;* but he who takes the same method, which *Homer* took, for arriving at a capacity of accomplishing a work so great. Tread in his steps to the sole fountain of immortality; drink where he drank, at the true *Helicon,*[13] that is, at the breast of nature: Imitate; but imitate not the *Composition,* but the *Man.* For may not this paradox pass into a maxim? *viz.* "The less we copy the renowned antients, we shall resemble them the more."

But possibly you may reply, that you must either imitate *Homer,* or depart from nature. Not so: For suppose you was to change place, in time, with *Homer;* then, if you write naturally, you might as well charge *Homer* with an imitation of you. Can you be said to imitate *Homer* for writing *so,* as you would have written, if *Homer* had never been? As far as a regard to nature, and sound sense, will permit a departure from your great predecessors; so far, ambitiously, depart from them; the farther from them in *similitude,* the nearer are you to them in *excellence;* you rise by it into an *Original;* become a noble collateral, not an humble descendant from them. Let us build our Compositions with the spirit, and in the taste, of the antients; but not with their materials: Thus will they resemble the structures of *Pericles* at *Athens,* which *Plutarch* commends for having had an air of antiquity as soon as they were built. All eminence, and distinction, lies out of the beaten road; excursion, and deviation, are necessary to find it; and the more remote your path from the highway, the more reputable; if, like poor *Gulliver* (of whom anon) you fall not into a ditch, in your way to glory.

What glory to come near, what glory to reach, what glory (presumptuous thought!) to surpass, our predecessors? And is that then in nature absolutely impossible? Or is it not, rather, contrary to nature to fail in it? Nature herself sets the ladder, all wanting is our ambition to climb. For by the bounty of nature we are as strong as our predecessors; and by the favour of time (which is but another round in nature's scale) we stand on higher ground. As to the *first,* were *they* more than men? Or are *we* less? Are not our minds cast in the same mould with those before the flood? The flood affected matter; mind escaped. As to the *second;* though we are moderns, the world is an antient; more antient far, than when they, whom we most admire, filled it with their fame. Have we not their beauties, as stars, to guide; their defects, as rocks, to be shunn'd; the judgment of ages on both, as a chart to conduct, and a sure helm to steer us in our passage to greater perfection than theirs? And shall we be stopt in our rival pretensions to fame by this just reproof?

Stat contra, dicitque tibi tua pagina,
　Fur es.

MART.[14]

It is by a sort of noble contagion, from a general familiarity with their writings, and not by any particular sordid theft, that we can be the better for those who went before us. Hope we, from a plagiarism, any dominion in literature; as that of *Rome* arose from a nest of thieves?

Rome was a powerful ally to many states; antient authors are our powerful allies; but we must take heed, that they do not succour, till they enslave, after the manner of *Rome.* Too formidable an idea of their superiority, like a spectre, would fright us out of a proper use of our wits; and dwarf our understanding, by making a giant of theirs. Too great awe for them lays genius under restraint, and denies it that free scope, that full

---

[13] Mountain sacred to the Greek Muses from which issued inspiring waters.

[14] "Your page itself says you are a thief" (*Epigrams,* I, liv, 12).

elbow-room, which is requisite for striking its most masterly strokes. Genius is a master-workman, learning is but an instrument; and an instrument, tho' most valuable, yet not always indispensable. Heaven will not admit of a partner in the accomplishment of some favourite spirits; but rejecting all human means, assumes the whole glory to itself. Have not some, tho' not famed for erudition, *so* written, as almost to persuade us, that they shone brighter, and soared higher, for escaping the boasted aid of that proud ally?

Nor is it strange; for what, for the most part, mean we by genius, but the power of accomplishing great things without the means generally reputed necessary to that end? A *genius* differs from a *good understanding,* as a magician from a good architect; *that* raises his structure by means invisible; *this* by the skilful use of common tools. Hence genius has ever been supposed to partake of something divine. *Nemo unquam vir magnus fuit, sine aliquo afflatu divino.*[15]

Learning, destitute of this superior aid, is fond, and proud, of what has cost it much pains; is a great lover of rules, and boaster of famed examples: As beauties less perfect, who owe half their charms to cautious art, learning inveighs against natural unstudied graces, and small harmless inaccuracies, and sets rigid bounds to that liberty, to which genius often owes its supreme glory; but the no-genius its frequent ruin. For unprescribed beauties, and unexampled excellence, which are characteristics of *genius,* lie without the pale of *learning's* authorities, and laws; which pale, genius must leap to come at them: But by that leap, if genius is wanting, we break our necks; we lose that little credit, which possibly we might have enjoyed before. For rules, like crutches, are a needful

aid to the lame, tho' an impediment to the strong. A *Homer* casts them away; and, like his *Achilles,*

Jura negat sibi nata, nihil non arrogat,[16]

by native force of mind. There is something in poetry beyond prose-reason; there are mysteries in it not to be explained, but admired; which render mere prose-men infidels to their divinity. And here pardon a second paradox; *viz.* *"Genius* often then deserves most to be praised, when it is most sure to be condemned; that is, when its excellence, from mounting high, to weak eyes is quite out of sight."

If I might speak farther of learning, and genius, I would compare genius to virtue, and learning to riches. As riches are most wanted where there is least virtue; so learning where there is least genius. As virtue without much riches can give happiness, so genius without much learning can given renown. As it is said in *Terence, Pecuniam negligere interdum maximum est lucrum;*[17] so to neglect of learning, genius sometimes owes its greater glory. Genius, therefore, leaves but the second place, among men of letters, to the learned. It is their merit, and ambition, to fling light on the works of genius, and point out its charms. We most justly reverence their informing radius for that favour; but we must much more admire the radiant stars pointed out by them.

A star of the first magnitude among the moderns was *Shakespeare;* among the antients, *Pindar;* who (as *Vossius*[18] tells us) boasted of his no-learning, calling himself the eagle, for his flight above it. And such genii as these may, indeed, have much reliance on their own native powers. For genius may be compared to the natural strength of the body; learn-

---

[15] "No one was ever great without a touch of divinity" (Cicero, *De Natura Deorum,* II, lvi, 167).

[16] "Let him spurn all laws, and . . . assert his cause" (Horace, *Ars Poetica,* l. 122, tr. *Francis*).

[17] "Often it is most profitable to be careless with money" (*Adelphi,* II, ii, 8).

[18] Probably Gerhard Johannes Vossius (1577-1649), a German classical scholar who wrote widely on classical literature.

ing to the superinduced accoutrements of arms: if the first is equal to the proposed exploit, the latter rather encumbers, than assists; rather retards, than promotes, the victory. *Sacer nobis inest Deus,*[19] says *Seneca.* With regard to the moral world, *conscience,* with regard to the intellectual, *genius,* is that god within. Genius can set us right in Composition, without the rules of the learned; as conscience sets us right in life, without the laws of the land: *This,* singly, can make us good, as men: *that,* singly, as writers, can, sometimes, make us great.

I say, sometimes, because there is a genius, which stands in need of learning to make it shine. Of genius there are two species, an earlier, and a later; or call them *infantine,* and *adult.* An adult genius comes out of nature's hand, as *Pallas* out of *Jove's* head, at full growth, and mature: *Shakespeare's* genius was of this kind: On the contrary, *Swift* stumbled at the threshold, and set out for distinction on feeble knees: His was an infantine genius; a genius, which, like other infants, must be nursed, and educated, or it will come to nought: Learning is its nurse, and tutor; but this nurse may overlay with an indigested load, which smothers common sense; and this tutor may mislead, with pedantic prejudice, which vitiates the best understanding: As too great admirers of the fathers of the church have sometimes set up their authority against the true sense of Scripture; so too great admirers of the classical fathers have sometimes set up their authority, or example, against reason.

Neve minor, neu sit quinto productior actu Fabula.[20]

So says *Horace,* so says antient example. But reason has not subscribed. I know but one book[21] that can justify our implicit acquiescence in it: And (by the way) on that book a noble disdain of undue deference to prior opinion has lately cast, and is still casting, a new and inestimable light.

But, superstition for our predecessors set aside, the classics are for ever our rightful and revered masters in *Composition;* and our understandings bow before them: But when? When a master is wanted; which, sometimes, as I have shown, is not the case. Some are pupils of nature only, nor go farther to school: From such we reap often a double advantage; they not only rival the reputation of the great antient authors, but also reduce the number of mean ones among the moderns. For when they enter on subjects which have been in former hands, such is their superiority, that, like a tenth wave, they overwhelm, and bury in oblivion all that went before: And thus not only enrich and adorn, but remove a load, and lessen the labour, of the letter'd world.

"But, you say, since *Originals* can arise from genius only, and since genius is so very rare, it is scarce worth while to labour a point so much, from which we can reasonably expect so little." To show that genius is not so very rare as you imagine, I shall point out strong instances of it, in a far distant quarter from that mentioned above. The minds of the schoolmen were almost as much cloistered as their bodies; they had but little learning, and few books; yet may the most learned be struck with some astonishment at their so singular natural sagacity, and most exquisite edge of thought. Who would expect to find

[19] "Sacred is the God within us." Young is apparently quoting from memory as the nearest approach to this statement in Seneca's extant writings is "Sacer intra nos spiritus sedet" (*Ep.,* xli, 2), a passage discussed at length by Charles Pomeroy Parker in *Harvard Studies in Classical Philology,* XVII (1906), 149–160.

[20] If you would have your play deserve success, / Give it five acts complete; no more, nor less. (*Ars Poetica,* l. 190, tr. Francis.)

[21] The allusion is to the Bible and the commentary Robert Lowth's *Praelectiones Academicae de Sacra Poesi Hebraeorum* (1753), which treats of the Bible as literature and poetry.

Pindar and *Scotus,*[22] *Shakespeare* and *Aquinas,* of the same party? Both equally shew an *original,* unindebted, energy; the *vigor igneus,* and *cœlestis origo,*[23] burns in both; and leaves us in doubt whether genius is more evident in the sublime flights and beauteous flowers of poetry, or in the profound penetrations, and marvelously keen and minute distinctions, called the thorns of the schools. There might have been more able consuls called from the plough, than ever arrived at that honour: Many a genius, probably, there has been, which could neither write, nor read. So that genius, that supreme lustre of literature, is less rare than you conceive.

By the praise of genius we detract not from learning; we detract not from the value of gold, by saying that diamond has greater still. He who disregards learning, shows that he wants its aid; and he that overvalues it, shows that its aid has done him harm. Overvalued indeed it cannot be, if genius, as to *Composition,* is valued more. Learning we thank, genius we revere; That gives us pleasure, This gives us rapture; That informs, This inspires; and is itself inspired; for genius is from heaven, learning from man: *This* sets us above the low, and illiterate; *That,* above the learned, and polite. Learning is borrowed knowledge; genius is knowledge innate, and quite our own. Therefore, as *Bacon* observes,[24] it may take a nobler name, and be called Wisdom; in which sense of wisdom, some are born wise.

But here a caution is necessary against the most fatal of errors in those automaths, those self-taught philosophers of our age, who set up genius, and often, mere *fancied* genius, not only above human learning, but divine truth. I have called genius wisdom; but let it be remembered, that in the most renowned ages of the most refined heathen wisdom (and theirs is not Christian) *"the world*

by wisdom knew not God, and it pleased God by the foolishness of preaching to save those that believed."[25] In the fairy-land of fancy, genius may wander wild; there it has a creative power, and may reign arbitrarily over its own empire of chimeras. The wide field of nature also lies open before it, where it may range unconfined, make what discoveries it can, and sport with its infinite objects uncontrouled, as far as visible nature extends, painting them as wantonly as it will: But what painter of the most unbounded and exalted genius can give us the true portrait of a seraph? He can give us only what by his own, or others eyes, has been seen; tho' that indeed infinitely compounded, raised, burlesqued, dishonoured, or adorned: In like manner, who can give us divine truth unrevealed? Much less should any presume to set aside divine truth when revealed, as incongruous to their own sagacities.—Is this too serious for my subject? I shall be more so before I close.

Having put in a caveat against the most fatal of errors, from the too great indulgence of genius, return we now to that too great suppression of it, which is detrimental to Composition; and endeavour to rescue the writer, as well as the man. I have said, that some are born wise; but they, like those that are born rich, by neglecting the cultivation and produce of their own possessions, and by running in debt, may be beggared at last; and lose their reputations, as younger brothers estates, not by being born with less abilities than the rich heir, but at too late an hour.

Many a great man has been lost to himself, and the publick, purely because great ones were born before him. *Hermias,*[26] in his collections on *Homer's* blindness, says, that *Homer* requesting the gods to grant him a sight of *Achilles,* that hero rose, but in armour so bright, that it struck *Homer* blind with the

---

[22] John Duns Scotus (1265?–1308), Scottish scholastic philosopher, who opposed the ideas of St. Thomas Aquinas.

[23] "fiery vigor" and "heavenly origin."

[24] Francis Bacon, *The Advancement of* *Learning* (1605).

[25] I Cor. 1:21.

[26] A Greek philosopher of the Alexandrian school.

blaze. Let not the blaze of even *Homer's* muse darken us to the discernment of our own powers; which may possibly set us above the rank of *Imitators;* who, though most excellent, and even immortal (as some of them are) yet are still but *Dii minorum gentium,*[27] nor can expect the largest share of incense, the greatest profusion of praise, on their secondary altars.

But farther still: a spirit of *Imitation* hath many ill effects; I shall confine myself to three. *First,* It deprives the liberal and politer arts of an advantage which the mechanic enjoy: In these, men are ever endeavouring to go beyond their predecessors; in the former, to follow them. And since copies surpass not their *Originals,* as streams rise not higher than their spring, rarely so high; hence, while arts mechanic are in perpetual progress, and increase, the liberal are in retrogradation, and decay. *These* resemble pyramids, are broad at bottom, but lessen exceedingly as they rise; *Those* resemble rivers which, from a small fountain-head, are spreading ever wider and wider, as they run. Hence it is evident, that different portions of understanding are not (as some imagine) allotted to different periods of time; for we see, in the same period, understanding rising in one set of artists, and declining in another. Therefore *nature* stands absolved, and our inferiority in Composition must be charged on ourselves.

Nay, so far are we from complying with a necessity, which nature lays us under, that, *Secondly,* by a spirit of *Imitation* we counteract nature, and thwart her design. She brings us into the world all *Originals:* No two faces, no two minds, are just alike; but all bear nature's evident mark of separation on them. Born *Originals,* how comes it to pass that we die *Copies?* That meddling ape *Imitation,* as soon as we come to years of *Indiscretion* (so let me speak), snatches the pen, and blots out nature's

mark of separation, cancels her kind intention, destroys all mental individuality; the letter'd world no longer consists of singulars, it is a medly, a mass; and a hundred books, at bottom, are but One. Why are Monkies such masters of mimickry? Why receive they such a talent at imitation? Is it not as the *Spartan* slaves received a licence for ebriety;[28] that their betters might be ashamed of it?

The *Third* fault to be found with a spirit of *Imitation* is, that with great incongruity it makes us poor, and proud: makes us think little, and write much; gives us huge folios, which are little better than more reputable cushions to promote our repose. Have not some sevenfold volumes put us in mind of *Ovid's* sevenfold channels of the *Nile* at the conflagration?

> *Ostia septem*
> *Pulverulenta vacant septem sine flumine valles.*[29]

Such leaden labours are like *Lycurgus's* iron money, which was so much less in value than in bulk, that it required barns for strong-boxes, and a yoke of oxen to draw five hundred pounds.

But notwithstanding these disadvantages of *Imitation,* imitation must be the lot (and often an honourable lot it is) of most writers. If there is a famine of *invention* in the land, like *Joseph's* brethren, we must travel far for food; we must visit the remote, and rich, Antients; but an inventive genius may safely stay at home; that, like the widow's cruse,[30] is divinely replenished from within; and affords us a miraculous delight. Whether our own genius be such, or not, we diligently should inquire; that we may not go a begging with gold in our purse. For there is a mine in man, which must be deeply dug ere we can conjecture its contents. Another often sees that in us, which we see not ourselves; and may there not be that in us which is unseen

---

[27] "gods of lower rank." Source unknown. Cicero mentions *majorum gentium dii* (*Tusc.* I, xiii, 23) which Young may have in mind.

[28] drunkenness.

[29] His seven divided currents are all dry,

And where they rolled seven gaping trenches lie.
   (*Metamorphoses,* II, 255, tr. Addison.)

[30] I Kings 17.

by both? That there may, chance often discovers, either by a luckily chosen theme, or a mighty premium, or an absolute necessity of exertion, or a noble stroke of emulation from another's glory; as that on *Thucydides* from hearing *Herodotus* repeat part of his history at the *Olympic* games: Had there been no *Herodotus,* there might have been no *Thucydides,* and the world's admiration might have begun at *Livy* for excellence in that province of the pen. *Demosthenes* had the same stimulation on hearing *Callistratus;* or Tully[31] might have been the first of consummate renown at the bar.

Quite clear of the dispute concerning *antient and modern learning,* we speak not of performance, but powers. The modern powers are equal to those before them; modern performance in general is deplorably short. How great are the names just mentioned? Yet who will dare affirm, that as great may not rise up in some future, or even in the present age? Reasons there are why talents may not *appear,* none why they may not *exist,* as much in one period as another. An evocation of vegetable fruits depends on rain, air, and sun; an evocation of the fruits of genius no less depends on externals. What a marvellous crop bore it in *Greece,* and *Rome?* And what a marvellous sunshine did it there enjoy? What encouragement from the nature of their governments, and the spirit of their people? *Virgil* and *Horace* owed their divine talents to Heaven; their immortal works, to men; thank *Maecenas* and *Augustus*[32] for them. Had it not been for these, the genius of those poets had lain buried in their ashes. *Athens* expended on her theatre, painting, sculpture, and architecture, a tax levied for the support of a war. *Caesar* dropt his papers when *Tully* spoke; and *Philip* trembled at the voice of *Demosthenes:* And has there arisen but one *Tully,* one *Demosthenes,* in so long a course of years? The powerful eloquence of them both in one stream, should never bear me down into the melancholy persuasion, that several have not

been born, tho' they have not emerged. The sun as much exists in a cloudy day, as in a clear; it is outward, accidental circumstances that with regard to genius either in nation, or age,

Collectas fugat nubes, solemque reducit.[33]
VIRG.

As great, perhaps, greater than those mentioned (presumptuous as it may sound) may, possibly, arise; for who hath fathomed the mind of man? Its bounds are as unknown, as those of the creation; since the birth of which, perhaps, not One has so far exerted, as not to leave his possibilities beyond his attainments, his powers beyond his exploits. Forming our judgments, altogether by what *has* been done, without knowing, or at all inquiring, what possibly *might* have been done, we naturally enough fall into too mean an opinion of the human mind. If a sketch of the divine Iliad before *Homer* wrote, had been given to mankind, by some superior being, or otherwise, its execution would, probably, have appeared beyond the power of man. Now, to surpass it, we think impossible. As the first of these opinions would evidently have been a mistake, why may not the second be so too? Both are founded on the same bottom; on our ignorance of the possible dimensions of the mind of man.

Nor are we only ignorant of the dimensions of the human mind in general, but even of our own. That a man may be scarce less ignorant of his own powers, than an oyster of its pearl, or a rock of its diamond; that he may possess dormant, unsuspected abilities, till awakened by loud calls, or stung up by striking emergencies, is evident from the sudden eruption of some men, out of perfect obscurity, into publick admiration, on the strong impulse of some animating occasion; not more to the world's great surprize, than their own. Few authors of distinction but have experienced something of this nature, at the first beamings

---

[31] Cicero.
[32] Roman patrons of the arts.

[33] "Dispell'd the darkness, and restored the day" (Vergil, *Aeneid,* I, 143, tr. Dryden).

of their yet unsuspected genius on their hitherto dark Composition: The writer starts at it, as at a lucid meteor in the night; is much surprized; can scarce believe it true. During his happy confusion, it may be said to him, as to *Eve* at the lake,

What there thou seest, fair creature, is thyself.[34]

MILT.

Genius, in this view, is like a dear friend in our company under disguise; who, while we are lamenting his absence, drops his mask, striking us, at once, with equal surprize and joy. This sensation, which I speak of in a writer, might favour, and so promote, the fable of poetic inspiration: A poet of a strong imagination, and stronger vanity, on feeling it, might naturally enough realize the world's mere compliment, and think himself truly inspired. Which is not improbable; for enthusiasts of all kinds do no less.

Since it is plain that men may be strangers to their own abilities; and by thinking meanly of them without just cause, may possibly lose a name, perhaps a name immortal; I would find some means to prevent these evils. Whatever promotes virtue, promotes something more, and carries its good influence beyond the *moral* man: To prevent these evils, I borrow two golden rules from *ethics,* which are no less golden in *Composition,* than in life. 1. *Know thyself;* 2dly, *Reverence thyself.* I design to repay ethics in a future letter, by two rules from rhetoric for its service.

1st. *Know thyself.* Of ourselves it may be said, as *Martial* says of a bad neighbour,

Nil tam prope, proculque nobis.[35]

Therefore dive deep into thy bosom; learn the depth, extent, biass, and full fort of thy mind; contract full intimacy with the stranger within thee; excite and cherish every spark of intellectual light and heat, however smothered under for-

mer negligence, or scattered through the dull, dark mass of common thoughts; and collecting them into a body, let thy genius rise (if a genius thou hast) as the sun from chaos; and if I should then say, like an *Indian, Worship it,* (though too bold) yet should I say little more than my second rule enjoins, (*viz.*) *Reverence thyself.*

That is, let not great examples, or authorities, browbeat thy reason into too great a diffidence of thyself: Thyself so reverence, as to prefer the native growth of thy own mind to the richest import from abroad; such borrowed riches make us poor. The man who thus reverences himself, will soon find the world's reverence to follow his own. His works will stand distinguished; his the sole property of them; which property alone can confer the noble title of an *author;* that is, of one who (to speak accurately) *thinks,* and *composes;* while other invaders of the press, how voluminous, and learned soever, (with due respect be it spoken) only *read,* and *write.*

This is the difference between those two luminaries in literature, the well-accomplished scholar, and the divinely-inspired enthusiast; the *first* is, as the bright morning star; the *second,* as the rising sun. The writer who neglects those two rules above will never stand alone; he makes one of a group, and thinks in wretched unanimity with the throng: Incumbered with the notions of others, and impoverished by their abundance, he conceives not the least embryo of new thought; opens not the least vista thro' the gloom of ordinary writers, into the bright walks of rare imagination, and singular design; while the true genius is crossing all publick roads into fresh untrodden ground; he, up to the knees in antiquity, is treading the sacred footsteps of great examples, with the blind veneration of a bigot saluting the papal toe; comfortably hoping full absolution for the sins of his own understanding, from the powerful charm of touching his idol's infallibility.

[34] Milton, *Paradise Lost,* IV, 468.
[35] "Nothing so intimate and at the same time so removed from us" (*Epigrams,* I, lxxxvii, 10).

Such meanness of mind, such prostration of our own powers, proceeds from too great admiration of others. Admiration has, generally, a degree of two very bad ingredients in it; of ignorance, and of fear; and does mischief in Composition, and in life. Proud as the world is, there is more superiority in it *given,* than *assumed:* And its grandees of all kinds owe more of their elevation to the littleness of others minds, than to the greatness of their own. Were not prostrate spirits their voluntary pedestals, the figure they make among mankind would not stand so high. *Imitators* and *Translators* are somewhat of the pedestal-kind, and sometimes rather raise their *Original's* reputation, by showing him to be by them inimitable, than their own. *Homer* has been translated into most languages; *Ælian* tells us,[36] that the *Indians,* (hopeful tutors!) have taught him to speak their tongue. What expect we from them? Not *Homer's Achilles,* but something, which, like *Patroclus,*[37] assumes his name, and, at its peril, appears in his stead; nor expect we *Homer's Ulysses,* gloriously bursting out of his cloud into royal grandeur, but an *Ulysses* under disguise, and a beggar to the last. Such is that inimitable father of poetry, and oracle of all the wise, whom *Lycurgus* transcribed; and for an annual public recital of whose works *Solon* enacted a law[38]; that it is much to be feared, that his so numerous translations are but as the publish'd testimonials of so many nations, and ages, that this author so divine is untranslated still.

But here,

> *Cynthius aurem*
> *Vellit,* . . .
>
> VIRG.[39]

and demands justice for his favourite, and ours. Great things he has done; but he might have done greater. What a fall is it from *Homer's* numbers, free as air, lofty and harmonious as the spheres, into childish shackles, and tinkling sounds! But, in his fall, he is still great—

> *Nor appears*
> *Less than archangel ruin'd, and the excess*
> *Of glory obscur'd.* . . .
>
> MILT.[40]

Had *Milton* never wrote, *Pope* had been less to blame:[41] But when in *Milton's* genius, *Homer,* as it were, personally rose to forbid *Britons* doing him that ignoble wrong; it is less pardonable, by that *effeminate* decoration, to put *Achilles* in petticoats a second time: How much nobler had it been, if his numbers had rolled on in full flow, through the various modulations of *masculine* melody, into those grandeurs of solemn sound, which are indispensably demanded by the native dignity of heroick song? How much nobler, if he had resisted the temptation of that Gothic dæmon, which modern poesy tasting, became mortal? O how unlike the deathless, divine harmony of three great names (how justly join'd!), of *Milton, Greece,* and *Rome?* His verse, but for this little speck of mortality, in its extreme parts, as his hero had in his heel; like him, had been invulnerable, and immortal. But, unfortunately, *that* was undipt in *Helicon;* as *this,* in *Styx.* Harmony as well as eloquence is essential to poesy; and a murder of his musick is putting half *Homer* to death. *Blank* is a term of diminution; what we mean by blank verse, is, verse unfallen, uncurst; verse reclaim'd, reinthron'd in the true *language of the gods;* who never thunder'd, nor suffer'd their *Homer* to thunder, in rhime; and therefore, I beg you, my Friend, to crown it with some nobler term; nor let the greatness of the thing lie under the defamation of such a name.

---

[36] Claudius Aelianus (d. *c.* 222) in his *Variae Historiae.*

[37] In the *Iliad,* Patroclus was killed fighting in the armor of his friend Achilles.

[38] Young's assumption of a share that the law-givers of Sparta (Lycurgus) and Athens (Solon) may have had in the transmission of the Homeric poems, now largely discredited, was conventional in his time.

[39] "Apollo tweaks my ear" (*Eclogues,* vi, 4–5).

[40] *Paradise Lost,* I, 592–594.

[41] Young is referring to the rhymed couplets of Pope's translations of the *Iliad* and *Odyssey.*

But supposing *Pope's Iliad* to have been perfect in its kind; yet it is a *Translation* still; which differs as much from an *Original,* as the moon from the sun.

　　. . . *Phoeben alieno jusserat igne*
Impleri, solemque suo.[42]
　　　　　　　CLAUD.

But as nothing is more easy than to write originally wrong; Originals are not here recommended, but under the strong guard of my first rule—*Know thyself.* *Lucian,* who was an Original, neglected not this rule, if we may judge by his reply to one who took some freedom with him. He was, at first, an apprentice to a statuary; and when he was reflected on as such, by being called *Prometheus,* he replied, "I am indeed the inventor of new work, the model of which I owe to none; and, if I do not execute it well, I deserve to be torn by twelve vulturs, instead of one."

If so, O *Gulliver!*[43] dost thou not shudder at thy brother *Lucian's* vulturs hovering o'er thee? Shudder on! they cannot shock thee more, than decency has been shock'd by thee. How have thy *Houyhnhunms* thrown thy judgment from its seat, and laid thy imagination in the mire? In what ordure hast thou dipt thy pencil? What a monster hast thou made of the

　　. . . *Human face divine?*
　　　　　　MILT.[44]

This writer has so satirised human nature, as to give a demonstration in himself, that it deserves to be satirised. But, say his wholesale admirers, Few could *so* have written; true, and Fewer *would.* If it required great abilities to commit the fault, greater still would have saved him from it. But whence arise such warm advocates for such a performance? From hence, *viz.* before a character is established, merit makes fame; afterwards fame makes merit. *Swift* is not commended for this piece, but this piece for *Swift.* He has given us some beauties which deserve all our praise; and our comfort is, that his faults will not become common; for none can be guilty of them, but who have wit as well as reputation to spare. His wit had been less wild, if his temper had not jostled his judgment. If his favourite *Houyhnhunms* could write, and *Swift* had been one of them, every horse with him would have been an ass, and he would have written a panegyrick on mankind, saddling with much reproach the present heroes of his pen: On the contrary, being born amongst men, and, of consequence, piqued by many, and peevish at more, he has blasphemed a nature little lower than that of angels, and assumed by far higher than they: But surely the contempt of the world is not a greater virtue, than the contempt of mankind is a vice. Therefore I wonder that, though forborn by others, the laughter-loving *Swift* was not reproved by the venerable Dean, who could sometimes be very grave.

For I remember, as I and others were taking with him an evening's walk, about a mile out of *Dublin,* he stopt short; we passed on; but perceiving that he did not follow us, I went back; and found him fixed as a statue, and earnestly gazing upward at a noble elm, which in its uppermost branches was much withered, and decayed. Pointing at it, he said, "I shall be like that tree, I shall die at top." As in this he seemed to prophesy like the Sybils; if, like one of them, he had burnt part of his works, especially *this* blasted branch of a noble genius, like her too, he might have risen in his demand for the rest.

---

[42] "He had asked the vacillating moon to shine with borrowed light, the sun with its own" (Claudian, *First Book against Rufinus,* III, 9).

[43] i.e., Swift, by his satire of man in the character of the Yahoos in the fourth book of *Gulliver's Travels,* "A Voyage to the Houyhnhnms," or the land of the horses.

[44] *Paradise Lost,* III, 44.

Would not his friend *Pope* have succeeded better in an *original* attempt? Talents untried are talents unknown. All that I know, is, that, contrary to these sentiments, he was not only an avowed professor of imitation, but a zealous recommender of it also. Nor could he recommend any thing better, except emulation, to those who write. One of these all writers must call to their aid; but aids they are of unequal repute. Imitation is inferiority confessed; emulation is superiority contested, or denied; imitation is servile, emulation generous; that fetters, this fires; that may give a name; this, a name immortal: This made *Athens* to succeeding ages the rule of taste, and the standard of perfection. Her men of genius struck fire against each other; and kindled, by conflict, into glories, which no time shall extinguish. We thank *Eschylus* for *Sophocles;*[45] and *Parrhasius* for *Zeuxis;*[46] emulation, for both. That bids us fly the general fault of *imitators;* bids us not be struck with the loud report of former fame, as with a knell, which damps the spirits; but, as with a trumpet, which inspires ardour to rival the renown'd. Emulation exhorts us, instead of learning our discipline for ever, like raw troops, under antient leaders in composition, to put those laurel'd veterans in some hazard of losing their superior posts in glory.

Such is emulation's high-spirited advice, such her immortalizing call. *Pope* would not hear, pre-engaged with imitation, which blessed him with all her charms. He chose rather, with his namesake of *Greece,* to triumph in the old world, than to look out for a new. His taste partook the error of his religion; it denied not worship to saints and angels; that is, to writers, who, canonized for ages, have received their apotheosis from established and universal fame. True poesy, like true religion, abhors idolatry; and though it honours the memory of the exemplary, and takes them willingly (yet cautiously) as guides in the way to glory; real, though unexampled, excellence is its only aim; nor looks it for any inspiration less than divine.

Though *Pope's* noble muse may boast her illustrious descent from *Homer, Virgil, Horace,* yet is an *Original* author more nobly born. As *Tacitus* says of *Curtius Rufus,*[47] an *Original* author is born of himself, is his own progenitor, and will probably propagate a numerous offspring of imitators, to eternize his glory; while mule-like imitators die without issue. Therefore, though we stand much obliged for his giving us an *Homer,* yet had he doubled our obligation, by giving us—a *Pope.* Had he a strong imagination, and the true sublime? That granted, we might have had two *Homers* instead of one, if longer had been his life; for I heard the dying swan talk over an epic plan a few weeks before his decease.

Bacon, under the shadow of whose great name I would shelter my present attempt in favour of *Originals,* says, "Men seek not to know their own stock, and abilities; but fancy their possessions to be greater, and their abilities less, than they really are."[48] Which is, in effect, saying, "That we ought to exert more than we do; and that, on exertion, our probability of success is greater than we conceive."

Nor have I *Bacon's* opinion only, but his assistance too, on my side. His mighty mind travelled round the intellectual world; and, with a more than eagle's eye, saw, and has pointed out, blank spaces, or dark spots in it, on which the human mind never shone: Some of these have been enlightened since; some are benighted still.

Moreover, so boundless are the bold excursions of the human mind, that in the vast void beyond real existence, it can call forth shadowy beings, and unknown worlds, as numerous, as bright, and, perhaps, as lasting, as the stars; such quite-

---

45 Greek classical dramatists.
46 Greek classical painters.
47 Cornelius Tacitus (*c.* 55–*c.* 120), speaking of Quintus Curtius Rufus, first-century Roman biographer of Alexander the Great, in *Annalia,* XI, xxi, 10–11.
48 In *The Advancement of Learning.*

original beauties we may call paradisaical,

Natos sine semine flores.
OVID.[49]

When such an ample area for renowned adventure in *original* attempts lies before us, shall we be as mere leaden pipes, conveying to the present age small streams of excellence from its grand reservoir in antiquity; and those too, perhaps, mudded in the pass? *Originals* shine, like comets; have no peer in their path; are rival'd by none, and the gaze of all: All other compositions (if they shine at all) shine in clusters; like the stars in the galaxy; where, like bad neighbours, all suffer from all; each particular being diminished, and almost lost in the throng.

If thoughts of this nature prevailed; if antients and moderns were no longer considered as masters and pupils, but as hard-matched rivals for renown; then moderns, by the longevity of their labours, might, one day, become antients themselves: And old time, that best weigher of merits, to keep his balance even, might have the golden weight of an *Augustan* age in both his scales: Or rather our scale might descend; and that of antiquity (as a modern match for it strongly speaks) might *kick the beam.*

And why not? For, consider, *since* an impartial Providence scatters talents indifferently, as thro' all orders of persons, so thro' all periods of time; *since,* a marvellous light, unenjoy'd of old, is pour'd on us by revelation, with larger prospects extending our understanding, with brighter objects enriching our imagination, with an inestimable prize setting our passions on fire, thus strengthening every power that enables composition to shine; *since,* there has been no fall in man on this side *Adam,* who left no works, and the works of all other antients are our auxiliars against themselves, as being perpetual spurs to our ambition, and shining lamps in our path to fame; *since,* this world is a school, as

well for intellectual, as moral, advance; and the longer human nature is at school, the better scholar it should be; *since,* as the moral world expects its glorious millennium, the world intellectual may hope, by the rules of analogy, for some superior degrees of excellence to crown her later scenes; nor may it only hope, but must enjoy them too; for *Tully, Quintilian,* and all true critics allow, that virtue assists genius, and that the writer will be more able, when better is the man—All these particulars, I say, considered, why should it seem altogether impossible, that heaven's latest editions of the human mind may be the most correct, and fair; that the day may come, when the moderns may proudly look back on the comparative darkness of former ages, on the children of antiquity; reputing *Homer* and *Demosthenes,* as the dawn of divine genius; and *Athens* as the cradle of infant fame; what a glorious revolution would this make in the rolls of renown?

What a rant, say you, is here?— I partly grant it: Yet, consider, my friend! knowledge physical, mathematical, moral, and divine, increases; all arts and sciences are making considerable advance; with them, all the accommodations, ornaments, delights, and glories of human life; and these are new food to the genius of a polite writer; these are as the root, and composition, as the flower; and as the root spreads, and thrives, shall the flower fail? As well may a flower flourish, when the root is dead. It is prudence to read, genius to relish, glory to surpass, antient authors; and wisdom to try our strength, in an attempt in which it would be no great dishonour to fail.

Why condemn'd *Maro*[50] his admirable epic to the flames? Was it not because his discerning eye saw some length of perfection beyond it? And what he saw, may not others reach? And who bid fairer than our countrymen for that glory? Something new may be expected from *Britons* particularly; who seem not to be more sever'd from the rest of mankind by the surrounding sea, than by the

---

[49] "Flowers come into being without seed" (*Metamorphoses*, I, 108).

[50] Vergil, who expressed a desire on his deathbed to destroy the *Aeneid.*

current in their veins; and of whom little more appears to be required, in order to give us *Originals,* than a consistency of character, and making their compositions of a piece with their lives. May our genius shine; and proclaim us in that nobler view!

. . . *minimâ contentos nocte Britannos.*
VIRG.[51]

And so it does; for in polite composition, in natural, and mathematical, knowledge, we have great *Originals* already; *Bacon, Boyle,*[52] *Newton, Shakespeare, Milton,* have showed us, that all the winds cannot blow the British flag farther, than an original spirit can convey the *British* fame; their names go round the world; and what foreign genius strikes not as they pass? Why should not their posterity embark in the same bold bottom of new enterprize, and hope the same success? Hope it they may; or you must assert, either that those *Originals,* which we already enjoy, were written by angels, or deny that we are men. As *Simonides* said to *Pausanias,*[53] reason should say to the writer, "Remember thou art a man." And for man not to grasp at all which is laudable within his reach, is a dishonour to human nature, and a disobedience to the divine; for as heaven does nothing in vain, its gift of talents implies an injunction of their use.

A friend of mine[54] has obeyed that injunction; he has relied on himself, and with a genius, as well *moral,* as *original* (to speak in bold terms), has cast out evil spirits; has made a convert to virtue of a species of composition, once most its foe. As the first christian emperors expell'd dæmons, and dedicated their temples to the living God.

But you, I know, are sparing in your praise of this author; therefore I will speak of one, which is sure of your applause. *Shakespeare* mingled no water with his wine, lower'd his genius by no vapid imitation. *Shakespeare* gave us a *Shakespeare,* nor could the first in antient fame have given us more. *Shakespeare* is not their son, but brother; their equal; and that, in spite of all his faults. Think you this too bold? Consider, in those antients what is it the world admires? Not the fewness of their faults, but the number and brightness of their beauties; and if *Shakespeare* is their equal (as he doubtless is) in that, which in them is admired, then is *Shakespeare* as great as they; and not impotence, but some other cause, must be charged with his defects. When we are setting these great men in competition, what but the comparative size of their genius is the subject of our inquiry? And a giant loses nothing of his size, tho' he should chance to trip in his race. But it is a compliment to those heroes of antiquity to suppose *Shakespeare* their equal only in dramatic powers; therefore, though his faults had been greater, the scale would still turn in his favour. There is at least as much genius on the *British* as on the *Grecian* stage, tho' the former is not swept so clean; so clean from violations not only of the *dramatic,* but *moral* rule; for an honest heathen, on reading some of our celebrated scenes, might be seriously concerned to see, that our obligations to the religion of nature were cancel'd by Christianity.

Johnson,[55] in the serious drama, is as much an imitator, as *Shakespeare* is an original. He was very learned, as *Sampson* was very strong, to his own hurt: Blind to the nature of tragedy, he pulled down all antiquity on his head, and buried himself under it; we see nothing of *Johnson,* nor indeed, of his admired (but also murdered) antients; for what shone

---

[51] "Britons content with the very briefest night." Young was mistaken in attributing this phrase to Virgil. It is from Juvenal (*Saturae,* II, 161).
[52] Robert Boyle (1627–1691), British chemist.
[53] Simonides of Ceos (*c.* 556–469 B.C.), a Greek lyric poet and intimate friend of Pausanias, a Spartan general.
[54] A complimentary allusion to Richardson for his accomplishments in the field of the novel.
[55] Ben Jonson (1573?–1637).

in the historian is a cloud on the poet; and *Cataline* might have been a good play, if *Salust* had never writ.[56]

Who knows whether *Shakespeare* might not have thought less, if he had read more? Who knows if he might not have laboured under the load of *Johnson's* learning, as *Enceladus* under *Ætna?*[57] His mighty genius, indeed, through the most mountainous oppression would have breathed out some of his inextinguishable fire; yet, possibly, he might not have risen up into that giant, that much more than common man, at which we now gaze with amazement, and delight. Perhaps he was as learned as his dramatic province required; for whatever other learning he wanted, he was master of two books, unknown to many of the profoundly read, though books, which the last conflagration alone can destroy; the book of nature, and that of man. These he had by heart, and has transcribed many admirable pages of them, into his immortal works. These are the fountain-head, whence the *Castalian*[58] streams of *original* composition flow; and these are often mudded by other waters, tho' waters in their distinct channel, most wholesome and pure: As two chymical liquors, separately clear as crystal, grow foul by mixture, and offend the sight. So that he had not only as much learning as his dramatic province required, but, perhaps, as it could safely bear. If *Milton* had spared some of his learning, his muse would have gained more glory, than he would have lost, by it.

Dryden, destitute of *Shakespeare's* genius, had almost as much learning as *Johnson,* and, for the buskin,[59] quite as little taste. He was a stranger to the pathos, and, by numbers, expression, sentiment, and every other dramatic cheat, strove to make amends for it; as if a saint could make amends for the want of conscience; a soldier, for the want of valour; or a vestal, of modesty. The noble nature of tragedy disclaims an equivalent; like virtue, it demands the heart; and *Dryden* had none to give. Let epic poets *think,* the tragedian's point is rather to *feel;* such distant things are a tragedian and a poet, that the latter indulged, destroys the former. Look on *Barnwell,* and *Essex,*[60] and see how as to these distant characters *Dryden* excells, and is excelled. But the strongest demonstration of his no-taste for the buskin, are his tragedies fringed with rhyme; which, in epic poetry, is a sore disease, in the tragic, absolute death. To *Dryden's* enormity, *Pope's* was a light offence. As lacemen are foes to mourning, these two authors, rich in rhyme, were no great friends to those solemn ornaments, which the noble nature of their works required.

Must rhyme then, say you, be banished? I wish the nature of our language could bear its intire expulsion; but our lesser poetry stands in need of a toleration for it; it raises that, but sinks the great; as spangles adorn children, but expose men. Prince *Henry* bespangled all over in his oylet-hole suit, with glittering pins; and an *Achilles,* or an *Almanzor,* in his *Gothic* array; [61] are very much on a level, as to the majesty of the poet, and the prince. *Dryden* had a great, but a general capacity; and as for a general genius, there is no such thing in nature: A genius implies the rays of the mind concenter'd, and determined to some particular point; when they are scatter'd widely, they act feebly, and strike not with sufficient force, to fire, or dissolve, the heart. As what comes from the writer's heart, reaches ours; so what comes from his head, sets our brains at work, and our hearts at ease. It makes a circle of thoughtful critics, not of distressed

---

[56] Sallust, the Roman historian from whom Jonson would ultimately have derived the story on which his tragedy of *Catiline* (1611) is based.

[57] The punishment Enceladus was subjected to for participating in the revolt of the Titans against Jupiter in classical mythology.

[58] The fountain at the foot of Mount Parnassus, sacred to the Muses.

[59] tragedy.

[60] Characters in plays of Young's time: George Lillo, *The London Merchant: or, the History of George Barnwell* (1731) and Henry Brooke, *The Earl of Essex* (1750).

[61] Characters in plays by Dryden.

patients; and a passive audience, is what tragedy requires. Applause is not to be given, but extorted; and the silent lapse of a single tear, does the writer more honour, than the rattling thunder of a thousand hands. Applauding hands, and dry eyes (which during *Dryden's* theatrical reign often met) are a satire on the writer's talent, and the spectator's taste. When by such judges the laurel is blindly given, and by such a poet proudly received, they resemble an intoxicated hoste, and his tasteless guests, over some sparkling adulteration, commending their Champaign.

But *Dryden* has his glory, tho' not on the stage: What an inimitable *original* is his ode? A small one, indeed, but of the first lustre, and without a flaw; and, amid the brightest boasts of antiquity, it may find a foil.

Among the brightest of the moderns, Mr. *Addison* must take his place. Who does not approach his character with great respect? They who refuse to close with the public in his praise, refuse at their peril. But, if men will be fond of their own opinions, some hazard must be run. He had, what *Dryden* and *Johnson* wanted, a warm, and feeling heart; but, being of a grave and bashful nature, thro' a philosophic reserve, and a sort of moral prudery, he conceal'd it, where he should have let loose all his fire, and have show'd the most tender sensibilities of heart. At his celebrated *Cato*,[62] few tears are shed, but *Cato's* own; which, indeed, are truly great, but unaffecting, except to the noble few, who love their country better than themselves. The bulk of mankind want virtue enough to be touched by them. His strength of genius has reared up one glorious image, more lofty, and truly golden, than that in the plains of *Dura*,[63] for cool admiration to gaze at, and warm patriotism (how rare!) to worship; while those two throbbing pulses of the drama, by which alone it is shown to live, *terror* and *pity*, neglected thro' the whole, leave our unmolested

hearts at perfect peace. Thus the poet, like his hero, thro' mistaken excellence, and virtue overstrain'd, becomes a sort of suicide; and that which is most dramatic in the drama, dies. All his charms of poetry are but as funeral flowers, which adorn; all his noble sentiments but as rich spices, which embalm, the tragedy deceased.

Of tragedy, pathos is not only the life and soul, but the soul inextinguishable; it charms us thro' a thousand faults. Decorations, which in this author abound, tho' they might immortalize other poesy, are the *splendida peccata*[64] which damn the drama; while, on the contrary, the murder of all other beauties is a venial sin, nor plucks the laurel from the tragedian's brow. Was it otherwise, *Shakespeare* himself would run some hazard of losing his crown.

Socrates frequented the plays of *Euripides;* and, what living *Socrates* would decline the theatre, at the representation of *Cato?* *Tully's* assassins found him in his litter, reading the *Medea* of the *Grecian* poet,[65] to prepare himself for death. Part of *Cato* might be read to the same end. In the weight and dignity of moral reflection, *Addison* resembles that poet, who was called the dramatic philosopher; and is himself, as he says of *Cato, ambitiously sententious*. But as to the singular talent so remarkable in *Euripides,* at melting down hearts into the tender streams of grief and pity, there the resemblance fails. His beauties sparkle, but do not warm; they sparkle as stars in a frosty night. There is, indeed, a constellation in his play; there is the philosopher, patriot, orator, and poet; but where is the tragedian? And, if that is wanting,

Cur in theatrum Cato severe venisti?
                                        MART.[66]

And, when I recollect what passed between him and *Dryden,* in relation to this drama, I must add the next line,

---

[62] A tragedy first produced in 1713.

[63] In the vicinity of Babylon, where Nebuchadnezzar erected a golden image (Dan., 3, 1).

[64] "sparkling sins."

[65] Euripides.

[66] "Grave Cato, why do you enter the theatre?" The next line: "Did you come just so that you can leave?" (*Epigrams*, I, 3-4.)

An ideo tantum veneras, ut exires?

For, when *Addison* was a student at *Oxford,* he sent up this play to his friend *Dryden,* as a proper person to recommend it to the theatre, if it deserved it; who returned it, with very great commendation; but with his opinion, that, on the stage, it could not meet with its deserved success. But tho' the performance was denied the theatre, it brought its author on the public stage of life. For persons in power inquiring soon after of the head of his college for a youth of parts, *Addison* was recommended, and readily received, by means of the great reputation which *Dryden* had just then spread of him above.

There is this similitude between the poet and the play; as this is more fit for the closet than the stage; so, that shone brighter in private conversation than on the public scene. They both had a sort of *local* excellency, as the heathen gods a local divinity; beyond such a bound *they,* unadmired; and *these,* unadored. This puts me in mind of *Plato,* who denied *Homer* to the public;[67] that *Homer,* which, when in his closet, was rarely out of his hand. Thus, tho' *Cato* is not calculated to signalize himself in the warm emotions of the theatre, yet we find him a most amiable companion, in our calmer delights of recess.

Notwithstanding what has been offered, this, in many views, is an exquisite piece. But there is so much more of art, than nature in it, that I can scarce forbear calling it, an exquisite piece of statuary,

Where the smooth chisel all its skill has shown,
To soften into flesh the rugged stone.
                              ADDISON.[68]

That is, where art has taken great pains to labour undramatic matter into dramatic life; which is impossible. However, as it is, like *Pygmalion,* we cannot but fall in love with it, and wish it was alive. How would a *Shakespeare,* or an *Otway,*[69] have answered our wishes? They would have outdone *Prometheus,* and, with their heavenly fire, have given him not only life, but immortality. At their dramas (such is the force of nature) the poet is out of sight, quite hid behind his *Venus,* never thought of, till the curtain falls. Art brings our author forward, he stands before his piece; splendidly indeed, but unfortunately; for the writer must be forgotten by his audience, during the representation, if for ages he would be remembered by posterity. In the theatre, as in life, delusion is the charm; and we are undelighted, the first moment we are undeceived. Such demonstration have we, that the theatre is not yet opened, in which solid happiness can be found by man; because none are more than comparatively good; and folly has a corner in the heart of the wise.

A genius fond of *ornament* should not be wedded to the tragic muse, which is in *mourning:* We want not to be diverted at an entertainment, where our greatest pleasure arises from the depth of our concern. But whence (by the way) this odd generation of pleasure from pain? The movement of our melancholy passions is pleasant, when we ourselves are safe: We love to be at once, miserable, and unhurt: So are we made; and so made, perhaps, to show us the divine goodness; to show that none of our passions were designed to give us pain, except when being pain'd is for our advantage on the whole; which is evident from this instance, in which we see, that passions the most painful administer greatly, sometimes, to our delight. Since great names have accounted otherwise for this particular, I wish this solution, though to me probable, may not prove a mistake.

To close our thoughts on *Cato:* He who sees not much beauty in it, has no taste for poetry; he who sees nothing else, has no taste for the stage. Whilst it justifies censure, it extorts applause. It is

---

[67] In *The Republic,* from which the poet is banished.

[68] *A Letter from Italy* (1704), ll. 85–86.

[69] Thomas Otway (1652–1685), author of two tragedies in blank verse, still popular in Young's day: *The Orphan* (1680) and *Venice Preserved* (1682).

much to be admired, but little to be felt. Had it not been a tragedy, it had been immortal; as it is a tragedy, its uncommon fate somewhat resembles his, who, for conquering gloriously, was condemn'd to die. Both shone, but shone fatally; because in breach of their respective laws, the laws of the drama, and the laws of arms. But how rich in reputation must that author be, who can spare a *Cato,* without feeling the loss?

That loss by our author would scarce be felt; it would be but dropping a single feather from a wing, that mounts him above his cotemporaries. He has a more refined, decent, judicious, and extensive genius, than *Pope,* or *Swift.* To distinguish this triumvirate from each other, and, like *Newton,* to discover the different colours in these genuine and meridian rays of literary light,[70] *Swift* is a singular wit, *Pope* a correct poet, *Addison* a great author. *Swift* looked on wit as the *jus divinum*[71] to dominion and sway in the world; and considered as usurpation, all power that was lodged in persons of less sparkling understandings. This inclined him to tyranny in wit; *Pope* was somewhat of his opinion, but was for softening tyranny into lawful monarchy; yet were there some acts of severity in his reign. *Addison's* crown was elective, he reigned by the public voice:

. . . *Volentes*
Per populos dat jura, viamque affectat Olympo.

VIRG.[72]

But as good books are the medicine of the mind, if we should dethrone these authors, and consider them, not in their royal, but their medicinal capacity, might it not then be said, that *Addison* prescribed a wholesome and pleasant regimen, which was universally relished, and

did much good; that *Pope* preferred a purgative of satire, which, tho' wholesome, was too painful in its operation; and that *Swift* insisted on a large dose of ipecacuanha,[73] which, tho' readily swallowed from the fame of the physician, yet, if the patient had any delicacy of taste, he threw up the remedy, instead of the disease?

Addison wrote little in verse, much in sweet, elegant, *Virgilian,* prose; so let me call it,[74] since *Longinus* calls *Herodotus* most *Homeric,* and *Thucydides* is said to have formed his style on *Pindar. Addison's* compositions are built with the finest materials, in the taste of the antients, and (to speak his own language) on truly *Classic ground:* And tho' they are the delight of the present age, yet am I persuaded that they will receive more justice from posterity. I never read him, but I am struck with such a disheartening idea of perfection, that I drop my pen. And, indeed, far superior writers should forget his compositions, if they would be greatly pleased with their own.

And yet (perhaps you have not observed it) what is the common language of the world, and even of his admirers, concerning him? They call him an *elegant* writer: That elegance which shines on the surface of his compositions, seems to dazzle their understanding, and render it a little blind to the depth of sentiment, which lies beneath: Thus (hard fate!) he loses reputation with them, by doubling his title to it. On subjects the most interesting, and important, no author of his age has written with greater, I had almost said, with equal weight: And they who commend him for his elegance, pay him such a sort of compliment, by their abstemious praise, as they would pay to *Lucretia,*[75] if they should commend her only for her beauty.

But you say, that you know his value

---

[70] Newton's *Opticks* (1704) had explained the separation of light into various colors by prismatic defraction.

[71] "divine right."

[72] With arts of peace the willing people draws;
On the glad Earth the golden age renews,
And his great father's path to Heaven pursues.

(*Georgics,* IV, 561–562, tr. Dryden.)

[73] Root of a South American plant used as an emetic.

[74] i.e., attributing poetic quality to a prose writer.

[75] A Roman heroine whose name implies preference for death to dishonor.

already—You know, indeed, the value of his writings, and close with the world in thinking them immortal; but, I believe, you know not, that his name would have deserved immortality, tho' he had never written; and that, by a better title than the pen can give: You know too, that his life was amiable; but, perhaps, you are still to learn, that his death was triumphant: That is a glory granted to very few: And the paternal hand of Providence, which, sometimes, snatches home its beloved children in a moment, must convince us, that it is a glory of no great consequence to the dying individual; that, when it is granted, it is granted chiefly for the sake of the surviving world, which may profit by his pious example, to whom is indulged the strength, and opportunity to make his virtue shine out brightest at the point of death: And, here, permit me to take notice, that the world will, probably, profit more by a pious example of lay-extraction, than by one born of the church; the latter being, usually, taxed with an abatement of influence by the bulk of mankind: Therefore, to smother a bright example of this superior good influence, may be reputed a sort of murder injurious to the living, and unjust to the dead.

Such an example have we in *Addison;* which, tho' hitherto suppressed, yet, when once known, is insuppressible, of a nature too rare, too striking to be forgotten. For, after a long, and manly, but vain struggle with his distemper, he dismissed his physicians, and with them all hopes of life: But with his hopes of life he dismissed not his concern for the living, but sent for a youth nearly related, and finely accomplished, yet not above being the better for good impressions from a dying friend: He came; but life now glimmering in the socket, the dying friend was silent: After a decent, and proper pause, the youth said, "Dear Sir! you sent for me: I believe, and I hope, that you have some commands; I shall hold them most sacred:" May distant ages not only hear, but feel, the reply!

Forcibly grasping the youth's hand, he softly said, "See in what peace a Christian can die." He spoke with difficulty, and soon expired. Thro' grace divine, how great is man! Thro' divine mercy, how stingless death! Who would not thus expire?

What an inestimable legacy were those *few dying words* to the youth beloved? What a glorious supplement to his own valuable fragment on the truth of Christianity? What a full demonstration, that his fancy could not feign beyond what his virtue could reach? For when he would strike us most strongly with the grandeur of *Roman* magnanimity, his dying hero is ennobled with this sublime sentiment,

While yet I live, let me not live in vain.
CATO.[76]

But how much more sublime is that sentiment when realized in life; when dispelling the languors, and appeasing the pains of a last hour; and brightening with illustrious action the dark avenue, and all-awful confines of an eternity? When his soul scarce animated his body, strong faith, and ardent charity, animated his soul into divine ambition of saving more than his own. It is for our honour, and our advantage, to hold him high in our esteem: For the better men are, the more they will admire him; and the more they admire him, the better will they be.

By undrawing the long-closed curtain of his deathbed, have I not showed you a stranger in him whom you knew so well? Is not this of your favourite author,

. . . Notâ major imago?
VIRG.[77]

His compositions are but a noble preface; the grand work is his death: That is a work which is read in heaven: How has it join'd the final approbation of angels to the previous applause of men? How gloriously has he opened a splendid path, thro' fame immortal, into eternal peace?

---

[76] Addison's *Cato*, V, i, 172.

[77] "Larger than life" (*Aeneid*, II, 773, tr. Dryden).

How has he given religion to triumph amidst the ruins of his nature? And, stronger than death, risen higher in virtue when breathing his last?

If all our men of genius had *so* breathed their last; if all our men of genius, like him, had been men of genius for *eternals; then,* had we never been pained by the report of a latter end—oh! how unlike to this? But a little to balance our pain, let us consider, that such reports as make us, at once, adore, and tremble, are of use, when too many there are, who must tremble before they will adore; and who convince us, to our shame, that the surest refuge of our endanger'd virtue is in the fears and terrors of the disingenuous human heart.

"But reports, you say, may be false; and you farther ask me, If all reports were true, how came an anecdote of so much honour to human nature, as mine, to lie so long unknown? What inauspicious planet interposed to lay its lustre under so lasting and so surprising an eclipse?"

The fact is indisputably true; nor are you to rely on me for the truth of it: My report is but a second edition: It was published before, tho' obscurely, and with a cloud before it. As clouds before the sun are often beautiful; so, this of which I speak. How finely pathetic are those two lines, which this so solemn and affecting scene inspired?

He taught us how to live; and, oh! too high
A price for knowledge, taught us how to die.

TICKELL.[78]

With truth wrapped in darkness, so sung our oracle to the public, but explained himself to me: He was present at his patron's death, and that account of it here given, he gave to me before his eyes were dry: By what means *Addison taught us how to die,* the poet left to be made known by a late, and less able hand; but one more zealous for his patron's glory: Zealous, and impotent, as

[78] Thomas Tickell, *To the Earl of Warwick on the Death of Mr. Addison* (1721), ll. 81–82.

the poor *Ægyptian,* who gather'd a few splinters of a broken boat, as a funeral pile for the great *Pompey,* studious of doing honour to so renown'd a name: Yet had not this poor plank (permit me, here, so to call this imperfect page) been thrown out, the chief article of his patron's glory would probably have been sunk for ever, and late ages have received but a fragment of his fame: A fragment glorious indeed, for his genius how bright! But to commend him for composition, tho' immortal, is detraction *now;* if there our encomium ends: Let us look farther to that concluding scene, which spoke human nature not unrelated to the divine. To that let us pay the long, and large arrear of our greatly posthumous applause.

This you will think a long digression; and justly; if that may be called a digression, which was my chief inducement for writing at all: I had long wished to deliver up to the public this sacred deposit, which by Providence was lodged in my hands; and I entered on the present undertaking partly as an introduction to that, which is more worthy to see the light; of which I gave an intimation in the beginning of my letter: For this is the *monumental marble* there mentioned, to which I promised to conduct you; this is the *sepulchral lamp,* the long-hidden lustre of our accomplished countryman, who now rises, as from his tomb, to receive the regard so greatly due to the dignity of his death; a death to be distinguished by tears of joy; a death which angels beheld with delight.

And shall that, which would have shone conspicious amid the resplendent lights of Christianity's glorious morn, by these dark days be dropped into oblivion? Dropped it is; and dropped by our sacred, august, and ample register of renown, which has entered in its marble-memoirs the dim splendor of far inferior worth: Tho' so lavish of praise, and so talkative of the dead, yet is it silent on a subject, which (if any) might have taught its unletter'd stones to speak: If powers were not wanting, a monument more durable than those of marble, should proudly rise in this ambitious page, to the new, and far nobler *Addison,* than that which you, and the public, have so long, and so much admired: Nor this nation only; for it is *Europe's Addison,* as well as ours; tho' *Europe* knows not half his title to her esteem; being as yet unconscious that the *dying Addison* far outshines her *Addison immortal:* Would we resemble him? Let us not limit our ambition to the least illustrious part of his character; heads, indeed, are crowned on earth; but hearts only are crowned in heaven: A truth, which, in such an *age of authors,* should not be forgotten.

It is piously to be hoped, that this narrative may have some effect, since all listen, when a death-bed speaks; and regard the person departing as an actor of a part, which the great master of the drama has appointed us to perform to-morrow: This was a *Roscius*[79] on the stage of life; his exit how great? Ye lovers of virtue! *plaudite:*[80] And let us, my friend! ever "remember his end, as well as our own, that we may never do amiss." I am,

> *Dear* SIR,
> *Your most obliged,*
> *humble Servant.*

P.S. How far *Addison* is an *Original,* you will see in my next; where I descend from this consecrated ground into his sublunary praise: And great is the descent, tho' into noble heights of *intellectual* power.

---

[79] A celebrated Roman actor.   [80] "applaud."

Oliver Goldsmith
1728-1774

THE CITIZEN OF THE WORLD

LETTERS FROM A CHINESE PHILOSOPHER RESIDING IN LONDON TO HIS FRIENDS IN THE EAST

LETTERS I–III [POINT OF VIEW]

To Mr.————, *Merchant in* London

Amsterdam.

Sir,

Yours of the 13th instant, covering two bills, one on Messrs. R. and D. value 478 *l.* 10s. and the other on Mr.————, value 285 *l.* duly came to hand, the former of which met with honour, but the other has been trifled with, and I am afraid will be returned protested.

The bearer of this is my friend, therefore let him be yours. He is a native of Honan in China, and one who did me signal services when he was a mandarine,[1] and I a factor[2] at Canton. By frequently conversing with English there, he has learned the language, though intirely a stranger to their manners and customs. I am told he is a philosopher, I am sure he is an honest man; that to you will be his best recommendation, next to the consideration of his being the friend of, Sir,

Yours, &c.

Lond.   From Lien Chi Altangi to ————, *Merchant in Amsterdam*

Friend of my heart,

May the wings of peace rest upon thy dwelling, and the shield of conscience preserve thee from vice and misery: for all thy favours accept my gratitude and esteem, the only tributes a poor philosophic wanderer can return; sure fortune is resolved to make me unhappy, when she gives others a power of testifying their friendship by actions, and leaves me only words to express the sincerity of mine.

I am perfectly sensible of the delicacy by which you endeavour to lessen your own merit and my obligations. By calling your late instances of friendship only a return for former favours, you would induce me to impute to your justice what I owe to your generosity.

The services I did you at Canton, justice, humanity, and my office bade me perform; those you have done me since my arrival at Amsterdam, no laws obliged you to, no justice required, even half your favours would have been

---

Text from the first collected edition, 2 vols., 1762. Originally published serially in *The Public Ledger* between June 24, 1760, and August 14, 1761.

[1] A Chinese official; used generally to signify one of the upper class.

[2] agent.

greater than my most sanguine expectations.

The sum of money therefore which you privately conveyed into my baggage, when I was leaving Holland, and which I was ignorant of till my arrival in London, I must beg leave to return. You have been bred a merchant, and I a scholar; You consequently love money better than I. You can find pleasure in superfluity, I am perfectly contented with with is sufficient; take therefore what is yours, it may give you some pleasure, even though you have no occasion to use it; my happiness it cannot improve, for I have already all that I want.

My passage by sea from Rotterdam to England, was more painful to me than all the journies I ever made on land. I have traversed the immeasurable wilds of Mogul Tartary; felt all the rigours of Siberian skies; I have had my repose an hundred times disturbed by invading savages, and have seen without shrinking the desart sands rise like a troubled ocean all around me; against these calamities I was armed with resolution; but in my passage to England, though nothing occurred that gave the mariners any uneasiness, yet to one who was never at sea before, all was a subject of astonishment and terror. To find the land disappear, to see our ship mount the waves quick as an arrow from the Tartar bow, to hear the wind howling through the cordage, to feel a sickness which depresses even the spirits of the brave; these were unexpected distresses, and consequently assaulted me unprepared to receive them.

You men of Europe think nothing of a voyage by sea. With us of China, a man who has been from sight of land is regarded upon his return with admiration. I have known some provinces where there is not even a name for the ocean. What a strange people therefore am I got amongst, who have founded an empire on this unstable element, who build cities upon billows that rise higher than the mountains of Tipartala,[3] and make the deep more formidable than the wildest tempest.

Such accounts as these, I must confess, were my first motives for seeing England. These induced me to undertake a journey of seven hundred painful days, in order to examine its opulence, buildings, sciences, arts and manufactures on the spot. Judge then how great is my disappointment on entering London, to see no signs of that opulence so much talked of abroad; wherever I turn, I am presented with a gloomy solemnity in the houses, the streets and the inhabitants; none of that beautiful gilding which makes a principal ornament in Chinese architecture. The streets of Nankin are sometimes strewed with gold leaf; very different are those of London: in the midst of their pavements, a great lazy puddle moves muddily along; heavy laden machines with wheels of unweildy thickness crowd up every passage; so that a stranger, instead of finding time for observation, is often happy if he has time to escape from being crushed to pieces.

The houses borrow very few ornaments from architecture; their chief decoration seems to be a paltry piece of painting,[4] hung out at their doors or windows, at once a proof of their indigence and vanity. Their vanity, in each having one of those pictures exposed to public view; and their indigence, in being unable to get them better painted. In this respect, the fancy of their painters is also deplorable. Could you believe it? I have seen five black lions and three blue boars in less than a circuit of half a mile; and yet you know that animals of these colours are no where to be found except in the wild imagination of Europe.

From these circumstances in their buildings, and from the dismal looks of the inhabitants, I am induced to conclude that the nation is actually poor; and that like the Persians, they make a splendid figure every where but at home. The proverb of Xixofou[5] is, that a man's riches may be seen in his eyes; if we

---

[3] This, like a few other names used by Goldsmith, has not been identified but probably had its source in some of the contemporary accounts of China and Asiatic Russia.

[4] i.e., shop signs.

[5] Not identified.

judge of the English by this rule, there is not a poorer nation under the sun.

I have been here but two days, so will not be hasty in my decisions; such letters as I shall write to Fipsihi in Moscow, I beg you'll endeavour to forward with all diligence; I shall send them open, in order that you may take copies or translations, as you are equally versed in the Dutch and Chinese languages. Dear friend, think of my absence with regret, as I sincerely regret yours; even while I write, I lament our separation.

Farewell.

From Lien Chi Altangi, to the care of Fipsihi, resident in Moscow; to be forwarded by the Russian caravan to Fum Hoam, first president of the ceremonial academy at Pekin in China

Think not, O thou guide of my youth, that absence can impair my respect, or interposing trackless desarts blot your reverend figure from my memory. The farther I travel I feel the pain of separation with stronger force, those ties that bind me to my native country, and you, are still unbroken. By every remove, I only drag a greater length of chain.

Could I find aught worth transmitting from so remote a region as this to which I have wandered, I should gladly send it; but instead of this, you must be contented with a renewal of my former professions, and an imperfect account of a people with whom I am as yet but superficially acquainted. The remarks of a man who has been but three days in the country can only be those obvious circumstances which force themselves upon the imagination: I consider myself here as a newly created Being introduced into a new world; every object strikes with wonder and surprise. The imagination still unsated, seems the only active principle of the mind. The most trifling occurrences give pleasure, till the gloss of novelty is worn away. When I have ceased to wonder, I may possibly grow wise; I may then call the reasoning principle to my aid, and compare those objects with each other, which were before examined without reflection.

Behold me then in London, gazing at the strangers, and they at me; it seems they find somewhat absurd in my figure; and had I been never from home it is possible I might find an infinite fund of ridicule in theirs; but by long travelling I am taught to laugh at folly alone, and to find nothing truly ridiculous but villainy and vice.

When I had just quitted my native country, and crossed the Chinese wall, I fancied every deviation from the customs and manners of China was a departing from nature: I smiled at the blue lips and red foreheads of the Tonguese;[6] and could hardly contain myself when I saw the Daures[7] dress their heads with horns. The Ostiacs[8] powdered with red earth; and the Calmuck[9] beauties tricked out in all the finery of sheep-skin appeared highly ridiculous; but I soon perceived that the ridicule lay not in them but in me; that I falsely condemned others of absurdity, because they happened to differ from a standard originally founded in prejudice or partiality.

I find no pleasure therefore in taxing the English with departing from nature in their external appearance, which is all I yet know of their character; it is possible they only endeavour to improve her simple plan, since every extravagance in dress proceeds from a desire of becoming more beautiful than nature made us; and this is so harmless a vanity that I not only pardon but approve it: A desire to be more excellent than others is what ac-

---

[6] Inhabitants of eastern Siberia between the Sea of Okotsk, the Yablonoi Mountains, and the Yenisei River.

[7] Inhabitants of the territory east of the Caspian Sea along the River Amu Darya in Afghanistan. In Letter X, Goldsmith described certain customs of the Daures. It has been shown to be a translation of Letter XXVIII of *Lettres Chinoises* (1739) by Jean Baptiste de Boyer, Marquis d'Argens, from whom Goldsmith borrowed considerably (see Ronald S. Crane and Hamilton Jewett Smith, "A French Influence on Goldsmith's 'Citizen of the World'," in *Modern Philology*, XIX, 83–92).

[8] Ustiacs; inhabitants of western Siberia.

[9] People of Kalmyk, a province of European Russia, north of the Caspian Sea.

tually makes us so, and as thousands find a livelihood in society by such appetites, none but the ignorant inveigh against them.

You are not insensible, most reverend Fum Hoam, what numberless trades, even among the Chinese, subsist by the harmless pride of each other. Your nose-borers, feet-swathers, tooth-stainers, eye-brow pluckers, would all want bread, should their neighbours want vanity. These vanities, however, employ much fewer hands in China than in England; and a fine gentleman, or a fine lady, here dressed up to the fashion, seems scarcely to have a single limb that does not suffer some distortions from art.

To make a fine gentleman, several trades are required, but chiefly a barber: you have undoubtedly heard of the Jewish champion, whose strength lay in his hair:[10] one would think that the English were for placing all wisdom there: To appear wise, nothing more is requisite here than for a man to borrow hair from the heads of all his neighbours, and clap it like a bush on his own: the distributors of law and physic stick on such quantities,[11] that it is almost impossible, even in idea, to distinguish between the head and the hair.

Those whom I have been now describing, affect the gravity of the lion: those I am going to describe more resemble the pert vivacity of smaller animals. The barber, who is still master of the ceremonies, cuts their hair close to the crown; and then with a composition of meal and hog's lard, plaisters the whole in such a manner, as to make it impossible to distinguish whether the patient wears a cap or a plaister; but to make the picture more perfectly striking, conceive the tail of some beast, a greyhound's tail, or a pig's tail for instance, appended to the back of the head, and reaching down to that place where tails in other animals are generally seen to begin; thus betailed and bepowdered, the man of taste fancies he improves in beauty, dresses up his hard-featured face in

smiles, and attempts to look hideously tender. Thus equipped, he is qualified to make love, and hopes for success more from the powder on the outside of his head, than the sentiments within.

Yet when I consider what sort of a creature the fine lady is, to whom he is supposed to pay his addresses, it is not strange to find him thus equipped in order to please. She is herself every whit as fond of powder, and tails, and hog's lard as he: to speak my secret sentiments, most reverend Fum, the ladies here are horridly ugly; I can hardly endure the sight of them; they no way resemble the beauties of China: the Europeans have a quite different idea of beauty from us; when I reflect on the small footed perfections of an Eastern beauty, how is it possible I should have eyes for a woman whose feet are ten inches long. I shall never forget the beauties of my native city of Nangfew. How very broad their faces; how very short their noses; how very little their eyes; how very thin their lips; how very black their teeth; the snow on the tops of Bao is not fairer than their cheeks; and their eye-brows are small as the line by the pencil of Quamsi. Here a lady with such perfections would be frightful; Dutch and Chinese beauties indeed have some resemblance, but English women are entirely different; red cheeks, big eyes, and teeth of a most odious whiteness, are not only seen here, but wished for; and then they have such masculine feet, as actually serve *some* for walking!

Yet uncivil as nature has been, they seem resolved to outdo her in unkindness; they use white powder, blue powder, and black powder for their hair, and a red powder for the face on some particular occasions.

They like to have the face of various colours, as among the Tartars of Koreki, frequently sticking on, with spittle, little black patches on every part of it, except on the tip of the nose, which I have never seen with a patch. You'll have a better idea of their manner of placing

---

[10] Samson; Judg. 13–16.

[11] i.e., the wigs of members of the legal and medical professions.

these spots, when I have finished a map of an English face patch'd up to the fashion, which shall shortly be sent to encrease your curious collection of paintings, medals, and monsters.

But what surprizes more than all the rest, is, what I have just now been credibly informed by one of this country; "Most ladies here, says he, have two faces; one face to sleep in, and another to shew in company: the first is generally reserv'd for the husband and family at home, the other put on to please strangers abroad; the family face is often indifferent enough, but the out-door one looks something better; this is always made at the toilet, where the looking-glass, and toad-eater[12] sit in council and settle the complexion of the day."

I can't ascertain the truth of this remark; however, it is actually certain, that they wear more cloaths within doors than without; and I have seen a lady who seem'd to shudder at a breeze in her own apartment, appear half naked in the streets.

Farewell.

LETTER XXI   [AN EVENING AT THE THEATRE]

To the same

The English are as fond of seeing plays acted as the Chinese; but there is a vast difference in the manner of conducting them. We play our pieces in the open air, the English theirs under cover; we act by day-light, they by the blaze of torches. One of our plays continues eight or ten days successively; an English piece seldom takes up above four hours in the representation.

My companion in black,[13] with whom I am now beginning to contract an intimacy, introduced me a few nights ago to the play-house, where we placed ourselves conveniently at the foot of the stage. As the curtain was not drawn before my arrival, I had an opportunity of observing the behaviour of the spectators,

and indulging those reflections which novelty generally inspires.

The rich in general were placed in the lowest seats, and the poor rose above them in degrees proportioned to their poverty. The order of precedence seemed here inverted; those who were undermost all the day, now enjoyed a temporary eminence, and became masters of the ceremonies. It was they who called for the music, indulging every noisy freedom, and testifying all the insolence of beggary in exaltation.

They who held the middle region seemed not so riotous as those above them, nor yet so tame as those below; to judge by their looks, many of them seem'd strangers there as well as myself. They were chiefly employed during this period of expectation in eating oranges, reading the story of the play, or making assignations.

Those who sat in the lowest rows, which are called the pit, seemed to consider themselves as judges of the merit of the poet and the performers; they were assembled partly to be amused, and partly to shew their taste; appearing to labour under that restraint which an affectation of superior discernment generally produces. My companion, however, informed me, that not one in an hundred of them knew even the first principles of criticism; that they assumed the right of being censors because there was none to contradict their pretensions; and that every man who now called himself a connoisseur, became such to all intents and purposes.

Those who sat in the boxes appeared in the most unhappy situation of all. The rest of the audience came merely for their own amusement; these rather to furnish out a part of the entertainment themselves. I could not avoid considering them as acting parts in dumb shew, not a curtesy or nod, that was not the result of art; not a look nor a smile that was not designed for murder. Gentlemen and ladies ogled each other through spectacles; for my companion observed, that

---

[12] flatterer.

[13] The "companion in black," who is never otherwise identified but who is frequently re-

ferred to, comes from D'Argens's *Lettres Chinoises*. See note 7 above.

blindness was of late become fashionable, all affected indifference and ease, while their hearts at the same time burned for conquest. Upon the whole, the lights, the music, the ladies in their gayest dresses, the men with chearfulness and expectation in their looks, all conspired to make a most agreeable picture, and to fill an heart that sympathises at human happiness with an expressible serenity.

The expected time for the play to begin at last arrived, the curtain was drawn, and the actors came on. A woman, who personated a queen, came in curtesying to the audience, who clapped their hands upon her appearance. Clapping of hands is, it seems, the manner of applauding in England: the manner is absurd; but every country, you know, has its peculiar absurdities. I was equally surprised, however, at the submission of the actress, who should have considered herself as a queen, as at the little discernment of the audience who gave her such marks of applause before she attempted to deserve them. Preliminaries between her and the audience being thus adjusted, the dialogue was supported between her and a most hopeful youth, who acted the part of her confidant. They both appeared in extreme distress, for it seems the queen had lost a child some fifteen years before and still kept its dear resemblance next her heart, while her kind companion bore a part in her sorrows.

Her lamentations grew loud. Comfort is offered, but she detests the very sound. She bids them preach comfort to the winds. Upon this her husband comes in, who, seeing the queen so much afflicted, can himself hardly refrain from tears or avoid partaking in the soft distress. After thus grieving through three scenes, the curtain dropped for the first act.

Truly, said I to my companion, these kings and queens are very much disturbed at no very great misfortune; certain I am were people of humbler stations to act in this manner, they would be thought divested of common sense. I had scarce finished this observation, when the curtain rose, and the king came on in a violent passion. His wife had, it seems, refused his proffered tenderness, had spurned his royal embrace; and he seemed resolved not to survive her fierce disdain. After he had thus fretted, and the queen had fretted through the second act, the curtain was let down once more.

Now, says my companion, you perceive the king to be a man of spirit, he feels at every pore; one of your phlegmatic sons of clay would have given the queen her own way, and let her come to herself by degrees; but the king is for immediate tenderness, or instant death: death and tenderness are leading passions of every modern buskin'd[14] heroe; this moment they embrace, and the next stab, mixing daggers and kisses in every period.

I was going to second his remarks, when my attention was engrossed by a new object; a man came in balancing a straw upon his nose, and the audience were clapping their hands in all the raptures of applause. To what purpose, cried I, does this unmeaning figure make his appearance; is he a part of the plot? Unmeaning do you call him, replied my friend in black; this is one of the most important characters of the whole play; nothing pleases the people more than the seeing a straw balanced; there is a great deal of meaning in the straw; there is something suited to every apprehension in the sight; and a fellow possessed of talents like these is sure of making his fortune.

The third act now began with an actor, who came to inform us that he was the villain of the play, and intended to shew strange things before all was over. He was joined by another, who seem'd as much disposed for mischief as he; their intrigues continued through this whole division. If that be a villain, said I, he must be a very stupid one, to tell his secrets without being ask'd; such soliloquies of late are never admitted in China.

The noise of clapping interrupted me once more; a child of six years old was learning to dance on the stage, which gave the ladies and mandarines infinite satisfaction. I am sorry, said I, to see the

_____

[14] tragic.

pretty creature so early learning so very bad a trade. Dancing being, I presume, as contemptible here as it is in China. Quite the reverse, interrupted my companion; dancing is a very reputable and genteel employment here; men have a greater chance for encouragement from the merit of their heels than their heads. One who jumps up and flourishes his toes three times before he comes to the ground, may have three hundred a year; he who flourishes them four times, gets four hundred; but he who arrives at five is inestimable, and may demand what salary he thinks proper. The female dancers too are valued for this sort of jumping and crossing; and 'tis a cant[15] word among them, that she deserves most who shews highest. But the fourth act is begun, let us be attentive.

In the fourth act the queen finds her long lost child, now grown up into a youth of smart parts[16] and great qualifications; wherefore she wisely considers that the crown will fit his head better than that of her husband, whom she knows to be a driveler. The king discovers her design, and here comes on the deep distress; he loves the queen, and he loves the kingdom; he resolves therefore, in order to possess both, that her son must die. The queen exclaims at his barbarity; is frantic with rage, and at length overcome with sorrow, falls into a fit;[17] upon which the curtain drops, and the act is concluded.

Observe the art of the poet, cries my companion; when the queen can say no more, she falls into a fit. While thus her eyes are shut, while she is supported in the arms of Abigail, what horrors do we not fancy, we feel it in every nerve; take my word for it, that fits are the true aposiopeisis of modern tragedy.

The fifth act began, and a busy piece it was. Scenes shifting, trumpets sounding, mobs hallooing, carpets spreading, guards bustling from one door to another; gods, dæmons, daggers, racks[18]

and ratsbane.[19] But whether the king was killed, or the queen was drowned, or the son was poisoned, I have absolutely forgotten.

When the play was over, I could not avoid observing, that the persons of the drama appeared in as much distress in the first act as the last: how is it possible, said I, to sympathize with them through five long acts; pity is but a short-lived passion; I hate to hear an actor mouthing trifles, neither startings, strainings, nor attitudes affect me unless there be cause: after I have been once or twice deceived by those unmeaning alarms, my heart sleeps in peace, probably unaffected by the principal distress. There should be one great passion aimed at by the actor as well as the poet, all the rest should be subordinate, and only contribute to make that the greater; if the actor therefore exclaims upon every occasion in the tones of despair, he attempts to move us too soon; he anticipates the blow, he ceases to affect though he gains our applause.

I scarce perceived that the audience were almost all departed; wherefore, mixing with the crowd, my companion and I got into the street; where essaying an hundred obstacles from coach wheels and palanquin[20] poles, like birds in their flight through the branches of a forest, after various turnings, we both at length got home in safety.

Adieu.

LETTER LXIII [THE DIFFERENCE BE-
TWEEN GRATITUDE AND LOVE]

From Lien Chi Altangi to Hingpo, by the way of Moscow

Generosity properly applied will supply every other external advantage in life, but the love of those we converse with; it will procure esteem and a conduct resembling real affection, but actual love is the spontaneous production of the mind, no generosity can purchase, no re-

---

[15] "barbarous jargon" (Johnson's *Dictionary*).

[16] bearing, appearance.

[17] faint, collapse.

[18] Instruments of torture.

[19] A poison.

[20] Covered litter of the orient; Lien Chi Altangi's word for the English conveyance by covered chair borne on two poles by porters.

wards encrease, nor no liberality continue it, the very person who is obliged, has it not in his power to force his lingring affections upon the object he should love, and voluntarily mix passion with gratitude.

Imparted fortune, and well-placed liberality, may procure the benefactor good will, may load the person obliged, with the sense of the duty he lies under to retaliate; this is gratitude: and simple gratitude untinctured with love, is all the return an ingenuous mind can bestow for former benefits.

But gratitude and love are almost opposite affections; love is often an involuntary passion, placed upon our companions without our consent, and frequently conferred without our previous esteem. We love some men, we know not why; our tenderness is naturally excited in all their concerns; we excuse their faults with the same indulgence, and approve their virtues with the same applause with which we consider our own. While we entertain the passion[21] it pleases us, we cherish it with delight, and give it up with reluctance, and love for love is all the reward we expect or desire.

Gratitude, on the contrary, is never conferred, but where there have been previous endeavours to excite it; we consider it as a debt, and our spirits wear a load till we have discharged the obligation. Every acknowledgment of gratitude is a circumstance of humiliation; and some are found to submit to frequent mortifications of this kind; proclaiming what obligations they owe, merely because they think it in some measure cancels the debt.

Thus love is the most easy and agreeable, and gratitude the most humiliating affection of the mind; we never reflect on the man we *love,* without exulting in our choice, while he who has bound us to him by *benefits* alone, rises to our idea as a person to whom we have in some measure, forfeited our freedom. Love and gratitude are seldom therefore found in the same breast without impairing each other; we may tender the one or the other singly to those we converse with, but cannot command both together. By attempting to encrease, we diminish them; the mind becomes bankrupt under too large obligations; all additional benefits lessen every hope of future return, and bar up every avenue that leads to tenderness.

In all our connexions with society therefore, it is not only generous, but prudent, to appear insensible of the value of those favours we bestow, and endeavour to make the obligation seem as slight as possible. Love must be taken by stratagem, and not by open force: We should seem ignorant that we oblige, and leave the mind at full liberty to give or refuse its affections; for constraint may indeed leave the receiver still grateful, but it will certainly produce disgust.

If to procure gratitude be our only aim, there is no great art in making the acquisition; a benefit conferred demands a just acknowledgment, and we have a right to insist upon our due.

But it were much more prudent to forego our right on such an occasion, and exchange it, if we can, for love. We receive but little advantage from repeated protestations of gratitude, but they cost him very much from whom we exact them in return; exacting a grateful acknowledgement is demanding a debt by which the creditor is not advantaged, and the debtor pays with reluctance.

As *Mencius*[22] the Philosopher was travelling in the pursuit of wisdom, night overtook him at the foot of a gloomy mountain, remote from the habitations of men. Here as he was straying, while rain and thunder conspired to make solitude still more hideous, he perceived a hermit's cell, and approaching, asked for shelter: Enter, cries the hermit, in a severe tone, men deserve not to be obliged, but it would be imitating their ingratitude to treat them as they deserve. Come

---

[21] emotion.

[22] Mengtse, a Chinese philosopher, follower of Confucius, of the fourth century B. C., who traveled widely and spent the last years of his life writing a treatise on morality.

in: examples of vice may sometimes strengthen us in the ways of virtue.

After a frugal meal, which consisted of roots and tea, Mencius could not repress his curiosity to know why the hermit had retired from mankind, the actions of whom taught the truest lessons of wisdom. Mention not the name of man, cries the hermit, with indignation; here let me live retired from a base ungrateful world; here among the beasts of the forest, I shall find no flatterers; the lion is a generous enemy, and the dog a faithful friend, but man, base man, can poison the bowl, and smile while he presents it. *You have been used ill by mankind?* interrupted the philosopher shrewdly. Yes, returned the hermit, on mankind I have exhausted my whole fortune, and this staff, and that cup, and those roots are all that I have in return. *Did you bestow your fortune, or did you only lend it?* returned Mencius. I bestowed it, undoubtedly, replied the other, for where were the merit of being a money lender? *Did they ever own that they received it?* still adds the philosopher. A thousand times, cries the hermit, they every day loaded me with professions of gratitude, for obligations received, and solicitations for future favours. *If then,* says Mencius, smiling, *you did not lend your fortune, in order to have it returned, it is unjust to accuse them of ingratitude; they own'd themselves obliged, you expected no more, and they certainly earn'd each favour by frequently acknowledging the obligation.* The hermit was struck with the reply, and surveying his guest with emotion, [said] I have heard of the great Mencius, and you certainly are the man; I am now fourscore years old, but still a child in wisdom, take me back to the school of man, and educate me as one of the most ignorant and the youngest of your disciples!

Indeed, my son, it is better to have friends in our passage through life than grateful dependents; and as love is a more willing, so it is a more lasting tribute than extorted obligation. As we are uneasy when greatly obliged, gratitude once refused, can never after be recov-

ered: the mind that is base enough to disallow the just return, instead of feeling any uneasiness upon recollection, triumphs in its new acquired freedom, and in some measure is pleased with conscious baseness.

Very different is the situation of disagreeing friends, their separation produces mutual uneasiness: Like that divided being in fabulous creation, their sympathetic souls once more desire their former union, the joys of both are imperfect, their gayest moments tinctured with uneasiness; each seeks for the smallest concessions to clear the way to a wished for explanation; the most trifling acknowledgement, the slightest accident serves to effect a mutual reconciliation.

But instead of pursuing the thought, permit me to soften the severity of advice, by an European story which will fully illustrate my meaning.

A fidler and his wife, who had rubbed through life, as most couples usually do, sometimes good friends, at others not quite so well; one day happened to have a dispute, which was conducted with becoming spirit on both sides. The wife was sure she was right, and the husband was resolved to have his own way. What was to be done in such a case? the quarrel grew worse by explanations, and at last the fury of both rose to such a pitch, that they made a vow never to sleep together in the same bed for the future. This was the most rash vow that could be imagined, for they still were friends at bottom, and besides they had but one bed in the house; however, resolved they were to go through with it, and at night the fiddle-case was laid in bed between them, in order to make a separation. In this manner they continued for three weeks; every night the fiddle-case being placed as a barrier to divide them.

By this time, however, each heartily repented of their vow, their resentment was at an end, and their love began to return; they wished the fiddle-case away, but both had too much spirit to begin. One night, however, as they were both lying awake with the detested fiddle-case between them, the husband happened to sneeze; to which the wife, as is usual in such cases, bid God bless him; *Ay, but,* returns the husband, *woman, do you say that from your heart?* Indeed I do, my poor Nicholas, cries his wife, I say it with all my heart. *If so then,* says the husband, *we had as good remove the fiddle-case.*

LETTER CXIV [CITY STEETS AT 2 A. M.]

To [*Fum Hoam*]

The clock just struck two, the expiring taper rises and sinks in the socket, the watchman forgets the hour in slumber, the laborious and the happy are at rest, and nothing wakes but meditation, guilt, revelry and despair. The drunkard once more fills the destroying bowl, the robber walks his midnight round, and the suicide lifts his guilty arm against his own sacred person.

Let me no longer waste the night over the page of antiquity, or the sallies of cotemporary genius, but pursue the solitary walk, where vanity, ever changing, but a few hours past, walked before me, where she kept up the pageant, and now, like a froward child, seems hushed with her own importunities.

What a gloom hangs all around! the dying lamp feebly emits a yellow gleam, no sound is heard but of the chiming clock, or the distant watch-dog. All the bustle of human pride is forgotten, an hour like this may well display the emptiness of human vanity.

There will come a time when this temporary solitude may be made continual, and the city itself, like its inhabitants, fade away, and leave a desart in its room.

What cities, as great as this, have once triumphed in existence, had their victories as great, joy as just, and as unbounded, and with short-sighted presumption, promised themselves immortality. Posterity can hardly trace the situation of some. The sorrowful traveller wanders over the awful ruins of others; and as he beholds, he learns wisdom, and feels the transience of every sublunary possession.

Here, he cries, stood their citadel, now grown over with weeds, there their senate-house, but now the haunt of every noxious reptile; temples and theatres stood here, now only an undistinguished heap of ruin. They are fallen, for luxury and avarice first made them feeble. The rewards of state were conferred on amusing, and not on useful, members of society. Their riches and opulence invited the invaders, who, though at first repulsed, returned again, conquered by perseverance, and at last swept the defendants into undistinguished destruction.

How few appear in those streets, which but some few hours ago were crowded; and those who appear, now no longer wear their daily mask, nor attempt to hide their lewdness or their misery.

But who are those who make the streets their couch, and find a short repose from wretchedness at the doors of the oppulent? These are strangers, wanderers, and orphans, whose circumstances are too humble to expect redress, and whose distresses are too great even for pity. Their wretchedness excites rather horror than pity. Some are without the covering even of rags, and others emaciated with disease; the world has disclaimed them; society turns its back upon their distress, and has given them up to nakedness and hunger. These poor shivering females have once seen happier days, and been flattered into beauty. They have been prostituted to the gay luxurious villain, and are now turned out to meet the severity of winter. Perhaps, now lying at the doors of their betrayers, they sue to wretches whose hearts are insensible, or debauchees who may curse, but will not relieve them.

Why, why was I born a man, and yet see the sufferings of wretches I cannot relieve! Poor houseless creatures! the world will give you reproaches, but will not give you relief. The slightest misfortunes of the great, the most imaginary uneasiness of the rich, are aggravated with all the power of eloquence, and held up to engage our attention and sympathetic sorrow. The poor weep unheeded, persecuted by every subordinate species of tyranny; and every law, which gives others security, becomes an enemy to them.

Why was this heart of mine formed with so much sensibility! or why was not my fortune adapted to its impulse! Ten-derness, without a capacity of relieving, only makes the man who feels it more wretched than the object which sues for assistance.

Adieu.

THE LIFE OF RICHARD NASH, OF BATH, ESQ.

. . . Non ego paucis
Offendar Maculis. . . .[23]
HOR.

[THE MAKING OF BEAU NASH]

History owes its excellence more to the writer's manner than the materials of which it is composed. The intrigues of courts, or the devastation of armies are regarded by the remote spectator with as little attention as the squabbles of a village, or the fate of a malefactor, that fall under his own observation. The great and the little, as they have the same senses, and the same affections, generally present the same picture to the hand of the draughtsman; and whether the heroe or the clown be the subject of the memoir, it is only man that appears with all his native minuteness about him, for nothing very great was ever yet formed from the little materials of humanity.

Thus none can properly be said to write history, but he who understands the human heart, and its whole train of affections and follies. Those affections and follies are properly the materials he has to work upon. The relations of great events may surprize indeed; they may be calculated to instruct those very few, who govern the million beneath, but the generality of mankind find the most real improvement from relations which are levelled to the general surface of life; which tell, not how men learned to conquer, but how they endeavoured to live; not how they gained the shout of the admiring croud, but how they acquired the esteem of their friends and acquaintance.

Every man's own life would perhaps furnish the most pleasing materials for history, if he only had candour enough to be sincere, and skill enough to select such parts as once making him more prudent, might serve to render his readers more cautious. There are few who do not prefer a page of *Montaigne*[24] or *Colley Cibber,* who candidly tell us what they thought of the world, and the world thought of them, to the more stately memoirs and transactions of *Europe,* where we see Kings pretending to immortality, that are now almost forgotten, and statesmen planning frivolous negociations, that scarce outlive the signing.

It were to be wished that ministers and Kings were left to write their own histories; they are truly useful to few but themselves; but for men who are contented with more humble stations, I fancy such truths only are serviceable as

---

Text from first edition, 1762.

[23] I am not angry when a casual line . . . human frailty shows.

(Horace, *Ars Poetica,* ll. 351–352, tr. Francis.)
[24] Michel de Montaigne (1533–1592), French essayist and philosopher.

may conduct them safely through life. That knowledge which we can turn to our real benefit should be most eagerly pursued. Treasures which we cannot use but little encrease the happiness or even the pride of the possessor.

I profess to write the history of a man placed in the middle ranks of life; of one, whose vices and virtues were open to the eye of the most undiscerning spectator, who was placed in public view without power to repress censure, or command adulation, who had too much merit not to become remarkable, yet too much folly to arrive at greatness. I attempt the character of one, who was just such a man as probably you or I may be, but with this difference, that he never performed an action which the world did not know, or ever formed a wish which he did not take pains to divulge. In short I have chosen to write the life of the noted Mr. *Nash*, as it will be the delineation of a mind without disguise, of a man ever assiduous without industry, and pleasing to his superiors without any superiority of genius or understanding.

Yet if there be any who think the subject of too little importance to command attention, and had rather gaze at the actions of the great, than be directed in guiding their own, I have one undeniable claim to their attention. Mr. *Nash* was himself a King. In this particular, perhaps no Biographer has been so happy as I. They who are for a delineation of men and manners may find some satisfaction that way, and those who delight in adventures of Kings and Queens, may perhaps find their hopes satisfied in another.

It is a matter of very little importance who were the parents, or what was the education of a man who owed so little of his advancement to either. He seldom boasted of family or learning, and his father's name and circumstances were so little known, that Doctor *Cheyne*[25] used frequently to affirm that Nash had no father. The Dutchess of *Marlborough* one day rallying him in public company upon

the obscurity of his birth, compared him to *Gil-Blas*,[26] who was ashamed of his father: No, Madam, replied *Nash*, I seldom mention my father in company, not because I have any reason to be ashamed of him; but because he has some reason to be ashamed of me.

However, though such anecdotes be immaterial, to go on in the usual course of history, it may be proper to observe that *Richard Nash* Esq; the subject of this memoir, was born in the town of *Swansea*, in *Glamorganshire*, on the 18th of *October*, in the year 1674. His father was a gentleman, whose principal income arose from a partnership in a glass-house; his mother was niece to Colonel *Poyer*, who was killed by *Oliver Cromwell*, for defending *Pembroke* castle against the rebels. He was educated under Mr. *Maddocks* at *Carmarthan* school, and from thence sent to *Jesus* college, in *Oxford*, in order to prepare him for the study of the law. His father had strained his little income to give his son such an education, but from the boy's natural vivacity, he hoped a recompence from his future preferment. In college, however, he soon shewed that though much might be expected from his genius, nothing could be hoped from his industry. A mind strongly turned to pleasure, always is first seen at the university, there the youth first finds himself freed from the restraint of tutors, and being treated by his friends in some measure as a man, assumes the passions and desires of riper age, and discovers in the boy, what are likely to be the affections of his maturity.

The first method Mr. *Nash* took to distinguish himself at college was not by application to study, but by his assiduity in intrigue. In the neighbourhood of every university there are girls who with some beauty, some coquettry, and little fortune, lie upon the watch for every raw amorous youth, more inclined to make love than to study. Our Heroe was quickly caught, and went through all the mazes and adventures of a college in-

---

[25] George Cheyne (1671–1743), famous physician, author of *The English Malady* (1733) and of the earlier *Observations on Gout and on the Bath Waters* (1720), which helped to celebrate the medicinal virtues of Bath.

[26] Hero of a popular French novel, *The Adventures of Gil Blas of Santilane* (4 Vols., 1715–1735), by Alain René Lesage.

trigue, before he was seventeen; he offered marriage, the offer was accepted, but the whole affair coming to the knowledge of his tutors, his happiness, or perhaps his future misery, was prevented, and he was sent home from college, with necessary advice to him, and proper instructions to his father.

When a man knows his power over the fair sex, he generally commences their admirer for the rest of life. That triumph which he obtains over one, only makes him the slave of another, and thus he proceeds conquering and conquered, to the closing of the scene. The army seemed the most likely profession in which to display this inclination for gallantry; he therefore purchased a pair of colours,[27] commenced a professed admirer of the sex, and dressed to the very edge of his finances. But the life of a soldier is more pleasing to the spectator at a distance than to the person who makes the experiment. Mr. *Nash* soon found that a red coat alone would never succeed, that the company of the fair sex is not to be procured without expence, and that his scanty commission could never procure him the proper reimbursements. He found too that the profession of arms required attendance and duty, and often encroached upon those hours he could have wished to dedicate to softer purposes. In short, he soon became disgusted with the life of a soldier, quitted the army, entered his name as a student in the temple books,[28] and here went to the very summit of second-rate luxury. Though very poor he was very fine; he spread the little gold he had, in the most ostentatious manner, and though the gilding was but thin, he laid it on as far as it would go. They who know the town, cannot be unacquainted with such a character as I describe; one, who though he may have dined in private upon a banquet served cold from a cook's shop, shall dress at six for the side box; one of those, whose wants are only known to their

laundress, and tradesmen, and their fine cloaths to half the nobility; who spend more in chair hire, than housekeeping; and prefer a bow from a Lord, to a dinner from a Commoner.

In this manner Mr. *Nash* spent some years about town, till at last his genteel appearance, his constant civility, and still more, his assiduity, gained him the acquaintance of several persons qualified to lead the fashion both by birth and fortune. To gain the friendship of the young nobility little more is requisite than much submission and very fine cloaths; dress has a mechanical influence upon the mind, and we naturally are awed into respect and esteem at the elegance of those, whom even our reason would teach us to contemn. He seemed early sensible of human weakness in this respect, he brought a person genteely dressed to every assembly, he always made one of those who are called very good company, and assurance gave him an air of elegance and ease.

When King *William* was upon the throne,[29] Mr. *Nash* was a member of the *Middle Temple*. It had been long customary for the Inns of court[30] to entertain our Monarchs upon their accession to the crown, or some such remarkable occasion, with a revel and pageant. In the earlier periods of our history, Poets were the conductors of these entertainments; plays were exhibited, and complimentary verses were then written; but by degrees the pageant alone was continued, Sir *John Davies*[31] being the last poet that wrote verses upon such an occasion in the reign of *James* I.

This ceremony which has been at length totally discontinued, was last exhibited in honour of King *William,* and Mr. *Nash* was chosen to conduct the whole with proper decorum. He was then but a very young man, but we see at how early an age he was thought proper to guide the amusements of his country, and be the *Arbiter Elegantiarum*[32] of his

[27] i.e., obtained a military commission.
[28] i.e., to study law.
[29] William III (1689–1702).
[30] Legal societies for the admission of law-

yers to the English bar: Inner Temple, Middle Temple, Lincoln's Inn, and Gray's Inn.
[31] 1569–1626.
[32] "master of ceremonies."

time; we see how early he gave proofs of that spirit of regularity, for which he afterwards became famous, and shewed an attention to those little circumstances, of which tho' the observance be trifling, the neglect has often interrupted men of the greatest abilities in the progress of their fortunes.

In conducting this entertainment, *Nash* had an opportunity of exhibiting all his abilities, and King *William* was so well satisfied with his performance, that he made him an offer of knighthood. This, however, he thought proper to refuse, which in a person of his disposition seems strange. *Please your Majesty,* replied he, when the offer was made him, *if you intend to make me a Knight, I wish it may be one of your poor Knights of* Windsor,[33] *and then I shall have a fortune, at least able to support my title.* Yet we do not find, that the King took the hint of encreasing his fortune, perhaps he could not, he had at that time numbers to oblige, and he never cared to give money without important services.

But though *Nash* acquired no riches by his late office, yet he gained many friends, or what is more easily obtained, many acquaintance, who often answer the end as well. In the populous city where he resided, to be known was almost synonimous with being in the road to fortune. How many little Things do we see, without merit, or without friends, push themselves forward into public notice, and by self-advertizing, attract the attention of the day. The wise despise them, but the public are not all wise. Thus they succeed, rise upon the wing of folly, or of fashion, and by their success give a new sanction to effrontery.

But beside his assurance, Mr. *Nash* had in reality some merit and some virtues. He was, if not a brilliant, at least an easy companion. He never forgot good manners, even in the highest warmth of familiarity, and as I hinted before, never went in a dirty shirt to disgrace the table of his patron or his friend. These qualifications might make the furniture of his head; but for his heart, that seemed an assemblage of the virtues which display an honest benevolent mind; with the vices which spring from too much good nature. He had pity for every creature's distress, but wanted prudence in the application of his benefits. He had generosity for the wretched in the highest degree, at a time when his creditors complained of his justice. He often spoke falshoods, but never had any of his harmless tales tinctured with malice.

An instance of his humanity is told us in the Spectator,[34] though his name is not mentioned. When he was to give in his accompts to the masters of the temple, among other articles, he charged *For making one man happy* 10 l. Being questioned about the meaning of so strange an item, he frankly declared, that happening to over-hear a poor man declare to his wife and a large family of children, that 10 l. would make him happy, he could not avoid trying the experiment. He added, that if they did not chuse to acquiesce in his charge, he was ready to refund the money. The masters struck with such an uncommon instance of good nature, publicly thanked him for his benevolence, and desired that the sum might be doubled as a proof of their satisfaction.

Another instance of his unaccountable generosity, and I shall proceed. In some transactions with one of his friends, Mr. *Nash* was brought in debtor twenty pounds. His friend frequently asked for the money, and was as often denied. He found at last, that assiduity was likely to have no effect, and therefore contrived an honourable method of getting back his money without dissolving the friendship that subsisted between them. One day, returning from *Nash's* chamber with the usual assurance of being paid to morrow, he went to one of their mutual acquaintance, and related the frequent disappointments he had received, and the little hopes he had of being ever paid. "My design, continues he, is that you should go, and try to borrow twenty pounds from *Nash,* and bring me the money. I am apt to think, he will lend to you, tho' he will

33 pensioners.   34 No. 248.

not pay me. Perhaps we may extort from his generosity, what I have failed to receive from his justice." His friend obeys, and going to Mr. *Nash,* assured him, that, unless relieved by his friendship, he should certainly be undone; he wanted to borrow twenty pounds; and had tried all his acquaintance without success. Mr. *Nash,* who had but some minutes before, refused to pay a just debt, was in raptures at thus giving an instance of his friendship, and instantly lent what was required. Immediately upon the receipt, the pretended borrower goes to the real creditor, and gives him the money, who met Mr. *Nash* the day after: our heroe upon seeing him, immediately began his usual excuses, that the billiard room had stript him, that he was never so damnably out of cash, but that in a few days —My dear Sir, be under no uneasiness, replied the other, I would not interrupt your tranquillity for the world, you lent twenty pounds yesterday to our friend of the back stairs, and he lent it to me, give him your receipt, and you shall have mine. "Perdition seize thee, cried *Nash,* thou hast been too many for me. You demanded a debt, he asked a favour; to pay thee, would not encrease our friendship, but to lend him, was procuring a new friend, by conferring a new obligation."

Whether men at the time I am now talking of, had more wit than at present, I will not take upon me to determine; but certain it is, they took more pains to shew what they had. In that age, a fellow of high humour would drink no wine, but what was strained through his mistresses smock. He would eat a pair of her shoes tossed up in a fricasee. He would swallow tallow-candles instead of toasted cheese, and even run naked about town, at it was then said, to divert the ladies. In short, that was the age of such kind of wit as is the most distant of all others from wisdom.

Mr. *Nash,* as he sometimes played tricks with others, upon certain occasions, received very severe retaliations. Being at *York,* and having lost all his money; some of his companions agreed to equip him with fifty guineas, upon this proviso, that he would stand at the great door of the Minster, in a blanket, as the people were coming out of church. To this proposal he readily agreed, but the Dean passing by unfortunately knew him. What, cried the Divine, Mr. *Nash* in masquerade? *Only a* Yorkshire *penance, Mr. Dean, for keeping bad company,* says *Nash,* pointing to his companions.

Some time after this, he won a wager of still greater consequence, by riding naked through a village upon a cow. This was then thought an harmless frolic, at present it would be looked upon with detestation.

He was once invited by some gentlemen of the navy, on board a man of war, that had sailing orders for the mediterranean. This was soon after the affair of the revels, and being ignorant of any design against him, he took his bottle with freedom. But he soon found, to use the expression then in fashion, that he was absolutely *bitten.* The ship sailed away before he was aware of his situation, and he was obliged to make the voyage in the company where he had spent the night.

Many lives are often passed without a single adventure, and I do not know of any in the life of our hero, that can be called such, except what we are now relating. During this voyage, he was in an engagement, in which his particular friend was killed by his side, and he himself wounded in the leg. For the anecdote of his being wounded, we are solely to trust to his own veracity; but most of his acquaintance were not much inclined to believe him, when he boasted on those occasions. Telling one day of the wound he had received for his country, in one of the public rooms at *Bath,* (*Wiltshire's* if I don't forget) a lady of distinction, that sat by, said it was all false. I protest, Madam, replied he, it is true, and if I cannot be believed, your Ladyship may, if you please, receive farther information and feel the ball in my leg.

Mr. *Nash* was now fairly for life entered into a new course of gaiety and dissipation, and steady in nothing but in pursuit of variety. He was thirty years old, without fortune, or useful talents to acquire one. He had hitherto only led a life of expedients, he thanked chance alone for his support, and having been long precariously supported, he became, at length, totally a stranger to prudence, or precaution. Not to disguise any part of his character, he was now, by profession a gamester, and went on from day to day, feeling the vicissitudes of rapture and anguish, in proportion to the fluctuations of fortune.

At this time, *London* was the only theatre in *England,* for pleasure, or intrigue. A spirit of gaming, had been introduced in the licentious age of *Charles* II. and had by this time thriven surprizingly. Yet all its devastations were confined to *London* alone. To this great mart of every folly, sharpers from every country daily arrived, for the winter, but were obliged to leave the kingdom at the approach of summer, in order to open a new campaign at *Aix, Spaw,* or the *Hague. Bath, Tunbridge, Scarborough,* and other places of the same kind here, were then frequented only by such as really went for relief; the pleasures they afforded were merely rural, the company splenetic, rustic, and vulgar. In this situation of things, people of fashion had no agreeable summer retreat from the town, and usually spent that season amidst a solitude of country squires, parsons wives, and visiting tenants, or farmers; they wanted some place where they might have each others company, and win each others money, as they had done during the winter in town.

To a person, who does not thus calmly trace things to their source, nothing will appear more strange, than how the healthy could ever consent to follow the sick to those places of spleen, and live with those, whose disorders are ever apt to excite a gloom in the spectator. The truth is, the gaming table was properly the salutary font, to which such numbers flocked. Gaming will ever be the pleasure of the rich, while men continue to be men, while they fancy more happiness in

being possessed of what they want, than they experience pleasure in the fruition of what they have. The wealthy only stake those riches, which give no real content, for an expectation of riches, in which they hope for satisfaction. By this calculation, they cannot lose happiness, as they begin with none; and they hope to gain it, by being possessed of something they have not had already.

Probably upon this principle; and by the arrival of Queen *Anne* there for her health, About the year 1703, the city of *Bath* became in some measure frequented by people of distinction. The company was numerous enough to form a country dance upon the bowling green; they were amused with a fiddle and hautboy,[35] and diverted with the romantic walks round the city. They usually sauntered in fine weather in the grove, between two rows of sycamore trees. Several learned Physicians, Doctor *Jordan,* and others had even then praised the salubrity of the wells, and the amusements were put under the direction of a master of the ceremonies.

Captain *Webster* was the predecessor of Mr. *Nash:* This I take to be the same gentleman, whom Mr. *Lucas* describes in his history of the lives of the gamesters,[36] by which it appears, that *Bath,* even before the arrival of Mr. *Nash,* was found a proper retreat for men of that profession. This gentleman, in the year 1704, carried the balls to the town hall, each man paying half a guinea each ball.

Still however, the amusements of this place were neither elegant, nor conducted with delicacy. General society among people of rank or fortune was by no means established. The nobility still preserved a tincture of *Gothic* haughtiness, and refused to keep company with the gentry at any of the public entertainments of the place. Smoking in the rooms was permitted; gentlemen and ladies appeared in a disrespectful manner at public entertainments in aprons and

---

[35] oboe.

[36] Theophilus Lucas, *Memoirs of the Lives, Intrigues, and Comical Adventures of the most famous Gamesters and celebrated Sharpers . . .* *the Whole Calculated for the Meridians of London, Bath, Tunbridge, and the Groom-Porters* (1714).

boots. With an eagerness common to those, whose pleasures come but seldom, they generally continued them too long, and thus they were rendered disgusting by too free an enjoyment. If the company liked each other they danced till morning, if any person lost at cards, he insisted on continuing the game till luck should turn. The lodgings for visitants were paltry, though expensive, the dining rooms and other chambers were floored with boards coloured brown with soot and small beer, to hide the dirt; the walls were covered with unpainted wainscot, the furniture corresponded with the meanness of the architecture; a few oak chairs, a small looking glass, with a fender and tongs, composed the magnificence of these temporary habitations. The city was in itself mean and contemptible, no elegant buildings, no open streets, nor uniform squares. The Pumphouse[37] was without any director; the chairmen permitted no gentlemen or ladies to walk home by night without insulting them; and to add to all this, one of the greatest Physicians of his age conceived a design of ruining the city, by writing against the efficacy of the waters. It was from a resentment of some affronts he had received there, that he took this resolution; and accordingly published a pamphlet, by which he said, *he would cast a toad into the spring.*

In this situation of things it was, that Mr. *Nash* first came into that city, and hearing the threat of this Physician, he humorously assured the people that if they would give him leave, he would charm away the poison of the Doctor's toad, as they usually charmed the venom of the Tarantula, by music. He therefore was immediately empowered to set up the force of a band of music, against the poison of the Doctor's reptile; the company very sensibly encreased, *Nash* triumphed, and the sovereignty of the city was decreed to him by every rank of people.

We are now to behold this gentleman as arrived at a new dignity for which nature seemed to have formed him; we are to see him directing pleasures, which none had better learned to share; placed over rebellious and refractory subjects that were to be ruled only by the force of his address, and governing such as had been long accustomed to govern others. We see a kingdom beginning with him, and sending off *Tunbridge*[38] as one of its colonies.

But to talk more simply, when we talk at best of trifles. None could possibly conceive a person more fit to fill this employment than *Nash:* He had some wit, as I have said once or twice before; but it was of that sort which is rather happy than permanent. Once a week he might say a good thing, this the little ones about him took care to divulge; or if they happened to forget the joke, he usually remembered to repeat it himself: In a long intercourse with the world he had acquired an impenetrable assurance; and the freedom with which he was received by the Great, furnished him with vivacity which could be commanded at any time, and which some mistook for wit. His former intercourse among people of fashion in town, had let him into most of the characters of the nobility; and he was acquainted with many of their private intrigues. He understood rank and precedence, with the utmost exactness, was fond of shew and finery himself, and generally set a pattern of it to others. These were his favourite talents, and he was the favourite of such as had no other.

But to balance these which some may consider as foibles, he was charitable himself, and generally shamed his betters into a similitude of sentiment, if they were not naturally so before. He was fond of advising those young men, who, by youth and too much money, are taught to look upon extravagance as a virtue. He was an enemy to rudeness in others, though in the latter part of his life he did not much seem to encourage a dislike of it by his own example. None talked with more humanity of the foibles of oth-

---

[37] Where the waters of the spring were taken for medicinal purposes.

[38] Tunbridge Wells, a resort similar to Bath, south of London.

ers, when absent, than he, nor kept those secrets with which he was entrusted more inviolably. But above all (if moralists will allow it among the number of his virtues) tho' he gamed high, he always played very fairly. These were his qualifications. Some of the nobility regarded him as an inoffensive, useful companion, the size of whose understanding was, in general, level with their own; but their little imitators admired him as a person of fine sense, and great good breeding. Thus people became fond of ranking him in the number of their acquaintance, told over his jests, and Beau *Nash* at length became the fashionable companion.

His first care when made master of the ceremonies, or king of *Bath,* as it is called, was to promote a music subscription, of one guinea each, for a band which was to consist of six performers, who were to receive a guinea a week each for their trouble. He allowed also two guineas a week for lighting and sweeping the rooms, for which he accounted to the subscribers by receipt.

The Pump-house was immediately put under the care of an officer, by the name of the *Pumper;* for which he paid the corporation an annual rent. A row of new houses was begun on the south side of the gravel walks, before which a handsome pavement was then made for the company to walk on. Not less than seventeen or eighteen hundred pounds was raised this year, and in the beginning of 1706, by subscription, and laid out in repairing the roads near the city. The streets began to be better paved, cleaned and lighted, the licenses of the Chairmen were repressed, and by an act of parliament procured on this occasion, the invalids, who came to drink or bathe, were exempted from all manner of toll, as often as they should go out of the city for recreation.

The houses and streets now began to improve, and ornaments were lavished upon them even to profusion. But in the midst of this splendor the company still were obliged to assemble in a booth to drink tea and chocolate, or to game. Mr. *Nash* undertook to remedy this inconvenience. By his direction, one *Thomas Har-* *rison* erected a handsome Assembly-house for these purposes. A better band of music was also procured, and the former subscription of one guinea, was raised to two. *Harrison* had three guineas a week for the room and candles, and the music two guineas a man. The money Mr. *Nash* received and accounted for with the utmost exactness and punctuality. To this house were also added gardens for people of rank and fashion to walk in; and the beauty of the suburbs continued to encrease, notwithstanding the opposition that was made by the corporation, who at that time, looked upon every useful improvement particularly without the walls, as dangerous to the inhabitants within.

His dominion was now extensive and secure, and he determined to support it with the strictest attention. But in order to proceed in every thing like a king, he was resolved to give his subjects a law, and the following rules were accordingly put up in the Pump-room.

RULES *to be observ'd at* BATH

1. That a visit of ceremony at first coming and another at going away, are all that are expected or desired, by ladies of quality and fashion,—except impertinents.
2. That ladies coming to the ball appoint a time for their footmen coming to wait on them home, to prevent disturbance and inconveniencies to themselves and others.
3. That gentlemen of fashion never appearing in a morning before the ladies in gowns and caps, shew breeding and respect.
4. That no person take it ill that any one goes to another's play, or breakfast, and not theirs;—except captious by nature.
5. That no gentleman give his ticket for the balls, to any but gentlewomen.
    N.B.   Unless he has none of his acquaintance.
6. That gentlemen crowding before the ladies at the ball, shew ill manners; and that none do so for the future,—except such as respect nobody but themselves.

7. That no gentleman or lady takes it ill that another dances before them;—except such as have no pretence to dance at all.

8. That the elder ladies and children be content with a second bench at the ball, as being past or not come to perfection.

9. That the younger ladies take notice how many eyes observe them.

N.B. This does not extend to the *Have-at-alls*.

10. That all whisperers of lies and scandal, be taken for their authors.

11. That all repeaters of such lies, and scandal be shun'd by all company;—except such as have been guilty of the same crime.

N.B. *Several men of no character, old women and young ones, of question'd reputation, are great authors of lies in these places, being of the sect of levellers.*[39]

These laws were written by Mr. *Nash* himself, and by the manner in which they are drawn up, he undoubtedly designed them for wit. The reader, however, it is feared, will think them dull. Poor *Nash* was not born a writer; for whatever humour he might have in conversation, he used to call a pen his torpedo, whenever he grasped it, it numbed all his faculties.

But were we to give laws to a nursery, we should make them childish laws; his statutes, tho' stupid, were addressed to fine gentlemen and ladies, and were probably received with sympathetic approbation. It is certain, they were in general religiously observed by his subjects, and executed by him with impartiality, neither rank nor fortune shielded the refractory from his resentment.

The balls by his directions were to begin at six, and to end at eleven. Nor would he suffer them to continue a moment longer, lest invalids might commit irregularities, to counteract the benefit of the waters. Every thing was to be performed in proper order. Each ball was to open with a minuet, danced by two persons of the highest distinction present. When the minuet concluded, the lady was to return to her seat, and Mr. *Nash* was to bring the gentleman a new partner. This ceremony was to be observed by every succeeding couple, every gentleman being obliged to dance with two ladies till the minuets were over, which generally continued two hours. At eight the country dances were to begin, ladies of quality, according to their rank, standing up first. About nine o'clock a short interval was allowed for rest, and for the gentlemen to help their partners to tea. That over, the company were to pursue their amusements till the clock struck eleven. Then the master of the ceremonies entering the ball-room, ordered the music to desist by lifting up his finger. The dances discontinued, and some time allowed for becoming cool, the ladies were handed to their chairs.

Even the royal family themselves had not influence enough to make him deviate from any of these rules. The princess *Amelia* once applying to him for one dance more, after he had given the signal to withdraw, he assured her royal highness, that the established rules of *Bath* resembled the laws of *Lycurgus*,[40] which would admit of no alteration, without an utter subversion of all his authority.

He was not less strict with regard to the dresses, in which ladies and gentlemen were to appear. He had the strongest aversion to a white apron, and absolutely excluded all who ventured to appear at the assembly dressed in that manner. I have known him on a ball night strip even the dutchess of Q———,[41] and throw her apron at one of the hinder benches among the ladies women; observing, that none but *Abigails* appeared in white aprons. This from another would be insult, in him it

---

[39] Members of a seventeenth-century movement to abolish all social distinctions. The term came into bad repute in the Restoration. Johnson defines a leveller as "one who destroys superiority."

[40] Plutarch says Lycurgus gave the senate of Sparta power equal to the king's (in the sixth century B.C.).

[41] The Duchess of Queensbury (d. 1777) was a celebrated beauty and eccentric hostess, known to many men of letters including Congreve, Thomson, Pope, Prior, Gay, and Horace Walpole. The *abigails* to whom she is here compared were "ladies' maids."

was considered as a just reprimand; and the good-natured dutchess acquiesced in his censure.

But he found more difficulty in attacking the gentlemens irregularities; and for some time strove, but in vain, to prohibit the use of swords. Disputes arising from love or play, were sometimes attended with fatal effects. To use his own expression, he was resolved to hinder people from doing, *what they had no mind to,* but for some time without effect. However, there happened about that time, a duel between two gamesters, whose names were *Taylor* and *Clarke,* which helped to promote his peaceable intentions. They fought by torch-light in the grove; *Taylor* was run through the body, but lived seven years after, at which time his wound breaking out afresh, it caused his death. *Clarke* from that time pretended to be a Quaker, but the orthodox brethren never cordially received him among their number; and he died at *London,* about eighteen years after, in poverty and contrition. From that time it was thought necessary to forbid the wearing of swords at *Bath,* as they often tore the ladies cloaths, and frighted them, by sometimes appearing upon trifling occasions. Whenever therefore *Nash* heard of a challenge given, or accepted, he instantly had both parties arrested. The gentlemen's boots also made a very desperate stand against him, the country 'squires were by no means submissive to his usurpations; and probably his authority alone would never have carried him thro', had he not reinforced it with ridicule. He wrote a song upon the occasion, which, for the honour of his poetical talents, the world shall see.

FRONTINELLA'S *invitation to the Assembly.*

Come, one and all, to *Hoyden* hall,
For there's the assembly this night;
   None but prude fools,
   Mind manners and rules;
We *Hoydens* do decency slight.

Come Trollops and Slatterns,
Cockt hats and white aprons,
This best our modesty suits;
   For why should not we,
   In dress be as free,
As *Hogs-Norton* 'squires in boots.

The keenness, severity and particularly the good rhymes of this little *morceau,*[42] which was at that time highly relished by many of the nobility at *Bath,* gained him a temporary triumph. But to push his victories, he got up a puppet shew, in which punch came in booted and spurred, in the character of a country 'squire. He was introduced as courting his mistress, and having obtained her consent to comply with his wishes, upon going to bed, he is desired to pull off his boots. My boots, replies punch, why, madam, you may as well bid me pull off my legs. I never go without boots, I never ride, I never dance without them; and this piece of politeness is quite the thing at *Bath.* We always dance at our town in boots, and the ladies often move minuets in riding-hoods. Thus he goes on, till his mistress, grown impatient, kicks him off the stage.

From that time few ventured to appear at the assemblies in *Bath* in a riding-dress; and whenever any gentleman, thro' ignorance, or haste, appeared in the rooms in boots, *Nash* would make up to him, and bowing in an arch manner, would tell him, that he had forgot his horse. Thus he was at last completely victorious.

Dolisq; coacti
Quos neque Tydides nec Larissaeus
   Achilles
Non anni domuere decem.[43]

He began therefore to reign without a rival, and like other kings had his mistresses, flatterers, enemies and calumniators; the amusements of the place however wore a very different aspect from what they did formerly. Regularity repressed pride, and that lessened, people of fortune became fit for society. Let the

[42] artistic fragment.
[43] "Tears produced what neither the son of Tydeus nor Achilles of Larissa was able to do in ten years" (Vergil, *Aeneid,* II, 196–198).

morose and grave censure an attention to forms and ceremonies, and rail at those, whose only business it is to regulate them; but tho' ceremony is very different from politeness, no country was ever yet polite, that was not first ceremonious. The natural gradation of breeding begins in savage disgust, proceeds to indifference, improves into attention, by degrees refines into ceremonious observance, and the trouble of being ceremonious at length produces politeness, elegance and ease. There is therefore some merit in mending society, even in one of the inferior steps of this gradation; and no man was more happy in this respect than Mr. *Nash*. In every nation there are enough who have no other business or care but that of buying pleasure; and he taught them, who bid at such an auction, the art of procuring what they sought without diminishing the pleasure of others.

The city of *Bath*, by such assiduity, soon became the theatre of summer amusements for all people of fashion; and the manner of spending the day there must amuse any, but such as disease or spleen had made uneasy to themselves. The following is a faint picture of the pleasures that scene affords. Upon a stranger's arrival at *Bath* he is welcomed by a peal of the Abbey bells, and in the next place, by the voice and music of the city waits.[44] For these civilities the ringers have generally a present made them of half a guinea, and the waits of half a crown, or more, in proportion to the person's fortune, generosity or ostentation. These customs, tho' disagreeable, are however generally liked, or they would not continue. The greatest incommodity attending them is the disturbance the bells must give the sick. But the pleasure of knowing the name of every family that comes to town recompences the inconvenience. Invalids are fond of news, and upon the first sound of the bells, every body sends out to enquire for whom they ring.

After the family is thus welcomed to *Bath*, it is the custom for the master of

it to go to the public places, and subscribe two guineas at the assembly-houses towards the balls and music in the pump-house, for which he is entitled to three tickets every ball night. His next subscription is a crown, half a guinea, or a guinea, according to his rank and quality, for the liberty of walking in the private walks belonging to *Simpson's* assembly-house; a crown or half a guinea is also given to the booksellers, for which the gentleman is to have what books he pleases to read at his lodgings. And at the coffee-house another subscription is taken for pen, ink and paper, for such letters as the subscriber shall write at it during his stay. The ladies too may subscribe to the booksellers, and to an house by the pump-room, for the advantage of reading the news, and for enjoying each other's conversation.

Things being thus adjusted, the amusements of the day are generally begun by bathing, which is no unpleasing method of passing away an hour, or so.

The baths are five in number. On the south-west side of the abbey church is the King's Bath; which is an oblong square, the walls are full of niches, and at every corner are steps to descend into it: this bath is said to contain 427 tons and 50 gallons of water; and on its rising out of the ground over the springs, it is sometimes too hot to be endured by those who bathe therein. Adjoining to the King's Bath there is another, called the Queen's Bath; this is of more temperate warmth, as borrowing its water from the other.

In the south-west part of the city are three other baths, viz. The Hot Bath, which is not much inferior in heat to the King's Bath, and contains 53 tons 2 hogsheads, and 11 gallons of water. The Cross Bath, which contains 52 tons 3 hogsheads, and 11 gallons; and the Leper's Bath, which is not so much frequented as the rest.

The King's Bath (according to the best observations) will fill in about nine hours and a half; the Hot Bath in about eleven hours and a half; and the Cross Bath in about the same time.

The hours for bathing are commonly between six and nine in the morning; and

---

[44] itinerant musicians.

the Baths are every morning supplied with fresh water; for when the people have done bathing, the sluices in each Bath are pulled up, and the water is carried off by drains into the river Avon.

In the morning the lady is brought in a close chair, dressed in her bathing cloaths, to the Bath; and, being in the water, the woman who attends, presents her with a little floating dish like a bason; into which the lady puts an handkerchief, a snuff-box, and a nosegay. She then traverses the Bath; if a novice with a guide, if otherwise by herself; and having amused herself thus while she thinks proper, calls for her chair, and returns to her lodgings.

The amusement of bathing is immediately succeeded by a general assembly of people at the pump-house, some for pleasure, and some to drink the hot waters. Three glasses, at three different times, is the usual portion for every drinker; and the intervals between every glass are enlivened by the harmony of a small band of music, as well as by the conversation of the gay, the witty, or the forward.

From the pump-house the ladies, from time to time, withdraw to a female coffee-house, and from thence return to their lodgings to breakfast. The gentlemen withdraw to their coffee-houses, to read the papers, or converse on the news of the day, with a freedom and ease not to be found in the metropolis.

People of fashion make public breakfasts at the assembly-houses, to which they invite their acquaintances, and they sometimes order private concerts; or when so disposed, attend lectures upon the arts and sciences, which are frequently taught there in a pretty superficial manner, so as not to teize the understanding, while they afford the imagination some amusement. The private concerts are performed in the ball-rooms, the tickets a crown each.

Concert breakfasts at the assembly-house, sometimes make also a part of the morning's amusement here, the expences of which are defrayed by a subscription among the men. Persons of rank and fortune who can perform are admitted into the orchestra, and find a pleasure in joining with the performers.

Thus we have the tedious morning fairly over. When noon approaches, and church (if any please to go there) is done, some of the company appear upon the parade, and other public walks, where they continue to chat and amuse each other, 'till they have formed parties for the play, cards, or dancing for the evening. Another part of the company divert themselves with reading in the booksellers shops, or are generally seen taking the air and exercise, some on horseback, some in coaches. Some walk in the meadows round the town, winding along the side of the river Avon, and the neighbouring canal; while others are seen scaling some of those romantic precipices that overhang the city.

When the hour of dinner draws nigh, and the company is returned from their different recreations, the provisions are generally served with the utmost elegance and plenty. Their mutton, butter, fish, and fowl, are all allowed to be excellent, and their cookery still exceeds their meat.

After dinner is over, and evening prayers ended, the company meet a second time at the pump-house. From this they retire to the walks, and from thence go to drink tea at the assembly-houses, and the rest of the evenings are concluded either with balls, plays or visits. A theatre was erected in the year 1705 by subscription, by people of the highest rank, who permitted their arms to be engraven on the inside of the house, as a public testimony of their liberality towards it. Every tuesday and friday evening is concluded with a public ball, the contributions to which are so numerous, that the price of each ticket is trifling. Thus Bath yields a continued rotation of diversions, and people of all ways of thinking, even from the libertine to the methodist, have it in their power to complete the day with employments suited to their inclinations.

In this manner every amusement soon improved under Mr. *Nash's* administration. The magistrates of the city found, that he was necessary and useful, and took every opportunity of paying the same respect to his fictitious royalty, that is generally extorted by real power. The same satisfaction a young lady finds upon being singled out at her first appearance; or an applauded poet, on the success of his first tragedy, influenced him. All admired him as an extraordinary character; and some who knew no better, as a very fine gentleman; he was perfectly happy in their little applause, and affected at length something particular in his dress, behaviour and conversation.

His equipage was sumptuous, and he usually travelled to *Tunbridge,* in a post chariot and six greys, with out-riders, footmen, *French* horns, and every other appendage of expensive parade. He always wore a white hat, and, to apologize for this singularity, said, he did it purely to secure it from being stolen; his dress was tawdry, tho' not perfectly genteel; he might be considered as a beau of several generations, and in his appearance he, in some measure, mixed the fashions of the last age with those of the present. He perfectly understood elegant expence, and generally passed his time in the very best company, if persons of the first distinction deserve that title.

[HIS GAMBLING ACTIVITIES]

But I hear the reader now demand, what finances were to support all this finery, or where the treasures, that gave him such frequent opportunities of displaying his benevolence, or his vanity? To answer this, we must now enter upon another part of his character, his talents as a gamester; for by gaming alone at that period, of which I speak, he kept up so very genteel an appearance. When he first figured at *Bath,* there were few laws against this destructive amusement. The gaming-table was the constant resource of despair and indigence, and the frequent ruin of opulent fortunes. Wherever people of fashion came, needy adventurers were generally found in waiting. With such *Bath* swarmed, and among this class Mr. *Nash* was certainly

to be numbered in the beginning, only with this difference, that he wanted the corrupt heart, too commonly attending a life of expedients; for he was generous, humane and honourable, even tho' by profession a gamester.

A thousand instances might be given of his integrity, even in this infamous profession; where his generosity often impelled him to act in contradiction to his interest. Wherever he found a novice in the hands of a sharper, he generally forewarned him of the danger; whenever he found any inclined to play, yet ignorant of the game, he would offer his services, and play for them. I remember an instance to this effect, tho' too nearly concerned in the affair to publish the gentleman's name of whom it is related. In the year 1725, there came to *Bath* a giddy youth, who had just resigned his fellowship at *Oxford.* He brought his whole fortune with him there, it was but a trifle, however he was resolved to venture it all. Good fortune seemed kinder than could be expected. Without the smallest skill in play, he won a sum sufficient to make any unambitious man happy. His desire of gain encreasing with his gains, in the *October* following he was *at all,* and added four thousand pounds to his former capital. Mr. *Nash* one night, after losing a considerable sum to this undeserving son of fortune, invited him to supper. Sir, cried this honest, tho' veteran gamester, perhaps you may imagine I have invited you, in order to have my revenge at home; but, sir! I scorn so inhospitable an action. I desired the favour of your company to give you some advice, which you will pardon me, Sir, you seem to stand in need of. You are now high in spirits, and drawn away by a torrent of success. But there will come a time, when you will repent having left the calm of a college life for the turbulent profession of a gamester. Ill runs, will come, as sure as day and night succeed each other. Be therefore advised, remain content with your present gains; for be persuaded, that had you the bank of *England,* with your present ignorance of gaming, it would vanish like a fairy dream. You are a stranger to me, but to convince you of the part I take in your welfare, I'll give you fifty guineas, to forfeit twenty, every time you lose two hundred at one sitting. The young gentleman refused his offer, and was at last undone!

The late duke of *B.* being chagrined at losing a considerable sum, pressed Mr. *Nash* to tie him up for the future from playing deep. Accordingly, the beau gave his grace an hundred guineas to forfeit ten thousand, whenever he lost a sum to the same amount at play, in one sitting. The duke loved play to distraction, and soon after at hazard lost eight thousand guineas, and was going to throw for three thousand more; when *Nash,* catching hold of the dice-box, entreated his Grace to reflect upon the penalty if he lost; the Duke for that time desisted; but so strong was the furor of play upon him, that soon after, losing a considerable sum at *New-market,* he was contented to pay the penalty.

When the late earl of T——d was a youth, he was passionately fond of play, and never better pleased than with having Mr. *Nash* for his antagonist. *Nash* saw with concern his lordship's foible, and undertook to cure him, tho' by a very disagreeable remedy. Conscious of his own superior skill, he determined to engage him in single play for a very considerable sum. His lordship, in proportion as he lost his game, lost his temper too; and as he approached the gulph, seemed still more eager for ruin. He lost his estate; some writings were put into the winner's possession; his very equipage was deposited as a last stake, and he lost that also. But, when our generous gamester had found his lordship sufficiently punished for this temerity, he returned all; only stipulating, that he should be paid five thousand pound whenever he should think proper to make the demand. However, he never made any such demand during his lordship's life; but some time after his decease, Mr. *Nash's* affairs, being in the wane, he demanded the money of his lordship's heirs, who honourably paid it without any hesitation.

But whatever skill *Nash* might have

acquired by long practice in play, he was never formed by nature for a successful gamester. He was constitutionally passionate and generous. To acquire a perfection in that art, a man must be natturally phlegmatic, reserved and cool; every passion must learn to obey controul; but he frequently was unable to restrain the violence of his, and was often betrayed by this means into unbecoming rudeness, or childish impertinence; was sometimes a minion of fortune, and as often deprest by adversity. While others made considerable fortunes at the gaming-table, he was ever in the power of chance; nor did even the intimacy with which he was received by the great, place him in a state of independance.

The considerable inconveniencies that were found to result from a permission of gaming, at length attracted the attention of the legislature, and in the twelfth year of his late majesty,[45] the most prevalent games at that time were declared fraudulent and unlawful. Every age has had its peculiar modes of gaming. The games of Gleek, Primero, In and In, and several others now exploded, employed our sharping ancestors; to these succeeded the Ace of hearts, Pharaoh, Basset, and Hazard, all games of chance like the former. But tho' in these the chances seemed equal to the novice; in general those who kept the bank were considerable winners. The act therefore, passed upon this occasion, declared all such games and lotteries illicit, and directed, that all who should set up such games, should forfeit two hundred pounds, to be levied by distress on the offender's goods; one third to go to the informer, the residue to the poor.

The act further declared, that every person who played in any place, except in the royal palace where his majesty resided, should forfeit fifty pounds, and should be condemned to pay treble costs in case of an appeal.

This law was scarcely made, before it was eluded by the invention of divers fraudulent and deceitful games; and a particular game, called Passage, was

[45] i.e., 1726.

daily practised, and contributed to the ruin of thousands. To prevent this, the ensuing year it was enacted, that this and every other game invented, or to be invented with one die, or more, or any other instrument of the same nature, with numbers thereon, should be subject to a similar penalty; and at the same time, the persons playing with such instruments should be punished as above.

This amendment of the law soon gave birth to new evasions; the game of Rolly Polly, Marlborough's Battles, but particularly the E O,[46] were set up; and strange to observe! several of those very noblemen, who had given their voices to suppress gaming, were the most ready to encourage it. This game was at first set up at *Tunbridge*. It was invented by one *C——k,* and carried on between him and one Mr. *A——e,* proprietor of the assembly-room at that place; and was reckoned extremely profitable to the bank, as it gained two and an half per cent. on all that was lost or won.

As all gaming was suppressed but this, Mr. *Nash* was now utterly destitute of any resource that he could expect from his superior skill, and long experience in the art. The money to be gained in private gaming is at best but trifling, and the opportunity precarious. The minds of the generality of mankind shrink with their circumstances; and *Nash,* upon the immediate prospect of poverty, was now mean[47] enough (I will call it no worse) to enter into a base confederacy with those low creatures to evade the law, and to share the plunder. The occasion was as follows. The profits of the table were, as I observed, divided between *C——k* the inventor, and *A——e* the room-keeper. The first year's profits were extraordinary, and *A——e* the room-keeper now began to wish himself sole proprietor. The combinations of the worthless are ever of short duration. The next year therefore *A——e* turned *C——k* out of his room, and set up the game for himself. The gentlemen and ladies who frequented the wells, unmindful of the immense profit gained by these reptiles, still continued to game as before; and *A——e* was triumphing in the success of his politics, when he was informed, that *C——k* and his friends hired the crier to cry the game down. The consequences of this would have been fatal to *A——e's* interest, for by this means frauds might have been discovered, which would deter even the most ardent lovers of play. Immediately, therefore, while the crier was yet upon the walks, he applied to Mr. *Nash* to stop these proceedings, and at the same time offered him a fourth share of the bank, which Mr. *Nash* was mean enough to accept. This is the greatest blot in his life, and this it is hoped will find pardon.

The day after, the inventor offered an half of the bank; but this Mr. *Nash* thought proper to refuse, being pre-engaged to *A——e.* Upon which, being disappointed, he applied to one Mr. *J——e,* and under his protection another table was set up, and the company seemed to be divided equally between them. I cannot reflect, without surprize, at the wisdom of the gentlemen and ladies, to suffer themselves to be thus parcelled out between a pack of sharpers, and permit themselves to be defrauded, without even the shew of opposition. The company thus divided, Mr. *Nash* once more availed himself of their parties, and prevailed upon them to unite their banks, and to divide the gains into three shares, of which he reserved one to himself.

Nash had hitherto enjoyed a fluctuating fortune; and had he taken the advantage of the present opportunity, he might have been for the future not only above want, but even in circumstances of opulence. Had he cautiously employed himself in computing the benefits of the table, and exacting his stipulated share, he might have soon grown rich; but he entirely left the management of it to the people of the rooms; he took them (as he says in one of his memorials upon this occasion) to be honest, and never enquired what was won or lost; and, it is

[46] A game in which the object is to guess whether a ball will fall into a slot marked E or one marked O; the use of letters instead of numbers was one means of evading the law.

[47] i.e., sufficiently below the character of one who should protect the laws by his leadership.

probable, they were seldom assiduous in informing him. I find a secret pleasure in thus displaying the insecurity of friendships among the base. They pretended to pay him regularly at first, but he soon discovered, as he says, that at *Tunbridge* he had suffered to the amount of two thousand guineas.

In the mean time, as the E O table thus succeeded at *Tunbridge,* Mr. *Nash* was resolved to introduce it at *Bath,* and previously asked the opinion of several lawyers, who declared it no way illegal. In consequence of this, he wrote to Mrs. *A———,* who kept one of the great rooms at *Bath,* acquainting her with the profits attending such a scheme, and proposing to have a fourth share with her, and Mr. *W———,* the proprietor of the other room, for his authority, and protection. To this Mr. *W———* and she returned him for answer, that they would grant him a fifth share; which he consented to accept. Accordingly he made a journey to *London,* and bespoke two tables, one for each room, at the rate of fifteen pounds each table.

The tables were no sooner set up at *Bath,* than they were frequented with a greater concourse of gamesters than those at *Tunbridge.* Men of that infamous profession, from every part of the kingdom, and even other parts of *Europe,* flocked here to feed on the ruins of each other's fortune. This afforded another opportunity for Mr. *Nash* to become rich; but, as at *Tunbridge,* he thought the people here also would take care of him, and therefore he employed none to look after his interest. The first year they paid him what he thought just; the next, the woman of the room dying, her son paid him, and shewed his books. Sometime after the people of the rooms offered him one hundred pounds a year each for his share; which he refused; every succeeding year they continued to pay him less and less; 'till at length he found, as he pretends, that he had thus lost not less than twenty thousand pounds.

Thus they proceeded, deceiving the public and each other, 'till the legislature thought proper to suppress these seminaries of vice. It was enacted, that after the 24th of *June,* 1745, none should be permitted to keep an house, room or place, for playing, upon pain of such forfeitures, as were declared in former acts instituted for that purpose.

The legislature likewise amended a law, made in the reign of queen *Anne,* for recovering money lost at play, on the oath of the winner. By this act no person was rendered incapable of being a witness; and every person present at a gaming-table might be summoned by the magistrate, who took cognizance of the affair. No privilege of parliament was allowed, to those convicted of having gaming tables in their houses. Those who lost ten pounds at one time, were liable to be indicted within six months after the offence was committed; and being convicted, were to be fined five times the value of the sum won or lost, for the use of the poor. Any offender before conviction, discovering another, so as to be convicted, was to be discharged from the penalties incurred by his own offences.

By this wise and just act, all *Nash's* future hopes of succeeding by the tables were blown up. He had now only the justice and generosity of his confederates to trust to; but that he soon found to be a vain expectation; for, if we can depend on his own memorials, what at one time they confessed, they would at another deny; and tho' upon some occasions they seemed at variance with each other, yet when they were to oppose him, whom they considered as a common enemy, they generally united with confidence and success. He now therefore had nothing but a law-suit to confide in for redress; and this is ever the last expedient to retrieve a desperate fortune. He accordingly threw his suit into Chancery, and by this means the public became acquainted with what he had long endeavoured to conceal. They now found that he was himself concerned in the gaming-tables, of which he only seemed the conductor; and that he had shared part of the spoil, tho' he complained of having been defrauded of a just share.

The success of his suit was what might have been naturally expected; he had but at best a bad cause, and as the oaths of the defendants were alone sufficient to cast him in Chancery, it was not surprizing that he was nonsuited.[48] But the consequence of this affair was much more fatal than he had imagined, it lessened him in the esteem of the public, it drew several enemies against him, and in some measure diminished the authority of any defence he could make. From that time (about the year 1745) I find this poor, good-natured, but misguided man involved in continual disputes, every day calumniated with some new slander, and continually endeavouring to obviate its effects.

Upon these occasions his usual method was, by printed bills handed about among his acquaintance, to inform the public of his most private transactions with some of those creatures, with whom he had formerly associated; but these apologies served rather to blacken his antagonists, than to vindicate him. They were in general extremely ill written, confused, obscure, and sometimes unintelligible. By these however it appeard, that W——— was originally obliged to him for the resort of company to his room; that lady H———, who had all the company before W———'s room was built, offered Mr. *Nash* an hundred pound for his protection; which he refused, having previously promised to support Mrs. W———. It appears by these apologies, that the persons concerned in the rooms made large fortunes, while he still continued in pristine indigence; and that his nephew, for whom he had at first secured one of the rooms, was left in as great distress as he.

His enemies were not upon this occasion contented with aspersing him, as a confederate with sharpers, they even asserted, that he spent, and embezzled the subscriptions of gentlemen and ladies, which were given for useful or charitable purposes. But to such aspersions he answered, by declaring, to use his own expression, before God and man, that he never diverted one shilling of the said subscriptions to his own use; nor was he

ever thought to have done it, till new enemies started up against him. Perhaps the reader may be curious to see one of these memorials, written by himself; and I will indulge his curiosity, merely to shew a specimen of the stile and manner of a man, whose whole life was past in a round of gaiety and conversation, whose jests were a thousand times repeated, and whose company was courted by every son and daughter of fashion. The following is particularly levelled against those who, in the latter part of his life, took every opportunity to traduce his character.

A Monitor.[49]

For the Lord hateth lying and deceitful lips.

PSAL.[50]

The curse denounced in my motto, is sufficient to intimidate any person, who is not quite abandoned in their evil ways, and who have any fear of God before their eyes; everlasting burnings are a terrible reward for their misdoings; and nothing but the most hardened sinners will oppose the judgments of heaven, being without end. This reflection must be shocking to such, as are conscious to themselves, of having erred from the sacred dictates of the Psalmist, and who following the blind impulse of passion, daily forging lies and deceit, to annoy their neighbour. But there are joys in heaven which they can never arrive at, whose whole study is to destroy the peace and harmony, and good order of society, in this place.

This carries little the air of a bagatelle, it rather seems a sermon in miniature, so different are some men in the closet, and in conversation. The following I have taken at random from an heap of other memorials, all tending to set his combination with the afore-mentioned partners in a proper light.

E O was first set up in *A———e* room,

---

[48] i.e., the case was dismissed as untenable.
[49] reminder, warning.
[50] Ps. 120:2. The text of the King James version reads: "Deliver my soul, O Lord, from lying lips, and from a deceitful tongue."

the profits divided between one *C——k* (the inventor of the game) and *A——e.*

The next year, *A——e* finding the game so advantageous, turned *C——k* out of his room, and set the game up himself; but *C——k* and his friends hired the crier to cry the game down; upon which *A——e* came running to me to stop it, after he had cried it once, which I immediately did, and turned the crier off the walks.

Then *A——e* asked me to go a fourth with him in the bank, which I consented to; *C——k* next day took me into his room which he had hired, and proffered me to go half with him, which I refused, being engaged before to *A——e.*

J——e then set up the same game, and complained that he had not half play at his room; upon which I made them agree to join their banks, and divide equally the gain and loss, and I to go the like share in the bank.

I taking them to be honest, never enquired what was won or lost; and thought they paid me honestly, 'till it was discovered, that they had defrauded me of 2000 guineas.

I then arrested *A——e,* who told me I must go into Chancery, and that I should begin with the people of *Bath,* who had cheated me of ten times as much; and told my attorney, that *J——e* had cheated me of 500, and wrote me word that I had not under his hand, which never was used in play.

Upon my arresting *A——e,* I received a letter not to prosecute *J——e,* for he would be a very good witness: I writ a discharge to *J——e* for 125 l. in full, though he never paid me a farthing, upon his telling me, if his debts were paid he was not worth a shilling.

Every article of this I can prove from *A——e's* own mouth, as a reason that he allowed the bank keepers but 10 *per cent.* because I went 20; and his suborning —— to alter his informations.

RICHARD NASH.

This gentleman's simplicity, in trusting persons whom he had no previous reasons to place confidence in, seems to be one of those lights into his character, which, while they impeach his understanding, do honour to his benevolence. The low and timid are ever suspicious; but a heart impressed with honourable sentiments, expects from others sympathetic sincerity.

[PROTECTOR OF WOMEN]

But now that we have viewed his conduct as a gamester, and seen him on that side of his character, which is by far the most unfavourable, seen him declining from his former favour and esteem, the just consequence of his quitting, tho' but ever so little, the paths of honour; let me turn to those brighter parts of his life and character, which gained the affection of his friends, the esteem of the corporation which he assisted, and may possibly attract the attention of posterity. By his successes we shall find, that figuring in life, proceeds less from the possession of great talents, than from the proper application of moderate ones. Some great minds are only fitted to put forth their powers in the storm; and the occasion is often wanting during a whole life for a great exertion: but trifling opportunities of shining, are almost every hour offered to the little sedulous mind; and a person thus employed, is not only more pleasing, but more useful in a state of tranquil society.

Tho' gaming first introduced him into polite company, this alone could hardly have carried him forward, without the assistance of a genteel address, much vivacity, some humour, and some wit. But once admitted into the circle of the Beau Monde, he then laid claim to all the privileges by which it is distinguished. Among others, in the early part of his life, he entered himself professedly into the service of the fair sex; he set up for a man of gallantry and intrigue; and if we can credit the boasts of his old age, he often succeeded. In fact, the business of love somewhat resembles the business of physic; no matter for qualifications, he that makes vigorous pretensions to either is surest of success. Nature had by no means formed Mr. *Nash* for a Beau

Garçon;[51] his person was clumsey, too large and aukward, and his features harsh, strong, and peculiarly irregular; yet even, with those disadvantages, he made love, became an universal admirer of the sex, and was universally admired. He was possessed, at least, of some requisites of a lover. He had assiduity, flattery, fine cloaths, and as much wit as the ladies he addressed. Wit, flattery, and fine cloaths, he used to say, were enough to debauch a nunnery. But my fair readers of the present day are exempt from this scandal; and it is no matter now, what he said of their grandmothers.

As *Nestor*[52] was a man of three ages, so *Nash* sometimes humorously called himself a beau of three generations. He had seen flaxen bobs succeeded by majors, which in their turn gave way to negligents, which were at last totally routed by bags and ramilees.[53] The manner in which gentlemen managed their amours, in these different ages of fashion, were not more different than their perriwigs. The lover in the reign of king *Charles* was solemn, majestic and formal. He visited his mistress in state. Languished for the favour, kneeled when he toasted his goddess, walked with solemnity, performed the most trifling things with decorum, and even took snuff with a flourish. The beau of the latter part of queen *Ann*'s reign was disgusted with so much formality, he was pert, smart and lively; his billet-doux were written in a quite different stile from that of his antiquated predecessor; he was ever laughing at his own ridiculous situation; till at last, he persuaded the lady to become as ridiculous as himself. The beau of the third age, in which Mr. *Nash* died, was still more extraordinary than either; his whole secret in intrigue consisted in perfect indifference. The only way to make love now, I have heard Mr. *Nash* say, was to take no manner of notice of the lady, which method was found the surest way to secure her affections.

However these things be, this gentleman's successes in amour were in reality very much confined in the second and third age of intrigue; his character was too public for a lady to consign her reputation to his keeping. But in the beginning of life it is said, he knew the secret history of the times, and contributed himself to swell the page of scandal. Were I upon the present occasion to hold the pen of a novelist, I could recount some amours, in which he was successful. I could fill a volume with little anecdotes, which contain neither pleasure nor instruction; with histories of professing lovers, and poor believing girls deceived by such professions. But such adventures are easily written, and as easily atchieved. The plan even of fictitious novel is quite exhausted; but truth, which I have followed here, and ever design to follow, presents in the affair of love scarce any variety. The manner in which one reputation is lost, exactly resembles that by which another is taken away. The gentleman begins at timid distance, grows more bold, becomes rude, till the lady is married or undone; such is the substance of every modern novel; nor will I gratify the pruriency of folly, at the expence of every other pleasure my narration may afford.

Mr. *Nash* did not long continue an universal gallant; but in the earlier years of his reign, entirely gave up his endeavours to deceive the sex, in order to become the honest protector of their innocence, the guardian of their reputation, and a friend to their virtue.

This was a character he bore for many years, and supported it with integrity, assiduity and success. It was his constant practice to do every thing in his power to prevent the fatal consequences of rash and inconsiderate love; and there are many persons now alive, who owe their present happiness to his having interrupted the progress of an amour, that threatened to become unhappy, or even criminal, by privately making their guardians or parents acquainted with what he could discover.

I shall beg leave to give some instances

---

[51] ladies' man.
[52] A wise old Homeric hero.
[53] Styles of hairdress.

of Mr. *Nash's* good-nature on these occasions, as I have had the accounts from himself. At the conclusion of the treaty of peace at *Utrecht,* colonel *M——* was one of the thoughtless, agreeable, gay creatures, that drew the attention of the company at *Bath.* He danced and talked with great vivacity; and when he gamed among the ladies, he shewed, that his attention was employed rather upon their hearts than their fortunes. His own fortune however was a trifle, when compared to the elegance of his expence; and his imprudence at last was so great, that it obliged him to sell an annuity, arising from his commission, to keep up his splendor a little longer.

However thoughtless he might be, he had the happiness of gaining the affections of Miss *L——,* whose father designed her a very large fortune. This lady was courted by a nobleman of distinction, but she refused his addresses, resolved upon gratifying rather her inclinations than her avarice. The intrigue went on successfully between her and the colonel, and they both would certainly have been married, and been undone, had not Mr. *Nash* apprized her father of their intentions. The old gentleman recalled his daughter from *Bath,* and offered Mr. *Nash* a very considerable present, for the care he had taken, which he refused.

In the mean time colonel *M——* had an intimation how his intrigue came to be discovered; and by taxing Mr. *Nash,* found that his suspicions were not without foundation. A challenge was the immediate consequence, which the king of *Bath,* conscious of having only done his duty, thought proper to decline. As none are permitted to wear swords at *Bath,* the colonel found no opportunity of gratifying his resentment, and waited with impatience to find Mr. *Nash* in town, to require proper satisfaction.

During this interval, however, he found his creditors become too importunate for him to remain longer at *Bath;* and his finances and credit being quite exhausted, he took the desperate resolution of going over to the *Dutch* army in *Flanders,* where he enlisted himself a volunteer. Here he underwent all the fatigues of a private centinel,[54] with the additional misery of receiving no pay, and his friends in *England* gave out, that he was shot at the battle of ——.

In the mean time the nobleman pressed his passion with ardour, but during the progress of his amour, the young lady's father died, and left her heiress to a fortune of fifteen hundred a year. She thought herself now disengaged from her former passion. An absence of two years had in some measure abated her love for the colonel; and the assiduity, the merit, and real regard of the gentleman who still continued to solicit her, were almost too powerful for her constancy. Mr. *Nash,* in the mean time, took every opportunity of enquiring after colonel *M——,* and found, that he had for some time been returned to *England,* but changed his name, in order to avoid the fury of his creditors; and that he was entered into a company of strolling players, who were at that time exhibiting at *Peterborough.*

He now therefore thought he owed the colonel, in justice, an opportunity of promoting his fortune, as he had once deprived him of an occasion of satisfying his love. Our Beau therefore invited the lady to be of a party to *Peterborough,* and offered his own equipage, which was then one of the most elegant in *England,* to conduct her there. The proposal being accepted, the lady, the nobleman, and Mr. *Nash,* arrived in town just as the players were going to begin.

Colonel *M——,* who used every means of remaining *incognito,* and who was too proud to make his distresses known to any of his former acquaintance, was now degraded into the character of *Tom* in the *Conscious Lovers.*[55] Miss *L——* was placed in the foremost row of the spectators, her lord on one side, and the impatient *Nash* on the other; when the unhappy youth appeared in that despicable situation upon the stage. The moment he came on, his

---

[54] soldier.   [55] By Sir Richard Steele (1722).

former mistress struck his view, but his amazement was encreased, when he saw her fainting away in the arms of those who sate behind her. He was incapable of proceeding, and scarce knowing what he did, he flew and caught her in his arms.

Colonel, cried *Nash,* when they were in some measure recovered, you once thought me your enemy, because I endeavoured to prevent you both from ruining each other, you were then wrong, and you have long had my forgiveness. If you love well enough now for matrimony, you fairly have my consent, and d——n him, say I, that attempts to part you. Their nuptials were solemnized soon after, and affluence added a zest to all their future enjoyments. Mr. *Nash* had the thanks of each, and he afterwards spent several agreeable days in that society, which he had contributed to render happy.

I shall beg the reader's patience, while I give another instance, in which he ineffectually offered his assistance and advice. This story is not from himself; but told us partly by Mr. *Wood,* the architect of *Bath,* as it fell particularly within his own knowledge; and partly from another memoir, to which he refers.

Miss *Sylvia S——* was descended from one of the best families in the kingdom, and was left a large fortune upon her Sister's decease. She had early in life been introduced into the best company, and contracted a passion for elegance and expence. It is usual to make the heroine of a story very witty, and very beautiful, and such circumstances are so surely expected, that they are scarce attended to. But whatever the finest poet could conceive of wit, or the most celebrated painter imagine of beauty, were excelled in the perfections of this young lady. Her superiority in both was allowed by all, who either heard, or had seen her. She was naturally gay, generous to a fault, good-natured to the highest degree, affable in conversation, and some of her letters, and other writings, as well in verse as prose, would have shone amongst those of the most celebrated wits of this, or any other age, had they been published.

But these great qualifications were marked by another, which lessened the value of them all. She was imprudent! But let it not be imagined, that her reputation or honour suffered by her imprudence; I only mean, she had no knowledge of the use of money, she relieved distress, by putting herself into the circumstances of the object whose wants she supplied.

She was arrived at the age of nineteen, when the croud of her lovers, and the continual repetition of new flattery, had taught her to think she could never be forsaken, and never poor. Young ladies are apt to expect a certainty of success, from a number of lovers; and yet I have seldom seen a girl courted by an hundred lovers, that found an husband in any. Before the choice is fixed, she has either lost her reputation, or her good sense; and the loss of either is sufficient to consign her to perpetual virginity.

Among the number of this young lady's lovers was the celebrated *S———,* who, at that time, went by the name of *the good-natured man.* This gentleman, with talents that might have done honour to humanity, suffered himself to fall at length into the lowest state of debasement. He followed the dictates of every newest passion, his love, his pity, his generosity, and even his friendships were all in excess; he was unable to make head against any of his sensations or desires, but they were in general worthy wishes and desires; for he was constitutionally virtuous. This gentleman, who at last died in a goal,[56] was at that time this lady's envied favourite.

It is probable that he, thoughtless creature, had no other prospect from this amour, but that of passing the present moments agreeably. He only courted dissipation, but the lady's thoughts were fixed on happiness. At length, however, his debts amounting to a considerable sum, he was arrested, and thrown into prison. He endeavoured at first to conceal his situation from his beautiful mistress; but she soon came to a knowledge of his distress, and took a fatal resolution

---

[56] Variant spelling of *gaol,* i.e., jail.

of freeing him from confinement by discharging all the demands of his creditors.

Mr. *Nash* was at that time in *London,* and represented to the thoughtless young lady, that such a measure would effectually ruin both; that so warm a concern for the interests of Mr. *S———,* would in the first place quite impair her fortune, in the eyes of our sex; and what was worse, lessen her reputation in those of her own. He added, that thus bringing Mr. *S———* from prison, would be only a temporary relief; that a mind so generous as his, would become bankrupt under the load of gratitude; and instead of improving in friendship or affection, he would only study to avoid a creditor he could never repay; that tho' small favours produce good-will, great ones destroy friendship. These admonitions however were disregarded, and she too late found the prudence and truth of her adviser. In short, her fortune was by this means exhausted, and, with all her attractions, she found her acquaintance began to disesteem her, in proportion as she became poor.

In this situation she accepted Mr. *Nash's* invitation of returning to *Bath;* he promised to introduce her to the best company there, and he was assured that her merit would do the rest; upon her very first appearance, ladies of the highest distinction courted her friendship and esteem; but a settled melancholy had taken possession of her mind, and no amusements that they could propose were sufficient to divert it. Yet still, as if from habit, she followed the crowd in its levities, and frequented those places, where all persons endeavour to forget themselves in the bustle of ceremony and shew.

Her beauty, her simplicity, and her unguarded situation, soon drew the attention of a designing wretch, who at that time kept one of the rooms at *Bath,* and who thought, that this lady's merit, properly managed, might turn to good account. This woman's name was dame *Lindsey,* a creature who, though vicious, was in appearance sanctified; and though designing, had some wit and humour. She began by the humblest assiduity to ingratiate herself with Miss *S———;* shewed, that she could be amusing as a companion, and by frequent offers of money, proved, that she could be useful as a friend. Thus by degrees she gained an entire ascendant over this poor, thoughtless, deserted girl; and in less than one year, namely about 1727, Miss *S,* without ever transgressing the laws of virtue, had entirely lost her reputation. Whenever a person was wanting to make up a party for play at dame *Lindsey's, Sylvia,* as she was then familiarly called, was sent for, and was obliged to suffer all those slights, which the rich but too often let fall upon their inferiors in point of fortune.

In most, even the greatest minds, the heart at last becomes level with the meanness of its condition; but in this charming girl, it struggled hard with adversity, and yielded to every encroachment of contempt with sullen reluctance.

But tho' in the course of three years she was in the very eye of public inspection, yet, Mr. *Wood* the architect, avers, that he could never, by the strictest observations, perceive her to be tainted with any other vice, than that of suffering herself to be decoyed to the gaming-table, and at her own hazard, playing for the amusement and advantage of others. Her friend Mr. *Nash,* therefore, thought proper to induce her to break off all connections with dame *Lindsey,* and to rent part of Mr. *Wood's* house, in *Queen square,* where she behaved with the utmost complaisance, regularity and virtue.

In this situation her detestation of life still continued; she found, that time would infallibly deprive her of part of her attractions, and that continual solicitude would impair the rest. With these reflections she would frequently entertain herself, and an old faithful maid in the vales of *Bath,* when ever the weather would permit them to walk out. She would even sometimes start questions in company, with seeming unconcern, in order to know what act of suicide was easiest, and which was attended with the smallest pain. When tired with exercise, she generally retired to meditation, and she became habituated to early hours of sleep and rest. But when the weather prevented her usual exercise, and her sleep was thus more difficult, she made it a rule to rise from her bed, and walk about her chamber, till she began to find an inclination for repose.

This custom made it necessary for her to order a burning candle to be kept all night in her room. And the maid usually, when she withdrew, locked the chamber door, and pushing the key under it beyond reach, her mistress by that constant method lay undisturbed till seven o'clock in the morning, then she arose, unlocked the door, and rang the bell, as a signal for the maid to return.

This state of seeming piety, regularity, and prudence continued for some time, till the gay, celebrated toasted miss *Silvia* was sunk into an housekeeper to the gentleman at whose house she lived. She was unable to keep company for want of the elegancies of dress, that are the usual passport among the polite, and she was too haughty to seem to want them. The fashionable, the amusing, and the polite in society now seldom visited her, and from being once the object of every eye, she was now deserted by all, and preyed upon by the bitter reflections of her own imprudence.

Mr. *Wood,* and part of his family, were gone to *London.* Miss *Silvia* was left with the rest as a governess at *Bath.* She sometimes saw Mr. *Nash,* and acknowledged the friendship of his admonitions, tho' she refused to accept any other marks of his generosity than that of advice. Upon the close of the day, in which Mr. *Wood* was expected to return from *London,* she expressed some uneasiness at the disappointment of not seeing him; took particular care to settle the affairs of his family, and then as usual sate down to meditation. She now cast a retrospect over her past misconduct, and her approaching misery; she saw, that even affluence gave her no real happiness, and from indigence she thought nothing could be hoped but lingering calamity. She at length conceived the fatal resolution of leaving a life, in which she could see no corner for comfort, and terminating a scene of imprudence in suicide.

Thus resolved, she sate down at her dining-room window, and with cool intrepidity, wrote the following elegant lines on one of the panes of the window.

O death; thou pleasing end of human woe!
Thou cure for life! Thou greatest good below!
Still may'st thou fly the coward, and the slave,
And thy soft slumbers only bless the brave.

She then went into company with the most chearful serenity; talked of indifferent subjects till supper, which she ordered to be got ready in a little library belonging to the family. There she spent the remaining hours, preceding bed-time, in dandling two of Mr. *Wood's* children on her knees. In retiring from thence to her chamber she went into the nursery, to take her leave of another child, as it lay sleeping in the cradle. Struck with the innocence of the little babe's looks, and the consciousness of her meditated guilt, she could not avoid bursting into tears, and hugging it in her arms; she then bid her old servant a good night, for the first time she had ever done so, and went to bed as usual.

It is probable she soon quitted her bed, and was seized with an alternation of passions, before she yielded to the impulse of despair. She dressed herself in clean linen, and white garments of every kind, like a bride-maid. Her gown was pinned over her breast, just as a nurse pins the swaddling cloaths of an infant. A pink silk girdle was the instrument with which she resolved to terminate her misery, and this was lengthened by another made of gold thread. The end of the former was tied with a noose, and the latter with three knots, at a small distance from one another.

Thus prepared, she sate down again, and read; for she left the book open at that place, in the story of *Olympia,* in the *Orlando Furioso*[57] of *Ariosto,* where,

---

[57] Chivalric epic poem (1516 and 1532) by Lodovico Ariosto.

by the perfidy and ingratitude of her bosom friend, she was ruined, and left to the mercy of an unpitying world. This tragical event gave her fresh spirits to go through her fatal purpose; so standing upon a stool, and flinging the girdle, which was tied round her neck, over a closet-door that opened into her chamber, she remained suspended. Her weight however broke the girdle, and the poor despairer fell upon the floor with such violence, that her fall awakened a workman that lay in the house about half an hour after two o'clock.

Recovering herself, she began to walk about the room, as her usual custom was when she wanted sleep; and the workman imagining it to be only some ordinary accident, again went to sleep. She once more, therefore, had recourse to a stronger girdle made of silver thread, and this kept her suspended till she died.

Her old maid continued in the morning to wait as usual for the ringing of the bell, and protracted her patience, hour after hour, till two o'clock in the afternoon; when the workmen at length entering the room through the window, found their unfortunate mistress still hanging, and quite cold. The coroner's jury being impanelled, brought in their verdict lunacy; and her corpse was next night decently buried in her father's grave, at the charge of a female companion, with whom she had for many years an inseparable intimacy.

Thus ended a female wit, a toast, and a gamester; loved, admired, and forsaken. Formed for the delight of society, fallen by imprudence into an object of pity. Hundreds in high life lamented her fate, and wished, when too late, to redress her injuries. They who once had helped to impair her fortune, now regretted that they had assisted in so mean a pursuit. The little effects she had left behind were bought up with the greatest avidity, by those who desired to preserve some token of a companion, that once had given them such delight. The remembrance of every virtue she was possessed of was now improved by pity. Her former follies were few, but the last swelled them to a large amount. And she

remains the strongest instance to posterity, that want of prudence alone, almost cancels every other virtue.

In all this unfortunate lady's affairs Mr. *Nash* took a peculiar concern, he directed her when they played, advised her when she deviated from the rules of caution, and performed the last offices of friendship after her decease, by raising the auction of her little effects.

But he was not only the assistant and the friend of the fair sex, but also their defender. He secured their persons from insult, and their reputations from scandal. Nothing offended him more, than a young fellow's pretending to receive favours from ladies he probably never saw; nothing pleased him so much, as seeing such a piece of deliberate mischief punished. Mr. *Nash* and one of his friends, being newly arrived at *Tunbridge* from *Bath,* were one day on the walks, and seeing a young fellow of fortune, with whom they had some slight acquaintance, joined him. After the usual chat and news of the day was over, Mr. *Nash* asked him, how long he had been at the wells, and what company was there? The other replied, he had been at *Tunbridge* a month; but as for company, he could find as good at a *Tyburn* ball. Not a soul was to be seen, except a parcel of gamesters and whores, who would grant the last favour, for a single stake at the Pharaoh bank. "Look you there, continued he, that Goddess of midnight, so fine, at t'other end of the walks, by Jove, she was mine this morning for half a guinea. And she there, who brings up the rear with powdered hair and dirty ruffles, she's pretty enough, but cheap, perfectly cheap; why, my boys, to my own knowledge, you may have her for a crown, and a dish of chocolate into the bargain. Last *Wednesday* night we were happy." Hold there, sir, cried the gentleman; as for your having the first lady, it is possible it may be true, and I intend to ask her about it, for she is my sister; but as to your lying with the other last *Wednesday,* I am sure you are a lying rascal— she is my wife, and we came here but last night. The Buck vainly asked pardon; the gentleman was going to give him proper chastisement; when Mr. *Nash* interposed in his behalf, and obtained his pardon, upon condition that he quitted *Tunbridge* immediately.

But Mr. *Nash* not only took care, during his administration, to protect the ladies from the insults of our sex, but to guard them from the slanders of each other. He, in the first place, prevented any animosities that might arise from place and precedence, by being previously acquainted with the rank and quality of almost every family in the *British* dominions. He endeavoured to render scandal odious, by marking it as the result of envy and folly united. Not even *Solon*[58] could have enacted a wiser law in such a society as *Bath.* The gay, the heedless, and the idle, which mostly compose the groupe of water-drinkers, seldom are at the pains of talking upon universal topics, which require comprehensive thought, or abstract reasoning. The adventures of the little circle of their own acquaintance, or of some names of quality and fashion, make up their whole conversation. But it is too likely, that when we mention those, we wish to depress them, in order to render ourselves more conspicuous; scandal must therefore have fixed her throne at *Bath,* preferable to any other part of the kingdom. However, tho' these endeavours could not totally suppress this custom among the fair, yet they gained him the friendship of several ladies of distinction, who had smarted pretty severely under the lash of censure. Among this number was the old duchess of *Marlborough,*[59] who conceived a particular friendship for him, and which continued during her life. She frequently consulted him in several concerns of a private nature. Her letting leases, building bridges, or forming canals, were often carried on under his guidance; but she advised with him particularly in purchasing liveries for the footmen; a business to which she thought his genius best adapted. As any thing relative to her may please the curiosity of such as delight in the anecdotes and letters of the great,

however dull and insipid, I shall beg leave to present them with one or two of her letters, collected at a venture from several others to the same purpose.

To Mr. Nash, *at the* Bath.

Blenheim, Sept. 18, 1724.

Mr. *Jennens* will give you an account how little time I have in my power, and that will make my excuse for not thanking you sooner for the favour of your letter, and for the trouble you have given yourself in bespeaking the cloth, which I am sure will be good, since you have undertaken to order it. Pray ask Mrs. *Jennens* concerning the cascade, which will satisfy all your doubts in that matter; she saw it play, which it will do in great beauty, for at least six hours together, and it runs enough to cover all the stones constantly, and is a hundred feet broad, which I am told is a much greater breadth than any cascade is in *England;* and this will be yet better than it is, when it is quite finished; this water is a great addition to this place, and the lake being thirty acres, out of which the cascade comes and falls into the canal that goes through the bridge, it makes that look as if it was necessary, which before seemed so otherwise.

> I am
> Your most humble Servant,
> S. MARLBOROUGH.

To Mr. Nash, *at the* Bath.

Marlborough-house, May 17, 1735.
Sir,

I have received the favour of yours of the tenth of *May,* with that from Mr. *Harvey.* And by last post I received a letter from Mr. *Overton,* a sort of a bailiff and a surveyor, whom I have employed a great while upon the estates in *Wiltshire.* He is a very active and very useful man of his sort. He writes to me, that Mr. *Harvey* has been with him, and brought him a paper, which I sent you. He says, that finding he was a man that

---

[58] Lawmaker of ancient Greece.

[59] Sarah Jennings, Duchess of Marlborough (1660–1744).

was desirous to serve me, he had assisted him all he could, by informations which he has given; and that he should continue to assist him. I have writ to him that he did mighty well. There is likewise a considerable tenant of my lord *Bruce's,* his name is *Cannons,* who has promised me his assistance towards recommending tenants for these farms. And if Mr. *Harvey* happens to know such a man, he may put him in mind of it. I am sure you will do me all the good you can. And I hope you are sure that I shall always be sensible of the obligations I have to you, and ever be

Your most thankful and obliged humble Servant,
S. MARLBOROUGH.

Mr. *Harvey* may conclude to take any prices that were given you in the paper. But as I know that we have been scandalously cheated, if he finds that any thing can be let better than it has been let, I do not doubt but he will do it.

The duchess of *Marlborough* seems to be not a much better writer than Mr. *Nash;* but she was worth many hundred thousand pounds, and that might console her. It may give splenetic philosophy, however, some scope for meditation, when it considers, what a parcel of stupid trifles the world is ready to admire.

[KING OF BATH]

Whatever might have been Mr. *Nash's* other excellencies, there was one in which few exceeded him; I mean his extensive humanity. None felt pity more strongly, and none made greater efforts to relieve distress. If I were to name any reigning and fashionable virtue in the present age, I think it should be charity. The numberless benefactions privately given, the various public solicitations for charity, and the success they meet with, serve to prove, that tho' we may fall short of our ancestors in other respects, yet in this instance we greatly excel them. I know not whether it may not be spreading the influence of Mr. *Nash* too widely to say, that he was one of the principal causes of introducing this noble emulation among the rich; but certain it is, no private man ever relieved the distresses of so many as he.

Before gaming was suppressed, and in the meridian of his life and fortune, his benefactions were generally found to equal his other expences. The money he got without pain, he gave away without reluctance; and whenever unable to relieve a wretch, who sued for assistance, he has been often seen to shed tears. A gentleman of broken fortune, one day standing behind his chair, as he was playing a game of picquet for two hundred pounds, and observing with what indifference he won the money, could not avoid whispering these words to another who stood by; "heavens! how happy would all that money make me!" *Nash,* overhearing him, clapp'd the money into his hand; and cried, *go and be happy.*

About six and thirty years ago, a clergyman brought his family to *Bath* for the benefit of the waters. His wife laboured under a lingering disorder, which it was thought nothing but the Hot Wells could remove. The expences of living there soon lessened the poor man's finances; his cloaths were sold, piece by piece, to provide a temporary relief for his little family; and his appearance was at last so shabby, that, from the number of holes in his coat and stockings, *Nash* gave him the name of doctor *Cullender.* Our beau, it seems, was rude enough to make a jest of poverty, tho' he had sensibility enough to relieve it. The poor clergyman combated his distresses with fortitude; and, instead of attempting to solicit relief, endeavoured to conceal them. Upon a living of thirty pounds a year he endeavoured to maintain his wife and six children; but all his resources at last failed him, and nothing but famine was seen in the wretched family. The poor man's circumstances were at last communicated to *Nash;* who, with his usual chearfulness, undertook to relieve him. On a sunday evening, at a public tea-drinking at *Harrison's,* he went about to collect a subscription, and began it himself, by giving five guineas. By this means two hundred guineas were collected in less than two hours, and the poor family raised from the lowest despondence into affluence and felicity. A bounty so unexpected, had a better influence even upon the woman's constitution, than all that either the physicians or the waters of *Bath* could produce, and she recovered. But his good offices did not rest here. He prevailed upon a nobleman of his acquaintance, to present the Doctor with a living of an hundred and sixty pounds a year, which made that happiness, he had before produced, in some measure permanent.

In the severe winter, which happened in the year 1739 his charity was great, useful, and extensive. He frequently, at that season of calamity, entered the houses of the poor, whom he thought too proud to beg, and generously relieved them.

The colliers were at this time peculiarly distressed; and in order to excite compassion, a number of them yoked themselves to a waggon loaded with coals, and drew it into *Bath,* and presented it to Mr. *Nash.* Their scheme had the proper effect. Mr. *Nash* procured them a subscription, and gave ten guineas towards it himself. The weavers also shared his bounty at that season. They came begging in a body into *Bath,* and he provided a plentiful dinner for their entertainment, and gave each a week's subsistence at going away.

There are few public charities to which he was not a subscriber, and many he principally contributed to support. Among others, Mr. *Annesly,*[60] that strange example of the mutability of fortune, and the inefficacy of our Laws, shared his interest and bounty. I have now before me a well written letter, addressed to Mr. *Nash,* in order to obtain his interest for that unhappy gentleman; it comes from Mr. *Henderson,* a quaker, who was Mr. *Annesly's* father's agent. This gentleman warmly espoused the young adventurer's interest, and, I am told, fell with him.

London, October 23, 1756.
My Good Friend,
When I had the honour of conversing with thee at *Tunbridge,* in *September* last, concerning that most singular striking case of Mr. *Annesley,* whom I have known since he was about six years old, I being then employed by the late Lord Baron of *Altham,* his father, as his agent. From what I know of the affairs of that family, I am well assured, that Mr. Annesley is the legitimate son of the late Lord Baron of *Altham,* and in consequence thereof, is intitled to the honours and estates of *Anglesey.* Were I not well assured of his right to those honours and estates, I would not give countenance to his claim.—I well remember, that thou then madest me a promise to assist him in soliciting a subscription, that was then begun at *Tunbridge;* but as that place was not within the limits of thy province, thou couldest not promise to do much there. But thou saidst, that in case he would go to *Bath* in the season, thou wouldest then and there shew how much thou wouldest be his friend.

And now, my good friend, as the season is come on, and Mr. *Annesley* now at *Bath,* I beg leave to remind thee of that promise; and that thou wilt keep in full view the honour, the everlasting honour, that will naturally redound to thee from thy benevolence, and crown all the good actions of thy life.—I say, now in the vale of life, to relieve a distressed young nobleman, to extricate so immense an estate, from the hands of oppression; to do this, will fix such a ray of glory on thy memory, as will speak forth thy praise to future ages.—This with great respect is the needful,
from thy assured Friend,
WILLIAM HENDERSON.
Be pleased to give my respects to Mr. *Annesley* and his spouse.

Mr. *Nash* punctually kept his word with this gentleman; he began the subscription himself with the utmost liber-

---

[60] James Annesley (1715–1760), disclaimed by his father, sold into slavery in the American colonies, devoted the last twenty years of his life to efforts at proving his claim as heir of the Annesley fortunes. His story was used in Smollett's *Peregrine Pickle,* Scott's *Guy Mannering,* and Reade's *Wandering Heir.*

ality, and procured such a list of encouragers, as at once did honour to Mr.
Annesly's cause, and their own generosity. What a pity it was, that this money,
which was given for the relief of indigence only, went to feed a set of reptiles,
who batten upon our weakness, miseries
and vice.

It may not be known to the generality
of my readers, that the last act of the
comedy, called *Esop*,[61] which was added
to the *French* plot of *Boursault,* by Mr.
Vanbrugh, was taken from a story told
of Mr. *Nash* upon a similar occasion. He
had in the early part of life made proposals of marriage to miss *V*———, of
D———; his affluence at that time, and
the favour which he was in with the nobility, readily induced the young lady's
father to favour his addresses. However,
upon opening the affair to herself, she
candidly told him, her affections were
placed upon another, and that she could
not possibly comply. Tho' this answer
satisfied Mr. *Nash,* it was by no means
sufficient to appease the father; and he
peremptorily insisted upon her obedience.
Things were carried to the last extremity; when Mr. *Nash* undertook to settle
the affair; and desiring his favoured
rival to be sent for, with his own hand
presented his mistress to him, together
with a fortune equal to what her father
intended to give her. Such an uncommon
instance of generosity had an instant effect upon the severe parent; he considered such disinterestedness as a just reproach to his own mercenary disposition,
and took his daughter once more into favour. I wish, for the dignity of history,
that the sequel could be concealed, but
the young lady ran away with her footman, before half a year was expired; and
her husband died of grief.

In general, the benefactions of a generous man are but ill bestowed. His heart
seldom gives him leave to examine the
real distress of the object which sues for
pity; his good-nature takes the alarm too
soon, and he bestows his fortune on only
apparent wretchedness. The man natu-

rally frugal, on the other hand, seldom
relieves, but when he does, his reason,
and not his sensations, generally find out
the object. Every instance of his bounty
is therefore permanent, and bears witness
to his benevolence.

Of all the immense sums which *Nash*
lavished upon real or apparent wretchedness, the effects, after a few years, seemed
to disappear. His money was generally
given to support immediate want, or to
relieve improvident indolence, and therefore it vanished in an hour. Perhaps towards the close of life, were he to look
round on the thousands he had relieved,
he would find but few made happy, or
fixed by his bounty in a state of thriving
industry; it was enough for him, that he
gave to those that wanted; he never considered, that charity to some might im-
poverish himself without relieving them;
he seldom considered the merit or the industry of the petitioner; or he rather
fancied, that misery was an excuse for
indolence and guilt. It was an usual saying of his, when he went to beg for any
person in distress, that they who could
stoop to the meanness of solicitation,
must certainly *want* the favour for which
they petitioned.

In this manner therefore he gave
away immense sums of his own, and still
greater, which he procured from others.
His way was, when any person was proposed to him as an object of charity, to
go round with his hat first among the
nobility, according to their rank, and so
on, till he left scarce a single person un-
solicited. They who go thus about to beg
for others, generally find a pleasure in
the task. They consider, in some measure, every benefaction they procure, as
given by themselves, and have at once the
pleasure of being liberal, without the self
reproach of being profuse.

But of all the instances of Mr. *Nash's*
bounty, none does him more real honour,
than the pains he took in establishing an
hospital at *Bath,* in which benefaction,
however, Doctor *Oliver*[62] had a great
share. This was one of those well guided

---

[61] By Sir John Vanbrugh (1697).

[62] William Oliver (1695–1764) physician
prominent in Bath from 1725.

charities, dictated by reason, and supported by prudence. By this institution the diseased poor might recover health, when incapable of receiving it in any other part of the kingdom. As the disorders of the poor, who could expect to find relief at *Bath,* were mostly chronical, the expence of maintaining them there was found more than their parishes thought proper to afford. They therefore chose to support them in a continual state of infirmity, by a small allowance at home, rather than be at the charge of an expensive cure. An hospital therefore at *Bath* it was thought would be an assylum, and a place of relief to those disabled creatures, and would, at the same time, give the physician more thorough insight into the efficacy of the waters, from the regularity, with which such patients would be obliged to take them. These inducements therefore influenced Doctor *Oliver,* and Mr. *Nash,* to promote a subscription towards such a benefaction. The design was set on foot so early as the year 1711, but not completed till the year 1742. This delay, which seems surprizing, was in fact owing to the want of a proper fund for carrying the work into execution. What I said above, of charity being the characteristic virtue of the present age, will be more fully evinced, by comparing the old and new subscriptions for this hospital. These will shew the difference between ancient and modern benevolence. When I run my eye over the list of those who subscribed in the year 1723, I find the subscription in general seldom rise above a guinea each person; so that, at that time, with all their efforts, they were unable to raise four hundred pounds; but in about twenty years after, each particular subscription was greatly encreased, ten, twenty, thirty pounds, being the most ordinary sums then subscribed, and they soon raised above two thousand pounds for the purpose.

Thus chiefly by the means of Doctor

Oliver and Mr. *Nash,* but not without the assistance of the good Mr. *Allen,*[63] who gave them the stone for building and other benefactions, this hospital was erected, and it is at present fitted up for the reception of one hundred and ten patients, the cases mostly paralytic or leprous. The following conditions are observed previous to admittance.

I.　The case of the patient must be described by some physician, or person of skill, in the neighbourhood of the place where the patient has resided for some time; and this description, together with a certificate of the poverty of the patient, attested by some persons of credit, must be sent in a letter post-paid, directed to the register of the *General Hospital* at *Bath.*

II.　After the patient's case has been thus described, and sent, he must remain in his usual place or residence 'till he has notice of a vacancy, signified by a letter from the register.

III.　Upon the receipt of such a letter, the patient must set forward for *Bath,* bringing with him this letter, the parish certificate duly executed, and allowed by two justices, and three pounds caution-money,[64] if from any part of *England* or *Wales;* but if the patient comes from *Scotland* or *Ireland,* then the caution-money, to be deposited before admission, is the sum of five pounds.

IV.　Soldiers may, instead of parish certificates, bring a certificate from their commanding officers, signifying to what corps they belong, and that they shall be received into the same corps, when discharged from the Hospital, in whatever condition they are. But it is necessary, that their cases be described, and sent previously, and that they bring with them three pounds caution-money.

Note, The intention of the caution-money is to defray the expences of returning the patients after they are discharged from the Hospital, or of their

---

[63] Ralph Allen (1694–1764), wealthy philanthropist, friend of the poet Pope and the novelist Fielding, possessed of an elaborate country residence, Prior Park, three miles from Bath, built between the years 1736 and 1743. See

note 120 to Johnsons *Life of Pope* above.

[64] Ordinarily, a deposit as security for good conduct, but in this instance, the purpose is explained later.

burial in case they die there. The remainder of the caution-money, after these expences are defrayed, will be returned to the person who made the deposit.

I am unwilling to leave this subject of his benevolence, because it is a virtue in his character, which must stand almost single against an hundred follies; and it deserves the more to be insisted on, because it was large enough to outweigh them all. A man may be an hypocrite safely in every other instance, but in charity; there are few who will buy the character of benevolence at the rate for which it must be acquired. In short, the sums he gave away were immense; and in old age, when at last grown too poor to give relief, *he gave,* as the poet has it, *all he had, a tear;*[65] when incapable of relieving the agonies of the wretched, he attempted to relieve his own by a flood of sorrow.

From the hospital erected for the benefit of the poor, it is an easy transition to the monuments erected by him in honour of the great. Upon the recovery of the Prince of *Orange,* by drinking the *Bath* waters, Mr. *Nash* caused a small obelisk, thirty feet high, to be erected in a grove near the Abbey church, since called *Orange Grove.* This Prince's arms adorn the west side of the body of the pedestal. The inscription is on the opposite side, in the following words:

In memoriam
Sanitatis
Principi Auriaco
Aquarum thermalium potu.
Favente Deo,
Ovante Britannia,
Feliciter restitutae,
M. DCC. XXXIV.
In English thus.
In memory
Of the happy restoration
Of the health of the
Prince of *Orange,*
Through the favour of God,
And to the great joy of Britain,

---

[65] Thomas Gray, *Elegy Written in a Country Churchyard* (1751), l. 123.

By drinking the *Bath* waters.
1734.

I find it a general custom, at all Baths and Spaws, to erect monuments of this kind to the memory of every Prince, who has received benefit from the waters. *Aix, Spau,* and *Pisa,* abound with inscriptions of this nature, apparently doing honour to the Prince, but in reality celebrating the efficacy of their springs. It is wrong, therefore, to call such monuments instances of gratitude, tho' they may wear that appearance.

In the year 1738, the Prince of *Wales* came to *Bath,* who presented Mr. *Nash* with a large gold enamelled snuff-box; and upon his departure, *Nash,* as king of *Bath,* erected an obelisk in honour of this Prince, as he had before done for the Prince of *Orange.* This handsome memorial in honour of that good-natured Prince is erected in *Queen square.* It is enclosed with a stone balustrade, and in the middle of every side there are large iron gates. In the center is the obelisk, seventy feet high, and terminating in a point. The expences of this were eighty pounds; and Mr. *Nash* was determined, that the inscription should answer the magnificence of the pile. With this view he wrote to Mr. *Pope,* at *London,* requesting an inscription. I should have been glad to have given Mr. *Nash's* letter upon this occasion; the reader, however, must be satisfied with *Pope's* reply; which is as follows.

Sir,
I have received yours, and thank your partiality in my favour. You say words cannot express the gratitude you feel for the favour of his R. H. and yet you would have me express what you feel, and in a few words. I own myself unequal to the task; for even, granting it possible to express an inexpressible idea, I am the worst person you could have pitched upon for this purpose, who have received so few favours from the great myself, that I am utterly unacquainted with what kind of thanks they like best. Whether the P——— most loves poetry or prose, I protest I do not know; but

this I dare venture to affirm, that you can give him as much satisfaction in either as I can.

I am,
Sir,
Your affectionate Servant,
A. POPE.

What Mr. *Nash's* answer to this billet was, I cannot take upon me to ascertain, but it was probably a perseverance in his former request. The following is the copy of Mr. *Pope's* reply to his second letter.

Sir,
I had sooner answered yours, but in the hope of procuring a properer hand than mine; and then in consulting with some, whose office about the P——— might make them the best judges, what sort of inscription to set up? Nothing can be plainer than the inclosed; it is nearly the common sense of the thing, and I do not know how to flourish upon it. But this you would do as well, or better yourself, and I dare say may mend the expression. I am truly,
Dear Sir,
Your affectionate Servant,
A. POPE.
I think I need not tell you my name should not be mentioned.

Such a letter as this was what might naturally be expected from Mr. *Pope.* Notwithstanding the seeming modesty towards the conclusion, the vanity of an applauded writer bursts through every line of it. The difficulty of concealing his hand from the clerks at the Post-office, and the solicitude to have his name concealed, were marks of the consciousness of his own importance. It is probable, his hand was not so very well known, nor his letters so eagerly opened by the clerks of the Office, as he seems always to think. But in all his letters, as well as those of *Swift,* there runs a strain of pride, as if the world talked of nothing but themselves. *Alas,* says he, in one of them, *the day after I am dead, the sun will shine as bright as the day before, and the world will be as merry as usual!*

Very strange, that neither an eclipse nor an earthquake should follow the loss of a Poet!

The inscription referred to in this letter, was the same which was afterwards engraved on the obelisk; and is as follows.

In memory of honours bestow'd,
And in gratitude for benefits conferred
in this city,
By his Royal Highness
Frederick, Prince of *Wales,*
And his Royal Consort,
In the Year 1738,
This obelisk is erected by
Richard Nash, Esq.

I dare venture to say, there was scarce a common-council-man in the corporation of *Bath,* but could have done this as well. Nothing can be more frigid; though the subject was worthy of the utmost exertions of Genius.

About this period every season brought some new accession of honour to Mr. *Nash;* and the corporation now universally found, that he was absolutely necessary for promoting the welfare of the city; so that this year seems to have been the meridian of his glory. About this time he arrived at such a pitch of authority, that I really believe *Alexander* was not greater at *Persepolis.* The countenance he received from the Prince of *Orange,* the favour he was in with the Prince of *Wales,* and the caresses of the nobility, all conspired to lift him to the utmost pitch of vanity. The exultation of a little mind, upon being admitted to the familiarity of the Great is inexpressible. The Prince of *Orange* had made him a present of a very fine snuff-box. Upon this some of the nobility thought it would be proper to give snuff-boxes too; they were quickly imitated by the middling gentry, and it soon became the fashion to give Mr. *Nash* snuff-boxes.

To add to his honours, the corporation of *Bath* placed a full length statue of him, in the pump-room, between the busts of *Newton* and *Pope.* It was upon this occasion that the Earl of *Chesterfield* wrote that severe, but witty epigram; the last lines, of which were so deservedly admired, and ran thus;

> The statue placed, the busts between,
>   Adds to the satire strength;
> *Wisdom* and *Wit* are little seen,
>   But *Folly* at full length.

The example of the corporation was followed by all his acquaintance, of inferior rank. He was treated in every respect like a great man; he had his levee, his flatterers, his buffoons, his good-natured creatures, and even his dedicators. A trifling ill-supported vanity was his foible, and while he received the homage of the vulgar, and enjoyed the familiarity of the great, he felt no pain for the unpromising view of poverty that lay before him; he enjoyed the world as it went, and drew upon content for the deficiencies of fortune. If a cringing wretch called him his Honour, he was pleased; internally conscious, that he had the justest pretensions to the title. If a beggar called him my Lord, he was happy, and generally sent the flatterer off happy too. I have known him, in *London,* wait a whole day at a window in the *Smyrna* coffee-house, in order to receive a bow from the Prince, or the Dutchess of *Marlborough,* as they passed by where he was standing; and he would then look round upon the company for admiration and respect.

But perhaps the reader desires to know, who could be low enough to flatter a man, who himself lived in some measure by dependance. Hundreds are ready upon those occasions. The very needy are almost ever flatterers. A man in wretched circumstances forgets his own value, and feels no pain in giving up superiority to every claimant. The very vain are ever flatterers; as they find it necessary to make use of all their arts, to keep company with such as are superior to themselves. But particularly the prodigal are prone to adulation, in order to open new supplies for their extravagance. The poor, the vain, and the extravagant, are chiefly addicted to this vice; and such hung upon his good nature. When these three characters are

found united in one person, the composition generally becomes a great man's favourite. It was not difficult to collect such a groupe in a city, that was the center of pleasure. *Nash* had them of all sizes, from the half pay captain in laced cloaths, to the humble boot-catcher at the *Bear.*

I have before me a bundle of letters, all addressed from a pack of flattering reptiles, to his *Honour;* and even some printed dedications, in the same servile strain. In these *his Honour* is complimented as the great encourager of the polite arts, as a gentleman of the most accomplished taste, of the most extensive learning, and in short of every thing in the world. But perhaps it will be thought wrong in me, to unveil the blushing muse, to brand learning with the meanness of its professors, or to expose scholars in a state of contempt.—For the honour of letters, the dedications to Mr. *Nash* are not written by scholars or poets, but by people of a different stamp.

Among this number was the highwayman, who was taken after attempting to rob and murder Doctor *Handcock.* He was called *Poulter,* alias *Baxter,* and published a book, exposing the tricks of gamblers, thieves and pick-pockets. This he intended to have dedicated to Mr. *Nash,* but the generous patron, tho' no man loved praise more, was too modest to have it printed. However, he took care to preserve the manuscript, among the rest of his papers. The book was entitled, *The discoveries of John Poulter, alias Baxter, who was apprehended for robbing Doctor Handcock, of Salisbury, on Clarken Down near Bath; and who has since been admitted king's evidence, and discovered a most numerous gang of villains. Being a full account of all the robberies he committed, and the surprizing tricks and frauds he has practised for the space of five years last past, in different parts of England, particularly in the West. Written wholly by himself.*[66] The dedication intended to be prefixed is as follows, and will give a specimen of the stile of an highwayman and a gambler.

---

[66] A copy in the British Museum is dated 1753.

To the Honourable *Richard Nash,* Esq;
May it please your Honour,

With humblest submission, I make
bold to present the following sheets to
your Honour's consideration, and well
known humanity. As I am industriously
careful, in respect to his Majesty, and
good subjects, to put an end to the unfortunate misconducts of all I know, by
bringing them to the gallows. To be sure
some may censure, as if from self-preser-
vation I made this ample discovery; but
I communicate this to your Honour and
gentry, whether the life of one person being taken away, would answer the end,
as to let escape such a number of villains,
who has been the ruining of many a poor
family, for whom my soul is now much
concerned. If my inclinations was ever so
roguish enclined, what is it to so great a
number of villains, when they consult together. As your Honour's wisdom, humanity and interest are the friend of the
virtuous, I make bold to lay, at your
Honour's feet, the following lines, which
will put every honest man upon his defence against the snares of the mischievous; and am, with greatest gratitude,
honoured Sir,
    Your Honour's
        Most truly devoted and obedient
        Servant,
            John Poulter, *alias* Baxter,
Taunton Goal
June 2d.

Flattery from such a wretch as this,
one would think but little pleasing; however, certain it is, that *Nash* was pleased
with it, he loved to be called your Honour, and Honourable; and the highwayman more than once experienced his generosity.

But since I have mentioned this fellow's book, I cannot repress an impulse
to give an extract from it, however foreign from my subject. I take the following picture to be a perfectly humorous
description of artful knavery affecting
ignorance on one hand, and rustic simplicity pretending to great wisdom and
sagacity on the other. It is an account of
the manner in which countrymen are deceived by gamblers, at a game called

Pricking in the Belt, or the Old Nob.
This is a leathern strop, folded up double, and then laid upon a table; if the
person who plays with a bodkin pricks
into the loop of the belt he wins; if otherwise, he loses. However, by slipping
one end of the strop, the sharper can
win at pleasure.

There are generally four persons concerned in this fraud, one to personate a
Sailor, called a *Legg Cull,* another called
the *Capper,* who always keeps with the
Sailor; and two pickers up, or *Money-
Droppers,* to bring in *Flats* or *Bubbles.*
The first thing they do at a fair, is to
look for a room clear of company, which
the *Sailor* and *Capper* immediately take,
while the *Money-Droppers* go out to
look for a *Flat.* If they see a countryman, whose looks they like, one drops a
shilling, or half a crown, just before
him, and picking it up again, looks the
man in the face, and says, I have found
a piece of money, friend, did you see me
pick it up? The man says, yes: Then says
the sharper, if you had found it, I would
have had half, so I will do as I would be
done unto; come honest friend, we will
not part with dry lips. Then taking him
into the room where the other two are,
he cries, By your leave gentlemen, I hope
we don't disturb the company. No, cries
the *Sailor;* no brothers; Will you drink
a glass of brandy, I don't like your weak
liquors; and then begins a discourse, by
asking the *Capper* how far it is to *London;* who replies, I don't know; perhaps
the gentleman there can tell you, directing his discourse to th*e Flat;* perhaps the
Flat will answer, a hundred miles; the
Sailor cries, I can ride that in a day, ay,
in four or five hours; for, says he, my
horse will run twenty nots an hour for
twenty-four hours together: *Capper,* or
the *Sailor's* supposed companion, says, I
believe *Farmer* you have not got such a
horse as the *Sailor* has; the *Farmer* cries
No, and laughs; and then the *Sailor* says,
I must go and get half a pint of brandy,
for I am griped, and so leaves them. The
Capper, affecting a look of wisdom in his
absence observes, that it is an old saying,
and a true one, *that Sailors get their*

money like horses, and spend it like asses; as for that there *Sailor* I never saw him till now, buying a horse of any man; he tells me he has been at *Sea,* and has got about four hundred pounds prize-money, but I believe he will squander it all away, for he was gaming just now with a sharping fellow, and lost forty shillings, at a strange game of pricking in a string. Did either of you ever see it, gentlemen? continued the *Capper;* if you two are willing, I will ask him to shew it, for we may as well win some of his money as any body else: The *Flat* and the *Dropper* cry, Do. Then in comes the *Sailor,* staggering as if drunk, and cries, What cheer, brothers? I have just seen a pretty girl in the fair, and went in to drink with her, we made a bargain, and I gave her a six and thirty shilling piece, but an old b——h her mother came and called her away, but I hope she will come back to me presently; then the *Capper* laughs, and says, Have you got your money of her again? The *Sailor* says, No; but she will come to me I'm sure; then they all laugh. This is done to deceive the *Flat:* then says the *Capper,* What have you done with the stick and the string, *Sailor?* he answers, What, that which I bought of the boys; I have got it here, but will not sell it, and then he pulls out the Old Nobb, saying, What do you think I gave for it? I gave but six-pence, and as much brandy as the two boys could drink; it is made out of a monkey's hide, as the boys told me, and they told me, there is a game to be played at it, which no body can do twice together; I will go down aboard ship, and play with my Captain, and I do not fear but I shall win his ship and cargo: then they all laugh, and the *Sailor* makes up the Old Nobb, and the *Capper* lays a shilling, and pricks himself and wins; the *Sailor* cries, You are a dab, I will not lay with you, but if you will call a stranger, I will lay again; why if you think me a dab, as you call it, I will get this strange gentleman, or this (pointing to the *Flat*). Done, cries the *Sailor,* but you shall not tell him; then he makes up the Nob, and *Capper* lays a shilling, *Flat* pricks, being

permitted to go six-pence; to which he agreeing, wins; and *Capper* says to the *Flat,* Can you change me half a crown? This is done to find the depth of his pocket; if they see a good deal of gold, *Flat* must win three or four times; if no gold, but twice. Sometimes, if the *Flat* has no money, the *Sailor* cries, I have more money than any man in the fair, and pulls out his purse of gold, and saith, Not one of you can beg, borrow or steal half this sum in an hour for a guinea. *Capper* cries, I have laid out all mine; *Farmer,* Can you? I'll go your halves, if you think you can do it. The *Sailor* saith, you must not bring any body with you; then the *Dropper* goes with the *Flat,* and saith, you must not tell your friend it is for a wager; if you do, he will not lend it you. *Flat* goes and borrows it, and brings it to the *Sailor,* shews it him, and wins the wager; then the *Sailor* pinches the Nob again, and the *Capper* whispers to the *Flat,* to prick out purposely this time, saying, it will make the *Sailor* more eager to lay on; we may as well win his money as not, for he will spend it upon whores: *Flat,* with all the wisdom in the world, loses on purpose; upon which the *Sailor* swears, pulls out all his money, throws it about the room, and cries, I know no man can win for ever, and then lays a guinea, but will not let him prick, but throws down five guineas; and the *Capper* urging the *Flat,* and going his halves, the *Sailor* saith, my cabbin boy will lay as much as that, I'll lay no less than twenty guineas; the *Capper* cries, lay *Farmer* and take up forty; which, being certain of winning, he instantly complies with, and loses the whole. When he has lost, in order to advise him, the *Dropper* takes him by the arm, and hauls him out of doors; and the reckoning being in the mean time paid within, the *Capper* and *Sailor* follow after, and run another way. When they are out of sight, the *Dropper* saith to the *Flat,* go you back, and play with the *Sailor* for a shilling, whilst I go and borrow money; but when the *Flat* goes to the house, he finds them gone, and then he knows that he is bit, but not till he has dearly paid for it.

By this fellow's discoveries Mr. *Nash* was enabled to serve many of the nobility and gentry of his acquaintance; he received a list of all those houses of ill fame which harboured or assisted rogues, and took care to furnish travellers with proper precautions to avoid them. It was odd enough to see a gamester thus employed, in detecting the frauds of gamblers.

Among the Dedications, there is one from a Professor of Cookery, which is more adulatory than the preceding. It is prefixed to a work, entituled, *The complete preserver, or a new method of preserving fruits, flowers, and other vegetables, either with or without sugar, vinegar or spirits, &c.*

To the very Honourable *Richard Nash,*
      Esq;
Honoured Sir,

As much as the oak exceeds the bramble, so much do you exceed the rest of mankind, in benevolence, charity, and every other virtue that adorns, enobles, and refines the human species. I have therefore made bold to prefix your name, tho' without permission, to the following work, which stands in need of such a patron, to excuse its errors, with a candour, only known to such an heart as your own; the obligations I have received at your hands, it is impossible for me ever to repay, except by my endeavours, as in the present case, to make known the many excellent virtues which you possess. But what can my wit do to recommend such a genius as yours, a single word, a smile from yourself, outweighs all that I, or perhaps the best of our poets could express in writing in the compass of a year. It would ill become my sex, to declare what power you have over us, but your generosity is, even in this instance, greater than your desire to oblige. The following sheets were drawn up at my hours of leisure, and may be serviceable to such of my sex, as are more willing to employ their time in laudable occupations, and domestic economy, than in dress and dissipation. What reception they may receive from your honour, I am

incapable of telling; However, from your known candour and humanity, I expect the most favourable.
  I am, Honoured Sir,
   Your most obedient,
   and obliged humble Servant,
    H. W.

A musician in his dedication still exceeds the other two in adulation. However, tho' the matter may be some impeachment on his sincerity, the manner in which it is written reflects no disgrace upon his understanding.

   To *Richard Nash,* Esq;
Sir,

The kind partiality of my friends, prevailed with me to present to the world these my first attempts in musical composition; and the generous protection you have been pleased to afford me, makes it my indispensable duty to lay them at your feet. Indeed, to whom could I presume to offer them, but to the great encourager of all polite arts; for your generosity knows no bounds; nor are you more famed for that dignity of mind, which enobles and gives a grace to every part of your conduct, than for that humanity and beneficence, which makes you the friend and benefactor of all mankind. To you, the poor and the rich, the diseased and the healthy, the aged and the young, owe every comfort, every conveniency, and every innocent amusement, that the best heart, the most skilful management, and the most accomplished taste can furnish. Even this age, so deeply practised in all the subtleties of refined pleasure, gives you this Testimony: even this age, so ardently engaged in all the ways of the most unbounded charity, gives you this praise. Pardon me then, if, amidst the croud of votaries, I make my humble offering, if I seize this first opportunity of publickly expressing the grateful sentiments of my own heart and profound respect, with which.
  I am, Sir,
   Your most obliged, most devoted,
   and most obedient Servant,
    J. G.

I fancy I have almost fatigued the reader, and I am almost fatigued myself, with the efforts of those elegant panegyrists; however, I can't finish this run of quotation, without giving a specimen of poetry, addressed to him upon a certain occasion; and all I shall say in its defence is, that those, who are pleased with the prose dedications, will not dislike the present attempt in poetry.

To *Richard Nash,* Esq;
On his sickness at *Tunbridge.*

Say, must the friend of human kind,
Of most refin'd—of most diffusive mind;
Must *Nash* himself beneath these ailments grieve?
He felt for all—He felt—but to relieve,
To heal the sick—the wounded to restore,
And bid desponding nature mourn no more.
Thy quickning warmth, O let thy patron feel,
Improve thy springs with double power to heal:
Quick, hither all inspiring health, repair,
And save the gay—and wretched from despair;
Thou only Esra's drooping sons can'st chear,
And stop the soft-ey'd virgin's trickling tear;
In murmurs who their monarch's pains deplore;
While sickness faints—and pleasure is no more;
O let not death, with hasty strides advance,
Thou, mildest charity, avert the lance;
His threatning power, cœlestial maid! defeat;
Nor take him with thee, to thy well known feat;
Leave him on earth some longer date behind,
To bless,—to polish,—and relieve mankind:
Come then kind health, O quickly come away,
Bid *Nash* revive—and all the world be gay.

[THE DECLINE OF THE KING]

Such addresses as these were daily offered to our titular King. When in the meridian of power, scarce a morning passed, that did not encrease the number of his humble admirers, and enlarge the sphere of his vanity.

The man who is constantly served up with adulation, must be a first-rate philosopher, if he can listen without contracting new affectations. The opinion we form of ourselves, is generally measured by what we hear from others; and when they conspire to deceive, we too readily concur in the delusion. Among the number of much applauded men in the circle of our own friends, we can recollect but few that have heads quite strong enough to bear a loud acclamation of public praise in their favour; among the whole list, we shall scarce find one, that has not thus been made, on some side of his character, a coxcomb.

When the best head turns and grows giddy with praise, is it to be wondered that poor *Nash,* should be driven by it almost into a phrenzy of affectation? Towards the close of life he became affected. He chiefly laboured to be thought a sayer of good things; and by frequent attempts was now and then successful, for he ever lay upon the lurch.

There never perhaps was a more silly passion, than this desire of having a man's jests recorded. For this purpose, it is necessary to keep ignorant or ill-bred company, who are only fond of repeating such stories; in the next place, a person must tell his own jokes, in order to make them more universal; but what is worst of all, scarce a joke of this kind succeeds, but at the expence of a man's good nature; and he who exchanges the character of being thought agreeable, for that of being thought witty, makes but a very bad bargain.

The success *Nash* sometimes met with led him on, when late in life, to mistake his true character. He was really agreeable, but he chose to be thought a wit. He therefore indulged his inclination, and never mattered how rude he was, provided he was thought comical. He thus got the applause he sought for, but too often found enemies, where he least expected to find them. Of all the jests recorded of him, I scarce find one that is not marked with petulance; he said whatever came uppermost, and in the number of his remarks it might naturally be expected that some were worth repeating; he threw often, and sometimes had a lucky cast.

In a life of almost ninety years, spent in the very point of public view, it is not strange, that five or six sprightly things of his have been collected, particularly as he took every opportunity of repeating them himself. His usual way, when he thought he said any thing clever, was to strengthen it with an oath, and to make up its want of sentiment by asseveration and grimace. For many years he thus entertained the company at the coffee-house with old stories, in which he always made himself the principal character. Strangers liked this well enough; but they who were used to his conversation found it insupportable. One story brought on another, and each came in the same order that it had the day preceding. But this custom may be rather ascribed to the peculiarity of age, than a peculiarity of character; it seldom happens, that old men allure, at least by novelty; age that shrivels the body contracts the understanding; instead of exploring new regions, they rest satisfied in the old, and walk round the circle of their former discoveries. His manner of telling a story, however, was not displeasing, but few of those he told are worth transcribing. Indeed it is the manner, which places the whole difference between the wit of the vulgar, and of those who assume the name of the polite; one, has in general as much good sense as the other; a story transcribed from the one, will be as entertaining as that copied from the other; but in conversation, the manner will give charms even to stupidity. The following is the story which he most frequently told, and pretty much in these words.

Suppose the company to be talking of a *German* war, or *Elizabeth Canning,*[67] he would begin thus. "I'll tell you something to that purpose, that I fancy will make you laugh. A covetous old parson, as rich as the Devil, scraped a fresh acquaintance with me several years ago at *Bath.* I knew him when he and I were students at *Oxford,* where we both studied damnationly hard, but that's neither here nor there. Well. Very well. I entertained him at my house in *John's Court.* (No, my house in *John's Court* was not built then) but I entertained him with all that the city could afford; the rooms, the music, and every thing in the world. Upon his leaving *Bath,* he pressed me very hard to return the visit; and desired me to let him have the pleasure of seeing me at his house in *Devonshire.* About six months after, I happened to be in that neighbourhood, and was resolved to see my old friend, from whom I expected a very warm reception. Well: I knocks at his door, when an old queer creature of a maid, came to the door, and denied him. I suspected, however, that he was at home; and going into the parlour, what should I see, but the Parson's legs up the chimney, where he had thrust himself to avoid entertaining me. This was very well. My dear, says I to the maid, it is very cold, extreme cold indeed, and I am afraid I have got a touch of my ague, light me the fire, if you please. La, sir, says the maid, who was a modest creature to be sure, the chimney smokes monstrously; you could not bear the room for three minutes together. By the greatest good luck there was a bundle of straw in the hearth, and I called for a candle. The candle came. Well, good woman, says I, since you won't light me a fire, I'll light one for myself, and in a moment the straw was all in a blaze. This quickly unkennelled the old fox; there he stood in an old rusty night gown, blessing himself, and looking like —a—hem —egad."

He used to tell surprizing stories of his activity when young. "Here I stand,

[67] The mystery of the whereabouts of Elizabeth Canning, a nineteen-year-old serving girl, during the month of January 1753 has been retold by Lillian De La Torre in *Elizabeth Is Missing* (1945).

gentlemen, that could once leap forty two feet upon level ground, at three standing jumps, backward or forward. One, two, three, dart like an arrow out of a bow. But I am old now. I remember I once leaped for three hundred guineas with Count *Klopstock,* the great leaper, leaping-master to the Prince of *Passau;* you must all have heard of him. First he began with the running jump, and a most damnable bounce it was, that's certain: Every body concluded that he had the match hollow; when only taking off my hat, stripping off neither coat, shoes, nor stockings, mind me, I fetches a run, and went beyond him one foot, three inches and three quarters measured, upon my soul, by Captain *Pately's* own standard."

But in this torrent of insipidity, there sometimes were found very severe satire, strokes of true wit, and lines of humour, *cum fluerent lutulentus,*[68] *&c.* He rallied very successfully, for he never felt another's joke; and drove home his own without pity. With his superiors he was familiar and blunt, the inferiority of his station secured him from their resentment; but the same bluntness which they laughed at, was by his equals regarded as insolence. Something like a familiar boot-catcher at an inn, a gentleman would bear that joke from him, for which a brother boot-catcher would knock him down.

Among other stories of *Nash's* telling, I remember one, which I the more chearfully repeat, as it tends to correct a piece of impertinence that reigns in almost every country assembly. The principal inhabitants of a market-town, at a great distance from the capital, in order to encourage that harmony which ought to subsist in society, and to promote a mutual intercourse between the sexes, so desirable to both, and so necessary for all, had established a monthly assembly in the Town Hall, which was conducted with such decency, decorum and politeness, that it drew the attention of the gentlemen and ladies in the neighbourhood; and a nobleman and his family contin-

ually honoured them with their presence. This naturally drew others, and in time the room was crouded with, what the world calls, good company, and the assembly prospered, till some of the new admitted ladies took it into their heads, that the tradesmens daughters were unworthy of their notice, and therefore refus'd to join hands with them in the dance. This was complained of by the town ladies, and that complaint was resented by the country gentlemen, who, more pert than wise, publickly advertised, that they would not dance with tradesmens daughters. This the most eminent tradesmen considered as an insult on themselves, and being men of worth, and able to live independently, they in return advertised that they would give no credit out of their town, and desired all others to discharge their accounts. A general uneasiness ensued; some writs were actually issued out, and much distress would have happened, had not my Lord, who sided with no party, kindly interfered and composed the difference. The assembly however was ruined, and the families I am told are not friends yet, tho' this affair happened thirty years ago.

Nothing debases human nature so much as pride.—This *Nash* knew, and endeavoured to stifle every emotion of it at *Bath.* When he observed any ladies so extremely delicate and proud of a pedigree, as to only touch the back of an inferior's hand in the dance, he always called to order, and desired them to leave the room, or behave with common decency; and when any Ladies and Gentlemen drew off, after they had gone down a dance, without standing up till the dance was finished, he made up to them, and after asking whether they had done dancing, told them, they should dance no more unless they stood up for the rest; and on these occasions he always was as good as his word.

Nash, tho' no great wit, had the art of sometimes saying rude things with decency, and rendering them pleasing by an uncommon turn.—But most of the good things attributed to him, which have found their way into the jest books, are no better than puns; the smartest things

I have seen are against him. One day in the grove, he joined some ladies, and asking one of them, who was crooked, whence she came? She replied, strait from *London.* Confound me, madam, said he, then you must have been damnably warpt by the way.

She soon, however, had ample revenge. Sitting the following evening in one of the rooms, he once more joined her company, and with a sneer and a bow, asked her, if she knew her Catechism, and could tell the name of *Tobit's* dog? His name, Sir, was *Nash,* replied the lady, and an impudent dog he was. This story is told in a celebrated romance; I only repeat it here to have an opportunity of observing, that it actually happened.

Queen *Anne* once asked him, why he would not accept of knighthood? To which he replied, lest Sir *William Read,*[69] the mountebank, who had been just knighted, should call him brother.

An house in *Bath* was said to be haunted by the Devil, and a great noise was made about it, when *Nash* going to the Minister of St. *Michael's,* intreated him to drive the Devil out of *Bath* for ever, if it were only to oblige the ladies.

Nash used sometimes to visit the great Doctor *Clarke.*[70] The Doctor was one day conversing with *Locke,* and two or three more of his learned and intimate companions, with that freedom, gaiety and chearfulness, which is ever the result of innocence. In the midst of their mirth and laughter, the Doctor, looking from the window, saw *Nash's* chariot stop at the door. Boys, boys, cried the philosopher, to his friends, let us now be wise, for here is a fool coming.

Nash was one day complaining in the following manner to the Earl of *Chesterfield* of his bad luck at play. Would you think it, my Lord, that damned bitch fortune, no later than last night, tricked me out of 500. Is it not surprizing, continued he, that my luck should never turn, that I should thus eternally be mauled? I don't wonder at your losing

money *Nash,* says his lordship, but all the world is surprized where you get it to lose.

Doctor *Cheney* once, when *Nash* was ill, drew up a prescription for him, which was sent in accordingly. The next day the Doctor coming to see his patient, found him up and well; upon which he asked, if he had followed his prescription? Followed your prescription, cried *Nash,* No.—Egad, If I had, I should have broke my neck, for I flung it out of the two pair of stairs window.

It would have been well, had he confined himself to such sallies; but as he grew old he grew insolent, and seemed, in some measure, insensible of the pain his attempts to be a wit gave others. Upon asking a lady to dance a minuet; if she refused, he would often demand, if she had got bandy legs. He would attempt to ridicule natural defects; he forgot the deference due to birth and quality, and mistook the manner of settling rank and precedence upon many occasions. He now seemed no longer fashionable among the present race of gentry, he grew peevish and fretful, and they who only saw the remnant of a man, severely returned that laughter upon him, which he had once lavished upon others.

Poor *Nash* was no longer the gay, thoughtless, idly industrious creature he once was; he now forgot how to supply new modes of entertainment, and became too rigid, to wind with ease through the vicissitudes of fashion. The evening of his life began to grow cloudy. His fortune was gone, and nothing but poverty lay in prospect. To embitter his hopes, he found himself abandoned by the great, whom he had long endeavoured to serve; and was obliged to fly to those of humbler stations for protection, whom he once affected to despise. He now began to want that charity, which he had never refused to any; and to find, that a life of dissipation and gaiety, is ever terminated by misery and regret.

Even his place of master of the cere-

---

[69] Notorious as a quack empiric, he was knighted for his services as oculist in ordinary to Queen Anne. He died in 1715.

[70] Samuel Clarke (1675–1729), a prominent theological writer.

monies (if I can trust the papers he has left behind him) was sought after. I would willingly be tender of any living reputation; but these papers accuse Mr. *Quin*[71] of endeavouring to supplant him. He has even left us a letter, which he supposed was written by that gentleman, soliciting a Lord for his interest upon the occasion. As I chuse to give Mr. *Quin* an opportunity of disproving this, I will insert the letter, and, to shew the improbability of its being his, with all its faults, both of style and spelling. I am the less apt to believe it written by Mr. *Quin,* as a gentleman, who has mended *Shakespear's* plays so often, would surely be capable of something more correct than the following. It was sent, as it should seem, from Mr. *Quin* to a nobleman, but left open for the perusal of an intermediate friend. It was this friend who sent a copy of it to Mr. *Nash,* who caused it to be instantly printed, and left among his other papers.

The letter from the intermediate friend to Nash, *is as follows.*

London, October 8, 1760.

Dear *Nash,*

Two posts ago I received a letter from *Quin,* the old player, covering one to my Lord, which he left open for my perusal, which after reading he desired I might seal up and deliver. The request he makes is so extraordinary, that it has induced me to send you the copy of his letter to my Lord, which is as follows.

Bath, October 3, 1760.

My dear Lord,

Old beaux *Knash* has mead himselfe so dissagreeable to all the company that comes here to *Bath* that the corperatian of this city have it now under their consideration to remove him from beeing master of the cereymonies, should he be continuead the inhabitants of thiss city will be rueind, as the best companey declines to come to *Bath* on his acc[tt].

Give me leave to show to your Lords'hip how he beheaved at the firs't ball he had here thiss' season which was *Tus'day* las't. A younge Lady was as'ked to dance a minueat she begg the gent[m] would be pleased to exquise here, as' she did not chuse to dance; upon thiss' old *Nash* called out so as to be head by all the company in the room G—dam yo Madam what buisness have yo here if yo do not dance, upon which the Lady was so afrighted, she rose and danced, the ress'et of the companey was so much offended at the rudness of *Nash* that not one Lady more, would dance a minueat that night. In the country dances' no person of note danced except two boys' Lords S——— and T———, the res't of the companey that danced waire only the families of all the habberdas'hers' machinukes and inkeepers in the three kingdoms' brushed up and colexted together.

I have known upon such an occasion as' thiss' seventeen Dutchess' and Contiss' to be at the opening of the ball at *Bath* now not one. This man by his' pride and extravigancis has out lived his' reasein it would be happy for thiss' city that he was ded; and is, now only fitt to reed *Shirlock*[72] upon death by which he may seave his soul and gaine more than all the proffits he can make, by his white hatt, suppose it was to be died red;

The fav[r] I have now to reques't by what I now have wrote yo; is' that your Lordship will be so kind as to speke to Mr. *Pitt,* for to recommend me to the corperatian of this city to succede this old sinner as master of the cerremonies and yo will much oblige,

My Lord your
Lord[s] and Hu[e]
Ob[t] Ser[t].

N.B. There were some other private matters and offers in *Quin's* letter to my Lord, which do not relate to you.

Here *Nash,* if I may be permitted the use of a polite and fashionable phrase, was humm'd[73]; but he experienced such rubs as these, and a thousand other mor-

---

[71] James Quin (1693–1766) popular actor.
[72] William Sherlock, *A Practical Discourse upon Death* (1689).
[73] i.e., hoaxed (colloquial).

tifications every day. He found poverty now denied him the indulgence not only of his favourite follies, but of his favourite virtues. The poor now solicited him in vain; he was himself a more pitiable object than they. The child of the public seldom has a friend, and he who once exercised his wit at the expence of others, must naturally have enemies. Exasperated at last to the highest degree, an unaccountable whim struck him; poor *Nash* was resolved to become an author; he, who in the vigour of manhood, was incapable of the task, now at the impotent age of eighty-six, was determined to write his own history! from the many specimens already given of his style, the reader will not much regret that the historian was interrupted in his design. Yet as *Montaigne* observes, the adventures of an infant, if an infant could inform us of them, would be pleasing; so the life of a Beau, if a beau could write, would certainly serve to regale curiosity.

Whether he really intended to put this design in execution, or did it only to alarm the nobility, I will not take upon me to determine; but certain it is, that his friends went about collecting subscriptions for the work, and he received several encouragements from such as were willing to be politely charitable. It was thought by many, that this history would reveal the intrigues of a whole age; that he had numberless secrets to disclose; but they never considered, that persons of public character, like him, were the most unlikely in the world to be made partakers of those secrets which people desired the public should not know. In fact, he had few secrets to discover, and those he had, are now buried with him in the grave.

He was now past the power of giving or receiving pleasure, for he was poor, old and peevish; yet still he was incapable of turning from his former manner of life to pursue happiness. The old man endeavoured to practise the follies of the boy, he spurred on his jaded passions after every trifle of the day; tottering with age he would be ever an unwelcome guest in the assemblies of the youthful and gay; and he seemed willing to find

lost appetite among those scenes where he was once young.

An old man thus striving after pleasure is indeed an object of pity; but a man at once old and poor, running on in this pursuit, might excite astonishment. To see a Being both by fortune and constitution rendered incapable of enjoyment, still haunting those pleasures he was no longer to share in; to see one of almost ninety settling the fashion of a lady's cap, or assigning her place in a country dance; to see him unmindful of his own reverend figure, or the respect he should have for himself, toasting demireps,[74] or attempting to entertain the lewd and idle; a sight like this might well serve as a satire on humanity; might shew that man is the only preposterous creature alive, who pursues the shadow of pleasure without temptation.

But he was not permitted to run on thus without severe and repeated reproof. The clergy sent him frequent calls to reformation; but the asperity of their advice in general abated its intended effects; they threatened him with fire and brimstone, for what he had long been taught to consider as foibles, and not vices; so like a desperated debtor, he did not care to settle an account, that, upon the first inspection, he found himself utterly unable to pay. Thus begins one of his monitors:

This admonition comes from your friend, and one that has your interest deeply at heart: It comes on a design altogether important, and of no less consequence than your everlasting happiness: so that it may justly challenge your careful regard. It is not to upbraid or reproach, much less to triumph and insult over your misconduct or misery; no, 'tis pure benevolence, it is disinterested goodwill prompts me to write; I hope therefore I shall not raise your resentment. Yet be the consequence what it will, I cannot bear to see you walk in the paths that lead to death, without warning you of the danger, without sounding in your

---

[74] Persons with a reputation for worldiness and pursuit of pleasure.

ear the lawful admonition, "Return and live! Why do you such things? I hear of your evil dealings by all this people?" I have long observed and pitied you; and must tell you plainly, Sir, that your present behaviour is not the way to reconcile yourself to God. You are so far from making atonement to offended justice, that each moment you are aggravating the future account, and heaping up an increase of his anger. As long as you roll on in a continued circle of sensual delights and vain entertainments, you are dead to all the purposes of piety and virtue. You are as odious to God as a corrupt carcase that lies putrefying in the church-yard. You are as far from doing your duty, or endeavouring after salvation, or restoring yourself to the divine favour, as a heap of dry bones nailed up in a coffin is from vigour and activity.— Think, Sir, I conjure you, think upon this, if you have any inclination to escape the fire that will never be quenched. Would you be rescued from the fury and fierce anger of God? Would you be delivered from weeping and wailing, and incessant gnashing of teeth? sure you would! But be certain, that this will never be done by amusements, which at best are trifling and impertinent; and for that, if for no other reason, foolish and sinful. 'Tis by seriousness; 'tis by retirement and mourning, you must accomplish this great and desirable deliverance. You must not appear at the head of every silly diversion, you must enter into your closet, and shut the door; commune with your own heart, and search out its defects. The pride of life, and all its superfluity of follies must be put away. You must make haste, and delay not to keep every injunction of heaven. You must always remember, that mighty sinners must be mightily penitent; or else mightily tormented. Your example, and your projects have been extremely *prejudicial;* I wish I could not say, *fatal* and *destructive* to many: For this there is no amends but an alteration of your conduct, as signal and remarkable as your *person* and *name.*

If you do not by this method remedy in some degree the evils that you have sent abroad, and prevent the mischievous consequences that may ensue—wretched will you be, wretched above all men, to eternity. The blood of souls will be laid to your charge; God's jealousy, like a consuming flame, will smoke against you; as you yourself will see in that day, when the mountains shall quake, and the hills melt, and the earth be burnt up at his presence.

Once more then I exhort you as a friend; I beseech you as a brother; I charge you as a messenger from God, in his own most solemn words; "Cast away from you your transgressions; make you a new heart, and a new spirit; so iniquity shall not be your ruin."

Perhaps you may be disposed to contemn this, and its serious purport; or to recommend it to your companions as a subject for raillery—Yet let me tell you before-hand, that for this, as well as for other things, God will bring you to judgment. He sees me now I write: He will observe you while you read. He notes down my words; he will also note down your consequent procedure. Not then upon me, not upon me; but upon your own soul, will the neglecting or despising my sayings turn. "If thou be wise, thou shalt be wise for thy self; if thou scornest, thou alone shall bear it."

Such repeated admonitions as these served to sting, without reforming him; they made him morose, but not pious. The dose was too strong for the patient to bear. He should have been met with smiles, and allured into reformation, if indeed he was criminal. But in the name of piety, what was there criminal in his conduct; he had long been taught to consider his trifling profession as a very serious and important business. He went through his office with great gravity, solemnity, and care; why then denounce peculiar torments against a poor harmless creature, who did a thousand good things, and whose greatest vice was vanity. He deserved ridicule, indeed, and he found it, but scarce a single action of his life, except one, deserves the asperity of reproach.

Thus we see a variety of causes concurred to embitter his departing life. The weakness and infirmities of exhausted nature, the admonitions of the grave, who aggravated his follies into vices; the ingratitude of his dependants, who formerly flattered his fortunes; but particularly the contempt of the great, who quite forgot him in his wants; all these hung upon his spirits and soured his temper, and the poor man of pleasure might have terminated his life very tragically, had not the corporation of *Bath* charitably resolved to grant him ten guineas the first *Monday* of every month. This bounty served to keep him from actual necessity, tho' far too trifling, to enable him to support the character of a gentleman. Habit, and not nature, makes almost all our wants; and he who had been accustomed in the early parts of life to affluence and prodigality, when reduced to an hundred and twenty-six pounds a year, must pine in actual indigence.

In this variety of uneasiness his health began to fail. He had received from nature a robust and happy constitution, that was scarce even to be impaired by intemperance. He even pretended, among his friends, that he never followed a single prescription in his life; however, in this he was one day detected on the parade; for boasting there of his contempt and utter disuse of medicine, unluckily the water of two blisters, which Dr. *Oliver* had prescribed, and which he then had upon each leg, ouzed through his stockings, and betrayed him. His aversion to physic, however, was frequently a topic of raillery between him and Doctor *Cheney,* who was a man of some wit and breeding. When *Cheney* recommended his vegetable diet, *Nash* would swear, that his design was to send half the world grazing like *Nebuchadnezzar.*[75] Ay, *Cheney* would reply, *Nebuchadnezzar* was never such an infidel as thou art. It was but last week, gentlemen, that I attended this fellow in a fit of sickness; there I found him rolling up his eyes to heaven, and crying for mercy; he would

then swallow my drugs like breast-milk, yet you now hear him, how the old dog blasphemes the faculty. What *Cheney* said in jest was true, he feared the approaches of death more than the generality of mankind, and was generally very devout while it threatened him. Tho' he was somewhat the libertine in action, none believed or trembled more than he; for a mind neither schooled by philosophy, nor encouraged by conscious innocence, is ever timid at the appearance of danger.

For some time before his decease nature gave warning of his approaching dissolution. The worn machine had run itself down to an utter impossibility of repair; he saw, that he must die, and shuddered at the thought. His virtues were not of the great, but the amiable kind; so that fortitude was not among the number. Anxious, timid, his thoughts still hanging on a receding world, he desired to enjoy a little longer that life, the miseries of which he had experienced so long. The poor unsuccessful gamester husbanded the wasting moments, with an encreased desire to continue the game, and to the last eagerly wished for one yet more happy throw. He died at his house in St. *John's Court, Bath,* on the 3d of *February,* 1761[76], aged eighty-seven years, three months, and some days.

His death was sincerely regretted by the city, to which he had been so long, and so great a benefactor. The day after he died, the Mayor of *Bath* called the corporation together, where they granted fifty pounds towards burying their Sovereign with proper respect. After the corpse had lain four days, it was conveyed to the abbey church in that city, with a solemnity somewhat peculiar to his character. About five the procession moved from his house; the charity girls two and two preceded, next the boys of the charity school singing a solemn occasional hymn. Next marched the city music, and his own band sounding at proper intervals a dirge. Three clergymen im-

---

[75] The reference is to Daniel 4: Nebuchadnezzar, in fulfillment of a dream, ". . . was driven from men, and did eat grass as oxen" (Dan. 4:33).

[76] Goldsmith's date is a year early. Perhaps he was still thinking of the old style calendar by which he would be correct.

mediately preceded the coffin, which was adorned with sable plumes, and the pall supported by the six senior Aldermen. The masters of the assembly-rooms followed as chief mourners; the beadles of that hospital, which he had contributed so largely to endow, went next, and last of all, the poor patients themselves, the lame, the emaciated, and the feeble, followed their old benefactor to his grave, shedding unfeigned tears, and lamenting themselves in him.

The crowd was so great, that not only the streets were filled but, as one of the journals in a *Rant* expresses it, "even the tops of houses were covered with spectators, each thought the occasion affected themselves most; as when a real King dies, they asked each other, *where shall we find such another;* sorrow sate upon every face, and even children lisped that their Sovereign was no more. The awfulness of the solemnity made the deepest impression on the minds of the distressed inhabitants. The peasant discontinued his toil, the ox rested from the plough, all nature seemed to sympathize with their loss, and the muffled bells rung a peal of Bob Major."

Our deepest solemnities have something truly ridiculous in them: there is somewhat ludicrous in the folly of historians, who thus declaim upon the death of Kings and Princes, as if there was any thing dismal, or any thing unusual in it. "For my part, says Poggi[77] the Florentine, I can no more grieve for another's death than I could for my own. I have ever regarded death as a very trifling affair; nor can black staves, long cloaks, or mourning coaches, in the least influence my spirits. Let us live here as long, and as merrily as we can, and when we must die, why let us die merrily too, but die so as to be happy."

The few things he was possessed of were left to his relations. A small library of well chosen books, some trinkets and pictures, were his only inheritance. Among the latter were a gold box, given by the late Countess of *Burlington,* with Lady *Euston's* picture in the lid. An agate etui,[78] with a diamond on the top, by the Princess Dowager of *Wales,* and some other things of no great value. The rings, watches, and pictures, which he formerly received from others, would have come to a considerable amount; but these his necessities had obliged him to dispose of: Some family pictures, however, remained, which were sold by advertisement, for five guineas each, after Mr. *Nash's* decease.

It was natural to expect, that the death of a person so long in the eye of the public, must have produced a desire in several to delineate his character, or deplore his loss. He was scarce dead, when the public papers were filled with elegies, groans and characters; and before he was buried, there were epitaphs ready made to inscribe on his stone. I remember one of those character writers, and a very grave one too, after observing, alass! that *Richard Nash,* Esq; was no more, went on to assure us, that he was *sagacious, debonair,* and *comode;* and concluded with gravely declaring, *that impotent posterity would in vain fumble to produce his fellow.* Another, equally sorrowful, gave us to know, *that he was indeed a man;* an assertion, which I fancy none will be so hardy as to contradict. But the merriest of all the lamentations made upon this occasion was, that where he is called, *A constellation of the heavenly sphere.*

[A few pages, including testimonial verses, have been omitted.]

---

[77] Giovanni Francesco Poggio Bracciolini (1380–1459), an Italian scholar famous for his vigorous invective.

[78] A case for pocket instruments.

Richard Hurd,
Bishop of Worcester
1720-1808

LETTERS ON CHIVALRY AND ROMANCE

LETTER VI [ON THE ENCHANTED GROUND OF GOTHIC ROMANCE]

Let it be no surprize to you that, in the close of my last Letter, I presumed to bring the *Gierusalemme liberata*[1] into competition with the Iliad.

So far as the heroic[2] and Gothic manners are the same, the pictures of each, if well taken, must be equally entertaining. But I go further, and maintain that the circumstances, in which they differ, are clearly to the advantage of the Gothic designers.

You see, my purpose is to lead you from this forgotten chivalry[3] to a more amusing subject, I mean the *Poetry* we still read, and which was founded upon it.

Much has been said, and with great truth, of the felicity of Homer's age, for poetical manners. But as Homer was a citizen of the world, when he had seen in Greece, on the one hand, the manners he has described, could he,[4] on the other hand, have seen in the west the manners of the feudal ages, I make no doubt but he would certainly have preferred the latter. And the grounds of this preference would, I suppose, have been *"The improved gallantry of the feudal times; and the superior solemnity of their superstitions."*

If any great poet, like Homer, had lived amongst and sung of, the Gothic knights (for after all Spenser and Tasso came too late, and it was impossible for them to paint truly and perfectly what was no longer seen or believed) this preference, I persuade myself, had been very sensible. But their fortune was not so happy.

> . . . omnes illacrymabiles
> Urgentur, ignotique longâ
> Nocte, carent quia vate sacro.[5]

As it is, we may take a guess of what the subject was capable of affording to

---

Text from the first edition, 1762.

[1] *Jerusalem Delivered* (1575), a Christian epic poem by the Italian Torquato Tasso.

[2] i.e., of the classical epic.

[3] i.e., the code of behavior in the feudal ages.

[4] if he could.

[5] In endless night they sleep, unwept, unknown,
No bard had they to make all time their own.
(Horace, *Odes*, IV, ix, 26–28, tr. Francis.)

real genius from the rude sketches we have of it, in the old Romancers. And it is but looking into any of them to be convinced that the *gallantry,* which inspirited the feudal times, was of a nature to furnish the poet with finer scenes and subjects of description in every view, than the simple and uncontrolled barbarity of the Grecian.

The principal entertainment arising from the delineation of these consists in the exercise of the boisterous passions, which are provoked and kept alive from one end of the Iliad to the other, by every imaginable scene of rage, revenge, and slaughter. In the other, together with these, the gentler and more humane affections are awakened in us by the most interesting displays of love and friendship; of love, elevated to it's noblest heights; and of friendship, operating on the purest motives. The mere variety of these paintings is a relief to the reader, as well as writer. But their beauty, novelty, and pathos give them a vast advantage, on the comparison.

Consider, withall, the surprizes, accidents, adventures which probably and naturally attend on the life of wandering knights; the occasion there must be for describing the wonders of different countries, and of presenting to view the manners and policies of distant states: all which make so conspicuous a part of the materials of the greater poetry.

So that, on the whole, tho' the spirit, passions, rapin,[6] and violence of the two sets of manners were equal, yet there was a dignity, a magnificence, a variety in the feudal, which the other wanted.

As to *religious machinery,*[7] perhaps the popular system of each was equally remote from reason, yet the latter had something in it more amusing, as well as more awakening to the imagination.

The current popular tales of Elves and Fairies were even fitter to take the credulous mind, and charm it into a willing admiration of the *specious miracles,* which wayward fancy delights in, than those of the old traditionary rabble of pagan divinities. And then, for the more solemn fancies of witchcraft and incantation, the horrors of the Gothic were above measure striking and terrible. The mummeries of the pagan priests were childish, but the Gothic Enchanters shook and alarmed all nature.

We feel this difference very sensibly in reading the antient and modern poets. You would not compare the Canidia[8] of Horace with the Witches in Macbeth. And what are Virgil's myrtles dropping blood, to Tasso's enchanted forest?

Ovid indeed, who had a fancy turn'd to romance, makes Medea, in a rant, talk wildly. But was this the common language of their other writers? The enchantress in Virgil says cooly of the very chiefest prodigies of her charms and poisons,

His ego saepe lupum fieri, & se condere sylvis
Moerin; saepe animas imis excire sepulchris,
Atque satas ali vidi traducere messes.[9]

The admirable poet has given an air of the marvellous to his subject, by the magic of his expression. Else, what do we find here, but the ordinary effects of *melancholy,* the vulgar superstition of *evoking Spirits,* and the supposed influence of *fascination* on the hopes of rural industry.

Non isthic obliquo oculo mihi commoda quisquam
Limat. . . .[10]

says the poet of his country-seat, as if

---

[6] plundering.

[7] Religious beliefs used as a framework to the stories.

[8] A detestable female character delineated in Horace's *Epodes* V and XVII and in his *Satires,* I, iii.

[9] And oft with Moeris, tasting them, become A wolf and prowl the woods, or by their power Call spirits out of graves, or charm away A planted crop to fill some stranger's field. (*Eclogues,* VIII, 97–99, tr. Williams.)

[10] "None there with eye askance my pleasure views" (Horace, *Epistles,* I, xiv, 37–38, tr. Francis).

this security from a *fascinating Eye* were a singular privilege, and the mark of a more than common good fortune.

Shakespear, on the other hand, with a terrible sublime (which not so much the energy of his genius, as the nature of his subject drew from him) gives us another idea of the *rough magic,* as he calls it, of fairy enchantment.

> . . . I have bedimm'd
> The noon-tide Sun, call'd forth the mu-
> tinous winds,
> And 'twixt the green sea and the azure
> vault
> Set roaring war; to the dread rattling
> thunder
> Have I giv'n fire, and rifted Jove's stout
> oak
> With his own bolt: The strong-bas'd
> promontory
> Have I made shake, and by the spurrs
> pluck'd up
> The Pine and Cedar: Graves, at my
> command,
> Have open'd, and let forth their sleep-
> ers. . . .[11]

The last circumstance, you will say, is but the *animas imis excire sepulchris*[12] of the latin poet. But a very significant word marks the difference. The pagan necromancers had a hundred little tricks by which they pretended to call up the ghosts, or shadows of the dead: but these, in the ideas of paganism, were quite another thing from Shakespear's *Sleepers.*

This may serve for a cast of Shake-spear's magic. And I can't but think that, when Milton wanted to paint the horrors of that night (one of the noblest parts in his *Paradise Regained*) which the Devil himself is feigned to conjure up in the wilderness, the Gothic language and ideas helped him to work up his tempest with such terror. You will judge from these lines:

> . . . nor staid the terror there;
> Infernal ghosts and hellish furies round

> Environ'd; some howl'd, some yell'd,
> some shriek'd,
> Some bent at thee their fiery darts. . . .

But above all from the following,

> Thus pass'd the night so foul, till morn-
> ing fair
> Came forth with pilgrim steps in amice
> gray,
> Who with her *radiant finger* still'd the
> roar
> Of thunder, chas'd the clouds, and laid
> the winds
> And *griesly specters.* . . .[13]

Where the *radiant finger* points at the potent wand of the Gothic magicians, which could reduce the calm of nature, upon occasion, as well as disturb it; and the *griesly specters laid* by the approach of morn were apparently of their raising, as a sagacious critic perceived when he took notice "how very injudicious it was to retail the *popular superstition* in this place."

After all, the conclusion is not to be drawn so much from particular passages, as from the *general impression* left on our minds in reading the antient and modern poets. And this is so much in fa-vour of the *Latter,* that Mr. Addison scruples not to say, "The Antients have not much of this poetry among them; for, indeed (continues he) almost the whole substance of it owes it's original to the darkness and superstition of later ages—Our forefathers looked upon na-ture with more reverence and horror, be-fore the world was enlightened by learn-ing and philosophy, and loved to astonish themselves with the apprehensions of Witchcraft, Prodigies, Charms, and In-chantments. There was not a village in England, that had not a Ghost in it, the churchyards were all haunted, every large common had a circle of fairies be-longing to it, and there was scarce a Shepherd to be met with who had not seen a spirit."[14]

---

[11] *The Tempest,* V, i, 42–50.
[12] "call spirits out of graves"; part of the passage from Vergil's *Eclogues* quoted above (see note 9).
[13] Bk. IV, ll. 421–430.
[14] *The Spectator,* No. 419.

We are upon enchanted ground, my friend; and you are to think yourself well used that I detain you no longer in this fearful circle. The glympse, you have had of it, will help your imagination to conceive the rest. And without more words you will readily apprehend that the fancies of our modern bards are not only more gallant, but, on a change of the scene, more sublime, more terrible, more alarming, than those of the classic fablers. In a word, you will find that the *manners* they paint, and the *superstitions* they adopt, are the more poetical for being Gothic.

James Boswell
1740-1795

From JOURNAL OF MY JAUNT, Harvest 1762

THURSDAY 7 OCTOBER.

I got up before breakfast a good time and was carried by Mr. William to his room which was the sweetest in the house.[1] There he has his Books of devotion, and there does perform his penances and all the other rites of his severe Religion. He made me just think myself in a monastery abroad. We then went and took a walk. I was surprised to find him very chearfull and realy facetious. At ten Mr. Irvine[2] and I left Kilhead and came to Annan, where we went to a back court which belonged to a Mr. Blair, lately dead, and saw a stone which made formerly a part of an old Castle here. I read plainly upon it *Robert de Bruss* 1300.[3] I am at a loss to account for the pleasure which many People have in Antiquities and yet I have it in a very strong degree. I am apt to imagine that there is realy an original principle which

stamps a value upon every thing that is ancient except an old woman, which is a byword for the reverse, and often indeed very unjustly. We din'd at Bonshaw, where Mr. Irvine lives with his Nephew, who was not at home. It is situated on a Bank and has a pretty river[4] and a good deal of Wood about it. We had here two Maiden Aunts, one of whom was very kind, and the other a sort of a reserved Gentlewoman. We had also two sisters, very genteel girls who played a little on the Spinet, and Miss Jeanie the youngest, who is a tall good-looking Woman, sung well enough. I got for my guide to Springkell, Mr. Currie, the young Laird of Bridekirk, and a writer in Edinburgh, a genteel, obliging young man. We got to Springkell in good time. Sir William Maxwell[5] is a man of a handsom figure and genteel air and carries in his external appearance the character which is much talked about and seldom found, a Gen-

Text reprinted with permission of Yale University and McGraw-Hill Book Company, Inc., from *The Private Papers of James Boswell from Malahide Castle in the Collection of Lt-Colonel Ralph Heyward Isham* (1928). Professor Frederick A. Pottle, Chairman of the Committee for the Yale Editions of the Boswell Papers, has kindly given his permission for the use of his notes first published in 1951 in an edition of the *Journal* published by William Heinemann Ltd. of London. "Harvest," according to Pottle, was "the usual Scots term for autumn."

[1] Boswell has been visiting Kelhead, as he said, "surrounded with cousins," among whom was William Douglas.

[2] Robert Irvine, described earlier by Boswell as "a writer in Edinburgh and a very good plain man and more genteel than usual."

[3] "This stone may now be seen in the Town Hall at Annan" (Pottle).

[4] The Kirtle.

[5] "Another cousin, for his mother was Catherine Douglas, sister to Sir John Douglas of Kelhead and daughter of Helen (Erskine) Douglas, half-sister to Boswell's mother" (Pottle).

tleman. He has a great deal of good sense, sweetness of Disposition and delicacy of taste. He is perfectly easy and polite and may be stiled in every sense of the word, a pretty man. Miss Maxwell, his sister, is an honest-hearted, merry, jocular girl, of size somewhat corpulent but has a very agreable countenance and can walk and dance with all imaginable cleverness. She plays with taste upon the Guitar, which she chiefly employs in accompanying her voice with a thorough bass. Indeed her singing is so excellent that I should wish to reward her with due praise in this, my Journal, but that I own is difficult to do. This acknowledgment I believe is a tollerable sort of a Compliment. However I will for my own satisfaction say a little more. Her voice is clear, strong and sweet. She has great command of it and sings with uncommon spirit and taste. She obliged us with several Italian airs and English Ballads. She likewise gave us *Gallowshiels, I'll never leave thee, O the broom,* and some others of the best Scotch Songs in which she exprest more tenderness of feeling than I ever heard. We had here with us, too, Mr. George Henderson, a good honest fellow, cousin to Sir William, and Doctor Garie,[6] a Physician, who has been Tutor to the Knights of this family for two Generations, a man upwards of seventy, nonjurant and High-church, but is a quiet peacable creature and never mentions Principles. He lives in the house and seems to be very happy. I was exceedingly high-spirited this night and was very merry and much relished.

has great Capabilitys.[7] There is a fine walk for near two miles upon the side of a river, and a pretty variety of grounds about his house, which is a very good one. Sir William has a turn for improving and will probably make Springkell much better. He has here a good many old trees, particularly about the old Churchyard of Kirkonnel, which parish is now joined with another. There are here a great many tomb-Stones; as also the family Burial Place, with a little chapel above the Vault. The Place has a pleasing melancholy about it and is admirably suited for calm Meditation. A tradition goes that there lived a pretty Woman of the name of Helen here who had two lovers, one of whom discovered her one day walking with his rival and immediately levelled his Gun at him, which Helen perceived, ran in between them to save Him, but from the same shot they both received death. The unfortunate lover went abroad to relieve his mind from thought, where he composed a mournfull Ditty—

I wish I were where Helen lies
In fair Kirkonnel Ley.

He was afterwards buried in the same grave with them.[8] I am happy to find my journal going on pretty well at present. A while ago, I found myself like a horse whose legs are stock'd, but now by a little exercise I am warmed and have got well and am moving with ease and pleasure. Long may it be so! In the afternoon Mr. Goldie[9] came here too. Things went on well.

FRIDAY 8 OCTOBER.

Sir William and I walked about the place which, as Lork Chalkstone says,

SATURDAY 9 OCTOBER.

Walking, music, chatting and indolent lolling employed the forenoon. Miss

---

6 "The correct spelling is probably Garioch" (Pottle).

7 "Lord Chalkstone is a character in Garrick's farce *Lethe*. In Lord Chalkstone's patter about 'capabilities' Garrick is satirising the famous landscape-architect Launcelot Brown, who used the expression so freely that it became his nickname" (Pottle).

8 "Boswell's account of the story on which this famous ballad is based appears to have

been written down some years before any other on record. As the story is usually told, only Helen is killed by the jealous suitor's bullet or arrow; the preferred lover takes bloody vengeance on his rival, and after long wanderings in Spain returns to die on Helen's grave" (Pottle).

9 George Goldie, whom Boswell had met earlier on his trip and described as "a neat young man, very cheerful and very friendly."

Maxwell told me that Lord and Lady Traquair had a very good opinion of me, and represented their Place and manner of life as so very agreable that I wished much to be there, and, as Miss Maxwell was to visit them in a few weeks, I agreed to meet her there. A much more agreable meeting than the Genius of Brutus with that Hero at Philippi.[10] At night Lord and Lady Kames arrived.[11]

SUNDAY 10 OCTOBER.

Sir William and Lord Kames went and surveyed the Place. And I sat in the house and read a little and wrote a little. It gives me some concern that I have no sort of turn for farming, for it is a pity that a Being who will probably posess a part of the earth should not know how to cultivate it. Indeed I have lived so much in a town, and have so high a relish of Society and other amusements, that my Attention has had little chance of being employed upon Ploughs and Harrows. But what I regret more is my want of taste for planting or gardening, which are realy noble and elegant Employments. I flatter myself that I may be able to acquire that taste by attention and Study. I shall have fine opportunities of learning the best methods in and about London. In the afternoon Miss Maxwell and I had some conversation about the Roman Catholic Religion.[12] Conversations of this kind I am very fond of. For there is something very pleasing to the human mind in thinking upon futurity and upon the various ways of securing happiness to itself in that State, about which indeed numberless conjectures have been formed.

MONDAY 11 OCTOBER.

We walked about all the forenoon in that sort of agreable sauntering way, which when the sun shines and the weather is gentle disposes much to serenity and good-humoured dispositions. In the afternoon, arrived from Carlisle, Mr. Benson,[13] a genteel sensible man who has an estate in Cumberland, and is a Steward to the Duke of Portland. Doctor Coltart,[14] an Apothecary, a true-looking Englishman with a round-cut head and leather bretches, a jolly dog who sung us a Song that the Boy sings, who sweeps Drurylane Stage, before the candles are lighted to the tune of *ballance a Straw*.

Tho' I sweep to and fro', yet I'd have you to know
There are sweepers in high life as well as in low.

Miss Yates, a Clergyman's Daughter in Yorkshire, a good humoured girl, sensible and well-looking enough, And Miss Kitty Gilpin, daughter to a Captain Gilpin, a fine lively creature, not pretty but of an agreable countenance. I soon made myself acquainted with her, and in a few minutes had her repeating Ossian's address to the Sun, which she did with much propriety and grace. After supper she sung us several songs, and among the rest, a little smart Ballad of her own Composition, which I got a copy of.[15] I

---

[10] "Shakespeare's *Julius Caesar*, IV, iii and V, v. Boswell (if he means anything) must mean that he agreed to be with Miss Maxwell in spirit. She died at Traquair on 15 April 1763" (Pottle).

[11] Henry Home, Lord Kames (1696–1782), had just published *The Elements of Criticism*, with which Boswell shows his acquaintance by paraphrasing it in his journal a few days earlier. Boswell had seen Lord and Lady Kames earlier on the jaunt and was to be accompanied by them from this point on his trip to their residence.

[12] Boswell could not reveal his own secret conversion to Catholicism two years earlier without being deprived of many civil rights including that of inheritance of his father's estate. His conversion was perhaps more a matter of esthetic experience or of moral rebellion from the ways of his family than of religion.

[13] Thomas Benson of Carlisle, steward to William Henry Cavendish-Bentinck, third Duke of Portland.

[14] Maurice Coulthard, M.D.

[15] "Miss Gilpin won some recognition for her verse in the Cumbrian dialect. Her father, Capt. John Bernard Gilpin, was commandant at Carlisle in 1745. Boswell had a pleasant meeting with her sixteen years later" (Pottle).

was in great spirits. Finding myself well taken I gave great scope and sung an infinite number of Songs, particularly from the *Jovial Crew*[16] which met with uncommon Applause. After I was in bed, My friend Doctor Coltart pay'd me a visit with his candle in his hand, took leave of me as he and Benson were to set off early, and hoped we shou'd sweep[17] at Carlisle.

TUESDAY 12 OCTOBER.

Sir William entertained me with the character of a Genius, a Mr. Stockdale who was a fellow Student of his at St. Andrews. He was very lively and had a pretty poetical turn. He was exceedingly wild and had an intrigue with the wife of an old Captain upon whom he wrote the following Epitaph.

Epitaph on Captain ———
Here, far from slaughter and the din of arms,
From brandy's comfort and Clarinda's charms,
By heav'n's high will and fate's allmighty doom
A Son of thunder slumbers in his tomb.
O mother earth, revenge the marriage vows,
Revenge the province of a slighted Spouse,
Press this inglorious wretch depriv'd of life,

For, when alive, he ne'er could press his wife.

He afterwards went into the Army where he continued for sometime, but tiring of it, and having allways had an enthusiastic turn, he lay'd aside the sword, and is now a Methodist Clergyman in England. What a curious creature is Man! how changeable is he! how inconsistent! Where is the resemblance between Stockdale the Buck, drinking, whoring and giving a loose to whim, and Stockdale the Parson, in his gown and cassoc, showing an example of Sobriety and austere virtue and preaching with vehement warmth against the horrid nature of Sin and Iniquity? Is there any identity of Person here? Yes, there is. They are in reality the same Person. The same vivacity which formerly hurried him into Vice, now renders him superlatively religious. He has got a disgust at the former, and, his eyes being opened, he is violently enamoured of the latter.[18]

We walked for an hour or two very pleasantly. After dinner we sung as before; and in the evening, we had a dance. I discovered that Miss Gilpin was an excellent mimic. So I made a fair exchange with her, and gave her Logan and Lord Dundonald and Sir George Preston and Lord Drumfries [sic], for as many of her acquaintances.[19] I contrived to make our personages talk together which was a most ludicrous scene. She learn't me a method of quarrelling to Prince Eugene's

[16] "By Richard Brome; first acted in 1642; altered to a very successful comic opera by additional songs and brought again on the stage in 1731" (Pottle).

[17] A pun on *sleep* in allusion to the words of the song with which the doctor had entertained the company.

[18] "Percival Stockdale gives a guarded account of the St. Andrews affair in his *Memoirs*, where it appears that the lady was a Mrs. Henderson, *née* Graham. Stockdale was a friend of Boswell's friend Temple, who later furnished Boswell with several other details of his life that do not appear in *The Dictionary of National Biography*. It seems that he married an old woman for her money, deserted her, and ran off to France with a young lady named Buck. When his wife died (apparently in 1769) he

returned to London, married Miss Buck, and 'commenced translator and author'. He managed *The Critical Review*, published a great quantity of miscellaneous writings, was chaplain of the Fleet Prison and later chaplain of a guardship, the *Resolution*. He was intimate with Johnson, who repeated for his benefit the remark (first made on the tour to the Hebrides) that a ship was worse than a jail" (Pottle).

[19] "Hugh Logan of that ilk was a bacchanalian laird whose extravagant humour and hospitality became a byword in the country; Thomas, eighth Earl of Dundonald (Boswell's grand-uncle), was a blustering, profane old soldier; William, fourth Earl of Dumfries, had a pompous manner. We do not know what Sir George Preston's peculiarity was" (Pottle).

March, by alternately singing Bars and half bars of it and varying our tones and countenances till we gradually rose to the highest pitch of rage. This had a most wonderfull effect upon the company, who were quite distrest with laughing. We likewise took off[20] the Italian Opera and altho' we neither knew a word of the language nor a single tune, we thrilled away the most pathetic expression, set to the tenderest Music which we succeeded in to a degree that was surprising. While we sat at table we agreed to humbug the Company and accordingly I whispered something to her with great earnestness, at which she seemed to be much shocked, started from me and said, "I don't understand, Sir—such usage, Sir, and I am sure you must mean to affront me—". This and two three more little exclamations of the same kind delivered with the proper Emphasis, joined with the disconcerted sheepiness of look, which I nicely affected, fairly took in[21] the whole Company, who were realy concerned, and could scarcely be perswaded that we were in joke.[22] She is likewise a girl of great good-nature, and is never severe and is quite free from the conceit and forwardness that is often to be met with in a Girl of wit and cleverness in a Country-town. She has likewise a simplicity of manners that pleased me much and convinced me of her being perfectly innocent. I promised to send her some little pieces of entertainment from London,[23] and she promised me what she cou'd send from Carlisle.

WEDNESDAY 13 OCTOBER.

Fortune seemed to declare that buying Horses was not my talent or at least should not be so, for my poor six-pounder had received a good many kicks from another horse that had been loose in the stable, so that she was lame and could not travel. I was therefore obliged to leave her at Springkell till she shou'd recover and either be sold or sent to me. I bought from Miss Maxwell, a strong grey horse fit for a plough or a Journey, for which I gave £10, and thus was necessitated to venture still farther in the horse trade. We left Springkell at 11 o'clock. Sir William and My Lord rode and I went in the chaise with My Lady to Langtown, where we dined and Sir William left us. In the afternoon we went to Brampton, a very good little village prettily situated. I was happy to find myself in Old England for which I have a great affection.[24] And in a town too, where Mankind are to be seen more spirited than in the country. And here it may not be amiss to give the reason of our being in this part of the country. It seems the road thro' England to Berwick-shire is much better and takes us but a day longer to travel than the road by Edinburgh would have done. Therefore when we considered the Question impartialy we determined to take this as the best. I thought proper to mention this; by way of rendering my Journal more perspicuous, and by way of rendering it more entertaining, as Mankind are very fond to

---

[20] parodied.

[21] tricked.

[22] For this prank Boswell's father reprimanded him severely in a letter of May 30, 1763, saying in part: "From Jedburgh I came to Dumfries, where I found that while you were in that country you had given yourself up to mimicry, and had at different times and places taken off (as you called it) Lord Dumfries, Sir George Preston, and Logan. This, too, you may believe behoved to give me vast pain. To make a mock of others is not praiseworthy; besides, such things are seldom concealed. You create enemies to yourself and even to your friends, it being the way of the world to resent such impertinences against all who show any

countenance to the person guilty of them. To all which I may add that mimicry has been justly considered as the lowest and meanest kind of wit." Quoted from Appendix II of *The Yale Editions of the Private Papers of James Boswell*, prepared for the Press, with Introduction and Notes by Frederick A. Pottle (London, William Heinemann Ltd., 1951).

[23] Boswell's tour of Scotland was preparatory to a visit to London described in his *Journal from the Time of My Leaving Scotland 15 November 1762*, now popularly known as his *London Journal*.

[24] Longtown and Brampton are in Cumberland, near the city of Carlisle.

know cause as well as effect upon most occasions, and will study very hard on that account. When we entered the Village, we were met by a crowd huzzaing a Man who was beating a drum for a Puppet-show and had, moreover, another man with him who carried, high elevated on a lofty pole, a hat and four halfpenny Cakes. This last circumstance puzled me a good deal; but I learnt that as many Boys were to eat the loaves and he who was first done eating was to have the hat. We had here an excellent inn—I was happy and chearfull; and I resolved to see the Show which raised my curiosity, as I had never seen Punch which indeed is unaccountable. Accordingly at seven I went to the town's hall where the exhibition was to be, full of vivacity and that kind of feeling which we carry to the Theatre when we expect to see a diverting play. The room was pretty well filled with a very curious Collection of human beings. An impudent dog sat by me who wanted much to cultivate an acquaintance with me; but *I repudiated him.* Next to him sat a jolly gentleman in black whose name was dean. As I had my bath[25] great-coat with a gold binding, my gold-lac'd hat smartly set upon my head, and twirled my cane switch with a good deal of gentility, I looked exceedingly like an officer of the Army. Mr. Dean therefore showed me respect; "Come Captain, take a snuff"—which I received with a hearty nod, and a "thank you, Mr. Dean." We bought Apples, and carried about in our hats to the company with inimitable civility and address, and so were very principal People. The Showman then attracted our notice. His scenes were painted on the wings with figures too strange to be described and on the middle division was painted an English officer of a royal Regiment on a bay horse, a figure of dignity and even ter-

ror. The stage was illuminated with a few small candle[s] stuck into white-iron chandeliers, with unlighted ones ballanced accross their rims, waiting like recruits to be formed into the Corps. By way of Preludio,[26] a Dulcimer was laid upon a drum and, the Showman being seated upon a Barrel, *Ballance a Straw* was immediately struck up, which gave great satisfaction. He next touched the tunefull fiddle with equal success, and at last had recourse to the spirit-stirring Drum, which he rattled away to great admiration. When he had satisfied himself of this, he proceeded to the contention for the Prize. The Boys had their hands tied behind their backs, and being placed upon their knees and the Cakes laid upon the ground, the signal was given. Never have I seen a more ludicrous sight. Their eagerness made them often stoop quickly and then their noses rap'd against the floor, while they had no way of defending against it. The Audience were all in a tumult, and that unlimited vent of feeling which is peculiar to the common people of England had it's full course. At last silence was imposed by the wave of a stick in the hand of the showman's wife, who delivered the hat to the victorious Boy, who I am sure felt as much satisfaction as he could hold. The Showman came near me, so I thought proper to shave[27] him a little. "This sir," says I (with a most important countenance) "was very entertaining," "Ay sir," say'd he, "I allways give some such thing as this for the encouragement of the Place that I am in." This I very gravely acquiesced in. Little did I think when I entered this scene of rude Amusement that the gentle Goddess of love was laying snares for me. However that was the case; on the bench behind me sat a young Lady in a red cloak and black hat very like, but younger and

---

25 "A woolen fabric formerly much used for making overcoats: baize with a long nap" (Pottle).

26 prelude.

27 "A cant term of the Soaping Club [a group of Boswell's friends interested, as Professor Pottle says on another occasion, in 'giggling and making giggle']. The approximate meaning is, 'to affect deep interest so as to lead another person on to make himself ridiculous'. The first procedure is 'soaping [the victim's] beard'; the second, 'shaving' or 'applying the razor'" (Pottle).

handsomer, than Lady Dunmore.[28] I instantly addrest myself to her in the most engaging manner that I could, and found her tender enough, and during the hubub, I obtained from her the sweetest kiss that virgin ever gave. She told me that she was Maid to an Inkeeper in the town, and that she could not have an opportunity of seeing me. However she agreed that she wou'd go to London with me, if I would take her. Dear little creature! How fond was I of her. Punch and the other Puppets next appeared, who diverted me much but my girl went to another seat, and when I follow'd her was excessively prudish. Whether she observed some acquaintance that she stood in awe of, or for what other reason I cou'd not imagine, but while my mind was occupied with mingled concern and merriment, I was sent for by my fellow travellers to supper and was obliged to leave my charmer. This adventure tho', pleased me at the time and does well for my Journal. At supper I fell much in love with the chambermaid who served us who was a handsom Girl, with an insinuating wantoness of look. I made her light me to my room and when I had her there, she indulged me in many endearments, but would by no means consent to the main Object of my ardent desires and seemed affraid of the People in the house hearing us make noise. So I was obliged to sleep by myself. However, I discovered that sleep has prevented me from felicity, for Lord Kames's servant jok'd me next morning and told me seriously that he saw her go into my room and shut the door after I was gone to bed. This was going pretty far, but I suppose she had not assurance enough to wake me.

THURSDAY 14 OCTOBER.

We breakfasted at Glenwhelt, a very handsom Inn. This forenoon My Lord and I walked about four miles and had a great deal of conversation. He told me that my greatest disadvantage was a too great avidity of Pleasure, by which he understood elevation of spirits and high relish of Company, which rendered me idle and made me unhappy in a calm situation. Just as a man who is accustomed to fine seasoned dishes, has no taste of plain and wholesom food. He said Mr. Hamilton of Bangour,[29] who was exceedingly lively and had the finest taste, was ruined on that very account; that he once made an attempt to cure him of it; he carried him out to Kames, and for a day or two did every thing to amuse him. After he had been there some days My Lord told him, "Mr. Hamilton I am obliged to be busy, you must excuse me. But there are Books for you." My Lord kept an eye upon him and saw him lift book after book in a listless way, and seem very wearied and very miserable, as he could fall upon no pretence to get away. He allowed him to suffer in this way for a week when he began to look into Davila's *History of france*,[30] read one Page the first day and two the second, till at last he became as diligent, as eager and as happy a Student as his Lordship. He kept him in this way for sometime and thought he had got him established in a good habit; but whenever he returned to Edinburgh he fell back to his former state which jaded him so much that his spirits were quite exhausted and in the latter part of his life he was good for nothing till enlivened by a Bottle. "Now," said he, "Boswell, take care of splitting upon the same rock. You are going to London. You are very agreable; your company will be much sought after. Be upon your guard in time. Be your own Master. Keep the reins in your own hand. Resolve to be able to live at times by yourself." In reality it is a matter of infinite conse-

[28] "Lady Charlotte Stewart, daughter of the Earl of Galloway. She later accompanied her husband, John, fourth Earl of Dunmore, to Virginia, of which he was the last royal governor" (Pottle).

[29] William Hamilton of Bangour (1704–1754), Scottish poet, one of whose poems Boswell mentioned earlier on the jaunt.
[30] Enrico Caterino Davila (1576–1631), Italian historian.

quence to be able to support retirement with satisfaction. I am resolved to be in earnest to attain this, while in London. I shall see how my resolution is performed. We talked upon Books and the inclination which many People, especialy when young, have to be Authors; which to be sure is an agreable wish, and if one succeeds must be very pleasing. It is making another self, which can be present in many places, and is not subject to the inconstancies of Passion which the man himself is. I told him that I should like much to be distinguished in that way, that I was sure that I had genius, and was not deficient in easiness of expression; but was at a loss for something to say, and, when I set myself seriously to think of writing, that I wanted a Subject. He said that he thought me well calculated for writing lively periodical papers and insisted that I should begin at Kames to do something in that way, and said he should asist me and put me upon a method of improving. He told me that he had once a scheme for the Publication of a Work of that kind at Edinburgh, but found a want of witty and humorous writers, which he said Captain Erskine and I would sufficiently make up. He said he had composed about a couple of dozen of Essays which he intended for that purpose, and he promised to exchange with me. I wish I may be able to do some good in this way. We dined at Chollingfoord, where there was a numerous meeting of the Gentlemen of Northumberland; well-drest people, plump and vivacious. We went at night to Cambo, a village very small and very poor. The Inn was indeed exceedingly bad. When we entered we first beheld a Company in the Parlour mortaly drunk. We were shown into the only other room, which was raw and confused. The Landlady was a Shrew and the Maids were slovenly and dirty. Everything was worse than the worst Inn in Scotland. I now felt the disadvantage of too much delicacy of taste. I was shocked and realy put out of humour and exprest my uneasiness and rage very strongly. Lady Kames grumbled a little, but My Lord said not a word. He thought it below a Philosopher to be affected by such trivial Inconveniences. But I imputed his silence to the excess of his anguish and declared that he put me in mind of the Picture of the sacrifice of Iphigenia, in which the Father's countenance is concealed, as beyond the power of the Painter to give an idea of his grief on so mournfull an occasion.[31] I felt much for our Landlord, who was a decent discreet man much resembling Mr. Love,[32] and seemed anxious to have things right for us. I had a bed in the Parlour which I had a great aversion at; I kept on all my cloaths except my Coat and Boots and made the best of it.

FRIDAY 15 OCTOBER.

I got up stupid and discontented enough. I was reduced to that ebb of Understanding as to produce the following compositions which I wrote with a diamond pen upon a window:

David Hume, the Historian, on Christmas did eat
A rabbit alive as it stood on it's feet.
                              T. Smollet M.D.

Howt owt Tobie Smallet maun ye lauch at me
Tho' ye in your garret be liken to dee.
                              D. Hume[33]

---

[31] "A famous lost painting by Timanthes, *c.* 400 B.C." (Pottle).

[32] "James Dance, who took the name of Love when he went on the stage, had formerly been manager of the theatre in Edinburgh. He taught Boswell English pronunciation and had long been his confidential friend. Boswell wrote his first journal (not yet recovered) at Love's request, and lent him money, as the London journal somewhat tediously iterates. Love had recently joined the company at Drury Lane, London" (Pottle).

[33] "Smollett and Hume were authors of rival histories of England, but there seems to have been no personal enmity between them" (Pottle). David Hume's six-volume *History of Great Britain*, begun in 1754, had just been completed in 1761; *The Complete History of England* by the Scottish novelist, Tobias Smollett, had appeared in 1757–1758. The two Scotsmen were in amiable correspondence as late as 1768.

Gentlemen, I am no Poet but I laugh at you both.

H. Home[34]

Alas! alas! am I reduced to this state! We dined at Rothbury, a tollerable village situated in a hollow surrounded with wild mountains, and went at night to Whittingham, where we had a charming Inn which seemed doubly agreable by being contrasted with our last night's quarters. I was satisfied and pleased and disposed to do every thing that was good. I am realy astonished to find myself so mechanical. External conveniences and elegance render me not only happy but benevolent. There was a dance of common labourers in the house, who were as jolly as mortals could be, drank and joked and laugh'd, and shook the floor with a vigorous northumbrian thump to a very good fiddle.

SATURDAY 16 OCTOBER.

We dined at Millfield a very poor Inn, where we got little or nothing. But I don't mind bad entertainment in the day, provided I am comfortable at night. We got to Kames about five o'clock, where we found Mr. Drummond of Blair, Brother to My Lady, a Gentleman who is reckoned very proud and has been nicknamed the Prince of Blair.[35] He has indeed a little haughtiness which renders him not very agreeable at first sight. So much for the shade of his character. He is at the same time a man of sense, very honest and very friendly when he has an attachment. He has done several generous things. He loves company and has humour, tho' it is sometimes a little dry. Lord Kames is a man of uncommon Genius, great Application and extensive knowledge of which his various works are a standing proof. It is indeed astonishing to find a man so much master of Law, Philosophy and the *Belles Lettres,* and posest of so great Insight into human

Nature and, at the same time, a good companion, chearfull and lively. Altho' he is now and then a little whimsical, and impatient of contradiction, he is honest, friendly and public-spirited, and is upon the whole a great character. Lady Kames was very handsom and still has a very good presence. She is a woman of good understanding and very well bred. Regulates her family with accuracy, and has in her house and at her table a remarkable degree of elegance. She has a great fund of humour, and a peculiar turn of strong and brilliant propriety of Expression. She has now and then a little lowness of spirits, which renders her more apt to be disturbed and offended than one could wish, and makes her say pretty severe things. But take her all in all, she is an excellent Woman. I greatly admire the manner in which Lord and Lady Kames live. Seldom have I seen a stronger picture of conjugal felicity. I have observed with pleasure the mutual confidence and Affection which subsists between them, after having lived together upwards of twenty years. Could I see many more such instances I should have a higher idea of Marriage. We were very hearty this night, and I rejoyced much at finding myself lodged in a sweet handsom Bed-room.

SUNDAY 17 OCTOBER.

What shall I say for myself for not going to Church? Public worship is surely decent and is at least a duty that a Man should perform as a good Subject, abstracting from Religion altogether. But I will not give up Religion. I adore with humility and gratitude the Lord of the Universe. I have strong feelings of devotion at times. They are now clouded with other Passions; I hope they shall be stronger and clearer sometime hence. Why then do I absent myself from Public Worship? Because I am not a Presbyterian, and do not find myself ben-

---

[34] Henry Home, Lord Kames, with whom Boswell was traveling; Boswell evidently was moved to recording one of Kames's criticisms of the two historians as a jest.

[35] George Drummond; "Lady Kames succeeded him in the estate of Blair in 1766; thereafter she was styled 'Mrs. Drummond'" (Pottle).

efited by extempore prayers. I wish there may not be another cause stronger than this; which is Indolence. I shall judge when I am in London. We walked and chatted all the day. At night arrived Mr. Ralph Carre, an uncle of My Lady's, who has been upwards of twenty years an Attorney in London, a round man with a Bob wig, and his coat buttoned, of manners plain and somewhat vulgar. I am told he is a very worthy man and very active in Business. He is also called sensible, but I thought he spoke too much and too minutely, took too much snuff and raised too often a kind of an alehouse laugh.[36]

From BOSWELL ON THE GRAND TOUR

[A DAY WITH ROUSSEAU][37]

Friday 14 December [1764].

At eight I got on horseback and had for my guide a smith called Dupuis. I said, "Since when (*depuis quand*)[38] have you had that name?" I passed the Mountain Lapidosa,[39] which is monstrously steep and in a great measure covered with snow. I was going to Rousseau, which consideration levelled the roughest mountains. I arrived at Môtiers before noon. I alighted at Rousseau's door. Up and I went and found Mademoiselle Le Vasseur,[40] who told me, "He is very ill." "But can I see him for a moment?" "I will find out. Step in, Sir." I found him sitting in great pain.

ROUSSEAU. "I am overcome with ailments, disappointments, and sorrows. I am using a probe.[41]—Every one thinks it my duty to attend to him." BOSWELL. "That is most natural; and are you not pleased to find you can be of so much help to others?" ROUSSEAU. "Why—"

I had left with him when I was last here what I called a "Sketch of My Life," in which I gave him the important incidents of my history and my melancholy apprehensions, and begged his advice and friendship. It was an interesting piece. He said, "I have read your Memoir. You have been gulled. You ought never to see a priest." BOSWELL. "But can I yet hope to make something of myself?" ROUSSEAU. "Yes. Your great difficulty is that you think it so difficult a matter. Come back in the afternoon. But put your watch on the table." BOSWELL. "For how long?" ROUSSEAU. "A quarter of an hour, and no longer." BOSWELL. "Twenty minutes." ROUSSEAU. "Be off with you!—Ha! Ha!" Notwithstanding the pain he was in, he was touched with my singular sally and laughed most really. He had a gay look immediately.

I dined in my old room with the two

Text reprinted with permission of McGraw-Hill Book Company, Inc., from *Boswell on the Grand Tour: Germany and Switzerland, 1764*, edited by Frederick A. Pottle. Copyright, 1928, 1953, by Yale University.

[36] Boswell left Kames for Edinburgh October 26.

[37] Jean Jacques Rousseau (1712–1778), the French philosopher, who had fled to Switzerland in 1762 because of government and church reaction to his writing, especially *Emile, ou traité de l'Education* (1762).

[38] Boswell is punning in French on the resemblance of the guide's name, Dupuis, and the French word for *since, depuis*.

[39] "... Mountain Lapidosa ('Rocky Mountain') would probably be Mont Chasseron (5285 ft.), one of the more spectacular peaks of the region" (Pottle).

[40] Thérèse le Vasseur, Rousseau's common-law wife.

[41] "French, 'J'ai un Sond'. Boswell had arrived at one of the crises of Rousseau's complaint. He had given up doctors, but sometimes tried to relieve the condition himself by the use of a probe or urethral dilator. The journal implies that when Boswell called the instrument was actually *in situ*. The memoranda read 'Sond toujours', which is perhaps more plausible, though it may be noted that Rousseau seems not on this occasion to have walked about the room, nor even to have risen" (Pottle).

boarders. After dinner I walked out. There had fallen much rain, and the *vallon*[42] was all overflowed. Nature looked somewhat different from the time that I was first here. I was sorry that such a scene was subject to any change.

At four I went to Monsieur Rousseau. "I have but a moment allowed me; I must use it well.—Is it possible to live amongst other men, and to retain singularity?" ROUSSEAU. "Yes, I have done it." BOSWELL. "But to remain on good terms with them?" ROUSSEAU. "Oh, if you want to be a wolf, you must howl.— I attach very little importance to books." BOSWELL. "Even to your own books?" ROUSSEAU. "Oh, they are just rigmarole." BOSWELL. "Now you are howling." ROUSSEAU. "When I put my trust in books, I was tossed about as you are—though it is rather by talking that you have been tossed. I had nothing stable here" (striking his head) "before I began to meditate." BOSWELL. "But you would not have meditated to such good purpose if you had not read." ROUSSEAU. "No. I should have meditated to better purpose if I had begun sooner." BOSWELL. "But I, for example, would never have had the agreeable ideas I possess of the Christian religion, had I not read 'The Savoyard's Creed'.[43] —Yet, to tell the truth, I can find no certain system. Morals appear to me an uncertain thing. For instance, I should like to have thirty women. Could I not satisfy that desire?" ROUSSEAU. "No!" BOSWELL. "Why?" ROUSSEAU. "Ha! Ha! If Mademoiselle were not here, I would give you a most ample reason why." BOSWELL. "But consider: if I am rich, I can take a number of girls; I get them with child; propagation is thus increased. I give them dowries, and I marry them off to good peasants who are very happy to have them. Thus they become wives at the same age as would have been the case if they had remained virgins, and I, on my side, have had the benefit of enjoying a great variety of women." ROUSSEAU. "Oh, you will be landed in jealousies, betrayals, and treachery." BOSWELL. "But cannot I follow the Oriental usage?" ROUSSEAU. "In the Orient the women are kept shut up, and that means keeping slaves. And, mark you, their women do nothing but harm, whereas ours do much good, for they do a great deal of work." BOSWELL. "Still, I should like to follow the example of the old Patriarchs, worthy men whose memory I hold in respect." ROUSSEAU. "But are you not a citizen? You must not pick and choose one law here and another law there; you must take the laws of your own society. Do your duty as a citizen, and if you hold fast, you will win respect. I should not talk about it, but I would do it.—And as for your lady,[44] when you go back to Scotland you will say, 'Madam, such conduct is against my conscience, and there shall be no more of it.' She will applaud you; if not, she is to be despised." BOSWELL. "Suppose her passion is still lively, and she threatens to tell her husband what has happened unless I agree to continue our intrigue?" ROUSSEAU. "In the first place, she will not tell him. In the second, you have no right to do evil for the sake of good." BOSWELL. "True. None the less, I can imagine some very embarrassing situations. And pray tell me how I can expiate the evil I have done?" ROUSSEAU. "Oh, Sir, there is no expiation for evil except good."

A beautiful thought this. Nevertheless, I maintained my doctrine of satisfaction by punishment. Yes, I must ever think that immutable justice requires atonement to be made for transgressions, and this atonement is to be made by suffering. This is the universal idea of all nations, and seems to be a leading principle of Christianity. I gave myself full scope; for since I left England I have not had anybody to whom I could lay open entirely my mind till I found Monsieur Rousseau.

[42] A little valley.
[43] Rousseau's *Profession de foi du Vicaire Savoyard*, in *Emile, ou traité de l'Education*.
[44] Wife of an unidentified Scottish friend of Boswell referred to in the "Sketch of My Life" given earlier to Rousseau.

I asked him, "When I get to France and Italy, may I not indulge in the gallantries usual to those countries, where the husbands do not resent your making love to their wives? Nay, should I not be happier as the citizen of such a nation?" ROUSSEAU. "They are corpses. Do you want to be a corpse?" He was right. BOSWELL. "But tell me, has a virtuous man any true advantages, is he really better off than a man given up to sensuality?" ROUSSEAU. "We cannot doubt that we are spiritual beings; and when the soul escapes from this prison, from this flesh, the virtuous man will find things to his liking. He will enjoy the contemplation of happy souls, nobly employed. He will say, 'I have already lived a life like that.' Whereas those who experience nothing but the vile passions which have their origin in the body will be dissatisfied by the spectacle of pleasures which they have no means of enjoying."

BOSWELL. "Upon my word, I am at a loss how to act in this world; I cannot determine whether or not I should adopt some profession." ROUSSEAU. "One must have a great plan." BOSWELL. "What about those studies on which so much stress is laid? Such as history, for instance?" ROUSSEAU. "They are just amusements." BOSWELL. "My father desires me to be called to the Scottish bar; I am certainly doing right in satisfying my father; I have no such certainty if I follow my light inclinations. I must therefore give my mind to the study of the laws of Scotland." ROUSSEAU. "To be sure; they are your tools. If you mean to be a carpenter, you must have a plane." BOSWELL. "I do not get on well with my father. I am not at my ease with him." ROUSSEAU. "To be at ease you need to share some amusement." BOSWELL. "We look after the planting together." ROUSSEAU. "That's too serious a business. You should have some amusement that puts you more on an equal footing: shooting, for example. A shot is missed and a joke is made of it, without any infringement of respect. You enjoy a freedom which you take for granted.—Once you are involved in a profession, you must keep on with it even though another, and apparently better, should present itself. If you keep changing, you can achieve nothing."

(I should have observed that when I pushed the conversation on women, Mademoiselle went out, and Monsieur Rousseau said, "See now, you are driving Mademoiselle out of the room." She was now returned.) He stopped, and looked at me in a singular manner. "Are you greedy?" BOSWELL. "Yes." ROUSSEAU. "I am sorry to hear it." BOSWELL. "Ha! Ha! I was joking, for in your books you write in favour of greed. I know what you are about to say, and it is just what I was hoping to hear. I wanted to get you to invite me to dinner. I had a great desire to share a meal with you." ROUSSEAU. "Well, if you are not greedy, will you dine here tomorrow? But I give you fair warning, you will find yourself badly off." BOSWELL. "No, I shall not be badly off; I am above all such considerations." ROUSSEAU. "Come then at noon; it will give us time to talk." BOSWELL. "All my thanks." ROUSSEAU. "Good evening."

Mademoiselle carried me to the house of a poor woman with a great many children whom Monsieur Rousseau aids with his charity. I contributed my part. I was not pleased to hear Mademoiselle repeat to the poor woman just the common consolatory sayings. She should have said something singular.

LETTER TO TEMPLE[45]

Château de Ferney,[46] 28 December 1764.

My Dear Temple,—Think not that I insult you when you read the full tale of my supreme felicity. After thanking

[45] William Johnson Temple (1739–1796), intimate friend of Boswell from their first meeting in the University of Edinburgh. He was at this time studying law in the Inner Temple, London.

[46] Residence in Switzerland of the French writer Voltaire (1694–1778).

you for your two letters of the month of October, I must pour forth the exultation of a heart swelling with joy. Call me bombast. Call me what you please. Thus will I talk. No other style can give the most distant expression of the feelings of Boswell. If I appear ridiculous, it is because our language is deficient.

I completed my tour through the German courts. At all of them I found state and politeness. At Baden-Durlach I found worth, learning, and philosophy united in the Reigning Margrave. He is a prince whose character deserves to be known over Europe. He is the best sovereign, the best father, the most amiable man. He has travelled a great deal. He has been in England and he speaks the language in amazing perfection. During the time that I stayed at his court, I had many, many conversations with him. He showed me the greatest distinction. The inspector of his cabinet, his library-keeper, and the officers of his court had orders to do everything in their power to render my stay agreeable. Madame la Margrave, who paints in perfection and has a general taste for the fine arts, treated me in the most gracious manner. The Margrave told me how happy he was to have me with him. I asked him if I could do anything that might show my gratitude. He replied, "I shall write to you sometimes. I shall be very happy to receive your letters." He was in earnest. I have already been honoured with a letter from His Most Serene Highness. I have promised to return and pass some weeks at his court. He is not far from France.

I have been with Rousseau. He lives in the village of Môtiers-Travers in a beautiful valley surrounded with immense mountains. I went thither from Neuchâtel. I determined to put my real merit to the severest test by presenting myself without any recommendation before the wild illustrious philosopher. I wrote him a letter in which I told him all my worth, and claimed his regard as what I had a title to. "Open your door, Sir, to a man who dares to tell you that he deserves to enter it." Such was my bold and manly style. He received me, although he was very ill. "I am ill, in pain, really in no state to receive visits. Yet I cannot deprive myself of Mr. Boswell's, provided that out of consideration for the state of my health, he is willing to make it short." I found him very easy and unaffected. At first he complained and lamented the state of humanity. But I had address enough to bring him upon subjects which pleased him, and he grew very animated, quite the amiable Saint-Preux[47] at fifty. He is a genteel man, has a fine countenance and a charming voice. You may believe I had a difficult task enough to come up to the idea which I had given him of myself. I had said all that my honest pride believed. My letter was a piece of true oratory. You shall see it when we meet. No other man in Europe could have written such a letter and appeared equal to all its praise. I stayed at this time three days in the village, and was with Monsieur Rousseau every day. A week after, I returned and stayed two days. He is extremely busy. The Corsicans have actually applied to him to give them a set of laws. What glory for him! He said, "It exceeds my powers but not my zeal." He is preparing to give a complete and splendid edition of all his works. When I was sure of his good opinion on my own merit, I showed him a recommendation which my Lord Marischal[48] had given me. I talked to him with undisguised confidence. I gave him a written sketch of my life. He studied it, and he loved me with all my failings. He gave me some advice which will influence the rest of my existence. He is to correspond with me while he lives. When I took leave of him, he embraced me with an elegant cordiality and said, "Don't ever forget me. There are points where our souls are bound." On my arrival at Geneva I received a letter from him, with a letter of recom-

[47] The hero of Rousseau's *La Nouvelle Héloïse*.

[48] George Keith, tenth Earl Marischal (1693?–1778).

mendation to an intimate friend of his at the Court of Parma, a man of uncommon value. He has left the letter open for me to read, although it contains his most important concerns and the kindest effusions of his heart. Is not this treating me with a regard which my soul must be proud of? I must give you a sentence of this letter. "I am glad that Mr. Boswell and you are to make each other's acquaintance. I think you will both be grateful to me for bringing you together. In the first letter he wrote me, he told me that he was a man 'of singular merit.' I was curious to see a man who spoke of himself in such a fashion, and I found that he had told me the truth."

And whence do I now write to you, my friend? From the château of Monsieur de Voltaire. I had a letter for him from a Swiss colonel at The Hague. I came hither Monday and was presented to him. He received me with dignity and that air of a man who has been much in the world which a Frenchman acquires in perfection. I saw him for about half an hour before dinner. He was not in spirits. Yet he gave me some brilliant sallies. He did not dine with us, and I was obliged to post away immediately after dinner, because the gates of Geneva shut before five and Ferney is a good hour from town. I was by no means satisfied to have been so little time with the monarch of French literature. A happy scheme sprung up in my adventurous mind. Madame Denis, the niece of Monsieur de Voltaire, had been extremely good to me. She is fond of our language. I wrote her a letter in English begging her interest to obtain for me the privilege of lodging a night under the roof of Monsieur de Voltaire, who, in opposition to our sun, rises in the evening. I was in the finest humor and my letter was full of wit. I told her, "I am a hardy and a vigorous Scot. You may mount me to the highest and coldest garret. I shall not even refuse to sleep upon two chairs in the bedchamber of your maid. I saw her pass through the room where we sat before dinner." I sent my letter on Tuesday by an ex-

press. It was shown to Monsieur de Voltaire, who with his own hand wrote this answer in the character of Madam Denis: "You will do us much honour and pleasure. We have few beds. But you will (*shall*) not sleep on two chairs. My uncle, though very sick, hath guessed at your merit. I know it better; for I have seen you longer." Temple, I am your most obedient. How do you find yourself? Have you got such a thing as an old friend in this world? Is he to be valued or is he not?

I returned yesterday to this enchanted castle. The magician appeared a little before dinner. But in the evening he came into the drawing-room in great spirits. I placed myself by him. I touched the keys in unison with his imagination. I wish you had flashes of wit. I got him to speak English, which he does in a degree that made me now and then start up and cry, "Upon my soul this is astonishing!" When he talked our language he was animated with the soul of a Briton. He had bold flights. He had humour. He had an extravagance; he had a forcible oddity of style that the most comical of our *dramatis personae* could not have exceeded. He swore bloodily, as was the fashion when he was in England. He hummed a ballad; he repeated nonsense. Then he talked of our Constitution with a noble enthusiasm. I was proud to hear this from the mouth of an illustrious Frenchman. At last we came upon religion. Then did he rage. The company went to supper. Monsieur de Voltaire and I remained in the drawing-room with a great Bible before us; and if ever two mortal men disputed with vehemence, we did. Yes, upon that occasion he was one individual and I another. For a certain portion of time there was a fair opposition between Voltaire and Boswell. The daring bursts of his ridicule confounded my understanding. He stood like an orator of ancient Rome. Tully[49] was never more agitated than he was. He went too far. His aged frame trembled beneath him. He

---

[49] Marcus Tullius Cicero, most famous of Roman orators (106–43 B.C.).

cried, "Oh, I am very sick; my head turns round," and he let himself gently fall upon an easy chair. He recovered. I resumed our conversation, but changed the tone. I talked to him serious and earnest. I demanded of him an honest confession of his real sentiments. He gave it me with candour and with a mild eloquence which touched my heart. I did not believe him capable of thinking in the manner that he declared to me was "from the bottom of his heart." He expressed his veneration—his love—of the Supreme Being, and his entire resignation to the will of Him who is All-wise. He expressed his desire to resemble the Author of Goodness by being good himself. His sentiments go no farther. He does not inflame his mind with grand hopes of the immortality of the soul. He says it may be, but he knows nothing of it. And his mind is in perfect tranquillity. I was moved; I was sorry. I doubted his sincerity. I called to him with emotion, "Are you sincere? are you really sincere?" He answered, "Before God, I am." Then with the fire of him whose tragedies have so often shone on the theatre of Paris, he said, "I suffer much. But I suffer with patience and resignation; not as a Christian—but as a man."

Temple, was not this an interesting scene? Would a journey from Scotland to Ferney have been too much to obtain such a remarkable interview? I have given you the great lines. The whole conversation of the evening is fully recorded, and I look upon it as an invaluable treasure. One day the public shall have it. It is a present highly worthy of their attention. I told Monsieur de Voltaire that I had written eight quarto pages of what he had said. He smiled and seemed pleased. Our important scene must not appear till after his death. But I have a great mind to send over to London a little sketch of my reception at Ferney, of the splendid manner in which Monsieur de Voltaire lives, and of the brilliant conversation of this celebrated author at the age of seventy-two. The sketch would be a letter, addressed to you, full of gaiety and full of friendship. I would send it to one of the best public papers or magazines. But this is probably a flight of my over-heated mind. I shall not send the sketch unless you approve of my doing so.

Before I left Britain, I was idle, dissipated, ridiculous, and regardless of reputation. Often was I unworthy to be the friend of Mr. Temple. Now I am a very different man. I have got a character which I am proud of. Speak, thou who hast known me from my earliest years! Couldst thou have imagined eight years ago that thy companion in the studies of Antiquity, who was debased by an unhappy education in the smoke of Edinburgh, couldst thou have imagined him to turn out the man that he now is? We are now, my friend, united in the strictest manner. Let us do nothing of any consequence without the consent of each other.

And must I then marry a Dutchwoman? Is it already marked in the rolls of heaven? Must the proud Boswell yield to a tender inclination? Must he in the strength and vigour of his youth resign his liberty for life to one woman? Rather (say you) shall not my friend embrace the happiness which fortune presents to him? Will not his pride be gratified by the attachment of a lady who has refused many advantageous offers? Must he not marry to continue his ancient family? and where shall he find a more amiable wife? Is he not a man of a most singular character? and would not an ordinary woman be insupportable to him? Should he not thank the Powers Above for having shown him Zélide,[50] a young lady free from all the faults of her sex, with genius, with good humour, with elegant accomplishments? But, my dear Temple, she is not by half so rich as I thought. She has only £400 a year. Besides, I am not pleased with her conduct. We had agreed to correspond, and she directed me to send my

[50] Belle de Zuylen, a fashionable young lady whom Boswell had met in Holland and to whom he had proposed marriage without success.

letters to the care of her bookseller. I wrote to her from Berlin a long letter. She did not answer it. I was apprehensive that I had talked too severely of her faults, and wrote from Anhalt-Dessau begging pardon for my too great freedom. Still I remain unanswered. Her father is a very worthy man. He and I correspond, and we write each other of his daughter in a strange, mysterious manner. I have trusted him upon honour with a letter to her. So I shall be sure that she received it, and shall see how she behaves. After all, when I consider my unhappy constitution, I think I should not marry, at least for some time; and when I do, should choose a healthy, cheerful woman of rank and fortune.[51] I am now well, because I am agitated by a variety of new scenes. But when I shall return to the uniformity of Scotland, I dread much a relapse into the gloomy distemper. I must endeavour by some scheme of ambition, by elegant study, and by rural occupations to preserve my mind. Yet I own that both of us are sadly undetermined. However, I hope the best.

My worthy father has consented that I shall go to Italy. O my friend, what a rich prospect spreads before me! My letter is already so long that I shall restrain my enthusiastic sallies. Imagine my joy. On Tuesday morning I set out for Turin. I shall pass the rigorous Alps with the resolution of Hannibal.[52] I shall be four months in Italy and then return through France. I expect to pass some time at Paris.

Forgive me, Temple, for having delayed to mention your concerns till almost at the end of my letter. You are sure how much I suffer from your uneasiness. I wish I could be as sure of relieving you. I know well the great, and can have no confidence in them. Lord Eglinton[53] would forget to do anything. I have written to Lady Northumberland[54] begging she may get Bob[55] put upon whole pay. Lord Warkworth[56] was in General Craufurd's regiment, and both my Lord and my Lady had a great esteem of the General. I have told her Ladyship that the General had promised to take care of the young lieutenant, and that if her Ladyship puts him again in commission, "in so doing you will fulfil the intentions of him who is no more, whose memory you must ever regard. May I add that your Ladyship will give me a pleasure—a comfort—which I can hardly express? Were I at present as rich as I shall probably be, the brother of my friend should not depend for a commission on the uncertain favour of any great person alive." (She may be angry at this last period. It ought to please, it ought to rouse her.) "O Madam! be truly great. Be generous to the unfortunate. If your Ladyship will befriend the young man sincerely, I beg to be honoured with a line," &c. I own to you I have but little hopes from her Ladyship. We shall see. I have not been mean enough to flatter her. That I am determined never to practise. I have also written to Mr. Mitchell, late Envoy at the Court of Berlin, who is just recalled. He is an old friend of my father's, and a man of the strictest probity and the warmest generosity. I have told him your story as I did to Lady Northumberland. O my Temple! how do I glory in displaying the conduct of my friend! If Mr. Mitchell can aid us, he will. I would hope he may serve either your father or brother. I have solicited him for both. Why am I not in power? I may be so perhaps yet, before I die.

Temple, I am again as loyal as ever. I abhor a despotic tyrant. But I revere a limited monarch. Shall I be a British

---

[51] Boswell married a first cousin, Margaret Montgomerie, in 1769.

[52] Carthaginian general who brought a great army across the Alps in 218 B.C. to descend on the Romans.

[53] Alexander Montgomerie, tenth Earl of Eglinton (1723–1769), who had introduced Boswell to London society in 1762 and who had encouraged him in rakish habits.

[54] Elizabeth Seymour, Duchess of Northumberland (1716–1776). She had befriended Boswell during his earlier stay in London.

[55] Brother of William Temple, a lieutenant in the army, apparently on reduced pay at the time.

[56] Lady Northumberland's eldest son.

courtier? Am I worthy of the confidence of my king? May George the Third choose that the most honest and most amiable of his subjects should stand continually in his royal presence? I will if he says, "You shall be independent." . . . Temple, this is a noble letter. Fare you well, my ever dear friend.

JAMES BOSWELL.

From JOURNAL of a Tour to the Hebrides

[A VISIT TO THE ISLE OF COLL][57]

Monday, October 4 [1773].

About eight o'clock we went in the boat to Mr. Simpson's vessel, and took in Dr. Johnson.[58] He was quite well, though he had tasted nothing but a dish of tea since Saturday night. On our expressing some surprise at this, he said, that, "when he lodged in the Temple,[59] and had no regular system of life, he had fasted for two days at a time, during which he had gone about visiting, though not at the hours of dinner or supper; that he had drunk tea, but eaten no bread; that this was no intentional fasting, but happened just in the course of a literary life."

There was a little miserable publick-house close upon the shore, to which we should have gone, had we landed last night: but this morning Col[60] resolved to take us directly to the house of Captain Lauchlan M'Lean, a descendant of his family, who had acquired a fortune in the East-Indies, and taken a farm in Col. We had about an English mile to go to it. Col and Joseph[61], and some others, ran to some little horses, called here *Shelties*[62], that were running wild on a heath, and catched one of them. We had a saddle with us, which was clapped upon it, and a straw halter was put on its head. Dr. Johnson was then mounted, and Joseph very slowly and gravely led the horse. I said to Dr. Johnson, "I wish, sir, *the club*[63] saw you in this attitude."

It was a very heavy rain, and I was wet to the skin. Captain M'Lean had but a poor temporary house, or rather hut; however, it was a very good haven to us. There was a blazing peat-fire, and Mrs. M'Lean, daughter of the minister of the parish, got us tea. I felt still the motion of the sea. Dr. Johnson said, it

---

Text from the sixth edition, 1813, substantially identical with the third and last edition to receive Boswell's corrections. The *Journal* was first published in 1785. Comparison with the version published in 1936 by Frederick A. Pottle and Charles H. Bennett from a manuscript found at Malahide Castle shows that Boswell edited the journal meticulously and widely for publication.

[57] An island off the west coast of Scotland among the Inner Hebrides.

[58] Samuel Johnson (1709–1784), the famous Dr. Johnson of Boswell's *Life*, an excerpt of which begins on p. 501.

[59] Johnson occupied rooms at No. 1, Inner Temple Lane, from 1760 to 1765.

[60] i.e., the laird of Col. The house to which he took his quests was probably near the village of Achamore, according to L. F. Powell who revised the George Birkbeck Hill edition of the *Journal* in 1950.

[61] Joseph Ritter was Boswell's servant, who was described earlier by Boswell as "a Bohemian, a fine stately fellow above six feet high, who had been over a great part of Europe, and spoke many languages. He was the best servant I ever saw. . . . Dr. Johnson gave him this character: 'Sir, he is a civil man, and a wise man'."

[62] Shetland ponies.

[63] Boswell here refers to the London club to which he had been elected on April 30th of this year at the nomination of Dr. Johnson (see note 148).

was not in imagination, but a continuation of motion on the fluids, like that of the sea itself after the storm is over.

There were some books on the board which served as a chimney-piece. Dr. Johnson took up *Burnet's History of his own Times*[64]. He said, "The first part of it is one of the most entertaining books in the English language; it is quite dramatick: while he went about every where, saw every where, and heard every where. By the first part, I mean so far as it appears that Burnet himself was actually engaged in what he has told; and this may be easily distinguished." Captain M'Lean censured Burnet, for his high praise of Lauderdale in a dedication,[65] when he shews him in his history to have been so bad a man. JOHNSON. "I do not myself think that a man should say in a dedication what he could not say in a history. However, allowance should be made; for there is a great difference. The known style of a dedication is flattery: it professes to flatter. There is the same difference between what a man says in a dedication, and what he says in a history, as between a lawyer's pleading a cause, and reporting it."

The day passed away pleasantly enough. The wind became fair for Mull in the evening, and Mr. Simpson resolved to sail next morning: but having been thrown into the island of Col, we were unwilling to leave it unexamined, especially as we considered that the Campbell-town vessel would sail for Mull in a day or two, and therefore we determined to stay.

Tuesday, October 5.

I rose, and wrote my Journal till about nine; and then went to Dr. Johnson, who sat up in bed and talked and laughed. I said, it was curious to look back ten years, to the time when we first thought of visiting the Hebrides.[66] How distant and improbable the scheme then appeared! Yet here we were actually among them.—"Sir, (said he,) people may come to do any thing almost, by talking of it. I really believe, I could talk myself into building a house upon island Isa,[67] though I should probably never come back again to see it. I could easily persuade Reynolds[68] to do it; and there would be no great sin in persuading him to do it. Sir, he would reason thus: 'What will it cost me to be there once in two or three summers?—Why, perhaps, five hundred pounds; and what is that, in comparison of having a fine retreat, to which a man can go, or to which he can send a friend?' He would never find out that he may have this within twenty miles of London.—Then I would tell him, that he may marry one of the Miss M'Leod's, a lady of great family.—Sir, it is surprising how people will go to a distance for what they may have at home. I knew a lady who came up from Lincolnshire to Knightsbridge with one of her daughters, and gave five guineas a week for a lodging and a warm bath; that is, mere warm water. That, you know, could not be had in *Lincolnshire!* She said, it was made either too hot or too cold there."

After breakfast, Dr. Johnson and I, and Joseph, mounted horses, and Col and the Captain walked with us about a short mile across the island. We paid a visit to the Reverend Mr. Hector M'Lean. His parish consists of the islands of Col and Tyr-yi.[69] He was

---

[64] Gilbert Burnet (1643–1715), whose *History of my Own Time* appeared posthumously (1723–1734).

[65] While Professor of Theology at Glasgow University, Burnet had dedicated *A Vindication of the Authority . . . of the Church and State of Scotland* (1673) to Charles II's Secretary to Scotland, John Maitland, the first Duke of Lauderdale.

[66] The project was broached during the first month of Boswell's acquaintance with Johnson

and is described in the *Life of Johnson* for July 21, 1763.

[67] The Isle of Isay off the northwest coast of Skye had been proposed humorously in a toast to Dr. Johnson two weeks earlier by his host, Alexander MacLeod of Ullinish, to encourage Johnson's expressed whim of "becoming owner of an island."

[68] Sir Joshua Reynolds (1723–1792), portrait artist and friend of Johnson's.

[69] Tiree, southwest of Col.

about seventy-seven years of age, a decent ecclesiastick, dressed in a full suit of black clothes, and a black wig. He appeared like a Dutch pastor, or one of the assembly of divines at Westminster. Dr. Johnson observed to me, afterwards, "that he was a fine old man, and was as well-dressed, and had as much dignity in his appearance as the dean of a cathedral." We were told, that he had a valuable library, though but poor accommodation for it, being obliged to keep his books in large chests. I was curious to see him and Dr. Johnson together. Neither of them heard very distinctly; so each of them talked in his own way, and at the same time. Mr. M'Lean said, he had a confutation of Bayle, by Leibnitz.[70] JOHNSON. "A confutation of Bayle, sir! What part of Bayle do you mean? The greatest part of his writings is not confutable: it is historical and critical."—Mr. M'Lean said, "the irreligious part;" and proceeded to talk of Leibnitz's controversy with Clarke,[71] calling Leibnitz a great man. JOHNSON. "Why, sir, Leibnitz persisted in affirming that Newton called space *sensorium numinis*,[72] notwithstanding he was corrected, and desired to observe that Newton's words were QUASI[73] *sensorium numinis*. No, sir; Leibnitz was as paltry a fellow as I know. Out of respect to Queen Caroline, who patronised him, Clarke treated him too well."

During the time that Dr. Johnson was thus going on, the old minister was standing with his back to the fire, cresting up erect, pulling down the front of his periwig, and talking what a great man Leibnitz was. To give an idea of the scene, would require a page with two columns; but it ought rather to be represented by two good players. The old gentleman said, Clarke was very wicked, for going so much into the Arian system.[74] "I will not say he was wicked, said Dr. Johnson; he might be mistaken." M'LEAN. "He was wicked, to shut his eyes against the Scriptures; and worthy men in England have since confuted him to all intents and purposes." JOHNSON. "I know not *who* has confuted him to *all intents and purposes.*" —Here again there was a double talking, each continuing to maintain his own argument, without hearing exactly what the other said.

I regretted that Dr. Johnson did not practise the art of accommodating himself to different sorts of people. Had he been softer with this venerable old man, we might have had more conversation; but his forcible spirit, and impetuosity of manner, may be said to spare neither sex nor age. I have seen even Mrs. Thrale[75] stunned; but I have often maintained, that it is better he should retain his own manner. Pliability of address I conceive to be inconsistent with that majestick power of mind which he possesses, and which produces such noble effects. A lofty oak will not bend like a supple willow.

He told me afterwards, he liked firmness in an old man, and was pleased to see Mr. M'Lean so orthodox. "At his age, it is too late for a man to be asking himself questions as to his belief."

We rode to the northern part of the island, where we saw the ruins of a church or chapel. We then proceeded to a place called Grissipol, or the rough Pool.

At Grissipol we found a good farm house, belonging to the Laird of Col, and possessed by Mr. M'Sweyn. On the beach here there is a singular variety of curious stones. I picked up one very like

---

[70] Pierre Bayle (1647–1706), French philosopher and author of *Dictionnaire historique et critique* (1697–1702); Gottfried Wilhelm von Leibniz (1646–1716), German philosopher, posited a pre-existent harmony between body and soul.
[71] Samuel Clarke (1675–1729), English theologian.
[72] "seat of sensation of the Divine Being."

[73] "as if it were."
[74] Arius, a fourth-century Greek patriarch whose followers opposed the orthodox belief in the divinity of Christ.
[75] Mrs. Hester Lynch Salusbury Thrale (later Piozzi) (1741–1821), great friend of Johnson's and second only to Boswell in fame among writers on Johnson.

a small cucumber. By the by, Dr. Johnson told me, that Gay's Line in the *Beggar's Opera,* "As men should serve a cucumber," &c. has no waggish meaning, with reference to men flinging away cucumbers as too *cooling,* which some have thought; for it has been a common saying of physicians in England, that a cucumber should be well sliced, and dressed with pepper and vinegar, and then thrown out, as good for nothing.[76]—Mr. M'Sweyn's predecessors had been in Sky from a very remote period, upon the estate belonging to M'Leod; probably before M'Leod had it. The name is certainly Norwegian, from *Sueno,* King of Norway. The present Mr. M'Sweyn left Sky upon the late M'Leod's raising his rents. He then got this farm from Col.

He appeared to be near fourscore; but looked as fresh, and was as strong as a man of fifty. His son Hugh looked older; and, as Dr. Johnson observed, had more the manners of an old man than he. I had often heard of such instances, but never saw one before. Mrs. M'Sweyn was a decent old gentlewoman. She was dressed in Tartan, and could speak nothing but Erse.[77] She said, she taught Sir James M'Donald Erse, and would teach me soon. I could now sing a verse of the song *Hatyin foam'eri,*[78] made in honour of Allan, the famous Captain of Clanranald,[79] who fell at Sherrif-muir; whose servant, who lay on the field watching his master's dead body, being asked next day who that was, answered, "He was a man yesterday."

We were entertained here with a primitive heartiness. Whiskey was served round in a shell,[80] according to the ancient Highland custom. Dr. Johnson would not partake of it; but, being desirous to do honour to the modes "of other times," drank some water out of the shell.

In the forenoon Dr. Johnson said, "it would require great resignation to live in one of these islands." BOSWELL. "I don't know, sir; I have felt myself at times in a state of almost mere physical existence, satisfied to eat, drink, and sleep, and walk about, and enjoy my own thoughts; and I can figure a continuation of this." JOHNSON. "Ay, sir; but if you were shut up here, your own thoughts would torment you. You would think of Edinburgh or London, and that you could not be there."

We set out after dinner for *Breacacha,* the family seat of the Laird of Col, accompanied by the young laird, who had now got a horse, and by the younger Mr. M'Sweyn, whose wife had gone thither before us, to prepare every thing for our reception, the laird and his family being absent at Aberdeen. It is called *Breacacha,* or the Spotted Field, because in summer it is enamelled with clover and daisies, as young Col told me. We passed by a place where there is a very large stone, I may call it a *rock;*—"a vast weight for Ajax."[81] The tradition is, that a giant threw such another stone at his mistress, up to the top of a hill, at a small distance; and that she in return, threw this mass down to him. It was all in sport.

Malo me petit lasciva puella.[82]

As we advanced, we came to a large extent of plain ground. I had not seen such a place for a long time. Col and I took a gallop upon it by way of race. It was very refreshing to me, after having been so long taking short steps in hilly

---

[76] The line from John Gay's *The Beggar's Opera* (1728) is from the song by Polly Peachum's mother lamenting her daughter's marriage to a highwayman. It begins "Our Polly is a sad slut," and ends, "As men should serve a cucumber, she flings herself away."

[77] Scottish Gaelic.

[78] Phonetic spelling for *Tha tighinn fodham éiridh* ("It comes upon me to arise").

[79] Allan Macdonald, killed in the Jacobite Rebellion of 1715; the song is thus a symbol of the Stuart cause against the Hanoverian succession of British monarchs, which began in 1714.

[80] A clam shell, according to Boswell's manuscript.

[81] From Pope's *Essay on Criticism,* l. 370.

[82] "My Phyllis me with pelted apples plied" (Vergil, *Eclogues,* III, 64, tr. Dryden).

countries. It was like stretching a man's legs after being cramped in a short bed. We also passed close by a large extent of sand-hills, near two miles square. Dr. Johnson said, "he never had the image before. It was horrible, if barrenness and danger could be so." I heard him, after we were in the house of *Breacacha,* repeating to himself, as he walked about the room,

And smother'd in the dusty whirlwind, dies.[83]

Probably he had been thinking of the whole of the simile in *Cato,* of which that is the concluding line; the sandy desart had struck him so strongly. The sand has of late been blown over a good deal of meadow; and the people of the island say, that their fathers remembered much of the space which is now covered with sand, to have been under tillage. Col's house is situated on a bay called *Breacacha* Bay. We found here a neat new-built gentleman's house, better than any we had been in since we were at Lord Errol's.[84] Dr. Johnson relished it much at first, but soon remarked to me, that "there was nothing becoming a Chief about it: it was a mere tradesman's box." He seemed quite at home, and no longer found any difficulty in using the Highland address; for as soon as we arrived, he said, with a spirited familiarity, "Now, *Col,* if you could get us a dish of tea."—Dr. Johnson and I had each an excellent bed-chamber. We had a dispute which of us had the best curtains. His were rather the best, being of linen; but I insisted that my bed had the best posts, which was undeniable. "Well, (said he,) if you *have* the best *posts,* we will have you tied to them and whipped."—I mention this slight cir-

cumstance, only to shew how ready he is, even in mere trifles, to get the better of his antagonist, by placing him in a ludicrous view. I have known him sometimes use the same art, when hard pressed in serious disputation. Goldsmith,[85] I remember, to retaliate for many a severe defeat which he has suffered from him, applied to him a lively saying in one of Cibber's[86] comedies, which puts this part of his character in a strong light.— "There is no arguing with Johnson; for, *if his pistol misses fire, he knocks you down with the but end of it."*

Wednesday, October 6.

After a sufficiency of sleep, we assembled at breakfast. We were just as if in barracks. Every body was master. We went and viewed the old castle of Col, which is not far from the present house, near the shore, and founded on a rock. It has never been a large feudal residence, and has nothing about it that requires a particular description. Like other old inconvenient buildings of the same age, it exemplified Gray's picturesque lines,

Huge windows that exclude the light, And passages that lead to nothing.[87]

It may however be worth mentioning, that on the second story we saw a vault, which was, and still is, the family prison. There was a woman put into it by the laird, for theft, within these ten years; and any offender would be confined there yet; for, from the necessity of the thing, as the island is remote from any power established by law, the laird must exercise his jurisdiction to a certain degree.

We were shewn, in a corner of this vault, a hole, into which Col said greater criminals used to be put. It was

[83] Act II of Addison's *Cato* ends with the lines:
So, where our wide Numidian wastes extend,
Sudden the impetuous hurricanes descend,
Wheel through the air, in circling eddies play,
Tear up the sands, and sweep whole plains away.
The helpless traveller, with wild surprise,
Sees the dry desert all around him rise,

And, smothered in the dusty whirlwind, dies.
[84] On August 24, at the outset of their tour, Boswell and Johnson had visited Slains Castle, near Aberdeen, the seat of James Hay, fifteenth Earl of Erroll.
[85] Oliver Goldsmith (1728–1774).
[86] Colley Cibber (1671–1757).
[87] Thomas Gray, *A Long Story,* l. 7.

now filled up with rubbish of different kinds. He said, it was of a great depth. "Ay, (said Dr. Johnson, smiling,) all such places, that *are filled up* were of a great depth." He is very quick in shewing that he does not give credit to careless or exaggerated accounts of things. After seeing the castle, we looked at a small hut near it. It is called *Teigh Franchich,* i.e. the Frenchman's House. Col could not tell us the history of it. A poor man with a wife and children now lived in it. We went into it, and Dr. Johnson gave them some charity. There was but one bed for all the family, and the hut was very smoky. When he came out, he said to me, *"Et hoc secundum sententiam philosophorum est esse beatus."*[88] BOSWELL. "The philosophers, when they placed happiness in a cottage, supposed cleanliness and no smoke." JOHNSON. "Sir, they did not think about either."

We walked a little in the laird's garden, in which endeavours have been used to rear some trees; but, as soon as they got above the surrounding wall, they died. Dr. Johnson recommended sowing the seeds of hardy trees, instead of planting.[89]

Col and I rode out this morning, and viewed a part of the island. In the course of our ride, we saw a turnip-field, which he had hoed with his own hands. He first introduced this kind of husbandry into the Western islands. We also looked at an appearance[90] of lead, which seemed very promising. It has been long known; for I found letters to the late laird, from Sir John Areskine and Sir Alexander Murray, respecting it.

After dinner came Mr. M'Lean, of Corneck, brother to Isle of Muck,[91] who is a cadet of the family of Col. He possesses the two ends of Col, which belong to the Duke of Argyll. Corneck had lately taken a lease of them at a very advanced rate, rather than let the Campbells get a footing in the island, one of whom had offered nearly as much as he. Dr. Johnson well observed, that, "landlords err much when they calculate merely what their land *may* yield. The rent must be in a proportionate ratio of what the land may yield, and of the power of the tenant to make it yield. A tenant cannot make by his land, but according to the corn and cattle which he has. Suppose you should give him twice as much land as he has, it does him no good, unless he gets also more stock. It is clear then, that the Highland landlords, who let their substantial tenants leave them, are infatuated; for the poor small tenants cannot give them good rents, from the very nature of things. They have not the means of raising more from their farms." Corneck, Dr. Johnson said, was the most distinct man that he had met with in these isles; he did not shut his eyes, or put his fingers in his ears, which he seemed to think was a good deal the mode with most of the people whom we have seen of late.

Thursday, October 7.

Captain M'Lean joined us this morning at breakfast. There came on a dreadful storm of wind and rain, which continued all day, and rather increased at night. The wind was directly against our getting to Mull. We were in a strange state of abstraction from the world: we could neither hear from our friends, nor write to them. Col had brought Daille *on the Fathers,*[92] Lucas *on Happiness,*[93] and More's *Dialogues,*[94] from the Reverend Mr. M'Lean's, and Burnet's *History of his own Times,* from Captain M'Lean's; and he had of his own some books of farming, and Gregory's *Geometry.*[95] Dr. Johnson read a good deal of

---

[88] "And that, according to the philosophers, is happiness."

[89] i.e., setting out young trees.

[90] outcropping.

[91] i.e., the laird of Muck.

[92] Jean Daillé, *A Treatise concerning the Right Use of the Fathers, in the Decision of the Controversies that are at this Day in Re-*ligion (1651).

[93] Richard Lucas, *Inquiry after Happiness* (1685).

[94] Henry More, *Divine Dialogues; concerning Sundry Disquisitions and Instructions concerning the Attributes and Providence of God* (1668).

[95] David Gregory of Aberdeen (1661–1708);

Burnet, and of Gregory, and I observed he made some geometrical notes in the end of his pocket-book. I read a little of Young's Six Weeks Tour through the Southern Counties;[96] and Ovid's Epistles, which I had bought at Inverness, and which helped to solace many a weary hour.

We were to have gone with Dr. Johnson this morning to see the mine; but were prevented by the storm. While it was raging, he said, "We may be glad we are not *damnati ad metalla*."[97]

Friday, October 8.

Dr. Johnson appeared to-day very weary of our present confined situation. He said, "I want to be on the main land, and go on with existence. This is a waste of life."

I shall here insert, without regard to chronology, some of his conversation at different times.

"There was a man some time ago, who was well received for two years, among the gentlemen of Northamptonshire, by calling himself my brother. At last he grew so impudent as by his influence to get tenants turned out of their farms. Allen the Printer,[98] who is of that county, came to me, asking, with much appearance of doubtfulness, if I had a brother; and upon being assured I had none alive, he told me of the imposition, and immediately wrote to the country, and the fellow was dismissed. It pleased me to hear that so much was got by using my name. It is not every name that can carry double; do both for a man's self and his brother (laughing). I should be glad to see the fellow. However, I could have done nothing against him. A man can have no redress for his name being used, or ridiculous stories being told of him in the news-papers, except he can shew that he has suffered damage.—Some years ago a foolish piece was published, said to be written '*by S. Johnson.*' Some of my friends wanted me to be very angry about this. I said, it would be in vain; for the answer would be, '*S. Johnson* may be Simon Johnson, or Simeon Johnson, or Solomon Johnson;' and even if the full name, Samuel Johnson, had been used, it might be said; 'it is not you; it is a much cleverer fellow.'[99]

"Beauclerk and I, and Langton,[100] and Lady Sydney Beauclerk, mother to our friend, were one day driving in a coach by Cuper's Gardens,[101] which were then unoccupied. I, in sport, proposed that Beauclerk and Langton, and myself should take[102] them; and we amused ourselves with scheming how we should all do our parts. Lady Sydney grew angry, and said, 'an old man should not put such things in young people's heads.' She had no notion of a joke, sir; had come late into life, and had a mighty unpliable understanding.

"*Carte's Life of the Duke of Ormond*[103] is considered as a book of authority; but it is ill-written. The matter is diffused in too many words; there is no animation, no compression, no vigour. Two good volumes in duodecimo might be made out of the two in folio."

Talking of our confinement here, I observed, that our discontent and impatience could not be considered as very unreasonable; for that we were just in the state of which Seneca complains so grievously, while in exile in Corsica. "Yes, (said Dr. Johnson,) and he was not farther from home than we are." The truth is, he was much nearer.[104]

There was a good deal of rain to-day,

one of his geometries was translated into English in 1745 as *A Treatise of Practical Geometry.*

[96] Arthur Young, *Six Weeks Tour through the Southern Counties of England and Wales* (1768).

[97] "condemned to the mines."

[98] Edmund Allen (1726–1784), who is mentioned frequently in the *Life of Johnson.*

[99] It has been suggested that the "foolish piece" may have been *A Compleat Introduction to the Art of Writing Letters* (1758), by an otherwise unidentified "S. Johnson."

[100] Topham Beauclerk (1739–1780) and Bennet Langton (1737–1801) were two of Johnson's closest friends of Boswell's age.

[101] A public resort south of the Thames opposite Somerset House.

[102] lease.

[103] Thomas Carte, *The History of the Life of James Duke of Ormond* (1735–1736).

[104] Corsica is approximately 150 miles from

and the wind was still contrary. Corneck attended me, while I amused myself in examining a collection of papers belonging to the family of Col. The first laird was a younger son of the Chieftain M'Lean, and got the middle part of Col for his patrimony. Dr. Johnson having given a very particular account of the connection between this family and a branch of the family of Camerons, called M'Lonich, I shall only insert the following document, (which I found in Col's cabinet,) as a proof of its continuance, even to a late period:

To The Laird Of Col.

Dear Sir,

The long-standing tract of firm affectionate friendship 'twixt your worthy predecessors and ours affords us such assurance, as that we may have full relyance on your favour and undoubted friendship, in recommending the bearer, Ewen Cameron, our cousin, son to the deceast Dugall M'Connill of Innermaillie, sometime in Glenpean, to your favour and conduct, who is a man of undoubted honesty and discretion, only that he has the misfortune of being alledged to have been accessory to the killing of one of M'Martin's family about fourteen years ago, upon which alledgeance the M'Martins are now so sanguine on revenging, that they are fully resolved for the deprivation of his life; to the preventing of which you are relyed on by us, as the only fit instrument, and a most capable person. Therefore your favour and protection is expected and intreated, during his good behaviour; and failing of which behaviour, you'll please to use him as a most insignificant person deserves.

Sir, he had, upon the alledgeance aforesaid, been transported, at Lochiel's desire, to France, to gratify the M'Martins, and upon his return home, about five years ago, married: But now he is so much threatened by the M'Martins, that he is not secure enough to stay where he is, being Ardmurchan, which occasions this trouble to you. Wishing prosperity and happiness to attend still yourself, worthy Lady, and good family, we are, in the most affectionate manner, Dear sir,

Your most obliged, affectionate,
and most humble servants,
Dugall Cameron, *of Strone.*
Dugall Cameron, *of Barr.*
Dugall Cameron, *of Inveriskvouilline.*
Dugall Cameron, *of Invinvalie.*
Strone, 11th March, 1737.

Ewen Cameron was protected, and his son has now a farm from the Laird of Col, in Mull.

The family of Col was very loyal in the time of the great Montrose,[105] from whom I found two letters in his own hand-writing. The first is as follows.

For My Very Loving Friend the Laird of Coall.

Sir,

I must heartily thank you for all your willingness and good affection to his Majesty's service, and particularly the sending alongs of your son, to who I will heave ane particular respect, hoping also that you will still continue ane goode instrument for the advancing ther of the King's service, for which, and all your former loyal carriages, be confident you shall find the effects of his Mas favour, as they can be witnessed you by

Your very faithful friende,
Montrose.
Strethearne,
10 Jan. 1646.

The other is,

For the Laird of Col.

Sir,

Having occasion to write to your fields, I cannot be forgetful of your will-

---

Rome; Col is approximately 135 miles from Boswell's home in Edinburgh and 190 miles from Johnson's home in London. In the manuscript version the last sentence in the paragraph is included within the quotation, pro-

ducing an entirely different possibility of interpretation. It is perhaps best to say the passage is ambiguous.

[105] James Graham, the first Marquis and fifth Earl of Montrose, was executed in 1650.

ingness and good affection to his Majesty's service. I acknowledge to you, and thank you heartily for it, assuring, that in what lies in my power, you shall find the good. Mean while, I shall expect that you will continue your loyal endeavours, in wishing those slack people that are about you, to appear more obedient than they do, and loyal in their prince's service; whereby I assure you, you shall find me ever

Your faithful friend,
Montrose.

Petty,
17 April, 1646.

I found some uncouth lines on the death of the present laird's father, intituled "Nature's Elegy upon the Death of Donald Maclean of Col." They are not worth insertion. I shall only give what is called his Epitaph, which Dr. Johnson said, "was not so very bad."

Nature's minion, Virtue's wonder,
Art's corrective here lyes under.

I asked, what "Art's corrective" meant. "Why sir, (said he,) that the laird was so exquisite, that he set art right, when she was wrong."

I found several letters to the late Col, from my father's old companion at Paris, Sir Hector M'Lean, one of which was written at the time of settling the colony in Georgia. It dissuades Col from letting people go there, and assures him there will soon be an opportunity of employing them better at home. Hence it appears that emigration from the Highlands, though not in such numbers at a time as of late, has always been practised. Dr. Johnson observed, that, "the Lairds, instead of improving their country, diminished their people."

There are several districts of sandy desart in Col. There are forty-eight lochs of fresh water; but many of them are very small,—mere pools. About one half of them, however, have trout and eel. There is a great number of horses in the island, mostly of a small size. Being over stocked, they sell some in Tir-yi, and on the main land. Their black cattle, which are chiefly rough-haired, are reckoned remarkably good. The climate being very mild in winter, they never put their beasts into any house. The lakes are never frozen so as to bear a man; and snow never lies above a few hours. They have a good many sheep, which they eat mostly themselves, and sell but a few. They have goats in several places. There are no foxes; no serpents, toads, or frogs, nor any venomous creature. They have otters and mice here; but had no rats till lately that an American vessel brought them. There is a rabbit-warren on the north-east of the island belonging to the Duke of Argyle. Young Col intends to get some hares, of which there are none at present. There are no blackcock, muir-fowl, nor partridges; but there are snipe, wild-duck, wild-geese, and swans, in winter; wild-pidgeons, plover, and great number of starlings; of which I shot some, and found them pretty good eating. Woodcocks come hither, though there is not a tree upon the island. There are no rivers in Col; but only some brooks, in which there is a great variety of fish. In the whole isle there are but three hills, and none of them considerable for a Highland country. The people are very industrious. Every man can tan. They get oak, and birch-bark, and lime, from the main land. Some have pits; but they commonly use tubs. I saw brogues very well tanned; and every man can make them. They all make candles of the tallow of their beasts, both moulded and dipped; and they all make oil of the livers of fish. The little fish called Cuddies produce a great deal. They sell some oil out of the island, and they use it much for light in their houses, in little iron lamps, most of which they have from England; but of late their own blacksmith makes them. He is a good workman; but he has no employment in shoeing horses, for they all go unshod here, except some of a better kind belonging to young Col, which were now in Mull. There are two carpenters in Col; but most of the inhabitants can do something as boat-carpenters. They can all dye. Heath[106]

---

[106] heather.

is used for yellow; and for red, a moss which grows on stones. They make broad-cloth, and tartan, and linen, of their own wool and flax, sufficient for their own use; as also stockings. Their bonnets come from the main land. Hardware and several small articles are brought annually from Greenock,[107] and sold in the only shop in the island, which is kept near the house, or rather hut, used for publick worship, there being no church in the island.—The inhabitants of Col have increased considerably within these thirty years, as appears from the parish registers. There are three considerable tacksmen[108] on Col's part of the island: the rest is let to small tenants, some of whom pay so low a rent as four, three, or even two guineas. The highest is seven pounds, paid by a farmer, whose son goes yearly on foot to Aberdeen for education, and in summer returns, and acts as a school-master in Col. Dr. Johnson said, "There is something noble in a young man's walking two hundred miles and back again, every year, for the sake of learning."

This day a number of people came to Col, with complaints of each others' trespasses. Corneck, to prevent their being troublesome, told them, that the lawyer[109] from Edinburgh was here, and if they did not agree, he would take them to task. They were alarmed at this; said, they had never been used to go to law, and hoped Col would settle matters himself.—In the evening Corneck left us.

Saturday, October 9

As, in our present confinement, any thing that had even the name of curious was an object of attention, I proposed that Col should shew me the great stone, mentioned in a former page, as having been thrown by a giant to the top of a mountain. Dr. Johnson, who did not like to be left alone, said, he would accompany us as far as riding was practicable. We ascended a part of the hill on horseback, and Col and I scrambled up the rest. A servant led our horses, and Dr. Johnson placed himself on the ground, with his back against a large fragment of rock. The wind being high, he let down the cocks of his hat, and tied it with his handkerchief under his chin. While we were employed in examining the stone, which did not repay our trouble in getting to it, he amused himself with reading *Gataker on Lots and on the Christian Watch,*[110] a very learned book, of the last age, which had been found in the garret of Col's house, and which he said was a treasure here. When we descried him from above, he had a most eremitical appearance; and on our return told us, he had been so much engaged by Gataker, that he had never missed us. His avidity for variety of books, while we were in Col, was frequently expressed; and he often complained that so few were within his reach. Upon which I observed to him, that it was strange he should complain of want of books, when he could at any time make such good ones.

We next proceeded to the lead mine. In our way we came to a strand of some extent, where we were glad to take a gallop, in which my learned friend joined with great alacrity. Dr. Johnson mounted on a large bay mare without shoes, and followed by a foal, which had some difficulty in keeping up with him, was a singular spectacle.

After examining the mine, we returned through a very uncouth district, full of sand hills; down which, though apparent precipices, our horses carried us with safety, the sand always gently sliding away from our feet. Vestiges of houses were pointed out to us, which Col, and two others who had joined us, asserted had been overwhelmed with sand blown over them. But, on going close to one of them, Dr. Johnson shewed the absurdity of the notion, by remarking, that "it was evidently only a house aban-

---

[107] South of Glasgow.
[108] Contractors who lease tracts of land for subletting to farmers.
[109] i.e., Boswell.

[110] This was evidently a book based on two works by Thomas Gataker: *On the Nature and Use of Lots* (1619) and *The Spirituall Watch, or Christ's generall Watch-word* (1619); or possibly the two were bound together.

doned, the stones of which had been taken away for other purposes; for the large stones, which form the lower part of the walls, were still standing higher than the sand. If *they* were not blown over, it was clear nothing higher than they could be blown over." This was quite convincing to me; but it made not the least impression on Col and the others, who were not to be argued out of a Highland tradition.

We did not sit down to dinner till between six and seven. We lived plentifully here, and had a true welcome. In such a season good firing was of no small importance. The peats were excellent, and burned cheerfully. Those at Dunvegan, which were damp, Dr. Johnson called "a sullen fuel."—Here a Scottish phrase was singularly applied to him. One of the company having remarked that he had gone out on a stormy evening, and brought in a supply of peats from the stack, old Mr. M'Sweyn said, "that was *main honest!*"

Blenheim[111] being occasionally mentioned, he told me he had never seen it: he had not gone formerly; and he would not go now, just as a common spectator, for his money: he would not put it in the power of some man about the Duke of Marlborough to say, "Johnson was here; I knew him, but I took no notice of him." He said, he should be very glad to see it, if properly invited, which in all probability would never be the case, as it was not worth his while to seek for it.— I observed, that he might be easily introduced there by a common friend of ours, nearly related to the duke.[112] He answered, with an uncommon attention to delicacy of feeling, "I doubt whether our friend be on such a footing with the duke as to carry any body there; and I would not give him the uneasiness of seeing that I knew he was not, or even of being himself reminded of it."

Sunday, October 10.
There was this day the most terrible storm of wind and rain that I ever remember. It made such an awful impression on us all, as to produce, for some time, a kind of dismal quietness in the house. The day was passed without much conversation: only, upon my observing that there must be something bad in a man's mind, who does not like to give leases to his tenants, but wishes to keep them in a perpetual wretched dependance on his will, Dr. Johnson said, "You are right: it is a man's duty to extend comfort and security among as many people as he can. He should not wish to have his tenants mere *Ephemerae*,— mere beings of an hour." BOSWELL. "But, sir, if they have leases, is there not some danger that they may grow insolent? I remember you yourself once told me, an English tenant was so independent, that, if provoked, he would *throw* his rent at his landlord." JOHNSON. "Depend upon it, sir, it is the landlord's own fault, if it is thrown at him. A man may always keep his tenants in dependence enough, though they have leases. He must be a good tenant indeed, who will not fall behind in his rent, if his landlord will let him; and if he does fall behind, his landlord has him at his mercy. Indeed, the poor man is always much at the mercy of the rich; no matter whether landlord or tenant. If the tenant lets his landlord have a little rent before-hand, or has lent him money, then the landlord is in his power. There cannot be a greater man than a tenant who has lent money to his landlord; for he has under subjection the very man to whom he should be subjected."

Monday, October 11.
We had some days ago engaged the Campbelltown vessel to carry us to Mull, from the harbour where she lay. The morning was fine, and the wind fair and moderate; so we hoped at length to get away.

Mrs. M'Sweyn, who officiated as our landlady here, had never been on the

---

[111] A country mansion, designed by Sir John Vanbrugh and built at government expense near Woodstock in Oxfordshire for the Duke of Marlborough in honor of his victory over the French at Blenheim in 1704.

[112] Topham Beauclerk had married the Duke's sister.

main land. On hearing this, Dr. Johnson said to me, before her, "That is rather being behind-hand with life. I would at least go and see Glenelg."[113] BOSWELL. "You yourself, sir, have never seen, till now, any thing but your native island."[114] JOHNSON. "But, sir, by seeing London, I have seen as much of life as the world can shew." BOSWELL. "You have not seen Pekin." JOHNSON. "What is Pekin? Ten thousand Londoners would *drive* all the people of Pekin: they would drive them like deer."

We set out about eleven for the harbour; but, before we reached it, so violent a storm came on, that we were obliged again to take shelter in the house of Captain M'Lean, where we dined, and passed the night.

Tuesday, October 12.

After breakfast, we made a second attempt to get to the harbour; but another storm soon convinced us that it would be in vain. Captain M'Lean's house being in some confusion, on account of Mrs. M'Lean being expected to lie in, we resolved to go to Mr. M'Sweyn's, where we arrived very wet, fatigued, and hungry. In this situation, we were somewhat disconcerted by being told that we should have no dinner till late in the evening, but should have tea in the mean time. Dr. Johnson opposed this arrangement; but they persisted, and he took the tea very readily. He said to me afterwards, "You must consider, sir, a dinner here is a matter of great consequence. It is a thing to be first planned, and then executed. I suppose the mutton was brought some miles off, from some place where they knew there was a sheep killed."

Talking of the good people with whom we were, he said, "Life has not got at all forward by a generation in M'Sweyn's family; for the son is exactly formed upon the father. What the father says, the son says; and what the father looks, the son looks."

There being little conversation to-night, I must endeavour to recollect what I may have omitted on former occasions.—When I boasted, at Rasay, of my independency of spirit, and that I could not be bribed, he said, "Yes, you may be bribed by flattery."—At the Reverend Mr. M'Lean's, Dr. Johnson asked him, if the people of Col had any superstitions. He said, "No." The cutting peats at the increase of the moon was mentioned as one; but he would not allow it, saying, it was not a superstition, but a whim. Dr. Johnson would not admit the distinction. There were many superstitions, he maintained, not connected with religion; and this was one of them.—On Monday we had a dispute at the Captain's, whether sand-hills could be fixed down by art. Dr. Johnson said, "How *the devil* can you do it?" but instantly corrected himself, "How can you do it?"—I never before heard him use a phrase of that nature.

He has particularities which it is impossible to explain. He never wears a night-cap, as I have already mentioned; but he puts a handkerchief on his head in the night.—The day that we left Talisker, he bade us ride on. He then turned the head of his horse back towards Talisker, stopped for some time; then wheeled round to the same direction with ours, and then came briskly after us. He sets open a window in the coldest day or night, and stands before it. It may do with his constitution; but most people, amongst whom I am one, would say, with the frogs in the fable, "This may be sport to you; but it is death to us."—It is in vain to try to find a meaning in every one of his particularities, which, I suppose, are mere habits, contracted by chance; of which every man has some

[113] The town on the mainland from which Boswell and Johnson had embarked for the Hebrides; it is not over 50 miles from Col.

[114] Two years later Dr. Johnson visited France for two months with his friends the Thrales, and wrote Boswell at that time that "Paris is, indeed, a place very different from the Hebrides, but it is to a hasty traveller not so fertile of novelty, nor affords so many opportunities of remark."

that are more or less remarkable. His speaking to himself, or rather repeating, is a common habit with studious men accustomed to deep thinking; and, in consequence of their being thus rapt, they will even laugh by themselves, if the subject which they are musing on is a merry one. Dr. Johnson is often uttering pious ejaculations, when he appears to be talking to himself; for sometimes his voice grows stronger, and parts of the Lord's Prayer are heard. I have sat beside him with more than ordinary reverence on such occasions.

In our Tour, I observed that he was disgusted whenever he met with coarse manners. He said to me, "I know not how it is, but I cannot bear low life: and I find others, who have as good a right as I to be fastidious, bear it better, by having mixed more with different sorts of men. You would think that I have mixed pretty well too."

He read this day a good deal of my Journal, written in a small book with which he had supplied me, and was pleased, for he said, "I wish thy books were twice as big." He helped me to fill up blanks which I had left in first writing it, when I was not quite sure of what he had said, and he corrected any mistakes that I had made. "They call me a scholar, (said he,) and yet how very little literature is there in my conversation." BOSWELL. "That, sir, must be according to your company. You would not give literature to those who cannot taste it. Stay till we meet Lord Elibank."[115]

We had at last a good dinner, or rather supper, and were very well satisfied with our entertainment.[116]

From THE LIFE OF SAMUEL JOHNSON, LL.D.

[INTRODUCTION ON THE ART OF BIOGRAPHY]

To write the life of him who excelled all mankind in writing the lives of others, and who, whether we consider his extraordinary endowments, or his various works, has been equalled by few in any age, is an arduous, and may be reckoned in me a presumptuous task.

Had Dr. Johnson written his own life, in conformity with the opinion which he has given, that every man's life may be best written by himself;[117] had he employed in the preservation of his own history, that clearness of narration and elegance of language in which he has embalmed so many eminent persons, the world would probably have had the most perfect example of biography that was ever exhibited. But although he at different times, in a desultory manner, committed to writing many particulars of the progress of his mind and fortunes, he never had persevering diligence enough to form them into a regular composition. Of these memorials a few have been preserved; but the greater part was consigned by him to the flames, a few days before his death.

As I had the honour and happiness of enjoying his friendship for upwards

---

Text from that of the second edition, revised, 1793.

[115] Patrick Murray (1703–1778), fifth Baron Elibank, army officer and economist; the meeting took place a month later in Edinburgh.

[116] The next day Boswell and Johnson went aboard ship for passage to the Isle of Mull. They visited Boswell's home at Auchenleck the first week of November. The tour ended in Edinburgh with Johnson's departure for London November 22.

[117] "Idler, No. 84" (Boswell).

of twenty years; as I had the scheme of writing his life constantly in view; as he was well apprised of this circumstance, and from time to time obligingly satisfied my inquiries, by communicating to me the incidents of his early years; as I acquired a facility in recollecting and was very assiduous in recording his conversation, of which the extraordinary vigour and vivacity constituted one of the first features of his character; and as I have spared no pains in obtaining materials concerning him, from every quarter where I could discover that they were to be found, and have been favoured with the most liberal communications by his friends; I flatter myself that few biographers have entered upon such a work as this, with more advantages; independent of literary abilities, in which I am not vain enough to compare myself with some great names who have gone before me in this kind of writing.

Since my work was announced, several Lives and Memoirs[118] of Dr. Johnson have been published, the most voluminous of which is one compiled for the booksellers of London, by Sir John Hawkins, Knight, a man, whom, during my long intimacy with Dr. Johnson, I never saw in his company, I think but once, and I am sure not above twice. Johnson might have esteemed him for his decent, religious demeanour, and his knowledge of books and literary history; but from the rigid formality of his manners, it is evident that they never could have lived together with companionable ease and familiarity; nor had Sir John Hawkins that nice perception which was necessary to mark the finer and less obvious parts of Johnson's character. His being appointed one of his executors, gave him an opportunity of taking possession of such fragments of a diary and other papers as were left; of which, before delivering them up to the residuary legatee, whose property they were, he endeavoured to extract the substance. In this he has not been very successful, as I have found upon a perusal of those papers, which have been since transferred to me. Sir John Hawkins's ponderous labours, I must acknowledge, exhibit a *farrago*,[119] of which a considerable portion is not devoid of entertainment to the lovers of literary gossiping; but besides its being swelled out with long unnecessary extracts from various works, (even one of several leaves from Osborne's Harleian Catalogue, and those not compiled by Johnson, but by Oldys,[120] a very small part of it relates to the person who is the subject of the book; and, in that, there is such an inaccuracy in the statement of facts, as in so solemn an authour is hardly excusable, and certainly makes his narrative very unsatisfactory. But what is still worse, there is throughout the whole of it a dark uncharitable cast, by which the most unfavourable construction is put upon almost every circumstance in the character and conduct of my illustrious friend; who, I trust, will, by a true and fair delineation, be vindicated both from the injurious misrepresentations of this authour, and from the slighter aspersions of a lady who once lived in great intimacy with him.[121]

There is, in the British Museum, a letter from Bishop Warburton to Dr.

---

118 Seven accounts of Johnson's life had appeared between his death in 1784 and the first edition of Boswell's *Life* in 1791: *A Biographical Sketch* (1784) by Thomas Tyers, a *Life* (1785) published by Kearsley and attributed to William Cook, *Memoirs of the Life and Writings* (1785) printed for Walker and attributed to the Rev. William Shaw, *A Poetical Review of the Literary and Moral Character* (1786) by John Courtenay, *Anecdotes . . . during the Last Twenty Years of His Life* (1786) by Hester Lynch Piozzi (Mrs. Thrale), and *An Essay on the Life, Character, and* *Writings* (1786) by Joseph Towers, as well as the *Life* (1787) by Sir John Hawkins which Boswell discusses below.

119 hodgepodge.

120 Boswell later attributed to Johnson *Proposals for Printing Bibliotheca Harleiana* (1742) in connection with a library purchased by the bookseller Thomas Osborne; William Oldys (1696–1761) edited a collection of pamphlets from the library in 1745 to which Johnson contributed an introductory essay.

121 Mrs. Thrale, of course, for whom see note 118.

Birch,[122] on the subject of biography; which, though I am aware it may expose me to a charge of artfully raising the value of my own work, by contrasting it with that of which I have spoken, is so well conceived and expressed, that I cannot refrain from here inserting it:

"I shall endeavour (says Dr. Warburton) to give you what satisfaction I can in any thing you want to be satisfied in any subject of Milton, and am extremely glad you intend to write his life. Almost all the life-writers we have had before Toland and Desmaiseaux,[123] are indeed strange insipid creatures; and yet I had rather read the worst of them, than be obliged to go through with this of Milton's, or the other's life of Boileau, where there is such a dull, heavy succession of long quotations of disinteresting passages, that it makes their method quite nauseous. But the verbose, tasteless Frenchman seems to lay it down as a principle, that every life must be a book, and what's worse, it proves a book without a life; for what do we know of Boileau, after all his tedious stuff? You are the only one, (and I speak it without a compliment) that by the vigour of your stile and sentiments, and the real importance of your materials, have the art (which one would imagine no one could have missed) of adding agreements to the most agreeable subject in the world, which is literary history.

Nov. 24, 1737."

Instead of melting down my materials into one mass, and constantly speaking in my own person, by which I might have appeared to have more merit in the execution of the work, I have resolved to adopt and enlarge upon the excellent plan of Mr. Mason, in his Memoirs of Gray.[124] Wherever narrative is necessary to explain, connect, and supply, I furnish it to the best of my abilities; but

in the chronological series of Johnson's life, which I trace as distinctly as I can, year by year, I produce, wherever it is in my power, his own minutes, letters, or conversation, being convinced that this mode is more lively, and will make my readers better acquainted with him, than even most of those were who actually knew him, but could know him only partially; whereas there is here an accumulation of intelligence from various points, by which his character is more fully understood and illustrated.

Indeed I cannot conceive a more perfect mode of writing any man's life, than not only relating all the most important events of it in their order, but interweaving what he privately wrote, and said, and thought; by which mankind are enabled as it were to see him live, and to "live o'er each scene"[125] with him, as he actually advanced through the several stages of his life. Had his other friends been so diligent and ardent as I was, he might have been almost entirely preserved. As it is, I will venture to say that he will be seen in this work more completely than any man who has ever yet lived.

And he will be seen as he really was; for I profess to write, not his panegyrick, which must be all praise, but his life, which, great and good as he was, must not be supposed to be entirely perfect. To be as he was, is indeed subject of panegyrick enough to any man in this state of being; but in every picture there should be shade as well as light, and when I delineate him without reserve, I do what he himself recommended, both by his precept and his example.

"If the biographer writes from personal knowledge, and makes haste to gratify the publick curiosity, there is danger lest his interest, his fear, his gratitude, or his tenderness overpower his fidelity, and tempt him to conceal,

[122] "Brit[ish] Mus[eum] 4320, Ayscough's Catal[ogue], Sloane Mss" (Boswell); William Warburton (1698–1779), Bishop of Gloucester, literary critic, to Thomas Birch (1705–1766), editor of Biographia Britannica.

[123] John Toland (1670–1722), author of a

life of Milton, and Pierre Des Maizeaux (1666–1745), author of a life of Boileau.

[124] William Mason (1724–1797), author of a life of the poet Thomas Gray (1775).

[125] From Pope's "Prologue to Mr. Addison's Tragedy of Cato," l. 4.

if not to invent. There are many who think it an act of piety to hide the faults or failings of their friends, even when they can no longer suffer by their detection; we therefore see whole ranks of characters adorned with uniform panegyrick, and not to be known from one another but by extrinsick and casual circumstances. 'Let me remember, (says Hale,[126]) when I find myself inclined to pity a criminal, that there is likewise a pity due to the country.' If we owe regard to the memory of the dead, there is yet more respect to be paid to knowledge, to virtue, and to truth."[127]

What I consider as the peculiar value of the following work, is, the quantity it contains of Johnson's conversation; which is universally acknowledged to have been eminently instructive and entertaining; and of which the specimens that I have given upon a former occasion,[128] have been received with so much approbation, that I have good grounds for supposing that the world will not be indifferent to more ample communications of a similar nature.

That the conversation of a celebrated man, if his talents have been exerted in conversation, will best display his character, is, I trust, too well established in the judgement of mankind, to be at all shaken by a sneering observation of Mr. Mason, in his Memoirs of Mr. William Whitehead,[129] in which there is literally no Life, but a mere dry narrative of facts. I do not think it was quite necessary to attempt a depreciation of what is universally esteemed, because it was not to be found in the immediate object of the ingenious writer's pen; for in truth, from a man so still and so tame, as to be contented to pass many years as the domestick companion of a superan-

nuated lord and lady,[130] conversation could no more be expected, than from a Chinese mandarin on a chimney-piece,[131] or the fantastick figures on a gilt leather skreen.

If authority be required, let us appeal to Plutarch, the prince of ancient biographers. "Nor is it always in the most distinguished atchievements that men's virtues or vices may be best discerned; but very often an action of small note, a short saying, or a jest, shall distinguish a person's real character more than the greatest sieges, or the most important battles."[132]

To this may be added the sentiments of the very man whose life I am about to exhibit. "The business of the biographer is often to pass slightly over those performances and incidents which produce vulgar greatness, to lead the thoughts into domestick privacies, and display the minute details of daily life, where exteriour appendages are cast aside, and men excel each other only by prudence and by virtue. The account of Thuanus is with great propriety said by its authour to have been written, that it might lay open to posterity the private and familiar character of that man, *cujus ingenium et candorem ex ipsius scriptis sunt olim semper miraturi,*[133] whose candour and genius will to the end of time be by his writings preserved in admiration.

"There are many invisible circumstances, which whether we read as enquirers after natural or moral knowledge, whether we intend to enlarge our science, or increase our virtue, are more important than publick occurrences. Thus Sallust,[134] the great master of nature, has not forgot in his account of Catiline to remark, that his walk was

---

[126] Sir Matthew Hale (1609–1676), judge.
[127] "Rambler, No. 60" (Boswell).
[128] In *Journal of a Tour to the Hebrides* (1785).
[129] In *Poems* (1788) by William Whitehead, III, 128.
[130] William Villiers (1704?–1769), third Earl of Jersey, and Anne Egerton (d. 1762), his Countess.
[131] A tapestry over a fireplace.

[132] "Plutarch's Life of Alexander, Langhorne's Translation" (Boswell); Boswell also prefaces the translation with the original Greek.
[133] The translation follows in the same sentence. Thuanus is the Latin name of the French historian, Jacques Auguste de Thou (1553–1617), author of *Historia sui Temporis* (1604–1608) from which Johnson is quoting.
[134] Roman historian (86–34 B.C.).

now quick, and again slow, as an indication of a mind revolving [something] with violent commotion. Thus the story of Melancthon[135] affords a striking lecture on the value of time, by informing us, that when he had made an appointment, he expected not only the hour, but the minute to be fixed, that the day might not run out in the idleness of suspence; and all the plans and enterprises of De Wit[136] are now of less importance to the world than that part of his personal character, which represents him as careful of his health, and negligent of his life.

"But biography has often been allotted to writers, who seem very little acquainted with the nature of their task, or very negligent about the performance. They rarely afford any other account than might be collected from publick papers, but imagine themselves writing a life, when they exhibit a chronological series of actions or preferments; and have so little regard to the manners or behaviour of their heroes, that more knowledge may be gained of a man's real character, by a short conversation with one of his servants, than from a formal and studied narrative, begun with his pedigree, and ended with his funeral.

"There are indeed, some natural reasons why these narratives are often written by such as were not likely to give much instruction or delight, and why most accounts of particular persons are barren and useless. If a life be delayed till interest and envy are at an end, we may hope for impartiality, but must expect little intelligence; for the incidents which give excellence to biography are of a volatile and evanescent kind, such as soon escape the memory, and are [rarely] transmitted by tradition. We know how few can pourtray a living acquaintance, except by his most prominent and observable particularities, and the grosser features of his mind; and it

may be easily imagined how much of this little knowledge may be lost in imparting it, and how soon a succession of copies will lose all resemblance of the original."[137]

I am fully aware of the objections which may be made to the minuteness on some occasions of my detail of Johnson's conversation, and how happily it is adapted for the petty exercise of ridicule, by men of superficial understanding, and ludicrous fancy; but I remain firm and confident in my opinion, that minute particulars are frequently characteristick, and always amusing, when they relate to a distinguished man. I am therefore exceedingly unwilling that any thing, however slight, which my illustrious friend thought it worth his while to express, with any degree of point, should perish. For this almost superstitious reverence, I have found very old and venerable authority, quoted by our great modern prelate, Secker, in whose tenth sermon there is the following passage:

"*Rabbi David Kimchi,* a noted Jewish Commentator, who lived about five hundred years ago, explains that passage in the first Psalm, *His leaf also shall not wither,* from Rabbins yet older then himself, thus: That *even the idle talk,* so he expresses it, *of a good man ought to be regarded;* the most superfluous things he saith are always of some value. And other ancient authours have the same phrase, nearly in the same sense."[138]

Of one thing I am certain, that considering how highly the small portion which we have of the table-talk and other anecdotes of our celebrated writers is valued, and how earnestly it is regretted that we have not more, I am justified in preserving rather too many of Johnson's sayings, than too few; especially as from the diversity of dispositions it cannot be known with certainty beforehand, whether what may seem trifling to some, and perhaps to the col-

---

135 Philipp Melanchthon (1497–1560), German theologian of the Reformation.
136 Jan DeWitt (1625–1672), Dutch statesman; an English version of his *The True Interest and Political Maxims of the Republick of Holland* appeared in 1743.

137 "Rambler, No. 60" (Boswell). The significance of Boswell's suppression of one paragraph is discussed by H. W. Hamilton (*Modern Language Notes,* LXXVI, 218–20).
137 "Rambler, No. 60" (Boswell).
138 Thomas Secker, *Sermons* (1770), II, 233.

lector himself, may not be most agreeable to many; and the greater number that an authour can please in any degree, the more pleasure does there arise to a benevolent mind.

To those who are weak enough to think this a degrading task, and the time and labour which have been devoted to it misemployed, I shall content myself with opposing the authority of the greatest man of any age, Julius Caesar, of whom Bacon observes, that "in his book of Apothegms which he collected, we see that he esteemed it more honour to make himself but a pair of tables, to take the wise and pithy words of others, than to have every word of his own to be made an apothegm or an oracle."[139]

Having said thus much by way of introduction, I commit the following pages to the candour of the publick.

[JOURNAL OF A VISIT TO ASHBOURNE
SEPTEMBER 1777]

[This passage in the *Life* describes a visit Boswell made the home of one of Johnson's lifelong friends, John Taylor, LL.D. (1711–1788), of Ashbourne, Derbyshire, a town about 25 miles north of Johnson's birthplace and childhood home in Lichfield. The letters with which the account is prefaced refer to mutual acquaintances, some made on Johnson's trip to Scotland in 1773, and to the recent trial of a famous London clergyman, William Dodd, which is related in more detail during the visit.]

To James Boswell, *Esq.*
Dear Sir,

Your notion of the necessity of an yearly interview is very pleasing to both my vanity and tenderness. I shall, perhaps, come to Carlisle another year; but my money has not held out so well as it

used to do. I shall go to Ashbourne, and I purpose to make Dr. Taylor invite you. If you live awhile with me at his house, we shall have much time to ourselves, and our stay will be no expence to us or him. I shall leave London, the 28th; and after some stay at Oxford and Lichfield, shall probably come to Ashbourne about the end of your Session,[140] but of all this you shall have notice. Be satisfied we will meet somewhere.

What passed between me and poor Dr. Dodd you shall know more fully when we meet.

Of lawsuits there is no end; poor Sir Allan[141] must have another trial, for which, however, his antagonist cannot be much blamed, having two Judges on his side. I am more afraid of the debts than of the House of Lords. It is scarcely to be imagined to what debts will swell, that are daily increasing by small additions, and how carelessly in a state of desperation debts are contracted. Poor Macquarry was far from thinking that when he sold his islands he should receive nothing. For what were they sold? And what were their yearly value? The admission of money into the Highlands will soon put an end to the feudal modes of life, by making those men landlords who were not chiefs. I do not know that the people will suffer by the change; but there was in the patriarchal authority something venerable and pleasing. Every eye must look with pain on a *Campbell* turning the *Macquarries* at will out of their *sedes avitae*,[142] their hereditary island.

Sir Alexander Dick is the only Scotsman liberal enough not to be angry that I could not find trees, where trees were not. I was much delighted by his kind letter.[143]

I remember Rasay with too much pleasure not to partake of the happiness of any part of that amiable family. Our

139 "Bacon's Advancement of Learning, Book I [chap. vii, sec. 25]" (Boswell).

140 Meeting of the Scottish Court of Session in which Boswell was an advocate.

141 Johnson was referring to a law case of which Boswell had spoken in the letter to which this is in answer; Johnson had met both

Sir Allan Maclean and Macquarry (who is mentioned further on) in the Hebrides four years earlier. Boswell had mentioned that the estates of the Macquarry family had been purchased by a Campbell.

142 "ancestral abodes."

143 Sir Alexander Dick (1703–1785), Scot-

ramble in the islands hangs upon my imagination, I can hardly help imagining that we shall go again. Pennant[144] seems to have seen a great deal which we did not see: When we travel again let us look better about us.

You have done right in taking your uncle's house. Some change in the form of life, gives from time to time a new epocha[145] of existence. In a new place there is something new to be done, and a different system of thoughts rises in the mind. I wish I could gather currants in your garden. Now fit up a little study, and have your books ready at hand; do not spare a little money, to make your habitation pleasing to yourself.

I have dined lately with poor dear ———.[146] I do not think he goes on well. His table is rather coarse, and he has his children too much about him. But he is a very good man.

Mrs. Williams[147] is in the country to try if she can improve her health; she is very ill. Matters have come so about that she is in the country with very good accommodation; but age and sickness, and pride, have made her so peevish that I was forced to bribe the maid to stay with her, by a secret stipulation of half a crown a week over her wages.

Our club[148] ended its session about six weeks ago. We now only meet to dine once a fortnight. Mr. Dunning,[149] the great lawyer, is one of our members. The Thrales[150] are well.

I long to know how the Negro's cause will be decided. What is the opinion of Lord Auchinleck, or Lord Hailes, or Lord Monboddo?[151] I am, dear Sir,

Your most affectionate, &c.

Sam. Johnson.

July 22, 1777.

Dr. Johnson *to Mrs.* Boswell[152]

Madam,

Though I am well enough pleased with the taste of sweetmeats, very little of the pleasure which I received at the arrival of your jar of marmalade arose from eating it. I received it as a token of friendship, as a proof of reconciliation, things much sweeter than sweetmeats, and upon this consideration I return you, dear Madam, my sincerest thanks. By having your kindness I think I have a double security for the continuance of Mr. Boswell's, which it is not to be expected that any man can long keep, when the influence of a lady so highly and so justly valued operates against him. Mr. Boswell will tell you that I was always faithful to your interest, and always endeavoured to exalt

---

tish physician, to whom Johnson had presented a copy of his *Journey to the Western Islands of Scotland.* Sir Alexander wrote Johnson February 17, 1777, saying that the demand for trees and hedges had lately multiplied, implying that Johnson's book had stirred interest in planting.

[144] Thomas Pennant, *Tour in Scotland* (1769); Boswell and Johnson had visited the Isle of Raasay on their tour of the Hebrides.

[145] Variant of *epoch* in Johnson's *Dictionary.*

[146] Bennet Langton (1737–1801). See notes 100 above and 242 below.

[147] Anna Williams (1706–1783), an intimate friend of Johnson's.

[148] The Club, the most illustrious in the history of English literature, met weekly; it had been founded in 1764 at the suggestion of Sir Joshua Reynolds and included such distinguished members as Edmund Burke, Oliver Goldsmith, David Garrick, and Adam Smith; Boswell had been admitted in 1773.

[149] John Dunning, first Baron Ashburton (1731–1783).

[150] Henry Thrale (1728–1781), a London brewer, and his wife Hester (see notes 75 and 121) were friends and patrons of Johnson.

[151] A suit for freedom from slavery, which was successful despite the negative vote of James Burnett, Lord Monboddo (1714–1799); Lord Auchinleck was Boswell's father; Lord Hailes (Sir David Dalrymple) was a judge and writer whom Johnson had met in Edinburgh through Boswell before the tour of the Hebrides.

[152] Margaret Montgomerie (d. 1789), Boswell's wife. Of the circumstances requiring "reconciliation," Boswell said of Johnson's visit to the Boswell home: "The truth is, that his irregular hours and uncouth habits, such as turning the candles with their heads downwards, when they did not burn bright enough, and letting the wax drop upon the carpet, could not but be disagreeable to a lady. Besides . . . she thought he had too much influence over her husband."

you in his estimation. You must now do the same for me. We must all help one another, and you must now consider me, as, dear Madam,

> Your most obliged,
> And most humble servant,
> Sam. Johnson.

July 22, 1777.

Mr. Boswell *to Dr.* Johnson
> Edinburgh, July 28, 1777.

My Dear Sir,

This is the day on which you were to leave London, and I have been amusing myself in the intervals of my law-drudgery, with figuring you in the Oxford post-coach. I doubt, however, if you have had so merry a journey as you and I had in that vehicle last year, when you made so much sport with Gwyn, the architect.[153] Incidents upon a journey are recollected with peculiar pleasure; they are preserved in brisk spirits, and come up again in our minds, tinctured with that gaiety, or at least that animation with which we first perceived them.

I added, that something had occurred, which I was afraid might prevent me from meeting him; and that my wife had been affected with complaints which threatened a consumption, but was now better.

To James Boswell, *Esq.*
Dear Sir,

Do not disturb yourself about our interviews; I hope we shall have many; nor think it any thing hard or unusual, that your design of meeting me is interrupted. We have both endured greater evils, and have greater evils to expect. Mrs. Boswell's illness makes a more serious distress. Does the blood rise from her lungs or from her stomach? From little vessels broken in the stomach there

is no danger. Blood from the lungs is, I believe, always frothy, as mixed with wind. Your physicians know very well what is to be done. The loss of such a lady would, indeed, be very afflictive, and I hope she is in no danger. Take care to keep her mind as easy as is possible.

I have left Langton in London. He has been down with the militia,[154] and is again quiet at home, talking to his little people, as, I suppose, you do sometimes. Make my compliments to Miss Veronica.[155] The rest are too young for ceremony.

I cannot but hope that you have taken your country-house at a very seasonable time, and that it may conduce to restore, or establish Mrs. Boswell's health, as well as provide room and exercise for the young ones. That you and your lady may both be happy, and long enjoy your happiness, is the sincere and earnest wish of, dear Sir,

> Your most, &c.
> Sam. Johnson.

Oxford, Aug. 4, 1777.

Mr. Boswell to Dr. Johnson.

Informing him that my wife had continued to grow better, so that my alarming apprehensions were relieved; and that I hoped to disengage myself from the other embarrassment which had occurred, and therefore requesting to know particularly when he intended to be at Ashbourne.

To James Boswell, Esq.
Dear Sir,

I am this day come to Ashbourne, and have only to tell you, that Dr. Taylor says you shall be welcome to him, and you know how welcome you will be to me. Make haste to let me know when you may be expected.

---

[153] John Gwynn (d. 1786), architect, with whom Boswell and Johnson had been accompanied on a jaunt to Oxford in March 1776. It was upon a witticism of Gwynn's that Johnson had remarked in high spirits: "Speak no more. Rest your colloquial fame upon **this.**"

[154] Bennet Langton was a captain in the Lincolnshire militia which was active in these years as a result of war with the American colonies and threat of war with France and Spain.

[155] The oldest (4 years) of Boswell's three children then living.

Make my compliments to Mrs. Boswell, and tell her, I hope we shall be at variance no more. I am, dear Sir,

Your most humble servant,
Sam. Johnson.

August 30, 1777.

To James Boswell, Esq.
Dear Sir,

On Saturday I wrote a very short letter, immediately upon my arrival hither, to shew you that I am not less desirous of the interview than yourself. Life admits not of delays; when pleasure can be had it is fit to catch it: Every hour takes away part of the things that please us, and perhaps part of our disposition to be pleased. When I came to Lichfield, I found my old friend Harry Jackson[156] dead. It was a loss, and a loss not to be repaired, as he was one of the companions of my childhood. I hope we may long continue to gain friends, but the friends which merit or usefulness can procure us, are not able to supply the place of old acquaintance, with whom the days of youth may be retraced, and those images revived which gave the earliest delight. If you and I live to be much older, we shall take great delight in talking over the Hebridean Journey.

In the mean time it may not be amiss to contrive some other little adventure, but what it can be I know not; leave it, as Sidney says,

To virtue, fortune, wine, and woman's breast;[157]

for I believe Mrs. Boswell must have some part in the consultation.

One thing you will like. The Doctor, so far as I can judge, is likely to leave us enough to ourselves. He was out to-day before I came down, and, I fancy, will stay out till dinner. I have brought the papers about poor Dodd, to show you, but you will soon have dispatched them.

Before I came away I sent poor Mrs. Williams into the country, very ill of a pituitous defluxion,[158] which wastes her gradually away, and which her physician declares himself unable to stop. I supplied her as far as could be desired, with all conveniences to make her excursion and abode pleasant and useful. But I am afraid she can only linger a short time in a morbid state of weakness and pain.

The Thrales, little and great, are all well, and purpose to go to Brighthelmstone at Michaelmas. They will invite me to go with them, and perhaps I may go, but I hardly think I shall like to stay the whole time; but of futurity we know but little.

Mrs. Porter[159] is well; but Mrs. Aston,[160] one of the ladies at Stowhill, has been struck with a palsy, from which she is not likely ever to recover. How soon may such a stroke fall upon us!

Write to me, and let us know when we may expect you. I am, dear Sir,

Your most humble servant,
Sam. Johnson.

Ashbourne, Sept. 1, 1777.

Mr. Boswell to Dr. Johnson.
Edinburgh, Sept. 9, 1777.

After informing him that I was to set out next day, in order to meet him at Ashbourne:—

I have a present for you from Lord Hailes; the fifth book of "Lactantius,"[161] which he has published with Latin notes. He is also to give you a few anecdotes for your "Life of Thomson," who I find was private tutor to the present Earl of

---

[156] Boswell had met him the year before in Lichfield and thought "he seemed to be a low man, dull and untaught."

[157] From Sir Philip Sidney's sonnet in the second edition of *Arcadia*, although *wine* has been substituted for *time*. R. W. Chapman, who has edited *The Letters of Samuel Johnson* (3 vols., 1952), assumes that Johnson's handwriting was mistaken by the printer of Boswell's *Life*.

[158] mucous discharge.

[159] Lucy Porter (1715–1786), daughter of Johnson's wife by her first husband.

[160] Elizabeth Aston (1708–1785), a friend of Johnson's, whom Boswell had met at Peter Garrick's house a year earlier.

[161] A fourth-century Christian apologist.

Hadington, Lord Hailes's cousin, a circumstance not mentioned by Dr. Murdoch.[162] I have keen expectations of delight from your edition of the English Poets.[163]

I am sorry for poor Mrs. Williams's situation. You will, however, have the comfort of reflecting on your kindness to her. Mr. Jackson's death, and Mrs. Aston's palsy, are gloomy circumstances. Yet surely we should be habituated to the uncertainty of life and health. When my mind is unclouded by melancholy, I consider the temporary distresses of this state of being, as "light afflictions," by stretching my mental view into that glorious after existence, when they will appear to be as nothing. But present pleasures and present pains must be felt. I lately read "Rasselas" over again with great satisfaction.

Since you are desirous to hear about Macquarry's sale I shall inform you particularly. The gentleman who purchased Ulva is Mr. Campbell, of Auchnaba: our friend Macquarry was proprietor of two-thirds of it, of which the rent was 156l. 5s. 1d.½. This parcel was set up at 4,069l. 15s. 1d. but it sold for no less than 5,540l. The other third of Ulva, with the island of Staffa, belonged to Macquarry of Ormaig. Its rent, including that of Staffa, 83l. 12s. 2d.⅔—set up at 2178l. 16s. 4d.—sold for no less than 3,540l. The Laird of Col, wished to purchase Ulva, but he thought the price too high. There may, indeed, be great improvements made there, both in fishing and agriculture; but the interest of the purchase-money exceeds the rent so very much, that I doubt if the bargain will be profitable. There is an island called Little Colonsay, of 10l. yearly rent, which I am informed has belonged to the Macquarrys of Ulva for many ages, but which was lately claimed by the Presbyterian Synod of Argyll, in consequence of a grant made to them by

Queen Anne. It is believed that their claim will be dismissed, and that Little Colonsay will also be sold for the advantage of Macquarry's creditors. What think you of purchasing this island, and endowing a school or college there, the master to be a clergyman of the Church of England? How venerable would such an institution make the name of DR. SAMUEL JOHNSON in the Hebrides! I have, like yourself, a wonderful pleasure in recollecting our travels in those islands. The pleasure is, I think, greater than it reasonably should be, considering that we had not much either of beauty and elegance to charm our imaginations, or of rude novelty to astonish. Let us, by all means, have another expedition. I shrink a little from our scheme of going up the Baltick.[164] I am sorry you have already been in Wales; for I wish to see it. Shall we go to Ireland, of which I have seen but little? We shall try to strike out a plan when we are at Ashbourne. I am ever

Your most faithful humble servant,
James Boswell.

To James Boswell, Esq.
Dear Sir,

I write to be left at Carlisle, as you direct me; but you cannot have it. Your letter, dated Sept. 6, was not at this place till this day, Thursday, Sept. 11; and I hope you will be here before this is at Carlisle. However, what you have not going, you may have returning; and as I believe I shall not love you less after our interview, it will then be as true as it is now, that I set a very high value upon your friendship, and count your kindness as one of the chief felicities of my life. Do not fancy that an intermission of writing is a decay of kindness. No man is always in a disposition to write; nor has any man at all times something to say.

That distrust which intrudes so often

[162] Patrick Murdoch (d. 1774), author of a life of James Thomson, the English poet.

[163] "Dr. Johnson was not the *editor* of this Collection of the English Poets; he merely furnished the biographical prefaces with which it is enriched" (Edmond Malone).

[164] "It seems that Johnson, now in his sixty-eighth year, was seriously inclined to realise the project of our going up the Baltick, which I had started when we were in the isle of Sky" (Boswell).

on your mind is a mode of melancholy, which, if it be the business of a wise man to be happy, it is foolish to indulge; and if it be a duty to preserve our faculties entire for their proper use, it is criminal. Suspicion is very often an useless pain. From that, and all other pains, I wish you free and safe; for I am, dear Sir,

Most affectionately yours,
Sam. Johnson.
Ashbourne, Sept. 11, 1777.

On[165] Sunday evening Sept. 14, I arrived at Ashbourne, and drove directly up to Dr. Taylor's door. Dr. Johnson and he appeared before I had got out of the post-chaise, and welcomed me cordially.

I told them that I had travelled all the preceding night, and gone to bed at Leek, in Staffordshire; and that when I rose to go to church in the afternoon, I was informed there had been an earthquake, of which, it seems, the shock had been felt in some degree, at Ashbourne. JOHNSON. "Sir, it will be much exaggerated in popular talk: for, in the first place, the common people do not accurately adapt their thoughts to the objects; nor, secondly, do they accurately adapt their words to their thoughts: they do not mean to lie; but, taking no pains to be exact, they give you very false accounts. A great part of their language is proverbial. If any thing rocks at all, they say *it rocks like a cradle;* and in this way they go on."

The subject of grief for the loss of relations and friends being introduced, I observed that it was strange to consider how soon it in general wears away. Dr. Taylor mentioned a gentleman of the neighbourhood as the only instance he had ever known of a person who had endeavoured to *retain* grief. He told Dr. Taylor, that after his Lady's death,

which affected him deeply, he *resolved* that the grief, which he cherished with a kind of sacred fondness, should be lasting; but that he found he could not keep it long. JOHNSON. "All grief for what cannot in the course of nature be helped, soon wears away; in some sooner, indeed, in some later; but it never continues very long, unless where there is madness, such as will make a man have pride so fixed in his mind, as to imagine himself a King; or any other passion in an unreasonable way: for all unnecessary grief is unwise, and therefore will not be long retained by a sound mind. If, indeed, the cause of our grief is occasioned by our own misconduct, if grief is mingled with remorse of conscience, it should be lasting." BOSWELL. "But, Sir, we do not approve of a man who very soon forgets the loss of a wife or a friend." JOHNSON. "Sir, we disapprove of him, not because he soon forgets his grief; for the sooner it is forgotten the better, but because we suppose, that if he forgets his wife or his friend soon, he has not had much affection for them."

I was somewhat disappointed in finding that the edition of the English Poets, for which he was to write Prefaces and Lives, was not an undertaking directed by him; but that he was to furnish a Preface and Life to any poet the booksellers pleased. I asked him if he would do this to any dunce's works, if they should ask him. JOHNSON. "Yes, Sir; and *say* he was a dunce." My friend seemed now not much to relish talking of this edition.[166]

On Monday, September 15, Dr. Johnson observed, that every body commended such parts of his "Journey to the Western Islands," as were in their own way. "For instance, (said he,) Mr. Jackson[167] (the all-knowing) told me, there was more good sense upon trade in it, than he should hear in the House of Com-

---

[165] The journal which Boswell kept while at Ashbourne is among the Malahide Papers in Yale University Library; comparison of passages in the journal with relation of the same events in the *Life* reveals that Boswell made only stylistic changes in adapting his journal for the published *Life* (cf. *Boswell Papers,*

VI, 186 ff.).

[166] The edition was published two years later.

[167] Richard Jackson (d. 1787), a politician known as Omniscient Jackson; Johnson, while respecting his knowledge, thought "omniscient" should be reserved for the deity; hence Boswell's use of "the all-knowing."

mons in a year, except from Burke.[168] Jones[169] commended the part which treats of language; Burke that which describes the inhabitants[170] of mountainous countries."

After breakfast, Johnson carried me to see the garden belonging to the school of Ashbourne, which is very prettily formed upon a bank, rising gradually behind the house. The Reverend Mr. Langley,[171] the head master, accompanied us.

While we sat basking in the sun upon a seat here, I introduced a common subject of complaint, the very small salaries which many curates have, and I maintained, "that no man should be invested with the character of a clergyman, unless he has a security for such an income as will enable him to appear respectable; that, therefore, a clergyman should not be allowed to have a curate, unless he gives him a hundred pounds a year; if he cannot do that, let him perform the duty himself." JOHNSON. "To be sure, Sir, it is wrong that any clergyman should be without a reasonable income; but as the church revenues were sadly diminished at the Reformation, the clergy who have livings cannot afford, in many instances, to give good salaries to curates, without leaving themselves too little; and, if no curate were to be permitted, unless he had a hundred pounds a year, their number would be very small, which would be a disadvantage, as then there would not be such choice in the nursery for the church, curates being candidates for the higher ecclesiastical offices, according to their merit and good behaviour." He explained the system of the English Hierarchy exceedingly well. "It is not thought fit (said he) to trust a man with the care of a parish, till he has given proof as a curate that he shall deserve such a trust." This is an excellent *theory;* and if the *practice* were according to it, the Church

of England would be admirable indeed. However, as I have heard Dr. Johnson observe as to the Universities, bad practice does not infer that the *constitution* is bad.

We had with us at dinner several of Dr. Taylor's neighbours, good civil gentlemen, who seemed to understand Dr. Johnson very well, and not to consider him in the light that a certain person[172] did, who being struck, or rather stunned by his voice and manner, when he was afterwards asked what he thought of him, answered, "He's a tremendous companion."

Johnson told me, that "Taylor was a very sensible acute man, and had a strong mind; that he had great activity in some respects, and yet such a sort of indolence, that if you should put a pebble upon his chimney-piece, you would find it there, in the same state, a year afterwards."

And here is the proper place to give an account of Johnson's humane and zealous interference in behalf of the Reverend Dr. William Dodd, formerly Prebendary of Brecon, and chaplain in ordinary to his Majesty; celebrated as a very popular preacher, an encourager of charitable institutions, and authour of a variety of works, chiefly theological. Having unhappily contracted expensive habits of living, partly occasioned by licentiousness of manners, he in an evil hour, when pressed by want of money, and dreading an exposure of his circumstances, forged a bond of which he attempted to avail himself to support his credit, flattering himself with hopes that he might be able to repay its amount without being detected. The person, whose name he thus rashly and criminally presumed to falsify, was the Earl of Chesterfield,[173] to whom he had been tutor, and who, he perhaps, in the warmth of his feelings, flattered himself would have generously paid the money

---

[168] Edmund Burke (1729–1797), the statesman and orator.

[169] Sir William Jones (1746–1794), an Orientalist of linguistic attainments.

[170] Alluding to Burke's interest in people.

[171] William Langley (1722?–1795), headmaster of Ashbourne Grammar School.

[172] George Garrick (1723–1779), an elder brother of David, the actor.

[173] Not the famous Chesterfield, but his successor, the fifth Earl.

in case of an alarm being taken, rather than suffer him to fall a victim to the dreadful consequences of violating the law against forgery, the most dangerous crime in a commercial country; but the unfortunate divine had the mortification to find that he was mistaken. His noble pupil appeared against him, and he was capitally convicted.

Johnson told me that Dr. Dodd was very little acquainted with him, having been but once in his company, many years previous to this period (which was precisely the state of my own acquaintance with Dodd;) but in his distress he bethought himself of Johnson's persuasive power of writing, if haply it might avail to obtain for him the royal mercy. He did not apply to him directly, but, extraordinary as it may seem, through the late Countess of Harrington,[174] who wrote a letter to Johnson, asking him to employ his pen in favour of Dodd. Mr. Allen,[175] the printer, who was Johnson's landlord and next neighbour in Bolt-court, and for whom he had much kindness, was one of Dodd's friends, of whom, to the credit of humanity be it recorded, that he had many who did not desert him, even after his infringement of the law had reduced him to the state of a man under sentence of death. Mr. Allen told me that he carried Lady Harrington's letter to Johnson, that Johnson read it walking up and down his chamber, and seemed much agitated, after which he said, "I will do what I can;—" and certainly he did make extraordinary exertions.

He this evening, as he had obligingly promised in one of his letters, put into my hands the whole series of his writings upon this melancholy occasion, and I shall present my readers with the abstract which I made from the collection; in doing which I studied to avoid copying what had appeared in print, and now make part of the edition of "Johnson's Works," published by the Booksellers of London, but taking care to mark John-son's variations in some of the pieces there exhibited.

Dr. Johnson wrote in the first place, Dr. Dodd's "Speech to the Recorder of London," at the Old-Bailey,[176] when sentence of death was about to be pronounced upon him.

He wrote also "The Convict's Address to his unhappy Brethren," a sermon delivered by Dr. Dodd, in the chapel of Newgate. According to Johnson's manuscript it began thus after the text, *What shall I do to be saved?*[177]— "These were the words with which the keeper, to whose custody Paul and Silas were committed by their prosecutors, addressed his prisoners, when he saw them freed from their bonds by the perceptible agency of divine favour, and was, therefore, irresistibly convinced that they were not offenders against the laws, but martyrs to the truth."

Dr. Johnson was so good as to mark for me with his own hand, on a copy of this sermon which is now in my possession, such passages as were added by Dr. Dodd. They are not many: Whoever will take the trouble to look at the printed copy, and attend to what I mention, will be satisfied of this.

There is a short introduction by Dr. Dodd, and he also inserted this sentence, "You see with what confusion and dishonour I now stand before you;—no more in the pulpit of instruction, but on this humble seat with yourselves." The *notes* are entirely Dodd's own, and Johnson's writing ends at the words, "the thief whom he pardoned on the cross." What follows was supplied by Dr. Dodd himself.

The other pieces written by Johnson in the above-mentioned collection, are two letters,[178] one to the Lord Chancellor Bathurst, (not Lord North, as is erroneously supposed,) and one to Lord Mansfield;—A Petition from Dr. Dodd to the King;—A Petition from Mrs. Dodd to the Queen;—Observations of some length inserted in the newspapers,

---

[174] Caroline, Countess of Harrington (1722–1784).

[175] See note 98.

[176] Old Bailey Sessions House was the crimi-nal court, connected with Newgate Prison.

[177] Acts 16:30.

[178] To judges concerned in the case.

on occasion of Earl Percy's[179] having presented to his Majesty a petition for mercy to Dodd, signed by twenty thousand people, but all in vain. He told me that he had also written a petition from the city of London; "but (said he, with a significant smile) they *mended* it."

The last of these articles which Johnson wrote is "Dr. Dodd's last solemn Declaration," which he left with the sheriff at the place of execution. Here also my friend marked the variations on a copy of that piece now in my possession. Dodd inserted, "I never knew or attended to the calls of frugality, or the needful minuteness of painful œconomy;" and in the next sentence he introduced the words which I distinguish by *Italicks;* "My life for some *few unhappy* years past has been *dreadfully erroneous.*" Johnson's expression was *hypocritical;* but his remark on the margin is "With this he said he could not charge himself."

Having thus authentically settled what part of the "Occasional Papers," concerning Dr. Dodd's miserable situation, came from the pen of Johnson, I shall proceed to present my readers with my record of the unpublished writings relating to that extraordinary and interesting matter.

I found a letter to Dr. Johnson from Dr. Dodd, May 23, 1777, in which "The Convict's Address" seems clearly to be meant:

"I am so penetrated, my ever dear Sir, with a sense of your extreme benevolence towards me, that I cannot find words equal to the sentiments of my heart. . . .

"You are too conversant in the world to need the slightest hint from me, of what infinite utility the Speech on the aweful day has been to me. I experience, every hour, some good effect from it. I am sure that effects still more salutary and important, must follow from *your kind and intended favour.* I will labour —GOD being my helper,—to do justice to it from the pulpit. I am sure, had I

[179] Hugh, Earl Percy, later Duke of Northumberland (1742–1817), military man and politician.

your sentiments constantly to deliver from thence, in all their mighty force and power, not a soul could be left unconvinced and unpersuaded. . . .'"

He added, "May GOD ALMIGHTY bless and reward, with his choicest comforts, your philanthropick actions, and enable me at all times to express what I feel of the high and uncommon obligations which I owe to the *first man* in our times."

On Sunday, June 22, he writes, begging Dr. Johnson's assistance in framing a supplicatory letter to his Majesty:

"If his Majesty could be moved of his royal clemency to spare me and my family the horrours and ignominy of a *publick death,* which the *publick* itself is solicitous to wave, and to grant me in some silent distant corner of the globe, to pass the remainder of my days in penitence and prayer, I would bless his clemency and be humbled."

This letter was brought to Dr. Johnson when in church. He stooped down and read it, and wrote, when he went home, the following letter for Dr. Dodd to the King:

Sir,

May it not offend your Majesty, that the most miserable of men applies himself to your clemency, as his last hope and his last refuge; that your mercy is most earnestly and humbly implored by a clergyman, whom your Laws and Judges have condemned to the horrour and ignominy of a publick execution.

I confess the crime, and own the enormity of its consequences, and the danger of its example. Nor have I the confidence to petition for impunity; but humbly hope, that publick security may be established, without the spectacle of a clergyman dragged through the streets, to a death of infamy, amidst the derision of the profligate and profane; and that justice may be satisfied with irrevocable exile, perpetual disgrace, and hopeless penury.

My life, Sir, has not been useless to mankind. I have benefited many. But my offences against GOD are numberless, and I have had little time for repentance.

Preserve me, Sir, by your prerogative of mercy, from the necessity of appearing unprepared at that tribunal before which Kings and Subjects must stand at last together. Permit me to hide my guilt in some obscure corner of a foreign country, where, if I can ever attain confidence to hope that my prayers will be heard, they shall be poured with all the fervour of gratitude for the life and happiness of your Majesty. I am, Sir,

Your Majesty's, &c.

Subjoined to it was written as follows:

To Dr. Dodd

Sir,

I most seriously enjoin you not to let it be at all known that I have written this letter, and to return the copy to Mr. Allen in a cover to me. I hope I need not tell you, that I wish it success.— But do not indulge hope.—Tell nobody.

It happened luckily that Mr. Allen was pitched on to assist in this melancholy office, for he was a great friend of Mr. Akerman, the keeper of Newgate. Dr. Johnson never went to see Dr. Dodd. He said to me, "it would have done *him* more harm, than good to Dodd, who once expressed a desire to see him, but not earnestly."

Dr. Johnson, on the 20th of June, wrote the following letter:

To the Right Honourable
Charles Jenkinson[180]

Sir,

Since the conviction and condemnation to Dr. Dodd, I have had, by the intervention of a friend, some intercourse with him, and I am sure I shall lose nothing in your opinion by tenderness and commiseration. Whatever be the crime, it is not easy to have any knowledge of the delinquent, without a wish that his life may be spared; at least when no life has been taken away by him. I will, therefore, take the liberty of suggesting some reasons for which I wish this unhappy being to escape the utmost rigour of his sentence.

He is, so far as I can recollect, the first clergyman of our church who has suffered publick execution for immorality; and I know not whether it would not be more for the interest of religion to bury such an offender in the obscurity of perpetual exile, than to expose him in a cart, and on the gallows, to all who for any reason are enemies to the clergy.

The supreme power has, in all ages, paid some attention to the voice of the people; and that voice does not least deserve to be heard, when it calls out for mercy. There is now a very general desire that Dodd's life should be spared. More is not wished; and, perhaps, this is not too much to be granted.

If you, Sir, have any opportunity of enforcing these reasons, you may, perhaps, think them worthy of consideration: but whatever you determine, I most respectfully intreat that you will be pleased to pardon for this intrusion, Sir,

Your most obedient
And most humble servant,
Sam. Johnson.

It has been confidently circulated, with invidious remarks, that to this letter no attention whatever was paid by Mr. Jenkinson, now Lord Hawkesbury; and that he did not even deign to shew the common civility of owning the receipt of it. I could not but wonder at such conduct in the noble Lord, whose own character and just elevation in life, I thought, must have impressed him with all due regard for great abilities and attainments. As the story had been much talked of, and apparently from good authority, I could not but have animadverted upon it in this work, had it been as was alledged; but from my earnest love of truth, and having found reason to think that there might be a mistake,

---

[180] Charles Jenkinson (1727–1808), first Baron Hawkesbury and first Earl of Liverpool, a politician with whom Johnson had had dealings a few years earlier and whose help apparently he thought might be available.

I presumed to write to his Lordship, requesting an explanation; and it is with the sincerest pleasure that I am enabled to assure the world, that there is no foundation for it, the fact being, that owing to some neglect, or accident, Johnson's letter never came to Lord Hawkesbury's hands. I should have thought it strange indeed, if that noble Lord had undervalued my illustrious friend; but instead of this being the case, his Lordship, in the very polite answer with which he was pleased immediately to honour me, thus expresses himself:—"I have always respected the memory of Dr. Johnson, and admire his writings; and I frequently read many parts of them with pleasure and great improvement."

All applications for the Royal Mercy having failed, Dr. Dodd prepared himself for death; and, with a warmth of gratitude, wrote to Dr. Johnson as follows:

June 25, Midnight.

Accept, thou *great* and *good* heart, my earnest and fervent thanks and prayers for all thy benevolent and kind efforts in my behalf.—Oh! Dr. Johnson! as I sought your knowledge at an early hour in life, would to heaven I had cultivated the love and acquaintance of so excellent a man!—I pray GOD most sincerely to bless you with the highest transports—the infelt satisfaction of *humane* and benevolent exertions!—And admitted, as I trust I shall be, to the realms of bliss before you, I shall hail *your* arrival there with transport, and rejoice to acknowledge that you was my Comforter, my Advocate and my *Friend!* GOD *be ever* with *you!*

Dr. Johnson lastly wrote to Dr. Dodd this solemn and soothing letter:

To the Reverend Dr. Dodd

Dear Sir,

That which is appointed to all men is now coming upon you. Outward circumstances, the eyes and the thoughts of men, are below the notice of an immortal being about to stand the trial for eternity, before the Supreme Judge of heaven and earth. Be comforted: your crime, morally or religiously considered, has no very deep dye of turpitude. It corrupted no man's principles; it attacked no man's life. It involved only a temporary and reparable injury. Of this, and of all other sins, you are earnestly to repent; and may GOD, who knoweth our frailty, and desireth not our death, accept your repentance, for the sake of his Son JESUS CHRIST our Lord.

In requital of those well-intended offices which you are pleased so emphatically to acknowledge, let me beg that you make in your devotions one petition for my eternal welfare. I am, dear Sir,

Your affectionate servant,
Sam. Johnson.
June 26, 1777.

Under the copy of this letter I found written, in Johnson's own hand, "Next day, June 27, he was executed."

To conclude this interesting episode with an useful application, let us now attend to the reflections of Johnson at the end of the "Occasional Papers," concerning the unfortunate Dr. Dodd.— Such were the last thoughts of a man whom we have seen exulting in popularity, and sunk in shame. For his reputation, which no man can give to himself, those who conferred it are to answer. Of his publick ministry the means of judging were sufficiently attainable. He must be allowed to preach well, whose sermons strike his audience with forcible conviction. Of his life, those who thought it consistent with his doctrine, did not originally form false notions. He was at first what he endeavoured to make others; but the world broke down his resolution, and he in time ceased to exemplify his own instructions.

"Let those who are tempted to his faults, tremble at his punishment; and those whom he impressed from the pulpit with religious sentiments, endeavour to confirm them, by considering the regret and self-abhorrence with which he reviewed in prison his deviations from rectitude."

Johnson gave us this evening, in his happy discriminative manner, a portrait of the late Mr. Fitzherbert,[181] of Derbyshire. "There was (said he) no sparkle, no brilliancy in Fitzherbert; but I never knew a man who was so generally acceptable. He made every body quite easy, overpowered nobody by the superiority of his talents, made no man think worse of himself by being his rival, seemed always to listen, did not oblige you to hear much from him, and did not oppose what you said. Every body liked him; but he had no friend, as I understand the word, nobody with whom he exchanged intimate thoughts. People were willing to think well of every thing about him. A gentleman was making an affected rant, as many people do, of great feelings about 'his dear son,' who was at school near London; how anxious he was lest he might be ill, and what he would give to see him. 'Can't you (said Fitzherbert) take a post-chaise and go to him?' This, to be sure, *finished* the affected man, but there was not much in it. However this was circulated as wit for a whole winter, and I believe part of a summer too; a proof that he was no very witty man. He was an instance of the truth of the observation, that a man will please more upon the whole by negative qualities than by positive; by never offending, than by giving a great deal of delight. In the first place, men hate more steadily than they love; and if I have said something to hurt a man once, I shall not get the better of this, by saying many things to please him."

Tuesday, September 16, Dr. Johnson having mentioned to me the extraordinary size and price of some cattle reared by Dr. Taylor, I rode out with our host, surveyed his farm, and was shown one cow which he had sold for a hundred and twenty guineas, and another for which he had been offered a hundred and thirty. Taylor thus described to me his old schoolfellow and friend, Johnson: "He is a man of a very clear head, great power of words, and a very gay imagination; but there is no disputing with him. He will not hear you, and having a louder voice than you, must roar you down."

In the afternoon I tried to get Dr. Johnson to like the Poems of Mr. Hamilton of Bangour,[182] which I had brought with me: I had been much pleased with them at a very early age; the impression still remained on my mind: it was confirmed by the opinion of my friend the Honourable Andrew Erskine,[183] himself both a good poet and a good critick, who thought Hamilton as true a poet as ever wrote, and that his not having fame was unaccountable. Johnson, upon repeated occasions, while I was at Ashbourne, talked slightingly of Hamilton. He said there was no power of thinking in his verses, nothing that strikes one, nothing better than what you generally find in magazines; and that the highest praise they deserved was, that they were very well for a gentleman to hand about among his friends. He said the imitation of *Ne sit ancillæ tibi amor*,[184] &c. was too solemn; he read part of it at the beginning. He read the beautiful pathetick song, "Ah the poor shepherd's mournful fate," and did not seem to give attention to what I had been used to think tender elegant strains, but laughed at the rhyme, in Scotch pronunciation, *wishes* and *blushes*, reading *wushes*—and there he stopped. He owned that the epitaph on Lord Newhall was pretty well done. He read the "Inscription in a Summer-house," and a little of the imitations of Horace's Epistles; but said, he found nothing to make him desire to read on. When I urged that there were some good poetical passages in the book, "Where (said he) will you find so large

---

[181] William Fitzherbert (1712–1772), a Member of Parliament who had once defended Johnson in Parliament as "my friend . . . a pattern of morality."

[182] Hamilton's poetry (see note 29) had been edited by Adam Smith in 1748.

[183] In 1763, Erskine and Boswell had published a volume of their correspondence with one another.

[184] Horace, *Odes,* II, 4.

a collection without some?" I thought the description of Winter might obtain his approbation:

See Winter, from the frozen north,
Drives his iron chariot forth!
His grisly hand in icy chains
Fair Tweeda's silver flood constrains, &c.

He asked why an *"iron* chariot?" and said "icy chains" was an old image. I was struck with the uncertainty of taste, and somewhat sorry that a poet whom I had long read with fondness, was not approved by Dr. Johnson. I comforted myself with thinking that the beauties were too delicate for his robust perceptions. Garrick maintained that he had not a taste for the finest productions of genius: but I was sensible, that when he took the trouble to analyse critically, he generally convinced us that he was right.

In the evening, the Reverend Mr. Seward,[185] of Lichfield, who was passing through Ashbourne in his way home, drank tea with us. Johnson described him thus:—"Sir, his ambition is to be a fine talker; so he goes to Buxton, and such places, where he may find companies to listen to him. And, Sir, he is a valetudinarian, one of those who are always mending themselves. I do not know a more disagreeable character than a valetudinarian, who thinks he may do any thing that is for his ease, and indulges himself in the grossest freedoms: Sir, he brings himself to the state of a hog in a stye."

Dr. Taylor's nose happening to bleed, he said, it was because he had omitted to have himself blooded four days after a quarter of a year's interval. Dr. Johnson, who was a great dabbler in physick, disapproved much of periodical bleeding. "For (said he) you accustom yourself to an evacuation which Nature cannot perform of herself, and therefore she cannot help you, should you, from forgetfulness or any other cause, omit it; so you may be suddenly suffocated. You may accustom yourself to other periodical evacuations, because should you omit them, Nature can supply the omission; but Nature cannot open a vein to blood you."—"I do not like to take an emetick, (said Taylor,) for fear of breaking some small vessels."—"Poh! (said Johnson) if you have so many things that will break, you had better break your neck at once, and there's an end on't. You will break no small vessels." (blowing with high derision.)

I mentioned to Dr. Johnson, that David Hume's persisting in his infidelity, when he was dying, shocked me much.[186] JOHNSON. "Why should it shock you, Sir? Hume owned he had never read the New Testament with attention. Here then was a man who had been at no pains to inquire into the truth of religion, and had continually turned his mind the other way. It was not to be expected that the prospect of death would alter his way of thinking, unless GOD should send an angel to set him right." I said, I had reason to believe that the thought of annihilation gave Hume no pain. JOHNSON. "It was not so, Sir. He had a vanity in being thought easy. It is more probable that he should assume an appearance of ease, than that so very improbable a thing should be, as a man not afraid of going (as, in spite of his delusive theory, he cannot be sure but he may go,) into an unknown state, and not being uneasy at leaving all he knew. And you are to consider, that upon his own principle of annihilation he had no motive to speak the truth." The horrour of death which I had always observed in Dr. Johnson, appeared strong to-night. I ventured to tell him, that I had been, for moments of my life, not afraid of death; therefore I could suppose another man in that state of

---

[185] Thomas Seward (1708–1790), Canon of Lichfield, whom Boswell had met a year earlier and described as "a genteel well-bred dignified clergyman" and "an ingenious and literary man"; he was the father of Anna Seward, "the Swan of Lichfield," a poetess.

[186] A few weeks before the death of the philosopher David Hume, in the summer of 1776, Boswell had interviewed him and recorded in his journal that Hume believed "it was a most unreasonable fancy that we should exist for ever" (*Boswell Papers,* XII, 232).

mind for a considerable space of time. He said, "he never had a moment in which death was not terrible to him." He added, that it had been observed, that almost no man dies in publick, but with apparent resolution; from that desire of praise which never quits us. I said, Dr. Dodd seemed to be willing to die, and full of hopes of happiness. "Sir, (said he,) Dr. Dodd would have given both his hands and both his legs to have lived. The better a man is, the more afraid is he of death, having a clearer view of infinite purity." He owned, that our being in an unhappy uncertainty as to our salvation, was mysterious; and said, "Ah! we must wait till we are in another state of being, to have many things explained to us." Even the powerful mind of Johnson seemed foiled by futurity. But I thought, that the gloom of uncertainty in solemn religious speculation, being mingled with hope, was yet more consolatory than the emptiness of infidelity. A man can live in thick air, but perishes in an exhausted receiver.[187]

Dr. Johnson was much pleased with a remark which I told him was made to me by General Paoli:[188]—"That it is impossible not to be afraid of death; and that those who at the time of dying are not afraid, are not thinking of death, but of applause, or something else, which keeps death out of their sight: so that all men are equally afraid of death when they see it; only some have a power of turning their sight away from it better than others."

On Wednesday, September 17, Dr. Butter,[189] physician at Derby, drank tea with us; and it was settled that Dr. Johnson and I should go on Friday and dine with him. Johnson said, "I'm glad of this." He seemed weary of the uniformity of life at Dr. Taylor's.

Talking of biography, I said, in writing a life a man's peculiarities should be mentioned because they mark his character. JOHNSON. "Sir, there is no doubt as to peculiarities: the question is, whether a man's vices should be mentioned; for instance, whether it should be mentioned that Addison and Parnell[190] drank too freely: for people will probably more easily indulge in drinking from knowing this; so that more ill may be done by the example, than good by telling the whole truth." Here was an instance of his varying from himself in talk; for when Lord Hailes and he sat one morning calmly conversing in my house at Edinburgh, I well remember that Dr. Johnson maintained, that "If a man is to write *A Panegyrick,* he may keep vices out of sight; but if he professes to write *A Life,* he must represent it really as it was:" and when I objected to the danger of telling that Parnell drank to excess, he said, that "it would produce an instructive caution to avoid drinking, when it was seen, that even the learning and genius of Parnell could be debased by it." And in the Hebrides he maintained, as appears from my "Journal," that a man's intimate friend should mention his faults, if he writes his life.

He had this evening, partly, I suppose, from the spirit of contradiction to his Whig friend, a violent argument with Dr. Taylor, as to the inclinations of the people of England at this time towards the Royal Family of Stuart. He grew so outrageous as to say, "that, if England were fairly polled, the present King would be sent away to-night, and his adherents hanged to-morrow." Taylor, who was as violent a Whig as Johnson was a Tory, was roused by this to a pitch of bellowing. He denied, loudly, what Johnson said; and maintained, that there was an abhorrence against the Stuart family, though he admitted that the people were not much attached to the present King. JOHNSON. "Sir, the state of the country is this: the people knowing it to be agreed on all hands that this King has not the hereditary right to the crown, and there being no

---

[187] i.e., a vacuum.

[188] Pasquale di Paoli (1725–1807), Corsican general and patriot, whom Boswell had visited on the Grand Tour and for whose cause he had raised help in England.

[189] William Butter (1726–1805), who was to attend Johnson in his last illness.

[190] Joseph Addison (1672–1719) and Thomas Parnell (1679–1718), poets and essayists.

hope that he who has it can be restored, have grown cold and indifferent upon the subject of loyalty, and have no warm attachment to any King. They would not, therefore, risk any thing to restore the exiled family. They would not give twenty shillings a piece to bring it about. But, if a mere vote could do it, there would be twenty to one; at least, there would be a very great majority of voices for it. For, Sir, you are to consider, that all those who think a King has a right to his crown, as a man has to his estate, which is the just opinion, would be for restoring the King who certainly has the hereditary right, could he be trusted with it; in which there would be no danger now, when laws and every thing else are so much advanced; and every King will govern by the laws. And you must also consider, Sir, that there is nothing on the other side to oppose to this; for it is not alledged by any one that the present family has any inherent right: so that the Whigs could not have a contest between two rights."

Dr. Taylor admitted, that if the question as to hereditary right were to be tried by a poll of the people of England, to be sure the abstract doctrine would be given in favour of the family of Stuart; but he said, the conduct of that family, which occasioned their expulsion, was so fresh in the minds of the people, that they would not vote for a restoration. Dr. Johnson, I think, was contented with the admission as to the hereditary right, leaving the original point in dispute, viz. what the people upon the whole would do, taking in right and affection; for he said, people were afraid of a change, even though they think it right. Dr. Taylor said something of the slight foundation of the hereditary right of the house of Stuart. "Sir, (said Johnson,) the house of Stuart succeeded to the full right of both the houses of York and Lancaster, whose common source had the undisputed right. A right to a throne is like a right to any thing else. Possession is sufficient, where no better right can be shown. This was

the case with the Royal Family of England, as it is now with the King of France: for as to the first beginning of the right, we are in the dark."

Thursday, September 18. Last night Dr. Johnson had proposed that the crystal lustre, or chandelier, in Dr. Taylor's large room, should be lighted up some time or other. Taylor said, it should be lighted up next night. "That will do very well, (said I,) for it is Dr. Johnson's birth-day." When we were in the Isle of Sky, Johnson had desired me not to mention his birth-day. He did not seem pleased at this time that I mentioned it, and said (somewhat sternly) "he would *not* have the lustre lighted the next night."

Some ladies, who had been present yesterday when I mentioned his birth-day, came to dinner to-day, and plagued him unintentionally, by wishing him joy. I know not why he disliked having his birth-day mentioned, unless it were that it reminded him of his approaching nearer to death, of which he had a constant dread.

I mentioned to him a friend of mine who was formerly gloomy from low spirits, and much distressed by the fear of death, but was now uniformly placid, and contemplated his dissolution without any perturbation. "Sir, (said Johnson,) this is only a disordered imagination taking a different turn."

We talked of a collection being made of all the English Poets who had published a volume of poems. Johnson told me, "that a Mr. Coxeter,[191] whom he knew, had gone the greatest length towards this; having collected, I think, about five hundred volumes of poets whose works were little known; but that upon his death Tom Osborne[192] bought them, and they were dispersed, which he thought a pity, as it was curious to see any series complete; and in every volume of poems something good may be found."

He observed, that a gentleman of eminence in literature had got into a bad style of poetry of late. "He puts (said

---

191 Thomas Coxeter (1689–1747), an antiquarian.

192 A bookseller; see note 120 above.

he) a very common thing in a strange dress till he does not know it himself, and thinks other people do not know it." BOSWELL. "That is owing to his being so much versant in old English Poetry." JOHNSON. "What is that to the purpose, Sir? If I say a man is drunk, and you tell me it is owing to his taking much drink, the matter is not mended. No, Sir, ——[193] has taken to an odd mode. For example; he'd write thus:

Hermit hoar, in solemn cell,
Wearing out life's evening gray.

"*Gray evening* is common enough; but *evening gray* he'd think fine.—Stay;—we'll make out the stanza:

Hermit hoar, in solemn cell,
    Wearing out life's evening gray;
Smite thy bosom, sage, and tell,
    What is bliss? and which the way?"

BOSWELL. "But why smite his bosom, Sir?" JOHNSON. "Why to shew he was in earnest," (smiling).—He at an after period added the following stanza:

Thus I spoke; and speaking sigh'd;
    —Scarce repress'd the starting tear;—
When the smiling sage reply'd—
    —Come, my lad, and drink some beer.

I cannot help thinking the first stanza very good solemn poetry, as also the three first lines of the second. Its last line is an excellent burlesque surprize on gloomy sentimental enquirers. And, perhaps, the advice is as good as can be given to a low-spirited dissatisfied being.—"Don't trouble your head with sickly thinking: take a cup, and be merry."

Friday, September 19, after breakfast, Dr. Johnson and I set out in Dr. Taylor's chaise to go to Derby. The day was fine, and we resolved to go by Keddlestone, the seat of Lord Scarsdale,[194] that I might see his Lordship's fine house. I was struck with the magnificence of the building; and the extensive park, with the finest verdure, covered with deer, and cattle, and sheep, delighted me. The number of old oaks, of an immense size, filled me with a sort of respectful admiration: for one of them sixty pounds was offered. The excellent smooth gravel roads; the large piece of water formed by his Lordship from some small brooks, with a handsome barge upon it; the venerable Gothick church, now the family chapel, just by the house; in short, the grand groupe of objects agitated and distended my mind in a most agreeable manner. "One should think (said I) that the proprietor of all this *must* be happy."—"Nay, Sir, (said Johnson,) all this excludes but one evil—poverty."

Our names were sent up, and a well-drest elderly house-keeper, a most distinct articulator, shewed us the house; which I need not describe, as there is an account of it published in "Adam's Works in Architecture." Dr. Johnson thought better of it to-day than when he saw it before; for he had lately attacked it violently, saying, "It would do excellently for a town-hall. The large room with the pillars (said he) would do for the Judges to sit in at the assizes; the circular room for a jury chamber; and the room above for prisoners." Still he thought the large room ill lighted, and of no use but for dancing in; and the bed-chambers but indifferent rooms; and that the immense sum which it cost was injudiciously laid out. Dr. Taylor had put him in mind of his *appearing* pleased with the house. "But (said he) that was when Lord Scarsdale was present. Politeness obliges us to appear pleased with a man's works when he is present. No man will be so ill bred as to question you. You may therefore pay compliments without saying what is not true. I should say to Lord Scarsdale of his large room, 'My Lord, this is the most *costly* room that I ever saw;' which is true."

Dr. Manningham,[195] physician in

---

[193] Probably Thomas Warton, the younger, who had just published a volume of poems; one of his lines ends with "evening chill."
[194] Nathaniel Curzon (1726–1804), first

Baron Scarsdale; Kedleston House had been designed by the famous architect Robert Adam and construction begun in 1761.
[195] Thomas Manningham (d. 1794).

London, who was visiting at Lord Scarsdale's, accompanied us through many of the rooms, and soon afterwards my Lord himself, to whom Dr. Johnson was known, appeared, and did the honours of the house. We talked of Mr. Langton. Johnson, with a warm vehemence of affectionate regard, exclaimed, "The earth does not bear a worthier man than Bennet Langton." We saw a good many fine pictures, which I think are described in one of "Young's Tours."[196] There is a printed catalogue of them which the housekeeper put into my hand; I should like to view them at leisure. I was much struck with Daniel interpreting Nebuchadnezzar's dream by Rembrandt. We were shown a pretty large library. In his Lordship's dressing-room lay Johnson's small Dictionary: he shewed it to me, with some eagerness, saying, "Look'ye! *Quae terra nostri non plena laboris.*"[197] He observed, also, Goldsmith's "Animated Nature;"[198] and said, "Here's our friend! The poor Doctor would have been happy to hear of this."

In our way, Johnson strongly expressed his love of driving fast in a post-chaise. "If (said he) I had no duties, and no reference to futurity, I would spend my life in driving briskly in a post-chaise with a pretty woman; but she should be one who could understand me, and would add something to the conversation." I observed, that we were this day to stop just where the Highland army did in 1745.[199] JOHNSON. "It was a noble attempt." BOSWELL. "I wish we could have an authentick history of it." JOHNSON. "If you were not an idle dog you might write it, by collecting from every body what they can tell, and putting down your authorities." BOSWELL. "But I could not have

the advantage of it in my lifetime." JOHNSON. "You might have the satisfaction of its fame, by printing it in Holland; and as to profit, consider how long it was before writing came to be considered in a pecuniary view. Baretti[200] says, he is the first man that ever received copy-money in Italy." I said that I would endeavour to do what Dr. Johnson suggested; and I thought that I might write so as to venture to publish my "History of the Civil War in Great-Britain in 1745 and 1746," without being obliged to go to a foreign press.

When we arrived at Derby, Dr. Butter accompanied us to see the manufactory of china there. I admired the ingenuity and delicate art with which a man fashioned clay into a cup, a saucer, or a tea-pot, while a boy turned round a wheel to give the mass rotundity. I thought this as excellent in its species of power, as making good verses in *its* species. Yet I had no respect for this potter. Neither, indeed, has a man of any extent of thinking for a mere versemaker, in whose numbers, however perfect, there is no poetry, no mind. The china was beautiful, but Dr. Johnson justly observed it was too dear; for that he could have vessels of silver, of the same size, as cheap as what were here made of porcelain.

I felt a pleasure in walking about Derby such as I always have in walking about any town to which I am not accustomed. There is an immediate sensation of novelty; and one speculates on the way in which life is passed in it, which, although there is a sameness every where upon the whole, is yet minutely diversified. The minute diversities in every thing are wonderful. Talking of shaving the other night at Dr. Taylor's,

---

[196] Boswell was wrong about this reference, if he meant Arthur Young's *Six Months' Tour through the North of England* (1770–1771), as he was about Kedleston being described in Adam's *Works in Architecture;* Kedleston is described in *Vitruvius Britannicus* (1767) and the pictures in Pilkington's *View of the Present State of Derbyshire* (1789).

[197] "Where on earth may not our work be found?" (Vergil, *Aeneid*, I, 460).

[198] *An History of the Earth and Animated Nature* (1774); Goldsmith had died in the year of its publication.

[199] The army of ill-fated Jacobites had stopped at Derby.

[200] Guiseppe Baretti (1719–1789), an Italian writer who had come to England in 1751 and formed an acquaintance with Johnson.

Dr. Johnson said, "Sir, of a thousand shavers, two do not shave so much alike as not to be distinguished." I thought this not possible, till he specified so many of the varieties in shaving;—holding the razor more or less perpendicular;—drawing long or short strokes;—beginning at the upper part of the face, or the under;—at the right side or the left side. Indeed, when one considers what variety of sounds can be uttered by the wind-pipe, in the compass of a very small aperture, we may be convinced how many degrees of difference there may be in the application of a razor.

We dined with Dr. Butter, whose lady is daughter of my cousin Sir John Douglas, whose grandson is now presumptive heir of the noble family of Queensberry. Johnson and he had a good deal of medical conversation. Johnson said, he had somewhere or other given an account of Dr. Nichols's discourse "*De Animâ Medicâ*."[201] He told us "that whatever a man's distemper was, Dr. Nichols would not attend him as a physician, if his mind was not at ease; for he believed that no medicines would have any influence. He once attended a man in trade, upon whom he found none of the medicines he prescribed had any

effect; he asked the man's wife privately whether his affairs were not in a bad way? She said no. He continued his attendance some time, still without success. At length the man's wife told him, she had discovered that her husband's affairs *were* in a bad way. When Goldsmith was dying, Dr. Turton[202] said to him, 'Your pulse is in greater disorder than it should be, from the degree of fever which you have: is your mind at ease?' Goldsmith answered it was not."

After dinner, Mrs. Butter went with me to see the silk-mill which Mr. John Lombe had had a patent for, having brought away the contrivance from Italy.[203] I am not very conversant with mechanicks; but the simplicity of this machine, and its multiplied operations, struck me with an agreeable surprize. I had learnt from Dr. Johnson, during this interview, not to think with a dejected indifference of the works of art, and the pleasures of life, because life is uncertain and short; but to consider such indifference as a failure of reason, a morbidness of mind; for happiness should be cultivated as much as we can, and the objects which are instrumental to it should be steadily considered as of importance, with a reference not only to

---

[201] Frank Nicholls, physician to George III; his medical treatise appeared first in 1750.

[202] Dr. John Turton (1735–1806).

[203] "This Town [Derby] has a Curiosity to boast of, perhaps the only one in the three Kingdoms, *viz.* a Machine erected in 1734, by the late Sir *Thomas Lambe,* for the Manufactury of Silk, which he brought from *Italy* at the Hazard of his Life: It is a Mill, in an Island of the *Derwent,* which works the three Capital Engines for making Arganzine, or thrown Silk; by which Invention, one Hand will twist as much Silk as before could be done by fifty, and that in a truer and better Manner. This Engine contains 26586 Wheels, and 97746 Movements, which work 73726 Yards of Silk-thread every Time the Water-wheel goes round, which is 3 Times in a Minute, and 318, 504, 960 Yards in one Day and Night. One Water-wheel gives Motion to all the rest of the Wheels and Movements, of which, any one may be stopped separately: One Fire-engine likewise conveys warm Air to every individual Part of the Machine, and the whole Work is governed by one Regulator. The House which contains this Engine is 5 or 6 Stories high, and half a Quarter of a Mile in Length. This Machine was thought of such Importance to this Kingdom, that the Legislature voted, by the Parliament, 14000 *l.* as a Reward to Sir *Thomas* for the Expence and Risque he had run, especially, as during his 14 Year's Patent, it had been of very little Advantage to him, partly through the King of *Sardinia's* prohibiting any Silk to be imported into his Dominions that had been manufactured by such a Machine, and likewise from the great Expence attending it, and the extraordinary Skill and Attention requisite to the conducting it" (Benjamin Martin, *The Natural History of England,* 1763, II, 231). In the first edition of the *Life* Boswell had spoken of Sir Thomas Lombe as the owner of the patent, but substituted Mr. John Lombe in the second edition.

ourselves, but to multitudes in successive ages. Though it is proper to value small parts, as

Sands make the mountain, moments make the year;[204]

yet we must contemplate, collectively, to have a just estimation of objects. One moment's being uneasy or not, seems of no consequence; yet this may be thought of the next, and the next, and so on, till there is a large portion of misery. In the same way one must think of happiness, of learning, of friendship. We cannot tell the precise moment when friendship is formed. As in filling a vessel drop by drop there is at last a drop which makes it run over; so in a series of kindnesses there is at last one which makes the heart run over. We must not divide objects of our attention into minute parts, and think separately of each part. It is by contemplating a large mass of human existence, that a man, while he sets a just value on his own life, does not think of his death as annihilating all that is great and pleasing in the world, as if actually *contained in his mind,* according to Berkeley's reverie.[205] If his imagination be not sickly and feeble, it "wings its distant way" far beyond himself, and views the world in unceasing activity of every sort. It must be acknowledged, however, that Pope's plaintive reflection, that all things would be as gay as ever, on the day of his death, is natural and common. We are apt to transfer to all around us our own gloom, without considering that at any given point of time there is, perhaps, as much youth and gaiety in the world as at another. Before I came into this life, in which I have had so many pleasant scenes, have not thousands and ten thousands of deaths and funerals happened, and have not families been in grief for their nearest relations? But have those dismal circumstances at all affected *me?* Why then should the gloomy scenes which I experience, or which I know, affect others? Let us guard against imagining that there is an end of felicity upon earth, when we ourselves grow old, or are unhappy.

Dr. Johnson told us at tea, that when some of Dr. Dodd's pious friends were trying to console him by saying that he was going to leave "a wretched world," he had honesty enough not to join in the cant:—"No, no (said he,) it has been a very agreeable world to me." Johnson added, "I respect Dodd for thus speaking the truth; for, to be sure, he had for several years enjoyed a life of great voluptuousness."

He told us, that Dodd's city friends stood by him so, that a thousand pounds were ready to be given to the gaoler, if he would let him escape. He added, that he knew a friend of Dodd's, who walked about Newgate for some time on the evening before the day of his execution, with five hundred pounds in his pocket, ready to be paid to any of the turnkeys who could get him out: but it was too late; for he was watched with much circumspection. He said, Dodd's friends had an image of him made of wax, which was to have been left in his place; and he believed it was carried into the prison.

Johnson disapproved of Dr. Dodd's leaving the world persuaded that "The Convict's Address to his unhappy Brethren," was of his own writing. "But, Sir, (said I,) you contributed to the deception, for when Mr. Seward[206] expressed a doubt to you that it was not Dodd's own, because it had a great deal more force of mind in it than any thing known to be his, you answered,—'Why should

---

[204] Think nought a *trifle,* though it small appear;

　　　Small sands the mountain, moments make the year,

　　　And trifles life.

(Edward Young, *The Universal Passion,* VI, 205–207.)

The passage, following shortly one describing the spinning of "the subtle thread" (VI, 181),

possibly came to Boswell's mind while he inspected the spinning factory.

[205] George Berkeley (1685–1753), Irish philosopher; Boswell was impressed with what he spoke of on another occasion as "Berkeley's ingenious philosophy, that nothing exists but as perceived by some mind."

[206] William Seward (1747–1799), author of *Anecdotes of Some Distinguished Persons.*

you think so? Depend upon it, Sir, when a man knows he is to be hanged in a fortnight, it concentrates his mind wonderfully." JOHNSON. "Sir, as Dodd got it from me to pass as his own, while that could do him any good, there was an *implied promise* that I should not own it. To own it, therefore, would have been telling a lie, with the addition of breach of promise, which was worse than simply telling a lie to make it be believed it was Dodd's. Besides, Sir, I did not *directly* tell a lie: I left the matter uncertain. Perhaps I thought that Seward would not believe it the less to be mine for what I said; but I would not put it in his power to say I had owned it."

He praised Blair's sermons:[207] "Yet," said he, (willing to let us see he was aware that fashionable fame, however deserved, is not always the most lasting,) "perhaps, they may not be reprinted after seven years; at least not after Blair's death."

He said, "Goldsmith was a plant that flowered late. There appeared nothing remarkable about him when he was young; though when he had got high in fame, one of his friends began to recollect something of his being distinguished at College. Goldsmith in the same manner recollected more of that friend's early years, as he grew a greater man."

I mentioned that Lord Monboddo[208] told me, he awaked every morning at four, and then for his health got up and walked in his room naked, with the window open, which he called taking *an air bath;* after which he went to bed again, and slept two hours more. Johnson, who was always ready to beat down any thing that seemed to be exhibited with disproportionate importance, thus observed: "I suppose, Sir, there is no more in it than this, he awakes at four, and cannot sleep till he chills himself, and makes the warmth of the bed a grateful sensation."

I talked of the difficulty of rising in the morning. Dr. Johnson told me, "that the learned Mrs. Carter, at that period when she was eager in study, did not awake as early as she wished, and she therefore had a contrivance, that, at a certain hour, her chamber-light should burn a string to which a heavy weight was suspended, which then fell with a strong sudden noise: this roused her from sleep, and then she had no difficulty in getting up." But I said *that* was my difficulty; and wished there could be some medicine invented which would make one rise without pain, which I never did, unless after lying in bed a very long time. Perhaps there may be something in the stores of Nature which could do this. I have thought of a pulley to raise me gradually; but that would give me pain, as it would counteract my internal inclination. I would have something that can dissipate the *vis inertiae,*[209] and give elasticity to the muscles. As I imagine that the human body may be put, by the operation of other substances, into any state in which it has ever been; and as I have experienced a state in which rising from bed was not disagreeable, but easy, nay, sometimes agreeable; I suppose that this state may be produced, if we knew by what. We can heat the body, we can cool it; we can give it tension or relaxation; and surely it is possible to bring it into a state in which rising from bed will not be a pain.

Johnson observed, that "a man should take a sufficient quantity of sleep, which Dr. Mead[210] says is between seven and nine hours." I told him, that Dr. Cullen[211] said to me, that a man should not take more sleep than he can take at once. JOHNSON. "This rule, Sir, cannot hold in all cases; for many people have their sleep broken by sickness; and surely,

[207] The first volume of what eventually became a five-volume collection of *Sermons* by Hugh Blair (1718–1800), Professor of Literature at the University of Edinburgh, had just been published.
[208] Lord Monboddo, the Scottish jurist and author, was interested in primitive behavior.

[209] "[the restraining] power of inactivity."
[210] Richard Mead (1673–1754), a famous physician of London.
[211] William Cullen (1710–1790), Scottish physician, Professor of Physic at the University of Edinburgh, whom Johnson had met on his tour to the Hebrides.

Cullen would not have a man to get up, after having slept but an hour. Such a regimen would soon end in a *long sleep.*" Dr. Taylor remarked, I think very justly, that "a man who does not feel an inclination to sleep at the ordinary time, instead of being stronger than other people, must not be well; for a man in health has all the natural inclinations to eat, drink, and sleep, in a strong degree."

Johnson advised me to-night not to *refine* in the education of my children. "Life (said he) will not bear refinement: you must do as other people do."

As we drove back to Ashbourne, Dr. Johnson recommended to me, as he had often done, to drink water only: "For (said he) you are then sure not to get drunk; whereas if you drink wine you are never sure." I said, drinking wine was a pleasure which I was unwilling to give up. "Why, Sir, (said he,) there is no doubt that not to drink wine is a great deduction from life; but it may be necessary." He however owned, that in his opinion a free use of wine did not shorten life; and said, he would not give less for the life of a certain Scotch Lord (whom he named) celebrated for hard drinking, than for that of a sober man. "But stay, (said he, with his usual intelligence, and accuracy of enquiry,) does it take much wine to make him drunk?" I answered, "a great deal either of wine or strong punch."—"Then (said he) that is the worse." I presume to illustrate my friend's observation thus: "A fortress which soon surrenders has its walls less shattered, than when a long and obstinate resistance is made."

I ventured to mention a person who was as violent a Scotsman as he[212] was an Englishman; and literally had the same contempt for an Englishman compared with a Scotsman, that he had for a Scotsman compared with an Englishman; and that he would say of Dr. Johnson, "Damned rascal! to talk as he does of the Scotch." This seemed, for a moment,

"to give him pause."[213] It, perhaps, presented his extreme prejudice against the Scotch in a point of view somewhat new to him, by the effect of *contrast.*

By the time when we returned to Ashbourne, Dr. Taylor was gone to bed. Johnson and I sat up a long time by ourselves.

He was much diverted with an article which I shewed him in the "Critical Review"[214] of this year, giving an account of a curious publication, entitled, "A Spiritual Diary and Soliloquies, by John Rutty, M.D." Dr. Rutty was one of the people called Quakers, a physician of some eminence in Dublin, and authour of several works. This Diary, which was kept from 1753 to 1775, the year in which he died, and was now published in two volumes octavo, exhibited, in the simplicity of his heart, a minute and honest register of the state of his mind; which, though frequently laughable enough, was not more so than the history of many men would be, if recorded with equal fairness.

The following specimens were extracted by the Reviewers:

"Tenth month, 1753.

"23. Indulgence in bed an hour too long.

"Twelfth month, 17. An hypochondriack obnubilation[215] from wind and indigestion.

"Ninth month, 28. An over-dose of whisky.

"29. A dull, cross, cholerick day.

"First month, 1757—22. A little swinish at dinner and repast.

"31. Dogged on provocation.

"Second month, 5. Very dogged or snappish.

"14. Snappish on fasting.

"26. Cursed snappishness to those under me, on a bodily indisposition.

"Third month, 11. On a provocation, exercised a dumb resentment for two days, instead of scolding.

"22. Scolded too vehemently.

---

212 i.e., Dr. Johnson.
213 Boswell's adaptation of Hamlet's "must give us pause" (III, i, 130).

214 *The Critical Review,* an important monthly literary magazine begun in 1756 with the assistance of the novelist Tobias Smollett.
215 i.e., a morbid depression of spirits.

"23. Dogged again.

"Fourth month, 29. Mechanically and sinfully dogged."

Johnson laughed heartily at this good Quietist's[216] self-condemning minutes; particularly at his mentioning, with such a serious regret, occasional instances of *"swinishness* in eating, and *doggedness of temper."* He thought the observations of the Critical Reviewers upon the importance of a man to himself so ingenious and so well expressed, that I shall here introduce them.

After observing, that "There are few writers who have gained any reputation by recording their own actions," they say,

"We may reduce the egotists to four classes. In the *first* we have Julius Caesar: he relates his own transactions; but he relates them with peculiar grace and dignity, and his narrative is supported by the greatness of his character and atchievements. In the *second* class we have Marcus Antoninus: this writer has given us a series of reflections on his own life; but his sentiments are so noble, his morality so sublime, that his meditations are universally admired. In the *third* class we have some others of tolerable credit, who have given importance to their own private history by an intermixture of literary anecdotes, and the occurrences of their own times: the celebrated *Huetius*[217] has published an entertaining volume upon this plan, *'De rebus ad eum pertinentibus.'* In the *fourth* class we have the journalists, temporal and spiritual: Elias Ashmole,[218] William Lilly,[219] George Whitefield, John Wesley,[220] and a thousand other old women and fanatick writers of memoirs and meditations."

I mentioned to him that Dr. Hugh Blair, in his lectures on Rhetorick and Belles Lettres, which I heard him deliver at Edinburgh, had animadverted on the Johnsonian style as too pompous; and attempted to imitate it, by giving a sentence of Addison in "The Spectator," No. 411, in the manner of Johnson. When treating of the utility of the pleasures of imagination in preserving us from vice, it is observed of those "who know not how to be idle and innocent," that "their very first step out of business is into vice or folly;" which Dr. Blair supposed would have been expressed in "The Rambler," thus: "Their very first step out of the regions of business is into the perturbation of vice, or the vacuity of folly." JOHNSON. "Sir, these are not the words I should have used. No, Sir; the imitators of my style have not hit it. Miss Aikin[221] has done it the best; for she has imitated the sentiment as well as the diction."

I intend, before this work is concluded, to exhibit specimens of imitation of my friend's style in various modes; some caricaturing or mimicking it, and some formed upon it, whether intentionally or with a degree of similarity to it, of which, perhaps, the writers were not conscious.

In Baretti's Review, which he published in Italy, under the title of *"Frusta Letteraria,"*[222] it is observed, that Dr. Robertson the historian had formed his style upon that of *"Il celebre Samuele Johnson."* My friend himself was of that opinion; for he once said to me, in a pleasant humour, "Sir, if Robertson's style be faulty, he owes it to me; that is, having too many words, and those too big ones."

I read to him a letter which Lord Monboddo had written to me, contain-

---

[216] Quietism, which is associated with the Society of Friends, emphasizes self-discipline.

[217] Pierre Daniel Huet (1630–1721), French theologian.

[218] An English antiquarian (1617–1692), whose collections are housed in the Ashmolean Museum at Oxford.

[219] an English astrologer (1602–1681).

[220] Rev. George Whitefield (1714–1770) and John Wesley (1703–1791) were leaders in the Methodist movement.

[221] Anna Letitia Aikin (1743–1825), Mrs. Barbauld, teacher and author of children's books; Johnson alludes to her *Miscellaneous Pieces in Prose* (1773).

[222] The journal ran to 25 numbers, 1763–1765; Boswell's reference is to No. 9, in which the Scottish historian, William Robertson (1721–1793), is compared to Dr. Johnson.

ing some critical remarks upon the style of his "Journey to the Western Islands of Scotland." His Lordship praised the very fine passage upon landing at Icolm-kill; but his own style being exceedingly dry and hard, he disapproved of the richness of Johnson's language, and of his frequent use of metaphorical expressions. JOHNSON. "Why, Sir, this criticism would be just, if in my style, superfluous words, or words too big for the thoughts, could be pointed out; but this I do not believe can be done. For instance: in the passage which Lord Monboddo admires, 'We were now treading that illustrious region,' the word *illustrious,* contributes nothing to the mere narration; for the fact might be told without it: but it is not, therefore, superfluous; for it wakes the mind to peculiar attention, where something of more than usual importance is to be presented. 'Illustrious!'—for what? and then the sentence proceeds to expand the circumstances connected with Iona. And, Sir, as to metaphorical expression, that is a great excellence in style, when it is used with propriety, for it gives you two ideas for one;—conveys the meaning more luminously, and generally with a perception of delight."

He told me, that he had been asked to undertake the new edition of the *Biographia Britannica,*[223] but had declined it; which he afterwards said to me he regretted. In this regret many will join, because it would have procured us more of Johnson's most delightful species of writing; and although my friend Dr. Kippis[224] has hitherto discharged the task judiciously, distinctly, and with more impartiality than might have been expected from a Separatist,[225] it were to have been wished that the superintendance of this literary Temple of Fame, had been assigned to "a friend to the constitution in Church and State." We

should not then have had it too much crowded with obscure dissenting teachers, doubtless men of merit and worth, but not quite to be numbered amongst "the most eminent persons who have flourished in Great-Britain and Ireland."

On Saturday, September 20, after breakfast, when Taylor was gone out to his farm, Dr. Johnson and I had a serious conversation by ourselves on melancholy and madness; which he was, I always thought, erroneously inclined to confound together. Melancholy, like "great wit," may be "near allied to madness;"[226] but there is, in my opinion, a distinct separation between them. When he talked of madness, he was to be understood as speaking of those who were in any great degree disturbed, or as it is commonly expressed, "troubled in mind." Some of the ancient philosophers held, that all deviations from right reason were madness; and whoever wishes to see the opinions both of ancients and moderns upon this subject, collected and illustrated with a variety of curious facts, may read Dr. Arnold's very entertaining work.[227]

Johnson said, "A madman loves to be with people whom he fears; not as a dog fears the lash; but of whom he stands in awe." I was struck with the justice of this observation. To be with those of whom a person, whose mind is wavering and dejected, stands in awe, represses and composes an uneasy tumult of spirits, and consoles him with the contemplation of something steady, and at least comparatively great.

He added, "Madmen are all sensual in the lower stages of the distemper. They are eager for gratifications to sooth their minds, and divert their attention from the misery which they suffer: but when they grow very ill, pleasure is too

---

[223] The first edition had appeared in 1747.

[224] Andrew Kippis (1725–1795); his revision of the *Biographia Britannica* was published in the years 1778 to 1793.

[225] Member of a sect which withdrew from the Church of England on the grounds that it did not sufficiently maintain its Protestant character.

[226] Great Wits are sure to Madness near ally'd;
And thin Partitions do their Bounds divide.
(John Dryden, *Absalom and Achitophel,* ll. 162–163.)

[227] "'Observations on Insanity,' by Thomas Arnold, M.D. London, 1782" (Boswell).

weak for them, and they seek for pain. Employment, Sir, and hardships, prevent melancholy. I suppose in all our army in America there was not one man who went mad."

We entered seriously upon a question of much importance to me, which Johnson was pleased to consider with friendly attention. I had long complained to him that I felt myself discontented in Scotland, as too narrow a sphere, and that I wished to make my chief residence in London, the great scene of ambition, instruction, and amusement: a scene, which was to me, comparatively speaking, a heaven upon earth. JOHNSON. "Why, Sir, I never knew any one who had such a *gust* for London as you have; and I cannot blame you for your wish to live there: yet, Sir, were I in your father's place, I should not consent to your settling there; for I have the old feudal notions, and I should be afraid that Auchinleck would be deserted, as you would soon find it more desirable to have a country-seat in a better climate. I own, however, that to consider it as a *duty* to reside on a family estate is a prejudice; for we must consider, that working-people get employment equally, and the produce of land is sold equally, whether a great family resides at home or not; and if the rents of an estate be carried to London, they return again in the circulation of commerce; nay, Sir, we must perhaps allow, that carrying the rents to a distance is a good, because it contributes to that circulation. We must, however, allow, that a well-regulated great family may improve a neighbourhood in civility and elegance, and give an example of good order, virtue, and piety; and so its residence at home may be of much advantage. But if a great family be disorderly and vicious, its residence at home is very pernicious to a neighbourhood. There is not now the same inducement to live in the country as formerly; the pleasures of social life are much better enjoyed in town; and there is no longer in the country that

power and influence in proprietors of land which they had in old times, and which made the country so agreeable to them. The Laird of Auchinleck now is not near so great a man as the Laird of Auchinleck was a hundred years ago."

I told him, that one of my ancestors never went from home without being attended by thirty men on horseback. Johnson's shrewdness and spirit of enquiry were exerted upon every occasion. "Pray (said he,) how did your ancestor support his thirty men and thirty horses, when he went at a distance from home, in an age when there was hardly any money in circulation? I suggested the same difficulty to a friend, who mentioned Douglas's[228] going to the Holy Land with a numerous train of followers. Douglas could, no doubt, maintain followers enough while living upon his own lands, the produce of which supplied them with food; but he could not carry that food to the Holy Land; and as there was no commerce by which he could be supplied with money, how could he maintain them in foreign countries?"

I suggested a doubt, that if I were to reside in London, the exquisite zest with which I relished it in occasional visits might go off, and I might grow tired of it. JOHNSON. "Why, Sir, you find no man, at all intellectual, who is willing to leave London. No, Sir, when a man is tired of London, he is tired of life; for there is in London all that life can afford."

To obviate his apprehension, that by settling in London I might desert the seat of my ancestors, I assured him, that I had old feudal principles to a degree of enthusiasm; and that I felt all the *dulcedo* of the *natale solum*.[229] I reminded him, that the Laird of Auchinleck had an elegant house, in front of which he could ride ten miles forward upon his own territories, upon which he had upwards of six hundred people attached to him; that the family seat was rich in natural romantick beauties of

---

[228] Sir James Douglas (1286–?1330).
[229] "charm of the native soil" (Ovid, *Epis-* *tulae ex Ponto*, I, iii, 25).

rock, wood, and water; and that in my "morn of life" I had appropriated the finest descriptions in the ancient Classicks, to certain scenes there, which were thus associated in my mind. That when all this was considered, I should certainly pass a part of the year at home, and enjoy it the more from variety, and from bringing with me a share of the intellectual stores of the metropolis. He listened to all this, and kindly "hoped it might be as I now supposed."

He said, "A country gentleman should bring his lady to visit London as soon as he can, that they may have agreeable topicks for conversation when they are by themselves."

As I meditated trying my fortune in Westminster Hall,[230] our conversation turned upon the profession of the law in England. JOHNSON. "You must not indulge too sanguine hopes, should you be called to our bar. I was told, by a very sensible lawyer, that there are a great many chances against any man's success in the profession of the law; the candidates are so numerous, and those who get large practice so few. He said, it was by no means true that a man of good parts and application is sure of having business, though, he, indeed, allowed that if such a man could but appear in a few causes, his merit would be known, and he would get forward; but that the great risk was, that a man might pass half a life-time in the Courts, and never have an opportunity of shewing his abilities."

We talked of employment being absolutely necessary to preserve the mind from wearying and growing fretful, especially in those who have a tendency to melancholy; and I mentioned to him a saying which somebody had related of an American savage, who, when an European was expatiating on all the advantages of money, put this question: "Will it purchase *occupation?*" JOHNSON. "Depend upon it, Sir, this saying is too refined for a savage. And, Sir, money *will* purchase occupation; it will purchase all the conveniences of life; it will purchase variety of company; it will purchase all sorts of entertainment."

I talked to him of Forster's "Voyage to the South Seas,"[231] which pleased me; but I found he did not like it. "Sir, (said he,) there is a great affectation of fine writing in it." BOSWELL. "But he carries you along with him." JOHNSON. "No, Sir; he does not carry *me* along with him: he leaves me behind him: or rather, indeed, he sets me before him; for he makes me turn over many leaves at a time."

On Sunday, September 21, we went to the church of Ashbourne, which is one of the largest and most luminous that I have seen in any town of the same size. I felt great satisfaction in considering that I was supported in my fondness of solemn publick worship by the general concurrence and munificence of mankind.

Johnson and Taylor were so different from each other, that I wondered at their preserving an intimacy. Their having been at school and college together, might, in some degree, account for this; but Sir Joshua Reynolds has furnished me with a stronger reason; for Johnson mentioned to him, that he had been told by Taylor he was to be his heir. I shall not take upon me to animadvert upon this; but certain it is, that Johnson paid great attention to Taylor. He now, however, said to me, "Sir, I love him; but I do not love him more; my regard for him does not increase. As it is said in the Apocrypha, 'his talk is of bullocks:'[232] I do not suppose he is very fond of my company. His habits are by

230 "Here are always held, since *Henry* the IIId, at the four Terms of the Year, the three great Courts of Chancery, King's Bench, and Common Pleas" (Benjamin Martin, *The Natural History of England*, 1763, II, 311).

231 *Voyage round the World* (1777) by George Forster (1754–1794), a naturalist who accompanied Captain James Cook on his second voyage.

232 "Ecclesiasticus, chap. xxxviii. v. 25. The whole chapter may be read as an admirable illustration of the superiority of cultivated minds over the gross and illiterate" (Boswell).

no means sufficiently clerical: this he knows that I see; and no man likes to live under the eye of perpetual disapprobation."

I have no doubt that a good many sermons were composed for Taylor by Johnson. At this time I found, upon his table, a part of one which he had newly begun to write: and *Concio pro Tayloro* appears in one of his diaries. When to these circumstances we add the internal evidence from the power of thinking and style, in the collection which the Reverend Mr. Hayes has published, with the *significant* title of "Sermons *left for publication* by the Reverend John Taylor, LL.D." our conviction will be complete.[233]

I, however, would not have it thought, that Dr. Taylor, though he could not write like Johnson, (as, indeed, who could?) did not sometimes compose sermons as good as those which we generally have from very respectable divines. He shewed me one with notes on the margin in Johnson's hand-writing; and I was present when he read another to Johnson, that he might have his opinion of it, and Johnson said it was "very well." These, we may be sure, were not Johnson's; for he was above little arts, or tricks of deception.

Johnson was by no means of opinion, that every man of a learned profession should consider it as incumbent upon him, or as necessary to his credit, to appear as an author. When in the ardour of ambition for literary fame, I regretted to him one day that an eminent Judge had nothing of it, and therefore would leave no perpetual monument of himself to posterity. "Alas, Sir, (said Johnson) what a mass of confusion should we have, if every Bishop, and every Judge, every Lawyer, Physician, and Divine, were to write books."

I mentioned to Johnson a respectable person of a very strong mind, who had little of that tenderness which is common to human nature; as an instance of which, when I suggested to him that he should invite his son, who had been settled ten years in foreign parts, to come home and pay him a visit, his answer was, "No, no, let him mind his business." JOHNSON. "I do not agree with him, Sir, in this. Getting money is not all a man's business: to cultivate kindness is a valuable part of the business of life."

In the evening, Johnson being in very good spirits, entertained us with several characteristical portraits. I regret that any of them escaped my retention and diligence. I found, from experience, that to collect my friend's conversation so as to exhibit it with any degree of its original flavour, it was necessary to write it down without delay. To record his sayings, after some distance of time, was like preserving or pickling long-kept and faded fruits, or other vegetables, which, when in that state, have little or nothing of their taste when fresh.

I shall present my readers with a series of what I gathered this evening from the Johnsonian garden.

"My friend, the late Earl of Corke,[234] had a great desire to maintain the literary character of his family: he was a genteel man, but did not keep up the dignity of his rank. He was so generally civil, that nobody thanked him for it."

"Did we not hear so much said of Jack Wilkes,[235] we should think more highly of his conversation. Jack has great variety of talk, Jack is a scholar, and Jack has the manners of a gentleman. But after hearing his name sounded from pole to pole, as the phoenix of convivial felicity, we are disappointed in his com-

---

233 Rev. Samuel Hayes (1749?–?1795) published the *Sermons* in two volumes, 1788–1789; the edition included one sermon attributed directly to Johnson, and it is known that Johnson wrote sermons for other clergymen as well.

234 Hamilton Boyle (1730–1764), sixth Earl of Cork and Orrery; his father was author of

Remarks on the Life and Writings of Swift; they both contributed essays to *The World.*

235 John Wilkes (1727–1797), politician and Boswell's "classical companion"; Boswell had brought Wilkes and Johnson together on a memorable occasion the year before.

pany. He has always been *at me:* but I would do Jack a kindness, rather than not. The contest is now over."

"Garrick's gaiety of conversation has delicacy and elegance: Foote[236] makes you laugh more; but Foote has the air of a buffoon paid for entertaining the company. He, indeed, well deserves his hire."

"Colley Cibber once consulted me as to one of his birth-day Odes, a long time before it was wanted. I objected very freely to several passages. Cibber lost patience, and would not read his Ode to an end. When we had done with criticism, we walked over to Richardson's, the authour of 'Clarissa,' and I wondered to find Richardson displeased that I 'did not treat Cibber with more *respect.'* Now, Sir, to talk of *respect* for a *player!'* (smiling disdainfully). Boswell. "There, Sir, you are always heretical: you never will allow merit to a player." Johnson. "Merit, Sir! what merit? Do you respect a rope-dancer, or a ballad-singer?" Boswell. "No, Sir: but we respect a great player, as a man who can conceive lofty sentiments, and can express them gracefully." Johnson. "What, Sir, a fellow who claps a hump on his back, and a lump on his leg, and cries, *'I am Richard the Third?'* Nay, Sir, a ballad-singer is a higher man, for he does two things; he repeats and he sings: there is both recitation and musick in his performance: the player only recites." Boswell. "My dear Sir! you may turn any thing into ridicule. I allow, that a player of farce is not entitled to respect; he does a little thing: but he who can represent exalted characters, and touch the noblest pas-

sions, has very respectable powers; and mankind have agreed in admiring great talents for the stage. We must consider, too, that a great player does what very few are capable to do: his art is a very rare faculty. *Who* can repeat Hamlet's soliloquy, 'To be, or not to be,' as Garrick does it?" Johnson. "Any body may. Jemmy, there (a boy about eight years old, who was in the room)[237] will do it as well in a week." Boswell. "No, no, Sir: and as a proof of the merit of great acting, and of the value which mankind set upon it, Garrick has got a hundred thousand pounds." Johnson. "Is getting a hundred thousand pounds a proof of excellence? That has been done by a scoundrel commissary."[238]

This was most fallacious reasoning. I was *sure,* for once, that I had the best side of the argument. I boldly maintained the just distinction between a tragedian and a mere theatrical droll; between those who rouse our terrour and pity, and those who only make us laugh. "If (said I) Betterton[239] and Foote were to walk into this room, you would respect Betterton much more than Foote." Johnson. "If Betterton were to walk into this room with Foote, Foote would soon drive him out of it. Foote, Sir, *quatenùs*[240] Foote, has powers superiour to them all."

On Monday, September 22, when at breakfast, I unguardedly said to Dr. Johnson, "I wish I saw you and Mrs. Macaulay[241] together." He grew very angry; and, after a pause, while a cloud gathered on his brow, he burst out, "No, Sir; you would not see us quarrel, to make you sport. Don't you know that it is very uncivil to *pit* two people against one another?" Then, checking himself, and wishing to be more gentle, he added,

---

[236] Samuel Foote (1720–1777), famous actor. Garrick is of course David (1717–1779), the leading English actor of the day and, like his brother George mentioned earlier (see note 172), a former student in Dr. Johnson's Latin school at Edial, near Lichfield.

[237] James Walter Fieldhouse, the 10-year-old son of a farmer who was visiting Dr. Taylor at this time.

[238] Business representative of a bishop.

[239] Thomas Betterton (1635?–1710), famous actor.

[240] "even"; at Foote's death a month later, Johnson wrote to Mrs. Thrale: "He was a fine fellow in his way; and the world is really impoverished by his sinking glories."

[241] Mrs. Catharine Macaulay (1731–1791), author of a *History of England* (1763–1783) and a political controversialist.

"I do not say you should be hanged or drowned for this; but it *is* very uncivil." Dr. Taylor thought him in the wrong, and spoke to him privately of it; but I afterwards acknowledged to Johnson that I was to blame, for I candidly owned, that I meant to express a desire to see a contest between Mrs. Macaulay and him; but then I knew how the contest would end; so that I was to see him triumph. JOHNSON. "Sir, you cannot be sure how a contest will end; and no man has a right to engage two people in a dispute by which their passions may be inflamed, and they may part with bitter resentment against each other. I would sooner keep company with a man from whom I must guard my pockets, than with a man who contrives to bring me into a dispute with somebody that he may hear it. This is the great fault of ———,[242] (naming one of our friends) endeavouring to introduce a subject upon which he knows two people in the company differ." BOSWELL. "But he told me, Sir, he does it for instruction." JOHNSON. "Whatever the motive be, Sir, the man who does so, does very wrong. He has no more right to instruct himself at such risk, than he has to make two people fight a duel, that he may learn how to defend himself."

He found great fault with a gentleman of our acquaintance for keeping a bad table. "Sir, (said he,) when a man is invited to dinner, he is disappointed if he does not get something good. I advised Mrs. Thrale, who has no card-parties at her house, to give sweet meats, and such good things, in an evening, as are not commonly given, and she would find company enough come to her; for every body loves to have things which please the palate put in their way, without trouble or preparation." Such was his attention to the *minutiae* of life and manners.

He thus characterised the Duke of Devonshire,[243] grandfather of the present representative of that very respecta-

ble family: "He was not a man of superiour abilities, but he was a man strictly faithful to his word. If, for instance, he had promised you an acorn, and none had grown that year in his woods, he would not have contented himself with that excuse; he would have sent to Denmark for it. So unconditional was he in keeping his word; so high as to the point of honour." This was a liberal testimony from the Tory Johnson to the virtue of a great Whig nobleman.

Mr. Burke's "Letter to the Sheriffs of Bristol, on the affairs of America," being mentioned, Johnson censured the composition much, and he ridiculed the definition of a free government, *viz.* "For any practical purpose, it is what the people think so."—"I will let the King of France govern me on those conditions, (said he,) for it is to be governed just as I please." And when Dr. Taylor talked of a girl being sent to a parish workhouse, and asked how much she could be obliged to work, "Why, (said Johnson,) as much as is reasonable: and what is that? as much as *she thinks* reasonable."

Dr. Johnson obligingly proposed to carry me to see Islam, a romantick scene, now belonging to a family of the name of Port, but formerly the seat of the Congreves. I suppose it is well described in some of the Tours. Johnson described it distinctly and vividly, at which I could not but express to him my wonder; because, though my eyes, as he observed, were better than his, I could not by any means equal him in representing visible objects. I said, the difference between us in this respect was as that between a man who has a bad instrument, but plays well on it, and a man who has a good instrument, on which he can play very imperfectly.

I recollect a very fine amphitheatre, surrounded with hills covered with woods, and walks neatly formed along the side of a rocky steep, on the quarter

---

[242] This, and the "gentleman" in the next paragraph, is now known to be Johnson's friend Bennet Langton, whom Boswell is shielding by a blank as he was living at the time the *Life* appeared. See note 146 above.

[243] William Cavendish (1698–1755), third Duke of Devonshire; Dr. Taylor, a Whig, supported the Devonshire family political interests.

next the house, with recesses under projections of rock, overshadowed with trees; in one of which recesses, we were told, Congreve wrote his "Old Bachelor."[244] We viewed a remarkable natural curiosity at Islam; two rivers bursting near each other from the rock, not from immediate springs, but after having run for many miles under ground. Plott,[245] in his "History of Staffordshire," gives an account of this curiosity; but Johnson would not believe it, though we had the attestation of the gardener, who said, he had put in corks, where the river *Manyfold* sinks into the ground, and had catched them in a net, placed before one of the openings where the water bursts out. Indeed, such subterraneous courses of water are found in various parts of our globe.

Talking of Dr. Johnson's unwillingness to believe extraordinary things, I ventured to say, "Sir, you come near Hume's argument against miracles, That it is more probable witnesses should lie, or be mistaken, than that they should happen." JOHNSON. "Why, Sir, Hume, taking the proposition simply, is right. But the Christian revelation is not proved by the miracles alone, but as connected with prophesies, and with the doctrines in confirmation of which the miracles were wrought."

He repeated his observation, that the differences among Christians are really of no consequence. "For instance, (said he,) if a Protestant objects to a Papist, 'You worship images;' the Papist can answer, 'I do not insist on *your* doing it; you may be a very good Papist without it: I do it only as a help to my devotion.'" I said, the great article of Christianity is the revelation of immortality. Johnson admitted it was.

In the evening, a gentleman-farmer,[246] who was on a visit at Dr. Taylor's attempted to dispute with Johnson in favour of Mungo Campbell,[247] who shot Alexander, Earl of Eglintoune, upon his having fallen, when retreating from his Lordship, who he believed was about to seize his gun, as he had threatened to do. He said, he should have done just as Campbell did. JOHNSON. "Whoever would do as Campbell did, deserves to be hanged; not that I could, as a juryman, have found him legally guilty of murder; but I am glad they found means to convict him." The gentleman-farmer said, "A poor man has as much honour as a rich man; and Campbell had *that* to defend." Johnson exclaimed, "A poor man has no honour." The English yeoman, not dismayed, proceeded: "Lord Eglintoune was a damned fool to run on upon Campbell, after being warned that Campbell would shoot him if he did." Johnson, who could not bear any thing like swearing, angrily replied, "He was *not* a *damned* fool: he only thought too well of Campbell. He did not believe Campbell would be such a *damned* scoundrel, as to do so *damned* a thing." His emphasis on *damned,* accompanied with frowning looks, reproved his opponent's want of decorum in *his* presence.

Talking of the danger of being mortified by rejection, when making approaches to the acquaintance of the great, I observed, "I am, however, generally for trying, 'Nothing venture, nothing have.'" JOHNSON. "Very true, Sir; but I have always been more afraid of failing, than hopeful of success." And, indeed, though he had all just respect for rank, no man ever less courted the favour of the great.

During this interview at Ashbourne, Johnson seemed to be more uniformly social, cheerful, and alert, than I had almost ever seen him. He was prompt on great occasions and on small. Taylor, who praised every thing of his own to excess, in short, "whose geese were all swans," as the proverb says, expatiated on the excellence of his bull-dog, which he told us, was "perfectly well shaped." Johnson, after examining the animal attentively, thus repressed the vain-glory

---

[244] William Congreve's first comedy (1693).
[245] Robert Plot (1640–1696), English antiquarian.
[246] Father of Jemmy; see note 237 above.

[247] In 1769, Campbell, an exciseman, had shot Lord Eglinton and had been convicted of murder; he took his own life the day after his conviction.

of our host:—"No, Sir, he is *not* well shaped; for there is not the quick transition from the thickness of the fore-part, to the *tenuity*—the thin part—behind, —which a bull-dog ought to have." This *tenuity,* was the only *hard word* that I heard him use during this interview, and it will be observed, he instantly put another expression in its place. Taylor said, a small bull-dog was as good as a large one. JOHNSON. "No, Sir; for, in proportion to his size, he has strength: and your argument would prove, that a good bull-dog may be as small as a mouse." It was amazing how he entered with perspicuity and keenness upon every thing that occurred in conversation. Most men, whom I know, would no more think of discussing a question about a bull-dog, than of attacking a bull.

I cannot allow any fragment whatever that floats in my memory concerning the great subject of this work to be lost. Though a small particular may appear trifling to some, it will be relished by others; while every little spark adds something to the general blaze: and to please the true, candid, warm admirers of Johnson, and in any degree increase the splendour of his reputation, I bid defiance to the shafts of ridicule, or even of malignity. Showers of them have been discharged at my "Journal of a Tour to the Hebrides;" yet it still sails unhurt along the stream of time, and, as an attendant upon Johnson,

Pursues the triumph, and partakes the gale.[248]

One morning after breakfast, when the sun shone bright, we walked out together, and "pored" for some time with placid indolence upon an artificial waterfall, which Dr. Taylor had made by building a strong dyke of stone across the river behind the garden. It was now somewhat obstructed by branches of trees and other rubbish, which had come down the river, and settled close to it.

Johnson, partly from a desire to see it play more freely, and partly from that inclination to activity which will animate, at times, the most inert and sluggish mortal, took a long pole which was lying on a bank, and pushed down several parcels of this wreck with painful assiduity, while I stood quietly by, wondering to behold the sage thus curiously employed, and smiling with an humorous satisfaction each time when he carried his point. He worked till he was quite out of breath; and having found a large dead cat so heavy that he could not move it after several efforts, "Come, said he, (throwing down the pole,) *you* shall take it now;" which I accordingly did, and being a fresh man, soon made the cat tumble over the cascade. This may be laughed at as too trifling to record; but it is a small characteristick trait in the Flemish picture which I give of my friend, and in which, therefore, I mark the most minute particulars. And let it be remembered, that "Æsop at play"[249] is one of the instructive apologues of antiquity.

I mentioned an old gentleman of our acquaintance whose memory was beginning to fail. JOHNSON. "There must be a diseased mind, where there is a failure of memory at seventy. A man's head, Sir, must be morbid, if he fails so soon." My friend, being now himself sixty-eight, might think thus: but I imagine, that *threescore and ten,* the Psalmist's period of sound human life, in later ages may have a failure, though there be no disease in the constitution.

Talking of Rochester's Poems, he said, he had given them to Mr. Steevens[250] to castrate for the edition of the poets, to which he was to write Prefaces. Dr. Taylor (the only time I ever heard him say any thing witty) observed, that "if Rochester had been castrated himself, his exceptionable poems would not have been written." I asked if Burnet[251] had not given a good Life of Rochester. JOHNSON. "We have a good *Death:*

248 Pope's *Essay on Man,* IV, 383.
249 Phaedrus's *Fables,* III, 14.
250 George Steevens (1736–1800), Shake-spearian editor.
251 Gilbert Burnet; see note 64.

there is not much *Life*." I asked whether Prior's Poems were to be printed entire: Johnson said they were. I mentioned Lord Hailes's censure of Prior, in his Preface to a collection of "Sacred Poems," by various hands, published by him at Edinburgh a great many years ago, where he mentions, "those impure tales which will be the eternal opprobrium of their ingenious authour." JOHNSON. "Sir, Lord Hailes has forgot. There is nothing in Prior that will excite to lewdness. If Lord Hailes thinks there is, he must be more combustible than other people." I instanced the tale of "Paulo Purganti and his Wife." JOHNSON. "Sir, there is nothing there, but that his wife wanted to be kissed, when poor Paulo was out of pocket. No, Sir, Prior is a lady's book. No lady is ashamed to have it standing in her library."

The hypochondriack disorder[252] being mentioned, Dr. Johnson did not think it so common as I supposed. "Dr. Taylor (said he) is the same one day as another. Burke and Reynolds are the same. Beauclerk, except when in pain, is the same. I am not so myself; but this I do not mention commonly."

I complained of a wretched changefulness, so that I could not preserve, for any long continuance, the same views of any thing. It was most comfortable to me to experience, in Dr. Johnson's company, a relief from this uneasiness. His steady vigorous mind held firm before me those objects which my own feeble and tremulous imagination frequently presented, in such a wavering state, that my reason could not judge well of them.

Dr. Johnson advised me to-day, to have as many books about me as I could; that I might read upon any subject upon which I had a desire for instruction at the time. "What you read *then* (said he) you will remember; but if you have not a book immediately ready, and the sub-ject moulds in your mind, it is a chance if you again have a desire to study it." He added, "If a man never has an eager desire for instruction, he should prescribe a task for himself. But it is better when a man reads from immediate inclination."

He repeated a good many lines of Horace's Odes, while we were in the chaise. I remember particularly the Ode *"Eheu fugaces."*[253]

He said, the dispute as to the comparative excellence of Homer or Virgil was inaccurate. "We must consider (said he) whether Homer was not the greatest poet, though Virgil may have produced the finest poem. Virgil was indebted to Homer for the whole invention of the structure of an epick poem, and for many of his beauties."

He told me, that Bacon was a favourite authour with him; but he had never read his works till he was compiling the English Dictionary, in which, he said, I might see Bacon very often quoted. Mr. Seward recollects his having mentioned, that a Dictionary of the English Language might be compiled from Bacon's writings alone, and that he had once an intention of giving an edition of Bacon, at least of his English works, and writing the Life of that great man. Had he executed this intention, there can be no doubt that he would have done it in a most masterly manner. Mallet's Life of Bacon[254] has no inconsiderable merit as an acute and elegant dissertation relative to its subject; but Mallet's mind was not comprehensive enough to embrace the vast extent of Lord Verulam's[255] genius and research. Dr. Warburton therefore observed, with witty justness, "that Mallet in his Life of Bacon had forgotten that he was a philosopher; and if he should write the Life of the Duke of Marlborough, which he had undertaken to do, he would probably forget that he was a General."

Wishing to be satisfied what degree of

---

252 In October of this year, Boswell began publishing anonymously in the *London Magazine* a series of essays entitled: "The Hypochondriack"; they have been edited by Margery Bailey (1928).

253 "Alas, the transitory . . ." (II, 14).

254 David Mallet, *Life of Bacon* (1740).

255 Francis Bacon was the Baron Verulam, Viscount St. Albans.

truth there was in a story which a friend of Johnson's and mine had told me to his disadvantage, I mentioned it to him in direct terms; and it was to this effect: that a gentleman who had lived in great intimacy with him, shewn him much kindness, and even relieved him from a spunging-house,[256] having afterwards fallen into bad circumstances, was one day, when Johnson was at dinner with him, seized for debt, and carried to prison; that Johnson sat still undisturbed, and went on eating and drinking; upon which the gentleman's sister, who was present, could not suppress her indignation: "What, Sir, (said she,) are you so unfeeling, as not even to offer to go to my brother in his distress; you who have been so much obliged to him?" And that Johnson answered, "Madam, I owe him no obligation; what he did for me he would have done for a dog."

Johnson assured me, that the story was absolutely false: but like a man conscious of being in the right, and desirous of completely vindicating himself from such a charge, he did not arrogantly rest on a mere denial, and on his general character, but proceeded thus:—"Sir, I was very intimate with that gentleman, and was once relieved by him from an arrest; but I never was present when he was arrested, never knew that he was arrested, and I believe he never was in difficulties after the time when he relieved me. I loved him much; yet, in talking of his general character, I may have said, though I do not remember that I ever did say so, that as his generosity proceeded from no principle, but was a part of his profusion, he would do for a dog what he would do for a friend: but I never applied this remark to any particular instance, and certainly not to his kindness to me. If a profuse man, who does not value his money, and gives a large sum to a whore, gives half as much, or an equally large sum to relieve a friend, it cannot be esteemed as virtue. This was all that I could say of that gentleman; and, if said at all, it must have been said after his death. Sir,

I would have gone to the world's end to relieve him. The remark about the dog, if made by me, was such a sally as might escape one when painting a man highly."

On Tuesday, September 23, Johnson was remarkably cordial to me. It being necessary for me to return to Scotland soon, I had fixed on the next day for my setting out, and I felt a tender concern at the thought of parting with him. He had, at this time, frankly communicated to me many particulars, which are inserted in this work in their proper places; and once, when I happened to mention that the expence of my jaunt would come to much more than I had computed, he said, "Why, Sir, if the expence were to be an inconvenience, you would have reason to regret it: but, if you have had the money to spend, I know not that you could have purchased as much pleasure with it in any other way."

During this interview at Ashbourne, Johnson and I frequently talked with wonderful pleasure of mere trifles which had occurred in our tour to the Hebrides; for it had left a most agreeable and lasting impression upon his mind.

He found fault with me for using the phrase to *make* money. "Don't you see (said he) the impropriety of it? To *make* money is to *coin* it: you should say *get* money." The phrase, however, is, I think, pretty current. But Johnson was at all times jealous of infractions upon the genuine English language, and prompt to repress colloquial barbarisms; such as, *pledging myself,* for *undertaking; line,* for *department,* or *branch,* as, the *civil line,* the *banking line.* He was particularly indignant against the almost universal use of the word *idea* in the sense of *notion* or *opinion,* when it is clear that *idea* can only signify something of which an image can be formed in the mind. We may have an *idea* or *image* of a mountain, a tree, a building; but we cannot surely have an *idea* or *image* of an *argument* or *proposition.* Yet we hear the sages of the law "delivering their *ideas* upon the question under consideration;" and the first speakers in parliament "entirely coinciding in the

---

[256] A house in which debtors were confined.

idea which has been ably stated by an honourable member;"—or "reprobating an *idea* unconstitutional, and fraught with the most dangerous consequences to a great and free country." Johnson called this "modern cant."

I perceived that he pronounced the word *heard,* as if spelt with a double *e, heerd,* instead of sounding it *herd,* as is most usually done. He said, his reason was, that if it was pronounced *herd,* there would be a single exception from the English pronunciation of the syllable *ear,* and he thought it better not to have that exception.

He praised Grainger's "Ode on Solitude," in Dodsley's collection,[257] and repeated, with great energy, the exordium:

O Solitude, romantick maid,
Whether by nodding towers you tread;
Or haunt the desart's trackless gloom,
Or hover o'er the yawning tomb;
Or climb the Andes' clifted side,
Or by the Nile's coy source abide;
Or, starting from your half-year's sleep,
From Hecla view the thawing deep;
Or, at the purple dawn of day,
Tadnor's[258] marble wastes survey.

observing, "This, Sir, is very noble."

In the evening our gentleman-farmer, and two others, entertained themselves and the company with a great number of tunes on the fiddle. Johnson desired to have "Let ambition fire thy mind," played over again, and appeared to give a patient attention to it; though he owned to me that he was very insensible to the power of musick. I told him, that it affected me to such a degree, as often to agitate my nerves painfully, producing in my mind alternate sensations of pathetick dejection, so that I was ready to shed tears; and of daring resolution, so

that I was inclined to rush into the thickest part of the battle. "Sir, (said he,) I should never hear it, if it made me such a fool."

Much of the effect of musick, I am satisfied, is owing to the association of ideas. That air,[259] which instantly and irresistibly excites in the Swiss, when in a foreign land, the *maladie du pais,*[260] has, I am told, no intrinsick power of sound. And I know from my own experience, that Scotch reels, though brisk, make me melancholy, because I used to hear them in my early years, at a time when Mr. Pitt called for soldiers "from the mountains of the north," and numbers of brave Highlanders were going abroad, never to return.[261] Whereas the airs in "The Beggar's Opera," many of which are very soft, never fail to render me gay, because they are associated with the warm sensations and high spirits of London. This evening, while some of the tunes of ordinary composition were played with no great skill, my frame was agitated, and I was conscious of a generous attachment to Dr. Johnson, as my preceptor and friend, mixed with an affectionate regret that he was an old man, whom I should probably lose in a short time. I thought I could defend him at the point of my sword. My reverence and affection for him were in full glow. I said to him, "My dear Sir, we must meet every year, if you don't quarrel with me." JOHNSON. "Nay, Sir, you are more likely to quarrel with me, than I with you. My regard for you is greater almost than I have words to express; but I do not choose to be always repeating it; write it down in the first leaf of your pocket-book, and never doubt of it again."

I talked to him of misery being "the doom of man," in this life, as displayed

---

[257] James Grainger (1721?–1766), Scottish physician and poet, and friend of Dr. Johnson's; Robert Dodsley (1703–1764) edited *A Collection of Poems by Several Hands* (3 vols., 1748).

[258] Tadmor (Palmyra); the spelling is correct in Dodsley's *Collection* (1755).

[259] The Swiss military were forbidden to play the air *Ranz des Vaches,* as it was said to

bring tears, desertion, and death.

[260] "homesickness."

[261] In 1757, at the beginning of the Seven Years' War, William Pitt (1708–1778), first Earl of Chatham, raised two battalions of Highlanders and sent them to America where they drove the French from Fort Duquesne and renamed it Pittsburgh.

in his "Vanity of Human Wishes." Yet I observed that things were done upon the supposition of happiness; grand houses were built, fine gardens were made, splendid places of publick amusement were contrived, and crowded with company. JOHNSON. "Alas, Sir, these are all only struggles for happiness. When I first entered Ranelagh,[262] it gave an expansion and gay sensation to my mind, such as I never experienced any where else. But, as Xerxes wept when he viewed his immense army, and considered that not one of that great multitude would be alive a hundred years afterwards, so it went to my heart to consider that there was not one in all that brilliant circle, that was not afraid to go home and think; but that the thoughts of each individual there, would be distressing when alone." This reflection was experimentally just. The feeling of languor, which succeeds the animation of gaiety, is itself a very severe pain; and when the mind is then vacant, a thousand disappointments and vexations rush in and excruciate. Will not many even of my fairest readers allow this to be true?

I suggested, that being in love, and flattered with hopes of success; or having some favourite scheme in view for the next day, might prevent that wretchedness of which we have been talking. JOHNSON. "Why, Sir, it may sometimes be so as you suppose; but my conclusion is in general but too true."

While Johnson and I stood in calm conference by ourselves in Dr. Taylor's garden, at a pretty late hour, in a serene autumn night, looking up to the heavens, I directed the discourse to the subject of a future state. My friend was in a placid and most benignant frame. "Sir, (said he,) I do not imagine that all things will be made clear to us immediately after death, but that the ways of Providence will be explained to us very gradually." I ventured to ask him whether although the words of some texts of Scripture seemed strong in support of the dreadful doctrine of an eternity of punishment, we might not hope that the denunciation was figurative, and would not literally be executed. JOHNSON. "Sir, you are to consider the intention of punishment in a future state. We have no reason to be sure that we shall then be no longer liable to offend against GOD. We do not know that even the angels are quite in a state of security; nay we know that some of them have fallen. It may, therefore, perhaps be necessary, in order to preserve both men and angels in a state of rectitude, that they should have continually before them the punishment of those who have deviated from it; but we may hope that by some other means a fall from rectitude may be prevented. Some of the texts of Scripture upon this subject are, as you observe, indeed strong; but they may admit of a mitigated interpretation." He talked to me upon this awful and delicate question in a gentle tone, and as if afraid to be decisive.

After supper I accompanied him to his apartment, and at my request he dictated to me an argument in favour of the negro who was then claiming his liberty, in an action in the Court of Session in Scotland. He had always been very zealous against slavery in every form, in which I with all deference thought that he discovered "a zeal without knowledge." Upon one occasion, when in company with some very grave men at Oxford, his toast was, "Here's to the next insurrection of the negroes in the West Indies." His violent prejudice against our West Indian and American settlers appeared whenever there was an opportunity. Towards the conclusion of his "Taxation no Tyranny," he says, "how is it that we hear the loudest *yelps* for liberty among the drivers of negroes?" and in his conversation with Mr. Wilkes, he asked, "Where did Beckford and Trecothick learn English?"[263] That Trecothick could both speak and write

---

[262] A place of public entertainment in Chelsea, London, with a rotunda 150 feet in diameter (1742–1802); see note 2 to the selection from Fanny Burney's *Evelina*, p. 574.

[263] William Beckford (1709–1770) and Barlow Trecothik (d. 1775) were merchants and participants in London politics.

good English is well known. I myself was favoured with his correspondence concerning the brave Corsicans. And that Beckford could speak it with a spirit of honest resolution even to his Majesty, as his "faithful Lord-Mayor of London," is commemorated by the noble monument erected to him in Guildhall.

[Here a short passage is omitted in which Johnson dictates to Boswell an argument in favor of freeing the Negro slave in the case Boswell is engaged with at the moment. The passage is not present in the first edition, but was added to the second.]

When I said now to Johnson, that I was afraid I kept him too late up, "No, Sir, (said he,) I don't care though I sit all night with you." This was an animated speech from a man in his sixty-ninth year.

Had I been as attentive not to displease him as I ought to have been, I know not but this vigil might have been fulfilled; but I unluckily entered upon the controversy concerning the right of Great-Britain to tax America, and attempted to argue in favour of our fellow-subjects on the other side of the Atlantick. I insisted that America might be very well governed, and made to yield sufficient revenue by the means of *influence,* as exemplified in Ireland, while the people may be pleased with the imagination of their participating of the British constitution, by having a body of representatives without whose consent money could not be exacted from them. Johnson could not bear my thus opposing his avowed opinion, which he had exerted himself with an extreme degree of heat to enforce; and the violent agitation into which he was thrown, while answering, or rather reprimanding me, alarmed me so that I heartily repented of my having unthinkingly introduced the subject. I myself however grew warm, and the change was great, from the calm state of philosophical discussion in which we had a little before been pleasingly employed.

I talked of the corruption of the British parliament, in which I alledged that any question, however unreasonable or unjust, might be carried by a venal majority; and I spoke with high admiration of the Roman Senate, as if composed of men sincerely desirous to resolve what they should think best for their country. My friend would allow no such character to the Roman Senate; and he maintained that the British parliament was not corrupt, and that there was no occasion to corrupt its members, asserting, that there was hardly ever any question of great importance before parliament, any question in which a man might not very well vote either upon one side or the other. He said there had been none in his time except that respecting America.

We were fatigued by the contest, which was produced by my want of caution; and he was not then in the humour to slide into easy and cheerful talk. It therefore so happened, that we were after an hour or two very willing to separate and go to bed.

On Wednesday, September 24, I went into Dr. Johnson's room before he got up, and finding that the storm of the preceding night was quite laid, I sat down upon his bed-side, and he talked with as much readiness and good-humour as ever. He recommended to me to plant a considerable part of a large moorish farm which I had purchased, and he made several calculations of the expence and profit, for he delighted in exercising his mind on the science of numbers. He pressed upon me the importance of planting at the first in a very sufficient manner, quoting the saying *"In bello non licet bis errare:"*[264] and adding, "this is equally true in planting."

I spoke with gratitude of Dr. Taylor's hospitality; and as evidence that it was not on account of his good table alone that Johnson visited him so often, I mentioned a little anecdote which had escaped my friend's recollection, and at

---

[264] "No mistakes are permitted in warfare" (Plutarch, *Regum et Imperatum Apophthegmata, Moralia,* ll. 186 ff.).

hearing which repeated, he smiled. One evening when I was sitting with him, Frank[265] delivered this message, "Sir, Dr. Taylor sends his compliments to you, and begs you will dine with him to-morrow. He has got a hare."—"My compliments (said Johnson) and I'll dine with him, hare or rabbit."

After breakfast I departed, and pursued my journey northwards. I took my post-chaise from the Green Man, a very good inn at Ashbourne, the mistress of which, a mighty civil gentlewoman, courtseying very low, presented me with an engraving of the sign of her house; to which she had subjoined, in her own hand-writing, an address in such singular simplicity of style, that I have preserved it pasted upon one of the boards of my original Journal at this time, and shall here insert it for the amusement of my readers:

M. Killingley's duty waits upon Mr. Boswell, is exceedingly obliged to him for this favour; whenever he comes this way, hopes for a continuance of the same. Would Mr. Boswell name the house to his extensive acquaintance, it would be a singular favour conferr'd on one who has it not in her power to make any other return but her most grateful thanks, and sincerest prayers for his happiness in time, and in a blessed eternity.
Tuesday morn.

From this meeting at Ashbourne I derived a considerable accession to my Johnsonian store. I communicated my original Journal to Sir William Forbes,[266] in whom I have always placed deserved confidence; and what he wrote to me concerning it is so much to my credit as the biographer of Johnson, that my readers will, I hope, grant me their indulgence for here inserting it. "It is not once or twice going over it (says Sir William) that will satisfy me; for I find in it a high degree of instruction as well as entertainment; and I derive more benefit from Dr. Johnson's admirable discussions than I should be able to draw from his personal conversation; for, I suppose there is not a man in the world to whom he discloses his sentiments so freely as to yourself."

I cannot omit a curious circumstance which occurred at Edensor-inn, close by Chatsworth,[267] to survey the magnificence of which I had gone a considerable way out of my road to Scotland. The inn was then kept by a very jolly landlord, whose name I think was Malton. He happened to mention that "the celebrated Dr. Johnson had been in his house." I inquired *who* this Dr. Johnson was, that I might hear mine host's notion of him. "Sir, (said he,) Johnson, the great writer; *Oddity*, as they call him. He's the greatest writer in England; he writes for the ministry; he has a correspondence abroad, and lets them know what's going on."

My friend, who had a thorough dependance upon the authenticity of my relation without any *embellishment*, as *falsehood* or *fiction* is too gently called, laughed a good deal at this representation of himself.

Mr. Boswell to Dr. Johnson.
My Dear Sir,
                    Edinburgh, Sept. 29, 1777.
By the first post I inform you of my safe arrival at my own house, and that I had the comfort of finding my wife and children all in good health.

When I look back upon our late interview, it appears to me to have answered expectation better than almost any scheme of happiness that I ever put in execution. My Journal is stored with wisdom and wit; and my memory is filled with the recollection of lively and affectionate feelings, which now, I think, yield me more satisfaction than at the time when they were first excited. I have experienced this upon other occasions. I

[265] Francis Barber (1745?–1801), Johnson's Negro servant.
[266] Scottish banker and author (1739–1806), one of the executors of Boswell's estate.
[267] Chatsworth and Edensor are on opposite banks of the River Derwent some 20 miles north of Derby; Chatsworth, the seat of the Duke of Devonshire, was too famous a mansion for Boswell to miss.

will be obliged to you if you will explain it to me; for it seems wonderful that pleasure should be more vivid at a distance than when near. I wish you may find yourself in a humour to do me this favour; but I flatter myself with no strong hope of it; for I have observed, that unless upon very serious occasions, your letters to me are not *answers* to those which I write.

I then expressed much uneasiness that I had mentioned to him the name of the gentleman who had told me the story so much to his disadvantage, the truth of which he had completely refuted; for that my having done so might be interpreted as a breach of confidence, and offend one whose society I valued:—therefore earnestly requesting that no notice might be taken of it to any body, till I should be in London, and have an opportunity to talk it over with the gentleman.

To James Boswell, Esq.
Dear Sir,

You will wonder, or you have wondered, why no letter has come from me. What you wrote at your return, had in it such a strain of cowardly caution as gave me no pleasure. I could not well do what you wished; I had no need to vex you with a refusal. I have seen Mr. ———, and as to him have set all right, without any inconvenience, so far as I know, to you. Mrs. Thrale had forgot the story. You may now be at ease.

And at ease I certainly wish you, for the kindness that you showed in coming so long a journey to see me. It was pity to keep you so long in pain, but, upon reviewing the matter, I do not see what I could have done better than as I did.

I hope you found at your return my dear enemy and all her little people quite well, and had no reason to repent of your journey. I think on it with great gratitude.

I was not well when you left me at the Doctor's, and I grew worse; yet I staid on, and at Lichfield was very ill. Travelling, however, did not make me worse; and when I came to London I complied with a summons to go to Brighthelmston, where I saw Beauclerk, and staid three days.

Our club has recommenced last Friday, but I was not there. Langton has another wench. Mrs. Thrale is in hopes of a young brewer. They got by their trade last year a very large sum, and their expences are proportionate.

Mrs. Williams's health is very bad. And I have had for some time a very difficult and laborious respiration, but I am better by purges, abstinence, and other methods. I am yet however much behind-hand in my health and rest.

Dr. Blair's sermons are now universally commended, but let him think that I had the honour of first finding and first praising his excellencies. I did not stay to add my voice to that of the publick.

My dear friend, let me thank you once more for your visit; you did me great honour, and I hope met with nothing that displeased you. I staid long at Ashbourne, not much pleased, yet aukward at departing. I then went to Lichfield, where I found my friend at Stowhill very dangerously diseased.[268] Such is life. Let us try to pass it well, whatever it be, for there is surely something beyond it.

Well, now I hope all is well, write as soon as you can to, dear Sir,
Your affectionate servant,
Sam. Johnson.
London, Nov. 25, 1777.

---

[268] "Mrs. [Elizabeth] Aston [1708–1785]" (Boswell); Johnson said of her in 1781: "We have known each other long, and, by consequence, are both old."

William Shenstone
1714-1763

ESSAYS ON MEN & MANNERS

ON WRITING AND BOOKS

Fine writing is generally the effect of spontaneous thoughts and a laboured style.

Long sentences in a short composition are like large rooms in a little house.

The world may be divided into people that read, people that write, people that think, and fox-hunters.

Instead of whining complaints concerning the imagined cruelty of their mistresses, if poets would address the same to their Muse, they would act more agreeably to nature and to truth.

Superficial writers, like the mole, often fancy themselves deep, when they are exceeding near the surface.

There is no word in the Latin language, that signifies a female friend. "Amica," means a mistress: and perhaps there is no friendship betwixt the sexes wholly disunited from a degree of love.

The chief advantage that ancient writers can boast over modern ones, seems owing to simplicity. Every noble truth & sentiment was expressed by the former in the natural manner; in word and phrase, simple, perspicuous, and incapable of improvement. What then re-

Selected from first edition, 1764.

mained for later writers but affectation, witticism, and conceit?

One can, now and then, reach an author's head when he stoops; and, induced by this circumstance, aspire to measure height with him.

Perhaps, an acquaintance with men of genius is rather reputable than satisfactory. It is as unaccountable, as it is certain, that fancy heightens sensibility; sensibility strengthens passion; and passion makes people humorists.

Yet a person of genius is often expected to shew more discretion than another man; this on account of that very vivacity, which is his greatest impediment. This happens for want of distinguishing betwixt the fanciful talents and the dry mathematical operations of the judgment, each of which indiscriminately give the denomination of a man of genius.

It is often observed of wits, that they will lose their best friends for the sake of a joke. Candour may discover, that it is their greater degree of the love of fame, not the less degree of their benevolence, which is the cause.

People in high or in distinguished life ought to have a greater circumspection in regard to their most trivial actions. For instance, I saw Mr. Pope—and what was he doing when you saw him? —why, to the best of my memory, he was picking his nose.

Even Joe Miller[1] in his jests has an eye to poetical justice; generally gives the victory or turns the laugh on the side of merit. No small compliment to mankind!

To say a person writes a good style, is originally as pedantic an expression as to say he plays a good fiddle.

The first line of Virgil seems to patter like an hailstorm—"Tityre, tu patulae,"[2] &c.

The vanity and extreme self-love of the French is no where more observable than in their authors; and among these, in none more than Boileau;[3] who, besides his rhodomontades, preserves ever the most insipid reading in his notes, though he has removed it from the text for the sake of one ever so much better.

The writer who gives us the best idea of what may be called the genteel in style and manner of writing, is, in my opinion, my Lord Shaftesbury.[4] Then Mr. Addison and Dr. Swift.

A plain narrative of any remarkable fact, emphatically related, has a more striking effect without the author's comment.

I think nothing truly poetic, at least no poetry worth composing, that does not strongly affect one's passions: and this is but slenderly effected by fables, allegories, and lies.

Incredulus odi.
HOR.[5]

I hate a style, as I do a garden, that is wholly flat and regular; that slides along like an eel, and never rises to what one can call an inequality.

It is obvious to discover that imperfections of one kind have a visible tendency to produce perfections of another. Mr. Pope's bodily disadvantages must incline him to a more laborious cultivation of his talent, without which he foresaw that he must have languished in obscurity. The advantages of person are a good deal essential to popularity in the grave world as well as the gay. Mr. Pope, by an unwearied application to poetry, became not only the favourite of the learned, but also of the ladies.

Pope, I think, never once mentions Prior; though Prior speaks so handsomely of Pope in his Alma.[6] One might imagine that the latter, indebted as he was to the former for such numberless beauties, should have readily repaid this poetical obligation. This can only be imputed to pride or party-cunning. In other words, to some modification of selfishness.

Pope seems to me the most correct writer since Virgil; the greatest genius only, since Dryden.

Pope's talent lay remarkably in what one may naturally enough term the condensation of thoughts. I think no other English poet ever brought so much sense into the same number of lines with equal smoothness, ease, and poetical beauty. Let him who doubts of this peruse his Essay on Man with attention. Perhaps, this was a talent from which he could not easily have swerved: Perhaps, he could not have sufficiently rarified his thoughts to produce that flimziness

---

[1] *Joe Miller's Jest-book, or The Wit's Vade Mecum* (1739) was prepared and published by John Mottley (1692–1750) after the death of an actor of the name Josias Miller (1684–1738); the name has since become synonymous with an old chestnut.

[2] *Eclogues*, I, 1.

[3] The famous critic Nicolas Boileau-Despréaux (1636–1711). By his "rhodomontades,"

Shenstone seems to imply pompous loquacity.

[4] Anthony Ashley Cooper, 3rd Earl of Shaftesbury (1670–1713), author of *Characteristicks*. For Addison and Swift, see text above.

[5] "They shock our faith, our indignation raise" (Horace, *Ars Poetica*, l. 188, tr. Francis).

[6] Matthew Prior (1664–1721) twice refers favorably to Pope in the *Alma* (1718), the second time in praise of his *Eloisa to Abelard*.

which is required in a ballad or love-song. His monster of Ragusa[7] & his translations from Chaucer have some little tendency to invalidate this observation.

I durst not have censured Mr. Pope's writings in his life-time, you say. True. A writer surrounded with all his fame, engaging with another that is hardly known, is a man in armour attacking another in his night-gown and slippers.

There is a vast beauty (to me) in using a word of a particular nature in the eighth and ninth syllables of an English verse. I mean what is virtually a dactyl. For instance,

And pikes, the tyrants of the Watry plains.

Let any person of an ear substitute "liquid" instead of "watry" and he will find the disadvantage. Mr. Pope (who has improved our versification through a judicious disposition of the pause) seems not enough aware of this beauty.

Prudes allow no quarter to such ladies as have fallen a sacrifice to the gentle passion; either because themselves, being borne away by the malignant ones, perhaps never felt the other so powerful as to occasion them any difficulty; or because no one has tempted them to transgress that way themselves. It is the same case with some critics, with regard to the errors of ingenious writers.

Poetry and consumptions are the most flattering of diseases.

Every person insensibly fixes upon some degree of refinement in his discourse, some measure of thought which he thinks worth exhibiting. It is wise to fix this pretty high, although it occasions one to talk the less.

Some men use no other means to acquire respect, than by insisting on it; and it sometimes answers their purpose, as it does an highwayman's in regard to money.

Perfect characters in a poem make but little better figure than regular hills, perpendicular trees, uniform rocks, and level sheets of water, in the formation of a landskip. The reason is, they are not natural, and moreover want variety.

Trifles discover a character more than actions of importance. In regard to the former, a person is off his guard, and thinks it not material to use disguise. It is, to me, no imperfect hint towards the discovery of a man's character, to say he looks as though you might be certain of finding a pin upon his sleeve.

A poet that fails in writing, becomes often a morose critic. The weak and insipid white-wine makes at length excellent vinegar.

Every single observation that is published by a man of genius, be it ever so trivial, should be esteemed of importance; because he speaks from his own impressions; whereas common men publish common things, which they have, perhaps, gleaned from frivolous writers.

The time of life when fancy predominates, is youth; the season when judgment decides best, is age. Poets therefore, are always, in respect of their disposition, younger than other persons: a circumstance that gives the latter part of their lives some inconsistency. The cool phlegmatic tribe discover it in the former.

A poet hurts himself by writing prose; as a racehorse hurts his motions by condescending to draw in a team.

The superior politeness of the French is in nothing more discernible than in the phrases used by them and us to express an affair being in agitation. The former says "sur la tapis";[8] the latter "upon the anvil." Does it not shew also the sincerity & serious face with which we enter upon business, and the negligent and jaunty air with which they perform even the most important?

A poetical genius seems the most ele-

---

[7] The *Monster of Ragusa,* a ballad, appeared in the third edition of Pope's *Miscellanies*

(1720).
[8] "on the carpet."

gant of youthful accomplishments; but it is entirely a youthful one.

Flights of fancy, gaiety of behaviour, sprightliness of dress, and a blooming aspect, conspire very amicably to their mutual embellishment; but the poetic talent has no more to do with age, than it would avail his Grace of Canterbury to have a knack at country dances, or a genius for a catch.

The most obsequious Muses, like the fondest and most willing courtezans, seldom leave us any reason to boast much of their favors.

It should seem, the many lies, discernible in books of travels, may be owing to accounts collected from improper people. Were one to give a character of the English, from what the vulgar act & believe, it would convey[9] a strange idea of the English understanding.

Critics must excuse me, if I compare them to certain animals called asses; who, by gnawing vines, originally taught the great advantage of pruning them.

Every good poet includes a critic; the reverse will not hold.

We want a word to express the "Hospes" or "Hospita" of the antients; among them, perhaps, the most respectable of all characters; yet with us translated "Host," which we apply also to an Innkeeper. Neither have we any word to express "Amica," as if we thought a woman always was somewhat more or less than a friend.

The philosopher, who considered the world as one vast animal,[10] could esteem himself no other than a louse upon the back of it.

Every thing disgusts, but mere simplicity; the scriptural writers describe their heroes using only some such phrase as this: "Alas! my brother!"[11] "O Absalom my son! my son!"[12] &c. The lamentation of Saul over Jonathan is more diffuse, but at the same time entirely simple.

Respect is the general end for which riches, power, place, title, and fame, are implicitly desired. When one is possessed of the end, through any one of these means, is it not wholly unphilosophical to covet the remainder?

Lord Shaftesbury, in the genteel management of some familiar ideas, seems to have no equal. He discovers an eloignment[13] from vulgar phrases much becoming a person of quality. His sketches should be studied, like those of Raphael. His Enquiry is one of the shortest and clearest systems of morality.

The question is, whether you distinguish me, because you have better sense than other people; or whether you seem to have better sense than other people because you distinguish me.

One feels the same kind of disgust in reading Roman history, which one does in novels, or even epic poetry. We too easily foresee to whom the victory will fall. The hero, the knight errant, and the Roman, are too seldom overcome.

I wish but two editions of all books whatsoever. One of the simple text, published by a society of able hands: another with the various readings, and remarks of the ablest commentators.

To endeavour, all one's days, to fortify our minds with learning & philosophy, is to spend so much in armour that one has nothing left to defend.

---

[9] "Missionaries clap a tail to every Indian nation that dislikes them" (Shenstone).

[10] An allusion to Thomas Hobbes, author of *The Leviathan* (1651).

[11] I Kings 13:30; said of the man of God from Judah by the prophet.

[12] II Sam. 19:4.

[13] Remoteness in feeling or taste.

Laurence Sterne
1713-1768

From A SENTIMENTAL JOURNEY
through France and Italy

[INTRODUCTION]

—They order, said I, this matter better in France—

—You have been in France? said my gentleman, turning quick upon me with the most civil triumph in the world.— Strange! quoth I, debating the matter with myself, That one and twenty miles sailing, for 'tis absolutely no further from Dover to Calais, should give a man these rights—I'll look into them: so giving up the argument—I went straight to my lodgings, put up half a dozen shirts and a black pair of silk breeches—"the coat I have on, said I, looking at the sleeve, will do"—took a place in the Dover stage; and the packet sailing at nine the next morning—by three I had got sat down to my dinner upon a fricassee'd chicken so incontestably in France, that had I died that night of an indigestion, the whole world could not have suspended the effects of the *Droits d'aubaine*[1]—my shirts, and black pair of silk breeches—portmanteau and all must have gone to the King of France—even the little picture which I have so long worn, and so often have told thee, Eliza,[2] I would carry with me into my grave, would have been torn from my neck.— Ungenerous!—to seize upon the wreck of an unwary passenger, whom your subjects had beckon'd to their coast—by heaven! Sire, it is not well done; and much does it grieve me, 'tis the monarch of a people so civilized and courteous, and so renown'd for sentiment and fine feelings, that I have to reason with—

But I have scarce set foot in your dominions—

CALAIS

When I had finish'd my dinner, and drank the King of France's health, to satisfy my mind that I bore him no spleen, but, on the contrary, high honour for the humanity of his temper—I rose up an inch taller for the accommodation.

—No—said I—the Bourbon is by no means a cruel race: they may be misled like other people; but there is a mildness in their blood. As I acknowledge this, I

Text from first edition, 1768.

[1] Laws by which the goods of a stranger who died in France were lost to his heirs.

[2] Sterne's Eliza was Mrs. Eliza Draper, a young married woman from India whom he had met in London just before embarking on his tour of the continent.

felt a suffusion of a finer kind upon my cheek—more warm and friendly to man, than what Burgundy (at least of two livres[3] a bottle, which was such as I had been drinking) could have produced.

—Just God! said I, kicking my portmanteau aside, what is there in this world's goods which should sharpen our spirits, and make so many kind-hearted brethren of us, fall out so cruelly as we do by the way?

When man is at peace with man, how much lighter than a feather is the heaviest of metals in his hand! he pulls out his purse, and holding it airily and uncompress'd, looks round him, as if he sought for an object to share it with— In doing this, I felt every vessel in my frame dilate—the arteries beat all chearily together, and every power which sustained life, perform'd it with so little friction, that 'twould have confounded the most *physical precieuse*[4] in France: with all her materialism, she could scarce have called me a machine—

I'm confident, said I to myself, I should have overset her creed.

The accession of that idea, carried nature, at that time, as high as she could go—I was at peace with the world before, and this finish'd the treaty with myself—Now, was I a King of France, cried I—what a moment for an orphan to have begg'd his father's portmanteau of me!

THE MONK
CALAIS

I had scarce utter'd the words, when a poor monk of the order of St. Francis came into the room to beg something for his convent. No man cares to have his virtues the sport of contingencies—or one man may be generous, as another man is puissant—*sed non, quo ad hanc*[5] —or be it as it may—for there is no reg-

ular reasoning upon the ebbs and flows of our humours; they may depend upon the same causes, for ought I know, which influence the tides themselves—'twould oft be no discredit to us, to suppose it was so: I'm sure at least for myself, that in many a case I should be more highly satisfied, to have it said by the world, "I had had an affair with the moon, in which there was neither sin nor shame," than have it pass altogether as my own act and deed, wherein there was so much of both.

—But be this as it may. The moment I cast my eyes upon him, I was predetermined not to give him a single sous;[6] and accordingly I put my purse into my pocket—button'd it up—set myself a little more upon my centre, and advanced up gravely to him: there was something, I fear, forbidding in my look: I have his figure this moment before my eyes, and think there was that in it which deserved better.

The monk, as I judged from the break in his tonsure, a few scatter'd white hairs upon his temples, being all that remained of it, might be about seventy— but from his eyes, and that sort of fire which was in them, which seemed more temper'd by courtesy than years, could be no more than sixty—Truth might lie between—He was certainly sixty-five; and the general air of his countenance, notwithstanding something seem'd to have been planting wrinkles in it before their time, agreed to the account.

It was one of those heads, which Guido[7] has often painted—mild, pale— penetrating, free from all common-place ideas of fat contented ignorance looking downwards upon the earth—it look'd forwards; but look'd, as if it look'd at something beyond this world. How one of his order came by it, heaven above, who let it fall upon a monk's shoulders, best knows: but it would have suited a Bramin, and had I met it upon the

---

[3] Slightly less than two shillings English sterling.

[4] One who carries to an extreme of refinement a materialistic or rather mechanistic view of life.

[5] "but no, as to that."

[6] The smallest French coin.

[7] Guido Reni (1575–1642), of Bologna, noted for softness of style.

plains of Indostan, I had reverenced it.

The rest of his outline may be given in a few strokes; one might put it into the hands of any one to design, for 'twas neither elegant or otherwise, but as character and expression made it so: it was a thin, spare form, something above the common size, if it lost not the distinction by a bend forwards in the figure—but it was the attitude of Intreaty; and as it now stands presented to my imagination, it gain'd more than it lost by it.

When he had enter'd the room three paces, he stood still; and laying his left hand upon his breast, (a slender white staff with which he journey'd being in his right)—when I had got close up to him, he introduced himself with the little story of the wants of his convent, and the poverty of his order—and did it with so simple a grace—and such an air of deprecation was there in the whole cast of his look and figure—I was bewitch'd not to have been struck with it—

—A better reason was, I had predetermined not to give him a single sous.

THE MONK
CALAIS

—'Tis very true, said I, replying to a cast upwards with his eyes, with which he had concluded his address—'tis very true—and heaven be their resource who have no other but the charity of the world, the stock of which, I fear, is no way sufficient for the many *great claims* which are hourly made upon it.

As I pronounced the words *great claims,* he gave a slight glance with his eye downwards upon the sleeve of his tunick—I felt the full force of the appeal—I acknowledge it, said I—a coarse habit, and that but once in three years, with meagre diet—are no great matters; and the true point of pity is, as they can be earn'd in the world with so little industry, that your order should wish to procure them by pressing upon a fund which is the property of the lame, the blind, the aged and the infirm—the cap-

tive who lies down counting over and over again the days of his afflictions, languishes also for his share of it; and had you been of the *order of mercy,* instead of the order of St. Francis, poor as I am, continued I, pointing at my portmanteau, full chearfully should it have been open'd to you, for the ransom of the unfortunate—The monk made me a bow—but of all others, resumed I, the unfortunate of our own country, surely, have the first rights; and I have left thousands in distress upon our own shore —The monk gave a cordial wave with his head—as much as to say, No doubt, there is misery enough in every corner of the world, as well as within our convent—But we distinguish, said I, laying my hand upon the sleeve of his tunick, in return for his appeal—we distinguish, my good Father! betwixt those who wish only to eat the bread of their own labour—and those who eat the bread of other people's, and have no other plan in life, but to get through it in sloth and ignorance, *for the love of God.*

The poor Franciscan made no reply: a hectic of a moment pass'd across his cheek, but could not tarry—Nature seemed to have had done with her resentments in him; he shewed none—but letting his staff fall within his arm, he press'd both his hands with resignation upon his breast, and retired.

THE MONK
CALAIS

My heart smote me the moment he shut the door—Psha! said I with an air of carelessness, three several times—but it would not do: every ungracious syllable I had utter'd, crouded back into my imagination: I reflected, I had no right over the poor Franciscan, but to deny him; and that the punishment of that was enough to the disappointed without the addition of unkind language—I consider'd his grey hairs—his courteous figure seem'd to re-enter and gently ask me what injury he had done me?—and why I could use him thus—I would have given twenty livres for an advocate—I have behaved very ill; said I within myself; but I have only just set out upon my travels; and shall learn better manners as I get along.

THE DESOBLIGEANT[8]
CALAIS

When a man is discontented with himself, it has one advantage however, that it puts him into an excellent frame of mind for making a bargain. Now there being no travelling through France and Italy without a chaise—and nature generally prompting us to the thing we are fittest for, I walk'd out into the coach yard to buy or hire something of that kind to my purpose: an old Desobligeant in the furthest corner of the court, hit my fancy at first sight, so I instantly got into it, and finding it in tolerable harmony with my feelings, I ordered the waiter to call Monsieur Dessein the master of the hotel—but Monsieur Dessein being gone to vespers, and not caring to face the Franciscan whom I saw on the opposite side of the court, in conference with a lady just arrived, at the inn—I drew the taffeta curtain betwixt us, and being determined to write my journey, I took out my pen and ink, and wrote the preface to it in the *Disobligeant*.

PREFACE
IN THE DESOBLIGEANT

It must have been observed by many a peripatetic philosopher, That nature has set up by her own unquestionable authority certain boundaries and fences to circumscribe the discontent of man: she has effected her purpose in the quietest and easiest manner by laying him under almost insuperable obligations to work out his ease, and to sustain his sufferings at home. It is there only that she

has provided him with the most suitable objects to partake of his happiness, and bear a part of that burden which in all countries and ages, has ever been too heavy for one pair of shoulders. 'Tis true we are endued with an imperfect power of spreading our happiness sometimes beyond *her* limits, but 'tis so ordered, that from the want of languages, connections, and dependencies, and from the difference in education, customs and habits, we lie under so many impediments in communicating our sensations out of our own sphere, as often amount to a total impossibility.

It will always follow from hence, that the balance of sentimental commerce is always against the expatriated adventurer: he must buy what he has little occasion for at their own price—his conversation will seldom be taken in exchange for theirs without a large discount—and this, by the by, eternally driving him into the hands of more equitable brokers for such conversation as he can find, it requires no great spirit of divination to guess at his party—

This brings me to my point; and naturally leads me (if the see-saw of this *Desobligeant* will but let me get on) into the efficient as well as the final causes of travelling—

Your idle people that leave their native country and go abroad for some reason or reasons which may be derived from one of these general causes—

> Infirmity of body,
> Imbecility of mind, or
> Inevitable necessity.

The first two include all those who travel by land or by water, labouring with pride, curiosity, vanity or spleen, subdivided and combined *in infinitum*.[9]

The third class includes the whole army of peregrine[10] martyrs; more especially those travellers who set out upon their travels with the benefit of the clergy, either as delinquents travelling

---

[8] A "disobliging" or uninviting carriage; it seated only one, a "fitting" carriage at this juncture.

[9] "to infinity."
[10] wayfaring.

under the direction of governors recommended by the magistrate—or young gentlemen transported by the cruelty of parents and guardians, and travelling under the direction of governors recommended by Oxford, Aberdeen and Glasgow.

There is a fourth class, but their number is so small that they would not deserve a distinction, was it not necessary in a work of this nature to observe the greatest precision and nicety, to avoid a confusion of character. And these men I speak of, are such as cross the seas and sojourn in a land of strangers with a view of saving money for various reasons and upon various pretences: but as they might also save themselves and others a great deal of unnecessary trouble by saving their money at home—and as their reasons for travelling are the least complex of any other species of emigrants, I shall distinguish these gentlemen by the name of

Simple Travellers.

Thus the whole circle of travellers may be reduced to the following *Heads*.

Idle Travellers,
Inquisitive Travellers,
Lying Travellers,
Proud Travellers,
Vain Travellers,
Splenetic Travellers.
Then follow the Travellers of Necessity.
The delinquent and felonious Traveller,
The unfortunate and innocent Traveller,
The simple Traveller,
And last of all (if you please) The
Sentimental Traveller (meaning thereby myself)

who have travell'd, and of which I am now sitting down to give an account—as much out of *Necessity,* and the *besoin de* Voyager,[11] as any one in the class.

I am well aware, at the same time, as both my travels and observations will be altogether of a different cast from any

11 "need for traveling."

of my fore-runners; that I might have insisted upon a whole nitch entirely to myself—but I should break in upon the confines of the *Vain* Traveller, in wishing to draw attention towards me, till I have some better grounds for it, than the mere *Novelty of my Vehicle.*

It is sufficient for my reader, if he has been a traveller himself, that with study and reflection hereupon he may be able to determine his own place and rank in the catalogue—it will be one step towards knowing himself; as it is great odds, but he retains some tincture and resemblance, of what he imbibed or carried out, to the present hour.

The man who first transplanted the grape of Burgundy to the Cape of Good Hope (observe he was a Dutch man) never dreamt of drinking the same wine at the Cape, that the same grape produced upon the French mountains—he was too phlegmatic for that—but undoubtedly he expected to drink some sort of vinous liquor; but whether good, bad, or indifferent—he knew enough of this world to know, that it did not depend upon his choice, but that what is generally called *chance* was to decide his success: however, he hoped for the best; and in these hopes, by an intemperate confidence in the fortitude of his head, and the depth of his discretion, *Mynheer* might possibly overset both in his new vineyard; and by discovering his nakedness, become a laughing-stock to his people.

Even so it fares with the poor Traveller, sailing and posting through the politer kingdoms of the globe in pursuit of knowledge and improvements.

Knowledge and improvements are to be got by sailing and posting for that purpose; but whether useful knowledge and real improvements, is all a lottery—and even where the adventurer is successful, the acquired stock must be used with caution and sobriety to turn to any profit—but as the chances run prodigiously the other way both as to the acquisition and application, I am of opinion, That a man would act as wisely, if he could prevail upon himself, to live contented without foreign knowledge or foreign improvements, especially if he lives in a country that has no absolute want of either—and indeed, much grief of heart has it oft and many a time cost me, when I have observed how many a foul step the inquisitive Traveller has measured to see sights and look into discoveries; all which, as Sancho Panca said to Don Quixote, they might have seen dry-shod at home. It is an age so full of light, that there is scarce a country or corner of Europe whose beams are not crossed and interchanged with others— Knowledge in most of its branches, and in most affairs, is like music in an Italian street, whereof those may partake, who pay nothing—But there is no nation under heaven—and God is my record, (before whose tribunal I must one day come and give an account of this work)—that I do not speak it vauntingly—But there is no nation under heaven abounding with more variety of learning—where the sciences may be more fitly woo'd, or more surely won than here—where art is encouraged, and will so soon rise high—where Nature (take her all together) has so little to answer for—and, to close all, where there is more wit and variety of character to feed the mind with—Where then, my dear countrymen, are you going—

—We are only looking at this chaise, said they—Your most obedient servant, said I, skipping out of it, and pulling off my hat—We were wondering, said one of them, who, I found, was an *inquisitive traveller*—what could occasion its motion.—'Twas the agitation, said I coolly, of writing a preface—I never heard, said the other, who was a *simple traveller,* of a preface wrote in a *Desobligeant.*—It would have been better, said I, in a *Vis a Vis.*[12]

As an English man does not travel to see English men, I retired to my room.

---

[12] A carriage in which two are face to face.

Thomas Gray
1716-1771

JOURNAL

30 Sept: 1769[1]

W^d at N:W. clouds & sunshine. a mile & ½ from Brough on a hill lay a great army encamp'd.[2] to the left open'd a fine valley with green meadows & hedge-rows, a Gentleman's house peeping forth from a grove of old trees. on a nearer approach appear'd myriads of horses & cattle in the road itself & in all the fields round me, a brisk stream hurrying cross the way, thousands of clean healthy People in their best party-color'd apparel, Farmers & their families, Esquires & their daughters, hastening up from the dales & down the fells on every side, glittering in the sun & pressing forward to join the throng: while the dark hills, on many of whose tops the mists were yet hanging, served as a contrast to this gay & moving scene, wch continued for near two miles more along the road, and the crowd (coming towards it) reach'd on as far as Appleby.

On the ascent of the hill above Appleby the thick hanging wood & the long reaches of the Eden (rapid, clear, & full as ever) winding below with views of the Castle & Town gave much employment to the mirror:[3] but the sun was wanting & the sky overcast. oats & barley cut every where, but not carried in. passed Kirby-thore, S^r W: Dalston's house at Acorn-bank, Whinfield-park, Harthorn - oaks, Countess - pillar, Brougham-Castle, Mr Brown (one of ye six Clerks)[4] his large new house, cross'd the Eden & the Eimot (pro-

---

Text and notes from *Correspondence of Thomas Gray*, ed. Paget Toynbee and Leonard Whibley, Oxford, Clarendon Press (3 vols., 1935), by courtesy of the directors of the Clarendon Press.

---

[1] "This letter contains the beginning of Gray's *Journal*, written during his tour in the Lakes and Yorkshire. For the first time since he went with Walpole to France and Italy in 1739 Gray wrote a continuous and detailed account of his travels and doings day by day. [William] Mason explains its purpose in a note [in his *Life and Letters of Gray* (1775)]: 'Dr. Wharton, who had intended to accompany Mr. Gray to Keswick, was seized at Brough with a violent fit of his asthmas, which obliged him to return home. This was the reason that Mr. Gray undertook to write the following journal of his tour for his friend's amusement. He sent it under different covers' " (Toynbee-Whibley).

[2] "There is a great fair for cattle kept on the hill near Brough, on this day and the preceding" (Mason).

[3] "Mr. Gray carried usually with him on these tours a Plano-convex Mirror of about four inches diameter on a black foil, and bound up like a pocketbook. A glass of this sort is perhaps the best and most convenient substitute for a Camera Obscura, of anything that has hitherto been invented" (Mason).

[4] "The six official clerks formerly connected with the Court of Chancery; their office was abolished in 1843" (Toynbee-Whibley).

nounce *Eeman*)[5] with its green vale, & at 3 o'clock dined with Mrs Buchanan, at *Penrith* on trout & partridge. in the afternoon walk'd up the *Beacon-hill* a mile to the top, saw Whinfield and Lowther-parks, & thro' an opening in the bosom of that cluster of mountains, wch the Doctor well remembers, the Lake of Ulz-water, with the craggy tops of a hundred nameless hills. these to W: & S:, to the N: a great extent of black & dreary plains, to E: *Cross-fell* just visible thro' mists & vapours hovering round it.

Oct: 1. W^d at S:W: a grey autumnal day, air perfectly calm & gentle. went to see *Ulz-water* 5 miles distant. soon left the Keswick-road & turn'd to the left thro' shady lanes along the Vale of *Eeman*, wch runs rapidly on near the way, ripling over the stones. to the right is *Delmaine*, a large fabrick of pale red stone with 9 windows in front & 7 on the side built by Mr Hassel, behind it a fine lawn surrounded by woods & a long rocky eminence rising over them. a clear & brisk rivulet runs by the house to join the Eeman, whose course is in sight & at a small distance.

Farther on appears *Hatton St John*, a castle-like old mansion of Mr Huddleston. approach'd *Dunmallert*, a fine pointed hill, cover'd with wood planted by old Mr Hassle beforemention'd, who lives always at home & delights in planting. walk'd over a spungy meadow or two & began to mount this hill thro' a broad & strait green alley among the trees, & with some toil gain'd the summit. from hence saw the Lake opening directly at my feet majestic in its calmness, clear & smooth as a blew mirror with winding shores & low points of land cover'd with green inclosures, white farm-houses looking out among the trees, & cattle feeding. the water is almost every where border'd with cultivated lands gently sloping upwards till they reach the feet of the mountains, wch rise very rude & aweful with their broken

tops on either hand. directly in front at better than 3 mile's distance, *Place-Fell*, one of the bravest among them, pushes its bold broad breast into the midst of the Lake & forces it to alter it's course, forming first a large bay to the left & then bending to the right.

I descended *Dunmallert* again by a side avenue, that was only not perpendicular, & came to *Barton*-bridge over the *Eeman*, then walking thro' a path in the wood round the bottom of the hill came forth, where the *Eeman* issues out of the lake, & continued my way along it's western shore close to the water, & generally on a level with it. Saw a cormorant flying over it & fishing. . . . (to be continued)

Aston. 18 Oct: 1769.
Dear D^r

I hope you got safe and well home after that troublesome night: I long to hear you say so. for me I have continued well, been so favour'd by the weather, that my walks have never once been hinder'd till yesterday, (that is during a fortnight & 3 or 4 days, & a journey of 300 miles, & more) & am now at Aston for two days. tomorrow I go towards Cambridge: Mason is not here, but Mr Alderson receives me. my best respects to the family! Adieu! I am ever

Yours (pray, tell me about
Stonehewer).[6]

Journal continued. 1 Oct: 1769.

The figure of *Ulz-water* nothing resembles that laid down in our maps: it is 9 miles long, & (at widest) under a mile in breadth. after extending itself 3 m: & ½ in a line to S: W: it turns at the foot of *Place-Fell*, almost due West, and is here not twice the breadth of the Thames at London. it is soon again interrupted by the roots of *Helvellyn*, a lofty & very rugged mountain, & spreading again turns off to S: E:, & is lost among the deep recesses of the hills. to this second turning I pursued my way

---

[5] "The Eamont, which flows out of the north end of Ullswater, forming the boundary between Westmorland and Cumberland" (Toynbee-Whibley).

[6] A mutual friend whose father was ill.

about four miles along its borders beyond a village scatter'd among trees &
call'd *Water-malloch,*[7] in a pleasant
grave day, perfectly calm & warm, but
without a gleam of sunshine: then the
sky seeming to thicken, the valley to
grow more desolate, & evening drawing
on, I return'd by the way I came to
Penrith.

Oct: 2. W^d at S: E:, sky clearing,
Cross-fell misty, but the outline of the
other hills very distinct. set out at 10
for *Keswick,* by the road we went in
1767. saw *Greystock*-town & castle to
the right, wch lie only 3 miles (over the
Fells) from *Ulz-water.* pass'd through
Penradock & Threlcot at the feet of *Sad-
dleback,* whose furrow'd sides were gilt
by the noon-day Sun, while its brow appear'd of a sad purple from the shadow
of the clouds, as they sail'd slowly by it.
the broad & green valley of *Gardies* and
Lowside, with a swift stream glittering
among the cottages & meadows lay to
the left; & the much finer (but nar-
rower) valley of St *John's* opening into
it: Hill-top the large, tho' low, mansion
of the Gaskarths,[8] now a Farm-house,
seated on an eminence among woods under a steep fell, was what appear'd the
most conspicuous, & beside it a great
rock like some antient tower nodding to
its fall. pass'd by the side of *Skiddaw*
& its cub call'd *Latter-rig,* & saw from
an eminence at two miles distance the
Vale of *Elysium* in all its verdure, the
sun then playing on the bosom of the
lake, & lighting up all the mountains
with its lustre.

Dined by two o'clock at the Queen's
Head, & then straggled out alone to the
Parsonage, fell down on my back across
a dirty lane with my glass open in one
hand, but broke only my knuckles: stay'd
nevertheless, & saw the sun set in all its
glory.

Oct: 3. W^d at S: E:, a heavenly
day. rose at seven, & walk'd out under
the conduct of my Landlord to *Borro-
dale.* the grass was cover'd with a hoar-

frost, wch soon melted, & exhaled in a
thin blewish smoke. cross'd the meadows obliquely, catching a diversity of
views among the hills over the lake &
islands, & changing prospect at every
ten paces, left *Cockshut* & Castle-hill
(wch we formerly mounted) behind me,
& drew near the foot of *Walla-crag,*
whose bare & rocky brow, cut perpen-
dicularly down above 400 feet, as I
guess, awefully overlooks the way: our
path here tends to the left, & the ground
gently rising, & cover'd with a glade of
scattering trees & bushes on the very
margin of the water, opens both ways
the most delicious view, that my eyes
ever beheld. behind you are the magnificent heights of *Walla*-crag; opposite
lie the thick hanging woods of Ld Egre-
mont, & *Newland*-valley with green &
smiling fields embosom'd in the dark
cliffs; to the left the jaws of *Borodale,*
with that turbulent Chaos of mountain
behind mountain roll'd in confusion; beneath you, & stretching far away to the
right, the shining purity of the *Lake,*
just ruffled by the breeze enough to shew
it is alive, reflecting rocks, woods, fields,
& inverted tops of mountains, with the
white buildings of *Keswick, Crosthwait-*
church, & *Skiddaw* for a back-ground
at distance. oh Doctor! I never wish'd
more for you; & pray think, how the
glass played its part in such a spot, w^ch
is called *Carf-close-reeds:* I chuse to set
down these barbarous names, that any
body may enquire on the place, & easily
find the particular station, that I mean.
this scene continues to *Barrow-gate,* & a
little farther, passing a brook called
Barrow-beck, we enter'd *Borodale.* the
crags, named *Lodoor-banks* now begin
to impend terribly over your way; &
more terribly, when you hear, that three
years since an immense mass of rock
tumbled at once from the brow, & bar'd
all access to the dale (for this is the only
road) till they could work their way
thro' it. luckily no one was passing at the
time of this fall; but down the side of

---

[7] "Watermillock, seven miles south-west from
Penrith" (Toynbee-Whibley).

[8] The home of Joseph Gaskarth, Fellow of
Pembroke College, Cambridge, and therefore an
acquaintance of Gray's

the mountain & far into the lake lie dispersed the huge fragments of this ruin
in all shapes & in all directions. something farther we turn'd aside into a cop-
pice, ascending a little in front of *Lodoor* water-fall. the height appears to be
about 200 feet, the quantity of water
not great, tho' (these three days excepted) it had rain'd daily in the hills
for near two months before: but then
the stream was nobly broken, leaping
from rock to rock, & foaming with fury.
on one side a towering crag, that spired
up to equal, if not overtop, the neighbouring cliffs (this lay all in shade &
darkness) on the other hand a rounder
broader projecting hill shag'd with wood
& illumined by the sun, wch glanced side-
ways on the upper part of the cataract.
the force of the water wearing a deep
channel in the ground hurries away to
join the lake. we descended again, &
passed the stream over a rude bridge.
soon after we came under *Gowder-crag,*
a hill more formidable to the eye & to
the apprehension than that of *Lodoor:*
the rocks atop, deep-cloven perpendicu-
larly by the rains, hanging loose & nodding forwards, seem just starting from
their base in shivers: the whole way
down & the road on both sides is strew'd
with piles of the fragments strangely
thrown across each other & of a dreadful
bulk. the place reminds one of those
passes in the Alps, where the Guides tell
you to move on with speed, & say nothing, lest the agitation of the air should
loosen the snows above, & bring down a
mass, that would overwhelm a caravan.
I took their counsel here and hasten'd on
in silence.

Non ragioniam di lor; ma guarda, e
passa!⁹

(to be continued)

Dear D^r
   Have you lost the former part of my
journal? it was dated from *Aston,* 18

Oct:. How does Stonhewer doe? will
his Father's condition allow him to return as yet? I beg my respects to all the
family at Old-Park, & am ever
                              Yours
                                 T G:
   29 Oct: 1769.   Cambridge.

   Oct: 3. The hills here are cloth'd
all up their steep sides with oak, ash,
birch, holly, &c; some of it has been cut
40 years ago, some within these 8 years,
yet all is sprung again green, flourishing,
& tall for its age, in a place where no
soil appears but the staring rock, &
where a man could scarce stand upright.
   Met a civil young Farmer overseeing
his reapers (for it is oat-harvest here)
who conducted us to a neat white house
in the village of Grange, wch is built on
a rising ground in the midst of a valley.
round it the mountains form an aweful
amphitheatre, & thro' it obliquely runs
the Darwent clear as glass, & shewing
under it's bridge every trout, that passes.
beside the village rises a round eminence
of rock cover'd entirely with old trees,
& over that more proudly towers *Castle-
crag,* invested also with wood on its
sides, & bearing on its naked top some
traces of a fort said to be Roman. by the
side of this hill, wch almost blocks up the
way, the valley turns to the left & contracts its dimensions, till there is hardly
any road but the rocky bed of the river.
the wood of the mountains increases &
their summits grow loftier to the eye, &
of more fantastic forms: among them
appear *Eagle's-cliff, Dove's-nest, White-
dale-pike,* &c: celebrated names in the
annals of Keswick. the dale opens about
four miles higher till you come to *Sea-
Whaite* (where lies the way mounting
the hills to the right, that leads to the
Wadd-mines)¹⁰ all farther access is here
barr'd to prying Mortals, only there is a
little path winding over the Fells, & for
some weeks in the year passable to the
Dale's-men; but the Mountains know
well, that these innocent people will not

⁹ "Dante, *Inferno,* III, 51: 'Let us not speak
of them; but look, and pass on' " (Toynbee-
Whibley).

¹⁰ "Wadd, or Wad, is the local name for
plumbago or graphite, commonly known as
blacklead" (Toynbee-Whibley).

reveal the mysteries of their ancient kingdom, the reign of Chaos & old Night.[11] only I learn'd, that this dreadful road dividing again leads one branch to *Ravenglas,* & the other to *Hawkshead.*

For me I went no farther than the Farmer's (better than 4 m: from Keswick) at *Grange:* his Mother & he brought us butter, that Siserah[12] would have jump'd at, tho' not in a lordly dish, bowls of milk, thin oaten-cakes, & ale; & we had carried a cold tongue thither with us. our Farmer was himself the Man, that last year plunder'd the Eagle's eirie: all the dale are up in arms on such an occasion, for they lose abundance of lambs yearly, not to mention hares, partridge, grous, &c: he was let down from the cliff in ropes to the shelf of rock, on w[ch] the nest was built, the people above shouting & hollowing to fright the old birds, w[ch] flew screaming round, but did not dare to attack him. he brought off the eaglet (for there is rarely more than one) & an addle egg. the nest was roundish & more than a yard over, made of twigs twisted together. seldom a year passes but they take the brood or eggs, & sometimes they shoot one, sometimes the other Parent, but the surviver has always found a mate (probably in Ireland) & they breed near the old place. by his description I learn, that this species is the *Erne* (the Vultur *Albicilla* of Linnaeus[13] in his last edition, but in

yours *Falco Albicilla*) so consult him & Pennant[14] about it.

Walk'd leisurely home the way we came, but saw a new landscape: the features indeed were the same in part, but many new ones were disclosed by the mid-day Sun, & the tints were entirely changed. take notice this was the best or perhaps the only day for going up Skiddaw, but I thought it better employ'd: it was perfectly serene, & hot as mid-summer.

In the evening walk'd alone down to the Lake by the side of *Crow-Park* after sunset & saw the solemn colouring of night draw on, the last gleam of sunshine fading away on the hill-tops, the deep serene of the waters, & the long shadows of the mountains thrown across them, till they nearly touch'd the hithermost shore. at distance heard the murmur of many waterfalls not audible in the day-time.[15] wish'd for the Moon, but she was *dark to me & silent, hid in her vacant interlunar cave.*[16]

Oct: 4. W[d] E:, clouds & sunshine, & in the course of the day a few drops of rain. Walk'd to *Crow-park,* now a rough pasture, once a glade of ancient oaks, whose large roots still remain on the ground, but nothing has sprung from them. if one single tree had remain'd, this would have been an unparallel'd spot, & Smith[17] judged right, when he took his print of the Lake from hence,

---

[11] "Milton, *Par. Lost,* I, 543" (Toynbee-Whibley).

[12] Judg. 5:25: "[Sisera] asked water, and [Jael] gave him milk; she brought forth butter in a lordly dish."

[13] "The twelfth edition of [the Swedish botanist Carolus Linnaeus's] *Systema Naturae* had been published at Stockholm in 1766-8" (Toynbee-Whibley).

[14] "Thomas Pennant (1726–98), the well-known traveller and naturalist, a friend of Gilbert White. . . . The work in question here was his *British Zoology* (Lond., fol., 1766; and 2 vols. 8vo., 1768)" (Toynbee-Whibley).

[15] "Wordsworth's lines in the *White Doe of Rylstone:*
A soft and lulling sound is heard
Of streams inaudible by day (*Canto* IV)—
may have been suggested by this passage"

(Toynbee-Whibley).

[16] "Milton, *Samson Agonistes:*
The Sun to me is dark
And silent as the Moon
When she deserts the night,
Hid in her vacant interlunar cave.
(ll. 86-9)" (Toynbee-Whibley).

[17] "The landscape painter, Thomas Smith (d. 1767), known from his birthplace as 'Smith of Derby', was one of the earliest delineators of the beauties of English scenery, and had a great reputation in his day. Many of his drawings were engraved by Vivares . . . and others; he himself engraved in 1767 from his own pictures a set of four views of the lakes of Cumberland, one of which doubtless was the print to which Gray here refers" (Toynbee-Whibley).

for it is a gentle eminence, not too high, on the very margin of the water & commanding it from end to end, looking full into the *gorge* of *Borodale*. I prefer it even to *Cockshut-hill,* wch lies beside it, & to wch I walk'd in the afternoon: it is cover'd with young trees both sown & planted, oak, spruce, scotch-fir, &c: all wch thrive wonderfully. There is an easy ascent to the top, & the view far preferable to that on Castle-hill (wch you remember) because this is lower & nearer to the Lake: for I find all points, that are much elevated, spoil the beauty of the valley, & make its parts (wch are not large) look poor & diminutive. While I was here, a little shower fell, red clouds came marching up the hills from the east,[18] & part of a bright rainbow seem'd to rise along the side of Castle-hill.

From hence I got to the *Parsonage* a little before Sunset, & saw in my glass a picture, that if I could transmitt to you, & fix it in all the softness of its living colours, would fairly sell for a thousand pounds. this is the sweetest scene I can yet discover in point of pastoral beauty. the rest are in a sublimer style.

(to be continued *without end*.)

P:S: I beg your pardon, but I have no franks.[19] the quill arrived very safe, & doubtless is a very snug and commodious method of travelling, for one of the rarities was alive & hearty, & was three times plunged in spirits, before I could get it to die. you are much improved in observation, for a common eye would certainly take it for a pismire. the place of its birth, form of ye antennae, & abdomen, particularly the long *aculeus* under it, shew it to be a *Cynips* (look among the *Hymenoptera*) not yet compleat, for the 4 wings do not yet appear, that I see. it is not a species described by Linnaeus, tho' he mentions others, that breed on the leaves, footstalks, buds, flowers & bark of the Oak. remember me to Mrs Wharton & the family. my love to S^tr, if he has not left Durham.

Adieu!

[Cambridge, Nov. 1769]

---

[18] "A reminiscence of Cowley, as appears from Gray's own note on l. 52 of his *Progress of Poesy:*
Or seen the Morning's well-appointed Star
Come marching up the eastern hills afar.
              Cowley—
which is a quotation (slightly altered) from stanza IV of Cowley's *Brutus, An Ode"* (Toynbee-Whibley).

[19] i.e., permits for free carriage of mail; hence, Gray apologizes because Wharton must pay the postage on receipt of the letter. Prepaid postage, other than by "franks," was not available. Gray's reference to a "quill" is to a species of gnat, known especially now in America to fly-fisherman who use imitations of the quill for artificial lures.

Thomas Warton, the Younger 1728-1790

THE HISTORY OF ENGLISH POETRY

VOLUME I, SECTION XVIII [A VIEW OF CONTINENTAL POETRY IN THE TIME OF CHAUCER]

It is not my intention to dedicate a volume to Chaucer, how much soever he may deserve it; nor can it be expected, that, in a work of this general nature, I should enter into a critical examination of all Chaucer's pieces. Enough has been said to prove, that in elevation, and elegance, in harmony and perspicuity of versification, he surpasses his predecessors in an infinite proportion: that his genius was universal, and adapted to themes of unbounded variety: that his merit was not less in painting familiar manners with humour and propriety, than in moving the passions, and in representing the beautiful or the grand objects of nature with grace and sublimity. In a word, that he appeared with all the lustre and dignity of a true poet, in an age which compelled him to struggle with a barbarous language, and a national want of taste; and when to write verses at all, was regarded as a singular qualification. It is true indeed, that he lived at a time when the French and Italians had made considerable advances and improvements in poetry: and although proofs have already been occasionally given of his imitations from these sources, I shall close my account of him with a distinct and comprehensive view of the nature of the poetry which subsisted in France and Italy when he wrote: pointing out in the mean time, how far and in what manner the popular models of those nations contributed to form his taste, and influence his genius.

I have already mentioned the troubadours of Provence, and have observed that they were fond of moral and allegorical fables. A taste for this sort of composition they partly acquired by reading Boethius,[1] and the PSYCHOMACHIA of Prudentius,[2] two favorite classics of the dark ages; and partly from the Saracens their neighbours in Spain, who were great inventors of apologues.[3] The French have a very early metrical romance DE FORTUNE ET DE FELICITE, a translation from Boethius's book DE CONSOLATIONE, by Reynault de Louens a Dominican friar.[4] From this source,

---

Text from first edition, 1774.

[1] Anicius Manlius Severinus Boethius (c. 480–524), Roman philosopher whose Latin work De Consolatione Philosophiae, of the consolations of philosophy, was widely popular.

[2] Aurelius Clemens Prudentius (348–?410), describes in allegory the struggle between paganism and Christianity in his most influential work, the Psychomachia.

[3] Moral fables, often of the incredible variety and thus distinguished from parables.

among many others of the Provencial poems, came the Tournament of ANTI- CHRIST[5] above-mentioned, which contains a combat of the Virtues and Vices: the Romaunt of Richard de Lisle, in which MODESTY fighting with LUST is thrown into the river Seine at Paris: and, above all, the ROMAUNT OF THE ROSE,[6] translated by Chaucer, and already mentioned at large in its proper place. Visions were a branch of this species of poetry, which admitted the most licentious excursions of fancy in forming personifications, and in feigning imaginary beings and ideal habitations. Under these we may rank Chaucer's HOUSE OF FAME, which I have before hinted to have been probably the production of Provence.

But the principal subject of their poems, dictated in great measure by the spirit of chivalry, was love: especially among the troubadours of rank and distinction, whose castles being crowded with ladies, presented perpetual scenes of the most splendid gallantry. This passion they spiritualised into various metaphysical refinements, and filled it with abstracted notions of visionary perfection and felicity. Here too they were perhaps influenced by their neighbours the Saracens, whose philosophy chiefly consisted of fantastic abstractions. It is manifest, however, that nothing can exceed the profound pedantry with which they treated this favorite argument. They defined the essence and characteristics of true love with all the parade of a Scotist[7] in his professorial chair: and bewildered their imaginations in speculative questions concerning the most desperate or the most happy situations of a sincere and sentimental heart. But it would be endless, and indeed ridiculous, to describe at length the systematical solemnity with which they cloathed this passion. The ROMAUNT OF THE ROSE

which I have just alleged as a proof of their allegorising turn, is not less an instance of their affectation in writing on this subject: in which the poet, under the agency of allegorical personages, displays the gradual approaches and impediments to fruition, and introduces a regular disputation conducted with much formality between Reason and a lover. Chaucer's TESTAMENT OF LOVE is also formed on this philosophy of gallantry. It is a lover's parody of Boethius's book DE CONSOLATIONE mentioned above. His poem called LA BELLE DAME SANS MERCY, and his ASSEMBLE OF LADIES, are from the same school. Chaucer's PRIORESSE and MONKE, whose lives were devoted to religious reflection and the most serious engagements, and while they are actually travelling on a pilgrimage to visit the shrine of a sainted martyr, openly avow the universal influence of love. They exhibit, on their apparel, badges entirely inconsistent with their profession, but easily accountable for from these principles. The Prioresse wears a bracelet on which is inscribed, with a crowned A, *Amor vincit omnia.*[8] The Monke ties his hood with a true- lover's knot. The early poets of Provence, as I before hinted, formed a society called the COURT OF LOVE, which gave rise to others in Gascony, Languedoc, Poictou, and Dauphiny: and Picardy, the constant rival of Provence, had a similar institution called *Plaids et Gieux sous l'Ormel.*[9] These establishments consisted of ladies and gentlemen of the highest rank, exercised and approved in courtesy, who tried with the most consummate ceremony, and decided with supreme authority, cases in love brought before their tribunal. Martial d'A- vergne,[10] an old French poet, for the diversion and at the request of the countess of Beaujeu, wrote a poem entitled ARRESTA AMORUM, or the De-

---

[4] Renaut de Louhans, French poet of the fourteenth century.

[5] By Huon de Meri, 1235.

[6] A French poem of the thirteenth century by Guillaume de Lorris, completed by Jean de Meung.

[7] A follower of the thirteenth-century Scottish philosopher, John Duns Scotus, who so abused his conception of reality that his name became the byword for a fool—*dunce.*

[8] "Love conquers all."

[9] "Assemblies and games under the elm."

[10] Martial d'Auvergne (1440?–1508).

crees of Love, which is a humourous description of the *Plaids* of Picardy. Fontenelle[11] has recited one of their processes, which conveys an idea of all the rest. A queen of France was appealed to from an unjust sentence pronounced in the love-pleas, where the countess of Champagne presided. The queen did not chuse to interpose in a matter of so much consequence, nor to reverse the decrees of a court whose decision was absolute and final. She answered, "God forbid, that I should presume to contradict the sentence of the countess of Champagne!" This was about the year 1206. Chaucer has a poem called the COURT OF LOVE, which is nothing more than the love-court of Provence: it contains the twenty statutes which that court prescribed to be universally observed under the severest penalties. Not long afterwards, on the same principle, a society was established in Languedoc, called the *Fraternity of the Penitents of Love*. Enthusiasm was here carried to as high a pitch of extravagance as ever it was in religion. It was a contention of ladies and gentlemen, who should best sustain the honour of their amorous fanaticism. Their object was to prove the excess of their love, by shewing with an invincible fortitude and consistency of conduct, with no less obstinacy of opinion, that they could bear extremes of heat and cold. Accordingly the resolute knights and esquires, the dames and damsels, who had the hardiness to embrace this severe institution, dressed themselves during the heat of summer in the thickest mantles lined with the warmest fur. In this they demonstrated, according to the antient poets, that love works the most wonderful and extraordinary changes. In winter, their love again perverted the nature of the seasons: they then cloathed themselves in the lightest and thinnest stuffs which could be procured. It was a crime to wear fur on a day of the most piercing cold; or to appear with a hood, cloak, gloves, or muff. The flame of love kept them sufficiently warm. Fires, all the winter, were utterly banished from their houses; and they dressed their apartments with evergreens. In the most intense frost their beds were covered only with a piece of canvass. It must be remembered, that in the mean time they passed the greater part of the day abroad, in wandering about from castle to castle; insomuch, that many of these devotees, during so desperate a pilgrimage, perished by the inclemency of the weather, and died martyrs to their profession.

The early universality of the French language greatly contributed to facilitate the circulation of the poetry of the troubadours in other countries. The Frankish language was familiar even at Constantinople and its dependent provinces in the eleventh century, and long afterwards. Raymond Montaniero, an historian of Catalonia, who wrote about the year 1300, says, that the French tongue was as well known in the Morea and at Athens as at Paris. "E parlavan axi belle Francis com dins en Paris."[12] The oldest Italian poetry seems to be founded on that of Provence. The word SONNET was adopted from the French into the Italian versification. It occurs in the ROMAN DE LA ROSE, "Lais d'amour et SONNETS courtois."[13] Boccacio[14] copied many of his best Tales from the troubadours. Several of Dante's[15] fictions are derived from the same fountain. Dante has honoured some of them with a seat in his Paradise: and in his tract DE VULGARI ELOQUENTIA, has mentioned Thiebault king of Navarre[16] as a pattern for writing poetry. With

[11] Bernard Le Bovier de Fontenelle (1657–1757), probably in *Discours sur l'origine des fables*.
[12] *History of Aragon:* "There French is as well spoken as it is in Paris."
[13] "lays of love and courtly sonnets."
[14] Giovanni Boccaccio (1313–1375), Italian author of, among other works, the *Decameron*.
[15] Dante Alighieri (1265–1321), Italian poet; the *De Vulgari Eloquentia*, written in Latin, is a defense of a hypothetical universalized Italian language as a literary and philosophical medium.
[16] Thibaud, fourth Count of Champagne (1201–1253), king of Navarre under the name Thibaud I; author of *Chansons*.

regard to Dante's capital work the IN-FERNO, Raoul de Houdane, a Provencial bard about the year 1180, wrote a poem entitled, LE VOYE OU LE SONGE D'EN-FER.[17] Both Boccacio and Dante studied at Paris, where they much improved their taste by reading the songs of Thiebauld king of Navarre, Gaces Brules, Chatelain de Coucy,[18] and other antient French fabulists. Petrarch's[19] refined ideas of love are chiefly drawn from those amorous reveries of the Provencials which I have above described; heightened perhaps by the Platonic system, and exaggerated by the subtilising spirit of Italian fancy. Varchi and Pignatelli[20] have written professed treatises on the nature of Petrarch's love. But neither they, nor the rest of the Italians who, to this day, continue to debate a point of so much consequence, consider how powerfully Petrarch must have been influenced to talk of love in so peculiar a strain by studying the poets of Provence. His TRIUMFO DI AMORE has much imagery copied from Anselm Faydditt,[21] one of the most celebrated of these bards. He has likewise many imitations from the works of Arnaud Daniel,[22] who is called the most eloquent of the troubadours. Petrarch, in one of his sonnets, represents his mistress Laura sailing on the river Rhone, in company with twelve Provencial ladies, who at that time presided over the COURT OF LOVE.

Pasquier observes,[23] that the Italian poetry arose as the Provencial declined. It is a proof of the decay of invention among the French in the beginning of the fourteenth century, that about that period they began to translate into prose their old metrical romances: such as the fables of king Arthur, of Charlemagne, of Oddegir the Dane, of Renaud of Montauban, and other illustrious champions, whom their early writers had celebrated in rhyme. At length, about the year 1380, in the place of the Provencial a new species of poetry succeeded in France, consisting of Chants Royaux, Balades, Rondeaux, and Pastorales. This was distinguished by the appellation of the NEW POETRY: and Froissart,[24] who has been mentioned above chiefly in the character of an historian, cultivated it with so much success, that he has been called its author. The titles of Froissart's poetical pieces will alone serve to illustrate the nature of this NEW POETRY: but they prove, at the same time, that the Provencial cast of composition still continued to prevail. They are, *The Paradise of Love, A Panegyric on the Month of May, The Temple of Honour, The Flower of the Daisy, Amorous Lays, Pastorals, The Amorous Prison, Royal Ballads in honour of our Lady, The Ditty of the Amourous Spinett, Virelais, Rondeaus, and The Plea of the Rose and Violet.* Whoever examines Chaucer's smaller pieces will perceive that they are altogether formed on this plan, and often compounded of these ideas. Chaucer himself declares, that he wrote

. . . Many an hymne for your holidaies
That hightin balades, rondils, virelaies.[25]

But above all, Chaucer's FLOURE AND THE LEAFE,[26] in which an air of rural description predominates, and where the allegory is principally conducted by mysterious allusions to the virtues or beauties of the vegetable world, to flowers and plants, exclusive of its general romantic and allegoric vein, bears a strong resemblance to some of these subjects.

---

[17] "The Sight or the Thought of Hell."
[18] Gace Brulé (end twelfth century) and Châtelain de Coucy (late twelfth and early thirteenth centuries), French trouvères.
[19] Petrarch (Francesco Petrarca or Petracco) (1304–1374), Italian poet.
[20] Benedetto Varchi (1503–1565) and Giovan Battista Pigna (1530–1575).
[21] Anselme Faydit (d. 1220).

[22] Of the twelfth century.
[23] "Etienne Pasquier, *Les Recherches de la France* (VII, 5, 609, 611, edit. 1633, fol.)" (Warton).
[24] Jean Froissart (1333?–?1400), French chronicler.
[25] "Prol[ogue to the] Leg[end of] G[ood] W[omen] V, 422" (Warton).
[26] The poem is no longer ascribed to Chaucer.

The poet is happily placed in a delicious arbour, interwoven with eglantine. Imaginary troops of knights and ladies advance: some of the ladies are crowned with flowers, and others with chaplets of agnus castus, and these are respectively subject to *a Lady of the Flower, and a Lady of the Leaf.* Some are cloathed in green, and others in white. Many of the knights are distinguished in much the same manner. But others are crowned with leaves of oak or of other trees: others carry branches of oak, laurel, hawthorn, and woodbine. Besides this profusion of vernal ornaments, the whole procession glitters with gold, pearls, rubies, and other costly decorations. They are preceded by minstrels cloathed in green and crowned with flowers. One of the ladies sings a bargaret, or pastoral, in praise of the daisy.

A bargaret in praising the daisie,
For as methought among her notis swete
She said *si douce est le margaruite.*[27]

This might have been Froissart's song: at least this is one of his subjects. In the mean time a nightingale, seated in a laurel-tree, whose shade would cover an hundred persons, sings the whole service, "longing to May." Some of the knights and ladies do obeysance to the leaf, and some to the flower of the daisy. Others are represented as worshipping a bed of flowers. Flora is introduced "of these flouris goddesse." The lady of the leaf invites the lady of the flower to a banquet. Under these symbols is much morality couched. The leaf signifies perseverance and virtue: the flower denotes indolence and pleasure. Among those who are crowned with the leaf, are the knights of king Arthur's round table, and Charlemagne's Twelve Peers; together with the knights of the order of the garter now just established by Edward the third.

But these fancies seem more immediately to have taken their rise from the FLORAL GAMES instituted in France in the year 1324, which filled the French poetry with images of this sort. They were founded by Clementina Isaure countess of Tholouse, and annually celebrated in the month of May. She published an edict, which assembled all the poets of France in artificial arbours dressed with flowers: and he that produced the best poem was rewarded with a violet of gold. There were likewise inferior prizes of flowers made in silver. In the mean time the conquerors were crowned with natural chaplets of their own respective flowers. During the ceremony, degrees were also conferred. He who had won a prize three times was created a doctor *en gaye Science,*[28] the name of the poetry of the Provencial troubadours. The instrument of creation was in verse. This institution, however fantastic, soon became common through the whole kingdom of France: and these romantic rewards, distributed with the most impartial attention to merit, at least infused an useful emulation, and in some measure revived the languishing genius of the French poetry.

The French and Italian poets, whom Chaucer imitates, abound in allegorical personages: and it is remarkable, that the early poets of Greece and Rome were fond of these creations. Homer[29] has given us, STRIFE, CONTENTION, FEAR, TERROR, TUMULT, DESIRE, PERSUASION, and BENEVOLENCE. We have in Hesiod,[30] DARKNESS, and many others, if the Shield of Hercules be of his hand. COMUS occurs in the Agamemnon of Eschylus;[31] and in the Prometheus of the same poet, STRENGTH and FORCE are two persons of the drama, and perform the capital parts. The fragments of Ennius[32] indicate, that his poetry consisted much of personifications. He says, that in one of the Carthaginian wars, the gigantic image of SORROW appeared in every place: "Omnibus endo locis ingens

---

[27] "so gentle is the marguerite."
[28] "of pleasant wisdom."
[29] The poet of the *Iliad* and the *Odyssey.*
[30] Greek poet of the eighth century B.C.

[31] Aeschylus, Greek tragic dramatist (525–456 B.C.).
[32] Quintus Ennius (239–?169 B.C.), Roman poet.

apparet imago TRISTITIAS."[33] Lucretius[34] has drawn the great and terrible figure of SUPERSTITION, "Quae caput e cœli regionibus ostendebat."[35] He also mentions, in a beautiful procession of the Seasons, CALORARIDUS, HYEMS, and ALGUS.[36] He introduces MEDICINE *muttering with silent fear,* in the midst of the deadly pestilence at Athens. It seems to have escaped the many critics who have written on Milton's noble but romantic allegory of SIN and DEATH, that he took the person of Death from the Alcestis of his favorite tragedian Euripides,[37] where ΘΑΝΑΤΟΣ [38] is a principal agent in the drama. As knowledge and learning encrease, poetry begins to deal less in imagination: and these fantastic beings give way to real manners and living characters.

---

[33] Translated in the preceding clause.

[34] Titus Lucretius Carus (96?–55 B.C.), Roman philosophical poet.

[35] "Who showed her head in the region of heaven" (*De Rerum Natura,* I, 64).

[36] "heat, ice, and chill."

[37] Greek playwright of the fifth century B.C.

[38] "death"; cf. the American William Cullen Bryant's *Thanatopsis,* a name directly from the Greek word Warton cites.

Edward Gibbon
1737-1794

THE DECLINE AND FALL
OF THE ROMAN EMPIRE

CHAPTER III

OF THE CONSTITUTION OF THE ROMAN
EMPIRE, IN THE AGE OF THE ANTONINES[1]

The obvious definition of a monarchy seems to be that of a state, in which a single person, by whatsoever name he may be distinguished, is intrusted with the execution of the laws, the management of the revenue, and the command of the army. But unless public liberty is protected by intrepid and vigilant guardians, the authority of so formidable a magistrate will soon degenerate into despotism. The influence of the clergy, in an age of superstition, might be usefully employed to assert the rights of mankind; but so intimate is the connexion between the throne and the altar, that the banner of the church has very seldom been seen on the side of the people. A martial nobility and stubborn commons, possessed of arms, tenacious of property, and collected into constitutional assemblies, form the only balance capable of preserving a free constitution against enterprises of an aspiring prince.

Every barrier of the Roman constitution had been levelled by the vast ambition of the dictator; every fence had been extirpated by the cruel hand of the Triumvir.[2] After the victory of Actium, the fate of the Roman world depended on the will of Octavianus, surnamed Caesar, by his uncle's adoption, and afterwards Augustus, by the flattery of the senate. The conqueror was at the head of forty-four veteran legions,[3] conscious of their own strength, and of the weakness of the constitution, habituated, during twenty years civil war, to every act of blood and violence, and passionately devoted to the house of Caesar, from whence alone they had received, and expected, the most lavish rewards. The provinces, long oppressed by the ministers of the republic, sighed for the government of a single person, who would be the master, not the accomplice, of those petty tyrants. The people of Rome, viewing, with a secret pleasure, the humiliation of the aristocracy, demanded only bread and public shows; and were supplied with both by the liberal hand

Text from third edition, 1777; first published in 1776.

[1] A.D 138–180.

[2] The first triumvirate of Julius Caesar, Pompey, and Crassus had ended with Julius Caesar as dictator; after his murder in 44 B.C., Antony, Octavianus, and Lepidus had formed a second triumvirate which ended with the defeat of Antony and Cleopatra at Actium in 31 B.C. and the emergence of Octavianus (b. 63 B.C.) as sole dictator.

[3] "Orosius, vi, 18" (Gibbon). Paulus Orosius (fl. c. 400), Christian Historian, author of *Historiarum adversus Paganos.*

of Augustus. The rich and polite Italians, who had almost universally embraced the philosophy of Epicurus, enjoyed the present blessings of ease and tranquillity, and suffered not the pleasing dream to be interrupted by the memory of their old tumultuous freedom. With its power, the senate had lost its dignity; many of the most noble families were extinct. The republicans of spirit and ability had perished in the field of battle, or in the proscription. The door of the assembly had been designedly left open, for a mixed multitude of more than a thousand persons, who reflected disgrace upon their rank, instead of deriving honour from it.[4]

The reformation of the senate, was one of the first steps in which Augustus laid aside the tyrant, and professed himself the father of his country. He was elected censor; and, in concert with his faithful Agrippa, he examined the list of the senators, expelled a few members, whose vices or whose obstinacy required a public example, persuaded near two hundred to prevent the shame of an expulsion by a voluntary retreat, raised the qualification of a senator to about ten thousand pounds, created a sufficient number of Patrician families, and accepted for himself, the honourable title of Prince of the Senate, which had always been bestowed, by the censors, on the citizen the most eminent for his honours and services.[5] But whilst he thus restored the dignity, he destroyed the independence of the senate. The principles of a free constitution are irrecoverably lost, when the legislative power is nominated by the executive.

Before an assembly thus modelled and prepared, Augustus pronounced a studied oration, which displayed his patriotism, and disguised his ambition. "He lamented, yet excused, his past conduct. Filial piety had required at his hands the revenge of his father's murder; the humanity of his own nature had sometimes given way to the stern laws of necessity, and to a forced connexion with two unworthy colleagues: as long as Antony lived, the republic forbade him to abandon her to a degenerate Roman, and a barbarian queen. He was now at liberty to satisfy his duty and his inclination. He solemnly restored the senate and people to all their ancient rights; and wished only to mingle with the crowd of his fellow-citizens, and to share the blessings which he had obtained for his country."[6]

It would require the pen of Tacitus[7] (if Tacitus had assisted at this assembly) to describe the various emotions of the senate; those that were suppressed, and those that were affected. It was dangerous to trust the sincerity of Augustus; to seem to distrust it, was still more dangerous. The respective advantages of monarchy and a republic have often divided speculative inquirers; the present greatness of the Roman state, the corruption of manners, and the licence of the soldiers, supplied new arguments to the advocates of monarchy; and these general views of government were again warped by the hopes and fears of each individual. Amidst this confusion of sentiments, the answer of the senate was unanimous and decisive. They refused to accept the resignation of Augustus; they conjured him not to desert the republic, which he had saved. After a decent resistance, the crafty tyrant submitted to the orders of the senate; and consented to receive the government of the provinces, and the general command of the

4 "Julius Caesar introduced soldiers, strangers, and half-barbarians, into the senate (Suetonius in Caesar, c, 77, 80). The abuse became still more scandalous after his death" (Gibbon). Gaius Suetonius Tranquillus (c. 70–c. 140), Roman historian, author of De Vita Caesarum, of which the Caesar here referred to and the Augustus in the next note are taken.

5 "Dion Cassius [Cassius Dio Cocceianus (c. 155–c. 235), Greek historian, author of a history of Rome], I, iii, 693. Suetonius in Augustus, c, 55" (Gibbon).

6 "Dion (l. liii. p. 698.) gives us a prolix and bombast speech on this great occasion. I have borrowed from Suetonius and Tacitus the general language of Augustus" (Gibbon).

7 Cornelius Tacitus (55?–?117), famous Roman historian.

Roman armies, under the well-known names of PROCONSUL and IMPERATOR.[8] But he would receive them only for ten years. Even before the expiration of that period, he hoped that the wounds of civil discord would be completely healed, and that the republic, restored to its pristine health and vigour, would no longer require the dangerous interposition of so extraordinary a magistrate. The memory of this comedy, repeated several times during the life of Augustus, was preserved to the last ages of the empire, by the peculiar pomp with which the perpetual monarchs of Rome always solemnized the tenth years of their reign.[9]

Without any violation of the principles of the constitution, the general of the Roman armies might receive and exercise an authority almost despotic over the soldiers, the enemies, and the subjects of the republic. With regard to the soldiers, the jealousy of freedom had, even from the earliest ages of Rome, given way to the hopes of conquest, and a just sense of military discipline. The dictator, or consul, had a right to command the service of the Roman youth; and to punish an obstinate or cowardly disobedience by the most severe and ignominious penalties, by striking the offender out of the list of citizens, by confiscating his property, and by selling his person into slavery.[10] The most sacred rights of freedom, confirmed by the Porcian and Sempronian laws, were suspended by the military engagement. In his camp the general exercised an absolute power of life and death; his jurisdiction was not confined by any forms of trial, or rules of proceeding, and the execution of the sentence was immediate and without appeal.[11] The choice of the enemies of Rome was regularly decided by the legislative authority. The most important resolutions of peace and war were seriously debated in the senate, and solemnly ratified by the people. But when the arms of the legions were carried to a great distance from Italy, the generals assumed the liberty of directing them against whatever people, and in whatever manner, they judged most advantageous for the public service. It was from the success, not from the justice, of their enterprises, that they expected the honours of a triumph. In the use of victory, especially after they were no longer controlled by the commissioners of the senate, they exercised the most unbounded despotism. When Pompey commanded in the east, he rewarded his soldiers and allies, dethroned princes, divided kingdoms, founded colonies, and distributed the treasures of Mithridates. On his return to Rome, he obtained, by a single act of the senate and people, the universal ratification of all his proceedings.[12] Such was the power over the soldiers, and over the enemies of Rome, which was either granted to, or assumed by, the generals of the republic. They

---

[8] *Imperator* (from which we have derived Emperor) signified under the republic no more than *general*, and was emphatically bestowed by the soldiers, when on the field of battle they proclaimed their victorious leader worthy of that title. When the Roman *emperors* assumed it in that sense, they placed it after their name, and marked how often they had taken it" (Gibbon).

[9] "Dion, l. liii. p. 703, etc." (Gibbon).

[10] "Livy Epitom. l. xiv. Valer. Maxim vi, 3" (Gibbon). Titus Livius (59 B.C.–A.D. 17), Roman historian who devoted a long life to producing a *History of Rome,* which now exists only in parts. Valerius Maximus (fl. A.D. 30), was the author of a book of rhetoric with examples from Livy among others.

[11] "See in the viiith book of Livy, the con-

duct of Manlius Torquatus and Papirius Cursor. They violated the laws of nature and humanity, but they asserted those of military discipline; and the people, who abhorred the action, was obliged to respect the principle" (Gibbon).

[12] "By the lavish but unconstrained suffrages of the people, Pompey had obtained a military command scarcely inferior to that of Augustus. Among the extraordinary acts of power executed by the former, we may remark the foundation of twenty-nine cities, and the distribution of three or four million sterling to his troops. The ratification of his acts met with some opposition and delays in the senate. See Plutarch, Appian, Dion Cassius, and the first book of the epistles to Atticus" (Gibbon).

were, at the same time, the governors, or rather monarchs, of the conquered provinces, united the civil with the military character, administered justice as well as the finances, and exercised both the executive and legislative power of the state.

From what has been already observed in the first chapter of this work, some notion may be formed of the armies and provinces thus intrusted to the ruling hand of Augustus. But as it was impossible that he could personally command the legions of so many distant frontiers, he was indulged by the senate, as Pompey had already been, in the permission of devolving the execution of his great office on a sufficient number of lieutenants. In rank and authority these officers seemed not inferior to the ancient proconsuls; but their station was dependent and precarious. They received and held their commissions at the will of a superior, to whose *auspicious* influence the merit of their actions was legally attributed.[13] They were the representatives of the emperor. The emperor alone was the general of the republic, and his jurisdiction, civil as well as military, extended over all the conquests of Rome. It was some satisfaction, however, to the senate, that he always delegated his power to the members of their body. The Imperial lieutenants were of consular or praetorian dignity; the legions were commanded by senators, and the praefecture of Egypt was the only important trust committed to a Roman knight.

Within six days after Augustus had been compelled to accept so very liberal a grant, he resolved to gratify the pride of the senate by an easy sacrifice. He represented to them, that they had enlarged his powers, even beyond that degree which might be required by the melancholy condition of the times. They had not permitted him to refuse the laborious command of the armies and the

frontiers; but he must insist on being allowed to restore the more peaceful and secure provinces, to the mild administration of the civil magistrate. In the division of the provinces, Augustus provided for his own power, and for the dignity of the republic. The proconsuls of the senate, particularly those of Asia, Greece, and Africa, enjoyed a more honourable character than the lieutenants of the emperor, who commanded in Gaul or Syria. The former were attended by lictors,[14] the latter by soldiers. A law was passed, that wherever the emperor was present, his extraordinary commission should supersede the ordinary jurisdiction of the governor, a custom was introduced, that the new conquests belonged to the Imperial portion, and it was soon discovered, that the authority of the *Prince,* the favourite epithet of Augustus, was the same in every part of the empire.

In return for this imaginary concession, Augustus obtained an important privilege, which rendered him master of Rome and Italy. By a dangerous exception to the ancient maxims, he was authorized to preserve his military command, supported by a numerous body of guards, even in time of peace, and in the heart of the capital. His command, indeed, was confined to those citizens who were engaged in the service by the military oath; but such was the propensity of the Romans to servitude, that the oath was voluntarily taken by the magistrates, the senators, and the equestrian order, till the homage of flattery was insensibly converted into an annual and solemn protestation of fidelity.

Although Augustus considered a military force, as the firmest foundation, he wisely rejected it, as a very odious instrument, of government. It was more agreeable to his temper, as well as to his policy, to reign under the venerable names of ancient magistracy, and art-

---

[13] "Under the commonwealth, a triumph could only be claimed by the general, who was authorized to take the Auspices in the name of the people. By an exact consequence drawn from this principle of policy and religion, the triumph was reserved to the emperor, and his most successful lieutenants were satisfied with some marks of distinction, which, under the name of triumphal honours, were invented in their favour" (Gibbon).

[14] Men who carried the fasces, symbols of authority.

fully to collect, in his own person, all the scattered rays of civil jurisdiction. With this view he permitted the senate to confer upon him, for his life, the powers of the consular[15] and tribunitian offices,[16] which were, in the same manner, continued to all his successors. The consuls had succeeded to the kings of Rome, and represented the dignity of the state. They superintended the ceremonies of religion, levied and commanded the legions, gave audience to foreign ambassadors, and presided in the assemblies both of the senate and people. The general control of the finances was intrusted to their care, and though they seldom had leisure to administer justice in person, they were considered as the supreme guardians of law, equity, and the public peace. Such was their ordinary jurisdiction; but whenever the senate empowered the first magistrate to consult the safety of the commonwealth, he was raised by that degree above the laws, and exercised, in the defence of liberty, a temporary despotism.[17] The character of the tribunes was, in every respect, different from that of the consuls. The appearance of the former was modest and humble; but their persons were sacred and inviolable. Their force was suited rather for opposition than for action. They were instituted to defend the oppressed, to pardon offences, to arraign the enemies of the people, and when they judged it necessary, to stop, by a single word, the whole machine of government. As long as the republic subsisted, the dangerous influence, which either the consul[18] or the tribune[19] might derive from their respective jurisdiction, was diminished by several important restrictions. Their authority expired with the year in which they were elected; the former office was divided between two, the latter among ten persons; and, as both in their private and public interest they were averse to each other, their mutual conflicts contributed, for the most part, to strengthen rather than to destroy the balance of the constitution. But when the consular and tribunitian powers were united, when they were vested for life in a single person, when the general of the army was, at the same time, the minister of the senate and the representative of the Roman people, it was impossible to resist the exercise, nor was it easy to define the limits, of his imperial prerogative.

To these accumulated honours, the policy of Augustus soon added the splendid as well as important dignities of supreme pontiff, and of censor. By the former he acquired the management of the religion, and by the latter a legal inspection over the manners and fortunes, of the Roman people. If so many distinct and independent powers did not exactly unite with each other, the complaisance of the senate was prepared to supply every deficiency by the most ample and extraordinary concessions. The emperors, as the first ministers of the republic, were exempted from the obligation and penalty of many inconvenient laws: they were authorized to convoke the senate, to make several motions in the same day, to recommend candidates for the honours of the state, to enlarge the bounds

---

[15] "Cicero (de Legibus, iii. 3) gives the consular office the name of *Regia potestas:* and Polybius (l. vi. c. 3.) observes three powers in the Roman constitution. The monarchical was represented and exercised by the Consuls" (Gibbon). Marcus Tullius Cicero (106–43 B.C.), Roman orator and consul, prolific and versatile writer.

[16] "As the tribunitian power (distinct from the annual office) was first invented for the dictator Caesar (Dion, l. xliv. p. 384), we may easily conceive, that it was given as a reward for having so nobly asserted, by arms, the sacred rights of the tribunes and people. See his own Commentaries, de Bell. Civil. l. i"

(Gibbon). Gaius Julius Caesar (100–44 B.C.), Roman politician and writer on contemporary affairs, particularly, as here, in the military.

[17] "Augustus exercised nine annual consulships without interruption. He then most artfully refused that magistracy as well as the dictatorship, absented himself from Rome, and waited till the fatal effects of tumult and faction forced the senate to invest him with a perpetual consulship. Augustus, as well as his successors, affected, however, to conceal so invidious a title" (Gibbon).

[18] Highest officer of the state.

[19] Civil representative of the plebeians.

of the city, to employ the revenue at their discretion, to declare peace and war, to ratify treaties; and by a most comprehensive clause, they were empowered to execute whatsoever they should judge advantageous to the empire, and agreeable to the majesty of things private or public, human or divine.[20]

When all the various powers of executive government were committed to the *Imperial magistrate,* the ordinary magistrates of the commonwealth languished in obscurity, without vigour, and almost without business. The names and forms of the ancient administration were preserved by Augustus with the most anxious care. The usual number of consuls, praetors, and tribunes,[21] were annually invested with their respective ensigns of office, and continued to discharge some of their least important functions. Those honours still attracted the vain ambition of the Romans, and the emperors themselves, though invested for life with the powers of the consulship, frequently aspired to the title of that annual dignity, which they condescended to share with the most illustrious of their fellow-citizens.[22] In the election of these magistrates, the people, during the reign of Augustus, were permitted to expose all the inconveniencies of a wild democracy. That artful prince, instead of discovering the least symptom of impatience, humbly solicited their suffrages for himself or his friends, and scrupulously practised all the duties of an ordinary candidate.[23] But we may venture to ascribe to his councils, the first measure of the succeeding reign, by which the elections were transferred to the senate.[24] The assemblies of the people were for ever abolished, and the emperors were delivered from a dangerous multitude, who, without restoring liberty, might have disturbed, and perhaps endangered, the established government.

By declaring themselves the protectors of the people, Marius and Caesar had subverted the constitution of their country. But as soon as the senate had been humbled and disarmed, such an assembly, consisting of five or six hundred persons, was found a much more tractable and useful instrument of dominion. It was on the dignity of the senate, that Augustus and his successors founded their new empire; and they affected, on every occasion, to adopt the language and principles of Patricians.[25] In the administration of their own powers, they frequently consulted the great national

[20] "See a fragment of a Decree of the Senate, conferring on the emperor Vespasian, all the powers granted to his predecessors, Augustus, Tiberius, and Claudius. This curious and important monument is published in Gruter's Inscriptions. No. ccxlii" (Gibbon). Gibbon's reference is to *Inscriptiones antiquae totius orbis Romani in absolutissimum* by Janus Gruterus (1560–1627).

[21] "Two consuls were created on the Calends of January; but in the course of the year others were substituted in their places, till the annual number seems to have amounted to no less than twelve. The praetors were usually sixteen or eighteen (Lipsius in Excurs. D. ad Tacit. Annal. l. i.). I have not mentioned the Ædiles or Quaestors. Officers of the police or revenue easily adapt themselves to any form of government. In the time of Nero, the tribunes legally possessed the right of *intercession,* though it might be dangerous to exercise it (Tacit. Annal. xvi. 26.). In the time of Trajan, it was doubtful whether the tribuneship was an office or a name (Plin. Epist. i. 23.)" (Gibbon). Gaius Plinius Caecilius Secundus (*c.* 61–

c. 114), author of many letters, adopted by the elder Pliny known for his *Natural History.*

[22] "The tyrants themselves were ambitious of the consulship. The virtuous princes were moderate in the pursuit, and exact in the discharge of it. Trajan revived the ancient oath, and swore before the consul's tribunal, that he would observe the laws (Plin. Panegyric. c. 64.)" (Gibbon).

[23] "Quoties Magistratuum Comitiis interesset, Tribus cum candidatis suis circuibat: supplicabatque more solemni. Ferebat et ipse suffragium in tribubus, ut unus e populo. Suetonius in August. c. 56." (Gibbon). ("Whenever he took part in the selection of magistrates, he went about the tribe with his candidates, appealing for them ceremoniously. He also voted as one of the people himself.")

[24] "Tum primum Comitia e campo ad patres translata sunt. Tacit. Annal. i. 15. [Translated in effect in the text.] The word *primum* seems to allude to some faint and unsuccessful efforts, which were made towards restoring them to the people" (Gibbon).

[25] People of noble birth.

council, and *seemed* to refer to its decision the most important concerns of peace and war. Rome, Italy, and the internal provinces were subject to the immediate jurisdiction of the senate. With regard to civil objects, it was the supreme court of appeal; with regard to criminal matters, a tribunal, constituted for the trial of all offences that were committed by men in any public station, or that affected the peace and majesty of the Roman people. The exercise of the judicial power became the most frequent and serious occupation of the senate; and the important causes that were pleaded before them, afforded a last refuge to the spirit of ancient eloquence. As a council of state, and as a court of justice, the senate possessed very considerable prerogatives; but in its legislative capacity, in which it was supposed virtually to represent the people, the rights of sovereignty were acknowledged to reside in that assembly. Every power was derived from their authority, every law was ratified by their sanction. Their regular meetings were held on three stated days in every month, the Calends, the Nones, and the Ides.[26] The debates were conducted with decent freedom; and the emperors themselves, who gloried in the name of senators, sat, voted, and divided with their equals.

To resume, in a few words, the system of the Imperial government; as it was instituted by Augustus, and maintained by those princes who understood their own interest and that of the people, it may be defined an absolute monarchy disguised by the forms of a commonwealth. The masters of the Roman world surrounded their throne with darkness, concealed their irresistible strength, and humbly professed themselves the accountable ministers of the senate, whose supreme decrees they dictated and obeyed.[27]

The face of the court corresponded with the forms of the administration. The emperors, if we except those tyrants whose capricious folly violated every law of nature and decency, disdained that pomp and ceremony which might offend their countrymen, but could add nothing to their real power. In all the offices of life, they affected to confound themselves with their subjects, and maintained with them an equal intercourse of visits and entertainments. Their habit, their palace, their table, were suited only to the rank of an opulent senator. Their family, however numerous or splendid, was composed entirely of their domestic slaves and freedmen.[28] Augustus or Trajan would have blushed at employing the meanest of the Romans in those menial offices, which, in the household and bedchamber of a limited monarch, are so eagerly solicited by the proudest nobles of Britain.

The deification of the emperors[29] is the only instance in which they departed from their accustomed prudence and modesty. The Asiatic Greeks were the first inventors, the successors of Alexander the first objects, of this servile and impious mode of adulation. It was easily transferred from the kings to the governors of Asia; and the Roman magistrates very frequently were adored as provincial deities, with the pomp of altars and temples, of festivals and sacrifices.[30] It

[26] i.e., the first, the fifth or seventh depending on the month, and the thirteenth or fifteenth.

[27] "Dion Cassius (l. liii. p. 703–714.) has given a very loose and partial sketch of the Imperial system. To illustrate and often to correct him, I have meditated Tacitus, examined Suetonius, and consulted the following moderns: the Abbè de la Bleterie, in the Memoires de l'Academie des Inscriptions, tom. xix. xxi. xxiv. xxv. xxvii. Beaufort Republique Romaine, tom. i. p. 255–275. Two Dissertations of Noodt and Grovonius, *de lege Regia;* printed at Leyden, in the year 1731. Gravina de Imperio Romano, p. 479–544 of his Opuscula. Masei Verona Illustrata, p. i. p. 245, etc." (Gibbon).

[28] "A weak prince will always be governed by his domestics. The power of slaves aggravated the shame of the Romans; and the senate paid court to a Pallas or a Narcissus. There is a chance that a modern favourite may be a gentleman" (Gibbon).

[29] "See a treatise of Vandale de Consecratione Principum. It would be easier for me to copy, than it has been to verify, the quotations of that learned Dutchman" (Gibbon).

[30] "See a dissertation of the Abbè Mongault

was natural that the emperors should not refuse what the proconsuls had accepted, and the divine honours which both the one and the other received from the provinces, attested rather the despotism than the servitude of Rome. But the conquerors soon imitated the vanquished nations in the arts of flattery; and the imperious spirit of the first Caesar too easily consented to assume, during his life-time, a place among the tutelar[31] deities of Rome. The milder temper of his successor declined so dangerous an ambition, which was never afterwards revived, except by the madness of Caligula and Domitian. Augustus permitted indeed some of the provincial cities to erect temples to his honour, on condition that they should associate the worship of Rome with that of the sovereign; he tolerated private superstition, of which he might be the object;[32] but he contented himself with being revered by the senate and people in his human character, and wisely left to his successor, the care of his public deification. A regular custom was introduced, that on the decease of every emperor who had neither lived nor died like a tyrant, the senate by a solemn decree should place him in the number of the gods: and the ceremonies of his Apotheosis were blended with those of his funeral. This legal, and as it should seem, injudicious profanation, so abhorrent to our stricter principles, was received with a very faint murmur,[33] by the easy nature of Polytheism; but it was received as an institution, not of religion but of policy. We should disgrace the virtues of the Antonines, by comparing them with the vices of Hercules or Jupiter. Even the character of Caesar or Augustus were far superior to those of the popular deities. But it was the misfortune of the former to live in an en-

lightened age, and their actions were too faithfully recorded to admit of such a mixture of fable and mystery, as the devotion of the vulgar requires. As soon as their divinity was established by law, it sunk into oblivion, without contributing either to their own fame, or to the dignity of succeeding princes.

In the consideration of the Imperial government, we have frequently mentioned the artful founder, under his well-known title of Augustus, which was not however conferred upon him, till the edifice was almost completed. The obscure name of Octavianus, he derived from a mean family, in the little town of Aricia. It was stained with the blood of the proscription: and he was desirous, had it been possible, to erase all memory of his former life. The illustrious surname of Caesar, he had assumed, as the adopted son of the dictator; but he had too much good sense, either to hope to be confounded, or to wish to be compared, with that extraordinary man. It was proposed in the senate, to dignify their minister with a new appellation; and after a very serious discussion, that of Augustus was chosen among several others, as being the most expressive of the character of peace and sanctity, which he uniformly affected.[34] *Augustus* was therefore a personal, *Caesar* a family distinction. The former should naturally have expired with the prince, on whom it was bestowed; and however the latter was diffused by adoption and female alliance, Nero was the last prince who could alledge any hereditary claim to the honours of the Julian line. But, at the time of his death, the practice of a century had inseparably connected those appellations with the Imperial dignity, and they have been preserved by a long succession of emperors, Romans, Greeks,

---

in the first volume of the Academy of Inscriptions" (Gibbon).

[31] protective.

[32] "Jurandasque tuum per nomen ponimus *aras*, says Horace to the emperor himself, and Horace was well acquainted with the court of Augustus" (Gibbon). "By thee we swear, to thee our altars raise" (*Epistles*, II, 16, tr. Francis).

[33] "See Cicero in Philippic. i. 6. Julian in Caesaribus. In que Deum templis jurabit Roma per umbras, is the indignant expression of Lucan, but it is a patriotic, rather than a devout indignation" (Gibbon). "And Rome shall swear by ghosts in the temples of the gods" (*De Bello Civili*, vii, 459).

[34] "Dion Cassius, l. liii. p. 710, with the curious annotations of Reymar" (Gibbon).

Franks, and Germans, from the fall of the republic to the present time. A distinction was, however, soon introduced. The sacred title of Augustus was always reserved for the monarch, whilst the name of Caesar was more freely communicated to his relations; and, from the reign of Hadrian,[35] at least, was appropriated to the second person in the state, who was considered as the presumptive heir of the empire.

The tender respect of Augustus for a free constitution which he had destroyed, can only be explained by an attentive consideration of the character of that subtle tyrant. A cool head, an unfeeling heart, and a cowardly disposition, prompted him, at the age of nineteen, to assume the mask of hypocrisy, which he never afterwards laid aside. With the same hand, and probably with the same temper, he signed the proscription of Cicero,[36] and the pardon of Cinna.[37] His virtues, and even his vices, were artificial; and according to the various dictates of his interest, he was at first the enemy, and at last the father, of the Roman world.[38] When he framed the artful system of the Imperial authority, his moderation was inspired by his fears. He wished to deceive the people by an image of civil liberty, and the armies by an image of civil government.

---

[35] 117–138.

[36] Cicero was murdered in 43 B.C.

[37] Cinna had plotted against him; the general subject of Octavianus's pardon would have been familiar to Gibbon and to many of his contemporaries through the brilliant French dramatization by Corneille in the preceding century.

[38] "As Octavianus advanced to the banquet of the Caesars, his colour changed like that of the camelion; pale at first, then red, afterwards black, he at last assumed the mild livery of Venus and the Graces (Caesares, p. 309.). This image employed by Julian, in his ingenious fiction, is just and elegant; but when he considers this change of character as real, and ascribes it to the power of philosophy; he does too much honour to philosophy, and to Octavianus" (Gibbon).

Frances Burney, Mme. d'Arblay 1752-1840

From EVELINA, or a Young Lady's Entrance into the World

LETTER VIII   EVELINA TO THE REV. MR. VILLARS.

Howard Grove, March 26.

This house seems to be the house of joy; every face wears a smile, and a laugh is at everybody's service. It is quite amusing to walk about, and see the general confusion; a room leading to the garden is fitting up for Captain Mirvan's study. Lady Howard does not sit a moment in a place; Miss Mirvan is making caps;[1] every body so busy!—such flying from room to room!—so many orders given, and retracted, and given again!—nothing but hurry and perturbation.

Well but, my dear Sir, I am desired to make a request to you. I hope you will not think me an incroacher; Lady Howard insists upon my writing!—yet I hardly know how to go on; a petition implies a want,—and have you left me one? No, indeed.

I am half ashamed of myself for beginning this letter. But these dear ladies are so pressing—I cannot, for my life, resist wishing for the pleasures they offer me,—provided you do not disapprove them.

They are to make a very short stay in town. The Captain will meet them in a day or two. Mrs. Mirvan and her sweet daughter both go;—what a happy party! Yet I am not *very* eager to accompany them: at least, I shall be contented to remain where I am, if you desire that I should.

Assured, my dearest Sir, of your goodness, your bounty, and your indulgent kindness, ought I to form a wish that has not your sanction? Decide for me, therefore, without the least apprehension that I shall be uneasy, or discontented. While I am yet in suspense, perhaps I may *hope,* but I am most certain, that when you have once determined, I shall not repine.

They tell me that London is now in full splendour. Two Play-houses are open,—the Opera-House,—Ranelagh,—and the Pantheon.[2]—You see I have learned all their names. However, pray don't suppose that I make any point of

---

Text from the second edition, 1778; first published in the same year.

---

[1] ladies' hats.

[2] The two playhouses were Drury Lane and Covent Garden; opera was usually performed at the King's Theatre in the Haymarket. Ranelagh and the Pantheon were public assemblies. Ranelagh, opened in 1742, was described at the time as "a vast Amphitheatre,

going, for I shall hardly sigh to see them depart without me; though I shall probably never meet with such another opportunity. And, indeed, their domestic happiness will be so great,—it is natural to wish to partake of it.

I believe I am bewitched! I made a resolution when I began, that I would not be urgent; but my pen—or rather my thoughts, will not suffer me to keep it—for I acknowledge, I must acknowledge, I cannot help wishing for your permission.

I almost repent already that I have made this confession; pray forget that you have read it, if this journey is displeasing to you. But I will not write any longer; for the more I think of this affair, the less indifferent to it I find myself.

Adieu, my most honoured, most reverenced, most beloved father! for by what other name can I call you? I have no happiness or sorrow, no hope or fear, but what your kindness bestows, or your displeasure may cause. You will not, I am sure, send a refusal, without reasons unanswerable, and therefore I shall chearfully acquiesce. Yet I hope—I hope you will be able to permit me to go! I am,

> With the utmost affection,
> gratitude, and duty,
> Your
> Evelina ———.

I cannot to *you* sign *Anville,*[3] and what other name may I claim?

LETTER IX   MR. VILLARS TO EVELINA.

Berry-Hill, March 28.

To resist the urgency of entreaty, is a power which I have not yet acquired: I aim not at an authority which deprives you of liberty, yet I would fain guide myself by a prudence which should save me the pangs of repentance. Your impatience to fly to a place which your imagination has painted to you in colours so attractive, surprises me not; I have only to hope that the liveliness of your fancy may not deceive you: to refuse, would be raising it still higher. To see my Evelina happy, is to see myself without a wish: go then, my child, and may that Heaven which alone can, direct, preserve, and strengthen you! To That, my love, will I daily offer prayers for your felicity; O may it guard, watch over you! defend you from danger, save you from distress, and keep vice as distant from your person as from your heart! And to Me, may it grant the ultimate blessing of closing these aged eyes in the arms of one so dear—so deservedly beloved!

> Arthur Villars.

LETTER X   EVELINA TO THE REV. MR. VILLARS.

Queen-Ann-Street, London, Saturday, April 2.

This moment arrived. Just going to

---

for structure *Roman;* for Decorations of Paint and Gilding, gay as the *Asiatic;* four grand Portals, in the manner of the antient triumphal Arches, and four Times twelve Boxes, in a double Row, with suitable Pilasters between, form the whole Interior of this wonderful Fabrick, save that, in the Middle, a magnificent Orchestre arises to the Roof, from which depend several large Branches, which contain a great Number of Candles enclosed in Chrystal Glasses, at once to light and adorn this spacious Rotund" (*The Champion*, August 5, 1742). The Pantheon, opened in 1772, was described as follows: "Imagination cannot well surpass the elegance and magnificence of the apartments, the boldness of the paintings, or the disposition of the lights, which last are suspended by gilt chains. Besides the splendid ornaments that decorate the rotundo, a great room, there are a number of statues, in niches below the dome, representing most of the Heathen Gods and Goddesses, supposed to be in the Pantheon of Rome. To these are added three more of white porphyry, the two first representing the present King and Queen, the last Britannia. The whole building is composed of a suite of fourteen rooms, all of which are adapted to particular uses, and each affording a striking instance of the splendor and profusion of modern times" (*The Gentleman's Magazine*, XLIV, 44).

3 At this point in the novel there is a mystery about the origin of Evelina.

Drury-Lane theatre. The celebrated Mr. Garrick performs Ranger.[4] I am quite in extacy. So is Miss Mirvan. How fortunate, that he should happen to play! We would not let Mrs. Mirvan rest till she consented to go; her chief objection was to our dress, for we have had no time to *Londonize* ourselves; but we teized her into compliance, and so we are to sit in some obscure place, that she may not be seen. As to me, I should be alike unknown in the most conspicuous or most private part of the house.

I can write no more now. I have hardly time to breathe—only just this, the houses and streets are not quite so superb as I expected. However, I have seen nothing yet, so I ought not to judge.

Well, adieu, my dearest Sir, for the present; I could not forbear writing a few words instantly on my arrival; though I suppose my letter of thanks for your consent is still on the road.

Saturday Night.

O my dear Sir, in what raptures am I returned! Well may Mr. Garrick be so celebrated, so universally admired—I had not any idea of so great a performer.

Such ease! such vivacity in his manner! such grace in his motions! such fire and meaning in his eyes!—I could hardly believe he had studied a written part, for every word seemed to be uttered from the impulse of the moment.

His action—at once so graceful and so free!—his voice—so clear, so melodious, yet so wonderfully various in its tones—such animation!—every look *speaks!*

I would have given the world to have had the whole play acted over again. And when he danced—O how I envied Clarinda![5] I almost wished to have jumped on the stage and joined them.

I am afraid you will think me mad, so I won't say any more; yet I really believe Mr. Garrick would make you mad too, if you could see him. I intend to ask

Mrs. Mirvan to go to the play every night while we stay in town. She is extremely kind to me, and Maria, her charming daughter, is the sweetest girl in the world.

I shall write to you every evening all that passes in the day, and that in the same manner as, if I could see, I should tell you.

Sunday.

This morning we went to Portland chapel, and afterwards we walked in the Mall of St. James's Park, which by no means answered my expectations: it is a long straight walk, of dirty gravel, very uneasy to the feet; and at each end, instead of an open prospect, nothing is to be seen but houses built of brick. When Mrs. Mirvan pointed out the *Palace* to me—I think I was never much more surprised.

However, the walk was very agreeable to us; every body looked gay, and seemed pleased, and the ladies were so much dressed, that Miss Mirvan and I could do nothing but look at them. Mrs. Mirvan met several of her friends. No wonder, for I never saw so many people assembled together before. I looked about for some of *my* acquaintance, but in vain, for I saw not one person that I knew, which is very odd, for all the world seemed there.

Mrs. Mirvan says we are not to walk in the Park again next Sunday, even if we should be in town, because there is better company in Kensington Gardens. But really if you had seen how much every body was dressed, you would not think that possible.

Monday.

We are to go this evening to a private ball, given by Mrs. Stanley, a very fashionable lady of Mrs. Mirvan's acquaintance.

We have been *a shopping,*[6] as Mrs. Mirvan calls it, all this morning, to buy silks, caps, gauzes, and so forth.

---

[4] Romantic lead in a popular comedy, *The Suspicious Husband* (1747) by Benjamin Hoadly; it was one of David Garrick's favorite parts. Garrick (1717–1779) had already played his last season two years before *Evelina* was

published.

[5] The feminine lead in *The Suspicious Husband.*

[6] *Shop* is a noun only in Johnson's *Dictionary.*

The shops are really very entertaining, especially the mercers;[7] there seem to be six or seven men belonging to each shop, and every one took care, by bowing and smirking, to be noticed; we were conducted from one to another, and carried from room to room, with so much ceremony, that at first I was almost afraid to go on.

I thought I should never have chosen a silk, for they produced so many I knew not which to fix upon, and they recommended them all so strongly, that I fancy they thought I only wanted persuasion to buy every thing they shewed me. And, indeed, they took so much trouble, that I was almost ashamed I could not.

At the milliners,[8] the ladies we met were so much dressed, that I should rather have imagined they were making visits than purchases. But what most diverted me was, that we were more frequently served by men than by women; and such men! so finical, so affected! they seemed to understand every part of a woman's dress better than we do ourselves; and they recommended caps and ribbands with an air of so much importance, that I wished to ask them how long they had left off wearing them!

The dispatch with which they work in these great shops is amazing, for they have promised me a compleat suit of linen against the evening.

I have just had my hair dressed. You can't think how oddly my head feels; full of powder and black pins, and a great *cushion* on the top of it. I believe you would hardly know me, for my face looks quite different to what it did before my hair was dressed. When I shall be able to make use of a comb for myself I cannot tell, for my hair is so much entangled, *frizled* they call it, that I fear it will be very difficult.

I am half afraid of this ball to-night, for, you know, I have never danced but at school; however, Miss Mirvan says there is nothing in it. Yet I wish it was over.

Adieu, my dear Sir; pray excuse the wretched stuff I write, perhaps I may improve by being in this town, and then my letters will be less unworthy your reading. Mean time I am,

Your dutiful and affectionate,
though unpolished,
Evelina.

Poor Miss Mirvan cannot wear one of the caps she made, because they dress her hair too large for them.

LETTER XI   EVELINA IN CONTINUATION.

Queen-Ann-Street, April 5,
Tuesday morning.

I have a vast deal to say, and shall give all this morning to my pen. As to my plan of writing every evening the adventures of the day, I find it impracticable; for the diversions here are so very late, that if I begin my letters after them, I could not go to bed at all.

We past a most extraordinary evening. A *private* ball this was called, so I expected to have seen about four or five couple; but Lord! my dear Sir, I believe I saw half the world! Two very large rooms were full of company; in one, were cards for the elderly ladies, and in the other, were the dancers. My mama Mirvan, for she always calls me her child, said she would sit with Maria and me till we were provided with partners, and then join the card-players.

The gentlemen, as they passed and repassed, looked as if they thought we were quite at their disposal, and only waiting for the honour of their commands; and they sauntered about, in a careless indolent manner, as if with a view to keep us in suspense. I don't speak of this in regard to Miss Mirvan and myself only, but to the ladies in general; and I thought it so provoking, that I determined, in my own mind, that, far from humouring such airs, I would rather not dance at all, than with any one who should seem to think me ready to accept the first partner who would condescend to take me.

Not long after, a young man, who

<hr />

[7] "mercer . . . one who sells silks" (Johnson's *Dictionary*).

[8] "milliner . . . one who sells ribands and dresses for women" (Johnson's *Dictionary*).

had for some time looked at us with a kind of negligent impertinence, advanced, on tiptoe, towards me; he had a set smile on his face, and his dress was so foppish, that I really believe he even wished to be stared at; and yet he was very ugly.

Bowing almost to the ground, with a sort of swing, and waving his hand with the greatest conceit, after a short and silly pause, he said, "Madam—may I presume?"—and stopt, offering to take my hand. I drew it back, but could scarce forbear laughing. "Allow me, Madam," (continued he, affectedly breaking off every half moment) "the honour and happiness—if I am not so unhappy as to address you too late—to have the happiness and honour—"

Again he would have taken my hand, but, bowing my head, I begged to be excused, and turned to Miss Mirvan to conceal my laughter. He then desired to know if I had already engaged myself to some more fortunate man? I said No, and that I believed I should not dance at all. He would keep himself, he told me, disengaged, in hopes I should relent; and then, uttering some ridiculous speeches of sorrow and disappointment, though his face still wore the same invariable smile, he retreated.

It so happened, as we have since recollected, that during this little dialogue, Mrs. Mirvan was conversing with the lady of the house. And very soon after another gentleman, who seemed about six-and-twenty years old, gayly, but not foppishly, dressed, and indeed extremely handsome, with an air of mixed politeness and gallantry, desired to know if I was engaged, or would honour him with my hand. So he was pleased to say, though I am sure I know not what honour he could receive from me; but these sort of expressions, I find, are used as words of course, without any distinction of persons, or study of propriety.

Well, I bowed, and I am sure I coloured; for indeed I was frightened at the thoughts of dancing before so many people, all strangers, and, which was worse, *with* a stranger; however, that was unavoidable, for though I looked round the room several times, I could not see one person that I knew. And so, he took my hand, and led me to join in the dance.

The minuets were over before we arrived, for we were kept late by the milliner's making us wait for our things.

He seemed very desirous of entering into conversation with me; but I was seized with such a panic, that I could hardly speak a word, and nothing but the shame of so soon changing my mind, prevented my returning to my seat, and declining to dance at all.

He appeared to be surprised at my terror, which I believe was but too apparent: however, he asked no questions, though I fear he must think it very strange; for I did not choose to tell him it was owing to my never before dancing but with a school-girl.

His conversation was sensible and spirited; his air and address were open and noble; his manners gentle, attentive, and infinitely engaging; his person is all elegance, and his countenance, the most animated and expressive I have ever seen.

In a short time we were joined by Miss Mirvan, who stood next couple to us. But how was I startled, when she whispered me that my partner was a nobleman! This gave me a new alarm; how will he be provoked, thought I, when he finds what a simple rustic he has honoured with his choice! one whose ignorance of the world makes her perpetually fear doing something wrong!

That he should be so much my superior every way, quite disconcerted me; and you will suppose my spirits were not much raised, when I heard a lady, in passing us, say, "This is the most difficult dance I ever saw."

"O dear, then," cried Maria to her partner, "with your leave, I'll sit down till the next."

"So will I too, then," cried I, "for I am sure I can hardly stand."

"But you must speak to your partner first," answered she; for he had turned aside to talk with some gentlemen. However, I had not sufficient courage to address him, and so away we all three tript, and seated ourselves at another end of the room.

But, unfortunately for me, Miss Mirvan soon after suffered herself to be prevailed upon to attempt the dance; and just as she rose to go, she cried, "My dear, yonder is your partner, Lord Orville, walking about the room in search of you."

"Don't leave me, then, dear girl!" cried I; but she was obliged to go. And now I was more uneasy than ever; I would have given the world to have seen Mrs. Mirvan, and begged of her to make my apologies; for what, thought I, can I possibly say to him in excuse for running away? he must either conclude me a fool, or half mad; for any one brought up in the great world, and accustomed to its ways, can have no idea of such sort of fears as mine.

My confusion encreased when I observed that he was every where seeking me, with apparent perplexity and surprise; but when, at last, I saw him move towards the place where I sat, I was ready to sink with shame and distress. I found it absolutely impossible to keep my seat, because I could not think of a word to say for myself, and so I rose, and walked hastily towards the card-room, resolving to stay with Mrs. Mirvan the rest of the evening, and not to dance at all. But before I could find her, Lord Orville saw and approached me.

He begged to know if I was not well? You may easily imagine how much I was embarrassed. I made no answer, but hung my head, like a fool, and looked on my fan.

He then, with an air the most respectfully serious, asked if he had been so unhappy as to offend me?

"No, indeed!" cried I: and, in hopes of changing the discourse, and preventing his further inquiries, I desired to know if he had seen the young lady who had been conversing with me?

No;—but would I honour him with any commands to her?

"O by no means!"

Was there any other person with whom I wished to speak?

I said *no,* before I knew I had answered at all.

Should he have the pleasure of bringing me a refreshment?

I bowed, almost involuntarily. And away he flew.

I was quite ashamed of being so troublesome, and so much *above* myself as these seeming airs made me appear; but indeed I was too much confused to think or act with any consistency.

If he had not been swift as lightning, I don't know whether I should not have stolen away again; but he returned in a moment. When I had drunk a glass of lemonade, He hoped, he said, that I would again honour him with my hand, as a new dance was just begun. I had not the presence of mind to say a single word, and so I let him once more lead me to the place I had left.

Shocked to find how silly, how childish a part I had acted, my former fears of dancing before such a company, and with such a partner, returned more forcibly than ever. I suppose he perceived my uneasiness, for he intreated me to sit down again, if dancing was disagreeable to me. But I was quite satisfied with the folly I had already shewn, and therefore declined his offer, tho' I was really scarce able to stand.

Under such conscious disadvantages, you may easily imagine, my dear Sir, how ill I acquitted myself. But, though I both expected and deserved to find him very much mortified and displeased at his ill fortune in the choice he had made, yet, to my very great relief, he appeared to be even contented, and very much assisted and encouraged me. These people in high life have too much presence of mind, I believe, to *seem* disconcerted, or out of humour, however they may feel: for had I been the person of the most consequence in the room, I could not have met with more attention and respect.

When the dance was over, seeing me still very much flurried, he led me to a seat, saying that he would not suffer me to fatigue myself from politeness.

And then, if my capacity, or even if my spirits had been better, in how animated a conversation might I have been engaged! It was then I saw that the rank of Lord Orville was his least recommendation, his understanding and his manners being far more distinguished. His remarks upon the company in general were so apt, so just, so lively, I am almost surprised myself that they did not re-animate me; but indeed I was too well convinced of the ridiculous part I had myself played before so nice an observer, to be able to enjoy his pleasantry: so self-compassion gave me feeling for others. Yet I had not the courage to attempt either to defend them, or to rally in my turn, but listened to him in silent embarrassment.

When he found this, he changed the subject, and talked of public place, and public performers; but he soon discovered that I was totally ignorant of them.

He then, very ingeniously, turned the discourse to the amusements and occupations of the country.

It now struck me, that he was resolved to try whether or not I was capable of talking upon *any* subject. This put so great a constraint upon my thoughts, that I was unable to go further than a monosyllable, and not even so far, when I could possibly avoid it.

We were sitting in this manner, he conversing with all gaiety, I looking down with all foolishness, when that fop who had first asked me to dance, with a most ridiculous solemnity, approached, and after a profound bow or two, said, "I humbly beg pardon, Madam,—and of you too, my Lord,—for breaking in upon such agreeable conversation— which must, doubtless, be much more delectable—than what I have the honour to offer—but—"

I interrupted him—I blush for my folly,—with laughing; yet I could not help it, for, added to the man's stately foppishness, (and he actually took snuff between every three words) when I looked round at Lord Orville, I saw such extreme surprise in his face,—the cause of which appeared so absurd, that I could not for my life preserve my gravity.

I had not laughed before from the time I had left Miss Mirvan, and I had much better have cried then; Lord Orville actually stared at me; the beau, I know not his name, looked quite enraged. "Refrain—Madam," (said he, with an important air,) "a few moments refrain!—I have but a sentence to trouble you with.—May I know to what accident I must attribute not having the honour of your hand?"

"Accident, Sir!" repeated I, much astonished.

"Yes, accident, Madam—for surely, —I must take the liberty to observe— pardon me, Madam,—it ought to be no common one—that should tempt a lady —so young a one too,—to be guilty of ill manners."

A confused idea now for the first time entered my head, of something I had heard of the rules of an assembly; but I was never at one before,—I have only danced at school,—and so giddy and heedless I was, that I had not once considered the impropriety of refusing one partner, and afterwards accepting another. I was thunderstruck at the recollection: but, while these thoughts were rushing into my head, Lord Orville, with some warmth, said, "This lady, Sir, is incapable of meriting such an accusation!"

The creature—for I am very angry with him,—made a low bow, and with a grin the most malicious I ever saw, "My Lord," said he, "far be it from me to *accuse* the lady, for having the discernment to distinguish and prefer—the superior attractions of your Lordship."

Again he bowed, and walked off.

Was ever any thing so provoking? I was ready to die with shame. "What a coxcomb!" exclaimed Lord Orville; while I, without knowing what I did, rose hastily, and moving off, "I can't imagine," cried I, "where Mrs. Mirvan has hid herself!"

"Give me leave to see," answered he. I bowed and sat down again, not daring to meet his eyes; for what must he think of me, between my blunder, and the supposed preference?

He returned in a moment, and told me that Mrs. Mirvan was at cards, but would be glad to see me; and I went immediately. There was but one chair vacant, so, to my great relief, Lord Orville presently left us. I then told Mrs. Mirvan my disasters, and she good-naturedly blamed herself for not having better instructed me, but said she had taken it for granted that I must know such common customs. However, the man may, I think, be satisfied with his pretty speech, and carry his resentment no farther.

In a short time, Lord Orville returned. I consented, with the best grace I could, to go down another dance, for I had had time to recollect myself, and therefore resolved to use some exertion, and, if possible, appear less a fool than I had hitherto done; for it occurred to me that, insignificant as I was, compared to a man of his rank and figure, yet, since he had been so unfortunate as to make choice of me for a partner, why I should endeavour to make the best of it.

The dance, however, was short, and he spoke very little; so I had no opportunity of putting my resolution in practice. He was satisfied, I suppose, with his former successless efforts to draw me out: or, rather, I fancied, he had been inquiring *who I was.* This again disconcerted me, and the spirits I had determined to exert, again failed me. Tired, ashamed, and mortified, I begged to sit down till we returned home, which we did soon after. Lord Orville did me the honour to hand me to the coach, talking all the way of the honour *I* had done *him!* O these fashionable people!

Well, my dear Sir, was it not a strange evening? I could not help being thus particular, because, to me, every thing is so new. But it is now time to conclude. I am, with all love and duty,

Your

Evelina.

Gilbert White
1720-1793

From THE NATURAL HISTORY AND ANTIQUITIES OF SELBORNE

LETTER XLIX [DISCOVERY OF A LONG-LEGGED BIRD]

Selborne,[1] May 7, 1779.

It is now more than forty years that I have paid some attention to the ornithology of this district, without being able to exhaust the subject: new occurrences still arise as long as any inquiries are kept alive.

In the last week of last month five of those most rare birds, too uncommon to have obtained an *English* name, but known to naturalists by the terms of *himantopus,* or *loripes,* and *charadrius himantopus,*[2] were shot upon the verge of *Frinsham-pond,* a large lake belonging to the Bishop of *Winchester,* and lying between *Woolmer-forest,* and the town of *Farnham,* in the county of *Surrey.* The pond keeper says there were three brace in the flock; but that, after he had satisfied his curiosity, he suffered the sixth to remain unmolested. One of these specimens I procured, and found the length of the legs to be so extraordinary, that, at first sight, one might have supposed the shanks had been fastened on to impose on the credulity of the beholder: they were legs in *caricatura;* and had we seen such proportions on a *Chinese* or *Japan* screen we should have made large allowances for the fancy of the draughtsman. These birds are of the *plover* family, and might with propriety be called the *stilt plovers. Brisson,*[3] under that idea, gives them the apposite name of *l'echasse.*[4] My specimen, when drawn and stuffed with pepper, weighed only four ounces and a quarter, though the *naked* part of the thigh measured three inches and an half, and the legs four inches and an half. Hence we may safely assert that these birds exhibit, weight for inches, incomparably the greatest length of legs of any known bird. The *flamingo,* for instance, is one of the most long legged birds, and yet it bears no manner of proportion to the *himantopus;* for a cock *flamingo* weighs, at an average, about four pounds avoirdupois; and his legs and thighs measure usually about twenty inches. But four pounds are fifteen times and a fraction more than four ounces, and one quarter; and if four ounces and a quarter have

Text from the first edition, 1788.

[1] A village in Hampshire.
[2] *himantopus,* from the Greek, means *thong-foot; loripes* is the Latin equivalent; *charadrius himantopus, wading birds,* are mentioned in the Bible (Lev. 11:19, and Deut. 14:18).
[3] Mathurin Jacques Brisson (1723–1806), French zoölogist and natural philosopher; White refers to his *Ornithologie* (1760).
[4] "stilt" (generically).

eight inches of legs, four pounds must have one hundred and twenty inches and a fraction of legs; *viz.* somewhat more than ten feet; such a monstrous proportion as the world never saw! If you should try the experiment in still larger birds the disparity would still increase. It must be matter of great curiosity to see the *stilt plover* move; to observe how it can wield such a length of lever with such feeble muscles as the thighs seem to be furnished with. At best one should expect it to be but a bad walker: but what adds to the wonder is, that it has no back toe. Now without that steady prop to support it's steps it must be liable, in speculation, to perpetual vacillations, and seldom able to preserve the true center of gravity.

The old name of *himantopus* is taken from *Pliny;*[5] and, by an aukward metaphor, implies that the legs are as slender and pliant as if cut out of a *thong* of leather. Neither *Willughby* nor *Ray,*[6] in all their curious researches, either at

home or abroad, ever saw this bird. Mr. *Pennant*[7] never met with it in all *Great-Britain,* but observed it often in the cabinets of the curious at *Paris. Hasselquist*[8] says that it migrates to *Egypt* in the autumn: and a most accurate observer of Nature has assured me that he has found it on the banks of the streams in *Andalusia.*[9]

Our writers record it to have been found only twice in *Great-Britain.* From all these relations it plainly appears that these long legged *plovers* are birds of *South Europe,* and rarely visit our island; and when they do are wanderers and stragglers, and impelled to make so distant and northern an excursion from motives or accidents for which we are not able to account. One thing may fairly be deduced, that these birds come over to us from the continent, since nobody can suppose that a species not noticed once in an age, and of such a remarkable make, can constantly breed unobserved in this kingdom.

[5] *The Natural History* of Pliny the Elder (A.D. 23–79), X, lxiv, 130.

[6] Francis Willughby's *Ornithologia* (1676) was translated into English in 1678 by John Ray, who was also the author of *A Collection of English Words . . . with Catalogues of English Birds and Fishes* (1674).

[7] Thomas Pennant, compiler of *British Zoology* (1766); it was to Pennant that White

first wrote regarding the natural history of Selborne.

[8] Frederik Hasselquist, *Voyages and Travels in the Levant in the Years 1749–52 containing Observations in Natural History,* English translation (1766) of a work first published in 1757 by Carolus Linnaeus.

[9] Southern Spain.

William Cowper
1731-1800

TWO LETTERS to Lady Hesketh

Olney,[1] May 15, 1786.

I have at length, my Cousin, found my way into my summer abode.[2] I believe that I described it to you some time since, and will therefore now leave it undescribed. I will only say that I am writing in a band-box, situated, at least in my account, delightfully, because it has a window in one side that opens into that orchard, through which as I am sitting here, I shall see you often pass, and which, therefore, I already prefer to all the orchards in the world. You do well to prepare me for all possible delays, because in this life all sorts of disappointments are possible, and I shall do well, if any such delay of your journey should happen, to practice that lesson of patience which you inculcate. But it is a lesson, which even with you for my teacher, I shall be slow to learn. Being sure however that you will not procrastinate without cause, I will make myself as easy as I can about it, and hope the best. To convince you how much I am under discipline, and good advice, I will lay aside a favourite measure,[3] influenced in doing so by nothing but the good sense of your contrary opinion. I had set my heart on meeting you at Newport. In my haste to see you once again, I was willing to overlook many awkwardnesses, I could not but foresee would attend it. I put them aside so long as I only foresaw them myself, but since I find that you foresee them too, I can no longer deal so slightly with them. It is therefore determined that we meet at Olney. Much I shall feel, but I will not die if I can help it, and I beg that you will take all possible care to outlive it likewise, for I know what it is to be balked in the moment of acquisition, and should be loth to know it again.

Last Monday in the evening, we walked to Weston,[4] according to our usual custom. It happened, owing to a mistake of time, that we set out half an hour sooner than usual. This mistake we discovered while we were in the wilderness, so, finding that we had time before us, as they say, Mrs. Unwin proposed that we should go into the village, and take a view of the house that I had just

---

Text from *The Life and Posthumous Writings of William Cowper* by William Hayley (Chichester, 1803, vol. I). Lady Hesketh is Cowper's cousin Harriet, then a widow living in London; it was her sister, Theodora, with whom Cowper had been infatuated as a youth.

[1] Town in the northern part of Buckinghamshire on the River Ouse.

[2] A greenhouse in the garden.

[3] A reference to his writing in blank verse; he was at the moment engaged in translating Homer's *Iliad*.

[4] i.e., Cowper and Mary Unwin, widow of a clergyman, with whom Cowper made his home; Weston is a neighboring village, where they visited the Throckmorton family, described later in the letter as "our Weston neighbors."

mentioned to you.[5] We did so, and found it such a one as in most respects would suit you well. But Moses Brown, our Vicar, who, as I told you, is in his eighty-sixth year, is not bound to die for that reason. He said himself, when he was here last summer, that he should live ten years longer, and for aught that appears, so he may. In which case, for the sake of its near neighbourhood to us, the Vicarage has charms for me, that no other place can rival. But this, and a thousand things more, shall be talked over when you come.

We have been industriously cultivating our acquaintance with our Weston neighbours, since I wrote last, and they on their part have been equally diligent in the same cause. I have a notion that we shall all suit well. I see much in them both that I admire. You know perhaps that they are Catholics.

It is a delightful bundle of praise,[6] my Cousin, that you have sent me. All jasmine and lavender. Whoever the Lady is, she has evidently an admirable pen, and a cultivated mind. If a person reads, it is no matter in what language, and if the mind be informed, it is no matter whether that mind belongs to a man or a woman. The taste and the judgment will receive the benefit alike in both.— Long before the Task was published, I made an experiment one day, being in a frolicksome mood, upon my friend:— We were walking in the garden, and conversing on a subject similar to these lines:—

The few that pray at all, pray oft' amiss,
And seeking grace t'improve the present
*   good,*
Would urge a wiser suit than asking
*   more.*[7]

I repeated them, and said to him with an air of non-chalance, "Do you recollect those lines? I have seen them some-

where, where are they?" He put on a considering face, and after some deliberation replied—"Oh, I will tell you where they must be—in the Night-Thoughts."[8] I was glad my trial turned out so well, and did not undeceive him. I mention this occurrence only in confirmation of the letter-writer's opinion; but at the same time I do assure you, on the faith of an honest man, that I never in my life designed an imitation of Young, or of any other writer; for mimicry is my abhorrence, at least in poetry.

Assure yourself, my dearest Cousin, that both for your sake, since you make a point of it, and for my own, I will be as philosophically careful as possible that these fine nerves of mine shall not be beyond measure agitated, when you arrive. In truth, there is much greater probability that they will be benefitted, and greatly too. Joy of heart, from whatever occasion it may arise, is the best of all nervous medicines, and I should not wonder if such a turn given to my spirits, should have even a lasting effect, of the most advantageous kind, upon them. You must not imagine, neither, that I am on the whole in any great degree subject to nervous affections, occasionally I am, and have been these many years, much liable to dejection. But at intervals, and sometimes for an interval of weeks, no creature would suspect it. For I have not that which commonly is a symptom of such a case, belonging to me: I mean extraordinary elevation in the absence of Mr. Blue-Devil.[9] When I am in the best health, my tide of animal sprightliness flows with great equality, so that I am never, at any time, exalted in proportion as I am sometimes depressed. My depression has a cause, and if that cause were to cease, I should be as cheerful thenceforth, and perhaps for ever, as any man need be. But as I have often said, Mrs. Unwin shall be my expositor.

---

[5] They were attempting to find a suitable house to accommodate Lady Hesketh, as their own Orchard Side was thought too small.

[6] *The Task* had just been published (1785), and Cowper was by now accustomed to being showered with praise.

[7] *The Task*, VI, 54–56.

[8] Edward Young's *The Complaint; or, Night-Thoughts on Life, Death, and Immortality* (1742–1746) enjoyed a wide popularity for many years.

[9] i.e., the blues.

Adieu, my beloved Cousin. God grant that our friendship, which while we could see each other, never suffered a moment's interruption, and which so long a separation has not in the least abated, may glow in us to our last hour, and be renewed in a better world, there to be perpetuated for ever.

For you must know that I should not love you half so well, if I did not believe you would be my friend to Eternity. There is not room enough for friendship to unfold itself in full bloom, in such a nook of life as this. Therefore I am, and must, and will be,

Yours for ever,
W. C.

Olney, May 29, 1786.

Thou dear, comfortable Cousin, whose Letters among all that I receive, have this property peculiarly their own, that I expect them without trembling, and never find any thing in them that does not give me pleasure! for which, therefore, I would take nothing in exchange that the world could give me, save, and except that, for which I must exchange them soon, (and happy shall I be to do so) your own company. That, indeed, is delayed a little too long, to my impatience at least it seems so, who find the spring backward as it is, too forward because many of its beauties will have faded before you will have an opportunity to see them. We took our customary walk yesterday in the wilderness at Weston, and saw with regret, the laburnums, syringas, and guelder-roses, some of them blown,[10] and others just upon the point of blowing, and could not help observing—all these will be gone before Lady Hesketh comes. Still, however, there will be roses and jasmine, and honey-suckle, and shady walks, and cool alcoves, and you will partake them with us. But I want you to have a share of every thing that is delightful here, and cannot bear that the advance of the season should steal away a single pleasure before you can come to enjoy it.

Every day I think of you, and almost all the day long; I will venture to say, that even *you* were never so expected in your life. I called last week at the Quaker's to see the furniture[11] of your bed, the fame of which had reached me. It is, I assure you, superb, of printed cotton, and the subject classical. Every morning you will open your eyes on Phaeton kneeling to Apollo, and imploring his father to grant him the conduct of his chariot for a day. May your sleep be as sound, as your bed will be sumptuous, and your nights, at least, will be well provided for.

I shall send up the sixth and seventh books of the Iliad shortly, and shall address them to you. You will forward them to the General.[12] I long to shew you my workshop, and to see you sitting on the opposite side of my table. We shall be as close packed as two wax figures in an old fashioned picture frame. I am writing in it now. It is the place in which I fabricate all my verse in summer time. I rose an hour sooner than usual this morning, that I might finish my sheet before breakfast, for I must write this day to the General.

The grass under my windows is all bespangled with dew-drops, and the birds are singing in the apple-trees among the blossoms. Never Poet had a more commodious oratory in which to invoke his Muse.

I have made your heart ache too often, my poor dear Cousin, with talking about my fits of dejection. Something has happened that has led me to the subject, or I would have mentioned them more sparingly. Do not suppose, or suspect, that I treat you with reserve, there is nothing in which I am concerned that you shall not be made acquainted with. But the tale is too long for a letter. I will only add for your present satisfaction, that the cause is not exterior, that it is not within the reach of human aid, and that yet I have a hope myself, and Mrs. Un-

---

[10] in flower.
[11] i.e., the covers; the "Quaker" was apparently a seamstress.

[12] Another cousin, Lady Hesketh's uncle, Spencer Cowper (d. 1797).

win a strong persuasion, of its removal. I am indeed even now, and have been for a considerable time, sensible of a change for the better, and expect, with good reason, a comfortable lift from you. Guess then, my beloved Cousin, with what wishes I look forward to the time of your arrival, from whose coming I promise myself, not only pleasure, but peace of mind, at least an additional share of it. At present it is an uncertain and transient guest with me, but the joy with which I shall see and converse with you at Olney, may, perhaps, make it an abiding one.

W. C.

Sir Joshua Reynolds
1723-1792

From DISCOURSES Delivered to the Students of the Royal Academy

DISCOURSE XIV   CHARACTER OF GAINS-
BOROUGH ; HIS EXCELLENCIES AND
DEFECTS[1]

Gentlemen,

In the study of our Art, as in the study of all Arts, something is the result of *our own* observation of Nature; something, and that not little, the effect of the example of those who have studied the same nature before us, and who have cultivated before us the same Art, with diligence and success. The less we confine ourselves in the choice of those examples, the more advantage we shall derive from them; and the nearer we shall bring our performances to a correspondence with nature and the great general rules of Art. When we draw our examples from remote and revered antiquity, —with some advantage undoubtedly in that selection, we subject ourselves to some inconveniences. We may suffer ourselves to be too much led away by great names, and to be too much subdued by overbearing authority. Our learning, in that case, is not so much an exercise of our judgement, as a proof of our docility. We find ourselves, perhaps, too much overshadowed; and the character of our pursuits is rather distinguished by the tameness of the follower, than animated by the spirit of emulation. It is sometimes of service, that our examples should be *near* us; and such as raise a reverence, sufficient to induce us carefully to observe them, yet not so great as to prevent us from engaging with them in something like a generous contention.

We have lately lost Mr. Gainsborough,[2] one of the greatest ornaments of our Academy. It is not our business here, to make panegyricks on the living, or even on the dead who were of our body. The praise of the former might bear appearance of adulation; and the latter, of untimely justice; perhaps of envy to those whom we have still the happiness to enjoy, by an oblique suggestion of invidious comparisons. In discoursing therefore on the talents of the late Mr. Gainsborough, my object is, not so much to praise or to blame him, as to draw from his excellencies and defects, matter of instruction to the Students in our academy. If ever this nation should produce genius sufficient to acquire to us the honourable distinction of an English School, the name of Gainsborough will

---

Text from Reynolds's *Works*, ed. Edmond Malone, 3 vols., third edition corrected, 1801.

---

[1] Delivered to the students of the Royal Academy on the distribution of the prizes, December 10, 1788.

[2] Thomas Gainsborough (1727–1788) had died four months earlier, on August 2.

be transmitted to posterity, in the history of the Art, among the very first of that rising name. That our reputation in the Arts is now only rising, must be acknowledged; and we must expect our advances to be attended with old prejudices, as adversaries, and not as supporters; standing in this respect in a very different situation from the late artists of the Roman School, to whose reputation ancient prejudices have certainly contributed: the way was prepared for them, and they may be said rather to have lived in the reputation of their country, than to have contributed to it; whilst whatever celebrity is obtained by English Artists, can arise only from the operation of a fair and true comparison. And when they communicate to their country a share of their reputation, it is a portion of fame not borrowed from others, but solely acquired by their own labour and talents. As Italy has undoubtedly a prescriptive right to an administration bordering on prejudice, as a soil peculiarly adapted, congenial, and, we may add, destined to the production of men of great genius in our Art, we may not unreasonably suspect that a portion of the great fame of some of their late artists has been owing to the general readiness and disposition of mankind, to acquiesce in their original prepossessions in favour of the productions of the Roman School.

On this ground, however unsafe, I will venture to prophesy, that two of the last distinguished Painters of that country, I mean Pompeio Battoni,[3] and Raffaelle Mengs,[4] however great their names may at present sound in our ears, will very soon fall into the rank of Imperiale, Sebastian Concha, Placido Constanza, Massuccio,[5] and the rest of their immediate predecessors; whose names, though equally renowned in their lifetime, are now fallen into what is little

short of total oblivion. I do not say that those painters were not superior to the artist I allude to, and whose loss we lament, in a certain routine of practice, which, to the eyes of common observers, has the air of a learned composition, and bears a sort of superficial resemblance to the manner of the great men who went before them. I know this perfectly well; but I know likewise, that a man, looking for real and lasting reputation, must unlearn much of the common-place method so observable in the works of the artists whom I have named. For my own part, I confess, I take more interest in, and am more captivated with, the powerful impression of nature, which Gainsborough exhibited in his portraits and in his landscapes, and the interesting simplicity and elegance of his little ordinary beggar-children, than with any of the works of that School, since the time of Andrea Sacchi,[6] or perhaps, we may say Carlo Maratti;[7] two painters who may truly be said to be ULTIMI ROMANORUM.[8]

I am well aware how much I lay myself open to the censure and ridicule of the academical professors of other nations, in preferring the humble attempts of Gainsborough to the works of those regular graduates in the great historical style. But we have the sanction of all mankind in preferring genius in a lower rank of art, to feebleness and insipidity in the highest.

It would not be to the present purpose, even if I had the means and materials, which I have not, to enter into the private life of Mr. Gainsborough. The history of his gradual advancement, and the means by which he acquired such excellence in his art, would come nearer to our purposes and wishes, if it were by any means attainable; but the slow progress of advancement is in general imperceptible to the man himself who

---

[3] Pompeo Girolamo Batoni (1708–1787).

[4] Anton Raphael Mengs (1728–1779).

[5] Francesco Ferdinandi (called Imperiali) was active in Rome about 1730; Sebastian Concha (1676–1764); Placido Constanza (1688–1759); Agostina Masuccio (1691–1758). All were Italian painters of the early part of the century.

[6] Andrea Sacchi (1599–1661), an Italian painter praised for his genuineness.

[7] Carlo Maratti (1625–1713), known for the affected manner of his paintings.

[8] "the last of the Romans."

makes it; it is the consequence of an accumulation of various ideas which his mind has received, he does not perhaps know how or when. Sometimes indeed it happens, that he may be able to mark the time when from the sight of a picture, a passage in an author, or a hint in conversation, he has received, as it were, some new and guiding light, something like inspiration, by which his mind has been expanded; and is morally sure that his whole life and conduct has been affected by that accidental circumstance. Such interesting accounts we may however sometimes obtain from a man who has acquired an uncommon habit of self-examination, and has attended to the progress of his own improvement.

It may not be improper to make mention of some of the customs and habits of this extraordinary man; points which come more within the reach of an observer; I however mean such only as are connected with his art, and indeed were, as I apprehend, the causes of his arriving to that high degree of excellence, which we see and acknowledge in his works. Of these causes we must state, as the fundamental, the love which he had to his art; to which, indeed, his whole mind appears to have been devoted, and to which every thing was referred; and this we may fairly conclude from various circumstances of his life, which were known to his intimate friends. Among others he had a habit of continually remarking to those who happened to be about him, whatever peculiarity of countenance, whatever accidental combination of figure, or happy effects of light and shadow, occurred in prospects, in the sky, in walking the streets, or in company. If, in his walks, he found a character that he liked, and whose attendance was to be obtained, he ordered him to his house: and from the fields he brought into his painting-room, stumps of trees, weeds, and animals of various kinds; and designed them, not from memory, but immediately from the objects. He even framed a kind of model of landscapes on his table; composed of broken stones, dried herbs, and pieces of looking glass, which he magnified and improved into rocks, trees and water. How far this latter practice may be useful in giving hints, the professors of landscape can best determine. Like every other technical practice, it seems to me wholly to depend on the general talent of him who uses it. Such methods may be nothing better than contemptible and mischievous trifling; or they may be aids. I think upon the whole, unless we constantly refer to real nature, that practice may be more likely to do harm than good. I mention it only, as it shows the solicitude and extreme activity which he had about every thing that related to his art; that he wished to have his objects embodied as it were, and distinctly before him; that he neglected nothing which could keep his faculties in exercise, and derived hints from every sort of combination.

We must not forget whilst we are on this subject, to make some remarks on his custom of painting by night, which confirms what I have already mentioned, —his great affection to his art; since he could not amuse himself in the evening by any other means so agreeable to himself. I am indeed much inclined to believe that it is a practice very advantageous and improving to an artist; for by this means he will acquire a new and a higher perception of what is great and beautiful in Nature. By candle-light, not only objects appear more beautiful, but from their being in a greater breadth of light and shadow, as well as having a greater breadth and uniformity of colour, nature appears in a higher style; and even the flesh seems to take a higher and richer tone of colour. Judgment is to direct us in the use to be made of this method of study; but the method itself is, I am very sure, advantageous. I have often imagined that the two great colourists, Titian and Correggio,[9] though I do not know that they painted by night, formed their high ideas of colouring

---

[9] Titian (1477–1576), Tiziano Vecelli, famous representative of the Venetian school of painting; Correggio (1494–1534), Antonio Allegri da Correggio, known for his vivid expression, also of the Venetian school.

from the effects of objects by this artificial light: but I am more assured, that whoever attentively studies the first and best manner of Guercino,[10] will be convinced that he either painted by this light, or formed his manner on this conception.

Another practice Gainsborough had, which is worth mentioning, as it is certainly worthy of imitation; I mean his manner of forming all the parts of his picture together; the whole going on at the same time, in the same manner as nature creates her works. Though this method is not uncommon to those who have been regularly educated, yet probably it was suggested to him by his own natural sagacity. That this custom is not universal appears from the practice of a painter whom I have just mentioned, Pompeio Battoni, who finished his historical pictures part after part; and in his portraits completely finished one feature before he proceeded to another. The consequence was, as might be expected; the countenance was never well expressed; and, as the painters say, the whole was not well put together.

The first thing required to excel in our art, or I believe in any art, is, not only a love for it, but even an enthusiastick ambition to excel in it. This never fails of success proportioned to the natural abilities with which the artist has been endowed by Providence. Of Gainsborough, we certainly know, that his passion was not the acquirement of riches, but excellence in his art; and to enjoy that honourable fame which is sure to attend it.—That *he felt this ruling passion strong in death,* I am myself a witness. A few days before he died, he wrote me a letter, to express his acknowledgements for the good opinion I entertained of his abilities, and the manner in which (he had been informed) I always spoke of him; and desired he might see me, once more, before he died. I am aware how flattering it is to myself to be thus connected with the dying testimony which this excellent painter bore

to his art. But I cannot prevail on myself to suppress, that I was not connected with him, by any habits of familiarity: if any little jealousies had subsisted between us, they were forgotten, in those moments of sincerity; and he turned towards me as one, who was engrossed by the same pursuits, and who deserved his good opinion, by being sensible of his excellence. Without entering into a detail of what passed at this last interview, the impression of it upon my mind was, that his regret at losing life, was principally the regret of leaving his art; and more especially as he now began, he said, to see what his deficiencies were; which, he said, he flattered himself in his last works were in some measure supplied.

When such a man as Gainsborough arrives to great fame, without the assistance of an academical education, without travelling to Italy, or any of those preparatory studies which have been so often recommended, he is produced as an instance, how little such studies are necessary; since so great excellence may be acquired without them. This is an inference not warranted by the success of any individual; and I trust it will not be thought that I wish to make this use of it.

It must be remembered that the style and department of art which Gainsborough chose, and in which he so much excelled, did not require that he should go out of his own country for the objects of his study; they were every where about him; he found them in the streets, and in the fields; and from the models thus accidentally found, he selected with great judgement such as suited his purpose. As his studies were directed to the living world principally, he did not pay a general attention to the works of the various masters, though they are, in my opinion, always of great use, even when the character of our subject requires us to depart from some of their principles. It cannot be denied, that excellence in the department of the art which he professed may exist without them; that in such subjects, and in the manner that belongs to them, the want of them is supplied, and more than supplied, by natural

---

[10] Guercino (1591–1666), Giovanni Francesco Barbieri, Italian painter.

sagacity, and a minute observation of particular nature. If Gainsborough did not look at nature with a poet's eye, it must be acknowledged that he saw her with the eye of a painter; and gave a faithful, if not a poetical, representation of what he had before him.

Though he did not much attend to the works of the great historical painters of former ages, yet he was well aware that the language of the art,—the art of imitation,—must be learned somewhere; and as he knew that he could not learn it in an equal degree from his contemporaries, he very judiciously applied himself to the Flemish School, who are undoubtedly the greatest masters of one necessary branch of art; and he did not need to go out of his own country for examples of that school: from that he learnt the harmony of colouring, the management and disposition of light and shadow, and every means which the masters of it practised, to ornament and give splendour to their works. And to satisfy himself as well as others, how well he knew the mechanism and artifice which they employed to bring out that tone of colour which we so much admired in their works, he occasionally made copies from Rubens, Teniers, and Vandyck,[11] which it would be no disgrace to the most accurate connoisseur to mistake, at the first sight, for the works of those masters. What he thus learned, he applied to the originals of nature, which he saw with his own eyes; and imitated, not in the manner of those masters, but in his own.

Whether he most excelled in portraits, landscapes, or fancy-pictures, it is difficult to determine: whether his portraits were most admirable for exact truth of resemblance, or his landscapes for a portrait-like representation of nature, such as we see in the works of Rubens, Ruysdaal,[12] and others of those schools. In his fancy-pictures, when he had fixed on his object of imitation, whether it was the mean and vulgar form of a wood-cutter, or a child of an interesting character, as he did not attempt to raise the one, so neither did he lose any of the natural grace and elegance of the other; such a grace, and such an elegance, as are more frequently found in cottages than in courts. This excellence was his own, the result of his particular observation and taste; for this he was certainly not indebted to the Flemish School, nor indeed to any School; for his grace was not academical or antique, but selected by himself from the great school of nature; and there are yet a thousand modes of grace, which are neither theirs, nor his, but lie open in the multiplied scenes and figures of life, to be brought out by skilful and faithful observers.

Upon the whole, we may justly say, that whatever he attempted he carried to a high degree of excellence. It is to the credit of his good sense and judgement, that he never did attempt that style of historical painting, for which his previous studies had made no preparation.

And here it naturally occurs to oppose the sensible conduct of Gainsborough in this respect, to that of our late excellent Hogarth,[13] who, with all his extraordinary talents, was not blessed with this knowledge of his own deficiency; or of the bounds which were set to the extent of his own powers. After this admirable artist had spent the greatest part of his life in an active, busy, and we may add, successful attention to the ridicule of life; after he had invented a new species of dramatick painting, in which probably he will never be equalled, and had stored his mind with infinite materials to explain and illustrate the domestick and familiar scenes of common life, which were generally, and ought to have been always, the subject of his pen-

---

[11] Flemish painters: Peter Paul Rubens (1577–1640); either of two Teniers, father (1582–1649) and son (1610–1690), both named David; Sir Anthony Vandyck (1599–1641), who settled in London, was knighted by Charles I, and left many of his paintings in England.

[12] Jacob van Ruisdael (*c.* 1628–1682), most celebrated of the Dutch painters of landscape.

[13] William Hogarth (1697–1764), pictorial satirist of the English scene.

cil; he very imprudently, or rather presumptuously, attempted the great historical style, for which his previous habits had by no means prepared him: he was indeed so entirely unacquainted with the principles of this style, that he was not even aware that any artificial preparation was at all necessary. It is to be regretted, that any part of the life of such a genius should be fruitlessly employed. Let his failure teach us not to indulge ourselves in the vain imagination, that by a momentary resolution we can give either dexterity to the hand, or a new habit to the mind.

I have, however, little doubt, but that the same sagacity, which enabled those two extraordinary men, to discover their true object, and the peculiar excellence of that branch of art which they cultivated, would have been equally effectual in discovering the principles of the higher style; if they had investigated those principles with the same eager industry, which they exerted in their own department. As Gainsborough never attempted the heroick style, so neither did he destroy the character and uniformity of his own style, by the idle affectation of introducing mythological learning in any of his pictures. Of this boyish folly we see instances enough, even in the works of great painters. When the Dutch School attempt this poetry of our art in their landscapes, their performances are beneath criticism; they become only an object of laughter. This practice is hardly excusable, even in Claude Lorrain,[14] who had shown more discretion, if he had never meddled with such subjects.

Our late ingenious Academician, Wilson,[15] has I fear, been guilty, like many of his predecessors, of introducing gods and goddesses, ideal beings, into scenes which were by no means prepared to receive such personages. His landscapes were in reality too near common nature to admit supernatural objects. In consequence of this mistake, in a very admirable picture of a storm, which I have seen of his hand, many figures are introduced in the fore ground, some in apparent distress, and some struck dead, as a spectator would naturally suppose, by the lightning; had not the painter injudiciously (as I think) rather chosen that their death should be imputed to a little Apollo, who appears in the sky, with his bent bow, and that those figures should be considered as the children of Niobe.

To manage a subject of this kind, a peculiar style of art is required; and it can only be done without impropriety, or even without ridicule, when we adapt the character of the landscape, and that too, in all its parts, to the historical or poetical representation. This is a very difficult adventure, and it requires a mind thrown back two thousand years, and as it were naturalized in antiquity, like that of Nicolo Poussin,[16] to atchieve it. In the picture alluded to, the first idea that presents itself is that of wonder, at seeing a figure in so uncommon a situation as that in which the Apollo is placed; for the clouds on which he kneels have not the appearance of being able to support him; they have neither the substance nor the form fit for the receptacle of a human figure; and they do not possess in any respect that romantick character which is appropriated to such an object, and which alone can harmonize with poetical stories.

It appears to me, that such conduct is no less absurd, than if a plain man, giving a relation of a real distress, occasioned by an inundation accompanied with thunder and lightning, should, instead of simply relating the event, take it into his head, in order to give a grace to his narration, to talk of Jupiter Pluvius,[17] or Jupiter and his thunderbolts, or any other figurative idea; an inter-

---

[14] 1600–1682, French landscape painter.

[15] Richard Wilson (1714–1782), one of the first members of the Royal Academy who contributed paintings regularly to its exhibitions until 1780; his picture of the children of Niobe, a tragic character of Greek myth, first brought to Wilson public attention in 1760.

[16] Nicolas Poussin (1594–1665), a French painter whose art is reasoned and intellectual.

[17] Name under which Jupiter was worshiped as god of rain.

mixture which, though in poetry, with its proper preparations and accompaniments, it might be managed with effect, yet in the instance before us would counteract the purpose of the narrator, and instead of being interesting, would be only ridiculous.

The Dutch and Flemish style of landscape, not even excepting those of Rubens, is unfit for poetical subjects; but to explain in what this ineptitude consists, or to point out all the circumstances that give nobleness, grandeur, and the poetick character, to style, in landscape, would require a long discourse of itself; and the end would be then perhaps but imperfectly attained. The painter who is ambitious of this perilous excellence, must catch his inspiration from those who have cultivated with success the poetry, as it may be called, of the art; and they are few indeed.

I cannot quit this subject without mentioning two examples which occur to me at present, in which the poetical style of landscape may be seen happily executed; the one is Jacob's Dream by Salvator Rosa,[18] and the other the Return of the Arc from captivity, by Sebastian Bourdon.[19] With whatever dignity those histories are presented to us in the language of Scripture, this style of painting possesses the same power of inspiring sentiments of grandeur and sublimity, and is able to communicate them to subjects which appear by no means adapted to receive them. A ladder against the sky has no very promising appearance of possessing a capacity to excite any heroick ideas; and the Arc, in the hands of a second-rate master, would have little more effect than a common waggon on the highway; yet those subjects are so poetically treated throughout, the parts have such a correspondence with each other, and the whole and every part of the scene is so visionary, that it is impossible to look at them, without feeling, in some measure,

the enthusiasm which seems to have inspired the painters.

By continual contemplation of such works, a sense of the higher excellencies of art will by degrees dawn on the imagination; at every review that sense will become more and more assured, until we come to enjoy a sober certainty of the real existence (if I may so express myself) of those almost ideal beauties; and the artist will then find no difficulty in fixing in his mind the principles by which the impression is produced; which he will feel, and practise, though they are perhaps too delicate and refined, and too peculiar to the imitative art, to be conveyed to the mind by any other means.

To return to Gainsborough: the peculiarity of his manner, or style, or we may call it—the language in which he expressed his ideas, has been considered by many as his greatest defect. But without altogether wishing to enter into the discussion—whether this peculiarity was a defect or not, intermixed, as it was, with great beauties, of some of which it was probably the cause, it becomes a proper subject of criticism and enquiry to a painter.

A novelty and peculiarity of manner, as it is often a cause of our approbation, so likewise it is often a ground of censure; as being contrary to the practice of other painters, in whose manner we have been initiated, and in whose favour we have perhaps been prepossessed from our infancy; for, fond as we are of novelty, we are upon the whole creatures of habit. However, it is certain, that all those odd scratches and marks, which on a close examination, are so observable in Gainsborough's pictures, and which even to experienced painters appear rather the effect of accident than design; this chaos, this uncouth and shapeless appearance, by a kind of magick, at a certain distance assumes form, and all the parts seem to drop into their proper places; so that we can hardly refuse acknowledg-

---

[18] 1615–1673, Italian painter of the Neapolitan school.

[19] 1616–1671, a painter who drew much from the work of Poussin and Lorrain; Reynolds had the picture of which he speaks in his possession at the time. It is now in the National Gallery in London.

ing the full effect of diligence, under the appearance of chance and hasty negligence. That Gainsborough himself considered this peculiarity in his manner and the power it possesses of exciting surprise, as a beauty in his works, I think may be inferred from the eager desire which we know he always expressed, that his pictures, at the Exhibition, should be seen near, as well as at a distance.

The slightness which we see in his best works, cannot always be imputed to negligence. However they may appear to superficial observers, painters know very well that a steady attention to the general effect takes up more time, and is much more laborious to the mind, than any mode of high finishing or smoothness, without such attention. His *handling, the manner of leaving the colours,* or in other words, the methods he used for producing the effect, had very much the appearance of the work of an artist who had never learned from others the usual and regular practice belonging to the art; but still, like a man of strong intuitive perception of what was required, he found out a way of his own to accomplish his purpose.

It is no disgrace to the genius of Gainsborough, to compare him to such men as we sometimes meet with, whose natural eloquence appears even in speaking a language which they can scarce be said to understand; and who, without knowing the appropriate expression of almost any one idea, contrive to communicate the lively and forcible impressions of an energetick mind.

I think some apology may reasonably be made for his manner, without violating truth, or running any risk of poisoning the minds of the younger students, by propagating false criticism, for the sake of raising the character of a favourite artist. It must be allowed, that this hatching manner of Gainsborough did very much contribute to the lightness of effect which is so eminent a beauty in his pictures; as on the contrary, much smoothness, and uniting the colours, is apt to produce heaviness. Every artist must have remarked, how often that lightness of hand which was in his dead-colour, or first painting, escaped in the finishing, when he had determined the parts with more precision: and another loss he often experiences, which is of greater consequence; whilst he is employed in the detail, the effect of the whole together is either forgotten or neglected. The likeness of a portrait, as I have formerly observed, consists more in preserving the general effect of the countenance, than in the most minute finishing of the features, or any of the particular parts. Now Gainsborough's portraits were often little more, in regard to finishing, or determining the form of the features, than what generally attends a dead colour; but as he was always attentive to the general effect, or whole together, I have often imagined that this unfinished manner contributed even to that striking resemblance for which his portraits are so remarkable. Though this opinion may be considered as fanciful, yet I think a plausible reason may be given, why such a mode of painting should have such an effect. It is presupposed that in this undetermined manner there is the general effect; enough to remind the spectator of the original; the imagination supplies the rest, and perhaps more satisfactorily to himself, if not more exactly, than the artist, with all his care, could possibly have done. At the same time it must be acknowledged there is one evil attending this mode; that if the portrait were seen; previous to any knowledge of the original, different persons would form different ideas, and all would be disappointed at not finding the original correspond with their own conceptions; under the great latitude which indistinctness gives to the imagination to assume almost what character or form it pleases.

Every artist has some favourite part, on which he fixes his attention, and which he pursues with such eagerness, that it absorbs every other consideration; and he often falls into the opposite error of that which he would avoid, which is always ready to receive him. Now Gainsborough having truly a painter's eye for colouring, cultivated those effects of the art which proceed from colours; and sometimes appears to be indifferent to or to neglect other excellencies. Whatever defects are acknowledged, let him still experience from us the same candour that we so freely give upon similar occasions to the ancient masters; let us not encourage that fastidious disposition, which is discontented with every thing short of perfection, and unreasonably require, as we sometimes do, a union of excellencies, not perhaps quite compatible with each other.—We may, on this ground, say even of the divine Raffaelle,[20] that he might have finished his picture as highly and as correctly as was his custom, without heaviness of manner; and that Poussin might have preserved all his precision without hardness or dryness.

To show the difficulty of uniting solidity with lightness of manner, we may produce a picture of Rubens in the Church of St. Judule, at Brussels, as an example; the subject is, *Christ's charge to Peter;*[21] which, as it is the highest, and smoothest, finished picture I remember to have seen of that master, so it is by far the heaviest; and if I had found it in any other place, I should have suspected it to be a copy; for painters know very well, that it is principally by this air of facility, or the want of it, that originals are distinguished from copies. —A lightness of effect, produced by colour, and that produced by facility of handling, are generally united; a copy may preserve something of the one, it is true, but hardly ever of the other; a connoisseur therefore finds it often necessary to look carefully into the picture before he determines on its originality. Gainsborough possessed this quality of lightness of manner and effect, I think, to an unexampled degree of excellence; but it must be acknowledged, at the same time, that the sacrifice which he made to this ornament of our art, was too great; it was, in reality, preferring the lesser excellencies to the greater.

To conclude. However we may apologize for the deficiencies of Gainsborough, (I mean particularly his want of precision and finishing,) who so ingeniously contrived to cover his defects by his beauties;[22] and who cultivated that department of art, where such defects are more easily excused; you are to remember, that no apology can be made for this deficiency, in that style which this academy teaches, and which ought to be the object of your pursuit. It will be necessary for you, in the first place, never to lose sight of the great rules and principles of the art, as they are collected from the full body of the best general practice, and the most constant and uniform experience; this must be the ground-work of all your studies: afterwards you may profit, as in this case I wish you to profit, by the peculiar experience and personal talents of artists living and dead; you may derive lights, and catch hints, from their practice; but the moment you turn them into models, you fall infinitely below them; you may be corrupted by excellencies, not so much belonging to the art, as personal and appropriated to the artist; and become bad copies of good painters, instead of excellent imitators of the great universal truth of things.

---

[20] Raphael (Raffaello Santi) (1483–1520).

[21] Roger Fry (1866–1934), the English painter and critic, remarked that if the picture to which Reynolds here refers is one now to be found in the Wallace Collection, "it justifies his dislike."

[22] Roger Fry's comment on this remark was that "there was, perhaps, only one other artist who showed a greater ingenuity in this respect, and that was Reynolds himself." This is said by a critic highly sympathetic of Reynolds's accomplishments both as an artist and as a critic, who said on another occasion of Reynolds that he "had the gift, an unusual one among artists, of rising to a general view of art as a whole, and of regarding his own performance with objective impartiality."

Edmund Burke
1729-1797

A LETTER from the Right Honourable
Edmund Burke to a Noble Lord

ON THE ATTACKS MADE UPON HIM AND HIS PENSION, IN
THE HOUSE OF LORDS, BY THE DUKE OF BEDFORD AND THE EARL OF LAUDERDALE,
EARLY IN THE PRESENT SESSIONS OF PARLIAMENT

My Lord,

I could hardly flatter myself with the hope, that so very early in the season I should have to acknowledge obligations to the Duke of Bedford[1] and to the Earl of Lauderdale.[2] These noble persons have lost no time in conferring upon me, that sort of honour, which it is alone within their competence, and which it is certainly most congenial to their nature and their manners to bestow.

To be ill spoken of, in whatever language they speak, by the zealots of the new sect in philosophy and politics, of which these noble persons think so charitably, and of which others think so justly, to me, is no matter of uneasiness or surprise. To have incurred the displeasure of the Duke of Orleans[3] or the Duke of Bedford, to fall under the censure of Citizen Brissot[4] or of his friend the Earl of Lauderdale, I ought to consider as proofs, not the least satisfactory, that I have produced some part of the effect I proposed by my endeavours. I have laboured hard to earn, what the noble Lords are generous enough to pay.[5] Personal offence I have given them none. The part they take against me is from zeal to the cause. It is well! It is perfectly well! I have to do homage to their justice. I have to thank the Bedfords and the Lauderdales for having so faithfully and so fully acquitted towards me whatever arrear of debt was left undischarged by the Priestleys and the Paines.[6]

Some, perhaps, may think them execu-

Text from first edition, 1796; the "noble lord" to whom the letter was addressed was William Wentworth, second Earl Fitzwilliam (1748–1833), nephew and heir to the Marquis of Rockingham, under whose patronage Burke had entered Parliament.

[1] Francis Russell, fifth Duke of Bedford (1765–1802).

[2] James Maitland, eighth Earl of Lauderdale (1759–1839).

[3] Louis Philippe Joseph, Duke of Orleans (1747–1793), voted for the execution of the French king at the Revolution and was himself guillotined during the ensuing Reign of Terror.

[4] Jacques Pierre Brissot (1754–1793), another of the French revolutionists who was guillotined.

[5] i.e., his pension on retiring from Parliament.

[6] Joseph Priestley (1733–1804) and Thomas Paine (1737–1809) had vigorously opposed Burke's conservative position on the French Revolution.

tors in their own wrong: I at least have nothing to complain of. They have gone beyond the demands of justice. They have been (a little perhaps beyond their intention) favourable to me. They have been the means of bringing out, by their invectives, the handsome things which Lord Grenville[7] has had the goodness and condescension to say in my behalf. Retired as I am from the world, and from all it's affairs and all it's pleasures, I confess it does kindle, in my nearly extinguished feelings, a very vivid satisfaction to be so attacked and so commended. It is soothing to my wounded mind, to be commended by an able, vigorous, and well informed statesman, and at the very moment when he stands forth with a manliness and resolution, worthy of himself and of his cause, for the preservation of the persons and government of our Sovereign, and therein for the security of the laws, the liberties, the morals, and the lives of his people. To be in any fair way connected with such things, is indeed a distinction. No philosophy can make me above it: no melancholy can depress me so low, as to make me wholly insensible to such an honour.

Why will they not let me remain in obscurity and inaction? Are they apprehensive, that if an atom of me remains, the sect has something to fear? Must I be annihilated, lest, like old *John Zisca's*,[8] my skin might be made into a drum, to animate Europe to eternal battle, against a tyranny that threatens to overwhelm all Europe, and all the human race?

My Lord, it is a subject of aweful meditation. Before this of France, the annals of all time have not furnished an instance of a *compleat* revolution. That revolution seems to have extended even to the constitution of the mind of man. It has this of wonderful in it, that it resembles what Lord Verulam[9] says of the operations of nature: It was perfect, not only in all its elements and princi-

ples, but in all it's members and it's organs from the very beginning. The moral scheme of France furnishes the only pattern ever known, which they who admire will *instantly* resemble. It is indeed an inexhaustible repertory of one kind of examples. In my wretched condition, though hardly to be classed with the living, I am not safe from them. They have tygers to fall upon animated strength. They have hyenas to prey upon carcasses. The national menagerie is collected by the first physiologists of the time; and it is defective in no description of savage nature. They pursue, even such as me, into the obscurest retreats, and haul them before their revolutionary tribunals. Neither sex, nor age—not the sanctuary of the tomb is sacred to them. They have so determined a hatred to all privileged orders, that they deny even to the departed, the sad immunities of the grave. They are not wholly without an object. Their turpitude purveys to their malice; and they unplumb[10] the dead for bullets to assassinate the living. If all revolutionists were not proof against all caution, I should recommend it to their consideration, that no persons were ever known in history, either sacred or profane, to vex the sepulchre, and by their sorceries, to call up the prophetic dead, with any other event, than the prediction of their own disastrous fate.— "Leave me, oh leave me to repose!"

In one thing I can excuse the Duke of Bedford for his attack upon me and my mortuary pension. He cannot readily comprehend the transaction he condemns. What I have obtained was the fruit of no bargain; the production of no intrigue; the result of no compromise; the effect of no solicitation. The first suggestion of it never came from me, mediately or immediately, to his Majesty or any of his Ministers. It was long known that the instant my engagements would permit it, and before the heaviest of all calamities had for ever condemned me to obscurity and sorrow, I had re-

---

[7] William Wyndham Grenville (1759–1834), Secretary of Foreign Affairs and Chancellor of the University of Oxford, who had spoken out in Burke's behalf.

[8] A fourteenth-century Moravian hero.
[9] Francis Bacon, first Baron Verulam (1561–1626), the English essayist and philosopher.
[10] Literally, "take the lead out of."

solved on a total retreat. I had executed that design. I was entirely out of the way of serving or of hurting any statesman, or any party, when the Ministers so generously and so nobly carried into effect the spontaneous bounty of the Crown. Both descriptions have acted as became them. When I could no longer serve them, the Ministers have considered my situation. When I could no longer hurt them, the revolutionists have trampled on my infirmity. My gratitude, I trust, is equal to the manner in which the benefit was conferred. It came to me indeed, at a time of life, and in a state of mind and body, in which no circumstance of fortune could afford me any real pleasure. But this was no fault in the Royal Donor, or in his Ministers, who were pleased, in acknowledging the merits of an invalid servant of the publick, to assuage the sorrows of a desolate old man.

It would ill become me to boast of any thing. It would as ill become me, thus called upon, to depreciate the value of a long life, spent with unexampled toil in the service of my country. Since the total body of my services, on account of the industry which was shewn in them, and the fairness of my intentions, have obtained the acceptance of my Sovereign, it would be absurd in me to range myself on the side of the Duke of Bedford and the Corresponding Society,[11] or, as far as in me lies, to permit a dispute on the rate at which the authority appointed by *our* Constitution to estimate such things, has been pleased to set them.

Loose libels ought to be passed by in silence and contempt. By me they have been so always. I knew that as long as I remained in public, I should live down the calumnies of malice, and the judgments of ignorance. If I happened to be now and then in the wrong, as who is not, like all other men, I must bear the consequence of my faults and my mis-takes. The libels of the present day, are just of the same stuff as the libels of the past. But they derive an importance from the rank of the persons they come from, and the gravity of the place where they were uttered. In some way or other I ought to take some notice of them. To assert myself thus traduced is not vanity or arrogance. It is a demand of justice; it is a demonstration of gratitude. If I am unworthy, the Ministers are worse than prodigal. On that hypothesis, I perfectly agree with the Duke of Bedford.

For whatever I have been (I am now no more) I put myself on my country. I ought to be allowed a reasonable freedom, because I stand upon my deliverance; and no culprit ought to plead in irons. Even in the utmost latitude of defensive liberty, I wish to preserve all possible decorum. Whatever it may be in the eyes of these noble persons themselves, to me, their situation calls for the most profound respect. If I should happen to trespass a little, which I trust I shall not, let it always be supposed, that a confusion of characters may produce mistakes; that in the masquerades of the grand carnival of our age, whimsical adventures happen; odd things are said and pass off. If I should fail a single point in the high respect I owe to those illustrious persons, I cannot be supposed to mean the Duke of Bedford and the Earl of Lauderdale of the House of Peers, but the Duke of Bedford and the Earl of Lauderdale of Palace Yard;[12]— The Dukes and Earls of Brentford.[13] There they are on the pavement; there they seem to come nearer to my humble level; and, virtually at least, to have waved their high privilege.

Making this protestation, I refuse all revolutionary tribunals, where men have been put to death for no other reason, than that they had obtained favors from the Crown. I claim, not the letter, but the spirit of the old English law, that is, to be tried by my peers. I decline his

---

[11] A political organization founded in London in 1792, sympathetic with the French revolutionists.

[12] The Palace Yard implied the place of pillory or execution of notorious members of Parliament or its enemies.

[13] Two kings of Brentford appear in Buckingham's *The Rehearsal* (1671) as effeminate characters.

Grace's jurisdiction as a judge. I challenge[14] the Duke of Bedford as a juror to pass upon the value of my services. Whatever his natural parts[15] may be, I cannot recognize in his few and idle years, the competence to judge of my long and laborious life.[16] If I can help it, he shall not be on the inquest of my *quantum meruit*.[17] Poor rich man! He can hardly know any thing of public industry in it's exertions, or can estimate it's compensations when it's work is done. I have no doubt of his Grace's readiness in all the calculations of vulgar arithmetic; but I shrewdly suspect, that he is very little studied in the theory of moral proportions; and has never learned the Rule of Three[18] in the arithmetic of policy and state.

His Grace thinks I have obtained too much. I answer, that my exertions, whatever they have been, were such as no hopes of pecuniary reward could possibly excite; and no pecuniary compensation can possibly reward them. Between them and money there is no common measurer. Such services, if done by abler men than I am, are, quantities incommensurable. Money is made for the comfort and convenience of animal life. It cannot be a reward for what, mere animal life must indeed sustain, but never can inspire. With submission to his Grace, I have not had more than sufficient. As to any noble use, I trust I know how to employ, as well as he, a much greater fortune than he possesses. In a more confined application, I certainly stand in need of every kind of relief and easement much more than he does. When I say I have not received more than I deserve, is this the language I hold to Majesty? No! Far, very far, from it! Before that presence, I claim no merit at all. Every thing towards me is favour, and bounty.

One style to a gracious benefactor; another to a proud and insulting foe.

His Grace is pleased to aggravate my guilt, by charging my acceptance of his Majesty's grant as a departure from my ideas, and the spirit of my conduct with regard to œconomy. If it be, my ideas of œconomy were false and ill founded. But they are the Duke of Bedford's ideas of œconomy I have contradicted, and not my own. If he means to allude to certain bills brought in by me on a message from the throne in 1782,[19] I tell him, that there is nothing in my conduct that can contradict either the letter or the spirit of those acts.—Does he mean the pay-office act? I take it for granted he does not. The act to which he alludes is, I suppose, the establishment act. I greatly doubt whether his Grace has ever read the one or the other. The first of these systems cost me, with every assistance which my then situation gave me, pains incredible. I found an opinion common through all the offices, and general in the publick at large, that it would prove impossible to reform and methodize the office of Paymaster General. I undertook it, however; and I succeeded in my undertaking. Whether the military service, or whether the general œconomy of our finances have profited by that act, I leave to those who are acquainted with the army, and with the treasury, to judge.

An opinion full as general prevailed also at the same time, that nothing could be done for the regulation of the civil-list establishment. The very attempt to introduce method into it, and any limitations to it's services, was held absurd. I had not seen the man, who so much as suggested one œconomical expedient, upon that subject. Nothing but coarse amputation, or coarser taxation, were then talked of, both of them without de-

---

[14] take exception to.

[15] abilities.

[16] Bedford was 31 years of age; Burke, at 67, was over twice his age.

[17] i.e., shall not be a judge of the extent of my value to the state.

[18] A method of finding from three known terms an unknown fourth related to the third as the second is to the first: e.g., $1:2::3:x$, in which x is found to equal 6.

[19] Burke refers to various portions of what became known as the Economic Reform Bill of 1782, which reduced government expenses by £72,000 annually by purging the pension lists of grants for political favors.

sign, combination, or the least shadow of principle. Blind and headlong zeal, or factious fury, were the whole contribution brought by the most noisy on that occasion, towards the satisfaction of the publick, or the relief of the Crown.

Let me tell my youthful Censor, that the necessities of that time required something very different from what others then suggested, or what his Grace now conceives. Let me inform him, that it was one of the most critical periods in our annals.

Astronomers[20] have supposed, that if a certain comet, whose path intersected the eclipstick, had met the earth in some (I forget what) sign, it would have whirled us along with it, in it's excentric course, into God knows what regions of heat and cold. Had the portentous comet of the rights of man, (which "from it's horrid hair shakes pestilence, and war," and "with fear of change perplexes Monarchs") had that comet crossed upon us in that internal state of England, nothing human could have prevented our being irresistibly hurried, out of the highway of heaven, into all the vices, crimes, horrors and miseries of the French revolution.

Happily, France was not then jacobinized.[21] Her hostility was at a good distance. We had a limb cut off;[22] but we preserved the body: We lost our Colonies; but we kept our Constitution. There was, indeed, much intestine heat; there was a dreadful fermentation. Wild and savage insurrection quitted the woods, and prowled about our streets in the name of reform.[23] Such was the distemper of the publick mind, that there was no madman, in his maddest ideas, and maddest projects, that might not count upon numbers to support his principles and execute his designs.

Many of the changes, by a great misnomer called parliamentary reforms, went, not in the intention of all the professors and supporters of them, undoubtedly, but went in their certain, and, in my opinion, not very remote effect, home to the utter destruction of the Constitution of this kingdom. Had they taken place, not France, but England, would have had the honour of leading up the death-dance of Democratick Revolution. Other projects, exactly coincident in time with those, struck at the very existence of the kingdom under any constitution. There are who remember the blind fury of some, and the lamentable helplessness of others; here, a torpid confusion, from a panic fear of the danger; there, the same inaction from a stupid insensibility to it; here, well-wishers to the mischief; there, indifferent lookers-on. At the same time, a sort of National Convention, dubious in its nature, and perilous in its example, nosed Parliament in the very seat of its authority; sat with a sort of superintendance over it; and little less than dictated to it, not only laws, but the very form and essence of Legislature itself. In Ireland things ran in a still more eccentrick course. Government was unnerved, confounded, and in a manner suspended. It's equipoise was totally gone. I do not mean to speak disrespectfully of Lord North.[24] He was a man of admirable parts; of general knowledge; of a versatile understanding fitted for every sort of business; of infinite wit and pleasantry; of a delightful temper; and with a mind most perfectly disinterested. But it would be only to degrade myself by a weak adulation, and not to honour the memory of a great man, to deny that he wanted something of the vigilance, and spirit of command, that the time required. In-

---

[20] It is interesting to note that the astronomer, Sir William Herschel (1738–1822), who had a crown pension of £200, had identified a comet in 1795, later known as Encke's Comet.

[21] The Jacobins were French revolutionists who met in a Jacobin Convent in Paris until the dissolution of their society in 1794; their name became identified with violent revolution.

[22] The loss of the American colonies.

[23] The Gordon riots occurred in 1780.

[24] Frederick North, second Earl of Guilford ("Lord North" was a courtesy title until 1790), Prime Minister from 1770 to 1782; he had died in 1792. His resignation signalized the end of the attempt at personal rule by George III.

deed, a darkness, next to the fog of this awful day, loured[25] over the whole region. For a little time the helm appeared abandoned—

Ipse diem noctemque negat discernere cœlo
Nec meminisse viæ mediâ Palinurus in undâ.[26]

At that time I was connected with men of high place in the community. They loved Liberty as much as the Duke of Bedford can do; and they understood it at least as well. Perhaps their politicks, as usual, took a tincture from their character, and they cultivated what they loved. The Liberty they pursued was a Liberty inseparable from order, from virtue, from morals, and from religion, and was neither hypocritically nor fanatically followed. They did not wish, that Liberty, in itself, one of the first of blessings, should in it's perversion become the greatest curse which could fall upon mankind. To preserve the Constitution entire, and practically equal to all the great ends of it's formation, not in one single part, but in all it's parts, was to them the first object. Popularity and power they regarded alike. They were with them different means of obtaining that object; and had no other preference over each other in their minds, than as they furnished the surer or the less certain means of arriving at that end. It is some consolation to me in the chearless gloom, which darkens the evening of my life, that with them I commenced my political career, and never for a moment, in reality, nor in appearance, for any length of time, was separated from their good wishes and good opinion.

By what accident it matters not, nor upon what desert, but just then, and in the midst of that hunt of obloquy, which ever has pursued me with a full cry through life, I had obtained a very considerable degree of publick confidence. I know well enough how equivocal a test this kind of popular opinion forms of the merit that obtained it. I am no stranger to the insecurity of it's tenure. I do not boast of it. It is mentioned, to shew, not how highly I prize the thing, but my right to value the use I made of it. I endeavoured to turn that short-lived advantage to myself into a permanent benefit to my Country. Far am I from detracting from the merit of some Gentlemen, out of office or in it, on that occasion. No!—It is not my way to refuse a full and heaped measure of justice to the aids that I receive. I have, through life, been willing to give every thing to others; and to reserve nothing for myself, but the inward conscience, that I had omitted no pains, to discover, to animate, to discipline, to direct the abilities of the Country for it's service, and to place them in the best light to improve their age, or to adorn it. This conscience I have. I have never suppressed any man; never checked him for a moment in his course, by any jealousy, or by any policy. I was always ready, to the height of my means, which were always infinitely below my desires, to forward those abilities that overpowered my own. He is an ill-furnished undertaker,[27] who has no machinery but his own hands to work with. Poor in my own faculties, I thought myself rich in theirs. I then consulted, and sincerely coöperated with men of all parties, who seemed disposed to the same ends, or to any main part of them. Nothing, to prevent disorder, was omitted: when it appeared, nothing to subdue it, was left uncounselled, nor unexecuted, as far as I could prevail. At the time I speak of, and having a momentary lead, so aided and so encouraged, and as a feeble instrument in a mighty hand—I do not say, I saved my Country; I am sure I did my Country important serv-

---

[25] descended.
[26] Cast from our course, we wander in the dark;
    No stars to guide, no point of land to mark.
    Ev'n Palinurus no distinction found

Betwixt the night and day, such darkness reign'd around.
(Vergil, *Aeneid*, III, 201–202, tr. Dryden.)
[27] contractor; the term had a special political significance at the time.

ice. There were few, indeed, that did not at that time acknowledge it, and that time was thirteen years ago. It was but one voice, that no man in the kingdom better deserved an honourable provision should be made for him.

So much for my general conduct through the whole of the portentous crisis from 1780 to 1782, and the general sense then entertained of that conduct by my country. But my character, as a reformer, in the particular instances which the Duke of Bedford refers to, is so connected in principle with my opinions on the hideous changes, which have since barbarized France, and spreading thence, threaten the political and moral order of the whole world, that it seems to demand something of a more detailed discussion.

My œconomical reforms were not, as his Grace may think, the suppression of a paltry pension or employment, more or less. Œconomy in my plans was, as it ought to be, secondary, subordinate, instrumental. I acted on state principles. I found a great distemper in the commonwealth; and, according to the nature of the evil and of the object, I treated it. The malady was deep; it was complicated, in the causes and in the symptoms. Throughout it was full of contraindicants.[28] On one hand Government, daily growing more invidious for an apparent increase of the means of strength, was every day growing more contemptible by real weakness. Nor was this dissolution confined to Government commonly so called. It extended to Parliament; which was losing not a little in it's dignity and estimation, by an opinion of it's not acting on worthy motives. On the other hand, the desires of the People, (partly natural and partly infused into them by art) appeared in so wild and inconsiderate a manner, with regard to the œconomical object (for I set aside for a moment the dreadful tampering with the body of the Constitution itself) that if their petitions had literally been complied with, the State would have been convulsed; and a gate would have been opened, through which all

property might be sacked and ravaged. Nothing could have saved the Publick from the mischiefs of the false reform but it's absurdity; which would soon have brought itself, and with it all real reform, into discredit. This would have left a rankling wound in the hearts of the People, who knew they had failed in the accomplishment of their wishes, but who, like the rest of mankind in all ages, would impute the blame to any thing rather than to their own proceedings. But there were then persons in the world, who nourished complaint; and would have been thoroughly disappointed if the people were ever satisfied. I was not of that humour. I wished that they *should* be satisfied. It was my aim, to give to the People the substance of what I knew they desired, and what I thought was right whether they desired it or not, before it had been modified for them into senseless petitions. I knew that there is a manifest marked distinction, which ill men, with ill designs, or weak men incapable of any design, will constantly be confounding, that is, a marked distinction between Change and Reformation. The former alters the substance of the objects themselves; and gets rid of all their essential good, as well as of all the accidental evil annexed to them. Change is novelty; and whether it is to operate any one of the effects of reformation at all, or whether it may not contradict the very principle upon which reformation is desired, cannot be certainly known beforehand. Reform is, not a change in the substance, or in the primary modification of the object, but a direct application of a remedy to the grievance complained of. So far as that is removed, all is sure. It stops there; and if it fails, the substance which underwent the operation, at the very worst, is but where it was.

All this, in effect, I think, but am not sure, I have said elsewhere. It cannot at this time be too often repeated; line upon line; precept upon precept; until it comes into the currency of a proverb, *To innovate is not to reform.* The French revolutionists complained of every thing; they refused to reform any thing; and they left nothing, no, nothing

---

[28] misleading symptoms.

at all *unchanged*. The consequences are *before* us,—not in remote history; not in future prognostication: they are about us; they are upon us. They shake the publick security; they menace private enjoyment. They dwarf the growth of the young; they break the quiet of the old. If we travel, they stop our way. They infest us in town; they pursue us to the country. Our business is interrupted; our repose is troubled; our pleasures are saddened; our very studies are poisoned and perverted, and knowledge is rendered worse than ignorance, by the enormous evils of this dreadful innovation. The revolution harpies of France, sprung from night and hell, or from that chaotick anarchy, which generates equivocally "all monstrous, all prodigious things,"[29] cuckoo-like, adulterously lay their eggs, and brood over, and hatch them in the nest of every neighbouring State. These obscene harpies, who deck themselves, in I know not what divine attributes, but who in reality are foul and ravenous birds of prey (both mothers and daughters) flutter over our heads, and souse down upon our tables, and leave nothing unrent, unrifled, unravaged, or unpolluted with the slime of their filthy offal.[30]

If his Grace can contemplate the result of this compleat innovation, or, as some friends of his will call it *reform,* in the whole body of it's solidity and compound mass, at which, as Hamlet[31] says, the face of Heaven glows with horror and indignation, and which, in truth, makes every reflecting mind, and every feeling heart, perfectly thought-sick, without a thorough abhorrence of every thing they say, and every thing they do, I am amazed at the morbid strength, or the natural infirmity of his mind.

It was then not my love, but my hatred to innovation, that produced my Plan of Reform. Without troubling myself with the exactness of the logical diagram, I considered them as things substantially opposite. It was to prevent

that evil, that I proposed the measures, which his Grace is pleased, and I am not sorry he is pleased, to recall to my recollection. I had (what I hope that Noble Duke will remember in all his operations) a State to preserve, as well as a State to reform. I had a People to gratify, but not to inflame, or to mislead. I do not claim half the credit for what I did, as for what I prevented from being done. In that situation of the publick mind, I did not undertake, as was then proposed, to new model the House of Commons or the House of Lords; or to change the authority under which any officer of the Crown acted, who was suffered at all to exist. Crown, Lords, Commons, judicial system, system of administration, existed as they had existed before; and in the mode and manner in which they had always existed. My measures were, what I then truly stated them to the House to be, in their intent, healing and mediatorial. A complaint was made of too much influence in the House of Commons; I reduced it in both Houses; and I gave my reasons article by article for every reduction, and shewed why I thought it safe for the service of the State. I heaved the lead[32] every inch of way I made. A disposition to expence was complained of; to that I opposed, not mere retrenchment, but a system of œconomy, which would make a random expence without plan or foresight, in future not easily practicable. I proceeded upon principles of research to put me in possession of my matter; on principles of method to regulate it; and on principles in the human mind and in civil affairs to secure and perpetuate the operation. I conceived nothing arbitrarily; nor proposed any thing to be done by the will and pleasure of others, or my own; but by reason, and by reason only. I have ever abhorred, since the first dawn of my understanding to this it's obscure twilight, all the operations of opinion, fancy, inclination, and will, in the affairs of Government, where only a

[29] Milton's *Paradise Lost*, II, 625.
[30] The allusion is to Vergil's *Aeneid*, III, 214–218.
[31] Shakespeare's *Hamlet*, III, iv, 48–51.
[32] took soundings (to avoid running on rocks or shoals).

sovereign reason, paramount to all forms of legislation and administration, should dictate. Government is made for the very purpose of opposing that reason to will and to caprice, in the reformers or in the reformed, in the governors or in the governed, in Kings, in Senates, or in People.

On a careful review, therefore, and analysis of all the component parts of the Civil List,[33] and on weighing them each against other, in order to make, as much as possible, all of them a subject of estimate (the foundation and corner-stone of all regular provident œconomy) it appeared to me evident, that this was impracticable, whilst that part, called the Pension List, was totally discretionary in it's amount. For this reason, and for this only, I proposed to reduce it, both in it's gross quantity, and it's larger individual proportions, to a certainty: lest, if it were left without a *general* limit, it might eat up the Civil List service; if suffered to be granted in portions too great for the fund, it might defeat it's own end; and by unlimited allowances to some, it might disable the Crown in means of providing for others. The Pension List was to be kept as a sacred fund; but it could not be kept as a constant open fund, sufficient for growing demands, if some demands could wholly devour it. The tenour of the Act will shew that it regarded the Civil List *only,* the reduction of which to some sort of estimate was my great object.

No other of the Crown funds did I meddle with, because they had not the same relations. This[34] of the four and a half per cents does his Grace imagine had escaped me, or had escaped all the men of business, who acted with me in those regulations? I knew that such a fund existed, and that pensions had been always granted on it, before his Grace was born. This fund was full in my eye.

It was full in the eyes of those who worked with me. It was left on principle. On principle I did what was then done; and on principle what was left undone was omitted. I did not dare to rob the nation of all funds to reward merit. If I pressed this point too close, I acted contrary to the avowed principles on which I went. Gentlemen are very fond of quoting me; but if any one thinks it worth his while to know the rules that guided me in my plan of reform, he will read my printed speech on that subject; at least what is contained from page 230 to page 241 in the second Volume of the collection which a friend has given himself the trouble to make of my publications.[35] Be this as it may, these two Bills (though atchieved with the greatest labour, and management of every sort, both within and without the House) were only a part, and but a small part, of a very large system, comprehending all the objects I stated in opening my proposition, and indeed many more, which I just hinted at in my Speech to the Electors of Bristol, when I was put out of that representation.[36] All these, in some state or other of forwardness, I have long had by me.

But do I justify his Majesty's grace on these grounds? I think them the least of my services! The time gave them an occasional value: What I have done in the way of political œconomy was far from confined to this body of measures. I did not come into Parliament to con my lesson. I had earned my pension before I set my foot in St. Stephen's Chapel.[37] I was prepared and disciplined to this political warfare. The first session I sat in Parliament, I found it necessary to analyze the whole commercial, financial, constitutional and foreign interests of Great Britain and it's Empire. A great deal was then done; and more, far more would have been done, if more

---

[33] Parliamentary allowance for the expenses of the crown.

[34] Bedford had thought to make an issue of a part of the crown disbursements left unmodified by Burke's reform.

[35] French Laurence (1757–1809) had begun the collection and publication of Burke's writings and speeches by the issuance of three volumes in 1792.

[36] In 1780, during the Gordon riots, Burke advocated toleration and free trade with Catholic Ireland with the result that his Bristol supporters deserted him.

[37] Meeting place of the House of Commons.

had been permitted by events. Then in the vigour of my manhood, my constitution sunk under my labour. Had I then died, (and I seemed to myself very near death) I had then earned for those who belonged to me, more than the Duke of Bedford's ideas of service are of power to estimate. But in truth, these services I am called to account for, are not those on which I value myself the most. If I were to call for a reward (which I have never done) it should be for those in which for fourteen years, without intermission, I shewed the most industry, and had the least success; I mean in the affairs of India.[38] They are those on which I value myself the most; most for the importance; most for the labour; most for the judgment; most for constancy and perseverance in the pursuit. Others may value them most for the *intention*. In that, surely, they are not mistaken.

Does his Grace think, that they who advised the Crown to make my retreat easy, considered me only as an œconomist? That, well understood, however, is a good deal. If I had not deemed it of some value, I should not have made political œconomy an object of my humble studies, from my very early youth to near the end of my service in parliament, even before, (at least to any knowledge of mine) it had employed the thoughts of speculative men in other parts of Europe. At that time, it was still in it's infancy in England, where, in the last century, it had it's origin. Great and learned men thought my studies were not wholly thrown away, and deigned to communicate with me now and then on some particulars of their immortal works. Something of these studies may appear incidentally in some of the earliest things I published. The House has been witness to their effect, and has profited of them more or less, for above eight and twenty years.

To their estimate I leave the matter. I was not, like his Grace of Bedford, swaddled, and rocked, and dandled into a Legislator; *"Nitor in adversum"*[39] is the motto for a man like me. I possessed not one of the qualities, nor cultivated one of the arts, that recommend men to the favour and protection of the great. I was not made for a minion or a tool. As little did I follow the trade of winning the hearts, by imposing on the understandings, of the people. At every step of my progress in life (for in every step was I traversed and opposed), and at every turnpike I met, I was obliged to shew my passport, and again and again to prove my sole title to the honour of being useful to my Country, by a proof that I was not wholly unacquainted with it's laws, and the whole system of it's interests both abroad and at home. Otherwise no rank, no toleration even, for me. I had no arts, but manly arts. On them I have stood, and, please God, in spite of the Duke of Bedford and the Earl of Lauderdale, to the last gasp will I stand.

Had his Grace condescended to enquire concerning the person, whom he has not thought it below him to reproach, he might have found, that in the whole course of my life, I have never, on any pretence of œconomy, or on any other pretence, so much as in a single instance, stood between any man and his reward of service, or his encouragement in useful talent and pursuit, from the highest of those services and pursuits to the lowest. On the contrary I have, on an hundred occasions, exerted myself with singular zeal to forward every man's even tolerable pretensions. I have more than once had good-natured reprehensions from my friends for carrying the matter to something bordering on abuse. This line of conduct, whatever it's merits might be, was partly owing to natural disposition; but I think full as much to reason and principle. I looked on the consideration of publick service, or publick ornament, to be real and very justice: and I ever held, a scanty and penurious justice to partake of the nature of a wrong. I held it to be, in its consequences, the worst œconomy in the

---

[38] Impeachment proceedings against Warren Hastings, Governor of India, had been dismissed in 1795.

[39] "I make my way against opposition" (Ovid, *Metamorphoses*, II, 72).

world. In saving money, I soon can count up all the good I do; but when by a cold penury, I blast the abilities of a nation, and stunt the growth of it's active energies, the ill I may do is beyond all calculation. Whether it be too much or too little, whatever I have done has been general and systematick. I have never entered into those trifling vexations and oppressive details, that have been falsely, and most ridiculously laid to my charge.

Did I blame the pensions given to Mr. Barré and Mr. Dunning[40] between the proposition and execution of my plan? No! surely, no! Those pensions were within my principles. I assert it, those gentlemen deserved their pensions, their titles,—all they had; and if more they had, I should have been but pleased the more. They were men of talents; they were men of service. I put the profession of the law out of the question in one of them. It is a service that rewards itself. But their *publick service,* though, from their abilities unquestionably of more value than mine, in it's quantity and in it's duration was not to be mentioned with it. But I never could drive a hard bargain in my life, concerning any matter whatever; and least of all do I know how to haggle and huckster with merit. Pension for myself I obtained none; nor did I solicit any. Yet I was loaded with hatred for every thing that was with-held, and with obloquy for every thing that was given. I was thus left to support the grants of a name ever dear to me, and ever venerable to the world, in favour of those, who were no friends of mine or of his, against the rude attacks of those who were at that time friends to the grantees, and their own zealous partizans. I have never heard the Earl of Lauderdale complain of these pensions. He finds nothing wrong till he comes to me. This is impartiality, in the true modern revolutionary style.

Whatever I did at that time, so far as it regarded order and œconomy, is stable and eternal; as all principles must be. A particular order of things may be altered; order itself cannot lose its value. As to other particulars, they are variable by time and by circumstances. Laws of regulation are not fundamental laws. The publick exigencies are the masters of all such laws. They rule the laws, and are not to be ruled by them. They who exercise the legislative power at the time must judge.

It may be new to his Grace, but I beg leave to tell him, that mere parsimony is not œconomy. It is separable in theory from it; and in fact it may, or it may not, be a *part* of œconomy, according to circumstances. Expence, and great expence, may be an essential part in true œconomy. If parsimony were to be considered as one of the kinds of that virtue, there is however another and an higher œconomy. Œconomy is a distributive virtue, and consists not in saving, but in selection. Parsimony requires no providence, no sagacity, no powers of combination, no comparison, no judgment. Mere instinct, and that not an instinct of the noblest kind, may produce this false œconomy in perfection. The other œconomy has larger views. It demands a discriminating judgment, and a firm sagacious mind. It shuts one door to impudent importunity, only to open another, and a wider, to unpresuming merit. If none but meritorious service or real talent were to be rewarded, this nation has not wanted, and this nation will not want, the means of rewarding all the service it ever will receive, and encouraging all the merit it ever will produce. No state, since the foundation of society, has been impoverished by that species of profusion. Had the œconomy of selection and proportion been at all times observed, we should not now have had an overgrown Duke of Bedford, to oppress the industry of humble men, and to limit by the standard of his own conceptions, the justice, the bounty, or, if he pleases, the charity of the Crown.

His Grace may think as meanly as he will of my deserts in the far greater part of my conduct in life. It is free for him

[40] In 1782, Burke had been succeeded by Colonel Barré in a change of ministry, and both Barré and John Wilkes's counsel, John Dunning, had received pensions.

to do so. There will always be some difference of opinion in the value of political services. But there is one merit of mine, which he, of all men living, ought to be the last to call in question. I have supported with very great zeal, and I am told with some degree of success, those opinions, or if his Grace likes another expression better, those old prejudices which buoy up the ponderous mass of his nobility, wealth, and titles. I have omitted no exertion to prevent him and them from sinking to that level, to which the meretricious French faction, his Grace at least coquets with, omit no exertion to reduce both. I have done all I could to discountenance their enquiries into the fortunes of those, who hold large portions of wealth without any apparent merit of their own. I have strained every nerve to keep the Duke of Bedford in that situation, which alone makes him my superiour. Your Lordship has been a witness of the use he makes of that pre-eminence.

But be it, that this is virtue! Be it, that there is virtue in this well selected rigour; yet all virtues are not equally becoming to all men and at all times. There are crimes, undoubtedly there are crimes, which in all seasons of our existence, ought to put a generous antipathy in action; crimes that provoke an indignant justice, and call forth a warm and animated pursuit. But all things, that concern, what I may call, the preventive police of morality, all things merely rigid, harsh and censorial, the antiquated moralists, at whose feet I was brought up, would not have thought these the fittest matter to form the favourite virtues of young men of rank. What might have been well enough, and have been received with a veneration mixed with awe and terror, from an old, severe, crabbed Cato, would have

wanted something of propriety in the young Scipios, the ornament of the Roman Nobility, in the flower of their life. But the times, the morals, the masters, the scholars have all undergone a thorough revolution. It is a vile illiberal school, this new French academy of the *sans culottes*.[41] There is nothing in it that is fit for a Gentleman to learn.

Whatever it's vogue may be, I still flatter myself, that the parents of the growing generation will be satisfied with what is to be taught to their children in Westminster, in Eaton, or in Winchester: I still indulge the hope that no *grown* Gentleman or Nobleman of our time will think of finishing at Mr. Thelwall's[42] lecture whatever may have been left incomplete at the old Universities of his country. I would give to Lord Grenville and Mr. Pitt[43] for a motto, what was said of a Roman Censor or Praetor (or what was he), who in virtue of a Senatus consultum[44] shut up certain academies,

Cludere Ludum Impudentiæ jussit.[45]

Every honest father of a family in the kingdom will rejoice at the breaking up for the holidays, and will pray that there may be a very long vacation in all such schools.

The awful state of the time, and not myself or my own justification, is my true object in what I now write; or in what I shall ever write or say. It little signifies to the world what becomes of such things as me, or even as the Duke of Bedford. What I say about either of us is nothing more than a vehicle, as you, my Lord, will easily perceive, to convey my sentiments on matters far more worthy of your attention. It is when I stick to my apparent first subject that I ought to apologize, not when I

---

[41] "without breeches"; a term applied to the French revolutionists.

[42] John Thelwall (1764–1834), a political agitator and lecturer on elocution; he replied to Burke in *Sober Reflections on the Seditious and Inflammatory Letter of the Right Honourable Edmund Burke to a Noble Lord* (1796).

[43] William Pitt, as leader of the Tories, was

Prime Minister; Lord Grenville, as leader of a group of Whig-Tory followers, had thrown in his lot with Pitt.

[44] decree.

[45] "He ordered the game of shamelessness to come to an end." There is a play on *ludus* which meant both *game* and the place where games are common, *school*.

depart from it. I therefore must beg your Lordship's pardon for again resuming it after this very short digression; assuring you that I shall never altogether lose sight of such matter as persons abler than I am may turn to some profit.

The Duke of Bedford conceives, that he is obliged to call the attention of the House of Peers to his Majesty's grant to me, which he considers as excessive and out of all bounds.

I know not how it has happened, but it really seems, that, whilst his Grace was meditating his well considered censure upon me, he fell into a sort of sleep. Homer nods; and the Duke of Bedford may dream; and as dreams (even his golden dreams) are apt to be ill-pieced and incongruously put together, his Grace preserved his idea of reproach to *me,* but took the subject-matter from the Crown-grants *to his own family.* This is "the stuff of which his dreams are made." In that way of putting things together his Grace is perfectly in the right. The grants to the House of Russel[46] were so enormous, as not only to outrage œconomy, but even to stagger credibility. The Duke of Bedford is the Leviathan among all the creatures of the Crown. He tumbles about his unwieldy bulk; he plays and frolicks in the ocean of the Royal bounty. Huge as he is, and whilst "he lies floating many a rood,"[47] he is still a creature. His ribs, his fins, his whalebone, his blubber, the very spiracles through which he spouts a torrent of brine against his origin, and covers me all over with the spray,—every thing of him and about him is from the Throne. Is it for *him* to question the dispensation of the Royal favour?

I really am at a loss to draw any sort of parallel between the public merits of his Grace, by which he justifies the grants he holds, and these services of mine, on the favourable construction of which I have obtained what his Grace so much disapproves. In private life, I have not at all the honour of acquaintance with the noble Duke. But I ought to presume, and it costs me nothing to do so, that he abundantly deserves the esteem and love of all who live with him. But as to public service, why truly it would not be more ridiculous for me to compare myself in rank, in fortune, in splendid descent, in youth, strength, or figure, with the Duke of Bedford, than to make a parallel between his services, and my attempts to be useful to my country. It would not be gross adulation, but uncivil irony, to say, that he has any publick merit of his own to keep alive the idea of the services by which his vast landed Pensions were obtained. My merits, whatever they are, are original and personal; his are derivative. It is his ancestor, the original pensioner, that has laid up this inexhaustible fund of merit, which makes his Grace so very delicate and exceptious about the merit of all other grantees of the Crown. Had he permitted me to remain in quiet, I should have said 'tis his estate; that's enough. It is his by law; what have I to do with it or it's history? He would naturally have said on his side, 'tis this man's fortune.—He is as good now, as my ancestor was two hundred and fifty years ago. I am a young man with very old pensions; he is an old man with very young pensions,—that's all?

Why will his Grace, by attacking me, force me reluctantly to compare my little merit with that which obtained from the Crown those prodigies of profuse donation by which he tramples on the mediocrity of humble and laborious individuals? I would willingly leave him to the Herald's College,[48] which the philosophy of the Sans culottes, (prouder by far than all the Garters, and Norroys and Clarencieux, and Rouge Dragons that ever pranced in a procession of what his friends call aristocrates and despots) will abolish with contumely and scorn. These historians, recorders, and blazoners of virtues and arms, differ wholly from that other description of historians, who never assign any act of politicians to a good motive. These gentle histori-

---

[46] Bedford's family.
[47] Milton's description of Satan in *Paradise Lost,* I, 196.

[48] An institution for keeping the records of aristocracy; the names in the following parenthesis refer to orders of chivalry.

ans, on the contrary, dip their pens in nothing but the milk of human kindness. They seek no further for merit than the preamble of a patent, or the inscription on a tomb. With them every man created a peer is first an hero ready made. They judge of every man's capacity for office by the offices he has filled; and the more offices the more ability. Every General-officer with them is a Marlborough;[49] every Statesman a Burleigh;[50] every Judge a Murray or a Yorke.[51] They, who alive, were laughed at or pitied by all their acquaintance, make as good a figure as the best of them in the pages of Guillim, Edmonson, and Collins.[52]

To these recorders, so full of good nature to the great and prosperous, I would willingly leave the first Baron Russel, and Earl of Bedford, and the merits of his grants. But the aulnager,[53] the weigher, the meter of grants, will not suffer us to acquiesce in the judgment of the Prince reigning at the time when they were made. They are never good to those who earn them. Well then; since the new grantees have war made on them by the old, and that the word of the Sovereign is not to be taken, let us turn our eyes to history, in which great men have always a pleasure in contemplating the heroic origin of their house.

The first peer of the name, the first purchaser of the grants, was a Mr. Russel,[54] a person of an ancient gentleman's family raised by being a minion of Henry the Eighth. As there generally is some resemblance of character to create these relations, the favourite was in all likelihood much such another as his master. The first of those immoderate grants was not taken from the antient demesne of the Crown, but from the recent confiscation of the ancient nobility of the land. The lion having sucked the blood of his prey, threw the offal carcase to the jackall in waiting. Having tasted once the food of confiscation, the favourites became fierce and ravenous. This worthy favourite's first grant was from the lay nobility. The second, infinitely improving on the enormity of the first, was from the plunder of the church.[55] In truth his Grace is somewhat excusable for his dislike to a grant like mine, not only in its quantity, but in it's kind so different from his own.

Mine was from a mild and benevolent sovereign; his from Henry the Eighth.

Mine had not it's fund in the murder of any innocent person of illustrious rank, or in the pillage of any body of unoffending men. His grants were from the aggregate and consolidated funds of judgments iniquitously legal, and from possessions voluntarily surrendered by the lawful proprietors with the gibbet at their door.

The merit of the grantee whom he derives from, was that of being a prompt and greedy instrument of a *levelling* tyrant, who oppressed all descriptions of his people, but who fell with particular fury on every thing that was *great and noble.* Mine has been, in endeavouring to screen every man, in every class, from oppression, and particularly in defending the high and eminent, who in the bad times of confiscating Princes, confiscating chief Governors, or confiscating Demagogues, are the most exposed to jealousy, avarice and envy.

The merit of the original grantee of his Grace's pensions, was in giving his hand to the work, and partaking the spoil with a Prince, who plundered a part of his national church of his time and country. Mine was in defending the

---

[49] John Churchill, first Duke of Marlborough (1650–1722), victor of Blenheim.

[50] William Cecil, first Baron Burleigh (1520–1598), one of the chief advisers to Elizabeth I.

[51] William Murray, first Earl of Mansfield (1705–1793), and Philip Yorke, first Earl of Hardwicke (1690–1764), famous chief justices.

[52] Authors of volumes on the peerage of England.

[53] official inspector.

[54] John Russel (1486?–1555) for service in foreign affairs was rewarded richly by Henry VIII and created Earl of Bedford under Edward VI in 1550.

[55] i.e., from property which was seized by the crown at the dissolution of the monasteries; incidentally, under Mary, Bedford opposed the restoration of the monasteries.

whole of the national church of my own time and my own country, and the whole of the national churches of all countries, from the principles and the examples which lead to ecclesiastical pillage, thence to a contempt of *all* prescriptive titles, thence to the pillage of *all* property, and thence to universal desolation.

The merit of the origin of his Grace's fortune was in being a favourite and chief adviser to a Prince, who left no liberty to their native country. My endeavour was to obtain liberty for the municipal country in which I was born, and for all descriptions and denominations in it.—Mine was to support with unrelaxing vigilance every right, every privilege, every franchise, in this my adopted, my dearer and more comprehensive country; and not only to preserve those rights in this chief seat of empire, but in every nation, in every land, in every climate, language and religion, in the vast domain that still is under the protection, and the larger that was once under the protection, of the British Crown.

His founder's merits were, by arts in which he served his master and made his fortune, to bring poverty, wretchedness and depopulation on his country. Mine were under a benevolent Prince, in promoting the commerce, manufactures and agriculture of his kingdom; in which his Majesty shews an eminent example, who even in his amusements is a patriot, and in hours of leisure an improver of his native soil.

His founder's merit, was the merit of a gentleman raised by the arts of a Court, and the protection of a Wolsey,[56] to the eminence of a great and potent Lord. His merit in that eminence was by instigating a tyrant to injustice, to provoke a people to rebellion.—My merit was, to awaken the sober part of the country, that they might put themselves on their guard against any one potent Lord, or any greater number of potent Lords, or any combination of great leading men of any sort, if ever they should attempt to proceed in the same courses, but in the reverse order, that is, by instigating a corrupted populace to rebellion, and, through that rebellion, should introduce a tyranny yet worse than the tyranny which his Grace's ancestor supported, and of which he profited in the manner we behold in the despotism of Henry the Eighth.

The political merit of the first pensioner of his Grace's house, was that of being concerned as a counsellor of state in advising, and in his person executing the conditions of a dishonourable peace with France; the surrendering the fortress of Boulogne, then our out guard on the Continent. By that surrender, Calais, the key of France, and the bridle in the mouth of that power, was, not many years afterwards,[57] finally lost. My merit has been in resisting the power and pride of France, under any form of it's rule; but in opposing it with the greatest zeal and earnestness, when that rule appeared in the worst form it could assume; the worst indeed which the prime cause and principle of all evil could possibly give it. It was my endeavour by every means to excite a spirit in the house, where I had the honour of a seat, for carrying on with early vigour and decision, the most clearly just and necessary war,[58] that this or any nation ever carried on; in order to save my country from the iron yoke of it's power, and from the more dreadful contagion of its principles; to preserve, while they can be preserved pure and untainted, the ancient, inbred integrity, piety, good nature, and good humour of the people of England, from the dreadful pestilence which beginning in France, threatens to lay waste the whole moral, and in a great degree the whole physical world, having done both in the focus of it's most intense malignity.

The labours of his Grace's founder merited the curses, not loud but deep, of the Commons of England, on whom *he* and his master had effected a *complete Parliamentary Reform,* in making them

---

[56] Thomas Cardinal Wolsey (1475?–1530), powerful religious and secular aide to Henry VIII.

[57] In 1558.

[58] With France, 1778–1783.

in their slavery and humiliation, the true and adequate representatives of a debased, degraded, and undone people. My merits were, in having had an active, though not always an ostentatious share, in every one act, without exception, of undisputed constitutional utility in my time, and in having supported on all occasions, the authority, the efficiency, and the privileges of the Commons of Great Britain. I ended my services by a recorded and fully reasoned assertion on their own journals of their constitutional rights, and a vindication of their constitutional conduct. I laboured in all things to merit their inward approbation, and (along with the assistants of the largest, the greatest, and best of my endeavours) I received their free, unbiassed, publick, and solemn thanks.

Thus stands the account of the comparative merits of the Crown grants which compose the Duke of Bedford's fortune as balanced against mine. In the name of common sense, why should the Duke of Bedford think, that none but of the House of Russel are entitled to the favour of the Crown? Why should he imagine that no King of England has been capable of judging of merit but King Henry the Eighth? Indeed, he will pardon me; he is a little mistaken; all virtue did not end in the first Earl of Bedford. All discernment did not lose it's vision when his Creator closed his eyes. Let him remit his rigour on the disproportion between merit and reward in others, and they will make no enquiry into the origin of his fortune. They will regard with much more satisfaction, as he will contemplate with infinitely more advantage, whatever in his pedigree has been dulcified[59] by an exposure to the influence of heaven in a long flow of generations, from the hard, acidulous, metallic tincture of the spring. It is little to be doubted, that several of his forefathers in that long series, have degenerated into honour and virtue. Let the Duke of Bedford (I am sure he will) reject with scorn and horror, the counsels of the lecturers, those wicked panders to avarice and ambition, who would tempt him in the troubles of his country, to seek another enormous fortune from the forfeitures of another nobility, and the plunder of another church. Let him (and I trust that yet he will) employ all the energy of his youth, and all the resources of his wealth, to crush rebellious principles which have no foundation in morals, and rebellious movements, that have no provocation in tyranny.

Then will be forgot the rebellions, which, by a doubtful priority in crime, his ancestor had provoked and extinguished. On such a conduct in the noble Duke, many of his countrymen might, and with some excuse might, give way to the enthusiasm of their gratitude, and in the dashing style of some of the old declaimers, cry out, that if the fates had found no other way in which they could give a Duke of Bedford and his opulence as props to a tottering world, then the butchery of the Duke of Buckingham might be tolerated;[60] it might be regarded even with complacency, whilst in the heir of confiscation they saw the sympathizing comforter of the martyrs, who suffer under the cruel confiscation of this day; whilst they beheld with admiration his zealous protection of the virtuous and loyal nobility of France, and his manly support of his brethren, the yet standing nobility and gentry of his native land. Then his Grace's merit would be pure and new, and sharp, as fresh from the mint of honour. As he pleased he might reflect honour on his predecessors, or throw it forward on those who were to succeed him. He might be the propagator of the stock of honour, or the root of it, as he thought proper.

Had it pleased God to continue to me the hopes of succession, I should have been, according to my mediocrity, and the mediocrity of the age I live in, a sort of founder of a family; I should have

[59] softened.
[60] In 1521, under Henry VIII, the Duke of Buckingham was accused of treason and, after a mock trial, summarily executed merely to strengthen the King's hand abroad by suppressing all signs of opposition at home.

left a son,[61] who, in all the points in which personal merit can be viewed, in science, in erudition, in genius, in taste, in honour, in generosity, in humanity, in every liberal sentiment, and every liberal accomplishment, would not have shewn himself inferior to the Duke of Bedford, or to any of those whom he traces in his line. His Grace very soon would have wanted all plausibility in his attack upon that provision which belonged more to mine than to me. He would soon have supplied every deficiency, and symmetrized every disproportion. It would not have been for that successor to resort to any stagnant wasting reservoir of merit in me, or in any ancestry. He had in himself a salient, living spring, of generous and manly action. Every day he lived he would have re-purchased the bounty of the crown, and ten times more, if ten times more he had received. He was made a public creature; and had no enjoyment whatever, but in the performance of some duty. At this exigent moment, the loss of a finished man is not easily supplied.

But a disposer whose power we are little able to resist, and whose wisdom it behoves us not at all to dispute; has ordained it in another manner, and (whatever my querulous weakness might suggest) a far better. The storm has gone over me; and I lie like one of those old oaks which the late hurricane has scattered about me. I am stripped of all my honours; I am torn up by the roots, and lie prostrate on the earth! There, and prostrate there, I most unfeignedly recognize the divine justice, and in some degree submit to it. But whilst I humble myself before God, I do not know that it is forbidden to repel the attacks of unjust and inconsiderate men. The patience of Job is proverbial. After some of the convulsive struggles of our irritable nature, he submitted himself, and repented in dust and ashes. But even so, I do not find him blamed for reprehending, and with a considerable degree of verbal asperity, those ill-natured neighbours of his, who visited his dunghill to read moral, political, and œconomical lectures on his misery. I am alone. I have none to meet my enemies in the gate. Indeed, my Lord, I greatly deceive myself, if in this hard season I would give a peck of refuse wheat for all that is called fame and honour in the world. This the appetite but of a few. It is a luxury; it is a privilege; it is an indulgence for those who are at their ease. But we are all of us made to shun disgrace, as we are made to shrink from pain, and poverty, and disease. It is an instinct; and under the direction of reason, instinct is always in the right. I live in an inverted order. They who ought to have succeeded me are gone before me. They who should have been to me as posterity are in the place of ancestors. I owe to the dearest relation (which ever must subsist in memory) that act of piety, which he would have performed to me; I owe it to him to shew that he was not descended, as the Duke of Bedford would have it, from an unworthy parent.

The Crown has considered me after long service: the Crown has paid the Duke of Bedford by advance. He has had a long credit for any service which he may perform hereafter. He is secure, and long may he be secure, in his advance, whether he performs any services or not. But let him take care how he endangers the safety of that Constitution which secures his own utility or his own insignificance; or how he discourages those, who take up, even puny arms, to defend an order of things, which, like the Sun of Heaven, shines alike on the useful and the worthless. His grants are engrafted on the public law of Europe, covered with the awful hoar of innumerable ages. They are guarded by the sacred rules of prescription, found in that full treasury of jurisprudence from which the jejuneness and penury of our municipal law has, by degrees, been enriched and strengthened. This prescrip-

---

[61] Richard Burke, his only son, had died in 1794 at the age of 36. A man of promise, a member of Johnson's Club as early as 1782, he had succeeded his father as a member of Parliament just two weeks before his sudden death.

tion I had my share (a very full share) in bringing to it's perfection. The Duke of Bedford will stand as long as prescriptive law endures; as long as the great stable laws of property, common to us with all civilized nations, are kept in their integrity, and without the smallest intermixture of the laws, maxims, principles, or precedents of the Grand Revolution. They are secure against all changes but one. The whole revolutionary system, institutes, digest, code, novels, text, gloss, comment, are, not only not the same, but they are the very reverse, and the reverse fundamentally, of all the laws, on which civil life has hitherto been upheld in all the governments of the world. The learned professors of the Rights of Man regard prescription, not as a title to bar all claim, set up against old possession—but they look on prescription as itself a bar against the possessor and proprietor. They hold an immemorial possession to be more than a long continued, and therefore an aggravated injustice.

Such are *their* ideas; such *their* religion, and such *their* law. But as to *our* country and *our* race, as long as the well compacted structure of our church and state, the sanctuary, the holy of holies of that ancient law, defended by reverence, defended by power, a fortress at once and a temple, shall stand inviolate on the brow of the British Sion—as long as the British Monarchy, not more limited than fenced by the orders of the State, shall, like the proud Keep of Windsor, rising in the majesty of proportion, and girt with the double belt of it's kindred and coeval towers, as long as this awful structure shall oversee and guard the subjected land—so long the mounds and dykes of the low, fat, Bedford level will have nothing to fear from all the pick-axes of all the levellers of France. As long as our Sovereign Lord the King, and his faithful subjects, the Lords and Commons of this realm,—the triple cord, which no man can break; the solemn, sworn, constitutional frank-pledge of this nation; the firm guarantees of each others being, and each others rights; the joint and several securities, each in it's

place and order, for every kind and every quality, of property and of dignity— As long as these endure, so long the Duke of Bedford is safe: and we are all safe together—the high from the blights of envy and the spoliations of rapacity; the low from the iron hand of oppression and the insolent spurn of contempt. Amen! and so be it: and so it will be,

Dum domus Æneæ Capitoli immobile
   saxum
Accolet; imperiumque pater Romanus
   habebit.—[62]

But if the rude inroad of Gallick tumult, with it's sophistical Rights of Man, to falsify the account, and it's sword as a makeweight to throw into the scale, shall be introduced into our city by a misguided populace, set on by proud great men, themselves blinded and intoxicated by a frantick ambition, we shall, all of us, perish and be overwhelmed in a common ruin. If a great storm blow on our coast, it will cast the whales on the strand as well as the periwinkles. His Grace will not survive the poor grantee he despises, no not for a twelvemonth. If the great look for safety in the services they render to this Gallick cause, it is to be foolish, even above the weight of privilege allowed to wealth. If his Grace be one of these whom they endeavour to proselytize, he ought to be aware of the character of the sect, whose doctrines he is invited to embrace. With them, insurrection is the most sacred of revolutionary duties to the state. Ingratitude to benefactors is the first of revolutionary virtues. Ingratitude is indeed their four cardinal virtues compacted and amalgamated into one; and he will find it in every thing that has happened since the commencement of the philosophic revolution to this hour. If he pleads the merit of having performed the duty of insurrection against the order he lives in (God forbid he ever should), the merit of others

---

[62] Fixt as the capitol's foundation lies;
And spread where'er the Roman eagle flies.
(Vergil, *Aeneid*, IX, 448–449, tr. Dryden.)

will be to perform the duty of insurrection against him. If he pleads (again God forbid he should, and I do not suspect he will) his ingratitude to the Crown for it's creation of his family, others will plead their right and duty to pay him in kind. They will laugh, indeed they will laugh, at his parchment and his wax. His deeds will be drawn out with the rest of the lumber of his evidence room, and burnt to the tune of *ça ira*[63] in the courts of Bedford (then Equality) House.

Am I to blame, if I attempt to pay his Grace's hostile reproaches to me with a friendly admonition to himself? Can I be blamed, to point out to him in what manner he is like to be affected, if the sect of the cannibal philosophers of France should proselytize any considerable part of this people, and, by their joint proselytizing arms, should conquer that Government, to which his Grace does not seem to me to give all the support his own security demands? Surely it is proper, that he, and that others like him, should know the true genius of this sect, what their opinions are; what they have done: and to whom; and what, (if a prognostick is to be formed from the dispositions and actions of men) it is certain they will do hereafter. He ought to know, that they have sworn assistance, the only engagement they ever will keep, to all in this country, who bear a resemblance to themselves, and who think as such, that *The whole duty of man* consists in destruction. They are a misallied and disparaged branch of the house of Nimrod. They are the Duke of Bedford's natural hunters; and he is their natural game. Because he is not very profoundly reflecting, he sleeps in profound security: they, on the contrary, are always vigilant, active, enterprizing, and though far removed from any knowledge, which makes men estimable or useful, in all the instruments and resources of evil, their leaders are not meanly instructed, or insufficiently fur-

nished. In the French Revolution every thing is new; and, from want of preparation to meet so unlooked for an evil, every thing is dangerous. Never, before this time, was a set of literary men, converted into a gang of robbers and assassins. Never before, did a den of bravoes and banditti, assume the garb and tone of an academy of philosophers.

Let me tell his Grace, that an union of such characters, monstrous as it seems, is not made for producing despicable enemies. But if they are formidable as foes, as friends they are dreadful indeed. The men of property in France confiding in a force, which seemed to be irresistible, because it had never been tried, neglected to prepare for a conflict with their enemies at their own weapons. They were found in such a situation as the Mexicans were, when they were attacked by the dogs, the cavalry, the iron, and the gunpowder of an handful of bearded men, whom they did not know to exist in nature.[64] This is a comparison that some, I think, have made; and it is just. In France they had their enemies within their houses. They were even in the bosoms of many of them. But they had not sagacity to discern their savage character. They seemed tame, and even caressing. They had nothing but *douce humanité*[65] in their mouth. They could not bear the punishment of the mildest laws on the greatest criminals. The slightest severity of justice made their flesh creep. The very idea that war existed in the world disturbed their repose. Military glory was no more than, with them, a splendid infamy. Hardly would they hear of self defence, which they reduced within such bounds, as to leave it no defence at all. All this while they meditated the confiscations and massacres we have seen. Had any one told these unfortunate Noblemen and Gentlemen, how, and by whom, the grand fabrick of the French monarchy under which they flourished would be subverted, they would not have pitied him as a vision-

[63] opening words to a French song of the Revolution, meaning: "All will come right at last."
[64] Within two years of landing in Mexico in 1519 with fewer than 600 men, Cortez had brought the country under the dominion of Spain.
[65] "human kindness."

ary, but would have turned from him as what they call a *mauvais plaisant*.[66] Yet we have seen what has happened. The persons who have suffered from the cannibal philosophy of France, are so like the Duke of Bedford, that nothing but his Grace's probably not speaking quite so good French, could enable us to find out any difference. A great many of them had as pompous titles as he, and were of full as illustrious a race: some few of them had fortunes as ample; several of them, without meaning the least disparagement to the Duke of Bedford, were as wise, and as virtuous, and as valiant, and as well educated, and as compleat in all the lineaments of men of honour as he is: And to all this they had added the powerful outguard of a military profession, which, in it's nature, renders men somewhat more cautious than those, who have nothing to attend to but the lazy enjoyment of undisturbed possessions. But security was their ruin. They are dashed to pieces in the storm, and our shores are covered with the wrecks. If they had been aware that such a thing might happen, such a thing never could have happened.

I assure his Grace, that if I state to him the designs of his enemies, in a manner which may appear to him ludicrous and impossible, I tell him nothing that has not exactly happened, point by point, but twenty-four miles from our own shore. I assure him that the Frenchified faction, more encouraged, than others are warned, by what has happened in France, look at him and his landed possessions, as an object at once of curiosity and rapacity. He is made for them in every part of their double character. As robbers, to them he is a noble booty: as speculatists, he is a glorious subject for their experimental philosophy. He affords matter for an extensive analysis, in all the branches of their science, geometrical, physical, civil and political. These philosophers are fanaticks; independent of any interest, which if it operated alone would make them much more

tractable, they are carried with such an headlong rage towards every desperate trial, that they would sacrifice the whole human race to the slightest of their experiments. I am better able to enter into the character of this description of men than the noble Duke can be. I have lived long and variously in the World. Without any considerable pretensions to literature in myself, I have aspired to the love of letters. I have lived for a great many years in habitudes with those who professed them. I can form a tolerable estimate of what is likely to happen from a character, chiefly dependent for fame and fortune, on knowledge and talent, as well in it's morbid and perverted state, as in that which is sound and natural. Naturally men so formed and finished are the first gifts of Providence to the World. But when they have once thrown off the fear of God, which was in all ages too often the case, and the fear of man, which is now the case, and when in that state they come to understand one another, and to act in corps, a more dreadful calamity cannot arise out of Hell to scourge mankind. Nothing can be conceived more hard than the heart of a thorough bred metaphysician. It comes nearer to the cold malignity of a wicked spirit than to the frailty and passion of a man. It is like that of the principle of Evil himself, incorporeal, pure, unmixed, dephlegmated, defecated evil. It is no easy operation to eradicate humanity from the human breast. What Shakespeare calls "the compunctious visitings of nature,"[67] will sometime knock at their hearts, and protest against their murderous speculations. But they have a means of compounding with their nature. Their humanity is not dissolved. They only give it a long prorogation.[68] They are ready to declare, that they do not think two thousand years too long a period for the good that they pursue. It is remarkable, that they never see any way to their projected good but by the road of some evil. Their imagination is not fatigued, with the contemplation of

[66] "practical joker."

[67] *Macbeth*, I, v, 46.

[68] "continuance . . . interruption of the session of parliament by the regal authority" (Johnson's *Dictionary*).

human suffering thro' the wild waste of centuries added to centuries, of misery and desolation. Their humanity is at their horizon—and, like the horizon, it always flies before them. The geometricians, and the chymists bring, the one from the dry bones of their diagrams, and the other from the foot of their furnaces, dispositions that make them worse than indifferent about those feelings and habitudes, which are the supports of the moral world. Ambition is come upon them suddenly; they are intoxicated with it, and it has rendered them fearless of the danger, which may from thence arise to others or to themselves. These philosophers consider men in their experiments, no more than they do mice in an air pump, or in a recipient of mephitic[69] gas. Whatever his Grace may think of himself, they look upon him, and every thing that belongs to him, with no more regard than they do upon the whiskers of that little long-tailed animal, that has been long the game of the grave, demure, insidious, spring-nailed, velvet-pawed, green-eyed philosophers, whether going upon two legs, or upon four.

His Grace's landed possessions are irresistibly inviting to an *agrarian* experiment. They are a downright insult upon the Rights of Man. They are more extensive than the territory of many of the Grecian republicks; and they are without comparison more fertile than most of them. There are now republicks in Italy, in Germany and in Swisserland, which do not possess any thing like so fair and ample a domain. There is scope for seven philosophers to proceed in their analytical experiments, upon Harrington's[70] seven different forms of republicks, in the acres of this one Duke. Hitherto they have been wholly unproductive to speculation; fitted for nothing but to fatten bullocks, and to produce grain for beer, still more to stupify the dull English understanding. Abbé

Sieyes[71] has whole nests of pigeon-holes full of constitutions ready made, ticketed, sorted, and numbered; suited to every season and every fancy; some with the top of the pattern at the bottom, and some with the bottom at the top; some plain, some flowered; some distinguished for their simplicity; others for their complexity; some of blood colour; some of *boue de Paris;*[72] some with directories, others without a direction; some with councils of elders, and councils of youngsters; some without any council at all. Some where the electors choose the representatives; others, where the representatives choose the electors. Some in long coats, and some in short cloaks; some with pantaloons; some without breeches. Some with five shilling qualifications; some totally unqualified. So that no constitution-fancier may go unsuited from his shop, provided he loves a pattern of pillage, oppression, arbitrary imprisonment, confiscation, exile, revolutionary judgment, and legalised premeditated murder, in any shapes into which they can be put. What a pity it is, that the progress of experimental philosophy should be checked by his Grace's monopoly! Such are their sentiments, I assure him; such is their language when they dare to speak; and such are their proceedings, when they have the means to act.

Their geographers, and geometricians, have been some time out of practice. It is some time since they have divided their own country into squares. That figure has lost the charms of it's novelty. They want new lands for new trials. It is not only the geometricians of the republick that find him a good subject, the chymists have bespoke him after the geometricians have done with him. As the first set have an eye on his Grace's lands, the chymists are not less taken with his buildings. They consider mortar as a very anti-revolutionary invention in it's

69 noxious.

70 James Harrington's *Oceana* (1656) envisioned various republican utopias as alternatives to the absolute monarchy of Hobbes's *Leviathan.*

71 Emmanuel Joseph Sieyès (1748–1836), a

French priest and political pamphleteer whose propaganda had been instrumental in provoking the Revolution and who continued to draw up constitutions which eventually made way for the military dictatorship of Napoleon.

72 "Parisian mud."

present state; but properly employed, an admirable material for overturning all establishments. They have found that the gunpowder of *ruins* is far the fittest for making other *ruins,* and so *ad infinitum.* They have calculated what quantity of matter convertible into nitre is to be found in Bedford House, in Woburn Abbey, and in what his Grace and his trustees have still suffered to stand of that foolish royalist Inigo Jones, in Covent Garden.[73] Churches, play-houses, coffee-houses, all alike are destined to be mingled, and equalized, and blended into one common rubbish; and well sifted, and lixiviated,[74] to chrystalize into true democratick explosive insurrectionary nitre. Their Academy del *Cimento* (per antiphrasin)[75] with Morveau and Hassenfrats at it's head, have computed that the grave Sans-culottes may make war on all the aristocracy of Europe for a twelvemonth, out of the rubbish of the Duke of Bedford's buildings.

While these experiments are going on upon the Duke of Bedford's houses by the Morveaux and Priestleys,[76] the Sieyes, and the rest of the analytical legislators, and constitution-venders, are quite as busy in their trade of decomposing organization, in forming his Grace's vassals into primary assemblies, national guards, first, second and third requisitioners, committees of research, conductors of the travelling guillotine, judges of revolutionary tribunals, legislative hangmen, supervisors of domiciliary visitation, exactors of forced loans, and assessors of the maximum.

The din of all this smithery may some time or other possibly wake this noble Duke, and push him to an endeavour to save some little matter from their experimental philosophy. If he pleads his grants from the Crown, he is ruined at the outset. If he pleads he has received them from the pillage of superstitious corporations, this indeed will stagger them a little, because they are enemies to all corporations, and to all religion. However, they will soon recover themselves, and will tell his Grace, or his learned council, that all such property belongs to the *nation;* and that it would be more wise for him, if he wishes to live the natural term of a *citizen,* (that is, according to Condorcet's[77] calculation, six months on an average,) not to pass for an usurper upon the national property. This is what the *Serjeants* at law of the Rights of Man, will say to the puny *apprentices* of the common law of England.

Is the Genius of Philosophy not yet known? You may as well think the Garden of the Tuilleries was well protected with the cords of ribbon insultingly stretched by the National Assembly to keep the sovereign canaille from intruding on the retirement of the poor King of the French,[78] as that such flimsy cobwebs will stand between the savages of the Revolution and their natural prey. Deep Philosophers are no triflers; brave Sans culottes are no formalists. They will no more regard a Marquis of Tavistock[79] than an Abbot of Tavistock; the Lord of Wooburn[80] will not be more respectable in their eyes than the Prior of Wooburn: they will make no difference between the Superior of a Covent Garden of nuns and of a Covent Garden of

---

[73] Covent Garden belonged to the Bedford family; the theater was designed by the seventeenth-century architect, Inigo Jones.

[74] blended with lye.

[75] A Florentine academy of science ("of cement," as Burke says, ironically); Morveau and Hassenfrats were French scientists who perfected the military machine for the Revolution.

[76] Joseph Priestley (see note 6), the clergyman and scientist, was made a French citizen for his espousal of the French Revolution; he had been among those who attempted to re-

fute Burke's *Reflections on the Revolution in France.*

[77] The Marquis de Condorcet, an eminent mathematician whose sympathies lay with the revolutionists, was driven to suicide in 1794 by the ironic turn of political events.

[78] Louis XVI had been granted temporary asylum; the garden of the Tuilleries, now a public park, was the limit of his bounds.

[79] A title of long standing in the Bedford family.

[80] Another part of the Bedford estate.

another description. They will not care a rush whether his coat is long or short; whether the colour be purple or blue and buff. They will not trouble *their* heads, with what part of *his* head, his hair is cut from; and they will look with equal respect on a tonsure and a crop. Their only question will be that of their *Legendre*[81], or some other of their legislative butchers, How he cuts up? how he tallows in the cawl[82] or on the kidneys?

Is it not a singular phœnomenon, that whilst the Sans culotte Carcase Butchers, and the Philosophers of the shambles, are pricking their dotted lines upon his hide, and like the print of the poor ox that we see in the shop windows at Charing Cross, alive as he is, and thinking no harm in the world, he is divided into rumps, and sirloins, and briskets, and into all sorts of pieces for roasting, boiling, and stewing, that all the while they are measuring *him,* his Grace is measuring *me;* is invidiously comparing the bounty of the Crown with the deserts of the defender of his order, and in the same moment fawning on those who have the knife half out of the sheath—poor innocent!

Pleas'd to the last, he crops the flow'ry food,
And licks the hand just rais'd to shed his blood.[83]

No man lives too long, who lives to do with spirit, and suffer with resignation, what Providence pleases to command or inflict: but indeed they are sharp incommodities which beset old age. It was but the other day, that on putting in order some things which had been brought here on my taking leave of London for ever, I looked over a number of fine portraits, most of them of persons now dead, but whose society, in my better days, made this a proud and happy place. Amongst these was the picture of Lord Keppel.[84] It was painted by an artist worthy of the subject,[85] the excellent friend of that excellent man from their earliest youth, and a common friend of us both, with whom we lived for many years without a moment of coldness, of peevishness, of jealousy, or of jar, to the day of our final separation.

I ever looked on Lord Keppel as one of the greatest and best men of his age; and I loved, and cultivated him accordingly. He was much in my heart, and I believe I was in his to the very last beat. It was after his trial at Portsmouth that he gave me this picture. With what zeal and anxious affection I attended him through that his agony of glory, what part my son in the early flush and enthusiasm of his virtue, and the pious passion with which he attached himself to all my connections, with what prodigality we both squandered ourselves in courting almost every sort of enmity for his sake, I believe he felt, just as I should have felt, such friendship on such an occasion. I partook indeed of this honour, with several of the first, and best, and ablest in the kingdom, but I was behind hand with none of them; and I am sure, that if to the eternal disgrace of this nation, and to the total annihilation of every trace of honour and virtue in it, things had taken a different turn from what they did, I should have attended him to the quarter-deck with no less good will and more pride, though with far other feelings, than I partook of the general flow of national joy that attended the justice that was done to his virtue.

Pardon, my Lord, the feeble garrulity of age, which loves to diffuse itself in discourse of the departed great. At my years we live in retrospect alone: and, wholly unfitted for the society of vigorous life, we enjoy, the best balm to all

---

[81] Louis Legendre (1752–1833), a French mathematician, active in introducing the metric system.

[82] "the omentum; the integument in which the guts are inclosed" (Johnson's *Dictionary*).

[83] Alexander Pope's *Essay on Man*, I, 83–84.

[84] Augustus, Viscount Keppel (1725–1786), a famous British admiral, was absolved of infamous charges in a celebrated court-martial; uncle to the Duke of Bedford.

[85] Sir Joshua Reynolds painted several portraits of Admiral Keppel; the one he presented to Burke now hangs in the National Gallery in London.

wounds, the consolation of friendship, in those only whom we have lost for ever. Feeling the loss of Lord Keppel at all times, at no time did I feel it so much as on the first day when I was attacked in the House of Lords.

Had he lived, that reverend form would have risen in its place, and with a mild, parental reprehension to his nephew the Duke of Bedford, he would have told him that the favour of that gracious prince, who had honoured his virtues with the government of the navy of Great Britain, and with a seat in the hereditary great council of his kingdom, was not undeservedly shewn to the friend of the best portion of his life, and his faithful companion and counsellor under his rudest trials. He would have told him, that to whomever else these reproaches might be becoming, they were not decorous in his near kindred. He would have told them that when men in that rank lose decorum, they lose every thing.

On that day I had a loss in Lord Keppel; but the publick loss of him in this aweful crisis—! I speak from much knowledge of the person, he never would have listened to any compromise with the rabble rout of this Sans Culotterie of France. His goodness of heart, his reason, his taste, his publick duty, his principles, his prejudices, would have repelled him for ever from all connection with that horrid medley of madness, vice, impiety, and crime.

Lord Keppel had two countries; one of descent, and one of birth. Their interests and their glory are the same; and his mind was capacious of both. His family was noble and it was Dutch. That is, he was of the oldest and purest nobility that Europe can boast, among a people renowned above all others for love of their native land. Though it was never shewn in insult to any human being, Lord Keppel was something high. It was a wild stock of pride, on which the tenderest of all hearts had grafted the milder virtues. He valued ancient nobility; and he was not disinclined to augment it with new honours. He valued the old nobility and the new, not

as an excuse for inglorious sloth, but as an incitement to virtuous activity. He considered it as a sort of cure for selfishness and a narrow mind; conceiving that a man born in an elevated place, in himself was nothing, but every thing in what went before, and what was to come after him. Without much speculation, but by the sure instinct of ingenuous feelings, and by the dictates of plain unsophisticated natural understanding, he felt, that no great Commonwealth could by any possibility long subsist, without a body of some kind or other of nobility, decorated with honour, and fortified by privilege. This nobility forms the chain that connects the ages of a nation, which otherwise (with Mr. Paine) would soon be taught that no one generation can bind another. He felt that no political fabrick could be well made without some such order of things as might, through a series of time, afford a rational hope of securing unity, coherence, consistency, and stability to the state. He felt that nothing else can protect it against the levity of courts, and the greater levity of the multitude. That to talk of hereditary monarchy without any thing else of hereditary reverence in the Commonwealth, was a low-minded absurdity; fit only for those detestable "fools aspiring to be knaves," who began to forge in 1789, the false money of the French Constitution—That it is one fatal objection to all *new* fancied and *new fabricated* Republicks, (among a people, who, once possessing such an advantage, have wickedly and insolently rejected it,) that the *prejudice* of an old nobility is a thing that *cannot* be made. It may be improved, it may be corrected, it may be replenished: men may be taken from it, or aggregated to it, but the *thing itself* is a matter of *inveterate* opinion, and therefore *cannot* be matter of mere positive institution. He felt, that this nobility, in fact does not exist in wrong of other orders of the state, but by them, and for them.

I knew the man I speak of; and, if we can divine the future, out of what we collect from the past, no person living would look with more scorn and horror on the impious parricide committed on all their ancestry, and on the desperate attainder passed on all their posterity, by the Orleans, and the Rochefoucaults, and the Fayettes, and the Viscomtes de Noailles, and the false Perigords, and the long *et cetera* of the perfidious Sans Culottes of the court, who like demoniacs, possessed with a spirit of fallen pride, and inverted ambition, abdicated their dignities, disowned their families, betrayed the most sacred of all trusts, and by breaking to pieces a great link of society, and all the cramps and holdings of the state, brought eternal confusion and desolation on their country. For the fate of the miscreant parricides themselves he would have had no pity. Compassion for the myriads of men, of whom the world was not worthy, who by their means have perished in prisons, or on scaffolds, or are pining in beggary and exile, would leave no room in his, or in any well-formed mind, for any such sensation. We are not made at once to pity the oppressor and the oppressed.

Looking to his Batavian descent, how could he bear to behold his kindred, the descendants of the brave nobility of Holland, whose blood prodigally poured out, had, more than all the canals, meers,[86] and inundations of their country, protected their independence, to behold them bowed in the basest servitude, to the basest and vilest of the human race; in servitude to those who in no respect, were superior in dignity, or could aspire to a better place than that of hangmen to the tyrants, to whose sceptered pride they had opposed an elevation of soul, that surmounted, and overpowered the loftiness of Castile, the haughtiness of Austria, and the overbearing arrogance of France?

Could he with patience bear, that the children of that nobility, who would have deluged their country and given it to the sea, rather than submit to Louis

XIV. who was then in his meridian glory, when his arms were conducted by the Turennes, by the Luxembourgs, by the Bouffiers; when his councils were directed by the Colberts, and the Louvois; when his tribunals were filled by the Lamoignons and the Daguessaus—that these should be given up to the cruel sport of the Pichegru's, the Jourdans, the Santerres, under the Rollands, and Brissots, and Gorsas, and Robespierres, the Reubels, the Carnots, and Talliens, and Dantons, and the whole tribe of Regicides, robbers, and revolutionary judges, that, from the rotten carcase of their own murdered country, have poured out innumerable swarms of the lowest, and at once the most destructive of the classes of animated nature, which like columns of locusts, have laid waste the fairest part of the world?

Would Keppel have borne to see the ruin of the virtuous Patricians, that happy union of the noble and the burgher, who with signal prudence and integrity, had long governed the cities of the confederate Republick, the cherishing fathers of their country, who, denying commerce to themselves, made it flourish in a manner unexampled under their protection? Could Keppel have borne that a vile faction should totally destroy this harmonious construction, in favour of a robbing Democracy, founded on the spurious rights of man?

He was no great clerk, but he was perfectly well versed in the interests of Europe, and he could not have heard with patience, that the country of Grotius,[87] the cradle of the Law of Nations, and one of the richest repositories of all Law, should be taught a new code by the ignorant flippancy of Thomas Paine, the presumptuous foppery of La Fayette, with his stolen rights of man in his hand, the wild profligate intrigue and turbulency of Marat, and the impious sophistry of Condorcet, in his insolent addresses to the Batavian Republick?[88]

[86] lakes.
[87] Hugo Grotius (1583–1645), the Dutch jurist and statesman, who laid the foundations of international law in his *De Jure Belli et Pacis* (1625), published in France.

[88] France was at war with Austria at this time; Marat, the French radical, was dead, and La Fayette was in "protective custody" of the Austrians.

Could Keppel, who idolized the house of Nassau,[89] who was himself given to England, along with the blessings of the British and Dutch revolutions; with revolutions of stability; with revolutions which consolidated and married the liberties and the interests of the two nations for ever, could he see the fountain of British liberty itself in servitude to France? Could he see with patience a Prince of Orange expelled as a sort of diminutive despot, with every kind of contumely, from the country, which that family of deliverers had so often rescued from slavery, and obliged to live in exile in another country, which owes it's liberty to his house?

Would Keppel have heard with patience, that the conduct to be held on such occasions was to become short by the knees[90] to the faction of the homicides, to intreat them quietly to retire? or if the fortune of war should drive them from their first wicked and unprovoked invasion, that no security should be taken, no arrangement made, no barrier formed, no alliance entered into for the security of that, which under a foreign name is the most precious part of England? What would he have said, if it was even proposed that the Austrian Netherlands (which ought to be a barrier to Holland, and the tie of an alliance, to protect her against any species of rule that might be erected, or even be restored in France) should be formed into a republick under her influence and dependent upon her power?

But above all, what would he have said, if he had heard it made a matter of accusation against me, by his nephew the Duke of Bedford, that I was the author of the war? Had I a mind to keep that high distinction to myself, as from pride I might, but from justice I dare not, he would have snatched his share of it from my hand, and held it with the grasp of a dying convulsion to his end.

It would be a most arrogant presumption in me to assume to myself the glory of what belongs to his Majesty, and to his Ministers, and to his Parliament, and to the far greater majority of his faithful people: But had I stood alone to counsel, and that all were determined to be guided by my advice, and to follow it implicitly—then I should have been the sole author of a war. But it should have been a war on my ideas and my principles. Whatever his Grace may think of my demerits with regard to the war with Regicide, he will find my guilt confined to that alone. He never shall, with the smallest colour of reason, accuse me of being the author of a peace with Regicide. But that is high matter; and ought not be mixed with any thing of so little moment, as what may belong to me, or even to the Duke of Bedford.

I have the honour to be, &c.
Edmund Burke.

---

[89] The hereditary Dutch royalty.　　　　　　[90] i.e., to stoop.

Bibliography

PART I. THE CONTEXT OF LITERATURE

BIBLIOGRAPHIES OF HISTORY

Davies, Godfrey. *Bibliography of British History, Stuart Period, 1603–1714*. 1928.

Grose, Clyde Leclare. *A Selected Bibliography of British History, 1660–1760*. 1939.

Morgan, William T. *A Bibliography of British History, 1700–1715*. 1934–1942. 5 vols.

Pargellis, Stanley McCrory, and D. J. Medley. *Bibliography of British History: The Eighteenth Century, 1714–1789*. 1951.

POLITICAL AND CULTURAL HISTORIES

Ashley, Maurice. *England in the Seventeenth Century*. 1952.

Butterfield, Herbert. *George III, Lord North, and the People*. 1949.

Clark, George N. *The Later Stuarts, 1660–1714*. 2nd ed. 1955.

Feiling, Keith Grahame. *A History of the Tory Party, 1640–1714*. 1924.

Feiling, Keith Grahame. *The Second Tory Party, 1714–1832*. 1938.

Jeudwine, J. W. *Religion, Commerce, Liberty: A Record of a Time of Storm and Change, 1683–1793*. 1925.

Laprade, William T. *Public Opinion and Politics in Eighteenth Century England to the Fall of Walpole*. 1936.

Laski, Harold J. *Political Thought in England from Locke to Bentham*. 1920.

Lecky, William E. H. *A History of England in the Eighteenth Century*. 1878–1890. 8 vols.

Mahan, Alfred Thayer. *The Influence of Sea Power upon History, 1660–1783*. 1890.

Michael, Wolfgang. *Englische Geschichte im Achtzehnten Jahrhundert*. 1896–1945. 5 vols.

Namier, Sir Lewis. *Structure of Politics at the Accession of George III*. 1929.

Pares, Richard. *King George III and the Politicians*. 1953.

Petrie, Charles A. *The Jacobite Movement*. 1932.

Petrie, Charles A. *The Jacobite Movement*. Vol. II: *The Last Phase, 1716–1807*. 1950.

Porritt, Edward. *The Unreformed House of Commons*. 1903. 2 vols.

Robertson, Charles Grant. *England under the Hanoverians*. 1930.

Smith, Preserved. *A History of Modern Culture*. Vol. II: *The Enlightenment, 1687–1776*. 1930.

Trevelyan, George M. *England under Queen Anne*. 1930–1934. 3 vols.

Trevelyan, George M. *England under the Stuarts*. 1930.

Walcott, R. *English Politics in the Early Eighteenth Century*. 1956.

Williams, Basil. *The Whig Supremacy, 1714–1760.* 1939.

Wrong, Edward Murray. *History of England: 1688–1815.* 1927.

Zagorin, Perez. *A History of Political Thought in the English Revolution.* 1954.

ACCOUNTS OF THE ARTS AND CRAFTS

Allen, B. Sprague. *Tides in English Taste, 1619–1800.* 1937. 2 vols.

Appleton, William W. *A Cycle of Cathay: The Chinese Vogue in England during the Seventeenth and Eighteenth Centuries.* 1951.

Binyon, Robert Laurence. *English Water-Colours.* 1933.

Blom, Eric. *Music in England.* 1947.

Carse, Adam Von Ahn. *The Orchestra in the XVIIIth Century.* 1940.

Chancellor, Edwin Beresford. *The Lives of the British Sculptors and Those Who have Worked in England from the Earliest Days to Sir Francis Chantrey.* 1911.

Dent, Edward J. *Opera.* 1940.

Dixon, J. L. *English Porcelain of the Eighteenth Century.* 1952.

Fassini, Sesto. *Il Melodramma Italiano a Londra nella prima Metà del Settecento.* 1914.

Frankau, Julia. *Eighteenth Century Colour Prints: An Essay on Certain Stipple Engravers and their Work in Colour.* 1900.

Grundy, C. Reginald. *English Art in the Eighteenth Century.* 1928.

Heal, Sir Ambrose. *The London Furniture Makers: From the Restoration to the Victorian Era, 1660–1840.* 1953.

Hudson, Derek, and Kenneth W. Luckhurst. *The Royal Society of Arts, 1754–1954.* 1954.

Jourdain, M. *English Interior Decoration, 1500–1830.* 1950.

Jourdain, Margaret, and Fred Rose. *English Furniture: The Georgian Period (1750–1830).* 1953.

King, William. *English Porcelain Figures of the Eighteenth Century.* 1925.

Lengyon, Francis. *The Decoration and Furniture of English Mansions during the Seventeenth and Eighteenth Centuries.* 1909.

Maitland, John Alexander Fuller. *The Oxford History of Music.* 1931.

Manwaring, Elizabeth W. *Italian Landscape in Eighteenth Century England.* 1925.

Marillier, Henry Currie. *English Tapestries of the Eighteenth Century.* 1930.

Meyer, Ernst H. *English Chamber Music: The History of a Great Art from the Middle Ages to Purcell.* 1951.

Molesworth, H. D. *Sculpture in England: Renaissance to Early XIXth Century.* 1951.

O'Brien, Donough. *Miniatures in the 18th and 19th Centuries.* 1951.

Oman, Charles Chichele. *English Domestic Silver.* 1934.

Paston, George. *Social Caricature in the Eighteenth Century.* 1905.

Quennell, Peter. *Hogarth's Progress.* 1955.

Ritchie, Andrew C. *English Painters, Hogarth to Constable.* 1942.

Salaman, Malcolm Charles. *The Old Engravers of England in their Relation to Contemporary Life and Art, 1540–1800.* 1907.

Savage, George. *Eighteenth-Century English Porcelain.* 1952.

Sirén, Osvald. *China and Gardens of Europe of the Eighteenth Century.* 1950.

Sitwell, Sacheverell. *British Architects and Craftsmen: A Survey of Taste, Design, and Style during Three Centuries, 1600 to 1830.* 1945.

Sitwell, Sacheverell. *Old Fashioned Flowers.* 1939.

Summerson, John N. *Architecture in Britain, 1530–1830.* 1953.

Summerson, John N. *Georgian London.* 1945.

Tinker, Chauncey Brewster. *Painter and Poet.* 1938.

Waterhouse, E. K. *Painting in Britain, 1530–1790.* 1953.

Whiffen, M. *Stuart and Georgian Churches.* 1948.

Bibliography

Whitley, William Thomas. *Artists and their Friends in England, 1700–1799.* 1928. 2 vols.

Yorke-Long, Alan. *Music at Court: Four Eighteenth Century Studies.* 1954.

ECONOMIC HISTORIES

Ashton, T. S. *An Economic History of England: The Eighteenth Century.* 1955.

Clapham, Sir John. *A Concise Economic History of Britain from the Earliest Times to 1750.* 1949.

Mantoux, Paul Joseph. *The Industrial Revolution in the Eighteenth Century.* Tr. Marjorie Vernon. 1928.

Toynbee, Arnold. *Lectures on the Industrial Revolution in England.* 1884.

HISTORIES OF EDUCATION AND SCHOLARSHIP

Adams, E. N. *Old English Scholarship in England.* 1917.

Bayne-Powell, Rosamund. *The English Child in the Eighteenth Century.* 1939.

Brauer, George C., Jr. *The Education of a Gentleman: Theories of Gentlemanly Education in England, 1660–1775.* 1959.

Clarke, M. L. *Greek Studies in England, 1700–1830.* 1945.

Dobbs, A. E. *Education and Social Movements, 1700–1850.* 1919.

Douglas, David. *English Scholars 1660–1730.* Rev. ed. 1951.

Hans, Nicholas. *New Trends in Education during the Eighteenth Century.* 1951.

Heal, A. *The English Writing-Masters and their Copy-Books, 1570–1800.* 1931.

Jones, Mary Gwladys. *The Charity School Movement.* 1938.

McLachlan, Herbert. *English Education under the Test Acts: Being the History of the Nonconformist Academies, 1662–1820.* 1931.

Mallett, Charles Edward. *A History of the University of Oxford.* 1924–1927. 3 vols.

Mead, William E. *The Grand Tour in the Eighteenth Century.* 1914.

Murphy, H. L. *A History of Trinity College, Dublin, from its Foundation to 1702.* 1951.

Pons, Jacques. *L'éducation en Angleterre entre 1750 et 1800.* 1919.

Reynolds, Myra. *The Learned Lady in England, 1650–1760.* 1920.

Walters, H. B. *The English Antiquaries of the Sixteenth, Seventeenth, and Eighteenth Centuries.* 1934.

Winstanley, D. A. *The University of Cambridge in the Eighteenth Century.* 1922.

Winstanley, D. A. *Unreformed Cambridge.* 1935.

Wormald, Francis, and C. E. Wright (eds.). *The English Library before 1700.* 1958.

INTELLECTUAL HISTORIES

Becker, Carl L. *The Heavenly City of the Eighteenth Century Philosophers.* 1932.

Benn, Alfred W. *A History of English Rationalism.* 1906. 2 vols.

Bonar, James. *Moral Sense.* 1930.

Bredvold, Louis I. *The Intellectual Milieu of John Dryden.* 1935.

Bury, John Bagnell. *The Idea of Progress.* 1920.

Cassirer, Ernst. *The Philosophy of the Enlightenment.* Tr. Fritz C. A. Koelln and James P. Pettegrove. 1951.

Fairchild, Hoxie N. *The Noble Savage.* 1928.

Fink, Z. S. *The Classical Republicans: An Essay in the Recovery of a Pattern of Thought in Seventeenth Century England.* 1945.

Hazard, Paul. *La crise de la conscience européenne 1680–1715.* 1935.

Hazard, Paul. *European Thought in the Eighteenth Century from Montesquieu to Lessing.* 1954.

Hearnshaw, Fossey John Cobb (ed.).

The Social and Political Ideas of Some Representative Thinkers of the Revolutionary Era. 1931.

James, D. J. *The Life of Reason.* 1949.

Jones, Richard Foster. *Ancients and Moderns.* 1936.

Kliger, Samuel. *The Goths in England: A Study in Seventeenth and Eighteenth Century Thought.* 1952.

Lovejoy, Arthur O. *Essays in the History of Ideas.* 1949.

Lovejoy, Arthur O. *The Great Chain of Being.* 1936.

Seeger, O. *Die Auseinandersetzung zwischen Antike und Moderne in England bis zum Tode Dr Johnsons.* 1927.

Stephen, Leslie. *A History of English Thought in the Eighteenth Century.* 1892. 2 vols.

Tinker, Chauncey Brewster. *Nature's Simple Plan: A Phase of Radical Thought in the Mid-Eighteenth Century.* 1922.

Vaughan, C. E. *Studies in the History of Political Philosophy before and after Rousseau.* 1925. 2 vols.

Whitney, Lois. *Primitivism and the Idea of Progress in English Popular Literature of the Eighteenth Century.* 1934.

Wiley, Margaret L. *The Subtle Knot: Creative Scepticism in Seventeenth-Century England.* 1952.

Willey, Basil. *The Eighteenth Century Background.* 1940.

Willey, Basil. *The Seventeenth Century Background.* 1934.

CONDITIONS OF PRINTING AND
PUBLISHING

Bond, Richmond P. (ed.) *Studies in the Early English Periodical.* 1957.

Bronson, Bertrand H. *Printing as an Index of Taste in Eighteenth-century England.* 1959.

Carlson, Carl Lennart. *The First Magazine: A History of the Gentleman's Magazine.* 1938.

Collins, Arthur Simons. *Authorship in the Days of Johnson.* 1927.

Collins, Arthur Simons. *The Profession of Letters, 1780–1800.* 1927.

Ewald, W. B. *Rogues, Royalty, and Reporters (Newsmen of Queen Anne).* 1956.

Gaskell, Philip. *John Baskerville: A Bibliography.* 1959.

Graham, Walter. *The Beginnings of English Literary Periodicals: A Study of Periodical Literature, 1668–1715.* 1926.

Graham, Walter. *English Literary Periodicals.* 1930.

Hanson, Laurence. *Government and the Press, 1695–1763.* 1936.

Heawood, Edward. *Watermarks Mainly of the 17th and 18th Centuries.* 1950.

Hofer, Philip (ed.). *Eighteenth-Century Book Illustration.* 1956.

Howe, Ellic. *A List of London Bookbinders, 1648–1815.* 1950.

Longman, Charles James. *The House of Longman, 1724–1800.* 1936.

Morison, Stanley. *The English Newspaper: Some Account of the Physical Development of Journals printed in London between 1622 and the Present Day.* 1932.

Nangle, Benjamin. *The Monthly Review: First Series; Index of Contributors and Articles.* 1924.

Philip, I. G. *William Blackstone and the Reform of the Oxford University Press in the Eighteenth Century.* 1957.

Plomer, Henry Robert. *A Dictionary of the Printers and Booksellers who were at Work in England, Scotland, and Ireland from 1668 to 1725.* 1922.

Plomer, Henry Robert, George Herbert Bushnell, and Ernest Reginald McClintock Dix. *A Dictionary of the Printers and Booksellers who were at Work in England, Scotland, and Ireland from 1726 to 1775.* 1932.

Roberts, S. C. *A History of the Cambridge University Press, 1521–1921.* 1921.

Sale, William Merritt. *Samuel Richardson: Master Printer.* 1950.

Siebert, F. S. *Freedom of the Press in England, 1476–1776.* 1952.

Simpson, Percy. *Proof-Reading in the*

Sixteenth, Seventeenth, and Eighteenth Centuries. 1935.

Strauss, Ralph. *Robert Dodsley, Poet, Publisher, and Playwright.* 1910.

Symonds, Robert Vincent. *The Rise of English Journalism.* 1953.

Todd, William B. *New Adventures Among Old Books: An Essay in Eighteenth Century Bibliography.* 1958.

Watson, Melvin R. *Magazine Serials and the Essay Tradition, 1746–1820.* 1956.

Wiles, R. M. *Serial Publication in England before 1750.* 1957.

HISTORIES OF RELIGIOUS THOUGHT
AND ORGANIZATION

Abbey, Charles J., and John Henry Overton. *The English Church in the Eighteenth Century.* 1887.

Cameron, Richard M. *The Rise of Methodism.* 1954.

Clark, Henry W. *A History of English Non-Conformity.* Vol. II: *From the Restoration to the Close of the Nineteenth Century.* 1913.

Clarke, W. K. L. *Eighteenth Century Piety.* 1944.

Colie, Rosalie L. *Light and Enlightenment: A Study of the Cambridge Platonists and the Dutch Arminians.* 1957.

Cragg, Gerald Robertson. *From Puritanism to the Age of Reason: A Study of Changes in Religious Thought within the Church of England, 1660–1700.* 1950.

Creed, J. N., and J. S. Boys Smith (eds.). *Religious Thought in the Eighteenth Century.* 1934.

Davies, Horton. *Worship and Theology in England From Watts and Wesley To Maurice, 1690–1850.* 1961.

Gill, F. C. *The Romantic Movement and Methodism.* 1937.

Hunt, John. *Religious Thought in England from the Reformation to the End of the Last Century.* 1870–1873. 3 vols.

Hutton, W. H. *The English Church from the Accession of Charles I to the Death of Anne.* 1903.

Knox, Ronald Arbuthnott. *Enthusiasm: A Chapter in the History of Religion with Special Reference to the 17th and 18th Centuries.* 1950.

Legg, J. W. *English Church Life from the Restoration to the Tractarian Movement.* 1914.

Lloyd, Arnold. *Quaker Social History, 1669–1738.* 1950.

Manuel, Frank E. *The Eighteenth Century Confronts the Gods.* 1959.

Mossner, Ernest C. *Bishop Butler and the Age of Reason.* 1936.

Overton, John Henry. *The English Church from the Accession of George I to the End of the Eighteenth Century.* 1906.

Overton, John Henry. *Life in the English Church, 1660–1714.* 1885.

Overton, John Henry. *The Nonjurors, Their Lives, Principles, and Writings.* 1902.

Schöffler, H. *Protestantismus und Literatur: Neue Wege zur Englischen Literatur des 18. Jahrhunderts.* 1922.

Shepherd, T. B. *Methodism and the Literature of the Eighteenth Century.* 1940.

Simpson, Alan. *Puritanism in Old and New England.* 1955.

Stromberg, Roland N. *Religious Liberalism in Eighteenth-Century England.* 1954.

Sykes, N. *Church and State in England in the XVIIIth Century.* 1934.

Thompson, H. P. *Into All Lands: The History of the Society for the Propagation of the Gospel in Foreign Parts, 1701–1950.* 1951.

Warner, Wellman Joel. *The Wesleyan Movement in the Industrial Revolution.* 1930.

HISTORIES OF SCIENCE

Boring, Edwin G. *Sensation and Perception in the History of Experimental Psychology.* 1942.

Burtt, Edwin Arthur. *Metaphysical Foundations of Modern Physical Science.* 1925.

Butterfield, H. *The Origins of Modern Science.* 1949.

Dampier, William Cecil. *A History of Science and its Relations with Philosophy and Religion.* 3rd ed. 1952.

Dampier, William Cecil. *A Shorter History of Science.* 1957.

Evans, B. Ifor. *Literature and Science.* 1954.

Gunther, R. T. *Early Science in Cambridge.* 1937.

Gunther, R. T. *Early Science in Oxford.* 1923–1945. 14 vols.

Hall, A. R. *The Scientific Revolution, 1500–1800.* 1954.

Literature and Science: Proceedings of the Sixth Triennial Congress of the International Federation for Modern Languages and Literatures. 1955.

Lyons, H. *The Royal Society, 1660–1940.* 1944.

MacLean, Kenneth. *John Locke and English Literature of the Eighteenth Century.* 1936.

Meyer, Gerald D. *The Scientific Lady in England, 1650–1750.* 1955.

Nicolson, Marjorie. *The Microscope and English Imagination.* 1935.

Nicolson, Marjorie. *Science and Imagination.* 1956.

Nussbaum, Frederick Louis. *The Triumph of Science and Reason, 1660–1685.* 1953.

Philosophical Transactions of the Royal Society. 1666–.

Pledge, H. T. *Science Since 1500.* 1939.

Shorr, Philip. *Science and Superstition in the Eighteenth Century.* 1932.

A Short History of Science: A Symposium. 1959. (Anchor)

Whitehead, Alfred North. *Science and the Modern World.* 1926.

Wolf, A. *A History of Science, Technology, and Philosophy in the Eighteenth Century.* Rev. ed. D. McKie. 1952.

SOCIAL HISTORIES

Ashton, John. *Social Life in the Reign of Queen Anne.* 1883.

Ashton, John. *Old Times: A Picture of Social Life at the End of the Eighteenth Century.* 1885.

Bayne-Powell, Rosamund. *Housekeeping in the Eighteenth Century.* 1956.

Bayne-Powell, Rosamund. *Travellers in 18th Century England.* 1951.

Bethell, S. L. *The Cultural Revolution of the Seventeenth Century.* 1951.

Botsford, Jay B. *English Society in the Eighteenth Century as Influenced from Oversea.* 1924.

Frantz, Ray W. *The English Traveller and the Movement of Ideas, 1660–1732.* 1934.

George, Mary Dorothy. *England in Johnson's Day, 1709–1784.* 1928.

Hartley, Dorothy, and Margaret Elliot. *Life and Work of the People of England: A Pictorial Record from Contemporary Sources.* 1931.

Hole, Christina. *The English Housewife in the Seventeenth Century.* 1953.

Humphreys, A. R. *The Augustan World: Life and Letters in 18th Century England.* 1954.

Lockitt, Charles Henry. *The Relations of French and English Society, 1763–93.* 1920.

MacDiarmid, Hugh. *Scottish Eccentrics.* 1936.

Marshall, Dorothy. *The English People in the Eighteenth Century.* 1957.

Plumb, J. H. *England in the Eighteenth Century: A Study of the Development of English Society.* 1950.

Quennell, Marjorie, and Charles Henry Bourne. *A History of Everyday Things in England.* 1918–1934. 4 vols.

Quinlan, Maurice J. *Victorian Prelude: A History of English Manners 1700–1830.* 1941.

Richardson, Albert Edward. *Georgian England: A Survey of Social Life, Trades, Industries, and Art from 1700 to 1820.* 1931.

Smith, Warren Hunting. *Originals Abroad: The Foreign Careers of Some Eighteenth-Century Britons.* 1952.

Sutherland, James R. *Background for Queen Anne.* 1939.

Sydney, William Connor. *England and*

the English in the Eighteenth Century. 1891. 2 vols.

Traill, Henry Duff, and James S. Mann. *Social England*. 1893–1897. 6 vols.

Trevelyan, George M. *Illustrated English Social History*. Vol. III: *The Eighteenth Century*. 1951.

Turberville, A. S. *English Men and Manners in the Eighteenth Century*. 1929.

Turberville, A. S. *Johnson's England*. 1933. 2 vols.

Wilson, John Harold. *The Court Wits of the Restoration*. 1948.

Wormald, Francis, and C. E. Wright (eds.). *The English Library before 1700: Studies in its History*. 1958.

ACCOUNTS OF CITY AND COUNTRY LIFE

Allen, Robert J. *The Clubs of Augustan London*. 1933.

Bayne-Powell, Rosamund. *Eighteenth-Century London Life*. 1937.

Bayne-Powell, Rosamund. *English Country Life in the Eighteenth Century*. 1935.

Boulton, William Biggs. *The Amusements of Old London*. 1901. 2 vols.

Chancellor, E. B. *The Eighteenth Century in London*. 1920.

Colson, Percy. *White's, 1693–1950*. 1951.

Ellis, Aytoun. *The Penny Universities: A History of the Coffee-Houses*. 1957.

Fussell, G. E. *Village Life in the Eighteenth Century*. 1947.

George, Mary Dorothy. *London Life in the Eighteenth Century*. 1925.

Hughes, Edward. *North Country Life in the Eighteenth Century: The North-East, 1700–1750*. 1952.

McCormick, Donald M. *The Hell-Fire Club*. 1958.

Patton, Julia. *The English Village, 1750–1850*. 1919.

Phillips, Hugh. *The Thames about 1750*. 1951.

Southworth, James Granville. *Vauxhall Gardens: A Chapter in the Social History of England*. 1941.

PART II. THE LITERARY SCENE

BIBLIOGRAPHIES OF LITERATURE

General

Annual Bibliography. Published by the Modern Language Association of America as a supplement to *PMLA*. 1921–.

Annual Bibliography of English Language and Literature. Published for the Modern Humanities Research Association. 1920–.

Arber, E. (ed.). *The Term Catalogues*. Vol. III (1668–1709), 1906.

Bateson, F. W. (ed.). *The Cambridge Bibliography of English Literature*. Vol. II (1660–1800), 1941. Vol. V (Supplement: 600–1950, ed. George Sampson), 1957.

Clifford, James L. (ed.). *Johnsonian News Letter*. 1940–.

Crane, Ronald S., Louis I. Bredvold, Richmond P. Bond, Arthur Friedman, and Louis A. Landa (eds.). *English Literature, 1660–1800: A Bibliography of Modern Studies Compiled for 'Philological Quarterly.'* 1950–1952. 2 vols.

Dyson, H. V. D., and J. E. Butt. *Augustans and Romantics*. 2nd ed. 1950.

"English Literature of the Restoration and Eighteenth Century: A Current Bibliography." Annually in *Philological Quarterly*. 1926–.

Ewen, Frederic. *Bibliography of 18th Century English Literature*. 1935.

Eyre, G. E. (ed.). *A Transcript of the Registers of the Stationers, 1640–1708*. 1913–1914. 3 vols.

Leary, Lewis (ed.). *Contemporary Literary Scholarship: A Critical Review*. 1958.

Lowndes, William Thomas. *The Bibliographer's Manual of English Litera-*

ture. Rev. ed. Henry G. Bohn. 1864. 4 vols.

Tobin, James E. *Eighteenth Century English Literature and Its Cultural Background: A Bibliography.* 1939.

Watson, George. *The Concise Cambridge Bibliography of English Literature, 600–1950.* 1958.

Watt, Robert. *Bibliotheca Britannica, or a General Index to British and Foreign Literature.* 1824. 4 vols.

Wing, Donald. *Short-Title Catalogue of Books, 1641–1700.* 1955. 3 vols.

The Year's Work in English Studies. Published by the English Association. 1919–.

Special

Block, A. *The English Novel, 1740–1850.* 1939.

Cordasco, Francesco. *The 18th Century Novel.* 1950.

Cox, Edward Godfrey. *A Reference Guide to the Literature of Travel.* 1935–1949. 3 vols.

Crane, Ronald S., and Fred B. Kaye. *A Census of British Newspapers and Periodicals, 1620–1800.* 1927.

Draper, J. W. *Eighteenth Century English Aesthetics: A Bibliography.* 1931.

Dudley, Fred A., Norbert Fuerst, Francis R. Johnson, and Hyatt H. Waggoner (eds.). *The Relations of Literature and Science: A Selected Bibliography, 1930–1949.* 1949.

Esdaile, Arundell. *A List of English Tales and Prose Romances Printed before 1740.* 1912.

Greenough, Chester Noyes. *A Bibliography of the Theophrastian Character in English with Several Portrait Characters.* 1947.

Kennedy, A. G. *A Bibliography of Writings on the English Language.* 1927.

Matthews, William. *British Diaries: An Annotated Bibliography of British Diaries written between 1442 and 1942.* 1950.

Rochedieu, Charles Alfred. *Bibliography of French Translations of English Works, 1700–1800.* 1948.

Summers, Montague. *A Gothic Bibliography.* 1941.

Weed, Katherine Kirtley, and Richmond Pugh Bond. *Studies of British Newspapers and Periodicals from their Beginning to 1800: A Bibliography.* 1946.

MODERN EDITIONS OF SOURCE MATERIALS

Augustan Reprint Society. *Publications.*

Barchilon, Jacques, and Henry Pettit (eds.). *The Authentic Mother Goose Fairy Tales and Nursery Rhymes.* 1960.

Boynton, H. (ed.). *The Beginnings of Modern Science: Scientific Writings of the Sixteenth, Seventeenth, and Eighteenth Centuries.* 1948.

Bredvold, Louis I., Alan Dugald McKillop, and Lois Whitney (eds.). *Eighteenth Century Poetry and Prose.* 1939.

Bredvold, Louis I., Robert Kilburn Root, and George Sherburn (eds.). *Eighteenth Century Prose.* 1932.

Browning, Andrew (ed.). *English Historical Documents.* Vol. VIII (1660–1714), 1953.

Burtt, Edwin A. (ed.). *The English Philosophers from Bacon to Mill.* 1939.

Carritt, E. F. (ed.). *A Calendar of English Taste.* 1949.

Carver, George (ed.). *Periodical Essays of the Eighteenth Century.* 1930.

Clifford, James L. (ed.). *Eighteenth Century English Literature: Modern Essays in Criticism.* 1959.

Davy, Norman (ed.). *British Scientific Literature in the Seventeenth Century.* 1954.

de Beer, E. S. (ed.). *The Diary of John Evelyn.* 1955. 6 vols.

Durham, Willard H. (ed.). *Critical Essays of the Eighteenth Century, 1700–25.* 1915.

Jefferson, D. W. (ed.). *Eighteenth Century Prose, 1700–1780.* 1956.

Mandeville, Bernard. *The Fable of the*

Bees: or Private Vices, Publick Benefits. Ed. F. B. Kaye. 1924. 2 vols.

Mendenhall, John C. (ed.). *English Literature, 1650–1800.* 1940.

Moore, Cecil A. (ed.). *English Prose of the Eighteenth Century.* 1933.

Needham, Harold Alfred (ed.). *Taste and Criticism in the Eighteenth Century: A Selection of Texts Illustrating the Evolution of Taste and the Development of Critical Theory.* 1952.

Saintsbury, George (ed.). *A Letter Book: Selected with an Introduction on the History and Art of Letter-Writing.* 1922.

Shaaber, M. A. (ed.). *Seventeenth-Century English Prose.* 1957.

Shepard, Odell, and Paul Spencer Wood (eds.). *English Prose and Poetry, 1660–1800.* 1934.

Smith, David Nichol (ed.). *Eighteenth Century Essays on Shakespeare.* 1903.

Spingarn, Joel E. (ed.). *Critical Essays of the Seventeenth Century.* 1908–1909. 3 vols.

Sypher, Feltus Wylie (ed.). *Enlightened England: An Anthology of Eighteenth Century Literature.* 1947.

Walbank, F. A. (ed.). *The English Scene in the Works of Prose Writers since 1700.* 1941.

GENERAL HISTORIES OF LITERATURE

Bredvold, Louis I. "The Literature of the Restoration and the Eighteenth Century 1660–1798." In *A History of English Literature,* ed. Hardin Craig. 1950.

Burton, K. M. P. *Restoration Literature.* 1958.

Butt, John. *The Augustan Age.* 1950.

Cazamian, Louis. "Modern Times, 1660–1932." In *A History of English Literature,* by Pierre Legouis and Louis Cazamian. Tr. W. D. MacInnes, rev. Donald Davie. 1957.

Churchill, R. C. *English Literature of the Eighteenth Century.* 1953.

Dobrée, Bonamy. *English Literature in the Early Eighteenth Century, 1700–1740.* 1959.

Elton, Oliver. *A Survey of English Literature, 1730–1780.* 1928. 2 vols.

Elton, Oliver. *A Survey of English Literature, 1780–1830.* 1912. 2 vols.

Ford, B. *From Dryden to Johnson.* 1957.

Grierson, Sir H. J. C. *Cross Currents in English Literature of the Seventeenth Century.* 1929.

Kunitz, S. J., and H. Haycraft. *British Authors before 1800.* 1952.

McCutcheon, Roger. *Eighteenth Century English Literature.* 1949.

McKillop, Alan Dugald. *English Literature: Dryden to Burns.* 1949.

Nichols, John. *Illustrations of the Literary History of the Eighteenth Century.* 1817–1858. 8 vols.

Nichols, John. *Literary Anecdotes of the Eighteenth Century.* 1812–1816. 9 vols.

Sampson, George. *The Concise Cambridge History of English Literature.* 1941.

Sherburn, George. "The Restoration and Eighteenth Century (1660–1789)." In *A Literary History of England,* ed. Albert C. Baugh. 1948.

Stephen, Leslie. *English Literature and Society in the Eighteenth Century.* 1904.

Stephen, Leslie, and Sidney Lee (eds.). *Dictionary of National Biography.* 1885–1900. Supplements.

Sutherland, James R., and Ian Watt. *Restoration and Augustan Prose.* 1957.

Vines, Sherard. *The Course of English Classicism.* 1930.

Ward, A. W., and A. R. Waller (eds.). *The Cambridge History of English Literature.* Vols. VIII–XI, 1912–1917.

Wedgwood, C. V. *Seventeenth-Century English Literature.* 1950.

STUDIES OF SPECIAL ASPECTS OF
LITERATURE

Beljame, Alexandre. *Men of Letters and*

the English Public in the Eighteenth Century, 1660–1714. 1953.

Cazamian, Louis. The Development of English Humor. 1952.

Cruse, Amy. The Shaping of English Literature and the Readers' Share in the Development of its Forms. 1927.

Gallaway, Francis. Rule, Reason, and Revolt in English Classicism. 1940.

Irving, William Henry. The Providence of Wit in the English Letter Writers. 1955.

Kitchin, George. A Survey of Burlesque and Parody in English. 1931.

Leonard, S. A. The Doctrine of Correctness in English Usage, 1700–1800. 1929.

MacLean, Kenneth. John Locke and English Literature of the Eighteenth Century. 1936.

Mason, John E. Gentlefolk in the Making: Studies in the History of English Courtesy Literature from 1531 to 1774. 1934.

Mathews, M. M. A Survey of English Dictionaries. 1933.

Meigs, Cornelia, Anne Eaton, Elizabeth Nesbitt, and Ruth Hill Viguers. A Critical History of Children's Literature: A Survey of Children's Books in English from the Earliest Times to the Present. 1953.

Mitchell, W. F. English Pulpit Oratory from Andrewes to Tillotson. 1932.

Muir, Percival Horace. English Children's Books, 1600 to 1900. 1954.

Saintsbury, George. The Peace of the Augustans. 1916.

Snyder, Edward Douglas. The Celtic Revival in English Literature: 1760–1800. 1923.

Starnes, D. T., and G. E. Noyes. The English Dictionary from Cawdrey to Johnson. 1946.

Stern, Bernard Herbert. The Rise of Romantic Hellenism in English Literature, 1732–1786.

Sutherland, James R. English Satire. 1958.

Symonds, E. M. Social Caricature in the Eighteenth Century. 1905.

Sypher, Wylie. Guinea's Captive Kings: British Anti-Slavery Literature of the XVIIIth Century. 1942.

Tinker, Chauncey Brewster. The Salon and English Letters. 1915.

Turner, F. M. C. The Element of Irony in English Literature. 1926.

COLLECTIONS OF SHORT STUDIES OF LITERATURE

The Age of Johnson: Essays Presented to Chauncey Brewster Tinker. 1949.

Boys, Richard C. (ed.). Studies in the Literature of the Augustan Age: Essays Collected in Honor of Arthur Ellicott Case. 1950.

Chapman, Ralph W. Johnsonian and Other Essays and Reviews. 1953.

Clifford, James L., and Louis A. Landa (eds.). Pope and His Contemporaries: Essays Presented to George Sherburn. 1949.

Dobrée, Bonamy (ed.). From Anne to Victoria. 1937.

Dobrée, Bonamy. A Variety of Ways. 1932.

Dobson, Austin. Eighteenth Century Vignettes. 1892–1896. 3 vols.

Dobson, Austin. Philanthropy and Other Papers. 1899.

Dobson, Austin. At Prior Park and Other Papers. 1912.

Dobson, Austin. Side-Walk Studies. 1902.

Eighteenth Century Literature: An Oxford Miscellany. 1909.

Jones, Richard Foster. The Seventeenth Century: Studies in the History of English Thought and Literature from Bacon to Pope. 1951.

Lucas, F. L. The Search for Good Sense: Four Eighteenth - Century Characters: Johnson, Chesterfield, Boswell, Goldsmith. 1958.

Moore, Cecil A. Backgrounds of English Literature, 1700–1760. 1953.

Quennell, Peter. The Profane Virtues: Boswell, Gibbon, Sterne, and Wilkes. 1945.

Sutherland, James R., and F. P. Wilson (eds.). Essays on the Eighteenth Century Presented to David Nichol Smith. 1945.

Tinker, Chauncey Brewster. Essays in Retrospect. 1948.

STUDIES OF AESTHETICS AND LITERARY CRITICISM

Abrams, Meyer Howard. *The Mirror and the Lamp: Romantic Theory and the Critical Tradition.* 1953.

Atkins, John W. H. *English Literary Criticism: 17th and 18th Centuries.* 1951.

Babcock, R. W. *The Genesis of Shakespearean Idolatry, 1766–1799.* 1931.

Bate, Walter Jackson. *From Classic to Romantic: Premises of Taste in Eighteenth-Century England.* 1946.

Bosker, A. *Literary Criticism in the Age of Johnson.* 1930.

Brett, Raymond Laurence. *The Third Earl of Shaftesbury: A Study in Eighteenth-Century Literary Theory.* 1951.

Clark, Kenneth. *The Gothic Revival: An Essay in the History of Taste.* 1928.

Folkierski, W. *Entre le classicisme et le romantisme: Étude sur l'esthétique et les esthéticiens du XVIII siècle.* 1925.

Hipple, Walter John. *The Beautiful, the Sublime, and the Picturesque in Eighteenth-Century British Aesthetic Theory.* 1957.

Monk, Samuel H. *The Sublime: A Study of Critical Theories in XVIII-Century England.* 1935.

Read, Herbert. *Reason and Romanticism.* 1926.

Robertson, J. G. *Studies in the Genesis of Romantic Theory in the Eighteenth Century.* 1923.

Saintsbury, George. *A History of Criticism and Literary Taste in Europe.* 1902. 3 vols.

Smith, David Nichol. *Shakespeare in the Eighteenth Century.* 1928.

Wellek, René. *A History of Modern Criticism: 1750–1950.* Vol. I: *The Later Eighteenth Century.* 1955.

Wimsatt, William K., and Cleanth Brooks. *Literary Criticism: A Short History.* 1957.

STUDIES OF PROSE

Baum, Paull F. *The Other Harmony of Prose.* 1952.

Boulton, M. *The Anatomy of Prose.* 1954.

Read, Herbert. *English Prose Style.* Rev. ed. 1952.

Sutherland, James R. *On English Prose.* 1957.

Tempest, N. R. *The Rhythm of English Prose.* 1930.

Thomson, J. A. K. *Classical Influences in English Prose.* 1956.

Williamson, George. *The Senecan Amble: A Study in Prose Form from Bacon to Collier.* 1951.

Wilson, F. P. *Seventeenth Century Prose: Five Lectures.* 1960.

STUDIES OF BIOGRAPHY

Dunn, Waldo Hilary. *English Biography.* 1916.

Longaker, Mark. *English Biography in the Eighteenth Century.* 1931.

Nicolson, Harold George. *Development of English Biography.* 1928.

Shumaker, Wayne. *English Autobiography: Its Emergence, Materials, and Form.* 1954.

Stauffer, Donald Alfred. *The Art of Biography in Eighteenth-Century England.* 1941. 2 vols.

Stauffer, Donald Alfred. *English Biography before 1700.* 1930.

STUDIES OF THE ESSAY

Boyce, Benjamin. *The Polemic Character, 1640–1661.* 1955.

Dobrée, Bonamy. *English Essayists.* 1946.

Marr, G. S. *The Periodical Essayists of the Eighteenth Century.* 1923.

Walker, Hugh. *The English Essay and Essayists.* 1915.

Withington, R. *Essays and Characters: Montaigne to Goldsmith.* 1933.

STUDIES OF PROSE FICTION

Baker, Ernest A. *The History of the English Novel.* 1924–1939. 10 vols.

Barry, F. V. *A Century of Children's Books.* 1922.

Conant, Martha Pike. *The Oriental Tale in England in the Eighteenth Century.* 1908.

Darton, F. J. H. *Children's Books in England.* 1932.

Foster, J. R. *History of the Pre-Romantic Novel in England.* 1949.

Gove, Philip Babcock. *The Imaginary Voyage in Prose Fiction: A History of its Criticism and a Guide for its Study, with an Annotated Check List of 215 Imaginary Voyages from 1700 to 1800.* 1941.

Horner, J. M. *The English Women Novelists and their Connection with the Feminist Movement, 1688–1797.* 1930.

Kettle, Arnold. *An Introduction to the English Novel.* 1951.

Lubbock, Percy. *The Craft of Fiction.* 1921.

McKillop, Alan D. *The Early Masters of English Fiction.* 1956.

Morgan, C. E. *The Rise of the Novel of Manners.* 1911.

Pons, Emile. *Le Voyage, genre littéraire au XVIIIᵉ siècle.* 1926.

Railo, Eino. *The Haunted Castle: A Study of the Elements of English Romanticism.* 1927.

Raleigh, Walter. *The English Novel.* 1894.

Saintsbury, George. *The English Novel.* 1913.

Singer, Godfrey F. *The Epistolary Novel.* 1933.

Summers, Montague. *The Gothic Quest: A History of the Gothic Novel.* 1939.

Tieje, A. J. *The Theory of Characterization in Prose Fiction prior to 1740.* 1916.

Tompkins, J. M. S. *The Popular Novel in England, 1770–1800.* 1932.

Varma, Devendra P. *The Gothic Flame, Being a History of the Gothic Novel in England.* 1957.

Watt, Ian. *The Rise of the Novel: Studies in Defoe, Richardson, and Fielding.* 1957.

STUDIES OF FOREIGN LITERARY
RELATIONS

Babbitt, Irving. *Rousseau and Romanticism.* 1919.

Clark, A. F. B. *Boileau and the French Classical Critics in England, 1660–1830.* 1925.

Goad, Caroline. *Horace in the English Literature of the Eighteenth Century.* 1918.

Green, F. C. *Minuet: A Critical Survey of French and English Literary Ideas in the Eighteenth Century.* 1935.

Heilman, Robert Bechtold. *America in English Fiction, 1760–1800.* 1940.

Herrick, Marvin T. *The Poetics of Aristotle in England.* 1930.

Mayo, T. F. *Epicurus in England, 1650–1725.* 1934.

Price, Lawrence Marsden. *The Reception of English Literature in Germany.* 1932.

Price, Mary B., and L. M. Price. *The Publication of English Humaniora in Germany in the Eighteenth Century.* 1955.

Reichwein, Adolf. *China and Europe: Intellectual and Artistic Contacts in the Eighteenth Century.* 1925.

Texte, Joseph J. *Rousseau et les origines du cosmopolitanisme littéraire.* 1899.

Torrey, Norman L. *Voltaire and the English Deists.* 1930.

Van Tieghem, Paul. *Le Préromantisme.* 1930.

Wheatley, K. E. *Racine and English Classicism.* 1956.

PART III. AUTHORS

ADDISON

Writings

Aitken, George A. (ed.). *The Tatler.* 1898–1899. 4 vols.

Bohn, Henry G. (ed.). *Works.* 1863–1869. 6 vols.

Graham, Walter (ed.). *Letters.* 1941.

Guthkelch, A. C. (ed.). *The Miscellaneous Works of Joseph Addison.* 1914. 2 vols.

Smith, G. Gregory (ed.). *The Spectator.* 1907. 4 vols.

Commentary

Smithers, Peter. *The Life of Joseph Addison.* 1954.

BERKELEY

Bibliography

Jessop, T. E., and A. A. Luce. *Bibliography.* 1934.

Writings

Luce, A. A., and T. E. Jessop (eds.). *Works.* 1948–1957. 9 vols.

Commentary

Hone, J. M., and M. M. Rossi. *Bishop Berkeley: His Life, Writings, and Philosophy.* 1931.

Luce, A. A. *The Life of Berkeley.* 1949.

Wild, John. *Berkeley: A Study of his Life and Philosophy.* 1936.

BOSWELL

Bibliography

Abbott, C. C. *A Catalogue of Papers relating to Boswell, Johnson, and Sir William Forbes, found at Fettercairn House.* 1936.

Pottle, Frederick A. *The Literary Career of James Boswell, Esq., being the Bibliographical Materials for a Life of Boswell.* 1929.

Pottle, Frederick A., and M. S. Pottle. *The Private Papers of James Boswell from Malahide Castle in the Collection of Lt. Colonel Ralph Heyward Isham: A Catalogue.* 1931.

Writings

Brady, Frank, and Frederick A. Pottle (eds.). *Boswell on the Grand Tour: Italy, Corsica, and France, 1765–1766.* 1955.

Brady, Frank, and Frederick A. Pottle (eds.). *Boswell in Search of a Wife, 1766–1769.* 1957.

Hill, G. Birkbeck (ed.). *The Life of Samuel Johnson.* Rev. ed. L. F. Powell. 1934–1950. 6 vols.

Pottle, Frederick A. (ed.). *Boswell on the Grand Tour: Germany and Switzerland 1764.* 1953.

Pottle, Frederick A. (ed.). *Boswell in Holland, 1763–1764.* 1952.

Pottle, Frederick A. (ed.). *Boswell's London Journal, 1762–1763.* 1950.

Pottle, Frederick A., and C. H. Bennett (eds.). *The Journal of a Tour to the Hebrides.* 1936.

Scott, Geoffrey, and Frederick A. Pottle (eds.). *The Private Papers of James Boswell from Malahide Castle in the Collection of Lt. Colonel Ralph Heyward Isham.* 1928–1934. 18 vols.

Tinker, Chauncey Brewster (ed.). *Letters.* 1924. 2 vols.

Wimsatt, William K., and Frederick A. Pottle (eds.). *Boswell for the Defence, 1769–1774.* 1959.

Commentary

Lewis, Dominic Bevan Wyndham. *James Boswell, a Short Life.* 1952. (English title: *The Hooded Hawk.* 1946.)

Lucas, F. L. *The Search for Good Sense: Four Eighteenth Century Characters: Johnson, Chesterfield, Boswell, Goldsmith.* 1958.

McLaren, Moray. *The Highland Jaunt: A Study of James Boswell and Samuel Johnson upon their Highland Hebridean Tour of 1773.* 1954.

Quennell, Peter. *The Profane Virtues: Boswell, Gibbon, Sterne, Wilkes.* 1945.

Tinker, Chauncey Brewster. *Young Boswell.* 1922.

BUNYAN

Bibliography

Harrison, F. M. *Bibliography of the Works of John Bunyan.* 1932.

Writings

Wharey, James Blanton (ed.). *The Pilgrim's Progress.* Rev. ed. Roger Sharrock. 1960.

Commentary

Brown, John. *Bunyan: His Life, Times, and Works.* Rev. ed. F. M. Harrison. 1928.

Frye, Roland M. *God, Man, and Satan.* 1960.

Harrison, G. B. *Bunyan: A Study in Personality.* 1928.

Mackaill, J. W. *John Bunyan.* 1924.

Sharrock, Roger. *John Bunyan.* 1954.

Talon, Henri. *John Bunyan.* 1951.

Tindall, William York. *John Bunyan: Mechanick Preacher.* 1934.

Wharey, J. B. *A Study of the Sources of Bunyan's Allegories.* 1904.

BURKE

Writings

Copeland, Thomas W. (ed.). *The Correspondence of Edmund Burke.* Vol. I (1744–1766), 1958.

Willis, W., and F. W. Rafferty (eds.). *Works.* 1906–1907. 6 vols.

Commentary

Copeland, Thomas W. *Our Eminent Friend Burke: Six Essays.* 1949.

Magnus, Philip. *Burke: A Life.* 1939.

Murray, Robert H. *Edmund Burke.* 1931.

Stanlis, Peter J. *Edmund Burke and the Natural Law.* 1958.

BURNEY

Writings

Barrett, Charlotte, and Austin Dobson (eds.). *Diary and Letters, 1778–1840.* 1904–1905. 6 vols.

Mackinnon, F. D. (ed.). *Evelina.* 1930.

Commentary

Hahn, Emily. *A Degree of Prudery.* 1951.

Hemlow, Joyce. *The History of Fanny Burney.* 1958.

Scholes, Percy. *The Great Dr Burney.* 1948. 2 vols.

Tourtelot, A. B. *Be Loved No More.* 1938.

BUTLER

Writings

Waller, A. R., and René Lamar (ed.). *Collected Works.* 1905–1928. 3 vols.

Commentary

Veldkamp, Jan. *Samuel Butler, the Author of 'Hudibras.'* 1924.

CHESTERFIELD

Bibliography

Gulick, Sidney L. *A Chesterfield Bibliography to 1800.* 1935.

Writings

Dobrée, Bonamy (ed.). *Letters.* 1932. 6 vols.

Commentary

Coxon, R. *Chesterfield and his Critics.* 1925.

Lucas, F. L. *The Search for Good Sense: Four Eighteenth Century Characters: Johnson, Chesterfield, Boswell, Goldsmith.* 1958.

Shellabarger, Samuel. *Lord Chesterfield and his World.* 1951.

CIBBER

Writings

Lowe, R. W. (ed.). *An Apology for the Life of Mr. Colley Cibber.* 1889. 2 vols.

Commentary

Barker, R. H. *Mr Cibber of Drury Lane.* 1939.
Senior, Dorothy. *The Life and Times of Colley Cibber.* 1928.

COWPER

Bibliography

Hartley, Lodwick C. *Cowper: A List of Critical and Bibliographical Studies, 1895–1949.* 1950.
Hartley, Lodwick C. *William Cowper, the Continuing Revaluation: An Essay and Bibliography of Cowperian Studies from 1895–1960.* 1960.

Writings

Wright, Thomas (ed.). *Correspondence.* 1904. 4 vols.

Commentary

Cecil, David. *The Stricken Deer.* 1929.
Hartley, Lodwick C. *Cowper, Humanitarian.* 1938.
Quinlan, Maurice J. *Cowper.* 1953.
Ryskamp, Charles. *William Cowper of the Inner Temple, Esq.; A Study of his Life and Works to the Year 1768.* 1959.
Thomas, Gilbert. *Cowper and the Eighteenth Century.* 1948.

DEFOE

Bibliography

Hutchins, Henry C. *Robinson Crusoe and its Printing, 1719–1731.* 1925.

Writings

Healey, George H. (ed.). *Letters.* 1955.

Novels and Selected Writings. 1927–1928. 14 vols.

Commentary

Dottin, Paul. *Daniel De Foe et ses romans.* 1924. 3 vols. Tr. 1929.
Moore, John Robert. *Daniel Defoe, Citizen of the World.* 1958.
Secord, A. W. *Studies in the Narrative Method of Defoe.* 1924.
Sutherland, James. *Defoe.* 1937.
Trent, W. P. *Defoe and How to Know Him.* 1916.

DRYDEN

Bibliography

Macdonald, Hugh. *Dryden: A Bibliography of Early Editions and of Drydeniana.* 1939.
Monk, Samuel H. *John Dryden: A List of Critical Studies, 1895–1948.* 1950.

Writings

Ker, W. P. (ed.). *Essays of John Dryden.* 1900. 2 vols.
Noyes, G. R. (ed.). *The Poetical Works of John Dryden.* 1950.
Ward, C. E. (ed.). *Letters.* 1942.

Commentary

Bredvold, Louis I. *The Intellectual Milieu of John Dryden.* 1934.
Frost, William. *Dryden and the Art of Translation.* 1955.
Osborn, James M. *John Dryden: Facts and Problems.* 1942.
Smith, D. Nichol. *Dryden.* 1950.
Verrall, A. W. *Lectures on Dryden.* 1914.
Young, Kenneth. *John Dryden: A Critical Biography.* 1954.

FIELDING

Writings

Saintsbury, George. *Works.* 1900. 12 vols.

Commentary

Blanchard, F. T. *Fielding the Novelist.* 1926.
Cross, W. L. *The History of Henry Fielding.* 1918. 3 vols.
Digeon, Aurélien. *The Novels of Henry Fielding.* 1925.
Dudden, F. Homes. *Fielding: His Life, Works, and Times.* 1952. 2 vols.
Iser, Wolfgang. *Die Weltanschauung Henry Fieldings.* 1952.

GIBBON

Bibliography

Norton, J. E. *Bibliography of the Works of Gibbon.* 1940.

Writings

Bury, J. B. (ed.). *The History of the Decline and Fall of the Roman Empire.* 1896–1900. 7 vols.
Morley, Henry (ed.). *Memoirs.* 1914.
Norton, J. E. (ed.). *The Letters of Edward Gibbon.* 1956. 3 vols.

Commentary

Black, J. B. *The Art of History: A Study of Four Great Historians of the Eighteenth Century.* 1926.
Bond, Harold L. *The Literary Art of Edward Gibbon.* 1960.
Fuglum, Per. *Edward Gibbon: His View of Life and Conception of History.* 1953.
Joyce, Michael. *Edward Gibbon.* 1953.
Low, D. M. *Edward Gibbon.* 1937.
Oliver, E. J. *Gibbon and Rome.* 1958.
Quennell, Peter. *The Profane Virtues: Boswell, Gibbon, Sterne, Wilkes.* 1945.
Young, G. M. *Gibbon.* 1932.

GOLDSMITH

Bibliography

Williams, Iola A. *Seven XVIIIth Century Bibliographies.* 1924.

Writings

Balderston, Katharine C. (ed.). *Collected Letters.* 1928.
Church, Richard (ed.). *The Citizen of the World and The Bee.* 1934.
Crane, Ronald S. (ed.). *New Essays.* 1927.
The Life of Richard Nash of Bath. 1914.

Commentary

Forster, John. *The Life and Adventures of Oliver Goldsmith.* 1848.
Kent, Elizabeth E. *Goldsmith and his Booksellers.* 1933.
Lucas, F. L. *The Search for Good Sense: Four Eighteenth Century Characters: Johnson, Chesterfield, Boswell, Goldsmith.* 1958.

GRAY

Bibliography

Northup, Clark S. *A Bibliography of Gray.* 1917.

Writings

Toynbee, Paget, and Leonard Whibley (eds.). *Correspondence.* 1953. 3 vols.

Commentary

Cecil, David. *Two Quiet Lives.* 1948.
Jones, W. P. *Thomas Gray, Scholar: The True Tragedy of an Eighteenth-Century Gentleman, with Two Youthful Notebooks now published for the First Time.* 1937.
Ketton-Cremer, R. W. *Gray: A Biography.* 1955.
Norton, Charles E. *The Poet Gray as a Naturalist.* 1903.

HERVEY

Writings

Sedgwick, Romney (ed.). *Memoirs of*

the Reign of George the Second. 1931.
3 vols.

Commentary

Earl of Ilchester (ed.). *Lord Hervey and his Friends, 1726–38; based on Letters from Holland House, Melbury, and Ickworth.* 1950.
Quennell, Peter. *Caroline of England: An Augustan Portrait.* 1940.

HUME

Bibliography

Jessop, T. E. *A Bibliography of Hume and of Scottish Philosophy from Hutcheson to Balfour.* 1938.

Writings

Greig, J. Y. T. (ed.). *Letters.* 1932. 2 vols.
Klibansky, Raymond, and Ernest C. Mossner (eds.). *New Letters.* 1954.
Selby-Bigge, L. A. (ed.). *Essays and Treatises.* 1902.

Commentary

Brunius, Teddy. *David Hume on Criticism.* 1952.
Mossner, Ernest C. *The Forgotten Hume.* 1943.
Mossner, Ernest C. *Life of Hume.* 1954.
Smith, Norman Kemp. *The Philosophy of Hume.* 1941.

HURD

Writings

Morley, Edith J. (ed.). *Letters on Chivalry and Romance.* 1911.

Commentary

Kilvert, F. *Memoirs of the Life and Writings of the Right Rev. Richard Hurd.* 1860.
Montague, E. *Bishop Hurd's Association with Thomas Warton.* 1941.

JOHNSON

Bibliography

The R. B. Adam Library relating to Johnson and his Era. 1929–1930. 4 vols.
Clifford, James L. *Johnsonian Studies, 1887–1950: A Survey and Bibliography.* 1951.
Courtney, W. P. *A Bibliography of Samuel Johnson.* Rev. ed. D. Nichol Smith. 1915.

Writings

Chapman, R. W. (ed.). *A Journey to the Western Isles of Scotland.* 1924.
Chapman, R. W. (ed.). *The Letters of Samuel Johnson.* 1952. 3 vols.
Hazen, Allen, T., *et al.* (eds.). *The Yale Edition of the Works of Samuel Johnson.* Vol. I: *Diaries, Prayers, and Annals.* 1958.
Hill, G. Birkbeck (ed.). *The Lives of the English Poets.* 1905. 3 vols.
Keast, W. R. (ed.). *Critical Essays, Exclusive of the Lives of the Poets.* 1955.

Commentary

Balderston, Katharine C. (ed.). *Thraliana: The Diary of Mrs. Thrale, 1776–1809.* 1951. 2 vols.
Bate, Walter J. *The Achievement of Samuel Johnson.* 1955.
Bloom, Edward A. *Samuel Johnson in Grub Street.* 1957.
Boswell, James. *Life of Samuel Johnson, LL.D.* Ed. George Birkbeck Hill, rev. L. F. Powell. 1934–1950. 6 vols.
Bronson, Bertrand H. *Johnson Agonistes & Other Essays.* 1946.
Christie, O. F. *Johnson the Essayist.* 1923.
Clifford, James L. *Hester Lynch Piozzi.* 1952.
Clifford, James L. *Young Samuel Johnson.* 1955.
Greene, Donald J. *The Politics of Samuel Johnson.* 1960.
Hagstrum, Jean. *Samuel Johnson's Literary Criticism.* 1952.
Hilles, Frederick W. (ed.). *New Light*

on Dr. Johnson: Essays on the Occasion of his 250th Birthday. 1959.

Hoover, Benjamin B. *Samuel Johnson's Parliamentary Reporting.* 1953.

Hopkins, Mary Alden. *Dr. Johnson's Lichfield.* 1952.

Krutch, Joseph Wood. *Samuel Johnson.* 1944.

Lucas, F. L. *The Search for Good Sense: Four Eighteenth Century Characters: Johnson, Chesterfield, Boswell, Goldsmith.* 1958.

McAdam, Edward Lippincott. *Dr Johnson and the English Law.* 1951.

Raleigh, Walter. *Six Essays on Johnson.* 1910.

Scholes, Percy A. *The Life and Activities of Sir John Hawkins, Musician, Magistrate, and Friend of Johnson.* 1953.

Sherbo, Arthur. *Samuel Johnson, Editor of Shakespeare.* 1956.

Sledd, James H., and Gwin J. Kolb. *Dr. Johnson's Dictionary: Essays in the Biography of a Book.* 1955.

Wimsatt, William K. *Philosophic Words: A Study of Style and Meaning in the 'Rambler' and Dictionary by Johnson.* 1948.

Wimsatt, William K. *The Prose Style of Johnson.* 1941.

LAW

Writings

Sykes, Norman (ed.). *A Serious Call to a Devout and Holy Life.* 1955.

Commentary

Baker, E. W. *A Herald of the Evangelical Revival: A Critical Enquiry into the Relationship of William Law to Wesley.* 1948.

Overton, J. H. *William Law, Nonjuror and Mystic.* 1881.

Talon, Henri. *Law: A Study in Literary Craftsmanship.* 1948.

MONTAGU

Writings

Johnson, R. Brimley (ed.). *Letters.* 1906.

Commentary

Halsband, Robert. *The Life of Lady Mary Wortley Montagu.* 1956.

PEPYS

Bibliography

Tanner, J. R., *et al.* (eds.). *Bibliotheca Pepysiana: A Descriptive Catalogue of the Library of Pepys.* 1919–1940. 4 vols.

Writings

Heath, Helen (ed.). *Letters of Pepys and his Family Circle.* 1955.

Tanner, J. R. (ed.). *Private Correspondence of Samuel Pepys.* 1926–1929. 3 vols.

Wheatley, Henry B. (ed.). *Diary.* 1893–1899. 10 vols.

Commentary

Abernethy, Cecil. *Mr Pepys of Seething Lane.* 1957.

Bryant, Arthur. *Samuel Pepys, the Man in the Making.* 1933.

Bryant, Arthur. *Samuel Pepys, the Saviour of the Navy.* 1938.

Bryant, Arthur. *Samuel Pepys, the Years of Peril.* 1935.

Hunt, Percival. *Samuel Pepys in the Diary.* 1958.

Latham, R. C. *Samuel Pepys, Diarist.* 1953.

Tanner, J. R. *Mr Pepys: An Introduction to the Diary.* 1925.

Weiss, David G. *Samuel Pepys, Curioso.* 1957.

PHILIPS

Writings

The Free-Thinker. 1722. 3 vols.

Commentary

Johnson, Samuel. "Ambrose Philips." In *Lives of the English Poets,* Vol. III, ed. G. Birkbeck Hill. 1905.

POPE

Bibliography

Griffith, R. H. *Pope: A Bibliography.* 1922–1927. 2 vols.

Tobin, James Edward. *Alexander Pope: A List of Critical Studies Published from 1895 to 1944.* 1945.

Writings

Ault, Norman (ed.). *Prose Works.* Vol. I (1711–20), 1935.

Sherburn, George (ed.). *Correspondence.* 1956. 5 vols.

Commentary

Ault, Norman. *New Light on Pope.* 1949.

Sherburn, George. *The Early Career of Alexander Pope.* 1934.

Tillotson, Geoffrey. *Pope and Human Nature.* 1958.

REYNOLDS

Writings

Fry, Roger (ed.). *Discourses.* 1905.

Hilles, Frederick W. (ed.). *Letters.* 1929.

Hilles, Frederick W. (ed.). *Portraits.* 1952.

Olson, Elder (ed.). *Discourses on Art.* 1945.

Commentary

Hilles, Frederick W. *The Literary Career of Sir Joshua Reynolds.* 1936.

Hudson, Derek. *Sir Joshua Reynolds: A Personal Study.* 1958.

RICHARDSON

Bibliography

Cordasco, Francesco. *Richardson: A List of Critical Studies, 1896–1946.* 1948.

Sale, William M. *Samuel Richardson: A Bibliographical Record of his Literary Career with Historical Notes.* 1936.

Writings

Saintsbury, George (ed.). *Pamela: or Virtue Rewarded.* 1914. 2 vols.

Commentary

McKillop, Alan D. *Samuel Richardson, Printer and Novelist.* 1936.

Sale, William M. *Samuel Richardson: Master Printer.* 1950.

SHENSTONE

Bibliography

Williams, Iola A. *Seven XVIIIth Century Bibliographies.* 1924.

Writings

Ellis, Havelock (ed.). *Men and Manners.* 1927.

Gordon, Ian A. (ed.). *Shenstone's Miscellany, 1759–63, now first edited from the Manuscript.* 1952.

Mallam, Duncan (ed.). *Letters.* 1939.

Williams, Marjorie (ed.). *Letters.* 1939.

Commentary

Humphreys, A. R., *William Shenstone: An Eighteenth Century Portrait.* 1937.

Williams, Marjorie. *William Shenstone.* 1935.

Williams, Marjorie. *William Shenstone and his Friends.* 1933.

SMOLLETT

Bibliography

Cordasco, Francesco. *Smollett Criticism, 1770–1924.* 1948.

Cordasco, Francesco. *Smollett Criticism, 1925–45.* 1947.

Writings

Noyes, E. S. (ed.). *The Letters of To-bias Smollett, M.D.* 1926.
Saintsbury, George (ed.). *Works.* 1925. 12 vols.
Seccombe, Thomas (ed.). *Travels through France and Italy.* 1907.

Commentary

Boege, F. W. *Smollett's Reputation as a Novelist.* 1947.
Goldberg, M. A. *Smollett and the Scottish School.* 1959.
Jones, Claude E. *Smollett Studies.* 1942.
Kahrl, George M. *Smollett: Traveler-Novelist.* 1945.
Knapp, Lewis M. *Smollett: Doctor of Men and Manners.* 1949.
Martz, Louis L. *The Later Career of Smollett.* 1942.
Whitridge, Arnold. *Tobias Smollett: A Study of his Miscellaneaus Works.* 1925.

STEELE

Writings

Aitken, G. A. (ed.). *The Tatler.* 1898. 4 vols.
Blanchard, Rae (ed.). *Correspondence.* 1941.
Smith, G. Gregory (ed.). *The Spectator.* 1907. 4 vols.

Commentary

Aitken, G. A. *Richard Steele.* 1889. 2 vols.

STERNE

Writings

Curtis, Lewis Parry (ed.). *The Letters of Laurence Sterne.* 1935.
Woolf, Virginia (ed.). *A Sentimental Journey through France and Italy.* 1928.

Commentary

Cross, Wilbur L. *Life and Times of Laurence Sterne.* 3rd ed. 1929. 2 vols.
Dilworth, Ernest N. *The Unsentimental Journey of Laurence Sterne.* 1948.
Fredman, Alice G. *Diderot and Sterne.* 1955.
Homes, Alan B. *Yorick and the Critics: Sterne's Reputation in England, 1760–1868.* 1958.
Quennell, Peter. *The Profane Virtues: Boswell, Gibbon, Sterne, Wilkes.* 1945.
Shaw, Margaret R. B. *Laurence Sterne: The Making of a Humorist, 1713–1762.* 1957.

SWIFT

Bibliography

Landa, Louis A., and James Edward Tobin. *Jonathan Swift: A List of Critical Studies Published from 1895 to 1945.* 1945.
Teerink, Herman. *A Bibliography of Swift.* 1937.
Williams, Sir Harold. *Dean Swift's Library.* 1932.
Williams, Sir Harold. *The Text of 'Gulliver's Travels.'* 1952.

Writings

Case, A. E. (ed.). *Gulliver's Travels.* 1938.
Davis, Herbert (ed.). *Prose Works.* 1939–1960. 14 vols.
Guthkelch, A. C., and D. Nichol Smith (eds.). *A Tale of a Tub; to which is added An Account of a Battel between Antient and Modern Books.* 1958.
Smith, D. Nichol (ed.). *Letters to Charles Ford.* 1935.
Williams, Harold (ed.). *Journal to Stella.* 1948. 2 vols.

Commentary

Berwick, Donald M. *The Reputation of Jonathan Swift, 1781–1882.* 1941.
Bullitt, John M. *Jonathan Swift and the Anatomy of Satire: A Study of Satiric Technique.* 1953.

Case, Arthur E. *Four Essays on 'Gulliver's Travels.'* 1945.

Craik, Henry. *The Life of Swift.* 1894. 2 vols.

Davis, Herbert. *The Satire of Jonathan Swift.* 1947.

Ehrenpreis, Irvin. *The Personality of Swift.* 1958.

Ewald, William Bragg. *The Masks of Jonathan Swift.* 1954.

Landa, Louis A. *Swift and the Church of Ireland.* 1954.

Leyburn, Ellen D. *Satiric Allegory: Mirror of Man.* 1956.

Murry, John Middleton. *Jonathan Swift: A Critical Biography.* 1954.

Paulson, Ronald. *Theme and Structure in Swift's* Tale of a Tub. 1960.

Price, Martin. *Swift's Rhetorical Art: A Study in Structure and Meaning.* 1953.

Quintana, Ricardo. *The Mind and Art of Jonathan Swift.* 1936.

Quintana, Ricardo. *Swift: An Introduction.* 1955.

Starkman, Miriam Kosh. *Swift's Satire on Learning in 'A Tale of a Tub.'* 1950.

Williams, Kathleen. *Jonathan Swift and the Age of Compromise.* 1958.

TEMPLE

Writings

Moore Smith, G. C. (ed.). *The Letters of Dorothy Osborne to William Temple.* 1928.

Commentary

Marburg, Clara. *Sir William Temple: Seventeenth Century 'Libertin.'* 1929.

Woodbridge, Homer E. *Temple: The Man and his Work.* 1940.

WALPOLE

Bibliography

Hazen, Allen T. *A Bibliography of the Strawberry Hill Press.* 1942.

Hazen, Allen T. *A Bibliography of Walpole.* 1948.

Writings

Lewis, Wilmarth S. (ed.). *The Yale Edition of Horace Walpole's Correspondence.* 1937–.

Commentary

Dobson, Austin. *Horace Walpole, a Memoir.* Rev. ed. Paget Toynbee. 1927.

Ketton-Cremer, R. W. *Horace Walpole: A Biography.* Rev. ed. 1946.

Lewis, Wilmarth S. *Collector's Progress.* 1951.

Lewis, Wilmarth S. *Horace Walpole.* 1961.

Lewis, Wilmarth S. *Horace Walpole's Library.* 1958.

Stuart, Dorothy M. *Horace Walpole.* 1927.

Yvon, Paul. *La vie d'un dilettante: Horace Walpole, Essai de biographique psychologique et littéraire.* 1924.

JOSEPH WARTON

Bibliography

McClintock, W. D. *Joseph Warton's 'Essay on Pope': A History of the Five Editions.* 1933.

THOMAS WARTON

Writings

Hazlitt, W. C. (ed.). *The History of English Poetry.* 1871. 4 vols.

Commentary

Rinaker, Clarissa. *Thomas Warton, A Biographical and Critical Study.* 1916.

Smith, D. Nichol. *Warton's History of English Poetry.* 1929.

Wellek, René. *The Rise of English Literary History.* 1941.

WESLEY

Bibliography

Green, Richard. *Works of John and*

Charles Wesley: A Bibliography. 1896.

Writings

Curnock, Nehemiah (ed.). *Journal.* 1909–1916. 8 vols.
Telford, John (ed.). *Letters.* 1931. 8 vols.

Commentary

Baker, E. W. *A Herald of the Evangelical Revival: A Critical Enquiry into the Relation of William Law to Wesley.* 1948.
Birrell, Augustine. *John Wesley: Some Aspects of the Eighteenth Century in England.* 1938.
Dobrée, Bonamy. *John Wesley.* 1933.
Sargant, William. *Battle for the Mind.* 1957.
Schmidt, M. *John Wesley.* Vol. I (1703–38), 1953.
Warner, W. J. *The Wesleyan Movement in the Industrial Revolution.* 1930.

WHITE

Bibliography

Martin, E. A. *A Bibliography of Gilbert White, with a Biography and a Descriptive Account of the Village of Selborne.* Rev. ed. 1934.

Writings

Fisher, James (ed.). *The Natural History of Selborne.* Illus. Claire Oldham. 1947.

Johnson, Walter (ed.). *Journals.* 1931.
Scott, W. S. (ed.). *The Antiquities of Selborne.* Illus. Samuel Grimm (1776). 1950.

Commentary

Emden, Cecil S. *Gilbert White in his Village.* 1956.
Johnson, Walter. *Gilbert White: Pioneer, Poet, and Stylist.* 1928.
Scott, W. S. *White of Selborne.* 1950.
White, Rashleigh Holt. *Life and Letters of Gilbert White.* 1901. 2 vols.

YOUNG

Bibliography

Cordasco, Francesco. *Young: A Handlist of Critical Notices and Studies.* 1950.

Writings

Morley, Edith J. (ed.). *Conjectures on Original Composition.* 1918.

Commentary

Kind, J. L. *Edward Young in Germany.* 1906.
Shelley, Henry C. *Life and Letters of Edward Young.* 1914.
Steinke, Martin W. *Edward Young's 'Conjectures on Original Composition' in England and Germany.* 1917.
Thomas, Walter. *Le Poète Edward Young: Etude sur la vie et ses œuvres.* 1901.

Index of Authors
and Titles